CW00696951

New Zealand

Paul Smitz, Martin Robinson, Nina Rousseau, Richard Watkins, James Belich,

Julie Biuso, Russell Brown, Vaughan Yarwood, David Millar

Contents

Highlights	6	The West Coast	466
Getting Started	13	Canterbury	501
Itineraries	16	Otago	555
The Authors	21	Southland	612
Snapshot	24	Stewart Island & Outer Islands	643
History	25	Directory	658
The Culture	34	Transport	678
Maori Culture	47	Health	693
Environment	54	World Time Zones	697
New Zealand Outdoors	61	Language	698
Food & Drink	85	Glossary	701
Auckland Region	92	Behind the Scenes	704
Northland	146	Index	710
Coromandel Region	193	Legend	724
Waikato & the King Country	216		
Taranaki	246		
Wanganui & the Manawatu	262		
Central Plateau	280		
Bay of Plenty	312		
The East Coast	351		
Wellington Region	382		
Marlborough & Nelson	416		

Northland
p146

Coromandel Region
p193

Auckland Region
p92

Waikato & the King Country
p216

Bay of Plenty
p312

Central Plateau
p280

The East Coast
p351

Taranaki
p246

Wanganui & the Manawatu
p262

Wellington Region
p382

Marlborough & Nelson
p416

The West Coast
p466

Canterbury
p501

Otago
p555

Southland
p612

Stewart Island & Outer Islands
p643

Destination New Zealand

You're winding your way along a valley etched into the earth by an ancient, industrious glacier, continually crisscrossing a broad, pebble-bottomed river that couldn't look fresher if it had just splashed its way out of a cloud, and drinking in views of variegated rock-hills, the knotted greenery of unkempt arboretums, and snow-dipped peaks crowding before an expansive blue backdrop… Such memory-filling vistas are commonplace in New Zealand, but truth be told, overblown descriptions don't do the country justice – this is one of those rare places where superlatives fight a losing battle to match the actual stature of the land, not the other way around.

And it's not just the living landscapes of New Zealand that conquer the expectations of contemporary explorers. Desires are also fulfilled (and fuelled) by restaurant plates decorated with home-grown edibles, glasses spilling over with fine local wines, entrancing Maori stories, and an overwhelming choice of inventive activities ranging from the impossible-made-easy allure of bungy jumping to the panoramic excitement of a river-skimming jetboat ride.

The wild, rough-cut beauty of this faraway country, where travellers tread paths of ice, lava, sand and rimu-sheltered dirt on their way around the pairing of main islands and across pristine satellite islets, has fittingly gained cult status as the celluloid setting for one of the most inspired stories ever told. But unlike *Lord of the Rings*, New Zealand is real – this is not Middle-earth, so forget the fictional comparisons and confront the country's magnificent geography, as well as its ever-evolving culture, on its own authentic terms.

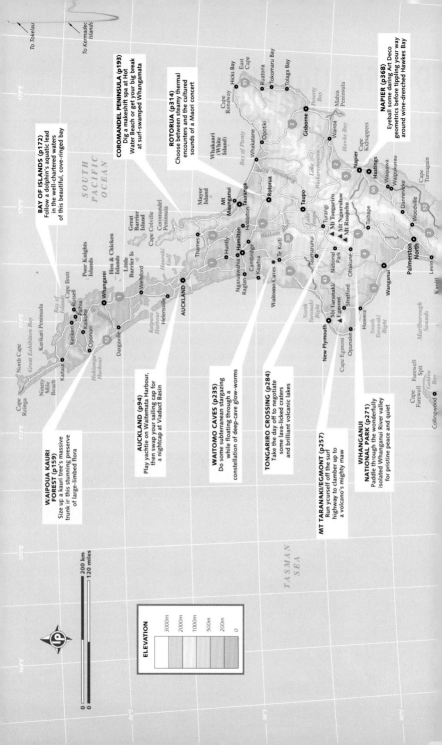

WAIPOUA KAURI FOREST (p159)
Size up a kauri tree's massive trunk in this stunning preserve of large-limbed flora

BAY OF ISLANDS (p172)
Follow a dolphin's aquatic lead in the well-chartered waters of this beautiful, cove-ringed bay

COROMANDEL PENINSULA (p193)
Dig a makeshift spa at Hot Water Beach or get your big break at surf-swamped Whangamata

ROTORUA (p314)
Choose between steamy thermal encounters and the cultured sounds of a Maori concert

NAPIER (p368)
Eyeball some daring Art Deco geometrics before tippling your way around wine-drenched Hawkes Bay

AUCKLAND (p94)
Play yachtie on Waitemata Harbour, then swap your sailing cap for a nightcap at Viaduct Basin

WAITOMO CAVES (p235)
Do some subterranean stargazing while floating through a constellation of deep-cave glow-worms

TONGARIRO CROSSING (p284)
Take the day off to negotiate some lava-licked craters and brilliant volcanic lakes

MT TARANAKI/EGMONT (p257)
Run yourself off the surf highway to clamber up to a volcano's mighty maw

WHANGANUI NATIONAL PARK (p271)
Paddle through the wonderfully isolated Whanganui River valley for pristine peace and quiet

ELEVATION
3000m
2000m
1000m
500m
200m
0

200 km
120 miles

SOUTH PACIFIC OCEAN

TASMAN SEA

To Tokelau

To Kermadec Islands

Yield to philosophical monologues and a penchant for wearing black in an arts-inspired, espresso-powered café

To Chatham Islands

To Bounty Islands; Antipodes Islands

SOUTH PACIFIC OCEAN

CHRISTCHURCH (p503)
Gentrify your senses with a cosmopolitan indulgence in a city eager to wine and dine

AORAKI/MT COOK (p549)
Watch the clouds part to make way for one of NZ's most spectacularly uplifting sights

QUEENSTOWN (p581)
Throw your sanity (and body) to the wind in a town that loves playing outdoors

OTAGO PENINSULA (p567)
Walk (or cruise) on the wild side amid the animal-rich splendour of this ocean-rimmed sanctuary

THE CATLINS (p638)
Veer down untrammelled byways into the sandy seclusion of this mesmerising coastal getaway

STEWART ISLAND (p645)
Pay your respects to remote wildlife under skies suffused with a legendary glow

To Campbell Island

To Snares Islands; Auckland Islands

NATIONAL PARK (p456)
Tramp the magnificent tidal flats and sun-tinged beaches of a seaside national park

FRANZ JOSEF GLACIER (p492) & FOX GLACIER (p495)
Surround yourself with the frosty majesty of some gloriously tumbledown ice flows

MILFORD SOUND (p624)
Kayak atop a mountain-hedged fiord or follow an unforgettable rainforested track from a reflective lake

TASMAN SEA

WELLINGTON
Lower Hutt
Cape Palliser
Cook Strait
Picton
Blenheim
Nelson
Richmond
Kaikoura
Kaikoura Peninsula
Murchison
St Arnaud
Karamea
Westport
Reefton
Lewis Pass
Hanmer Springs
Pegasus Bay
Punakaiki
Greymouth
Arthur's Pass
Hokitika
Ross
Mt Arrowsmith
Whataroa
Franz Josef
Fox Glacier
Aoraki/Mt Cook
Mt Cook Village
CHRISTCHURCH
Lyttelton
Akaroa
Banks Peninsula
Methven
Mt Hutt
Ashburton
Haast Pass
Haast
Jackson Bay
Mt Aspiring
Lake Wanaka
Lake Hawea
Lake Tekapo
Twizel
Temuka
Timaru
Waimate
Canterbury Bight
Oamaru
Milford Sound
Lake Te Anau
Te Anau
Manapouri
Lake Manapouri
Glenorchy
Queenstown
Arrowtown
Wanaka
Cromwell
Alexandra
Lumsden
Palmerston
DUNEDIN
Otago Peninsula
Milton
Balclutha
George Sound
Doubtful Sound
Dusky Sound
West Cape
Puysegur Point
Winton
Gore
Invercargill
Bluff
Foveaux Strait
Oban (Halfmoon Bay)
Mason Bay
Stewart Island (Rakiura)
Chaslands Mistake

NZ's national parks encapsulate undulating coastal dunes, lush rainforest, steep-sided volcanoes and creeping ice fields. Hug a towering conifer in **Waipoua Kauri Forest** (p159), see Mt Taranaki's lava-coloured cone in **Egmont National Park** (p257) and ride a river wild in **Whanganui National Park** (p271). Scale glaciers in the magnificent Milford Sound in **Fiordland National Park** (p615) or explore the beautiful bush of **Rakiura National Park** (p645). **Arthur's Pass National Park** (p535) makes a spectacular pit stop on your way across the South Island.

MICHAEL LAANELA

Fearlessly tramp your way across the Southern Circuit Track on Stewart Island (p645)

Experience the awesome volcano of Mt Ngauruhoe in Tongariro National Park (p282)
OLIVER STREWE
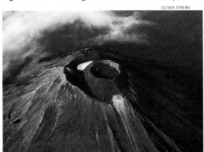

Invigorate yourself with a tramp to Welcome Flat (p498), through the Copland Valley in Westland National Park
GRANT DIXON

GARETH MCCORMACK

Navigate your way through the splendid alpine scenery of Mt Aspiring National Park (p606)

GARETH MCCORMACK

Be overwhelmed by the sheer enormity of Aoraki/Mt Cook National Park (p549)

Explore the lush coastal beauty of the Abel Tasman National Park (p456)

MARK PARKES

NZ's indigenous culture, the Maori, are a vibrant part of the country's cultural makeup, their influence prevalent in society from the very traditional (dance performances and museum artefacts) to the very modern (the names of government departments!) Increasingly, international visitors look to Maori culture as part of the attractions NZ has to offer. Traditional Maori performances of dance and song, such as those in **Rotorua** (p319), are a uniquely NZ experience, and visitors are also welcome to visit many *marae* (meeting places), including the national *marae* in **Christchurch** (p510). Visits to museums and sites such as the **Waitangi National Reserve** (p178), Wellington's **Te Papa** (p390) and Dunedin's **Otago Museum** (p559) provide fascinating insights into Maori culture and history and a close-up look at some beautifully carved Maori artefacts. For more about the Maori, see Maori Culture (p47).

See Maori war canoes in Ngaruawahia (p220), Waikato

JENNY & TONY ENDERBY

Experience Maori culture
with the *hongi* (pressing of noses; p51)

ANDERS BLOMQVIST

DENNIS JOHNSON

Check out traditional carvings
at Te Whakarewarewa (p318),
Rotorua

You could come to New Zealand and just laze around, or you could slap some sense into yourself and engage in some decidedly unreal activities. Take a chaperoned trip underwater and **swim with dolphins** (p66), **surf** (p70) some world-famous swells, or let a **jetboat** (p66) speed you through otherwise untrafficked wilderness. **Bungy jumping** (p63) is the safest near-death experience you can have, while NZ has spectacular places to **ski** (p71) and **snowboard** (p71). You might even choose to create your own cliff-hanger with a spot of **rock climbing** (p68).

Abseil (p237) into the glow-worm-lit depths of the Waitomo Caves in the King Country

Spin the wheels with a spot of mountain biking (p67) at St Kilda beach, Dunedin

Raft (p469) down a gorgeful of rapids on the Buller near Murchison

NZ's urban areas offer visitors many memorable encounters within city limits and in settled reaches of the countryside. Urbane **Christchurch** (p503) mixes the formality of old-empire architecture with a bohemian appreciation of arts and nightlife. You can join Maori festivities and plunge into thermal pools in **Rotorua** (p314), and feel the Celtic connection amid the Victorian buildings of pretty **Dunedin** (p557).

JOHN HAY

Indulge in the pastel-plastered celebration of Art Deco style in Napier (p368)

PAUL KENNEDY

Embrace activity-obsessed, extro-verted Auckland (p94) and its multi-cultural social scene

Take in the high-culture personality of Wellington (p384), with its numerous galleries and theatres

DAVID WALL

NZ has enough edible attractions to keep your stomach as occupied as your eyes and energy levels while you tour the country. Connoisseurs of **seafood** (p86) can eat delicious green-lipped mussels, smoked slabs of serpentine eels and patties mashed together from seasonal catches of that West Coast delicacy, whitebait. There's also plenty of **farm produce** (p86) to sample, including locally reared lamb, pork, beef and cervena (deer), plus gourmet cheeses and unique orchard goods like kiwi fruit. Liquid goodies are in abundance too, with plenty of frothy island-brewed **beers** (p87) and regional vineyards producing internationally recognised **wine** (p87), from the sauvignon blanc of Marlborough and the chardonnay of Hawkes Bay to the produce of 70 vineyards in Central Otago.

For more about NZ cuisine, see the Food & Drink chapter (p85).

Climb the giant kiwi fruit at
Kiwi Fruit Country (p342),
Te Puke

DAVID WALL

Delight your tastebuds at one of
New Zealand's many food and wine
festivals (p665)

JOHN HAY

Sample a succulent lamb dish in one of
Gisborne's restaurants (p363)

OLIVER STREWE

The remarkable, varied landscapes of NZ makes the country heaven for film-makers (a skilled workforce and favourable exchange rate have helped of course!) Most famously, Peter Jackson's *Lord of the Rings* (p42) trilogy cast NZ as Middle-earth for the better part of a decade, and inspired thousands of travellers down under on their own journeys from Hobbiton (**Matamata**; p232) to Mordor. The thriving local film industry (p42) has produced such treats as *Whale Rider* (**East Coast**; p357) and *Once Were Warriors* (**Otara, South Auckland**; p126). Meanwhile a number of Hollywood productions have used the country as a backdrop. Recent examples include *Vertical Limit* (**Queenstown region**; p581) and *The Lion, the Witch & the Wardrobe* (**Auckland**, p94; **Christchurch**, p503; and **Queenstown**, p581).

CHRIS MELLOR

Visit Mt Taranaki/Egmont (p257), the stand-in for Mt Fuji in *The Last Samurai* (2003)

PAUL

Ponder Piha Beach (p131) in the Waitakeres, where grand pianos were treated poorly (*The Piano;* 1993)

Walk among the alien landscapes of Tongariro National Park (p282), with its smoking volcanoes and steep cliffs above desolate plains – a natural choice for Mordor in the *Lord of the Rings* trilogy (2001–03)

GARETH MC

Getting Started

The relative ease of travel in New Zealand and its established network of all-budgets accommodation and organised activities make this country easy to explore. That said, look beyond the idyllic, hassle-free persona pushed by tourism brochures and videos or you'll end up taking NZ's idiosyncratic people and landscapes for granted.

There's a lot to see and do, so think about your priorities and allow enough time to achieve them. But don't forget to factor some space into your itinerary for those serendipitous moments that can make your trip.

WHEN TO GO

The warmer months between November and April are the catalyst for outdoor exploration and this is the official high season, with the slightly cooler and less tourist-trafficked months of October/November and April/May the best times to visit. The period around summer (December to February) is also when Kiwis lift their spirits with numerous food and wine festivals, concerts and sports events. If you're a fan of pointing your feet downhill, visit when snow is thick on the ground over winter (June to August), the high season in skiing areas.

See Climate (p662) in the Directory for more information.

Hat lovers beware: NZ is in the Roaring Forties and so has a prevailing wind blowing over it from west to east year-round, ranging from gentle breezes to the odd raging gale. On both main islands it gets wetter in the west than in the east because the mountains block the moisture-laden winds blowing in from the Tasman Sea. It's usually a few degrees cooler on the South Island than the North Island (p662). When concocting your travel plans, remember that NZ has a maritime climate, meaning the weather can change very quickly – anyone tramping at high altitudes must be fully prepared for this climatic unpredictability.

If you're serious about having a holiday – as opposed to engaging in modern-day gladiatorial contests with flotillas of campervans, queues of high-strung parents and inexhaustible platoons of children for the right to stay and eat in your accommodation and restaurant of choice – then try not to visit key sites during local school holidays (particularly mid-December to mid-January) and public holidays (p667).

COSTS & MONEY

In recent years the NZ dollar has made up some ground against stronger international currencies such as the greenback, and the country's growing

---

DON'T LEAVE HOME WITHOUT...

- Double checking the visa situation (see p674)
- Knowing what your embassy/consulate in NZ can and can't do to help you if you're in trouble (see p665)
- A travel insurance policy specifically covering you for any planned high-risk activities (see p667)
- Insect repellent to dissuade sandflies from dropping by for lunch (see p664)
- Packing a range of clothing to suit the changeability of the weather
- Preparing yourself for the fact that every kea (parrot) in NZ is apparently born with a gene that makes it 'cheeky'

tourist popularity has seen some prices rise in line with demand. However, it's still a fairly economical destination – unless you throw yourself out of a plane or cling to a jetboat every day of your trip, that is. In fact, the cost of activities figures prominently in the expense of every visit, and it helps to decide in advance what you'd prefer to spend your money on. Travellers who intend being very active should consider staying in cheaper accommodation to help finance their exertions, while more sedentary types who prefer sitting in front of a meal to dangling at the end of a bungy cord should limit their organised activities. Gastronomes will find that food is sometimes surprisingly pricey.

If you do a fair amount of sightseeing, eat out once or twice a day and stay in the least expensive motels or B&Bs, you should budget at least $90 to $110 per day (per person travelling as a pair), not including car hire or extra activities. Packing kids into your suitcases obviously means greater expense, but museums, cinemas and tour and activity organisers usually offer reasonable discounts for children, and there are plenty of open-air attractions available free of charge (see p661).

Self-catering travellers who camp, sleep in hired campervans or frequent hostels, and who tackle attractions independently, can explore NZ for as little as $50 per day. But if you want to enjoy the occasional restaurant-cooked meal and sip of beer or wine, then $70 per day is far more realistic.

LONELY PLANET INDEX

Litre of petrol $1.05

Litre of bottled water $2-3

Beer (DB) $3-5

Souvenir T-shirt $20

Hot pie $2.50-3.50

TRAVEL LITERATURE

There's a noticeable dearth of dedicated travel literature on NZ, but the country's ability to inspire its explorers is obvious in most published accounts of local wanderings.

Greenstone Trails (1994) by Barry Brailsford retraces with descriptive zeal the arduous journeys undertaken by Maoris into the wild tangle of the Southern Alps in search of the highly prized *pounamu* (greenstone).

Though it recounts a fictitious journey to a nonsensical land in order to satirise Victorian-era hypocrisy, Samuel Butler's *Erewhon* (written in 1872 and an anagram of 'nowhere') nonetheless has some appropriately rough-cut descriptions of Canterbury's mountainous west, where Butler once ran a sheep farm.

Chris Duff's *Southern Exposure* (2003) details a 2700km sea-kayak circumnavigation of the South Island. It's written in a style reserved for self-obsessed sportspeople who regard their own exploits as spiritual revelations, but has some interesting descriptions of NZ's coastline.

If you like the way Paul Theroux cheers himself up by denigrating everything around him, leaf through the ultra-brief NZ entry in *The Happy Isles of Oceania* (1993), where Theroux flees to the Routeburn Track after Christchurch apparently makes him contemplate suicide.

INTERNET RESOURCES

Destination New Zealand (www.url.co.nz/nzl.html) Resourceful site with an excellent listing of informative websites.

Lonely Planet (www.lonelyplanet.com) Get started with summaries on NZ and travellers trading info on the Thorn Tree.

NZ Government (www.govt.nz) Everything you ever wanted to know about NZ bureaucracy, including services and regulations.

Pure New Zealand (www.purenz.com) NZ's official tourism site has comprehensive info for visitors.

Stuff (www.stuff.co.nz) Pages of NZ news, though all of it sourced from Fairfax New Zealand publications.

Te Puna Web Directory (http://webdirectory.natlib.govt.nz) Exhaustive directory of domestic websites, maintained by the National Library of New Zealand.

TOP TENS
MUST-SEE MOVIES

Spending an evening or three reeling off some classic NZ films doesn't just reward you with advance screenings of some much-publicised scenery. It also allows you to dig past the country's distractingly grand surface and get right under its skin to an often-bleak mysticism that's been well-captured on celluloid. See Cinema (p42) for reviews of these and other locally produced films.

- *An Angel at My Table* (1990) Director: Jane Campion
- *Heavenly Creatures* (1994) Director: Peter Jackson
- *Lord of the Rings: The Fellowship of the Ring* (2001) Director: Peter Jackson
- *Once Were Warriors* (1994) Director: Lee Tamahori
- *The Piano* (1993) Director: Jane Campion
- *Rain* (2001) Director: Christine Jeffs
- *Sleeping Dogs* (1977) Director: Roger Donaldson
- *Smash Palace* (1977) Director: Roger Donaldson
- *Vigil* (1984) Director: Vincent Ward
- *Whale Rider* (2003) Director: Niki Caro

TOP READS

Be it through escapist plots, multilayered fiction, reinvented realities or character-driven social commentary, the significant body of Kiwi literature presents an opportunity to learn much about the islands. NZ's unsettled history, its burgeoning cultural awareness and the physical power of the landscape go well beyond a camera lens. See Literature (p41) for reviews of these and other books.

- *Bone People* (1988) Keri Hulme
- *The Book of Fame* (2000) Lloyd Jones
- *The Carpathians* (1988) Janet Frame
- *Dreams Lost Never Walked* (2003) Raumoa Ormsby
- *Electric* (2003) Chad Taylor
- *Going West* (1993) Maurice Gee
- *In a Fishbone Church* (1998) Catherine Chidgey
- *The Season of the Jew* (1987) Maurice Shadbolt
- *The Vintner's Luck* (2000) Elizabeth Knox
- *Whale Rider* (1987) Witi Ihimaera

Itineraries
CLASSIC ROUTES

TOP TO BOTTOM

4–6 weeks / Auckland to Christchurch
(1–2 weeks minimum travel time)

After cruising inner-city **Auckland** (p94), follow SH1 north to the glorious **Bay of Islands** (p172) to juggle surfboards, kayaks and scuba gear. Cross the island on SH12 and loop through the ancient **Waipoua Kauri Forest** (p159) on your way back to Auckland. Take SH1 to the gush and bubble of **Rotorua** (p314) after a sidetrip into the glow-worm-lit depths of **Waitomo Caves** (p235). Continue south into the triple-peaked **Tongariro National Park** (p282) and then on towards the capital hills of **Wellington** (p384).

After navigating Cook Strait, hug the east coast on SH1 to dolphin-friendly **Kaikoura** (p435) and cathedral-centred **Christchurch** (p503). Further south are the faunal sanctuary of the **Otago Peninsula** (p567) and the Victorian façades of **Dunedin** (p557). Mix-and-match highways across the island to reach **Te Anau** (p615) for the beguiling side-road to **Milford Sound** (p624), then backtrack to SH6 and head north into the frenzy of **Queenstown** (p581). Swap SH6 for SH8 for an eyeful of **Aoraki/Mt Cook** (p549) before veering east to regain the coast road to Christchurch.

For transport tips see Getting Around (p682).

Go loopy as you join the main attraction dots on this city-sampling, surf-riding, mountain-spotting tour of the country. You can go down this well-travelled road in a mere week, but we advise you to take at least a month and really savour the pleasures of dual-island travel.

SOUTHERN EXPOSURE

1 month / Christchurch to Christchurch
(1–2 weeks minimum travel time)

The rough-hewn South Island, with its mountainous spine, glaciers and vast fiords, coupled with a quilt of green meadows and an unhurried pace of life, affords a popular, visually inspiring circuit.

From **Christchurch** (p503) travel north up the east coast to the marvellous marine life of **Kaikoura** (p435) and then onto the grape-wreathed vineyards around **Blenheim** (p430). Swing past Marlborough Sounds to the stunning bays of **Abel Tasman National Park** (p456) before traversing formidable **Buller Gorge** (p470) to reach the rugged west coast at **Westport** (p470). Heading south on SH6 are the strikingly layered rocks of **Punakaiki** (p476), the greenstone-polishing town of **Hokitika** (p484) and the magnificent sèracs of **Franz Josef Glacier** (p492) and **Fox Glacier** (p495). Further south, over the Haast Pass, are the perpetually active towns of **Wanaka** (p604) and **Queenstown** (p581).

After heading south, detour off SH6 to **Te Anau** (p615) and then on to the divine **Milford Sound** (p624). Backtrack via Te Anau to **Manapouri** (p627) to access the fantastically remote **Doubtful Sound** (p627). Doubling back, the road south ends at low-rise **Invercargill** (p632), but a secondary road skirts the captivating coastal ecology of **The Catlins** (p638). Rejoin SH1 and forge north to Scottish-bred **Dunedin** (p557) and the stately limestone of **Oamaru** (p577) before ducking inland on SH83 towards **Aoraki/Mt Cook** (p549). Continue past the turquoise brilliance of **Lake Tekapo** (p545) back to Christchurch.

If you prefer, do this route in a clockwise direction. For more transport info, browse Getting Around (p682) in the Transport chapter.

Expose yourself (in a socially acceptable way) to mountain highs, valley lows, icy vistas and indomitable wilderness on this journey around the deep south. Why flail around the island in a week when you can stretch your environmental enjoyment over a whole month?

ROADS LESS TRAVELLED

DUE NORTH

1 month / Auckland to Wellington
(1–2 weeks minimum travel time)

A full exploration of the North Island's volcanic, river-swept landscape doesn't always occur to visitors, who leapfrog large swathes of terrain between prominent features like the Bay of Islands and Rotorua. But a circumnavigation of this ragged island's secluded beaches and secret forests won't disappoint.

Depart **Auckland** (p94) for a snorkel off **Goat Island Beach** (p153). Continue on to the iconic **Bay of Islands** (p172) to peruse the historic confines of **Russell** (p181) and to see where a landmark treaty was signed at **Waitangi** (p176). After sprawling on the gorgeous sands of **Matai Bay** (p168), swing north to the desolate dunes of **Ninety Mile Beach** (p166). Snake back through Auckland and head east to roam the splendidly forested **Coromandel Peninsula** (p196), then follow SH26 to the equine paradise of **Cambridge** (p231) before heading to 'Sulphur City', **Rotorua** (p314).

Take SH30 to the karst (limestone) glory of **Waitomo Caves** (p235), then SH3 to the dormant cone of **Mt Taranaki/Egmont** (p257). Further south, detour up the scenic **Whanganui River Rd** (p271) before trundling north via the still-smoking volcanoes of **Tongariro National Park** (p282) to sparkling **Lake Taupo** (p295). The SH5 visits **Napier** (p368) and its roaring '30s wardrobe, while SH2 terminates in the windy cosmopolitanism of **Wellington** (p384).

See Getting Around (p682) for more transport info.

Hot springs, mud baths, variegated volcanic lakes, untramped native forests and tracts of sand with nary a footprint in sight will be encountered as you range northwards on this diverse trail. The itinerary can be done in a week, but a month of travel will be just as busy and far more fulfilling.

KIWI EXTREMITIES

1–2 months / Auckland to Christchurch
(2 weeks minimum travel time)

Journey to the ends of NZ earth and experience locales far removed from man-made bustle on this all-points-of-the-compass tour.

Head north from **Auckland** (p94) to diminutive **Tutukaka** (p188) to arrange a visit to the fish-rich waters and rocky underwater labyrinths of the **Poor Knights Islands** (p188). Beyond the **Bay of Islands** (p172) is rugged Aupouri Peninsula, at the tip of which is **Cape Reinga** (p166), wrapped in eerie solitude and Maori legend.

Venture back south past Auckland and through **Rotorua** (p314) and the lush greenery of **Te Urewera National Park** (p366) to the narrow roads and wilderness-choked ranges of **East Cape** (p353).

Hop across Cook Strait to pretty **Picton** (p420), then lose yourself in the myriad waterways of **Marlborough Sounds** (p425).

Detour to the west, past the artful environs of **Nelson** (p442), to the enormous, species-dense **Kahurangi National Park** (p463). Travel southwest, where a memorable road north of **Westport** (p470) accesses the fabulous caverns of **Oparara Basin** (p474). South-bound, divert to the superb inland extremity of **Arthur's Pass National Park** (p535). Stop at **Milford Sound** (p624), but don't miss a voyage to the ocean mouth of utterly isolated **Doubtful Sound** (p627), accessible from **Manapouri** (p627). Ferry yourself to paradisal **Stewart Island** (p645), then sojourn in the peacefully overgrown **Catlins** (p638) before journeying north to **Christchurch** (p503).

For more transport info, look up Getting Around (p682) in the Transport chapter.

It's hard to find less-travelled paths in NZ nowadays, but this varied route from the country's northernmost fingernail to its detached southern toe takes in plenty of minimally touristed landscapes. You could spend just a fortnight reaching these far reaches, but why would you in lieu of a longer stay?

TAILORED TRIPS

FINE WINES

If your palate has a fine appreciation of fermented grape juice, or you want to make an impressive splash in a spittoon with connoisseur friends back home, then consider an intoxicating tour of some of NZ's 400-odd vineyards.

On the North Island there's accomplished viticulture west of **Auckland** (p94), where speciality fruit wines can be sampled, and east of the city on **Waiheke Island** (p134), where numerous wineries compete for vintage accolades. The fertile plains around **Gisborne** (p360) are devoted to char-

donnay, while **Hawkes Bay** (p378) also loves its chardy but squeezes out some premier cabernet sauvignon and merlot too. **Martinborough** (p413) in the Wairarapa region creates outstanding pinot noir flavours.

The country's most notable bouquet-sniffing realm is on the South Island in **Marlborough** (p432), where crisp sauvignon blanc and fruity riesling is guzzled with wild yet refined abandon. Also barrelling down the road to commercial success are the wineries of **Central Otago** (p576), specialising in fine pinots. The **Waipara Valley** (p530) is a relatively new grape-growing region now producing over 90,000 cases of wine annually.

YOUTHFUL DISTRACTIONS

A child would have a fantastic time customising their own NZ itinerary considering the country's overwhelming variety of activities, awesome visuals and wild animal encounters.

Man-made amusements are exemplified by the corkscrew rollercoaster at Auckland's **Rainbow's End Adventure Park** (p106) and the totally cool storm chamber at Christchurch's **International Antarctic Centre** (p510). High spirits are in abundance during sundry urban celebrations, such as Wellington's **Summer City Festival** (p394), while geysers and Maori performers put on sensational shows at Rotorua's **Te Whakarewarewa** (p318).

Unique perspectives on NZ's stupendous landscape are provided by aerial sightseeing over the fuming spires of **Tongariro National Park** (p282) and the frozen contours of the **Franz Josef Glacier** (p492) and **Fox Glacier** (p495). And what child could resist clattering across the mountainous backbone of the South Island on the **TranzAlpine railway** (p484)? There's open-air excitement aplenty while swimming with seals and dolphins or watching whales at **Kaikoura** (p435), or while high-stepping it down well-beaten paths in one of NZ's many national parks, like the quartet that make up the sublime **Southwest New Zealand (Te Wahipounamu) World Heritage Area** (p615).

The Authors

PAUL SMITZ
Coordinating Author & the West Coast, Canterbury, Otago, Southland, Outer Islands

A native of Australia with an inbred appreciation of all things Pacific and vaguely island-shaped, Paul has long wanted to follow the contours of New Zealand and got his chance with this book. Equipped with the requisite love of the great (and even the humble) outdoors and an eerie ability to drive for hours without being distracted by a single coherent thought (similar to what happens while he's working), he enjoyed touring a fold-out map of NZ and sketching the country in with three-dimensional experiences. He thinks the so-called Frodo Economy has its place, but that it's far inferior to real-life encounters with the gamut of human and environmental moods on these extraordinary islands.

The Coordinating Author's Favourite Trip

The South Island's West Coast is an exceptional stretch of turf. I rolled into Westport (p470) fresh from clambering across Buller Gorge Swingbridge (p470) and drove north along a fantastic road squeezed between hills hiding ghost towns and the ocean to remote Karamea (p474), not far from Oparara Basin (p474). South of Westport I was treated to a view of the Pancake Rocks (p476) getting lashed by an ocean storm, and the glow-worm dell at Hokitika (p484). I regret not taking a paddle around the beautiful Okarito Lagoon (p489), but cheered myself up with a squiz at Franz Josef (p492) and Fox glaciers (p495) and a hike around Lake Matheson (p496).

MARTIN ROBINSON
Auckland, Northland, Coromandel Region, Waikato & the King Country

Born in the UK, Martin taught his way around the world several times, writing about his travels for magazines and newspapers. He first visited NZ in 1989 and has lived and worked there off and on ever since, attracted by the country's outdoor lifestyle and compact and diverse landscapes. He has contributed to *Outback Australia* and other Lonely Planet guides and enjoys the nomadic life of an information hunter and gatherer.

NINA ROUSSEAU
Taranaki, Wanganui & the Manawatu, Wellington Region, Marlborough & Nelson

Nina is a freelance writer who has written for international print media, online publications and other Lonely Planet guidebooks, including *Australia* and *Southeast Asia on a Shoestring*. She isn't afraid to load up a chilly-bin full of Speight's, slip into a pair of jandals and feast on some kumara chips and battered scallops to be 100% pure New Zealand.

RICHARD WATKINS

Central Plateau, Bay of Plenty, the East Coast

Richard's first experience of New Zealand was as an over-encumbered backpacker in 1998, when he toured the length and breadth of both islands, and was immediately captivated by the sheer variety of landscapes this small country has to offer. An Oxford history graduate, Richard has written for a number of Lonely Planet titles, as well as other guidebooks and travel websites. Currently based in the UK, he was more than happy to escape the Northern Hemisphere winter to bask in the antipodean sun and write for this book. His only regret is that he never did get to meet any hobbits.

CONTRIBUTING AUTHORS

Professor James Belich wrote the History chapter (p25). James is one of NZ's pre-eminent historians, award-winning author of *The New Zealand Wars*, *Making Peoples* and *Paradise Reforged*. He has also worked in television – *NZ Wars* was screened in NZ in 1998. James is currently head of the History Department at the University of Auckland.

Julie Biuso wrote the Food & Drink chapter (p85). After a successful stint teaching at the prestigious London School of Cordon Bleu, and setting up and running the franchised school in NZ, Julie chucked in the toque to take up the pen and set off on a hedonistic life of eating, drinking, travelling and writing, hoping someone would pay for it. She has been, and still is, food editor at a number of NZ magazines and newspapers, has written 12 food books, is a regular on television and radio and runs a website (www.juliebiuso.com). For relaxation she strokes her cat while watching her goldfish Jacob swimming in his bowl.

Russell Brown wrote the Culture chapter (p34). Russell is one of New Zealand's most prolific journalists. He is the host of *Mediawatch*, a weekly media commentary show on National Radio, and has written the weekly 'Computers' column in the *New Zealand Listener* since its inception. He also writes columns for New Zealand's leading business magazine, *Unlimited*, and the music magazine *Real Groove*. And when he's not doing any of that he's mentoring at Auckland college radio station 95bFM, and tending to the award-winning website publicaddress.net, where his popular weblog, *Hard News*, is hosted. He lives in Auckland's Pt Chevalier with his family and likes playing and watching sport, cooking, listening to music and drinking wine in moderation.

Tony Horwitz wrote the 'Captain James Cook' boxed text in the History chapter (p28). Tony is a Pulitzer-winning author of fiction and nonfiction. His fascination with James Cook, and with travel, took him around NZ, Australia and the Pacific while researching *Blue Latitudes* (alternatively titled *Into the Blue*): part biography of Cook and part travelogue.

Josh Kronfeld wrote the 'Surfing in New Zealand' boxed text in the New Zealand Outdoors chapter (p70). Josh is an ex–All Black flanker, whose passion for surfing NZ's beaches is legendary and who found travelling for rugby a way to surf other great breaks around the world.

Dr David Millar wrote the Health chapter (p693). David is a travel-medicine specialist, diving doctor and lecturer in wilderness medicine. He is currently a medical director with the Travel Doctor in Auckland.

Nandor Tanczos MP wrote the 'Environmental Issues in Aotearoa New Zealand' boxed text (p55). New Zealand's first Rastafarian member of parliament (NZ Greens Party), and the first to enter Parliament in dreadlocks and a hemp suit, he's also the Greens' spokesperson on Treaty of Waitangi issues and a high-profile grassroots campaigner on genetic engineering and cannabis law reform.

Vaughan Yarwood wrote the Environment chapter (p54). Vaughan is an Auckland-based writer whose most recent book, *The History Makers: Adventures in New Zealand Biography*, is published by Random House. Earlier work includes *The Best of New Zealand*, a collection of essays on NZ life and culture by prominent Kiwis, which he edited, and the regional history *Between Coasts: from Kaipara to Kawau*.

He has written widely for NZ and international publications and is the former associate editor of *New Zealand Geographic*, for which he continues to write. International assignments have taken him to many countries in Europe, Asia and the Pacific. Most recently he travelled to Antarctica to research a book on polar exploration.

Thanks also for contributions from **Sir Ian McKellen** ('Sandflies' boxed text, p664) and **Errol Hunt** ('Land Wars' boxed text, p30; 'New Zealand's *Lord of the Rings*' boxed text, p42; and Maori Culture, p47).

Snapshot

Recently it's been impossible to spend a single day in New Zealand without hearing the words 'Lord of the Rings' (p42). Even if you don't encounter one of the thousands of people who worked on Peter Jackson's film trilogy, you'll inevitably bear the brunt of someone shamelessly announcing the most tenuous connection to the Tolkien-derived spectaculars – 'My best friend's husband's hairdresser played an orc, you know.' Kiwis claim the movies as their own and the tourism industry is milking the concept of NZ as legendary realm for all it's worth.

Arguably due to the mass advertising of its landscape in the *Rings* flicks, and also to a widespread international perception of it as a haven far removed (geographically and historically) from global mayhem, NZ received a record 2.1 million visitors in 2003, up 3% on 2002. A common talking point in NZ is the potential boost to its relatively stable economy (p34) if its profile remains as 'pure' as is suggested by the successful international tourism marketing campaign of the same name.

A divisive contemporary issue has been the ownership of, and access to, NZ's foreshores and seabeds. After a mid-2003 court decision paved the way for Maori peoples (p47) to claim customary title over this coastal *whenua* (land), NZ's Labour government asserted that the Crown was the true owner, reigniting a land rights debate that's as old as the 1840 Treaty of Waitangi (p29). After an unhappy reaction from indigenous groups, the government floated the concept of a 'public domain', giving all NZ citizens responsibility (as opposed to notions of ownership) for the territory in question. But this compromise solution hasn't placated those positioned at the issue's extremes.

In politics, the National Party has been pre-campaigning for the 2005 national election on a platform of restricting race-based funding and policies. In early 2004, National's leader Don Brash engineered a huge opinion poll swing towards his party primarily because of this stance on so-called indigenous concessions. This was significant considering that in 2002 the Nationals recorded their worst election result in 70 years when a Labour government headed by Prime Minister Helen Clark was voted in for its second term. The right-wing New Zealand First Party (the country's third-largest political group) has also played the race card, citing the deeply xenophobic social equation that immigration equals an increase in violent crime plus economic hardship.

Rugby (p39) is always a hot topic in NZ. Late-2003 brought the good, the bad and the ugly in quick succession, starting with the reverential invocation of All Blacks names like Spencer, Mealamu and McCaw in the early stages of the prized World Cup. This was followed by a pride-thumping semi-final loss to less-fancied Australia, and then gutter-press attacks on a team that had apparently let a nation down. Reason gained the upper hand, however, and the country took the loss with far more dignity than its 1999 World Cup semi-final loss to France, when NZ temporarily became 'Land of the Long Black Cloud'.

FAST FACTS

Population: 3.95 million humans, 39.2 million sheep

GDP growth: 3.3%

Inflation: 2.7%

Unemployment: 5.3%

Average weekly full-time wage for males: $857

Average weekly full-time wage for females: $685

Roads: NZ has 92,000km of main roads, 62% of which are paved

Life expectancy: the tuatara (lizard) can live for 100 years, while the totara (tree) can live for 1000

0 minutes: the amount of screen time an inconsolable Christopher Lee got in *Lord of the Rings: The Return of the King*

History James Belich

New Zealand's history is not long, but it is fast. In less than a thousand years these islands have produced two new peoples: the Polynesian Maori and European New Zealanders. The latter are often known by their Maori name, 'Pakeha' (though not all like the term). NZ shares some of its history with the rest of Polynesia, and with other European settler societies, but has unique features as well. It is the similarities that make the differences so interesting, and vice versa.

MAKING MAORI

Despite persistent myths (see the boxed text on p26), there is no doubt that the first settlers of NZ were the Polynesian forebears of today's Maori. Beyond that, there are a lot of question marks. Exactly where in east Polynesia did they come from – the Cook Islands, Tahiti, the Marquesas? When did they arrive? Solid archaeological evidence points to about 1200, but much earlier dates have been suggested for the first human impact on the environment. Did the first settlers come in one group or several? Some evidence, such as the diverse DNA of the Polynesian rats that accompanied the first settlers, suggest multiple founding voyages. On the other hand, only rats and dogs brought by the founders have survived, not the more valuable pigs and chickens. The survival of these cherished animals would have had high priority, and their failure to be successfully introduced suggests fewer voyages. See the boxed texts on p229 and p343 for the tales of just two of the great migratory canoes that made the voyage.

NZ seems small compared to Australia, but it is bigger than Britain, and very much bigger than other Polynesian islands. Its regions vary wildly in environment and climate. Prime sites for first settlement were warm coastal gardens for the food plants brought from Polynesia (kumara or sweet potato, gourd, yam and taro); sources of workable stone for knives and adzes; and areas with abundant big game. NZ has no native land mammals apart from a few species of bat, but 'big game' is no exaggeration: the islands were home to a dozen species of moa (a large flightless bird), the largest of which weighed up to 240kg, about twice the size of an ostrich. There were also other species of flightless bird and large sea-mammals such as fur seals, all unaccustomed to being hunted. For people from small Pacific islands, this was like hitting the jackpot. The first settlers spread far and fast, from the top of the North Island to the bottom of the South Island within the first 100 years. High protein diets are likely to have boosted population growth.

By about 1400, however, the big-game supply was in rapid decline. Except in the far south, fur-seal breeding colonies were hunted out, and moa were extinct or close to it. Rumours of late survivals abound, but none have been authenticated. So if you see a moa in your travels, photograph it – you have just made the greatest zoological discovery of the last 100 years. Maori economics turned from big game to small game – forest birds and rats – and from hunting to gardening and fishing. A good living

One of NZ's foremost modern historians, James Belich has written a number of books on NZ history and hosted the TV documentary series *NZ Wars*. James is currently Professor of History at Auckland University.

AD 1000–1200	1642
Range of possible dates for Maori settlement	First European visit, by Abel Tasman

THE MORIORI & THEIR MYTH

One of NZ's most persistent legends is that Maoris found mainland NZ already occupied by a more peaceful and racially-distinct Melanesian people, known as the Moriori, whom they exterminated. This myth has been regularly debunked by scholars since the 1920s, but somehow hangs on.

To complicate matters, there were real 'Moriori', and Maoris did treat them badly. The real Moriori were the people of the Chatham Islands, a windswept group about 900km east of the mainland. They were, however, fully Polynesian, and descended from Maoris – 'Moriori' was their version of the same word. Mainland Maoris arrived in the Chathams in 1835, as a spin-off of the Musket Wars, killing some Moriori and enslaving the rest (see the boxed text on p652). But they did not exterminate them. The mainland Moriori remain a myth.

could still be made, but it required detailed local knowledge, steady effort and complex communal organisation – hence the rise of the Maori tribes. Competition for resources increased, conflict did likewise, and this led to the building of increasingly sophisticated fortifications, known as *pa*. Vestiges of *pa* earthworks can still be seen around the country – on the hilltops of Auckland for example.

The Maori had no metals and no written language (and no alcoholic drinks or drugs). But their culture and spiritual life was rich and distinctive. Below Ranginui (sky father) and Papatuanuku (earth mother), were various gods of land, forest and sea, joined by deified ancestors over time. The mischievous demi-god Maui was particularly important. In legend, he vanquished the sun and fished up the North Island before meeting his death between the thighs of the goddess Hine-nui-te-po in an attempt to conquer the human mortality embodied in her. Maori traditional performance art, the group singing and dancing known as *kapa haka*, has real power, even for modern audiences. Visual art, notably woodcarving, is something special – 'like nothing but itself', in the words of 18th-century explorer-scientist Joseph Banks.

For more about Maui and other mythological figures, Maori tribal structure and performing arts, see 'Maori Culture' on p47.

ENTER EUROPE

NZ became an official British colony in 1840, but the first authenticated contact between Maoris and the outside world took place almost two centuries earlier – in 1642, in Golden Bay at the top of the South Island. Two Dutch ships sailed from Indonesia, then the 'Dutch East Indies', to search for the legendary 'Great South Land' and anything valuable it might contain. The commander, Abel Tasman, was instructed to pretend to any natives he might meet 'that you are by no means eager for precious metals, so as to leave them ignorant of the value of the same'.

When Tasman's ships anchored in the bay, local Maori came out in their canoes to make the traditional challenge: friends or foes? Misunderstanding this, the Dutch challenged back, by blowing trumpets. When a boat was lowered to take a party between the two ships, it was attacked. Four crewmen were killed. Tasman sailed away and did not come back; nor did any other European for 127 years. But the Dutch did leave a name: 'Nieuw Zeeland' or 'New Sealand'.

Contact between Maoris and Europeans was renewed in 1769, when both English and French explorers arrived, under James Cook (see the

1769	1814
European contact recommences with visits by James Cook and Jean de Surville	First European mission station and settlement

boxed text on p28) and Jean de Surville. Despite some violence, both managed to communicate with Maoris, and this time NZ's link with the outside world proved permanent. Another French expedition arrived in 1772, under Marion du Fresne, and stayed for some weeks at the Bay of Islands to rest and refit. At first, relations with Maoris were excellent, but a breach of Maori *tapu* (sacred law) led to violence. Marion and two dozen of his men were killed, and the rest retaliated by destroying a Maori *pa*, which may or may not have belonged to the offenders.

Captain James Cook
MILK WELDON

Exploration continued, motivated by science, profit and great power rivalry. Cook made two more visits between 1773 and 1777, and there were further French expeditions. Unofficial visits, by whaling ships in the north and sealing gangs in the south, began in the 1790s. The first mission station was founded in 1814, in the Bay of Islands, and followed by dozens of others: Anglican, Methodist and Catholic. Trade in flax and timber generated small European-Maori settlements by the 1820s. Surprisingly, the most numerous category of European visitor was probably American. New England whaling ships favoured the Bay of Islands for rest and recreation; 271 called there between 1833 and 1839 alone. To whalers, 'rest and recreation' meant sex and drink. Their favourite haunt, the little town of Kororareka (now Russell) was known to the missionaries as 'the hellhole of the Pacific'. New England visitors today might well have distant relatives among the local Maoris.

One or two dozen bloody clashes dot the history of Maori-European contact before 1840 but, given the number of visits, inter-racial conflict was modest. Europeans needed Maori protection, food and labour, and Maoris came to need European articles, especially muskets. Whaling stations and mission stations were linked to local Maori groups by intermarriage, which helped keep the peace. Most warfare was between Maori and Maori: the terrible intertribal 'Musket Wars' of 1818–36. Because Northland had the majority of early contact with Europe, its Ngapuhi tribe acquired muskets first. Under their great general Hongi Hika, Ngapuhi then raided south, winning bloody victories against tribes without muskets. Once they acquired muskets, these tribes saw off Ngapuhi, but also raided further south in their turn. The domino effect continued to the far south of the South Island in 1836. The missionaries claimed that the Musket Wars then tapered off through their influence, but the restoration of the balance of power through the equal distribution of muskets was probably more important.

Europe brought such things as pigs (at last) and potatoes, which benefited Maoris, while muskets and diseases had the opposite effect. The negative effects have been exaggerated, however. Europeans expected peoples like the Maori to simply fade away at contact, and some early estimates of Maori population were overly-high – up to one million. Current estimates are between 85,000 and 110,000 for 1769. The Musket Wars killed perhaps 20,000, and new diseases did considerable damage too (although NZ had the natural quarantine of distance: infected Europeans usually recovered or died during the long voyage and smallpox, for example, which devastated native Americans, did not make it here). By 1840, the Maoris had been reduced to about 70,000, a decline of at least 20%. Maoris bent under the weight of European contact, but they certainly did not break.

1840	1845–46
Treaty of Waitangi; NZ becomes a nominal British colony	Northland War (Hone Heke's war)

CAPTAIN JAMES COOK *Tony Horwitz*

If aliens ever visit earth, they may wonder what to make of the countless obelisks, faded plaques, and graffiti-covered statues of a stiff, wigged figure gazing out to sea from Alaska to Australia, from New Zealand to North Yorkshire, from Siberia to the South Pacific. James Cook (1728–79) explored more of the earth's surface than anyone in history, and it's impossible to travel the Pacific without encountering the captain's image and his controversial legacy in the lands he opened to the West.

For a man who travelled so widely, and rose to such fame, Cook came from an extremely pinched and provincial background. The son of a day labourer in rural Yorkshire, he was born in a mud cottage, had little schooling, and seemed destined for farm work – and for his family's grave plot in a village churchyard. Instead, Cook went to sea as a teenager, worked his way up from coal-ship servant to naval officer, and attracted notice for his exceptional charts of Canada. But Cook remained a little-known second lieutenant until, in 1768, the Royal Navy chose him to command a daring voyage to the South Seas.

In a converted coal ship called *Endeavour*, Cook sailed to Tahiti, then became the first European to land at New Zealand and the east coast of Australia. Though the ship almost sank after striking the Great Barrier Reef, and 40% of the crew died from disease and accidents, the *Endeavour* limped home in 1771 with eye-opening reports on curiosities, including erotic Tahitian dances and, from Australia, a leaping, pouched quadruped so difficult for Europeans to classify that Cook's botanist called it an 'eighty-pound mouse'.

On a return voyage (1772–75), Cook became the first navigator to pierce the Antarctic Circle and circled the globe near its southernmost latitude, demolishing the ancient myth that a vast, populous, and fertile continent surrounded the South Pole. Cook also crisscrossed the Pacific from Easter Island to Melanesia, charting dozens of islands between. Though Maoris killed and cooked 10 sailors, the captain remained strikingly sympathetic to islanders. 'Notwithstanding they are cannibals,' he wrote, 'they are naturally of a good disposition'.

On Cook's final voyage (1776–79), in search of a Northwest Passage between the Atlantic and Pacific, he became the first European to visit Hawaii, and coasted America from Oregon to Alaska. Forced back by Arctic pack ice, Cook returned to Hawaii, where he was killed during a skirmish with islanders who had initially greeted him as a Polynesian god. In a single decade of discovery, Cook had filled in the map of the Pacific and, as one French navigator put it, 'left his successors with little to do but admire his exploits'.

Cook's legacy extends far beyond his Pacific charts, some of them so accurate that they remained in use until the 1990s. His sails were the first true voyages of scientific discovery, aboard ships filled with trained observers: artists, astronomers, botanists – even poets. Their observations helped lay the foundation for modern disciplines such as anthropology and museum science, and inspired Western writers and artists to romanticise the South Pacific as an innocent paradise. The plant and animal specimens Cook's men collected also revolutionised Western understanding of nature, seeding the notion of biodiversity and blazing a trail for Charles Darwin's voyage on the *Beagle*.

But Cook's travels also spurred colonisation of the Pacific, and within a few decades of his death, missionaries, whalers, traders and settlers began transforming – and often devastating – island cultures. As a result, many indigenous people now revile Cook as an imperialist villain who introduced disease, dispossession and other ills to the Pacific (hence the frequent vandalising of Cook monuments). However, as islanders revive traditional crafts and practices, from tattooing to *tapa*, they have turned to the art and writing of Cook and his men as a resource for cultural renewal. For good and ill, a Yorkshire farm boy remains the single most significant figure in the shaping of the modern Pacific.

Tony Horwitz is a Pulitzer-winning reporter and nonfiction author. In researching Blue Latitudes *(or* Into the Blue*), Tony travelled the Pacific – 'boldly going where Captain Cook has gone before'.*

1853–56	1861
Provincial and central elected governments established	Gold discovered in Otago

MAKING PAKEHA

By 1840, Maori tribes described local Europeans as 'their Pakeha', and valued the profit and prestige they brought. They wanted more, and concluded that accepting nominal British authority was the way to get them. At the same time, the British government was overcoming its reluctance to undertake potentially expensive intervention in NZ. It too was influenced by profit and prestige, but also by humanitarian considerations. It believed, wrongly but sincerely, that Maoris could not handle the increasing scale of unofficial European contact. In 1840, the two peoples struck a deal, symbolised by the treaty first signed at Waitangi on 6 February that year. The Treaty of Waitangi now has a standing not dissimilar to that of the Constitution in the US, but is even more contested. The original problem was a discrepancy between British and Maori understandings of it. The English version promised Maoris full equality as British subjects in return for complete rights of government. The Maori version also promised that Maoris would retain their chieftainship, which implied local rights of government. The problem was not great at first, because the Maori version applied outside the small European settlements. But as those settlements grew, conflict brewed.

The Waitangi National Reserve, where the Treaty of Waitangi was first signed in 1840, is now a tourist attraction for Kiwis and non-Kiwis alike. Each year on 6 February, Waitangi hosts treaty commemorations and protests.

In 1840, there were only about 2000 Europeans in NZ, with the shanty town of Kororareka (Russell) as the capital and biggest settlement. By 1850, six new settlements had been formed (Auckland, Wellington, New Plymouth, Nelson, Christchurch and Dunedin), with 22,000 settlers between them. About half of these had come under the auspices of the New Zealand Company and its associates. The company was the brainchild of Edward Gibbon Wakefield, who also influenced the settlement of South Australia. Wakefield hoped to short-circuit the barbarous frontier phase of settlement with 'instant civilisation', but his success was limited. From the 1850s, his settlers, who included a high proportion of upper-middle-class gentlefolk, were swamped by succeeding waves of immigrants that continued to wash in until the 1880s. These people were part of the great British and Irish diaspora that also populated Australia and much of North America, but the NZ mix was distinctive. Lowland Scots settlers were more prominent in NZ than elsewhere, for example, with the possible exception of parts of Canada. NZ's Irish, even the Catholics, tended to come from the north of Ireland. NZ's English tended to come from the counties close to London. Small groups of Germans, Scandinavians and Chinese made their way in, though the last faced increasing racial prejudice from the 1880s, when the Pakeha population reached half a million.

Season of the Jew by Maurice Shadbolt is the first in a series of novels about the NZ Wars. This book covers the second Taranaki war (1865–69) and the exploits of the remarkable one-eyed general Titokowaru, who for a short while brought imperial NZ to its knees.

Much of the mass immigration of the 1850s to the 1870s was assisted by the provincial and central governments, which also mounted large-scale public works schemes, especially in the 1870s under Julius Vogel. In 1876, Vogel abolished the provinces on the grounds that they were hampering his development efforts. The last imperial governor with substantial power was the talented but Machiavellian George Grey, who ended his second governorship in 1868. Thereafter, the governors (governors-general from 1917) were largely just nominal heads of state. The head of government, the premier or prime minister, had more power. The central government, originally weaker than the provincial governments, the imperial governor and the Maori tribes, eventually exceeded the power of all three.

1860–72	1882
NZ land wars (Taranaki, Waikato, Taranaki again, East Coast)	First refrigerated cargo to Britain

The Maori tribes did not go down without a fight, however. Indeed, their resistance was one of the most formidable ever mounted against European expansion, comparable to that of the Sioux and Seminole in the USA. The first clash took place in 1843 in the Wairau Valley, now a wine-growing district. A posse of settlers set out to enforce the myth of British control, but encountered the reality of Maori control. Twenty-two settlers were killed, including Wakefield's brother, Arthur, along with about six Maoris (see the boxed text on p422). In 1845, more serious fighting broke out in the Bay of Islands, where the young Ngapuhi chief, Hone Heke, challenged British sovereignty, first by cutting down the British flag at Russell, and then by sacking the town itself. Heke and his ally Kawiti baffled three British punitive expeditions, using a modern variant of the traditional *pa* fortification. Vestiges of these innovative earthworks can still be seen at Ruapekapeka (south of Kawakawa). Governor Grey claimed victory in the north, but few were convinced at the time. Grey had more success in the south, where he arrested the formidable Ngati Toa chief Te Rauparaha, who until then wielded great influence on both sides of Cook Strait. Pakeha were able to

---

LAND WARS *Errol Hunt*

Five separate major conflicts made up what are now collectively known as the New Zealand Wars (also referred to as the Land Wars or Maori Wars). Starting in Northland and moving throughout the North Island, the wars had many complex causes, but *whenua* (land), was the one common factor. In all five wars, Maoris fought both for and against the government, on whose side stood the Imperial British Army, Australians and NZ's own Armed Constabulary. Land confiscations imposed on the Maoris as punishment for involvement in these wars are still the source of conflict today, with the government struggling to finance compensation for what are now acknowledged to have been illegal seizures.

Northland war (1844–46) 'Hone Heke's War' began with the famous chopping of the flagpole at Kororareka (now Russell, p181) and 'ended' at Ruapekapeka (south of Kawakawa) – although massive concessions from the 'victorious' government towards the 'vanquished' Heke made many at the time doubt who had really won! In many ways, this was almost a civil war between rival Ngapuhi factions, with the government taking one side against the other.

First Taranaki war (1860–61) Starting with the controversial swindling of Maori land by the government at Waitara (p256), the first Taranaki war (p248) inflamed the passions of Maoris across the North Island and involved many military participants from the Waikato tribes (despite being traditional enemies of the Taranaki Maoris).

Waikato war (1863–64) The largest of the five wars. Predominantly involving Maoris of the King Movement (p219), the Waikato war was caused in part by what the government saw as a challenge to sovereignty. However it was land, again, that was the real reason for friction. Following defeats such as Rangiriri (p220), the Waikato people were pushed entirely from their own lands, south into what became known as the King Country. Massive confiscations of land followed, for which the country is still paying now.

Second Taranaki war (1865–69) Caused by Maori resistance to land confiscations stemming from the first Taranaki war, this was perhaps the war in which the Maoris came closest to victory, under the brilliant, one-eyed prophet/general Titokowaru. However, once he lost the respect of his warriors (probably through an indiscretion with the wife of one of his warriors) the war too was lost.

East Coast war (1868–72) Te Kooti's holy guerrilla war: see the boxed text on p361.

---

swamp the few Maoris living in the South Island, but the fighting of the 1840s confirmed that the North Island at that time comprised a European fringe around an independent Maori heartland.

In the 1850s, settler population and aspirations grew, and fighting broke out again in 1860. The wars burned on sporadically until 1872 over much of the North Island. In the early years, a Maori nationalist organisation, the King Movement (see the boxed text on p219), was the backbone of resistance. In later years, some remarkable prophet-generals, notably Titokowaru and Te Kooti (see the boxed text on p361), took over. Most wars were small-scale, but the Waikato War of 1863–64 was not. Up to 5000 Maori resisted an invasion mounted by 20,000 imperial, colonial and 'friendly' Maori troops. This conflict, fought at the same time as the American Civil War, involved armoured steamships, ultra-modern heavy artillery, telegraph and 10 proud British regular regiments. Despite the odds, the Maoris won several battles, such as that at Gate Pa, near Tauranga, in 1864. But in the end they were ground down by European numbers and resources. Maori political, though not cultural, independence ebbed away in the last decades of the 19th century. It finally expired when police invaded its last sanctuary, the Urerewa Mountains, in 1916.

See the 'Land Wars' boxed text on p30 for the major areas of conflict.

WELFARE & WARFARE

From the 1850s to the 1880s, despite conflict with Maoris, the Pakeha economy boomed on the back of wool exports, gold rushes and massive overseas borrowing for development. The crash came in the 1880s, when NZ experienced its Long Depression. In 1890, the Liberals came to power, and stayed there until 1912, helped by a recovering economy. Their major leader was Richard John Seddon, 'King Dick, as I am usually known'. The Liberals were NZ's first organised political party, and the first of several governments to give NZ a reputation as 'the world's social laboratory'. NZ became the first country in the world to give women the vote in 1893, and introduced old age pensions in 1898. The Liberals also introduced a long-lasting system of industrial arbitration, but this was not enough to prevent bitter industrial unrest in 1912–13. A striker was killed by police at the gold mining town of Waihi in 1912, and riots and a gunfight took place between unionists and the forces of the law in Wellington the following year. This happened under the conservative 'Reform' government, which had replaced the Liberals in 1912. Reform remained in power until 1928, and later transformed itself into the National Party. Renewed depression struck in 1929, and the NZ experience of it was as grim as any. The derelict little farm houses still seen in rural areas often date from this era.

In 1935, a second reforming government took office: the First Labour Government, led by Michael Joseph Savage, easily NZ's favourite Australian. This government created NZ's pioneering version of the welfare state, and also took some independent initiatives in foreign policy. For a time, it was considered the most socialist government outside Soviet Russia. But, when the chips were down in Europe in 1939, Labour had little hesitation in backing Britain.

NZ had also backed Britain in the Boer War (1899–1902) and WWI (1914–18). Indeed, in the latter conflict, NZ's contribution was quite

1935–49	1977
First Labour government	First edition of Lonely Planet *New Zealand* published!

staggering for a country of just over one million people: about 100,000 NZ men served overseas, and close on 60,000 became casualties, mostly on the Western Front in France. You can count the cost in almost any little NZ town. A central square or park will contain a memorial lined with names – more for WWI than WWII. Even in WWII, however, NZ did its share of fighting: a hundred thousand or so New Zealanders fought in Europe and the Middle East, while a hundred thousand or so Americans arrived from 1942 to protect NZ from the Japanese. NZ, a peaceful-seeming country, has spent much of its history at war. In the 19th century it fought at home; in the 20th, overseas.

BETTER BRITONS?

British visitors have long found NZ hauntingly familiar. This is not simply a matter of the British and Irish origin of most Pakeha. It also stems from the tightening of NZ links with Britain from 1882, when refrigerated cargoes of food were first shipped to London. By the 1930s, 100 giant ships carried frozen meat, cheese and butter, as well as wool, on regular voyages taking about five weeks one way. The NZ economy adapted to the feeding of London, and cultural links were also enhanced. NZ children studied British history and literature, not their own. NZ's leading scientists and writers, such as Ernest Rutherford and Katherine Mansfield (see the boxed text, p391), gravitated naturally to Britain. This tight relationship has been described as 'recolonial', but it is a mistake to see NZ as an exploited colony. Average living standards in NZ were normally better than in Britain, as were the welfare and lower-level education systems. New Zealanders had access to British markets and culture, and they contributed their share to the latter as equals. The list of 'British' writers, academics, scientists, military leaders, publishers and the like who were actually New Zealanders is long. Indeed, New Zealanders, especially in war and sport, sometimes saw themselves as a superior version of the British – the Better Britons of the south. The NZ-London relationship was rather like that of the American Midwest and New York.

'Recolonial' NZ prided itself, with some justice, on its affluence, equality and social harmony. But it was also conformist, even puritanical. Until the 1950s, it was technically illegal for farmers to allow their cattle to mate in fields fronting public roads, for moral reasons. The 1954 American movie, *The Wild One*, was banned until 1977. Sunday newspapers were illegal until 1969, and full Sunday trading was not allowed until 1989. Licensed restaurants hardly existed in 1960, nor did supermarkets or television. Notoriously, from 1917 to 1967, pubs were obliged to shut at 6pm. Yet the puritanical society of Better Britons was never the whole story. Opposition to Sunday trading stemmed, not so much from belief in the sanctity of the Sabbath, but from the belief that workers should have weekends too. Six o'clock closing was a standing joke in rural areas, notably the marvellously idiosyncratic region of South Island's west coast. There was always something of a Kiwi counter-culture, even before imported counter-cultures took root from the 1960s.

There were also developments in cultural nationalism, beginning in the 1930s but really flowering from the 1970s. Writers, artists and filmmakers were by no means the only people who 'came out' in that era.

DID YOU KNOW?

Travellers can stay in the former primary-school building in Havelock where NZ's Ernest Rutherford, the 'Father of the Atom', first studied.

1981	1985
Springbok rugby tour divides the nation	*Rainbow Warrior* sunk in Auckland harbour by French government agents

COMING IN, COMING OUT

The 'recolonial' system was shaken several times after 1935, but managed to survive until 1973, when Mother England ran off and joined the Franco-German commune now known as the EU. NZ was beginning to develop alternative markets to Britain, and alternative exports to wool, meat and dairy products. Wide-bodied jet aircraft were allowing the world and NZ to visit each other on an increasing scale. NZ had only 36,000 tourists in 1960, compared with over two million a year now. Women were beginning to penetrate first the upper reaches of the workforce and then the political sphere. Gays came out of the closet, despite vigorous efforts by moral conservatives to push them back in. University-educated youths were becoming more numerous and more assertive.

From 1945, Maoris experienced both a population explosion and massive urbanisation. In 1936, Maoris were 17% urban and 83% rural. Fifty years later, these proportions had reversed. The immigration gates, which until 1960 were pretty much labelled 'whites only', widened, first to allow in Pacific Islanders for their labour, and then to allow in (East) Asians for their money. These transitions would have generated major socio-economic change whatever happened in politics. But most New Zealanders associate the country's recent 'Big Shift' with the politics of 1984.

In 1984, NZ's third great reforming government was elected – the Fourth Labour government led nominally by David Lange and in fact by Roger Douglas, the Minister of Finance. This government adopted an anti-nuclear foreign policy, delighting the left, and a more-market economic policy, delighting the right. NZ's numerous economic controls were dismantled with breakneck speed. Social restrictions were removed almost as fast as economic ones – the pubs still closed at six, but am, not pm. Middle NZ was uneasy about the anti-nuclear policy, which threatened NZ's Anzus alliance with Australia and the USA. But in 1985, French spies sank the anti-nuclear protest ship *Rainbow Warrior* (see the boxed text on p171) in Auckland Harbour, killing one crewman. The lukewarm American condemnation of the French act brought middle NZ in behind the anti-nuclear policy, which became associated with national independence. Other New Zealanders were uneasy about the more-market economic policy, but failed to come up with a convincing alternative. Revelling in their new freedom, NZ investors engaged in a frenzy of speculation, and suffered even more than the rest of the world from the economic crash of 1987.

The economy remained fairly stagnant until the late 1990s, when a recovery began. In politics, a National (conservative) government replaced Labour in 1990, and introduced proportional representation in 1996. A Labour government (now technically a Labour-led coalition), led by Helen Clark, returned to office in 1999, and was re-elected in 2002.

The early 21st century is an interesting time for NZ. Like NZ food and wine, film and literature are flowering as never before, and the new ethnic mix is creating something very special in popular music. There are continuities, however – the pub, the sports ground, the quarter-acre section, the bush, the beach and the bach – and they too are part of the reason people like to come here. Realising that NZ has a great culture, and an intriguing history, as well as a great natural environment, will double the bang for your buck.

INTERNET RESOURCES

www.nzhistory.net.nz
Ministry for Culture & Heritage's history resource

www.dnzb.govt.nz
Dictionary of NZ Biography

www.teara.govt.nz
Te Ara online encyclopedia

1992

Government begins reparations for land confiscated in the Land Wars of 1844–72

2004

Lord of the Rings: The Return of the King wins 'best film' at the Oscars

The Culture
Russell Brown

NATIONAL IDENTITY

Russell Brown is one of New Zealand's most prolific journalists. He hosts National Radio's weekly Mediawatch programme and the Wednesday Wire on 95bFM, writes on a variety of issues for the *Listener* and *Unlimited* magazines, and keeps a popular weblog at publicaddress.net. He lives in Auckland's Pt Chevalier with his family.

'So, what do you think of New Zealand?'… That, by tradition, is the question that visitors, especially important ones, were once asked within an hour of disembarking in NZ. Sometimes they might be granted an entire day's research before being asked to pronounce, but asked they would be. The question – composed equally of great pride and creeping doubt – was symbolic of the national consciousness.

When George Bernard Shaw visited for four weeks in 1934, he was deluged with what-do-you-think-of questions from newspaper reporters the length of the country. Although he never saw fit to write a word about NZ, his answers to those newspaper questions were collected and reprinted as *What I Saw in New Zealand: the Newspaper Utterances of George Bernard Shaw in New Zealand*. Yes, people really were that keen for vindication.

Other visitors were willing to pronounce in print, including the British Liberal MP, David Goldblatt, who came to NZ to convalesce from a heart attack in 1955, became fascinated with the place and wrote an intriguing and prescient little book called *Democracy At Ease: a New Zealand Profile*.

Goldblatt found New Zealanders a blithe people; kind, prosperous, fond of machines, frequently devoid of theory. In 'a land in which the practice of neighbourliness is most strongly developed', no one went wanting, yet few seemed to aspire. He admired the country's education system and its newspapers, despaired of its tariffs and barriers and wondered at laws that amounted to 'the complete control of the individual by the government'.

He was far from the first visitor to muse about NZ's contradictions – the American academic Leslie Lipson, who weathered the WWII years at Wellington's Victoria University, admired NZ's 'passion for social justice' but fretted about its 'restraint on talent' and 'lack of cultural achievement'.

For the *bon vivant* Goldblatt, the attitude to food and drink was all too telling. Apart from one visit to a clandestine European-style restaurant in Auckland, where the bottles were hidden under tables, he found only 'the plain fare and even plainer fetch and carry of the normal feeding machine of this country' and shops catering 'in the same pedestrian fashion for a people never fastidious – the same again is the order of the day'.

Thus, a people with access to some of the best fresh ingredients on earth tended to boil everything to death. A nation strewn almost its entire length with excellent microclimates for viticulture produced only fortified plonk. Material comfort was valued, but was a plain thing indeed.

It took New Zealanders a quarter of a century more to shuck 'the same dull sandwiches', and embrace a national awareness – and, as Goldblatt correctly anticipated, it took 'hazards and misfortunes' to spur the 'divine discontent' for change.

But when it did happen, it *really* happened. Modern NZ culture pivots on a few years in the early 1980s. First, the unquestioned primacy of rugby football as a source of social cohesion (which rivalled the country's commitment to the two world wars as a foundation of nation-building) was stripped away when tens of thousands of New Zealanders took to the streets to protest a tour by the South African rugby side in 1981. They held that the politics of apartheid not only had a place in sport, they trumped it.

The country was starkly divided; there were riots in Paradise. The mark is still strong enough that most New Zealanders over 30 will recognise the simple phrase 'The Tour' or even just '1981' as referring to those events.

The tour protests both harnessed and nourished a political and cultural renaissance among the country's native people, the Maori, which had already been rolling for a decade. Three years later, that renaissance found its mark, when a reforming Labour government gave statutory teeth to the Waitangi Tribunal, an agency that has since guided a process of land return, compensation for past wrongs and interpretation of the Treaty of Waitangi – the 160-year-old compact between Maoris and the Crown – as a living document.

New Zealand's fondness for social experiment also came roaring back in 1984, this time to blast away the accretions of the decades since the democracy was first constructed. The bloated public sector was slashed with sweeping privatisations, regulation was removed from many sectors, trade barriers dismantled.

If there is broad agreement that the economy had to be restructured, the reforms remain controversial. The old social guarantees no longer apply: there is poverty in NZ, and South Auckland sees Third World diseases such as tuberculosis. And yet there is a dynamism about NZ that was rare in the 'golden weather' years before the reforms. New Zealand farmers take on the world without the massive subsidies of yore, and Wellington's inner city – once virtually closed after dark by oppressive licensing laws – now thrives with great bars and restaurants.

As with the economic reforms, the 'Treaty process' of redress and reconciliation with Maoris makes some New Zealanders uneasy more in their uncertainty about its extent than that it has happened at all. A court decision suggesting that some Maoris might have unforeseen traditional rights to stretches of the country's seabed and foreshore (not the beaches themselves, but the area from the high tide outwards) hit a particularly raw nerve. Although its basis in law proved to be shaky, the assumption had long been that access to the beach was a NZ birthright. The conservative National Party, ailing in Opposition, tapped into public unease over this new and unexpected dimension to the Treaty process, claiming the country was moving towards 'separatism' – and shot up in the opinion polls. The Labour government, spooked by the public response, passed a law that confirmed the seabed and foreshore in Crown (public) ownership but offered Maori groups the chance to explore their 'customary rights' to places they had traditionally used. Many Maoris, feeling they had been denied due process, were angry, and a *hikoi* (march) of 15,000 protested at Parliament, amid speculation that political allegiances with Maoris were being re-drawn.

And yet, for all the change, key elements of the NZ identity are an unbroken thread. If it can hardly be claimed that this is a country where all are equal, fortune is still a matter of economics rather than class. If you are well served in a restaurant or shop, it will be out of politeness or pride in the job, rather than servility.

You might on your travels hear the phrase 'number-eight wire' and wonder what on earth it means. It's a catchphrase New Zealanders still repeat to themselves to encapsulate a national myth: that NZ's isolation and its pioneer stock created a culture in which ingenuity allowed problems to be solved and tools to be built from scratch. A NZ farmer, it was said, could solve pretty much any problem with a piece of number-eight wire (the gauge used for fencing on farms).

It's actually largely true – NZ farms are full of NZ inventions. And in a wider sense, New Zealanders have always operated best at the intersection of practicality and creativity, as designers rather than artists.

One reason big offshore film and TV producers bring their projects here – apart from the more modest costs and huge variety of locations –

'New Zealanders have operated best at the intersection of practicality and creativity, as designers rather than artists' is that they like the can-do attitude and ability to work to a goal of NZ technical crews. Many more New Zealanders have worked as managers, roadies, or chefs for famous recording artists (everyone from Led Zeppelin and U2 to Madonna) than have enjoyed the spotlight themselves.

Although the national anthem, *God Defend New Zealand*, is an appeal to the Almighty, and Parliament begins every day with prayers, New Zealanders are not a particularly pious people – far less so, according to polls, than Australians. A New Zealander is more likely to be spiritually fulfilled in the outdoors than in church. The land and sea were spiritual constants in pre-European Maori culture and they are scarcely less so today.

This can be seen in the work of another major artist, the late Colin McCahon, which can be found in the major public galleries. His paintings might seem inscrutable, even forbidding, to the visitor, but, even where McCahon lurched into Catholic mysticism or quoted screeds from the *Bible*, his spirituality was rooted in geography. His bleak, brooding landscapes evoke the sheer power of NZ's terrain.

'The land and sea were spiritual constants in pre-European Maori culture and they are scarcely less so today'

But McCahon's work is also riven with doubt. And culturally speaking, doubt is what separates New Zealanders from the Australians, makes them less likely to wave the flag, less confident, but also more subtle, more measured and in some ways more interesting.

New Zealand's cultural development was stultified for decades by the way it was walled off from the outside world. That is no longer the case. New cultures are flowing in and becoming established. Born and bred Kiwis – always great travellers, but now more inclined to return to the nest – adopt the best of what they see elsewhere. A 54-page feature in *Time* magazine in 2003 hailed what the magazine saw as a new determination among New Zealanders to seek their destinies at home rather than abroad. Perhaps Lipson's 'restraint on talent' has finally eased.

So what, as diversity grows, will remain central to the NZ cultural identity? It's instructive here to look at a failed project. Eddie Rayner, a former member of NZ's most celebrated pop group, Split Enz, led a project several years ago to devise a new national anthem to replace *God Defend New Zealand*, which is not greatly loved by New Zealanders. The song, *This Land*, was written and recorded, but did not displace the incumbent. It's pretty hard to change anthems.

And yet Rayner's explanation of the new song's theme still resonates. He and his collaborators had looked at ideas of culture, race, patriotism, history – all of them were not quite right. The one thing, they decided, on which everyone could agree, and which united all New Zealanders, was the land. And it seems likely that for future New Zealanders, it will be a defining belief that it is the land – moody, beautiful, endlessly varied – to which they belong, rather than the reverse.

LIFESTYLE

For most of its history, NZ's small population and plentiful land has seen its people live in stand-alone houses on large, green sections. And while that's still the rule, for a number of reasons it has started to change.

In Auckland, concern about suburban sprawl and poor public transport, and the gentrification of once-poor inner-city suburbs, has seen a boom in terraced housing and apartments, either in the central city or on its fringes. As immigration-fuelled population growth continues to put pressure on space, more Auckland citizens are learning to do without the birthright of a back yard.

Wellington's inner-city boom is slightly different. There, as the public service has shrunk and large companies have moved their head offices away, old office buildings and warehouses have been converted for apartment living.

At the same time, a parallel trend has seen a rush to the coastlines, and to beautiful areas such as Nelson, at the top of the South Island, where property values have rocketed and orchards have been ploughed under to make way for more housing. In the process, an icon of the Kiwi lifestyle, the bach (pronounced 'batch') – a rough beach house, often passed down through families – has begun to disappear. Many New Zealanders feel this as a loss, especially when the land goes to foreign buyers, and the fear that coastal land is getting beyond the reach of ordinary families is a significant political issue.

The growth in economic inequality in recent decades has seen a serious problem with overcrowding in a few poor urban areas, such as South Auckland. Two or three families can share a single house, with attendant public health problems. A partial return to the public housing policies that created a chunk of the country's current housing stock aims to address this problem.

Family trends, meanwhile, are similar to those in other Western countries: New Zealanders are marrying later – the median age for marriage has increased from just over 20 to about 30 years of age in the last 20 years – or not marrying at all. For those under 25 years of age, de facto unions are now more common than formal marriage, and about a third of all people between the ages of 15 and 44 who are living in partnerships are not legally married. About 20,000 couples still get married every year, and half that many get divorced.

Law changes in recent years have aimed to extend matrimonial property principles to unmarried couples, including same-sex couples. The growth in the number of sole-parent families (which tend to be poorer than two-parent households) has not been without controversy, but the majority of NZ children are still raised in the traditional family unit.

As regards wealth, NZ sits 21st among the 30 OECD countries on a measure of GDP per head in terms of 'purchasing power parity', indicating that its people are nearly a third less affluent than those of Canada or Ireland, or roughly as wealthy as the average Spaniard.

Average weekly household income is in excess of $1000, but wealth is far less evenly spread than it was 25 years ago – some households get by on half or less of that figure.

New Zealand's GDP growth (still driven largely by farm incomes) has outperformed that of the rest of the OECD in the last few years, and consumers have been in a fairly buoyant mood. The proportion of New Zealanders earning $60,000 per annum doubled from 5% to 10% between late 1999 and 2003. The wealthiest region is Wellington, where one in 25 of income earners reaps more than $100,000 per annum.

New Zealand's geographical isolation means that young New Zealanders in particular have for some time been highly mobile – 'OE' (overseas experience) is still considered a rite of passage, but the primary destination has, in recent years, become Australia rather than Britain. In a notable development the 'brain drain' that has persisted for much of the country's history has recently been reversed, but it remains to be seen whether this trend will persist.

Although incomes are lower in NZ, returning expats seem to be attracted by the lifestyle. An international survey in 2003 named Auckland as the fifth-best city in the world for quality of life, rating the city highly for recreational opportunities and quality of housing and public services, less so for its overstretched transport system.

'Overseas experience is still considered a rite of passage, but the primary destination has become Australia rather than Britain'

Much of New Zealanders' leisure time has traditionally been spent outdoors. About two-thirds of New Zealanders list walking and gardening among their leisure pursuits, around 40% enjoy swimming at some point every year, and more than a quarter go fishing. Access to beaches and wilderness areas continues to be regarded as an essential part of their heritage.

The old image of life in NZ as a cultural desert no longer applies. A recent government survey on cultural activities found that 1.2 million people, or more than a third of adult New Zealanders, had bought a book in the previous month – making reading the nation's most popular cultural activity – and about the same number had used a library or purchased recorded music, with video and DVD hire and cinema attendance not far behind.

Over the past year, just over a million people had attended a live popular music performance, and 750,000 had been to the theatre, and more than half a million had visited a *marae*. Wellingtonians' claim to be the country's most culturally active people was also borne out.

DEMOGRAPHICS & CULTURES

There are just over four million resident New Zealanders, and almost one in three of them now live in the largest city, Auckland, where growth has been fuelled both by a 'drift north' that has been going on for half a century, and more recent waves of immigration. The general drift to the cities means that urban areas now account for 72% of the population.

Auckland is effectively the capital of the South Pacific, and is home to more Pacific Islanders now than the Pacific Island nations themselves. People of Pacific Island heritage make up about 6% of the population.

Auckland has also been the prime destination for ethnic Chinese since immigration rules were relaxed in 1987. While many (East) Asian immigrants have chosen to cluster in Auckland's distant eastern suburbs, visitors are often startled by the 'Asianisation' of its central city, where thousands of Asian students reside, either studying at Auckland University, learning English, or both.

Occasional incidents involving Asians – usually Asian-on-Asian crimes such as kidnapping or driving offences – have added to disquiet about Asian immigration in some parts of the country. But recent opinion polls indicate that most Aucklanders tend to value the contribution of new migrants. Now, more than 13% of Aucklanders are Asian and 6% of these are Chinese. About 20% of Auckland Chinese were born in NZ.

The Maori population was somewhere between 100,000 and 200,000 at the time of first European contact 200 years ago. Disease and warfare subsequently brought the population near to collapse, but a high birth rate now sees about 15% of New Zealanders identify as Maori, and that proportion is likely to grow.

Maori is, along with English, an official language, and many Maoris believe the clear implication of the Treaty of Waitangi is one of a partnership with the Crown, representing the 80% of New Zealanders who are 'Pakeha', or of European heritage – forging a bicultural nation.

Yet somewhere within that bicultural nation, room will have to be found to accommodate the diversity, the developing multiculturalism of NZ. How will the strong claim of a cultural stake by the growing Pacific population be accommodated in coming years? The country has, over the years, absorbed and assimilated earlier waves of migrants – English, Dutch, Polynesian – but will it also do so with the more varied and, to some, exotic cultures now taking root? Will 'new' New Zealanders settle more widely, or stay in the urban north?

Department of Conservation www.doc.govt.nz 'DOC' as it is universally known, states its mission thus: 'To conserve NZ's natural and historic heritage for all to enjoy now and in the future.' Its site has a wealth of information on the things that make NZ what it is.

NZ never had an official 'white' immigration policy as Australia did, but its people for decades tended to regard it as an outpost of Britain. In the years to come, other influences – NZ's role in the Pacific, its burgeoning economic links to Asia, its offering of sanctuary to refugees – will now inevitably help shape what it is to be a New Zealander.

SPORT

New Zealanders not only watch sport, they play it: and although golf can claim more participants than any other sport, no one doubts that the national game is rugby union. The game is interwoven with NZ's history and culture, and the national side, the All Blacks, have, even in the professional era, an almost mythical status.

The All Blacks are, however, the subject of extraordinary expectations; it frequently seems that nothing less than 100% success will satisfy the public. When the All Blacks dip out of the Rugby World Cup at semi-final stage (as they have done no fewer than three times) there is national mourning.

Below top international level, the Super 12 competition with teams from Australia and South Africa offers the world's best rugby, although local purists still prefer the National Provincial Championship, which takes place later in the winter.

For all rugby's influence on the culture, don't go along to a game expecting to be caught up in an orgy of noise and cheering. Rugby crowds at Auckland's Eden Park (p125) are as restrained as their teams are cavalier, but they get noisier as you head south. Fans at Canterbury's excellent Jade Stadium (p521) are reputed to be most one-eyed in the land.

Auckland is home to the NZ Warriors rugby league team, which plays in the Australian NRL (National Rugby League). Supporting the Warriors has become a way into the culture for South Auckland immigrant communities, and a Warriors home game at Ericsson Stadium (p125) is a noisy spectacle. The on-field action, however, is not for the faint of heart.

You need to go to the other end of the country to find the heartland of netball, the leading winter sport for women (and the one in which the national team, the Silver Ferns, perpetually vies for world supremacy with the Australians). The Invercargill-based Southern Sting (p635) attracts a fanatical following from the local community – and repay the support by winning most of the time.

Cricket is the established summer team sport, and the State Shield (one-day) and State Championship provincial competitions take place alongside international matches involving the national side, the Black Caps, through the summer months. Wellington's Basin Reserve (p390) is the last sole-use test cricket venue in the main centres (and only a few minutes' walk from the bars and restaurants of Courtenay Place) and New Plymouth's Pukekura Park (p250) is simply one of the prettiest cricket grounds in the world.

MEDIA

Almost all NZ cities have their own morning newspapers, sometimes co-existing with the likes of the Auckland-based *New Zealand Herald*, which cover wider regions, and they're fairly good.

The magazine market is more varied, and dominated by independent publishers. The *Listener*, the country's leading left-liberal periodical, is published weekly and also offers TV and radio listings. Auckland's own magazine, *Metro*, is a good-looking guide to the style of the city, while Wellington has the hipper, more streety, *Staple* magazine. *Cuisine* is a sleek, popular and authoritative guide to food and wine.

Cycling NZ
www.cyclingnz.com
/cnz_content.phtml
A big site with downloadable maps, links and club contact information.

NZXsports.com
nzxsports.com
An award-winning site that offers a way into surf and ski information, webcams and many other land and water-based sports. Highly recommended.

Sports.co.nz
www.sports.co.nz
Links to everything.

Free-to-air TV is dominated by the two publicly owned Television New Zealand channels (TV One and TV2), versus the Canadian-owned TV3 and its sibling music channel C4. Regional TV struggles, but is stronger on the South Island, where Nelson's Mainland TV and Invercargill's Southland TV are part of their communities. The country's only access TV station, Triangle, reflects Auckland's cultural and ethnic diversity.

The only TV show you really need to know about is the nightly national soap, *Shortland Street*, a hospital drama which has had its ups and downs over the years, but often does an uncanny job of anticipating the zeitgeist.

Radio Sport carries one of the true sounds of the NZ summer: cricket commentaries. The public broadcaster, Radio New Zealand, is based in Wellington: its flagship, National Radio, offers strong news and feature programming and is available nationwide.

The network of student stations, the bNet, offers an engaging and adventurous alternative (they're also the best place to hear about local gigs), and the most sophisticated of the stations, Auckland's 95bFM, is surprisingly influential.

There is also a nationwide network of *iwi* (tribal) stations, some of which, including Waikato's Radio Tainui, offer welcome respite from the commercial networks – others, such as Auckland's Mai FM, take on the commercial broadcasters at their own game. Also worth noting are the national Pacific Island station Niu FM and the dance station, George FM, which can be heard in central Auckland and Queenstown.

RELIGION

Reflecting its English heritage, NZ is nominally of the Anglican-Protestant denomination, and where religion has a place in public affairs, it will be of that flavour. The Catholic church claims about 470,000 adherents to the Anglican church's 630,000.

But the number of people actively identifying with the major Christian denominations has been falling, and a 1998 survey indicated that fewer than a third of New Zealanders were 'certain' of a belief in God. Census figures show that more than a quarter of New Zealanders claim no religious affiliation. Immigrants have brought their faiths with them, but religions such as Islam and Hinduism account for less than 1% of the population.

New Pentecostal churches have grown strongly in the past decade, and churchgoing remains strong in the Pacific Island communities. Maori spirituality has historically been fused with Christianity in messianic movements such as Ratana and Ringatu, but is increasingly expressed in its own right – most notably when a planned motorway route in Waikato was held up because a local tribe said it disturbed a *taniwha* (a kind of river dragon).

WOMEN IN NEW ZEALAND

Although NZ has prided itself on being the first country in the world, in 1893, to introduce universal suffrage, for many years the real role for women in public life was modest.

That can hardly be said now, with three of the most important roles in civil society – prime minister, governor general and chief justice – filled by women; Helen Clark, Dame Sylvia Cartwright and Dame Sian Elias respectively. The country's second-largest company, Telecom NZ, is also steered by a woman, Theresa Gattung.

Yet, even with the presence of a Ministry of Women's Affairs, some benefits have been slower to come to ordinary NZ women: paid parental leave was only instituted in 2002, for example. As in most other countries, women's wages tend to be lower than men's, although the gap is closing.

There is a very strong tradition of women's sport, and the world-champion Silver Ferns netball side and individuals such as Olympic boardsailor Barbara Kendall are household names. There is even a women's national rugby side, the Black Ferns, which labours under the same expectations as the All Blacks – the team must beat all comers, all the time – albeit with a much lower profile.

Nowhere is women's contribution to NZ stronger than in the arts and creative industries. Niki Caro, director of *Whale Rider*, is but one in a line of accomplished film-makers that includes directors Jane Campion (*The Piano, In the Cut*), Christine Jeffs (*Rain, Sylvia*) and Gillian Ashurst (*Snakeskin*), Peter Jackson's longtime collaborator Fran Walsh and top-flight costume designer Ngila Dickson, and actors Anna Paquin, Kerry Fox and Lucy (*Xena*) Lawless. In literature, Janet Frame, Fiona Kidman, Elizabeth Knox, and Stephanie Johnson enjoy a stature equal to or greater than their male counterparts.

ARTS
Literature
New Zealand literature was dominated for a long time by an important nationalist movement that arose in the 1930s to address the challenge of defining independence from the 'mother country', Britain, whose identity had been adopted virtually by proxy until then.

Some writers who appeared then – especially the poets Allen Curnow, Denis Glover, ARD Fairburn – RAK Mason – became commanding figures in the definition of a new culture, and were still around in the 1950s to be part of what the country's most prominent historian, Keith Sinclair (himself a poet), called the time 'when the NZ intellect and imagination came alive'.

Katherine Mansfield's work began a NZ tradition in short fiction, and for years the standard was carried by novelist Janet Frame, whose dramatic life was depicted in Jane Campion's film of her autobiography, *An Angel at My Table*. A new era of international recognition began in 1985 when Keri Hulme's haunting *The Bone People* won a Booker Prize (the world is still waiting for the follow-up, *Bait*).

The centre of NZ's literary universe now is undoubtedly Bill Manhire's creative-writing course at Victoria University of Wellington, which has produced most of the country's most prominent new writers in the past decade, including novelists Catherine Chidgey, Elizabeth Knox (pick up *The Vintner's Luck*, avoid *Black Oxen*), and Emily Perkins, and playwrights and screenwriters Anthony McCarten and Duncan Sarkies. Chidgey was recently named the country's best novelist under 40, and her *In a Fishbone Church* is recommended.

Manhire, a poet himself, also compiled *100 NZ Poems*, which is widely regarded as the best anthology of NZ poetry, and with Marion McLeod, *The New Zealand Short Story Collection*.

But there are also writers who, consciously or not, buck the introspective style often associated with the Manhire school. Auckland-based Chad Taylor writes tight, spare, noir fiction that is urban in character yet defiantly indigenous. His *Electric* offers a seamy view of Auckland that might surprise visitors.

Much of the best nonfiction of recent years has concerned NZ history: Philip Temple's *A Sort of Conscience* (about the Wakefields, the family that drove the colonisation of NZ), the late Michael King's hugely popular *Penguin History of New Zealand* and James Belich's more academic *Making Peoples* are all fine works.

Architecture in NZ
user.chollian.net
/~ucnet2001/
A general architectural history site, with good photos and information about old churches of interest.

NZ literary links
http://www.piperpat.co
.nz/nz/society/writing.html
NZ Literary Tourism
www.bookcouncil.org.nz
/littourism/indexliterary
tourism.htm

Cinema

The commanding figure in NZ cinema is, without doubt, the director and screenwriter Peter Jackson, whose successful completion of the *Lord of the Rings* trilogy was not only a boon to the local industry but a significant morale boost to the country as a whole.

With his world-leading Weta post-production facility in Wellington firmly established, Jackson seems set to dominate the local industry for decades yet. His earlier works, including the shoestring splatter

NEW ZEALAND'S *LORD OF THE RINGS* Errol Hunt

Unless you've been living in a hole in the ground, you must have heard about New Zealand's Oscar-winning director, Peter Jackson, and his trilogy of films: *Lord of the Rings*: *Fellowship of the Ring* (2001), *Two Towers* (2002) and *The Return of the King* (2003).

From Exploding Sheep to Middle-Earth

Peter Jackson was a minor hero to NZ's small film industry long before *Rings*. From his very first film, *Bad Taste*, back in 1987, it was obvious that Jackson was a unique talent (even if some people didn't appreciate the exploding sheep). *Bad Taste* was followed by *Meet the Feebles* (1989), an hilarious Muppets-on-acid flick, and an even sicker splatter movie, *Brain Dead* (1992). Then there were two slightly-more-mainstream, but just as creative, films: *Heavenly Creatures* (1994) and *Frighteners* (1996), the success of which led to Jackson being awarded the *Lord of the Rings* contract in 1997.

One Movie to Rule Them All...

Once his Hollywood backers had given him the nod to film Tolkien's classic, Jackson endeared himself immediately to four million New Zealanders by insisting stubbornly that the films be shot and produced here in NZ. He also endeared himself to many million Tolkien fans worldwide by insisting just as stubbornly that the film be made in three parts (not one, as the studio preferred), as intended by the revered professor himself. The three films were filmed simultaneously over 16 months, with post-production of each film progressing separately after that.

Many of the crew (Kiwis and non-Kiwis alike) involved in the films were ardent Tolkien fans and the film-makers' attention to minor, often entirely unnoticeable details was as high as Tolkien's himself: documentaries on the post-release DVDs show some of the effort behind the scenes. Being faithful to the story was also essential, although the screenwriting team did take a few tactical liberties with JRR's story. In the long run some hard-core fans may have been infuriated, but most agreed that the end result on film was magnificent.

NZ as a nation had no reservations: the country embraced Jackson and the *Rings* films with a passion. The country pretty much declared ownership of Jackson's trilogy, with the films a vehicle for national pride. The excitement really started when *Fellowship* was released in late 2001: Wellington was renamed Middle-earth for the week, a Minister for the *Rings* was named in the NZ government and Jackson was made a Companion of the New Zealand Order of Merit for his services in the film industry. The frenzy only increased for the second and third films, especially when the world premiere (*world* premiere!) of *The Return of the King* was held in Wellington in December 2003, and of course went on to win a record-equalling 11 Oscars.

The pride that Kiwis felt in the films was not misplaced – the *Rings* films were undeniably a product of NZ. There was all that magnificent local scenery for a start: nowhere else in the world, Jackson had argued, was a film maker going to find such diverse and spectacular landscapes in one small country (after *Fellowship*, Tourism New Zealand jokingly awarded NZ the Oscar for 'Best Supporting Country in a Motion Picture').

Jackson himself, scruffy, barefoot and unapologetically 'not Hollywood', is the very picture of a Kiwi lad. To hear Jackson's, and others', NZ accents on the Oscars stage bought tears to many a Kiwis' eye (actually the NZ accent brings tears to some eyes anyway).

of *Bad Taste* and the thoroughly scabrous *Meet the Feebles*, are worth seeking out.

Notwithstanding the scale and success of *Rings*, the status of NZ cinema remains a matter of keen debate. In his BBC-funded documentary, *Cinema of Unease*, NZ actor Sam Neill described the country's 'uniquely strange and dark film industry' producing bleak, haunted work. The *Listener*'s film critic, Philip Matthews, offered his own characterisation, based on three celebrated recent local productions: 'Between (Niki

Many, many other Kiwis contributed to the films' success: in all, about 2000 New Zealanders had full-time jobs working on the films, and that's in addition to all the 'extras' (15,000 of them, including a few hundred New Zealand Army personnel pressed into costume and drafted into battle scenes for *Fellowship*).

The effect of the *Rings* films was not only on national morale: the films' very-concrete effect on NZ's economy was enormous. Of the $650 million spent on making the films, much stayed in NZ. The film industry in particular has gone from strength to strength, with the filming of other Hollywood blockbusters, such as *The Last Samurai*, in part due to Jackson and the trilogy paving the way. The effect on tourism was even greater. At a time when world tourism was suffering, following the USA's 'War on Terror' and SARS, all three films sparked massive world-wide interest in the country of their origin and helped boost NZ's important tourism industry. *Rings* tourism, with travellers specifically coming to see the locations filmed, has become a significant industry.

Middle-Earth Tourism

If you're one of those travellers inspired to come down under by the scenery of the *Rings* movies, you won't be disappointed. Jackson's decision to film here in NZ wasn't mere patriotism. Nowhere else on earth will you find such wildly varied, unspoiled landscapes.

However if you've come seeking scenes of Middle-earth itself, you might be let down. Although filming occurred at over 150 separate locations, there's very little concrete *Rings* scenery left to see anywhere. The Department of Conservation, which administered the public lands on which Jackson filmed, insisted that all the sets be dismantled immediately afterwards and the land returned to its previous state, including in some cases the original plants being replanted!

You will doubtless recognise some places from the films, however. For example, Hobbiton (near Matamata, the Waikato; p233), Mount Doom (instantly recognisable as towering Ngauruhoe, Central Plateau; p284) or the Misty Mountains (the South Island's Southern Alps). And if you're in Wellington (p387), Twizel (p548) or Queenstown (p583) the information centre should be able to direct you to local *Rings* sites of interest. If you're serious about finding the exact spots where scenes were filmed, you should invest in Ian Brodie's comprehensive *The Lord of the Rings: Location Guidebook*, which includes instructions, and even GPS coordinates, for finding all the important scenes. Also check the Film New Zealand website (www.filmnz.com/middleearth), which has an interesting online location guide.

If you make it down to Jackson's home town, Wellington (aka 'Wellywood'), you might as well go see the films a second time (third time, fourth time...) at their spiritual home – the Embassy Theatre (p403) – where *The Return of the King's* world premiere was shown.

If armchair travelling will do, you could get a few old Jackson films out on video to fill rainy nights at backpacker hostels (let's face it – any trip to NZ involves a few rainy nights) looking for Jackson's own performances. He stars as the chainsaw-wielding (beardless) Derek and vomit-eating Robert the Alien in *Bad Taste*, and has cameos as the undertaker's assistant in *Brain Dead*, a derelict hobo outside a cinema in *Heavenly Creatures*, and a clumsy, chain-wearing biker in *Frighteners*. In the *Rings*' films, Jackson appears as a belching hobbit outside a pub in *Fellowship*, a stone-throwing fighter in the battle of Helms Deep in *Two Towers* and captain of the Corsairs in *The Return of the King*.

The NZ Film Archive
www.filmarchive.org.nz
A superb online resource,
lovingly curated.

'The Waiting Room'
www.listener.co.nz
/default,893,879,0.sm
Philip Matthews' essay
from the *Listener*.

Caro's) *Whale Rider*, (Christine Jeffs') *Rain* and *Lord of the Rings*, you can extract the qualities that our best films possess. Beyond slick technical accomplishment, all share a kind of land-mysticism, an innately supernatural sensibility.'

Most of the other high points of NZ cinema fall somewhere on the two men's thematic axes: the 1977 speculative political thriller *Sleeping Dogs* (starring Neill), which is credited with kick-starting local production; Geoff Murphy's vigorous 'Maori western' *Utu*; Roger Donaldson's man-on-the-edge domestic drama *Smash Palace* ('the ultimate 'unease' film', according to Matthews); Vincent Ward's haunting image of a young girl and nature, *Vigil*; the anarchic road movie *Goodbye Pork Pie*; Jane Campion's Oscar-winning *The Piano* (a tale of erotic longing that has since functioned as a postcard for its location on Karekare Beach); Lee Tamahori's graphic, jarring *Once Were Warriors*; and of course Jackson's own *Heavenly Creatures*. An industry that sometimes doubts its own existence has more than its share of over-achievers.

Music

Amplifier
www.amplifier.co.nz
Local music news, free
and paid downloads
(including video) and
more.

Capital Recordings
www.capitalrecordin
gs.co.nz

Festival Mushroom
Records
www.fmrecords.co.nz
Aussie-owned company
with a strong NZ roster,
including the Flying Nun
and Dirty Records labels.

Maorimusic.com
www.maorimusic.com
'From *haka* to hip-hop' –
you can try and buy here.

NewZealandMusic.com
nzmusic.com
Comprehensive news and
information, lots of free
downloads and some
very robust discussion
forums.

There has been music in NZ since the first human occupation, more than 800 years ago – song, dance, rhythm and melody are woven tightly into Maori culture – but it has never been stronger or more varied than it is now.

New Zealand music has been on a roll for the past few years, in large part because the environment has become more supportive: a voluntary local music quota agreed between the government and commercial radio broadcasters has been hugely influential. Less than a decade ago, locally produced music accounted for about 2% of commercial radio schedules – now in some cases, it's well over 20%. The perennial local heroes, the Finn brothers, of Split Enz and Crowded House, have a lot more company on the airwaves these days.

At the same time, the influence of Maori and Pacific Island artists has been growing. Contemporary Maori music is flourishing on its own terms, and several leading artists, including the very popular singer-songwriter Bic Runga, have Maori heritage.

But brown faces show up nowhere more prominently than in the country's burgeoning hip-hop scene. The country's most popular MC, Scribe, has topped the national album and singles charts at the same time and sold triple platinum.

Mareko (like Scribe, of Samoan heritage) has recorded with various American rap stars, and is backed by Dawn Raid, a remarkable South Auckland enterprise that encompasses a record label, a clothing factory, a community trust and even a barbershop. Clubs situated around Auckland's Karangahape Rd (p124) feature the top local DJs and MCs till late.

Auckland is also home to the garage-rock scene that provided a springboard for the D4 and the Datsuns, and while those two are generally touring elsewhere, you can catch the next wave of would-be's at the King's Arms (p124) and various other small, local bars. The same city spawned the respected drum-and-bass (D&B) crews Concord Dawn and Bulletproof: the basement club Fu, in Queen St, is the best place to catch D&B.

In Wellington, it's all about groove, and no one grooves more than Fat Freddy's Drop, a remarkable live act which merges jazzy flights of improvisation with the heartbeat of dub. The group's prime mover, Mu, pops up in a variety of other ventures, most of them through the prolific

TRY THESE FOR SIZE

- **Dimmer** *You've Got to Hear the Music* (FMR) Slinky, downbeat songs from the soul of indie legend Shayne Carter.
- **Fat Freddy's Drop** *Live at the Matterhorn* (Fat Freddy's Drop) Great live band, great live album.
- **Goldenhorse** *Riverhead* (Siren/EMI) Intriguing, artful and eclectic pop music.
- **Toni Huata** *Maori To* (WaaHuu Creations) Huata recorded and re-interpreted a batch of traditional Maori *waiata* (songs), most written by her grandfather. Gentle and authentic.
- **Katchafire** *Revival* (Mai Music) Bob Marley's sole NZ concert in 1978 had a profound impact on many Maori musicians, and Katchafire are unabashed about their dedication to reggae, Bob-style. They're also very popular.
- **Pacifier** *Live* (Warner Music) An in-concert catch-up of the best of the thunderous rock band formerly known as Shihad.
- **Bic Runga** *Beautiful Collision* (Sony Music) A Maori-Malaysian singer-songwriter who crafts resonant songs that have worked their way into the nation's heart.
- **Scribe** *The Crusader* (Dirty/FMR) Debut by the national rap kingpin. The ladies love him and the boys want to be him.
- **Various Artists** *Dub Combinations Vol 3* (Kog Transmissions) The dub sound of Aotearoa.
- **Various Artists** *Sideways Too* (Round Trip Mars) What goes on in bedroom studios: intriguing, endlessly varied Kiwi downbeat.
- **Various Artists** *Speed of Sound* (Flying Nun) A selection from the last few years' releases by the venerable but lively Flying Nun Records.

Capital Recordings. The central city has two very good venues: Bar Bodega (p403) and the Matterhorn (p402).

Flying Nun, the record label at the centre of a creative boom in the 1980s (and still a source of cult fascination for indie music buffs the world over) is under corporate ownership now, but still releasing records by both its established artists, and new acts such as the Mint Chicks.

In Dunedin, the Flying Nun label's original creative wellspring, the scruffy, arty, independent vibe is alive and well. The Arc café (p566), the city's leading live venue, is owned and operated by an arts trust. You might also check out Records Records (p561), in a row of terraced houses just up the hill from the Octagon, where owner-operator Roy Colbert has shaped the tastes of successive generations of local musicians. In Christchurch, home of the downbeat masters Salmonella Dub (very popular with students), the venue to check out is the Dux De Lux (p520) on the edge of the city's arts centre, which has been presenting live bands for decades.

Not all the great music venues are in the city: indeed, some of the best are in beautiful country settings. The Leigh Sawmill Café (p153), in Leigh, on the east coast north of Auckland, has bands and DJs throughout the summer, and its dub reggae evenings are the stuff of legend. A newer place on the opposite coast, by the Kaipara Harbour, is the Grand Hotel (p132) in Helensville, an old pub restored as a family-friendly venue. Lyttelton, Christchurch's port town, boasts the Wunderbar (p525), which hosts anything from poetry readings to drag acts. In January, some good touring bills pass through the popular beach resorts.

Noizyland
noizyland.com
Bustling and literate music news and information site with many useful links.

Real Groovy Records
www.realgroovy.co.nz
The online counterpart of Real Groovy's vast Auckland shop and smaller Wellington store. Both used and new stock are searchable via the site.

SmokeCDs
smokecds.com
Efficient and nicely priced online record store, with a big range of local sounds.

ART OUT THERE

Not all the best galleries are in the cities. The energetic **Govett-Brewster Art Gallery** (www .govettb.org.nz; p250) – home to the legacy of sculptor and film-maker Len Lye – is worth a visit to New Plymouth in itself, and Gore's **Eastern Southland Gallery** (p637) has an important and growing collection of works by Ralph Hotere, Rita Angus and others.

Visual Arts

It should not be surprising that in a nation so defined by its natural environment, landscape painting constitutes the first (post-European) body of art. John Gully and Petrus van der Velden were among those to arrive and paint memorable (if sometimes over-dramatised) depictions of the land. Their modern successor is Graham Sydney, whose ultra-realist depictions of the grand, wide lands of Central Otago are highly sought-after.

A little later, Charles Frederick Goldie painted a series of compelling, realist portraits of Maoris, who were feared to be a dying race. Debate over the political propriety of Goldie's work raged for years, but its value is widely accepted now: not least because the Maoris themselves generally acknowledge and value them as ancestral representations.

As was the case in literature, nationalism was a driving force in art in the 1930s and '40s, notably in the work of Toss Woollaston and Colin McCahon, whose work can be widely seen in NZ galleries, particularly Nelson's Suter Gallery (Woolaston; p444) and the Auckland Art Gallery (McCahon; p101).

Maori art has a distinctive visual style with well-developed motifs, and a few Pakeha artists have tried to incorporate and adopt it: the most notable being the cool modernism of the work of Gordon Walters and the more controversial pop-art approach of Dick Frizzell's Tiki series. Leading contemporary Maori artists such as Shane Cotton and Peter Robinson are, in turn worldly and (especially in Robinson's case) fond of political humour. The dean of modern Maori artists is undoubtedly Ralph Hotere, an heir to McCahon who lives and works near Dunedin. The Auckland Museum (p99) has an amazing collection of historical Maori and Pacific treasures.

Auckland Art Gallery
www.aucklandart
gallery.govt.nz

Auckland Museum
www.akmuseum.org.nz

Museum of New Zealand
Te Papa Tongarewa
www.tepapa.govt.nz

New Zealand Museums
Online (includes galleries)
www.nzmuseums.co.nz

The Suter Art Gallery
www.thesuter.org.nz

Maori Culture

MYTHOLOGY
In the Beginning...

In the beginning there was Ranginui (Sky Father) and Papatuanuku (Earth Mother), who were united. They bore many children, the most important of which were Tawhiri-matea (God Of Winds and Storms), Tangaroa (God of the Ocean), Tane-mahuta (God of the Forests), Haumia-tike-tike (God of Wild Foods), Rongo-matane (God of Peace and Cultivated Food) and Tu-matauenga (God of War and Humans).

After aeons of living in darkness, because their parents were so tightly joined together that no light came between them, the children of Ranginui and Papatuanuku could take it no longer – they wanted light! They debated what they should do and eventually decided they should separate their parents so that light could enter the world. Each tried in turn, and failed, to separate Ranginui and Papatuanuku. Finally it was Tane-mahuta's turn to try, and by pushing and straining with his shoulders to the ground and his feet to the sky, Tane finally succeeded in forcing his parents apart: light flooded into the world at last.

Because all the gods were male, a woman needed to be created in order that the earth be inhabited. After a few unsuccessful tries with immortals, Tane created the first woman, Hine-ahuone, out of soil and gave her *tihe mauriora* (breath of life). Hine-ahuone and Tane had a daughter Hine-titama (Dawn Maid), who Tane then married, thus ensuring the birth of humanity (much to the shame of Hine-titama when she eventually found out her husband and father were one and the same).

...And Then along Came Maui

A long time after the creation of the world there lived the demigod Maui, a figure who features in myths right across the Pacific, from New Zealand to the Solomon Islands to Hawaii. One story of his exploits in particular is known in almost all Polynesian cultures. It began one day when Maui, who lived in ancient Hawaiki, went out fishing with his five brothers...

The brothers paddled their canoes far out to sea, where Maui took out his magic fish-hook (the jawbone of his sorcerer grandmother), baited it with blood from his own nose, tied it to a strong rope and dropped it over the side of the canoe. Soon Maui caught an immense fish and, struggling mightily, pulled it up to the surface. This fish became the North Island of NZ, called Te Ika a Maui (The Fish of Maui) by the an-cient Maori. Wellington Harbour is the fish's mouth, the Taranaki and East Coast areas are its two fins, Lake Taupo is its heart and the Northland peninsula its tail. Mahia Peninsula in the Hawkes Bay region is Te Matau a Maui (The Fish-hook of Maui) – the magic hook with which he fished up the island.

Maui fishing New Zealand out of the ocean

WILHELM DITTMER, 1866–1909
ALEXANDER TURNBULL LIBRARY,
WELLINGTON, NZ.
REF NO PUBL-0088-049

The South Island was known as Te Waka o Maui (The Canoe of Maui), the canoe in which Maui was sitting when he caught the fish. Kaikoura Peninsula was where Maui braced his foot while hauling up the fish and Stewart Island was the anchor stone that held the canoe steady as he hauled in the giant fish.

TRIBAL SOCIETY

Maori society was (and to some degree, still is) tribal – Maoris refer to themselves in terms of their *iwi* (tribe), often named after an ancestor, for example, Ngati Kahungunu (descendants of the ancestor Kahungunu) or Ngapuhi (descendants of Puhi). Two or more *iwi* can be grouped into larger alliances by their descent from one *waka*, or migratory canoe. For example, the Waikato and Ngati Maniapoto tribes have traditionally been allied because of their common descent from those who arrived on the *Tainui* canoe.

Traditionally of more relevance than the *iwi* was the *whanau* (extended family groups) and the village structure based around the *marae* (literally, the flat area in front of a meeting house, but more often now used to refer to the entire complex of buildings).

'Traditional society was hierarchical, with positions of leadership largely hereditary, and almost always male'

Traditional society was hierarchical, with positions of leadership largely hereditary, and almost always male. The tribes were headed by an *ariki* (supreme chief) while *hapu* (sub-tribes) were led by a *rangatira* (local chief). Right down at the bottom of the pecking order were the *taurekareka* (slaves) taken from opposing tribes in battle.

Within each *hapu* there were clear lines of responsibility between chiefs, men, women and slaves as to which daily tasks they would perform. Men prepared the agricultural plots (chiefs participated in this also), but women did the planting; men fished in the open sea and dived for shellfish, and the women were allowed to bring food out to them; only slaves and women were allowed to cook, weave and make cloaks; and only men were allowed to go to war, build canoes, become tattooists or carvers.

Wairua (Spirituality)

Traditional Maori religion for the most part followed that of the other Polynesian cultures. This religion was complex, with a pantheon of gods representing the sea, sky, war, agriculture etc.

The *tohunga* (priests) could communicate with the gods and knew the rituals associated with offerings, but were also responsible for maintaining the history, genealogy, stories and songs of the tribe. The *tohunga* were not just priests, but included many different experts; such as tattooists, woodcarvers and shipwrights.

IWI ON THE WEB

It's a sign of the incorporation of Maori society into modern NZ that one of the second-level Internet domain names in NZ (the same level as other countries' .com for commercial) is .iwi, for tribal websites:

Arawa (www.tearawa.iwi.nz) Rotorua *iwi*; 39,000 members.

Ngai Tahu (www.ngaitahu.iwi.nz) The main South Island *iwi*; over 30,000 members.

Ngapuhi (www.ngapuhi.iwi.nz) Northland *iwi* (tribe) has its main *marae* (tribal home) at Waitangi (p176); nearly 100,000 members.

Ngati Porou (www.ngatiporou.iwi.nz) East Cape, *iwi* represented in the film, *Whale Rider*; 55,000 members.

Waikato (www.waikato.iwi.nz) The *iwi* of the Maori King movement (p219) is based in Turangawaewae (p220); 25,000 members.

KO TONGARIRO TE MAUNGA

In this famous 1856 quote, Te Heuheu Iwikau, the hereditary *ariki* (high chief) of the Tuwharetoa tribe established his credentials by identifying himself and his tribe with his mountain and his 'sea':
Ko Tongariro te maunga, ko Taupo te moana, ko Ngati Tuwharetoa te iwi, ko Te Heuheu te tangata
'Tongariro is the mountain, (Lake) Taupo is the sea, Ngati Tuwharetoa is the tribe, Te Heuheu is the person'.

Essential to Maori beliefs and society were the notions of *tapu* (complex rules of sacredness and/or prohibition) and *mana* (personal spiritual power or prestige).

Tapu applied to sacred and/or forbidden objects, such as sacred ground or a chief's possessions, and also to actions prohibited by the tribe. Its application could be temporary or permanent; canoe builders could be made *tapu* in a special ceremony prior to commencing work, and war parties would be given a blood *tapu*, which was removed when they returned to their families.

Mana was possessed by chiefs (both via their ancestors and via deeds of their own) and from them it flowed through to their tribe. *Mana* could be lost – a chief captured in battle would lose his own *mana*, as well as that of his tribe. *Mana* could also be gained – the warrior who killed the first enemy in a battle would attain considerable *mana*.

Whenua (Land)

Geographical features such as *maunga* (mountains) and *awa* (rivers) often delineated tribal boundaries, and were an important genealogical indicator.

Some *maunga* were personified and, even today, each tribe has one or more sacred *maunga*. Tribal *whakapapa* (oral genealogies) always referred to the names of mountains, as they were an important part of the social grid (see the boxed text above).

On Pakeha (European) settlement, the government assigned European names to many *maunga* in an almost deliberate attempt to tame the 'wilderness'. This practice was more prevalent in areas with small Maori

Maori survivors of war

J COWAN, CIRCA 1914
ALEXANDER TURNBULL LIBRARY,
WELLINGTON, NZ, REF NO 1/1-017975

populations (such as the South Island), while locations in heartland Maori regions like King Country, Te Urewera and Taupo have retained their original Maori names.

Tipuna (Ancestors)

The proper reverence for ancestors was important to the ancient Maori and, in the absence of a written language, long *whakapapa* (oral genealogies), stretching back hundreds of years to people who arrived by *waka* from Hawaiki, were committed to memory. *Whakapapa* defined ancestral and family ties and determined everyone's place in the tribe. Maoris saw themselves not as individuals, but as part of the collective knowledge and experience of all of their ancestors.

'Maoris saw themselves not as individuals, but as part of the collective knowledge and experience of all of their ancestors'

Burial practices differed between tribes but the *tangi* (funeral) was similar. Traditionally, the soul of the departed travelled north to Te Rerenga-Wairua (Cape Reinga; p166), where it slid down the roots of a lone pohutukawa tree (which still stands) and then rejoined the ancestral spirits in Hawaiki (simultaneously the name for the underworld and the ancestral homeland).

Marae (Tribal Home)

Strictly, the *marae* is the flat area of grass in front of a *whare whakairo* (carved meeting house), but these days the term is used to describe the entire complex of buildings surrounding the meeting house – in most cases the major meeting spot for Maoris in that area. A *marae* complex contains several buildings but the most important are the meeting house (*whare whakairo*) and the building where food is served, the *whare kai*.

VISITING A MARAE

Probably the best way to gain some understanding of Maoritanga (Maori culture) is by visiting a *marae*. It's a place that is sacred to Maoris, and needs be treated with great respect.

A welcoming ritual called *te powhiri* is followed every time visitors come onto the *marae*. The hosts and visitors exchange welcoming calls, speeches,

MARAE VISITS

Rotorua (p319) in the Bay of Plenty probably has the most *marae* set up for tours, performances or visits. But there are other options around the country:

- Waitangi National Reserve (p178) in Northland – not an operating *marae* as such but fascinating to visit;
- Te Poho-o-Rawiri (p360) in Gisborne;
- Historic Parihaka (p261) in the Taranaki;
- Te Papa museum (see the boxed text, p390) in Wellington – again, not an operating *marae* in the traditional sense;
- Nga Hau e Wha (p510) in Christchurch.

In the Far North (p163), the Urewera region (p366) and around the East Cape (p353) you'll see many, many operating *marae*, but they're not usually set up for casual visitors. If someone's there, ask if you can have a look around, otherwise you'll just have to admire them from outside the gate (remember: they're private property). The Waikato region similarly holds some of NZ's most historically important *marae* – such as Turangawaewae (p220), Maketu (p228) and Te Tokanganui-o-noho (p241) – but they're not usually open for visitors.

Maori dancers, Rotorua
PETER HENDRIE

ceremonial challenges, more speeches, songs, a few speeches, perhaps one or two speeches...you get the idea: there's a fair bit of talking involved. Once the appropriate ancestors have been praised and lineages established, the *tapu* of the visitors is deemed lifted and hosts and visitors are permitted to interact with the locals with handshakes and the *hongi* (pressing of noses).

Ah, the *hongi* – evidently a problem area for some visitors. In some places the *hongi*, a sharing of life breath, is a single press, in others it is press, release, press. It is never a rubbing together of noses, a popular misconception. (Neither, never ever, is it a quick kiss on the nose, as was delivered by one confused Australian prime minister.)

Marae protocol varies around the country but a few things are common to all *marae*: Shoes must be removed before entering the meeting house. If you receive hospitality such as food and lodging, it is customary to offer a *koha* (donation), to help towards the upkeep of the *marae*. And long, long speeches could be said to be a tradition countrywide.

Visitors to New Zealand are increasingly being given the opportunity to enjoy *marae* hospitality, often on one of the *marae* tours that are becoming popular (see the boxed text opposite).

Pakanga (War)

Perhaps the greatest social change in Maori culture was the progression, since arrival from East Polynesia, from a peaceful society towards a far more warlike society as population and land pressures increased. Associated with this was the migration from open *kainga* (unfortified settlements) to *pa* (fortified enclosures), especially in the richer northern region where kumara and fern root thrived.

One of the best ways to promote the *mana* of a tribe was through battle, so the Maori had a highly developed warrior society. War had its own worship, sacrifices, rituals, dances and art forms. Tribes engaged in numerous battles over territory, for *utu* (revenge or payment) or for other reasons, with the losers often becoming slaves or food. Cooking and eating an enemy delivered the ultimate insult, destroying their personal *tapu*.

The *pa*, to which the Maori retreated when attacked, were built on terraced hill tops with concentric walls and elaborate earth defences. If the outer wall was breached the defenders could retreat to the next fortified inner terrace. Many of these earthworks are still visible, such as the sculpted hills that dot Auckland city. These elaborate earthworks were

successfully adapted to deal with cannon and musket fire during the New
Zealand Wars (Land Wars; p30) in the 1840s and 1860s – incidentally,
the world's first example of trench warfare.

ARTS
Waiata (Song) & Haka (Dance)

Traditionally Maori did not keep a written history; their history was kept
in long, specific and stylised songs and chants. As in many parts of the
world where oral history has been practised, song and chant developed
to become a magnificent art in the local culture.

The Maori arts of song and dance (see the boxed text opposite) include
some special features:

The highly expressive *waiata kori* (action song) is perhaps the most
beloved tradition, and a highlight of a visit to NZ could be learning some
songs with members of a Maori cultural group. Usually the men perform
with vigorous actions, whereas the movements of women are graceful and
flowing, reflecting some of the artistic forms of Asia.

The *poi* dance is distinctive to the NZ Maori, where the dancers swing
poi (balls tied on the end of a cord) to the rhythm of the music. The

most famous *poi* dance is the *waka
poi*, with the women sitting in a
row as if in a canoe (in other *poi*
dances, the performers do their
thing standing up).

Whakairo (Carving)

Woodcarving became increasingly
refined after the Maori arrived in
Aotearoa, and peaked in the period
immediately before the arrival of
Europeans. Ornate meeting houses

HAKA

Haka is Maori for any form of dance, but it's come to be associated with the chant (correctly the *haka taparahi*) that traditionally preceded a battle or challenged suspicious visitors. Delivered with fierce shouting, flexing arm movements that resemble fists pummelling the side of someone's head and thunderous stamping to grind whatever is left into the dust, it is indeed a frightening sight.

Each tribe had its own *haka*, but the most famous comes from Te Rauparaha (1768–1849), a chief of the Ngati Toa tribe. He was one of the last great warrior chiefs, carving a trail of mayhem from Kapiti near Wellington to the South Island, where he oversaw several rather nasty massacres. Te Rauparaha's *haka* is said to have originated when he was fleeing from his enemies (he had more than a few). A local chief hid him in an underground kumara store, where Te Rauparaha waited in the dark, expecting to be found. When the store was opened and the sun shone in, it was not his enemies but the (hairy) local chief telling him they had gone. Te Rauparaha climbed the ladder to perform this victorious *haka*. Made famous by the All Blacks, the *haka* is as follows:

> *Ka mate, ka mate* (It is death, it is death)
> *Ka ora, ka ora* (It is life, it is life)
> *Tenei te tangata puhuruhuru* (Behold the hairy man)
> *Nana nei i tiki mai i Whakawhiti te ra* (Who caused the sun to shine)
> *Upane, aupane* (Abreast, keep abreast)
> *Upane, ka aupane* (The rank, hold fast)
> *Whiti te ra* (Into the sunshine)

were built, with powerful wooden carvings depicting ancestors and the relevant gods. Human figures were the central motif in such carvings, usually with enlarged head, mouth and eyes. Another prevalent feature, often seen in window lintels and along the barge boards of canoes, is the *manaia*, a 'bird-headed man' identifiable by a human-shaped head with a beak.

Beautifully carved war canoes were (and are) a source of great *mana* for a tribe and were protected by *tapu*. Built of kauri or totara, they were up to 25m in length – the bow and stern pieces were elaborately carved.

Today in Rotorua you can check out woodcarvings, see artisans at work (such as at Whakarewarewa thermal village, p318) and in some cases buy direct from the artists. For more information see p671.

Maori bone carvings are another fine art form. Tiki, stylised human forms, are carved from *pounamu* (greenstone). Bone fish-hook pendants, carved in traditional Maori and modernised styles, are common (almost the badge of honour for an expat Kiwi), worn on a thong around the neck.

Paua (abalone) shell is carved into some beautiful ornaments and jewellery, as well as some impressively tacky souvenir ashtrays! It is also used as an inlay in many Maori carvings.

Moko (Tattoos)

Traditionally, the higher classes were decorated with intricate *moko* (tattoos) – women had *moko* only on their chins and lips, while high-ranking men not only had tattoos over their entire face, but also over other parts of their body (especially their buttocks). The tattoos were created using bone chisels, a mallet and blue pigment.

Maoris and Pakeha (and even visitors to NZ) now sport Maori patterns on their skin, and in some very rare cases you'll see Maori men or women with traditional full facial tattoos.

Environment Vaughan Yarwood

THE LAND

New Zealand is a young country – its present shape is less than 10,000 years old. Having broken away from the supercontinent of Gondwanaland (which included Africa, Australia, Antarctica and South America) in a stately geological dance some 130 million years ago, it endured eons of uplift and erosion, buckling and tearing, and the slow fall and rise of the sea as ice ages came and went. Straddling the boundary of two great colliding slabs of the earth's crust – the Pacific plate and the Indian/Australian plate – to this day NZ remains the plaything of nature's most powerful forces.

The result is one of the most varied and spectacular series of landscapes in the world, ranging from snow-dusted mountains and drowned glacial valleys to rainforests, dunelands and an otherworldly volcanic plateau. It is a diversity of landforms you would expect to find across an entire continent rather than a small archipelago of islands in the South Pacific.

Evidence of NZ's tumultuous past is everywhere. The mountainous spine of the South Island – the 650km-long ranges of the Southern Alps – is one product of the clash of the two plates; the result of a process of rapid lifting that, if anything, is accelerating. Despite the country's highest peak, Mt Cook (p549), losing 10m from its summit overnight in a 1991 landslide, the Southern Alps are on an express elevator that, without erosion and landslides, would see them reach 10 times their present height within just a few million years.

On the North Island, the most impressive changes have been wrought by volcanoes. Auckland is built on an isthmus peppered by scoria cones, on many of which you can still see the earthworks of *pa* (fortified villages) built by early Maori. The city's biggest and most recent volcano, 600-year old Rangitoto Island (p133), is just a short ferry ride from the downtown wharves. Some 300km further south, the classically shaped cone of snow capped Mt Taranaki/Egmont (p257) overlooks tranquil dairy pastures.

But the real volcanic heartland runs through the centre of the North Island, from the restless bulk of Mt Ruapehu in Tongariro National Park (p282) northeast through the Rotorua lake district (p316) out to the country's most active volcano, White Island (p346), in the Bay of Plenty. Called the Taupo Volcanic Zone, this great 250km-long rift valley – part of a great chain of volcanoes known as the 'Pacific Ring of Fire' – has been the seat of massive eruptions that have left their mark on the country both physically and culturally.

Most spectacular were the eruptions from the volcano which created Lake Taupo. Considered the world's most productive volcano in terms of the amount of material ejected, Taupo last erupted 1800 years ago in a display which was the most violent anywhere on the planet within the past 5000 years (see p306).

You can experience the aftermath of volcanic destruction on a smaller scale at Te Wairoa (the Buried Village; p330) near Rotorua on the shores of Lake Tarawera. Here, partly excavated and open to the public, lie the remains of a 19th-century Maori village overwhelmed when nearby Mt Tarawera erupted without warning (p329). The famous Pink and White Terraces (one of several claimants to the popular title 'eighth wonder of the world') were destroyed overnight by the same upheaval.

But when Nature sweeps the board clean with one hand she often rebuilds with the other: Waimangu Valley (p327), born of all that

Vaughan is a historian and travel writer who is widely published in NZ and internationally. His most recent book is *The History Makers: Adventures in New Zealand Biography* and he is currently researching a book on Antarctic exploration.

LAND OF THE RINGS

Forget hobbits, wizards and that gold trinket. The real star of Peter Jackson's epic film trilogy *Lord of the Rings* (p42) is the breathtaking NZ landscape. If nothing else, the movie makes a fine trip planner.

New Zealand *is* Middle-earth. It has every geological formation and geographical landscape you can imagine…and some you can't.

ELIJAH WOOD, 'FRODO BAGGINS'

ENVIRONMENTAL ISSUES IN AOTEAROA NEW ZEALAND *Nandor Tanczos*

Aotearoa New Zealand is famous for having won some significant environmental battles. Since the 1980s we have seen the NZ Forest Accord (developed to protect native forest) and the end of all native logging on public land. Our national parks and reserves now cover around a third of our land area, and the first few marine reserves have been established. We are also famous for our strong antinuclear stance.

To describe ourselves as 'clean and green', however, is 100% pure fantasy. A drive in the country soon reveals that much of our land is more akin to a green desert.

The importation of European sheep and cattle grazing systems to Aotearoa New Zealand has left many hillsides with marginal productivity; they are bare of trees and prone to erosion. In many areas grazing threatens our waterways, with stock causing damage to stream and lake margins and runoff leading to nutrient overload of waterways. Regional councils and farming groups are starting to fence and plant stream banks to protect water quality but their efforts may be outstripped by the growth in dairy farming.

Despite increasing international and local demand for organic food, most farming in Aotearoa New Zealand relies on high levels of chemical inputs in the form of fertilisers, pesticides and herbicides. In addition, the Labour government, backed by most other political parties, has voted to end the ban on the release of genetically engineered (GE) organisms into the environment, in the face of overwhelming public opposition. However, we are still GE free and many of us are determined to keep it that way.

Our record on waste is regrettable. The parliamentary commissioner for the environment recently stated that the average New Zealander generates 900kg of waste a year, which is more than the average American. Recycling facilities barely exist in some areas, although many local councils have been working with communities to combine waste reduction, job creation and reuse of reclaimed materials. Even so, some items, such as batteries, remain almost impossible to recycle, and the packaging industry has largely been left to 'self-regulate', with predicable consequences.

Energy consumption in Aotearoa New Zealand has grown three times more than population over the last 20 years. We are one of the most inefficient users of energy in the developed world and a staggering two-thirds of our energy comes from nonrenewable resources (although most other countries use an even higher proportion of nonrenewable resources!).

Add to that the ongoing battle being fought in many communities over the disposal of sewage and toxic waste, a conflict often spearheaded by *tangata whenua* (Maori), and the 'clean and green' label begins to look seriously compromised.

We do have a number of things in our favour. Our biggest saving grace is our small population, so the cumulative effect is reduced. Also, there are many national park and reserve areas set aside to protect native ecosystems making Aotearoa New Zealand a place well worth visiting. This is a beautiful land with enormous geographical and ecological diversity. Our forests are unique and magnificent, and the bird species that evolved in response to an almost total lack of mammalian life are spectacular, although now reduced in numbers.

The responsibility of New Zealanders is to make change, not just at a personal level, but at an institutional and infrastructural level, for ecological sustainability. The responsibility of visitors to Aotearoa New Zealand is to respect our unique biodiversity, and to query and question. Every time you ask where the recycling centre is; every time you express surprise at the levels of energy use, car use and water use; every time you demand organic food at a café or restaurant; you affect the person you talk to.

Aotearoa New Zealand has the potential to be a world leader in ecological wisdom. We have a strong tradition to draw from – the careful relationship the Maori developed with the natural world over the course of many, many generations. We live at the edge of the Pacific, on the Rim of Fire, a remnant of the ancient forests of Gondwanaland. We welcome conscious travellers.

Nandor is a Member of Parliament (NZ Greens), a high-profile campaigner on genetic engineering and a keen user of public transport.

geothermal violence, is the place to go to experience the hot earth up close and personal amid geysers, silica pans, bubbling mud pools and the world's biggest hot spring. Or you can wander around Rotorua's Whakarewarewa Thermal Village (p318) where descendants of Maori displaced by the eruption live in the middle of steaming vents and prepare food for visitors in boiling pools.

A second by-product of movement along the tectonic plate boundary is seismic activity – earthquakes. Not for nothing has NZ been called 'the Shaky Isles'. Though most quakes do little more than rattle the glassware, one was indirectly responsible for creating an internationally celebrated tourist attraction…

In 1931 an earthquake measuring 7.9 on the Richter scale levelled the Hawkes Bay city of Napier (p368) causing huge damage and loss of life. Napier was rebuilt almost entirely in the then-fashionable Art Deco architectural style, and walking its streets today you can relive its brash exuberance in what has become a mecca for lovers of Art Deco (p444).

Travellers to the South Island can also see some evidence of volcanism – if the remains of the old volcanoes of Banks Peninsula (p526) weren't there to repel the sea, the vast Canterbury Plains, built from alpine sediment washed down the rivers from the Alps, would have eroded away long ago.

But in the south it is the Southern Alps themselves that dominate, dictating settlement patterns, throwing down engineering challenges and offering outstanding recreational opportunities. The island's mountainous backbone also helps shape the weather, as it stands in the path of the prevailing westerly winds which roll in, moisture-laden, from the Tasman Sea. As a result bush-clad lower slopes of the western Southern Alps are among the wettest places on earth, with an annual precipitation of some 15,000mm. Having lost its moisture, the wind then blows dry across the eastern plains towards the Pacific coast.

The North Island has a more even rainfall and is spared the temperature extremes of the South – which can plunge when a wind blows in from Antarctica. The important thing to remember, especially if you are tramping at high altitude, is that NZ has a maritime climate. This means the weather can change with lightning speed, catching out the unprepared.

WILDLIFE

New Zealand may be relatively young, geologically speaking, but its plants and animals go back a long way. The tuatara, for instance, an ancient reptile unique to these islands, is a Gondwanaland survivor closely related to the dinosaurs, while many of the distinctive flightless birds (ratites) have distant African and South American cousins.

Due to its long isolation, the country is a veritable warehouse of unique and varied plants, most of which are found nowhere else. And with separation of the landmass occurring before mammals appeared on the scene, birds and insects have evolved in spectacular ways to fill the gaps.

The now extinct flightless moa, the largest of which grew to 3.5m tall and weighed over 200kg, browsed open grasslands much as cattle do today (skeletons can be seen at Auckland Museum, p99), while the smaller kiwi still ekes out a nocturnal living rummaging among forest leaf litter for insects and worms much as small mammals do elsewhere. One of the country's most ferocious looking insects, the mouse-sized giant weta, meanwhile, has taken on a scavenging role elsewhere filled by rodents.

As one of the last places on earth to be colonised by humans, NZ was for millennia a safe laboratory for such risky evolutionary strategies, but

Landforms: the Shaping of New Zealand, by L Molloy and R Smith takes digital modelling to its aesthetic limits to show nature at work. A delectable series of topographical 'snapshots' with explanatory text tells the story of how NZ became the way it is.

Lifestyles of New Zealand Forest Plants, by J Dawson and R Lucas, is a beautifully photographed foray into the world of NZ's forests. This guidebook will have you reaching for your boots.

DID YOU KNOW?

Found only in NZ, tuatara have a redundant third eye and are covered with scales. Unlike other reptiles, the male has no penis. Living wild now only on offshore islands, you can see them in captivity in the museum in Invercargill (p632).

with the arrival first of Maori and soon after of Europeans, things went downhill fast.

Many creatures, including moa and the huia, an exquisite songbird, were driven to extinction and the vast forests were cleared for their timber and to make way for agriculture. Destruction of habitat and the introduction of exotic animals and plants have taken a terrible environmental toll and New Zealanders are now fighting a rearguard battle to save what remains.

Birds & Animals

The first Polynesian settlers found little in the way of land mammals – just two species of bat – but forests, plains and coasts alive with birds. Largely lacking the bright plumage found elsewhere, NZ's birds – like its endemic plants – have an understated beauty which does not shout for attention.

Among the most musical are the bellbird, common in both native and exotic forests everywhere except Northland, though like many birds more likely to be heard than seen. Its call is a series of liquid bell notes, most often sounded at dawn or dusk.

The tui, another nectar eater and the country's most beautiful songbird, is a great mimic, with an inventive repertoire that includes clicks, grunts and chuckles. Notable for the white throat feathers which stand out against its dark plumage, the tui often feeds on flax flowers in suburban gardens but is most at home in densely tangled forest ('bush' to New Zealanders).

Fantails are commonly encountered on forest trails, swooping and jinking to catch insects stirred up by passing hikers, while pukeko, elegant swamp-hens with blue plumage and bright red beaks, are readily seen along wetland margins and even on the sides of roads nearby – be warned, they have little road sense.

If you spend any time in South Island high country, you are likely to come up against the fearless and inquisitive kea – an uncharacteristically drab green parrot with bright red underwings. Kea are common in the car parks of the Fox and Franz Josef Glaciers (p492 and p495) where they hang out for food scraps or tear rubber from car windscreens.

Then there is the takahe, a rare flightless bird thought extinct until a small colony was discovered in 1948, and the equally flightless kiwi, the country's national emblem and of course the nickname for New Zealanders themselves.

The kiwi has a round body covered in coarse feathers, strong legs and a long, distinctive bill with nostrils at the tip for sniffing out food. It is not easy to find them in the wild, but they can be seen in simulated environments at excellent nocturnal houses. One of the best is the Otorohanga

B Heather and H Robertson's *Field Guide to the Birds of New Zealand* is the most comprehensive guide for bird-watchers and a model of helpfulness for anyone even casually interested in the country's remarkable birdlife.

Herbert Guthrie-Smith's *Tutira* is a book like no other. Subtitled 'the story of a New Zealand sheep station', it is really much more: a teeming mix of geology, geography, botany, animal husbandry and natural history leavened with dry Scottish humour... an undisputed classic.

KIWI SPOTTING

The kiwi is a threatened species, and with the additional difficulty of them being nocturnal, it's only on Stewart Island (p645) that you easily see one in the wild. However, they can be observed in many artificially dark 'kiwi houses', such as:

- Otorohanga Kiwi House & Native Bird Park (p235)
- National Aquarium of New Zealand, Napier (p371)
- Wellington Zoo (p392)
- Willowbank Wildlife Reserve, Christchurch (p510)
- Kiwi & Birdlife Park, Queenstown (p585)

RESPONSIBLE TRAVEL

Toitu te whenua – Care for the land. Help protect the environment by following these guidelines:

■ Treat NZ's forests and native wildlife with respect. Damaging or taking plants is illegal in most parts of the country.

■ Remove rubbish. Litter is unsightly and can encourage vermin and disease. Rather than burying or burning, carry out what you carry in.

■ In areas without toilet facilities bury toilet waste in a shallow hole away from tracks, huts, camp sites and waterways.

■ Keep streams and lakes pure by cleaning away from water sources. Drain waste water into the soil to filter out soaps and detergent. If you suspect contamination, boil water for three minutes, filter or chemically treat it before use.

■ Where possible use portable fuel stoves. Keep open fire small, use only dead wood and make sure the fire is out by dousing it with water and checking the ashes before leaving.

■ Keep to tracks where possible. Get permission before crossing private land and move carefully around livestock.

Kiwi House (p235), which also has other birds, including native falcons, moreporks (owls) and weka, as well as tuatara.

To get a feel for what the bush used to be like, take a trip to Tiritiri Matangi Island (p145), not far from Auckland. This regenerating island is an open sanctuary and one of the country's most successful exercises in community-assisted conservation.

Encountering marine mammals is one of the great delights of a visit to NZ, now that well-regulated ecotourism has replaced the commercial whaling and sealing that drove many NZ species to the brink of extinction in the early 19th century. Sperm whales can be seen off the coast of Kaikoura (p437) and licensed companies offer swimming with wild dolphins in the Bay of Islands and elsewhere (p66); forget aquarium shows – sea encounters are the real thing.

Kiwi House (p235)

(p145)

(p437)

(p66)

Trees

No visitor to NZ (particularly Australians!) will go for long without hearing about the damage done to the bush by that bad-mannered Australian import, the brush-tailed possum. The long list of mammal pests introduced accidentally or for a variety of misguided reasons includes deer, rabbits, stoats, pigs and goats. But the most destructive by far is the possum, 70 million of which now chew through millions of tonnes of foliage a year despite the best efforts of the Department of Conservation (DOC) to control them.

Among favoured possum food are NZ's most colourful trees: the kowhai, a small-leaved tree growing to 11m, that in spring has drooping clusters of bright yellow flowers (NZ's national flower); the pohutukawa, a beautiful coastal tree of the northern North Island which bursts into vivid red flower in December, earning the nickname 'Christmas tree'; and a similar crimson-flowered tree, the rata. Species of rata are found on both islands; the northern rata starts life as a climber on a host tree (that it eventually chokes).

The few remaining pockets of mature centuries-old kauri are stately emblems of former days. Their vast hammered trunks and towering, epiphyte-festooned limbs, which dwarf every other tree in the forest, are reminders of why they were sought after in colonial days for spars and building

DID YOU KNOW?

The egg of the flightless kiwi can weigh as much as a quarter of the female bird and, not having an egg tooth, the chick uses its feet to break out of the shell. With whiskers, tiny hidden wings, a low metabolic rate, no tail feathers, hair-like plumage and a keen sense of smell, the ground-dwelling kiwi is more like a mammal than a bird.

timber. The best place to see the remaining giants is Northland's Waipoua Forest (p159), home to three-quarters of the country's surviving kauri.

Now, the pressure has been taken off kauri and other timber trees including the distinctive rimu, or red pine, and the long-lived totara (favoured for Maori war canoes), by one of the country's most successful imports – *pinus radiata*. Pine was found to thrive in NZ, growing to maturity in just 35 years, and plantation forests are now widespread through the central North Island – the Southern Hemisphere's biggest, Kaingaroa Forest, lies southeast of Rotorua.

You won't get far into the bush without coming across one of its most prominent features – tree ferns. NZ is a land of ferns (more than 80 species) and most easily recognised are the mamuka (black tree fern), which grows to 20m and can be seen in damp gullies throughout the country; and the 10m high ponga (silver tree fern) with its distinctive white underside. The silver fern is equally at home as part of corporate logos and on the clothing of many of the country's top sportspeople.

NATIONAL PARKS

A third of the country – more than five million hectares – is protected in environmentally important parks and reserves which embrace almost every conceivable landscape: from mangrove-fringed inlets in the north to the snow-topped volcanoes of the Central Plateau, and from the forested fastness of the Ureweras in the east to the Southern Alps' majestic mountains, glaciers and fiords. The 14 national parks, three maritime parks and two marine reserves, along with numerous forest parks, offer huge scope for wilderness experiences, ranging from climbing, snow skiing and mountain biking to tramping, kayaking and trout fishing.

Three places are World Heritage areas: NZ's sub-Antarctic islands (p645), Tongariro National Park (p282) and Te Wahipounamu, an amalgam of several national parks in southwest NZ (p615) which boast the world's finest surviving Gondwanaland plants and animals in their natural habitats.

Access to the country's wild places is relatively straightforward, though huts on walking tracks require passes and may need to be booked in advance. In practical terms, there is little difference for travellers between a national park and a forest park, though dogs are not allowed in national parks without a permit. Camping is possible in all parks, but may be restricted to dedicated camping grounds – check first. Permits are required for hunting (game birds) and licences needed for inland fishing (trout, salmon). Both can be bought online at www.fishandgame.org.nz.

DID YOU KNOW?

Tane-mahuta (p159), the biggest surviving kauri tree – 51m high and with a girth of 13m – is only a quarter the size of the largest known, a kauri that grew on the Coromandel Peninsula, said to have had a girth of over 26m.

The Department of Conservation website (www.doc.govt.nz) has useful information on the country's national parks, tracks and walkways. It also lists backcountry huts and camp sites.

TOP FIVE NATIONAL PARKS

- **Aoraki/Mt Cook** (p549) Alpine landscape. Home to the wonderfully naughty kea and NZ's highest mountain. Alpine trail, glacier flights, climbing.
- **Fiordland** (p615) Vast untouched fiords. Waterfalls, sandflies, pristine lakes. Outstanding walks including Milford (p624) and Keplar (p617) tracks.
- **Te Urewera** (p366) Rugged forested hills, steeped in Maori history. Lake Waikaremoana walking trail (p366).
- **Tongariro** (p282) Active volcanic wilderness. The world's fourth-oldest national park. Ski fields, rock climbing, Tongariro Northern Circuit (p284).
- **Whanganui** (p271) Primeval river valleys. Rich Maori and settler history. Canoe journeys, *marae* stays.

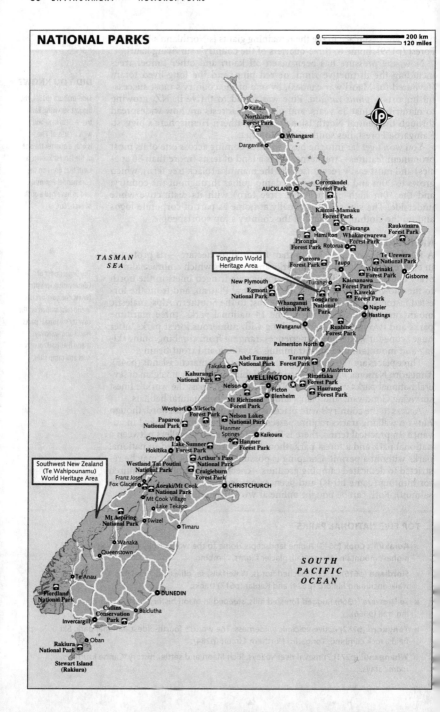

NATIONAL PARKS

0 ————— 200 km
0 ————— 120 miles

Kaitaia

Whangarei

Dargaville

Northland
Forest Park

Coromandel
Forest Park

AUCKLAND

Kaimai-Mamaku
Forest Park

Pirongia   Tauranga   Raukumara
Forest Park   Hamilton Whakarewarewa   Forest Park
                  Rotorua   Forest Park

TASMAN
SEA

Pureora
Forest Park   Te Urewera
                        Taupo   National Park
New Plymouth   Whirinaki   Gisborne
              Turangi Kaimanawa Forest Park
Egmont   Forest Park
National Park   Tongariro Kaweka
Whanganui   National   Forest Park
National Park   Park   Napier
                         Hastings
Wanganui   Ruahine
               Forest Park
Palmerston North

Tararua
Abel Tasman Forest Park
National Park
Takaka   Masterton
Kahurangi   Nelson Rimutaka
National Park   Forest Park
              Picton Haurangi
Nelson   Blenheim Forest Park
         Mt Richmond
Westport Victoria Forest Park
        Forest Park Nelson Lakes
Paparoa   National Park
National Park   Hanmer
          Springs   Kaikoura
Greymouth Lake Sumner
Hokitika Forest Park Hanmer
                Forest Park
         Arthur's Pass
Westland Tai Poutini National Park
National Park Craigieburn
Franz Josef   Forest Park
Fox Glacier   CHRISTCHURCH
       Aoraki/Mt Cook
        National Park
        Mt Cook Village
        Lake Tekapo

Mt Aspiring Twizel
National Park   Timaru
     Wanaka
   Queenstown
                      SOUTH
  Te Anau   PACIFIC
                      OCEAN
Fiordland
National Park
         Catlins
   Invercargill Conservation Balclutha
          Park   DUNEDIN

Rakiura
National Park   Oban

Stewart Island
(Rakiura)

Tongariro World
Heritage Area

Southwest New Zealand
(Te Wahipounamu)
World Heritage Area

New Zealand Outdoors

New Zealand's outstanding natural assets will prompt even the most hard-core armchair dweller to fire up the neurons and drag themselves outside. The country has an abundance of spacious, fresh-aired terrain, including surf-struck oceans, vast lakes and sounds, toehold-conducive mountains and trail-blazed parks (see map opposite), the majority of it reasonably accessible. There are also plenty of facilities and outdoor-enthused local operators to help immerse you in almost every conceivable kind of activity.

There's little that's off limits to those with energy to expend, a fact exemplified by the startling variety of ways in which Kiwis and visitors move over or through land, air and water. They jetboat, white-water sledge, raft, boogie board, canoe, kayak, surf, surf raft, scuba dive and ski through the water; they bungy jump, parapente, skydive, abseil, fly, helicopter and barrel roll through the air; and they tramp, mountain bike, ski, horse ride, rock climb, 'zorb' and ice climb across terra firma. Beneath the surface, caving, cave rafting, the exploration of *tomos* (the hole or entrance to a cave) and hydro-sliding are all undertaken.

The various adrenaline-pumping activities obviously have an element of risk, but the perception of danger is part of the thrill. Such risk is underlined in adventure sports, particularly rafting and kayaking on fast-flowing rivers. Chances of a mishap are arguably minuscule, but reassure yourself that the company you choose takes adequate safety precautions. Also make sure that you have travel insurance that fully covers you for any planned activities – for reasons why a comprehensive insurance policy is so important, including details of NZ's litigation-free approach to accidents, see Insurance (p667) in the Directory chapter.

AERIAL SIGHTSEEING

Planes and helicopters circle the skies on sightseeing trips (called 'flightseeing' by the locals) all over NZ, operating from local aerodromes. It's a great way to see the country's incredible contrast in landscapes, close-ups of its spectacular mountain ranges, and the remote and otherwise little-viewed terrain deep within national-park

Bay of Islands (p172)
DAVID WALL

forests and glacial valleys. Some of the most striking trips take place over the Bay of Islands, the Bay of Plenty, Tongariro National Park, Mt Taranaki, Mt Cook, the West Coast glaciers and the southern fiords.

A far more sedate way to see the countryside is from a hot-air balloon. A float above Methven snags you spectacular views of the Southern Alps and contrasting Canterbury Plains, and there are also early-morning balloon trips from Queenstown and Auckland.

BIRD-WATCHING

Twitchers have been known to flock (sorry) to NZ, because this relatively small country is home to an overwhelming number of endemic species and foreign feathered friends who fly by in waves. Unfortunately, NZ is as (in) famous for extinct and point-of-extinction species as it is for common species.

EXTREME (OR JUST EXTREMELY UNUSUAL) ACTIVITIES

The fact that an activity as patently terrifying and sanity-challenging as bungy jumping is now an everyday pursuit in NZ says a lot about how the concept of 'extreme sports' has evolved in this country. The truth is, the old days of hardcore, often-dangerous physical experimentation have more or less been replaced by safe variations on popular, well-tested themes.

The humble bungy, for example, has metamorphosed into the less scary **bungy rocket**, where you sit in a capsule that zooms skywards and then bounces around on several cords; these rockets take off in Wellington and Queenstown. A much more nerve-racking take on the bungy (but no less safe) is Auckland's **Sky Jump**, a 16-second freefall using a cable and 'fan descenders' (used by movie-industry stunt actors) – at 192m it's the world's highest tower-based jump. Then there's the **parabungy**, where you get lifted above Queenstown's Lake Wakatipu by a speedboat-towed parasail and test your cord's elasticity from between 150m and 180m above the water.

Another unusual above-ground activity is the **Shotover Canyon Swing**, a 109m-high rope swing (apparently the world's highest) concocted by those funsters in nearby Queenstown. There's also **Fly By Wire**, where you briefly 'fly' a cable-tethered plane at high speeds – wannabe pilots can try it in Queenstown; at the time of writing it was unclear if a second such device at Paekakariki near Wellington would remain open.

At the eccentric end of the activity scale is **zorbing**, which involves rolling downhill in a transparent plastic ball – sit it out if you're prone to motion sickness, otherwise try it at Rotorua. An alternative land-based activity is **quad biking**, where you roam the countryside around Ahipara, Taupo, Queenstown, Wanaka, Te Anau and Hanmer Springs on four-wheel farm bikes, sniffing out mud, sand dunes and water crossings as you go. Taupo is also where you can have a bruising bout of **mountainboarding** – just imagine you're snowboarding when suddenly the snow disappears and your board sprouts pneumatic tyres.

NZ also offers uncommon watersports. **Cave rafting** (called 'tumu tumu toobing' and 'blackwater rafting' at Waitomo, 'underworld rafting' at Westport and 'adventure caving' at Greymouth) is technically not rafting, as it involves donning a wet suit, a lighted hard hat and a black inner tube and floating along underground rivers. But it's still an entertaining if not captivating diversion, particularly when you encounter glow-worms in an otherwise pitch-black cavern.

For more aquatic manoeuvring, grab a polystyrene sled or a modified boogie board, flippers, a wet suit and a helmet and go **river sledging** (also called river surfing or white-water sledging). Rivers around Queenstown and Wanaka offer this wet thrill, as does Rotorua, where there's a sizable waterfall drop on the Kaituna River. In Taranaki, the concept has been tweaked to include 'dam dropping', where you slide down a 7m dam and proceed to sledge the Waingongoro River.

Kiteboarding, where a mini parachute drags you along on a surfboard, is touted as the successor to windsurfing and can be attempted at Paihia.

The flightless kiwi is the species most sought after by bird-watchers. Sightings of the Stewart Island subspecies are common at all times of the year. Elsewhere, wild sightings of this increasingly rare nocturnal species are difficult, but there are quite a few kiwi enclosures (Christchurch and Auckland both have 'kiwi houses') that allow dimly lit glimpses of this shy bird. Other birds that twitchers like to sight are the royal albatross, white heron, Fiordland crested penguin, yellow-eyed penguin, Australasian gannet and wrybill.

On the Coromandel Peninsula, the Firth of Thames (particularly Miranda) is a haven for migrating birds, while the Wharekawa Wildlife Refuge at Opoutere is a breeding ground of the endangered NZ dotterel and the variable oystercatcher. There's also a very accessible Australasian gannet colony at Muriwai, west of Auckland.

Two good guides are *The Reed Field Guide to New Zealand Birds*, by Geoff Moon, and *Birds of New Zealand – Locality Guide*, by Stuart Chambers. See p57 for more information about NZ's bird life.

BUNGY JUMPING

Bungy jumping (hurtling earthwards from bridges with nothing between you and kingdom come but a gigantic rubber cord strapped to your limbs) has a bit of daredevil panache about it and prompts a heady adrenaline rush, but the behind-the-scenes action could hardly be more organised, with jumper safety obviously of paramount importance. As for exhibitionist backpackers, the days of bungying nude for free are well and truly over – though you might still get a discount.

Queenstown is virtually surrounded by bungy cords, including a 43m-high jump off the Kawarau Bridge (which now has a bungy theatre and museum), a 102m plunge at Skippers Canyon and the 134m Nevis Highwire act (for an idea of what to expect, see the boxed text on p586). Another South Island bungy jump awaits you outside Hanmer Springs.

Jumping is also done on the North Island at Taupo (45m), above the scenic Waikato River, and from Auckland Harbour Bridge.

DID YOU KNOW?

Bungy jumping was made famous by Kiwi AJ Hackett's dive from the Eiffel Tower in 1986, after which he teamed up with NZ champion speed skier Henry van Asch to turn the endeavour into a profitable and safe commercial enterprise.

Bungy rocketer, Christchurch (p586)

DAVID WALL

CANOEING & KAYAKING

Just to prove their internationalism, Kiwis call an open two-person canoe a 'Canadian canoe'. A smaller, narrower one-person craft that's covered, except for a hole in which the paddler sits, is often called a 'kayak' but it can also be called a 'canoe', especially if it's of the sit-on-top variety. When organising waterborne trips in NZ with a local operator, specify exactly what type of vessel you're interested in.

Kayakers, Kawarau River Queenstown

DAVID WALL

Canoeing is especially popular on the Whanganui River on the North Island. It's also popular on northern lakes, notably Lake Taupo, as well as on many bodies of freshwater on the South Island.

For more info on canoeing and kayaking check out the website of the New Zealand Recreational Canoeing Association, www.rivers.org.nz.

Many backpacker hostels situated close to water will have kayaks for hire or free use, and loads of commercial guided trips (for those without equipment or experience) are offered on rivers and lakes throughout the country. Many trips have an eco element such as bird-watching – a good example is the beautiful Okarito Lagoon on the West Coast of the South Island.

Sea Kayaking

Highly rated sea-kayaking areas in NZ's north include the Hauraki Gulf (particularly off Waiheke and Great Barrier Islands), the Bay of Islands and Coromandel Peninsula; in the south, try the Marlborough Sounds and along the coast of Abel Tasman National Park, where this activity has become almost as big as walking. Fiordland is also a great destination, as evidenced by the number of tour operators in Te Anau, Milford and Manapouri arranging spectacular trips on local lakes and fiords.

CAVING

Caving opportunities abound in the honeycombed karst (limestone) regions of the islands. Auckland, Westport and Waitomo are all areas where you'll find active local clubs and organised tours – one of the most spectacular caving experiences is the 100m abseil into the Lost World *tomo* (cave) near Waitomo. Local underground organisations include the **Wellington Caving Group** (http://caving.wellington.net.nz/) and the **Auckland Speleo Group** (www.asg.org.nz).

FISHING

Thanks to the widespread introduction of exotic rainbow trout, brown trout, quinnat salmon, Atlantic salmon, perch, char and several other fishy species, NZ has become one of the world's great recreational fisheries. The lakes and rivers of the central North Island are famous for trout fishing, especially Lake Taupo and the rivers that feed it – the town of Turangi is a top base for trout fishing in this region. The rivers and lakes of the South Island also fare well on the trout index, most notably the Mataura River (Southland) and Lake Brunner and the Arnold River (the West Coast). The rivers of Otago and Southland also have some of the best salmon fishing in the world.

Interested in guided fishing trips? Check out the website of the New Zealand Professional Fishing Guides Association, www.nzpfga.com.

Saltwater fishing is another attraction for Kiwi anglers, especially in the warmer waters surrounding the North Island where surfcasting or fishing from boats can result in big catches of (deep breath) grey mullet, trevally, mao mao, porae, John Dory, snapper, gurnard, flounder, mackerel, hapuku (groper), tarakihi, moki and kahawai. Ninety Mile Beach (Northland) and the beaches of Hauraki Gulf are good for surfcasting. The Bay of Islands, Whangaroa, Tutukaka near Whangarei (all in Northland), Whitianga on the Coromandel and Tuhua (Mayor Island) in the Bay of Plenty are noted big-game fishing areas.

The colder waters of the South Island, especially around the Marlborough Sounds, are good for snapper, hake, hapuku, trumpeter, butterfish, ling, barracouta and blue cod. Kaikoura Peninsula is great for surfcasting.

Fishing gear can be hired in places such as Taupo and Rotorua, and at sports outlets in other main towns, but serious line-dangling enthusiasts might want to bring their own. Rods and tackle may have to be treated by NZ quarantine officials, especially if they're made with natural materials such as cane or feathers.

Surfcasting, Ngawi
(p414), Wairarapa Coast
PAUL KENNEDY

A fishing permit is required to fish in inland waters. Sold at sport shops, permits cover particular regions and are available for a day, a month or a season. Local visitors centres and **Department of Conservation** (DOC; www.doc.govt.nz) offices can provide information on fishing licences and regulations. For comprehensive online info on recreational fishing in NZ, including loads of links, visit www.fishing.net.nz. In terms of fishing tomes, John Kent has written the *North Island Trout Fishing Guide* and the *South Island Trout Fishing Guide*. Tony Orman, a renowned NZ fisherman and author, has written *21 Great New Zealand Trout Waters*, as well as *Fishing the Wild Places of New Zealand*, which not only explains how to catch fish but also relates some of the author's fishing exploits in wilderness areas.

GOLF

NZ has more golf courses per capita than any other country – though given the population, this isn't all that surprising. Among the more than 400 courses here are some spectacularly situated fairways and greens, such as Howick on Musick Pt in Auckland, swanky Gulf Harbour on the Whangaparaoa Peninsula north of Auckland, and Wairakei near Taupo. Paraparaumu, near Wellington, is regarded as the country's best course and is where Tiger Woods famously swung his clubs in 2002. Down south, there are a couple of grand courses at Arrowtown and Millbrook, both near Queenstown.

The average green fee for an 18-hole course usually ranges from $25 to $45, though Millbrook (which is a private resort) charges a whopping $125 for casual players.

HORSE RIDING

Horse riding is commonplace in NZ and, unlike some other parts of the world where beginners only get led by the nose around a paddock, here you really can get out into the countryside on farm, forest and beach rides. Rides can range from one-hour jaunts (from $50) to week-long, fully catered treks.

On the South Island, all-day adventure rides on horseback are a fine way to see the country around Kaikoura, Nelson, Mt Cook, Hanmer Springs, Wanaka, Glenorchy and Dunedin. Treks are also offered in Paparoa National Park on the West Coast.

On the North Island, Taupo has options for wilderness horse trekking and for rides in the hills overlooking thermal regions. The Coromandel

Peninsula, Waitomo, Pakiri, Ninety Mile Beach (from Ahipara) and the East Cape are also good places for horse trekking.

Where to Ride In New Zealand, a pamphlet produced by the Hamilton-based **International League for the Protection of Horses** (ILPH; ☎ 07-849 0678; www.horsetalk.co.nz/ilph/), is widely available from visitors centres; it can also be downloaded from the ILPH website. **Riding for the Disabled** (☎ 07-849 4727; Foreman Park) is another useful organisation based in Hamilton.

JETBOATING

The jetboat is a local invention, thought up by CWF Hamilton in 1957. An inboard engine sucks water into a tube in the bottom of the boat and an impeller driven by the engine blows it out of a nozzle at the stern in a high-speed stream. The boat is steered simply by directing the jet stream.

Jetboats make short work of shallow and white water because there are no propellers to damage, there's better clearance under the boat and the jet can be reversed instantly for quick braking. The instant response of the jet enables these craft to execute passenger-drenching 360° spins almost within the length of the boat.

On the South Island, the Shotover and Kawarau Rivers near Queenstown and the Buller River near Westport are renowned jetboating rivers. The Dart River is less travelled but also good, and the Waiatoto River near Haast is a superb wilderness experience, as is the Wilkin River in Mt Aspiring National Park.

On the North Island, the Whanganui, Motu, Rangitaiki and Waikato Rivers are excellent for jetboating, and there are sprint jets at the Agrodome in Rotorua and at Waitomo. Jetboating around the Bay of Islands in Northland is also popular, particularly the trips to Hole in the Rock.

Half-hour trips cost from $60 to $90 and sprints start at $35. Like many activities, jetboating seems to be marginally cheaper on the North Island than on the South.

MARINE-MAMMAL WATCHING

Kaikoura, on the northeast coast of the South Island, is NZ's nexus of marine-mammal watching. The main attraction here is whale-watching but this is dependent on weather conditions, so don't expect to just be able to rock up and head straight out on a boat for a dream encounter. The sperm whale, the largest toothed whale, is seen from October to August, while most of the other mammals are seen year-round.

Kaikoura is also an outstanding place to swim with dolphins. Pods of up to 500 playful dusky dolphins can be seen on any given day. Dolphin

Jetboaters, Shotover
River, Queenstown
(p586)
DAVID WALL

Mountain bikers, Moke
Creek, near Queenstown
(p588)

DAVID WALL

swimming is common elsewhere in NZ, with the animals gathering off
the North Island near Whakatane, Paihia, Tauranga, Whitianga and in
the Hauraki Gulf (from Auckland), and off Akaroa on the South Island's
Banks Peninsula. Seal swimming is possible at Kaikoura and Abel Tasman National Park.

Swimming with sharks is also popular, though with a protective cage
as a chaperone. You can do it at Tutukaka and Kaikoura.

MOUNTAIN BIKING & CYCLE TOURING

At any given time, but especially in summer, you will come across
plenty of pannier-laden cycle tourists pedalling Kiwi highways and
back roads, with one eye on the scenery and another looking out for
the plentiful off-road possibilities. Most towns offer bike hire, either
at backpacker hostels or specialist bike shops, but quality mountain
bikes can usually be hired only in major towns or adventure-sports
centres such as Queenstown, Nelson, Picton, Taupo and Rotorua. Bike
service and repair shops can be found in most big settlements and
some excellent cycling books are available, including Lonely Planet's
Cycling New Zealand.

For more info on
mountain biking
in NZ, check out
www.mountainbike.co.nz
or www.mountainbike.co
.nz/nzmba.

For wind-in-the-hair types, various companies will take you up to the
tops of mountains, hills and volcanoes (such as Christchurch's Port Hills,
Mt Ruapehu, Cardrona and the Remarkables) so that you can hurtle
down without the usual grunt of getting uphill beforehand. Rotorua's
Redwood Grove is a noted place for mountain biking, as is the 42nd
Traverse near National Park and Twizel near Mt Cook.

Some of the traditional tramping tracks are open to mountain bikes,
but DOC has restricted access in many cases due to track damage and the
inconvenience to walkers, especially at busy times. Never cycle on walking tracks in national parks unless it's permissible (check with DOC),
or risk heavy fines and the ire of hikers. The Queen Charlotte Track is a
good one to bike, but part of it is closed in summer.

MOUNTAINEERING

NZ has a rich history of mountaineering and has proved an ideal training ground for greater adventures overseas – this, after all, is the home
of Sir Edmund Hillary, who along with Tenzing Norgay became the first
to scale Mt Everest. The Southern Alps are studded with a number of
impressive peaks and offer many challenging climbs.

This very physical and highly challenging pursuit is not for the uninitiated, and the risks can be high due to fickle weather, storms, winds, extreme cold, rock falls and the like. The deaths of eight climbers on Mt Tasman and Mt Cook in December 2003 were a sad illustration of this. Proper instruction and training will enable you to make common-sense decisions that will enhance your safety and get you up among those beautiful mountain peaks.

The Mt Cook region is only one of many outstanding climbing areas in the country. Others extend along the spine of the South Island from Tapuaenuku (in the Kaikoura Ranges) and the Nelson Lakes peaks in the north to the rugged southern mountains of Fiordland. Another area with possibilities for all levels of climbs is Mt Aspiring National Park, centred on the 'Matterhorn of the South', Mt Aspiring, and the Volta, Therma and Bonar ice fields which cling to its sides. To the south in the Forbes Mountains is Mt Earnslaw, flanked by the Rees and Dart Rivers.

The Christchurch-based **New Zealand Alpine Club** (NZAC; ☎ 03-377 7595; www.alpineclub.org.nz) gives professional information and produces the annual *NZ Alpine Journal* as well as numerous other publications.

For those seeking to learn the necessary skills or just get climbing, there are companies in locales such as Wanaka, Mt Cook, Tekapo and Fox Glacier providing expert instruction, mountaineering courses and private guiding.

PARAGLIDING/PARAPENTING

Paragliding, also known as parapenting, is perhaps the easiest way for humans to achieve assisted flight. The sport involves taking to the skies in what is basically a parachute that's been modified so that it glides through the air. After a half-day of instruction you should be able to do limited solo flights, and before you know it you could be taking flights at a height of 300m. One of the best places to learn the skills necessary to operate your paraglider/parapente is the **Wanaka Paragliding School** (☎ 03-443 9193; www.wanakaparagliding.co.nz).

This is a sport where you need to be confident in the qualifications and safety record of your instructor – we've had some complaints over the years from readers about substandard operators.

Tandem flights, where you are strapped to an experienced paraglider, are offered all over the country. Popular tandem experiences include glides from the top of the gondola in Queenstown and from Te Mata Peak in Hawke's Bay.

ROCK CLIMBING

Want to find out more about rock climbing? An informative website is hosted by Climb New Zealand – www.climb.co.nz.

On the North Island, popular rock-climbing areas include the Mt Eden Quarry in Auckland, Whanganui Bay and Motuoapa in the vicinity of Lake Taupo, and Piarere, near Cambridge. Wharepapa, about 20km southeast of Te Awamutu, is regarded as one of the best places in the country for climbing.

On the South Island, the Port Hills area above Christchurch has many climbs, and 100km away on the road to Arthur's Pass is Castle Hill, with great friction climbs. West of Nelson, the marble and limestone mountains of Golden Bay and Takaka Hill provide prime climbing, and north of Dunedin is Long Beach.

SAILING

This island nation has a habit of throwing up some of the world's best mariners. There's also a good reason why Auckland is called the 'City of

Sails'. If you're keen on yacht racing, try visiting the country's various sailing clubs and ask if you can help crew in local competitions. Otherwise, there are plenty of sailing operators who allow you to just laze around on deck or play a more hands-on role.

The Bay of Islands (and Whangaroa to the north), the southern lakes (Te Anau and Wakatipu) and the cities of Auckland and Dunedin are good places to get some wind in your sails.

SCUBA DIVING

The Bay of Islands Maritime and Historic Park, the Hauraki Gulf Maritime Park, Great Barrier Island and the Marlborough Sounds Maritime Park are obvious diving locales, but there are many more deep-water possibilities around both islands. Even Invercargill, with its notoriously cold water, has a diving club.

The Poor Knights Islands, off the east coast of the North Island, are reputed to have the best diving in NZ, and the late and great Jacques Cousteau rated them among the top 10 diving spots in the world – nearby

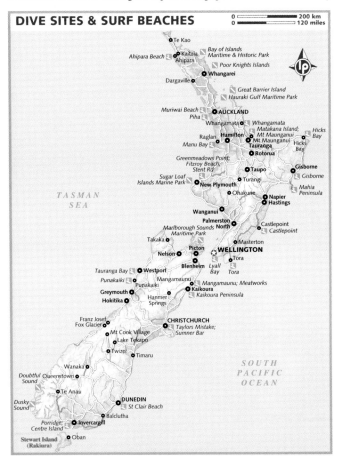

DIVE SITES & SURF BEACHES

SURFING IN NEW ZEALAND *Josh Kronfeld*

As a surfer I feel particularly guilty in letting the reader in on a local secret – NZ has a sensational mix of quality waves perfect for beginners and experienced surfers. As long as you're willing to travel off the beaten track, you can score some great, uncrowded waves. The islands of NZ are hit with swells from all points of the compass throughout the year. So, with a little weather knowledge and a little effort, numerous options present themselves. Point breaks, reefs, rocky shelves and hollow sandy beach breaks can all be found – take your pick!

Surfing has become increasingly popular in NZ and today there are surf schools up and running at most premier surf beaches. It's worth doing a bit of pretravel research: **Surfing New Zealand** (www.surfing.co.nz) recommends a number of schools on its website. If you're on a surf holiday in NZ, consider buying a copy of either *New Zealand Surfing Guide*, by Mike Bhana, or *Surf Riding in New Zealand*, by Wayne Warrick.

The Surfing New Zealand website also includes information on many great surf spots, but most NZ beaches hold good rideable breaks. Some of the ones I particularly enjoy are:

- **Waikato** Raglan (p226), NZ's most famous surf break and usually the first stop for overseas surfies.
- **Coromandel** Whangamata (p211)
- **Bay of Plenty** Mt Maunganui (p337), Matakana Island (p340)
- **Taranaki** Fitzroy Beach (p251), Stent Road and Greenmeadows Point all lie along the 'Surf Highway'.
- **The East Coast** Hicks Bay (p355), Gisborne city beaches (p362), Mahia Peninsula (p365)
- **Wellington region** Wellington city beaches such as Lyall Bay (p393), Castlepoint (p414) and Tora
- **Marlborough & Nelson** Kaikoura Peninsula (p435), Mangamaunu (p438), Meatworks
- **Canterbury** Taylors Mistake (p511), Sumner Bar
- **Otago** Dunedin is a good base for surfing on the South Island, with access to a number of superb breaks such as St Clair Beach (p561).
- **The West Coast** Punakaiki (p476), Tauranga Bay (p473)
- **Southland** Porridge (p631), Centre Island

New Zealand water temperatures and climate vary greatly from north to south. For comfort while surfing, wear a wet suit. In the summer on the North Island you can get away with a spring suit and boardies; on the South Island, a 2–3mm steamer. In winter on the North Island use a 2–3mm steamer, and on the South Island a 3–5mm with all the extras.

Josh is a keen surfer hailing originally from the Hawkes Bay region. While representing the All Blacks (1995–2000) he successfully juggled surfing, pop music and an international rugby career.

is the diveable wreck of the Greenpeace flagship *Rainbow Warrior*. You can also submerge yourself in the Sugar Loaf Islands Marine Park off Back Beach in New Plymouth.

The Marlborough Sounds have some interesting dives, including the *Mikhail Lermontov*, the largest diveable cruise-ship wreck in the world.

Fiordland on the South Island is highly unusual in that the region's extremely heavy rainfall and mountain runoff leaves a layer of often peaty brown fresh-water sitting on top of some of the saltwater fiords, notably Dusky and Doubtful Sounds. The fresh-water filters out light and discourages the growth of seaweed, so divers get to experience amazingly clear pseudo-deep-water conditions not far below the surface.

For more on NZ's explorable depths, pick up a copy of Lonely Planet's *Diving & Snorkeling New Zealand*, contact the **New Zealand Underwater Association** (☎ 09-623 3252) in Auckland, or visit www .divenewzealand.com.

SKIING & SNOWBOARDING

NZ is one of the most popular southern-hemisphere destinations for snow bunnies, with downhill (alpine), cross-country, ski touring and ski mountaineering all vigorously pursued. Heli-skiing is another popular activity, where choppers are used to lift skiers to the top of long, isolated stretches of virgin snow.

Unlike Europe, America or even Australia, NZ's commercial ski areas are generally not set up as resorts with chalets, lodges or hotels. Rather, accommodation and après-ski nightlife are often in surrounding towns that connect with the main ski areas via daily shuttles.

Club ski areas are publicly accessible and usually much less crowded and cheaper than commercial ski fields, even though nonmembers pay a slightly higher fee. Many such areas have lodges you can stay at, subject to availability – winter holidays and weekends will be fully booked, but midweek you'll be OK.

The variety of resorts and conditions makes it difficult to rate the ski fields in any particular order. Some people like to be near Queenstown's party scene or the classic volcanic scenery of Ruapehu, while others prefer the high slopes and quality runs of Mt Hutt, the less-crowded Rainbow Valley or the many club skiing areas.

At major ski areas, lift passes cost from $30 to $75 a day (roughly half for children and two-thirds for students). Lesson-and-lift packages are available at most resorts. Ski equipment rental starts at around $30 a day, while daily snowboard and boots hire starts at around $35; prices decrease for multiday hire. Try to rent equipment close to where you'll be skiing, so you can easily return your gear if there's a problem with the fit.

The ski season is generally from June to October, although it varies considerably from one ski area to another and can go as late as November.

Information centres in NZ, and the New Zealand Tourism Board (NZTB) internationally, have brochures on the various ski areas and packages, and can make bookings.

Useful snowphone services provide prerecorded information on weather, access and snow levels. Several websites (www.snow.co.nz and www.nzski.com, to name two) provide ski reports, employment updates, Web cams and virtual tours. The websites of various resorts (see the listings following) are also packed with up-to-date info.

The *NZ Ski & Snowboard Guide,* published by Brown Bear, is an excellent annual reference for snow lovers.

Left-facing page
Surfers, Manu Bay, Raglan (p226)
PAUL KENNEDY

Skiers, Mt Hutt (p537)
GRANT SOMERS

North Island

The North Island is dominated by volcanic cone skiing, with active Mt Ruapehu the premier ski area.

WHAKAPAPA & TUROA

The twin ski resorts of **Whakapapa** and **Turoa** (☎ 07-892 3738; www.whakapapa.co.nz; daily lift pass adult/child $62/31, 5-day passes $250/125), on either side of Mt Ruapehu, easily form NZ's largest ski area. Whakapapa, 6km above Whakapapa Village in Tongariro National Park, has more than 30 groomed runs. It includes a downhill course dropping nearly 722m over 4km, and the highest lift access in the country. There are plenty of snowboarding possibilities, including excellent pipes off the far western T-bar, cross-country, downhill and ski touring. You can drive yourself up to the slopes or take a shuttle minibus from Whakapapa Village, National Park township or Turangi.

Turoa has a 4km run, a beginners' lift, snowboarding and cross-country skiing. There's no road toll or parking fee and daily ski-area transport is available from Ohakune 17km away, which has the liveliest after-ski scene in the north.

For more information on the area, see Tongariro National Park (p282).

TUKINO

Club-operated **Tukino** (☎ 06-387 6294; www.tukino.co.nz; daily lift pass adult/child $30/10) is on the eastern side of Mt Ruapehu, 50km from Turangi. It's quite remote, situated 14km down a gravel road from the sealed Desert Rd (SH1), and you need a 4WD vehicle to get in (or make a prior arrangement to use club transport). Because access is so limited the area is uncrowded, but most runs are beginner or intermediate. Accommodation at the lodges must be arranged in advance: contact either **Desert Alpine Club** (☎ 09-575 8079) or **Aorangi Ski Club** (☎ 04-479 1194; www.aorangi.org).

See Tongariro National Park (p282) for more info.

MANGANUI SKI AREA

The **Manganui club ski area** (☎ 06-759 1119; http://snow.co.nz/manganui/; daily lift pass adult/child from $37/20) offers more volcano-slope skiing on the eastern slopes of Mt Taranaki in the Egmont National Park, 22km from Stratford. Skiing is possible off the summit; when conditions permit, it's an invigorating two-hour climb to the crater with an exhilarating 1300m descent.

For more info on the area, see Mt Taranaki/Egmont (p257).

South Island

NZ's best-known (and top-rated) skiing is on the South island, most of it revolving around the resort towns of Queenstown and Wanaka.

CORONET PEAK

The region's oldest ski field is **Coronet Peak** (☎ 03-442 4620; daily lift pass adult/child $77/39). The season here is reliable because of a multimillion dollar snow-making system, and the treeless slopes and good snow provide excellent skiing – the chairlifts run to altitudes of 1585m and 1620m. The consistent gradient and the many undulations make this a snowboarder's paradise.

Access is from Queenstown, 18km away, and there are shuttles in the ski season. See Queenstown (p581) for details of facilities in the area.

THE REMARKABLES

The visually impressive **Remarkables ski area** (☎ 03-442 4615; daily lift pass adult/child $72/37) is also near Queenstown (23km away), from where shuttle buses run during the season. It has beginner, intermediate and advanced runs, with chairlifts and beginners' tows. Look out for the sweeping run called Homeward Bound.

TREBLE CONE

The highest of the southern lake areas, **Treble Cone** (☎ 03-443 7443; www .treblecone.co.nz; daily lift pass adult/child $75/35) is in a spectacular location 29km from Wanaka and has steep slopes that are best for intermediate to advanced skiers. It also has a natural half-pipe for snowboarding.

For info on local facilities, see Wanaka (p604).

CARDRONA

Some 25km from Wanaka, **Cardrona** (☎ 03-443 7341, snowphone ☎ 0900 47669; www.cardrona.com; daily lift pass adult/child $68/34) has several high-capacity chair-lifts, beginners' tows and a radical half-pipe for snowboarders. Buses run from Wanaka during the ski season, and also from Queenstown.

Cardrona has acquired a reputation for the services it offers to disabled skiers, and it was the first resort on the South Island to have an on-field crèche. In summer it attracts mountain bikers.

WAIORAU NORDIC AREA

NZ's only commercial Nordic ski area, **Waiorau** (☎ 03-443 7542; www.snow farmnz.com; daily lift pass adult/child $29/10) is 26km from Wanaka on the Pisa Range, high above Lake Wanaka. There are 25km of groomed trails and thousands of hectares of open rolling country for the ski tourer. Huts with facilities are dotted along the top of the Pisa Range.

SOUTH CANTERBURY REGION

The commercial ski area **Ohau** (☎ 03-438 9885; www.ohau.co.nz; daily lift pass adult/child $48/16) is located on Mt Sutton some 52km from Twizel. It has the longest T-bar lift in NZ and a large percentage of intermediate and advanced runs, plus excellent terrain for snowboarding, cross-country and ski touring to Lake Dumb Bell. See Lake Ohau & Ohau Forests (p549) for info on accommodation.

The 3km-wide basin at **Mt Dobson** (☎ 03-685 8039; www.dobson.co.nz; daily lift pass adult/child $50/14), a commercial ski area 26km from Fairlie, caters for learners and has NZ's largest intermediate area. On a clear day you can see Mt Cook and the Pacific Ocean from the summit of Mt Dobson. For info on nearby facilities, see Fairlie (p545).

Fox Peak (☎ 03-688 0044; www.foxpeak.co.nz; daily lift pass $40, $35 if staying in lodge) is a club ski area situated 29km from Fairlie in the Two Thumb Range. Fox Peak has four rope tows and the learners' tow is free. There is good ski touring from the summit of Fox Peak and parapenting is also popular here. There is accommodation at Fox Lodge, 3km below the ski area.

MT HUTT

Mt Hutt (☎ 03-308 5074, snowphone ☎ 0900 99766; www.nzski.com/mthutt; daily lift pass adult/child $72/37) is one of the highest ski areas in the southern hemisphere, as well as one of NZ's best. It's close to Methven and can be reached by bus from Christchurch (118km to the west). Travellers have told us that the ski area's access road is a rough, unpaved ride and that drivers should be extremely cautious when the weather is poor.

Mt Hutt has beginner, intermediate and advanced slopes, with a quad and a triple chairlift, three T-bars, various other lifts and heli-skiing from the car park to slopes further afield. The wide open faces are good for those learning to snowboard.

For info on where to stay and eat in the area, see Methven (p537).

MT POTTS

The former Erewhon club ski area, **Mt Potts** (☎ 03-303 9060; www.mtpotts.co.nz) sits above the headwaters of the Rangitata River about 75km from Methven and is one of NZ's snow-white gems. It has a good mix of beginner, intermediate and advanced slopes, with snowboarding and cross-country also popular here, and serves as the base for a snow cat and heli-skiing operation.

Accommodation and meals are available at a lodge 8km from the ski area (DB&B from $80). Transport is by 4WD and can be arranged through the club. A day of skiing from the snow cat, including helicopter access, starts at $320. For info on the nearby Mt Somers, see p540.

PORTER HEIGHTS
The closest commercial ski area to Christchurch is **Porter Heights** (☎ 03-318 4002; www.porterheights.co.nz; daily lift pass adult/child $50/28), 96km away on the Arthur's Pass road. Its 720m-long Big Mama is the steepest run in NZ and there's a half-pipe for snowboarders, plus good cross-country areas and ski touring out along the ridge.

For accommodation in the area, see Craigieburn Forest Park (p534).

ARTHUR'S PASS & CRAIGIEBURN REGIONS
There are four ski areas in the Arthur's Pass and Craigieburn regions.

Temple Basin (☎ 03-377 7788; www.templebasin.co.nz; daily lift pass adult/child $38/26) is a club area 4km from the Arthur's Pass township, with half its terrain taken up by advanced runs. It's a 50-minute walk uphill from the car park to the ski-area lodges. There's floodlit skiing at night and good back-country runs for snowboarders. For info on local facilities, see Arthur's Pass (p535).

Craigieburn Valley (☎ 03-365 2514, snowphone 03-366 7766; www.craigieburn.co.nz; daily lift pass adult/child $44/25), centred on Hamilton Peak, is a ski area 40km from Arthur's Pass. It's one of NZ's most challenging club areas, with intermediate and advanced runs and a shredder's 'soggy dream'. It's a pleasant 10-minute walk through beech forest from the car park to the ski area. See Craigieburn Forest Park (p534) and Arthur's Pass (p536) for details of local places to stay and eat.

Another good club area in the Craigieburn Range is **Mt Cheeseman** (☎ 03-379 5315; www.mtcheeseman.com; daily lift pass adult/child $45/25), 112km from Christchurch. The ski area, based on Mt Cockayne, is in a wide, sheltered basin.

Also in Craigieburn and difficult to find, but worth the search, is **Mt Olympus** (☎ 03-318 5840; www.mtolympus.co.nz; daily lift pass adult/child $35/20), 66km from Methven and 12km from Lake Ida. This club area has four tows which lead to intermediate and advanced runs. Snowboarding is allowed, and there are good cross-country areas and ski-touring trails to other areas. Access by 4WD is advisable from the bottom hut.

HANMER SPRINGS REGION
There are two ski areas near Hanmer Springs. Accommodation is on-field, or you can stay in the township (p530).

Hanmer Springs Ski Area (☎ 025-341 806; www.snow.co.nz/hanmersprings/; daily lift pass adult/child $35/20) is based on Mt St Patrick, 17km from Hanmer Springs, and has mostly intermediate and advanced runs.

Skier, Cardrona (p611)
DAVID WALL

Mt Lyford (Amuri; ☎ 03-315 6178, snowphone ☎ 03-366 1220; www.mtlyford.co.nz; daily lift pass adult/child $45/25) is about 60km from Hanmer Springs or Kaikoura, and 4km from Mt Lyford Village, where accommodation is available. The Lake Stella field has skiing at all levels, basin and off-piste cross-country skiing, 15km of groomed trails for ski touring, and a natural pipe for snowboarding, while nearby **Terako Basin** has advanced skiing and is linked by rope tow to Mt Lyford.

NELSON REGION

Near St Arnaud in Nelson Lakes National Park are two ski areas. The closest accommodation is in St Arnaud (p451) but there's also transport to and from Nelson (p442) and Blenheim (p430).

The commercial ski area **Rainbow Valley** (☎ 03-521 1861) is just outside the park and offers good cross-country ski touring. Rainbow was closed during the 2003 season while new lifts and other equipment were installed; at the time of writing, lift prices hadn't yet been established.

Mt Robert (☎ 03-548 8336; www.mtrobert.co.nz; daily lift pass adult/child $25/20) is a club area inside the national park – from St Arnaud, drive 7km to the car park, then walk for two hours (8km) to reach the ski field. This area is known for its fine powder and cross-country opportunities, but only those suitably equipped need apply.

Heli-skiing & Glacier Skiing

NZ's remote snow-dusted heights are tailor-made for heli-skiing. From July to October, operators cover a wide off-piste area along the Southern Alps. The cost ranges from around $550 for a half-day trip (three runs), or from $700 to $950 for a full day (four to seven runs).

Some reliable heli-skiing companies:

Fox & Franz Josef Heliservices (☎ 0800 800 793, 03-752 0793; www.scenic-flights.co.nz; Fox and Franz Josef Glaciers)

Hanmer Springs Helicopters (☎ 0800 888 308, 03-315 7758; Hanmer Springs)

Harris Mountains Heli-Ski (☎ 03-442 6722; www.heliski.co.nz; Queenstown)

Heli Ski Queenstown (☎ 03-442 7733; Queenstown)

Methven Heliskiing (☎ 03-302 8108; www.heliskiing.co.nz/methven/about.htm; Methven)

Want to avoid the crowds? DOC offices and park headquarters can advise and help you plan some enjoyable tramps on lesser-known tracks. There are DOC offices in every city and in dozens of towns, providing free information about tramping in their areas, or you can check out the website, www.doc.govt.nz.

Snowboarder, Cardrona (p611)

GRANT SOMERS

SKYDIVING

Strangely enough, ejecting yourself from a plane at high altitude and plummeting earthwards with only a few metres of cloth strapped to your back is a popular activity in NZ. There are plenty of professional operators, and at most drop zones the views on the way up (not to mention on the way down) are breathtaking.

Some operators and clubs offer static-line jumps and Accelerated Free Fall courses, but for most first-timers a tandem skydive is the way to go. After bonding with a fully-qualified instructor, you get to experience up to 45 seconds of high-speed free fall before the chute opens. The thrill is worth every dollar (specifically as much as $245/295 for a 9000/12,000ft jump).

Tandem skydiving can be tried on the North Island at Parakai near Auckland, Paihia, Taupo and Rotorua. On the South Island there's tandem skydiving at Nelson, Christchurch, Fox Glacier, Wanaka and Queenstown.

TRAMPING

Tramping (that's Kiwi-speak for bushwalking, hiking or trekking) is a fine way to notch up first-hand experiences within NZ's natural beauty. There are thousands of kilometres of tracks, many well marked but some only a line on a map, as well as an excellent network of huts that enable trampers to avoid lugging tents and (in some cases) cooking gear. Before plodding along any track, you should get up-to-date information from the appropriate authority, usually the DOC. The DOC received a significant increase in government funding in 2002 and has embarked on an upgrade of many huts, tracks and national-park facilities.

The so-called Great Walks are the most popular tracks. Their beauty does indeed make them worth experiencing, but prepare yourself for the fact that they can get quite crowded, especially over summer, when people from all over the world come to follow them. On the Milford, Routeburn and Kepler Tracks, you have to prebook your tramp for specific days over summer, sometimes well in advance depending on demand; the Lake Waikaremoana Track requires booking year-round.

When tramping, consult and register your intentions with a DOC office before starting the longer walks and, above all, heed their advice.

Tracks that receive the highest numbers of feet are the Routeburn, Milford, Tongariro Northern Circuit (and the one-day Tongariro Crossing), Kepler, Lake Waikaremoana and Abel Tasman Coastal Tracks. Most people on these tracks are from outside NZ – Kiwis are keen trampers, but tend to avoid the most heavily promoted tracks in favour of wilder, less trafficked pathways gleaned from local knowledge.

When to Go

The high season for walking is during the school summer holidays, lasting from two weeks before Christmas until the end of January; avoid it if you can. The best weather is from January to March, though most tracks can be walked enjoyably at any time from about October through to April. June and July (midwinter) is not the time to be out on the tracks, especially at altitude – some paths close in winter because of avalanche danger.

What to Bring

For an enjoyable tramp the primary considerations are your feet and shoulders. Make sure your footwear is adequate and that your pack isn't too heavy. Adequate wet-weather gear is also very important, especially on the South Island's waterlogged West Coast, where your pores can be flooded in minutes if your gear is substandard. And don't forget insect repellent unless you want to dance the sandfly jig in coastal areas.

If you're camping, or staying in huts where there are no stoves (eg on the Abel Tasman Coastal Track), bring a camping stove. You can buy these, along with fuel and other camping gear, from sundry outdoor shops around NZ.

Books

DOC produces very good books with detailed information on the flora and fauna, geology and history of NZ's national parks. It also publishes leaflets (each usually costing 50c to $1.50) outlining thousands of walking tracks throughout the country.

Lonely Planet's *Tramping in New Zealand,* by Jim DuFresne, describes more than 50 walks of various lengths and degrees of difficulty. *101 Great Tramps,* by Mark Pickering and Rodney Smith, has suggestions for two- to six-day tramps around the country. Also worth scanning is John Cobb's *Walking Tracks of NZ's National Parks.*

Tramping in North Island Forest Parks, by Euan and Jennie Nicol, and *Tramping in South Island Forest Parks*, by Joanna Wright, outline shorter excursions, from half-hour walks to tramps taking several days. *Accessible Walks*, by Anna Jameson and Andrew Jameson, is an excellent guide for trampers with a disability (and elderly walkers) to more than 100 South Island walks.

Maps

Topographical maps produced by **Land Information New Zealand** (LINZ; www.linz.govt.nz) are best. Bookshops don't usually have a good selection of these, but LINZ has map-sales offices in main cities and towns, and DOC offices also often sell LINZ maps for tracks in their area. LINZ's map series includes park maps, covering national, state and forest parks; cartography for the more popular walking tracks; and the highly detailed 'Topomaps', though you may need two or three maps to cover one track.

Track Classification

Tracks are classified according to various features, including their level of difficulty. In this chapter we loosely refer to the level of difficulty as easy, medium, hard or difficult. The widely used track classification system is:

Path Easy and well formed; allows for wheelchair access or constructed to 'shoe' standard (ie walking boots not required). Suitable for people of all ages and fitness levels.

Walking Track Easy and well formed; constructed to 'shoe' standard. Suitable for people of most ages and fitness levels.

Tramping Track Requires skill and experience; constructed to 'boot' standard. Suitable for people of average physical fitness.

Route Requires a high degree of skill, experience and route-finding ability. Suitable for well-equipped trampers.

Track Safety

Thousands of people tramp in NZ every year without incident, but every year a few die in the mountains. Most fatalities could have been avoided if simple safety rules had been observed.

Some trails are only for the experienced and well-equipped – don't attempt such tracks if you don't fit the bill. NZ's climatic changeability subjects high-altitude walks to snow and ice even in summer, so always check weather conditions before setting off.

Right-facing page
Trekker, Matukituki River,
Mt Aspiring National Park
(p606)
GARETH MCCORMACK

The Great Walks

All nine Great Walks (one of which is actually a river trip) are described in this guidebook and in Lonely Planet's *Tramping in New Zealand*, and are also detailed in pamphlets provided by DOC offices and visitors centres.

To tramp them you'll need to buy a Great Walks hut or camping pass, sold at DOC offices and visitors centres in the vicinity of each walk – on some walks, regular back-country hut tickets and passes (p82) can be used to procure a bunk or camp site in the track's low (nonsummer) season. Hut prices vary from $10 to $35 per night depending on the track and the season; camping fees range from $6 to $15 per night. You can camp only at designated camping grounds; there's no camping on the Milford Track.

The Great Walks:

Abel Tasman Coastal Track (p456) An easy two- to three-day walk close to beaches and bays in Abel Tasman National Park (South Island). NZ's most popular walk is inundated with people, including sea kayakers.

Heaphy Track (p464) A four- to five-day, medium to hard 77km tramp through the forest and karst (limestone) landscape of Kahurangi National Park (South Island). The last day includes a magnificent beach walk.

Kepler Track (p617) This four- to five-day, 67km walk in Fiordland National Park (South Island) is a medium to hard tramp. Climb to the top of a mountain and enjoy alpine, lake and river-valley scenery.

Lake Waikaremoana Track (p366) A three- to four-day, easy to medium tramp in Te Urewera National Park (North Island), with great views of the lake and surrounding bush-clad slopes.

Milford Track (p624) This 54km, four-day walk in Fiordland National Park (South Island) is one of the world's best-known. It's an easy walk and includes an alpine-pass crossing and views of river valleys, glaciers and waterfalls.

GREAT WALKS

Rakiura Track (p648) A three-day tramp on Stewart Island, mostly on duckboards and requiring medium fitness. The track goes along the coast and through forest.
Routeburn Track (p600) A medium, three-day, 40km walk through the stunning alpine scenery of Mt Aspiring and Fiordland National Parks (South Island).
Tongariro Northern Circuit (p284) A four-day, medium to hard tramp through the active volcanic landscape of Tongariro National Park (North Island). Part of this tramp can be done as the one-day Tongariro Crossing (p284).
Whanganui Journey (p272) A canoe trip down the Whanganui River in Whanganui National Park (North Island). Designated a Great Walk even though it's obviously not a walk.

Other Tracks

There are numerous tramping possibilities besides the Great Walks in all forest and national parks. Most of the following walks are *not* described in detail in this book:

NORTH ISLAND
Coromandel Track A three-day, easy to medium walk in the Kauaeranga Valley in Coromandel Forest Park, Coromandel Peninsula.
Mt Holdsworth Circuit & Totara Flats Track Two three-day tramps in Holdsworth and Tararua Forest Park, respectively. The first is a medium to hard walk over the top of alpine Mt Holdsworth. The second is a medium tramp mostly along the Totara River Valley.
Ninety Mile Beach–Cape Reinga Walkway A 50km, three-day, easy beach tramp (camping only) in Northland.
Round the Mountain, Mt Taranaki/Egmont A 55km walk of four days or more in Egmont National Park, comprising medium to hard tramping through mountainous country.
Tongariro Crossing A brilliant, 17km, one-day, medium tramp through Tongariro National Park.

SOUTH ISLAND
Arthur's Pass There are many walks to choose from in Arthur's Pass National Park, most of which are rated difficult.
Banks Peninsula Walk A two-day (medium) or four-day (easy) walk over the hills and along the coast of Banks Peninsula, crossing private and public land near Akaroa.
Greenstone & Caples Tracks These two tracks are on stewardship land, just outside Fiordland National Park. They're close to the Routeburn Track and a good way to start or finish this popular track.
Hump Ridge Track Inaugurated in 2001, this is a three-day, 53km circuit beginning and ending at Bluecliffs Beach on Te Wae Wae Bay, 20km from Tuatapere.
Inland Pack Track A 30km medium tramp in Paparoa National Park, following river valleys through the karst landscape near Punakaiki on the West Coast.
Kaikoura Coast Track A three-day, easy walk over private and public land along the spectacular coastline 50km south of Kaikoura.
Matukituki Valley walks There are good medium-to-hard walks in the Matukituki Valley, in Mt Aspiring National Park, near Wanaka.
North-West Circuit This eight- to 10-day hard walk is just one of many wilderness possibilities on Stewart Island (Rakiura).
Queen Charlotte Track A three- to four-day medium walk in the Marlborough Sounds affording great views of the sounds and passing many historic places. There's accommodation and water transport on this track.
Rees-Dart Track A 70km, four- to five-day hard walk in Mt Aspiring National Park, through river valleys and traversing an alpine pass.
St James Walkway This 66km, five-day medium walk in Lake Sumner Forest Park/Lewis Pass Reserve passes through excellent subalpine scenery.
Wangapeka & Leslie-Karamea Tracks The Wangapeka is a four- to five-day medium tramp along river valleys and overpasses. The Leslie-Karamea is a 90km to 100km, five- to seven-day tramp for experienced walkers only, which negotiates river valleys, gorges and passes.

Back-country Hut & Camping Fees

DOC has a huge network of back-country huts (more than 1000) in NZ's national, maritime and forest parks. There are 'serviced huts' (with mattress-equipped bunks or sleeping platforms, water, heating, toilets and sometimes cooking facilities), 'standard huts' (no cooking equipment or heating) and 'basic huts' or bivvies. Back-country hut fees range from free to $25 per night for adults, paid with tickets purchased in advance at any DOC office or park visitors centre. Children under 11 years of age can use all huts free of charge. School children aged 11 and older are charged half-price. If you plan to do a lot of tramping, DOC also sells an annual hut pass (adult/child $65/32.50), applicable to all its huts bar those on the Great Walks.

Depending on the category of hut, a night's stay may use one or two tickets. When you arrive at a hut, date the tickets and put them in the box provided. Accommodation is on a first-come, first-served basis.

DOC also manages 200 vehicle-accessible camping grounds – the most basic of these ('informal' sites) are free, while 'standard' and 'serviced' grounds cost between $3 and $12 per person per night.

The Milford, Kepler and Routeburn tracks operate on a separate system and can be booked through **Te Anau DOC** (☎ 03-249 8514; greatwalks booking@doc.govt.nz). The booking centre for the Abel Tasman Coastal Track is the **Motueka visitors centre** (☎ 03-528 0005), but you can also buy passes at Takaka DOC and Nelson visitors centre.

Getting There & Away

Getting to and from tracks can be a real problem, except for the most popular trails, which are serviced by trampers' transport. Having a vehicle only simplifies the problem of getting to one end of the track. Otherwise you have to take public transport or hitch in, and if the track starts or ends at the terminus of a dead-end road, hitching will be difficult.

Of course, tracks that are easily accessed by public transport (such as Abel Tasman) are also the most crowded. An alternative is to arrange private transport, either with a friend or by chartering a vehicle to drop you off at one end and pick you up at the other. If you intend to leave

Kahurangi National Park
(p463), Nelson

GARETH MCCORMACK

RESPONSIBLE TRAMPING
To help preserve the ecology and beauty of NZ consider the following tips when tramping.

RUBBISH
- Carry out all your rubbish. Don't overlook easily forgotten items, such as silver paper, orange peel, cigarette butts and plastic wrappers. Empty packaging should be stored in a dedicated rubbish bag. Make an effort to carry out rubbish left by others.
- Never bury your rubbish: digging disturbs soil and ground cover and encourages erosion. Buried rubbish will likely be dug up by animals, who may be injured or poisoned by it. It may also take years to decompose.
- Minimise waste by taking minimal packaging and no more food than you will need. Take reusable containers or stuff sacks.
- Sanitary napkins, tampons, condoms and toilet paper should be carried out despite the inconvenience. They burn and decompose poorly.

HUMAN-WASTE DISPOSAL
- Contamination of water sources by human faeces can lead to the transmission of all sorts of nasties. Where there is a toilet, please use it. Where there is none, bury your waste. Dig a small hole 15cm (6in) deep and at least 100m (320ft) from any watercourse. Cover the waste with soil and a rock. In snow, dig down to the soil.
- Ensure that these guidelines are applied to a portable toilet tent if one is being used by a large tramping party. Encourage all party members to use the site.

WASHING
- Don't use detergents or toothpaste in or near watercourses, even if they are biodegradable.
- For personal washing, use biodegradable soap and a water container (or even a lightweight, portable basin) at least 50m (160ft) away from the watercourse. Disperse the waste water widely to allow the soil to filter it fully.
- Wash cooking utensils 50m (160ft) from watercourses using a scourer, sand or snow instead of detergent.

EROSION
- Hillsides and mountain slopes, especially at high altitudes, are prone to erosion. Stick to existing tracks and avoid short cuts.

- If a well-used track passes through a mud patch, walk through the mud so as not to increase the size of the patch.
- Avoid removing the plant life that keeps topsoils in place.

FIRES & LOW-IMPACT COOKING
- Don't depend on open fires for cooking. The cutting of wood for fires in popular tramping areas can cause rapid deforestation. Cook on a lightweight kerosene, alcohol or Shellite (white gas) stove and avoid those powered by disposable butane gas canisters.
- In alpine areas, ensure that all members are outfitted with enough clothing so that fires are not a necessity for warmth.
- If you patronise local accommodation, select those places that do not use wood fires to heat water or cook food.
- Fires may be acceptable below the tree line in areas that get very few visitors. If you light a fire, use an existing fireplace. Don't surround fires with rocks. Use only dead, fallen wood. Remember the adage 'the bigger the fool, the bigger the fire'. Use minimal wood, just what you need for cooking. In huts, leave wood for the next person.
- Ensure that you fully extinguish a fire after use. Spread the embers and flood them with water.

WILDLIFE CONSERVATION
- Do not engage in or encourage hunting. It is illegal in all parks and reserves.
- Don't buy items made from endangered species.
- Don't attempt to exterminate animals in huts. In wild places, they are likely to be protected native animals.
- Discourage the presence of wildlife by not leaving food scraps behind you. Place gear out of reach and tie packs to rafters or trees.
- Do not feed the wildlife as this can lead to animals becoming dependent on hand-outs, to unbalanced populations and to diseases.

CAMPING & WALKING ON PRIVATE PROPERTY
- Always seek permission to camp from landowners.

Kayakers, Buller River,
near Murchison (p468)
DAVID WALL

your own vehicle at a track-head car park and return for it later, don't leave anything of value inside – thefts from cars in these isolated areas is a significant problem.

WHITE-WATER RAFTING & KAYAKING

There are almost as many white-water rafting possibilities as there are rivers in NZ, and there's no shortage of companies to take you on an exhilarating ride down some magnificently wild watercourses.

Popular raft carriers on the South Island include the Shotover and Kawarau Rivers, while the Rangitata River is considered one of the country's best. The north of the island also has great rafting possibilities, such as the Buller, Karamea and Mohikinui Rivers; Westport and Murchison are the best bases from which to take these rivers on. Other West Coast possibilities include the Hokitika, Arnold and Waiho Rivers.

On the North Island there are plenty of raft-worthy rivers too, such as the Rangitaiki, Wairoa, Motu, Tongariro, Rangitikei and Ngaruroro. There are also the Kaituna Cascades near Rotorua – the highlight of this river is the 7m Okere Falls.

Rivers are graded from I to VI, with VI meaning 'unraftable'. The grading of the Shotover canyon varies from III to V+, depending on the time of year, while the Kawarau River is rated IV and the Wairoa River III to V. On the rougher stretches there's usually a minimum age limit of 12 or 13 years. All safety equipment is supplied by the operator.

For more info on windsurfing, check out the website of Windsurfing New Zealand, www.windsurfingnz.org.

Half-day and full-day rafting trips cost from $90 to $200 per person, with the highest prices involving helicopter access. Note that an excursion taking up most of a day often involves only an hour or two on the water, with the rest of the time taken up with travel to/from the river.

White-water kayaking is popular among enthusiasts but, unlike rafting, it's a solo activity requiring skills and training. The **New Zealand Kayak School** (☎ 03-523 9611; www.nzkayakschool.com) in Murchison offers intensive four-day courses for introductory to advanced levels from $595.

WINDSURFING

Windsurfing has thousands of Kiwi adherents and there are plenty of lakes and other popular spots on both islands to catch the wind. Auckland harbour, Hauraki Gulf, the Bay of Islands, Oakura near New Plymouth and 'windy' Wellington are just some of the outstanding coastal locations. There are many places where you can hire boards and receive high-standard instruction.

Food & Drink Julie Biuso

It's easier to capture the essence of 'being Kiwi' than to try to define the cuisine of this country. It's the beach and lake environment, barbecues, fresh air ruffling our feathers, and the space and climate to cook and eat outside. There is the chance to grow dinner in the back garden, find it in the countryside, and catch it in the wild or in the sea. All of these things are what is great about New Zealand.

We used to have 60 million cloven-hoofed woolly blankets on legs munching the lush grasslands and the dry country. Hardly any surprise then, that our national dinner was roast lamb, or more likely the longer-toothed brother, hogget.

We're still eating lamb, but something momentous has happened down on the farm, something which can't be blamed on the carnivores among us. In just over 20 years the number of sheep grown in NZ has dropped from 60 to 40 million. Who ate the other 20 million?

Deregulation hit NZ in the 1980s – which opened the farm gate to a lot more options than growing sheep and cattle. Some farmers stopped replacing animal stock and sold off their land, making way for kiwi fruit, grape vines and olive trees. It changed the look of the land and drastically altered what we put on our plates and our palates.

Shrugging off the image NZ had as a supplier of bulk frozen lamb and beef and blocks of yellow, all-purpose cheese, was not easy. But a new breed of producers and manufacturers entered the arena in the '80s and '90s with one goal in mind: excellence.

With a history of cooking rather than cuisine and eating the food of our British migrant ancestors, Kiwis have finally gone global. The past two decades have seen us embrace our unique blend of ethnic cultures and cuisines, drawing in Pacific and Asian influences and giving rise to Pacific Rim cookery.

The cultural freedom this generation enjoys has given birth to a free spirit in the kitchen, where experimentation and adaptation are now part of everyday cooking.

The most striking features about the food are its quality and its freshness. Prime cuts of meat from animals that graze freely outdoors, lakes of fresh milk and cream, orchards of tree-ripened fruit, fields of fresh vegetables, hundreds of vineyards producing sensational wines, all-around seas teaming with fish and skies abuzz with honey bees – no joking, this is as near to the land of milk and honey as you're likely to find.

For the visitor, it's all good news. The food and wine has never been better, and award-winning fare is easy and affordable in restaurants and cafés,

Julie Biuso's food career started with a great batch of hot cross buns at the age of 10. The following year, the buns flopped and she realised she had a lot to learn – 23 years as a magazine food editor and 12 award-winning books later, she reckons she's still learning.

DID YOU KNOW?

It's all to do with teeth. 'Lamb', which in NZ refers to animals up to 12 months old, should still have their first teeth. Once their second incisors pop into their mouths, from 12 to 18 months old, the meat is sold as 'hogget' and once they're sporting their third and final chompers, they're called 'mutton'.

NZ SCOOPS WINE AWARDS

New Zealand wine first gained international attention in 1985 in London with the success of Cloudy Bay Sauvignon Blanc in the Air New Zealand Export Awards held in association with *Decanter* magazine.

It was inconceivable at the time that a wine produced in a country that was known as a primary producer of meat, butter and cheese, with a fledgling wine industry, could win a top award in a prestigious wine competition.

This recognition proved to be a catalyst for the country's burgeoning wine industry, and was a catalyst for NZ's food world, too.

in specialist stores and well-stocked supermarkets. Well-cooked fresh food is in abundance in the cities and the variety there is impressive, but it's also surprisingly easy to dine on exceptional food and wines in the proverbial 'middle of nowhere'. NZ is a culinary adventure for the hungry traveller.

STAPLES & SPECIALITIES

We're still predominately a nation of meat eaters and the quality of our meat these days is outstanding. Sheep and cattle are reared outdoors and fed entirely on grass (in fact Kiwis struggle to believe that farms could be run any other way!). The climate, the breeds and the natural diet all combine to produce sweet-tasting lamb with particularly fine-grained meat, and beef of incomparable tenderness and flavour.

Roast lamb or hogget is a popular choice for a family meal. The classic vegetable accompaniments are roasted potatoes, kumara (sweet potato), greens and pumpkin. There's nothing quite like the sticky caramelised goo adhering to the meat, and chunks of kumara and pumpkin as you dish up a traditional Kiwi roast.

DID YOU KNOW?

The flesh of the male green shell mussel is creamy white, and the female is coral-coloured.

It's still possible to catch dinner from the sea without much effort, but you don't usually *need* to – fish farms are springing up everywhere. The most common mussel species is the green shell. It is farmed in abundance, and famed too for its anti-inflammatory properties that have spread from folklore to fact. It's a true Kiwi icon.

A NZ sauvignon blanc full of passionfruit, capsicum and gooseberry characters and the zing of crisp acid, may be out of place on a chilly night in the northern hemisphere. But try it on a beach in NZ, with the salty tang of the sea filling the nostrils, a whiff of barbecue smoke in the air, and a bowlful of plump mussels or scallops, which have met the heat for just a few seconds…and you'll quickly swoon and fall in love!

Luv 'em or loathe 'em, oysters are big time here, especially the Bluff oyster, dredged around the southern tip of the South Island.

Much of NZ's paua (abalone) finds its way overseas illegally, but it also appears on the menus of top-notch local seafood restaurants and seaside cafés.

New Zealand whitebait is a tiny thread-like fish with a deliciously sweet but delicate flavour. It features regularly on menus as whitebait fritters.

DID YOU KNOW?

When you order scallops – both the muscle and orange roe are served and eaten.

Other distinctive and expensive seafood offerings include the rare shellfish *toheroa* (a large clam that grows to around 15cm long), which is said to taste like oyster that has dined on asparagus, and crayfish, which is exported under the name of rock lobster.

And although you can't buy rainbow or brown trout, there are plenty of opportunities to fish for them, and plenty of places to stay with cooking facilities, or where the chef will cook your catch for you.

Cervena (farmed deer) features on menus throughout NZ and can be purchased fresh from specialist butchers. The meat is lean and better served rare.

Kiwi fruit takes pride of place on top of the eggwhite and sugar concoction known as pavlova. The Australians have long laid claim to this sweet meringue cake, but they garnish it with kiwi fruit, too, which shows that they copied us, so we must have invented it! The pav, as it is known, is the quintessential Kiwi dessert, touted around in plastic containers to family gatherings. At its best the sugar crust cracks with a tap giving way to a mass of foamy meringue. The whole lot is sunk under a mountain of cream and a ring of kiwi fruit. Not to be missed.

A recent industry is avocado oil. The emerald green oil is redolent of artichokes and celery when you sniff it, with a hint of mushroom. It also tastes a bit like artichoke, too, with no acidity or astringency, then, at the end, a bucket load of pure avocado flavour kicks in.

Kiwis usually start the day with cereal, fruit, yoghurt, toast, juice and coffee or tea. Although at weekends they might make more of an effort or eat out at a café.

A city lunch, unless it's a special occasion, is eaten at the desk, on the street, in the car, or at the park without any pomp and ceremony. It's usually a bread-based meal.

Dinner takes place anytime from 6pm through to 9.30pm (many restaurants close their kitchens at 10pm).

DRINKS
Alcohol

Kiwis like to drink. Whether it's a beer after work, a glass of bubbly to celebrate a special occasion, or a glass or two of wine around the barbecue or over dinner, alcohol is part of the social culture on all levels.

It's easy to find good wine and not that much harder to find excellent wine in NZ. Good bargains can be found in supermarket wine sections, but boutique wines have to be sought at wine stores or bought from the winery.

One of the best ways to get to know NZ wines, and NZ itself for that matter, is to visit wineries, which you can do independently or by taking a wine tour (see the boxed text p88).

There are still some restaurants, mainly ethnic and inexpensive, which hold a BYO (bring your own) license, allowing diners to bring in their own wine to consume in the restaurant. You'll be charged a small fee for corkage, but will have saved yourself the usual restaurant mark-up on the wine.

While beer consumption has dropped about 30% in 30 years, there's now more choice in beer styles. Boutique breweries are popping up all

---

TRAVEL YOUR TASTEBUDS

There are many interesting foods to try on your travels, some unique to NZ.

Piko piko (edible fern shoots) Like a down-under version of asparagus. Nutty in flavour, they can be served up in salads and cooked dishes.

Horopito (bush pepper) Has a hot peppery bite. Made into a rub for meats, or seafood before it is smoked.

Kawakawa (bush basil) Has a subtle flavour and scent. Best for white meats and fish, or added to fresh pasta.

Kelp salt Salt flavoured with lemon, chilli or lime and is fantastic sprinkled over pan-fried, barbecued or grilled fish, and on smoked fish or seafood pasta, as well as over vegetables such as tomatoes and cooked beans. Made from hand-harvested and sun-dried kelp, it's packed full of nutrients.

Karengo (a native seaweed) Also hand-harvested and sun-dried, *karengo* adds the nutrients of the sea and a fresh saline flavour to dishes.

We dare you:

- Kiwis are rather fond of an iron-rich, sticky brown yeast spread called Marmite, or the vegetable equivalent called Vegemite. Spread thinly on crackers, topped with a slice or two of tomato and a sprig of parsley it makes a homespun snack, which wards off the desire for something salty and savoury. The trick is to spread it thinly – a tablespoon of either has the strength of a cup of soy sauce.

- Kina, a species of sea urchin plentiful around NZ coastlines, looks like something from outer space with its spiny exterior. It is sweetest in spring, and best eaten straight out of the water. Cut it open and scoop or suck out the contents. An acquired taste.

WINE-TOURING

Wine touring may not seem as synonymous with NZ as it does with countries like France, Germany and Australia, but the country has nurtured some outstanding wine regions and its international reputation for quality wine continues to grow. In turn, this has fed an interest in wine-touring. There are dozens of tours available, many of which also visit food producers and places of interest.

Wineries are distributed from around Kaitaia and Kerikeri in the far north right down to Central Otago, which at a latitude of 45 degrees has some of the most southern vineyards in the world. You can cycle or drive between many of these vintage enterprises and taste at the cellar door. And many wineries are now equipped with fine cafés, restaurants, associated businesses such as cheese or preserve making, and accommodation. There are numerous operators willing to bus you around the main grape-littered regions on half- and full-day tours.

The best regions to tour are Marlborough (see the boxed text p432), Nelson, Martinborough in the Wairarapa, Hawkes Bay (p379), Gisborne, Henderson (west Auckland, p129), Waiheke Island (in the Hauraki Gulf, p135) and Central Otago (p576). Marlborough, Hawkes Bay and Martinborough all host big annual wine and food festivals.

---

over the country, and it's now considered as trendy to sip a fruity tasting beer as it is an unoaked chardonnay or pinot gris.

Coffee

You've got to give it to the Kiwis – when they decide to do something, they do it well. Take coffee. Ten years ago most places served up 'perked' coffee, coffee that was left to stew over an element set on low, or 'drip' coffee which was kept hot for hours.

But coffee in the big cities now rivals that of NZ's nearest coffee capital, Melbourne, and it's certainly better than coffee in Italy.

Unique perhaps to NZ is the penchant for oversized bowls of latte and cappuccino. No self-respecting Italian would order a cappuccino after 11am, but Kiwis lap up giant bowls of the frothy stuff day and night. And good it is, too. Practically any café that looks modern and clean will serve up a decent espresso or cappuccino.

Working as a barrista is considered sexy and something the young do with a great deal of panache.

CELEBRATIONS

Food and wine are celebrated throughout NZ, with many regions and cities holding festivals. It's generally a great day out, offering the visitor a chance to mingle with the locals and to sip and savour some of the best food, wine and hospitality that particular part of the country has to offer.

The Maori *hangi*, is an unusual method of cooking food in the ground over hot river stones. Potatoes, kumara, carrots, pumpkin, onion, corn, cabbage, poultry, fish and meats are thrown in together and steamed until tender, taking on some of the flavour of the earth. *Hangi* are a feature of almost any formal Maori occasion, from funerals to important meetings on the *marae*. They're also a great informal communal event: there's much exertion and nodding of wise heads as the hole is dug and food prepared, and plenty of time for sitting around talking while the stones are heated (with a few exploding stones adding moments of excitement) and while the food cooks. The Polynesian equivalent of the earth oven is the *umu*.

The most common form of entertaining and celebrating on a small scale is the backyard barbecue. Most Kiwis own a barbecue, probably gas-fired, although there is an increasing number of sophisticated outdoors kitchens-on-wheels. The NZ barbecue can either be dire – charred sausages and steak the texture of sawdust – or brilliant. With superb quality meat and seafood it can be as simple as firing up the barbie, slapping on a few pieces of aged beef and opening a bottle of chardonnay.

WHERE TO EAT & DRINK
You're spoilt for choice in the big cities, and you'll find some amazingly well-prepared fresh food all around NZ. You'll find some shockers, too, and the usual advice applies – it is a good idea to choose a clean, well-patronised place.

On the whole Auckland cafés are pavement-spilling affairs, often with cutting edge design, lots of chrome and glass, and stylish fit-outs. Even in the chill of a winter's evening, Aucklanders sit huddled outside under huge gas lamps. To see and be seen is part of the café culture.

In Wellington and further south they're not as silly. When the southerly winds come howling in from Antarctica they huddle around open fires in bars, cafés and restaurants. Recycled furniture and a homely welcoming feel sums up many of these unpretentious cafés.

The influences of the Pacific are as evident as those of Italy, the Mediterranean and Asia, and many restaurants and cafés seem unable to settle for one style or the other. Don't be surprised if on the same menu you find kokoda (raw fish marinated in lemon/lime juice and finished with coconut cream), and linguine dressed with prosciutto, parmigiano reggiano and rocket leaves.

When you make an evening reservation in a restaurant, you can pretty well rest assured that if it is for after 7.30pm, the table is yours for the night. If not, the restaurant will ask if you want an early or late seating. If you trawl through the courses, expect to stay two to three hours.

Quick Eats
A lot of Kiwis consume their working lunch on the go, out of a paper bag – street eating is a common sight, with pies and sandwiches of some description being the most popular. Cafés and delis offer good 'food to go' mostly based on a theme or style of cuisine. There's always plenty of vegetarian options for the lunch trade.

Fish and chips is the most popular takeout food and is usually done well. Kumara fritters and wedges are worth trying, as are scallops and paua if on offer. And if you overhear someone ordering feesh and cheeps while you're waiting for your order, don't worry, it's just an Aussie from over 'the Ditch'. Likewise, if you hear someone order a sex-pack in a booze store, it'll be another Aussie, this time ordering a six-pack of beer.

VEGETARIANS & VEGANS
Most cafés offer vegetarian food. Ethnic restaurants, particularly Indian and Middle Eastern, generally have plenty of vegetarian dishes. If you're a strict vegetarian you need to ask about the stocks and sauces to ensure that no meat or fish stocks have been used.

It's harder for vegans, but again, ethnic is the way to go.

Over 60% of NZ cheese is made from a natural rennet substitute, making it suitable for vegetarians.

WHINING & DINING
Kids in cafés are fine, especially during the day and early evening. Many places provide highchairs for toddlers, or a roped off area for them to play.

DID YOU KNOW?

'Six o'clock closing', a law that for 50 years forced pubs to close their doors at 6pm, was finally relaxed in 1967, extending the legal hours for serving alcohol to 10pm. It's now totally relaxed, with some supermarkets licensed to sell alcohol around the clock.

It's another matter in fine dining establishments which, like airlines with their business-class travel, rarely encourage patrons to bring along young children.

An exception would be ethnic restaurants, especially mid-range or inexpensive Italian and Chinese. Italians seem to accept children happily in most circumstances.

HABITS & CUSTOMS

New Zealand Food Lovers' Guide by Margaret Brooker is an excellent book, with unbiased opinions and discussions on the food specialities of various regions around the country.

When the 19th-century migrants arrived here from Britain, they found ample fertile land at their disposal. It bred an aura of generosity as there was plenty to go around. Cooks always added 'one more for the pot' just in case an unexpected visitor turned up. The tradition continues to this day and the visitor can't help but notice the Kiwis' genuine warmth, openness and hospitality.

If you receive an invitation with the words 'bring a plate', don't turn up with an empty plate or they'll hoot with laughter. What they really want is for you to contribute some food, like a 'pot-luck' dinner. If you don't have cooking facilities, it is quite acceptable to buy something ready-made.

COOKING COURSES

One good course option in Auckland is **Epicurean Workshop** (☎ 0800 555151; www.epicurean.co.nz), which runs short and snappy inexpensive lunchtime classes as well as evening demonstrations and hands-on weekend classes, including trips to the market. **Auckland Cooking Academy** (☎ 0800-200123; www.millyskitchen.co.nz) holds theatre-style and hands-on cooking classes during the day and evenings.

Further afield, **Somerset Cottage** (☎ 07-576 6889) in Tauranga has regular guest chefs giving demonstrations. **Sileni Estates** (p379) in Hawkes Bay

---

DOS & DON'TS

Do...

- take a bottle of wine, or a small gift of chocolates or flowers, if you're invited to someone's place for a meal.
- offer to bring some meat, or at least a salad, if you're invited for a barbecue.
- remember the drink-driving laws (see Legal Matters on p668). If you intend drinking more than the limit, organise a taxi (they cannot be hailed on the street) or a dial-a-driver (a twosome, one of which will drive you home in your car, followed by his or her mate in their car).
- turn up on time for a restaurant reservation; if you're late you may lose your table.
- ask for a corked wine (smells of dirt and cobwebs) to be replaced or return it to its source and exchange it for another.
- tip for good service – it's optional, not expected, but always appreciated.

Don't...

- light up a cigarette anywhere without checking first as you risk offending others, and it's now illegal to smoke in many public places (including restaurants, pubs and bars).
- belch at the table – it is considered the height of bad manners.
- call for another napkin on return to your seat after popping out for a smoke or a visit to the loo – you'll most likely find the waitperson has draped it on the back of your chair.
- tip for bad service – ever.

NEW ZEALAND'S TOP FIVE

- **Smokehouse** (p452; ☎ 03-540 2280; Mapua) A glorified bach (seaside house), idyllic on the water's edge. Fish smoked daily and the best fish and chips in a country mile – eat outside in courtyard for a cheap dining experience.

- **Flax** (p452; ☎ 03-540 2028; Mapua) Mapua is blessed with yet another great eating establishment. Flax features contemporary design and truly inspiring fresh food. Stylish and delicious.

- **SPQR** (p121; ☎ 09-360 1710; Auckland) With an Italian slant to the menu and consistently scrumptious food, SPQR has a cosmopolitan atmosphere. Excellent NZ wines by the glass.

- **Church Road Winery** (p379; ☎ 06-844 2053; Napier) Delicious fresh food with great wines and occasional live jazz can be found here at the home of NZ's only wine museum.

- **Eichardt's** (☎ 03-441 0450; www.eichardtshotel.co.nz; Marine Pde, Queenstown) Great attention to detail in this small lunchtime-only restaurant, with superb fresh food and gorgeous setting. And for around $1500 you can hunker down for a night in one of the five suites under the most luxurious possum throw imaginable.

---

run cookery demonstrations featuring the food and wine bounty of the bay.

On the South Island, **D'Urville Wine Bar & Brasserie** (☎ 03-577 9945; www .durville.co.nz) in Blenheim runs interesting cookery packages giving a full taste of Marlborough produce, including five-course dinner demonstrations prepared by the excellent chef.

Auckland Region

CONTENTS

Auckland	**94**
History	94
Orientation	94
Information	95
Sights	97
Activities	106
Walking Tours	109
Auckland for Children	109
Quirky Auckland	109
Tours	109
Festivals & Events	111
Sleeping	112
Eating	118
Drinking	123
Entertainment	123
Shopping	125
Getting There & Away	126
Getting Around	128
Around Auckland	**129**
Regional Parks	129
West of Auckland	129
Hauraki Gulf Islands	**133**
Rangitoto & Motutapu Islands	133
Waiheke Island	134
Great Barrier Island	139
Tiritiri Matangi Island	145
Other Islands	145

The name Auckland (in Maori, 'Tamaki Makaurau') refers both to a region, stretching roughly from the Bombay Hills in the south to the Whangaparaoa Peninsula in the north, and to a city, nestled between the Waitemata and Manukau Harbours.

On a narrow strip of land between two scenic harbours, Auckland is surrounded by more sandy beaches and attractive islands than probably any other city in the world. The city itself is splashed with green parks that include the terraced volcanic hills where Maoris once lived in *pa* (fortified villages). Out west of the city are vineyards, surf beaches and a regenerating Waitakere rainforest with reservoirs, waterfalls and hiking trails.

Wellington is the capital city, but the Auckland region is the economic capital and is challenging Queenstown as the country's adventure capital. There are enough daredevil leaps out of aeroplanes and off bridges, towers and rock faces, climbs up and down buildings and waterfalls, mountain bike, quad bike and rollercoaster rides to satisfy any thrill-seeker. The self-proclaimed 'City of Sails' has an outdoors culture with plenty of sailing, boating and kayaking opportunities around the Hauraki Gulf Islands, and masses of sports to play or watch. Swim with dolphins, sample the region's wines or beers, see the Maori show at the museum – Auckland has everything.

Central Auckland is an architectural mish-mash and an entertainment hub with theatres, concert halls, two comedy venues, a vibrant live music scene and late-night clubbing at the weekend. From Asian eateries and outdoor cafés to top-class Pacific Rim and European restaurants, the Auckland region serves up fresh, locally produced food, generally in a casual atmosphere.

HIGHLIGHTS

- **Boating** (p106) or **sailing** (p107) on Waitemata Harbour
- Visiting Viaduct Basin **restaurants** (p119) and **bars** (p123)
- Exploring Maori and other Polynesian cultures at **Auckland Museum** (p99)
- Taking a ferry to a nearby island – volcanic **Rangitoto** (p133), vineyard-laden **Waiheke** (p134) and bird paradise **Tiritiri Matangi** (p145)
- Taking a ferry to historical **Devonport** (p103) for art and craft shops
- **Base jumping** off Sky Tower (p107), **bungy jumping** (p107) off Auckland Harbour Bridge or **skydiving** (p107) at Parakai or Mercer
- **Canyoning** (p106) in the Waitakere Ranges or **surfing** (p131) on the black-sand beaches of Muriwai, Piha or Karekare

Map showing: ★ Tiritiri Matangi Island, ★ Parakai Airfield, Rangitoto Island, Waitemata Harbour, ★ Muriwai Beach, ★ Devonport, ★ Waiheke Island, ★ Auckland City, ★ Piha Beach, ★ Karekare Beach, ★ Waitakere Ranges, ★ Mercer Airfield

| ■ TELEPHONE CODE: 09 | ■ www.aucklandnz.com | ■ www.arc.govt.nz |

Climate

Summer months in the Auckland region have an average of eight days of rain, but the climate is fickle, with 'four seasons in a day' at any time of the year.

Getting There & Around

Auckland is the country's main transport hub, with an international and domestic airport, long-distance bus services and tours to all parts of the North Island and on to the South Island. There are trains to Wellington, and the local trains that service the Auckland region are being upgraded. Stagecoach provides a comprehensive bus service and the $8 day pass makes travelling around the Auckland region a bargain.

Everything from a brand-new Mercedes to a touring motorbike or elderly Toyota can be hired, and Auckland is the best place to buy or sell a cheap car. Ferries provide an escape to nearby islands.

AUCKLAND

pop 1.2 million

The country's primary international gateway, Auckland has accommodation to suit all credit card limits as well as a comprehensive bus network – but avoid the rush hours when vehicles pack the roads as tightly as an All Black scrum.

HISTORY

Maori settlement in the Auckland area dates back at least 800 years. Initial settlements were concentrated on the coastal regions of the Hauraki Gulf islands, but gradually the fertile isthmus became settled and land was cleared for growing food. From the 17th century tribes from outside the region challenged the local Ngati Whatua tribe for this desirable place. The locals in response built *pa* (fortified villages) on Auckland's numerous volcanic cones. But when the first Europeans arrived in the area in the 1830s they reported a land largely devoid of inhabitants. The Auckland isthmus (Tamaki Makaurau – literally, 'Tamaki Desired by Many') had largely been forsaken, either ravaged by war or the threat of it.

From early colonial times the country's administrative centre had been at Russell in Northland, but after the signing of the Treaty of Waitangi in 1840, Captain William Hobson, New Zealand's first governor, moved the capital south to Auckland because of its fine harbour (Waitemata, meaning 'Sparkling Waters'), fertile soil and more central location. Hobson named the settlement after his commanding officer, George Eden (Lord Auckland). Beginning with just a few tents on a beach at Official Bay, the settlement grew quickly and soon the port was kept busy exporting the region's produce, including kauri timber. However it lost its capital status to Wellington after just 25 years.

Since the beginning of the 20th century Auckland has been NZ's fastest-growing city and its main industrial centre. Political deals may be done in Wellington, but Auckland is the dominant commercial centre.

ORIENTATION

The commercial heart of the city is Queen St, which runs from the Britomart station near the waterfront up to Karangahape Rd (K Rd). On the way it passes Aotea Square, and comes within a few blocks of the landmark Skytower.

While the central district has accommodation, restaurants and nightlife, K Rd, with its ethnic restaurants, funky bars and clubs is a lively, bohemian alternative. Parnell Rd, just east of the city centre, is a street of renovated wooden villas converted into restaurants and boutiques, and continues to the fashion outlets in Newmarket. Just west of the city centre is Ponsonby Rd, packed with cafés, bars and more boutiques.

Further out, Mt Eden, Takapuna and Mission Bay are residential suburbs with restaurants, bars and cafés. Devonport, easily reached by ferry across the harbour, is a quaint waterside suburb on the southern tip of the residential North Shore, with beaches, art galleries and B&Bs. For bush walks, surf beaches and wineries, head west to the Waitakere Ranges.

The airport is 23km south of the city centre, but the airbus, shuttle minibuses and taxis can transport you to the city – see p129.

Maps

Auckland Map Centre (Map pp98-9; ☎ 09-309 7725; 209 Queen St; 🕙 9am-5.30pm Mon-Fri, 10am-4pm Sat, 10am-2pm Sun)

AUCKLAND IN...

Two Days

Breakfast in **Vulcan Lane** (p118), and take the Link bus to **Auckland Museum** (p99) for the Polynesian galleries and Maori culture show. You can step back to Victorian times at **Kinder House** (p103) or **Ewelme Cottage** (p102), or indulge in retail therapy in **Newmarket** (p126) and lunch somewhere down **Parnell Rd** (p120), with its quaint shops and varied eateries. Stroll down Parnell Rd to Viaduct Basin with its **Maritime Museum** (p100). Sail on an **Admiral's Cup boat** (p107) and have dinner overlooking the harbour (p119) followed by a **live comedy show** (p125).

Day two, view the **Auckland Art Gallery** (p101) and board a ferry to **Devonport** (p103) for lunch and a walk up one or two extinct **volcanoes** (p103). Come back to Britomart and take a bus to **Kelly Tarlton's Antarctic Encounter and Underwater World** (p101) followed by **kayaking** (p108) or other water sport at **Mission Bay** (p108) before dining there as the sun sets.

Four Days

Follow itinerary for two days then spend a day swimming with **dolphins** (p106), or learning to surf, sail, abseil, bungy jump or skydive (p107). Dine in **Ponsonby** (p121) then cruise around the bars, live music venues and dance clubs in **K Rd** (p124).

Spend day four on a **Hauraki Gulf Island** (p133) before visiting **Sky Tower** (p97) and a bar or theatre.

INFORMATION

Bookshops

Borders (Map pp98-9; ☎ 09-309 3377; 291 Queen St; ☽ 10am-10pm Sun-Thu, 10am-midnight Fri-Sat) For books, music and DVDs in the Sky City Metro Mall.

Hard to Find But Worth the Effort Secondhand Bookshop (Map p104; ☎ 09-446 0300; 81a Victoria Rd, Devonport; ☽ 9.30am-5.30pm)

Whitcoull's (Map pp98-9; ☎ 09-356 5400; 210 Queen St; ☽ 8am-6pm Mon-Thu, 8am-9pm Fri, 9am-6pm Sat, 10am-6pm Sun) Another large bookshop with good NZ, travel and fiction sections.

Women's Bookshop (Map p105; ☎ 09-376 4399; 105 Ponsonby Rd; ☽ 10am-6pm) A community resource as well as a bookshop.

Emergency

Ambulance, Fire Service & Police (☎ 111)
Auckland Central Police Station (Map pp98-9; ☎ 09-302 6400; cnr Vincent & Cook Sts)
Auckland Victim Support (☎ 09-302 6653)
AIDS Hotline (☎ 0800 802 437)

Internet Access

Expect to pay from $2 to $4 an hour at the numerous Internet cafés, a few of which are open 24 hours.

Internet Resources

www.arc.govt.nz Information about Auckland's parks and transport.
www.aucklandnz.com All the tourist information can be found here.

www.dineout.co.nz Customers' comments on local restaurants.
www.hotcity.co.nz Get the dirt on what's happening in Auckland.

Laundry

Clean Green Laundromat (Map pp98-9; ☎ 09-358 4370; 18b Fort St; ☽ 8am-6.30pm Mon-Fri, 8am-5pm Sat)

Left Luggage

Most hostels offer storage and there are some left-luggage lockers on the lower level of Britomart station (small lockers 50c an hour or $10 for 24 hours, big lockers $1 an hour or $15 for 24 hours).

Libraries

Central City Library (Map pp98-9; ☎ 09-377 0209; 44-46 Lorne St; ☽ 9.30am-8pm Mon-Fri, 10am-4pm Sat, noon-4pm Sun) Has NZ and world newspapers and magazines as well as books, CDs and DVDs. Newspapers can also be read online free of charge (top floor).

Devonport Library (Map p104; cnr Victoria Rd & Flagstaff Tce) Offers Internet access.

Medical Services

Ascot Accident & Medical Clinic (Map p96; ☎ 09-520 9555; 90 Greenlane East, Remuera; ☽ 24hr) It costs $55 to see a doctor in business hours.

Auckland City Hospital (Map pp98-9; ☎ 09-379 7440; Park Rd, Grafton; ☽ 24hr) This is the main accident and emergency hospital. ACC should cover any accident tourists have inside NZ, but non-accident medical services under

AUCKLAND REGION

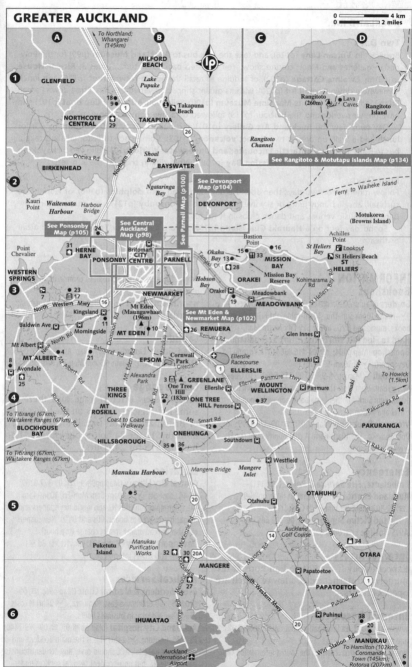

GREATER AUCKLAND

0 — 4 km
0 — 2 miles

A **B** **C** **D**

To Northland;
Whangarei
(145km)

MILFORD
BEACH

1

GLENFIELD

Lake
Pupuke

Rangitoto
(260m) △ Lava
Caves

Rangitoto
Island

NORTHCOTE
CENTRAL

18
9
29

TAKAPUNA

2
Takapuna
Beach

Rangitoto
Channel

See Rangitoto & Motutapu Islands Map (p134)

26

BIRKENHEAD

Onewa Rd

Shoal
Bay

BAYSWATER

2

Kauri
Point

Waitemata
Harbour

Harbour
Bridge

Ngataringa
Bay

See Devonport
Map (p104)

DEVONPORT

Ferry to Waiheke Island

Motukorea
(Browns Island)

See Ponsonby
Map (p105)

24

See Central
Auckland
Map (p98)

Bastion
Point

16

Achilles
Point

St Heliers
Bay

Lookout

Point
Chevalier

31

HERNE
BAY

PONSONBY

Britomart,
CITY
CENTRE

PARNELL

Okahu
Bay 13

15

33

28

MISSION
BAY

St Heliers Beach
ST
HELIERS

WESTERN
SPRINGS

7

23
17

North Western Mwy

16

NEWMARKET

Hobson
Bay

Mission Bay
Reserve

ORAKEI

Kohimarama
Rd

3

Kingsland

11

Mt Eden
(Maungawhau)
(196m)

10

Dominion Rd

See Mt Eden &
Newmarket Map (p102)

Orakei

19

Meadowbank

MEADOWBANK

Baldwin Ave

Morningside

MT EDEN

26

REMUERA

Remuera Rd

Glen Innes

Mt Albert

4

21

New North Rd

Balmoral Rd

EPSOM

Cornwall
Park

Greenlane Rd

Ellerslie
Racecourse

Tamaki

To Howick
(1.5km)

4

8

Avondale

25

Richardson Rd

Mt Albert Rd

Alexandra
Park

3

GREENLANE

Ellerslie

ELLERSLIE

1

Ellerslie Panmure Hwy

MOUNT
WELLINGTON

Panmure

Tamaki River

Pakuranga Rd

14

THREE
KINGS

MT
ROSKILL

One Tree
Hill
(183m)

22

ONE TREE
HILL

Penrose

37

PAKURANGA

To Titirangi (67km);
Waitakere Ranges (67km)

Coast to Coast
Walkway

Mt Smart Rd

5

Ti Rakau Dr

BLOCKHOUSE
BAY

HILLSBOROUGH

ONEHUNGA

12

Southdown

To Titirangi (67km);
Waitakere Ranges (67km)

35

36

Manukau Harbour

Mangere Bridge

Mangere
Inlet

Westfield

OTAHUHU

Harris Rd

5

5

20

Otahuhu

Great South Rd

Auckland
Golf Course

34

OTARA

Puketutu
Island

Manukau
Purification
Works

32

30

20A

MANGERE

14

McKenzie Rd

Massey Rd

Southern Mwy

Papatoetoe

PAPATOETOE

1

27

Puhinui Rd

6

IHUMATAO

George Bolt Memorial Dr

South-Western Mwy

20

Puhinui

38

20

MANUKAU

Auckland
International
Airport

Win Station Rd

To Hamilton (102km);
Coromandel
Town (145km);
Rotorua (207km)

6

INFORMATION
Ascot Accident & Medical...................1 C4
Takapuna Visitors Centre.....................2 B1

SIGHTS & ACTIVITIES   (pp97–109)
Acacia Cottage......................................3 B4
Alberton House......................................4 A4
Ambury Farm Park................................5 B5
Auckland Botanical Gardens.................6 D6
Auckland Zoo..7 A3
Avondale Racecourse............................8 A4
Dive Centre...9 B1
Eden Gardens......................................10 B3
Eden Park..11 A3
Ericsson Stadium.................................12 C4
Fergs Kayaks..13 C3
Gulfwind Sailing Academy..............(see 24)
Howick Historical Village....................14 D4
Kelly Tarlton's Antarctic Encounter &
   Underwater World 15 C3

Mission Bay Watersports....................16 C3
Motat..17 A3
North Shore Events Centre.................18 B1
Orakei Scuba Centre...........................19 C3
Penny Whiting Sailing.....................(see 24)
Rainbow's End Adventure Park...........20 D6
Rocknasium..21 A4
Stardome Observatory........................22 B4
Western Springs Stadium....................23 A3
Westhaven Marina..............................24 A2

SLEEPING   (pp112–18)
Avondale Motor Park..........................25 A4
Gateway Hotel.................................(see 30)
Hansen's...26 B3
Jet Inn...27 B6
Nautical Nook B&B.............................28 C3
North Shore Motels &   29 B1
   Holiday Park 29 B1
Oak Tree Lodge................................(see 26)

Pacific Inn...30 B6
Sea Breeze Motel...............................31 A3
Skyway Lodge.....................................32 B5
Traveller's International...................(see 30)
Tudor Court.....................................(see 26)

EATING   (pp118–23)
Hammerheads......................................33 C3

SHOPPING   (pp125–6)
Avondale Market................................(see 8)
Otara Markets.....................................34 D5

TRANSPORT   (pp126–9)
Car Warehouse....................................35 B4
Hammer Car Auctions.........................36 B4
Turner's Car Auctions.........................37 C4

OTHER
Manukau City Centre..........................38 D6

$500 have to be paid for, and the money later reclaimed from your insurance company. To see a doctor here costs $120 and there could be a three-hour wait.

Quay Med (Map p100; ☎ 09-919 2555; 68 Beach Rd; consultations adult $50-55, student $30-35, child under 6 $10-15; ☼ 8am-8pm Mon-Fri, 10am-2pm Sat, Sun & public holidays) Provides a wide range of medical services without the long queues at Auckland City Hospital. Free parking. There is a **pharmacy** (☼ 9am-6pm Mon-Fri) and a **dentist** (☼ 8am-8pm Mon-Fri).

Travel Care Medical Centre (Map pp98-9; ☎ 09-373 4621; 125 Queen St; ☼ 9am-5.30pm Mon-Fri, 10am-5pm Sat, noon-4pm Sun) Specialises in health care for travellers, such as vaccinations and travel consultations. It costs $55 to see a doctor.

Money
There are plenty of moneychangers, banks and ATMs on Queen St. The exchange rates offered at private moneychangers are usually similar but it pays to shop around. For weekend banking visit the **ASB Bank branch** (☼ 9am-4.30pm Mon-Fri, 9am-4pm Sat & Sun) in the Westfield Downtown Shopping Centre (p126).

Post
Wellesley St post office (Map pp98-9; ☼ 7.30am-5pm Mon-Fri) Near Aotea Sq. It's the place to pick up poste restante mail (ID is required).

Tourist Information
Auckland Visitors Centre (Map pp98-9; ☎ 09-979 2333; www.aucklandnz.com; cnr Victoria & Federal Sts; ☼ 8am-8pm Sun-Wed, 8am-10pm Thu-Sat) In the Sky Tower Atrium.
Automobile Association (AA; Map pp98-9; ☎ 09-377 4660; 99 Albert St; ☼ 9am-5pm Mon-Fri, 9am-3pm Sat) Has maps and accommodation directories.
Department of Conservation Information Centre (DOC; Map pp98-9; ☎ 09-379 6476; www.doc.govt.nz; Ferry Bldg, 99 Quay St; ☼ 10am-5.30pm Mon-Fri, 10am-3pm Sat)

Devonport i-SITE (Map p104; ☎ 09-446 0677; www .tourismnorthshore.org.nz; 3 Victoria Rd; ☼ 8.30am-5pm) Has a list of B&Bs and the *Old Devonport Walk* pamphlet, which guides you around the many historic buildings. For more information view www.devonport.co.nz.
Domestic Airport Visitors Centre (Map p96; ☎ 09-256 8480; ☼ 7am-5pm) Is in the Air New Zealand section of the domestic airport, which is a short walk from the international airport.
NZ Visitors Centre (Map pp98-9; ☎ 09-979 2333; nzvc@ aucklandnz.com; cnr Quay & Hobson Sts; ☼ 9am-5pm) At Viaduct Harbour; it covers the entire country.
Takapuna Visitors Centre (Map p96; ☎ 09-486 8670; www.tourismnorthshore.org.nz; 49 Hurstmere Rd; ☼ 8.30am-5pm Mon-Fri, 10am-3pm Sat & Sun) Covers the less touristy North Shore.
Visitors Information Centre (Map p96; ☎ 09-275 6467; international airport; ☼ 1st flight–last flight) It's on your left as you exit the customs hall and you can make free calls to Auckland accommodation providers.

The Waitakere Ranges (p130), Waiheke Island (p134) and Great Barrier Island (p139) also have tourist information centres. See those sections for details.

Travel Agencies
The following two agencies have several offices in Auckland:
Flight Centre (☎ 0800 354 448, 09-358 0074)
STA Travel (☎ 0508 782 872, 09-309 0458)

SIGHTS
Sky Tower
The imposing **Sky Tower** (Map pp98-9; ☎ 09-363 6400; www.skycity.co.nz; cnr Federal & Victoria Sts; adult/senior/backpacker/child $15/14/10/7.50; ☼ 8.30am-11pm Sun-Thu, 8.30am-midnight Fri & Sat) is part of the Sky City complex – a 24-hour casino with restaurants, cafés, bars and a hotel. At 328m

AUCKLAND REGION

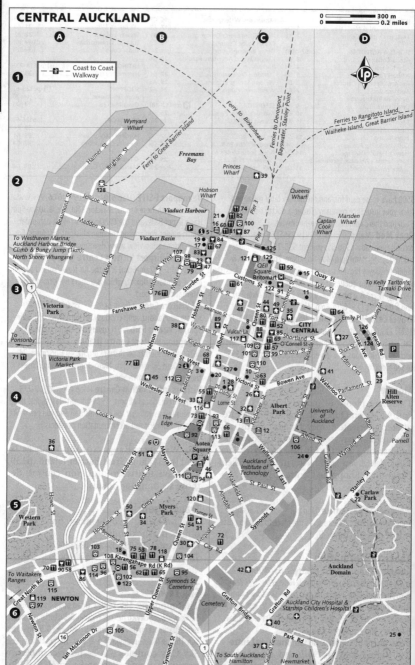

CENTRAL AUCKLAND

AUCKLAND •• Sights 99

AUCKLAND REGION

INFORMATION
Auckland Map Centre...........................1 C4
Auckland Visitors Centre.......................2 B4
Automobile Association (AA)...............3 B4
Borders Bookshop.........................(see 113)
Central City Library...............................4 C4
Clean Green Laundromat.................(see 49)
DOC Information Centre..................(see 125)
NZ Visitors Centre................................5 B2
Police Station......................................6 B4
Post Office & Poste Restante................7 B6
Travel Care Medical Centre..................8 C3
Wellesley Post Office...........................9 B4
Whitcoulls Bookshop.........................10 C4

SIGHTS & ACTIVITIES   (pp97–109)
Adventure Cycles...............................11 C3
Auckland Art Gallery (Main)...............12 C4
Auckland Art Gallery (New)................13 C4
Auckland Town Hall............................14 B5
Fullers Cruises................................(see 125)
Ground Rush (Mercure Hotel
   Abseiling)....................................(see 91)
Kawau Kat Cruises..........................(see 125)
Magic Travellers Network...................15 C3
National Maritime Museum.................16 C2
Ocean Rafting.....................................17 B3
Pride Centre.......................................18 B5
Pride of Auckland............................(see 16)
Sail NZL (America's Cup Sailing
   Yachts)..19 B3
Sky Jump..(see 112)
Sky Screamer......................................20 C4
Sky Tower..(see 112)
Sky Tower Climb..............................(see 112)
Soren Larsen......................................21 C2
Stanley St Tennis Courts.....................22 D5
Tepid Baths..23 B3
University Recreation Centre...............24 C5
Wintergarden......................................25 D6

SLEEPING   (pp112–18)
Albert Park Backpackers.....................26 C4
Aspen House.......................................27 D3
Auckland Central Backpackers.............28 C4
Auckland City Hotel............................29 D4
Auckland City YHA..............................30 B5
Auckland International YHA.................31 B5
Central City Backpackers.....................32 C4
City Central Hotel...............................33 B4
Duxton Hotel......................................34 B5
Fat Camel Hostel.................................35 C3
Freeman's B&B....................................36 A4
Grafton Hall of Residence....................37 C6
Heritage Auckland..............................38 B3
Hilton Hotel..39 C2
Huia Residence 40 C6
Hyatt Regency Hotel...........................41 D4
International House..............................42 C6
New President Hotel............................43 C4
Queen St Backpackers.........................44 C3

Sail City Hotel.....................................45 B4
Scenic Circle Airedale Hotel................46 B5
Sebel Suites..47 B3
Sky City Hotel.................................(see 112)
Stamford Plaza Hotel..........................48 C3
XBase...49 C3
YMCA...50 B5
YWCA...51 B5

EATING   (pp118–23)
A1 Sushi...52 C3
Alleliyah...53 B5
Asian Restaurants...............................54 B5
Atrium on Elliot..................................55 B4
Brazil..56 B6
Café Melba...57 C4
Café Midnight Express.....................(see 68)
Caluzzi...58 A6
Cin Cin on Quay.............................(see 125)
Daikoku Ramen.............................(see 59)
Daikoku...59 C3
Euro...60 C2
Food Alley..61 C3
Food for Life.......................................62 B6
Foodoo...63 C4
Fortuna...(see 112)
Good Fortune.....................................64 D3
Guranga's...65 B6
Harbourside Restaurant..................(see 125)
Kangnam Station Korean
   Restaurant...................................(see 94)
Kermedec Restaurant & Brasserie......(see 67)
Kiwi Music Bar & Café........................66 C4
Little Turkish Café...........................(see 75)
Loaded Hog..67 B3
Mai Thai...68 B4
Mecca Café...69 C3
Monkey House....................................70 A6
New World Supermarket......................71 A4
No.5 Wine Bistro.................................72 C5
Observatory.....................................(see 112)
Orbit...(see 112)
Pie Mania...73 B4
Princes Wharf Restaurants & Cafés......74 C2
Rasoi..75 B5
Raw Power.....................................(see 88)
Seamart Deli & Café............................76 B3
Toto...77 B4
Verona..78 B5
Wangthai..79 B3
White Lady...80 C3
Wildfire..81 C2
Y-Not..82 A6

DRINKING   (p123)
Bubble Champagne Bar.......................83 B3
Danny Doolans...................................84 C3
Embargo Bar...................................(see 32)
Globe Bar......................................(see 28)
Honey...85 C3
Kamo...86 A6

Lenin Bar...87 C2
Minus 5° Bar...................................(see 87)
O'Carrolls......................................(see 88)
Occidental Belgian Beer Café 88 C3
Shakespeare Tavern............................89 C3
Thirsty Dog..90 A6
Vertigo Bar...91 C3

ENTERTAINMENT   (pp123–5)
Academy Cinema..............................(see 4)
Aotea Centre......................................92 B4
Civic...93 C4
Classic Comedy Club...........................94 B5
Covert Theatre....................................95 B6
Cruising Rock Bar................................96 A6
Dogs Bollix...97 A6
Europa..98 B3
Flesh Bar & Nightclub.........................99 C4
Float...100 C2
Fu Bar..101 C4
Galatos...102 B6
Ibiza...103 A5
Khuja Lounge....................................104 B5
Kings Arms Tavern.............................105 B6
Maidment Theatre.............................106 C4
Mojo...107 B3
NZ Film Archives...............................108 B6
Papa Jack's Voodoo Lounge...............109 C4
Rakinos..110 C4
Silo Theatre......................................111 B5
Sky City..112 B4
Sky City Casino..............................(see 112)
Sky City Metro Centre.....................(see 113)
Sky City Theatre.............................(see 112)
Sky City Village Multiplex.................113 C4
Staircase...114 A6
Urge...115 A6

SHOPPING   (pp125–6)
Aotea Square Market.......................(see 92)
Illicit..116 B4
Kathmandu.......................................117 C3
Modus Operandi............................(see 110)
Paper Bag Princess............................118 B5
Pauanesia.....................................(see 110)
R&R Sport...119 A6
Real Groovy Records.........................120 B5
Westfield Downtown Shopping
   Centre..121 C3

TRANSPORT   (pp126–9)
Air New Zealand...............................122 C3
Backpackers Car Market....................123 B6
Car Rental Companies.......................124 D3
Ferry Building...................................125 C3
Fullers Ferries................................(see 125)
NZ Motorcycle Rentals......................126 D3
Qantas Travel Centre........................127 C4
Sky City Coach Terminal.................(see 112)
Subritzky Ferry Terminal...................128 A2
Tour Company Offices.......................129 C3

it is the tallest structure in the southern hemisphere and a lift takes you up to the observation decks in 40 seconds. It costs $3 extra to catch the skyway lift to the ultimate viewing level. Late afternoon is a good time to go up, and the Sky Lounge sells beer, wine and coffee, which you can sip as the sun sets. See the Activities section for the Sky Jump and the Sky Tower Climb (p108).

Auckland Museum

This **museum** (Te Papa Whakahiku; Map p100; ☎ 09-309 0443; www.akmuseum.org.nz; admission by donation, suggested donation adult/child $5/free; ☉ 10am-5pm) sits

atop a sweeping expanse of lawn that forms part of the Auckland Domain, one of Auckland's oldest parks. The museum has a comprehensive display on Pacific Island and Maori culture on the ground floor, including a 25m-long war canoe. The 1st floor is dedicated to the natural world and has a first-class activities centre for children. The 2nd floor focuses on New Zealanders at war – from the 19th century to the peace-keeping assignments of today, and includes a re-creation of 19th-century Auckland shops.

For many, the highlight is the performance of Maori song and dance by **Manaia** (☎ 09-306

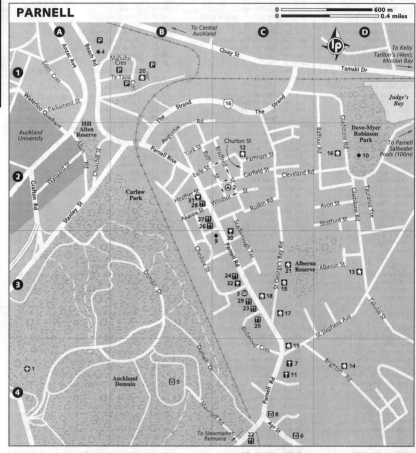

PARNELL

INFORMATION	
Auckland City	
Hospital	1 A4
Police Station	2 C2
Post Office	3 C3
Quay Med	4 A1

SIGHTS & ACTIVITIES	(pp97–109)
Auckland Museum	5 B4
Ewelme Cottage	6 C4
Holy Trinity Cathedral	7 C4
Kinder House	8 C4
Kiwi Experience	9 C3
Parnell Rose Gardens	10 D2
St Mary's Church	11 C4

SLEEPING	⋒ (pp112–18)
Auckland International Backpackers	12 C2
Barrycourt Motor Inn	13 D3
Chalet Chevron B&B	14 D4
City Garden Lodge	15 C3
Kingsgate Hotel	16 D2
Leadbetter Lodge	17 C3
Parnell Inn	18 C3
Parnell Village Motor Lodge	19 C4
Railway Campus	20 B1
St George's Bay Lodge	21 C3

EATING	🍴 (p120)
Al & Pete's	22 C4
Antoines	23 C3

Iguaçu	24 C3
Java Room	(see 29)
Kebab Kid	25 C3
La Porchetta	26 B2
Mink Cafe & Bar	(see 31)
Oh Calcutta	27 B2
Strawberry Alarm	
Clock	28 B2
Thai Friends	29 C3

DRINKING	🍷 (p123)
Bog	30 C3
Exchange Hotel	31 B2
Veranda Bar &	
Grill	32 C3

7048; adult/concession & child $15/12). The informal shows at 11am, noon and 1.30pm provide a good introduction to Maori culture.

It's about a 25-minute walk from Queen St through the domain to the museum or you can catch either the Link or Explorer

Bus to Parnell Rd, from where it's an easy short walk.

National Maritime Museum
This **museum** (Map pp98-9; ☎ 0800 725 897, 09-373 0800; www.nzmaritime.org; cnr Quay & Hobson Sts; adult/

student & child $12/6; 9am-6pm summer, 9am-5pm winter) is the place to learn about NZ's seafaring history. It's a well-designed, extensive display of dozens of boats, from Maori canoes and immigrant ships to jet boats, and includes the history of the America's Cup.

An old steamboat, *SS Puke*, is moored outside the museum and runs free 20-minute trips around the harbour on either Saturday or Sunday between 11am and 3pm. The **Ted Ashby** (adult/student & child $15/7, with museum admission $19/12), a flat-bottomed scow, operates one-hour cruises from the museum at noon and 2pm on Tuesday, Thursday, Saturday and Sunday.

Kelly Tarlton's Antarctic Encounter & Underwater World

Housed in old stormwater holding tanks is this unique **aquarium** (Map p96; 0800 805 050, 09-528 0603; www.kellytarltons.co.nz; 23 Tamaki Dr; adult/senior & student/child $25/18/10; 9am-8pm Dec-Feb, 9am-6pm Mar-Nov). A transparent tunnel runs along the centre of the aquarium, through which you travel on a conveyor belt, with the fish, including sharks and stingrays, swimming around you. You can step off at any time to take a closer look.

The big attraction, however, is the Antarctic Encounter, which includes a walk through a replica of Scott's 1911 Antarctic hut, and a ride aboard a heated Snow Cat through a frozen environment where a colony of King and Gentoo penguins lives at sub-zero temperatures. Displays include an Antarctic scientific base of the future and exhibits on the history of Antarctica.

To get there take bus Nos 74 to 76 from outside Britomart station, or the Explorer Bus. It's 6km from the city centre on the road to Mission Bay.

Auckland Art Gallery

The **Auckland Art Gallery** (Map pp98-9; 09-379 1349; www.aucklandartgallery.govt.nz; admission free, special exhibitions adult/child $7/3, Mon free; 10am-5pm) is housed in two neighbouring buildings and the admission fee covers both galleries. The **Main Gallery** (cnr Wellesley St E & Kitchener St), built in French chateau style, has an extensive permanent collection of NZ art, including Charles Goldie's stark Maori portraits of a vanished age. The Gallery café has a deck that overlooks Albert Park. The **New Gallery**

(cnr Wellesley & Lorne Sts) concentrates on contemporary art. Ten private art galleries can be found nearby these two public galleries.

Motat (Museum of Transport & Technology)

This 19-hectare **museum** (Map p96; 09-846 0199; www.motat.org.nz; Great North Rd; adult/child $10/5; 10am-5pm) is at Western Springs near the zoo. Motat is in two parts. **Motat I** has exhibits on transport, communications and energy, including vintage cars, a display about pioneer aviator Richard Pearse and the infotainment Science Centre, with hands-on displays.

Motat II features rare and historic aircraft as well as railway and military hardware. Exhibits include a V1 flying bomb and a Lancaster bomber from WWII, but pride of place goes to the huge Solent flying boat that ran a Pacific islands loop in the days of luxury flying. Electric trams (adult/child $2/1 return) run every 20 minutes from Motat I to Motat II and the zoo.

To get there, take the Explorer Bus, or bus Nos 042 to 045 from outside Britomart station.

Auckland Zoo

Although the **Auckland Zoo** (Map p96; 09-360 3819; Motions Rd; adult/child $13/7; 9.30am-5.30pm) is not huge, it has spacious, natural compounds. The primate exhibit is well done, and the African animals' enclosure, Pridelands, is excellent, as is the meerkat domain, which can be explored through tunnels. A nocturnal house has native birds such as kiwi, but they are hard to see. New additions to the zoo include a penguin enclosure and the sea lions, which you can watch through an underwater viewing window. The last admission to the zoo is at 4.15pm.

To get there take the Explorer Bus, or bus Nos 042 to 045 from outside Britomart station.

Lion Breweries

Lion Breweries (Map p102; 09-358 8366; www.lionzone.co.nz; 380 Khyber Pass Rd, Newmarket; adult/child $15/7.50) has turned its plain old brewery tours onto an interactive 'beer experience'. Two-hour tours are held daily at 9.30am, 12.15pm and 3pm and include a history of brewing, an audiovisual presentation, a

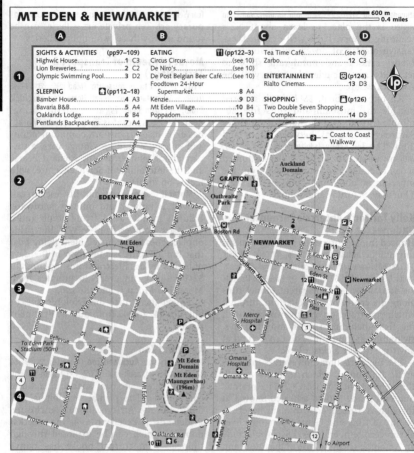

MT EDEN & NEWMARKET

0 — 600 m
0 — 0.4 miles

SIGHTS & ACTIVITIES (pp97–109)	**EATING** 🍴 (pp122–3)
Highwic House.........................1 C3	Circus Circus.....................(see 10)
Lion Breweries.......................2 C2	De Niro's...........................(see 10)
Olympic Swimming Pool..........3 D2	De Post Belgian Beer Café......(see 10)
	Foodtown 24-Hour
SLEEPING 🛏 (pp112–18)	Supermarket...................8 A4
Bamber House........................4 A3	Kenzie...............................9 D3
Bavaria B&B..........................5 A4	Mt Eden Village................10 B4
Oaklands Lodge......................6 B4	Poppadom.......................11 D3
Pentlands Backpackers............7 A4	
	Tea Time Café..................(see 10)
	Zarbo.............................12 C3
	ENTERTAINMENT 🎭 (p124)
	Rialto Cinemas..................13 D3
	SHOPPING 🛍 (p126)
	Two Double Seven Shopping
	Complex.........................14 D3

Coast to Coast Walkway

virtual tour of the brewing process and, of course, some quality time spent sampling Steinlager and Lion Red beers in a replica brew house.

Stardome Observatory

In the One Tree Hill Domain, off Manukau Rd, is the **Stardome Observatory** (Map p96; ☎ 09-624 1246; www.stardome.org.nz; adult/child $12/6). At the observatory, as well as viewing the sky inside the planetarium, on clear nights it is possible to view the night sky and stars through the courtyard telescopes. The night sky can also be viewed through a large 50cm telescope (adults per use $8). The hour-long Stardome Show in the planetarium is not dependent on Auckland's

fickle weather and is usually held on Wednesday to Saturday evenings (phone the observatory or check the website for scheduled times).

Historic Buildings

The NZ Historic Places Trust owns three 19th-century properties with period furnishings that give an insight into the lifestyle of wealthy pioneer families in Auckland. **Alberton House** (Map p96; ☎ 09-846 7367; 100 Mt Albert Rd; adult/child $7.50/free; ⏱ 10.30am-noon & 1-4.30pm Wed-Sun) is a classic colonial-style mansion. **Highwic House** (Map p102; ☎ 09-524 5729; 40 Gillies Ave; adult/child $7.50/free; ⏱ 10.30am-noon & 1-4.30pm Wed-Sun) is wooden and Gothic, and entry is via Mortimer Pass. **Ewelme Cottage** (Map p100; ☎ 09-379 0202; 14 Ayr St; adult/child $3/free; ☺ 10.30am-noon & 1-4.30pm Fri-Sun) was built for a clergyman in the 1860s.

Almost next door to Ewelme Cottage is the restored **Kinder House** (Map p100; ☎ 09-379 4008; 2 Ayr St; adult/child $2/50c; ☺ 11am-3pm Tue-Sun), which was built of stone in 1857 and displays the art and memorabilia of the Rev Dr John Kinder (1819–1903).

St Mary's Church (Map p100; Parnell Rd; ☺ 10am-4pm Mon-Sat, 11am-4pm Sun) is a perfect example of a wooden Gothic church (1886), and is next door to **Holy Trinity Cathedral**, which is worth seeing for its stained glass windows.

In southeastern Auckland, **Howick Historical Village** (Map p96; ☎ 09-576 9506; Bells Rd, Pakuranga; adult/student/child $10/8/5; ☺ 10am-4pm), is an interesting collection of 30 restored 19th-century buildings, including a thatched sod cottage, forge, school, toy museum and chapel. The guides wear period costumes and there is a café.

Devonport

Devonport is a quaint suburb on the tip of Auckland's North Shore peninsula, easily reached by ferry from the centre of Auckland. One of the earliest areas of European settlement, it retains a 19th-century atmosphere with many well-preserved Victorian and Edwardian buildings. Since it makes such an easy day trip from the city, it's touristy and has lots of small shops, high-quality art and craft galleries, bookshops and cafés. There are beaches and B&Bs and a great view of the Auckland city skyline from the foreshore, especially in the evening.

There are also several museums worth a look: the **Navy Museum** (☎ 09-445 5186; Spring St; admission by donation; ☺ 10am-4.30pm), covering the history of the NZ navy which is based in Devonport; **Jackson's Muzeum** (☎ 09-446 0466; Victoria Rd; adult/child $10/5; ☺ 11am-4pm), which is an eccentric collection of NZ historical memorabilia – a true testament to one man's passion for collectables; and **Devonport Museum** (☎ 09-445 2661; 31a Vauxhall Rd; ☺ 2-4pm Sat & Sun), which chronicles Devonport's history.

The 12-minute ferry ride departs from the Auckland Ferry Building every 30 minutes from 6.15am to 11pm (until 1am Friday and Saturday) and 7.30am to 10pm on Sunday and public holidays. The last

ferries back from Devonport are at 11.30pm Monday to Thursday, 1.15am Friday and Saturday, and 10.30pm Sunday. The fare is adult/child $5/2 for a one-way ticket, $8/4 for an open return. The last ferries from the city to Devonport are at 11pm Monday to Thursday, 1am Friday and Saturday, and 10pm Sunday.

You can hire a bicycle ($15 for four hours) outside the Auckland ferry ticket office and cycle around Devonport. Buses to Devonport run regularly from outside Britomart station, but you have to pass through Takapuna and traffic can be slow. The ferry crossing is much quicker and far more enjoyable.

Fullers has ferries to Waiheke and Rangitoto Islands that call in at Devonport – see p139.

Extinct Volcanoes

Auckland is punctuated by some 48 volcanoes, many of which provide parkland retreats and great views. The view from **Mt Eden** (Maungawhau), the highest volcanic cone in the area, at 196m, is superb. You can see the entire Auckland area – all the bays and the land between Manukau Harbour and Hauraki Gulf – and look 50m down into the volcano's crater. You can drive to the top or take bus Nos 274 to 277 and then walk.

The 183m **One Tree Hill**, or Maungakiekie (Mountain of the Kiekie Tree), is a distinctive bald hill, topped only by a huge obelisk and, until recently, a lone Monterey pine. It was the largest and most populous of the Maori *pa*, and the terracing and dugout storage pits are still visible.

The two volcanic cones in Devonport, Mt Victoria and North Head, were once Maori *pa*. **Mt Victoria** is the higher of the two, with a great 360-degree view and a gun emplacement at the top. It's a 10-minute walk to the summit from Victoria Rd. You can drive up but the gate is closed at 6.30pm in winter and 8.30pm in summer. **North Head**, on the other cone, is an historic reserve riddled with fortifications and old tunnels built at the end of the 19th century in response to fears of a Russian invasion. They were extended and enlarged during WWI and WWII, and some of the old guns are still here. The reserve is open to vehicles from 6am to 6pm daily and to pedestrians until

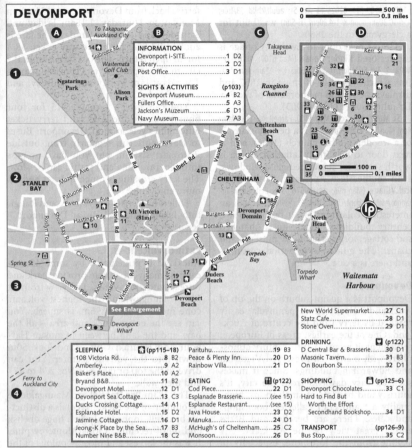

DEVONPORT

0 ————— 500 m
0 ————— 0.3 miles

INFORMATION	
Devonport i-SITE	1 D2
Library	2 D2
Post Office	3 D1

SIGHTS & ACTIVITIES	(p103)
Devonport Museum	4 B2
Fullers Office	5 A3
Jackson's Muzeum	6 D1
Navy Museum	7 A3

New World Supermarket	27	C1
Statz Cafe	28	D1
Stone Oven	29	D1

DRINKING		(p122)
D Central Bar & Brasserie	30	D1
Masonic Tavern	31	B3
On Bourbon St	32	D1

SLEEPING	(pp115–18)		Parituhu	19 B3
108 Victoria Rd	8 B2		Peace & Plenty Inn	20 D1
Amberley	9 A2		Rainbow Villa	21 D1
Baker's Place	10 A2			
Bryand B&B	11 B2		**EATING**	(p122)
Devonport Motel	12 D1		Cod Piece	22 D1
Devonport Sea Cottage	13 C3		Esplanade Brasserie	(see 15)
Ducks Crossing Cottage	14 A1		Esplanade Restaurant	(see 15)
Esplanade Hotel	15 D2		Java House	23 D1
Jasmine Cottage	16 D1		Manuka	24 D1
Jeong-K Place by the Sea	17 B3		McHugh's of Cheltenham	25 C2
Number Nine B&B	18 C2		Monsoon	26 D1

SHOPPING	(pp125–6)
Devonport Chocolates	33 C1
Hard to Find But	
Worth the Effort	
Secondhand Bookshop	34 D1

TRANSPORT	(pp126–9)
Bus Stop	35 C2

10pm. See Walking Tours (p110) for more information.

K Rd & Ponsonby

Just south of the central city area, straight up the hill from Queen St, is Karangahape Rd – known simply as **K Rd**. In recent years artists and media companies have moved in, and the street has a growing number of nightclubs, cafés and ethnic restaurants.

K Rd runs southwest to Ponsonby Rd and the fashionable suburb of **Ponsonby**. Behind historic shopfronts, Ponsonby Rd's many restaurants, bars and cafés are abuzz with the chatter of diners, the hiss of cappuccino machines and the ringing tones of mobile phones.

Tamaki Drive

This scenic coastal road, lined with pohutukawa trees, which turn red at Christmas time, crosses Hobson Bay to **Orakei**, where you can hire kayaks and inline skates at Fergs Kayaks (p108). It continues past **Kelly Tarlton's Antarctic Encounter & Underwater World** to **Bastion Point**, which was occupied by members of the Ngati Whatua tribe in a 1978 land protest. The garden **memorial** to an early Labour Party prime minister, Michael Joseph Savage, has a good viewpoint.

Tamaki Drive continues to **Mission Bay**, which has a popular beach with water sports gear for hire, sidewalk restaurants, bars and a cinema multiplex. Further on, **St Heliers Bay** is smaller and more relaxed. Further

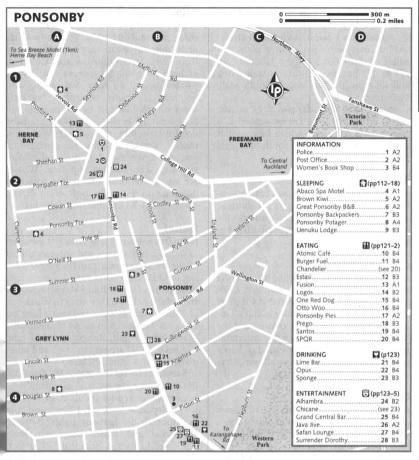

PONSONBY

INFORMATION	
Police	1 A2
Post Office	2 A2
Women's Book Shop	3 B4

SLEEPING	(pp112–18)
Abaco Spa Motel	4 A1
Brown Kiwi	5 A2
Great Ponsonby B&B	6 A2
Ponsonby Backpackers	7 B3
Ponsonby Potager	8 A4
Uenuku Lodge	9 B3

EATING	(pp121–2)
Atomic Café	10 B4
Burger Fuel	11 B4
Chandelier	(see 20)
Estasi	12 B3
Fusion	13 A1
Logos	14 B2
One Red Dog	15 B4
Otto Woo	16 B4
Ponsonby Pies	17 A2
Prego	18 B3
Santos	19 B4
SPQR	20 B4

DRINKING	(p123)
Lime Bar	21 B4
Opus	22 B4
Sponge	23 B3

ENTERTAINMENT	(pp123–5)
Alhambra	24 B2
Chicane	(see 23)
Grand Central Bar	25 B4
Java Jive	26 A2
Safari Lounge	27 B4
Surrender Dorothy	28 B3

east along Cliff Rd, the **Achilles Point lookout** has dramatic views of the city, harbour and Hauraki Gulf.

You can hire a bicycle and cycle along this route (p109), or else take a bus (Nos 74 to 76).

Parks & Gardens

Albert Park (Map pp98-9) is a good spot in the city centre to relax or have a picnic surrounded by flower beds and historical monuments such as the 1899 statue of Queen Victoria.

Covering about 80 hectares, the **Auckland Domain** (Map pp98-9), near the centre of the city, is a large public park that contains Auckland Museum, sports fields and the

Wintergarden (☎ 09-379 2020; admission free; ⊙ 9am-4.30pm), with its fernery, tropical house, cool house and café.

On Gladstone Rd in Parnell is the **Parnell Rose Gardens** (Map p100), which are in bloom from November to March.

The **Eden Gardens** (Map p96; ☎ 09-638 8395; 24 Omana Ave, Epsom; adult/child $5/free; ⊙ 9am-4.30pm), on the slopes of Mt Eden, are noted for camellias, rhododendrons and azaleas.

Popular for jogging, picnics and walks, **Cornwall Park** (Map p96) adjoins One Tree Hill on Greenlane Rd and is an extensive pastoral retreat only 6km south of the city centre. It has sports grounds, fields of grazing sheep, a visitors centre (Huia Lodge), historical Acacia Cottage and a restaurant.

The 65-hectare **Auckland Botanical Gardens** (Map p96; ☎ 09-267 1457; Hill Rd; admission free ⊗ 8am-dusk) has a café and visitors centre as well as rose, herb, cacti, native plant and edible gardens. To get there take bus No 471 or 472 but it's a 20-minute walk along Hill Rd from the bus stop in South Mall, Manurewa.

Ambury Farm Park (Map p96; ☎ 09-366 2000; Ambury; ⊗ 8am-5pm winter, 8am-8pm summer) is a coastal park-cum-farm which has animals and lots of bird life, 15km south of central Auckland.

ACTIVITIES

Auckland has become an adventure capital in recent years, so there's no shortage of challenging activities. Look around for backpacker reductions or special offers before booking anything.

Amusement Parks

Rainbow's End Adventure Park (Map p96; ☎ 09-262 2030; www.rainbowsend.co.nz; cnr Great South & Wiri Station Rds, Manukau; super pass adult/child 4-13 yrs old $37/27; ⊗ 10am-5pm) has enough rides (including a corkscrew roller coaster and the 'fear fall'), shows and interactive entertainment to keep the kids happy all day. Super passes allow unlimited rides while an entry-only pass is $10 at peak times.

Canyoning

Awol Canyoning (☎ 0800 462 965, 09-834 0501; www .awoladventures.co.nz; $135) offers abseiling down waterfalls, sliding down rocks and jumping into pools in the Waitakere Ranges. Pick-up from Auckland, lunch and snacks are included in the price. The whole trip takes from 10am to 5pm but the actual canyoning takes two to three hours. Night trips using headlamps can also be arranged.

Canyonz (☎ 0800 422 696, 09-815 9464; www .canyonz.co.nz; half-/full-day trips $125/145) also runs canyoning trips to the Waitakeres which include lunch and transport. A more challenging trip for experienced canyoners to the Kauaeranga Valley near Thames in the Coromandel costs $225.

Cliffhanger Adventures (☎ 09-827 0720; www .cliffhanger.co.nz; half-/full-day trips $95/145) runs abseiling and rock climbing trips in the Auckland area. Trips further afield cost $295, or $337 overnight. Sea kayaking and other adventures are also possible.

Dolphin Swimming

Dolphin Explorer (☎ 09-357 6032; www.dolphin explorer.com; adult/child $99/50; ⊗ 11am-4pm) has daily dolphin swimming trips departing from Pier 3 in central Auckland. Common or bottlenose dolphins, orcas and Bryde's whales can all be seen. Swimming with dolphins is strictly controlled (eg only common dolphin can be swum with and no swimming is allowed if there are baby dolphins sleeping or feeding). Wet suits, masks, snorkels and fins are provided. If you don't see any dolphins and whales you can take another trip free. Whales are sighted on over 60% of the trips and dolphins on 95%. The boat often carries researchers who are studying dolphins.

Cruises

Fullers Cruises (Map pp98-9; ☎ 09-367 9111; www.fullers .co.nz) has lots of cruises and operates almost all the ferries that run from the Ferry Building in Quay St. Fullers runs 1½-hour harbour cruises (adult/child $31/16, includes a free return ticket to Devonport), which run at 10.30am and 1.30pm and visit a long list of sights. Ferries go to many of the nearby islands in the gulf. Rangitoto (p133) and Waiheke (p134) are easy to reach and make good day trips from Auckland.

Kawau Kat Cruises (Map pp98-9; ☎ 0800 888 006, 09-425 8006; www.kawaukat.co.nz) also runs 1½-hour harbour cruises (adult/child $30/15), which depart at 10.30am, 1.30pm and 3pm and tour all the harbour sights. Between Christmas and Easter boats run from Auckland to Kawau Island (p152) and on varying days of the week to Coromandel Town (adult/child one way $45/25, return $100/45), on the other side of the Hauraki Gulf, which leave Auckland at 9am, arrive at Coromandel Town at 11am, and return at 3pm. A tour of the stamper battery and a ride on the Driving Creek Railway (p201) is included.

Ocean Rafting (Map p96; ☎ 0800 801 193, 09-577 3194; www.oceanrafting.co.nz) is a fast inflatable boat that whips you round the harbour or further out into the gulf. A 45-minute trip costs $45 (child $25), while a one-hour trip out to Rangitoto Island costs $70 (child $35) and a trip round Waiheke Island costs $130 (child $70). Based in the Viaduct Basin, bookings are essential for the Waiheke trip.

Sailing

This is the 'City of Sails' and nothing gets you closer to the heart and soul of Auckland than sailing on the harbour.

SAIL NZL (Map pp98-9; ☎ 0800 724 569, 09-359 5987; www.sailnewzealand.co.nz; adult/child $125/110) runs two-hour hands-on sailing trips around the harbour on *NZL40* and *NZL41*. Go on a breezy day for more excitement. These two multi-million dollar boats, built for America's Cup racing, leave from the Viaduct Basin, usually in the afternoon. Experience the speed and power of these elite yachts, and enjoy the thrill of match racing (twice a week, usually Wednesday and Saturday or Sunday) when the two yachts race against one another.

Pride of Auckland (Map pp98-9; ☎ 09-377 0459; www.prideofauckland.com; adult/child 45min cruises $45/25, 1½hr cruises $55/28), based next to the Maritime Museum, offers sailing trips round the harbour. The 1½-hour cruise with lunch costs $65 (child $35) and a 2½-hour dinner cruise is also available for $90 (child $55). Some Auckland tours include a sail on one of these yachts.

Based at Princes Wharf during summer, the tall ship **Soren Larsen** (Map pp98-9; ☎ 09-411 8755; www.sorenlarsen.co.nz; adult/senior, student & child day trips $95/80) offers hands-on sailing and four-day trips to the Bay of Islands for $200 a night. In the winter you can join them cruising around tropical South Pacific islands.

Gulfwind Sailing Academy (Map p96; ☎ 09-521 1564, 027-489 2462; www.gulfwind.co.nz; Westhaven Marina) can provide day sailing cruises ($400 for four people) as well as personalised tuition and flexible small-group sailing courses for beginners or experienced sailors. Courses run all year and a three-day competent crew certificate costs $600. Westhaven Marina is a 10-minute walk from Victoria Park.

Penny Whiting Sailing (Map p96; ☎ 09-376 1322; www.pennywhiting.com; Westhaven Marina; courses $600) runs courses that consist of five three-hour practical sailing lessons. They run from October to March, and small-group tuition can also be arranged.

Skydiving

Skydive Auckland (Map p130; ☎ 0800 865 567; www.skydiveauckland.com) offers a tandem skydive from 3660m (12,000ft; including a 50-second

free fall) for $250, or training followed by a solo jump for $350. A video costs $125 or a video and photos are $150. It all takes place at Mercer airfield, 55km south of Auckland.

Skydive Parakai (Map p130; ☎ 0800 425 867, 09-420 7327; www.nzskydive.com; Parakai Airfield, Greens Rd) runs tandem skydives for $185 from 2440m (8000ft), $400 from 4900m (16,000ft). Four to five hours of training followed by a 3660m (12,000ft) solo jump costs $390. A video and photos are $150.

Spiderman Activities

Auckland Harbour Bridge Bungy Jump (Map pp98-9; ☎ 0800 462 8649, 09-302 4561; www.ajhackett.com; Westhaven Marina) offers a 40m leap off the bridge and a quick dip in the harbour for $125 but discounts may be available. A video is $39, photos are $24, a T-shirt is $25 but the certificate is free.

Sky Jump (Map pp98-9; ☎ 0800 759 586, 09-368 1835; adult/backpacker & student $195/145; ☼ 10am-5.30pm) is a 192m, 16-second, 75kph base wire jump from the observation deck of the Sky Tower. It's more like a parachute jump than a bungy jump. Beware, it can be addictive – one guy has already jumped 87 times. Photos cost $25 and a second jump is $75.

Sky Screamer (Map pp98-9; ☎ 09-578 0818; cnr Albert St & Victoria St W; 1st/2nd rides $35/15; ☼ 10.30am-10pm Sun-Thu, 10.30am-2am Fri & Sat) involves being strapped into a seat and being hurled 70m up in the air. A video costs $20.

Ground Rush (Map pp98-9; ☎ 0800 727 586; www.groundrush.co.nz; tickets $80) offers rappelling (forward abseiling) down the Mercure Hotel in

Customs St. The price includes two walks down the building and a 20m freefall if you want to try it, and it all takes around 45 minutes.

Auckland Harbour Bridge Climb (Map pp98-9; ☎ 0800 462 5462, 09-377 6543; www.ajhackett.co.nz; Westhaven Marina; adult/child $110/55) is a 2½-hour guided climb involving walking to one of the support pylons, into which you descend, then climbing the arch itself up to the summit and back down the other side. You wear a climbing suit with a harness attached to a static line. Bookings are essential.

Sky Tower Climb (Map pp98-9; ☎ 0800 483 784, 09-368 1917; www.4vertigo.com; adult/child $145/75) involves climbing inside the Sky Tower mast up to the crows nest, 80m above the observation deck. These climbs take 1½ hours and run at 10am, noon, 2pm and 4pm, and a photo costs $17.

Swimming

Auckland is noted for its fine and varied **beaches**, which are dotted around the harbours and coastline. The east coast beaches along Tamaki Drive, including Mission and St Heliers Bays, are popular and can be crowded in summer. At most east coast and harbour beaches swimming is best at high tide. Popular North Shore beaches include Cheltenham (Map p104), Takapuna (Map p96), Milford (Map p130), and further north, Browns Bay (Map p130) and Long Bay (Map p130). The west coast beaches (Map p130) such as Piha and Muriwai are great for surfing but have dangerous currents and rips.

The **Tepid Baths** (Map pp98-9; ☎ 09-379 4754; 100 Customs St; adult/child $4.50/2; ☼ 6am-9pm Mon-Fri, 7am-7pm Sat & Sun) have two undercover pools, a sauna, spa bath and steam rooms. It's a bargain, and a work-out in the gym is an extra $11, or yoga/pilates is $15.

Olympic Swimming Pool (Map p102; ☎ 09-522 4414; 77 Broadway, Newmarket; adult/student/child $5/4/3; ☼ 5.45am-10pm Mon-Fri, 7am-8pm Sat & Sun) has a spa, steam room and sauna as well as a large indoor pool. Use of the fitness centre is $12 and the **creche** (☎ 09-522 1532) costs $12 for two hours.

Parnell Saltwater Pools (Map p100; ☎ 09-373 3561; Judges Bay Rd; adult/child $5/3; ☼ 6am-8pm Mon-Fri, 8am-8pm Sat & Sun Dec-Apr) are outdoors, and the pools and sunbathing areas are popular in summer.

Water Sports

Fergs Kayaks (Map p96; ☎ /fax 09-529 2230; www.fergs kayaks.co.nz; 12 Tamaki Dr, Okahu Bay; ☼ 8am-6pm Mon-Fri, 9am-6pm Sat & Sun, extended hrs Dec-Mar) sells and hires out kayaks ($9 to $15 per hour or $30 to $40 a day) and inline skates ($15 per hour, $30 a day). Day and night guided kayak trips are available to Devonport (8km, 4½ hours, $65) or Rangitoto Island (13km, six hours, $75).

Mission Bay Watersports (Map p96; ☎ 09-521 7245; Mission Bay Beach; ☼ 10am-evening Dec-Mar) has sailboard hire ($25 per hour) and tuition ($35 per hour), kayak hire ($10 per hour), kite surfing courses ($550 for three days), and wakeboarding ($30 for 15 minutes). Wetsuit hire is free.

For good surf less than 50km from the city, try Piha, Muriwai or Bethells Beach (Te Henga) on the west coast, where the water is often very rough. Most of the surfing beaches have surf clubs and lifeguards. The **Aloha Surf School** (☎ 09-489 2846; www.alohasurfschool.com; 1½-2hr lessons/practice $80/25, pick-up $30) is a long-running surf school with very experienced and safety-conscious instructors, which conducts lessons at Piha and elsewhere.

NZ Surf Tours (☎ /fax 09-832 9622; www.newzealand surftours.com; 1-/2-day $120/220) runs weekend surfing courses (October to June) that include transport, all equipment and three hours of lessons a day. A five-day course costs $700 and includes accommodation and food.

Dive Centre (Map p96; ☎ 09-444 6948; www.dive centre.co.nz; 128 Wairau Rd, Takapuna) has a large dive shop, runs PADI courses, and owns a 15m boat for local dive trips to Little Barrier Island ($155 for two dives), Mokohinau Island and the Hen and Chickens Islands ($170 for two dives).

Orakei Scuba Centre (Map p96; ☎ 09-524 2117; www.orakeidive.co.nz; 234 Orakei Rd) has a dive shop and runs PADI courses ($480 for five days) with practice dives at the Poor Knights Islands.

Scuba Blue (Map p100; ☎ 09-377 6929; Parnell Saltwater Pool; courses $400) offers scuba diving courses in summer to children over eight who have wealthy parents.

Other Activities

Extreme 4WD Adventures (☎ 0800 493 238; www .extreme4wd.co.nz; 1-2 drivers $120) offers driving a 4WD around a special two-hour adventure trail near Helensville behind a guiding vehicle. Training courses are also available.

4 Track Adventures (☎ 0800 487 225, 09-420 8104; 1hr/2hr/3hr tours $115/175/220) offers you a chance to drive a quad bike through Woodhill Forest (beach ride included on the two- and three-hour tours). Pick up from Auckland is $20 per person.

Howick Golf Course (☎ 09-535 1001; 32 Musick Point Rd, Bucklands Beach; affiliated/non-affiliated golfers $35/50) is located at the tip of a peninsula to the southeast of the city and has spectacular views. There are countless golf courses around Auckland.

Balloon Expeditions (☎ 09-416 8590; www.balloon expeditions.co.nz; adult/child $250/175) and **Balloon Safaris** (☎ 09-415 8289; adult/child $250/200) do early morning hot-air balloon flights that take about four hours (one hour in the air) with breakfast and a bottle of bubbles.

Rocknasium (Map p96; ☎ 09-630 5522; rocknasium@ clear.net.nz; 610 Dominion Rd; adult/child $20/15) is a funky indoor climbing centre with a café. The price covers all-day instruction and even free basic accommodation upstairs (a 14-bed dorm and two doubles) with a kitchen and lounge.

University Recreation Centre (Map pp98-9; ☎ 09-373 7999; 17 Symonds St; adult/child $11/5; 6am-9.30pm Mon-Thu, 9am-5.30pm Sat & Sun) is where you can play squash, badminton or basketball or work out in the gym.

Adventure Cycles (Map pp98-9; ☎ 09-309 5566; 36 Customs St E; 7am-7pm) hires out road and mountain bikes ($18 to $35 a day). Cycle along Tamaki Drive to Mission Bay, or put the bike on a ferry and cycle around Devonport.

WALKING TOURS

The visitors centres and the DOC office have pamphlets on walks in and around Auckland. DOC's *Auckland Walkways* pamphlet has a good selection of forest and coastal day walks outside the metropolitan area.

The **Coast to Coast Walkway** is a 16km north–south walk between the Viaduct Basin on Waitemata Harbour and Onehunga Bay on Manukau Harbour. The four-hour walk encompasses Albert Park, the university, the domain, Mt Eden, One Tree Hill and other points of interest, keeping as much as possible to reserves rather than city streets. Starting from the Viaduct Basin and heading south it's marked by yellow markers and milestones; heading north from Onehunga there are blue markers. The visitors centre has a detailed brochure and map showing the walk and describing sights along the way.

AUCKLAND FOR CHILDREN

Auckland is child-friendly, except for the traffic. It has plenty to keep the little darlings busy and uncomplaining. **Mission Bay** (p104) has a safe beach, water-sport gear for hire and a playground in sight of a café, while **Rainbow's End** (p106), **Kelly Tarlton's Antarctic Encounter & Underwater World** (p101), **Auckland Zoo** (p101) and **Parakai Aquatic Park** (p132) are other favourites.

The **Tepid Baths** (p108) has a children's pool and is cheap. **Ambury Park** (p106) is another more distant option, while **Scuba Blue** (p108) could be a popular Special Treat, and younger kids would enjoy the **Teddy Bear's picnic** (p111).

QUIRKY AUCKLAND

Minus 5° Bar (Map pp98-9; Princes Wharf; 2-10pm) is an extraordinary ice bar where everything from the seats to your glass is made of ice. Put on special clothing (including gloves and shoes), pay $20 and sip a vodka-based drink or a juice from an edible ice glass. You can only stay inside the shimmering ice world for 30 minutes. Lenin Bar next door offers a good view inside.

TOURS

You can spend a day touring the major Auckland attractions in the hop-on-hop-off **Explorer Bus** (☎ 0800 439 756; www.explorerbus.co.nz; adult/child $30/15). It departs daily from the Ferry Building every half-hour from 9am to 4pm from October to April and every hour from 10.30am to 4.30pm from May to September. The bus runs to Kelly Tarlton's, Mission Bay, Parnell, Auckland Museum, Sky Tower, Victoria Park Market, and back to the ferry building. At Auckland Museum you can pick up the Satellite Link (October to April only) to Mt Eden, Westfield St Lukes Shopping Mall, Auckland Zoo, Motat, Lionzone Brewery tour and Eden Park sports museum. This service also offers free pick-up from the airport and South Auckland.

Auckland has plenty of tour operators. Three-hour bus tours will typically take

TWO VOLCANOES WALK

This 5km walk takes 2½ hours, but can be extended to 6km and three hours by including the Navy Museum.

Take the ferry from central Auckland to Devonport, a quiet suburb of wooden Victorian villas which is almost entirely surrounded by water. You can detour left past the naval base to the **Navy Museum** (**1**; p103) if that interests you, or head up Victoria Rd with its many well-preserved historical buildings, and browse the art and craft galleries, cafés, bookshops, antique shops and **Jackson's Muzeum** (**2**; p103). Then walk up the extinct volcanic cone, **Mt Victoria** (**3**; p103), to the panoramic viewpoint and hidden artillery on the top.

Return to Kerr St and then walk along Vauxhall Rd to sandy **Cheltenham Beach** (**4**; p108). Enjoy the view of Rangitoto Island (Auckland's youngest volcano) as you walk along the beach before turning right into Cheltenham Rd and then left to **North Head** (**5**; p103). This is another volcanic cone with extensive defence relics and coastal views from the summit. Walk down and back along King Edward Pde, with views of central Auckland, to the ferry wharf.

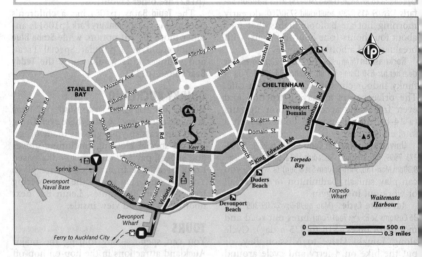

you around the city centre, over the harbour bridge and out along Tamaki Drive, including stops at Mt Eden, the Auckland Museum and Parnell, for about $50.

Scenic Pacific Tours (☎ 0800 698 687, 09-307 7880; 172 Quay St) and **Great Sights** (☎ 0800 744 487, 09-375 4700; www.greatsights.co.nz; 180 Quay St) are other major operators with city tours as well as tours to the Bay of Islands, Waitomo and Rotorua. Free hotel pick-up and drop-off is usually included with city tours.

ABC Tours (☎ 0800 222 868; adult/child half-day tours $65/33, full-day tours $95/50) has an afternoon tour covering Devonport, the Henderson wine region, Scenic Drive and the Waitakere Ranges, and Manukau Harbour. The full-day tour gives a good picture of the Auckland region.

Auckland Adventures (☎ 09-379 4545; www.aucklandactivities.co.nz/aa/; afternoon/day tours $65/100) runs good-value tours. The afternoon one (12.45pm to 5pm) includes Muriwai gannet colony, an orchard, wineries and Mt Eden, while the day tours (9am to 5pm) also include either a 1½-hour hike or a one-hour downhill mountain-bike ride.

Bush & Beach (☎ 09-575 1458; www.bushandbeach.co.nz) has a tour to the Waitakere Ranges (including hiking) and Karekare Beach for $75, or include a city tour and the cost is $125.

Devonport Tours (☎ 09-357 6366; 1hr/2hr/dinner tours $30/50/65) runs one-hour hop-on-hop-off bus tours of Devonport, including Mt Victoria and North Head, or a two-hour tour that includes lunch. Prices include the return ferry ticket from the Ferry Building. They operate from 10am to 3pm. Children are half-price and there's also a dinner tour.

Fine Wine Tours (☎ /fax 09-849 4519; 4hr tours $120) also tours the West Auckland wineries and has a Matakana tour for $240.

Geotours (☎ 09-525 3991; www.geotours.co.nz; half-/full-day tours $80/120) offers cerebral trips led by a geologist who can explain Auckland's volcanic cones and other geological features, as well as flora and fauna.

Volcano City Tours (☎ 09-838 0986; www.volcano citytours.co.nz; adult/child half-day tours $60/28, full-day tours $96/48) has small-group tours, including to the Waitakere Ranges.

Wine Trail Tours (☎ 09-630 1540; www.winetrail tours.co.nz; half-/full-day tours $90/135) has small-group tours around the West Auckland wineries and the Waitakere Ranges as well as trips further afield to Matakana ($130/155) and Bay of Plenty wineries ($185).

FESTIVALS & EVENTS

The visitors centre keeps a list of the many annual events held in Auckland, or view www.aucklandnz.com/VisitorInformation/Events.

JANUARY
ASB Open Tennis Championships (Women) Watch some leading players warm up for the Aussie Open.
Heineken Open Tennis Championships (Men) See some famous tennis names in action as the new season gets under way in Stanley St.

Auckland Anniversary Day Regatta The City of Sails lives up to its name.

FEBRUARY
Devonport Food & Wine Festival Sip and sup with the smart set at this two-day festival.
HERO Festival The gay parade has had financial problems but will no doubt continue.
Aotearoa Maori Performing Arts Festival A rare chance to see Maori culture in action.
Asian Lantern Festival Three days of Asian food and culture in Albert Park to welcome the lunar New Year.
Mission Bay Jazz & Blues Street Fest New Orleans comes to the Bay as jazz and blues bands line both sides of the street as the sun sets.
Teddy Bears Picnic Held in the Auckland Domain with all sorts of entertainment aimed at children.

MARCH/APRIL
Waiheke Jazz Festival The wine island is booked up months ahead for this annual music fest.
Pasifika Festival Western Springs Park hosts this giant Polynesian party with music, dancing and food.
Royal NZ Easter Show Fun for all the family with an agricultural flavour.

MAY
Comedy Festival Laughter is the medicine dispensed during two weeks of mayhem in early May, when local and international comedy talent guarantees to give you a good time.
NZ Boat Show One of the world's leading boatie nations shows off its wares – if it floats you can find it here.

GAY & LESBIAN AUCKLAND

Pride Centre (Map pp98-9; ☎ 09-302 0590; www.pride.org.nz; 281 K Rd; ☺ 10am-5pm Mon-Fri, 10am-3pm Sat) is the main contact point for the gay and lesbian community.

Express is a fortnightly magazine with masses of information on the Auckland gay scene. *Up* is a monthly magazine, while *New Zealand Gay Guide* (www.gogaynewzealand.com) is a new pocket-sized booklet with listings. Log on to www.gaynz.com for news and venue listings.

Auckland hosts a HERO festival every February with two weeks of events, including the Big Gay Out, the HERO parade and a Heroic Gardens weekend when 20 gay gardens go on view to the public to raise money for AIDS sufferers.

Urge (Map pp98-9; ☎ 09-307 2155; 490 K Rd; ☺ 9pm-late Thu-Sat) is a gay men's bar and club with a friendly owner, a DJ on Friday and Saturday nights and occasional theme nights. **Kamo** (Map pp98-9; ☎ 09-377 2313; 382 K Rd; mains $15-20; ☺ 10.30am-10.30pm Tue-Sun) is a low-key restaurant and bar. **Flesh Bar & Nightclub** (Map pp98-9; ☎ 09-336 1616; 15 O'Connell St; ☺ 6pm-late) is a dimly lit central lounge bar with free snacks and karaoke on Wednesday. The **nightclub** (☺ 11pm-late Fri & Sat) is downstairs, usually has no cover charge and features regular drag shows by the resplendent Ms Ribena. In Ponsonby, **Surrender Dorothy** (Map p105; ☎ 09-376 4446; 175 Ponsonby Rd; ☺ 5pm-midnight Tue-Sat) is a small, friendly gay bar that welcomes everyone. The crowd spills out onto the pavement during the Saturday night drag shows by Ms Onya Knees or Ms Bumper.

OCTOBER

Auckland to Russell Yacht Race Superb tall ships race from NZ's 'real' capital to its first capital.

Wine Waitakere Wet your whistle at the Westie wineries.

NOVEMBER

Ellerslie Flower Show Five days of flowers, music and food lure crowds of visitors to Auckland Botanical Gardens.

DECEMBER

Auckland Cup Try to spot the winner at the biggest horse race of the year.

Christmas in the Park This party is so big it has to be held in the Auckland Domain.

First Night (31 December) A free and alcohol-free music party in Aotea Square & Centre.

SLEEPING – BUDGET
City Centre   Map pp98-9
HOSTELS

Auckland has plenty of hostels and student-style rooms in the city centre and inner suburbs, but you will still need to book ahead in summer, especially if you want a private room. The city centre has the biggest hostels in town, mostly on or just off Queen St, but they tend to be crowded, some need upgrading and parking is a major problem. For easier parking, and a quieter and more pleasant environment, try the hostels in Parnell, Mt Eden or

---

THE AUTHOR'S CHOICE

Xbase (Map pp98-9; ☎ 09-300 9999; www.base backpackers.com; 16 Fort St; dm $22-24, tw $65, d & tw with bathroom $85; 🖳) This large, brand new and ultra-smart backpackers sets new standards, with a café (breakfasts under $5, other meals under $10), a cosy bar and nightclub, a quiet library room, a travel agency and a roof deck with a sauna and hot pool (payment required). Dorms have eight to 12 beds, and the immaculate en suite rooms have TVs, Sky TV, linen, heaters and hairdryers. One floor is reserved for females only. Everything is well-designed with bright colours, big windows and even big mirrors. The TVs in the washrooms are a bit overboard but the toilet seat wipes are a nice touch. This central haven has bubbly, well-trained staff and is the author's choice for trying the hardest to please its customers.

Ponsonby. Dorm prices range from $20 to $27, singles without bathrooms generally go for around $45 but can be hard to find, while doubles and twins without bathrooms usually cost $50 to $60 a night, and en suite rooms cost around $85. Prices can be a few dollars less if you have a backpacker card.

Auckland Central Backpackers (☎ 09-358 4877; www.acb.co.nz; cnr Queen & Darby Sts; dm $22-24, d & tw $62, d & tw with bathroom $85, f $120; 🖳) This almost brand-new backpackers with over 500 beds is so popular that it buzzes day and night like a beehive, so don't stay here if you don't like crowds. The dorms have four beds or four double bunks. Full linen is supplied except in bunk dorms. En-suite and family rooms have their own TV. Some rooms have no windows but all rooms have air-con and heating and a small fridge. Facilities include a large Internet area and a job-search agency, and downstairs is the Globe Bar which parties till late every night.

Auckland City YHA (☎ 09-309 2802; www.stayyha .com; cnr City Rd & Liverpool St; dm/s/d & tw $27/46/64; 🖳) On a quiet street just off the southern end of Queen St, this ever-popular, purpose-built, high-rise hostel is clean and well-run with artworks on the walls and linen supplied. Dorms have three to six beds, YHA members pay $4 less, and children pay reduced rates. **Tommy's Bistro** (breakfasts $7, dinner mains $10-12) is on the ground floor along with a tour desk. Upstairs is a sun deck.

Auckland International YHA (☎ 09-302 8200, www.stayyha.com; 5 Turner St; dm $27, d & tw $75, d & tw with bathroom $85; Ⓟ 🖳) This bright, modern and clean accommodation is the nearby City YHA's twin but has rooms with private bathrooms that are only available to members. It is child- and disabled-friendly, linen is supplied, and dorm rooms have individual lights and four or eight beds. YHA members pay $4 less except for the en-suite rooms. Some rooms only have small high windows, and the dining room is nicer than the windowless TV room. There is a travel desk and a board for job vacancies.

YWCA (☎ 09-377 8763; www.akywca.org.nz; 10 Vincent St; s/d & tw $40/50, per week $140/210; Ⓟ 🖳) Much better than most YWCAs, both men and women can stay here, although there are some female-only zones. The recently refurbished rooms have cheerful décor, linen, a fridge, heating and desk, and the staff are helpful and welcoming. Weekly rates apply only for a four-week minimum stay. Facilities include a new kitchen and a popular outdoor area. Fast Internet access is free.

YMCA (☎ 09-303 2068; www.nzymca.com; cnr Pitt St & Greys Ave; s/tw/d/tr $45/65/70/75, per week $250/360/420/450; P 🖳) The tidy rooms have linen, a table and chairs, fridge and splashes of colour, but only microwave cooking is available. It has an institutional feel and lacks a friendly welcome and atmosphere. It's open to men and women.

Queen St Backpackers (☎ 09-373 3471; www.qsb .co.nz; 4 Fort St; dm/s/d & tw $24/46/60; 🖳) A large lounge area with a bar and pool table makes this a sociable hotel-turned-backpackers. It is gradually being upgraded with new showers and carpets, most rooms have a sink and a table and chairs. Dorms vary from four to eight beds.

Others worth considering:

Albert Park Backpackers (☎ 09-309 0336; bakpak@ albertpark.co.nz; 27 Victoria St E; dm $21-23, s/d & tw $45/55; 🖳)

Central City Backpackers (☎ 09-358 5685; www.back packer.net.nz; 26 Lorne St; dm $22-25, d & tw $60; 🖳)

Fat Camel Hostel (☎ 0800 220 198, 09-307 0181; www.fatcamel.co.nz; 38 Fort St; dm/d &tw/d deluxe $22/50/60; 🖳)

UNIVERSITY ACCOMMODATION

Huia Residence (☎ 09-377 1345; fax 377 4871; 110 Grafton Rd; s/d & tw/apt $40/50/85; P 🖳) Available all year round to travellers, this student-style high-rise accommodation is a good deal with central heating, a fridge, linen and some furniture in the rooms. Each floor has a kitchen. The self-contained and spacious apartments with kitchens and TVs are a good deal, too.

Grafton Hall of Residence (☎ 09-373 3994; graf tonhall@auckland.ac.nz; 40 Seafield View Rd; s/tw $37/65; 🖳 P) Free breakfasts, laundry, Internet and tennis makes for a tempting offer at this spacious student accommodation in a quiet street. It is open to travellers from mid-November to mid-February.

International House (☎ 09-379 7192; 27 Whitaker Pl; s incl breakfast & dinner $30) A great deal is offered to solo travellers between mid-November and mid-February at these typical student rooms with linen, desk, chair and cupboard. It lacks a kitchen but meals are provided and there is a games

room and a lounge with TV, video and DVD player.

HOTELS

Auckland City Hotel (☎ 09-303 2463; www.auckland cityhotel.co.nz; 131 Beach Rd; backpacker dm/d $25/50, hotel s/d & tw/tr $65/80/90; 🖳) Stay here if you want cheap but clean rooms, with bathroom, in a central location. All rooms (except the backpacker ones) have a TV, a fridge, a table and chairs and en suite facilities. In the loft is a tiny backpacker section with a kitchen, TVs in the rooms, and shared facilities. The Mascot Café downstairs does a full breakfast for $5.50.

Aspen House (☎ 09-379 6633; www.aspenhouse .co.nz; 62 Emily Pl; s $50-55, d & tw $70-75; P 🖳) This is a budget hotel with 27 uninspiring rooms without ensuite, but the price includes breakfast and the plus points are a laundry and the lounge and outdoor areas where guests can relax and discuss the day's events, and a laundry. Triple rooms are also available. Next door 30 new rooms with bathrooms will soon be available for around $100 a night.

Parnell   Map p100

Stylish Parnell is a 30-minute walk to the city centre or you can take the frequent Link bus ($1.20).

City Garden Lodge (☎ 09-302 0880; 25 St Georges Bay Rd; dm $20-22, tw $46-50, d $60; P 🖳) Housed in an elegant two-storey palace built for the Queen of Tonga, this TV-less and well-run backpackers that has a courtyard and barbecue area is filled with character and decorative flair. The cheaper dorm has eight beds, the others have three or four.

Auckland International Backpackers (☎ 09-358 4584; international.bp@xtra.co.nz; 2 Churton St; camp sites $20, dm/d & tw $22/52; 🖳) Eat in the sunroom, the pleasant dining room or out in the small garden at this large and rambling but comfortable and friendly backpackers that used to be a YHA hostel.

Railway Campus (☎ 09-367 7100; rail camp@ auckland.ac.nz; 26 Te Taou Cres; studio $85-95 & apt winter $150-194, studio/3-bed apt summer $80/145) Auckland's spacious 1930s railway station has retained many period features but now offers en suite accommodation, which is available to travellers all year with plenty of vacancies from mid-November to mid-February. An odd mixture of grand architecture and budget student-style rooms, it's packed with facilities such as a large industrial kitchen, gym, games room, library, and a large-screen TV. Giant chess can be played in the impressive atrium concourse.

Mt Eden   Map p102
Mt Eden is a pleasant, quiet and leafy suburb of wooden villas that is a short bus journey from the city centre. All three of these backpackers are part of the Bamber empire.

Bamber House (☎/fax 09-623 4267; www.hostel backpacker.com; 22 View Rd; dm $20-23; s/d & tw $43/56; P ⬚ ⬚) One of Auckland's best backpackers, with young, personable staff, it consists of two smart, clean and colourful houses with a large garden, a pool and a trampoline. One house is colonial-style while the other is modern. Tennis courts are across the road. Dorms vary from three to eight beds, but singles are in outbuildings.

Oaklands Lodge (☎ 0800 220 725, 09-638 6545; www.oaklands.co.nz; 5a Oaklands Rd; dm/s/d & tw $23/45/60; ⬚) More smart and bright accommodation with a small garden and friendly staff can be found here, near Mt Eden village. The dorms have four and eight beds.

Pentlands Backpackers (☎/fax 09-638 7031; www.pentlands.co.nz; 22 Pentland Ave; dm $20-23, s/d & tw $45/60; P ⬚) Another colourful and comfortable place with small dorms, a large lounge, log fire, garden deck and tennis court.

Ponsonby   Map p105
Uenuku Lodge (☎ 09-378 8990; www.uenukulodge .co.nz; 217 Ponsonby Rd; dm $22-24, s/tw/d $45/52/54; P ⬚) This new, high-quality, gay-friendly backpackers has an outdoor area, a touch of style, and good views from most private rooms. There are dorms with four, six, eight and 10 beds. Rooms have a sink and bedside lamp, and all linen is supplied.

Brown Kiwi (☎ 09-378 0191; www.brownkiwi.co.nz; 7 Prosford St; dm $22-24, d & tw/tr $55/70; P ⬚) Another smart, gay-friendly backpackers where dorms have four or eight beds, and the triple rooms are set in the small garden courtyard.

Ponsonby Backpackers (☎ 0800 476 676, 09-360 1311; www.ponsonby-backpackers.co.nz; 2 Franklin Rd; camp sites $30, dm/d/tw $22/55/60, s $35-40; P ⬚) The biggest dorm has six beds in this laid-back,

slightly tatty colonial-style backpackers with a garden.

Airport   Map p96
Skyway Lodge (☎ 09-275 4443; skyway@ihug.co.nz; 30 Kirkbride Rd, Mangere; dm/s $23/45, d & tw $55, d & tw with bathroom $65; ⬚) This is the best budget option near the airport with a friendly and helpful owner, and a large communal lounge and kitchen. The dorms have four beds, and a ride to/from the airport is free.

Other Areas
A few hostels allow camping – see Auckland Backpackers (p100), Ponsonby Backpackers (p105) and Leadbetter Lodge (p100). Other camping grounds with cabins are outside the city centre.

North Shore Motels & Holiday Park (Map p96; ☎ 09-418 2578; info@nsmotels.co.nz; 52 Northcote Rd, Takapuna; camp sites $32, dm/tourist flats $35/90, cabins $55-70; ⬚ ⬚) An indoor pool, spa and 24-hour check-in are all available at this large Top 10 holiday park near Takapuna on North Shore, 4km north of the Harbour Bridge. It's the best in Auckland.

Avondale Motor Park (Map p96; ☎ 0800 100 542, 09-828 7228; www.aucklandmotorpark.co.nz; 46 Bollard Ave, Avondale; camp/campervan sites $20/24, cabins $55, cabins with bathroom $60, tourist flats $65) In a leafy and rural setting, the pink cabins are good but the camp's kitchen and TV lounge are poor.

SLEEPING – MID-RANGE
Auckland has masses of motels and costs start at around $85 to $100 for a studio double, though they can be higher. The best motel area close to the city centre is along Great South Rd in Remuera. A good area for mid-range B&Bs is Devonport, which is just a 12-minute ferry ride from Queen St.

City Centre   Map pp98-9
Freeman's B&B (☎ 0800 437 336, 09-376 5046; www .freemansbandb.co.nz; 65 Wellington St; s/d & tw/f $65/85/140; ⬚) Free Internet, free tea and coffee and a substantial continental breakfast is included in the price at this refurbished accommodation with new beds and hardworking owners. There are no en-suite rooms at present, but it's in a quiet street away from the central hubbub with a shady garden.

Sail City Hotel (☎ 0800 724 524, 09-356 7272; www.sailcityhotel.com; cnr Nelson & Wellesley Sts; d & tw $75-110) The spacious, en suite rooms in this brand-new hotel in a renovated Art Deco building still have a sparkle and all have a fridge, TV, cupboard, table and chairs. The cheaper rooms are smaller with no view.

New President (☎ 0800 321 333, 09-303 1333; www.newpresidenthotel.co.nz; 27 Victoria St W; studios $120-135, 1-bed apt $140-155; 🖳) The rather bare but modern studios have air-con and kitchenette, and a buffet breakfast is available, but the central location is the main reason people stay here.

City Central Hotel (☎ 0800 323 6000, 09-307 3388; www.citycentralhotel.co.nz; cnr Albert & Wellesley Sts; d & tw $95-115, tr & f $135; 🖳) Small but clean and tidy en-suite rooms with TV are available at this very central location, along with a buffet breakfast to set you up for the day.

Parnell   Map p100
Chalet Chevron B&B (☎ 09-309 0290; www.chalet chevron.co.nz; 14 Brighton Rd; s $80, d & tw $110-125; 🅿) The communal lounge and dining room are pleasant, as are the en-suite upstairs rooms that have views, but the single rooms, though with en-suite, are spartan. The hosts are friendly and prices can be reduced in winter. B&Bs are almost extinct around central Auckland so book ahead.

Parnell Inn (☎ 09-358 0642; parnelin@ihug.co .nz; 320 Parnell Rd; s winter/summer $75/85, d studios winter $80-110, summer $95-130; 🅿) The rooms are smallish in this small motel but they are clean and tidy with Sky TV and an en suite.

Parnell Village Motor Lodge (☎ 09-377 1463; www.parnellmotorlodge.co.nz; 2 St Stephens Ave; studios $95-105, apt $135-170; 🅿) An old and newer section is available in this motel where every unit is different, some have a bit of character, and they all have a kitchenette.

Barrycourt Motor Inn (☎ 0800 504 466, 09-303 3789; www.barrycourt.co.nz; 10 Gladstone Rd; lodge units/ studios/apt from $90/110/130; 🅿 🖳) A mixed bag of over a hundred motel rooms and units are available in this large complex. The lodge is spacious but very old-fashioned, and the modern wing starts at $135, although prices can be discounted in winter. It has a restaurant/bar/café and hot spa pools.

Kingsgate Hotel (☎ 0800 782 548, 09-377 3619; www.kingsgatehotels.co.nz; 92 Gladstone Rd; d & tw $125-

140, ste/1-/2-bed apt $190/350/440; 🅿 🖳 🌊) Opposite the Parnell Rose Gardens, this large hotel has smart rooms clustered in landscaped blocks, together with a restaurant and bar, an outdoor pool, hot spa pools and plenty of parking.

Mt Eden   Map p102
Bavaria B&B (☎ 09-638 9641; www.bavariabandbhotel .co.nz; 83 Valley Rd; s/d May-Sep $80/110, Oct-Apr $95/135; 🅿) This long-running B&B in a spacious villa offers almost luxurious en-suite rooms decorated in pastel shades, with a convivial TV lounge, dining room and deck where guests can mix and mingle.

Ponsonby   Map p105
Ponsonby Potager (☎ 09-378 7237; 43 Douglas St; s/d $90/120) This cluttered cottagey self-contained unit with a conservatory and a garden deck is unique. A DIY breakfast is supplied.

Abaco Spa Motel (☎ 0800 220 066, 09-360 6850; www.abacospamotel.com; 59 Jervois Rd; studios/1-bed apt from $110/120; 🅿) Prices could rise as units are being refurbished with earth tones and spa baths. Upper floor units have balconies and breakfast is available ($5 to $10).

Sea Breeze Motel (Map p96; ☎ 09-376 2139; www.seabreeze.co.nz; 213 Jervois Rd; s/d & tw $95/110, units $120-150; 🅿) This century-old building not far from a beach has been refurbished and contains a varied collection of boutique units. Some have balcony, one has a sea view and all have kitchen and central heating.

Devonport   Map p104
Devonport has a range of B&Bs ideal for those wanting a quiet and homely place to stay that is only a 12-minute ferry ride from Queen St. Some are in restored villas while others are modern units set in garden.

Rainbow Villa (☎ 09-445 3597; www.rainbow villa.co.nz; 17 Rattray St; B&B s/d & tw $100/130, Jan-Apr $120/150) Stay here for the period features in this 1885 Victorian villa, the elegant en-suite rooms, the spa pool in the garden and the healthy breakfasts.

108 Victoria Road (☎ 09-445 7565; 108 Victoria Rd; d $100-120; 🌊) The main feature here is a fairyland-style swimming pool just outside your front door if you stay in one of the comfortable and spacious, modern, two-storey units in the garden. A continental breakfast is $5.

Parituhu (☎ /fax 09-445 6559; www.parituhu.co.nz; 3 King Edward Pde; s/d $70/90) A modern en-suite room is available in this gay and lesbian-friendly family house with well-travelled and friendly hosts, a perfect seafront location, a sunny deck and a garden.

Bryand B&B (☎ 09-445 6037; selliott@hotmail.com; 98 Victoria Rd; s/d & tw $80/90) The comfortable rooms in this wooden villa don't have bathrooms but it's a genuine homestay with a kind and helpful hostess, access to the kitchen if you want to cook, and a small garden.

Jasmine Cottage (☎ 09-445 8825; 20 Buchanan St; B&B d & tw $100-110) The hostess pampers guests who stay in the cute little courtyard unit with a kitchenette and flowers, and the quality breakfast will fuel you up for the day.

Devonport Motel (☎ 09-445 1010; www.devonport motel.co.nz; 11 Buchanan St; units $120) This mini-motel has just two self-contained units in the back garden, but they are modern and clean.

Ducks Crossing Cottage (☎ /fax 09-445 8102; duckxing@splurge.net.nz; 58 Seabreeze Rd; B&B s $70, d & tw $110-120) A lovely modern cottage with friendly and experienced hosts who serve a generous breakfast. The rooms have patchwork quilts and a TV. A pick-up from the ferry and orientation tour is available.

Baker's Place (☎ 09-445 4035; thefleafm@clear.net.nz; 30 Hastings Pde; d $65) This is a fully self-contained unit in the garden that is reasonably priced and includes laundry and ironing facilities and use of the spa pool.

Devonport Sea Cottage (☎ 09-355 7117; leth abys@ihug.co.nz; 3a Cambridge Tce; d $120) This has a good self-contained unit in the garden, and weekly rates are available.

Number Nine B&B (☎ 09-445 3059; tainui@ xtra.co.nz; 9 Tainui Rd; d $130, Jan $160) There is lots of natural wood in this stylish villa where the rooms have private facilities.

Amberley (☎ 09-446 0506; amberley@xtra.co.nz; 3 Ewen Alison Ave; B&B s $80-110, d & tw $130-140) Facilities are shared but one bathroom has a double spa bath in this elegant Edwardian villa full of olde worlde features.

Airport   Map p96

Out near the airport, Mangere has dozens of motels, particularly along Kirkbride and McKenzie Rds. They're competitively priced, provide free airport transfers and often have a restaurant and bar.

Pacific Inn (☎ 0800 504 800, 09-275 1129; www.pacific-inn.co.nz; 210 Kirkbride Rd; s/d & tw/f $80/90/100; P 🖳) There are some good upgraded rooms here and the bar and restaurant are being refurbished, too.

Gateway Hotel (☎ 0800 651 110, 09-275 4079; www.kiwihotel.co.nz; 206 Kirkbride Rd; d & tw/tr/ste $90/105/150; P 🕱) A restaurant and bar are available here as well as an outdoor pool area.

Traveller's International (☎ 0800 800 564, 09-275 5082; www.travellersinternational.co.nz; 190 Kirkbride Rd; s/d & tw $90/100; P 🕱) Some of its units have kitchenettes; the motel also has a small pool and a restaurant.

Jet Inn (☎ 0800 538 466, 09-275 4100; www.jet inn.co.nz; 63 Westney Rd; r $125-170; P 🖳 🕱) This superior accommodation has a stylish restaurant and bar, an attractive pool area and a memorable décor of hundreds of authentic African carvings. Rates are negotiable, especially Friday to Sunday, each room has a safe and the airport is only 4km away.

Other Areas

Nautical Nook B&B (Map p96; ☎ 09-521 2544; www.nauticalnook.com; 23b Watene Cres, Orakei; s/d $85/130; 🖳) Very comfortable nautical-themed accommodation is offered in this modern house with sea and park views. The friendly retired owners are keen sailors and have been known to take their guests out for a sail on their boat.

Motels along the Great South Rd in Remuera offer good deals:

Hansen's (Map p96; ☎ 09-520 2804; hansens mot@xtra.co.nz; 96 Great South Rd; units $80-140; P 🕱) All the spacious units have a video player, most have a kitchen, and there's a small pool and an indoor spa.

Tudor Court (Map p96; ☎ 0800 826 878, 09-523 1069; stay@tudor.co.nz; 108 Great South Rd, Remuera units $80-85; P) Friendly owners here offer good-value, small but quiet units at the foot of Mt Hobson, some of which have a kitchenette.

Oak Tree Lodge (Map p96; ☎ 0800 625 8733, 09-524 2211; contact@oaktreelodge.co.nz; 104 Great South Rd; studios $85-95, units $120-160; P) Some large units are available in this modern and stylish yet reasonably priced motel.

DAVID WALL

Auckland Museum (p99)

WAYNE WALTON

Christmas window display,
Ponsonby (p104), Auckland

National Maritime Museum
(p100), Auckland

CHRIS MELLOR

CHRIS MELLOR

Auckland Harbour Bridge (p107)

Mission Bay (p104), Auckland

Sky Tower, Auckland (p97)

Viaduct Harbour (p119), Auckland

SLEEPING – TOP END
City Centre   Map pp98-9
Auckland's top business hotels often offer discounts on their official prices.

Hilton Hotel (☎ 09-978 2000; www.hilton.com; Princes Wharf, 147 Quay St; d & tw $310-390; 🖥 🏊) Perched at the tip of Princes Wharf, this stylish ship-shaped boutique luxury hotel is almost out to sea. The rooms are not as exciting as the overall design but have wide balconies, and there's a business centre, a slither of an outdoor pool, the classy White restaurant (mains $35) and a bar (beers $8). Neighbouring serviced apartments are also available, but harbour views plus style equals expensive.

Sky City Hotel (☎ 0800 759 2489, 09-363 6000; www.skycity.co.nz; cnr Victoria & Federal Sts; d & tw $180-240; 🅿 🖥 🏊) Rooms in this popular luxury hotel (an extension is being built) have large windows, TV, Internet, a bath and shower, and there's a pool, business centre, gym and sauna. But the big attraction is its brilliant location in Auckland's entertainment hub with a buzzing atrium foyer, surrounded by Sky Tower, restaurants, bars and a 24-hour casino. It's as near to Las Vegas as Auckland gets.

Heritage Auckland (☎ 09-379 8553; 35 Hobson St; r & apt $190-250; 🖥 🏊) What stands out at this hotel are the period features from when it was a high-class department store and the superb and unique atrium restaurant (mains $22 to $36). A range of accommodation, some with kitchen, dishwasher, washing machine and drier is offered together with a business centre, bar, gym, outdoor and indoor pool, and a sauna.

Sebel Suites (☎ 0800 937 373, 09-978 4000; www.mirvachotels.com.au; 85 Customs St; studio $230, 1-bed apt without/with harbour view $250/320) Stay here for the fantastic (but expensive) views of the Viaduct Basin harbour. The business-style rooms and apartments have kitchenette, washing machine, drier and dishwasher. Car parking is $20. Ask about weekend specials.

Stamford Plaza Hotel (☎ 09-309 8888; www.stamford.com.au; Albert St; d & tw $180-200; 🅿 🖥 🏊) A top hotel in the heart of the city, the quiet rooms have TV, Internet, local artworks on the walls and both a bath and shower. On the roof is a heated pool (more greenery please!), and elsewhere are a sauna, gym, business centre, champagne bar and cigar lounge. Valet parking is $25.

Duxton Hotel (☎ 0800 655 555, 09-375 1800; www.duxton.com; 100 Greys Ave; d & tw/studios/apt $180/240/400; 🅿 🖥 🏊) All rooms are deluxe and equipped with TV, Internet, air-con and heating, kitchenette, washing and drying machines and small balcony, and some have double spa baths and two TVs.

Hyatt Regency Hotel (☎ 09-355 1234; www.auckland.regency.hyatt.com; Princes St; d & tw $150-650; 🖥 🏊) This functional but elegant hotel has helpful staff and is equipped with a classy gym and a pool.

Scenic Circle Airedale Hotel (☎ 09-374 1741; www.scenic-circle.co.nz; 380 Queen St; standard/superior r $200/230) This landmark, tiled, Art Deco building in Queen St has been cleverly converted into a comfortable hotel where room sizes and shapes vary but they all have a kitchenette and neutral-toned décor, and fittings and furnishings are new. Valet parking costs $13 per night, and there is a gym and launderette.

Parnell
St George's Bay Lodge (Map p100; ☎ 09-303 1050; carol@stgeorge.co.nz; 43 St Georges Bay Rd; B&B d & tw $150-270, tr $300; 🖥) Enjoy top-quality accommodation and genuine Kiwi hospitality in this Edwardian villa B&B with masses of period charm which has underfloor heating, free Internet access and a free glass of port. Prices are greatly reduced in winter.

Ponsonby
Great Ponsonby B&B (Map p105; ☎ 0800 766 792, 09-376 5989; www.ponsonbybnb.co.nz; 30 Ponsonby Tce; d/penthouse $180/330, studios $230-280) Prices are high but the décor and furnishings are colourful and stylish with attractive Pacific art on the walls, and there is a very pleasant lounge and dining area where a full breakfast is served. En-suite rooms in the classy villa have Sky TV and the self-contained studios are in a line in the back garden. Limited off-street parking is available. Expect a $20 reduction in the off-season.

Devonport   Map p104
Peace & Plenty Inn (☎ 09-445 2925; www.peaceandplenty.co.nz; 6 Flagstaff Tce; B&B d & tw $270-300; 🖥) This perfectly located and wonderful period house is stocked with antique furnishings, and the luxury rooms have en suite, TV, flowers, free sherry and chocolates. Perfect

hosts and a memorable breakfast make this the number one choice.

Esplanade Hotel (☎ 09-445 1291; www.esplanade hotel.co.nz; 1 Victoria Rd; B&B d & tw $280-370, ste/penthouse $450/750) This boutique hotel in a 1903 heritage building has retained period features such as high ceilings and has far more style than luxury hotels in the city centre. Perfectly located, the prices are high but include breakfast.

Jeong-K Place by the Sea (☎ 09-445 1358; jeong-k@ihug.co.nz; 4 King Edward Pde; B&B s/d/tw $210/240/280) This is another quality B&B, with suave Asian Kiwi hosts and a green garden.

EATING

Because of its size and ethnic diversity, Auckland has the best range of dining options in the country. For good-value fast food, you can't beat the ready-made sushi lunch packs or the food at the cheap noodle and rice Asian eateries that have sprung up to cater for the numerous Asian students. Cheap takeaway kebab places are also common in central Auckland. Lorne St, High St and Vulcan Lane are lined with cafés of all shapes, sizes and philosophies. West of the city, Ponsonby Rd is by far the trendiest café strip, but Parnell, Mt Eden Village and Newmarket are other options. Ponsonby attracts a hip, young crowd who come to drink and dine before heading off to the late-night clubs on K Rd.

The attractive Princes Wharf and Viaduct Basin waterfront area is where some of the fanciest restaurants have sprung up. This area is popular with the 'after-five' crowd and is heaving on Friday and Saturday evenings, but tends to go quiet late at night.

Parnell has a more refined and compact eating scene, with a strip of good (some quite pricey) restaurants mingling with the fashion boutiques and gift shops. Along the coast, Mission Bay has a cluster of restaurants, while Devonport has a street of galleries, cafés, restaurants and bars, and is only a short ferry ride from the city centre.

City Centre   Map pp98-9
RESTAURANTS

A1 Sushi (☎ 09-377 8008; 18 Shortland St; lunch $13, dinner $7-30; ☉ lunch & dinner Mon-Sat) All sorts of freshly made Japanese lunch items come round on the mini-conveyor belt and you

---

AUTHOR'S CHOICE

Orbit (☎ 09-363 6000; mains $28-31; ☉ lunch & dinner daily, brunch Sat & Sun) This is the place for a special meal as the restaurant is 52 storeys up, revolves once an hour and has stunning views of the Auckland region. The food is not as good as the views, so avoid vegetarian dishes and stick to basic mains and a stylish dessert ($13). The service is leisurely so you can stay a couple of hours and revolve twice. There's a minimum charge of $25 per head. Bring a sunhat for the 6pm sitting or go to the 8pm sitting for a night view. Free entry to the observation deck (normally $15 for adults) is included and you need to book ahead.

---

can eat as much as you like for $13. Don't miss out! Dinner is sukiyaki and shabu shabu.

Wangthai (☎ 09-358 4131; 96 Custom St; mains $17-24; ☉ lunch Mon-Fri, dinner Mon-Sun) This reasonably priced Thai restaurant has cool and smart surroundings near the Viaduct Basin.

Café Midnight Express (☎ 09-303 0312; 59 Victoria St W; mains $8-16; ☉ lunch & dinner) This authentic ethnic restaurant offers Middle Eastern food, music and décor.

Mai Thai (☎ 09-366 6258; cnr Albert St & Victoria St W; mains $17-22; ☉ lunch Mon-Fri, dinner Mon-Sat) This elegant upstairs Thai restaurant has a soothing atmosphere and a bar, and has been serving up stylish food for years and years.

Daikoku (☎ 09-302 2432; 148 Quay St; meals $23-50; ☉ lunch Mon-Fri, dinner daily) Near Britomart station this Japanese Teppanyaki restaurant offers barbecue meals cooked on a hotplate at your table by dexterous chefs.

Toto (☎ 09-302 2665; 53 Nelson St; mains $24-30; ☉ lunch Mon, Fri dinner Mon-Sun) Italian and NZ wines accompany fine modern Italian cuisine and there are professional opera singers on Saturday and Thursday ($10 cover charge). Lunch is unique *Yum Ciao* – lots of small items.

No 5 Wine Bistro (☎ 09-309 9273; 5 City Rd; mains $24-35; ☉ dinner Mon-Sat) It's fine dining in this formal restaurant in an unusual red-brick heritage building with candles, a brief NZ and Euro menu and a choice of over a hundred local wines. Parking is available.

Sky City restaurants:

Observatory (☎ 09-363 6000; lunch/dinner buffet $38/50; ☺ lunch Wed-Sun, dinner daily) It is new and one floor higher than the Orbit restaurant but it doesn't revolve.

Fortuna (☎ 09-363 6000; breakfast/lunch/dinner buffet $18/23/28) This place is at ground level but has a good selection of NZ favourites.

CAFÉS

Join the locals in traffic-free Vulcan Lane:

Café Melba (☎ 09-377 0091; 33 Vulcan Lane; meals $11-15; ☺ breakfast & lunch) For breakfast try the egg or salmon Benedict, bagels, croissants or the porridge and plums in this small but lively café with indoor and outdoor seating.

Mecca Café (☎ 09-309 6300; Vulcan Lane; meals $6-17; ☺ breakfast & lunch) Opposite Café Melba, it also offers plenty of choice, including seafood hotpot and banana pancakes.

Vulcan Café (☎ 09-377 9899; 19 Vulcan Lane; meals $8-15; ☺ breakfast & lunch, closed Sun) Coffee, muffins and deli items star here and the owner claims the service is fast.

Raw Power (☎ 09-303 3624; 10 Vulcan Lane; meals $10; ☺ breakfast & lunch Mon-Fri, brunch Sat) Up on the 1st floor, this small no-frills vegetarian café is worth seeking out and is popular with young women. Fresh fruit juices are $5 and dishes such as tofu burgers and falafels in pitta bread with salad are tasty and carefully prepared.

Foodoo (☎ 09-373 2340; 62 High St; meals $10-13; ☺ breakfast & lunch, closed Sun) Lots of deli food and some more substantial items make a tempting display at this everything-home-cooked café and gourmet takeaway.

Seamart Deli & Café (☎ 09-302 8980; cnr Fanshawe St & Market Pl; ☺ 6am-6pm Mon-Sat, 7am-6pm Sun) This is a great place for fresh fish and seafood with a wide choice of sashimi, sushi and deli items to eat in or takeaway. There is lots of parking outside.

Kiwi Music Bar & Café (☎ 09-309 7717; 332 Queen St; regular/large pizzas $12/16; ☺ lunch Mon-Fri, dinner daily) This laid-back pizzeria and bar in Queen St plays NZ music only, so it's your chance to discover Scribe, Zed, Betchadupa…

QUICK EATS

Food Alley (☎ 09-373 4917; 9 Albert St; meals $7-9; ☺ 10.30am-10pm) For authentic Asian fare, you can't beat this large, no-frills food court where nearly every meal is under $9. Come here for *bibimbap*, *roti chanai*, laksa,

claypot, *okonomiyake*, Thai desserts and all your other Asian favourites.

Pie Mania (☎ 09-377 1984; 36 Wellesley St; pies $2.50-4.50; ☺ 8am-4pm Mon-Fri) Lovers of this wonderful food item can eat in or takeaway 30 varieties, including fruit ones, with weekly specials such as herb chicken, cranberry and camembert pie.

Kangnam Station Korean Restaurant (☎ 09-309 1588; 329 Queen St; meals $8-20; ☺ 10.30-2am Mon-Sat, 5pm-2am Sun) Lots of meals are under $10 at this authentic Korean restaurant with a jovial host.

Sushi Factory (☎ 09-307 3600; 15 Vulcan Lane; sushi plates $2-4; ☺ lunch & dinner, closed Sun) Try the female squid, which is apparently superior to the male squid.

Good Fortune (☎ 09-302 0928; 16 Emily Pl; ☺ lunch Mon-Fri, dinner daily) Twenty-four lunch choices for $5.50 and dinner specials from $5.50 to $9 makes this no-frills Chinese restaurant popular with Asian students who say it tastes just like it does at home.

Daikoku Ramen (☎ 09-309 2200; Tyler St; noodles $8-14; ☺ lunch & dinner) This small and almost funky Japanese fast-food joint doesn't waste money on décor and is the place for cheap and fast noodles.

White Lady (Shortland St; burgers $8-13; ☺ 7.30am-3am Mon-Thu, 24hr Fri-Sun) This long, white bus has been in business here serving fast food to late-night revellers since 1950.

Food courts in central Auckland are mostly open during shopping hours only because they're usually located in shopping centres. Westfield Downtown Shopping Centre (p126) and **Atrium on Elliot** (Elliot St) have international food courts.

SELF-CATERING

New World supermarket (☎ 09-307 8400; 2 College Hill Rd; ☺ 7am-midnight) This is the nearest supermarket for all your food and alcohol needs. The Link bus stops nearby.

Star Mart convenience stores are dotted around the central area and most are open 24 hours.

Viaduct Harbour & Princes Wharf
Map pp98-9

This great waterfront location is awash with some of Auckland's best restaurants and bars, most of which have outdoor areas.

Harbourside Restaurant (☎ 09-307 0486; Ferry Bldg, 99 Quay St; lunch $25, mains $30-33; ☺ lunch &

dinner) This well-established restaurant has the best views and great seafood. Try the fresh cockles, pipi or mussels, or the triple game-fish, although the seafood platter ($46) and John Dory are the usual choices. Vegetables are extra.

Cin Cin on Quay (☎ 09-307 6966; Ferry Bldg, 99 Quay St; mains $29; ☺ breakfast, lunch & dinner) This smart restaurant on the harbour has a new look with interesting contemporary cuisine that deserves to succeed.

Loaded Hog (☎ 09-366 6491; 204 Quay St; mains $22-26; ☺ 11am-late) This spacious and ever-popular restaurant bar overlooking the harbour has its own microbrewery (hog beers $5.50 a pint) and a meat-oriented menu. Cocktails are $10 and salads $12 to $15.

Euro (☎ 09-309 9866; Shed 22, Princes Wharf; mains $28-38; ☺ lunch & dinner) If you're not intimidated by the prices or by restaurants that are very serious about their food then give it a go, and expect a few surprises.

Kermedec Restaurant & Brasserie (☎ 09-309 0413; Quay St; restaurant mains $27-32, brasserie mains $15-24; ☺ lunch & dinner) This upstairs restaurant with Polynesian décor is run by one of the country's major fish companies. The restaurant and brasserie are next to each other but separate.

Wildfire (☎ 09-353 7595; Princes Wharf; lunch/dinner $27/40; ☺ lunch & dinner) This Brazilian *churrasco* (pronounced 'shoohasco') restaurant offers unlimited Brazilian barbecued meats which are brought to your table. At 11.30pm on Saturday night a Brazilian band takes over (no cover charge).

Y Not (☎ 09-359 9998; Shed 23, Princes Wharf; mains $25-36; ☺ lunch & dinner) International cuisine, including roast ostrich, snapper with tiger prawns or duck, is served here.

Parnell   Map p100
East of the city centre, Parnell Rd heads uphill and is lined with craft, gift and fashion shops as well as bars, cafés and restaurants which often have outdoor seating.

RESTAURANTS
Antoines (☎ 09-379 8756; 333 Parnell Rd; mains $30-39; ☺ lunch Wed-Fri, dinner Mon-Sat) Visit this hushed shrine to the culinary arts for fine French/Kiwi dining with discreet opera music in the background and suave service. The nostalgia menu items haven't changed since 1973!

Iguaçu (☎ 09-358 4804; 269 Parnell Rd; mains $18-29; ☺ 11am-late) This always popular, multi-level restaurant and bar complex has a great but relaxed atmosphere with live jazz music on Sunday afternoon and evening and on Wednesday and Thursday evening.

Java Room (☎ 09-366 1606; 317 Parnell Rd; mains $16-21; ☺ dinner Mon-Sat) This charming restaurant serves up Indonesian/Malaysian/Thai/Indian food at a reasonable price. The chilli prawns and orange duck curry are popular.

Thai Friends (☎ 09-373 5247; 311 Parnell Rd; mains $16-20; ☺ lunch Tue-Sat, dinner Mon-Sun) Sit on floor cushions in this cosy and reasonably priced BYOW Thai restaurant.

La Porchetta (☎ 09-309 0807; 167 Parnell Rd; mains $10-20; ☺ lunch Wed-Fri, dinner Mon-Sun) Join the crowds and tuck into bargain pizzas and pastas in this bright new BYOW diner and takeaway.

Oh Calcutta (☎ 09-377 9090; 151 Parnell Rd; mains $15-19; ☺ lunch & dinner) One of Auckland's best Indian restaurants with tandoori meals, lamb rogan josh, Goan fish curry and $15 vegetarian meals.

CAFÉS & QUICK EATS
Strawberry Alarm Clock (☎ 09-377 6959; 119 Parnell Rd; mains $10-15; ☺ breakfast & lunch) and **Min** (☎ 09-377 7035; 99 Parnell Rd; mains $17-25; ☺ breakfast, lunch & dinner) are two popular café bars.

Al & Pete's (☎ 09-377 5439; 496 Parnell Rd; burgers $4-9, meals $15; ☺ lunch & dinner) Legendary gourmet burgers (such as chicken and camembert or scotch fillet) as well as fish and chips, sandwiches and meals are available here.

Kebab Kid (☎ 09-373 4290; 363 Parnell Rd; dishes $8; ☺ lunch & dinner) This is the place for cheap shwarmas, pittas and kebabs.

K Rd   Map pp98-
K Rd is known for its late-night clubs but cafés and inexpensive ethnic restaurants are mixed in with the fashion boutiques, tattooists and adult shops.

RESTAURANTS
Verona (☎ 09-307 0508; 169 K Rd; lunch mains $14, dinner mains $16-24; ☺ 11am-late Mon-Sat, 3pm-late Su) The best restaurant on K Rd offers mainly organic food but it's also a bar and sells deli snacks. It's usually busy and service can be haphazard.

Caluzzi (☎ 09-357 0778; 461 K Rd; dinner & show $4; ☺ dinner Tue-Sat) A unique restaurant and ba with 'garden shed' décor where three drag queen waitresses put on a cabaret show as they serve you. Note that bookings are essential, and the thin-skinned should stay well away.

Rasoi (☎ 09-377 7780; 211 K Rd; meals $5-15; ☒ lunch & dinner Mon-Sat) Good cheap vegetarian *thali* and South Indian food can be found here together with *lassi* and Indian sweets such as *barfi* and *laddoo*.

CAFÉS

Brazil (☎ 09-302 2677; 256 K Rd; meals $8-14; ☒ breakfast, lunch & dinner) Unusual music ('electro-industrial soundscapes') and décor are the main attractions at this dark tunnel-like café. There's a DJ on Saturday afternoon.

Alleluya (☎ 09-377 8424; St Kevin's Arcade; meals $8-14; ☒ breakfast & lunch daily, dinner Tue-Sat) Super-thick pizza slices, Thai chicken pies, tuna bakes and home-made baked beans are included in the lengthy and eclectic menu at this relaxed licensed café with a view.

Monkey House (☎ 09-358 1884; 501 K Rd; breakfasts $3-14, lunch mains $9-15; ☒ 7am-7pm Mon-Thu, 7am-late Fri & Sat) K Rd's smartest and most spacious café/bar, it has an outside area, Euro beers on tap, some organic food, and Cuban dancing on Friday nights.

QUICK EATS

Little Turkish Café (☎ 09-302 0353; 217 K Rd; meals $5-9; ☒ 10.30am-late) Authentic Middle Eastern kebabs, salad and desserts are available here until late at night. Smoke a *shishe* pipe for $8.

Food for Life (☎ 09-300 7585; 268 K Rd; meals $5; ☒ lunch Mon-Sat, dinner Mon-Fri) This Hare Krishna vegetarian restaurant serves a bargain seven-item combination meal that may include lasagne, pizza and semolina pudding as well as the usual Indian items.

Guranga's (☎ 09-303 1560; 214 K Rd; meals $5; ☒ lunch Mon-Sat) A smaller rival Hare Krishna restaurant with Indian combination meals. Large juices cost only $3, and seating on floor cushions is available in the area upstairs.

Ponsonby   Map p105

Auckland's busiest restaurant/café/bar strip, Ponsonby (www.ponsonbyroad.co.nz) is well spread out and mixed with designer boutiques, hairdressers, delis and gift shops.

RESTAURANTS

One Red Dog (☎ 09-360 1068; 151 Ponsonby Rd; medium pizzas $18; ☒ 11am-late) As well as serving popular pizzas there are hog microbrewery beers and bare-brick décor.

Chandelier (☎ 09-360 9315; 152 Ponsonby Rd; mains $27-33; ☒ 5pm-late) A plush and palatial ambience prevails in this narrow restaurant with a bar at the end. The upmarket food has a French influence.

SPQR (☎ 09-360 1710; 150 Ponsonby Rd; mains $18-28; ☒ noon-2am Mon-Fri, 10am-2am Sat & Sun) This is a bar and a pricey but popular Italian restaurant with spartan décor and stylish staff.

Estasi (☎ 09-361 3222; 222 Ponsonby Rd; mains $20-30; ☒ lunch & dinner) and **Prego** (☎ 09-376 3095; 226 Ponsonby Rd; mains $20-30; ☒ lunch & dinner) are popular Italian/European restaurants-cum-bars.

CAFÉS

Atomic Café (☎ 09-376 4954; 121 Ponsonby Rd; meals $7-15; ☒ breakfast, lunch & dinner) Popular and long-established, this café (with a covered garden area) offers delights such as Atomic porridge ($6.50) and leafy greens with roast vegetables and feta ($11).

Santos (☎ 09-378 8431; 114 Ponsonby Rd; meals $4-15; ☒ breakfast & lunch) A popular café, with an outdoor area, it offers simple healthy food and fast service.

Fusion (☎ 09-378 4573; 32 Jervois Rd; breakfast $5-14, lunch $10-14; ☒ 7.30am-6pm) A licensed café with a garden and children's sandpit out the back, it has a menu that lives up to the café's name and at present includes *miso* soup, *lassi*, Turkish delight and curried banana salad.

Logos (☎ 09-376 2433; 265 Ponsonby Rd; lunch mains $7-15, dinner mains $12-16; ☒ 9.30am-midnight) This café/bar has mainly vegetarian food, including vegan muffins, and plays New Age music.

QUICK EATS

Ponsonby Pies (☎ 09-361 3685; 288 Ponsonby Rd; ☒ 8am-6pm Mon-Thu, 7am-7pm Fri & Sat, 9am-5pm Sun) More than 20 varieties of these famous-in-NZ pies are on sale for around $3 each, including fruit ones which cost $1 extra with ice cream.

Otto Woo (☎ 09-360 1989; www.ottowoo.com; 47 Ponsonby Rd; meals $6-13; ☒ lunch Mon-Fri, dinner daily) Eat in or take away at this clean, bright Asian-style eatery that serves its original fusion food in a neat white cardboard box. You can order online.

Burger Fuel (☎ 09-378 6466; 114 Ponsonby Rd; burgers $6-10; ⏰ noon-10pm/late) This is the place for gourmet burgers – try the Bastard for size.

Devonport   Map p104
Devonport has a great range of eateries and bars, mostly along Victoria Rd.

RESTAURANTS
Manuka (☎ 09-445 7732; 49 Victoria Rd; pizzas $18-23; ⏰ 11am-late Mon-Fri, 9am-late Sat & Sun) This licensed restaurant specialises in pizzas cooked in a manuka-fired oven.

Monsoon (☎ 09-445 4263; 71 Victoria Rd; takeaway mains $12-17; ⏰ dinner) Contemporary Thai/Malaysian food is available at a reasonable price, sit-down or take away at this BYO restaurant.

Esplanade Restaurant (☎ 09-445 1291; 1 Victoria Rd; mains $40; ⏰ breakfast, lunch & dinner) Fusion meals are served at this fine dining venue. Next door is a bar and brasserie (mains $19 to $24 excluding vegetables).

McHugh's of Cheltenham (☎ 09-445 0305; 46 Cheltenham Rd; lunch buffet adult/child $24/12; ⏰ lunch) Enjoy an excellent buffet lunch as well as splendid sea views at this long-running establishment.

On Bourbon St (☎ 09-445 0085; 59 Victoria Rd) This bar specialises in Cajun and Creole food such as *gumbo* and *jambalaya*, and has live jazz, blues and acoustic music on Friday and Saturday.

D Central Bar & Brasserie (☎ 09-445 3010; 14 Victoria Rd; mains $15-25; ⏰ 11.30am-late) This bar and eatery has various zones, pool, quiz nights, comedy shows and live bands.

Masonic Tavern (☎ 09-455 0485; 29 King Edward Pde) This beachside pub has 19 beers on tap and live music on Friday and Saturday.

CAFÉS
Stone Oven (☎ 09-445 3185; 5 Clarence St; meals $5-14; ⏰ breakfast & lunch) This café is just so good and so popular that queues can build up at weekends despite the legion of female staff.

Java House (☎ 09-446 1353; Scott Mall; salads $12; ⏰ breakfast & lunch) Visit this hidden gem for the coffee, smoked chicken, giant sausage rolls, apricot and camembert quiche and other goodies.

Statz Café (☎ 09-445 0478; 41 Victoria Rd) This welcoming café has Internet access and a muffin and coffee costs only $3.95.

QUICK EATS
Cod Piece (☎ 09-446 0877; 26 Victoria Rd; ⏰ 5pm-late Mon-Fri, noon-late Sat & Sun) has burgers ($6) and fish and chips (from $5). You can sit down or take away.

SELF-CATERING
Self-caterers can pop into the **New World supermarket** (Bartley Tce), which also sells wine and other alcohol.

Other Suburbs
NEWMARKET   Map p102
Zarbo (☎ 09-520 2721; 24 Morrow St; meals $12-14; ⏰ breakfast & lunch) A large and popular delicatessen/café with a delectable range of fodder on sale which has published its own recipe book.

Poppadom (☎ 09-529 1897; 471 Khyber Pass Rd; lunch mains from $5.50, dinner mains $10-18; ⏰ lunch Mon-Fri, dinner Mon-Sun) This reliable and modestly priced BYO Indian tandoori eatery is in an area of cheap ethnic restaurants. A vegetarian banquet is $20 per person (minimum two).

Kenzie (☎ 09-522 2647; 17a Remuera Rd; meals $11-16; ⏰ breakfast & lunch) Light meals, good coffee and slices of cake are available at this roadside café.

MT EDEN   Map p102
Compact Mt Eden Village has excellent cafés and a Baker's Delight (big custard scrolls $1.80).

Circus Circus (☎ 09-623 3883; 447 Mt Eden Rd; ⏰ 7am-11pm Tue-Sun, 7am-4.30pm Mon) An interesting chameleon café/bar with lively staff, various zones and food that varies from bagel towers and hotpots to waffles and *banoffee* pie.

De Post Belgian Beer Café (☎ 09-630 9330; 466 Mt Eden Rd; mains $12-17; ⏰ 8.30am-1am) A two-storey Belgian pub with good food. There's another branch in the Occidental Belgian Beer Café in Vulcan Lane (p123).

De Niro's (☎ 09-623 3450; 448 Mt Eden Rd; mains $14-18; ⏰ dinner Mon-Sat) Serves unpretentious but wholesome and fresh Italian food at affordable prices.

Tea Time Café (☎ 09-623 2319; 442 Mt Eden Rd; ⏰ breakfast & lunch) There are 130 teas to drink or buy here, as well as snacks and good coffee.

Self-caterers can forage for food and wine at the **Foodtown Supermarket** (Valley Rd; ⏰ 24hr).

MISSION BAY   Map p96
Along Tamaki Drive, Mission Bay has a line of restaurants, bars, fast-food outlets, ice cream parlours and cafés. On the way is **Hammerheads** (☎ 09-521 4400; 19 Tamaki Dr; mains $25-31; ⏰ lunch & dinner), a classy, mainly seafood, restaurant with great views, a deck and plenty of parking.

DRINKING
City Centre   Map pp98-9
Auckland's nightlife tends to be quiet during the week, but wakes up late on Friday and Saturday when most pubs and bars are open until 1am or later.

Globe Bar (☎ 09-357 3980; Darby St; ⏰ 4pm-late) This is the current backpacker favourite with $4.50 beers and wines, happy hour until 8pm, Miss Backpacker competitions, karaoke, theme parties, and a DJ most nights at 10pm currently playing funked-up house music.

Embargo Bar (26 Lorne St) This bar, below Central City Backpackers, hosts special events and theme nights aimed at backpackers.

Occidental Belgian Beer Café (☎ 09-300 6226; 6-8 Vulcan Lane; mains $12-17; ⏰ 7am-3am Mon-Fri, 9am-3am Sat & Sun) Belgian beer is on tap and Belgian food is on the menu at this smart and popular bar. Try the mussels with a blue cheese topping.

Shakespeare Tavern (☎ 09-373 5396; 61 Albert St; mains $12-19, platters $23; ⏰ 11.30am-late) This English-style pub does bar food and has 10 of its own brews, including Pucks, which packs a punch with an alcohol content of 11%. There's an upstairs balcony.

Vertigo Bar (☎ 09-302 9424; Mercure Hotel, 8 Customs St) Buy a beer here ($5) and you can sit back and enjoy the harbour and city views from up on the 13th floor.

Honey (☎ 09-369 5639; 5 O'Connell St; ⏰ 4pm-late) This champagne bar with sofas sells unique Kiwi drinks such as NZ-made gin (South) and NZ-made vodka (42 Below), which can be infused with feijoa or even manuka honey. Bubbly stuff costs from $10 a glass.

Viaduct Harbour & Princes Wharf   Map pp98-9
Lenin Bar (☎ 09-377 0040; Princes Wharf) This is a strange bar with a Russian theme, lots of vodkas and DJs from Thursday to Saturday. Next door is the even stranger Minus 5° Bar (p109).

Danny Doolans (☎ 09-358 2554; 204 Quay St; mains $15-22; ⏰ 11am-late) Behind the Loaded Hog, this Irish pub has Irish food and live music at 10pm from Thursday to Saturday.

Bubble Champagne Bar (☎ 09-358 2800; Quay St; ⏰ 4pm-late) This cosy bar has purple velvet décor and 30 types of champagne from $18 a glass.

Parnell   Map p100
Parnell is more a place for dining than drinking, but there is the **Bog** (☎ 09-377 1510; 196 Parnell Rd; mains $17-22), which serves hearty food and has live music on Thursday, Friday and Sunday, and Iguaçu, the Veranda Bar & Grill and the **Exchange Hotel** (☎ 09-377 4968; 99 Parnell Rd), which has DJs and pool competitions.

K Rd   Map pp98-9
Thirsty Dog (☎ 09-377 9190; 469 K Rd; bar meals $8-21; ⏰ closed Sun) This pub has Newcastle Brown, Tetleys (the beer not the tea), and Irish and Australian beers.

Ponsonby   Map p105
Along Ponsonby Rd, the line between café, restaurant, bar and club gets blurred. A lot of food places also have live music or become clubs later on.

Lime Bar (☎ 09-360 7167; 167 Ponsonby Rd; ⏰ 4pm-2am Mon-Fri, 6pm-2am Sat) A tiny, blink-and-you-miss-it bar which plays sing-along music for the older generation.

Opus (☎ 09-376 6373; 43 Ponsonby Rd; mains $15-27; ⏰ 11am-late) This large, smart brasserie/bar specialises in NZ wines. It also serves jugs of microbrewery beer such as Tall Blonde and Limburg.

Sponge (☎ 09-360 0098; 198 Ponsonby Rd; ⏰ 3pm-late) This is a trendy bar with a nightclub upstairs (see Chicane, p125).

ENTERTAINMENT
The *NZ Herald* has 'The Guide' section from Monday to Friday with local what's on and entertainment features, and a larger 'Time Out' section on Saturday. *Backpacker Xpress* (free every Thursday) has what's on

at some of Auckland pubs and bars. *The Fix* (www.thefix.co.nz) is a weekly brochure (also free every Thursday) with live music listings. See p111 for gay and lesbian venues.

Tickets for major events can be bought from **Ticketek** (☎ 09-307 5000; www.ticketek.co.nz), which has outlets at Aotea Centre and Sky City Atrium.

Cinemas

A **Sky City Village 13-screen multiplex** (Map pp98-9; ☎ 09-979 2400; www.villageskycity.co.nz; 291 Queen St) is part of Sky City Metro, a modernistic mall that includes Borders bookshop, Starbucks, bars and a food court. Most cinemas offer cheaper rates on weekdays before 5pm and all day on Tuesday.

In the basement of the Central City Library is the **Academy Cinema** (Map pp98-9; ☎ 09-373 2761; www.academy-cinema.co.nz; adult $10-13), which shows independent foreign and arthouse films. A glass of champagne with the film is $7. The **Rialto Cinemas** (Map p102; ☎ 09-529 2218; www.rialto.co.nz; 167 Broadway) in Newmarket shows similar films.

The **NZ Film Archives** (Map pp98-9; ☎ 09-379 0688; www.filmarchive.org.nz; 300 K Rd; ⏲ 11am-5pm Mon-Fri, 11am-4pm Sat) has a wonderful resource of over a thousand Kiwi feature films and documentaries, dating from 1905, which you can watch for free on a TV screen. See p42 for some recommended Kiwi feature films.

Live Music

O'Carrolls (Map pp98-9; ☎ 09-300 7118; 10 Vulcan Lane; mains $16-21; ⏲ 10am-late) This Irish pub has breakfasts ($14), Sunday roast ($12) and live acoustic music on Wednesday, Thursday and Saturday.

Rakinos (Map pp98-9; ☎ 09-358 3535; 35 High St; lunch meals $6-15; ⏲ 11am-6am Mon-Sat, 11am-3am Sun) Upstairs is this retro café/bar/music venue with $12 cocktails, live music and DJs. Come for the music rather than the off-hand staff.

Dogs Bollix (Map pp98-9; ☎ 09-376 4600; cnr K & Newton Rds; meals $10) This Irish pub is a live music venue at 9pm from Tuesday to Sunday. Monday is quiz night.

Kings Arms Tavern (Map pp98-9; ☎ 09-373 3240; 59 France St; ⏲ 11am-late) This is one of Auckland's leading small venues for live rock bands, which play most nights.

Galatos (Map pp98-9; ☎ 09-303 1928; 17 Galatos St; ⏲ 9pm-late Wed-Sat) Three venues in one here, with DJs, top local live bands, and hip-hop drum 'n' bass in the basement.

Java Jive (Map p105; ☎ 09-376 5870; Pompallier Tce; ⏲ 6pm-late) New owners have taken over but reasonably priced bar meals and live Kiwi rock/blues/jazz bands will continue.

Grand Central Bar (Map p105; ☎ 09-360 1260; 126 Ponsonby Rd; ⏲ 4pm-late Mon-Fri, 6pm-late Sat & Sun; ☐) This New York themed bar has live music from around 9.30pm on Wednesday, Thursday and Sunday.

Alhambra (Map p105; ☎ 09-376 2430; 283 Ponsonby Rd; tapas $3-6, dinner mains $12-23; ⏲ 5pm-late) Live jazz or blues is played from Wednesday to Sunday nights.

For big international bands and major local bands, the main venues in Auckland include **Western Springs Stadium** (Map p96; ☎ 09-849 3807), the **North Shore Events Centre** (Map p96; ☎ 09-443 8199; Porana Rd, Glenfield) and **Ericsson Stadium** (Map p96; ☎ 09-571 1699; Beasley Ave, Penrose).

Nightclubs

K Rd and Ponsonby Rd are the main places to find late-night clubs but there are a few around Vulcan Lane and the Viaduct Basin. Some clubs have a $5 to $20 cover charge depending on the night and the event.

Fu Bar (Map pp98-9; ☎ 09-309 3079; 166 Queen St; ⏲ 10pm-late Tue-Sat). This long-running basement dance club has live bands, house and techno DJ's with some drum and bass and hip-hop, plus pool tables.

Papa Jack's Voodoo Lounge (Map pp98-9; ☎ 09-358 4847; 9 Vulcan Lane; ⏲ 7pm-late Tue-Sat) This is the home of hard rock with skulls, ripped seats, a pool table, a live band on Wednesday and a DJ on Friday and Saturday.

Khuja Lounge (Map pp98-9; ☎ 09-377 3711; 536 Queen St; ⏲ 8pm-3am Wed-Sat) Above the Westpac building, this laid-back venue offers DJs and live jazz/soul/hip-hop bands.

Staircase (Map pp98-9; ☎ 09-374 4278; 340 K Rd; cover charge $10; ⏲ 10pm-late Thu-Sat) This large venue is into hard house dance.

Ibiza (Map pp98-9; ☎ 09-302 3354; 253 K Rd; ⏲ 24hr Fri & Sat) This is a nonstop house and trance venue.

Cruising Rock Bar (Map pp98-9; 262 K Rd; ⏲ 10pm-late Fri & Sat) This spacious black cellar with couches and a pool table has a DJ who plays rock, hard rock, and rock and roll.

Safari Lounge (Map p105; ☎ 09-378 7707; 116 Ponsonby Rd; ☼ 5pm-3am Tue-Sun) A dimly-lit den with bar football and pool tables, this place has a DJ on Wednesday, Friday and Saturday night from 9pm.

Chicane (Map p105; ☎ 09-360 0098; 198 Ponsonby Rd; ☼ 10pm-late Fri-Sat) Upstairs from the Sponge Bar, Chicane has a DJ, curtained booths and purple furniture.

Float (Map pp98-9; ☎ 09-307 1344; Shed 19, Princes Wharf) This venue has a black box area with a DJ on Friday and Saturday night.

Mojo (Map pp98-9; ☎ 09-374 4255; www.getmojo .co.nz; Custom St) and neighbouring **Europa** (Map pp98-9; ☎ 09-358 5060; Custom St) are venues for a night of R&B hip-hop – Polynesian style – on Friday or Saturday night. They operate a strict dress code and sometimes have a $5 cover charge.

Sport

Eden Park (Map p96; ☎ 09-815 5551; www.eden park.co.nz) It is the stadium for top rugby (winter) and cricket (summer) matches. The All Blacks, the Black Caps and the Auckland Blues all play here. To get there, take the train from Britomart to Kingsland station.

Ericsson Stadium (Map p96; ☎ 09-571 1699; www .ericssonstadium.co.nz; Beasley Ave, Penrose) This stadium hosts soccer, rugby league (NZ Warriors) and the Big Day Out, Auckland's largest concert, which is held every January.

Stanley St Tennis Courts (Map p98-9; ☎ 09-373 3623; 72 Stanley St) In January the Women's ASB Tennis Classic is followed by the men's Heineken Tennis Open. Some famous tennis names show up to battle it out at this venue.

Theatre & Musicals

Most theatrical and major musical events can be booked through **Ticketek** (☎ 09-307 5000; www.ticketek.co.nz) in the Sky City Atrium and the Aotea Centre. Aotea Square and the buildings that surround it comprise Auckland's main arts and entertainment complex.

Edge (Map pp98-9; ☎ 09-309 2677; www.the-edge .co.nz; Queen St) This is the collective name given to the other venues – the Town Hall, Civic and Aotea Centre.

Auckland Town Hall (Map pp98-9; ☎ 09-309 2677; 50 Mayoral Dr) This venue hosts concert

performances and is home to the NZ Symphony Orchestra and **Auckland Philharmonia** (☎ 0800 744 542; www.aucklandphil.co.nz).

Aotea Centre (Map pp98-9; ☎ 09-307 5060; 50 Mayoral Dr) It is Auckland's main venue for theatre, dance, ballet and opera. The excellent Auckland Theatre Company puts on a regular programme here.

Civic (Map pp98-9; ☎ 09-309 2677; cnr Queen St & Wellesley St W) This newly restored grand theatre, with a lavish Eastern-fantasy interior, is used by major touring productions, including opera, musicals and live theatre, as well as by the Auckland International Film Festival.

Classic Comedy Club (Map pp98-9; ☎ 09-373 4321; www.comedy.co.nz; 321 Queen St; tickets $8-15) This is Auckland's top venue for comedy. Shows run from Wednesday to Saturday from around 8pm with late shows on Friday and Saturday. Telephone or check the website for the schedule.

Covert Theatre (Map pp98-9; ☎ 09-366 6637; www.coverttheatre.com; 84 K Rd; tickets $15; ☼ Wed-Sun) This 50-seat venue specialises in improvised comedy, with shows at 8pm.

Sky City (Map pp98-9; ☎ 0800 759 2489; cnr Victoria & Hobson Sts) This is Auckland's biggest single entertainment venue. As well as restaurants, bars, the observation deck and a 700-seat theatre, it has two casinos – the huge 24-hour Sky City Casino (Level 2) and the smaller Alto Casino (Level 3), which are open 24 hours. Bars around the casinos offer nightly live music (mainly jazz and ballads) and a DJ.

Other theatres:

Maidment Theatre (Map pp98-9; ☎ 09-308 2383; University of Auckland, 8 Alfred St)

Silo Theatre (Map pp98-9; ☎ 09-373 5151; Lower Greys Ave) Specialises in youth and fringe dramas.

Sky City Theatre (Map pp98-9; ☎ 0800 759 2489, 09-363 6000; www.skycity.co.nz; cnr Victoria & Federal Sts)

SHOPPING

Followers of fashion should head to High St, Chancery Lane, Newmarket, Ponsonby Rd and possibly K Rd and Victoria Park Market. Hairdressers cluster in Ponsonby Rd. An official All Black rugby shirt costs $130.

Devonport Chocolates (☎ 09-445 6001; 17 Wynyard St; ☼ 9.30am-5pm Mon-Fri, 10am-4pm Sat & Sun) Sells handmade chocolates and you can taste one free.

Illicit (Map pp98-9; 41 Elliot St) This boutique stocks Misery and other local designer labels.

Kathmandu (Map pp98-9; 151 Queen St) This is a local brand of outdoor gear.

Modus Operandi (Map pp98-9; ☎ 09-309 4008; 51 High St; ☼ 8am-7pm) Check out the imaginative use of mirrors and lifelike mannequins at this hip boutique which showcases young NZ designers.

Paper Bag Princess (Map pp98-9; ☎ 09-307 3591; 145 K Rd) Second-hand designer clothes sell for under $20.

Pauanesia (Map pp98-9; ☎ 09-520 6359; 35 High St; ☼ daily) An Aladdin's cave of Polynesian-style craft and gifts.

R&R Sport (Map pp98-9; ☎ 09-309 6444; cnr K Rd & Grundy St; ☼ 9am-6pm Mon-Fri, 10am-4pm Sat & Sun) This huge shop has everything in the hiking, bicycling, skiing, surfing, camping and outdoor sports line, with some second-hand stuff.

Real Groovy Records (Map pp98-9; ☎ 09-302 3940; 438 Queen St; ☼ 9am-7pm Sat-Wed, 9am-9pm Thu & Fri) This megastore of new and second-hand music also sells concert tickets and stocks DVDs, books, magazines and clothing. Bands regularly play in-store.

Westfield Downtown Shopping Centre (Map pp98-9; QE Sq) It has a Flight Centre travel agency, post office, pharmacy, gift shops, Warehouse discount shop, a food court and a 24-hour Star Mart convenience store, and the ASB bank here is also open on the weekend.

Two Double Seven Shopping Complex (Map p102; ☎ 09-520 0277; Broadway; ☼ 9am-5.30pm Mon-Thu, 9am-9pm Fri, 9am-5.30pm Sat, 10am-5pm Sun) Where the fashion-conscious look over local and international brand name items. Try Lush, Max and Cue.

Markets

Victoria Park Market (Map pp98-9; ☎ 09-309 6911; 210 Victoria St W; ☼ 9am-6pm) Here you'll find mostly clothes, shoes, accessories, crafts and souvenirs but it includes a food court, cafés and a spacious pub. Massages ($10 for 10 minutes) and portraits ($20 to $25) are also available. It's a 20-minute walk west from the city centre, or you can take the Link or Explorer buses.

Aotea Square Market (Map pp98-9; Aotea Sq; ☼ 10am-6pm Fri & Sat) It has ethnic food stalls, arts and crafts and entertainment. There's live music on Saturday from noon to 3pm.

Otara Markets (Map p96; ☎ 09-274 0830; Newbury St; ☼ 6am-noon Sat) Held in the car park between the Manukau Polytech and the Otara town centre, this market has a real Polynesian atmosphere and you can buy South Pacific food, music and fashions. Take bus No 487 or 497 from outside Britomart station.

Avondale Market (Map pp98-9; ☎ 09-818 4931; Avondale Racecourse, Ash St; ☼ 8am-noon Sun) This is diverse and worth a visit.

GETTING THERE & AWAY
Air

Auckland is the major gateway to NZ, and a hub for domestic flights. See p678 for information on international flights.

Domestic airlines operating to/from Auckland:

Air New Zealand (☎ 09-357 3000; www.airnewzealand.co.nz; cnr Customs & Queen Sts; 9am-5pm Mon-Fri, 10am-1pm Sat)

Great Barrier Airlines (☎ 0800 900 600, 09-256 6500; www.greatbarrierairlines.co.nz; Auckland domestic terminal)

Mountain Air (☎ 09-256 7025; www.mountainair.co.nz; Auckland domestic terminal)

Origin Pacific (☎ 0800 302 302; www.originpacific.co.nz) Flies to nine local destinations from Auckland, including Wellington (from $75) and Christchurch (from $80).

Qantas (Map pp98-9; ☎ 09-357 8900; 191 Queen St; ☼ 9am-5pm Mon-Fri)

Bus

The main long-distance bus company in Auckland, as for the rest of NZ, is InterCity/Newmans. With a few exceptions, these buses go to almost all bigger towns and the main tourist areas.

There are services from Auckland to just about everywhere in NZ, and they operate from the **Sky City Coach Terminal** (☎ 09-916 6222; 102 Hobson St, Sky City Complex).

Northliner Express (☎ 09-307 5873) services Northland, with buses heading north from Auckland to Whangarei, the Bay of Islands and Kaitaia.

Backpacker buses operate in and from Auckland and have their main offices here: **Kiwi Experience** (☎ 09-366 9830; 195 Parnell Rd), **Magic Travellers Network** (☎ 09-358 5600; 136 Quay St) and **Stray** (☎ 07-824 3627 in Hamilton; www.straytravel.co.nz) offer a door-to-door service with pick-ups and drop-offs at any Auckland hostel.

Car

HIRING A CAR

Auckland has countless car-hire operators and is the best city in which to hire (or buy) a vehicle for touring NZ. Some good deals can be had for long-term hire, but be warned that cheapest is not necessarily the best.

A swag of car-hire companies can be found conveniently grouped together along Beach Rd, opposite the old train station. The major companies – Avis, Budget, Hertz and Thrifty – are reliable, offer full insurance and have offices at the airport and all over the country. They are more expensive, but rates are often negotiable for longer rentals or off-season.

If you are prepared to take limited insurance and risk losing an excess of around $700, then the cheaper operators offer some pretty good deals. Prices vary with the season, the age of the car and length of rental. Ignore prices quoted in brochures and shop around by phone. Always read the rental agreement thoroughly before you sign.

Some of the more reputable car rental companies are (*rents out sleeper vans or campervans as well as cars):

A2B (☎ 0800 222 929, 09-377 0825)
Ace* (☎ 0800 502 277, 09-303 3112)
Alternative Rental Cars* (☎ 09-373 3822)
Avis (☎ 0800 655 111, 09-526 2847)
Backpacker Campervans* (☎ 0800 422 267, 09-275 0200)
Britz NZ* (☎ 0800 831 900, 09-275 1834)
Budget* (☎ 0800 652 227, 09-375 2270)
Hertz (☎ 0800 654 321, 09-367 6350)
Hertz Campervans* (☎ 0800 525 5000, 09-256 9698)
Maui* (☎ 0800 651 080, 09-255 0620)
Thrifty (☎ 0800 737 070, 09-309 0111)

BUYING A CAR

For stays of two months or more, many people look at buying a car. You can buy through dealers on the buy-back scheme, at car fairs or auctions, or through ads at backpacker hostels. Before buying a car you must check that it is mechanically sound, has not been stolen, and does not have money owing on it to a finance company or bank.

Backpackers Car Market (Map pp98-9; ☎ 09-377 7761; 20 East St; ☻ 9.30am-5pm) can give you the A to Z of buying and selling cars in NZ. A full mechanical check with a one-month

guarantee is $110 and third-party insurance can be arranged (around $190 for three months with an $800 excess). To display a car to sell there costs $55 for three days.

Buy-backs, where the dealer agrees to buy back your car for an agreed price (usually 50% of what you pay), are not a great deal, but offer a safety net if you have trouble reselling the car. Dealers who work on this system:

Auckland Rentals & Buy-Backs (☎ 09-629 5455; 746 Dominion Rd) Has good, cheap vehicles that can be used as campervans.
Car Warehouse (Map p96; ☎ 0800 888 850, 09-636 9903; 34 Alfred St, Onehunga)
Matthew Minicoaches & Rental Cars (☎ 09-622 1592; 47 Nelson St)

A popular way to buy a car is through the car fairs where people bring their own cars to sell them. Arrive between 8.30am and 9.30am for the best choice; car fairs are over by about noon. For a credit check quote chassis and licence-plate numbers. Mechanical inspection services, credit agencies and Auto Check details are all on hand at the following car fairs:

Ellerslie Racecourse (Map p96; ☎ 09-529 2233; www .carfair.co.nz; ☻ 9am-noon Sun) Ellerslie is near the Greenlane roundabout. It's the largest car fair and it costs $30 to display your vehicle.
Manukau (Map p96; ☎ 09-358 5000; Manukau City Centre Car Park; ☻ 9am-1pm Sun) It costs $20 to display your car.

Alternatively, you could try the car auctions for a good deal. Auckland's two best-known car auctions:

Hammer Car Auctions (Map p96; ☎ 09-636 4900; cnr Neilson & Alfred Sts, Onehunga) Auctions are held daily except for Sunday and viewing is from 8am with 60 to 100 cars for sale. Vehicle checks are available and ownership/ finance company checks cost $250 for cars over $2000. Bring some ID. Selling a vehicle costs $25 per auction plus $250 and 3.5% of the sale price.
Turner's Car Auctions (Map p96; ☎ 09-525 1920; www.turners.co.nz; cnr Leonard & Penrose Rds, Penrose) Auctions are held daily except Monday. A mechanical inspection costs $95 and a $250 Protection Plan avoids any ownership or money-owing hassles. The website has details of upcoming cars for sale and auction and viewing times.

Motorcycle

NZ Motorcycle Rentals (☎ 09-377 2005; www.nzbike .com; 31 Beach Rd; ☻ 9am-6pm Mon-Fri, 10am-5pm Sat,

10am-3pm Sun) Motor bike hire costs $70 to $300 a day (insurance excess is $1000 upwards). Scooters cost $22 to $45 a day. Guided tours are also available.

Train

Trains arrive at and depart from **Britomart station** (Map pp98-9; ☎ 0800 872 467; www.tranz scenic.co.nz) on Quay St. You can book online, or else the booking office is open from 8am to 8.30pm daily.

Only two trains operate out of Auckland and both go to Wellington via Hamilton and Palmerston North. The *Overlander* runs daily, departing from Auckland at 9.15am and arriving in Wellington at 8.30pm (the return train leaves Wellington at 8.40am and arrives in Auckland at 7.50pm). The *Northerner* is a daily overnight train that departs from Auckland at 8.25pm (arriving 7.40am) and from Wellington at 8.50pm (arrives 8.50am). There are no sleeper carriages, just reclining seats.

The standard Auckland–Wellington adult fare on the *Overlander* is $145 (child $90), but a seat in an older carriage costs only $75. On the *Northerner* the standard adult fare is $130, but again an older carriage costs only $65. There are also reductions on standard fares for seniors (60 years and over), students and backpackers.

GETTING AROUND
To/From the Airport

Auckland airport (☎ 09-256 8899; www.auckland -airport.co.nz) is 21km south of the city centre. It has an international terminal and a domestic terminal, each with a tourist information centre. A free shuttle service operates every 20 minutes between the terminals and there's also a signposted footpath between them (about a 1km walk).

At the international terminal there's a freephone for accommodation bookings. Both terminals have left-luggage facilities and car-rental desks, though you get better rates from companies in town.

The **AirBus** (☎ 09-375 4702, 0508 247 287; adult one way/return $13/22, backpacker $11/18, child $6/12) runs every 20 or 30 minutes (from 6am to 10pm) between the international and domestic terminals and the city, stopping outside major hotels and backpacker hostels. Reservations are not required and you buy a ticket from the driver. The trip takes about 50 minutes one way (longer during rush hour).

Convenient door-to-door **shuttle minibuses** (1st person $20, each subsequent person $5) run to and from the airport. It pays to get a group together and all get off at the same place. The price increases if you want to go to an outlying suburb. Each shuttle is supposed to stay a maximum of 15 minutes, so you may be able to negotiate a lower price if one is about to leave. The main operator is **Super Shuttle** (☎ 09-306 3960).

A taxi to the airport from the city costs around $40.

Bicycle

Adventure Cycles (Map pp98-9; ☎ 09-309 5566; 36 Customs St E; ☼ 7am-7pm) hires out road and mountain bikes ($18 to $35 a day) and carries out repairs. It also hires out touring bikes long-term, and run a buy-back scheme. Bicycles can be also be hired ($15 for four hours) from the ticket office on the harbour side of the Ferry Building (Map pp98–9).

In Auckland cycling up to Mission Bay or around Devonport are both good options. The visitors centres have a useful *Bike Guide* for the Auckland region.

Boat

Fullers (☎ 09-367 9111; www.fullers.co.nz; adult $8.40-13.40, child $4.40-7.40) operates passenger ferries between the city and Devonport, Stanley Bay, Birkenhead and Bayswater on the North Shore, the gulf islands and Half Moon Bay near Howick.

Car & Motorcycle

Parking is a problem in central Auckland, but there are plenty of car parks off Beach Rd (Map pp98–9), which is at the eastern end of Customs St. They cost around $6 for 12 hours. Most on-street parking meters ($2 to $4 an hour) do not have to be fed money between 6pm and 8am or on Sunday.

Public Transport

Public Transport Information (☎ 09-366 6400; www .rideline.co.nz, text 3666wap.rideline.co.nz)

BUS

The Auckland city bus service is primarily run by **Stagecoach** (☎ 09-366 6400; www.rideline .co.nz). There is no central bus station, but most buses leave from bus stops that are scattered around the new Britomart station

(Map pp98–9). Useful information about bus routes and timetables are on bus stop notice boards. The Britomart Plaza has stalls selling crepes ($5), baguette rolls ($5) and sushi, a small convenience store and **Lotus foreign exchange** (🕒 9am-5pm), which offers competitive rates. Downstairs are plush toilets and left-luggage lockers. For lost property on buses phone ☎ 09-442 0555.

The **Link bus** (fares $1.20; 🕒 every 10-15min 6am-11.30pm Mon-Fri, 7am-11.30pm Sat & Sun) is a very handy bus service that travels clockwise and anticlockwise around a loop that includes Queen St, Sky City, Victoria Park Market, Ponsonby Rd, K Rd, Newmarket, Parnell and Britomart station.

The **City Circuit bus** (🕒 every 10min 8am-8pm) provides free transport around the inner city from Britomart station, up Queen St, past Albert Park to Auckland University and across to Sky Tower and back to Britomart.

Single-ride fares in the inner city are 50c for an adult and 30c for a child (you pay the driver when you board), but if you're travelling further afield there are fare stages from $1.20/70c to $7.90/4.70. A one-day pass (which includes the city centre to North Shore ferries) costs only $8, while a three-day pass costs $19, but there's no reduction for children.

The **Niterider** (☎ 09-366 6400; fares $4-6) runs from the Civic, on Queen St (Map pp98–9), along 10 routes between 1am and 3am on Friday and Saturday nights.

TRAIN

Tranz Metro (☎ 09-366 6400; www.rideline.co.nz; fares $1.10-5, bikes $1) runs just three routes from the smart new Britomart station (Map pp98–9); one runs west to Waitakere, while two routes run south to Pukekohe. Services are at least hourly and run from around 6am to 8pm from Monday to Saturday. A $12 Discovery Pass allows a day's travel on most bus, train and ferry services. All train carriages have wheelchair ramps.

Taxi

Auckland's many taxis usually work from ranks, but they also cruise popular areas. **Auckland Co-Op Taxis** (☎ 09-300 3000) is one of the biggest companies. Other taxi companies are listed in the *Yellow Pages*. Flagfall is $2 and then $1.85 per kilometre.

AROUND AUCKLAND

REGIONAL PARKS

The Auckland Regional Council (ARC) administers 21 regional parks around the Auckland region, all within 15km to 90km of the city. There are several coastal and beach parks with swimming and surfing beaches, plus bush parks, a kauri park, the Waitakere Ranges west of Auckland, the Hunua catchment southeast of Auckland and a gannet colony at Muriwai. The parks have good walking and tramping tracks, ranging from 20 minutes to several hours to walk, and camping is allowed in several of them.

An Auckland Regional Parks pamphlet, with a list of facilities in each park, is available from the Auckland visitor centre, or the DOC office in the ferry building in Auckland.

Auckland Regional Council has camping grounds in the regional parks, many in coastal areas. Some are accessible by vehicle, others are reached by tramping. Most tend to be heavily booked in summer – contact **Parksline** (☎ 09-303 1530) for information and bookings.

WEST OF AUCKLAND

Less than an hour's drive out west from the city centre is the Waitakere Ranges Regional Park, which has a dramatic, rugged coastline with iron-sand beaches backed by regenerating native bush. There are some fine bushwalks, surf beaches, golf courses and wineries. Obtain the *Art Out West* leaflet for information on the area's galleries and studios.

Wineries

The area west of Auckland has long been a wine-producing region and some wineries have excellent cafés or restaurants. The free *Winemakers of Auckland* brochure gives full details and is available from visitors centres.

Riverhead Winery & Brewery (Map p130; ☎ 09-412 8595; 1171 SH28; lunch mains $8-13, dinner mains $17-25; 🕒 11am-midnight Mon-Fri, 10am-midnight Sat & Sun) Beers and feijoa, kiwi fruit and other such wines can be tasted and purchased here, 3km from the main road. There's a restaurant and bar as well.

AUCKLAND REGION

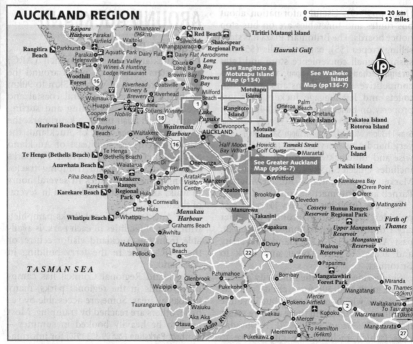

Soljans Winery (Map p130; ☎ 09-412 2680; 366 SH16, Kumeu; meals $7-21; �YO 9am-5.30pm) Tasting of up to a dozen wines, which cost from $13 a bottle, are available here. Cellar tours ($10) can be booked. The café is popular, with a menu that includes salmon, fish and venison.

Other wineries you might want to visit include:

Coopers Creek (Map p130; ☎ 09-412 8560; 601 SH16, Huapai; meals under $20; �YO 9am-5.30pm Mon-Fri, 10.30am-5.30pm Sat & Sun, meals Thu-Sun Dec-Feb) Wines to sample and buy here as well as attractive gardens with *pétanque* and outdoor chess.

Matua Valley Wines (Map p130; ☎ 09-411 8301; Waikoukou Valley Rd; �YO 9am-5pm Mon-Fri, 10am-5pm Sat, 11am-4.30pm Sun) This has wine tasting 3km from the main road and a restaurant, the **Hunting Lodge** (☎ 09-411 8259; mains $17-30; �YO lunch & dinner Wed-Sun).

Nobilo (Map p130; ☎ 09-412 9148; 45 Station Rd, Huapai; �YO 9am-5pm Mon-Fri, 10am-5pm Sat & Sun) Taste up to a dozen wines, which cost from $13 per bottle.

Winery tours are available (see p111).

Waitakere Ranges

This 18,000-hectare wilderness area once supported important kauri forests, but they were logged almost to extinction in the 19th century. A few stands of ancient kauri and other mature trees, such as rimu, survive amid the regenerating rainforest, which is now protected inside the **Waitakere Ranges Regional Park**. Bordered to the west by the beaches on the Tasman Sea, the park's sometimes rugged terrain with steep-sided valleys, is the most significant natural area close to Auckland. It's popular for picnics and walks, with 250km of tracks.

SCENIC DRIVE

The 28km State Hwy 24 (SH24), also known as the Scenic Drive, winds its way from Titirangi to Swanson, passing numerous falls and lookouts. The **Arataki Visitors Centre** (Map p96; ☎ 09-817 4941; www.waitakereranges.org.nz; Scenic Dr; �YO 9am-5pm) is 6km west of Titirangi along this road and is a good starting point for exploring the ranges. As well as providing a host of information on the 250km of trails in the area, this impressive centre with its Maori carvings and spectacular views is an attraction in its own right. The giant carving that greets visitors at the entrance depicts the ancestors of the Kawerau *iwi* (tribe). Inside there is a theatre showing a 20-minute video (adult/child $2/1) on the park and its wildlife. A 1.6km nature trail opposite the centre takes visitors past labelled native species, including mature kauri. Noted walks include the Cascades/ Kauri area to the north, which has three good walks, the Upper Kauri Track and the Pukematekeo Track.

There are a couple of miniature train rides through the ranges but both must be booked in advance. **Waitakere Tramline Society** (☎ 09-836 0900 evening only; adult/child $8/4) runs four scenic trips every Sunday which pass through a glow-worm tunnel. They start from the end of Christian Rd which runs south of Swanson station. The **Rain Forest Express** (☎ 0800 788 788; adult/child $16/8) departs from Jacobsons' Depot (off Scenic Drive) at 2pm on Sunday, and there's a special twilight trip at 5.30pm in summer. It runs along the 6km Nihotupu line.

The **Nikau Club** (☎ 09-814 8919; 473 Scenic Dr; mains $16-25; ⏱ lunch & dinner Mon-Fri, brunch & dinner Sat & Sun) has a global restaurant menu, café meals, a splendid view and a bar that makes this an ideal and popular place to stop.

Piha & Karekare Beaches

Note that swimming on these west coast beaches can be very dangerous because of strong undercurrents. Surf lifesaving clubs patrol the main beaches in summer – always swim between the flags where life-guards can provide help if you get into trouble.

Piha, 16km off Scenic Drive, with its rugged, iron-sand beach, has long been a favourite with Auckland holiday-makers and surfers, as well as with artists and al-ternative types. The view of the coast as you drive down on Piha Rd is quite spectacular. The distinctive **Lion Rock** (101m), which you can climb, sits just off the beach.

Surfing competitions are held in Piha in the summer and there is a horse race along the beach towards the end of sum-mer. You can hire surfboards and wet suits and surfing instruction is available. View www.pihasurf.co.nz for surf conditions. Numerous bush walks are also possible.

There is a small general store and café (try a Piha pie), two surf shops, two take-aways and two basic camp sites. The surfing club is a social centre with meals and a bar. There is no supermarket, liquor shop, bank or petrol station.

Just five minutes down Karekare Rd, off Piha Rd, is **Karekare Beach**, which is even more rugged, wild and pristine than Piha. Scenes from Jane Campion's *The Piano* were filmed there and it's an iconic NZ landscape that is worth a visit.

SIGHTS & ACTIVITIES
Piha Surf Shop & Crafts (☎ 09-812 8896; www.piha surf.co.nz; 122 Seaview Rd) sells crafts upstairs and surfboards downstairs. Surfboards (half-day $25), wet suits ($10) and body boards ($15) can also be hired. Surf lessons (two or three hours) can be arranged for around $50.

Lush Surf Shop, next to the general store, also sells and rents surfing gear.

SLEEPING
Piha Surf Shop Accommodation (☎ 09-812 8896; www.pihasurf.co.nz; 122 Seaview Rd; caravans per person $25) Each caravan has its own linen, TV, a fridge, cooker and long-drop toilet and they all share a very basic shower. It's on the right, 2km from the beach.

Piha Domain Motor Camp (☎ 09-812 8815; 21 Seaview Rd; camp sites $20, s/d on-site caravans $25/38; 🖳) It is on the beach but facilities are scruffy and basic.

Piha Lodge (☎ 09-812 8595; www.pihalodge.co.nz; 117 Piha Rd; units/apt $140/200; 🖳 🖳) This lodge has homely, fully-furnished self-contained units with a deck and splendid views. Bin-oculars, DVD players, stereos, Sky TV, a hot spa and complimentary breakfast are supplied by the bright and breezy hostess. The apartment requires a minimum stay of two nights.

EATING
Piha Life Saving Club (☎ 09-812 8896; Lion Rock Beachfront; mains $13-18; ⏱ dinner Wed-Sun) It has a bar and dining room with an ocean view and serves fish, chicken and pasta meals.

GETTING THERE & AWAY
A **shuttle bus** (☎ 09-627 2644; www.surfshuttle.co.nz; one-way/same-day return $20/30) leaves Auckland at around 8.30am for Piha and returns to

Auckland at 4pm daily from December to February. Booking is advisable.

Whatipu

Whatipu Beach is the most southerly beach and can be reached along Huia Rd. The last part is gravel but the beach has huge sand-flats at low tide and lagoons that attract unusual vegetation and birds, including the endangered dotterel (only 1500 in the world).

Te Henga (Bethells Beach)

Bethells Beach is reached by taking the Te Henga Rd at the northern end of Scenic Drive. It's another black-sand beach with surf, windswept dunes and bush walks, such as the popular one to Lake Wainamu and on to the Cascades.

Bethells Beach Cottages (☎ 09-810 9581; www .bethellsbeach.com; 267 Bethells Rd; cottages from $220) These two lovely, self-contained cottages are in a bush setting with sea and sunset views. Exotic meals can be arranged.

Muriwai Beach & Gannet Colony

Muriwai Beach, reached by turning off SH16 at Waimauku, is home to the **Takapu Refuge**, an Australasian gannet colony in the Muriwai Regional Park. The colony was once confined to a nearby rock stack but has now overflowed to the shore cliffs. There's an easy walking trail to two viewing platforms and this is a great opportunity to see (and smell) these beautiful birds at close range.

There's a **surf beach** stretching away into the distance, north of the refuge. You can go horse riding on the beach and through the bush with **Muriwai Beach Riding Centre** (☎ 09-411 8480; 1hr/2hr rides $50/70), which also runs lessons for beginners ($50 for 45 minutes). **Muriwai Beach Motor Camp** (☎ 09-411 9262; Motutara Rd; camp sites $20) is shady, clean and on the beachfront.

Helensville

pop 2200

Less than 50km from central Auckland, this small town has historical buildings, antique and curio shops, cafés, takeaways and a couple of excellent accommodation options.

Helensville visitor information centre (☎ 09-420 8060; www.helensville.co.nz; 27 Commercial Rd;

⊗ 9am-5pm Mon-Fri, 10am-1pm Sat & Sun) has details about kayaking, fishing, horse riding and mountain biking. The **Internet Café** (☎ 09-420 9105; 96a Commercial Rd; ⊗ 9am-6pm) charges $6 an hour.

The small **Pioneer Museum** (☎ 09-420 7881; admission by donation; ⊗ 1-3.30pm) was being relocated to Mill St at the time of writing, but should now be open. The town is a base for good-value **cruises** (☎ 09-420 8466; 3hr/7hr adult $15/45, child $7/15) around the huge Kaipara Harbour; telephone for the schedule. **Woodhill Mountain Bike Park** (☎ 09-479 9194; bike hire per hr $15-20; ⊗ 8am-5pm Sat & Sun) has many challenging tracks around Woodhill Forest, west of Helensville.

Malolo House (☎ 09-420 7262; malolo@xtra.co.nz; 110 Commercial Rd; camp sites $20, dm/d & tw $19/50, s with bathroom $75-85, d with bathroom $90-100; ▣) has smart, stylish and refurbished accommodation that includes a spa bath and a sunroom with views. The dorm has six beds with linen provided and one en-suite room has a four-poster bed.

Kaipara House B&B (☎ 09-420 7462; kaipara@ ihug.co.nz; cnr SH16 & Parkhurst Rd; s/d & tw $55/110) offers period rooms with bathroom in the house or equally excellent self-contained units in a garden setting. There's a spa pool, and breakfast is included for the inside rooms.

Café Regent (☎ 09-420 9148; 14 Bridge St; meals $4-10; ⊗ breakfast & dinner Wed-Mon) in the foyer of the old Art Deco cinema, has home-cooked food, and behind it is an amazing den of collectables.

Grand Hotel (☎ 09-420 8427; 1 Railway Rd; ⊗ 10am-1am) is a lively and child-friendly place, with five beers on tap, a garden area out the back and live bands at the weekend. Every other Thursday is an open mike evening (anyone can come and perform), but best of all there are no pokies (gambling machines).

Corridor Bar (☎ 09-420 6040; 88 Commercial Rd; meals $7-16; ⊗ Wed-Sun) is a smart bar with sofas and a view.

Parakai

pop 1100

Just 2km northwest of Helensville is **Parakai Aquatic Park** (☎ 09-420 8998; Parkhurst Rd; adult/child $12/8; ⊗ 10am-10pm), which has a large outdoor hot spring swimming pool and a couple of hydroslides. Private spa pools cost an extra

Bottle-nosed dolphins (p66)

Great Barrier Island (p139)

Waterfall and swimming hole, Karekare (p131)

Karekare Beach (p131)

DAVID WALL

Putiki Bay, Waiheke Island
(p134)

DAVID

Rangitoto Island (p133)

PAUL KENNEDY

Surfer (p70)

Waitakere Ranges, west of Auckland (p130)

DAV

$3 for 30 minutes. The **camping ground** (adult/child $15/10), next door, includes free entry to the hot pools.

At Parakai airfield, **tandem skydiving** is available – see p107. Another 11km on from the hot pools is **MacNuts Farms** (☎ 09-420 2853; 914 South Head Rd; ☽ 10am-4pm), which has a large macadamia orchard, a processing plant and a shop. There's also a **café** (☎ 09-420 2501; ☽ 10am-4pm Wed-Sun).

HAURAKI GULF ISLANDS

The Hauraki Gulf, off Auckland, is dotted with islands (in Maori, *motu*). Some are only minutes from the city and make popular day trips. Waiheke, a favourite weekend escape, and volcanic Rangitoto really should not be missed. Great Barrier, once a remote and little-visited island, still feels like a million miles from anywhere, and provides an escape from many aspects of modern life.

There are 47 islands in the Hauraki Gulf Maritime Park, administered by DOC. Some are good-sized islands, others are no more than rocks jutting out of the sea. The islands are loosely put into two categories: recreation and conservation. The recreation islands can easily be visited and their harbours are dotted with yachts in summer. The conservation islands, however, have restricted access. Special permits are required to visit some, and others cannot be visited at all as they are refuges for the preservation of rare plants and animals, especially birds.

For information on Kawau Island and Goat Island, see p152 and p153 respectively.

Information

The DOC information centre in Auckland's Ferry Building has the best information about walks and camping on the islands. The Auckland visitors centre is where you can find out about the more commercial aspects of the islands, such as accommodation and ferry services.

RANGITOTO & MOTUTAPU ISLANDS
pop 105

As recently as 600 years ago, Rangitoto (260m) erupted from the sea and was probably active for several years before settling down. It's now believed to be extinct. Maoris living on nearby Motutapu Island, to which Rangitoto is now joined by a causeway, certainly witnessed the eruptions as human footprints have been found embedded in the ash thrown out during the course of the mountain's creation. Rangitoto literally means 'Blood Red Sky' and is the largest and youngest of Auckland's volcanic cones.

Ten kilometres northeast of central Auckland, Rangitoto is a good place for a picnic. It has many pleasant walks, barbecues, a surprising amount of flora (including red flowering pohutukawa in summer) and a great view from the summit of the cone. There's an information board at the wharf with maps of the walks.

The hike from the wharf to the summit takes about an hour. Up at the top, a loop walk goes around the crater's rim. The walk to the lava caves branches off the summit walk and takes 30 minutes return. As the island's black volcanic rock can get hot in summer, you'll need good shoes and plenty of water.

Motutapu (www.motutapu.org.nz), in contrast to Rangitoto, is mainly covered in grassland which is grazed by sheep and cattle. Archaeologically, this is a very significant island – the traces of some 500 years of continuous human habitation are etched into its landscape.

A **DOC camping ground** (☎ 09-372 7348; adult/child $5/2.50) is at Home Bay on Motutapu. Facilities are basic, with only a water tap and flush toilet provided. Bring cooking equipment, as open fires are forbidden. It's a three-hour walk from Rangitoto wharf.

The **Outdoor Education Camp** (☎ 09-445 4486; www.motutapucamp.com; per person/cottage $15/150) has three-bedroom, self-contained cottages that sleep up to 12 people. Prices are reduced in winter and include free pick-up from the Rangitoto ferry. Kayaking, sailing, abseiling and other courses and activities are available.

Getting There & Around
The ferry trip to Rangitoto Island from Auckland's Ferry Building takes 20 minutes. **Fullers** (☎ 09-367 9111; adult/child return $20/10) has boats leaving at 9.15am and 2.15pm daily. Fullers also has one-day tours to Rangitoto. On the **Volcanic Explorer** (adult/child $50/25) you

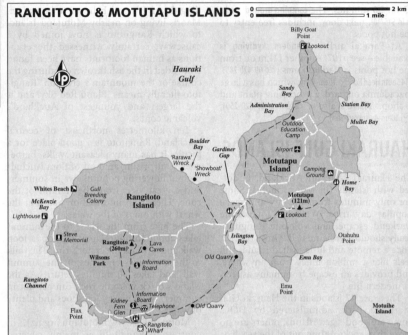

RANGITOTO & MOTUTAPU ISLANDS

ride in a canopied trailer, towed by a 4WD tractor, to a 900m boardwalk leading to the summit. The cost includes the return ferry trip.

WAIHEKE ISLAND
pop 8500

Waiheke is the most visited of the gulf islands and, at 93 sq km, is one of the largest. Though only a little over half an hour by ferry from Auckland, Waiheke enjoys a slow pace of life and a fine climate; its many picturesque bays and safe beaches make it a great place to relax, and vineyards and olive groves are scattered all over.

The island attracts artistic types who exhibit their work in local galleries and craft shops. It is still a relaxed, seaside retreat that deserves more than one day. Every house has its own water tank and the roads are narrow and winding. To experience Waiheke at its peaceful best, try to avoid weekends.

Waiheke has been inhabited since about AD 950 and oral legends relate that one of the pioneering canoes landed on the island. Traces of an old fortified *pa* can still be seen on the headland overlooking Putiki Bay. Europeans arrived with the missionary Samuel Marsden in the early 1800s and the island was soon stripped of its kauri forest.

The biggest event on the island is the annual **Waiheke Jazz Festival** (www.waihekejazz.co.nz), which draws up to 30,000 people over the Easter weekend.

Orientation & Information

Nearly 2km from Matiatia wharf, the main village is Oneroa and below it is a sandy beach. The eastern half of the island is lightly populated. There are petrol stations in Ostend and Onetangi, and banks in Oneroa have ATMs.

The helpful **Waiheke Island visitors centre** (☎ 09-372 1234; info@waiheke.co.nz; 2 Korora Rd; ⊙ 9am-5pm Mon-Sat, 9.30am-4pm Sun) is in the Artworks complex in Oneroa. **Netspace** (☎ 09-372 9920; Pendragon Mall; ⊙ 9am-6pm Mon-Sat, noon-5pm Sun) has Internet access.

Sights

The **Artworks complex** (☎ 09-372 6900; cnr Ocean View & Kororoa Rds; ⊙ daily) houses a library community theatre and cinema, art and craft galleries and second-hand bookshop as well as an Indian restaurant and the visitors centre. Also part of the complex is **Whittaker's Musical Experience** (☎ 09-372 5573; adult/child $3/free, with 1½hr show $10/5; 10am-4pm, closed Tue & Fri), a museum of antique concert instruments, which the owners play and talk about from 1pm to 2.30pm on opening days.

On the road to Onetangi, next to the golf club, is the **Waiheke Island Historic Village & Museum** (☎ 09-372 2970; admission by donation; noon-4pm Mon, Wed, Sat & Sun) with exhibits displayed in five restored buildings.

The free *Waiheke Island Art Map* gives details of over 30 photographers, potters, artists and jewellery designers who can be visited.

The colourful and bustling **Ostend market** is held inside and outside the Ostend Hall next to the RSA on Belgium St from 8am to 1pm every Saturday. Here you can find local organic produce, second-hand books and clothes, handicrafts, plants and much more.

It's possible to drive right around the scenic loop road at the eastern end of the island. At the end of Man o' War Bay Rd there's a car park and a 1.5km walk to **Stony Batter** where you can explore WWII tunnels and gun emplacements that were built in 1941 to defend Auckland's harbour. The tunnels are open from 9.30am to 3.30pm and admission costs $5. Bring a torch.

WINERIES

At last count Waiheke had 24 vineyards which you can visit for tasting and sales, and some of them have restaurants. Because of their emphasis on quality rather than quantity, the premium wine produced here is relatively expensive and nearly all the wineries charge for tastings ($10 or less). Some are spectacularly located and worth a visit for that reason alone. Pick up the free *Waiheke Island of Wine* brochure from the visitors centre. Their opening hours vary considerably.

Picturesque **Mudbrick** (☎ 09-372 9050; www.mudbrick.co.nz; 126 Church Bay Rd; mains $25-33; lunch & dinner) is open from 10am to 4pm for tours and wine tasting, which cost $8 (tasting only costs $5). Bookings are essential.

Te Whau (☎ 09-372 7191; www.tewhau.com; 218 Te Whau Dr; mains $23-29; lunch Wed-Mon summer,

Sat & Sun winter) is perched out on the end of Te Whau peninsula with superb views. It is open for tastings from 11am to 5pm Wednesday to Monday in summer, Saturday and Sunday in winter.

Stonyridge (☎ 09-372 8822; www.stonyridge.co.nz; 80 Onetangi Rd; mains $24; lunch daily summer, Sat & Sun winter) is one of the oldest and most famous wineries on Waiheke. Tours cost $10 and include cork trees, an olive grove and tasting and take place at 11.30am Saturday and Sunday, but daily during the peak season.

Onetangi Road (☎ 09-372 1014; www.onetangiroad.co.nz; 82 Onetangi Rd; platters $14-18; 11am-6pm daily Dec-Mar, 11am-4pm Wed-Sun Apr-Nov) has a winery and a microbrewery. Wine tasting (four wines), beer tasting (four beers), a wine-making tour and a beer-brewing tour each cost $6 per person.

BEACHES

Popular beaches with good sand and swimming include **Oneroa Beach** and the adjacent **Little Oneroa Beach**. **Palm Beach** is in a lovely little cove, and there's a long stretch of sand at Onetangi Bay, 12 km from Matiatia wharf. A number of the beaches have shady pohutukawa trees. There are nudist beaches at Palm Beach and Onetangi Bay – head west just past some rocks in both cases.

Activities

Waiheke has a good system of walkways outlined in the *Waiheke Islands Walkways* pamphlet, which has detailed maps and descriptions of eight hikes which take from 1½ to three hours and is available on the island or at the DOC office in Auckland.

In Onetangi there's a **forest and bird reserve** with several good walks. For coastal walks, a good, well-marked track leads right around the coast from Oneroa Bay to Palm Beach. It's about a two-hour walk; and at the Palm Beach end you can jump on a bus back to town. Another good coastal walk begins at the Matiatia ferry wharf.

Other walks are in the undeveloped eastern part of the island. The **Stony Batter Walk**, leading through private farmland, derives its name from the boulder-strewn fields. From there you can continue north to Hooks Bay or south to Opopo Bay.

Ross Adventures (☎ 09-372 5550; www.kayakwaiheke.co.nz; Matiatia; adult/child 2hr trips $45/30,

WAIHEKE ISLAND

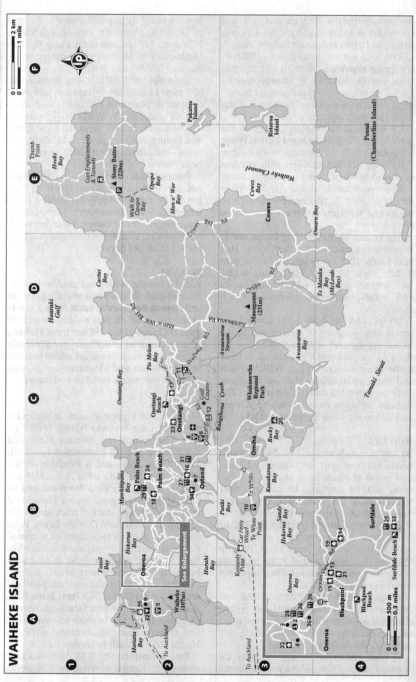

0   1 mile
0   2 km

F

Thumb
Point

Hooks
Bay

Gun Emplacements
& Tunnels

▲ Stony Batter
(220m)

Opopo
Bay

Walk to
Opopo Bay

Man o' War
Bay

Cowes Bay Rd

E

Waiheke Channel

Cowes
Bay

Cowes

Omaru Bay

Te Manuku
Bay
(McLeods
Bay)

Orapu Rd

Ponui
(Chamberlins Island)

Rotoroa
Island

Pakatoa
Island

D

Hauraki
Gulf

Cactus
Bay

Man o' War Bay Rd

Waiheke Rd

Awaawaroa Rd

Awaawaroa
Stream

▲ Maunganui
(231m)

Awaawaroa Bay

Tamaki Strait

C

Onetangi Bay

Pie Melon
Bay

Waiheke Rd

11
17

Onetangi
Beach

Onetangi

Rd

Golf
Course

23
8
16
Onetangi 12

Rangihoua Creek

Whakanewha
Regional Park

Omiha

Rocky
Bay

20

B

Mawhitipana
Bay

Palm Beach

24

29
18

27
31
16

34
7

Palm Beach

Oostend

10
Te Whau

Puaiki
Bay

Kauakarua
Bay

Te Whau
Point

A

Fossil
Bay

Hekerua
Bay

Oneroa

See Enlargement

35
32   9

5

▲ Waiheke
(107m)

Matiatia
Bay

To Auckland

Kennedy Point

Car Ferry
Wharf

Huruhi
Bay

1

2

3

4

0   0.3 miles
0   500 m

To Auckland

Oneroa

22
3
28
2
4
26
36

Oneroa
Bay

15
30
1

Blackpool

Blackpool
Beach

Ocean View Rd

13
21

19
14

Hekerua
Bay

Sandy
Bay

Surfdale

25
33

Surfdale Beach

INFORMATION			SLEEPING	🅰 🅖 (pp137–8)	Oneroa Fish & Chips..........................28 A3
Netspace.................................(see 36)			Boat Shed 13 A4		Salvage................................(see 36)
Post Office.................................1 A4			Hekerua Lodge....................................14 B4		Sticki Fingers......................29 B2
Waiheke Island Visitors Centre.....2 A3			Kiwi House...15 A4		Vino Vino...........................30 A3
			Midway Motel.....................................16 B2		Woolworth's Supermarket........31 B2
SIGHTS & ACTIVITIES	(pp134–7)		Onetangi Beachfront		Zora......................................(see 17)
Artworks Complex........................3 A3			Apartments......................................17 C2		
Blue Bikes Bicycle Hire.................4 A3			Palm Beach Lodge 18 B2		DRINKING 🅳 (pp138–9)
Mudbrick Vineyard &			Punga Lodge.......................................19 B4		Harbour Masters..................32 A2
Restaurant...............................5 A2			Rocky Bay Camping Ground.................20 C3		Malone's Place.....................33 B4
Onetangi Road Vineyard................6 C2			Tawa Lodge..21 A4		Rocks..................................34 B2
Ostend Hall.................................7 B2			Twin Gables.......................................22 A3		RSA.......................................(see 7)
Stonyridge..................................8 C2			Waiheke Island Hostel.........................23 C2		
Sunset Corral Horse Riding............9 A2			Waiheke Island Resort.........................24 B2		TRANSPORT (p139)
Te Whau....................................10 B3					Bicycle, Scooter or Car Hire..........(see 35)
Waiheke Forest & Bird Reserve,			EATING 🍴 (pp138–9)		Bus Depot................................(see 35)
Kauri Grove.............................11 C2			Belgium St Deli & Café..........................(see 7)		Matiatia Wharf.....................35 A2
Waiheke Island Historic Village &			Caffe Pizzeria da Stefano......................25 B4		
Museum..................................12 C2			Lazy Lounge Café Bar..........................26 A3		OTHER
Whittaker's Musical Experience..........(see 3)			Mangrove Pizza...................................27 B2		Pendragon Mall....................36 A3

4hr trips $65/45) runs short trips as well as overnight and all-day paddles ($125). Kayak hire starts at $10 per hour.

The **Kayak Company** (☎ 09-372 6127; www.the kayakcompany.co.nz; half-/full-day trips $60/95) operates day and moonlight excursions. Kayak hire is $55 a day.

Sunset Corral (☎/fax 09-372 6565; Matiatia; adult $55-75, child $45-65; ☯ 9am-5pm) runs horse treks at 11am, 1pm and 3pm which last one or two hours. Bookings are essential.

Flying Carpet (☎ 09-372 5621; www.flyingcarpet .co.nz; half-/full-day trips $50/95) offers outings on an ocean-going catamaran sailing boat.

Seabirds Tandem Paragliding (☎ 09-372 5556; www.seabirds.co.nz; Onetangi Beach; trips $160) operates in summer for a gentle rise and descent from around 2000ft.

Windsurfing Waiheke (☎ 09-372 6275; www.wind surfing-waiheke.co.nz; boards per hr $20-30, 2hr tuition $35-45) operates from different beaches depending on conditions.

Waiheke Air Services (☎ 09-372 5000; trips $25-55) offers scenic flights for a gannet's view of the island.

Tours
Fullers (☎ 09-367 7911) runs a Vineyard Explorer tour (adult $70, usually at noon) that visits three of the islands top wineries, a 1½-hour Explorer tour (adult/child $50/23, at 10am) and a Beyond & Back tour (adult/child $55/28, at 10am summer only) that includes Stony Batter. Bookings are essential.

Waiheke Island Adventure (☎ 09-372 6127; www waihekeislandadventures.com) runs customised tours such as one-hour scenic tours ($25), two-hour vineyard tours ($50), or Stony Batter tours ($35) in a 15-seater bus.

With **Ananda Tours** (☎ 09-372 7530; www.ananda .co.nz) you can do a guided walk on the eco tour ($40) or visit artists and their studios, or local wineries ($65 to $85). The informal minibus and 17-seater bus tours (three to four hours) can both be customised to suit your needs.

Sleeping
Waiheke has more than a hundred backpackers, B&Bs, lodges, baches or apartments for rent, costing anything from $20 to $700 a night. Prices at most places jump from mid-December to the end of January and at Easter (when you'd be lucky to get a bed anywhere).

HOSTELS & CAMP SITES
Hekerua Lodge (☎ 09-372 8990; www.hekerualodge .co.nz; 11 Hekerua Rd; camp sites $30, dm $21-25, s/units $35/90, d & tw $50-65; ☲) Nestled in native bush this small backpacker haven has a deck, garden, outdoor pool and hot spa pool. The atmosphere is relaxed and friendly and TV/videos can only be watched after 6pm. It's a 15-minute walk to Oneroa but buses stop nearby.

Waiheke Island Hostel (☎ 09-372 8971; www .waiheke.cjb.net; 419 Seaview Rd, Onetangi Bay; dm/s $24/36, d $50-70; ☲) This clean and colourful associate-YHA ($4 less for members), with a large garden, has helpful staff and overlooks Onetangi Beach. The dorms have only two bunk beds, linen is provided, mountain bikes can be hired ($20 a day) and other activities can be booked commission-free.

At the far end of Gordons Rd in the Whakanewha Regional Park is **Rocky Bay camping ground** (☎ 09-303 1530; adult/child $5/2). Telephone to make a reservation and for the combination number to unlock the gate. Only drinking water and long-drop toilets are provided.

B&BS & LODGES

Twin Gables (☎ 09-372 9877; 17 Tiri Rd, Oneroa; s/tw/d $60/80/90, tw/d Dec-Apr $90/100) Guest facilities are shared, but this excellent loft accommodation has wonderful views, and the retired owners provide a free continental breakfast and pick-ups from Matiatia Wharf.

Kiwi House (☎ 09-372 9123; kiwihouse@clear.net.nz; 23 Kiwi St; s $45, d & tw $80, d & tw with bathroom $95) This friendly guesthouse offers a filling continental breakfast, pleasant decks, a shared kitchen and reasonable prices.

Punga Lodge (☎ /fax 09-372 6675; 223 Ocean View Rd; d & tw $125, garden cottages $125-175, winter $100-130) Both the colourful en-suite rooms in the house and the self-contained garden units have access to decks in this very bushy setting. There's a spa pool and prices include home-made breakfast, afternoon tea and transfers from Matiatia Wharf.

Tawa Lodge (☎ 09-372 9434; tawalodge@hotmail .com; 15 Tawa St; s/d & tw/studio with bathroom $90/ 110/145, units $170-200) The B&B rooms have a TV and prices include a breakfast basket, but they are small and share bathroom and kitchen facilities. Prices include transfers, and there is a garden and sea views from this hillside location.

MOTELS, APARTMENTS & RESORTS

Midway Motel (☎ 09-372 8023; waihekemidway@ xtra.co.nz; 1 Whakarite Rd, Ostend; studio/1-bed unit/3-bed house $90/100/120; 🖳) Units have Sky TV and kitchens but the main attraction at this reasonably priced and centrally located motel is the heated covered pool and spa pool. Prices rise (less than $20) in the peak season.

Onetangi Beachfront Apartments (☎ 09-372 7051; www.onetangi.co.nz; 27 The Strand, Onetangi Beach; studio $130-170, 1- & 2-bed apt $160-210, luxury apt $220-350) The price variations are seasonal for this smart perfectly located accommodation with a spa and sauna.

Palm Beach Lodge (☎ 09-372 7763; palmbch@ orcon.net.nz; 23 Tiri View Rd; 2-bed apt $260) This quality self-contained accommodation overlooks Palm Beach and has kitchens, decks and sea views. Discounts are available in winter.

Waiheke Island Resort (☎ 0800 924 4353, 09-372 0011; www.waihekeresort.co.nz; 4 Bay Rd, Palm Beach; B&B chalets/villas $180/230; 🖳) These well-landscaped upmarket units are on a hillside overlooking Palm Beach, have Sky TV and decks, and most have sea views. Facilities include a restaurant, bar and tennis court, but prices rise 12% from December to February.

Boat Shed (☎ 09-372 3242; www.boatshed.co.nz; cnr Tawa & Huia Sts; units $460-700) Architect-designed with fine views and a telescope, this small, modern luxury resort has candles, flowers, music, a log fire, a bar and a restaurant ($80 for a four-course dinner). There are stylish rooms and a white Lighthouse penthouse. The price includes breakfast, transfers and sun hats, and are reduced by $100 in winter.

Eating & Drinking

The place for cafés, bars and restaurants is Oneroa's main street, but there are a few scattered around in Matiatia, Surfdale, Palm Beach, Ostend and Onetangi. For details on restaurants at wineries see p135.

Oneroa Fish & Chips (☎ 09-372 8752; 29 Waikare Rd; ☯ lunch & dinner) Hidden away between the police station and a café is this superior takeaway that also does burgers ($5 to $10).

Lazy Lounge Café Bar (☎ 09-372 5732; 139 Ocean View Rd; meals $8-22; ☯ breakfast, lunch & dinner) This funky laid-back place above the Rockit Gallery has varied indoor/outdoor areas, some of which have a 1960s feel, with scruffy sofas, a pool table, music, art on the walls, sea views and a great range of food from deli items to pizzas.

Salvage (☎ 09-372 2273; Pendragon Mall; ☯ 7am-late) Thin, crispy, minimalist but tasty pizzas ($14 to $20) and tapas ($8 each) are available in this smart bar with a pleasant outdoor area.

Vino Vino (☎ 09-372 9888; 153 Ocean View Rd; dinner mains $20-28; ☯ lunch & dinner summer) One of the island's best restaurants, with a bar, deck, great sea views and an emphasis on Mediterranean-style seafood.

Harbour Masters (☎ 09-372 2950; Matiatia Bay; dinner mains $15-22) This modern pub near the ferry has a beach volleyball court, a garden and deck area, weekly live entertainment and a DJ on Friday and Saturday.

Surfdale, between Oneroa and Ostend, has a café, restaurant/takeaway and a pub.

Malone's Place (☎ 09-372 8011; 6 Miami Ave; mains $12-25) This Irish pub has a garden area, hearty bistro meals and live music on Friday, Saturday and Sunday.

Caffe Pizzeria da Stefano (☎ 09-372 5309; 18 Hamilton Rd; dishes $15-25; ☺ dinner Tue-Sun) This is a locally recommended BYO indoor/ outdoor place for Italian pizza, pasta and even gelati.

Sticki Fingers (☎ 09-372 3068; 39 Palm Rd; mains $19-28; ☺ breakfast, lunch & dinner summer) This café/restaurant/bar at Palm Beach offers an interesting global menu as well as coffee, drinks and deli items. Next door is the general store, which sells giant $2 ice creams.

At Onetangi Beach there's a new seafood restaurant and bar, **Zora** (☎ 09-372 9672; 21 The Strand, Onetangi Beach; mains $8-22; ☺ 8-1am), as well as a café, takeaway and shop nearby.

Eateries in Ostend:

Belgium St Deli & Café (☺ breakfast & lunch Mon-Sat)
Mangrove Pizza (☎ 09-372 8789; 14 Belgium St; ☺ dinner) You can eat pizzas (large $18) or burgers ($5-8) inside or take away.

Rocks (☎ 09-372 3722; 11 Belgium St; meals $14-16) This modern pub has a nice outdoor area, Waiheke oysters on the menu (six for $14), a pool table and karaoke on Thursday.

RSA (☎ 09-372 9250; Belgium St; mains $8-18; ☺ lunch & dinner) In the centre of Ostend, it has little character but does have cheap food and beer.

Self-caterers should head to **Woolworth's Supermarket** (102 Ostend Rd, Ostend).

Getting There & Away

Waiheke Air Services (☎ 0800 372 5000, 09-372 5000) has flights between Waiheke and Auckland (one way $110, or $80 per person for two or more), Great Barrier Island (one way $90), Coromandel Town (one way $110, or $80 per person for two or more) and Whitianga (one way $160, or $90 per person for two or more).

Fullers (☎ 09-367 9111; adult/child return $25/13) runs frequent daily ferries between central Auckland and Matiatia Wharf. From Monday to Friday they operate approximately hourly from 5.30am to 11.45pm (on the hour between 9am and 5pm). On Saturday it's 6.30am to 11.45pm and on Sunday and public holidays 7am until 9.30pm (until 11.45pm December to February). They take 35 minutes and a few go via Devonport.

Subritzky Line (☎ 09-534 5663; www.subritzky.co .nz; car/motorcycle return $110/31, adult/child return $25/ 13) takes cars and passengers on its route from Half Moon Bay (Map p130) in Pakuranga to Kennedy Point on Waiheke. The

ferry runs at least every two hours between 6am and 8pm Monday to Friday, 6am and 6pm on Saturday and 8am and 6pm on Sunday. The journey takes 45 minutes and bookings are essential.

Getting Around
BUS
Fullers (☎ 09-366 6400) operates four bus routes on the island and all connect with the arriving and departing ferries. All buses go from Matiatia Wharf to Oneroa, then depending on the route you can get to Little Oneroa, Palm Beach, Ostend and Rocky Bay; or Blackpool, Surfdale, Ostend and Onetangi. Matiatia to Oneroa costs $1.10, Matiaitia Wharf to Palm Beach costs $2.70 and an all-day bus pass is $10.

CAR, SCOOTER & BICYCLE
The island is hilly and places to visit are spread out, and there are 12km, 25km and 70km loop bicycle routes. Mountain bikes can be hired at **Waiheke Bike Hire** (☎ 09-372 7937; Matiatia Wharf; ☺ 9am-5pm) for $20 or $30 a day. Walk 1.5km to Oneroa Village and **Blue Bikes** (☎ 09-372 3143; 113 Ocean View Rd; ☺ 9am-5pm, 9am-7pm Dec-Mar) is cheaper at $15 a day. The **general store** (☎ 09-372 7937) at Palm Beach also hires out bikes for $20 a day.

Waiheke Auto Rentals (☎ 09-372 8998) and **Waiheke Rental Cars** (☎ 09-372 8635), both at Matiatia Wharf, rent out cars from $50 a day and 4WDs from $75. You must be over 21, pay 50c a kilometre, and the insurance excess (deposit) is $750. A cheaper rate applies for two-hour hires. Waiheke Rental Cars also hires out 50cc scooters ($40 a day, $500 excess) and motorbikes ($65 a day, $750 excess) neither of which have a kilometre charge.

TAXI
There are lots of car and minibus taxis: Try **Waiheke Taxis** (☎ 09-372 8038), **Dial-a-Cab** (☎ 09-372 9666) or **Waiheke Island Shuttle Service** (☎ 09-372 7756).

GREAT BARRIER ISLAND
☎ 09 pop 1000
Great Barrier (Aotea), 88km from the mainland, is the largest island in the gulf. It's a rugged and scenic island, resembling the Coromandel Peninsula to which it was once joined. Named by James Cook, Great

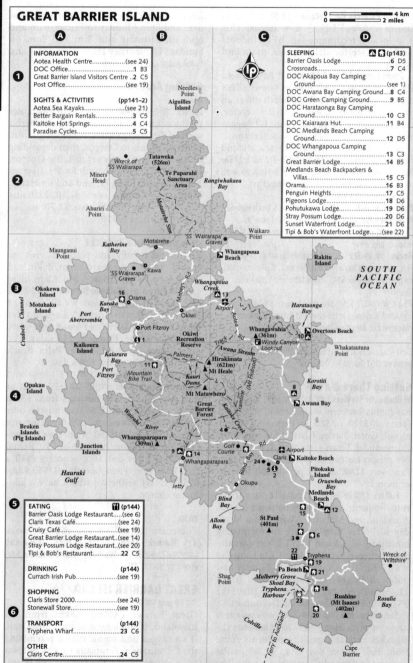

Barrier Island later became a whaling, mining and logging centre, but all these industries came to an end. Most of the island is publicly owned and managed by DOC.

Great Barrier has unspoilt beaches, hot springs, old kauri dams, a forest sanctuary and a network of tramping tracks. Because there are no possums on the island, the native bush is lush. The west coast has safe sandy beaches; while the east coast beaches are good for surfing. Mountain biking, swimming, fishing, diving, boating, sea kayaking and just relaxing are other popular activities on the island.

Although easily (but not cheaply) reached from Auckland, Great Barrier is a world – and a good 50 years – away. The island has no supermarket, no electricity supply (only private generators), no main drainage (only septic tanks), most roads are unsealed, and petrol costs nearly double the Auckland price. Mobile phone reception is very limited and there are no banks, ATMs or street lights. Still, the great god Internet has found its way here – practically everyone has their own website!

From around mid-December to mid-January is the peak season, so make sure you book transport, accommodation and activities in advance.

Orientation

Tryphena is the main settlement but is 3km away from the ferry wharf at Shoal Bay. Strung out along several kilometres of coastal road, it consists of a few dozen houses, a school and a handful of shops and accommodation places dotted around the harbour. From the wharf it is a couple of kilometres to Mulberry Grove, and then another 1km over the headland to Pa Beach and the Stonewall Store.

The airport and visitors centre are at Claris, a small settlement with a general store, bottle shop, launderette, vehicle repair garage, fuel, an adventure centre and a good café, about 16km north of Tryphena. Whangaparapara is an old timber town and the site of the island's 19th-century whaling activities. Port Fitzroy is the other main harbour on the west coast, a one-hour drive from Tryphena (roads are unsealed beyond Claris).

Information

The **Great Barrier Island visitors centre** (☎ 09-429 0033; www.greatbarrier.co.nz; Claris; ☽ 9am-4pm Mon-Fri, 9am-1pm Sat & Sun) is opposite the airfield and has shorter hours in winter. The staff know most of the people on the island and can help with fishing charters. The free *Great Barrier Island* booklet is full of useful and up-to-date information. The **DOC office** (☎ 09-429 0044; Port Fitzroy; ☽ 8am-4.30pm Mon-Fri) is 1km from the Port Fitzroy jetty and deals with the DOC huts, camp sites and hiking trails.

The **Aotea Health Centre** (☎ 09-429 0356; Claris) has a full-time doctor and dentist as well as nurses. A nurse is also stationed at Port Fitzroy. The post office is in Outpost, a gift shop, in Tryphena.

Activities
SWIMMING & SURFING

Beaches on the west coast are safe, but note that care needs to be taken on the surf-pounded eastern beaches. **Medlands Beach**, with its wide sweep of white sand, is one of the best beaches on the island and is easily accessible from Tryphena. Remote **Whangapoua** in the northeast requires more effort to get to, while **Kaitoke**, **Awana Bay** and **Harataonga** on the east coast are also worth a visit.

Okiwi Bar has an excellent right-hand break, while Awana has both left- and right-hand breaks. Tryphena's bay, lined with pohutukawa, has sheltered beaches.

PIGEON-GRAMS

Great Barrier's first pigeon-gram service took flight in 1897, a year after an enterprising Auckland newspaper reporter had used a pigeon to file a report from the island. From small beginnings the service expanded to include a good part of the Hauraki Gulf. Shopping lists, election results, mine claims and important pieces of news winged their way across land and sea tied to the legs of the canny birds. The arrival of the telegraph in 1908 grounded the service, but the pigeon-gram stamps are now prized collector's items.

DIVING

There's pinnacle diving, shipwreck diving, lots of fish and over 33m visibility at some times of the year.

Hooked on Barrier (☎ 09-429 0417; Claris) sells and hires out diving, snorkelling, fishing, surfing and kayak gear. You can dive from a beach or charter a boat.

Tryphena Mobile Dive Centre (☎ 09-429 0654; Tryphena Wharf). hires out dive tanks and weight belts and fills tanks.

HORSE TREKKING

Great Barrier Island Horse Treks (☎ 09-429 0274; Medlands; 1hr/2hr/half-day rides $35/75/95) offers beach riding and swimming with horses (the horses do the swimming).

Karaka Horse Treks (☎ 09-429 0063; 2hr/3hr rides $60/90) Does guided horse treks that go from Orama, north of Port Fitzroy, through regenerating bush for hilltop views and can include a beach ride.

MOUNTAIN BIKING

With rugged scenery and little traffic on the unsealed roads, mountain biking is a popular and not too difficult activity here. A good ride is from Tryphena to Whangaparapara: cycle about an hour to Medlands Beach where you can stop for a swim, then cycle another hour to the hot springs, from where it's another half-hour to accommodation in Whangaparapara. Spend another day cycling through the forest up to Port Fitzroy, stopping on the way for a hike up to the kauri dams on a good, well-marked 4WD track.

Paradise Cycles (☎ 09-429 0303; Claris) hires out mountain bikes and organises cycling tours.

GBI Adventure Rentals (☎ 09-429 0062; Mulberry Grove, Tryphena & Claris) hires out mountain bikes, sailboards, surfboards, jet skis, motor boats, kayaks and dinghies.

SEA KAYAKING

Aotea Sea Kayak (☎ 09-429 0664; aoteakayak@hotmail.com) runs sunset ($35), night ($50), snorkelling ($55), and overnight ($85) guided paddles. You can even paddle right round the island, but it takes 10 days. Night paddlers experience phosphorescence on the water surface.

WALKING

Many people come here for the walks but be aware that they are not always well sign-posted, although they are being upgraded. So be properly equipped with water and food, and be prepared for bad weather. The best tramping trails are in the Great Barrier Forest north of Whangaparapara, where there has been a great deal of reforestation.

The most spectacular short walk is from Windy Canyon to Hirakimata (Mt Hobson). **Windy Canyon**, which is only a 15-minute walk from the main Port Fitzroy–Harataonga (Aotea) road, has spectacular rock outcrops and affords great views of the island.

From Windy Canyon, an excellent trail continues for another 1½ hours through scrubby forest to **Hirakimata** (621m), the highest point on the island, with views across to the Coromandel and Auckland on a fine day. Near the top of the mountain are lush forests and a few mature kauri trees that survived the logging days. From Hirakimata it is two hours through forest to the hut closest to Port Fitzroy and then 45 minutes to Port Fitzroy itself.

Another very popular walk is the **Kaitoke Hot Springs Track**. The natural hot pools can be reached from Whangaparapara Rd (45 minutes).

A more challenging tramp is the **Tramline Track** which starts on Aotea Rd and follows old logging tramlines to Whangaparapara Harbour (five hours). The track is hilly and in some parts the clay becomes slippery after rain.

Many other trails traverse the forest, taking between 30 minutes and five hours – pick up a copy of DOC's fold-out *Great Barrier Island* hiking brochure ($2 donation) which has a detailed map and short descriptions of 23 hikes. It's available from the visitors centre and many accommodation places.

There is a good trampers bus service that will drop you at the start of a trail and pick you up at the other end – see p144.

OTHER ACTIVITIES

Barrier Adventures (☎ 09-429 0699; www.barrieradventures.co.nz; Claris, near the airport; adult/child $50/20) offers one-hour 8WD Argo tours around the Claris area that traverse beach, wetland and volcanic terrain. Mountain bikes can also be hired to ride on special tracks, and bouldering, abseiling and even archery are available.

Sleeping

There are half a dozen camp sites and backpacker hostels and more than 50 lodges, cottages and B&Bs spread around the island. Some accommodation places cater for a range of visitors from backpackers and campers to luxury-seeking honeymooners and also run restaurants and bars that are open to nonguests. Prices can be steep in summer, but rates can drop dramatically outside the peak period. Summer prices are quoted here.

HOSTELS, CAMP SITES & HUTS

Stray Possum Lodge (☎ 0800 767 786, 09-429 0109; www.straypossum.co.nz; camp sites $24, dm/d & tw/ chalets $20/60/125) Nestled in the bush south of Tryphena is this popular place with its own bar and restaurant (see p144). Dorms have six or eight beds and the chalets are self-contained and sleep up to six.

Crossroads (☎ 09-429 0889; xroads@ihug.co.nz; 1 Blind Bay Rd, Claris; dm/s/tw $25/35/60; 🖳) This comfortable backpackers is in the middle of the island, 2km from the airfield. Mountain bikes can be hired, and golf clubs can be borrowed free to play on the nearby nine-hole golf course ($10 to play all day).

Pohutukawa Lodge (☎ 09-429 0211; plodge@xtra .co.nz; Tryphena; dm/d & tw with bathroom $20/95) Dorms have two or four beds at this place. It's part of Currach Irish Pub, which has a big garden and play area.

Medlands Beach Backpackers & Villas (☎ 09-429 0320; www.medlandsbeach.com; 9 Mason Rd; dm $23, d & tw $50-70, f $70-90, 2-bed villa $150-200) Basic accommodation is provided at the cheaper rates but it's a five-minute walk to a beautiful beach and there's usually some water sport equipment.

Penguin Heights (☎ 09-429 0628; www.penguin heights.com; 41 Medland Rd; dm $21, units $140-200) North of Tryphena, this establishment offers modern self-contained accommodation and a rustic backpackers cottage. There's a Penguin gift shop that raises money to support the local blue penguin.

Orama (☎ 09-429 0063; www.orama.org.nz; Karaka Bay; camp sites $20, dm/cabin $18/35, units $100-140; 🖳) Surrounded by hectares of bush, plenty of diverse accommodation is available at this Christian community just north of Port Fitzroy. There's a small shop, and kayaks, rowing dinghies, fishing and snorkelling gear are available. Environmental projects

pursued here include protecting the endangered brown teal and kaka parrot.

DOC camping grounds (☎ 09-429 0044; adult/child $7/3.50) These are at Haratonga Bay, Medlands Beach, Akapoua Bay, Whangapoua, The Green (Whangaparapara) and Awana Bay. All have basic facilities, including water (cold showers) and chemical toilets. You need to bring your own gas cooking stove. Bookings are essential in December and January and camping is not allowed outside the camping grounds without a permit.

DOC Kaiaraara Hut ($20) This hut in the Great Barrier Forest is a 45-minute walk from Port Fitzroy wharf. The hut sleeps up to 30 in two bunkrooms, and facilities include cold water, chemical toilets and a kitchen with a wood stove. Bring your own sleeping bag and cooking equipment. It operates on a first-come, first-served basis, but is never full. You can also camp outside for $5 (child $2.50).

GUESTHOUSES, LODGES & MOTELS

Sunset Waterfront Lodge (☎ 09-429 0051; www .sunsetlodge.co.nz; Tryphena; dm/studios/A-frame villas $20/150/185; 🖳) The units have decks and views, and facilities include a games room and a 3-hole pitch and putt on the lawn. A small shop and café is next door.

Pigeons Lodge (☎ 09-429 0437; www.pigeons lodge.co.nz; 179 Shoal Bay Rd; d & tw with bathroom & self-contained cottages from $95) On the beachfront south of Tryphena, this mock-Tudor lodge has a bush setting, can provide breakfasts and other meals, and has a dinghy that is available free to guests.

Tipi & Bob's Waterfront Lodge (☎ 09-429 0550; www.waterfrontlodge.co.nz; Puriri Bay Rd, Tryphena; units $135-200) West of Tryphena, these modern units have sea views and the complex includes a restaurant and bar.

Great Barrier Lodge (☎ 09-429 0488; Whangaparapara Harbour; dm/studio units & cottages $50/145) This large modern place on the water's edge overlooks the inlet and is near the tramping tracks. There is a small shop, restaurant (p144) and bar, and mountain bikes and kayaks are available.

Barrier Oasis Lodge (☎ 09-429 0021; www.barrier oasis.net; B&B d/cottage $250/$180) This is pricey but has three bright, luxury en-suite rooms, plus a self-contained unit, on a property that includes a vineyard and winery that offers wine tasting. The restaurant here is worth a visit (p144).

Eating & Drinking

Cruisy Café (☎ 09-429 0997; Blackwell Dr, Tryphena) It sells bread, cakes, doughnuts and lunch items.

Claris Texas Café (☎ 09-429 0811; Claris Centre) This café is licensed and has a blackboard menu as well as deli food.

Stray Possum Lodge Restaurant (☎ 09-429 0109; meals under $20) Offers pizzas from $13 and a varied takeaway-style menu.

Tipi & Bob's Restaurant (☎ 09-429 0550; Puriri Bay Rd, Tryphena; mains $24-29; ☺ breakfast, lunch & dinner) This popular haunt has an inviting deck overlooking the harbour, with fresh fish, seafood and steaks on the menu. There's a bistro menu in the bar ($6 to $20), which is famous for fish and chips ($11).

Currach Irish Pub (☎ 09-429 0211; Blackwell Dr; Tryphena; mains $10-20) This lively and child-friendly pub has a changing menu of sea-food, steak and Asian-style meals and is the island's social centre. Thursday is the big music night when anyone can get up and perform, but there is also live music at the weekend in summer.

Barrier Oasis Restaurant (☎ 09-429 0021; Try-phena; lunch $25, dinner $65) This is a good place for a night of fine dining with a fixed-price two-course lunch or three-course dinner with fresh, local seafood a speciality.

Great Barrier Lodge Restaurant (☎ 09-429 0488; Whangaparapara Harbour; mains $18-28) The menu here is based around lamb, steak and fresh fish.

Claris Store 2000 (☎ 09-429 0852) is near the airport and well-stocked with groceries, bread, organic meat, pizzas and pies. In Tryphena, you'll find the **Stonewall Store** (☎ 09-429 0474; Blackwell Dr, Tryphena), which sells food and bait.

Getting There & Away

AIR

Great Barrier Airlines (☎ 0800 900 600, 09-275 9120; www.greatbarrierairlines.co.nz; adult/child one way $90/65, return $180/130) flies three times daily to Great Barrier Island from Auckland airport (Map p130) and twice daily from Dairy Flat aerodrome (Map pp98-9) on Portman Rd on the way to Orewa. Flights take 35 minutes. You can fly one way and take a Subritzky ferry the other way for $125 (children $85) or fly to Great Barrier Island from Whangarei (see p192) or Whitianga (see p207).

Mountain Air (Great Barrier Express; ☎ 0800 222 123, 09-256 7025; www.mountainair.co.nz; one way adult/child $105/70, return $175/115) flies three or four times a day to Great Barrier Island from Auckland airport, and four times a week from Whangarei and both trips cost the same. You can also fly one way and take a ferry the other way for $125 (children $85).

BOAT

Subritzky (☎ 09-373 4036; www.subritzky.co.nz; adult/senior & student/child one way $55/40/35, return $85/70/55) is the main ferry provider, usually operating daily except Tuesday and Saturday, although daily in December and January. The boats also take cars ($500 return December and January, $300 return February to November) and run from Wynyard Wharf (Map pp98-9) to Tryphena Shell Bay. Ring for times of sailings, which vary.

Fullers (☎ 09-367 9111; www.fullers.co.nz; adult/child one way $60/30, return $120/60) runs services, which take two hours, from Auckland Ferry Building (Map pp98-9) to Tryphena from mid-December to the end of January, usually at the weekend.

Getting Around

From Tryphena in the south to Port Fitzroy in the north is 47km by (mostly) unsealed road, or 40km via Whangaparapara using the walking tracks. The roads are sealed – but narrow and winding – from Tryphena to Claris. Elsewhere they are graded but quite rough.

Great Barrier Buses (☎ 09-429 0474) runs five buses a day from Stray Possum Lodge to Claris via Tryphena and Medlands Beach with two services continuing on to the hot pools and White Cliffs. It also offers an excellent trampers transport service, which can drop you off at any of the main trail heads and pick you up at the other end. A one-day pass that includes trampers transport or scheduled services is $30, and a three-day pass is $50.

GBI Rent-A-Car (☎ 09-429 0062; gbi.rentacar@xtra.co.nz; Mulberry Grove Bay, Tryphena & Claris) hires out a wide range of hardy vehicles, including mini mokes starting at $50. The company also hires out adventure gear.

Aotea Bus (☎ 09-429 0055) has airport and wharf transfers ($12 from Claris to Tryphena) and a bus service from Tryphena to Port Fitzroy ($15), which runs daily from

December to February, and from Monday to Friday the rest of the year. Tours of the island can also be arranged.

Better Bargain Rentals (☎ 09-429 0092; Tryphena) has cars from $65 a day and 4WDs from $85 a day.

Many of the accommodation places will pick you up from the airport or wharf if notified in advance.

TIRITIRI MATANGI ISLAND

This magical 210-hectare and predator-free island (www.tiritirimatangi.co.nz) is home to lots of endangered native birds, including the very rare and colourful takahe. Other birds that can be seen here are the bell bird (NZ's nightingale), the stitch bird, the saddleback, the whitehead, kakariki, kokako, little spotted kiwi, brown teal, NZ robin, fernbird and penguins. The saddleback was close to extinction with just 150 left, but now there are over 200 on Tiritiri alone.

The island was occupied by Maoris but was sold to the Crown in 1841 and farmers came in and cut down or burnt the forest. But since 1984 hundreds of volunteers have planted 250,000 native trees and the forest cover has regenerated. An 1865 lighthouse stands on the eastern end of the island.

The **bunkhouse** (☎ 09-479 4490; adult/child $15/10) has a kitchen, hot showers, and toilets.

Fullers (☎ 09-367 9111; adult/child from Auckland $45/23, from Whangaparaoa Peninsula $25/15) usually has ferries to the island from Auckland and Gulf Harbour on the Whangaparaoa Peninsula on Thursday, Saturday and Sunday but they run more often between December and March. The ferries leave central Auckland at 9am and Gulf Harbour at 9.45am, and arrive back in Gulf Harbour at 3.45pm and Auckland at 4.45pm. A guided walk on the island is a good deal at $5.

MOTUIHE ISLAND

Between Waiheke and Rangitoto Islands, the remote 176-hectare Motuihe Island can be enjoyed for a couple of nights at a bargain price. Regenerating bush, walking tracks and sandy beaches are features of this island which was a prison camp during WW1 and has only four permanent residents. A self-contained **farmhouse** (☎ 09-534 5419; 1-4 people $60) sleeps up to 10 and is only rented out to one group at a time. Bring your own linen, towels and food. **Camping** (adult/child $5/2) is possible but the only facilities are toilets and water.

Fullers (☎ 09-367 9111; adult/child return $20/10) runs a ferry to Motuihe every Friday which leaves Auckland at 7pm, and another ferry leaves Motuihe for Auckland every Sunday at around 5.15pm. A water taxi service will cost you a maximum of $110 one way – telephone the farmhouse on the island for details.

OTHER ISLANDS

Little Barrier, located 25km northeast of Kawau Island (see p152), is one of NZ's prime nature reserves, and the only area of NZ rainforest unaffected by humans, deer or possums. Several rare species of birds, reptiles and plants live in the varied habitats on the volcanic island. Access to the island is highly restricted and a DOC permit is required before landing can be made on this closely guarded sanctuary.

Motuora is halfway between Kawau and Tiritiri Matangi. There is a wharf and camping site on the west coast of the island, but there is no regular ferry service (you'll need your own motor boat). Get a camping permit from the **ranger** (☎ 09-422 8882; adult/child $5/2.50) on Kawau, or from the caretaker on Motuora.

Northland

CONTENTS

North of Auckland 149
Whangaparaoa Peninsula 149
Orewa 149
Around Orewa 150
Puhoi 151
Warkworth 151
Kawau Island 152
Warkworth to Leigh 152
Leigh 153
Goat Island Beach 153
Leigh to Waipu 154
Waipu & Bream Bay 154
Kauri Coast 155
Matakohe 155
Dargaville 156
Around Dargaville 157
Dargaville to Hokianga 158
Hokianga 160
Omapere & Opononi 160
Rawene 162
Kohukohu 162
Mitimiti 163
Puketi & Omahuta Forests 163
The Far North 163
Kaitaia 163
Around Kaitaia 165
Cape Reinga & Ninety
Mile Beach 166
Karikari Peninsula 168
Doubtless Bay 169
Doubtless Bay to Bay of Islands 170
Bay of Islands 172
Pewhairangi 176
Paihia & Waitangi 176
Russell 181
Kerikeri 183
Bay of Islands to Whangarei 187
Russell Road 187
Tutukaka Coast & Poor
Knights Islands 188
Whangarei 189
Around Whangarei 192

Northland is blessed with some of the world's most varied and spectacular coastal scenery: along the surf-pounded and pristine west coast are huge harbours, mountainous sand dunes and endless black-sand beaches, while scenic peninsulas, sheltered bays, small rocky islands, world-class dive sites and sandy beaches are scattered along the east coast. Spend two weeks in this aquatic playground and you could enjoy a different water sport or adventure activity every day, particularly in the Bay of Islands. Despite the clusters of seaside homes, much of the coastline is undeveloped and uninhabited with national parks and hundreds of wilderness areas to explore, particularly in the far north.

Waitangi is where the treaty between tattooed Maori chiefs and the British Crown was first signed in 1840 after a vigorous debate that still continues over 150 years later (see p29). With Maori settlement also starting in this region, Northland is 'the birthplace of the nation' and the strong Maori influence in Northland adds an extra cultural dimension to any visit.

Awesome kauri trees once covered much of the region but nearly all were chopped down and sawn up for financial gain. Fortunately a few centuries-old giant kauri can still be seen, mainly in the protected and jungly Waipoua Forest on the west coast.

Northland may not be as scenic as the South Island, but the so-called 'winterless north' is usually warmer and drier. There are no glaciers and the only ice you're likely to come across is in the bottom of your glass.

HIGHLIGHTS

- Jetboating, sailing or kayaking around the beautiful **Bay of Islands** (p187)
- Standing in awe of the ancient kauri trees of **Waipoua Kauri Forest** (p159)
- Taking a 4WD tour along **Ninety Mile Beach** to sacred **Cape Reinga** (p166)
- Scuba diving around the **Poor Knights Islands** (p188) and the Cavalli Islands, home to the **wreck of the Rainbow Warrior** (p171), and snorkelling or diving around **Goat Island** (p153)
- Exploring New Zealand's bicultural roots at **Waitangi** (p176)
- Seeking out pristine, remote beaches on the east coast at **Pakiri** (p154), **Matauri Bay** (p170) and **Matai** (p168)
- Stepping back in time at charming and historic **Russell** (p181), **Mangonui** (p169) and **Rawene** (p162)

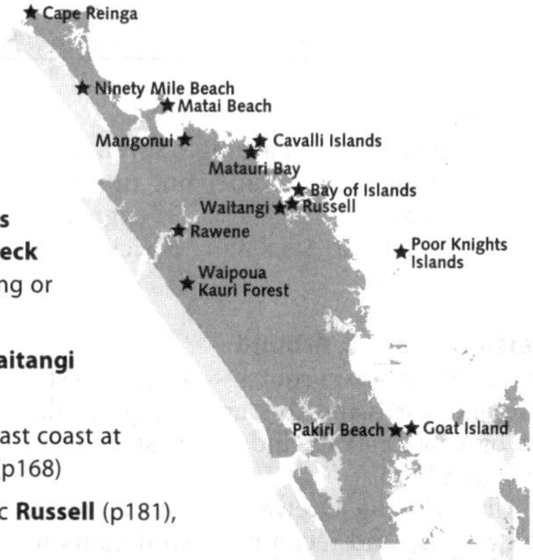

★ Cape Reinga
★ Ninety Mile Beach
★ Matai Beach
Mangonui ★   ★ Cavalli Islands
Matauri Bay
★ Bay of Islands
Waitangi ★★ Russell
★ Rawene
★ Poor Knights Islands
Waipoua ★
Kauri Forest
Pakiri Beach ★★ Goat Island

- TELEPHONE CODE: 03   - www.northland.org.nz

NORTHLAND

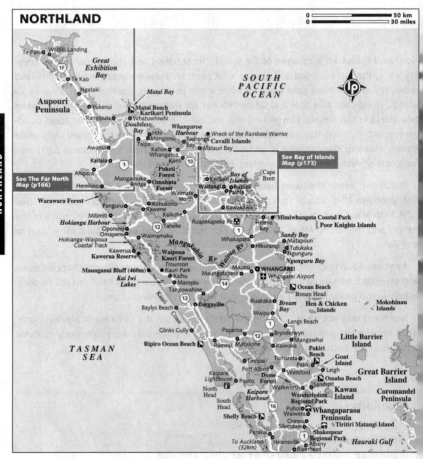

NORTHLAND

0 ————— 50 km
0 ————— 30 miles

Climate

The Northland region averages seven rainy days per month in summer but fifteen in winter. Temperatures can be a degree or two warmer than Auckland, especially on the east coast.

Getting There & Around

There are two main routes – east and west – through Northland to Cape Reinga at the top of New Zealand, and these can be travelled as a loop.

After visiting Orewa's beach, Waiwera Hot Springs and recommended detours to Puhoi historical village, Goat Island, Pakiri Beach and Waipu, take Hwy 12 and head west of Brynderwyn. The west coast route

then passes along the Kauri Coast through Matakohe, Dargaville, the beautiful Waipoua Kauri Forest and the remote and scenic Hokianga Harbour to Kaitaia and on to Cape Reinga. This chapter describes a clockwise (west coast) route, but the direction you take may depend on the prevailing weather – if it's fine in the Bay of Islands take advantage of it and head there first.

Northliner and InterCity are the main bus services in Northland. Both connect with the West Coaster, which has services from Auckland to Warkworth, Matakohe, Dargaville, Waipoua Forest, Omapere, Rawene and Paihia on Tuesday, Thursday and Saturday, and to Dargaville on Monday, Wednesday and Friday.

The Northliner runs daily from Auckland to Paihia in the Bay of Islands and on to Kaitaia. The standard fare to Paihia is $45, but backpackers and over 50s receive a 30% discount. Travel on Wednesday is discounted 20%. Buy a backpacker or YHA card and you are entitled to excellent-value passes. The Bay of Islands Pass ($55) takes you from Auckland to Paihia and back and you can get on and off anywhere along the way. The Loop Pass ($85) is similar but you go up to Paihia and across to Opononi on the southern shore of the Hokianga Harbour and down the west coast past the Waipoua Forest to Dargaville, Matakohe and back to Auckland. The Freedom Pass ($115) adds in Kerikeri, Mangonui (north of the Bay of Islands) and Kaitaia to the Loop Pass.

InterCity's bus service and basic prices are similar to Northliner, but backpackers receive only a 15% discount and passengers must be over 60 to receive a 20% discount. Its Twin Coast Discovery pass ($103) covers a similar route to Northliner's Loop Pass.

NORTH OF AUCKLAND

While many visitors, in their haste to get to the Bay of Islands, do this trip along State Highway 1 (SH1) in just a few hours, the east coast, north of Auckland, has a hot-spring resort and many delightful bays and beaches. A multi-lane motorway takes you as far as Orewa and the Hibiscus Coast between Whangaparaoa and Warkworth. This is a popular holiday area for Aucklanders over the Christmas season. Heading further north, the coast is less developed but no less beautiful with diving and snorkelling opportunities at Goat Island Marine Reserve.

WHANGAPARAOA PENINSULA
The Whangaparaoa (pronounced fa-nga-pa-ro-a) Peninsula – just north of Auckland off SH1 – is a heavily developed spit of land with a suburban feel and the 376-hectare **Shakespear Regional Park** at its tip. Windsurfers flock to Manly Beach, boaties leave from the Weiti River and Gulf Harbour, while swimmers head to one of the peninsula's fine beaches, and walkers and mountain bikers follow the trails around the park. Hiking trails take 1½ to 2½ hours. Many

native bush birds (especially pukeko) and waders can be seen here as well as native trees such as karaka, kowhai and puriri. Buses from Auckland run to the park.

Stagecoach (☎ 09-442 0555; www.stagecoach.co.nz) bus No 898 runs to the park from Wellesley St in central Auckland. The one-way fare is $7.90 so it's best to buy an $8 day pass.

The park is just beyond the impressive Gulf Harbour Marina development, which boasts a resort golf course and country club. **Gulf Harbour Ferries** (☎ 09-424 5561) go from here to and from Tiritiri Matangi Island on the regular service from central Auckland; taking this ferry is a good option for cyclists wanting to skip the boring road trip out of Auckland.

The **Whangaparaoa Steam Railway** (☎ 09-424 5018; www.rail.co.nz; 400 Whangaparaoa Rd; train rides $3.50, admission to railway & animal park $6; 10am-5pm Sat & Sun) is at Stanmore Bay on the main road into the peninsula. There are steam-train rides and an animal park.

OREWA
pop 4900
Just 38km north of Auckland, Orewa is the main town on the Hibiscus Coast and has a 3km-long sheltered and sandy beach that is patrolled by lifeguards in the peak season (December and January).

Information
The **Hibiscus Coast Information Centre** (☎ 09-426 0076; 214a Hibiscus Coast Hwy; 9am-5pm Mon-Sat, 10am-4pm Sun) is next to a mini-golf course and can help with fishing and horse-riding trips. Internet access is available at **PC Time** (Westpac Plaza; 20min $1).

Sights & Activities
The **Alice Eaves Scenic Reserve**, to the north of the town, is 10 hectares of native bush with labelled trees, easy short walks, a Maori *pa* (fortified village) and a lookout, while the **Millennium Walkway** is an 8km walk that takes in part of the reserve.

Orewa Cycle Works (☎ 09-426 6958; 12 Bakehouse Lane; 9am-5pm Mon-Fri, 9am-3pm Sat) hires out bikes for $25 a day ($50 deposit).

Sleeping
BUDGET
Pillows Travellers Lodge (☎ 09-426 6338; www .pillows.co.nz; 412 Hibiscus Coast Hwy; dm/d/d with

NORTHLAND

bathroom $20/45/60; 🖥) This clean and tidy backpackers has the best location with rooms around a pleasant garden as well as an outdoor spa pool, free tea and coffee, a piano and TVs in the private rooms.

Marco Polo Backpackers Inn (☎ 09-426 8455; www.marcopolo.co.nz; 2d Hammond Ave, Hatfields Beach; dm $20, d & tw $55-60; 🖥) This equally clean and tidy backpackers just north of Orewa is in a peaceful spot and has bananas growing in the garden. No TV is the policy here but there are hillside views to look at from the deck.

Puriri Park (☎ 09-426 4648; www.puriripark.com; 290 Centreway Rd; camp sites $28, cabins $50-70, units $90-110; 🐾) Peacocks roam around this large, well-equipped holiday park that borders Alice Eaves Scenic Reserve and has modern units with TVs, kitchens and linen. Facilities include a café, shop and a 25m heated pool.

MID-RANGE

Clipper Court Motel (☎ 09-426 4098; www.clipper court.co.nz; 420 Hibiscus Coast Hwy; units $85-110; 🖥) The well-maintained units here have two TVs and there's an indoor spa pool.

Orewa Motor Lodge (☎ 0800 267 392, 09-426 4027; www.orewamotorlodge.co.nz; 290 Hibiscus Coast Hwy; units $90-130; 🖥) This lodge is in a bunch of motels that line the main road. Units here have Sky TV, kitchens and pine décor and there's an outdoor covered spa pool.

Beachcomber Motel (☎ 0508 232 242, 09-426 5973; www.beachcombermotel.co.nz; 246 Hibiscus Coast Hwy; units $80-140) All units have Sky TV and some have spa baths and sea views. Palm trees add a sub-tropical touch.

TOP END

Orewa Bach B&B (☎ 09-426 3510; grahame.g@xtra .co.nz; 309a Hibiscus Coast Hwy; d winter/summer $150/ 200) This guesthouse opposite the shopping centre offers luxurious, modern, en suite beachfront rooms with a lounge, stunning views and fine breakfasts.

Eating

Plantation Café (☎ 09-426 5083; 226 Hibiscus Coast Hwy; meals $5-15; ☾ breakfast, lunch & dinner) At the entrance to town, this place has sea views and serves ice cream and home-made deli-type food including giant sausage rolls.

Kai Zen (☎ 09-427 5633; 350 Hibiscus Coast Hwy; meals $15-19; ☾ breakfast & lunch) This café has

good coffee and an ever-changing Italian-style menu.

Thai Orewa (☎ 09-426 9711; 328 Hibiscus Coast Hwy; lunch mains $7-14, dinner mains $12-24; ☾ lunch & dinner) This licensed Thai restaurant has a wide-ranging, reasonably priced menu.

Wishing Well of India (☎ 09-426 4499; 334 Hibiscus Coast Hwy; ☾ lunch & dinner) Special-deal meals at $10 and $12 are usually on offer at this Indian restaurant.

Rock Salt (☎ 09-426 5379; 2nd fl, 350 Hibiscus Coast Hwy; mains $18-27; ☾ dinner) This classy restaurant has sea views from its deck. Menu items include smoked fish pâté, vegetarian tartlets and teriyaki pork.

Self-caterers could try the **New World supermarket** (11 Moana Avenue; ☾ 7am-10pm).

Drinking & Entertainment

Muldoon Irish Bar & Brasserie (☎ 09-427 8000; West-pac Plaza, Moana Ave; meals $12; ☾ lunch & dinner) Try one of the huge burgers or the Ballydooly cider from Napier which is on tap. There's live music most Fridays (8pm) and Sundays (5pm).

Barnacles Bar (☎ 09-427 5127; Hibiscus Coast Hwy; ☾ 8.30pm-1am Thu-Sat) This nightclub has DJs and live music, and revs up on summer weekends. The entrance is on Bakehouse Lane.

Getting There & Away

Stagecoach (☎ 09-442 0555; www.stagecoach.co.nz) runs buses to Orewa (Nos 893 and 894) and the service to Waiwera (No 895) goes to Wenderholme Regional Park (below) in summer. Buses leave from Wellesley St in central Auckland and cost $7.90 one way (so it's better to buy an $8 day pass).

AROUND OREWA

Near Waiwera (literally 'warm water'), an unspoilt beach just 6km north of Orewa, is the **Waiwera Thermal Resort** (☎ 0800 924 9372; www.waiwera.co.nz; adult/student/child $18/14/10; ☾ 9am-10pm Sun-Thu, 9am-10.30pm Fri & Sat; 🖥) This resort boasts 19 pools, including a movie pool, 10 big slides, private spas ($25), a sauna, a sunbed, massages ($40), a gym ($8) and pizzas. All the pools use hot spring water from 1500m underground. A super pass is $35. An hourly bus service (No 895) runs here from Auckland.

Just north of Waiwera is the 134-hectare **Wenderholme Regional Park**, with a diverse ecology, abundant bird life, beaches, an estuary, and fine views and walks (one to two hours). **Couldrey House** (☎ 09-303 1530; adult/child $2/50c; ☼ 1-4pm daily Jan, 1-4pm Sat & Sun Feb-Dec), the original homestead, is now a museum. Bus No 895 from Auckland goes into the park, or you can walk there from Waiwera Thermal Resort.

PUHOI
pop 450

Only 1km off the main road, Puhoi ('slow water') is a quaint village that was founded by Bohemian peasants who spoke a German dialect. Around 200 of them settled here in the 1860s and were each given 40 acres of bush.

The **Bohemian Museum** (☎ 09-422 0816; Puhoi Rd; admission by donation; ☼ 1-4pm Christmas-Easter, school holidays & weekends) concentrates on the early days. Next door is the village's attractive **Catholic Church**, built in 1881, which is usually open.

Puhoi River Canoe Hire (☎ 09-422 0891; www .puhoirivercanoes.co.nz; single/double kayaks or canoes per hr $15/25) has been running trips on the tidal Puhoi River since 1991. Moonlight canoeing is also possible. Paddle 8km to 12km downstream to the estuary (two hours) and then get picked up ($30). Booking is essential.

In the **Puhoi Hotel** (☎ 09-422 0816; cnr Saleyards & Puhoi Rds; ☼ 11am-10pm) the bar walls are completely covered in old photos, animal heads and vintage household goods – an amazing sight. A Bohemian band plays every second and last Friday at 7pm and their musical instruments include a 'doodle-sac' – Bohemian bagpipes.

Five hundred metres beyond the village is **Puhoi Cottage** (☎ 09-422 0604; 50 Ahuroa Rd; ☼ 9.30am-5pm Thu-Mon), which is well known for its Devonshire teas ($6). Just 3km further on is the **Art of Cheese Café** (☎ 09-422 0670; 275 Ahuroa Rd; ☼ 9am-5pm Tue-Sun) where cheeses you can see being made are sold in the shop and the licensed café (platters $15, with wine $19).

WARKWORTH
pop 2800

Just off the main highway, beside the Mahurangi River, Warkworth has retained a village atmosphere with plenty of cafés and art and craft shops. A free Heritage Trail leaflet is available from the visitors centre and features the main historical buildings.

Information

The helpful **Warkworth visitors centre** (☎ 09-425 9081; www.warkworth-information.co.nz; 1 Baxter St; ☼ 8.30am-5pm Mon-Fri, 9am-4pm Sat & Sun) is near the bus stop and the New World supermarket, and can book boat tours along the river. Internet access is available at the **library** (☎ 09-425 9803; Baxter St) next door.

Sights & Activities

Just south of town, the 8.5-hectare **Parry Kauri Park** has a 15-minute forest boardwalk and a couple of giant old kauri, including the 800-year-old McKinney kauri. Also at the park, the small **Warkworth Museum** (☎ 09-425 7093; adult/child $5/1; ☼ 9am-4pm) features pioneer-era exhibits.

About 5km south of Warkworth, the **Honey Centre & Café** (☎ /fax 09-425 8003; SH1; ☼ 9am-5pm) has free honey tasting and glass-fronted hives where you can see thousands and thousands of bees at work. The shop sells all sorts of bee-related products from honey to beeswax candles. Try the delicious manuka-honey ice creams ($2).

Sheepworld (☎ 0800 227 433, 09-425 7444; www .sheepworldfarm.co.nz; adult/child incl sheep & dog show $13/7, without show $7/4; ☼ 9am-5pm), 4km north of Warkworth on SH1, demonstrates many aspects of NZ sheep farming. Popular sheep and dog shows include sheep shearing and are held at 11am and 2pm daily, and visitors can feed sheep and lambs in the mini farm and browse the large arts and crafts shop which includes wool products. There's also an adventure playground, an eco trail and a café.

Further north on SH1, the **Dome Forest** is a regenerating forest that was logged about 90 years ago. A walking track to the Dome summit (336m), which has great views across the Mahurangi Peninsula, leads from the carpark and takes about 1½ hours return. A three-hour return walk leads beyond the Dome summit to the **Waiwhiu Kauri Grove**, a stand of about 20 mature kauri trees. The start of the walkway is some 6km north of Warkworth.

Sleeping & Eating

Sheepworld Caravan Park (☎ /fax 09-425 9962; www.sheepworldcaravanpark.co.nz; SH1; camp sites/cabins/ chalets $25/50/80) Set on a large farm next to

NORTHLAND

Sheepworld, 4km north of Warkworth, this peaceful park with friendly owners has good facilities including a spa pool.

Bridge House Lodge & Bar (☎ 09-425 8351; www.bridgehouse.co.nz; 16 Elizabeth St; dm/s/d & tw $25/85/95) This lodge, next to the river, has bright en suite rooms. The refurbished bar and restaurant (mains $25) serves up pizza and pasta.

Burgers from off this Planet (58 Queen St; burgers $6-10; ☯ lunch & dinner) This superior fastfood outlet provides a wide range of popular gourmet burgers. Look for the rocket outside – it's hard to miss.

Ducks Crossing Café (☎ 09-425 9940; Riverview Plaza, Kapanui St; meals $4-16; ☯ breakfast & lunch) Overlooking the river and the new wharf is this café with a patio. It serves coffee and vegetarian and light meals.

Millstream Restaurant, Bar & Cinema (☎ 09-422 2292; 17 Elizabeth St; mains $19-22; ☯ lunch & dinner Tue-Sun) This smart and unusual restaurant opposite Bridge House Lodge serves Indian and Pacific-rim food and has a cinema downstairs that usually shows film-festival movies. A drink and a movie cost $10. Live jazz or piano music is on occasionally.

Top of the Dome Café (☎ 09-425 7794; all-day breakfast $6-11, mains $15-22, salads $16; ☯ breakfast & lunch daily, dinner Fri-Sun) This place is near the Dome Forest.

Getting There & Away

Auckland to Warkworth takes 50 minutes on the daily InterCity or Northliner bus and costs $19 one way.

There is no bus from Warkworth to Sandspit for Kawau Island; the only option is a taxi which costs about $15 one way. A taxi to Leigh costs around $45.

KAWAU ISLAND

pop 300

East of Warkworth is the scenic Mahurangi Peninsula and Sandspit, from where ferries depart for Kawau Island. The island's main attraction is **Mansion House** (☎ 09-422 8882; adult/child $4/2; ☯ 9.30am-3.30pm), an impressive historic house rebuilt from an earlier structure by Sir George Grey, a former governor of NZ, who purchased the island in 1862. It was a hotel for many years before being restored and turned into a museum. Inside is a collection of Victorian memorabilia including items once owned by Sir George.

HELPING THE AUSSIES

A particular type of tammar wallaby became extinct in Australia in the 1960s, but plenty survive on Kawau Island where they were introduced by Governor Grey. In an unusual reverse migration, 100 tammar wallabies will be re-exported back to Australia to re-establish them in the wild. Ironically DOC regards them as pests on Kawau Island and is glad to get rid of them.

Bush-tailed rock wallabies are also being sent from Kawau Island back to Australia where they are an endangered species.

Kawau has some beautiful walks, starting from Mansion House and leading to beaches, the old copper mine and a lookout. The *Kawau Island Historic Reserve* pamphlet ($1) published by the Department of Conservation (DOC) has a map of walking tracks. The pamphlet is available from the DOC office in Auckland.

Sleeping & Eating

Pah Farm Lodge (☎ 09-422 8765; fax 09-422 8794; Bon Accord Harbour; camp sites/dm/d & tw/f $20/20/45/100) Facilities include a kitchen, bar and restaurant (mains $16 to $20).

Beach House (☎ 09-422 8850; fax 09-422 8849; Vivian Bay; ste $320-480, chalet d incl breakfast & dinner $550) On the north of the island, on Kawau's only sandy beach, this upmarket place has suites and self-contained chalets. Water sports and *pétanque* are free, but lunch is extra.

Getting There & Away

Two ferry companies (Kawau Kat and Matata Cruises, see below) operate trips to Kawau from Sandspit (one hour) yearround. Car parking at Sandspit costs $6.50. Departures from central Auckland run from Christmas to Easter only.

The **Kawau Kat** (☎ 0800 888 006, 09-425 8006; www.kawaukat.co.nz) has a 3½-hour Royal Mail Run daily at 10.30am which stops at Mansion House and many coves, bays and inlets (adult/child $49/15, with BBQ lunch $59/20). A Coffee Cruise departing at 10.30am is $39/15 per adult/child. The Shipwreck Cruise (adult/child $39/15) leaves at noon and visits the *Rewa* shipwreck and Kawau Island. The Paradise Cruise only runs between Christmas and Easter, and departs from central Auckland at 9.30am on varying days of the week and visits the *Rewa* shipwreck en route to Kawau Island (adult/child $50/20, $60/24 with BBQ lunch).

Matata Cruises (☎ 0800 225 292, 09-425 6169; www.matata-cruises.co.nz) has a coffee cruise to Kawau for $25 at 10am daily (returning 2pm) and a combined three-hour Mansion House lunch cruise ($40). From December to April there is also a 2pm sailing. Bookings are essential.

WARKWORTH TO LEIGH

Less frequented than the main highway to Whangarei is the scenic Matakana Rd route from Warkworth out to Leigh, 22km away on the east coast, and then north via Mangawhai and Waipu to Bream Bay. This route has a number of attractions including scenic beaches, wineries, craft galleries and Goat Island Marine Reserve.

Excellent wineries along Matakana Rd include **Ascension Vineyard & Café** (☎ 09-422 9601; 480 Matakana Rd; set lunches $30 & $50; ⏰ lunch daily, dinner Fri & Sat) that has tours for $15 ($8 for diners), **Matanka Estate** (☎ 09-425 0494; 568 Matakana Rd) and **Heron's Flight & Café** (☎ /fax 09-422 7915; 49 Sharps Rd; platters $18; ⏰ 10am-6pm), which offer daily wine tastings from 10am to 5pm.

Morris & James Café, Bar & Tileworks (☎ 09-422 7116; 48 Tongue Farm Rd; meals $6-16; ⏰ breakfast & lunch) has a pleasant courtyard and colourful, practical ceramics are on sale. There are free weekday tours at 11.30am. It's just off the main road.

The first good beach, Omaha, is 6km off the Leigh road with a long stretch of white sand, good surf and holiday homes.

LEIGH

pop 450

The gateway to Goat Island, **Leigh** (www.leighbythesea.co.nz) is a small community perched above a picturesque harbour dotted with fishing boats.

Goat Island Dive (☎ 0800 348 369, 09-422 6925; www.goatislanddive.co.nz; 142a Pakiri Rd; ⏰ 8am-5.30pm summer, 9am-5pm winter) has a shop in Leigh and a boat that can take you diving anywhere in the Hauraki Gulf, including wreck dives and overnight trips ($300) at any time of year. Snorkel equipment hire is $12. Gear for a two-tank dive costs $90, dive trips are $65 to $100, and beach dives with instruc-

tion are $150. Professional Association of Diving Instructors (PADI) courses (four days including four sea dives) cost $480.

Leigh Motel (☎ 09-4226179; leigh.motel@xtra.co.nz; 15 Hill St; units $75-120) has eight comfortable hillside units with kitchens.

The rooms at the **Leigh Hotel & Bar** (☎ /fax 09-422 6036; Cumberland St; d & tw with bathroom $50) are a good deal and the pub has nightly happenings including DJs and live music.

Leigh Sawmill Café & Accommodation (☎ 09-422 6019; www.sawmillcafe.co.nz; 142 Pakiri Rd; mains $18-25; dm/d with bathroom $25/120; ⏰ lunch & dinner daily summer, Fri-Sun winter) is a funky bar and café, decorated with sawmill memorabilia, that puts on DJs and live music, including some top Kiwi bands on summer weekends. Accommodation includes backpacker rooms and separate smart modern units inside an old sawmill shed.

Fresh local fish and home-cooked food, including scotch eggs, are available at **Leigh Café Bar & Grill** (☎ 09-422 6033; 21 Hauraki Rd; meals $4-15; ⏰ breakfast, lunch & dinner), and for takeaways there is **Leigh Fish & Chips** (☎ 09-422 6035; 18 Cumberland St; meals $4-10; ⏰ 11am-7.30pm summer, closed Mon & Tue winter).

GOAT ISLAND BEACH

This is one of NZ's special places and only 3km from Leigh. The country's first marine reserve of 547 hectares was established here in 1978 and the sea has become a giant aquarium. Walk to the right over the rocks and you can usually see snapper (the big fish with blue dots and fins), blue maomao and stripy parore swimming around. You can snorkel or scuba dive from the black-sand beach, and there are dive areas all round Goat Island, which is just offshore. Colourful sponges, forests of brown seaweed, boarfish, crayfish, stingrays, and if you're very lucky orca and bottle-nosed dolphins can all be seen. Visibility is claimed to be 10m or more 75% of the time.

A glass-bottomed boat, the **Habitat Explorer** (☎ 09-422 6334; www.glassbottomboat.co.nz; adult/child summer $20/15, winter $15/10) provides a great all-year on-the-hour trip around Goat Island to see the underwater life. Trips last 45 minutes and run from the beach. When the sea is too rough the boat doesn't operate; ring to check.

Snorkelling, diving gear and wet suits can be hired at **Seafriends** (☎ 09-422 6212;

www.seafriends.org.nz; 7 Goat Island Rd; ⏰ 10am-5pm), 1km before Goat Island beach. You can hire a mask with a lens if you are short-sighted or a buoyant wet suit if you are a poor swimmer. Seafriends also runs a saltwater aquarium, marine education centre, café and restaurant.

LEIGH TO WAIPU

Instead of driving back to Warkworth from Leigh, you can make a loop to Wellsford via Pakiri, or carry on past Pakiri along good-quality gravel roads via Tomarata to Mangawhai, where the tarseal begins again. From there you can drive on to Bream Bay and Waipu, which is only 1km from SH1.

Pakiri, 11km from Leigh, is a secret paradise with a beautiful 9km white-sand beach, sand dunes and surf. **Pakiri Beach Holiday Park** (☎/fax 09-422 6199; 261 Pakiri River Rd; camp sites/campervan sites/cabins/cottages $24/26/40/90) has a shop and good units in a magical beachfront setting.

Just 6km on from Pakiri is **Pakiri Horse Riding** (☎ 09-422 6275; www.horseride-nz.co.nz; Rahuikiri Rd) which has over 100 horses with superb bush-and-beach rides ranging from one hour ($35) to all day ($165). Booking is essential. The **Stables Café** (snacks $5-12; ⏰ breakfast & lunch) serves baps, *panini* (focaccia), burgers and vegetarian food.

Another 12km on from Pakiri Horse Riding, turn left for Wellsford or turn right for Mangawhai and Waipu.

A long and winding gravel road goes to **Mangawhai** (www.mangawhai.org.nz) but the final 6km and the rest of the route to Waipu is sealed. The **Mangawhai Cliffs Walkway** (1½ to two hours one way) starts at the surf beach and affords extensive views inland and out to the Hauraki Gulf islands. Mangawhai has camping grounds, an Italian restaurant, a tavern, general store, petrol station and B&Bs. The **Smashed Pipi Café, Bar, Restaurant & Gallery** (☎ 09-431 4849; 40 Moir Rd; café meals $8-17, dinner mains $18-25; ⏰ breakfast & lunch daily, dinner Thu-Sun) has occasional live music in the bar, ceramics in the gallery, and delicious deli food in the café.

Mangawhai Heads is the next community where facilities include Sail Rock Café, an Internet café, a diving and fishing shop, a pharmacy, mini-golf and a golf club.

Milestone Cottages (☎/fax 09-431 4018; www .milestonecottages.co.nz; 27 Moir Pt Rd; cottages $115-230; 💻 🚣) are wonderful award-winning themed cottages set in superb gardens with a South Pacific feel near the sea. Free videos, kayaks, croquet and *pétanque* are available.

Mangawhai Lodge B&B (☎ 09-431 5311; www.sea viewlodge.co.nz; 4 Heather St; s/d winter $95/140, summer $135/160) is a boutique B&B with a commanding position and great views, and the rooms have access to the wraparound veranda.

Bunk 'N' Brekkie Backpackers (☎/fax 09-431 4939; dm/d $20/40; 💻) is a small but brand-new place with a full range of modern facilities just outside Mangawhai Heads on the road to Waipu. Breakfast is an additional $5 to $10. The owners live up the road.

From Mangawhai Heads, a particularly scenic road goes over the headland to Langs Beach and then on to Waipu.

WAIPU & BREAM BAY
pop 1980

Just before Waipu is Waipu Cove which has some accommodation. **Camp Waipu Cove** (☎ 09-432 0410; www.campwaipucove.com; Cove Rd; camp sites $25, cabins $50-100) is a large and comfortable camping ground on the beach. You can catch snapper off the rocks.

On the main road between Waipu Cove and Waipu is the **Stone House** (☎ 09-432 0432; loft $15, units $70-100), whose owners live in a unique Cornish-style house built of huge stone slabs in a lovely location. Guests are accommodated in separate units and can use a kayak or rowing boat to cross the saltwater lagoon and get to the beach which has shellfish and plenty of shore birds. The backpackers loft is basic but has TV and a stereo.

Waipu has motels, a pub, bank, petrol station and garage, Internet café, and shops.

The **House of Memories** (☎ 09-432 0746; 36 The Centre; adult/child $5/2; ⏰ 9.30am-4.30pm), a museum that doubles as the local information centre, tells the story of the 900 Scottish settlers who came to Waipu in six ships between 1853 and 1860 via Nova Scotia in Canada. Only 10% of locals are direct descendants, but there is a big get-together on 1 January every year when the Waipu **Highland Games** (www.highlandgames.co.nz), established in 1871, take place in Caledonian Park.

The **Old Waipu Firehouse Art Gallery** (☎/fax 09-432 0797; 7 The Braigh; ⏰ 10am-4pm) has displays that include the well-known hand-painted Waipu tiles.

Activities include surfing, fishing, boat trips and hiking to a cave with glow-worms. Just 10 minutes' drive west of Waipu is **North River Treks** (☎ 0800 743 344, 09-432 0565; www .northriver.co.nz; Helmsdale Rd; rides from $35) which offers a variety of horse rides through farmland and along rivers.

Waipu Wanderer Backpackers (☎ 09-432 0532; wanderers@xtra.co.nz; 25 St Marys Rd; dm, s & d per person $20) is a small, friendly backpackers in town – a real home from home – with free fruit in season.

Waihoihoi Lodge (☎ 09-432 1234; www.waihoihoi .co.nz; 219 Massey Rd; lodge s $60-120, d & tw $95-135, studio $110) is women-only, prices include a Pacific breakfast, and dinner with wine is available ($35). The separate self-contained studio is open to men and women, has a veranda and can sleep four. With a rural ambience 3km inland from Waipu both options are stylish and have great views of Bream Bay.

Pizza Barn 'n' Bar (☎ 09-432 1011; 2 Cove Rd) has popular platters and light fare as well as pizzas.

Waipu has a bus depot and Intercity, Northliner (see p148) and **Mainline** (☎ 09-278 8070) buses all stop here on the way from Auckland to Whangarei ($19, two hours 20 minutes).

From Waipu it's a 38km drive north to Whangarei, or you can head south to Brynderwyn and then west to the Kauri Coast.

KAURI COAST

Many people skip the west coast of Northland, but it's well worth including in a loop trip which takes you through rolling farmland – this is the area known as the Kauri Coast. The kauri forests are a natural highlight in this part of NZ.

Turn off SH1 at Brynderwyn and travel west along SH12. A must-see is the Kauri Museum (below) at Matakohe on the way to the west coast. From the northern end of Kaipara Harbour, extending along the west coast to Hokianga, the Kauri Coast is so-called because of the kauri timber and gum industry that flourished here in the 19th

century, generating much of NZ's wealth at the time. Those massive kauri forests are all but gone now, but the Waipoua Kauri Forest (p159) has untouched kauri stands and is the best place in NZ to see these magnificent trees.

Baylys Beach and Ahipara offer seaside fun and activities.

MATAKOHE
pop 400
At Matakohe, the superb **Kauri Museum** (☎ 09-431 7417; adult/student/child $10/8/2.50; ☼ 9am-5pm) will leave you amazed at how impressive wood can be. There's a scale exhibit of a working pioneer sawmill, clever static displays showing the lives of kauri bushmen, tradesmen and their families, and a gallery with a huge vertical cross section of kauri. But perhaps the most fascinating aspect is the **Gum Room**, a weird and wonderful collection of kauri gum or resin, the amber substance that can be carved, sculpted and polished to a jewel-like quality. The museum shop has plenty of excellent items crafted from kauri wood and gum.

Facing the museum is the tiny **Matakohe Pioneer Church**, built in 1867 of local kauri, which served both Methodists and Anglicans, and also acted as the town hall and school for the pioneer community.

Kauri Country Eco-tours (☎ 0800 246 528, 09-439 2394; www.kauricountry.co.nz; adult/child $85/45) has a descendant of one of the area's original pioneering families who provides explanations of the history of kauri logging and an insight into conservation efforts today. You can also dig for kauri gum and meet a bullock team. The three-hour trips leave from the museum and bookings are essential.

Sleeping & Eating
Matakohe Top 10 Holiday Park (☎ 09-431 6431; Church Rd; camp sites $26, s/d cabins $27/40, s/d units $50/80) This friendly small camp has modern amenities, plenty of space, good views and is only 350m from the museum.

Matakohe House (☎ 09-431 7091; 24 Church Rd; s/d incl breakfast $90/125-135) This lovely B&B and attached restaurant, a short walk from the museum, is built in colonial style. Rooms feature antique furnishings and open out onto a veranda. The licensed restaurant is a good spot for a meal (open 7.30am to 5pm, and by prior arrangement for dinner).

NORTHLAND

Gumdiggers Café (☎ 09-431 7075; Church Rd; meals $5-15; ✆ breakfast & lunch) This is licensed and opposite the museum.

Getting There & Away

The West Coaster bus provides a Monday to Saturday service down to Auckland ($32, three hours) and up to Dargaville, with buses continuing on to Rawene and Paihia on Tuesday, Thursday and Saturday.

DARGAVILLE

pop 4530

Founded in 1872 by a timber merchant, Joseph Dargaville, this once-important river port thrived on the export of kauri timber and gum. As the forests were decimated, it declined and today it is a quiet backwater servicing the agricultural Northern Wairoa area, which is the Kumara Capital of NZ, producing two-thirds of the country's output. In April a Kumara Festival is held in the town.

Information

The helpful **visitors centre** (☎ 09-439 8360; www.kauricoast.co.nz; cnr Normanby & Poto Sts; ✆ 8.30am-5pm Mon-Fri, 10am-4pm Sat & Sun) has Internet access and can help with booking tours, buses and accommodation. Next door is the **Sunset Laundry** (☎ 09-439 0005; 67 Normanby St). One block closer to the river is the **Bank of NZ** (☎ 09-439 3200; 72 Victoria St).

Dargaville (Maritime) Museum

Perched on top of a hill just out of town, the **Dargaville Museum** (☎ 09-439 7555; adult/child $5/1; ✆ 9am-4pm) houses pioneer artefacts plus a kauri gum-diggers display. There's also a maritime section that includes a vintage Maori canoe and the masts of the *Rainbow Warrior*, the Greenpeace flagship blown up by French agents in 1985.

Tours

Kaipara Action Experience (☎ 09-439 1400; www.kaiparaaction.co.nz; tours $95) Has an interesting adventure tour from Dargaville that includes a boat trip down the Kaipara Harbour, a quad-bike ride across the dunes to the lighthouse, and a 4WD trip up Ripiro Ocean Beach back to Dargaville. Fishing charters (from $75 per person) and boat cruises (from $50 per person) are also available.
Kewpie (☎ 09-420 8466; 3hr/day/3-day trips $15/45/300) Operates good-value cruises on the Kaipara Harbour to Helensville, Shelly Beach and Port Albert.

Taylor Made Tours (☎ 09-439 1576; tours $45) Runs 4WD tours along Ripiro beach to the lighthouse.

Sleeping

BUDGET

Greenhouse Backpackers Hostel (☎ 09-439 6342; fax 09-439 6327; 13 Portland St; dm/s/d & tw $19/28/45) This converted 1921 schoolhouse has large partitioned dorms, small new units in the back garden and a good atmosphere.

Dargaville Holiday Park (☎ 0800 114 441, 09-439 8296; www.kauriparks.co.nz; 10 Onslow St; camp sites/dm/cabins/units $22/20/40/80) This place has been recently renovated and the facilities are impressive – check out the BBQ area.

McLeans B&B (☎ 09-439 5915; westendnursery@xtra.co.nz; 136 Hokianga Rd; s/d incl breakfast $40/60) Guests share a large lounge in this spacious 1934 house originally built by the local mayor. The friendly hosts know all about the area and will take you on a day-long 4WD tour for around $110.

MID-RANGE

Kauri House Lodge (☎ /fax 09-439 8082; Bowen St; d incl breakfast $175-230; ✆) This grand colonial homestead, built by a kauri king in 1910 and now hosted by an entertaining cockney, is packed with amazing antiques and curios. It's a stately home with a snooker room, a study/library, extensive gardens and a long driveway. All rooms are en suite. Booking is essential.

Dargaville Motel (☎ /fax 09-439 7734; 217 Victoria St; low/high season d $70/95) These comfortable studio units with Sky TV and kitchenettes have views of the eternally muddy Wairoa River.

Motel Hobson's Choice (☎ 0800 158 786, 09-439 8551; hobsonschoice@xtra.co.nz; 212 Victoria St; units $100-165; ✆ ✆) This Spanish-villa-style motel has upmarket refurbished units and the relaxing pool area brings a splash of Fiji to dull Dargaville.

Eating & Drinking

Blah, Blah, Blah Café & Bar (☎ 09-439 6300; 101 Victoria St; café meals $5-16, dinner mains $18-28; ✆ breakfast & lunch daily, dinner Tue-Sat) Number one in Dargaville with a garden area, deli-style snacks, a global menu, great salads, pizzas, curried kumara, twice-cooked duck, mulled wine (spicy and warm) and rude cocktails.

RSA Club (☎ 09-439 8164; Hokianga Rd; mains $10-16; ✆ dinner Thu-Sat) This place serves top-value

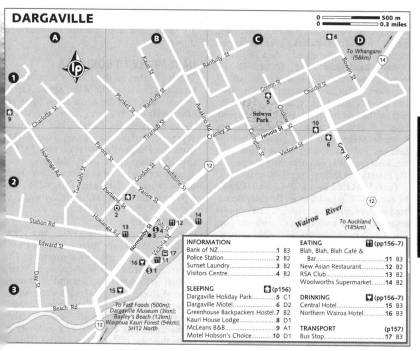

DARGAVILLE

INFORMATION		EATING	(pp156–7)
Bank of NZ...................................1	B3	Blah, Blah, Blah Café &	
Police Station...............................2	B2	Bar.....................................11	B3
Sunset Laundry............................3	B2	New Asian Restaurant............12	B2
Visitors Centre.............................4	B2	RSA Club.............................13	B2
		Woolworths Supermarket......14	B2
SLEEPING	(p156)		
Dargaville Holiday Park............5	C1	DRINKING	(pp156–7)
Dargaville Motel........................6	D2	Central Hotel.........................15	B3
Greenhouse Backpackers Hostel.7	B2	Northern Wairoa Hotel...........16	B3
Kauri House Lodge....................8	D1		
McLeans B&B............................9	A1	TRANSPORT	(p157)
Motel Hobson's Choice..........10	D1	Bus Stop..............................17	B3

roast and steak meals but only on three evenings a week.

New Asian Restaurant (☎ 09-439 8388; 114 Victoria St; mains $8-10; ☺ lunch & dinner Mon-Sat, dinner Sun) Here is Chinese food at budget prices, including a smorgasbord for $6 to $9.

Self-caterers should head to **Woolworths** (☎ 09-439 3035; 129 Victoria Street; ☺ 7am-9pm), while the best fish and chips is at **Fast Foods** (☎ 09-439 8497; 3 Murdoch St; meals $4-12; ☺ lunch & dinner) on the way out of town going north.

Pop into the **Northern Wairoa Hotel** (☎ 09-439 8923; cnr Victoria St & Hokianga Rd) or the **Central Hotel** (☎ 09-439 8034; cnr Victoria & Edward Sts) if you feel like a drink or meal in an old-fashioned pub.

Getting There & Away

The bus stop is on Kapia Street. **Main Coachlines** (☎ 09-278 8070) runs a bus to and from Auckland via Matakohe from Friday to Sunday ($37, three hours). **InterCity** (☎ 09-913 6100) does the same run every day except Sunday. Northliner runs from Dargaville to Auckland but not from Auckland to Dargaville. **East West Charters** (☎ 09-439 5151) runs

buses between Dargaville and Whangarei from Monday to Friday ($10; leaves Dargaville at 7.30am).

AROUND DARGAVILLE
Baylys Beach

Baylys Beach, 12km from Dargaville off SH12, lies on the 100km-long Ripiro Ocean Beach, and this stretch of surf-pounded coast has been the site of many shipwrecks. Ripiro Ocean Beach is a gazetted highway and you can drive along its hard sand at low tide, although it is primarily for 4WD vehicles. Several tour companies run tours along it; see opposite. Ripiro is NZ's longest drivable beach and less crowded than Ninety Mile Beach further north. Ask locals about conditions before venturing out onto the sand. Quad bikes can be hired at the holiday park; see p158.

Baylys Beach Horse Treks (☎ 09-439 4549; 2hr trek $50) offers regular beach rides.

SLEEPING & EATING

Hunky Dory Travellers Accommodation (☎ 09-439 0922; aymditch@paradise.net.nz; dm, s & d per person 1st night/subsequent nights $20/15) This bright and breezy small backpackers with friendly and helpful young owners has a creative corner, cacti, colourful décor and a deck.

Baylys Beach Holiday Park (☎ /fax 09-439 6349; www.baylysbeach.co.nz; 22 Seaview Rd; camp sites $20, campervan sites $22, cabins $35-50, units $80) This place has good facilities and quad-bikes for hire: $60 for the first half hour, $45 for subsequent hours. Ride north along the beach to view volcanic Maunganui Bluff (460m), but the hike up and down it takes five hours. Also available are 4WD van trips ($60 per person, 5½ hours) and fishing trips ($60 a day).

Funky Fish Café & Bar (☎ 09-439 8883; 34 Seaview Rd; mains $14-26; ☾ lunch & dinner) Brightly decorated with murals and mosaics, this popular restaurant, café and bar has a wide-ranging menu and bookings are advisable in summer. People drive from Dargaville just to eat here.

Sharky's (☎ 09-439 4549; 1 Seaview Rd; meals $5-19; ☾ breakfast, lunch & dinner) Fast food, all-day breakfasts and pizzas are available in this small bottle-shop-cum-general-store.

A taxi to Baylys Beach from Dargaville should cost around $20.

Pouto & Kaipara Lighthouse

Various 'sand buses' do tours 71km along the beach to the remote Kaipara Lighthouse (built with kauri in 1884) at Pouto Point. You go down along the sand and back along the inland road which is sealed for 30km south of Dargaville but gravel the rest of the way. If you have a 2WD stick to the inland road. Pouto (pronounced 'Poto') has a hostel and a luxury lodge for those who enjoy staying in wild and remote places. Quad-bike rides are available from Pouto to the lighthouse which you can climb up. Fishing from the beach is a popular and rewarding activity.

Pouto Marine Hall & Camping (☎ /fax 09-439 4298; camp sites $14, dm per person $10) This hall provides basic facilities and has a very small store. It's 7km from the lighthouse, but you can be driven there on a quad bike ($45 for an hour's ride). Ring this number if your vehicle gets stuck in the sand at this end of the beach and someone will tow you out!

Lighthouse Lodge B&B (☎ 0800 439 515, 09-439 5150; www.lighthouse-lodge.co.nz; d with/without bathroom $190/170) An architect-designed contemporary building in a remote spot, this lodge has light and stylish rooms with verandas

that have great sea views and there's Sky TV, a bar and dining room (three-course dinner $30).

DARGAVILLE TO HOKIANGA

The highlights of the Kauri Coast are the lakes and forests north of Dargaville – apart from several massive kauri trees, there are other walks in Waipoua Kauri Forest and the smaller reserves. Get the DOC brochure *Waipoua & Trounson Kauri Forests* ($1) from the Dargaville visitors centre (p156) If you're planning to overnight along here bring your own food as there are few stores or restaurants between Dargaville and Opononi, and no ATMs until Kaitaia.

Kai Iwi Lakes

Only 34km north of Dargaville, and 12km off the highway, are three beautiful fresh water lakes that are close together. The largest, Taharoa, has blue-coloured water fringed with sandy patches and pine trees Lake Waikere is popular with water skiers while Lake Kai Iwi is relatively untouched A half-hour walk takes you from the lake to the coast and it's another two hours to reach the base of Maunganui Bluff. There's also trout fishing and a mountain-bike trail

Pine Beach Camping Ground (☎ 09-439 0766 adult/child $8/4), a beautiful camping spot under the pine trees on Lake Taharoa, has flush toilets, but no electricity and only cold showers. A small shop is open from December to April when it gets busy. Canoes can be hired for one hour ($8) or a half day ($20).

Country Cottage (☎ 09-439 0303; fax 09-439 0302 49 Kai Iwi Lakes Rd; units $60-100) has value-for money modern self-contained units in an attractive garden 2km before the lakes.

Willowdale (☎ /fax 09-439 4645; www.willowdale .co.nz; 115 Kai Iwi Lakes Rd; B&B d & tw $135, cottage d $100) has en suite rooms and a self-contained cottage which sleeps up to eight. Meals are available.

Waterlea (☎ 09-439 0727; Kai Iwi Lakes Rd; studio unit $100, house for two $150, per extra person $20) offer self-contained options on this farm near the lakes, past the camping ground turn-off Mountain bikes and kayaks are free.

Trounson Kauri Park

The 450-hectare Trounson Kauri Park 40km north of Dargaville (turn off th highway at Kaihu), has an easy half-hour walk leading from the parking and picnic area by the road. It passes through a beautiful forest with streams and some fine kauri stands, a couple of fallen kauri trees and the Four Sisters – two trees each with two trunks. There's a ranger station and camping grounds.

Guided night-time **nature walks** (adult/child $15/9), organised by the Kauri Coast Top 10 Holiday Park (below), explain the flora and nocturnal wildlife that thrives here. This is a rare chance to see a kiwi in the wild. Trounson has a predator-eradication programme and has become a mainland refuge for threatened native bird species, so you should at least hear a morepork (a native owl) or a brown kiwi.

SLEEPING

Kauri Coast Top 10 Holiday Park (☎ /fax 0800 807 200, 09-439 0621; kauricoast.top10@xtra.co.nz; camp sites $26, cabins $38-60, units $85; 🖳) Just 2km from the main road and before Trounson Kauri Park carpark, this attractive riverside camping ground has good facilities, a small shop and organises night safaris (see above), horse rides, fishing and quad-bike trips.

Kaihu Farm Backpackers (☎ 09-439 4004; kaihu farm@clear.net.nz; SH2; camp sites/dm/s/d & tw $28/20/39/50) A cosy and well-kept farm-based hostel, 2km north of the Trounson turn-off, this place has farm produce for sale, a bush walk with glow-worms and a no TV policy. The hosts provide meals ($8) and a ride to local attractions ($5 to $10). West Coaster buses will stop outside.

Waipoua Kauri Forest

The highlight of the west coast, this superb forest sanctuary – proclaimed in 1952 after much public pressure and antagonism towards continued milling – is the largest remnant of the once extensive kauri forests of northern NZ.

The road through the jungly forest stretches for 18km and passes some huge kauri trees – a fully grown kauri can reach 60m in height and have a trunk 5m or more in diameter. Just after you enter the park turn off to the forest lookout, which offers a spectacular view, and the short Toatoa viewpoint walk is just 1km away. Back on the main road is a picnic spot and some youthful kauri trees. A little further

north, the **park visitors centre** (☎ 09-439 3011; 8.30am-5.30pm Mon-Fri, 9am-5pm Sat & Sun) has information and interpretive displays on kauri trees, the gum industry, native birds and other wildlife.

From the visitors centre, the highway winds through this lush forest of ferns and native trees for about 8km before the signposted turn-off to the kauri walks, where several giant trees are easily reached. The carpark here is guarded – theft from cars has been a problem – and a $2 donation pays for the protection service.

Te Matua Ngahere (The Father of the Forest) has a trunk over 5m in diameter, believed to be the widest girth of any kauri tree in NZ, and could be the oldest in NZ (probably 2000 years old). This massive tree, a 20-minute walk from the carpark, has to be seen to be believed. It presides over a clearing surrounded by mature trees that look like matchsticks in comparison. Close by are the **Four Sisters** (not to be confused with the kauri siblings of the same name in Trounson Kauri Park), a graceful stand of four tall trees clumped together.

From the same access path you can follow a half-hour walking track to the large **Yakas Tree**. You can also continue along this path for the popular two-hour, 6km forest trek to the visitors centre, but be warned that the track can be muddy after heavy rain.

Further north up the highway is **Tane-mahuta**, named for the Maori god of the forests. It's the largest kauri tree in NZ, standing close to the road and estimated to be between 1200 and 2000 years old. At 51m, it's much taller than Te Matua Ngahere but doesn't have the same impressive girth.

SLEEPING

Waipoua Lodge B&B (☎ 09-439 0422; www.waipoua lodge.co.nz; d incl breakfast $250-260) This fine old villa, run by hosts who work hard to please their guests, is on the highway at the southern edge of the forest, 48km north of Dargaville. The four luxurious apartments with imaginative décor were originally the stables, the woolshed and the calf-rearing pen! Dinner ($55) is available at the lodge restaurant.

Solitaire Homestay (☎ 09-405 4891; solitaire homestay@xtra.co.nz; s/d incl breakfast $65/105) A well-restored old kauri house on the main road

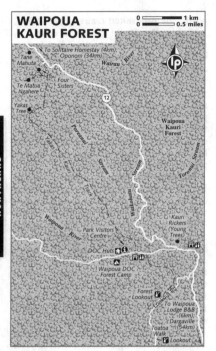

near Waimamaku and has a veranda and a pretty garden. Dinner is also available.

In the heart of the forest, next to the Waipoua River and just past the visitors centre is the **Waipoua DOC Forest Camp** (☎ 09-439 3011; camp sites $14, cabins $16-28) with cabins that are spacious but spartan. Bring your own bedding (BYOB) and book ahead for cabins in summer. There are hot showers, flush toilets and a separate kitchen. **InterCity** (☎ 09-913 6100) buses stop here on their way to Dargaville (one hour) and Omapere (50 minutes).

HOKIANGA

North of the Kauri Coast, the road winds down to Hokianga Harbour and the tiny twin towns of Omapere and Opononi. Hokianga is a 'Kiwi Outback' area with little development, but the harbour is unspoilt and beautiful. It's a good place to take time out to relax for a while, as plenty of alternative lifestylers have discovered. As you come up over the hill from the south,

the lookout point on **Pakia Hill** has a spectacular view of the harbour and the golden sand dunes.

Further down the hill, 2km west of Omapere, Signal Station Rd leads out to **Arai-Te-Uru Recreation Reserve**, on the South Head of Hokianga Harbour. It's about a 30-minute walk from Omapere or, if you're driving, a five-minute walk from the carpark to Signal Station Point. This overlooks the harbour entrance, the massive sand dunes of North Head and the turbulent confluence of the harbour and the open sea. There's a swimming beach, and it's also the northern end of the superb Hokianga–Waipoua Coastal Track (see below). But be wary – theft from cars is a problem.

OMAPERE & OPONONI
pop 630
These two tranquil settlements, on the southern shore of Hokianga Harbour, more or less run into one another.

Information
The very helpful **Hokianga visitors centre** (☎ 09-405 8869; visitorinfo@findc.govt.nz; SH12, Omapere; 🕑 8.30am-5pm) has Internet access.

Sights
Located in the same building as the information centre is a tiny local **museum** (☎ 09-405 8896; SH12; admission by donation; 🕑 9.30am-4.30pm) which tells the story of the hippie invasion of the 1970s and of 'Opo', a wild dolphin that played with children and learned to do tricks with beach balls back in the 1950s. Opo became a national celebrity but died of unknown causes a year after his arrival.

Activities
WALKING
The **Hokianga–Waipoua Coastal Track** leads south along the coast from South Head, at the entrance of Hokianga Harbour. It's four hours to the Waimamaku Beach exit, six hours to the Kawerua exit and 12 hours to the Kerr Rd exit. Or you can continue the entire 16 hours (allow about three days) to Kai Iwi Lakes. Pick up a brochure from any local visitors centre or DOC office. Hikers must carry all their own water and food, and cross the major rivers two hours either side of low tide.

From Cemetery Rd on the eastern outskirts of Opononi, a half-hour climb leads up **Mt Whiria**, a *pa* site with a splendid view of the harbour.

Two kilometres east of Opononi, Waiotemarama Gorge Rd turns south for 6km to the **Waiotemarama bush track** which climbs Mt Hauturu (680m). It's a four-hour walk to the summit (six hours return), but there's a shorter two-hour loop walk starting from the same place, passing kauri trees and a picturesque waterfall.

The **Six Foot Track** at the end of Mountain Rd (near Okopako Lodge; see below) gives access to many Waima Range walks.

OTHER ACTIVITIES

Hokianga Express (☎ 09-405 8872; adult/child $19/9) is a fast boat that leaves from Opononi Jetty and takes you across the harbour to the large golden sand dunes. You can **sandboard** down a 30m slope as often as you like and even skim over the water. The price includes hire of a sandboard and a return boat ride. Trips leave every hour.

Okopako Horse Trekking (☎ 09-405 8815) at Okopako Lodge (see below) has two-hour horse treks ($40) and longer rides through the bush of the Waima Range.

Sleeping

OMAPERE

Omapere Tourist Hotel & Motel (☎ 09-405 8737; www.omapere.co.nz; SH12; camp sites $20, units $85-135; ⬛) Both camping and classy harbourside units are available here with a choice restaurant and bar.

Hokianga Haven (☎ 09-405 8285; www.hokianga haven.co.nz; 226 SH12; d & tw incl breakfast $130-180; ⬛) This modern house with original Kiwi art on the walls offers exceptional accommodation on the harbour's edge. The room has private facilities and there is a hot tub.

OPONONI

House of Harmony (☎ /fax 09-405 8778; harmony@ grin.co.nz; SH12; dm/d & tw $20/45) This cosy and friendly backpackers with good facilities and a veranda is near the jetty. A haircut is $10.

Opononi Resort Hotel (☎ 0800 116 565, 09-405 8858; SH12; dm, s & d per person $15, d with bathroom $50, units $90-100; ⬛) This rambling and pleasant harbourside hotel has cheap but reasonable backpacker rooms, a separate motel section

out the back, plus a bar and a bistro restaurant; see below.

Okopako Lodge (☎ /fax 09-405 8815; 140 Mountain Rd; camp sites/dm/d $20/19/45) High up in the bush 5km east of Opononi and 2km down a reasonable gravel road, this comfortable YHA associate offers horse trekking ($20 per hour), hiking (the Six Foot Track begins here) and seasonal farm activities. Breakfast ($10) and dinner ($16) are available as well as pick-ups from the main road where buses can drop you off.

Opononi Dolphin Lodge (☎ 09-405 8451; cnr Fairlie Cres & SH12; campervan sites/dm/B&B s $20/25/55, d with/without bathroom $85/65) This large converted house has a range of modern accommodation with a lounge, kitchen and outside area from which to admire the harbour.

Opononi Lighthouse Motel (☎ /fax 09-405 8824; www.lighthousemotel.co.nz; SH12; units $75-135; ⬛) This refurbished motel has very comfortable harbourside units with kitchens and decks.

Koutu Lodge B&B (☎ 09-405 8882; Koutulodge bnb@xtra.co.nz; Kotu Loop Rd, Opononi; s incl breakfast $65, d & tw incl breakfast $90-100; ⬛) En suite or private facilities are offered at this homestay just north of Opononi and overlooking the harbour. You can explore the garden, share the lounge, or play pool or even a tune on the piano. Dinner is $35.

Eating

Harbourmaster's Restaurant (☎ 09-405 8737; mains $19-30; ☯ lunch & dinner) This very classy modern restaurant at the Omapere Tourist Hotel & Motel has a deck, great harbour views and fresh local crayfish for $45. Try the Kupe Kaimoana (squid, scallops and fish in a tomato, onion, wine and chili sauce) for something different. There's also a smart bar that does bar snacks and bistro meals ($13).

Opononi Resort Hotel (☎ 09-405 8858; bar meals & takeaways $4-15, bistro meals $12-22; ☯ breakfast, lunch & dinner) This is the centre of Opononi's social life; the pleasant restaurant has a terrace and serves bistro meals while the bar serves bar meals and takeaways and has live music some Saturdays.

Getting There & Away

West Coaster (☎ 09-913 6100) buses stop off at Omapere and Opononi from Paihia on Monday, Wednesday and Friday and from

Dargaville on Tuesday, Thursday and Saturday. It's a two-hour trip from Paihia to Omapere, and one hour and 50 minutes from Dargaville to Omapere.

RAWENE
pop 515

Rawene is a charming settlement from where a car ferry crosses Hokianga Harbour to Kohukohu. There is a surprising number of historical buildings, including six churches, from the time when kauri timber and gum was exported from here and the harbour was a lot busier than it is nowadays. There is a heritage trail with information boards.

Walk along the harbourfront to see around **Clendon House** (☎ 09-405 7874; adult/child $3/free; 10am-4pm Sat-Mon Nov-Apr), which was built in the bustling 1860s by James Clendon, a trader, shipowner and magistrate. A little further on are some mangroves with a short **mangrove boardwalk**.

Hokianga Blue Kayak Hire (☎ 09-405 7675; www .hokiangablue.co.nz; 49 Parnell St) runs guided tours for $35 to $75 per person and hires out kayaks for $25 per person for half a day or $40 for a full day. **Whirinaki Kayaking Tours** (☎ 09-405 8415; www.whirinakitours.com; trips $52) also runs kayaking trips but with a Maori flavour, mainly in summer.

Old Lane's Store Homestay (☎ /fax 09-405 7554; 9 Clendon Esplanade; s/d incl breakfast $85/110) is actually an attractive self-contained apartment with its own parking and courtyard. To stay at the **Postmaster's Lodgings** (☎ 09-405 7676; fax 09-405 7473; 3 Parnell St; r with bathroom $75-95), which has a lounge and kitchenette but no TV, contact the gentleman at the Ferry House.

You can eat on a deck over the water at the **Boatshed Café Gallery & Crafts** (☎ 09-405 7728; 8 Clendon Esplanade; meals $7-12; breakfast & lunch, closed part of Sep), a cute deli-style café with art on the walls and a wide range of excellent food.

Ferry House (☎ 09-405 7676; 1 Parnell St; lunch $9-15, dinner mains $22-30; lunch & dinner Tue-Sun;) is a quality restaurant opposite the ferry where you sit at tables surrounded by books and antiques.

Masonic Hotel (☎ 09-405 7822; Parnell St) is the local pub with occasional live country-and-western music shows.

If you opt to continue on the main highway heading towards the Bay of Islands,

you'll pass through **Kaikohe**, a centre for the Ngapuhi tribe and the scene of bloody battles during the Northland Land War (1844–46). Hone Heke eventually settled in Kaikohe and died there in 1850.

Trumps Café (☎ 09-401 2816; Station Rd; meals around $15; breakfast & lunch Mon-Fri) is the place for a drink, snack or meal. The **Mid North Motor Inn** (☎ 09-401 0149; 158 Broadway; units $85;) has tourist information, a shared kitchen, and a bar and restaurant.

Getting There & Away

The **car ferry** (☎ 09-405 2602; car & driver one-way/ return $14/19, passenger $2/4) operates hourly from 7.30am to 7.30pm. You can buy your ticket for this 15-minute ride on board. It runs more frequently if necessary so there shouldn't be a queue, and usually leaves Rawene on the half hour. The **InterCity** (☎ 09-913 6100) bus stops outside the Wharf House on its way to Paihia and Omapere.

KOHUKOHU
pop 220

Kohukohu, 4km from the ferry, was once a busy town (it was once at the heart of the kauri industry) with a sawmill, a shipyard, two newspapers and banks. These days it's a very quiet backwater on the north side of Hokianga Harbour. There are a number of historic kauri villas over 100 years old and other fine buildings including the Masonic Lodge, the Anglican Church and an old school, but you have to detour off the main road to see them. Some buildings are derelict.

Kohukohu Tree House (☎ 09-405 5855; www.tree house.co.nz; camp sites $28, dm/s/tw/d per person $20/36/ 24/26) A hint of budget paradise can be found here with friendly hosts and brightly painted little cottages set among exotic fruit and nut trees. This quiet retreat is 2km from the ferry terminus (turn sharp left as you come off the ferry). You can sleep in an old school bus ($20 per person), play volleyball in the macadamia orchard or just relax. Pick-ups are offered from the ferry.

Harbour Views Guest House (☎ 09-405 5815; Rakautapu Rd; B&B per person $40) This restored kauri home opposite the café has two rooms (one with a queen-sized bed, one twin) that share a large bathroom. Both of the rooms open onto a veranda with expansive harbour views. Dinner is available for $18.

Waterline Café (☎ 09-405 5552; meals $5-16; ⏰ 10am-5.30pm Tue-Sun but closes late Fri, closed Jul-Sep) At the waterfront is this excellent café and bar which has interesting pizzas, chickpea burgers and ever-changing blackboard offerings.

Palace Flophouse & Grill (☎ 09-405 5858; burgers $6; ⏰ lunch & dinner Tue-Sun) This fast-food restaurant serves great burgers, including vegetarian and fish varieties.

MITIMITI

About 40km west of Kohukohu, via Panguru on a rugged, wild stretch of coast, is the tiny isolated Maori settlement of Mitimiti, which consists of only 30 families and not even a shop. The last 20km of the road is gravel.

Stay at **Manaia Hostel** (☎ 09-409 5347; West Coast Rd; s, d & tw per person $25) to experience life in a remote Maori community. You can take the owner's flexible Maori culture tour (one hour, $10) that includes a *marae* (meeting house) visit, go on wilderness walks in Warawara Forest (NZ's second-largest kauri forest), fish off the rocks or try drag netting.

PUKETI & OMAHUTA FORESTS

North of Kaikohe, the Puketi and Omahuta Forests consist of one large forest area with kauri groves and other native trees, camping and picnic areas, streams and pools. Kauri milling in Puketi was stopped some years back to protect not only the kauri trees but also the rare kokako bird. It seems that the kokako here have their own dialect and won't breed with kokako from other areas.

The two forests are reached by several entrances and contain a network of walking tracks varying in length from 15 minutes (the Manginangina kauri walk) to two hours (the 2.6km Waihoanga Gorge kauri loop walk) and two days (the 20km Waipapa River track). A pamphlet detailing the tracks and features of the forests is available from any DOC office. Camping is permitted and there is a **camping ground** (☎ 09-407 8474; camp sites $14) at Puketi Recreation Area on Waiare Rd, 28km north of Kaikohe. It has hot showers, a kitchen with a stove and fridge, and composting toilets.

THE FAR NORTH

KAITAIA
pop 5630

Kaitaia (www.kaitaia.com) is mainly the jumping-off point for trips up Ninety Mile Beach to Cape Reinga. It's also a good place to learn about and participate in aspects of Maori culture. In the museum you'll see a welcome sign in three languages – welcome (English), *haere mai* (Maori) and *dobro dosli* (Dalmation) – as both Maoris and Dalmatians live in the area. Both groups are culturally active, with a Maori *marae* and the Dalmatian Cultural Club the focus of activities.

Each year in March a special marathon, the Te Houtawea Challenge, takes place along the length of Ninety Mile Beach, celebrating the legend of Te Houtaewa. This great runner ran the length of the beach from Te Kao to Ahipara to steal kumara from the Te Rarawa people, returning with two full baskets after being angrily pursued. The marathon celebrates the return of the kumara – reconciliation for a past deed. A Maori food festival and *waka* (canoe) racing are also held in March.

Information

The helpful **Far North Information Centre** (☎ 09-408 0879; www.topofnz.co.nz; South Rd; ⏰ 8.30am-5pm Sat-Thu) has Internet access and information on Kaitaia and the region, and books accommodation, tours and activities. Internet access is also available at **Hacker's Internet café** (84 Commerce St; 30 mins $5). ATMs are rare up north but the **Bank of New Zealand** (108 Commerce St) has one.

Sights & Activities

Te Wero Nui (☎ /fax 09-408 4884; 235a Commerce St; ⏰ varies) is an active Maori cultural centre which is based around a unique *whare* (house) where flax weaving and woodcarving take place. Informal tuition is available or you can just watch. A shop sells art and craft made on the premises. If Te Wero Nui is closed ask at Main Street Lodge next door.

The **Far North Regional Museum** (☎ 09-408 1403; 6 South Rd; adult/child $3.50/1; ⏰ 10am-4pm Mon-Fri) has among its exhibits a giant moa skeleton and a 1769 anchor.

NORTHLAND

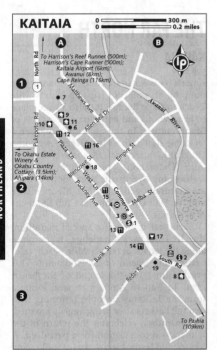

KAITAIA

INFORMATION	
Bank of NZ	1 B2
Far North Information Centre	2 B3
Hacker's Internet Cafe	3 B2
Post Office	4 B2

SIGHTS & ACTIVITIES	(pp163–4)
Far North Regional Museum	5 B3
Sand Safaris	6 A1
Te Wero Nui	7 A1

SLEEPING	(p164)
Kauri Lodge Motel	8 B3
Main Street Lodge	9 A1
Orana Motor Inn	10 A1
Wayfarer Motel	11 A1

EATING	(pp164–5)
Beachcomber	12 A2
Bushman's Hut Steakhouse	13 B2
C14	14 B3
Pak N Save	15 A2
Sea Dragon	16 A1

DRINKING	(pp164–5)
Kaitaia Hotel	17 B2

TRANSPORT	(p165)
Kaitaia Travel	18 A2

OTHER	
Dalmation Cultural Club	19 B3

Okahu Estate Winery (Map p166; ☎ 09-408 0888; okahuestate@xtra.co.nz; Ahipara Rd; ⏲ 10am-5pm), just south of Kaitaia on the road to Ahipara, has a range of wines and free tasting.

Harrisons Reef Runner (☎ 09-408 1033; 123 North Rd; tours adult/child $35/25) is a Unimog 4WD (a large all-terrain vehicle) tour of the Ahipara gumfields that includes sandboarding down the dunes.

Heather's Horse Treks (☎ 09-406 7133; 2hr rides $45), in Awanui, offers rides through a forest and along Ninety Mile Beach.

Blue Sky Scenics (☎ 09-406 7320; flights per person $55-135), based at the airport, 6km north of Kaitaia, operates a number of scenic flights over the Far North (minimum two people).

Kaitaia is a centre for popular tours up Ninety Mile Beach to Cape Reinga (see p167). The tours from Kaitaia are cheaper and travel a shorter distance than similar tours from Paihia in the Bay Of Islands.

Sleeping

Main Street Lodge (☎ 09-408 1275; www.tall-tale .co.nz; 235 Commerce St; camp sites $30, dm/s/d & tw $21/45/50, dm/s/d & tw with bathroom $29/55/60; 🖵)

There's lots of space and plenty of facilities in this large and popular YHA-associate backpackers which is upgrading with new en suite facilities. Peter, the live-in owner, is active in the local Maori community and will teach you bone carving for $25. He and his wife, Kerry, also run Te Wero Nui (see p163) which is nearby.

Okahu Country Cottage (☎ 09-408 0888; okahu estate@xtra.co.nz; Ahipara Rd; cottage incl breakfast $180) This lovely self-contained cottage at Okahu vineyard on the road to Ahipara comes with a free bottle of wine.

Kauri Lodge Motel (☎ 09-408 1190; kaurilodge motel@xtra.co.nz; 15 South Rd; units $55-70; 🏊) Conveniently located opposite the information centre, this motel offers kitchen units at a good price, some of which are more spacious than others.

Orana Motor Inn (☎ 0800 267 262, 09-408 1510; oranamotorinn@xtra.co.nz; 238 Commerce St; d from $90; 🏊) This smart motel also operates a restaurant that is open for dinner.

Wayfarer Motel (☎ 0800 118 100, 09-408 2600; wayfarermotel@xtra.co.nz; 231 Commerce St; units $80; 🏊) The units have been refurbished and facilities include an indoor spa, Sky TV and a games room.

Eating & Drinking

C14 (☎ 09-408 4935; 14 Commerce St; meals under $13; ⏲ breakfast & lunch daily, dinner Thu-Sat summer) An enticing new café which has *panini* and a wide-ranging blackboard menu.

Beachcomber (☎ 09-408 2010; 222 Commerce St; lunch $12-24, dinner mains $20-26; ✆ lunch Mon-Fri, dinner Mon-Sat) A popular restaurant where the menu includes duck, ostrich, venison and salmon.

Bushman's Hut Steakhouse (☎ 09-408 4320; 7 Bank St; mains $20-28; ✆ dinner) Barbecued meat is the speciality at this rustic licensed restaurant with indoor or outdoor seating.

Sea Dragon (☎ 09-408 0555; 185 Commerce St; mains $14; ✆ lunch & dinner) This inexpensive Chinese restaurant and takeaway has lunch specials ($10) and a Sunday evening buffet ($18 for 25 dishes).

The large **Pak N Save** (West Lane) is the cheapest place for self-caterers. For a drink head to the **Kaitaia Hotel** (Commerce St), which has been quenching thirsts since 1839.

Getting There & Away

Air New Zealand (☎ 0800 737 000 24hr; www.airnz .co.nz; one way $70-280) has daily flights (50 minutes) between Kaitaia and Auckland. The airport is 6km north of Kaitaia.

InterCity and Northliner buses (see p148) leave from Kaitaia Travel on Blencowe Street, and go daily to Auckland ($67, seven hours) via Paihia and Whangarei.

AROUND KAITAIA
Ahipara
pop 1000

Ahipara (www.ahipara.co.nz) is a small but growing community at the southernmost section of Ninety Mile Beach, only 14km southwest of Kaitaia. It's popular with locals and visitors and makes a good alternative to staying at Kaitaia. Beach activities include fishing, blowkarting (sand yachting), surfing and horse riding, but the area is also known for its mountainous sand dunes and massive gumfield where 2000 people once worked. Sand tobogganing, beach safaris and quad-bike rides are popular activities on the dunes above Ahipara and further around the Tauroa Peninsula.

Ahipara Adventure Centre (☎ 09-409 2055; www .ahipara.co.nz/adventure; 15 Takahe St; ✆ 9am-5pm) can book you on day-long Cape Reinga bus tours including a barge trip (adult/child $55/35) or 16-seater Unimog half-day trips to the gumfields and sand dunes (adult/child $45/25). The centre hires out

sandboards ($10 a day) and mountain bikes, kayaks and surfboards for $10 per hour or $12 per half-day. Blowkarts cost $30 for the first half hour (including instruction) and $20 for subsequent half-hours. Quad-bikes are $60 for the first hour and $40 for subsequent hours. Horse treks on the beach ($25 per hour) and fishing charters ($800 per day for five people) can also be booked at their office and fishing gear can be hired.

For horse rides on the beach and sand dunes contact **Jayar Horse Treks** (☎ 09-409 2055; 2hr ride $45).

On the beachfront is a superb kauri house, **Endless Summer Lodge** (☎ 09-409 4181; www.endlesssummer.co.nz; 245 Foreshore Rd; dm/s/d $20/35/50; 🖳), which has been beautifully restored with natural wood décor. Free boogie boards are available, surfboards can be hired for $20 a day and surfing instruction is usually available. Booking is advised.

Coastal Cabins (☎ 09-409 4839; 267 Foreshore Rd; cabins $40), also on the beachfront, is great value and has no TV. The bathroom facilities are shared and there's a barbecue and gas cooking outside, but each cabin has its own fridge and microwave. Experience the traditional Kiwi bach lifestyle.

Ahipara Motor Camp (☎ 09-409 4864; www.ahi para.co.nz/ahiparamotorcamp/index.html; 168 Takahe St; camp sites $20, cabins $25-45, tourist flats $60) is a bit basic but is being spruced up and is under the pine trees.

Opposite the motor camp and next to the golf course, **Baylinks Lodge Motel** (☎ 09-409 4694; baylinks@xtra.co.nz; 115 Takahe St; s/d from $70/100) has good clean units with kitchens.

Beachfront (☎ 09-409 4007; www.beachfront.net.nz; 14 Kotare St; d & tw $90-150) is a new upmarket two-bedroom en suite apartment with Sky TV, located as near to Ninety Mile Beach as you can get. Breakfast and dinner can be provided by arrangement.

Steak and seafood is on the menu at **Bayview Restaurant & Bar** (☎ 09-409 4888; 22 Reef View Rd; mains $19-25; ✆ lunch & dinner daily summer) at Adrian Lodge Motel, but the food and service are nowhere near as good as the view.

Gumdiggers Park

This **park** (☎ 09-406 7166; Heath Rd; adult/child $7/3; ✆ 9am-5pm) is 35km north of Kaitaia and 3km off the highway. It has a maze of footpaths around a major gum-digging site and an original gum-digger's hut, evidence

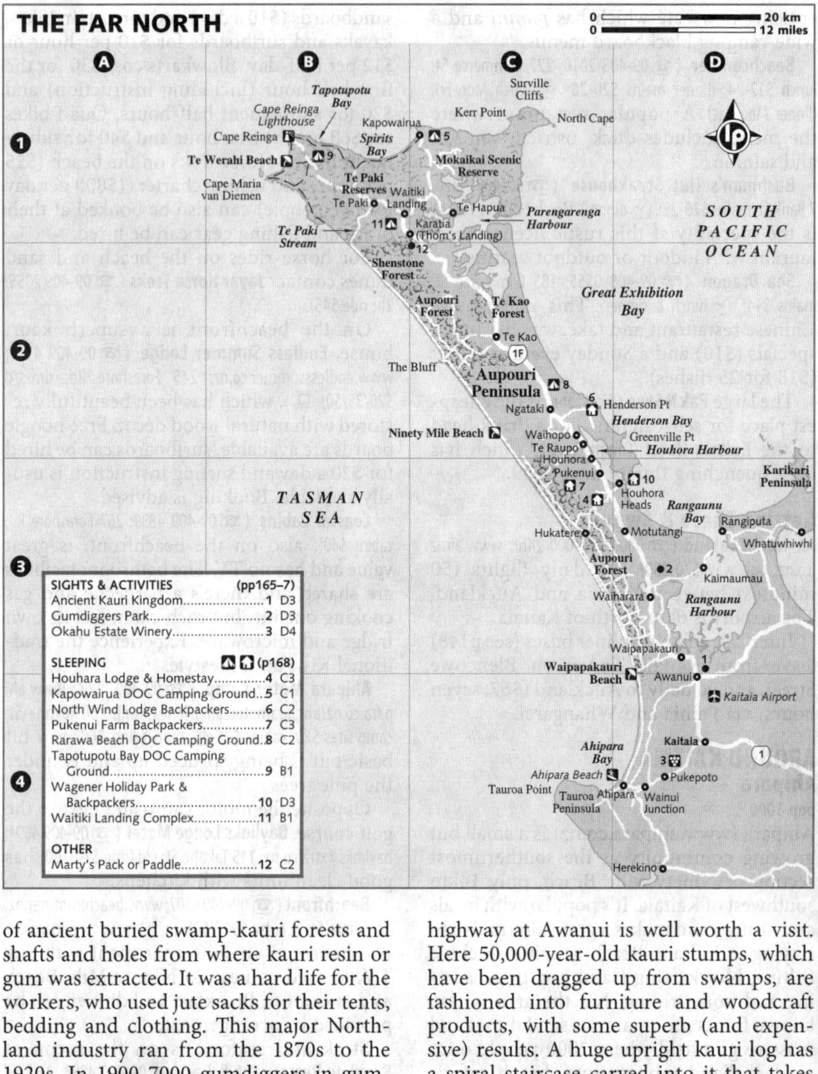
THE FAR NORTH
0 20 km
0 12 miles
A
B
C
D
1
2
3
4
Tapotupotu Bay
Cape Reinga Lighthouse
Cape Reinga
Te Werahi Beach
Cape Maria van Diemen
Kapowairua
Spirits Bay
Surville Cliffs
Kerr Point
North Cape
Mokaikai Scenic Reserve
Te Paki Reserves
Te Paki
Waitiki Landing
Te Hapua
Parengarenga Harbour
Te Paki Stream
Karatia (Thom's Landing)
Shenstone Forest
Aupouri Forest
Te Kao Forest
Te Kao
SOUTH PACIFIC OCEAN
Great Exhibition Bay
The Bluff
Aupouri Peninsula
Ngataki
Henderson Pt
Henderson Bay
Ninety Mile Beach
Waihopo
Te Raupo
Greenville Pt
Houhora Harbour
Houhora
Pukenui
Houhora Heads
Karikari Peninsula
TASMAN SEA
Rangaunu Bay
Rangiputa
Whatuwhiwhi
Hukatere
Motutangi
Kaimaumau
Waiharara
Rangaunu Harbour
Waipapakauri
Waipapakauri Beach
Awanui
Kaitaia Airport
Kaitaia
Ahipara Bay
Ahipara Beach
Pukepoto
Tauroa Point
Tauroa Peninsula
Ahipara
Wainui Junction
Herekino
SIGHTS & ACTIVITIES (pp165–7)
Ancient Kauri Kingdom 1 D3
Gumdiggers Park 2 D3
Okahu Estate Winery 3 D4
SLEEPING (p168)
Houhara Lodge & Homestay 4 C3
Kapowairua DOC Camping Ground 5 C1
North Wind Lodge Backpackers 6 C2
Pukenui Farm Backpackers 7 C3
Rarawa Beach DOC Camping Ground 8 C2
Tapotupotu Bay DOC Camping Ground 9 B1
Wagener Holiday Park & Backpackers 10 D3
Waitiki Landing Complex 11 B1
OTHER
Marty's Pack or Paddle 12 C2

of ancient buried swamp-kauri forests and shafts and holes from where kauri resin or gum was extracted. It was a hard life for the workers, who used jute sacks for their tents, bedding and clothing. This major Northland industry ran from the 1870s to the 1920s. In 1900 7000 gumdiggers in gumboots were digging holes all over Northland looking for buried kauri gum treasure. The gum was used in making varnish, linoleum and other products. The park has a small gift shop. If the site is unattended you can wander around on your own.

Ancient Kauri Kingdom

This impressive **workshop, café and gallery** (☎ 09-406 7172; Far North Rd; 🕑 9am-5pm) on the highway at Awanui is well worth a visit. Here 50,000-year-old kauri stumps, which have been dragged up from swamps, are fashioned into furniture and woodcraft products, with some superb (and expensive) results. A huge upright kauri log has a spiral staircase carved into it that takes you to the mezzanine level.

CAPE REINGA & NINETY MILE BEACH

At the top of the long Aupouri Peninsula, Cape Reinga (116km by road from Kaitaia) is almost at the northern tip of NZ. Standing at the windswept Cape Reinga lighthouse and looking out over the endless ocean has an end-of-the-world feel to it. The lighthouse is still in use, and directly below it is where the waters of the Tasman Sea and Pacific Ocean meet, generating waves up to 10m high in stormy weather. Still visible on the very tip of Cape Reinga is the 800-year-old pohutukawa tree whose roots hide the entrance to the mythical Maori Underworld; see p50. This point is known in Maori legend as Te Rerenga Wairua, where the spirits of the dead depart the earth.

Sights & Activities

From Cape Reinga you can walk along Te Werahi Beach to **Cape Maria van Diemen** which takes about five hours return. Beautiful **Tapotupotu Bay** is a two-hour walk east of Cape Reinga carpark, via Sandy Bay and the cliffs. From Tapotupotu Bay it is about an eight-hour walk to **Kapowairua** at the eastern end of Spirits Bay. Both Tapotupotu Bay and Kapowairua have basic camping grounds (see p168) and there is road access.

The **Aupouri Peninsula** is known to the Maori as Te Hiku o te Ika a Maui (The Tail of Maui's Fish) from the creation legend that tells of how Maui hauled a great fish from the sea, which became the North Island. The peninsula is a rugged, desolate landscape dominated by high sand dunes and flanked by Ninety Mile Beach – if it was metricated to Ninety Kilometre Beach the name would be more accurate.

The **Aupouri Forest**, about 75km long and 5km wide, covers two-thirds of the western side of the peninsula. Kauri forest used to cover the area but now it's mostly pine and planted for commercial timber.

Te Paki Reserves are public land with free access; just leave the gates as you found them and don't disturb the animals. There are about 7 sq km of giant sand dunes on either side of where Te Paki Stream meets the sea. A stop to take flying leaps off the dunes or toboggan down them is a highlight of locally operated tours.

Bus tours (see Tours below) travel along the hard sands of **Ninety Mile Beach** on their way from Kaitaia or Paihia to Cape Reinga, or vice versa, depending on the tides. Private vehicles can also do the beach trip but all hire-car agreements prohibit driving on the beach. The usual access point for vehicles is Waipapakauri, just north of Kaitaia. The beach 'road' is only for the well prepared with rugged vehicles. Cars have

hit soft sand before now and been swallowed by the tides – you may see the roof of an unfortunate vehicle poking through the sands. Check tide times before setting out, avoid it 2½ hours either side of high tide – and watch out for 'quicksand' on Te Paki Stream (keep moving).

Tours

Bus tours go to Cape Reinga from Kaitaia, Mangonui on Doubtless Bay (north of the Bay of Islands), and the Bay of Islands. It makes sense to take the tour from Kaitaia or Doubtless Bay since they are much closer to Cape Reinga and offer a cheaper deal.

Sand Safaris (Map p164; ☎ 0800 869 090, 09-408 1778; www.sandsafaris.co.nz; 221 Commerce St, Kaitaia; adult/child $50/25) in Kaitaia run 28-seater and 31-seater buses up to Cape Reinga including a picnic lunch and a guided tour of Gumdiggers Park.

Harrison's Cape Runner (☎ 0800 227 373, 09-408 1033; 123 North Rd; adult/child $40/20) has 19- to 45-seater buses for day trips that take in the main features of the cape as well as sand tobogganing.

The trips offered by Sand Safaris and Harrison's are pretty similar and include a picnic lunch.

Far North Outback Adventure (☎ 09-408 0927; www.farnorthtours.co.nz) runs small-group, flexible, day-long tours from Kaitaia for $100 per person (minimum two people) including lunch. As well as Cape Reinga, you can visit remote areas such as Great Exhibition Bay and Tauroa Point.

Paradise Connexion (☎ 0800 494 392, 09-406 0460; adult/child $55/25) operates from Mangonui on Doubtless Bay. Also available are personalised 4WD tours (including a seafood lunch and a bottle of wine) for $150 per person (minimum two people).

Fullers, King's Tours, Dune-Rider 4x4, Northern Exposure and Awesome Adventures operate long day trips from the Bay of Islands (see p175).

Marty's Pack or Paddle (☎ 09-409 8445; www.pack orpaddle.co.nz; half-/full-day trips $80/125), at Thom's Landing, offers combined sea kayaking and fishing trips around the superb Parengarenga Harbour. Kayaks can be hired for $55 a day, and sandboarding and horse rides are also available. There's also backpacker accommodation here and two-/three-day all-inclusive adventures cost $175/340.

NORTHLAND

Sleeping & Eating
FAR FAR NORTH
Waitiki Landing Complex (☎ /fax 09-409 7508; camp sites/campervan sites $18/14, dm/cabins $20/55) This accommodation, 21km south of Cape Reinga, is the northernmost in NZ and the road north is gravel. There is a camp kitchen, launderette and hot showers ($1). Waitiki Landing is also the last stop for fuel, and has a shop, liquor store and a restaurant that does good pizzas (medium/large $16/23) and ostrich burgers ($5.50 takeaway or $11 as a sit-down meal). Sandboard hire is $10 for 4 hours ($50 bond). Trips to Cape Reinga ($25 to $45), Te Paki sandboarding ($30), scenic flights, kayaking, fishing and tours to the white silica sand across Parengarenga Harbour ($10) can all be arranged. Drop-offs and pick-ups for hiking trips are possible – for example the three-day hike from Te Paki Stream to Spirits Bay.

North Wind Lodge Backpackers (☎ 09-409 8515; Otaipango Rd, Henderson Bay; dm/tw/d $18/40/50; 🖳) This unusual retreat with turrets is by the ocean, 6km down an unsealed road on the peninsula's east side. It is spacious and modern, and near a great stretch of beach. Boogie boards and sandboards are available to guests.

There are several **DOC camping grounds** (camp sites $10-12) in the Cape Reinga area. There's a site at **Kapowairua** on Spirits Bay, with cold water and limited toilet facilities, and another at **Tapotupotu Bay**, with toilets and showers; neither has electricity. Bring a cooker as fires are not allowed. Both bays have mosquitoes and biting sandflies, so come prepared with repellent. The **Rarawa Beach camping ground**, at the end of Rarawa Beach Rd, 3km north of Ngataki or 10km south of Te Kao, has water and toilet facilities only (no prior bookings, no open fires; open September to April).

PUKENUI
This village, on the highway about 45km north of Kaitaia, is situated on the Houhora Harbour and has shops, a café and a bar. Boats for fishing and cruising can be hired and there are a couple of budget places to stay.

Pukenui Lodge Motel & Youth Hostel (☎ 09-409 8837; pukenui@igrin.co.nz; dm $18, d & tw $45, units $70; 🛒) This YHA-associate backpackers is in a historic house, built in 1891, which has pleasant rooms and overlooks Houhora Harbour. Motel guests can also access a spa pool and the Internet.

Pukenui Farm Backpackers (☎ 09-409 7863; Lamb Rd; camp sites/dm/d $16/13/34) Just 2km down the mostly unsealed Lamb Rd is this modern, comfortable cottage with a six-bed dorm, a twin and double, and a veranda from which you see memorable sunsets. The owners will pick you up from the Pukenui shops, and guests can collect their own vegetables, and take part in farm activities.

Houhora Lodge & Homestay (☎ /fax 09-409 7884; www.topstay.co.nz; 3994 Far North Rd; s/d B&B May-Sep $80/125, Oct-Apr $90/140; 🖳) Rooms in this spacious and stylish architect-designed home, 2km south of the Pukenui village shops, have en suite or private facilities.

AROUND PUKENUI
Wagener Holiday Park & Backpackers (☎ 09-409 8564; www.northlandholiday.co.nz; Houhora Heads; camp sites/campervan sites $20/24, dm, s & d per person $18; 🖳) New accommodation is being built and kayaks, mountain bikes, surfboards and fishing gear can be hired at this beautiful waterfront spot at Houhora Heads, 2km off the main road. The complex includes a café, free local museum and the 15-room **Subritzky Homestead** (☎ 09-406 7298; 3 tours daily $7.50), an 1862 homestead constructed of local swamp kauri set in a pretty garden.

KARIKARI PENINSULA
Karikari Peninsula forms the northwestern end of Doubtless Bay. Roads are mostly sealed and sandy beaches along the peninsula face all directions. There are plenty of holiday homes as well as a luxury golf club and winery but few facilities in this out-of-the-way area.

Rangiputa has lovely white-sand beaches that are easy to reach. A turn-off on the road to Rangiputa takes you to remote **Puheke Beach** with white sand dunes and long, lonely windswept beaches. On the east coast of the peninsula, **Matai Bay** (21km from the turn-off), with its tiny 'twin coves', is the loveliest of the beaches. There is a large **DOC camping ground** (☎ 09-408 6014; camp sites $16) with chemical toilets and cold water.

Just 1km along the road up the peninsula is the **Rockhouse** (☎ 09-406 7151; rockhouse ian@clear.net.nz; r $30), which has unusual but comfortable en suite accommodation and a laid-back host. Meals can be served by arrangement.

Whatuwhiwhi Top 10 Holiday Park (☎ 0800 142 444, 09-408 7202; whatuwhiwhi@xtra.co.nz; Whatuwhiwhi Rd; camp sites $24, cabins $45-55, units $70-200) overlooks a beach, has good facilities and offers kayaks for hire.

Facing a beach on the north side of the peninsula, **Reef Lodge** (☎ 09-408 7100; reeflodge@ clear.net.nz; Rangiputa Beach; studios & units $75-195) has varied accommodation, and the prices vary with the seasons.

DOUBTLESS BAY

The bay gets its unusual name from an entry in Captain Cook's logbook, where he wrote that the body of water was 'doubtless a bay'. Lying east of the Karikari Peninsula, Doubtless Bay has picturesque coves and beaches. The whole area is great for fishing and shellfishing, boating, swimming and other water sports.

The main centre, Mangonui (its name means 'Great Shark'), is a fishing port and has a line of historical buildings along the waterfront that were constructed in the days when it used to be a centre of the whaling industry (1792–1850) and exported flax, kauri wood and gum. Nowadays the buildings are tourist-oriented with cafés, gift shops, high-quality art and craft shops, and accommodation. Stretching west along the bay are the beach resorts of Coopers Beach, Cable Bay and Taipa.

Information

The volunteers in the **Doubtless Bay Information Centre** (☎ 09-406 2046; www.doubtlessbay.com; Waterfront Rd; ⏱ 8am-6pm summer) are helpful and can arrange fishing trips. Internet access is provided by **Mangonui Stationery** (☎ 09-406 0233; 78 Waterfront Rd).

Sights & Activities

Mr Roosevelt (☎ 09-406 1554; www.sailingcharters .nz.co.nz; Mill Bay; per person $75) offers one-day sailing trips on a 12m boat, or overnight cruises further afield for $150 per person (overnight cruises maximum four or six people).

Crystal Coast Seabed Safaris (☎ 09-408 5885; trips $95-135) does dives around pinnacles in Doubtless Bay from $95, and trips to the *Rainbow Warrior* wreck further out near the Cavalli Islands for $135.

From Mangonui, **Paradise Connexion** (☎ 0800 494 392, 09-406 0460; www.paradisenz.co.nz; adult/child $55/25) operates 4WD bus tours up Ninety Mile Beach to Cape Reinga. Also available are personalised 4WD car tours (including a seafood lunch and a bottle of wine) for $150 per person (minimum two people).

A free **Heritage Trail** brochure is a guide to a 3km walk around 18 of the historical buildings in the village. Other walks are to attractive **Mill Bay**, west of Mangonui and **Rangikapiti Pa Historic Reserve**, with ancient Maori terracing and a spectacular view of Doubtless Bay. A walkway runs from Mill Bay to the top of the *pa*.

At Hihi, a 15km drive east of Mangonui, is **Butler Point**. A guided tour around the small **whaling museum** (☎ 09-406 0006; www .butlerpoint.co.nz; adult/child $10/2), an 1843 homestead furnished in the Victorian style, and the gardens is worthwhile. Captain Butler, who built the homestead, left Dorset in England when he was 14 years old and at 24 was captain of a whaling ship. He settled down here in 1839, had 13 children and became a trader, farmer, magistrate and Member of Parliament (MP). You must telephone to arrange a visit.

Swamp Palace Cinema (☎ 09-408 7040; Oruru) shows films regularly but is 7km inland off the main road.

BEACHES

The first beach west of Mangonui is **Coopers Beach**, a fine sweep of sand lined with pohutukawa trees. Coopers Beach is quite developed and has a small shopping centre that includes a shop with diving and fishing gear and a quality restaurant. The next bay along is the less-developed **Cable Bay**, and across the river is **Taipa**, another popular summer destination, which has a fine beach, a harbour where the Taipa River meets the sea, and several motels and motor camps.

Sleeping
BUDGET
Mangonui Hotel (☎ 09-406 0003; fax 09-406 0015; Waterfront Rd; dm $25, d with/without bathroom $80/40) Rooms in this fine 1905 heritage building are upstairs and comfortable with doors onto the veranda and splendid harbour views. Downstairs is a pub and restaurant (see p170).

NORTHLAND

Old Oak Inn (☎ /fax 09-406 0665; 66 Waterfront Rd; dm with/without bathroom $25/20, d & tw with bathroom $80-130, without bathroom $55-80) This inn is in an 1861 kauri building with a backpacker section and smarter accommodation upstairs with good en suite rooms. The pub has seafaring décor and offers bistro meals (roasts $15, steak $20).

Taipa Caravan Park (☎ /fax 09-406 0995; 47 Taipa Point Rd; camp & campervan sites/on-site caravans/cabins $22/35/45) This place is well-positioned on Taipa beach and by the river, but the facilities need improving. Try the cute cabivan ($45).

MID-RANGE

Heaths (☎ 09-406 0088; heaths.bandb@xtra.co.nz; Hihi Rd; s/d May-Oct $65/80, Nov-Apr $80/100) There are great views, kind hosts and meals on request at this B&B, 15km round the harbour from Mangonui on the way to Hihi.

Mac 'n' Mo's (☎ 09-406 0538; MacNMo@xtra.co.nz; 104 Main Rd; s $40, d with/without bathroom $80/70) On SH1 near Coopers Beach, Mac 'n' Mo's is a friendly and long-established B&B with tidy units and views over the harbour from the breakfast balcony.

Flores Cottage (☎ 09-406 1554; 51 Mill Bay Rd; cottage $100-170) This modern self-contained, wood-lined Lockwood house on the waterfront sleeps up to eight, and the owners run sailing trips.

Waterfront Apartments (☎ 09-406 0347; www .mangonuiwaterfront.co.nz; Waterfront Rd; apt winter/ summer $85/120) These apartments on the waterfront have loads of charm and character and each one is different; try to book Rua or Tahi.

Driftwood Lodge (☎ 09-406 0418; Cable Bay; units $95-115, peak season $190-230) These comfortable motel-style units with kitchens are right on the sandy beach at Cable Bay.

Taipa Bay Resort (☎ 09-406 0656; www.taipabay .co.nz; 22 Taipa Point Rd; studios $115-195, 1-bed apt $155-290; 🏊) Pricing is seasonal at these modern holiday units on the sandy beach at Taipa, and beach-facing units are $20 extra. Tennis, table tennis, croquet, volleyball and *pétanque* are all available and there is a spa pool and restaurant which is open for breakfast, lunch and dinner daily in summer and Wednesday to Sunday in winter.

Eating

Mangonui Fish Shop (☎ 09-406 0478; Waterfront Rd; meals $5-50; 🕑 breakfast, lunch & dinner) You can eat outdoors over the water in this licensed and famous fish-and-chip shop, which also sells smoked fish, seafood salads, raw fish and cooked crayfish.

Waterfront Café (☎ 09-406 0850; Waterfront Rd; mains $10-30; 🕑 breakfast, lunch & dinner) This café has fresh fish, seafood laksa, whitebait and lots more.

Café Al Marlin (☎ 09-406 1601; 12 Waterfront Rd; snacks & meals $3-10; 🕑 breakfast & lunch) Light home-cooked meals and snacks are available here.

Pamir (☎ 09-406 0860; Coopers Beach; mains $21-30; 🕑 lunch & dinner daily Dec-Apr, Wed-Sun May-Nov) There's excellent food in this classy restaurant, which tries hard with imaginative Pacific-rim mains and also does Indian meals ($17 to $20), pizzas ($14 to $20) and novelties like Turkish delight cheesecake with a chocolate base.

Slung Anchor Restaurant & Bar (☎ 09-406 1233; 10 Waterfront Rd; lunch mains $12, dinner mains $24-29; 🕑 brunch Sat-Mon, lunch Wed-Sun, dinner Mon & Wed-Sun) The seafood chowder ($13) is popular but sushi, smoked fish, scallops and crayfish are also available.

Mangonui Hotel (☎ 09-406 0003; Waterfront Rd; mains $10-20; 🕑 lunch & dinner) This pleasant restaurant has an ever-changing but good-deal menu that includes T-bone steaks ($20), scallops (five big ones $20) and flounder ($10).

Getting There & Away

InterCity and Northliner buses (see p148) stop at Wilton's BP Garage on Waterfront Road. It's 40 minutes to Kaitaia ($14) and one hour to Kerikeri ($17).

DOUBTLESS BAY TO BAY OF ISLANDS

From Mangonui it's about 44km to Kerikeri via the main highway (SH10), but about halfway along you can make a worthwhile scenic detour to busy Whangaroa Harbour and on to the very picturesque Matauri Bay (a mini Bay of Islands) before rejoining the highway.

Whangaroa Harbour

The small fishing village of Whangaroa is 6km off the main road. **Boyd Gallery** (☎ 09-405 0230; Whangaroa Rd; 🕑 8am-7pm) is the general store but also acts as a tourist information office.

For **game-fishing** (November to May), particularly for marlin, there are plenty

THE BOMBING OF THE RAINBOW WARRIOR

In 1985, a tragic, explosive event in Auckland Harbour made world headlines and put NZ on the map. The Greenpeace flagship *Rainbow Warrior* lay anchored in Auckland Harbour, preparing to sail to Moruroa near Tahiti to protest against French nuclear testing. But it never left Auckland because French saboteurs, in the employ of the French government, attached explosives to the side of the ship and sank her, killing a green campaigner, Fernando Pereira.

It took some time to find out exactly what had happened, but two of the saboteurs were captured, tried and found guilty, although the others have never been brought to justice.

The incident caused an uproar in France – not because the French government had conducted a deliberate and lethal act of terrorism on the soil of a friendly nation, but because the French secret service had bungled the operation and been caught. The French used all their political and economic might to force NZ to release the two saboteurs, and in a farcical turn of events the agents were imprisoned on a French Pacific island as if they had won a trip to Club Med. Within two years, and well before the end of their sentence, they returned to France to receive a hero's welcome.

Northland was the stage for this deadly mission involving several secret service agents. Explosives for the sabotage were delivered by a yacht (which had picked them up from a submarine) from Parengarenga Harbour in the Far North. They were driven to Auckland in a Kombi van by French agents posing as tourists. Bang! An innocent man dead, and international outrage – NZ was in the news.

The skeletal remains of the *Rainbow Warrior* were taken to the waters of Northland's beautiful Cavalli Islands, where it can now be explored by divers. The masts of this oceanic crusader were bought by the museum in Dargaville, where they are displayed outside. The memory of the Portuguese photographer and campaigner who died endures in a peaceful bird hide in Thames. A haunting memorial to the once-proud boat sits atop a Maori *pa* site at Matauri Bay, north of the Bay of Islands.

Attention again focused on the *Rainbow Warrior* in 1995. Ten years after the sinking the French announced they were resuming nuclear testing in the Pacific, and Greenpeace's new flagship bearing the name of its ill-fated predecessor set sail for the Moruroa test site. It entered the exclusion zone only to be stormed by French marines.

of charter boats and prices start at $850 a day.

Seabed Safari (☎ 09-408 5885) is based in Taipa, but runs diving trips out of Whangaroa harbour to the *Rainbow Warrior* ($135) and Doubtless Bay pinnacles ($125) as well as four-day PADI courses ($450).

Contact the owner of **Whangaroa Harbour Retreat** (☎ /fax 09-405 0306; http://whangaroa.tripod.com) for dive equipment hire and dive trips around the Cavalli Islands (including the wreck of the *Rainbow Warrior*), or for crayfish (maximum six) or scallops (maximum 20).

Snow Cloud (☎ 09-405 0523; day trips $80), an 11m yacht, makes day trips to the Cavalli Islands, where there are excellent beaches, diving spots, snorkelling opportunities and walks.

Sea Eagle (☎ 09-405 1963) is a large and comfortable 15m sailing boat that does harbour cruises for $45 and day trips with

lunch for $80. Overnight trips are possible (minimum four people) as well as diving and diving instruction.

An excellent 30-minute **hike** starts from the carpark at the end of Hospital Road and goes up **St Paul's Rock** (213m) which dominates the village. During the last part you have to use a wire cable to pull yourself up, but the views from the top make it worth the effort.

The Wairakau track north to Pekapeka Bay begins near the church hall on Campbell Rd in Totara North on the other side of the bay. The two-hour hike passes through farmland, hills and shoreline before arriving at DOC's **Lane Cove Cottage** (☎ 09-407 8474; per person Mon-Thu/Fri-Sun $10/12) which is a hut with 16 beds, cold showers and composting toilets. You need to bring your own cooker and no camping is permitted.

Up the hill in Whangaroa **Sunseeker Lodge** (☎ 09-405 0496; www.sunseekerlodge.co.nz; Old Hospital

Rd; dm/d & tw/units $20/50/90; 🖥) has friendly staff, a spa bath with a view, hires out kayaks ($20 a day) and will pick-up from Kaeo on SH10. The rooms in **Marlin Hotel** (☎ 09-405 0347; s/tw/d $50/55/60) are not en suite but are pleasant enough, and bar meals and drinks are available downstairs. **Whangaroa Motel** (☎ /fax 09-405 0022; whangaroamotel@xtra.co.nz; Church St; units winter/summer $70/90) is up the hill and the owner runs fishing trips.

On the main road north of the turn-off to Whangaroa, **Kahoe Farm Hostel** (☎ 09-405 1804; www.kahoefarms.co.nz; dm $20, s $35-40, d & tw $50; 🖥) is a smart place which serves up legendary pizzas and pasta and has kayaks, table soccer and a soccer pitch.

Located about 3km before Whangaroa wharf **Whangaroa Harbour Retreat** (☎ /fax 09-405 0306; http://whangaroa.tripod.com; camp sites/ campervan sites $24/27, cabins $42-50, cabins Dec-Feb $60-80; 🐾) has a small store and the owner hires out snorkelling and diving equipment and can organise boat charters.

Visitors are welcome to the bar and dining room of the **Big Game-fish Club** (☎ 09-405 0399; ⏱ 4.30-11pm daily summer, 4.30-11pm Thu-Sun winter).

Tauranga & Matauri Bays

For a drive passing beautiful bays and beaches, head back out of Whangaroa and turn east towards Tauranga Bay and Te Ngaire. The highlight is Matauri Bay, with the 17 Cavalli Islands scattered offshore and a sandy beach with surf. On top of the far headland is a monument to the *Rainbow Warrior* which was deliberately sunk off one of the islands and is a popular dive site. See p171 for more on the *Rainbow Warrior* story. Matauri Bay is about 25km from Whangaroa and it's another 18km back to SH10.

Based on the coast past Tauranga Bay **Northland Sea Kayaking** (☎ 09-405 0381; north landseakayaking@xtra.co.nz; tours per day $60) offers kayak tours to explore this magical coastline of bays, sea caves and islands. Accommodation is available for $10 extra and pick-up from Kaeo can be arranged.

There is accommodation at **Tauranga Bay Holiday Park** (☎ /fax 09-405 0436; www.tauranga bay.co.nz; camp sites $20, campervan sites $24, cabins $40-60), which is on the picturesque, sandy beach, but the park lacks trees. **Tauranga Bay Motel** (☎ 09-405 0222; etbmotel@ihug.co.nz; units

winter/summer $60/100) is clean and units have kitchens.

Also on a great beach is **Matauri Bay Holiday Park** (☎ /fax 09-405 0525; matauribayhp@act rix.co.nz; camp sites/campervan sites $24/27) and there is a shop with a liquor licence and a petrol station on the site.

At the end of the beach road at Matauri Bay, **Oceans Holiday Village** (☎ /fax 09-405 0417; www.matauribay.co.nz/oceans; units & lodges Apr-Nov $88-150, Dec-Mar $150-210) has cute cottages on their own little cove beach. Facilities include a bar and restaurant, and kayaks and dinghies are available.

BAY OF ISLANDS

Long famed for its stunning coastal scenery, the Bay of Islands is one of NZ's major attractions. The bay is punctuated by dozens of coves and when the sun is shining its clear waters range in hue from turquoise to deep blue. Although a hugely popular tourist and sailing destination, the 150 or so islands have thankfully escaped development; townships are all on the mainland.

The Bay of Islands is also of enormous historical significance. As the site of NZ's first permanent English settlement, it is the birthplace of European colonisation. It was here that the Treaty of Waitangi was drawn up and first signed by 46 Maori chiefs in 1840; the treaty remains the linchpin of race relations in NZ today (see p29).

Paihia is the hub of the Bay of Islands. Though only a small town, its population swells dramatically in summer and it has all the trappings of a thriving tourist centre. Waitangi National Reserve, with its historic Treaty House, is within walking distance.

Only a short passenger-ferry ride away, Russell has all the charm and character that Paihia lacks. Though also a popular side trip for Bay of Islands tourists, historic Russell is a smaller, sleepier town with many fine old buildings and a delightful waterfront.

To the north Kerikeri, famous for its orchards and outdoor Mediterranean-style cafés, is much less touristy, but still has a few attractions and a great deal of history.

Activities & Tours

The Bay of Islands has a mind-boggling array of activities and tours and it seems

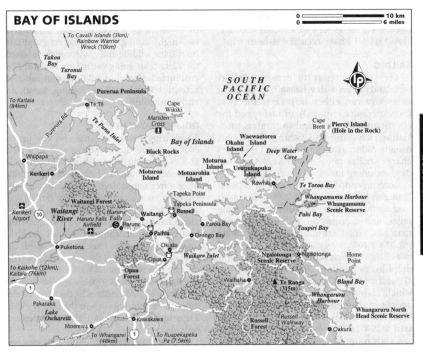

BAY OF ISLANDS

0 — 10 km
0 — 6 miles

like everyone is trying to sell you one. Many are water-based to make the most of the splendid natural surroundings. It's a competitive business and backpacker discounts are available for many activities and tours. Hostels can book all tours and can generally arrange cheap deals. Most of the following depart from Paihia, but pick-ups from Kerikeri can be arranged and most of the cruises call in at Russell.

CRUISING
You can't leave the Bay of Islands without taking some sort of cruise and there are plenty of operators keen to get you on board. They are dominated by the 'big two': **Fullers** (☎ 09-402 7422; www.fullers-bay-of-islands.co.nz) and **Kings Tours & Cruises** (☎ 0800 222 979, 09-402 8288; www.kings-tours.co.nz). There are also smaller operators, as well as sailing and fishing boat charters.

Fullers' **Cream Trip** (adult/child $85/45) is a day trip (10am to 4pm) which started back in 1920 when one Captain Lane picked up dairy products from the many farms around the bay. As more roads were built and the small

dairy farms closed, it became a mail delivery service. It is now part of the 'Supercruise', which incorporates the Hole in the Rock off Cape Brett, passing through it if conditions are right, and a one-hour stopover on Urupukapuka Island where Westerns writer Zane Grey went big-game fishing, and a tourist submarine, the **Nautilus** (adult/child $12/6), is submerged.

Other Fullers cruises include the **Hole in the Rock** (adult/child $62/31), with a stopover on Urupukapuka Island. The tour lasts four hours with one hour on the island.

Kings has a **Day in the Bay cruise** (adult/child $85/50), which combines the Cream Trip route and the Hole in the Rock with dolphin swimming. It also runs a **scenic cruise** (adult/child $60/30) that includes dolphin-watching and Maori culture.

JETBOATING
Also very popular are the high-speed Hole in the Rock trips on board a **jetboat** – good fun and handy if you're short on time. Put on the waterproof gear provided and fasten your seatbelts! **Excitor** (☎ 09-402 7020;

www.excitor.co.nz; adult/child $65/33) and **Mack Attack** (☎ 0800 622 528, 09-402 8180; www.mackattack.co.nz; adult/child $65/33) have regular 1½-hour trips.

SAILING

A very pleasant way to explore the Bay of Islands is on a day **sailing** trip. In most cases you can either help crew the boat (no experience required), or just spend the afternoon sunbathing and swimming, snorkelling, kayaking and fishing. The boats usually call in at various islands. Operators charge similar rates: $80 to $120 for a full day, including lunch.

Recommended boats include the **R Tucker Thompson** (☎ 0800 882 537, 09-402 8430; www.tucker .co.nz; adult/child $95/45) which offers a barbecue lunch and a cruise on a classic schooner that has sailed around the world; **Carino** (☎ 09-402 8040; www.sailinganddolphin.co.nz; adult/ child $70/35) which combines sailing and dolphin swimming; **Phantom** (☎ 0800 224 421; adult/child $80/40), a fast 50ft ocean racer, which claims to offer the best lunch (10 people maximum); **Gungha** (☎ 0800 478 900, 09-407 7930; adult $75), a 65ft maxi yacht; **Straycat** (☎ 09-402 6130; adult/child $75/45), a catamaran with room for 16 passengers; and **She's a Lady** (☎ 0800 724 584; www.bay-of-islands.com; adult $80), on which you can try your hand at kneeboarding or tubing.

If you're interested in learning to sail, **Great Escape Yacht Charters** (☎ 09-402 7143; www .greatescape.co.nz), based in Opua, has lessons, including a five-day course ($450) with training for two days after which you are on your own. One-day courses cost $140 and two-day courses are $260. Yachts can be hired for $70 to $390 a day.

OVERNIGHT CRUISES

The cheapest way to spend a possibly romantic night on the water is aboard the **Rock** (☎ 0800 762 527; www.rocktheboat.co.nz; 24hr cruises $140), an unlikely looking vessel set up for backpackers. A double room costs an extra $15 per person. The Rock was a vehicle ferry in a former life but now it's a comfortable floating hostel with four-bed dorms, twin and double rooms, and (of course) a bar. The cruise departs at about 5pm and includes an excellent barbecue and seafood dinner with live music, then a full day spent cruising around and visiting islands, fishing, kayaking, snorkelling and swimming.

Ecocruz (☎ 0800 432 627; www.ecocruz.co.nz; cruises dm/d $450/530) is a recommended three-day/ two-night sailing cruise with an emphasis on marine wildlife and environment, aboard the 72ft ocean-going yacht *Manawanui*. The cost includes accommodation, all meals and activities which include fishing, kayaking and snorkelling.

DOLPHIN SWIMMING

These trips operate all year and you get to cruise around the islands as well as watch and swim with the dolphins. They have a high success rate, and operators generally offer a free trip if dolphins are not sighted. Dolphin swims are subject to weather and sea conditions, with restrictions if the dolphins have young. As well as encountering bottlenose and common dolphins, whales, orcas and penguins may be seen. With all operators a portion of the cost goes towards marine research, via DOC.

Dolphin Discoveries (☎ 09-402 8234; dolphin@ igrin.co.nz; adult/child $95/50) was the first to do dolphin-swimming trips in the bay in 1991. Trips last 3½ hours and all equipment is provided.

Dolphin Adventures (☎ 09-402 6985; www.awe someadventures.co.nz; adult/child $95/50) has similar trips with an option to spend time on Urupukapuka Island.

Kings Cruises (☎ 09-402 8288; www.dolphincruises .co.nz; adult/child $85/50) runs dolphin-swimming trips daily that include boom netting. See p173 earlier for more information on Kings Cruises.

SEA KAYAKING

There are plenty of opportunities for kayaking around the bay, either on a guided tour or by renting a kayak and going it alone.

Coastal Kayakers (☎ 09-402 8105; www.coastal kayakers.co.nz; Te Karuwha Pde) runs a half-day guided tour for $50 per person ($70 for a full day), and a two-day budget harbour wilderness tour is $110. A minimum of two people is required. Kayaks can be rented for $28 (half-day) or $40 (full day).

New Zealand Sea Kayak Adventures (☎ 09-402 8596; nzakayak@clear.net.nz; 2-/3-/6-day trips $175/250/ 900) runs kayaking and camping trips and also has a day trip for $125 including lunch.

Island Kayaks (☎ 09-402 6078; Marsden Rd; trips $60) operates from **Bay Beach Hire** (☎ 09-402 6078; Marsden Rd; trips $50).

SCUBA DIVING

The Bay of Islands offers some fine subtropical diving and local operators all go out to the wreck of the *Rainbow Warrior* off the Cavalli Islands, about an hour from Paihia by boat.

Paihia Dive (☎ 0800 107 551, 09-402 7551; www .divenz.com; Williams Rd) offers *Rainbow Warrior* dive trips ($175 for two dives including gear) or you can do two adventure dives for the same price. Dive courses start at $210.

Dive North (☎ 09-402 7079; divenorth@xtra.co.nz) also has trips to the *Rainbow Warrior* and other popular dive sites such as Deep Water Cove and Cape Brett.

SURFING

NZ Surf Tours (☎ /fax 09-832 9622; www.newzealand surftours.com; $400) based in Auckland runs a three-day surfing course from Tuesday to Thursday at surf beaches near the Bay of Islands and includes meals, transport, surfboards, wet suits and lessons.

OTHER ACTIVITIES

The Bay of Islands is noted for its **fishing** and charter boats can be booked at the Maritime Building in Paihia (see p176) or at Russell wharf.

Bay of Islands Skydive Centre (☎ 0800 427 593, 09-402 6744) operates from the Haruru Falls airport. A tandem skydive costs $270, a video of it is $125, and a video and photographs cost $150.

Skywalk (☎ 021-415 556; skywalk@igrin.co.nz; 20-30min $150) offers passenger flights in a motorised hang glider that takes off from Haruru Falls airfield. You can learn to fly it yourself for $580.

Bay Beach Hire (☎ 09-402 6078; www.baybeach hire.co.nz; Marsden Rd, Paihia; ☉ 9am-5.30pm) hires out just about everything: kayaks ($35 half-day), small sailing catamarans ($125), mountain bikes ($15 half-day), boogie boards, fishing rods, wet suits and snorkelling gear. Guided kayak tours and overnight kayak tours are available. Bay Beach Hire also runs **Flying Kiwi Parasail** (☎ 09-402 6078; www.parasail-nz.co.nz; trips $75) which organises one-hour parasailing trips leaving from Paihia wharf hourly during summer.

Air Torn Kiteboarding (☎ 09-402 6236; www.air torn.co.nz) is a relatively new sport where the drag from a kite (a mini-parachute really) propels you along on a surfboard.

Described as the next big thing after windsurfing, you can get a full course of instruction on how to fly the kite and control the board for $400.

Salt Air (☎ 09-402 8338; www.saltair.co.nz) has scenic flights ranging from a 30-minute tour of the Bay of Islands ($95 per person) to a five-hour flight-and-4WD tour to Cape Reinga and Ninety Mile Beach ($330). Helicopter flights out to the Hole in the Rock and Cape Brett cost $170.

Paihia Duck (☎ 09-402 8681; www.paihiaduck.co.nz; adult/child $45/25) is a one-hour tour with a difference on an amphibious bus that leaves Paihia at 9am, 11am, 1.30pm and 3.30pm up to Waitangi, then across the water to Opua and back to Paihia.

Big Rock Springs Trail Rides (☎ 09-401 9923; half-/full-day ride $55/80) is in Okaihau, northwest of Paihia, but will pick up in Paihia. The full-day ride includes a river swim on horseback.

CAPE REINGA TOURS

It's cheaper and easier to do trips to Cape Reinga and Ninety Mile Beach from Kaitaia or Doubtless Bay if you're heading up that way. However, if you're short on time, it's possible to do a long day trip (10 to 12 hours) from the Bay of Islands with several operators. They're all pretty similar bus tours, driving one way along Ninety Mile Beach, with visits to Puketi forest, sandboarding on the dunes and other places on the way, but check the stops and whether lunch is included.

Awesome Adventures (☎ 09-402 6985; www.awe someadventures.co.nz; Maritime Building, Paihia; trips $95) has backpacker-oriented trips with sandboarding on the 85m dunes, swimming at Tapotupotu Bay and a visit to Puketi kauri forest.

Dune-Rider 4X4 (☎ 09-402 8681; www.dunerider .co.nz; adult/child $90/50) is popular among backpackers and younger travellers. The smaller group trips (20-seater buses) make plenty of stops for sandboarding and swimming.

Northern Exposure (☎ 0800 573 875, 09-402 8644; trips $85) also aims its trips at backpackers; for instance no children are allowed.

Fullers (☎ 09-402 7422; adult/child $95/50, trips with BBQ lunch $110/65) has all-day trips departing from Paihia and Kerikeri.

King's Tours (☎ 0800 222 979, 09-402 8288; adult/ child $90/50) has coach tours (no lunch).

NORTHLAND

Festivals & Events

Tall Ship Race (January) This takes place in Russell.

Waitangi Day (6 February) Various ceremonial events at Waitangi.

Country Music Festival (May) This is held over the second weekend.

Jazz & Blues Festival (August) Held over the second weekend.

Weekend Coastal Classic (October) Held during Labour Weekend, this is NZ's largest yacht race from Auckland to the Bay of Islands.

Wine & Food Festival (November) This popular festival is held in early November in Waimate.

Getting There & Away

AIR

Air New Zealand (☎ 0800 737 000 24hr; www.airnz .co.nz; one-way fares $70-250) operates three to four flights daily from Auckland to nearby Kerikeri.

BUS

All buses serving Paihia arrive at and depart from the Maritime Building by the wharf. InterCity and Northliner (see p148) have buses daily from Auckland to the Bay of Islands, via Whangarei. Paihia to Kerikeri ($10) takes 20 minutes, Paihia to Kaitaia ($29) takes two hours and 40 minutes, and Paihia to Auckland ($44) takes four hours.

Getting Around

Passenger ferries connect Paihia with Russell, running from around 7am to 7pm (to 10pm from October to June). Ferries operate on average every 20 minutes from Russell to Paihia in summer. The adult/child fare is $5/2.50 one way.

To get to Russell with your car, you have to drive down to Opua and cross to Okiato Point using the car ferry (see p183), or drive another 40km along mainly gravel roads via Waihaha.

There's also a **water taxi** (☎ 09-403 8823) for getting around the bay islands. For bicycle hire visit **Bay Beach Hire** (☎ 09-402 6078; Marsden Rd) in Paihia.

PEWHAIRANGI

This park consists of 40 separate areas which extend from Whangamumu Harbour in the south to Whangaroa in the north. Diverse hikes cover islands, *pa* sites and some spectacular scenery. The **DOC Pewhairangi Bay of Islands visitors centre** (☎ 09-

403 9003; www.doc.govt.nz; The Strand; ☺ 9am-4.30pm winter, 9am-5pm summer) in Russell can provide information.

The **Cape Brett hike** is famous but costs $30 on top of the cost of the **hut** (☎ 09-403 9003; per adult per night $12); see p187 for details.

Camping (☎ 09-403 9003; camp sites $12) is permitted at two other bays on **Urupukapuka Island**. Cable and Urupukapuka Bays have water supplies, cold showers and composting toilets but you need to bring food, a stove and fuel.

Zane Grey's Restaurant & Bar (☎ 09-403 7009; zanegrey@xtra.co.nz; mains $12-25; ☺ breakfast, lunch & dinner) at Otehei Bay also provides **accommodation** (camp sites $24, dm/d cabins/d cabins with bathroom per person $20/15/25). There's a small store and craft shop and kayaks can be hired ($10 an hour). Hikes on the island range up to five hours.

To get to Urupukapuka Island, take a **water taxi** (☎ 09-403 8823) or a Fullers tour boat, get off at Otehei Bay and arrange to catch the boat back on the day you want to return.

PAIHIA & WAITANGI

pop 7250

Paihia was first settled by Europeans as a mission station in 1823 with the arrival of Reverend Henry Williams. Paihia has a very pretty setting and is now a tourist town with countless activity and accommodation options.

Adjoining Paihia to the north is Waitangi, the site of the historic signing on 6 February 1840 of the treaty between mainly local Maori chiefs and the representatives of Queen Victoria's government. The treaty then toured the country and many other chiefs added their signatures or marks.

Information

The **Bay of Islands visitors centre** (☎ 09-402 7345; visitorinfo@fndc.govt.nz; ☺ 8am-5pm winter, 8am-late summer) is near the ferry launch and terminal. Alongside is the Maritime Building where Fullers, Kings, Awesome Adventures and other tour and activity companies have offices. Buses (see p176) stop outside.

Internet access is available in the **Maritime Building** (Marsden Rd; $6 per hr) and at **Boots Off Travellers Centre** (☎ 09-402 6632; Selwyn Rd; $9 per hr).

The **Post Shop** (☎ 09-402 7800; Shop 2, Williams Rd; ☺ 8am-5.30pm Mon-Fri, 8am-2pm Sat) will sell

PAIHIA & WAITANGI

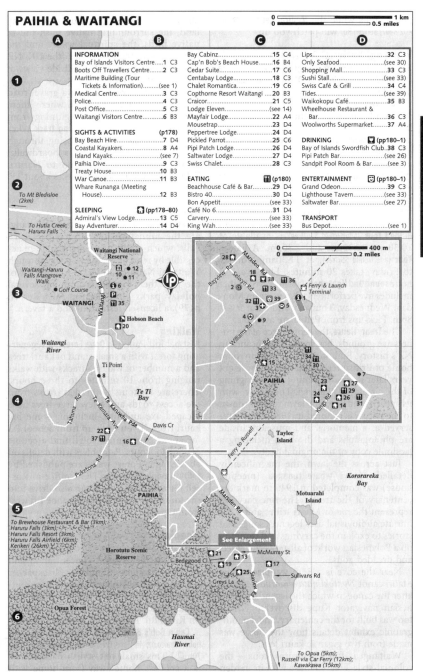

INFORMATION	
Bay of Islands Visitors Centre.....1	C3
Boots Off Travellers Centre......2	C3
Maritime Building (Tour Tickets & Information).........(see 1)	
Medical Centre.........................3	C3
Police....................................4	C3
Post Office.............................5	C3
Waitangi Visitors Centre..........6	B3

SIGHTS & ACTIVITIES	(p178)
Bay Beach Hire.......................7	D4
Coastal Kayakers.....................8	A4
Island Kayaks........................(see 7)	
Paihia Dive............................9	C3
Treaty House........................10	B3
War Canoe...........................11	B3
Whare Runanga (Meeting House)................................12	B3

SLEEPING	(pp178–80)
Admiral's View Lodge............13	C5
Bay Adventurer.....................14	D4

Bay Cabinz...........................15	C4
Cap'n Bob's Beach House......16	B4
Cedar Suite..........................17	C6
Centabay Lodge....................18	C3
Chalet Romantica..................19	C6
Copthorne Resort Waitangi ...20	B3
Craicor................................21	C5
Lodge Eleven......................(see 14)	
Mayfair Lodge......................22	A4
Mousetrap...........................23	D4
Peppertree Lodge.................24	D4
Pickled Parrot......................25	C6
Pipi Patch Lodge...................26	D4
Saltwater Lodge....................27	D4
Swiss Chalet.........................28	C3

EATING	(p180)
Beachhouse Café & Bar..........29	D4
Bistro 40.............................30	D4
Bon Appetit.........................(see 33)	
Café No 6............................31	D4
Carvery...............................(see 33)	
King Wah.............................(see 33)	

Lips.....................................32	C3
Only Seafood......................(see 30)	
Shopping Mall......................33	C3
Sushi Stall...........................(see 33)	
Swiss Café & Grill 34	C4
Tides...................................(see 39)	
Waikokopu Café...................35	B3
Wheelhouse Restaurant & Bar.................................36	C3
Woolworths Supermarket........37	A4

DRINKING	(pp180–1)
Bay of Islands Swordfish Club..38	C3
Pipi Patch Bar.....................(see 26)	
Sandpit Pool Room & Bar.....(see 3)	

ENTERTAINMENT	(pp180–1)
Grand Odeon.......................39	C3
Lighthouse Tavern...............(see 33)	
Saltwater Bar......................(see 27)	

TRANSPORT	
Bus Depot...........................(see 1)	

NORTHLAND

you stamps while the **Medical Centre** (☎ 09-402 8407; Selwyn Rd) will patch you up.

Waitangi National Reserve

A visit to the **Waitangi National Reserve** (☎ 09-402 7437; adult/child $10/free; 9am-6pm) is definitely a must for every itinerary. The **visitors centre** here shows an interesting 15-minute audiovisual that is played every half-hour from 9am. The centre also has a gallery of portraits, Maori weaponry and a gift shop.

A 30-minute **He Toho** (Cultural Performance; adult/child $10/free) takes place at 11.30am, 1.30pm and 2.30pm and includes *poi* (a women's formation dance that involves singing and manipulating a ball of woven flax), the *haka* (war dance), songs and dances. A **Maori guided tour** (adult/child $10/free) is available at 10.30am, 12.30pm and 2.30pm. A **Garden Tour** (adult/child $5/free), at 11.30am Monday to Friday, takes 20 minutes. Finally a 1½-hour **sound and light show** (adult/child $45/23) that includes live performers takes place on Monday, Wednesday, Thursday and Saturday at 8pm. Pick-ups from Paihia are available.

The **Treaty House**, the centrepiece of the impressive grounds, has special significance in NZ's history. Built in 1832 as the four-room home of British resident James Busby, eight years later it was the setting for the signing of the Treaty of Waitangi. The house, with its gardens and beautiful lawn running down to the bay, was restored in 1989 and is preserved as a memorial and museum. Inside are photographs and displays, including a facsimile copy of the original treaty.

Just across the lawn, the magnificently detailed Maori **whare runanga** (meeting house) was completed in 1940 to mark the centenary of the treaty. The fine carvings represent the major Maori tribes and a 15-minute audiovisual uses legends, songs and stories to explain the carvings and summon up a Polynesian world of all-powerful chiefs and dreaded gods.

Near the cove is a 35m **war canoe** – the Maori canoe *Ngatokimatawhaorua* – named after the canoe in which the legendary Polynesian navigator Kupe discovered NZ. It too was built for the centenary, and a photographic exhibit details how the canoe was made from two gigantic kauri logs.

Waitangi is full of cultural icons – the colonial-style Treaty House with its garden and lawns transplanted from a far away land, the surrounding native bush full of native birds, the spiritual *whare* and the warlike *waka*, the three flags (the UK, NZ and Maori flags), and the hillside views of a still-beautiful land.

Beyond the Treaty House a gravel road climbs Mt Bledisloe, from where there are commanding views. Beginning from the visitors carpark, a **walking track** takes off through the reserve, passing through the mangrove forest (over a boardwalk) around Hutia Creek and on to Haruru Falls. The walk to the falls takes about 1½ hours each way.

Haruru Falls

A few kilometres upstream from Waitangi are the miniature but attractive Haruru Falls, which are lit up at night and are accessible by road or via the walkway through Waitangi National Reserve. At the foot of the falls there's good swimming, several holiday parks (see Haruru Falls Resort, p179), a licensed restaurant and a tavern.

Walking

Just behind Paihia is **Opua Forest**, a regenerating forest with a small stand of kauri trees and a number of walking tracks with walks ranging from 10 minutes to three hours. There are lookouts up graded tracks from the access roads and a few large trees have escaped axe and fire, including some big kauri trees. If you walk up from School Rd for about 20 minutes, you'll find a couple of good lookouts. Pamphlets with details on all the Opua Forest walks are published by DOC (available at the DOC office in Russell for around $1). You can also drive into the forest by taking the Oromahoe Rd west from Opua.

Sleeping

BUDGET

Paihia has the greatest concentration and arguably the highest standard of backpacker hostels in Northland and some offer mid-range accommodation too; all make discount bookings for activities and most are on Kings Rd, Paihia's 'backpackers row'.

Cap'n Bob's Beach House (☎ 09-402 8668; capnbobs@xtra.co.nz; 44 Davis Cres; dm/d & tw/units $21/50/70;) This small but stylish backpackers is a spotless home-away-from-home with a hard-working owner, views from the veranda and a touch of luxury.

Bay Adventurer (☎ 09-402 5162; www.bayadventurer.co.nz; 28 Kings Rd; dm $20, d $55-85, studio $75-95, 1-bed apt $125-165; 🖳 🐾) A new, large and smart-to-luxurious establishment with a spa pool and good, very clean facilities, Bay Adventurer has comfy mattresses with linen included and free bikes.

Centabay Lodge (☎ 09-402 7466; www.centabay.co.nz; 27 Selwyn Rd; dm/d & tw/d & tw with bathroom/units $20/49/59/65; 🖳) This lodge is just behind the shops and the friendly owners maintain a high standard. The spa pool and kayaks are free, and the en suite rooms are a good deal.

Peppertree Lodge (☎ /fax 09-402 6122; www.peppertree.co.nz; 15 Kings Rd; dm $20-22, d & tw $60, units $75-85; 🖳) All rooms are heated and en suite in this clean, modern hostel which has free kayaks and bicycles.

Mousetrap (☎ 09-402 8182; www.mousetrap.co.nz; 11 Kings Rd; dm $19-22, d & tw $50-55; 🖳) There are plenty of small chill-out areas in this nautical-themed, natural-wood décor hostel where a mixed bag of rooms have wardrobes and central heating.

Pickled Parrot (☎ 0508 727 768, 09-402 6222; theparrot@paradise.net.nz; Greys Lane; camp sites $32, dm per person $20-22, d & tw per person $25-26; 🖳) Breakfast, free bikes and fishing rods are included in the price at this laid-back backpackers that is in a pleasant garden setting. The parrot nips.

Lodge Eleven (☎ /fax 09-402 7487; lodgeeleven@hotmail.com; cnr Kings Rd & MacMurray St; dm/d & tw $20/60; 🖳) This YHA-associate hostel is a converted motel and the rooms are all en suite, with bedding and heating, but the communal areas are not as good as the rooms.

Pipi Patch Lodge (☎ 09-402 7111; pipipatch@acb.co.nz; 18 Kings Rd; dm/d & tw/d & tw with bathroom $22/60/80; 🖳 🐾) This backpackers, popular with tour groups, has eight-bed dorms

(which are en suite with a sink and a fridge), a spa and the world's tiniest swimming pool. It's a party place with a bar (see p180).

Mayfair Lodge (☎ 09-402 7471; mayfair.lodge@xtra.co.nz; 7 Puketona Rd; camp sites $24, dm per person $20-22, s $40, d & tw $50; 🖳) This small, friendly backpackers is clean and colourful but a bit out of town.

MID-RANGE
Chalet Romantica (☎ /fax 09-402 8270; chalet-romantica@xtra.co.nz; 1 Bedggood Close; d with bathroom $115-165, apt $115-220; 🐾) A Swiss breakfast is included along with an indoor spa and gym in this luxury B&B. Try the loft for a romantic bird's-eye view.

Craicor (☎ 09-402 7882; www.craicor-accom.co.nz; 49 Kings Rd; units $120) This deluxe private accommodation is out in the wonderful garden and the price is negotiable in winter.

Cedar Suite (☎ 09-402 8516; fax 09-402 8555; 5 Sullivans Rd; studio ste from $85, B&B $95, ste with spa $120) Cedar Suite boasts a range of self-contained and B&B accommodation in a lovely, secluded bush setting.

Admiral's View Lodge (☎ 0800 247 234, 09-402 6236; www.admiralsviewlodge.co.nz; 2 McMurray St; studios $115-135, apt $175-250; 🖳) This refurbished lodge offers smart units, continental brekkie (included in the price) in the galley and free bikes and tennis.

Swiss Chalet (☎ 09-402 7615; www.swisschalet motel.co.nz; 3 Bayview Rd; studios & 1-/2-bed units $75-170/145-220; 🖳) This Swiss-style motel has a spa, Sky TV and good clean rooms with balconies.

Bay Cabinz (☎ 09-402 8534; www.baycabinz.co.nz; 32-34 School Rd; units $70-125; 🖳) The self-contained units are comfortable with decks and views.

Haruru Falls Resort (☎ 0800 757 525, 09-402 7525; resort@onenz.co.nz; Old Wharf Rd; camp sites/campervan sites $22-28, studios $90-110, units $100-130; 🐾 🖳) This resort has smart units with a bar, restaurant and a view of the Haruru Falls, which

---

AUTHOR'S CHOICE

Saltwater Lodge (☎ 0800 002 266, 09-402 7075; www.saltwaterlodge.co.nz; 14 Kings Rd; dm $21-23, d & tw $100-115; 🖳) This is an excellent, large, five-star, purpose-built backpackers. All rooms are en suite and heated with bedding and lockers, and dorms have four to six beds. There are large balconies, a lift for the disabled, a bar (see p180), all the usual facilities and free kayaks, bicycles and tennis racquets. A special feature is the gym which has a variety of weights. The dorms are a better deal than the pricey private rooms, but the private rooms are reduced when things are quiet.

NORTHLAND

Swiss Café & Grill (☎ 09-402 6701; 48 Marsden Rd; mains $17-24; ☺ dinner) This unpretentious but excellent European-style restaurant on the waterfront has indoor and outdoor options, and candles add a romantic touch. The wide-ranging and eclectic menu includes BBQ prawns, a hearty Swiss farmhouse plate and chocolate fondue. The owner works hard yet continues to smile, and the service is unbeatable.

is lit up at night. Fishing and diving trips can be arranged.

TOP END
Copthorne Resort Waitangi (☎ 09-402 7411; www .copthornebayofislands.co.nz; Tau Henare Dr; rooms winter $130-150, summer $150-170; ☐ ☒) A smart resort in Waitangi with low-rise units which are a good deal in summer. It has a bar and restaurant ($35 buffet).

Eating
RESTAURANTS
Only Seafood (☎ 09-402 6066; Upstairs, 40 Marsden Rd; mains $21-28; ☺ dinner) This is the place to go for local seafood, including fish, mussels, oysters and scallops.

Bistro 40 (☎ 09-402 7444; 40 Marsden Rd; mains $24-27; ☺ dinner winter, lunch & dinner summer) Downstairs from Only Seafood, Bistro 40 offers items such as venison and oyster pie, steaks and fish.

Tides (☎ 09-402 7557; Williams Rd; lunch mains $7-17, dinner mains $16-25; ☺ breakfast, lunch & dinner) Tides provides light but tasty meals with daily seafood specials.

Wheelhouse Restaurant & Bar (☎ 09-402 6281; Paihia Wharf; dinner mains $18-25; ☺ breakfast, lunch & dinner) The star at Wheelhouse, near the wharf, is the large aquarium, so you can watch the fish swim while you eat seafood (or drink).

Lips (☎ 09-402 7185; 14 Selwyn Rd; mains $18-24; ☺ breakfast, lunch & dinner) A café during the day Lips becomes a quality restaurant in the evening.

CAFÉS & QUICK EATS
Beachhouse Café & Bar (☎ 09-402 7345; 16 Kings Rd; ☺ breakfast, lunch & dinner, bar till 1am) This lively

place has fresh juices for $5.50, gourmet burgers for $6 to $10, all-day breakfasts, big beer glasses, and a DJ (Friday) live music (Saturday), and a jam session (Sunday).

Café No 6 (☎ 09-402 6797; 6 Marsden Rd; mains $11-20; ☺ breakfast, lunch & dinner; ☐) An informal café that serves mainly Mediterranean food including tapas and ciabatta bread but occasionally Bavarian meatballs sneak onto the menu.

Waikokopu Café (☎ 09-402 6275; Treay Ground, Waitangi; lunch mains $14, dinner mains $22-26; ☺ breakfast & lunch year-round, dinner summer) This excellent café near the Waitangi visitors centre offers deli snacks and light meals. You can sit inside or outside on a deck that borders a pond.

The Shopping Mall is the place for cheap eats. **Bon Appetit** (☎ 09-402 7867; ☺ lunch & dinner) offers lasagne ($4.50), seafood soup ($3) and a buffet selection ($12 for a large plastic container). Next door is a **carvery** (☺ lunch Mon-Sat, dinner Mon-Fri) that serves meat and salad rolls for $6 and meals for $12, and nearby is a **sushi stall** ($6.90 a packet) and **King Wah's** (☎ 09-402 7566; ☺ lunch & dinner) Chinese buffet dinner ($24).

Self-caterers can buy supplies at **Woolworth's Supermarket** (☎ 09 402 5524; 6 Puketona Rd; ☺ 7am-10pm).

Drinking & Entertainment
Saltwater Bar (☎ 09-402 7783; 14 Kings Rd; ☺ noon-1am) This bar at the Saltwater Lodge (p179) serves popular pizzas and has a shuffleboard and nightly karaoke, bar games and quizzes.

Pipi Patch Bar (☎ 09-402 7111; 18 Kings Rd; ☺ 5pm-midnight) This bar at Pipi Patch Lodge (p179) has a DJ on Saturday, Wild Wednesdays, a moist-mouth competition (not what you think it is) and other backpacker fun and games.

Bay of Islands Swordfish Club (☎ 09-402 7723; Marsden Rd; ☺ 4pm-1am) There are great views and tall tales at this club bar that welcomes visitors.

Sandpit Pool Room & Bar (☎ 09-402 6063; 16 Kings Rd; ☺ noon-1am) Pool tables are $10 an hour.

Grand Odeon (☎ 09-402 6677; 9 Williams Rd; dinner mains $4-45; ☺ 5pm-3am) This is a seafood restaurant but after 11pm it becomes a nightclub with a DJ.

Lighthouse Tavern (☎ 09-402 8324; above the Shopping Mall) There's a DJ in summer and a dance area.

Brewhouse Restaurant & Bar (☎ 09-402 7195; Haruru Falls; dinner mains $15-22) This historical tavern brews its own draught beers. It's a convivial place with an open fire, a restaurant and a DJ or live music on summer weekends. A courtesy coach operates to and from Paihia if there are enough passengers, but new owners may change things.

RUSSELL
pop 1140

Historic Russell is directly across the bay from Paihia. It was originally a fortified Maori settlement which spread over the entire valley, then known as Kororareka (Sweet Penguin).

Russell's early European history was turbulent. In 1830 it was the scene of the so-called War of the Girls, when two pairs of Maori girls (one pair from the northern Bay of Islands and one pair from the south) were vying for the wealth and attention of a whaling captain called Brind. The rivalry resulted in verbal abuse and fighting when they happened to meet on the beach. This minor conflict quickly escalated as fam- ily members rallied around to avenge the insult and harm done to their respective relatives. Hundreds were killed and injured over a two-week period before missionaries managed to broker a peace settlement.

In 1845, during the Northland Land War, government soldiers and marines garrisoned the town after the Ngapuhi leader Hone Heke threatened to chop down the flagstaff, a symbol of Pakeha authority, for the fourth time - he had already chopped it down three times. On 11 March 1845 the Ngapuhi staged a diversionary siege of Russell. It was a great tactical success, with Chief Kawiti at- tacking from the south and another Ngapuhi war party attacking from Long Beach. While the troops rushed off to protect the town- ship, Hone Heke felled the hated symbol of European authority on Maiki (Flagstaff Hill) for the fourth and final time. The Pakeha were forced to evacuate to ships lying at anchor off the settlement. The captain of HMS *Hazard* was wounded severely in the battle and his replacement ordered the ships' cannons to be fired on the town and most of the buildings were razed.

NORTHLAND

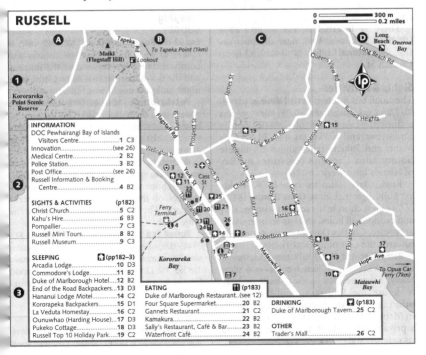

RUSSELL

0 — 300 m
0 — 0.2 miles

INFORMATION
DOC Pewhairangi Bay of Islands
  Visitors Centre.........................**1** C3
Innovation..............................(see 26)
Medical Centre..........................**2** B2
Police Station..........................**3** B2
Post Office.............................(see 26)
Russell Information & Booking
  Centre................................**4** B2

SIGHTS & ACTIVITIES   (p182)
Christ Church...........................**5** C2
Kahu's Hire.............................**6** B3
Pompallier.............................**7** C3
Russell Mini Tours......................**8** B2
Russell Museum.........................**9** C3

SLEEPING   (pp182–3)
Arcadia Lodge..........................**10** D3
Commodore's Lodge.....................**11** B2
Duke of Marlborough Hotel...........**12** B2
End of the Road Backpackers......**13** D3
Hananui Lodge Motel.................**14** C2
Kororapeka Backpackers.............**15** D1
La Veduta Homestay..................**16** C2
Ounuwhao (Harding House)...**17** D3
Pukeko Cottage........................**18** D3
Russell Top 10 Holiday Park.....**19** C2

EATING   (p183)
Duke of Marlborough Restaurant..(see 12)
Four Square Supermarket............**20** B2
Gannets Restaurant...................**21** C2
Kamakura................................**22** B2
Sally's Restaurant, Café & Bar......**23** B2
Waterfront Café.......................**24** B2

DRINKING   (p183)
Duke of Marlborough Tavern....**25** C2

OTHER
Trader's Mall..........................**26** C2

In its early days Russell was a magnet for rough elements like fleeing convicts, whalers, prostitutes and drunk sailors. Charles Darwin described it in 1835 as full of 'the refuse of society', but it was probably no worse than other ports.

Today cafés, gift shops and motels have replaced the grog shops and brothels. Russell is now a peaceful and pretty little place, which justifiably calls itself 'romantic' in promotional material. The waterfront is lined with stately colonial buildings and pohutukawa trees.

It's a marked contrast to the hustle of Paihia across the bay. Most Bay of Islands water-based tours pick up from here, so it's certainly an alternative base.

Information

The useful **Russell Information & Booking Centre** (☎ 09-403 8020; russell.information@xtra.co.nz; ⊙ 8.30am-5pm winter, 7.30am-9pm summer) is on the pier where the passenger ferry from Paihia docks.

The excellent **DOC Pewhairangi Bay of Islands visitors centre** (☎ 09-403 9003; www.doc.govt.nz; The Strand; ⊙ 9am-4.30pm winter, 9am-5pm summer) has information on Pewhairangi, a park that consists of 40 separate areas – see p176.

There is Internet access at **Innovation** (☎ 09-403 8843; Traders Mall), near the post office. The **Medical Centre** (☎ 09-403 7690) is on Church St.

Sights & Activities

The small but modern **Russell Museum** (☎ 09-403 7701; 2 York St; adult/child $5/1; ⊙ 10am-4pm) has a fine 1:5 scale model of Captain Cook's *Endeavour* and a 7kg crayfish as well as Maori and Pakeha relics and a 10-minute history video. Captain Cook visited the Bay of Islands for a week in 1769.

Russell lays claim to some of NZ's oldest buildings, including **Christ Church** (1847), NZ's oldest church; it's scarred with musket and cannonball holes, and has an interesting graveyard. Charles Darwin made a donation towards the cost of its construction.

Pompallier (☎ 09-403 9015; tours adult/student/child $7.50/3.50/free; ⊙ 10am-5pm Dec-Feb & school holidays, 5 tours a day Mar-Nov) was built in 1842 to house the Roman Catholic mission's printing press which printed 40,000 books in Maori. In the 1870s it was converted into a private home but it has been restored to its original state.

Overlooking Russell is **Maiki** (Flagstaff Hill), where Hone Heke chopped down the flagpole four times. The view is well worth the effort of the climb. By car take Tapeka Rd or if on foot, take the track west from the boat ramp along the beach at low tide, or up Wellington Street at high tide.

In good weather **Kahu's Hire** on the Strand rents kayaks or dinghies for $10 an hour.

The Information Centre at the end of the jetty rents out **bicycles** for $10 for an hour or $25 for half a day.

About 1½km behind Russell and an easy walk or cycle is **Long Beach** (Oneroa Bay Beach). Turn left (facing the sea) to visit Donkey Bay, a small cove that is an unofficial nudist beach.

Tours

Russell Mini Tours (☎ 09-403 7866; adult/child $17/8) departs from the Fullers office, which fronts Russell Wharf, six times daily on the hour and visits local sites of interest.

Many of the cruises out of Paihia pick up passengers at Russell about 15 minutes after their Paihia departure.

Sleeping
BUDGET
End of the Road Backpackers (☎ 09-403 7632; 24 Brind Rd; dm/d & tw $20/45) This is a homely and comfy cottage with views over the marina, and the dorm has just two beds. Come for a night and you might want to stay a week.

Pukeko Cottage (☎ 09-403 8498; 14 Brind Rd; barry mp@xtra.co.nz; dm/d $20/45; 🖳) This is a mini-hostel that's more like a homestay, where you can chat with the artistic owner over a cup of tea.

Kororareka Backpackers (☎ /fax 09-403 8494; korobp@xtra.co.nz; 22 Oneroa Rd; dm/d $20/50; 🖳) Learn about local Maori history from the owners of this comfortable, small backpackers. There are great views from the large deck.

Russell Top 10 Holiday Park (☎ 0800 148 671, 09-403 7826; russelltop10@xtra.co.nz; Long Beach Rd; camp sites $22-26, campervan sites $26-30, cabins $45-60, tourist flats $95-105) This park has a small store, good facilities, an attractive setting and refurbished tourist flats.

MID-RANGE
La Veduta Homestay (☎ 09-403 8299; laveduta@ xtra.co.nz; 11 Gould St; B&B d $130-180) You will soon

feel at home here (free tea and port) with the fine furnishings and views and rooms with en suite or private facilities.

Arcadia Lodge (☎ 09-403 7756; arcadialodge@ xtra.co.nz; Florance Ave; d $135-250) There is an antiquey, cottagey feel to this 1890 house; the rooms are all different but they have en suite or private facilities.

Two smart places on the waterfront:

Commodore's Lodge (☎ 09-403 7899; commodores .lodge@xtra.co.nz; 28 The Strand; studios $170-220, 1-bed units $130-170; 🖳)

Hananui Lodge Motel (☎ 09-403 7875; hananui@ xtra.co.nz; The Strand; units $85-250)

TOP END

Ounuwhao (Harding House; ☎ 09-403 7310; ounuwhao@ bay-of-islands.co.nz; 16 Hope Ave; d $170-230) This beautiful period house, where wonderful quilts are an outstanding decorative feature, is 1km from town. A gourmet breakfast is provided (included in the cost).

Duke of Marlborough Hotel (☎ 09-403 7829; www.theduke.co.nz; 35 The Strand; d $155-450) This fine hotel, situated right on the waterfront, has real old-fashioned charm and the rooms have been recently renovated. The harbour-facing rooms are the best (and most expensive). Prices include continental breakfast.

Eating & Drinking

Kamakura (☎ 09-402 7771; The Strand; mains $25-35; ☯ lunch & dinner) This restaurant usually has a top chef, such as Rick Rutledge-Manning (well-known locally due to his *Hell's Kitchen* TV programme), so expect meals to be something special.

Gannets Restaurant (☎ 09-403 7990; cnr York & Chapel Sts; mains $20-30; ☯ dinner Tue-Sun) This restaurant specialises in seafood dishes such as scallops and crab, as well as steak and venison, and the menu usually includes a few unusual dishes like smoked eel or Maori bread.

Duke of Marlborough Restaurant (☎ 09-403 7829; Duke of Marlborough Hotel, 35 The Strand; lunch mains $12-19, dinner mains $25; ☯ lunch & dinner) The grand old Duke has period charm with a veranda. Try the smoked venison if it's available.

Duke of Marlborough Tavern (☎ 09-403 7851; York St) This sports bar has live music most Fridays, a bistro restaurant, draught Guinness and a table-tennis table.

Cafés on the waterfront:

Sally's Restaurant, Café & Bar (☎ 09-403 7652; 25 The Strand; mains $18-28; ☯ lunch & dinner, bar till late)

Waterfront Café (☎ 09-403 7589; The Strand; ☯ breakfast & lunch, closed Mon winter)

Getting There & Around

From Paihia, the quickest and easiest way to reach Russell is on the regular **passenger ferry** (adult/child one-way $5/2.50). It runs from 7.20am to 7.30pm (until 10.30pm October to May), generally every 20 minutes. Buy your tickets on board.

The **car ferry** (one-way/return vehicle & driver $8/15, motorcycle & rider $4/7, additional passenger $1/2) runs every 10 minutes or so from Opua (about 8km from Russell) to Okiato Point, between 6.50am and 10pm. Buy your tickets on board.

KERIKERI

pop 5000

At the northern end of the Bay of Islands, Kerikeri has historical and natural attractions as well as a relaxed Mediterranean feel with its citrus orchards and café culture. Kerikeri means 'to dig' and the Maori grew kumara here before the Pakeha arrived; its fertile soils now produce kiwi fruit and oranges as well as vegetables. Picking and pruning go on virtually all year, and attract workers at wage rates that are around $9 an hour.

Information

The **visitors centre** (☎ 09-407 9297; www.kerikeri .co.nz; Cobham Rd; ☯ 9am-5pm Mon-Fri, 10am-noon Sat) is part of the new library complex which has Internet access. Net access is also available at **Kerikeri Computers** (☎ 09-407 7941; 88 Kerikeri Rd) for $6 an hour. Hiking information and brochures are available at **DOC** (☎ 09-407 8474; 34 Landing Rd).

The **post office** (☎ 09-407 9721; 6 Hobson Ave; ☯ 8.30am-5.30pm Mon-Fri, 9am-1.30pm Sat) is opposite the cinema.

Sights & Activities

The **Stone Store** (☎ 09-407 9236; adult/child $3.50/ free; ☯ 10am-5pm Nov-Apr, 10am-4pm May-Oct), on the banks of the Kerikeri River, was built between 1833 and 1836 and is the oldest stone building in NZ. It's full of the type of goods that used to be bartered in the store, including muskets and blankets, as well as diaries and other relics of missionary endeavour. At one

NORTHLAND

NORTHLAND

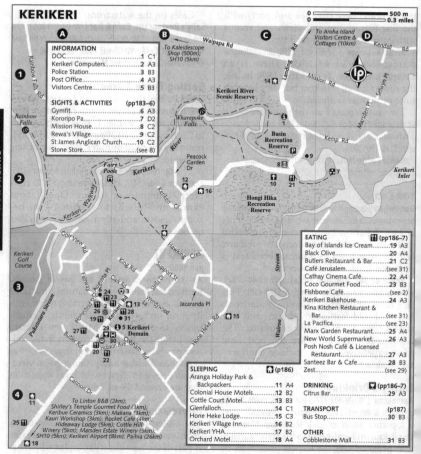

KERIKERI

INFORMATION	
DOC	.1 C1
Kerikeri Computers	.2 A3
Police Station	.3 B3
Post Office	.4 A3
Visitors Centre	.5 B3

SIGHTS & ACTIVITIES	(pp183–6)
Gymfit	.6 A3
Kororipo Pa	.7 D2
Mission House	.8 C2
Rewa's Village	.9 C2
St James Anglican Church	.10 C2
Stone Store	(see 8)

EATING	(pp186–7)
Bay of Islands Ice Cream	.19 A3
Black Olive	.20 A4
Butlers Restaurant & Bar	.21 C2
Café Jerusalem	(see 31)
Cathay Cinema Café	.22 A4
Coco Gourmet Food	.23 B3
Fishbone Café	(see 2)
Kerikeri Bakehouse	.24 A3
Kina Kitchen Restaurant & Bar	(see 31)
La Pacifica	(see 23)
Marx Garden Restaurant	.25 A4
New World Supermarket	.26 A3
Posh Nosh Café & Licensed Restaurant	.27 A3
Santeez Bar & Cafe	.28 B3
Zest	(see 29)

SLEEPING	(p186)
Aranga Holiday Park & Backpackers	.11 A4
Colonial House Motels	.12 B2
Cottle Court Motel	.13 B3
Glenfalloch	.14 C1
Hone Heke Lodge	.15 C3
Kerikeri Village Inn	.16 B2
Kerikeri YHA	.17 B2
Orchard Motel	.18 A4

DRINKING	(pp186–7)
Citrus Bar	.29 A3

TRANSPORT	(p187)
Bus Stop	.30 B3

OTHER	
Cobblestone Mall	.31 B3

time a blanket was worth a pig but a musket cost eight or ten pigs (or blankets). The role of missionaries in arming northern Maori with muskets is still a controversial topic.

Adjacent to the Stone Store, the **Mission House** (adult/child $5/free; 10am-4pm) is even older – erected in 1822 by Reverend Butler. It's the country's oldest wooden building and contains some original fittings and chattels. A ticket to visit both buildings is $7.

Just across the river from the Stone Store, **Rewa's Village** (09-407 6454; adult/child $3/50c; 9am-5pm summer, 10am-4pm winter) has a video, a mock-up of a pre-European Maori village, and information boards on plants that were used by Maoris. By all accounts some food plants like fern roots did not taste good.

Pick up the brochure on the **Art & Craft Trail** from the information centre to visit the many art, furniture, wool and pottery outlets, including an unusual **kaleidoscope shop** (09-407 4415; 256 Waipapa Rd).

On the road into Kerikeri from the south are orchards, fruit stalls and a cluster of shops: colourful crockery at **Keriblue Ceramics** (09-407 7158; 505 Kerikeri Rd); homemade food at **Shirley's Temple Gourmet Food** (09-403 7141; 55 Kerikeri Rd); expensive but delicious handmade-on-the-premises chocolate at **Makana** (09-407 6800; 9am-5.30pm); and kauri products at **Kauri Workshop** (09-407 9196).

Aroha Island visitors centre (09-407 5243; www.aroha.net.nz; Aroha Island; admission free; 9.30am-5.30pm Tue-Sun Sep-May) is located on a tiny five-hectare island, 12km northeast of Kerikeri. It is reached via a permanent causeway through mangrove bushes. The visitors centre has environmental displays and currently four adult North Island brown kiwi live on the island along with lots of other birds such as fantails and tui. Kayaks can be rented ($20 for two hours). The island is open all year for overnight stays; see p186.

Gymfit (☎ 09-407 7522; Fairway Dr; day pass $10; 6.30am-7.30pm Mon-Fri, 9-11am Sat & Sun) has every kind of exercise machine.

On SH10, just south of Kerikeri Rd, are a couple of wineries that offer wine-tasting. **Cottle Hill Winery** (☎ 09-407 5203; 10am-5pm) is a boutique winery that sells cheese and meat platters for lunch, while **Marsden Estate Winery** (☎ 09-407 9398; Wiroa Rd; 10am-5pm daily Sep-Jun, 10am-4pm Wed-Sun Jul & Aug) offers a range of meals and platters (from $12 to $20) on their deck.

WALKING

Just up the hill behind the Stone Store is a marked historical walk, which takes about 10 minutes and leads to **Kororipo Pa**, the fortress of the famous Ngapuhi chief Hongi Hika. Huge Ngapuhi warfaring parties led by Hika once departed from here on raids, terrorising much of the North Island during the so-called Musket Wars (see p27). The walk finally emerges near the St James Anglican church, which was built in 1878.

Across the river from the Stone Store is a scenic reserve with several marked tracks. There's a 4km Kerikeri River track leading to the 27m **Rainbow Falls**, passing by the Wharepoke Falls and the Fairy Pools along the way. Alternatively, you can reach the Rainbow Falls from Waipapa Rd, in which case it's only a 10-minute walk to the falls. The Fairy Pools are great for swimming and picnics and can be reached from the dirt

CAFÉ CULTURE IN KERIKERI

With its orange orchards, palm trees on the main street and indoor/outdoor café/restaurant/bars sprouting up everywhere, Kerikeri has a relaxed Mediterranean atmosphere and is the café capital of the North.

- **Posh Nosh Café & Licensed Restaurant** (☎ 09-407 7213; The Courtyard Homestead Rd) lives up to its promise of 'fabulous food and fun' with a great array of meals and live comedy and music at the weekend.
- **Fishbone Café** (☎ 09-407 6065; 88 Kerikeri Rd) specialises in coffee but also serves imaginative food (such as the dessert of sponge fingers soaked in espresso and Marsala wine, and layered with mascarpone and chocolate). It does breakfasts, $10 lunches and sometimes $20 dinners.
- **Santeez Bar & Café** (☎ 09-407 1185; 93 Kerikeri Rd) has mouth-watering food, some of it gluten-free. Try the kiwi fruit muffins or the big scones, but meals are served too.
- **La Pacifica** (☎ 09-407 1461; Hub Mall, Kerikeri Rd) has Internet access, Atomic coffee, mini pizzas, *paninis* and mussel fritters.
- **Zest** (☎ 09-407 7164; 73 Kerikeri Rd) serves moderately-priced home-made food and you can sit on pop-art chairs.
- **Kerikeri Bakehouse** (☎ 09-407 7266; Fairway Dr) has a huge range of popular café-style snacks. It's mainly takeaway but there are a few seats. Try an intriguingly named 'wasp nest'.
- **Coco Gourmet Food** (☎ 09-407 8826; Hub Mall, Kerikeri Rd) is always worth a look for an adventurous and never-before-tasted picnic item.
- **Cathay Cinema Café** (Hobson Ave) doesn't serve popcorn and chemical drinks, but is a restaurant serving top-notch meals. Ask about movie and meal deals.
- **Bay of Islands Ice Cream** (☎ 09-407 8136; Main Rd) offers generous helpings of its 'made on the premises' ice cream. All are 100% natural of course.
- **Rocket Café** (☎ 09-407 3100; Kerikeri Rd), just south of Kerikeri, has won a stack of awards, and serves up superb deli-style food and meals. Spinach roulade is popular.

NORTHLAND

road beside the YHA hostel, if you're not up to the hike along the river.

Sleeping
BUDGET
Kerikeri YHA (☎ 09-407 9391; yhakeri@yha.org.nz; 144 Kerikeri Rd; camp sites $36, dm/tw/d/cottages $23/55/60/80; ☐) This hostel has some character, a tranquil setting with a large garden leading down to the river, and you might see a kingfisher on the volleyball net. YHA members get a $4 discount.

Hone Heke Lodge (☎ /fax 09-407 8170; honeheke@xtra.co.nz; 65 Hone Heke Rd; dm/s/d & tw $18/35/45, s/d & tw with bathroom $45/50; ☒) Hone Heke has a line of single-storey units which caters mainly to those working in local orchards. Weekly rates range from $90 to $100 per person.

Hideaway Lodge (☎ 0800 562 746, 09-407 9773; www.hideawaylodge.co.nz; 111 Wiroa Rd; camp sites $20-26, dm per week $90, d per week $180-190; ☒ ☐) Hideaway is a good place to stay if you're looking for work as there's usually lots available year-round. The lodge is spacious with two of most things and is usually busy and lively. It's 5km out of Kerikeri, west of the SH10 junction, but there are free rides to town twice a day.

Aranga Holiday Park & Backpackers (☎ 0800 276 648, 09-407 9326; www.aranga.co.nz; Kerikeri Rd; camp sites/campervan sites $22/24, cabins/tourist flats/units $45/70/80; ☐) This is a large riverside camping ground with good facilities that is within walking distance of the town centre.

Linton B&B (☎ 09-407 7654; 518 Kerikeri Rd; s/d $40/60) Facilities are shared but there is a good cooked breakfast (included in the price) and a large garden at this B&B 2km out of Kerikeri.

Aroha Island Cottages (☎ 09-407 5243; www.aroha.net.nz; Aroha Island; camp sites $18, cottages d Mar-Nov/Dec-Apr $80/95, extra person $12) The modern self-contained cottages on this small kiwi island with a causeway sleep up to 10.

MID-RANGE
Glenfalloch (☎ /fax 09-407 5471; glenfall@ihug.co.nz; 48 Landing Rd; s $60, d $80-95; ☒) This relaxing homestay B&B with a beautiful garden and a tennis court is 500m north of the Stone Store. Rooms have en suite or private facilities and the hosts go out of their way to please.

Orchard Motel (☎ 09-407 8869; orchardmotel@xtra.co.nz; cnr Kerikeri & Hall Rds; units $75-110; ☒)

These units with kitchens and a spa are among the orchards less than 1km south of the town centre.

Colonial House Motels (☎ 0800 242 555, 09-407 9106; colonial.lodge@xtra.co.nz; 178 Kerikeri Rd; units Feb-Nov $85-130, Dec-Jan $125-180; ☒) A cut above your average motel, Colonial has an outdoor spa and a garden setting.

Cottle Court Motel (☎ 09-407 8867; cottlecourt@xtra.co.nz; Kerikeri Rd; units Apr-Dec/Jan-Mar $90/150; ☒) The plus point here is that it's in the middle of town.

TOP END
Kerikeri Village Inn (☎ 09-407 4666; kerikeri.village.inn@xtra.co.nz; 165 Kerikeri Rd; d $145-165, units summer only $195) This stylish B&B, decorated with cool Mediterranean colours and furnishings, has en suite rooms and a communal lounge. The price includes a gourmet breakfast.

Eating & Drinking
Café Jerusalem (☎ 09-407 1001; Cobblestone Mall; mains $13-20; ☒ lunch & dinner Mon-Fri, dinner Sat) Enjoy authentic Middle Eastern food such as *schwarma*, falafel and baklava that you can eat in or take away. A four-meat combo with yogurt, rice, pitta bread and salad is $20.

Black Olive (☎ 09-407 9693; Kerikeri Rd; meals $12-25; ☒ dinner Tue-Sun) This place serves up popular pasta and pizza takeaways or you can sit down and eat in the back.

Kina Kitchen Restaurant & Bar (☎ 09-407 7669; Cobblestone Mall; mains $20-28; ☒ lunch & dinner) The hardworking young chefs are on view in this classy restaurant where the carefully crafted food has more than a touch of originality.

Marx Garden Restaurant (☎ 09-407 6606; Kerikeri Rd; lunch mains $18, dinner mains $24-30; ☒ breakfast & lunch year-round, dinner summer) For fine dining, Marx is among Kerikeri's best. Set back off the road, the converted house is in a leafy garden, with an à la carte menu including steak, prawn laksa, mussels in wine, and pasta dishes.

Butler's Restaurant & Bar (☎ 09-407 8479; Stone Store Basin; lunch mains $8-14, dinner mains $22-25; ☒ lunch & dinner Wed-Sun winter, daily summer) There's beef, venison, lamb or fish for dinner on the veranda overlooking the river.

Citrus Bar (☎ 09-407 1050; Kerikeri Rd; meals $10-24; ☒ 10am-late) Citrus is a sports-music bar and the most popular nightspot in town with live bands or a DJ on Friday night. The bistro menu includes pizza and nachos.

The **New World Supermarket** (☎ 09-407 7440; Fairway Dr) has everything self-caterers might need.

Getting There & Away
Air New Zealand (☎ 0800 737 000 24hr; www .airnz.co.nz; one-way fares $70-250) operates three to four flights daily from Auckland to Kerikeri.

The InterCity and Northliner buses (see p148) arrive at and leave from a stop in Cobham Rd, opposite the new library and visitors centre. Kerikeri to Mangonui ($17) takes an hour, and Kerikeri to Auckland ($46) takes five hours.

BAY OF ISLANDS TO WHANGAREI

On the way from the Bay of Islands to Whangarei there are two scenic detour routes: the back road from Russell to SH1, and the drive out to Tutukaka from Hikurangi on SH1, which loops around to Whangarei. Out to sea are the Poor Knights Islands, a world-class marine reserve and a paradise for scuba divers.

RUSSELL ROAD
The back road from Russell skirts around the coast before joining SH1 at Whakapara. The scenic road is long, unsealed and rough

---

HUNDERTWASSER'S LOO

Kawakawa is just an ordinary Kiwi outback town, located just off SH1 south of Paihia, but the public toilets (60 Gillies St) were designed by Austrian-born artist and eco-architect, Friedensreich Hundertwasser. He lived near Kawakawa in an isolated house without electricity from 1973 until his death in 2000.

The most photographed toilets in NZ are typical Hundertwasser – lots of wavy lines, decorated with ceramic mosaics and brightly coloured bottles, and with grass and plants on the roof. Other examples of his work can be seen in cities as far apart as Vienna and Osaka. The café opposite was another of his designs, and inside are books and photographs of his work.

---

for most of the way – strictly for those with their own transport, plenty of time and a desire to get off the beaten track.

From Russell, the road starts near Orongo Bay and skirts along the Waikare Inlet before reaching the Waikare Road to Waihaha. This turn-off eventually leads back to the highway and Paihia. It's about a 90-minute drive from Russell.

Continuing along Russell Road past the Waihaha turn-off, there's access to the **Ngaio-tonga Scenic Reserve**, which conserves the mixed forest that once prevailed throughout Northland. There are two short walks – the 20-minute **Kauri Grove Nature Walk** and the 10-minute **Twin Bole Kauri Walk**.

Closer to the Rawhiti turn-off, a shorter one-hour walk leads through Maori land and over the headland to Whangamumu Harbour. At the main beach on the harbour, the **Whangamumu Scenic Reserve** has camping. There are over 40 prehistoric sites on the peninsula and the remains of an unusual whaling station. A net, fastened between the mainland and Net Rock, was used to ensnare or slow down whales so the harpooners could get an easy shot in.

Further north is the turn-off to isolated **Rawhiti**, a small Ngapuhi settlement where life still revolves around the *marae*. Rawhiti is also the starting point for the trek to **Cape Brett**, a hard 7½-hour 20km walk to the top of the peninsula, where overnight stays are possible in the Cape Brett Hut. You can book the hut and get information on the walk at the **DOC Pewhairangi Bay of Islands visitors centre** (☎ 09-403 9003; www.doc.govt.nz; The Strand; 9am-4.30pm winter, 9am-5pm summer) in Russell.

Further south, another side road leads to the **Whangaruru North Head Scenic Reserve**, which has beaches, camping grounds, walks and fine coastal scenery in a farmland park setting.

Whangaruru Beach Camp (☎ 09-433 6806) and, further south at Oakura, **Oakura Motels and Caravan Park** (☎ 09-433 6803;) both have camping, cabins and motel units.

At Helena Bay, Russell Road returns to tarseal and leads back to SH1. About 8km from Helena Bay along a rough, winding side road is the Mimiwhangata Coastal Park (p192). This is a truly scenic part of the coastline, with coastal dunes, pohutukawa trees, jutting headlands and picturesque beaches.

TUTUKAKA COAST & POOR KNIGHTS ISLANDS

At Hikurangi on SH1 you can turn off for the winding scenic but still sealed road to Whangarei via the Tutukaka Coast. After 25km you reach **Sandy Bay**, a small surf beach, followed by a succession of idyllic bays where you can surf, swim, walk, relax or fish.

Another 11km on from Sandy Bay is **Tutukaka**, which is 26km northeast of Whangarei. The marina is a hive of activity with yachts, dive boats and game-fishing boats moored together. It is the base for diving trips that run all year to the Poor Knights Islands which are 24km offshore. You can organise diving trips to the islands from Whangarei or Tutukaka.

Dive! Tutukaka (☎ 0800 288 882, 09-434 3867; www.diving.co.nz; ⏰ 8am-5pm) is the main operator, run by an ex-cabinet minister. The basic all-day trip costs $175 and runs from 8am to 4pm with two dives, and time for snorkelling and kayaking from the boat as well. Diving here is unique and world-class; see the boxed text below. Hot drinks are free but lunch is an extra $10. You can also explore two navy ships, the *Tui* and the *Waikato*, that were sunk on purpose outside the reserve for recreational diving ($175 or $100 with your own gear). A five-day PADI open-water course is $600 (medical certificate required). Tutukaka is a good place for first-time divers, too, with plenty of experienced instructors around.

Another very experienced operator is **Pacific Hideaway** (☎ 0800 693 483, 09-437 3632; www.divenz.co.nz; $170) which runs a large catamaran boat and will pick you up from Whangarei where the owner lives.

The owner of **Knight Diver Tours** (☎ 0800 766 756, 09-436 2584; 30 Heads Rd, Whangarei; www.poorknights.co.nz; 2 dives $170) has dived the Poor Knights over 10,000 times but still comes back for more!

Oceanblue Adventures (☎ 027 488 0459; www.oceanblue.co.nz; day/weekend/4-day trips $180/380/850), run by Glen and Tiana Edney specialises in overnight trips (one to four nights) for experienced divers, including night dives. Six is the maximum number taken.

Another small operator is **Yukon Dive** (☎ 021 261 7779; www.yukon.co.nz) who takes groups of four to eight. A resort dive (for a first-timer) costs $190. The boat also does fishing trips.

Delray Charters (☎ 09-434 3028; delray@igrin.co.nz) has a 45-ft boat for cruising, game-fishing or bottom fishing.

Shuttle buses leave Whangarei at 7.10am and 3pm and leave Tutukaka Marina at 8.15am and 4.30pm. In summer the shuttle also runs from Whangarei to Paihia at 5.30pm and leaves Paihia for Whangarei at 7.30pm.

Three kilometres north of Tutukaka Marina is **Bluewater Farm Park** (☎ 09-434 3423; Matapouri Rd; adult/child $6/4; ⏰ 10am-4pm) which has 25 different animals including alpacas,

---

WORLD-CLASS DIVING AT THE POOR KNIGHTS ISLANDS

This marine reserve, 24km off Northland's east coast near Tutukaka, was established in 1981. It is reputed to have the best scuba diving in NZ and has been rated as one of the world's top 10 diving spots.

The islands are bathed in a subtropical current from the Coral Sea, so varieties of tropical and subtropical fish not seen in other coastal waters are observed here. The waters are clear, with no sediment or pollution problems. The 40m to 60m underwater cliffs drop steeply to the sandy bottom, and are a labyrinth of archways, caves, tunnels and fissures that attract a wide variety of sponges and colourful underwater vegetation. Manta rays are common.

The two main volcanic islands, Tawhiti Rahi and Aorangi, were once home to members of the Ngai Wai tribe but, since a raiding-party massacre in the early 1800s the islands have been *tapu* (forbidden). Even today no-one is allowed to set foot on the islands in order to protect their pristine environment. Not only do tuatara and Butler's shearwater breed there, but there are unique species of flora and fauna, such as the Poor Knights red lily.

Dive trips can be organised from Whangarei or Tutukaka and cater for first-timers and experts. A comprehensive diving guide with excellent photographs is *Poor Knights Wonderland* ($26) by Glen Edney, available from local dive shops.

llamas, ostriches, emus, donkeys, miniature horses and birds along with arts and crafts and a café.

Sleeping

Tutukaka Holiday Park (☎/fax 09-434 3938; www .tutukaka-holidaypark.co.nz; Matapouri Rd; camp sites $20-24, dm $20, cabins $40-45) This park has modern facilities and is near the marina.

Bluewater Cottages (☎ 09-434 3423; www.blue waterparadise.co.nz; Matapouri Rd; cottages $120-175) These new self-contained, open-plan cottages with indoor/outdoor flow can sleep six and enjoy sea views from a hillside 3km north of Tutukaka marina. There's a spa pool and Bluewater Farm Park is part of the same property.

Eating & Drinking

Tutukaka has a couple of interesting eateries right on the marina.

Schnappa Rock Café (☎ 09-434 3774; lunch mains $10-22, dinner mains $13-28; ☺ lunch & dinner, bar till late) This is a relaxed and popular café/restaurant/bar where top NZ bands play on summer weekends.

Marina Pizzeria (☎ 09-434 3166; large pizzas $15-22; ☺ breakfast, lunch & dinner Thu-Sun) Further along the harbour this is an excellent takeaway and eatery where everything is homemade – the bread, the pasta, the pizza and the ice cream.

Whangarei Deep Sea Anglers Club (☎ 09-434 3818; Marina Rd, Tutukaka; mains $10-17; ☺ 4pm-late winter, noon-late summer) This is a large bar that has a big screen and serves bistro meals.

WHANGAREI
pop 45,800

Whangarei is the major city in Northland and is pleasant enough with an equable climate, parks and walks, and a busy river harbour and café area. The main local attractions are in the surrounding area: Whangarei Heads with its attractive beaches and scenery and diving around the Poor Knights Islands.

Information

Whangarei Information & Travel Centre (☎ 09-438 1079; www.whangareinz.org.nz; 92 Otaika Rd/SH1; ☺ 8.30am-5pm Mon-Fri, 9.30am-4.30pm Sat & Sun Feb-Dec, 8.30am-6.30pm daily Jan; ☐) is at Tarewa Park to the south of the city. In the same building is a café and the **DOC office** (☎/fax 09-438 2007; ☺ 9am-5pm Mon-Fri, 10am-4pm Sat & Sun

Mar-Nov, 8am-6pm daily Dec-Feb), which can help with information and advice on hiking, bush camping, maps and hut tickets.

The **Automobile Association** (AA; ☎ 09-438 4848; cnr Robert & John Sts) office has maps and advice. **Klosenet** (34 John St) has Internet access. The **Central Post Shop** (☎ 09-430 2761; 16-20 Rathbone St; ☺ 8.30am-5pm Mon-Fri, 9am-1pm Sat) is conveniently located.

Sights & Activities

Margie Maddren Fernery & Conservatory (☎ 09-430 4200; First Ave; admission free; ☺ 10am-4pm) has one of the best displays of native ferns in NZ. Each fern adapts to a different degree of shade. Next door are tropical plants and cacti in a heated conservatory. Nearby is **Whangarei Art Museum** (☎ 09-430 4240; admission by donation; ☺ 10am-4pm Tue-Fri, noon-4pm Sat & Sun) which showcases Northland arts and crafts. In front of the art gallery is a rose garden and alongside is delightful little **Cafler Park** which spans Waiarohia Stream.

The **Town Basin** is an attractive harbour full of yachts and fishing boats. Besides fine cafés and restaurants there is a home-made fudge shop, art and craft shops and a bicycle hire kiosk. In a modern building with a striking mural is **Clapham's Clocks** (☎ 09-438 3993; Town Basin; adult/child $8/4; ☺ 9am-5pm), which has an awesome 1300 timepieces inside, ticking and gonging away. Admission includes a guided tour and there are some music boxes too.

Quarry Craft Co-op (☎ 09-438 1215; www.the quarry.co.nz; 21 Selwyn Ave; admission free; ☺ 10am-4pm) is an artists' cooperative set in gardens with walkways.

Bushwacka Experience (☎ 09-434 7839; half-/full day tour incl lunch $45/80) runs fun and flexible 4WD adventure tours for small groups, which include farm activities, abseiling and bush walking.

West of Whangarei, 5km out on the road to Dargaville at Maunu, is the **Whangarei Museum** (☎ 09-438 9630; 4 SH14; 1 venue/3 venues $3/7; ☺ 10am-4pm). The museum includes a kiwi house, the 1885 Clarke Homestead and the Exhibition Centre Museum which houses European relics and an impressive collection of Maori artefacts, including superb feather cloaks.

Beside the museum is the **Native Bird Recovery Centre** (☎ 09-438 1457; admission by donation; ☺ 10am-Mon-Fri) which nurses sick and injured birds back to health.

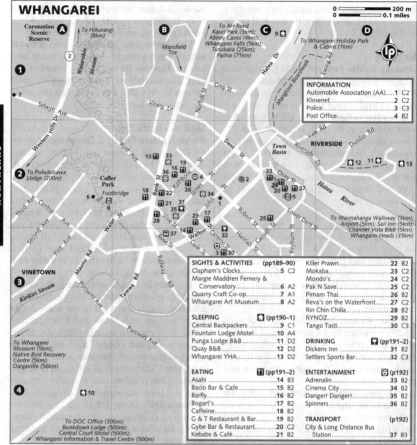

WHANGAREI

0 ————— 200 m
0 ————— 0.1 miles

INFORMATION
Automobile Association (AA).....1 C2
Klosenet.....................................2 C2
Police.......................................3 C3
Post Office................................4 B2

SIGHTS & ACTIVITIES (pp189–90)
Clapham's Clocks.......................5 C2
Margie Maddren Fernery &
  Conservatory...........................6 A2
Quarry Craft Co-op.....................7 A1
Whangarei Art Museum................8 A2

SLEEPING (pp190–1)
Central Backpackers....................9 C1
Fountain Lodge Motel.................10 A4
Punga Lodge B&B......................11 D2
Quay B&B...............................12 D2
Whangarei YHA........................13 D2

EATING (pp191–2)
Asahi......................................14 B3
Bacio Bar & Cafe.......................15 B2
Barfly....................................16 B2
Bogart's..................................17 B2
Caffeine..................................18 B2
G & T Restaurant & Bar..............19 B2
Gybe Bar & Restaurant...............20 C2
Kebabs & Café..........................21 B2

Killer Prawn............................22 B2
Mokaba..................................23 C2
Mondo's..................................24 C2
Pak N Save..............................25 C2
Pimarn Thai.............................26 B2
Reva's on the Waterfront............27 C2
Rin Chin Chilla.........................28 B2
RYNOZ...................................29 B2
Tango Tasti..............................30 C3

DRINKING (pp191–2)
Dickens Inn.............................31 B2
Settlers Sports Bar....................32 C3

ENTERTAINMENT (p192)
Adrenalin................................33 B2
Cinema City.............................34 B2
Danger! Danger!........................35 B2
Spinners.................................36 B2

TRANSPORT (p192)
City & Long Distance Bus
  Station.................................37 B3

The 26m-high **Whangarei Falls**, 5km north of town, are very photogenic, with water cascading over the edge of an old basalt lava flow. The falls can be reached on the Tikipunga bus (Monday to Friday only; see p192).

The **AH Reed Kauri Park** northeast of the city has short walks including a cleverly designed boardwalk high up in the tree tops.

Southeast of Whangarei, the **Waimahanga Walkway** in Onerahi is an easy walk along an old railway embankment. It takes two hours and passes through mangrove swamps and over a 300m-long timber truss harbour bridge. The free *Whangarei Walks*, available from the information centre, describes more walks.

Abbey Caves is an undeveloped network of limestone caves full of glow-worms and formations just off Abbey Caves Rd, about 4km east of town. It's possible to visit them alone for free (take a torch and wear strong shoes), but you'll get further with a guided tour. **Bunkdown Lodge** (☎ 09-438 8886; 23 Otaika Rd/SH1) organises cave tours for $40.

Whangarei is a popular centre for diving and fishing, mostly organised out of Tutukaka; see p188.

Sleeping
BUDGET
Bunkdown Lodge (☎ 09-438 8886; www.bunkdown lodge.co.nz; 23 Otaika Rd/SH1; dm/d $19/50) There's a homely atmosphere in this just-south-

of-town-backpackers with a garden aviary. The lodge runs Abbey Caves tours ($40) and bookings are taken for Bushwacka Experience tours. Pick-ups are available from the bus station.

Whangarei YHA (☎ 09-438 8954; yhawhang@yha .org.nz; 52 Punga Grove Ave; dm/d & tw $24/60, members $20/50) This small, easy-going hostel is up a hill just a short walk from the town centre and the manager does a free walk to a nearby cave and glow-worms.

Central Backpackers (☎ 09-437 6174; central back@xtra.co.nz; 67 Hatea Dr; dm $18, s $32-40, d $40-50; 🖳) It's a bit cramped but there are kayaks for hire and the river is over the road.

Whangarei Holiday Park & Cabins (☎ 09-437 6856; whangareiholiday@actrix.co.nz; 24 Mair St; camp sites $11, on-site caravans/cabins/cabins with bathroom/units $30/40/50/65) This holiday park has a better-than-average set of cabins and a variety of bush walks start from here.

Punga Lodge B&B (☎ 09-438 3879; 9 Punga Grove; s/d $45/60) This B&B has modern units with private facilities, a deck with views and is near the town centre.

MID-RANGE

Sail Inn (☎ 09-436 2356; sailinn@xtra.co.nz; 148 Beach Rd, Onerahi; d & tw $165-180) This is exceptional accommodation east of town with harbour views.

Quay B&B (☎ /fax 09-430 8882; quaybandb@xtra .co.nz; 6 Dundas Rd; d with bathroom $120-140) The price includes continental breakfast in this stylish contemporary accommodation, which is near the town centre.

Channel Vista B&B (☎ /fax 09-436 5529; tancred@ igrin.co.nz; 254 Beach Rd, Onerahi; s $90-100, d $120-150) This upmarket beachside accommodation east of town is self-contained or in-house. Dinner is $25.

Fountain Lodge Motel (☎ 0800 999 944, 09-438 3532; fountainlodge@clear.net.nz; 17 Tarewa Rd; studios $75, 1-/2-bed units $85/95) The hosts are friendly, the prices are reasonable and it's clean.

Central Court Motel (☎ /fax 09-438 4574; central court@xtra.co.nz; 54 Otaika Rd/SH1; s $60-80, d $65-90) This motel just south of town is a good deal at this price with a spa, Finnish sauna ($5) and Sky TV. Breakfasts are $8 to $12.

Pohutukawa Lodge (☎ 0800 200 355, 09-430 8634; www.pohutukawalodge.co.nz; 363 Western Hills Dr; units $100-135; 🖳) These superior motel units just west of town have Sky TV, fans and kitchens and some have spa baths.

Eating & Drinking
TOWN CENTRE

Caffeine (☎ 09-438 6925; 4 Water St; meals $13; 😊 breakfast & lunch) There's art on the walls, a seasonal menu, and coffee in a funky atmosphere.

Bacio Bar & Café (☎ 09-430 0446; 31 Bank St; meals from $12; 😊 lunch & dinner Mon-Sat, bar till late) This bar has a big screen, pizzas and other Italian food. The 'small' $12 pizzas are big!

Rin Chin Chilla (☎ 09-438 5882; 6 Vine St; meals $7-11; 😊 lunch & dinner) Rin Chin Chilla serves cheap but good Middle Eastern and Mexican food.

Kebabs & Café (☎ 09-438 8870; 25 Vine St; meals $12; 😊 lunch & dinner) This is a Turkish rival for Rin Chin Chilla.

Tango Tasti (☎ 09-438 1164; 99 Cameron St; 😊 breakfast, lunch & dinner Mon-Fri, brunch & dinner Sat, dinner Sun) This place has gourmet spuds, Mexican food, pasta and fresh juices.

Barfly (☎ 09-438 8761; 13 Rathbone St; mains $14-28; 😊 breakfast, lunch & dinner Tue-Sat, breakfast & lunch Sun & Mon) Barfly has wood-fired pizzas, imaginative desserts and a bar.

Pimarn Thai (☎ 09-430 0718; 12 Rathbone St; lunch mains $9-14, dinner mains $12-18; 😊 lunch & dinner) A centrally located restaurant with reasonably priced and well-prepared Thai food.

Killer Prawn (☎ 09-430 3333; 28 Bank St; prawn meals $29; 😊 lunch & dinner Mon-Sat) It's not just prawns at this smart and popular restaurant and bar, but the menu is mainly seafood.

G & T Restaurant & Bar (☎ 09-438 0999; 15a Rathbone St; mains $13-30; 😊 breakfast, lunch & dinner Mon-Sat, breakfast & lunch Sun) This restaurant has a menu that ranges from roast kangaroo to vegetarian crepes and bubble and squeak.

Bogart's (☎ 09-438 3088; cnr Cameron & Walton Sts; mains $15-27; 😊 dinner daily & lunch Fri) This bar and restaurant serves better than average pizzas, pasta, nachos, salads and more.

RYNOZ (☎ 09-438 1380; 79 Cameron St; mains $17-25; 😊 breakfast, lunch & dinner) There are stonegrill meals cooked at your table in this sports bar which has late-night live bands and DJs.

Dickens Inn (☎ 09-430 0406; cnr Cameron & Quality Sts; mains $22-29; 😊 breakfast, lunch & dinner) This English-style pub has Murphy's and Amstel beer, and a wide range of pub-style food is served all day.

Asahi (☎ 09-430 3005; cnr Vine & Quality Sts; mains $14-18; 😊 dinner Mon-Sat) This Japanese restaurant has plenty of space and a comprehensive menu.

Settlers Sports Bar (☎ 09-438 3838; Cameron St) This bar has a round pool table, a big screen and bar snacks.

TOWN BASIN
Mokaba (☎ 09-438 7557; Town Basin; meals $8-14; ✆ breakfast, lunch & afternoon tea) Mokaba has yummy, stylish food. For something unusual try a salmon muffin.

Mondo's (☎ 09-430 0467; Town Basin; meals $7-13; ✆ breakfast & lunch) The menu on the mega board has masses of deli snacks and weekend brunch items.

Reva's on the Waterfront (☎ 09-438 8969; Town Basin; lunch mains $15-25, dinner mains $23-28; ✆ lunch & dinner) This long-running casual restaurant serves pizzas, seafood and a global menu and has live music at the weekends. It sits right on the water overlooking the harbour.

Gybe Bar & Restaurant (☎ 09-430 0406; Town Basin; brunch $5-17, lunch meals $12, dinner mains $24-32; ✆ breakfast, lunch & dinner) This upmarket all-day eatery has stylish food to match the stylish décor. You can eat upstairs, downstairs, inside or outside.

Entertainment
Danger! Danger! (☎ 09-459 7461; 37 Vine St; lunch mains $6-12, dinner mains $7-18; ✆ 10.30am-very late) This huge barn has a giant screen, high tables and bar stools, surprisingly good food and a pool table. At around 10.30pm it becomes a nightclub.

Spinners (☎ 09-430 7458; cnr Bank St & Rust Ave; ✆ 8pm-late Wed-Sat) and the nearby **Adrenalin** (☎ 09-459 7512; 58 Bank St) are nightspots with live bands and DJs.

Head to **Cinema City** (☎ 09-438 8550) for the latest movies.

Getting There & Away
AIR
Air New Zealand (☎ 0800 737 000 24hr; www.airnz.co.nz; one way $60-200) operates four to six flights a day between Auckland and Whangarei.
Great Barrier Airlines (☎ 0800 900 600; 09-275 9120; one way adult/child $100/65) flies twice a week between Whangarei and Great Barrier Island. **Mountain Air** (☎ 0800 222 123, 09-256 7025; www.mountainair.co.nz; one way adult/child $105/70) flies between Whangarei and Great Barrier four times a week. The airport is at Onerahi, to the east of the town centre.

The **Whangarei Airport Shuttle** (☎ 09-437 0666) has a door-to-door service for $8.

BUS
The **City & Long Distance Bus Station** (☎ 09-438 2653) is on Rose St. InterCity has daily buses between Auckland and Whangarei ($32, two hours and 50 minutes), which continue north to Paihia ($19, 1½ hours from Whangarei). **Main Coachlines** (☎ 09-278 8070) runs a bus daily to and from Auckland (one way $27).

There is a local city bus service ($2 per trip) – a useful one can take you to Whangarei Falls.

AROUND WHANGAREI
Mimiwhangata Coastal Park
This park is 48km from Whangarei and 52km from Russell and can be reached via a gravel road from Helena Bay on the old Russell Rd. Accommodation can be booked at **Whangarei DOC office** (☎ /fax 09-438 2007; 92 Otaika Rd/SH1; ✆ 9am-5pm Mon-Fri, 10am-4pm Sat & Sun Mar-Nov, 8am-6pm daily Dec-Feb), which shares the same building as the Whangarei Information & Travel Centre. There is a luxurious **lodge** run by DOC, and a simpler but comfortable **cottage**; both sleep eight people. Self-contained accommodation must be booked for one week minimum, but camping ($12; the only facilities are water and toilets) is available at secluded Waikahoa Bay where there are cliffs and dunes and great hiking trails.

Whangarei Heads
From Whangarei, Heads Rd winds its way past picturesque coves and bays to the heads at the harbour entrance 35km away. This drive (there is no bus) passes small settlements and there are great views from the top of 419m **Mt Manaia**, a sheer rock outcrop above McLeod Bay, but it is a hard, steep 1½-hour climb.

From Woolshed Bay it is a 30-minute walk over the headland to the delightful beach at **Smugglers Bay**. You can also drive on to **Ocean Beach**.

A detour from Parua Bay takes you to beautiful **Pataua**, a small settlement that lies on a shallow inlet. A pedestrian footbridge crosses the inlet to a surf beach.

Coromandel Region

CONTENTS

Coromandel Peninsula	**196**
Thames	196
Coromandel Forest Park	200
Thames to Coromandel Town	200
Coromandel Town	201
Far North Coromandel	203
Coromandel Town to Whitianga	204
Whitianga	204
Around Whitianga	207
Hahei	207
Around Hahei	208
Hot Water Beach	209
Tairua	209
Around Tairua	210
Pauanui	210
Opoutere Beach	211
Whangamata	211
Waihi	212
Waihi Beach	212
Hauraki Region	**213**
Miranda	213
Paeroa	213
Te Aroha	214

Coromandel
Region

The spine of the Coromandel Peninsula is densely forested and mountainous, crisscrossed with hiking trails, around which narrow roads wind along the attractive coastline. The historical gold-mining towns of Thames and Coromandel Town on the west coast retain a pioneer atmosphere, and the area attracts city dropouts who have exchanged their mobile phones and stressful jobs for 10-hectare lifestyle properties with sea views.

The east coast has rapidly expanding patches of holiday homes around some beaches but most of the coast, particularly in the north, is much as it was when Captain Cook and his crew sailed by at the end of the eighteenth century. Whitianga and nearby Hahei are a mini Bay of Islands with plenty of activities in, on and below the water.

The star ecological attraction is the top bird-watching site at Miranda, southwest of the peninsula, where sharp-eyed waders feast on the tidal mud-flat banquet of worms and shellfish. Further east at Karangahake Gorge, rusting 19th-century relics of the gold-rush era can be compared with a modern mine in Waihi with its endless convoy of monster trucks that could squash you like a fly.

Life is quiet except from Christmas to February when local holiday-makers and their much-needed cash flood the peninsula. More remote communities are still accessed by gravel roads and an aura of rugged individualism hangs like mist over this compact and special region.

COROMANDEL REGION

HIGHLIGHTS

- Boating, scuba diving, snorkelling, kayaking and fishing around **Whitianga** (p204) or **Cathedral Cove** (p207)
- Relaxing in your own natural spa bath at **Hot Water Beach** (p209)
- Hiking up to the **Pinnacles** (p200) and along the **Coromandel Coastal Walkway** (p203)
- Exploring historic gold-mining relics at **Thames** (p196), **Coromandel Town** (p201) and **Karangahake Gorge** (p214)
- Enjoying the beautiful unspoilt east coast beaches at **Opito Bay** (p204) or **Opoutere** (p211) and surf at **Whangamata** (p211)
- Marvelling at the shore birds on the mudflats at **Miranda** (p213)
- Riding on the unique **Driving Creek Railway** (p201)

★ Coromandel Coastal Walkway
Driving Creek Railway ★
★ Opito
★ Coromandel Town
Whitianga ★   ★ Cathedral Cove
★ Hot Water Beach
★ The Pinnacles
★ Opoutere
★ Miranda   ★ Thames
★ Whangamata
★ Karangahake Gorge

| TELEPHONE CODE: 07 | www.thecoromandel.com | www.hauraki-dc.govt.nz |

COROMANDEL REGION

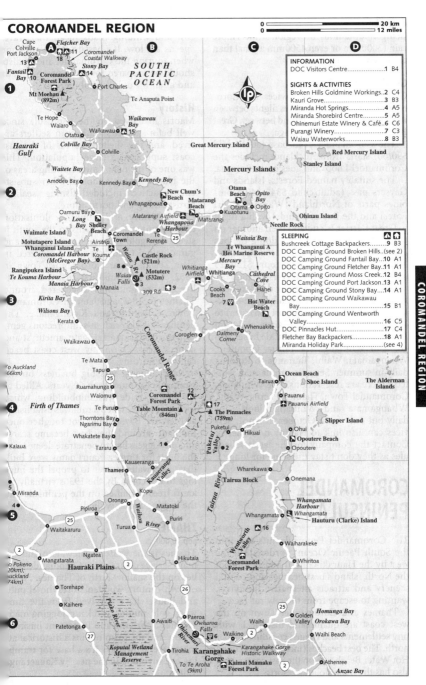

0 ____ 20 km
0 ____ 12 miles

INFORMATION
DOC Visitors Centre...................1   B4

SIGHTS & ACTIVITIES
Broken Hills Goldmine Workings..2   C4
Kauri Grove..............................3   B3
Miranda Hot Springs..................4   A5
Miranda Shorebird Centre..........5   A5
Ohinemuri Estate Winery & Café..6   C6
Purangi Winery.........................7   C3
Waiau Waterworks.....................8   B3

SLEEPING
Bushcreek Cottage Backpackers........9   B3
DOC Camping Ground Broken Hills..(see 2)
DOC Camping Ground Fantail Bay..10   A1
DOC Camping Ground Fletcher Bay..11   A1
DOC Camping Ground Moss Creek..12   B4
DOC Camping Ground Port Jackson..13   A1
DOC Camping Ground Stony Bay....14   A1
DOC Camping Ground Waikawau
  Bay..15   B1
DOC Camping Ground Wentworth
  Valley...16   C5
DOC Pinnacles Hut.......................17   C4
Fletcher Bay Backpackers...............18   A1
Miranda Holiday Park...................(see 4)

COROMANDEL REGION

Climate

Being mountainous, the region attracts more rain (3000mm or even 4500mm a year) than elsewhere on the east coast.

Getting There & Around

Great Barrier Airlines services the Coromandel Peninsula. It operates flights between Auckland and Whitianga, and between Great Barrier Island and Whitianga.

The Coromandel Trail pass (adult/child $90/60) starts from Auckland, includes the Coromandel Loop, and goes on to Rotorua.

The suitably named Forests, Islands and Geysers pass (adult/child $345/240) combines parts of Northland (Waipoua Kauri Forest and the Bay of Islands) with a flight to Great Barrier Island and then another on to Whitianga, before finally doing the bus journey on to Rotorua. A flexi pass (five hours of bus travel $50, 15 hours $150, 25 hours $240) is also worth considering.

Go Kiwi Shuttles operates door-to-door services. Shuttle buses run daily from Auckland city and Auckland airport ($6 extra) to Whitianga via Thames and Tairua, and from Auckland city to Thames. Shuttle buses also go from Whitianga via Tairua, Opoutere, Whangamata, Waihi, Tauranga to Rotorua daily in summer. Services run daily in winter if there are reservations. The Whitianga, Coromandel Town, Thames, Paeroa, Waihi, Whangamata and Whitianga loop runs daily but only from October to April. Services can also link to Hamilton at Paeroa. Contact the company for the latest schedules as they don't stay the same for long.

COROMANDEL PENINSULA

The Coromandel Peninsula juts out into the South Pacific Ocean, bordered on the west by the Hauraki Gulf. It boasts some of the North Island's best beaches and coastal scenery and attracts alternative lifestylers, wanting to escape from the city rat race.

Thames and Coromandel Town on the west coast are quaint and historical, with tiny settlements and rugged coastline further north. The best beaches (including the famed Hot Water Beach) are on the east coast which also has the main holiday resorts.

The peninsula is compact, but the narrow and winding roads mean that travel speeds are low. It's best to take your time when touring the Coromandel and cyclists should be prepared for some narrow roads and a fair bit of hill climbing.

History

Maoris had lived on the peninsula since well before the first European settlers arrived, and the sheltered areas of the east coast supported a large population. This was one of the major moa-hunting areas of the North Island, although other subsistence practices included fishing, sealing bird-hunting and horticulture.

The history of European colonisation of the peninsula and plains to the south is steeped in gold-mining, kauri logging and gumdigging. Gold was first discovered in New Zealand near Coromandel Town in 1852. Although this first rush was short-lived, more gold was discovered around Thames in 1867 and later in Coromandel Town, Kuaotunu and Karangahake. The peninsula is also rich in semiprecious gemstones, such as quartz, agate, amethyst and jasper. A fossick on any west coast beach can be rewarding.

Kauri logging was big business on the peninsula for more than 60 years. Allied to the timber trade was shipbuilding, which took off in 1832 when a mill was established at Mercury Bay. Things got tougher once the kauri around the coast became scarce and the loggers had to penetrate deeper into the bush for timber. Kauri dams were built that used water power to propel the huge logs to the coast. By the 1930s virtually no kauri trees remained on the peninsula and the logging industry died.

THAMES

pop 10,000

Thames is the western gateway to and the main service centre of the Coromandel, and lies on the shallow Firth of Thames. Plenty of 19th-century wooden stores, hotel pubs and houses have survived from the time when gold-mining and kauri logging made Thames a thriving and important business centre, and the town retains a historical atmosphere. Nowadays it's a base for tramping or canyoning in the nearby Kauaeranga Valley.

Information

The useful **Thames visitors centre** (☎ 07-868 7284; www.thames-info.co.nz; 206 Pollen St; ☒ 8.30am-5pm Mon-Fri, 9am-4pm Sat & Sun, extended hrs in summer) has Internet access, which is also available at **United Video & Internet** (456 Pollen St) and at **Laundromat Internet** (740 Pollen St), where you can surf the Web while you wash your clothes. In between the two is the **New Zealand Post Shop** (☎ 07-868 7850; Pollen St).

Sights & Activities

The **Gold Mine Experience** (☎ 07-868 8514; adult/child $10/4; ☒ 10am-4pm) is a worthwhile visit that includes walking through a gold-mine tunnel, watching a stamping battery crush rock, and also panning for gold ($2 extra).

The **Butterfly & Orchid Garden** (☎ 07-868 8080; Victoria St; adult/child $9/4; ☒ 10am-4pm summer), north of town next to the Dickson Holiday Park, is an indoor tropical jungle full of hundreds of colourful butterflies that allows visitors to observe the beauty of nature at close range. Call for winter opening hours.

Karaka Bird Hide is a great bird-watching hide that is easily reached by a boardwalk through the mangroves just off Brown St. It overlooks the Firth of Thames and the best viewing time is two hours either side of high tide.

The **School of Mines & Mineralogical Museum** (☎ 07-868 6227; cnr Brown & Cochrane Sts; adult/child $3.50/free; ☒ 11am-4pm Wed-Sun) has a full collection of NZ rocks, minerals and fossils.

The local **historical museum** (☎ 07-868 8509; cnr Cochrane & Pollen Sts; adult/child $2.50/1; ☒ 1-4pm) has pioneer relics, rocks and old photographs of the town.

Harley Davidson Motor Cycle Rides (☎ 07-867 5661; www.coromandelharleytours.co.nz; 1hr/half-day/full-day passenger rides $70/300/450) is the coolest way to tour the Coromandel. You can also hire Harleys for $380 a day and for an extra $150 a day you can have a guided tour. Fully inclusive four-day tours around other regions are also possible.

Paki Paki Bike Shop (☎ 07-867 9026; pakipaki@xtra.co.nz; Goldfields Mall) rents out fully equipped touring bikes for around $30 a day.

The **Saturday morning market** (☒ 9am-noon) has lots of organic produce and handicrafts. It's at the northern end of Pollen St, which is known as Grahamstown.

Young kids can enjoy a train ride on the **Thames Small Gauge Railway** (☎ 07-868 6678; tickets $1; ☒ 11am-3pm Sun), a 900m-loop small-gauge track.

Matatoki Farm Cheese (☎ 07-868 1284; ☒ 10am-4pm, Mon-Sat May-Oct) This cheese factory and shop, located 10km from Thames, on State Highway 26 (SH26) en route to Paeroa, is where you can taste and buy cheeses handmade from milk produced by the farm's cows.

Sleeping

BUDGET

Gateway Backpackers (☎ 07-868 6339; 209 MacKay St; dm $20, d & tw $50; ☐) This well-located, relaxed backpackers takes up two neighbouring houses, has light and airy rooms, plenty of facilities and a deck in the garden. The hard-working young owners also offer free bikes, free use of the washing machine and free tea and coffee.

Awakite (Valley View) B&B (☎ /fax 07-868 7213; 499 Kauaeranga Valley Rd; s/d $50/80) About 7km up the valley, this guesthouse has clean bright rooms, a lounge and friendly, enthusiastic hosts who grow their own organic fruit and vegetables.

Sunkist International Backpackers (☎ /fax 07-868 8808; sunkist@xtra.co.nz; 506 Brown St; camp sites $28, dm $18-20, d & tw $45; ☐) This heritage 1860s building has dorms with four to 10 beds, a garden, and offers free bikes, lots of information and a shuttle-bus service to the Kauaeranga Valley hikes (p200).

Brian Boru Hotel & Motel (☎ 07-868 6523; brian boru@xtra.co.nz; 200 Richmond St; s $25, d $60, units $80-135) The backpackers is above the pub which the owner is renovating, while the motel is a separate block out the back. For a bizarre experience try the kauri room, which is decorated like a forest.

Brookby Motel (☎ 07-868 6663; brookbymotel@xtra.co.nz; 102 Redwood Lane; units $65-90) It's worth searching out this reasonably priced brook-side gem where all the rooms have small decks and stylish furnishing.

Dickson Holiday Park (☎ 07-868 7308; www.dickson park.co.nz; camp sites $22, campervan sites $23, dm $18, cabins $45-65, units $90; ☐ ☒) Situated in a quiet valley, 4km north of Thames, this pleasant camping ground has a shop, free bikes and a three-hour bush hike up into the hills which are riddled with gold-mine tunnels.

COROMANDEL REGION

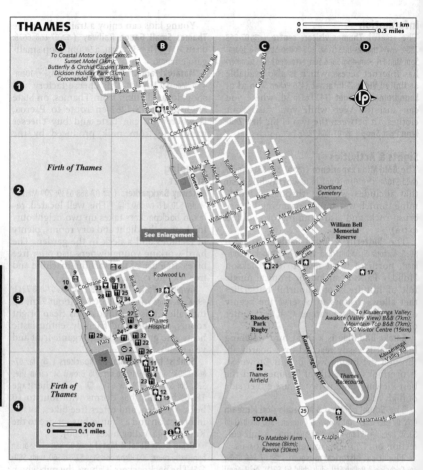

THAMES

Other backpackers in old gold-rush hotels include:

ABC Backpackers (☎ 0800 868 6200, ☎ /fax 07-868 6200; 476 Pollen St; dm/s/tw/d with bathroom $14/24/36/45; 🖳)

Thames Central Backpackers (☎ 07-868 5330; manager@thamescentralbackpackers.com; 330 Pollen St; dm $15, s $30, d & tw $40; 🖳)

MID-RANGE

Brunton House B&B (☎ /fax 07-868 5160; 210 Parawai Rd; s/d $60/95; 🛋) This very impressive two-storey kauri villa, encircled by verandas, has real historical charm and a tennis court as well as an outdoor pool.

Cotswold Cottage B&B (☎ /fax 07-868 6306; 36 Maramarahi Rd; s $70, d & tw $100-120) This pretty riverside villa has comfortable en suite rooms and helpful hosts.

Mountain Top B&B (☎ 07-868 9662; 452 Kauaeranga Valley Rd; tw/d $90/95) The breathtaking view is the special feature of this guesthouse, which is approximately 7km from town. It's run by experienced but slightly eccentric hosts.

Tuscany on Thames (☎ 07-868 5099; www.tuscany onthames.co.nz; Jellicoe Cres; units $125-150) All of the smart units have quality fittings and spa baths at this Italian-themed motel. Prices at Tuscany on Thames are negotiable in winter.

Grafton Cottage & Chalets (☎ /fax 07-868 9971; www.graftoncottage.co.nz; 304 Grafton Rd; d & tw incl breakfast $90-160; 🛋) Smart self-contained or studio chalets are available here. They come with decks and views, and there's an

INFORMATION			
Laundromat Internet...................1 B3	Brookby Motel..........................13 B3	Pak N Save Supermarket................29 A3
New Zealand Post Shop..............2 B3	Brunton House B&B....................14 C3	Sealey Café & Bar......................30 B4
Thames Visitors Centre...............3 B4	Cotswold Cottage B&B................15 D4	Sola Café................................31 B3
United Video & Internet..............4 B4	Gateway Backpackers.................16 B4	Twin Souls Café........................32 B3
	Grafton Cottage & Chalets............17 D3	
SIGHTS & ACTIVITIES (p197)	Sunkist International Backpackers......18 B1	**DRINKING** 🖥 (p199)
Gold Mine Experience.................5 B1	Thames Central Backpackers.........19 B4	Krazy Cow Bar........................(see 11)
Historical Museum.....................6 B3	Tuscany on Thames...................20 C3	Punters Sports Bar 33 A3
Karaka Bird Hide.......................7 A3		
Paki Paki Bike Shop..................(see 35)	**EATING** 🍴 (p199)	**ENTERTAINMENT** 🎭 (p200)
Saturday Morning Market.............8 B3	Billy Goat Café........................21 B4	Goldfields Cinemas....................(see 35)
School of Mines & Mineralogical	Food for Thought......................22 B3	Thames Multiplex Cinemas.............34 B3
Museum.............................9 A3	Gold Bar & Restaurant................23 B4	
Thames Small Gauge Railway 10 A3	Goldfields Café.......................(see 35)	**TRANSPORT** (p200)
	Goldmine.............................24 B3	Intercity Bus Depot...................(see 3)
SLEEPING 🛏 (pp197–9)	Green Cheese Café 25 B3	
ABC Backpackers......................11 B4	Kaveeta's.............................26 B3	**OTHER**
Brian Boru Hotel & Motel.............12 B4	Majestic Fish Shop...................27 B3	Goldfields Shopping
	Old Thames Restaurant...............28 A3	Centre..............................35 A4

outdoor pool and a spa pool. The Mexican (or other) breakfast can be served in your room if you wish.

Sunset Motel (☎ /fax 07-868 8573; www.sunset motel.co.nz; 1017 Tararu Rd; units $85-120) This standard motel, 3km north of Thames, is the only one right by the sea and has kayaks and a boat for hire.

Coastal Motor Lodge (☎ 07-868 6843; www.nz motels.co.nz/coastal; 608 Tararu Rd; chalets $125-135, family units $100-115) Superior accommodation is provided at these stylish modern chalets, 2km north of Thames, that overlook the sea and are good enough even for honeymooners.

Eating & Drinking

Thames has a handful of superb cafés.

Food for Thought (☎ 07-868 6065; 574 Pollen St; 🕑 breakfast & lunch Mon-Sat) This place has lots of deli snacks for under $5.

Green Cheese Café (☎ 07-868 3314; 710 Pollen St; meals $5-15; 🕑 breakfast & lunch) Offerings here include bagels, *panini* (focaccia), Italian-style meals, fresh juice and there's a charming garden at the back.

Twin Souls Café (☎ 07-868 5255; 578 Pollen St; meals $6-12; 🕑 breakfast & lunch Mon-Sat) Excellent home-cooked food and good coffee can be found here.

Sola Café (☎ 07-868 8781; 720b Pollen St; lunch mains $7-9, dinner mains $15-18; 🕑 breakfast & lunch daily, dinner Thu-Sun in summer, dinner Fri in winter) This is a brilliant vegetarian café with vegan, dairy-free and gluten-free food. The risotto cakes are popular.

Billy Goat Café (☎ 07-868 7384; 444 Pollen St; meals $5-8; 🕑 breakfast & lunch daily in summer, Mon-Fri in winter) Home-baked cakes as well as bagels, lasagne and salads are available at this newcomer.

Goldfields Café (☎ 07-867 9240; Goldfields Mall; 🕑 breakfast & lunch) This café has drinks and lots of snacks for under $4, and is in the mall near the food court which has sushi, kebab, Chinese and hamburger stalls.

Majestic Fish Shop (☎ 07-868 6204; 640 Pollen St; mains $13-21; 🕑 lunch & dinner) This popular fish and chip takeaway also sells chicken and steak. It has a restaurant at the back.

Kaveeta's (☎ 07-868 7049; 518 Pollen St; lunch mains $10, dinner mains $12; 🕑 lunch & dinner) The youthful owner serves up Indian food, pizzas (including Indian-style varieties), a herby lassi, and kulfi ice cream in this unusual and inexpensive restaurant which also has a tasty vegetarian selection.

Old Thames Restaurant (☎ 07-868 7207; 705 Pollen St; lunch mains under $15, dinner mains $21-26; 🕑 lunch & dinner) This smart and well-established place serves top NZ fare – try the local flounder – as well as pizzas.

Sealey Café & Bar (☎ 07-868 8641; 109 Sealey St; lunch mains $8-13, dinner mains $22-26; 🕑 breakfast, lunch & dinner) This all-day café/restaurant has a pleasant courtyard out the front and some unusual and tempting combinations and salads on its menu.

Goldmine (☎ 07-868 3180; 545 Pollen St; mains $10-28; 🕑 breakfast, lunch & dinner, bar open till late) This bar and grill has a surprisingly long and varied menu.

Gold Bar & Restaurant (☎ 07-868 5548; 404 Pollen St; mains $27-29; 🕑 dinner Wed-Sat winter, daily summer) This place serves up fancy-looking food based on fresh local produce.

Self-caterers might like to try **Pak N Save Supermarket** (☎ 07-868 9565; Mary St).

Popular places for an evening drink include the Gold Bar (above), **Krazy Cow Bar** (☎ 0800 868 6200; 76 Pollen St) and **Punters Sports Bar** (☎ 07-868 7033; 719 Pollen St).

Entertainment

There are two cinemas in town: **Thames Multiplex** (☎ 07-868 6600; 708 Pollen St) and **Goldfields Cinemas** (☎ 07-867 9100; Goldfields Shopping Centre).

Getting There & Around

Thames is the transport hub of the Coromandel. **InterCity** (☎ 09-913 6100 Auckland) has daily buses from Auckland to Thames ($19, two hours), from where you can continue on to Paeroa, Waihi, Tauranga and Rotorua. **Go Kiwi Shuttles** (☎ 0800 446 549, 07-866 0336; www.go-kiwi.co.nz) also has services from Auckland ($26). InterCity buses stop at the InterCity bus depot, while Go Kiwi Shuttles run door-to-door.

The Coromandel Loop pass (adult/child $55/36) allows you to travel around the peninsula from Thames to Coromandel Town, Whitianga and Tairua, then back to Thames.

COROMANDEL FOREST PARK

Over 30 walks and tramps crisscross the Coromandel Forest Park, which stretches from Paeroa up to Cape Colville. The most popular hike is the 3½-hour hike up to the dramatic Pinnacles (759m) in the Kauaeranga Valley behind Thames. There are old kauri dams in the valley, including the Tarawaere Waterfalls, Dancing Camp, Kauaeranga Main, Moss Creek and Waterfalls Creek dams. Other outstanding hikes include the Coromandel Coastal Walkway from Fletcher Bay to Stony Bay (see p203) in the far north, and the Puketui Valley (p210) walk to old gold-mine workings.

The **DOC visitors centre** (☎ 07-867 9080; Kauaeranga Valley Rd; ☽ 8am-4pm) has hiking information, maps and takes bookings for the Pinnacles hut. There are displays on kauri logging and nearby is a model of a kauri dam. The centre is 14km off the main road, and a further 9km along a gravel road is the start of the hiking trails. Sunkist International Backpackers (see p197) has transport from Thames to the hiking trails.

The **DOC Pinnacles hut** (☎ 07-867 9080; $30) has 80 beds, gas cookers, heaters, toilets and cold showers, and must be pre-booked. Very basic **DOC camping grounds** (sites $14) are scattered throughout Coromandel Forest Park at Fantail Bay, Port Jackson, Fletcher Bay, Stony Bay and Waikawau Bay in the north, further south at Broken Hills and Wentworth

---

BRING BACK THE KAURI TREES

The Coromandel Peninsula once supported magnificent stands of the long-lived kauri tree, but after continual logging between the 1870s and the 1930s, very few remain.

For a $10 donation you can help bring the kauri forests back to life, as a volunteer will plant a kauri seedling on your behalf. Pick up a leaflet at the DOC visitors centre or contact the **Kauri 2000 Trust** (☎ /fax 07-866 0468; Box 174, Whitianga, NZ).

Valley, and near the Pinnacles hut at Moss Creek. Expect chemical toilets and few, if any, other facilities. Camp sites are on a first-come, first-served basis but Waikawau Bay requires booking (☎ 07-866 1106) over Christmas and New Year.

THAMES TO COROMANDEL TOWN

As you travel north from Thames, the narrow SH25 snakes along the coast past pretty little bays and rocky beaches. Sea birds can be seen, especially around high tide, and you can fish, look for shellfish and fossick for quartz, jasper and even gold-bearing rocks on the beaches. The landscape turns crimson when the pohutukawa (often referred to as the 'NZ Christmas tree') blooms in late December. At Wilsons Bay the road leaves the coast and climbs over several hills and valleys before dropping down to Coromandel Town, 54km from Thames. A handful of stores, motels, B&Bs and camping grounds are spread around the tiny settlements that front the bays.

There are holiday parks with camping and cabins at regular intervals along the highway, including: **Waiomu Bay Holiday Park** (☎ 07-868 2777; Waiomu Valley Rd; camp & campervan sites $21, cabins $45-85; ☒) in Waiomu, which also has backpacker bunkrooms at $12 per person, and a pool; and **Tapu Motor Camp** (☎ 07-868 4837; Main Rd; camp/campervan sites $16/20), on the beach at Tapu, 22km north of Thames.

About 11km north of Thames **Te Puru Coast View Lodge** (☎ 07-868 2326; tepuru-lodge@xtra.co.nz; 468 Thames Coast Rd, Te Puru; s $110, d & tw $130-165) is a luxurious Mediterranean-style villa on a hill overlooking the Firth of Thames. There is a bar and restaurant and all meals can be provided (guests only).

Set on a cattle and deer farm at Te Kouma harbour, just past Manaia, **Te Kouma Harbour Farmstay** (☎ 07-866 8747; tekouma@xtra.co.nz; 1105a SH25; dm/units $20/80; ☒) has modern units with kitchens and TVs, a games room and kayaking and bushwalking opportunities in a secluded environment.

COROMANDEL TOWN

pop 1620

It was at Driving Creek, 3km north of the township, that Charles Ring discovered gold in 1852. At the height of the gold rush the town's population rose to over 10,000, but today it's a sleepy little township noted for its craft shops, alternative lifestylers and mussel fishing.

Information

The **visitors centre** (☎ 07-866 8598; www.coromandeltown.co.nz; 355 Kapanga Rd; ⏲ 9am-5pm daily summer, 9am-5pm Mon-Sat & 10am-2pm Sun winter) has Internet access and information on DOC hikes and camping grounds. Nearby are the **police station** (☎ 07-866 1190; 405 Kapanga Rd) and the **Post Shop** (☎ 07-866 8865; Kapanga Rd), while the **Bank of New Zealand** (BNZ; ☎ 0800 866 8865; cnr Tiki & Wharf Rds) is closer to the harbour.

Sights & Activities

The amazing **Driving Creek Railway & Pottery** (☎ /fax 07-866 8703; www.drivingcreekrailway.co.nz; 410 Driving Creek Rd; train trips adult/child $15/7) is 3km north of Coromandel Town. The unique trains run at 10.15am and 2pm (more often

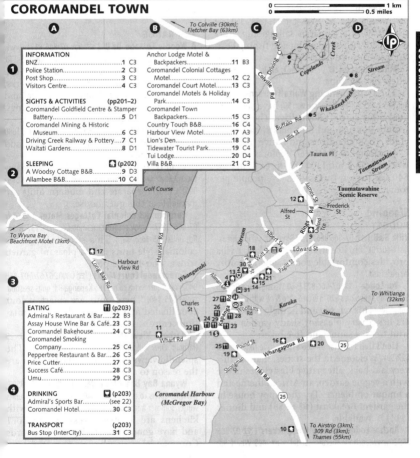

COROMANDEL TOWN

0 _____ 1 km
0 _____ 0.5 miles

INFORMATION	
BNZ	.1 C3
Police Station	.2 C3
Post Shop	.3 C3
Visitors Centre	.4 C3

SIGHTS & ACTIVITIES	(pp201-2)
Coromandel Goldfield Centre & Stamper Battery	.5 D1
Coromandel Mining & Historic Museum	.6 C3
Driving Creek Railway & Pottery	.7 C1
Waitati Gardens	.8 D1

SLEEPING	⊡ (p202)
A Woodsy Cottage B&B	.9 D3
Allambee B&B	.10 C4

Anchor Lodge Motel & Backpackers	.11 B3
Coromandel Colonial Cottages Motel	.12 C2
Coromandel Court Motel	.13 C3
Coromandel Motels & Holiday Park	.14 C3
Coromandel Town Backpackers	.15 C3
Country Touch B&B	.16 C3
Harbour View Motel	.17 A3
Lion's Den	.18 C3
Tidewater Tourist Park	.19 C4
Tui Lodge	.20 D4
Villa B&B	.21 C3

EATING	⊞ (p203)
Admiral's Restaurant & Bar	.22 B3
Assay House Wine Bar & Café	.23 C3
Coromandel Bakehouse	.24 C3
Coromandel Smoking Company	.25 C4
Peppertree Restaurant & Bar	.26 C3
Price Cutter	.27 C3
Success Café	.28 C3
Umu	.29 C3

DRINKING	⊡ (p203)
Admiral's Sports Bar	.(see 22)
Coromandel Hotel	.30 C3

TRANSPORT	(p203)
Bus Stop (InterCity)	.31 C3

To Colville (30km); Fletcher Bay (63km)

COROMANDEL REGION

Taumatawahine Scenic Reserve

Golf Course

To Wyuna Bay Beachfront Motel (3km)

To Whitianga (32km)

Coromandel Harbour (McGregor Bay)

To Airstrip (3km); 309 Rd (3km); Thames (55km)

in summer) up steep grades, across four trestle bridges, along two spirals and a double switchback, and through two tunnels, finishing at the 'Eye-full Tower'. The hour-long trip goes up into the hills, past artworks and through an area of recently planted native trees. The owner is a well-known NZ potter and ceramics are for sale at reasonable prices.

The **Coromandel Goldfield Centre & Stamper Battery** (☎ 07-866 7933; 410 Buffalo Rd; adult/child $6/3; ☼ 10am-4pm) has informative one-hour tours of this working 1899 rock-crushing plant with a water mill.

The small **Coromandel Mining & Historic Museum** (☎ 07-866 7251; 900 Rings Rd; adult/child $2/50c; ☼ 10am-1pm Mon-Fri, 10am-4pm Sat & Sun) provides a glimpse of life in the golden days.

Te Kaihau (☎ 07-868 7546; www.sailcoro.co.nz; day/overnight trips incl meals per adult $85/100, per child $30/50) is a trimaran sailing ship, fully equipped with snorkelling and fishing gear. Longer trips are possible.

Mussel Barge (☎ 07-866 7667; adult/child $35/20) offers fishing trips.

The award-winning **Waitaiti Gardens** (☎ 07-866 8659; 485 Buffalo Rd; admission $5) have been created either side of a long drive. The gardens feature unusual and rare plants, native orchids, rhododendrons and native trees.

Argo Tours (☎ 07-866 7667) explores old gold workings in a mini 8WD – three hours for $40 per person (maximum five people per tour).

Sleeping
BUDGET
Villa B&B (☎ 07-866 8862; 756 Rings Rd; s/d incl breakfast $40/70) This centrally located kauri villa provides comfortable rooms, and a healthy breakfast.

Tui Lodge (☎ 07-866 8237; 60 Whangapoua Rd; dm $18, camp sites $20, s $20, d & tw $40, d & tw with bathroom $60; ☐) This relaxed and homely backpackers has a very pleasant shady garden with fruit trees, a sauna and free bikes.

Lion's Den (☎ /fax 07-866 8157; 126 Te Tiki St; dm/d $22/50) 'Welcome to the sixties, man' at this very laid-back, alternative lifestyle residence with a veggie garden, an African theme and a unique ambience. Try the hippy house in the garden. Breakfast ($3 to $6) and dinner ($14) is available.

Anchor Lodge Motel & Backpackers (☎ 07-866 7992; www.anchorlodgecoromandel.co.nz; 448 Wharf Rd;

dm $20, d $50-70, units $80-185; ☐ ☒) New and smart accommodation is available in both the motel and backpacker sections, but the latter lacks the Tui Lodge's atmosphere.

Tidewater Tourist Park (☎ 07-866 8888; tide watr@world-net.co.nz; 270 Tiki Rd; camp sites $20, dm $20, d $45, units $75-120) Units are newish but small and dull at this YHA-associate with bicycles ($20 a day) and kayaks ($40 a day) for hire and a sauna ($5).

Coromandel Town Backpackers (☎ 07-866 8327; 732 Rings Rd; dm $17, d & tw $36) This central, relaxed hostel has small modern rooms that lack character.

Coromandel Motels & Holiday Park (☎ 07-866 8830; coromandelholidaypark@paradise.net.nz; 636 Rings Rd; camp sites $20, campervan sites $24, cabins $40-55, units $65-110) This park is small but clean and tidy with lots of facilities.

MID-RANGE
A Woodsy Cottage B&B (☎ /fax 07-866 8111; www .awoodsycottage.com; 2 Oxford Tce; d $75, cottages $75-140; ☒) This timber house, tucked away in a fairyland ferny garden with Asian artworks, is somewhere special and has a spa and cottages with Balinese or antique furnishings. An organic breakfast is an optional extra.

Allambee B&B (☎ 07-866 8011; fax 866 8611; 1680 Tiki Rd; s/d $55/85) This character house has good en suite rooms.

Country Touch B&B (☎ 07-866 8130; country touch@xtra.co.nz; 39 Whangapoua Rd; s $55, d & tw $85-105) Clean, separate and modern units are available at this guesthouse.

Coromandel Colonial Cottages Motel (☎ /fax 07-866 8857; www.corocottagesmotel.co.nz; 1737 Rings Rd; units $85-165; ☒) This street of separate colonial-style units is in a pleasant garden with a solar-heated pool.

Coromandel Court Motel (☎ 0800 267 626, 07-866 8402; corocourt@xtra.co.nz; 365 Kapanga Rd; units seasonal range $75-140) These units are smart, colour coordinated and just behind the information centre.

Harbour View Motel (☎ /fax 07-866 8690; 25 Harbour View Rd; units seasonal range $85-165) The splendid views overlooking the harbour are the reason to stay here.

Wyuna Bay Beachfront Motel (☎ 07-866 8507; www.nzmotels.co.nz/wyuna; 2640 Wyuna Bay Rd; units winter/summer from $65/130) Secluded units with kitchens are located across the harbour and have good views facing back towards Coromandel.

Eating & Drinking

Coromandel Smoking Company (☎ 07-866 8793; 70 Tiki Rd) This shop stocks a great range of smoked fish and seafood and the staff will smoke your catch too. Try the smoked fish pâté.

Coromandel Bakehouse (☎ 07-866 8554; 92 Wharf Rd) Nip in here for a quick snack.

Success Café (☎ 07-866 7100; 104 Kapanga Rd; lunch mains $5-10, dinner mains $16-22; ⏰ breakfast, lunch & dinner) This café goes à la carte in the evening, with an original mainly seafood menu.

Assay House Wine Bar & Café (☎ 07-866 7397; 2 Kapanga Rd; light meals around $8) This place features a blackboard menu, brightly coloured décor and a garden.

Umu (☎ 07-866 8618; 22 Wharf Rd; lunch mains $7-22, dinner mains $17-26; ⏰ breakfast, lunch & dinner) Umu has lots of indoor and outdoor seating and serves up classy food. Try the chunky vegetable mussel chowder or the fresh fish 'cooked to the chef's whim' with roasted veggies. The pizzas (large $16 to $20) and $7 lunch hotpots are also popular.

Admiral's Restaurant & Bar (☎ 07-866 8020; upstairs, 146 Wharf Rd; lunch mains $8-10, dinner mains $20-25; ⏰ lunch & dinner) An enthusiastic young chef has taken over at this refurbished restaurant which has harbour views from the veranda. There is live music once a week at the very flash Admiral's Sports Bar down below.

Peppertree Restaurant & Bar (☎ 07-866 8211; 31 Kapanga Rd; mains $20-25; ⏰ breakfast, lunch & dinner) The all-day and diverse menu at this place includes fresh local seafood such as mussel spring rolls and crayfish. Coromandel is famous for its mussels.

Coromandel Hotel (☎ 07-866 8760; 611 Kapanga Rd) is the local pub.

Self-caterers can browse in the **Price Cutter** (☎ 07-866 8669; 255 Kapanga Rd) supermarket.

Getting There & Away

Between Christmas and Easter the **Kawau Kat** (☎ 0800 888 006; adult/child one way $45/25) boat runs between central Auckland and Coromandel Town twice a week (trips take two hours). It's a good alternative to the bus.

InterCity (☎ 07-868 7284 Thames) runs daily buses to and from Thames ($16) and Whitianga ($17), which stop in the centre of town, while **Go Kiwi Shuttles** (☎ 0800 446 549, 07-866 0336; www.go-kiwi.co.nz) go door-to-door and cost $25 for each route.

FAR NORTH COROMANDEL

The road north is sealed up to the tiny settlement of **Colville** (25km north of Coromandel Town), which is home to a few alternative lifestylers. There is a Buddhist retreat; the **Colville Café** (☎ 07-866 6912; 2312 Colville Rd; ⏰ 9.30am-4pm), which has excellent carrot cake; and the quaint **Colville General Store** (☎ 07-866 6805; Colville Rd; ⏰ 8.30am-5pm) that sells just about everything, including organic food and petrol.

North of Colville, the gravel roads are narrow but in reasonable condition. Heading north along the west coast takes you to Fletcher Bay, but a detour over the ranges goes to **Port Charles** where there are holiday baches (cottages) on a pleasant bay beach and then on to the aptly named **Stony Bay** that has a DOC camping ground. From Stony Bay, hiking tracks lead north to Fletcher Bay and south to Mt Moehau (892m), the peninsula's highest peak.

Following the west coast road, 12km north of Colville is Te Hope, the start of the demanding eight-hour return hike to the top of Mt Moehau which rewards you with fine views of Coromandel and the Hauraki Gulf. The road stops at **Fletcher Bay** which is a real land's end and a magical get-away-from-it-all place with deserted beaches, forest and coastal hikes and splendid views across to Great Barrier, Little Barrier and Cuvier Islands.

The **Coromandel Coastal Walkway** is a scenic three-hour hike between Fletcher Bay and Stony Bay. It's a relatively easy walk with great coastal views and an ambling section across open farmland. **Strongman Coaches** (☎ 07-866 8175) will drive you from Coromandel Town up to Fletcher Bay and pick you up from Stony Bay three or four hours later. The cost is $65.

Mahamudra Centre (☎ 07-866 6851; www.mahamudra.org.nz; dm/s/tw/units $15/20/30/40) is a serene Buddhist retreat that has a stupa and a yoga and meditation hall. It offers simple but comfortable accommodation in a park-like setting, located 1km south of Colville. Buddhist teachers run courses that are open to all.

The 1260-hectare **Colville Farm** (☎ /fax 07-866 6820; 2140 Colville Rd; camp sites $14, campervan sites $18, dm $17, s $20, d $40, d with bathroom $50-55, units $60-75) has a wide range of accommodation and guests can milk cows by hand and try other types of farm work. Horse rides are $30 for two hours.

On a farm property on the tip of the peninsula, **Fletcher Bay Backpackers** (☎ 07-866 6712; js.lourie@xtra.co.nz; dm $14, camp sites $24) is a quiet, comfortable 16-bed cottage. There are four dorms with two double bunks in each room. It has all facilities but you must bring food as there are no shops and no meals are provided.

Very basic DOC **camping grounds** (per night $14) are at Waikawau Bay and Stony Bay on the eastern side of the peninsula, and at Fantail Bay, Port Jackson and Fletcher Bay which can be reached from the west coast road. There is no road between Fletcher Bay and Stony Bay.

COROMANDEL TOWN TO WHITIANGA

There are two routes from Coromandel Town southeast to Whitianga: the main road is the slightly longer SH25 which follows the coast, enjoys sea views and has short detours to pristine sandy beaches. The other route is via the mainly gravel 309 Road which has some fine forest walks along the way.

State Highway 25

First stop on the SH25 east of Coromandel Town is Te Rerenga, almost on the shore of Whangapoua Harbour. The road forks at the harbour, and if you detour north you can visit Whangapoua, from where you can walk along the rocky foreshore to the isolated and often deserted **New Chum's Beach** (30 minutes).

Also at Te Rerenga is the **Castle Rock Winery** (☎ 07-866 4542; units $75-110; ☉ wine-tasting 9am-6pm summer, 10am-5pm winter), which produces a range of fruit wines – try the feijoa. Platter lunches, jams, pickles and organic ale are also for sale.

Continuing east you soon reach **Kuaotunu**, a quaint settlement with a delightful beach and **Black Jack Backpackers** (☎ 07-866 2988; www.black-jack.co.nz; camp sites $30, dm $22, d $60-80), which is new and smart with bikes for hire and free kayaks for paddling on the river. Meals are provided by arrangement.

Heading off the highway at Kuaotunu takes you to an even more remote area where **Otama Beach** and **Opito Bay** have some of the finest stretches of sand on the east coast. At the end of Opito Bay there's a walk up to a viewpoint on the headland.

309 Road

This is the shorter route to Whitianga (45 minutes, 26km), and the well-maintained gravel road is being sealed bit by bit. The **Waiau Waterworks** (☎ 07-866 7191; 471 309 Rd; adult/child $8/4; ☉ 9am-5pm), 5km from SH25, is a family theme park with whimsical water-powered amusements, a flying fox and a playground.

Forest walks along the 309 Road include a two-hour return trail to the summit of **Castle Rock** (521m) and short walks to **Waiau Falls** and to a **kauri grove**.

Bushcreek Cottage Backpackers (☎ 07-866 5151; 1694 309 Rd; www.bushcreek.co.nz; camp sites $24, dm/d & tw $19/44) About 10km from Whitianga, this backpackers is a lovely 150-year-old kauri cottage beside a river with swimming holes. It's a relaxing place surrounded by bush and an organic farm. You can camp in a tepee for the same price as pitching your own tent.

WHITIANGA

pop 3580

The legendary Polynesian explorer and seafarer Kupe is said to have landed near here in about AD 800 and the area was called Te Whitianga a Kupe (the Crossing Place of Kupe). Whitianga is the main town on Mercury Bay and a popular resort with a harbour and plenty of marine activities such as scuba diving or kayaking around offshore islands, and on land, bone carving and horse riding. Nearby are two famous natural attractions, Cathedral Cove and Hot Water Beach.

Information

The well-organised **Whitianga i-SITE visitors centre** (☎ 07-866 5555; www.whitianga.co.nz; 66 Albert St; ☉ 9am-5pm Mon-Fri, 9am-4pm Sat & Sun) has Internet access and hires out bicycles ($25 a day). An Internet café has opened on Blacksmith Lane and there is a **Medical Centre** (☎ 07-866 5911 24hr; 87 Albert St; ☉ 8.30am-5pm Mon-Fri, 9-11am Sat & Sun, closed Sun in winter). The **Post Shop** (☎ 07-866 4006; 72 Albert St) is nearby.

Sights & Activities

The **museum** (☎ 07-866 0770; adult/child $3/50c; 12 The Esplanade; ☉ 10am-4pm summer, 11am-3pm Tue-Thu & Sun winter) has local history, nature displays and an interesting video about Maori and Pakeha views on Captain Cook.

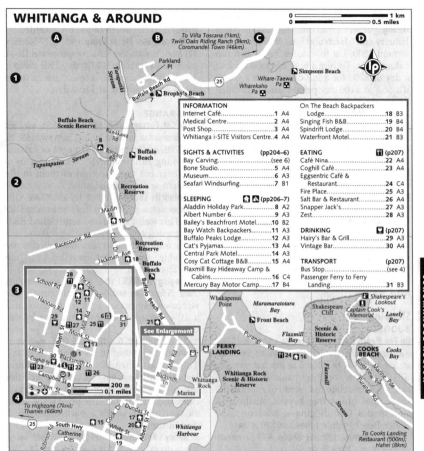

WHITIANGA & AROUND

INFORMATION
Internet Café..............................1 A4
Medical Centre..........................2 A4
Post Shop...................................3 A4
Whitianga i-SITE Visitors Centre..4 A4

SIGHTS & ACTIVITIES (pp204–6)
Bay Carving..........................(see 6)
Bone Studio................................5 A4
Museum.......................................6 A3
Seafari Windsurfing....................7 B1

SLEEPING (pp206–7)
Aladdin Holiday Park...................8 A2
Albert Number 6.........................9 A3
Bailey's Beachfront Motel.........10 B2
Bay Watch Backpackers...........11 A3
Buffalo Peaks Lodge.................12 A3
Cat's Pyjamas...........................13 A4
Central Park Motel....................14 A3
Cosy Cat Cottage B&B.............15 A4
Flaxmill Bay Hideaway Camp &
  Cabins....................................16 C4
Mercury Bay Motor Camp........17 B4

On The Beach Backpackers
  Lodge.....................................18 B3
Singing Fish B&B......................19 B4
Spindrift Lodge.........................20 B4
Waterfront Motel......................21 B3

EATING (p207)
Café Nina...................................22 A4
Coghill Café...............................23 A4
Eggsentric Café &
  Restaurant..............................24 C4
Fire Place...................................25 A4
Salt Bar & Restaurant...............26 A4
Snapper Jack's..........................27 A3
Zest..28 A3

DRINKING (p207)
Hairy's Bar & Grill.....................29 A4
Vintage Bar...............................30 A4

TRANSPORT (p207)
Bus Stop...............................(see 4)
Passenger Ferry to Ferry
  Landing...................................31 B3

Maurice Aukett of **Bay Carving** (☎ 07-866 4021; The Esplanade; 9am-4pm), next door to the museum, will help you create a high-quality Maori-style carving using a dentist drill and sandpaper. It takes about two hours, costs $35 and is recommended. **Bone Studio** (☎ 07-866 2158; 6b Bryce St) offers more in-depth bone-carving tuition ($80 a day).

The **Cave Cruzer** (☎ 0800 427 893, 07-866 2275; www.cavecruzer.co.nz; 1-3hr trips $45-85) is a rigid-hull inflatable boat that offers trips around the caves and islands with snorkelling, fishing, music and commentary.

The **Blue Boat** (☎ 07-866 4904; adult/child $30/5) operates a two-hour trip to Cathedral Cove at 10am and 2pm. In summer it also runs at 5pm (minimum four adults).

Playmaker Tours (☎ 07-866 4303; www.playmaker.co.nz; 1-1/2-hr tours $60/90) operates a fast boat around the scenic spots.

Ocean Wave Tours (☎ 0800 806 060; adult/child $45/35) run at 10am, 1pm and 3.30pm and take 1½ to two hours.

Seafari Glass Bottom Boat (☎ 021-478 290; www.glassbottomboatwhitianga.co.nz; adult/child $65/35) operates 2½-hour tours all year-round and you can see what's under the water as well as the limestone coastal scenery. Three trips a day are available in summer, snorkelling gear is available and bookings can be made at Whitianga i-SITE visitors centre.

Banana Boat (☎ 07-866 5617) has banana-boat rides from $10, but they only operate in January.

Whitianga marina is a base for **game-fishing** (particularly marlin and tuna) between January and March and boat charters start at around $800. Up to a dozen boats also run fishing trips. To hire a boat it's $350 for half a day or $700 for a full day; to join a group it's $60 to $100 per person on a scheduled departure.

Seafari Windsurfing (☎ 07-866 0677; Brophy's Beach), 4km north of Whitianga, hires out sailboards ($20 to $35 an hour) and kayaks ($10 to $20 an hour) and provides windsurfing lessons ($40 for 1½ hours). Wet suit hire is $5 and life jackets are free.

For horse trekking, the **Twin Oaks Riding Ranch** (☎ 07-866 5388; 2hr adult/child $30/25) is 9km north of Whitianga on the Kuaotunu Rd.

Highzone (☎ /fax 07-866 2113; www.highzone.co.nz; 49 Kaimarama Rd; activities $10-60) offers high adventure on a ropes course which involves nine challenges 12m above ground level, including a leap onto a trapeze. It's located 7km south of Whitianga, just off the main road. Call for times.

Sleeping
BUDGET

On The Beach Backpackers Lodge (☎ 07-866 5380; www.coromandelbackpackers.com; 46 Buffalo Beach Rd; dm $22, s $50, d & tw $55, d & tw with bathroom $80; 🖳) This large, brightly painted and well-run YHA-associate has plenty of rooms and space, and offers free kayaks, surfboards and spades (for digging a pool on Hot Water Beach) while bikes are $20 a day.

Cat's Pyjamas (☎ /fax 07-866 4663; www.cats-pyjamas.co.nz; 4 Monk St; dm $20, camp sites $24, d & tw $45, d & tw with bathroom $50; 🖳) A small and bright backpackers with friendly hosts who can arrange 30-minute scenic flights at a reasonable price.

Buffalo Peaks Lodge (☎ 07-866 2933; www.buffalopeaks.co.nz; 12 Albert St; dm/d $22/50; 🖳) This place has nine-bed, six-bed and four-bed dorms, is popular with backpacker tour groups and has a spa pool and a free pool table.

Bay Watch Backpackers (☎ 07-866 5481; www.whitianga.co.nz/baywatch; 22 The Esplanade; dm $18-22, d & tw $50-55, units $65-140; 🖳) This cosy backpackers on the seafront also has motel units and hires out kayaks.

Aladdin Holiday Park (☎ 07-866 5834; 6 Bongard Rd; camp sites & campervan sites $20-25, cabins $45-75, tourist flats $70-110) Bush walks for all energy

levels are available near this pleasant camp ground to the north of the town centre.

Mercury Bay Motor Camp (☎ /fax 07-866 5579; 121 Albert St; camp sites $20-26, campervan sites $26-34, cabins $40-80, tourist flats $60-120; 🖳) This camp is small and shady with a spa, clean facilities and kayaks for hire at $10 a day.

MID-RANGE

Cosy Cat Cottage B&B (☎ 07-866 4488; www.bed-and-breakfast.co.nz/cosycat.html; 41 South Hwy; s $50-75, d $85-105, units per person $45) Images of cats fill this long-running B&B cottage run by a cat-lover but there are less of them in the modern self-contained units.

Spindrift Lodge (☎ 0800 127 627, 07-866 5116; www.spindrift.co.nz; 129 Albert St; s/d incl breakfast $110/140) This well-located and refurbished B&B has garden or estuary views. Breakfast is a fresh fruit platter, kayaks and bicycles are available, and the well-travelled hosts are people-oriented.

Singing Fish B&B (☎ 07-866 2275; www.cavecruzer.co.nz; 25 South Hwy; units $65-95) This guesthouse is reasonably priced with a spa pool and a 10% discount on boat trips run by the owner.

Albert Number 6 (☎ 07-866 0036; www.albertnumbersix.co.nz; 6 Albert St; d & tw incl breakfast $85) These smart new units with colourful and stylish furnishings have no cooking facilities but there are plenty of nearby takeaways, cafés and restaurants. The price is the same all year-round, so it's a particularly good deal in summer.

Bailey's Beachfront Motel (☎ 07-866 5500; baileysmotel@xtra.co.nz; 66 Buffalo Beach Rd; units $80-150) The advantage of these self-contained holiday units is that they are on the seafront.

Central Park Motel (☎ 07-866 5471; centralparkmotel@wave.co.nz; 6 Mill Rd; s $40-70, d $50-80; 🖳) These reasonably priced units are within easy walking distance of the town and seafront.

Waterfront Motel (☎ 07-866 4498; www.waterfrontmotel.co.nz; 2 Buffalo Beach Rd; units $120-300) This boutique motel has stylish deluxe rooms with balconies and sea views.

TOP END

Villa Toscana (☎ 07-866 2293; www.villatoscana.co.nz; Ohuka Park, Whitianga; d & tw incl breakfast Nov-Mar $640, Apr-Oct $440) Experience stylish luxury and gracious hosts at this palatial Italian hillside villa just north of town. It has great views, a helipad, a hot spa and Italian antiques and wines. Kayaks and mountain bikes are available and the owners' game-fishing boat *Mamma Mia!* can be chartered.

Eating & Drinking

Café Nina (☎ 07-866 5440; 20 Victoria St; meals $4.50-11; breakfast, lunch & dinner summer, breakfast & lunch winter) BBQ breakfasts, an ever-changing lunch menu, afternoon tea and cakes, and dinner (in summer only) are available at this popular café in a cottage run by a talented and hard-working couple. It's worth seeking out.

Coghill Café (☎ 07-866 0592; 10 Coghill St; meals $8.50-14; breakfast & lunch) This café opens at 7am and provides homemade snacks, giant pies, date scones, smoothies and meals.

Snapper Jack's (☎ 07-866 5482; Albert St; lunch & dinner) This popular fast-food outlet serves up fish or chicken and chips, takeaway or sit-down.

Fire Place (☎ 07-866 4828; 9 The Esplanade; mains $20-27; lunch & dinner) The top place for pizzas and *nouvelle cuisine* with geometric, smallish portions and delicate sauces.

Salt Bar & Restaurant (☎ 07-866 5818; 1 Blacksmith Lane; mains $16-22; lunch & dinner) Thai dishes are served inside or on the terrace overlooking the marina. The sports bar has live music and DJs on a regular basis.

Zest (☎ 07-866 5127; 5 Albert St; mains $16-25; dinner daily summer, Wed-Sun winter) A global menu and blackboard desserts can be found in this licensed restaurant.

Stroll along The Esplanade for steak and seafood dinners.

Hairy's Bar & Grill (☎ 07-866 5249; 31 Albert St) This sports bar has table tennis, a big screen, a jukebox, a pool table, live bands at the weekend and, surprisingly, a swimming pool out the back.

Vintage Bar (☎ 07-866 5858; 69 Albert St; 3pm-1am daily summer, Tue-Sat winter) This small, smart bar plays mostly jazz music and offers a choice of 90 wines.

Getting There & Around

Go Kiwi (☎ 0800 446 549, 07-866 0336; www.go-kiwi .co.nz) has a daily shuttle bus from Whitianga to Thames ($30, 1½ hours), Coromandel Town ($25) and Tairua ($20). It also runs shuttle buses from Ferry Landing to Hahei and Hot Water Beach; see p207.

The **InterCity** (☎ 09-913 6100 Auckland) stops at the visitors centre on its Coromandel Loop (adult/child $55/36) every day. The range of InterCity services include Whitianga to Coromandel Town ($17), Whitianga to Tairua ($16), and Whitianga to Waihi ($44).

Great Barrier Airlines (☎ 0800 900 600, Auckland 09-275 9120; www.greatbarrierairlines.co.nz; one-way fare adult/child $100/65) operates flights four times a week between Auckland and Whitianga, and twice a week between Great Barrier Island and Whitianga (the cost is the same for both).

AROUND WHITIANGA

Ferry Landing

From the Narrows, on the southern end of Whitianga, a small passenger ferry crosses over to **Ferry Landing**, where there is a general store, a café, a motel and a B&B. From there you can travel on by foot, bike or shuttle bus to Flaxmill Bay, Shakespeare's Lookout, Captain Cook's Memorial, Lonely Bay, Cooks Bay and further afield to Cathedral Cove, Hahei and Hot Water Beach.

The **passenger ferry** (adult/child or bicycle one way $1/50c) takes five minutes, and runs continuously from 7am to 10.30pm in summer, and from 7am to 6.30pm, 7.30pm to 8.30pm and 9.30pm to 10.30pm in winter.

HAHEI

Hahei (www.hahei.co.nz) is a lovely white-sand beach with islands scattered out in the bay, and is 38km by road from Whitianga via Coroglen. The dramatic limestone coastline and small islands here make up the Te Whanganui a Hei Marine Reserve. Kayaking, snorkelling, diving and boat trips are all popular activities.

Sights & Activities

Just 1km north of Hahei is the carpark for the 45-minute walk to the impressive **Cathedral Cove** with its famous gigantic limestone arch. On the way you can visit the rocky cove at **Gemstone Bay**, which has an excellent snorkelling trail, and a sandy cove at **Stingray Bay**. It's a 70-minute walk along the coast from Hahei Beach to Cathedral Cove. At the southern end of Hahei Beach is a 20-minute walk up to an old Maori *pa* (fortified village), **Te Pare Point**, with splendid coastal views especially if you walk through the grass and look south.

Cathedral Cove Sea Kayaking (☎ 07-866 3877; www.seakayaktours.co.nz; 188 Hahei Beach Rd; half-day trips $65) has guided kayaking trips around the fascinating limestone arches, caves and islands in the Cathedral Cove area. The Remote Coast Tour heads the other way when conditions permit and is also highly recommended with caves, blow holes, a long tunnel and great limestone scenery. A free pick-up is available from Ferry Landing.

Hahei Explorer (☎ 07-866 3910; www.haheiexplorer .co.nz; Hahei Beach Rd; adult/child $50/25) is a rigid inflatable boat that makes daily hour-long scenic tours that cover 14km.

Cathedral Cove Dive (☎ 07-866 3955; 3 Margaret Place) has dives two or three times daily. Prices vary from $40 (own gear) to $80 (includes all gear). A Discover Scuba half-day course for first-timers is $120 and Professional Association of Diving Instructors (PADI) courses cost $500 including all the gear. Its shop in the shopping centre rents out scuba and snorkelling gear and boogie boards.

Snorkelling is best done in Gemstone Bay (on the walk to Cathedral Cove), which is a boulder beach but has a DOC snorkelling trail. You can hire snorkelling gear (including a wet suit) for $35 a day. Big snapper, crayfish and stingrays can be seen in this protected marine reserve.

Sleeping

Tatahi Lodge (☎ 07-866 3992; tatahi_lodge@xtra.co.nz; Grange Rd; dm $20, d & tw $55, units $100-165) This is a spotless and smart choice next to the shops and cafés and has an alpine chalet design, brightly coloured furnishings, pine-wood décor and views.

Hahei Beach Resort (☎ 07-866 3889; info@hahei holidays.co.nz; Harsant Ave; camp sites $22, campervan sites $24, backpacker dm $19, d & tw $45, cabins $45-55, tourist flats $80-90) Large and perfectly located on the beachfront, the accommodation is more modern than the kitchen and bathroom facilities. A good upmarket option in this resort are the beachfront Cathedral Lodge Villas (units Feb-Nov $125-180, Dec-Jan $150-330).

Fernbird (☎ 07-866 3080; fernbird@xtra.co.nz; 24 Harsant Ave; dm/d $19/45; 🖳) This place has two plain rooms but the accommodation is homely with a beautiful front garden.

Church (☎ 07-866 3533; 87 Beach Rd; cottages $90-145) These smart and self-contained timber

cottages have colourful and natural wood interiors in an attractive garden setting; smaller units have no kitchen but breakfast (included in the cost) is offered in the restaurant.

Eating

Church (☎ 07-866 3797; 87 Beach Rd; mains $18-31; ☽ dinner daily summer, Thu-Mon winter) Hahei's best restaurant is housed in a rebuilt church and the à la carte menu has a Mediterranean and Pacific-rim flavour. Accommodation is available in the garden behind; see above.

Grange Road Café (☎ /fax 07-866 3502; 7 Grange Rd; lunch mains $5-10, dinner mains $20-28; ☽ breakfast, lunch & dinner summer) The kitchen here turns out excellent and very original meals (such as giant bagel-like buns stuffed with minced lamb, spices and black-eyed beans). It caters for everyone including vegans and pizza lovers, with lots of NZ wines and beers as well as fresh juices. The café is open less frequently in winter. Call ahead first.

Luna Café (☎ 07-866 3016; 1 Grange Rd; mains $14-26; ☽ breakfast, lunch & dinner) This is another good restaurant-café that serves mainly Mediterranean-style food including $20 pizzas. Luna is open less frequently in winter – it's best to call ahead.

Getting There & Around

If you don't have a car the easiest way to get from Whitianga to Hahei is by using the ferry crossing. Go Kiwi Shuttles (☎ 0800 446 549, 07-866 0336; www.go-kiwi.co.nz) runs a bus three times daily from Ferry Landing to Cook's Beach ($3, 10 minutes), Hahei ($7, 35 minutes) and Hot Water Beach ($10, 45 minutes), with some services continuing to Dalmeny Corner on the highway for connections with buses to Auckland and Whitianga. A day pass costs $20 and a $35 explorer pass allows you to use the service as much as you like over a three-day period. You can pick up a timetable and make a booking at the Whitianga i-SITE visitors centre (p204).

AROUND HAHEI

Refer to the map on p195 for the location of the winery. For the location of the other items in this section refer to the map on p205.

On the way to Cook's Beach and Ferry Landing, taste wines made from kiwifruit, feijoa and manuka honey at **Purangi Winery** (☎ 07-866 3724; ⏱ 10am-5pm). Meals are also available.

At Cook's Beach, 14km from Hahei, **Cooks Landing Restaurant** (☎ 07-867 1015; 19 Captain Cook Rd; mains $16-20; ⏱ brunch & dinner) offers good kiwi fare with a touch of international flair at reasonable prices and is worth seeking out.

Further on is **Flaxmill Bay Hideaway Camp & Cabins** (☎ 07-866 2386; fax 866 2314; 1019 Purangi Rd; camp sites $24-32, campervan sites $27-37, cabins $40-130) and the wonderful **Eggsentric Café & Restaurant** (☎ 07-866 0307; 1047 Purangi Rd; lunch mains $8-13, dinner mains $19-30; ⏱ lunch & dinner) which has an innovative menu, live acoustic music every night, and a jam session on the first Sunday of the month from 3pm until late. You can also design your own plate ($10 to $50) and have it fired in a kiln and posted to you. A pick-up from Ferry Landing, 1½km away, is usually possible.

HOT WATER BEACH

Just 9km south of Hahei is the famous Hot Water Beach, where thermal waters brew just below the sand in front of a rocky outcrop. You can join the crowd on the beach two hours each side of low tide, dig a hole in the sand with a spade, and then relax in your own natural spa pool. Spades can be hired for $4 from the **Tarte Café** (☎ 07-866 3006; ⏱ 9am-5pm winter, 9am-7pm summer). See the boxed text below about the hidden dangers of swimming at this beach.

Opposite the café, the very very stylish **Moko** (☎ 07-866 3367; www.moko.co.nz; 24 Pye Pl; units $140-200) has modernist Pacific-rim décor and an art gallery out the back.

Another luxury pad, just up the road from the café, is **Hot Water Beach B&B** (☎ 07-866 3991; www.hotwaterbedandbreakfast.co.nz; 48 Pye Pl; incl breakfast s $140, d $160-200; 🖳), which has priceless views, a buffet breakfast, a spa bath on the deck and a snooker table.

Auntie Dawn's Place (☎ 07-866 3707; www.auntie dawn.co.nz; 15 Radar Rd; units $90-100) is a comfort-

able, spacious and homely place to stay with a big garden that includes ancient pohutukawa trees. Breakfast materials and homebrew beer supplied. Backpacker beds are available in garden huts in summer.

TAIRUA
pop 1566

Tairua is a small town on an estuary and has cafés, restaurants, water sports, walks and some good accommodation. Pauanui is its twin town on the other side of the harbour.

Information

Tairua information centre (☎ 07-864 7580; www .tairua.info; 223 Main Rd; ⏱ 9am-5pm summer, 9am-4pm winter) is friendly and helpful. Over the road, **Tairua Video** (☎ 07-864 8170; 228 Main Rd) has Internet access.

Sights & Activities

Tairua Dive & Fishing (☎ 07-864 8054; www.dive tairua.co.nz; Paku Boat Ramp; ⏱ 8am-5pm) hires out sailboards, sailing boats, dinghies and kayaks as well as scuba, snorkel and fishing gear. The company also runs dive trips out to the Aldermen Islands (dive and full gear $165, snorkelling $65) and PADI courses ($450).

A popular walk is the climb up **Paku**, an old *pa* site, which takes 30 minutes from the Esplanade and provides 360-degree views. If you climb Paku, legend has it that you will return in seven years.

For nature and wilderness walks in this area, **Kiwi Dundee Adventures** (☎ 07-865 8809; www.kiwidundee.co.nz; tours $180) has built up quite a reputation over the years. Guide Doug Johansen has been called NZ's answer to Crocodile Dundee, and he'll lead you on informative day-long adventure walks. The tours are not cheap, but you pay for experience.

Sleeping

Tairua Beach Villa Backpackers (☎ 07-864 8345; tairuabackpackers@xtra.co.nz; 200 Main Rd; camp sites $30, dm $22, s $25-35, tw $25-50, d $50; 🖳) This is an ideal harbour side backpackers in a beautiful garden setting south of the town centre and the owner works hard to keep everyone happy. Bunk beds have their own curtains and lights. Sailboards, bikes, kayaks, boogie boards and videos are all free, and windsurfing lessons are only $10.

BEACH WARNING!

Hot Water Beach has dangerous currents (also known as rips or undertows) year-round. It's one of the four most dangerous beaches in New Zealand in terms of drownings. Swimming there is not safe.

Pinnacles Backpackers (☎ 07-864 8448; flying .dutchman.bp@xtra.co.nz; 305 Main Rd; camp sites $24, dm $20, tw & d $50; ☑) North of the town centre, this place has bright rooms, a balcony, a free pool table, and bikes for hire.

Pacific Harbour Lodge (☎ 07-864 8581; www .pacificharbour.co.nz; Main Rd; s $100-180, d $120-180; ☑) This attractive upmarket 'island-style' resort in the town centre has very attractive chalets with natural wood and Gauguin décor inside and a South Seas garden outside. The Shells restaurant (see below) is part of the complex.

Pakuvista B&B (☎ 07-864 7999; cjcollier@wave .co.nz; 308 Main Rd; d $80-100) This place has smart rooms with a view.

Harbourview (☎ 07-864 7040; www.harbourview lodge.co.nz; 179 Main Rd; incl breakfast s $100-130, d $140-160; ☑ ☑) This spotless guesthouse has stylish en suite rooms, a lounge area and fine views. The owners will spoil you and also include a full breakfast. The lower prices are charged from May to September.

Eating & Drinking

Shells Restaurant & Bar (☎ 07-864 8811; Main Rd; mains $21-29; ☑ dinner daily in summer, Tue-Sat in winter) Next to the Pacific Harbour Lodge, the shell tables are a talking point and the food is high-quality Kiwi fare. The large restaurant is popular with German tour groups so it must be good.

Out of the Blue Café (☎ 07-864 8987; 227 Main Rd; meals $5-12; ☑ breakfast & lunch) This popular meeting place serves decent coffee, breakfast, deli snacks and light Mediterranean meals.

Tairua Landing Bar & Café (☎ 07-864 7774; 222 Main Rd; meals $5-15; ☑ breakfast, lunch & dinner) This establishment offers drinks, snacks and meals indoors or in a pleasant outdoor area that overlooks the estuary.

Punters Café & Bar (☎ 07-864 9370; Main Rd; ☑ lunch & dinner) This is primarily a bar but it also serves snacks and $12 burgers.

About 2km from the town centre along the estuary is the proposed Paku Marina (also known as the Paku Boat Ramp), where there are a couple of restaurants.

Upper Deck Restaurant & Bar (☎ 07-864 7499; mains $21-29; ☑ dinner daily summer, Thu-Mon winter) In the grounded SS *Ngorio*, this almost-floating restaurant is a former Auckland steamer ferry and an atmospheric place

for a meal or a drink with occasional live entertainment in summer.

Ikamata (☎ 07-864 7171; tapas $5-15; ☑ dinner) This is the place for a sundowner drink and snacks. It's next door to the Upper Deck.

Getting There & Away

InterCity (☎ 09-913 6100 Auckland) charges $16 to travel from Tairua to Whitianga, while **Kiwi Shuttles** (☎ 0800 446 549, 07-866 0336; www.go -kiwi.co.nz) charges $20.

AROUND TAIRUA
Puketui Valley

Located about 12km south of Tairua is the turn-off to Puketui Valley and the historical Broken Hills gold-mine workings, which are 8km from the main road along a mainly gravel road. There are short walks up to the sites of stamper batteries, but the best hike is through the 500m-long Collins Drive (mine tunnel). It takes between two to three hours return; remember to take a torch and a jacket with you. This is a wilderness area so take care and be properly prepared.

There is a **DOC camp site** (camp sites $14) but the only facilities are rubbish bins and a long-drop toilet. Water from the river should be boiled before drinking. It's hard to imagine that two hundred miners were living in this area a century ago.

Slipper Island

Off the coast, the privately owned **Slip-per Island** (☎ 07-298 8459; www.slipper.co.nz) has camp sites ($20) in South Bay and lodge and chalet accommodation (self-contained units $250 to $500 per weekend) in Home Bay. It's a beautiful little retreat, but the problem is actually getting out there; check with Tairua information centre (p209) about boat trips to the island.

PAUANUI
pop 950

Pauanui, on the other side of the harbour from Tairua, has a good sandy beach and expensive canal-side houses. A **passenger ferry** (☎ 07-864 8133; adult/child one way $3/1, return $5/2) links it with Tairua and the Paku Marina site (Paku Boat Ramp). It usually leaves Tairua at 9am, 11am, 1pm, 3pm and 5pm daily from November to April. The trip takes five minutes.

The distance from Tairua to Pauanui by road is 23km.

The **visitors centre** (☎ 07-864 7101; Jubilee Dr; ⌚ 9am-5pm daily summer, 10am-noon Mon-Fri, 10am-2pm Sat & Sun winter) is in the shopping centre.

OPOUTERE BEACH

Just 4km off the main road is the carpark for the 15-minute walk to the long, unspoilt and sandy Opoutere Beach, but swimming is dangerous, especially near Hikinui islet, which is close to the beach. On the sandspit is the **Wharekawa Wildlife Refuge**, a breeding ground for the endangered NZ dotterel. Only 1500 exist and around 18 pairs were breeding here in 2004. Lots of other birds can be seen in this unpopulated area.

Opoutere YHA (☎ 07-865 9072; www.stayyha.com; camp sites $32, dm $20-24, d & tw $55; 🖳) Located just before the carpark, this place has comfortable rooms in a wonderful get-away-from-it-all bush setting that is full of birdsong. Kayaks, hot-water bottles, alarm clocks, stilts, hoola hoops can all be borrowed free. You can harvest shellfish from the beach but other food you'll need to bring with you as there are no shops here.

Go Kiwi Shuttles (☎ 0800 446 549, 07-866 0336; www.go-kiwi.co.nz) runs between Opoutere and Whangamata ($15, 10 minutes), where you can connect with other services; bookings are essential.

WHANGAMATA
pop 3880
Whangamata (pronounced fa-nga-ma-ta) has a great 4km-long surf beach with an excellent break by the bar, which attracts a big influx of surfers and NZ holiday-makers in December and January, but it's quiet the rest of the year.

Information
Whangamata i-SITE visitors centre (☎ 07-865 8340; www.whangamatainfo.co.nz; 616 Port Rd; ⌚ 9am-5pm daily summer, 9am-5pm Mon-Sat, 10am-2pm Sun winter) can provide you with information, and **Bartley Internet & Graphics** (706 Port Rd) has Internet access.

Activities
Besides surfing, kayaking, fishing (game fishing runs from January to April), snorkelling near Hauturu (Clarke) Island, orienteering and mountain biking, there are

excellent walks. The **Wentworth Falls walk** takes 1½ hours one way and starts 3km south of the town and 4km down a good gravel road.

Sleeping
Garden Tourist Lodge (☎ /fax 07-865 9580; garden lodge@xtra.co.nz; cnr Port Rd & Mayfair Ave; dm $20, s $25, d & tw $50, units $80-150) This smart, clean complex in a garden setting north of the town centre has spacious and modern accommodation to suit just about everyone and provides free boogie boards and fishing gear.

DOC camping ground (☎ 07-865 7032; camp sites $16) This camping ground has toilets, hot showers and gas barbecues.

Whangamata Backpackers Hostel (☎ /fax 07-865 8323; 227 Beverley Tce; dm/s/d $17/22/45) This is a rather run-down surfers' hang-out.

Pinefield Top 10 Holiday Park (☎ 07-865 8791; www.pinefield.co.nz; 207 Port Rd; dm $15-28, camp sites $22-36, d $30-55, cabins $50-110, units $95-210; 🖳 🐾) Just north of the town centre, this place has good facilities and spacious accommodation with natural wood décor.

Copsefield B&B (☎ /fax 07-865 9555; www.copsefield.co.nz; 1055 SH25; incl breakfast s $100, d & tw $140) This peaceful villa with kind hosts and en suite rooms is 8km north of Whangamata. It has a spa pool, a six-hole pitch and putt course in the garden and bicycles and kayaks are available.

Whangamata Motel (☎ 07-865 8250; www.whangamatamotel.co.nz; 106 Barbara Ave; d $75-105) This motel, conveniently positioned behind the information centre near the shops and the beach, has a spa.

Eating & Drinking
Caffe Rossini (☎ 07-865 6117; 646 Port Rd; dinner mains $17-28; ⌚ breakfast & lunch daily in summer, Fri-Mon in winter, dinner Thu-Tue year-round) Delightful dishes, including steak in a champagny cream sauce.

Vibes Café (☎ 07-865 7121; 636 Port Rd; mains $8-15; ⌚ breakfast & lunch) Vibes is slightly funky and has good espresso and food (such as wholemeal spinach and feta quiche with salad).

Oceana's (☎ 07-865 7157; 328 Ocean Rd; mains $28-31; ⌚ dinner, closed Sun & Mon winter) The town's top restaurant specialises in seafood and venison.

Coast (☎ 07-865 6999; 501 Port Rd) and **Bach** (☎ 07-865 6301; 101 Casement Rd) are smart bar restaurants, while opposite Bach is a **carvery** (meals around $14) that has roast meals just like mum used to cook on Sundays.

Getting There & Away
Daily buses to Whitianga go via Waihi on **InterCity** (☎ 09-913 6100 Auckland) and cost $62, while **Go Kiwi Shuttles** (☎ 0800 446 549, 07-866 0336; www.go-kiwi.co.nz) charges $45.

WAIHI
pop 4700
Gold was first discovered here in 1878 and the Martha Mine became the richest in NZ. After closing down in 1952, open-cast mining restarted in 1988. The mine is still producing a million dollars of gold every week although it takes a ton of rock to yield 3g to 6g of gold. The existing mine is likely to run out soon, but permission is being sought to open a new mine in a nearby area.

Information
The **Waihi information centre** (☎ 07-863 6715; Seddon St; ☽ 9am-5pm summer, 9am-4.30pm winter) is helpful. The nearby **Farmhouse Café** (☎ 07-863 7654; 14 Haszard St) has Internet access.

Sights & Activities
Martha Gold-mine Tours (☎ 07-863 9880; admission by donation; ☽ 10am & 1.30pm Mon-Fri) last 1¼ hours (bookings essential). Find out how a modern mine is run and then compare it to the old days by taking the vintage train ride to Waikino.

You can see the 200m-deep hole that is Martha Mine from a **lookout** in Moresby Avenue near the Waihi information centre. A giant dump truck is on display there too.

The **Goldfields Vintage Train** (☎ 07-863 8251; www.goldfieldsrailway.org.nz; adult/child return $12/6) is run by volunteers. It leaves Waihi Station, in Wrigley St, daily at 11am, 12.30pm, 1.15pm and 2.00pm. The 7km-long scenic journey takes 25 minutes. See p214 for interesting hikes around Waikino.

Waihi Arts Centre & Museum (☎ 07-863 8386; 54 Kenny St; adult/child $4/2; ☽ 10am-4pm Mon-Fri, 1.30-4pm Sat & Sun) features displays and models of the region's gold-mining history.

Sleeping
Goldmine Motel (☎ 07-863 7111; fax 07-863 3084; 6 Victoria St; s/d $75/90) The pick of Waihi's

motels, it's near the railway station, with an indoor spa and air conditioning in all rooms.

Rob Roy Hotel (☎ 07-863 7025; fax 07-863 3147; cnr Seddon St & Rosemount Rd; s/d/d with bathroom $20/40/50) Cheap and reasonable rooms are available in this central pub that hasn't changed much in the last hundred years.

Westwind B&B (☎ 07-863 7208, 58 Adams St; s/d incl breakfast $35/70) On the way to Tauranga, this guesthouse has a nice garden. Their previous B&B fell into a hole (mining subsidence) but this one seems okay.

Eating
Farmhouse Café (☎ 07-863 7649; 14 Haszard St; mains $12-15; ☽ breakfast & lunch, dinner Fri & Sat; 🖳) This attractive café has a marvellous garden area, a blackboard menu, local wines and gluten-free goodies.

Chambers Wine Bar & Restaurant (☎ 07-863 7474; 22 Haszard St; light meals $12, mains $20-25; ☽ lunch & dinner) This restaurant in a heritage building offers an interesting dinner menu, good lunch meals and bar snacks.

Getting There & Away
Lots of buses come in and out of this transport hub, and they stop outside the BP petrol station in Rosemount Rd. **InterCity** (☎ 09-913 6100 Auckland) and **Go Kiwi Shuttles** (☎ 0800 446 549, 07-866 0336; www.go-kiwi.co.nz) run buses from Waihi to Whangamata for around $20. Long distance buses and shuttles go to Auckland, Hamilton, Tauranga and Rotorua.

WAIHI BEACH
pop 1700
Just 11km east of Waihi, the 9km-long sandy Waihi Beach is lined with holiday homes. The shopping area in Wilson Rd includes a supermarket, café, restaurant, chemist and surfing/fishing shop. There are ocean surfing beaches and sheltered harbour beaches such as beautiful Anzac Bay beyond Bowentown. A very popular 45-minute walk is north through bush to pristine Orokawa Bay, which has no road access.

Boating and game-fishing are popular, and out to sea is Mayor (Tuhua) Island with its Blue and Green crater lakes; contact **Waihi Beach Boat Charter** (☎ 07-863 5385) if you want to visit.

Another 8km south is **Athenree Hot Springs** (☎ 07-863 5600; adult/child $4.50/2.50; ⊙ 10am-7.30pm) with two bubbling outdoor hot pools. Stay in the **holiday park** (☎ 07-863 5600; camp sites/campervan sites/tourist flats/units $24/28/75/90) and entry to the hot pools is free.

There are four holiday parks at Waihi Beach as well as lots of B&Bs. Turn left when you reach the sea and go to the end of the road for **Waihi Beach Top 10 Holiday Park** (☎ 07-863 5504; www.waihibeach.com; 15 Main Rd; camp sites $22, campervan sites $26, cabins $38-50, units $80; 🖳) a large, clean and modern camping ground with a wide range of good accommodation. Kayaks, surfboards, boogie boards, bikes and even baby-sitters can be hired here.

Beachfront B&B (☎ 07-863 5393; 3 Shaw Rd; d $95) is absolute beachfront, has great sea views, and the tastefully furnished rooms have TV.

Waterfront Homestay B&B (☎ /fax 07-863 4342; 17 The Esplanade; s/d $75/90) has a comfortable, modern basement unit with underfloor heating close to the beach.

Cactus Jacks (☎ 07-863 5160; 31 Wilson Rd; mains $13-15) is an American-style diner that serves steaks, chicken and seafood.

HAURAKI REGION

The big drawcards on the mainly pancake-flat Hauraki Plains are the superb bird-watching at Miranda and the hot springs at Miranda and Te Aroha. Beyond the antique and second-hand shops of Paeroa is the historic and scenic Karangahake Gorge, with hikes around derelict gold-mine workings.

MIRANDA

Avid bird-watchers love this area – one of the most accessible for studying waders or shore birds all year round. It is 11km from Waitakaruru and the Thames–Pokeno road, and just an hour's drive from Auckland. The vast mudflat on the western side of the Firth of Thames is teeming with aquatic worms and crustaceans, which attract thousands of Arctic-nesting shore birds over the winter; 43 species of wader have been spotted here. The two main species that can be seen are the bar-tailed godwit and the lesser or red knot, but it isn't unusual to see turnstones, sandpipers and

the odd vagrant red-necked stint. Internal migrants include the pied oystercatcher and the threatened wrybill from the South Island, and banded dotterels and pied stilts from both main islands.

The **Miranda Shorebird Centre** (☎ 09-232 2781; www.miranda-shorebird.org.nz; ⊙ 9am-5pm; dm/d members $13/45, non-members $18/50) offers basic but clean accommodation with a kitchen. The centre also has displays on the birdlife, hires out binoculars and sells useful $2 pamphlets on birds you can see. Nearby is a bird-watching hide and there are walks that take half an hour to two hours.

Five kilometres south of Miranda Shorebird Centre is **Miranda Hot Springs** (☎ 07-867 3055; Front Miranda Rd; adult/child $8/5; ⊙ 8am-9.30pm) which has a large hot-spring swimming pool, a super-hot sauna pool, and private spa tubs ($5 extra).

Next door is **Miranda Holiday Park** (☎ 07-867 3205; www.mirandaholidaypark.co.nz; camp sites & campervan sites/cabins/units $30/50/100), which has sparkling clean and new units and facilities with its own hot-spring pool and floodlit tennis court.

Kaiaua, 8km north of Miranda Shorebird Centre, has a store, B&Bs, a popular fish-and-chip shop and a pub that serves bistro meals and has two accommodation units ($75 for a double).

PAEROA
pop 4000

Well known for its antique and curio shops, Paeroa was the birthplace of Lemon & Paeroa (L&P), the soft drink that describes itself as 'World famous in NZ'. Two giant L&P bottles are reminders that it was produced here from 1907 until 1980 when production was moved to Auckland.

The helpful **information centre** (☎ /fax 07-862 8636; www.hauraki-dc.govt.nz; 1 Belmont Rd/SH2; ⊙ 9am-5pm daily summer, 9am-5pm Mon-Fri, 10am-3pm Sat & Sun winter) is to the north of the town.

The small **museum** (☎ 07-862 8942; 37 Belmont Rd; ⊙ 10.30am-3pm Mon-Fri) has a splendid selection of Royal Albert porcelain and other pioneer and Maori artefacts – look in the drawers.

Casa Mexicana (☎ 0800 654 040, 07-862 8216; casa.mexicana@wave.co.nz; 71 Puke Rd; s/d $65/80), just north of town, has an obliging owner, has been recently refurbished and is the best place to stay.

COROMANDEL REGION

World Famous in NZ Café (☎ 07-862 7773; SH2; lunch mains $6-15, dinner mains $16-26; ☺ breakfast, lunch & dinner), opposite the information centre, serves a wide range of food, including pizzas ($18), L&P ice cream, and sometimes L&P muffins and L&P cheesecake.

Lazy Fish (☎ 07-862 8822; 56 Belmont Rd; meals $6-27; ☺ breakfast, lunch & dinner daily summer, Wed-Sun winter) has international cuisine, with good Mediterranean-style options, in the centre of town.

Karangahake Gorge

The 4.5km Karangahake Gorge Historic Walkway takes 1½ hours and starts from the carpark, 8km east of Paeroa. It follows the disused railway line and the Ohinemuri River to Owharoa Falls and Waikino Station, from where a veteran train runs to Waihi four times a day. The **Waikino Station Café** (☎ 07-863 8640; ☺ breakfast & lunch, snacks till 4pm) is a perfect lunch and snack stop before heading back.

A shorter walk from the carpark takes only an hour and crosses two bridges before following the boulder-strewn river for 20 minutes. Then turn left over another bridge and through a long tunnel where a torch is useful but not necessary. The track then loops back to the carpark and the delightful **Talisman Café** (☎ 07-862 8306; meals under $13; ☺ 9am-5pm).

The huge **Victoria Battery**, a five-minute walk from Waikino Station, operated from 1896 to 1952 and you can see eight large kilns and other gold-mining relics. **Tours** (☎ 07-863 8640; adult/child $10/5; ☺ 10am-4pm Sun Oct-Apr) include a visit to the battery's museum, a tram ride and a kiln visit.

Ohinemuri Estate Winery & Café (☎ 07-862 8874; Moresby St; ☺ 10am-5pm Oct-Apr, 10am-5pm Fri-Sun May-Sep; units $80; lunch mains $9-15) has free wine tasting just off the main road at Karangahake.

TE AROHA
pop 3800

Te Aroha, 31km south of Paeroa and 55km northeast of Hamilton on SH26, is nestled at the foot of bush-clad 952m-high Mt Te Aroha (literally 'the love'). Another natural attraction are the town's therapeutic hot springs which have a high soda content and have attracted visitors since the late 19th century.

Information

Cyber Café (☎ 07-884 9228; Whitaker St) Has Internet access.

Te Aroha visitors centre (☎ 07-884 8052; www.te-aroha.com; 102 Whitaker St; ☺ 9.30am-5pm Mon-Fri, 10am-4pm Sat & Sun)

Sights & Activities

At the top of the domain behind the visitors centre are the **Hot Spring Spa Pools** (☎ 07-884 8717; 30min sessions $10-15; ☺ 10am-10pm) which offers private tubs and aromatherapy. Children are half-price and booking is recommended. Nearby is **Mokena Geyser** that shoots 3m in the air every 40 minutes or so, but it can be temperamental.

Lower down the domain is the outdoor **Wyborn Leisure Pool** (☎ 07-884 4498; adult/child $5/3; ☺ 11am-7pm) which is heated but uses ordinary water. Next to it is the indoor **Hot Spa No 2** ($1 extra), a natural spa with hot water and bubbles rising directly from a spring. A **drinking fountain** has warm, soapy water which tastes better cold and mixed with whisky. It's good for constipation however you drink it.

The **museum** (☎ 07-884 4427; admission by donation; ☺ 11am-4pm Dec-Apr, 11am-4pm Mon-Fri & 1-4pm Sat & Sun May-Nov) is in a converted bath house on the domain. More interesting than most, the displays include souvenir ceramics.

The **hiking** trails up Mt Te Aroha start at the top of the domain. It takes an hour to climb up to the **Bald Spur/Whakapipi Lookout** (350m). Then it's another 2.7km or two hours climbing to the summit.

An easier one-hour hike (4km but flat) is around the **Howarth Wetlands Reserve**, which attracts plenty of birds, and is reached from the southern part of the town.

Sleeping

Te Aroha YHA (☎ 07-884 8739; tearoha.yha@xtra.co.nz; Miro St; dm/d $20/45) This unusual but long-running hostel is a cosy, TV-free, three-bedroom cottage. YHA members pay $4 less. Free bikes are available and a 10km mountain-bike track starts at the back door.

Te Aroha Holiday Park (☎ 07-884 9567; marta@xtra.co.nz; 217 Stanley Rd; camp sites $16, campervan sites $20, cabins $35-55; ☐ ☒) Wake up to a bird orchestra in the large oak trees at this gym-equipped site, 3km southwest of town.

Te Aroha Motel (☎ 07-884 9417; tearohamotel@xtra.co.nz; 108 Whitaker St; s/d $60/70) These are ood, reasonably priced units near the domain and the owners are very helpful.

Aroha Mountain Lodge B&B (☎ /fax 07-884 8134; Boundary St; s/d $90/110, incl breakfast $110/150) It's ight next to the Hot Spring Spa Pools and he en suite upmarket rooms are furnished with antiques.

ating & Drinking

onique Café, Restaurant & Bar (☎ 07-884 8489; 59 Whitaker St; lunch $10, dinner mains $14-27; ☼ lunch dinner) This retro café with décor of iron-work and totara wood serves stylish food and big coffees.

Banco (☎ 07-884 7574; 174 Whitaker St; mains $25 ☼ lunch Tue-Sun, dinner Thu-Sun) A popular licensed café and restaurant that is housed in an old bank building.

Getting There & Away

Turley-Murphy Buses (☎ 07-884 8208) has services from Thames to Te Aroha ($10, 1 hour 20 minutes) and from Te Aroha to Hamilton ($10, 1 hour 10 minutes).

Waikato & the King Country

CONTENTS

Waikato	**219**
Auckland to Hamilton	219
Hamilton	220
Waingaro Hot Springs	225
Raglan	225
Around Raglan	227
Raglan to Kawhia	228
Kawhia	228
Te Awamutu	229
Around Te Awamutu	230
Cambridge	231
Lake Karapiro	232
Matamata	232
Tirau	233
The King Country	**234**
Otorohanga	234
Waitomo	235
Marokopa Road	240
Te Kuiti	241
Te Kuiti to Mokau	242
Taumarunui	243

This region is the heart and soul of rural New Zealand. Iconic pastoral landscapes of grazing cattle, sheep, deer and thoroughbred horses unfold around every bend in the road. It was no surprise that Peter Jackson chose a farm here as the site to recreate the rustic paradise of Hobbiton village in his *Lord of the Rings* trilogy. The area's prosperity is the gift of the mighty 420km Waikato River, which flows from Lake Taupo to Port Waikato on the west coast. It still rolls on despite the eight hydroelectric dams that impede its flow.

The orderliness of the tamed landscape is reflected in its major city, Hamilton, the country's largest inland city and the 'capital of nice' with its careful town planning and mainly civic attractions. It livens up when the university students are around, but for more excitement head to Waitomo to abseil underground and explore or float along dark limestone caves and tunnels decorated by starry glow-worms. At the country's top rock-climbing site at Wharepapa South you can cling to rocky cliffs by your fingertips. Surfers travel thousands of kilometres to laid-back Raglan on the west coast to ride its world-famous left break, and surfing instruction is available.

To visit quaint remote communities and for more of a wilderness experience, follow the little-used roads to Kawhia Harbour or Marokopa, both tiny outposts in a natural wonderland.

HIGHLIGHTS

- Abseiling into deep glow-worm–studded caves, and tubing along underground rivers at **Waitomo** (p235)
- Surfing the world-famous waves at **Raglan** (p225)
- Enjoying remote unspoilt beaches at **Mokau** (p242) and **Marokopa** (p240), and the hot-water beach near **Kawhia** (p228)
- Visiting Middle-earth's Hobbiton outside **Matamata** (p232)
- Relaxing in the café and craft shops of horsey **Cambridge** (p231)
- Seeing the elusive kiwi and other native birds in **Otorohanga** (p234)
- Amusing yourself in the laid-back, riverside city of **Hamilton** (p220), with its famous gardens and student nightlife

WAIKATO & THE KING COUNTRY

- TELEPHONE CODE: 07
- www.waikatonz.co.nz

WAIKATO & THE KING COUNTRY

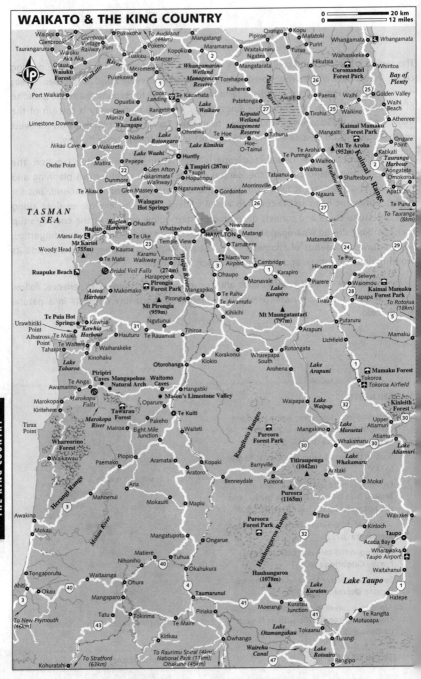

Climate

The southern area around Taumarunui is wetter and colder than the rest of the region, which can suffer summer droughts.

Getting There & Around

Hamilton is the transport hub and Inter-City buses link the city with Auckland and south to Te Awamutu, Otorohanga, Waitomo Caves, Te Kuiti, Taumarunui, Mokau and on to New Plymouth and Wanganui. Other bus services go from Hamilton to Cambridge, Matamata, Thames, Tauranga, Rotorua and Lake Taupo.

The Waitomo Wanderer links Rotorua, Waitomo Caves and Wharepapa South, a rock-climbing mecca. Other buses run to Raglan and Kawhia.

Trains are another option but they are infrequent. Hamilton's airport has flights to domestic destinations and Australia.

WAIKATO

History

The banks of the Waikato River were planted by the Maoris in pre-European times with kumara (sweet potatoes) and other crops. There was a *pa* and a chief at every bend of the river. In the 1830s missionaries introduced European crops and farming methods to the Waikato region, and by the 1840s Maoris were trading their agricultural produce with the European settlers in Auckland.

Relations between the two cultures soured during the 1850s, largely due to the Europeans' pressure to purchase Maori land for settlement. By the early 1860s the Waikato Maori had formed a 'King Movement' (see the boxed text, below) and united to elect a king. In July 1863 the Europeans sent soldiers on gunboats and small craft up the Waikato River to put down what they regarded as the open rebellion of the King Movement. After almost a year of battles and skirmishes, known as the Waikato Land War, the Kingites retreated south in 1864 to what became known as the King Country. Europeans dared not venture there for several decades and even today Maori influence is stronger there than elsewhere in the country.

AUCKLAND TO HAMILTON

The trip to Hamilton by road from Auckland takes about 1½ hours and there are a few points of interest along the way. Steam-train enthusiasts can detour to the **Glenbrook Vintage Railway** (☎ 09-235 8924; adult/child $12/6; 🕙 11am-4pm Sun & public holidays Oct-Jun) for a 12km steam-train ride. To get there leave the Southern Motorway at Drury, 31km south of Auckland, and follow the yellow signs west towards Waiuku.

Mercer, 65km south of Auckland, is the place for skydiving and for buying locally produced Pokeno bacon and sausages.

THE MAORI KING MOVEMENT

The King Movement stemmed from a need for greater unity and organisation of Maori tribes against the Pakeha and from a desire to have a Maori leader equivalent to the British queen when dealing with the Pakeha.

Potatau-te-wherowhero was a high chief of the Waikato tribes when he was made the first Maori king in 1858. He died in 1860 aged about 85 and was succeeded by his son, the second and most widely known Maori king, Matutaera-te-wherowhero – known as King Tawhiao – who held the position for the next 34 years until his death.

The King Movement was a nationalistic step for those Maori who were unwilling to sell or otherwise lose their land to the Europeans. Based in Te Kuiti, the king and his followers continued to resist Pakeha incursions. However, after the king and the chiefs agreed to the Auckland–Wellington railway being built through their land, Europeans were allowed to enter the King Country in the 1890s.

Te-arikinui-dame-te-atairangikaahu, the present 'Maori queen', is the sixth in line of succession, and has held the position since her father, Koroki-mahuta, died in 1966. She is head of the Tainui tribal confederation, which consists of four major tribes – the Waikato, Maniapoto, Hauraki and Raukawa – who are all descended from those who arrived in NZ on the *Tainui* canoe (see p229).

Cooks Landing (☎ 07-826 0004; Paddy Rd; meals $10-20; 🕒 10am-4pm Mon-Wed, 10am-5pm Thu-Sun) is on State Highway 1 (SH1), 67km south of Auckland, and has free wine tasting. Buy a bottle and enjoy it with a meat, seafood or cheese platter overlooking the vineyard.

A few kilometres south at Rangiriri, on SH1, the **Rangiriri Battle Site Heritage Centre** (☎ 07-826 3663; Talbot St; 🕒 9am-4pm) has displays about this decisive battle between British troops and Maori warriors. On 20 November 1863, 1500 British troops, backed by gunboats and artillery, were repulsed a number of times and lost 60 men, but overnight many of the 500 Maori defenders retreated and the remaining 180 were taken prisoner the next day. The centre has a café and the audiovisual show ($2) is worth seeing. On the other side of the road is the overgrown *pa* site where the battle took place.

Next to the heritage centre is the historic **Rangiriri Hotel** (☎ 07-826 3467), which has six beers and two ciders on tap.

From Rangiriri the road follows the Waikato River all the way to Hamilton. Along the way is **Huntly**, a coal-mining town with a large power station. The well-stocked **visitors centre** (☎ 07-828 6406; SH1; 🕒 9am-5pm Mon-Fri, 9am-3pm Sat & Sun) is next to a café, souvenir shop and toilet block.

The **Waikato Coalfields Museum** (☎ 07-828 8128; 26 Harlock Pl, Huntly; adult/child $3/1; 🕒 10am-4pm) is large and concentrates on the local mining industry. From near here you can walk around **Lake Hakanoa** (3.6km, one hour).

South of Huntly the road passes through a range and you can see the sacred mountain Taupiri and a Maori cemetery. **Ngaruawahia**, 19km north of Hamilton on SH1, is the site of the Maori Queen's (see the boxed text, p219) headquarters, the impressive **Turangawaewae Marae** (☎ 07-824 5189; River Rd), but visitors are only allowed inside on Regatta Day in March.

If you're fit, the top of Taupiri Mountain has excellent views (a sign on the track explains the appropriate etiquette near graves), and the **Hakarimata Walkway** also has good views. Its northern end leads off Parker Rd, which can be reached by crossing the river at Huntly and following the Ngaruawahia–Huntly West Road. The southern end meets the Ngaruawahia–Waingaro Road just out of Ngaruawahia. To walk the length of the track takes up to seven hours, but shorter hikes are possible. Easier to get to if you have no transport is the three-hour return trek from Brownlee Ave, Ngaruawahia, to Hakarimata Trig (371m). The top part is fairly steep but the view is rewarding. Tracks from each access point meet at the trig.

If you detour way out west along SH22, you reach **Nikau Cave** (☎ 09-233 3199; www.nikaucave.co.nz; 1779 Waikaretu Rd; 1½hr tours $20-25), where you can see glow-worms, limestone formations and subterranean streams. It's on a private farm and refreshments are included. Bookings are essential.

HAMILTON
pop 132,000
NZ's largest inland city, Hamilton is 129km south of Auckland and is the Waikato region's major centre. European settlement began in 1864 but the Waikato River was Hamilton's only transport and communication link with other towns until the railway arrived in 1878. Hamilton Gardens and its conservation zoo are the main attractions but there are walks, kayak trips and cruises along the river, and a hot-air balloon festival (www.balloonsoverwaikato.co.nz) in April. University students enliven the city during term time and theatres, cinemas, cafés, restaurants and bars crowd the city centre.

Information
The well-informed **Hamilton visitors centre** (☎ 07-839 3580; www.waikatonz.com; cnr Brice & Anglesea Sts; 🕒 8.30am-5pm Mon-Fri, 9am-4pm Sat, 10am-4pm Sun) is inside the Hamilton Transport Centre which also has a café and Internet access ($4 an hour). View www.hamiltonevent.co.nz for what's on locally and www.absorbed.co.nz for entertainment news.

The **Post Shop** (☎ 07-838 2233; 36 Bryce St 🕒 8am-5pm Mon-Fri, 9am-2pm Sat, 9am-noon Sun) is near the visitors centre.

Victoria Central Medical Centre (☎ 07-834 0333 750 Victoria St; 🕒 8am-10pm) offers walk-in service can take X-rays and sets fractures. Seeing a doctor costs $45; next door is a pharmacy **Anglesea Clinic** (☎ 07-858 0800; Anglesea St; 🕒 24hr charges $54 to see a doctor, $70 after 11pm. A dentist is available 8am to 5pm and the pharmacy is open 7.30am to 11pm.

Some recommendations:
Automobile Association (AA; ☎ 07-839 1397; 295 Barton St)
DOC (☎ 07-838 3363; 4th fl, 18 London St)

Hamilton City Library (☎ 07-838 6826; Garden Pl; ☯ 9am-8.30pm Mon-Fri, 9am-4pm Sat, noon-3.30pm Sun)

Sights

The splendid 50-hectare **Hamilton Gardens** (☎ 07-856 3200; www.hamiltongarden.co.nz; Cobham Dr; admission free; ☯ 7.30am-sunset) is a collection of themed gardens. The rose gardens, herb and scented garden, glasshouse garden, American garden, Renaissance garden and Asian garden are well worth a look, and there is a café, restaurant and shop.

The **Waikato Museum of Art & History** (☎ 07-838 6606; www.waikatomuseum.co.nz; 1 Grantham St; admission by donation; ☯ 10am-4.30pm) has an excellent permanent collection of Tainui Maori treasures

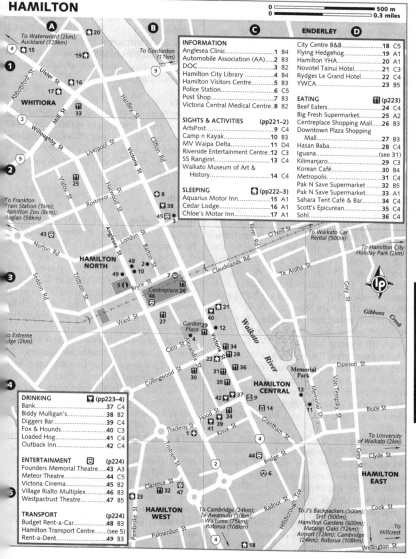

HAMILTON

0 _____ 500 m
0 _____ 0.3 miles

INFORMATION	
Anglesea Clinic	1 B4
Automobile Association (AA)	2 B3
DOC	3 B2
Hamilton City Library	4 B4
Hamilton Visitors Centre	5 B3
Police Station	6 C5
Post Shop	7 B3
Victoria Central Medical Centre	8 B2

SIGHTS & ACTIVITIES	(pp221–2)
ArtsPost	9 C4
Camp n Kayak	10 B3
MV Waipa Delta	11 D4
Riverside Entertainment Centre	12 C3
SS Rangiriri	13 C4
Waikato Museum of Art & History	14 C4

SLEEPING	(pp222–3)
Aquarius Motor Inn	15 A1
Cedar Lodge	16 A1
Chloe's Motor Inn	17 A1

City Centre B&B	18 C5
Flying Hedgehog	19 A1
Hamilton YHA	20 A1
Novotel Tainui Hotel	21 C3
Rydges Le Grand Hotel	22 C4
YWCA	23 B5

EATING	(p223)
Beef Eaters	24 C4
Big Fresh Supermarket	25 A2
Centreplace Shopping Mall	26 B3
Downtown Plaza Shopping Mall	27 B3
Hasan Baba	28 C4
Iguana	(see 31)
Kilimanjaro	29 C3
Korean Café	30 B4
Metropolis	31 C4
Pak N Save Supermarket	32 B5
Pak N Save Supermarket	33 A1
Sahara Tent Café & Bar	34 C4
Scott's Epicurean	35 C4
Sohl	36 C4

DRINKING	(pp223–4)
Bank	37 C4
Biddy Mulligan's	38 B2
Diggers Bar	39 C4
Fox & Hounds	40 C3
Loaded Hog	41 C4
Outback Inn	42 C4

ENTERTAINMENT	(p224)
Founders Memorial Theatre	43 A3
Meteor Theatre	44 C5
Victoria Cinema	45 B2
Village Rialto Multiplex	46 B3
Westpactrust Theatre	47 B5

TRANSPORT	(p224)
Budget Rent-a-Car	48 B3
Hamilton Transport Centre	(see 5)
Rent-a-Dent	49 B3

WAIKATO & THE KING COUNTRY

on display. They include exquisite weaving and woodcarving, which are well displayed in a darkened room. Other temporary exhibitions are held here (admission varies). The award-winning **Museum Café** (☎ 07-839 7209) has a classy menu.

ArtsPost (☎ 07-839 3857; 120 Victoria St; admission free; 🕙 10am-4.30pm), near the museum, is a contemporary art gallery that mainly focuses on local artists.

Hamilton Zoo (☎ 07-838 6720; www.hamilton zoo.co.nz; Brymer Rd; adult/child $7.50/4; 🕙 9am-5pm, last entry 3.30pm) has natural pens and a programme to breed endangered species from around the world. It is well laid out with spacious grounds and a large walk-through aviary of native birds, but is 8km from the city centre – take Norton Rd then SH23 west towards Raglan, turn right at Newcastle Rd and then left onto Brymer Rd. Buses run to the zoo but only on Saturdays and during school holidays, when some buses on Frankton Route 8 extend their trip to the zoo.

Activities

MV Waipa Delta (☎ 0800 472 3353; 🕙 cruises Thu-Sun) is a replica of an 1876 Waikato paddle steamer and runs popular river cruises from Memorial Park, on the river bank opposite the city centre. There are 1½-hour buffet lunch cruises ($39), one-hour afternoon-tea cruises ($20) and evening buffet and music cruises ($55). Children are half-price and reservations are recommended.

Riverside Entertainment Centre (☎ 07-834 4800; 346 Victoria St; 🕙 9am-11pm) is a new complex with a **casino** (admission free; 🕙 11am-3am), a buffet **restaurant** (lunches $18, dinners $28), bar and café. The **tenpin bowling centre** (adult/child $8/7) becomes a kind of disco in the evening from Tuesday to Saturday. **Mega-zone** (per person $8) is a strategy, tagging team game played in a maze with harmless laser guns.

Waterworld (☎ 07-849 4389; Garnett Ave; adult/child $3.50/1.50; 🕙 6am-9pm Mon-Fri, 7am-9pm Sat, 9am-9pm Sun), located 4km north of the city centre, has indoor and outdoor pools, water slides, a gym, spa and crèche. For $10 you can do most things.

Extreme Edge (☎ 07-847 5858; www.sportsclimber .co.nz; 90 Greenwood St; 🕙 10am-Tue-Sat, 10am-8.30pm Sun & Mon) offers a free introductory lesson and a day's unlimited indoor climbing

for $18. More expensive outdoor climbing courses are also available.

Max's Balloon Adventures (☎ 07-549 1614; rides $250) take off very early in the morning.

Camp n Kayak (☎ 07-847 5565; 386 Anglesea St, guided tours $20-55, kayak hire per day/weekend/week $30/50/100) takes guided tours and hires out kayaks – perfect for a trip down the scenic Waikato River.

Bush-covered **riverside walkways** run along both sides of the Waikato River and provide a green belt to the city. Memorial Park is particularly attractive and embedded in the river bank is part of **SS Rangiriri**, an iron-clad steam-powered gunboat that saw action in the Waikato Land War.

Tours

Archer Tours (☎ 07-855 2860; www.archertours.co.nz) runs three-hour tours of Hamilton for $40, day tours to Rotorua, Waitomo, Coromandel, Auckland and Taupo for $110 to $130, and usually includes lunch and some entry fees.

Sleeping
BUDGET

Flying Hedgehog (☎ 07-839 2800; maxfield@centra city.co.nz; 1157 Victoria St; dm $20, d & tw $50-80) Dorm have six or eight bunks in this converted motel where all rooms have Sky TV.

Hamilton YHA (☎ 07-838 0009; yhahamil@yha.or .nz; 1190 Victoria St; dm/s/d & tw $24/35/56; 🖳) Dorm have three to five beds and there are no en suites, but some rooms have tables, chair and cupboards. The garden, with native tre ferns, stretches down to the river.

YWCA (☎ 07-838 2219; www.ywcahamilton.org.nz; cr Pembroke & Clarence Sts; r without/with linen per person $20 25; 🖳) This three-storey hostel accepts men and women and the rooms are small with shared facilities, but carpeted and heated Each floor has a kitchen and a TV and video and reduced weekly rates are available. Nex door, the YMCA has a gym ($10).

J's Backpackers (☎ 07-856 8934; admin@jsbac packers.co.nz; 8 Grey St; dm/d & tw $18/40) This sma but relaxed and comfortable hostel is in converted suburban house, 1.5km south o the Hamilton East shops. It provides a fre pick-up service and there are buses int town ($1.70).

Hamilton City Holiday Park (☎ 07-855 825 www.hamiltoncityholidaypark.co.nz; 14 Ruakura Rd; can sites $24, cabins $20-45, tourist flats $50-60) This shad park with good cabins and facilities is 2km east of town.

MID-RANGE
City Centre B&B (☎ 07-838 1671; citycentrebb@hotm ail.com; 3 Anglesea St; s/tw from $50/80; 🐾) Stay in this cute self-contained unit with a pool at your front door. A continental breakfast is supplied and it's on a quiet cul-de-sac just a few minutes walk from the city centre.

Matangi Oaks (☎ 07-829 5765; www.matangioaks .co.nz; 634 Marychurch Rd, Matangi; s/d & tw $100/145) Private or en suite rooms are available in this attractive house, 12km from Hamilton on the way to Cambridge. Cattle and crops are farmed, a full breakfast is included and dinner can be provided.

Cedar Lodge (☎ 0800 105 252, 07-839 5569; 174 Ulster St; units $72-88; 💻) Comfortable, reasonably priced motel units with a spa pool.

Aquarius Motor Inn (☎ 0800 839 244, 07-839 2447; bookings@aquarius-motor-inn.co.nz; 230 Ulster St; studios/family units $89/120; 🐾) This smart motel with Sky TV and an indoor heated pool is at the city's northern end.

Chloe's Motor Inn (☎ 0800 245 637, 07-839 3410; www.chloes.co.nz; 181 Ulster St; studios/1-bed units $89/ 135; 🐾) Newly refurbished, these smart and spotless units have coffee plungers, share a spa pool and the owners are helpful.

TOP END
Rydges Le Grand Hotel (☎ 0800 534 7263, 07-839 1944; www.rydges.com; 237 Victoria St; s & d from $200; 💻) This small (38-room) boutique hotel in a heritage building with stylish furnishing and bright colours offers a range of rooms. Prices are negotiable and special B&B rates may be available. The bar (live jazz some evenings) and restaurant (buffet breakfast $12.95) are like the hotel – small but smart and chic.

Novotel Tainui Hotel (☎ 0800 444 442, 07-838 1366; www.novotel.co.nz; 7 Alma St; d & tw $135-225) Prices are cheaper at the weekend and depend on the occupancy rate. This modern river-side hotel has a bright and airy reception area and gym, massage, spa and sauna facilities.

Eating
CAFÉS & RESTAURANTS
The following are just a selection of the dining options, which include Indian, Chinese, Cambodian and Thai.

Kilimanjaro (☎ 07-839 2988; 337 Victoria St; meals $3.50-12.50; 🕐 breakfast & lunch) Delicious self-service, home-cooked food is available at this Garden Pl café.

Scott's Epicurean (☎ 07-839 6680; 181 Victoria St; breakfasts $9, lunches $7-13; 🕐 breakfast & lunch) Sample interesting international food with an individual twist at this popular and reasonably priced café with outdoor areas downstairs and upstairs. Try the *aglio olio* spaghetti ($7).

Metropolis (☎ 07-834 2081; 211 Victoria St; mains $18-24; 🕐 9am-midnight) A global and varied menu is offered at this casual and popular café.

Korean Café (☎ 07-838 9100; cnr Collingwood & Alexandra Sts; mains $8-13; 🕐 lunch & dinner Mon-Sat) All the Korean favourites are here – try the *dolsot bibimbap*, a rice, meat, vegetable and chilli-sauce hotpot.

Sahara Tent Café & Bar (☎ 07-839 3939; 237 Victoria St; mains $17-25; 🕐 lunch & dinner) Middle Eastern food served in Middle Eastern décor.

Hasan Baba (☎ 07-838 2002; 228 Victoria St; mains $17; 🕐 lunch & dinner) Turkish, Greek and Middle Eastern food is on the menu.

Sohl (☎ 07-839 1996; 236 Victoria St; mains $15-28; 🕐 dinner Mon-Sat) Classy food in this stylish bar-restaurant includes a wild-food meat and fish platter, rack of venison, game fish, Coromandel mussels and chocolate pheasant.

Iguana (☎ 07-834 2280; 203 Victoria St; medium pizzas/mains $17/25; 🕐 10am-late) This has a garden bar and serves up popular gourmet pizzas.

For picnic and other food items head to the Pak N Save or Big Fresh supermarkets.

QUICK EATS
Both the Centreplace and Downtown Plaza malls have small international food courts.

Beef Eaters (☎ 07-839 5374; 5 Hood St; burgers $5; 🕐 6pm-4am Tue-Sun) This is the place for late-night snacks.

Drinking
Nightspots in the Hood St area are lively on Friday and Saturday nights with live music and DJs.

Outback Inn (☎ 07-839 6354; 141 Victoria St) A large and popular student bar with screens, bar footy, music and DJs.

Loaded Hog (☎ 07-839 2777; 27 Hood St; mains $15-26; 🕐 10.30am-late) This restaurant and bar with a popular outdoor deck becomes a nightclub around 10pm.

Diggers Bar (☎ 07-834 2228; 17b Hood St; ☺ 5pm-late Tue-Sun) This bar has Murphy's on tap, $17 pizzas, and live music from around 8.30pm Wednesday to Saturday.

Bank (☎ 07-839 4740; cnr Victoria & Hood Sts; ☺ 11am-late) Inside this cream 1878 heritage building are eight beers on tap, good nachos and DJs on Friday and Saturday from 10pm.

Fox & Hounds (☎ 07-834 1333; 402 Victoria St) Boddington, Guinness, Kilkenny and cider are on tap and bands play on Friday.

Biddy Mulligan's (☎ 07-834 0306; 742 Victoria St; ☺ Tue-Sun) A cosy, genuine Irish pub with a round pool table (free on Thursdays) and occasional live Irish music.

Entertainment

Village Rialto Multiplex (☎ 07-834 1222; Centreplace Mall) has 10 screens, while **Victoria Cinema** (☎ 07-838 3036; 690 Victoria St) puts on festival and other interesting films and you can sip a glass of wine or beer in the cinema.

Live theatre and concerts can be enjoyed at the **Meteor Theatre** (☎ 07-838 6603; 1 Victoria St), **Founders Memorial Theatre** (☎ 07-838 6603; 221 Tristram St) and **Westpactrust Theatre** (☎ 07-838 6603; 59 Clarence St). The Gallagher Concert Chamber, the Telecom Playhouse, a dance studio and a Maori performing arts centre are all at the **University of Waikato** (☎ 07-858 5100).

Getting There & Away

AIR

Freedom Air (☎ 0800 600 500, 09-523 8686 if calling from Auckland; www.freedomair.com) has direct flights from Hamilton to Brisbane, Gold Coast, Melbourne and Sydney. **Air New Zealand** (☎ 0800 737 000; www.airnz.co.nz; ☺ 24hr) has two direct flights daily to and from Auckland ($46 to $186 one way) as well as direct and connecting flights to all domestic airports. Fares from Hamilton to Wellington range from $80 to $290, and Hamilton to Christchurch costs from $116 to $426. The cheapest flights must be booked online. **Origin Pacific** (☎ 0800 302 302) has direct flights from Hamilton to Wellington (from $79), Blenheim, Nelson, Christchurch (from $116), Dunedin and Invercargill. Most fly daily.

BUS

All local and long-distance buses arrive at and depart from the **Hamilton Transport Centre** (☎ 07-834 3457; cnr Anglesea & Bryce Sts).

InterCity/Newmans (☎ 07-834 3457) has an office in the transport centre. Buses run to Auckland ($20 to $25, two hours), Rotorua ($23 to $34, 1¾ hours), Thames ($24, 1¾ hours), Whakatane ($44, 3½ hours), Opotiki ($44, 4¼ hours), Gisborne ($64, 6¾ hours), Taupo ($33 to $55, 2½ hours), New Plymouth ($40, 4¼ hours), Wellington ($78 to $81, 8¼ hours) and Waitomo Caves ($29, two hours).

Guthreys (☎ 0800 759 999) operates services to Auckland ($20, two hours) and Rotorua ($23, 1½ hours).

Dalroy Express (☎ 0508 465 622; www.dalroy tours.co.nz) operates a daily service between Auckland ($18, two hours) and Hawera ($44, 4¾ hours) via Hamilton, stopping at most towns, including New Plymouth ($33, 3½ hours) and Te Kuiti ($14, 1¼ hours).

Local bus companies offer regular services to nearby towns such as Raglan, Huntly, Te Awamutu, Te Aroha and Thames.

TRAIN

Hamilton is on the main rail line between Auckland and Wellington (two trains a day in each direction). Trains stop at Hamilton's **Frankton train station** (☎ 07-846 8353; Queens Ave), located 1km west of the city centre. Dinsdale buses run between the Hamilton Transport Centre and near the train station ($2, every 30 minutes).

Getting Around

TO/FROM THE AIRPORT

Hamilton Airport (☎ 07-843 3623; www.hamiltonairport .co.nz) is 12km south of the city. Departure tax is $25 (12 years and over). The **Super Shuttle** (☎ 07-843 7778) offers a door-to-door service into the city ($10). A taxi costs around $35.

BUS

Hamilton's city bus system, **Busline** (☎ 0800 4287 5463), operates Monday to Saturday from around 7am to 5.45pm (later on Friday). All buses pass through Hamilton Transport Centre.

CAR

Budget Rent-A-Car (☎ 07-838 3585; www.budget .co.nz; 404 Anglesea St)

Rent-a-Dent (☎ 07-839 1049; www.rentadent.co.nz; 383 Anglesea St)

Waikato Car Rentals (☎ 0800 154 444, 07-855 0094; www.waikatocarrentals.co.nz; Brooklyn Rd)

WAINGARO HOT SPRINGS

A popular day trip from Hamilton are the **Waingaro Hot Springs** (☎ 07-825 4761; adult/child $5/3; ☒ 9am-10pm), which have three thermal mineral pools, private spa pools, giant water slides, bumper boats, children's play areas and barbecues. Kids love it! The **motel and caravan park** (☎ 07-825 4761; campervan sites $28, on-site caravans/units $48/85) here offers free entry to the hot pools. To get to the springs, turn west at Ngaruawahia, 19km north of Hamilton, and travel for 23km; they are clearly signposted.

RAGLAN

pop 2700

On the coast, 48km west of Hamilton, is the small community of Raglan, named after Lord Raglan, a British officer who seriously wiped out at the charge of the Light Brigade during the Crimea War. Nearby bays are internationally famous for their waves and attract surfers from around the world, especially in summer when surfing competitions are held. Bruce Brown's classic 1964 film *The Endless Summer* about surfies roaming the world in search of the perfect wave features footage shot at Manu Bay, west of Raglan.

Laid-back Raglan, with its art-and-craft shops and cafés, lies on a beautiful sheltered harbour, which is good for kayaking, boating and swimming.

Information

Health centre (☎ 07-825 0114; Wallis St; ☒ 9am-5pm Mon-Fri, 9am-1pm Sat)
Post Shop (☎ 07-825 8007; Bow St; ☒ 9am-5pm Mon-Fri)
Raglan Laundry (Wainui Rd; ☒ 7.30am-8.30pm) Coin-operated washers and driers.
Raglan Video (☎ 07-825 0008; 9 Bow St; Internet per 30 min $5; ☒ 10am-8.30pm) The surfing videos are upstairs.
Raglan visitors centre (☎ 07-825 0556; www.raglan .org.nz; 4 Wallis St; ☒ 10am-3pm Mon-Fri, 10am-4pm Sat & Sun May-Sep, 9am-5pm daily Oct-Apr) The very helpful staff can book many activities, including surfing lessons.

Sights & Activities
PIONEER MUSEUM

Visit the small **pioneer museum** (13 Wainui Rd; admission by donation; ☒ 1-3.30pm Sat & Sun) to

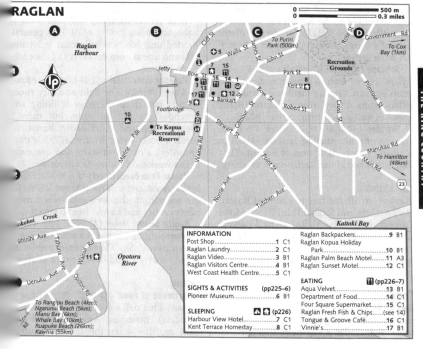

RAGLAN

0 _____ 500 m
0 _____ 0.3 miles

INFORMATION	
Post Shop	1 C1
Raglan Laundry	2 C1
Raglan Video	3 B1
Raglan Visitors Centre	4 B1
West Coast Health Centre	5 C1

SIGHTS & ACTIVITIES	(pp225-6)
Pioneer Museum	6 B1

SLEEPING	(p226)
Harbour View Hotel	7 C1
Kent Terrace Homestay	8 C1

Raglan Backpackers	9 B1
Raglan Kopua Holiday Park	10 B1
Raglan Palm Beach Motel	11 A3
Raglan Sunset Motel	12 B1

EATING	(pp226-7)
Aqua Velvet	13 B1
Department of Food	14 C1
Four Square Supermarket	15 C1
Raglan Fresh Fish & Chips	(see 14)
Tongue & Groove Café	16 C1
Vinnie's	17 B1

WAIKATO & THE KING COUNTRY

explore the stories of local Maori and Pakeha pioneers through their artefacts, photographs and newspapers.

BEACHES

Te Kopua Recreational Reserve, over the footbridge by the holiday park, is a safe, calm harbour beach that is popular with families despite the black sand. Other beaches are at **Cox Bay**, which is reached by a walkway from Government Rd or Bayview Rd, and at **Puriri Park**, towards the end of Wallis St, which is a safe swimming spot around high tide. See p227 for details of the surfing beaches.

SURFING

Learn to catch waves with the **Raglan Surfing School** (☎ 07-825 7873; www.raglansurfingschool.co.nz; Whale Bay; 3hr lesson $79) on soft surfboards that make it easier to stay upright. All equipment is provided and instructors pride themselves on getting 95% of first timers standing on a surfboard during their first lesson. If you're already experienced you can rent surfboards ($10 per hour), boogie boards ($5 per hour) and wet suits ($5 per hour). The school operates from Ngarunui Beach, 7km west of Raglan, and lessons can be booked at the Raglan visitors centre. See Whale Bay (p227) for details of the school's own accommodation in a beautiful bush setting.

Solscape (☎ 07-825 8268; 611 Wainui Rd, Manu Bay) offers lessons from a female surfie. It also rents out surfing equipment and kayaks and offers scuba diving trips to Gannet Island ($80) as well as accommodation (p227).

Skyrider (☎ 07-825 7453) offers 1½-hour, one-on-one kite-surfing lessons ($100) at Rangipu Beach, 6km west of Raglan. They can be booked at the Raglan visitors centre.

KAYAKING

Kayaks are offered free to guests at Raglan Backpackers and Raglan Palm Beach Motel (see opposite for both). Raglan Backpackers also hires out kayaks to nonguests ($8 for two or three hours). A 15-minute paddle brings you to the **Rocks**, which has limestone pinnacles and sea caves.

Tours

Raglan Scenic Tours (☎ 07-825 7805; www.raglan scenictours.co.nz) runs good-value, small-group tours. It includes a one-hour tour around Raglan for $10/7 per adult/child and th popular 2½-hour Round the Mountain tou which includes Te Toto Gorge, Ruapuk Beach and the Bridal Veil Falls and cost $25/15 per adult/child. Book at the visito centre.

Green Goose Cruises (☎ 07-825 8153; adult/chi $16.50/11; 🕙 noon & 5pm) runs trips around th harbour in summer. You can book at th visitors centre.

Sleeping

Contact the visitors centre (p225) for detai of local B&Bs.

Raglan Backpackers (☎ 07-825 0515; info@ragl backpackers.co.nz; 6 Nero St; dm/d & tw $18/40) On th water's edge, with sea views from som rooms, this excellent purpose-built hoste which surrounds a garden courtyard, h small but smart rooms and a helpful owne The dorm has eight beds and kayaks are fr for guests.

Raglan Kopua Holiday Park (☎ 07-825 8283; r lanholidaypark@xtra.co.nz; Marine Pde; camp & camperv sites $20, dm/cabins/cottages/tourist flats/houses $15/4 55/60/80) This is a well-kept facility situate on a sheltered, inner-harbour beach acro the inlet from town.

Kent Terrace Homestay (☎ 07-825 7858; r raglan@hotmail.com; Kent Tce; d $75) This central located unit has two bedrooms, a kitche ette and opens onto decks. It's at the end Kent Terrace.

Harbour View Hotel (☎ 07-825 8010; 14 Bow s/d & tw/f $50/70/85) The light and airy roon in this two-storey heritage building wi verandas are not en suite, but there plenty of natural kauri décor. Restaura meals (locals swear by the $8.50 seafo chowder), a bar downstairs and live mus at the weekends add to its attraction.

Raglan Palm Beach Motel (☎ /fax 07-825 8153; lanmotel@paradise.net.nz; 50 Wainui Rd; units $85-105) C the waterfront, this well-maintained mo offers canoes and kayaks free to guests.

Raglan Sunset Motel (☎ 07-825 0050; www. lansunsetmotel.co.nz; 7 Bankart St; r from $110) Bra new units with Sky TV, balconies overlool paved courtyard and have a touch of clas

Eating

Department of Food (☎ 07-825 7017; 35 Bow 🕙 lunch) This deli's goodies include pan (focaccia), hummus, Anzac biscuits a giant muffins – try the savoury muff which includes sun-dried tomatoes, olives and feta cheese for just $3.50.

Raglan Fresh Fish & Chips (☎ 07-825 8119; 33 Bow St; ☻ 11.30am-7.30pm) Choose your own fresh fish, including snapper.

Vinnie's (☎ 07-825 7273; 7 Wainui Rd; mains $18-24; ☻ breakfast, lunch & dinner Tue-Sun) Eat outside, downstairs or in the loft at this unpretentious café/restaurant, which serves up a wide range of excellent food and drink. Carnivores could try the Gamekeeper's Trophy ($22), which includes venison, spareribs and ostrich sausages.

Tongue & Groove Café (☎ 07-825 0027; 19 Bow St; lunch mains $10-16, dinner mains $20-26; ☻ breakfast, lunch & dinner) This café/restaurant has music, good atmosphere and art on the walls. Chicken roti is a surfer favourite but there is a stack of tasty food on offer.

Aqua Velvet (☎ 07-825 8588; www.aquavelvet.net.nz; 8 Bow St; lunch mains $8-13, dinner mains $13-25; ☻ lunch & dinner, closed Wed May-Nov) Mainly organic food is served in this smart new restaurant and bar. Unique surfboard art adorns the walls.

Self-caterers should visit the **Four Square** supermarket (Bow St).

Entertainment

Both Aqua Velvet and the Harbour View Hotel (p226) host live music most Saturday nights, with top Kiwi bands playing in summer at the Harbour View Hotel.

Getting There & Away

Busit (☎ 07-825 1975; adult/child $5.50/3.50) runs buses between Hamilton and Raglan three times daily Monday to Friday only. **Beach Express** (☎ 0800 021 130) is a new shuttle service that runs from Raglan to Hamilton ($15) and to Auckland airport or Auckland city centre (one way $55, return $85).

AROUND RAGLAN

Four Brothers Scenic Reserve

On the road between Hamilton and Raglan, the **Karamu Walkway** goes through the reserve. A 15-minute hike up a gully covered in native bush leads to a hilltop where cows and sheep enjoy panoramic views.

Rangipu Beach

Just 6km west of Raglan, down Riria Kerepa Memorial Drive, this beach with sand dunes at the mouth of the harbour is popular with windsurfers and kite surfers.

Ngarunui Beach

Seven kilometres west of Raglan, this black-sand beach is popular with surfers. On the cliff-top is the impressive club for the volunteer lifeguards who patrol part of the beach from late October until April. This is the only beach with lifeguards.

Manu Bay

Eight kilometres west of Raglan is this rocky but famous surfing beach, said to have the longest left-hand break in the world. The very long, uniform waves are created by the angle at which the ocean swell from the Tasman Sea meets the coastline.

Solscape (☎ 07-825 8268; 611 Wainui Rd; camp sites $20; dm/d & tw/f $20/60/120; ☐) is perched on a hilltop with some unusual units inside gaily-painted railway carriages. Scuba diving, surfing tuition, surfboard and sea-kayak hire are available in this surfie hang-out, which offers free pick-ups from Raglan.

Whale Bay

This famous surfing spot is a couple of kilometres further west.

Deep in native bush, **Karioi Outdoor Adventure Centre** (☎ 07-825 7873; www.raglanadventure .com; dm/d $22/59; dinner $12; ☐) offers basketball, a flying fox, mountain bikes, bush walks and surf lessons by Raglan Surfing School (p226). There are no en suite rooms available but it has a wonderful location and a good chef. **Sleeping Lady Lodging** (☎ 07-825 7873; www.sleepinglady.co.nz; lodges $120-210) has self-contained lodges nearby.

Indicators Beach House (☎ 07-825 8818; www .indicators.co.nz; d & tw $150, extra person $20) is a large self-contained and fully-equipped house that overlooks the beach and has a deck. Wood-lined, everything is modern and it can sleep up to seven.

Ruapuke Beach

Whale Bay marks the end of the sealed road, but a gravel road continues to Ruapuke Beach, 28km from Raglan, which is dangerous for swimmers but popular with surf-casting fisher folk. **Ruapuke Motor Camp** (☎ 07-825 6800; camp sites/campervan sites per person $15/19, cabins $25-30, units $40) is near the beach. The gravel road continues on round Mt Karioi and rejoins the inland road at Te Mata. The journey from Raglan to Te Mata takes around an hour.

RAGLAN TO KAWHIA

The back roads between Raglan and Kawhia, 55km south on the coast, are slow and winding but scenic, enjoyable and off the beaten track. The gravel roads take at least 1½ hours of driving time, not counting stops. Traffic is light.

There are two routes between Raglan and Kawhia. From Raglan you can head west along the coast, past Ngarunui Beach, Manu Bay and Whale Bay, until the road turns inland and meets the interior road at Te Mata, 20km south of Raglan. Along this route, starting from Te Toto car park, a strenuous but scenic track goes up the western side of **Mt Karioi** (755m). It takes 2½ hours to reach a lookout point, followed by an easier hour up to the summit. From the east side, the **Wairake Track** is a steeper 2½-hour climb to the summit, where it meets the Te Toto Track.

The alternative route from Raglan is to head towards Hamilton and take the signposted Te Mata–Kawhia turn-off. **Magic Mountain Farmstay** (☎ 07-825 6892; www.magic mountain.co.nz; 334 Houchen Rd; s/d B&B $100/150, self-contained lodge $250) has stunning views and provides horse rides from $30. Turn off 4km before Te Mata and it's 4km from the main road.

Located just 1km past Te Mata is the turn-off to the spectacular 55m **Bridal Veil Falls**, 4km from the main road. From the car park, it's an easy 10-minute walk through mossy native bush to the top of the falls, with a further 10-minute walk leading to the pool at the bottom, where it's possible to swim once you've admired the view. Unfortunately, theft from cars is a problem here.

The road is sealed until 7km beyond Te Mata and then it's gravel until Hwy 31, the Te Awamutu–Kawhia road.

KAWHIA

pop 670

Kawhia is a sleepy little fishing port on pretty Kawhia Harbour, which is large but has a narrow entrance – the occupants of the *Tainui* canoe missed it on their first trip down the coast in the 14th century and Captain Cook also missed it when he sailed past in 1770, naming Albatross Point on its southern side but failing to note the harbour itself. Kawhia (pronounced 'kar-fee-a') is quaint and quiet except in summer when accommodation can fill up.

Kawhia has a **general store/post office** (☒ 7am-7pm), a petrol station and fish bait is for sale near the wharf.

Sights & Activities

Kayaks can be hired from Kawhia Beachside S-Cape (p228) for $6.50 an hour. Quad bikes can be hired ($30 for two hours) from **Kawhia Camping Ground** (☎ 07-871 0863 www.kawhiacamping.co.nz; Moke St). For fishing trips contact **Dove Charters** (☎ 07-871 5854) or **Taylors Harbour Cruises** (☎ 07-871 0149).

The **Kawhia Museum** (☎ 07-870 0161; admission free; ☒ 11am-4pm Wed-Sun summer, noon-4pm Sat & Sun winter) is near the wharf, and serves as the visitors centre.

Six kilometres west of Kawhia, through the Tainui Kawhia Pine Forest is wind swept Ocean Beach and its high, black sand dunes. Swimming can be dangerous but one to two hours either side of low tide you can find the **Te Puia Hot Springs** in the sand – just dig a hole for your own natural hot pool. It's a lot less crowded than Hot Water Beach near Hahei on the Coromandel. You can walk from the car park or there's a driveable track over the dunes and quad bikes can be hired.

From the wharf, a pleasant walk extends along the coast to the **Maketu Marae,** which has an impressively carved meeting house Auaukiterangi. Through the *marae* ground and behind the wooden fence, two stones Hani and Puna, mark the burial place of the *Tainui* canoe (see the boxed text, opposite). You need permission from a local elder to visit this *marae*.

Sleeping

Kawhia Beachside S-Cape (☎ 07-871 0727; www .kawhiabeachscape.co.nz; 225 Pouewe St; camp sites campervan sites $20/22, bunk rooms s/d $26/36, cabins s/ $28/38, units s/d $80/95) Perfectly positioned on the water's edge at the entrance to Kawhia herons, godwits, oystercatchers and royal spoonbills sometimes visit.

Rosamond House (☎ 07-871 0681; Rosamond Te race; s/d half board $75/100; ☐ ☒) This historic colonial-style house has five bedrooms with shared facilities and is a quiet retreat. If backpackers turn up and there's an empty room, the owner will give them a good price as well as a continental breakfast.

THE AMAZING VOYAGE OF THE TAINUI CANOE

Though it's only a small settlement, Kawhia has an illustrious history as it was here that the *Tainui* canoe – one of the ancestral canoes that arrived in Aotearoa during the 14th century from the Maori homeland, Hawaiki, thousands of kilometres away – made its final landing. Kawhia, the Maketu Marae and the burial place of the *Tainui* canoe are all sacred to the Tainui people.

The leaders of the *Tainui* canoe – Hoturoa, the captain, and Rakataura, the *tohunga* or high priest – knew that the *Tainui's* home was destined to be on the west coast. They searched up and down the west coast, until they finally recognised their prophesied new home at Kawhia Harbour.

When they landed the canoe, they tied it to a pohutukawa tree on the shore, naming the tree Tangi te Korowhiti. Though the tree is not marked, it still grows with a few other pohutukawa trees on the shoreline between Kawhia and the Maketu Marae. At the end of its long and epic voyage, the *Tainui* canoe was dragged up onto a hill and buried. Hoturoa and Rakataura placed sacred stones at either end to mark its resting place. Hani, on higher ground, is the stone marking the bow of the canoe, and Puna, the lower stone, marks the stern.

Kawhia Motel (☎ 07-871 0865; fax 07-871 0165; nr Jervois & Tainui Sts; s/d & tw $65/75) Six freshly painted units with kitchens.

Blue Chook Inn (☎ 07-871 0778; Jervois St) A self-contained unit ($75) that sleeps up to six is available.

Eating & Drinking

Happy Flounder (Jervois St) Offers locally caught fish – feast on the flounder, chips and salad for $15.

Annie's Café & Restaurant (☎ 07-871 0198; 146 Jervois St; mains $17-22; ❧ 9.30am-4pm, closed Mon & Tue in winter) A pleasant place in the main street, serving espresso, *panini*, nachos, local flounder and chips, and steak and salad.

Blue Chook Inn (☎ 07-871 0778; Jervois St; ❧ 11am-midnight) A smart bar and café with good pizzas.

Getting There & Away

Kawhia Bus & Freight (☎ 07-871 0701) runs a service that leaves Kawhia at 7am for Te Awamutu, returning from Te Awamutu at 10.30am Monday to Friday and 10am on Saturday.

TE AWAMUTU
pop 9340

Te Awamutu (which means 'The River Cut Short' since the river above this point was unsuitable for large canoes) is a service town for the local dairy-farming community. It's noted for its rose garden and is the gateway to the rock-climbing centre of Wharepapa South, 23km southeast.

Information

Internet access is available at the **Redoubt Bar & Eatery** (☎ 07-871 4768; cnr Rewi & Alexandra Sts; per 15min $2.50).

Te Awamutu visitors centre (☎ 07-871 3259; www.teawamutu.co.nz; cnr Gorst Ave & SH3; ❧ 9am-4.30pm Mon-Fri, 9.30am-3pm Sat & Sun)

Sights & Activities

The **Rose Garden** is next to the visitors centre and has 2000 rose bushes with 50 varieties that usually bloom from November to April.

St John's Anglican Church is across the road from the visitors centre, where the key is kept. It opened in 1854 and is constructed of matai and rimu. The sanctuary's stained-glass window is one of the oldest in the country. Memorials relating to the Waikato Land War can be seen.

The **museum** (☎ 07-871 4326; www.tamuseum .org.nz; Civic Centre, 135 Roche St; admission by donation; ❧ 10am-4pm Mon-Fri, 10am-1pm Sat, 1-4pm Sun) has a fine collection of Maori *taonga* (treasures). Other displays tell the story of the Waikato Land War and of music heroes Tim and Neil Finn – a must for fans of Split Enz or Crowded House – who came from here.

Ask at the visitors centre for the **Te Awamutu Heritage Trail** brochure, a 1½-hour walk that takes in old fortifications and heritage buildings.

Behind the visitors centre and the Rose Garden is the Events Centre which has a large **indoor pool** (☎ 07-871 2080; cnr Mahoe & Selwyn Sts; adult/child $3.50/2; ❧ 6am-9pm Mon-Fri, 8am-7pm Sat & Sun). The hydroslide is an extra

$3 for adults and children. Spas and saunas are also available.

Sleeping

Road Runner Motel & Holiday Park (☎ 07-871 7420; fax 07-871 6664; 141 Bond Rd; camp sites/campervan sites $18/22, cabins s/d $25/30, units s/d $65/75) This small camping ground has modern facilities and the motel units are plain but comfortable.

Farmstay Guesthouse (☎ 07-871 3301; 296 Storey Rd; s/d & tw/d with bathroom $70/120/130; 🖳) Just 4km northeast of Te Awamutu is this 34-hectare farm with cows, horses, pigs, poultry, sheep, goats and pets. Horse riding and gig rides are $10 per person and there is a tennis court. The rooms are spacious and prices include a full breakfast. It's ideal for children.

Rosetown Motel (☎ 0800 767 386, 07-871 5779; bryants@ihug.co.nz; 844 Kihikihi Rd; units $80; 🖳) These comfortable units have kitchens and Sky TV, and share a spa pool.

Albert Park Motor Lodge (☎ 07-870 2995; albert.park@xtra.co.nz; 299 Albert Park Dr; units $95-120) Smart and modern, these units have Sky TV and some have spa baths.

Eating, Drinking & Entertainment

Rose & Thorn (☎ 07-871 8761; 32 Arawata St; mains $28) The smartest restaurant in town with a bar next door that has a mixed bag of live music on Thursday, Friday and Saturday nights.

Redoubt Bar & Eatery (☎ 07-871 4768; cnr Rewi & Alexandra Sts; bar meals under $10; 🖳) A relaxed, natural-wood bar with $6 cocktails, old photos on the walls and daily food specials.

Regency Cinema (☎ 07-871 6678; Alexandra St; tickets per adult $12) Built in 1932, this Art Deco cinema has four screens and movie memorabilia in the foyer.

Getting There & Away

InterCity (☎ 0508 424 368) buses and **Tranz Scenic** (☎ 0800 277 482) trains that run between Auckland and Wellington stop at Te Awamutu. The buses stop outside Stewart Law Motors in Mahoe St.

Dalroy (☎ 0508 465 622) runs buses daily to Auckland (10.35am departure) and New Plymouth (3.40pm), which leave from outside the visitors centre.

Hodgson Motors (☎ 07-871 6363; adult/child $5/3) runs buses from Te Awamutu to Hamilton and back five times daily Monday to Friday.

AROUND TE AWAMUTU
Wharepapa South

Wharepapa South, 25km southeast of Te Awamutu, is one of the best places for rock climbing in the North Island. Froggate Edge is a climbing mecca with more than 115 routes but there are plenty of other world-class climbs nearby. One of the best, Whanganui Bay at Lake Taupo, is only an hour's drive away.

Staff at **Bryce's** (Wharepapa Outdoor Centre; ☎ 07-872 2533; bryce@rockclimb.co.nz; 1424 Owairaka Valley Rd) have a wealth of knowledge and experience about climbing in the area and this is the place to come if you are a serious climber. There's a well-stocked shop that sells and hires out a full range of climbing gear, an indoor bouldering cave ($9 but free to guests) and a café. A day's instruction costs around $350. There's **accommodation** (dm/d $18/48) available at the centre or you can **camp** ($8) at the primary school next door.

Castle Rock Adventure (☎ 0800 225 462, 07-872 2509; www.castlerockadventure.co.nz; 1250 Owairaka Valley Rd; dm $25-30, s/d & tw $45/70; 🖳 🖳) provide accommodation and lots of fun activities. The cheaper dorm has ten beds while the more expensive one has four. A new feature is the Woolshed, which has hot showers and a small kitchen and you can sleep on a mattress on the floor for $10. Rock climbing or abseiling instruction for half a day is $79, and you can add in the 200m flying fox (normally $15) off a cliff for no extra charge. Mountain bike and helmet hire is $10 an hour and there are three tracks to try out. An adventure package that covers rock climbing, abseiling, the flying fox, a two-hour mountain bike ride and a night in a dorm costs $99.

The best way to get here is on the **Waitomo Wanderer** (☎ 07-349 2509), which runs daily from Rotorua ($10) and Waitomo ($10). Otherwise phone Castle Rock Adventure or Wharepapa Outdoor Centre for a pickup from Te Awamutu ($10).

Pirongia Forest Park

The main attraction of this park is **Mt Pirongia**, its 959m summit clearly visible from much of the Waikato region. The mountain is usually climbed from Corcoran Rd. There's a hut near the summit if you want to spend the night. Maps and information about Pirongia Forest Park are available

om DOC in Hamilton. You can go horse-
iding on the slopes of the mountain with **Mt
irongia Horse Treks** (☎ 07-871 9960; 394 Mangati Rd;
ir rides $20), southwest of Pirongia.

AMBRIDGE
op 11,300
in the Waikato River, 22km southeast of
Hamilton, Cambridge is a small town with a
harming rural-English atmosphere. Cricket
played on the village green and the avenues
re lined with broad, shady European trees,
t their best in autumn. The Cambridge re-
ion is famous for the breeding and training
f thoroughbred horses. One well-known
Cambridge-bred horse is Charisma, which
on the Olympic three-day equestrian event
n 1984 and 1988 (ridden by New Zealander
Mark Todd). Nearby Lake Karapiro (p232)
the place for watersports, and is where
he country's Olympic-champion rower
.ob Waddell honed his skills.

nformation
he **Cambridge visitors centre** (☎ 07-823 3456;
www.cambridge.net.nz; cnr Victoria & Queen Sts; ☺ 9am-
im Mon-Fri, 10am-4pm Sat & Sun) has details on
cal B&Bs and farm stays.

ights & Activities
Cambridge has a 1½-hour **heritage trail** that
ncludes the town's historical buildings, the
Waikato River and Te Koutu lake, which at-
acts water birds. Don't miss the interior
f **St Andrew's Anglican Church**. The visitors
entre has a leaflet with a map.
   The musty **Cambridge Museum** (☎ 07-827
19; Victoria St; admission by donation; ☺ 10am-4pm
 in-Sat, 10am-2pm Sun), housed in the former
ourthouse, has the usual pioneer relics and
scale model of the local Te Totara Pa before
was wiped out by Maoris from the north.
   The **Cambridge Thoroughbred Lodge** (☎ 07-
7 8118; www.racing.net.nz/cambridge; horse shows
ult/child $12/5; ☺ usually 10.30am), 6km south of
wn on SH1, is a top horse stud. The one-
our shows include tea and introduce you
the world of thoroughbred horses, which
ut on a show. Bookings are essential.
   Stud Tours (☎ 07-827 5910; www.barrylee.co.nz;
2½hr tours $60/120) offers visits to local stud
rms by a local bloodstock expert. Prices are
ir up to four people, which makes this a very
asonably priced and unique tour. Booking
usually essential, especially in January.

Cambridge Raceway (☎ 07-827 5506; www.cambrid
geraceway.co.nz; Taylor Rd) is the venue for trotting
and greyhound races three times a month.
Check the website for dates and times.
   Camjet (☎ 0800 226 538; fax 07-870 1090; Dominion
Ave; adult/student & child $50/35) offers exciting and
scenic jetboat rides along the Waikato River
to Lake Karapiro that last around 35 minutes. Reservations are necessary.
   Cambridge Country Store (☎ 07-827 8715; 92 Victoria St; ☺ 9am-5.30pm; ▣), housed in a former
'wooden Gothic' church, has a wide range
of mainly Kiwi-made gifts and souvenirs.

Sleeping
Cambridge Country Lodge Backpackers (☎ 07-827
8373; Peake Rd; camp site $18, dm/s/d & tw/self-contained
units $18/35/45/65) Rooms share bathrooms
and overlook horse paddocks but the camp-
ground-style facilities need upgrading and
heating is provided by hot-water bottles.
It's 3km north of the town centre but free
pick-ups from town are available.
   Cambridge Motor Camp (☎ 07-827 5649; 32 Scott
St, Leamington; camp sites & campervan sites $22, s/d
cabins from $20/30, tourist flats $65) A quiet, well-
maintained campground over the bridge
from Cambridge town centre, which is
1½km away.
   Pamades (☎ 07-827 4916; pamades@slingshot.co.nz;
229 Shakespeare St; s/d/d with bathroom $60/75/90; ▣)
Prices include continental breakfast, the en
suites are self-contained and there is a hot
spa as well as a pool.
   Park House (☎ 07-827 6368; www.parkhouse.co.nz;
70 Queen St; s/d & tw $120/160) Centrally located
and overlooking the cricket green, this
stately house is full of antiques, quilts and
period features. Experienced hosts serve an
ample breakfast in the formal dining room
and add their touch of old-worlde charm.
   Cambrian Lodge Motel (☎ 0800 886 886, 07-827
7766; www.cambrianlodge.net.nz; 63 Hamilton Rd; units
$75-110; ▣) An attractive pool-side area is
the main feature of this motel with Sky TV
and an indoor spa.
   Cambridge Mews (☎ 07-827 7166; www.cambridge
mews.co.nz; 20 Hamilton Rd; units from $130; ▣) All the
units in this boutique motel have double spa
baths, kitchens and Sky TV.
   Souter House (☎ 07-827 3610; www.souterhouse
.co.nz; 19 Victoria St; d from $120; ▣) Period ele-
gance with luxurious modern facilities such
as central heating and spa baths can be found
in this Victorian homestead with a veranda,

which also has a fine restaurant. It's on the main street near the town centre.

A novel place to spend a couple of nights is relaxing on a houseboat on Lake Karapiro – contact Houseboat Holidays (below).

Eating & Drinking

All Saints Café (☎ 07-827 7100; 92 Victoria St; ☯ breakfast & lunch) Savouries, cakes, sandwiches and speciality teas are served upstairs in the Cambridge Country Store.

Deli on the Corner (☎ 07-827 5370; 48 Victoria St; ☯ 9am-5pm Mon-Fri, 10am-4pm Sat, 10am-2pm Sun) This tiny, triangular café has character and offers a touch of gourmet home-cooking – try the crêpes or *mezze* platter for $9.

Rata (☎ 07-823 0999; 64c Victoria St; mains $20-25; ☯ 10am-3pm Sun & Mon, 9am-5pm Tue & Wed, 9am-late Thu-Sat) This funky bar/café/restaurant has a large blackboard menu that is a work of art and features lengthy items such as kumera ricotta and coriander chilli spring rolls.

Oasis Wine Bar & Restaurant (☎ 07-827 8004; 35 Duke St; mains $19-25; ☯ 11am-late; ▣) Stylish, modern cuisine is available here – vegetarians could try the *spanakopita* ($19).

Prince Albert Tavern & Restaurant (☎ 07-827 7900; Victoria Plaza, Halley's Lane; mains $19-24) This English-style pub has Boddington, Kilkenny, Guinness and Mac's cider on tap, dark ale pie ($17) and a DJ or live music Friday and Saturday nights.

Souter House (☎ 07-827 3610; 19 Victoria St; mains $20-30; ☯ dinner Mon-Sat) Enjoy old-worlde charm in this smart hotel restaurant that offers the classics: venison, ostrich, salmon and lamb.

Getting There & Away

Lying on SH1, Cambridge is well connected by bus. Most long-distance buses from Hamilton to Rotorua or the Bay of Plenty stop in the town.

Cambridge Travel Lines (☎ 07-827 7363; adult/child $5/3) runs buses to and from Hamilton, two or three times daily.

LAKE KARAPIRO

Karapiro, the furthest downstream of a chain of eight hydroelectric power stations on the Waikato River, was opened in 1947. It is 30km southeast of Hamilton, 8km from Cambridge, and 3km off SH1. The 21km-long lake is popular for all kinds of aquatic sports, especially kayaking and rowing.

Drive down Hydro Rd from SH1 for good café and to reach the dam wall. Driv on over the dam and walk to **Karapiro Lak Domain** (☎ 07-827 4178; camp sites/campervan site chalets $16/20/50).

Drive down Gorton Rd to reach the **Boa shed Café** (☎ 07-827 8286; www.theboatshed.net.n 21 Amber Lane; mains $9-14; ☯ 10am-4pm, closed mi Jun–Jul). This popular café on the lakesid sells mainly home-made food, some c which is gluten and dairy free. The rowin boat of Rob Waddel (NZ's Olympic gold medallist rower) is part of the décor – h used to practise here. Kayaks can be hire for $10/35 for half/full day. You can paddl to a couple of waterfalls in around an hou Sleek, speedy but tippy multisport canoe cost $30 for half a day.

Houseboat Holidays (☎ 07-827 2195; www.hous boatescape.co.nz; 2 nights $550, $600 Jan) hires out smart houseboat (sleeps seven) on the lak It's the perfect way to relax for a couple days, and you can load the boat up wit kayaks. Available all year, fuel will co around $35, and you can fish for trout you have a licence and fishing gear. Get group together to share the cost.

Birches (☎ 07-827 6556; birches@ihug.co.nz; 2 Maungatautari Rd; s/d $60/95; ▣ ▣) Stay in separate cottage or in the house with spa bath at this B&B with a wide range breakfast options, a tennis court and hos who enjoy waterskiing.

MATAMATA
pop 7800

This town, 23km northeast of Cambridg is famous for its thoroughbred stud farm but the local tourist industry has been give a boost by Peter Jackson's epic film trilog *Lord of the Rings*. A nearby farm was use to create Hobbiton and thousands of th film's fans have been taking the tour t visit the setting for the Hobbit villag Enough remains of the set for your im agination to fill in the holes and the guid are full of stories about the making of th film. Other attractions in the area includ tandem skydiving at the nearby airport, pioneer village, a hot-spring resort and a attractive waterfall.

Information

The **visitors centre** (☎ 07-888 7260; www.matama -info.co.nz; 45 Broadway; ☯ 8.30am-5pm Mon-Fri, 9.30a

3pm Sat & Sun) can book tickets, including the Hobbiton tour. Opposite the visitors centre is an Internet centre.

Sights & Activities
Visit Hobbiton with **Rings Scenic Tours** (☎ 07-888 6838; www.hobbitontours.com; adult $50, child 10-14 $25, child under 9 free). The two-hour tours have proved to be so popular (13,000 people went on them in 2003) that they have been running three times a day (note that the number may decrease). Book at the local visitors centre.

Skydive Waikato (☎ 0508 759 3483, 029-759 3483; www.freefall.co.nz; SH27) runs gravity-powered adventures, usually on Wednesday and Saturday, such as tandem skydiving from 3000m, which costs $220. See the website for other options. The airfield is 8km north of Matamata.

The **Firth Tower** (☎ 07-888 8369; Tower Rd; adult/child $5/1; ☻ 10am-4pm, Wed-Sun) was built in 1882 by Auckland businessman Josiah Firth. He acquired 56,000 acres from his friend Wiremu Tamihana, chief of the Ngati Haua. The tower was a fashionable status symbol rather than for defence as the Waikato Land War was long over by the time it was built. The concrete tower is filled with Maori and pioneer relics and around it are 10 other buildings including a pioneer school room, jail, cottage and 14m-deep bricked well – hard work to dig and build. It's 3km from town.

Opal Hot Springs (☎ 0800 800 198, 07-888 8198; Okauia Springs Rd; swimming pool adult/child $4.50/2, private spas 30min $5/2.50) is 2km down an access road off Tower Rd, just north of Firth Tower and 6km from Matamata. Try Ramaroa Spa, a private outdoor hot spa for a Garden of Eden experience. There's also a camping ground (see below).

Carry on past Opal Pools to visit the 150m-high **Wairere Falls**.

Sleeping
Maple Lodge (☎ /fax 07-888 8764; maplelodge@xtra.co.nz; 11 Mangawhero Rd; units $70; ☻) This motel is within walking distance of the town centre and also has a spa pool.

Opal Hot Springs Holiday Park (☎ 0800 800 198, 07-888 8198; Okauia Springs Rd; camp sites/campervan sites $22/24, cabins $40-53, tourist flats $63) Basic facilities but clean and offers free entry to the hot pools.

Broadway (☎ 07-888 8482; www.broadwaymatamata.co.nz; 128 Broadway; units from $80; ☻) In the town centre, these recently refurbished motel units have Sky TV and share a spa pool.

Southern Belle B&B (☎ 0800 244 233, 07-888 6804; 101 Firth St; d/tr $150/180) This quality B&B (breakfast is $7 to $15 extra) has three bedrooms, a lounge and bathroom facilities. A couple has the entire area to themselves for $150 or it can sleep up to five people ($210/240 for four/five people).

Other recommendations:

O'Reilly's Motor Inn (☎ 0800 358 352, 07-888 9126; oreillys@clear.net.nz; 187 Firth St; units from $90) Some units have spa baths.

Tower Lodge Motel (☎ 07-888 6112; Tower Rd; units from $82)

Eating & Drinking
Workman's Café & Bar (☎ 07-888 5498; 52 Broadway; mains $26; ☻ breakfast, lunch & dinner Tue-Sun) The menu here in this Retro café/bar/restaurant changes every two weeks but it has built itself a reputation that extends beyond Matamata.

Ronnie's Café (78 Broadway) This place has a huge self-service selection.

Lucky's (☎ 07-888 5630; 96 Broadway; ☻ Mon-Sat) This bar sometimes has live music.

Getting There & Away
InterCity (☎ 07-834 3457) runs daily buses that link Matamata with Cambridge, Hamilton and Tauranga.

TIRAU
pop 720

The small gift-shop town of Tirau, 54km southeast of Hamilton at the junction of SH1 and SH5, has fallen in love with corrugated iron. This material has been used to construct a **giant dog and sheep**, which are bigger than most buildings in town. The dog houses the **visitors centre** (☎ 07-883 1202; www.tirauinfo.co.nz), while the sheep houses a large gift shop. Other fun corrugated-iron art around the town includes a big cheese, a pukeko and a cow pushing a shopping trolley. For something equally outlandish, visit the **castle** at the southern end of town.

Just off SH27, 5km north of Tirau, is **Oraka Deer Park** (☎ 07-883 1382; www.oraka-deer.co.nz; 71 Bayly Rd; d & tw $160; ☻), which offers a self-contained cottage or en suite rooms in the house with your own entrance. The farm has 700 deer and a deer shop. Venison meals may be possible, and it's ideal for children; it includes a pool, spa pool and tennis court.

Many **InterCity** (☎ 07-834 3457) buses pass through Tirau and link it with just about everywhere.

THE KING COUNTRY

The King Country is named after the Maori King Movement (p219), which developed in the Waikato region in the late 1850s and early 1860s. When King Tawhiao and his people were forced to move from Waikato after being defeated by British troops during the Waikato Land War (1863–64), they came south to this region. Legend has it that King Tawhiao placed his top hat on a large map of NZ and declared that all the land it covered would be under his *mana*, or authority. It was only after 1884 that Pakeha were allowed into the district and it still retains a powerful Maori influence as Maoris are less outnumbered here than elsewhere.

OTOROHANGA
pop 2700

Otorohanga (often called 'Oto' by locals) is on SH3, 58km south of Hamilton and 16km from Waitomo. A farming community, the town's biggest attraction is the kiwi and native-bird house, but the main street is decorated with murals and displays of 'Kiwiana', including the All-Blacks, sheep, Maori carvings, gumboots, Anchor butter and pavlova. You can also learn about other Kiwi icons, such as Footrot Flats, 'the good old quarter acre', No 8 wire, Marmite and Buzzy Bees. Otorohanga itself is a perfect example of another Kiwi icon: a one-street town that services the local farming community.

Information

The useful **visitors centre** (☎ 07-873 8951; www .otorohanga.co.nz; 57 Maniapoto St; ☒ 9am-5.30pm Mon-Fri, 10am-4pm Sat & Sun) is the AA agent, and it also sells bus, ferry and train tickets. The **Post Shop** (☎ 07-873 8816; ☒ 8.30am-5pm Mon-Fri, 9am-7pm Sat) is conveniently located on the main street.

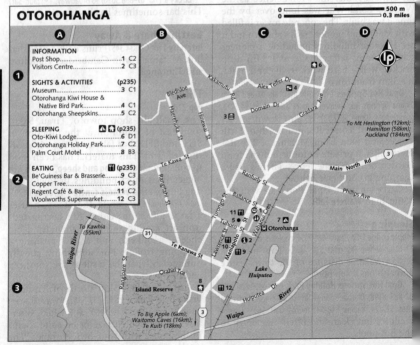

OTOROHANGA

0 — 500 m
0 — 0.3 miles

INFORMATION	
Post Shop	1 C2
Visitors Centre	2 C3

SIGHTS & ACTIVITIES	(p235)
Museum	3 C1
Otorohanga Kiwi House & Native Bird Park	4 C1
Otorohanga Sheepskins	5 C2

SLEEPING	(p235)
Oto-Kiwi Lodge	6 D1
Otorohanga Holiday Park	7 C2
Palm Court Motel	8 B3

EATING	(p235)
Be'Guiness Bar & Brasserie	9 C3
Copper Tree	10 C3
Regent Café & Bar	11 C2
Woolworths Supermarket	12 C3

Sights

The **Otorohanga Kiwi House & Native Bird Park** (☎ 07-873 7391; www.kiwihouse.org.nz; Alex Telfer Dr; adult/child $10/7; ⏰ 9am-5pm) is a must-see. In the kiwi house night and day are reversed and you are guaranteed to see active kiwi in their indoor enclosure – they are usually energetically digging with their long beaks, searching for food. Other native birds, such as kaka, kea, falcon, morepork and weka, can also be seen.

A small **museum** (Kakamutu Rd; ⏰ 2-4pm Sun) covers local history and **Otorohanga Sheepskins** (☎ 07-873 7799; 52 Maniapoto St) sells Kiwiana souvenirs.

Sleeping

Oto-Kiwi Lodge (☎ 07-873 6022; oto-kiwi@xtra.co.nz; Sangro Cres; camp sites $21, dm/d & tw $19/44; ▢) This small but tidy backpackers, near the kiwi house, has a log fire and a deck. Mountain bikes are for hire ($10 a day) and kayak trips are $30.

Otorohanga Holiday Park (☎ 07-873 7253; www .kiwiholidaypark.co.nz; 12 Huiputea Dr; sites $22, cabins/ cabins with bathrooms/tourist flats/units $40/50/60/80; ▢) The park's new facilities include a fitness centre.

Mt Heslington (☎ 07-873 1873; jean.phil-newman@ xtra.co.nz; 1375 SH3; s/d & tw $70/90; ▢ ▣) This 80-hectare farm, 12km north of Otorohanga, breeds cattle and racehorses, as well as growing vegetables and fruit. There are two rooms in a separate guest section, but only one group stays there at a time. Facilities include a pool table.

Palm Court Motel (☎ 07-873 7122; palmcourt@ xtra.co.nz; cnr Clarke & Maniapoto Sts; studio/1-bed units $95/110) These smart and modern units are at the southern end of town and some have spa baths.

Eating

Regent Café & Bar (☎ 07-873 7370; 48 Maniapoto St; ⏰ breakfast & lunch daily, dinner Fri-Sun) A spacious self-service café that offers lots of choice, mostly home-made.

Big Apple (☎ 07-873 8753; ⏰ breakfast, lunch & dinner) This huge barn-like restaurant is on the highway south of town.

Copper Tree (☎ 07-873 7777; 80 Maniapoto St; brunch $6-13, pizzas $12-19; ⏰ brunch & dinner) The Copper Tree specialises in gourmet pizzas.

Be'Guiness Bar & Brasserie (☎ 07-873 8010; Maniapoto St; mains $19-25; ⏰ dinner Tue-Sun) There's a Serious Seafood Platter ($23) or you can take on a double challenge – the Hog Slab ($25) followed by Addicted to Chocolate ($12.50).

Self-caterers should head to **Woolworths** (☎ 07-873 7378; 125 Maniapoto St; ⏰ 7am-10pm) at the southern end of town.

Getting There & Away

InterCity (☎ 09-913 6100) buses arrive at and depart from the visitors centre, which sells tickets. There are four buses to Rotorua ($30 to $47) and Auckland ($32 to $42) daily. The **Waitomo Shuttle** (☎ 0800 808 279) runs to Waitomo and Hamilton ($8).

Train services between Auckland and Wellington stop at Otorohanga station in the town centre.

WAITOMO

The name Waitomo, which comes from *wai* (water) and *tomo* (hole or shaft), is appropriate: dotted throughout the countryside are numerous shafts dropping abruptly into underground cave systems and streams. There are more than 300 mapped caves in the area and these limestone caves and accompanying limestone formations make up one of the premier attractions of the North Island.

Tours through the Glowworm Cave (also known as the Waitomo Cave) and the Aranui Cave have been feature attractions for decades, but in typical Kiwi fashion the list of things to do has grown and become more daring. Now you can abseil, raft and tube through the caves, or try your hand at a number of above-ground activities such as driving a jetboat, riding a horse or quad bike or swinging on a high-ropes course.

Information

The **visitors centre** (☎ 07-878 7640; www.waitomo caves.com; 21 Waitomo Caves Rd; ⏰ 8am-8pm Jan & Feb, 8am-5pm Mar-Dec) is in the Museum of Caves. It has Internet access, an ATM and bookshop, and acts as a post office and booking agent. Next door, in the general store, is the **Waitomo Adventures Luminosa information centre** (☎ 0800 924 866, 07-878 7788; Waitomo Caves Rd; ⏰ 7am-8pm summer, 7am-6pm winter).

Sights

WAITOMO CAVES

The **Glowworm Cave** had been known to the local Maoris for a long time, but the first European to explore it was an English

WAIKATO & THE KING COUNTRY

surveyor Fred Mace, who was shown the cave in December 1887 by Maori chief Tane Tinorau. Mace prepared an account of the expedition, a map was made and photographs given to the government, and before long Tane Tinorau was operating tours of the cave. The Glowworm Cave is just a big cave with the usual assortment of stalactites and stalagmites – until you board a boat and swing off onto the river. As your eyes grow accustomed to the dark, you'll see a Milky Way of little lights surrounding you – these are the glow-worms. You can see them in other caves and other places around Waitomo, and in other parts of NZ, but the ones in this cave are something special. Conditions for their growth are just about perfect in this cave, so there is a remarkable number of them. Try to avoid the big tour groups, most of which arrive between 10.30am and 2.30pm. Photography is not allowed.

Three kilometres west from the Glowworm Cave is the **Aranui Cave**. This cave has no river running through it and hence no glow-worms. It is a large cave with thousands of tiny 'straw' stalactites hanging from the ceiling. Various scenes in the colourful formations are pointed out and photography is permitted. It's an hour's walk to the cave or the ticket office can arrange transport.

Tickets for the two caves are sold at the entrance to the Glowworm Cave. Entry to one cave is $25/12 per adult/child, or a combined two-cave ticket costs $45/22.50. A 'museum-cave special' includes the Glowworm Cave tour and the informative Museum of Caves for $26/12.

To visit the caves you'll need to take a tour. The 45-minute tours of the Glowworm Cave leave daily on the half-hour from 9am to 5pm. From late October to Easter there's also a 5.30pm tour, with more at the height of the summer season. Aranui Cave tours leave at 10am, 11am, 1pm, 2pm and 3pm, and also take about 45 minutes.

The nearby **Ruakuri Cave** is open only for group tours (see Black-Water Rafting, p238).

MUSEUM OF CAVES

This **museum** (☎ 07-878 7640; 21 Waitomo Caves Rd; adult/child $5/free; ⏰ 8am-5pm, 8am-8pm Jan & Feb) has some excellent exhibits that explain

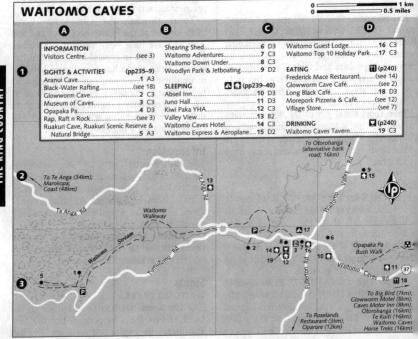

WAITOMO CAVES

0 ——————— 1 km
0 ——————— 0.5 miles

INFORMATION	
Visitors Centre.....................(see 3)	**Shearing Shed.................6** D3
	Waitomo Adventures.........7 C3
SIGHTS & ACTIVITIES (pp235–9)	**Waitomo Down Under.......8** C3
Aranui Cave.............................1 A3	**Woodlyn Park & Jetboating....9** D2
Black-Water Rafting............(see 18)	
Glowworm Cave.....................2 C3	**SLEEPING** 🏕 🏠 (pp239–40)
Museum of Caves....................3 C3	Abseil Inn.............................10 C3
Opapaka Pa............................4 D3	Juno Hall..............................11 C3
Rap, Raft n Rock.................(see 3)	Kiwi Paka YHA......................12 C3
Ruakuri Cave, Ruakuri Scenic Reserve &	Valley View..........................13 B2
Natural Bridge.....................5 A3	Waitomo Caves Hotel............14 C3
	Waitomo Express & Aeroplane....15 D2

Waitomo Guest Lodge..............16 C3	
Waitomo Top 10 Holiday Park.....17 C3	
EATING 🍴 (p240)	
Frederick Mace Restaurant.......(see 14)	
Glowworm Cave Café.............(see 2)	
Long Black Café.....................18 D3	
Morepork Pizzeria & Café........(see 12)	
Village Store.........................(see 7)	
DRINKING 🍷 (p240)	
Waitomo Caves Tavern............19 C3	

GLOW-WORM MAGIC

Glow-worms are the larvae of the fungus gnat, which looks much like a large mosquito without mouth parts. The larvae glow-worms have luminescent organs which produce a soft, greenish light. Living in a sort of hammock suspended from an overhang, they weave sticky threads which trail down and catch unwary insects attracted by their lights. When an insect flies towards the light, it gets stuck in the threads and becomes paralysed – the glow-worm reels in the thread and eats the insect.

The larval stage lasts for six to nine months, depending on how much food the glow-worm gets. When the glow-worm has grown to about the size of a matchstick it goes into a pupa stage, much like a cocoon. The adult fungus gnat emerges about two weeks later.

The adult insect does not live very long because it does not have a mouth. It emerges, mates, lays eggs and dies, all within about two or three days. The sticky eggs, laid in groups of 40 or 50, hatch in about three weeks to become larval glow-worms.

Glow-worms thrive in moist, dark caves but they can survive anywhere if they have the requisites of moisture, an overhang to suspend from, and insects to eat. Waitomo is famous for its glow-worms but you can see them in many other places around NZ, both in caves and outdoors.

When you come upon glow-worms, don't touch their hammocks or hanging threads, try not to make loud noises and don't shine a light right on them. In daylight their lights fade out, and if you shine a torch right on them they will dim their lights. It takes the lights a few hours to become bright again, during which time the glow-worm will catch no food. The glow-worms that shine most brightly are the hungriest.

---

exactly how caves are formed, the flora and fauna that thrive in them and the history of the caves and cave exploration. Displays include a cave model, fossils of extinct birds and animals that have been discovered in caves and a cave crawl. There are also audiovisual presentations about caving, glow-worms and other natural attractions in the Waitomo area.

Free entry is often included with various activities or you can get a 'museum-cave special' (see p236).

SHEARING SHED

The **Shearing Shed** (☎ 07-878 8371; admission free; ☼ 9am-4pm) is where big fluffy Angora rabbits are sheared rather than sheep. The store has top-quality Angora fur products.

Activities

If it's challenging underground adventures that you're after, then Waitomo is the place to be, with abseiling, rock climbing and cave tubing along underground rivers. You can pick and choose from a number of operators.

CAVING & ABSEILING

Waitomo Adventures (☎ 0800 924 866, 07-878 7788; www.waitomo.co.nz; Caveland Cafe) offers a range of cave adventures.

With 100m of abseiling to get into the Lost World Cave, its **Lost World** trip is amazing, and you don't even need prior abseiling or caving experience. The principal trip to Lost World is an all-day one ($355). Trips run from 10.30am to 5.30pm, followed by dinner. First you abseil 100m down into the cave (accompanied by your guide), then by a combination of walking, climbing, spider-walking, inching along narrow rock ledges, wading and swimming through a subterranean river, you take a three-hour journey through a 30m-high cave to get back out, passing glow-worms, amazing rock and cave formations, waterfalls and more. The price includes lunch (underground) and dinner.

The other option is a four-hour dry trip ($225) that involves a 100m abseil into the cave, with a guide beside you on another rope. At the bottom, you walk for about an hour into the cave and exit via another vertical cavern back to the surface, without doing the underground river trip. These trips depart at 7.10am, 11.30am and 3pm but can vary.

Haggas Honking Holes four-hour caving trip ($165) includes professional abseiling instruction followed by a caving trip with three abseils, rock climbing and travelling along a subterranean river with waterfalls.

Along the way you see glow-worms and a variety of cave formations – including stalactites, stalagmites, columns, flowstone and cave coral. It's a good way to see real caving action, using caving equipment and going through caverns of various sizes, from squeezing through tight, narrow passageways to traversing huge caverns.

The name of the adventure derives from a local farmer, 'Haggas', and characters in a Dr Seuss story, 'honking holers'. Trips depart at 10am and 3pm but can vary. The 'Gruesome Twosome' combines this with the four-hour Lost World trip ($370).

Tumu Tumu Toobing is a more physical four-hour tubing trip ($85) for the adventurous traveller. Trips leave at 10am and 3pm. 'Blackwater Fever', a combination of this trip and the Haggas Honking Holes adventure, costs $230. If you combine the Lost World and Tumu Tumu trips it will save you $20.

St Benedict's Cavern is a three-hour trip ($100) that includes abseiling, a subterranean flying fox and 1½ hours underground in this attractive cave with straw stalagmites.

Waitomo Down Under (☎ 0800 456 9676, 07-878 6577; www.waitomocavesfloatthrough.co.nz) is next door to the Museum of Caves. It operates 'float through' caving adventures for groups of up to 12 – three times daily in winter but six in summer. Prices include soup and toast.

In **Adventure I** (three-hour trip, 1½ hours underground; $75) you go through Te Anaroa (Long Cave) in inner tubes, going over two waterfalls (one on a slide) and getting a good close-up view of some glow-worms along the way.

Adventure II ($75) is a 50m abseil into the 'Baby Grand' *tomo* (you can do it at night as well for $85).

Rap, Raft n Rock (☎ 0800 228 372; www.cave raft.com; trips $85), next door to the Museum of Caves, runs a five-hour trip with small groups. It starts with abseil training, followed by a 27m abseil into a natural cave, and then involves floating along a subterranean river on an inner tube. How fast you float will depend on the season and the recent rainfall, but there are always plenty of glow-worms. After some caving you do a belayed rock climb up a stepped 20m pitch to the surface.

BLACK-WATER RAFTING

The **Legendary Black Water Rafting Company** (☎ 0800 228 464, 07-878 6219; Waitomo Caves Rd; www .blackwaterrafting.co.nz), with its headquarters at the Long Black Café, runs three different adventures. The cost of each trip includes admission into the Museum of Caves.

Black Labyrinth (three-hour trip, one hour underground; $75) involves floating on an inner tube down a subterranean river that flows through Ruakuri Cave. The high point is leaping off a small waterfall and then floating through a long, glow-worm–covered passage. The trip ends with hot showers, soup and bagels in the café. You wear a wet suit, which will keep you warm, but having something hot to eat or drink before the trip will make you feel more comfortable.

Black Abyss (five-hour trip, two to three hours underground; $145) is more adventurous and includes a 30m abseil into Ruakuri Cave and more glow-worms, tubing and cave climbing. Hot showers and snacks are included.

Spellbound (three-hour trip, one hour underground; $37) includes a boat trip and is a good option if you don't want to get wet. This guided tour goes through parts of the Mangawhitiakau cave system at Oparure, 12km south of Waitomo. You will learn all about the life cycle of glow-worms and gain an insight into other things that inhabit the caves. Tea/coffee and biscuits are included in the price.

WALKING

The Museum of Caves has free pamphlets on various walks in the area. The walk from the Aranui Cave to the Ruakuri Cave is an excellent short path. From the Glowworm Cave ticket office, it's a 15-minute forest walk to a grove of California redwood trees. Also from here, the 5km, three-hour-return **Waitomo Walkway** takes off through farmland, following Waitomo Stream to the Ruakuri Scenic Reserve, where a 30-minute return walk passes by the river, caves and a natural limestone bridge.

At night, drive to the Ruakuri Scenic Reserve car park and walk across the bridge where glow-worms put on a magical display. Bring a torch to find your way.

A one-hour return walk, the **Opapaka Pa Bush Walk**, leads up to a pre-European *pa* (fort) site on a hill. Plaques along the way describe traditional Maori medicines found in the forest, traditional forest lore and the *pa* site itself.

OTHER ACTIVITIES
Woodlyn Park (☎ 07-878 6666; www.woodlynpark.co .nz; 1177 Waitomo Valley Rd; adult/child $15/8; shows 1.30pm) has a rustic theatre where fair-dinkum Barry Woods puts on a helluva one-hour farm animal show that combines history and humour. Snowy the sheep, Trev the black pig and Big Mac the steer are other stars, but the audience takes part too. The **jetboating** (7 laps $47; ☯ 9.30am-6.30pm Nov-Apr, 9.30am-5pm May-Oct) at the park is unique because you get the chance to drive a jetboat around a figure-of-eight course instead of just being a passenger. There is also accommodation (p239) available in a train or a plane.

Waitomo Caves Horse Treks (☎ 07-878 5065; 1/2hr rides $40/50) offers a variety of different rides through bush or farmland. Longer treks are available and all levels are catered for, from beginners to adrenalin riders. The stables are a 15-minute drive west of Waitomo or pick-ups can be arranged from Waitomo.

Big Red (☎ 07-878 7640; 2hr trips $75) takes self-drive, quad-bike trips through bush and countryside. Book at the visitors centre.

Track n Paddle (☎ 07-957 0002; www.tracknpaddle .co.nz; tours $100-300) runs mountain-biking, hiking and kayaking tours from Waitomo to Marokopa and Kawhia Harbour three times a week with small groups (maximum eight).

Caving company **Rap, Raft n Rock** (☎ 0800 228 372; www.caveraft.com) also has a high-ropes course ($40, two hours), which are 9m above the ground.

Sleeping
BUDGET
Kiwi Paka YHA (☎ 07-878 3395; www.kiwipaka-yha .co.nz; School Rd; dm/d & tw/f/chalets $22/50/75/120; ▣) This jumbo-sized, excellent, new hostel is purpose-built in Alpine style and has four-bed dorms and a popular restaurant (see Eating & Drinking, p240) that serves mainly pizzas. YHA members and non-members pay the same.

Juno Hall (☎ /fax 07-878 7649; junohall@juno waitomo.com; 600 Waitomo Caves Rd; camp sites $20, dm/d & tw/d & tw with bathroom $20/48/58; ▣ ☒) A smaller purpose-built chalet-style hostel with lots of wood panelling and an outdoor

pool and tennis court. It can organise fishing, hunting and farm stays.

Waitomo Top 10 Holiday Park (☎ /fax 07-878 7639; stay@waitomopark.co.nz; sites $26, cabins/tourist flats $40/75; ▣ ☒) Opposite the museum, this modern and well-maintained park has an outdoor pool and spa. Ask for a free torch for the Ruakuri Scenic Reserve glow-worm walk.

MID-RANGE
Waitomo Express & Aeroplane (☎ 07-878 6666; billy@ woodlynpark.co.nz; 1177 Waitomo Valley Rd; f $90-100) Stay in comfortable, modern, motel-style en suite units housed inside a 1950s railway carriage or in the front or tail of a Bristol fighter aeroplane that saw action in the Vietnam War. Everything in this place is unusual!

Glowworm Motel (☎ 07-873 8882; fax 07-873 8856; Waitomo Caves Rd; units $65, Nov-Mar $80; ☒) These reasonably priced units, 8km before Waitomo, have kitchens.

Caves Motor Inn (☎ 07-873 8109; glow.worm@xtra .co.nz; SH3; backpacker r $25, motel s/d $75/85) This motel on the main road by the Waitomo turn-off is better than it looks from the outside, and has a backpacker section, a bar and a restaurant (dinner only).

Waitomo Caves Hotel (☎ 07-878 8204; www .waitomocaveshotel.co.nz; School Rd; d $70-130, f $150) All rooms are en suite and period charm rules in this old-fashioned hotel on a hill, parts of which date back to 1908. It has a bar, café, restaur-ant (mains $20 to $30) and Sky TV.

Waitomo Guest Lodge (☎ 07-878 7641; fax 07-878 7466; 7 Waitomo Caves Rd; s/d $50/70) All rooms are en suite in this well-located and comfortable B&B, but the fluffy toys in every room may not survive the new owners.

Abseil Inn (☎ 07-878 7815; abseilinn@xtra.co.nz; 709 Waitomo Caves Rd; d $120-140) This very stylish and modern B&B has spacious en suite rooms, a large communal lounge and a big breakfast. Take care as the driveway is short but steep.

Valley View (☎ /fax 07-878 7063; valley123@xtra .co.nz; 168 Te Anga Rd; self-contained unit $70) The garden unit has a great view from the double bed. Home comforts and a continental breakfast are provided.

Big Bird (☎ 0800 733 244, 07-873 7459; www .waitomobigbird.co.nz; 17 Waitomo Caves Rd; s/d/self-contained cottage $40/65/80) The price includes continental breakfast but an ostrich bacon, ostrich egg and ostrich sausage breakfast is $6 extra. With free tours of the ostrich farm and to the glow-worms at Ruakuri Scenic Reserve, this is a guesthouse with character at a good price.

Eating & Drinking

Long Black Café (Waitomo Caves Rd; meals $5-12; ☺ breakfast & lunch; 🖳) This popular and spacious café, run by one of the caving companies, has *panini*, bagels, pasta and all-day breakfasts.

Glowworm Cave Café (☺ 9am-5pm) This fine café is at the entrance to the Glowworm Cave – check out the *tortinos*.

Morepork Pizzeria & Café (☎ 07-878 8395; School Rd; mains $16-22; ☺ breakfast, lunch & dinner) Inside the upmarket Kiwi Paka YHA is this modern and popular restaurant, with an Alpine look and a balcony. Pizza is the main menu item.

Frederick Mace Restaurant (☎ 07-878 8204; School Rd; mains $26-30) In the Waitomo Caves Hotel, it has an à la carte menu.

Roselands Restaurant (☎ 07-878 7611; Fullerton Rd; BBQ lunches $22; ☺ lunch) This buffet restaurant has a garden setting 3km from Waitomo.

Waitomo Caves Tavern (☎ 07-878 8448; School Rd; mains $12-15) This tavern has 11 beers on tap, good-value bistro meals and bands on Friday and Saturday night. Relax here after a hard day of spelunking.

The village store beside the Museum of Caves is small but has an ice-cream parlour, a bar and Internet access.

Getting There & Away

The **Waitomo Shuttle** (☎ 0800 808 279) operates up to five times daily between Waitomo and Otorohanga ($8). Bookings are essential.

InterCity/Newmans (☎ 09-913 6100) runs a daily bus service to Waitomo from Auckland ($48) and Rotorua ($33 to $38).

The **Waitomo Wanderer** (☎ 07-349 2509; www .waitomotours.co.nz) operates a useful daily loop from Rotorua to Waitomo via the rock-climbing centre of Wharepapa South. The bus leaves Rotorua at 7.45am, arrives at Waitomo at 10am, then departs again at 3.45pm, arriving back in Rotorua at 6pm. The cost is $30 one-way. Packages including cave adventures are available ($120).

Guthreys (☎ 0800 732 528) runs buses daily between Auckland and Waitomo ($39), departing Auckland at 7am and Waitomo at 4pm.

MAROKOPA ROAD

Heading west from Waitomo, you start to enter a little-visited corner of NZ. Te Anga Rd becomes Marokopa Rd, and follows a rewarding and scenic route with a couple of natural attractions worth visiting. The useful *West to Marokopa* pamphlet ($1) is produced by DOC. There are no petrol stations on the Marokopa Rd.

The **Tawarau Forest**, about 20km west of Waitomo village, has various walks outlined in the DOC pamphlet, including a one-hour walk to the Tawarau Falls from the end of Appletree Rd.

The **Mangapohue Natural Bridge Scenic Reserve**, 26km west of Waitomo, is a 5.5-hectare reserve with a giant natural limestone arch. It's a 20-minute round-walk to the arch on a wheelchair-accessible pathway. You can easily walk atop the arch. On the far side, big rocks full of oyster fossils jut up from the grass, and at night you'll see glow-worms.

About 4km further west is **Piripiri Caves Scenic Reserve**, where a five-minute walk along a track leads to a large cave containing fossils of giant oysters. Bring a torch and be prepared to get muddy after heavy rain.

The impressive three-tier **Marokopa Falls** are located 32km west of Waitomo. A short track (10 minutes return) from the road leads to the bottom of the falls.

The falls are near Te Anga, where you can stop for a drink at the pleasant **Te Anga Tavern**. From Te Anga you can turn north to Taharoa or Kawhia, 53km away, or southwest to **Marokopa**, a small village on the coast, 48km from Waitomo. The whole Te Anga–Marokopa area is riddled with caves.

The bitumen ends just past Marokopa at Kiritehere, but it is possible to continue 60km further south on a difficult but scenic road, until you meet SH3 at Awakino (p242). About 20km south of Marokopa is the **Whareorino Forest**, which has forest walks.

From Monday to Friday **Perry's bus** (☎ 07-876 7570) runs between Te Waitere, at the southern end of Kawhia Harbour, and Te Kuiti (adult/child $8/4), passing through Waitomo, Te Anga and the other scenic attractions along the Marokopa Road. It leaves Te Waitere at 7.30am, arrives in Te Kuiti at 9.15am and makes the return journey at 1pm. Another weekday bus runs from Te Anga to Marokopa.

About 10km south of Te Anga, on the road to Marokopa, the friendly **Hepipi Farm** (☎ 07-876 7861; B&B per person $50) offers farm stay. It also manages three self-contained units ($50 per person) at the beach in Marokopa, each of which sleeps up to four people, but you need your own linen.

The **Marokopa Camping Ground** (☎ 07-876 7444; Rauparaha St; camp sites/campervan sites/cottages $18/20/50) is close to the coast and has a snack bar and small shop with a tennis court nearby.

There's also accommodation in the Whareorino Forest at **Leitch's Hut** (☎ 07-878 1050; dm $7).

TE KUITI
pop 4540

This small, provincial town, south of Otorohanga, is a base for visiting Waitomo, 19km away. The magnificently carved Te Tokanganui-o-noho Marae, overlooking the south end of Rora St, was Maori rebel leader Te Kooti's grateful gift to his hosts, the Ngati Maniapoto people, who looked after him once he had accepted the Maori

king's creed of pacifism. Te Kuiti hosts the annual NZ sheep shearing championships and has a 'Big Shearer' statue as its most prominent feature.

Information
The useful **Te Kuiti visitors centre** (☎ 07-878 8077; pellowe@xtra.co.nz; Rora St; ☼ 9am-5pm) can do transport bookings. There's Internet access at **Cabana** (☎ 07-878 8278; 129b Rora St; 30min/1hr $6/9). The **DOC office** (☎ 07-878 1050; 78 Taupiri St) can help with hiking information. The **Post Shop** (☎ 07-878 1121; ☼ 8.30am-5pm Mon-Fri, 9am-noon Sat) is on the main street.

Sights & Activities
The best time to visit is around the end of March or the beginning of April when the **Te Kuiti Muster** takes over the town. Sheep-shearing championships, sheep races, a parade, arts and crafts, Maori culture groups, live music, barbecues, *hangi* and lots of market stalls combine in this rural festival.

Near the Big Shearer statue is a **Japanese garden** and **Redwood Park**, which is full of dwarf conifers.

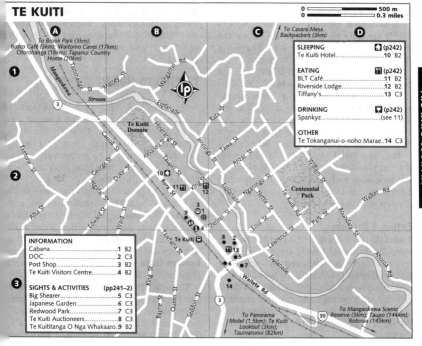

TE KUITI

```
0 ————————— 500 m
0 ————————— 0.3 miles
```

SLEEPING 🛏 (p242)
Te Kuiti Hotel.....................10 B2

EATING 🍴 (p242)
BLT Café............................11 B2
Riverside Lodge...................12 B2
Tiffany's............................13 C3

DRINKING 🍷 (p242)
Spankyz..........................(see 11)

OTHER
Te Tokanganui-o-noho Marae..14 C3

INFORMATION
Cabana.................................1 B2
DOC.....................................2 C3
Post Shop..............................3 B2
Te Kuiti Visitors Centre.............4 B2

SIGHTS & ACTIVITIES (pp241–2)
Big Shearer.............................5 C3
Japanese Garden......................6 C3
Redwood Park.........................7 C3
Te Kuiti Auctioneers..................8 C3
Te Kuititanga O Nga Whakaaro....9 B2

To Brook Park (3km);
Bosco Café (3km); Waitomo Caves (17km);
Otorohanga (18km); Tapanui Country
Home (20km)

To Casara Mesa
Backpackers (3km)

To Panorama
Motel (1.5km); Te Kuiti
Lookout (3km);
Taumarunui (82km)

To Mangaokewa Scenic
Reserve (3km); Taupo (144km);
Rotorua (145km)

WAIKATO & THE KING COUNTRY

Te Kuiti Auctioneers (☎ 07-878 8300; 237 Rora St) is an amazing Aladdin's cave of second-hand collectables. **Te Kuititanga O Nga Whakaaro** (Rora St) is a pavilion that illustrates the town's history.

The Mangaokewa Stream winds through the town, with a pleasant **walkway** along it. Beside the stream, the **Mangaokewa Scenic Reserve** (SH30), 3km south of town, has picnic and barbecue areas and a waterhole for safe swimming. **Te Kuiti Lookout** (Awakino Rd), as the road climbs out of town heading south, provides a great view over the town, especially at night with the sparkling lights stretching out below.

On the northwestern boundary of Te Kuiti, the attractive **Brook Park** has an excellent café (p242) and a 40-minute walk leading up a hill to the site of the historic Matakiora Pa, which was constructed in the 17th century by Rora, son of Maniapoto.

Sleeping

Casara Mesa Backpackers (☎ 07-878 6697; casara@ xtra.co.nz; Mangarino Rd; dm/d & tw/d & tw with bathroom $15/35/40) North of town, this farm stay has great views from its veranda and will pick up guests from town.

Te Kuiti Hotel (☎ 07-878 8172; Rora St; s/d & tw $35/50) En suite rooms with TV above the restaurant/pub/TAB complex. There's a disco on Friday and Saturday nights.

Tapanui Country Home (☎ 07-877 8549; www.tapa nui.co.nz; 1714 Oparure Rd; s $155, d & tw B&B $165) This 770-hectare working farm is 20km northwest of Te Kuiti, with sheep, cattle and pet animals. Children over 16 are welcome and guests are asked to arrive after 4pm. Dinner is by arrangement ($50, including NZ wine).

Panorama Motel (☎ 07-878 8051; glow.worm@ xtra.co.nz; 59 Awakino Rd; s/d from $75/85; 🖳) Decked out in cream and lilac, these slightly tired units have good views and a restaurant that is open all day every day.

Eating & Drinking

Bosco Café (☎ 07-878 3633; 57 Te Kumi Rd; light meals around $5; ⏱ breakfast & lunch) By Brook Park, this excellent and well-designed café has good coffee and wonderful delights such as custard squares and a gourmet muffin stack drizzled with cream and raspberry sauce.

BLT Café (King St; meals $8.50; ⏱ breakfast & lunch Mon-Fri) A small place with good pancakes for $7.50.

Tiffany's (☎ 07-878 8872; 241 Rora St; mains $15-22; ⏱ breakfast, lunch & dinner) Light meals under $10 are also offered in this large, pleasant café.

Riverside Lodge (☎ 07-878 8027; off Sheridan St; ⏱ 9.30am-late Tue-Sun) This is a smart bar and bistro (mussel steamers $13), with a deck that overlooks the stream.

Spankyz (☎ 07-878 8496; King St; mains $16-27) This den-like bar offers bistro meals, pool, karaoke, a DJ Thursday to Saturday and occasional live bands.

Getting There & Away

InterCity buses arrive at and depart from Tiffany's restaurant at the south end of Rora St; book and buy your tickets at the visitors centre. Long-distance buses stopping at Te Kuiti include those heading south to Taumarunui and New Plymouth and north to Hamilton and Auckland. Auckland–Wellington **Tranz Scenic** (☎ 0800 802 802) trains stop in Te Kuiti at the Rora St station.

Buses also operate in the local region. From Monday to Friday **Perry's bus** (☎ 07-876 7570) runs between Te Waitere, at the southern end of Kawhia Harbour, and Te Kuiti (adult/child $8/4), passing through Waitomo, Te Anga and the other scenic attractions along the Marokopa Road. It leaves Te Waitere at 7.30am, arrives in Te Kuiti at 9.15am, and makes the return journey at 1pm.

TE KUITI TO MOKAU
☎ 06

From Te Kuiti, SH3 runs southwest to Awakino on the rugged west coast before continuing on to New Plymouth in Taranaki. The road runs through a lightly populated farming area and is very scenic in parts. Buses between Hamilton and New Plymouth take this route.

The road passes through the small town of **Piopio**, which has a small museum, and then tiny **Mahoenui**, from where the road follows the Awakino River, which is the most spectacular part of the route. Through a short road tunnel you enter the steep **Awakino Gorge**, lined with dense bush and giant ponga tree ferns.

The road follows the river to **Awakino**, a small settlement on the coast where boats shelter on the estuary, away from the windswept coast. The **Awakino Hotel** (☎ 06-752 9815; SH3; s/d/d with bathroom $30/60/70) is a basic but friendly pub on the river and near the beach. It has rooms, a bar, pool table, garden, bistro meals and Sky TV. Awakino can also be reached via the Marokopa Rd (p240) from Waitomo.

Just south of Awakino is the **Manioroa Marae**, which contains the anchor stone of the *Tainui* canoe, whose descendants populated Waikato and the King Country. Ask at the organic farm opposite the *marae* on SH3 for permission to enter.

Five kilometres further south, the little fishing village of **Mokau** is at the border of the King Country and Taranaki. The town's **Tainui Museum** (10am-4pm) has a fascinating collection of old photographs from the time when this once-isolated outpost was a coal and lumber shipping port for pioneer Pakeha settlements along the Mokau River.

Mokau River Cruises (06-752 9775; adult/child $30/15) has three-hour trips up the river in the historic Cygnet. Reservations are essential.

Mokau has a fine stretch of black-sand beach and good surfing and fishing – the river mouth hides some of the best whitebait in the North Island. There's also a nine-hole golf course.

In Mokau township and a five-minute walk to the beach, **Palm House** (06-752 9081; palmhouse@taranaki-bakpak.co.nz; SH3; dm/s/tw/d $20/30/46/50) is a good little backpackers where the unisex dorm has nine beds. Inquire at the house opposite if no-one is around. Also five minutes from the beach is **Mokau Motel** (/fax 06-752 9725; SH3; s/d & tw $60/75), where all units have cooking facilities.

Just north of Mokau, **Seaview Holiday Park** (/fax 06-752 9708; seaview.holidaypark@xtra.co.nz; SH3; camp sites & campervan sites $20, cabins/tourist flats $35/60) is on the beach.

There are a couple of little stores in Mokau that do takeaways. The **Whitebait Inn** (06-752 9713; SH3) has takeaways and sit-down meals, with the area's famous whitebait on the menu in various forms. The whitebait season runs from August until November.

TAUMARUNUI
pop 4500

Taumarunui is a quiet little town on SH4, 82km south of Te Kuiti and 43km north of the township of National Park. The main reason for staying here is to kayak on the Whanganui River or as a cheaper alterna-tive to staying in the tramping/skiing resorts at Tongariro National Park. See p272 for details of kayaking and jetboat trips on the Whanganui River.

Information

The helpful **Taumarunui visitors centre** (07-895 7494; taumarunui.vic@xtra.co.nz; Hakiaha St; 9am-4.30pm Mon-Fri, 10am-4pm Sat & Sun) can book transport, accommodation and tours. It has a working model of the Raurimu Spiral (50c).

DOC (07-895 8201; Cherry Grove Domain; 8am-5pm Mon-Fri) has information on Whanganui National Park and canoeing. The town has a **Post Shop** (07-895 8149; Miriama St; 9am-5pm Mon-Fri), and the hospital is over the Ongarue River.

Sights & Activities

The **Maori Arts and Crafts Shop** (07-896 8560; 49 Hakiaha St) and Maata Gallery are worth a look. The **Hanaroa Whare** (hall) next to the police station has some beautiful carvings.

The **Raurimu Spiral** is a unique feat of railway engineering that was completed in 1908 after 10 years' work. Rail buffs can experience the spiral by taking the 2pm train to National Park township ($19) but at present there is no convenient way of returning.

For details on the **Stratford–Taumarunui Heritage trail** see p260 but note that 11km of it is unsealed.

You can **walk** along the Whanganui River from Cherry Grove Domain to the Taumarunui Holiday Park, 3km away, and continue further along the river through fine native bush. A shorter walk goes through native bush on the Domain and up the Incline, which provides good views over Rangaroa, the town, its rivers and mountains. Te Paka Lookout, across the Ongarue River on the western edge of town, is another good vantage point.

Sleeping

Accommodation here is well-priced as motels try to lure hikers and skiers away from Tongariro National Park.

Taumarunui Holiday Park (07-895 9345; www.taumarunuiholidaypark.co.nz; SH4; camp sites/campervan sites $16/18, cabins/tourist flats $29/45) On the banks of the Whanganui River, 3km east of town, the park has kayaks for hire.

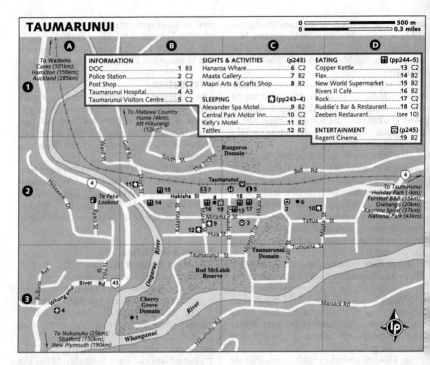

TAUMARUNUI

0 — 500 m
0 — 0.3 miles

INFORMATION	
DOC	1 B3
Police Station	2 C2
Post Shop	3 C2
Taumarunui Hospital	4 A3
Taumarunui Visitors Centre	5 C2

SIGHTS & ACTIVITIES	(p243)
Hanaroa Whare	6 C2
Maata Gallery	7 B2
Maori Arts & Crafts Shop	8 C2

SLEEPING	(pp243–4)
Alexander Spa Motel	9 B2
Central Park Motor Inn	10 C2
Kelly's Motel	11 B2
Tattles	12 B2

EATING	(pp244–5)
Copper Kettle	13 C2
Flax	14 B2
New World Supermarket	15 B2
Rivers II Café	16 B2
Rock	17 C2
Ruddie's Bar & Restaurant	18 C2
Zeebers Restaurant	(see 10)

ENTERTAINMENT	(p245)
Regent Cinema	19 B2

Matawa Country Home (☎ 07-896 7722; costley@ xtra.co.nz; 213 Taringamotu Rd; s/d & tw $70/110) This small farm, 4km north of town, has nice rooms leading on to a veranda but you may have to share facilities with other guests. A full breakfast is provided and there is an attractive garden with a stream. Dinner by arrangement.

Fernleaf B&B (☎ 0800 337 653, 07-895 4847; www .babs.co.nz/fernleaf/index.htm; 58 Tunanui Rd, Owhango; s/d/cottage $60/100/75) This characterful villa offers spacious rooms with Sky TV and shared guest facilities inside the house, or an outside cottage with just a room. It's a working cattle-and-sheep farm and the kind hostess enjoys cooking so the generous breakfast and $20 dinners are labours of love. It's just off SH4, 15km southeast of Taumarunui.

Tattles (☎ /fax 07-895 8063; tattles.motel@xtra.co.nz; 23 Marae St; s/d from $56/63) Good, cheap units with kitchens and the owners hire out fully equipped kayaks.

Kelly's Motel (☎ 07-895 8175; fax 07-895 9089; 10 River Rd; s/d/villas $55/75/95) Well-maintained and reasonably priced units with good showers.

Central Park Motor Inn (☎ 07-895 7132; Maata St; r $65-110; ☒) A wide range of good-quality units are available, some with spa baths but all guests can use the sauna, spa and gym. Zeebers Restaurant (opposite) is here.

Alexander Spa Motel (☎ 07-895 8501; 6 Marae St; s/d $70/90) Prices include continental breakfast, Sky TV and use of an indoor spa pool.

Eating & Drinking

Flax (☎ 07-895 6611; 1 Hakiaha St; mains $18-25; ☺ brunch & dinner Tue-Sun) Stylish natural-wood décor, a log fire and a large deck with shade are features of this new café-restaurant. Try the venison pâté or the seafood tower.

Copper Kettle (☎ 07-895 7541; Manuaute St; mains $15-19; ☺ breakfast, lunch & dinner) A huge range of interesting budget food can be found here, including such items as home-made soup, spinach macaroni, cranberry meat loaf, roasts, home-made chocolate-chip cheesecake, all-day breakfasts and takeaways.

Rivers II Café (☎ 07-895 5822; 43 Hakiaha St; mains $18; ☺ breakfast & lunch) The Rivers café has a good atmosphere where you can enjoy your meal both indoors or outside. The lamb and steak meals are popular at $18 and medium pizzas are $12.

Rock (☎ 07-895 8666; 111 Hakiaha St; mains $5-15; ⊙ breakfast & lunch) This café has an indoor and outdoor section. The Rock Breakfast ($12.50) is quite a challenge – you get two of everything.

Zeebers Restaurant (☎ 07-895 7132; Maata St; mains $16-25; ⊙ dinner Mon-Sat) This restaurant in a motel has retained its chef for some years and offers specialities such as ostrich in red-wine sauce.

Ruddie's Bar & Restaurant (☎ 07-896 7443; upstairs, 93 Hakiaha St; mains $17-25; ⊙ breakfast, lunch & dinner Mon-Fri) This licensed restaurant is opposite the train station.

Self-caterers can stroll the aisles of the **New World Supermarket** (☎ 07-896 0070; 10 Hakiaha St; ⊙ 8am-7pm Mon-Sat, 9am-7pm Sun).

Entertainment
Regent Cinema (Hakiaha St; adult $10; ⊙ Thu-Sun) shows the latest releases. Check out the Art Deco interior.

Getting There & Away
Buses travelling between Auckland and Wellington all stop outside the train station in Taumarunui, which also houses the visitors centre, where you can buy tickets.

Taranaki

CONTENTS

New Plymouth	248
Around New Plymouth	255
Mt Taranaki (Mt Egmont)	257
Around Mt Taranaki	259

TARANAKI

Taranaki juts out into the Tasman Sea on the west coast of the North Island, about halfway between Auckland and Wellington. The region is named after the Mt Taranaki volcano and its massive cone dominates the landscape. Conditions are excellent for agriculture, with rich volcanic soil and abundant rainfall.

It's a thoroughly enjoyable drive from Wellington, via Wanganui, through green pastures dotted with ubiquitous sheep, gently rolling hills, and glimpses of the striking coastline. The world-class beaches along the surf highway, State Highway 45 (SH45), are popular surfing and windsurfing destinations.

New Plymouth is the area's big smoke and the town has a lot to offer, with leafy and coastal walks and plenty of cafés, pubs and restaurants. It's also the best place to base yourself for exploring the region and organising a trip to Mt Taranaki, the major attraction and New Zealand's 'most climbed mountain'.

In 2003 the mountain made it onto the world stage when scenes were filmed for *The Last Samurai*, starring Tom Cruise and Ken Wantanabe. From certain angles Mt Taranaki looks like Mt Fuji, making it a perfect stand-in.

The names Taranaki and Egmont are both used throughout the region. Taranaki is the Maori name for the volcano and Egmont is the name James Cook gave it, after the Earl of Egmont. Today the region is called Taranaki, the cape is called Cape Egmont, and the waters around the cape are called the North and South Taranaki Bights. Egmont National Park retains its name but Taranaki and Egmont are both official names for the volcano.

HIGHLIGHTS

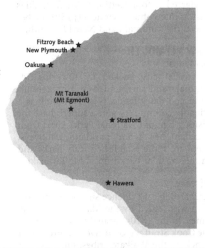

- Tackling the summit of the awe-inspiring **Mt Taranaki volcano** (p257) and skiing or tramping back down
- Expanding your vision of what art can be at the mind-blowing **Govett-Brewster Art Gallery** (p250) in New Plymouth
- Learning to **surf** (p251) or **windsurf** (p251) at Fitzroy Beach or Oakura – world-class surfing areas
- Taking a brisk, invigorating walk along **New Plymouth's Coastal Walkway** (p251)
- Experiencing old-fashioned hospitality during a farmstay near **Hawera** (p261)
- Taking a drive along the **Stratford–Taumarunui Heritage Trail** (p260) and visiting significant Maori historical sites

Fitzroy Beach
New Plymouth
Oakura
Mt Taranaki (Mt Egmont)
Stratford
Hawera

■ TELEPHONE CODE: 06   ■ www.taranakinz.org

TARANAKI

Climate

Taranaki has plenty of fertile farming land, however, its most prominent geological feature is the spectacular volcano cone Mt Taranaki (also known as Mt Egmont; p257). The mountain is one of the wettest spots in NZ, with about 7000mm of rain recorded annually at North Egmont (compared with about 1500mm in New Plymouth), as it catches the moisture-laden winds coming in from the Tasman Sea and sweeps them up to freezing heights. Weather on the mountain is extremely changeable (see the boxed text on p258) and snow is common, even in summer.

November to April are the region's warmer months and the best time to visit – temperatures during this time hover around 20°C. During May to August, the temperatures drop to around 5°C to 14°C.

Getting There & Around

Air New Zealand Link and Origin Pacific have domestic flights and onward connections to/from New Plymouth. InterCity runs several bus services that connect with New Plymouth; Dalroy Express and White Star City to City are smaller bus companies that run more localised services.

For comprehensive, local timetable and fare information check online at www.wrc .govt.nz/timetables. New Plymouth is easily navigated on foot. Getting to Mt Taranaki is easy as many shuttle services (p259) run between the mountain and New Plymouth.

NEW PLYMOUTH

pop 49,100

A coastal city backed by towering Mt Taranaki and surrounded by rich agricultural and dairy lands, New Plymouth is a friendly community and a superb base for visiting Egmont National Park. Apart from excellent beach and parkland walkways, there are some established leafy parks and the spectacular backdrop of Mt Taranaki.

History

Archaeological evidence shows that the region was settled by the Maoris from early times. In the 1820s Taranaki Maoris fled to the Cook Strait region to avoid a threatened attack by the Waikato tribes, but it wasn't until 1832 that the Waikato attacked and subdued the remaining Te Ati Awa tribe.

The Te Ati Awa remained only at Okoki Pa (New Plymouth), where whalers had joined in the battle. Thus when the first European settlers arrived in the district in 1841 the coast of Taranaki was almost deserted. Initially it seemed there would be no opposition to land claims, so the New Zealand Company managed to buy extensive tracts from the Te Ati Awa who had remained.

When other members of Te Ati Awa and other tribes returned after years of exile and slavery, they objected strongly to the sale of their land. Their claims were substantially upheld when Governor Fitzroy ruled that the New Zealand Company was only allowed to retain just over 10 sq km around New Plymouth of the 250 sq km it had claimed. The Crown slowly acquired more land from the Maoris, who became increasingly reluctant to sell. At the same time the European settlers became increasingly greedy for the fertile land around Waitara, just northeast of New Plymouth.

The settlers' determination finally forced the government to abandon its policy of negotiation, and in 1860 war broke out. For 10 years the Maoris kept them engaged in guerrilla warfare. During this time, settlers moved in on Waitara and took control, but the Maoris did as they pleased throughout the rest of the province. The Taranaki chiefs had not signed the Treaty of Waitangi and did not recognise the sovereignty of the British queen, so they were treated as rebels. By 1870 over 500 hectares of their land had been confiscated and much of the rest acquired through dubious transactions.

The Taranaki province experienced an economic boom with the discovery of natural gas and oil at Kapuni in 1959 and more recently at the Maui natural gas field off the coast in the South Taranaki Bight.

Orientation & Information

Devon St (East and West) is the city's hub. For information about the region pick up the *Taranaki* guide or check online at www .windwand.co.nz and www.taranakinz.org.

BOOKSHOPS
Whitcoull's Bookshop (☎ 06-758 4656; Centre City Shopping Centre, Gill St)

EMERGENCY
Police, fire & ambulance (☎ 111)

TARANAKI

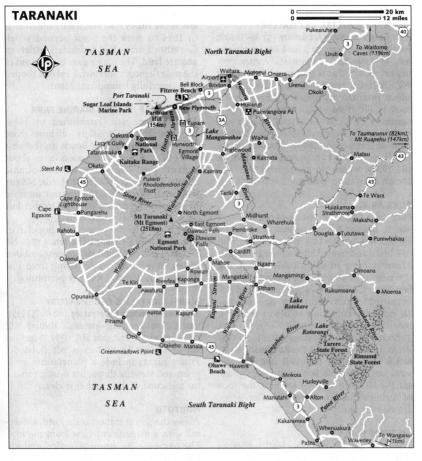

INTERNET ACCESS

Internet access is available at the visitors centre and at most backpackers.

Interplay Internet Cafe (☎ 06-758 1918; Top Town Complex; 30min/1hr $3/5)

MEDICAL SERVICES

Phoenix Urgent Doctors (☎ 06-759 4295; 95 Vivian St; ☎ 8am-10pm) Formerly New Plymouth Doctors.

MONEY

There are a number of banks along New Plymouth's main street and several foreign-exchange offices.

Bank of New Zealand (☎ 0800 275 269; 50-54 Devon St)

Harvey World Travel Foreign Exchange (☎ 06-757 5459; www.harveyworld.co.nz; 55-57 Devon St East)

TSB Foreign Exchange (☎ 06-968 3713; www.tsb.co.nz; Centre City Shopping Centre, Gill St)

POST

Main post office (☎ 06-759 8931; www.nzpost.co.nz; Currie St)

TOURIST INFORMATION

Automobile Association (AA; ☎ 06-759 4010; www.nzaa.co.nz; 49-55 Powderham St; ☺ 8.30am-5pm Mon & Wed-Fri, 9am-5pm Tue) Stocks Wise maps.

Department of Conservation (☎ 06-758 0433; www.doc.govt.nz; 220 Devon St West; ☺ 8am-4.30pm Mon-Fri)

New Plymouth visitors centre (☎ 06-759 6060; www.newplymouthnz.com; 1 Ariki St; ☺ 9am-6pm Mon, Tue, Thu & Fri, 9am-9pm Wed, 9am-5pm Sat & Sun) In the Puke Ariki building.

Sights

GOVETT-BREWSTER ART GALLERY

The **Govett-Brewster Art Gallery** (☎ 06-759 6060; www.govettbrewster.com; cnr Queen & King Sts; admission free; ⏱ 10.30am-5pm) is a fantastic contemporary art gallery that is renowned throughout NZ. It has a reputation for adventurous, often international, shows where artists look at life from unique and bizarre perspectives. Even if art's not your thang, a visit to the Govett-Brewster is totally worthwhile. Fans of abstract animation should seek out the films of Len Lye, pioneer animator of the 1930s, whose works are held here and shown from time to time.

PUKE ARIKI

Puke Ariki (☎ 06-759 6060; www.pukeariki.com; 1 Ariki St; admission free; ⏱ 9am-6pm Mon & Tue-Fri, 9am-9pm Wed, 9am-5pm Sat & Sun), meaning 'Hill of Chiefs' and named after a New Plymouth Maori *pa*, is a stunning complex housing the visitors centre (p249), **museum** (admission free), library, Daily News café (p254) and Arborio (p253) restaurant. The museum has an extensive collection of Maori artefacts, wildlife and colonial exhibits.

Bone and wood carvings from local students are on display at the **Rangimarie Maori Arts & Crafts Centre** (☎ 06-751 2880; www.windwand.co.nz; 80 Centennial Dr; admission free; ⏱ 9am-4pm Mon-Fri), 3km west of town at the foot of Paritutu Hill. Some of the smaller pieces are also for sale.

HISTORIC PLACES

The free *Heritage Walkway* leaflet, obtainable from the visitors centre, outlines an interesting self-guided tour of around 30 historic sites.

Richmond Cottage & Heritage Garden (☎ 06-759 6060; www.pukeariki.com; cnr Ariki & Brougham Sts; adult/child $1/20c) was built in 1853. Unlike most early cottages, which were made of timber, Richmond Cottage was sturdily built of stone. The interior is still under development, but the gardens are a mixture of old world and rare NZ natives. It is part of Puke Ariki.

St Mary's Church (Vivian St), built in 1846, is the oldest stone church in NZ. Its graveyard has the headstones of early settlers and of soldiers who died during the Taranaki Land Wars (1860–61 and 1865–69). Impressed by their bravery, the British also buried several Maori chiefs here.

On Devon St at the eastern end of the city is the **Fitzroy Pole**, erected by the Maoris in 1844 to mark the point beyond which Governor Fitzroy had forbidden settlers to acquire land. The carving on the bottom of the pole depicts a sorrowful Pakeha topped by a cheerfully triumphant Maori.

SUGAR LOAF ISLANDS MARINE PARK

This marine park, established in 1986, includes: the rocky islets offshore from the power station, Back Beach on the west side of Paritutu and the waters up to about 1km offshore. The islands, eroded volcanic remnants, are a refuge for sea birds, NZ fur seals and marine life; the greatest number of seals are there from June to October but some are there all year round.

Boat trips to the islands are popular in summer. **Happy Chaddy's Charters** (☎ 06-758 9133; www.windwand.co.nz/chaddiescharters/; adult/child charters $20/10) has boats departing from Lee Breakwater, tide and weather permitting.

MARSLAND HILL & OBSERVATORY

The **New Plymouth Observatory** (☎ 06-753 2358; http://shell.world-net.co.nz/~paulsueh/; Marsland Hill; suggested donation adult/child $3/2; ⏱ 7.30-9pm Tue Mar-Oct, 8-9.30pm Tue Nov-Mar) is off Robe St. Public nights include a planetarium program and viewing through a 6-inch refractor telescope, if the weather is clear.

PARITUTU

Above the power station is Paritutu, a steep hill with a magnificent view from the top. The name means 'rising precipice' and it's worth the tiring but quick scramble to the summit. Not only do you look down on the power station but also out over the city and the rocky Sugar Loaf Islands looming just offshore.

PARKS

New Plymouth is renowned for its superb parks. **Pukekura Park**, (☎ 06-759 6060; www.newplymouthnz.com), a 10-minute walk from the city centre, is worth a visit, with 49 hectares of gardens, bushwalks, streams, waterfalls, ponds and a kiosk. There are **display houses** (admission free; ⏱ 8am-4pm) with orchids and other exotic plants. At the lake, rowing **boats** (30min $5) can be hired at weekends and summer evenings. The lights and decorations in Pukekura Park from late December to early

February are worth making a special trip to see. The park also has a delightful cricket oval in the English tradition.

Adjoining Pukekura is the lovely **Brooklands Park** and, between them, the Bowl of Brooklands, an outdoor sound-shell in a bush and lake setting. Brooklands Park was once the land around an important early settler's home; the fireplace and chimney are all that remain of the house after the Maoris burnt it down. Highlights include a 2000-year-old puriri tree, a rhododendron dell with over 300 varieties, a great children's **zoo** (admission free; ☺ 8.30am-5pm), which has a walk-through monkey enclosure, and the **Gables** (admission free; ☺ 1-4pm Sat & Sun), one of the oldest hospitals in NZ, now converted into an art gallery and medical museum.

On the waterfront is **Kawaroa Park**, with green areas, squash courts and the Petrocorp Aquatic Centre, which has a waterslide, an outdoor pool and an indoor pool (open all year). Also on the waterfront in the central city area is **Puke Ariki Landing**, an historic area with sculptures.

Activities

AERIAL SIGHTSEEING
Several operators offer scenic flights around the area, including flights over the snow-capped summit of Mt Taranaki, which is superb if the weather's clear. Operators include **New Plymouth Aero Club** (☎ 06-755 0500; www.airnewplymouth.co.nz) and **Beck Helicopters** (☎ 06-764 7073).

SURFING & WINDSURFING
Besides being beautiful, the Taranaki coastline is a world-class surfing and windsurfing area. Fitzroy and East End beaches are both at the eastern end of New Plymouth. There's also decent surf at Back Beach, by Paritutu at the western end of the city, and at Oakura, about 15km west of New Plymouth. There are no buses to Oakura but hitching is easy. There are surf beaches all along SH45.

Vertigo (☎ 06-752 8283; vertigosurf@xtra.co.nz; 605 Surf Hwy 45, Oakura) hires out surfboards and sailboards and offers instruction. **Tangaroa Adventures** (☎ 021-701 904; tangaroa.adventures@xtra .co.nz; 25 Collins St, Hawera) and **Taranaki Coastal Surf Charters** (☎ 025-592 306) both provide guided surf tours of the area, and the inexperienced can try **Tandem Surfing** (☎ 06-752 7734;

www.hang20.com; 27 Maise Tce, Oakura) – they guarantee you'll stand up. **Carbon Art** (☎ 0508 946 376; carbonart@xtra.co.nz; Ngamotu beach) specialises in windsurfing hire and lessons.

WALKING
The visitors centre has leaflets about walks around New Plymouth, including coastal, local reserve and park walks, in addition to the Heritage Walkway (p250). The 7km Coastal Walkway, from Lake Rotomanu to Port Taranaki, is a personal favourite and Te Henui Walkway, extending from the coast at East End Reserve to the city's southern boundary, is one of the most interesting and varied walks. Huatoki Valley Walkway, following Huatoki Stream, makes an attractive walk to the city centre.

OTHER ACTIVITIES
Sugar Loaf Islands Marine Park (see p250) offers activities such as boating and sailing, diving, bird-watching, pole fishing, surfing and beach walks.

Tours
Cruise NZ Tours (☎ 06-758 3222; kirstall@xtra.co.nz; adult/child full-day $90/60) runs tours around the city and in the surrounding area.

Sleeping
New Plymouth has plenty of mid-range hotels and a wide range of budget accommodation. Many places have sea views.

BUDGET
Sunflower Lodge (☎ 06-759 0050; www.sunflower lodge.co.nz; 25 Ariki St; dm $20-22, s $40, tw & d $50-60; 🖳) Great single and double rooms with your own TV, cupboard, lounge chair (and footrest!). A fantastic balcony overlooks the ocean, there's Internet access, a homey lounge room, and big clean kitchen. Sunflower Lodge has friendly owners and is great value.

Shoestring Budget Backpackers (☎ 06-758 0404; shoestringb@xtra.co.nz; 48 Lemon St; dm/s $19/27, tw & d $40-50) Shoestring backpackers is friendly and central but the real drawcard is the beautiful heritage building, built in 1910 (they think), its interior made with rimu timber. Rooms are upstairs (away from the communal areas), there's a small kitchen and separate dining area, small sauna and mega-relaxing sunroom with superb ocean views.

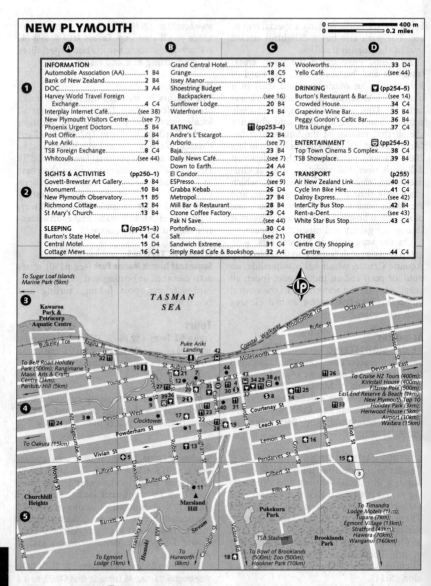

NEW PLYMOUTH

0 ___ 400 m
0 ___ 0.2 miles

INFORMATION
Automobile Association (AA)..........1 B4
Bank of New Zealand.................2 B4
DOC....................................3 A4
Harvey World Travel Foreign
 Exchange...........................4 C4
Interplay Internet Café............(see 38)
New Plymouth Visitors Centre.......(see 7)
Phoenix Urgent Doctors.............5 B4
Post Office..........................6 B4
Puke Ariki...........................7 B4
TSB Foreign Exchange................8 C4
Whitcoulls.........................(see 44)

SIGHTS & ACTIVITIES (pp250–1)
Govett-Brewster Art Gallery..........9 B4
Monument...........................10 B4
New Plymouth Observatory............11 B5
Richmond Cottage...................12 B4
St Mary's Church...................13 B4

SLEEPING (pp251–3)
Burton's State Hotel................14 C4
Central Motel......................15 D4
Cottage Mews.......................16 C4

Grand Central Hotel................17 B4
Grange.............................18 C5
Issey Manor........................19 C4
Shoestring Budget
 Backpackers....................(see 16)
Sunflower Lodge....................20 B4
Waterfront.........................21 B4

EATING (pp253–4)
Andre's L'Escargot.................22 B4
Arborio............................(see 7)
Baja...............................23 B4
Daily News Café....................(see 7)
Down to Earth......................24 A4
El Condor..........................25 C4
ESPresso...........................(see 9)
Grabba Kebab.......................26 D4
Metropol...........................27 B4
Mill Bar & Restaurant..............28 B4
Ozone Coffee Factory...............29 C4
Pak N Save.........................(see 44)
Portofino..........................30 C4
Salt...............................(see 21)
Sandwich Extreme...................31 C4
Simply Read Cafe & Bookshop........32 A4

Woolworths.........................33 D4
Yello Café.........................(see 44)

DRINKING (pp254–5)
Burton's Restaurant & Bar..........(see 14)
Crowded House......................34 C4
Grapevine Wine Bar.................35 B4
Peggy Gordon's Celtic Bar..........36 B4
Ultra Lounge.......................37 B4

ENTERTAINMENT (pp254–5)
Top Town Cinema 5 Complex..........38 C4
TSB Showplace......................39 B4

TRANSPORT (p255)
Air New Zealand Link...............40 C4
Cycle Inn Bike Hire................41 C4
Dalroy Express.....................(see 42)
InterCity Bus Stop.................42 B4
Rent-a-Dent........................(see 43)
White Star Bus Stop................43 C4

OTHER
Centre City Shopping
 Centre...........................44 C4

Egmont Lodge YHA (☎ 06-753 5720; www.taranaki-bakpak.co.nz; 12 Clawton St; camp sites/dm/s/tw & d/f $22/20/30/50/70) A tranquil hostel in large, park-like grounds with a stream running through it – you can even feed the eels. There are 10-bed mixed dorms, a small kitchen, and communal living area that opens onto a veranda surrounded by tree

ferns. It's a 15-minute walk from town on a pleasant streamside walkway or phone for a free pick-up from the bus station. The famous 'Mt Egmont' cake, made nightly, is a sight to behold.

Central Motel (☎ 06-758 6444; central.new.plymouth@xtra.co.nz; 86 Eliot St; s/d $65/75) Up the hill on Eliot St, Central Motel is indeed central and has tidy studio units with a small kitchen and optional Sky TV. Excellent value.

Burton's State Hotel (☎ 06-758 5373; statehotel@ burtons.org.nz; cnr Devon St East & Gover St; s/tw & d/tr $55/70/85) Above Burton's Restaurant and Bar, this is excellent pub accommodation at reasonable rates. Rooms have a bathroom and TV.

There are also camping areas close to the city centre.

Belt Road Holiday Park (☎ 0800 804 204, 06-758 0228; www.beltroad.co.nz; 2 Belt Rd; camp sites $20, cabins $30-75) This pohutukawa-covered Holiday Park is on a bluff overlooking the port, 1.5km west of the town centre. Cabin prices depend on facilities.

New Plymouth Top 10 Holiday Park (☎ 06-758 2566; www.nptop10.co.nz; 29 Princes St; camp sites/cabins $20/40, tourist flats $55-80, units $70-100) New Plymouth Park is in Fitzroy, 3.5km east of the centre with a shady camping area.

Hookner Park (☎ 06-753 6945; hooknerpark@ paradise.net.nz; 885 Carrington Rd; camp sites/on-site vans $18/32, cabins $30-45) A quiet, peaceful camp on a commercial dairy farm 10km south of the town centre. Campers are more than welcome to join in with the farm life.

MID-RANGE

Grand Central Hotel (☎ 06-758 7495; www.grandcentral hotel.co.nz; 42 Powderham St; r $115-120) A four-star hotel in the heart of New Plymouth with a range of business and executive rooms. King-sized beds have fat Italian mattresses, quality linen and some rooms have spas. Comfortable and stylish with modern décor, Grand Central is privately owned and great value.

Grange (☎ 06-758 1540; cathyt@clear.net.nz; 44b Victoria Rd; r $70-90) The Grange is a lovely, welcoming B&B. It's a contemporary home with decks and bush views, opposite beautiful Pukekura Park.

Henwood House (☎ 06-755 1212; henwood.house@ xtra.co.nz; 314 Henwood Rd; r $100-150) Henwood House B&B is 5km east of town. The beautifully restored Victorian home with lovely grounds has five rooms (three of them have en suites).

Issey Manor (☎ 06-758 2375; www.isseymanor.co.nz; 32 Carrington St; r $75-150) Central Issey Manor offers boutique lodge accommodation with contemporary, comfortable, self-contained rooms, designer bathrooms and spa baths. There's a big deck overlooking Huatoki Stream.

Kirkstall House (☎ 06-758 3222; www.kirkstall.co .nz; 8 Baring Tce; s $65-75, d $80-95) Two minutes' walk from the beach and with beautiful views of Mt Taranaki, Kirkstall House is a friendly B&B in a 1920s home.

Timandra Lodge Motels (☎ 06-758 6006; timandra@xtra.co.nz; 31b Timandra St; s/d $75/85) This secluded motel that's located in a large colonial style house south of town backs onto bush. There's lawn tennis and meals are available (on request).

Cottage Mews (☎ 06-758 0403; shoestringb@xtra .co.nz; 48 Lemon St; s/d $65/75) Cottage Mews is next door to the Shoestring Budget Backpackers (where you check in). One-bedroom units and studios are good value and well kept.

TOP END

Waterfront (☎ 06-769 5301; www.waterfront.co.nz; 1 Egmont St; r $155-400) If you want to treat yourself, the Waterfront is worth the splurge with excellent facilities and reasonable prices. The Waterfront is contemporary – minimalist design in greys and blacks – and themed throughout. A local artist painted the pictures in each room and murals in the restaurant, Salt (below).

Eating

Like so many of New Zealand's towns and cities, New Plymouth has embraced the coffee culture. Restaurants tend to be overpriced but are of a high quality.

RESTAURANTS

Baja (☎ 06-757 8217; 17 Devon St; mains $9.25-20) A great range of Mexican food with a delightful lack of sombreros. Feast on Tex-Mex quesadillas, enchiladas and fajitas with chicken, beef or veg fillings. There's a big screen for sport and Baja is also fun for a drink or two.

Salt (☎ 06-759 5304; 1 Egmont St; mains $13-30; breakfast, lunch & dinner) Part of the Waterfront hotel, Salt is a vast expanse of glass giving uninterrupted sea views. It's a sleek, smooth space serving quality Pacific Rim fare. It's also very civilised for an afternoon G&T.

Arborio (☎ 06-759 6060; 1 Ariki St; meals $5-10; breakfast, lunch & dinner) In a similar vein to Salt, Arborio has big glass windows and superb views of the Tasman Sea. Its Italian-inspired menu offers contemporary fare and a great wine list.

El Condor (☎ 06-757 5436; 170 Devon St East; meals $11-24; ☯ dinner Tue-Sat) El Condor, near the corner of Gover St, is a pizza and pasta place with a difference – it's Argentinean. Feast on homemade cannelloni and double-layered pizza.

Portofino (☎ 06-757 8686; 14 Gill St; pizza & pasta $15-19; ☯ dinner) This Italian restaurant has a huge selection of pasta dishes and steaming wood-fired pizzas with thick and tasty toppings. Takeaways are available and it's fully licensed.

Metropol (☎ 06-758 9788; cnr King & Egmont Sts; mains $16-28; ☯ lunch & dinner) This bar and grill is the place to taste NZ and Pacific Rim dishes (predominantly for carnivores) with a hint of international flavours. Meals are cheaper during the day.

Andre's L'Escargot (☎ 06-758 4812; 37-39 Brougham St; mains $23-35; ☯ lunch & dinner Mon-Sat) This is a 'genuinely French' restaurant with fine dining in a beautiful historical building.

Mill Bar & Restaurant (☎ 06-758 1935; 2 Courtenay St; meals $11-25; ☯ 10am-10pm Sun-Tue, 10am-midnight Wed, 10am-3am Thu-Sat) The Mill specialises in 'stonegrill' – a piping hot stone (supposedly heated to 400°C!) is used to cook your meat selection at your table. This way you get to cook your steak just the way you like it. The large bar is a popular place for a night out, and often has live bands at weekends.

CAFÉS
Simply Read Cafe & Bookshop (☎ 06-757 8667; cnr Dawson & Hine Sts; meals $6-12; ☯ breakfast, lunch & dinner) With beautiful water views, Simply Read is a cheerful, popular café with a small bookshop. Its blackboard menu changes regularly and home-style meals include mushroom strudel, chicken lasagne, vegetable filos plus a tempting selection of cakes and muffins.

Yello Café (☎ 06-759 4130; Centre City Shopping Centre, Gill St; meals $6.50-11; ☯ breakfast & lunch, until 8pm Fri) Yello has hefty sandwiches, soups, a kids menu and pre-schooler snacks. Breakfast is a no-nonsense affair and rich fudge brownies give you an afternoon sugar rush.

Daily News Café (☎ 06-759 6060; 1 Ariki St; meals $5-10; ☯ lunch) Where current affairs cost a cup of coffee. In the south wing of the Puke Ariki complex, you can select from a range of daily newspapers or listen to the radio through headphones while drinking espresso and eating fresh *panini* (focaccia).

Ozone Coffee Factory (☎ 06-779 9020; 121 Devon St East; meals $6.50-13; ☯ lunch) A terrific café for a strong heart-starting brew of aromatic Ozone coffee (these guys supply many of the cafés around New Plymouth). Lunchtime sandwiches and hot food are equally delicious.

ESPresso (☎ 06-759 9399; cnr Queen & King Sts; meals $5-10; ☯ lunch) Next to the Govett-Brewster Art Gallery, ESPresso is a great lunchtime café serving sandwiches, *panini*, cakes and strong coffee.

QUICK EATS
In the Centre City Shopping Centre there's a food hall with Chinese and Italian food, seafood, wholefood, sandwich and dessert counters.

Sandwich Extreme (☎ 06-759 6999; 52 Devon St East; dishes $5.50-7.50; ☯ lunch) This little eatery makes fresh, filling sandwiches, toasties and baked potatoes for eat-in or takeaway.

Grabba kebab (☎ 06-757 8158; 211a Devon St East; kebabs $7-9) Tasty kebabs are served at this ever-reliable takeaway.

SELF-CATERING
Pak N Save (☎ 06-758 1594; Centre City Shopping Centre, Gill St) is a supermarket selling cheap groceries. Another useful supermarket is **Woolworths** (☎ 06-759 7481; btwn Leach & Courtenay Sts). **Down to Earth** (☎ 06-758 3700; cnr Devon St West & Morley St) is an organic wholefood shop selling dry goods, dairy, honey etc.

Drinking & Entertainment
Ultra Lounge (☎ 06-758 8444; 75 Devon St East; lunch $5-14, dinner $17-30; ☯ lunch & dinner) Ultra Lounge falls into many different categories and does each one equally well – funky café with full-bodied coffee and sticks of loose-leaf tea, a superb restaurant, and mellow cocktail lounge bar. Food here is truly excellent. For brunch the bacon and egg butty with wholegrain mustard hollandaise cannot be beaten. DJs spin ambient house and mellow hip-hop on Friday nights.

Burton's Restaurant & Bar (☎ 06-758 5373; cnr Devon & Grover Sts; mains $17-22; ☯ breakfast, lunch & dinner) A pub that's popular with families and the after-work drink crowd. There's a sports bar, open fires, 'spin the wheel' between 5pm and 6pm, and live music on Thursday nights.

TARANAKI

Peggy Gordon's Celtic Bar (☎ 06-758 8561; cnr Devon St West & Egmont St) A relaxed Irish bar with live music at the weekends. It's a good place to come at night.

Some other popular nightspots include **Crowded House** (☎ 06-759 4921; www.crowdedhouse.co.nz; Devon St East; mains $13-22; ☺ 10am-late) popular with all ages, and the **Grapevine Wine Bar** (☎ 06-757 9355; cnr Currie & Devon Sts; ☺ 5pm-late Tue-Sun) catering largely to a more mature crowd.

Bowl of Brooklands (☎ 06-759 6080; www.bowl.co.nz; Brooklands Park) A large outdoor theatre. Check with the visitors centre for current concert schedules and prices.

TSB Showplace (☎ 06-758 4947; tsbshowplace.newplymouth@xtra.co.nz; Devon St West) Formerly the Opera House, TSB seats around 960 people and stages a variety of big performances.

Getting There & Away
You can book tickets for InterCity, Tran-Scenic and the Interislander Wellington–Picton ferry at **Travel Centre** (☎ /fax 06-759 9039; Level 2, Centre City Shopping Centre, Gill St).

AIR
Air New Zealand Link (☎ 06-737 3300; www.airnz.co.nz; 12-14 Devon St East) has daily direct flights to/from Auckland (one way $80 to $280, 45 minutes, three to four daily) and Wellington (one way $85 to $290, 55 minutes, four daily), with onward connections to Christchurch and Nelson. **Origin Pacific** (☎ 0800 302 302, 03-547 2020; www.originpacific.co.nz) also has direct flights to Wellington and Auckland with onward connections.

BUS
InterCity (☎ 06-759 9039; www.intercitycoach.co.nz; behind Centre City Shopping Centre, Gill St) runs buses to/from Hamilton (one way $33, four hours, one daily), Auckland (one way $55, six hours, one daily), and two buses daily (three on Friday and Sunday) to Wanganui (one way $16, three hours), Palmerston North (one way $45, four hours) and onto Wellington (one way $65, four hours). **Dalroy Express** (☎ 0508 465 622; www.dalroytours.co.nz; Erica Pl) operates a daily service between Auckland (one way $65, four hours) and Hawera (one way $13, four hours) via New Plymouth and Hamilton (one way $45, two hours). Buses depart from behind Centre City Shopping Centre.

White Star City to City (☎ 04-478 4734; 25 Liardet St) has two daily buses during weekdays and one at weekends to/from Wanganui (one way $22, 2½ hours), Palmerston North (one way $30, 3¾ hours), Wellington (one way $45, 6¼ hours) and many small towns in between.

Getting Around
New Plymouth airport (☎ 06-755 2250) is 11km east of the centre. **Withers** (☎ 0800 751 177, 06-751 1777; www.withers.co.nz; adult around $12) operates a door-to-door shuttle to and from the airport – you can book online.

Cycle Inn Bike Hire (☎ 06-758 7418; 133 Devon St; per day $20-30) rents bicycles. For cheap car hire, head to **Rent-a-Dent** (☎ 0800 736 822; 191 Devon St).

Okato Bus Lines (☎ 06-758 2799; okatobus@xtra.co.nz; Stanley St; timetables 50c) serves the city and its surrounding suburbs Monday to Saturday. The main bus stop is outside the Centre City Shopping Centre.

For details of shuttle services from New Plymouth to Mt Taranaki see p259.

AROUND NEW PLYMOUTH
Egmont National Park is the primary regional attraction, but there are several other places of interest, all within about 20km of New Plymouth.

Pukeiti Rhododendron Trust
This is a 4 sq km **garden** (☎ 06-752 4141; www.pukeiti.org.nz; 2290 Carrington Rd; adult/child $8/free; ☺ 9am-5pm Oct-Mar, 10am-3pm Apr-Sep) surrounded by native bush and renowned internationally for its collection of rhododendrons and azaleas. Peak flowering of rhododendrons generally takes place from September to November, although the garden is worth seeing at any time of year.

Pukeiti is 20km south of New Plymouth. To get there, just keep following Carrington Rd all the way from town. The road passes between the Pouakai and Kaitake Ranges, both part of Egmont National Park, but separated by the trust.

Tupare
Tupare (☎ 06-764 6544; 487 Mangorei Rd; admission by gold coin donation; ☺ garden 9am-5pm 1 Sep-31 Mar), 7km south of New Plymouth, is a fine three-storey Tudor-style house surrounded by 3.6 hectares of lush English garden. It's part of the National Trust; look for it on the Waiwhakaiho River.

Hurworth

This early **homestead** (☎ 06-753 3593; 06-759 6080; 906 Carrington Rd; adult/child $3.50/1; ☺ appointment only), about 8km south of New Plymouth, dates from 1856. Its pioneer builder and first occupant, Harry Atkinson, was to become NZ premier four times. The house was the only one at this site to survive the Taranaki Land Wars and is today owned by the Historic Places Trust.

Lake Mangamahoe & the Tatatm

If you're heading out towards Stratford or North Egmont on SH3, stop at Lake Mangamahoe, 9.5km south of New Plymouth. It's a great setting for photographs of Mt Taranaki (when it shows itself), reflected in the waters of the lake.

Opposite the lake, on the corner of SH3 and Kent Rd, is the **Taranaki Aviation, Transport & Technology Museum** (Tatatm; ☎ 06-758 0686; www.nzmuseums.co.nz/MuseumDetail.asp?MuseumID=263; adult/child $5/1; ☺ 10.30am-4pm Sun) with vehicles, railway and aviation exhibits, farm equipment and household items.

Inglewood

The small town of Inglewood, 13km southeast of New Plymouth, has a butcher, fruit and veg shop, and two pubs – the Railway Hotel and the Inglewood – and a ShopRite supermarket. It's a handy place for daytrippers to Egmont National Park.

Forrestal Lodge (☎ 06-756 7242; forrestallodge@xtra.co.nz; 23 Rimu St; dm $18, s/tw $30/60) This large house occupies a quiet corner in town. Cheap B&B rooms are available.

White Eagle Motel (☎ 06-756 8252; whiteeaglemotel@xtra.com.nz; 87b Rata St; s/d $60/90) Self-contained units have a kitchenette and Sky TV and make a great base for Mt Taranaki. The sizes of the units vary dramatically, so ask to look at more than one.

Macfarlanes (☎ 06-756 6665; www.macfarlanes.co.nz; 1 Kelly St; mains $9.50-25; ☺ breakfast, lunch & dinner Tue-Sun) Macfarlanes is in a charming colonial-style building dating from the late 1800s. It's an elegant fine-dining area lit by modern chandeliers and has a cosy café section.

North via SH3

Heading north towards Waikato from New Plymouth, SH3 is a scenic route. This is the route for Waitomo, and buses head-

ing north go this way to Hamilton. Get the free *Scenic 3 Highway* brochure from the Otorohanga (p234) or New Plymouth visitors centre (p249).

Waitara is 13km northeast of New Plymouth on SH3. If you turn off SH3 at Brixton, just before Waitara, and head 7km south, you'll reach the site of the Pukerangiora Pa. It's beautifully situated on a high cliff by the Waitara River, but historically it was a particularly bloody battle site.

Just beyond Waitara, on SH3 heading east from New Plymouth, is the **Methanex NZ's Motunui Plant** (☎ 06-754 9700; admission free; ☺ 8am-8pm summer, 8am-5pm winter). Opened in 1986, it was the world's first plant to convert natural gas to petrol (gasoline). The synthetic fuel produced here meets around a third of NZ's petrol needs.

Heading north the highway follows the west coast, with its high sand dunes and surf beaches. **Urenui**, 16km past Waitara, is a popular beach destination in summer.

About 5km past Urenui, you can sample natural beers at the **White Cliffs Brewing Company** (☎ 06-752 3676; www.brewing.co.nz/mikes.htm; Main Rd Nth; ☺ 9.30am-6pm) a boutique brewery.

The brewery is located near the turn-off to Pukearuhe and the **Whitecliffs**, huge cliffs resembling their namesake in Dover. The cliffs dominate the coastal landscape and contain two-million-year-old marine sediments. The **Whitecliffs walkway** along the cliffs leads from Pukearuhe to Tongaporutu River via a tunnel from the beach, accessible only at low tide. On a fine day the full-day walk has superb views of the coastline and of Mts Taranaki and Ruapehu.

Oakura

pop 1218

If you're starting round the mountain from New Plymouth, on the coast road SH45, the first settlement is tiny Oakura, 15km southwest of New Plymouth. It's known for its beautiful **beach**, which is great for swimming, surfing and windsurfing. **Crafty Fox** (☎ 06-752 7291; www.windwand.co.nz/thecraftyfox; Main Rd; ☺ 10.30am-4.30pm) is a fun arts and crafts shop in a beautiful church, dating from the 1800s. For surfing and windsurfing head to Vertigo (p251).

Oakura Beach Camp (☎ 06-752 7861; www.windwand.co.nz/oakurabeachcamp; 2 Jans Tce; camp/campervan sites $15/17, cabins $40) This basic camping ground is right on the beach with great views back towards the Sugar Loaf Islands.

Wave Haven (☎ 06-752 7800; www.thewavehaven .co.nz; 1518 Main Rd; dm/s/d $15/25/40) Wave Haven is a very chilled out and well-kept house with a deck on the corner of Ahu Ahu and Main South Rds. It isn't far from the beach and is extremely popular with wave riders.

Ahu Ahu Beach Villas (☎ 06-752 7370; www.ahu .co.nz; 321 Ahu Ahu Rd; units $135) At the beach end of Ahu Ahu Rd are these fantastic villas with views back towards New Plymouth. Recycled materials were used to construct the two villas and the result is rustic yet elegant, with large bay windows, stone floors and wood-beam ceilings.

Butler's Bar & Cafe (☎ 06-752 7765; South Rd; meals $7.50-10; ☾ lunch & dinner) This local bar has an attractive beer garden and small conservatory facing SH45.

Malaysian Restaurant & Cafe (☎ 06-752 1007; South Rd; mains $15-25; ☾ lunch & dinner) This Malaysian place serves traditional Malay food for dinner and a mix of European and Malay for lunch. It's housed in a former railway carriage behind the Crafty Fox.

MT TARANAKI (MT EGMONT)

The massive cone of 2518m Taranaki, a dormant volcano that looks remarkably like Japan's Mt Fuji or the Philippines' Mayon, dominates the Taranaki region.

Geologically, Mt Taranaki is the youngest of a series of three large volcanoes on one fault line, the others being Kaitake and Pouakai. Mt Taranaki last erupted 350 years ago, and is considered dormant rather than extinct. The top 1400m is covered in lava flows, some descend to 800m above sea level. An interesting feature is the small subsidiary cone on the flank of the main cone and 2km south of the main crater, called Fantham's Peak (1962m).

There's a saying in Taranaki that if you can see the mountain it's going to rain and if you can't see the mountain it's already raining! For more on Taranaki's climate, see p248. Still, it doesn't *always* rain there and the volcano is a spectacular sight on a clear day.

History

Mt Taranaki was supremely sacred to the Maoris, both as a burial site for chiefs and as a hide-out in times of danger.

According to legend, Taranaki was once a part of the group of volcanoes at Tongariro. He was forced to leave rather hurriedly when Tongariro caught him with the beautiful Pihanga, the volcano near Lake Taupo who was Tongariro's lover.

So angry was Tongariro at this betrayal that Taranaki made for the coast. The defeated Taranaki gouged a wide scar (the Whanganui River, p271) in the earth as he fled south in anger, pain and shame, moving west to his current position, where he's remained in majestic isolation ever since, hiding his face behind a cloud of tears.

The Maori did not settle the area between Taranaki and Pihanga very heavily, perhaps because they feared the lovers might be reunited with dire consequences. Most of the Maori settlements in this district were clustered along the coast between Mokau and Patea, concentrated particularly around Urenui and Waitara.

Egmont National Park was created in 1900 and is the second-oldest national park in the country.

Information

If you plan to tramp in Egmont National Park, it's essential that you have some local information about current track and weather conditions before you set off (see also Tramping & Skiing, following).

The best information sources are at New Plymouth DOC (p249) and **North Egmont visitors centre** (☎ 06-756 0990; www.doc.govt.nz; ☾ 8am-4pm Oct-Apr, 9am-4pm May-Sep), which has the most current information. At the centre, there are interactive displays on the mountain, an informative video and a small café. **Dawson Falls visitors centre** (☎ 025-430 248; www.doc.govt.nz; Rd 29; ☾ 8am-4.30pm Wed-Sun, Mon-Sun school summer holidays) is around the other side of the mountain and is periodically staffed.

Other information sources include:
Stratford DOC (☎ 06-765 5144; www.doc.govt.nz; Pembroke Rd; ☾ 8am to 4pm) On Pembroke Rd, coming up the mountain from Stratford.
Stratford visitors centre (☎ 06-765 6708; www.stratfordnz.co.nz; cnr Miranda & Prospero Sts; ☾ 8.30am-5pm Mon-Fri, 9.30am-noon Sat)

Tramping & Skiing

Due to its easy accessibility, Mt Taranaki ranks as the 'most climbed' mountain in NZ. Nevertheless, tramping on this mountain holds definite dangers and should not be undertaken lightly (see the boxed text below). It's *crucial* to get advice before departing and fill out the intentions book at a DOC office or visitors centre. If you intend to walk or climb for any distance or height be sure to have the appropriate map.

In winter the mountain is popular with skiers, while during the summer it can be climbed in one day. There are a number of excellent tramping possibilities, including hikes to the summit or right around the mountain. Shorter tracks ranging from easy to difficult, and in length from 30 minutes to several hours, start off from the three roads heading up the mountain. Some of the higher alpine tracks are suffering erosion and DOC is encouraging people to use the lower tracks, which are well maintained. At the time of writing an existing northern circuit was being upgraded – check with the North Egmont visitors centre.

Trips to North Egmont, Dawson Falls and East Egmont are worthwhile for the views, and there are numerous long and short tracks and tramps as well – pick up a copy of the DOC brochure *Short Walks in Egmont National Park*. Other walks include the York Loop Track, which follows part of a disused railway line (DOC produce a leaflet on the walk). York Rd provides access to the walk.

The round-the-mountain track, accessible from all three mountain roads, goes 55km around the mountain and takes from three to five days to complete. You can start or finish this track at any park entrance and there are a number of huts on the mountain. Purchase hut tickets and the handy *Around the Mountain Circuit* DOC brochure at visitor centres or DOC.

There is one main route to the summit, which starts at the North Egmont visitors centre; it's a pole route and you should allow about six to eight hours for the return trip. This route on the north side of the mountain loses its snow and ice earliest in the year – it's advisable not to make the climb in snow and ice conditions if you're inexperienced. Another route to the summit, taking off from the Dawson Falls visitors centre, requires more technical skill and keeps its ice longer; it's best attempted with an experienced guide.

GUIDES

You can hike without a guide from February to March when snowfall is at its lowest, but if you are an inexperienced climber, want other people to climb or tramp with or want to try your hand at rock climbing, DOC can put you in contact with tramping clubs and guides in the area. It generally costs around $300 per day to hire a guide. Reliable operators include:

MacAlpine Guides (☎ 025-417 042, 06-765 6234; www.macalpineguides.com; 30 Ceilia St, Stratford)

Top Guides (☎ 0800 448 433, 021-838 513; www.topguides.co.nz)

At the top of Pembroke Rd is Stratford Plateau, and from there it's a mere 1.5km walk to the small Manganui ski area. You can purchase ski passes for the day (adult/child $30/15), and skiing equipment can be hired at the **Mountain House Motor Lodge** (www.mountainhouse.co.nz) near Stratford. The Stratford visitors centre has useful daily weather and snow reports and there's also a **snow phone service** (☎ 06-765 7669).

THE DECEPTIVE MOUNTAIN

To many, Mt Taranaki may look for all intents and purposes an easy climb, but the mountain has claimed 63 lives. The principal hazard is the erratic weather, which can change from warm and sunny to raging gales and white-out conditions unexpectedly quickly and within a distance of 100m; snow can fall at any time of year on the mountain, even in summer. There are also precipitous bluffs and steep icy slopes. Don't be put off, but don't be deceived. Go at the pace set by the mountain, not the pace set by you.

In good conditions, tramping around the mountain, or even to the summit, can be reasonably easy – January to March is the best time for this. Be sure that you have up-to-date maps and consult a DOC officer for current weather and track conditions before you set off. It's also important to register your tramping intentions and some emergency contact numbers with a DOC office. Pick up the brochure *Taranaki: The Mountain* from DOC offices or local information centres for more information about safety tips.

Sleeping
BUDGET
There are many tramping huts scattered about the mountain, administered by DOC and reached only by trails. Most cost $10 a night (for two tickets, purchased from DOC offices), but two cost $5 (Syme and Kahui huts). You provide your own cooking, eating and sleeping gear, they provide bunks and mattresses, and no bookings are necessary. It's all on a first-come, first-served basis, but you must purchase tickets before starting the walks. Camping is permitted in the park, though it is not encouraged; you're supposed to use the tramping huts.

For DOC places (the first two places in the following list) bookings are essential, and you must carry out *all* your rubbish. You must also bring your own sleeping bag, food and cooking utensils.

Konini Lodge (☎ 025-430 248; Dawson Falls visitor centre; adult/child $20/10) Right by the Dawson Falls visitors centre, this lodge offers bunkhouse accommodation.

Camphouse (☎ 06-756 0990; adult/child $20/10) The Camphouse is located at North Egmont visitors centre and it offers bunkhouse-style accommodation.

Eco Inn (☎ 06-752 2765; www.homepages.paradise.net.nz/ecoinn; 671 Kent Rd; camp sites/s/tw & d $20/24/45) About 6.5km further south from Tatatm, this ultra ecofriendly place is small and made from recycled timber. A mixture of solar, wind and hydropower provides hot water and electricity. A hot tub is available for use. Eco Inn is 3km from the boundary of Egmont National Park and they provide transport to the mountain (for a price).

Missing Leg (☎ 06-752 2570; missingleg@xtra.co.nz; 1082 Junction Rd; dm/d $16/37) Missing Leg backpackers is a casual communal place where you can come in and brew yourself a cuppa. There are dorm beds only, a loft section, log fire and a pot-bellied stove. It's in Egmont Village and there's a swimming hole here.

MID-RANGE
Mountain House Motor Lodge (☎ 0800 668 682, 06-765 6100; www.mountainhouse.co.nz; Pembroke Rd; r from $115) This lodge, on the east side of the mountain, about 15km from Stratford, has rooms and chalets with kitchens. There's a restaurant, and you can hire skis in winter for use at the Manganui ski area.

Andersons Alpine Lodge (☎ 0800 668 682, 06-765 6620; www.mountainhouse.co.nz; 922 Pembroke Rd; r $150-190) The same management that runs Mountain House Motor Lodge also runs this place, further down the mountain not far from the DOC office. It's a modern place in pleasant surroundings.

TOP END
Dawson Falls Mountain Lodge (☎ 0800 695 6343, 06-765 5457; www.dawson-falls.co.nz; Upper Manaia Rd; s/d $150/250) Dawson Falls is beside the visitors centre and is an attractive Swiss-style lodge with lots of carved wood, good views, sitting rooms and a spacious dining room. All rooms have en suite and are individually decorated. Dinner and breakfast are included in the price.

Getting There & Away
There are several points of access to the park, but three roads lead almost right up to where the heavy bush ends. Closest to New Plymouth is Egmont Rd, turning off SH3 at Egmont Village, 12km south of New Plymouth, and heading another 14km up the mountain to the North Egmont visitors centre. Pembroke Rd enters the park from the east at Stratford and ascends 15km to East Egmont, Mountain House Motor Lodge, the Plateau car park and Manganui ski area. From the southeast, Upper Manaia Rd leads up to Dawson Falls, 23km from Stratford.

Public buses don't go to Egmont National Park but shuttle buses (one way $25 to $30, return $35 to $40) to/from New Plymouth to the mountain include **Mt Taranaki Shuttle** (☎ 06-758 9696), **Withers** (☎ 06-751 1777; www.withers.co.nz) and **Cruise NZ Tours** (☎ 06-758 3222; kirstall@xtra.co.nz).

Central Cabs (☎ 06-765 8395) provides a taxi service from Stratford.

AROUND MT TARANAKI
Mt Taranaki is the main attraction of the region. There are two principal highways around the mountain. SH3, on the inland side of the mountain, is the most travelled route, heading south from New Plymouth for 70km until it meets the coast again at Hawera. The coast road, SH45 (also known as the surf highway), heads 105km around the coast from New Plymouth to Hawera, where it meets up again with SH3.

An around-the-mountain trip on both highways is 175km, though short cuts can be taken. Get a *Taranaki Heritage Trails* booklet, free from visitors centres and DOC offices.

Stratford
pop 9730

Stratford, 40km southeast of New Plymouth on SH3, is named after Stratford-upon-Avon in England, Shakespeare's birthplace, and almost all of its streets are named after Shakespearian characters.

The town has an excellent visitors centre that is also the AA agent. It stocks heaps of brochures on walks in the area, including guided tramps and tours.

On SH3, 1km south of the centre, the **Taranaki Pioneer Village** (☎ 06-765 5399; adult/child $7/3; ⊙ 10am-4pm) is a 4-hectare outdoor museum with 50 historic buildings.

At Stratford is the turn-off for Pembroke Rd, heading up the mountain for 15km to East Egmont, the Mountain House Motor Lodge and the Manganui ski area. Stratford is also the southern end of the Stratford–Taumarunui Heritage Trail.

Stratford–Taumarunui Heritage Trail

From Stratford, the Whangamomona–Tangarakau Gorge route (SH43) heads off towards Taumarunui in central North Island. This has been designated a Heritage Trail, passing many historic sites, including **Whangamomona village**, **Maori pa sites**, **small villages**, **waterfalls**, **abandoned coal mines** and small **museums**. You can pick up a Heritage Trail booklet from visitors centres or DOC offices in Stratford, Taumarunui or New Plymouth that give details of places of interest along the way; keep an eye out for the blue-and-yellow Heritage Trail signs, with explanatory plaques.

It takes a minimum of 2½ to three hours to drive the 150km from Stratford to Taumarunui (or vice versa), as the road winds through hilly bush country and 19km of it is unsealed. Nevertheless, it's a good trip if you can put up with the road. It's best to start early in the day; allow at least five hours for the trip if you plan to make stops to see the historic sites. Fill up with petrol at either Stratford or Taumarunui, as petrol stations are limited once you're on the road. This road is definitely off the beaten track.

Kaieto Cafe (☎/fax 06-762 5858; dm $28, meals $14-20) This café, situated high on the Tahora Saddle 73km from Stratford, has panoramic views of the surrounding countryside. The food is mainly NZ orientated, but with Russian influences (try the pie). Accommodation consists of small but cosy cabins.

Hawera
pop 8740

Hawera is on the coast, 70km south of New Plymouth and 90km from Wanganui. It's the largest town on the southern coast of Taranaki.

INFORMATION
AA (☎ 06-278 5095; www.nzaa.co.nz; 121 Princes St)
Hawera visitors centre (☎ 06-278 8599; visitorinfo@stdc.govt.nz; 55 High St; ⊙ 8.30am-5pm Mon-Fri, 10am-3pm Sat & Sun)

SIGHTS & ACTIVITIES
Elvis fans might want to visit the **Kevin Wasley Elvis Presley Memorial Room** (☎ 06-278 7624, 025-982 942; elvisroom@xtra.co.nz; 51 Argyle St; admission by donation), which has a collection of Elvis records (over 2000) and souvenirs. Phone before you arrive.

The excellent **Tawhiti Museum** (☎ 06-278 6837; www.tawhitimuseum.co.nz; 401 Ohangai Rd; adult/child $6/2; ⊙ 10am-4pm daily late-Dec–Jan, 10am-4pm Fri-Mon Feb-May & Sep–mid-Dec, 10am-4pm Sun Jun-Aug) houses a private collection of remarkable exhibits, models and dioramas. The lifelike human figures were modelled on real people around the region; it's quite an unusual museum. It's near the corner of Tawhiti Rd, 4km from town. In the museum complex are arts and crafts **shops** and a **café** with an adorable collection of Wind in the Willows dioramas – chocolate muffins and tea are recommended, coffee is not.

One of the most exciting activities around is dam dropping and white-water sledging with **Kaitiaki Adventures** (☎/fax 06-278 4452, 025-249 9481; www.kaitiaki.co.nz; 3hr trips per person $80). The trips, which centre on the Waingongoro River, include sliding down a 7m dam on a board (more than once if you're game enough), then sledging a further 5km on the river (Grade II to III). This is one activity that rain can't spoil; in fact it can be more fun if it's rained hard the night before. Also included is a journey past **Okahutiti Pa**, birthplace of the Maori prophet

Tohu Kakahi, an advocate of passive resistance following the Taranaki Land Wars of the 1860s (see the boxed text above). All gear is provided. This group also does river trips in Rotorua (see pp320–1 for details). Kaitiaki also offers night trips.

Two kilometres north of Hawera, on Turuturu Rd, are the remains of the pre-European **Turuturumokai Pa**. The reserve is open to the public daily. The **Tawhiti Museum** has a model of the *pa*.

SLEEPING

Hawera has two farm backpackers places past the Tawhiti Museum.

Ohangai Farm Backpacker (☎ 06-272 2878; Urupa Rd; per person $15, linen $3) This place in Ohangai is a 350-cow dairy farm with a well-equipped backpackers in the paddocks. The friendly owners speak German and French and offer a short farm tour involving milking and

mustering cattle. Free pick-up from Hawera is offered, or take the Tawhiti Rd from Hawera, turn right in front of the museum and follow the signs for 8km.

Wheatly Downs (☎ 06-278 6523; www.taranaki-bakpak.co.nz/hawera.htm; 46 Ararata Rd; dm/s/tw/d $20/33/46/50) This is another good farmstay backpackers in the area, also past the Tawhiti Museum – don't turn right but keep going straight on the Ararata Rd (the extension of Tawhiti Rd) for 5.5km beyond the museum. There is also a free pick-up from Hawera.

Try either **Rough Habits Sports Bar and Cafe** (☎ 06-278 7333; 79 Regent St) or the more upmarket **White Elephant** (☎ 06-278 7424; 47 High St) for something to eat.

Opunake
pop 1500
Opunake is the largest town on the western side of the mountain. There's a fine beach in the sheltered Opunake Bay, a peaceful place, good for swimming and surfing even on the windiest of days.

The **Opunake visitors centre** (☎ 06-761 8663; opunakel@stdc.govt.nz; Main Rd; 9am-4pm) is in the Egmont Public Library & Cultural Centre.

Opunake Beach Camp (☎ 0800 758 009, 06-761 7525; www.holidayparks.co.nz/opunake; Beach Rd; camp sites/on-site caravan $21/37) This mellow resort is a stone's throw from the water's edge.

Opunake Motel & Backpackers Lodge (☎ 06-761 8330; opunakemotel@xtra.co.nz; 36 Heaphy Rd; lodge rooms $15, cottage for 2 people $50, s/d units $55/70) This place has a range of good accommodation options that should suit most travellers.

Opunake's main street hosts a couple of pleasant cafés, including the **Volcanic Cafe** (☎ 06-761 8848; Main Rd; meals $6-14), which doubles as a surf shop (surf boards can be rented here).

Wanganui & the Manawatu

CONTENTS

Wanganui Region	**264**
Wanganui	266
Whanganui National Park &	
River Road	271
Manawatu	**274**
Palmerston North	274

The Wanganui region and the Manawatu, its southern neighbour, make up much of the southwestern corner of the North Island, collectively running from Tongariro National Park to the Wellington region. It's a mellow, rural area with green rolling hills, gently curving roads and significant historical and cultural attractions.

A meandering drive through these relaxing, pastoral regions is the perfect antidote to NZ's tourism juggernaut and it's a great place to unwind and explore some of the beautiful national parks, rivers and gorges.

In the Wanganui region the beautiful Whanganui River, historically one of the most important rivers in New Zealand, lazily wends its way through Whanganui National Park. It's a stunning drive from Wanganui up the Whanganui River Rd to the town of Pipiriki and there's plenty of canoeing, tramping, kayaking and jetboating options in the park. The historic town of Wanganui is a pretty country town and an excellent place to base yourself for explorations into the national park.

The allure of the Manawatu is its rural nature and the dramatic Manawatu Gorge. Palmerston North, the region's main city, is a bustling university town and has a lively café scene, plenty of entertainment options, some excellent gourmet restaurants and old-fashioned pubs.

HIGHLIGHTS

- Tramping through the wilderness of Whanganui National Park on the **Matemateaonga** or **Mangapurua Tracks** (p273)
- Drinking an aromatic coffee blend at George St, the heart of the café culture of **Palmerston North** (p277)
- Taking an exhilarating jetboat ride on **Whanganui River** (p272), or paddling your way by canoe or kayak
- Admiring Palmerston North's magnificent rose garden at **Victoria Esplanade** (p276)
- Walking through the beautiful **Manawatu Gorge** (p276), steeped in Maori history
- Visiting **Te Manawa** (p276) for its comprehensive collections of art, science and history
- Feeling the raw emotion of rugby at Palmerston North's **New Zealand Rugby Museum** (p276)

- ★ Whanganui National Park
- ★ Whanganui River
- ★ Manawatu Gorge
- Palmerston North ★

- TELEPHONE CODE: 06   - www.wanganuinz.com   - www.manawatunz.co.nz

Climate

Wanganui and the Manawatu have temperatures ranging from 19°C to 24°C in the summer, and 10°C to 14°C in the winter. Winters are fairly mild in New Plymouth and Wanganui, but can be a bit chillier in and around Palmerston North.

There's plenty of sunshine – around 2000 hours per year – but it can be windy on the coast around New Plymouth.

Usually average rainfall for New Plymouth is around 100mm in summer and 140mm in winter; and, in Wanganui and Palmerston North, around 60mm in summer and 95mm in winter. However, in February 2004 the monthly rainfall was six times the average and the region experienced disastrous floods – the worst seen in decades. The floods caused power, gas and water supply outages and a state of civil emergency was declared.

Getting There & Around

Palmerston North has an international airport serviced by international and domestic flights from Air New Zealand; Freedom Air (from Australia); and domestic flights with Origin Pacific. Air New Zealand also has flights to/from Wanganui to Auckland.

InterCity and Newmans bus lines have a comprehensive network of routes that service Wanganui and the Manawatu regions. White Star City to City also runs buses to/from Wanganui to New Plymouth, Palmerston North and Wellington; and to/from Palmerston North to Wellington, Auckland, Wanganui, Napier and New Plymouth. Tranzit Coachlines operates a service from Palmerston North to Masterton in the Wairarapa. TranzScenic runs a rail service from Auckland to Wellington, which stops at Palmerston North.

Travelling north by car or motorcycle from Wanganui, there's a scenic drive to the centre of the North Island via State Highway 4 (SH4), or you can take the winding Whanganui River Rd. From the north, there's road access to Whanganui River at Taumarunui, Ohinepane and Whakahoro.

For getting around the scenic Whanganui National Park there's the Whanganui National Park Rural Mail Tour (p268), which travels along the Whanganui River Rd to/from Wanganui to Pipiriki. To travel up Whanganui River, you can go by canoe, kayak or jetboat.

To get to Manawatu Gorge from Palmerston North, take the SH2, about 15km northeast of Palmerston North.

WANGANUI REGION

The Wanganui region's main artery is the Whanganui River, and its main highlight is Whanganui National Park, based around the river and the parallel Whanganui River Rd. The estuary, over 30km long, was known to the early Maoris as Whanganui meaning 'Great Harbour' or 'Great Wait'.

The spelling difference between Whanganui and Wanganui causes much confusion. Both town and river were originally spelt Wanganui, because in the local dialect *whanga* (harbour) is pronounced 'whan-ga' not (as in the rest of the country) 'fan-ga'. However, to indicate that the 'wh' sound is aspirated the 'h' was officially restored to the name of the river and national park but not to the city or the region as a whole (the pronunciation of the two spellings is identical). The Pakeha-dominated town and region retain the old spelling, while the river area – very much Maori territory – takes the new spelling.

History

In Maori legend the Whanganui River was formed when Mt Taranaki, after his fight with Mt Tongariro over the lovely Mt Pihanga, fled the central North Island and headed for the sea, leaving a long gouge in his wake. When he reached the sea he turned westwards, finally coming to rest in the place where he stands today. Mt Tongariro sent cool water from his side, to flow down and heal the wound in the earth – and the Whanganui River was born.

Kupe, the great Polynesian explorer, is believed to have travelled up the Whanganui River for about 20km around AD 800, and there were Maoris living in the area around 1100. By the time the first European settlers arrived at the coast around the late 1830s there were numerous Maori settlements scattered up and down the river.

The European missionary settlements of Hiruharama (Jerusalem), Ranana (London), Koriniti (Corinth) and Atene (Athens) survive today, though the river population has dwindled.

WANGANUI & THE MANAWATU

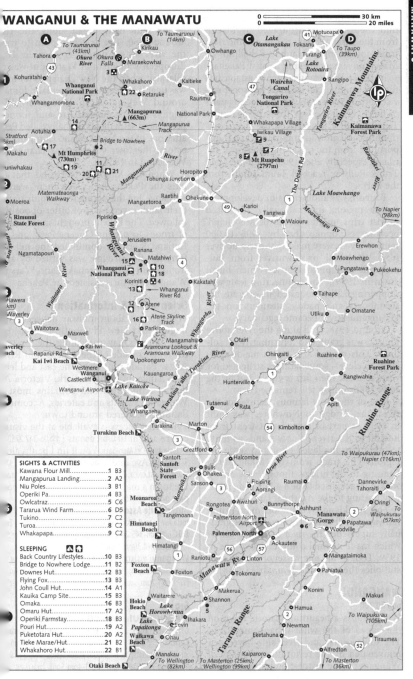

0 ————— 30 km
0 ————— 20 miles

SIGHTS & ACTIVITIES

Kawana Flour Mill	1	B3
Mangapurua Landing	2	A2
Niu Poles	3	B1
Operiki Pa	4	B3
Owlcatraz	5	C6
Tararua Wind Farm	6	D5
Tukino	7	C2
Turoa	8	C2
Whakapapa	9	C2

SLEEPING

Back Country Lifestyles	10	B3
Bridge to Nowhere Lodge	11	B2
Downes Hut	12	B3
Flying Fox	13	B3
John Coull Hut	14	A1
Kauika Camp Site	15	B3
Omaka	16	B3
Omaru Hut	17	A2
Operiki Farmstay	18	B3
Pouri Hut	19	A2
Puketotara Hut	20	A2
Tieke Marae/Hut	21	B2
Whakahoro Hut	22	B1

Steamers first voyaged up the river in the mid-1860s, when, encouraged by Maoris from the Taranaki region, some of the river tribes joined in the Hauhau Rebellion – a Maori movement seeking to oust Pakeha.

In 1886 a Wanganui company established the first commercial steamer transport service. Others soon followed, connecting parts of the river all the way from Wanganui to Taumarunui. They serviced the river communities and grew in importance as a transport link from the sea to the interior of the island, especially after 1903, when the Main Trunk Railway reached Taumarunui from the north.

Tourism was another major development in the region. Internationally advertised tourist trips on the 'Rhine of Maoriland' became so popular that by 1905 12,000 tourists a year were making the trip upriver from Wanganui, or downriver from Taumarunui to Pipiriki House (which burnt down in 1959). The engineering feats and skippering ability required to operate the steamboats and paddle steamers on the Whanganui River became legendary.

Around 1918, land along the river above Pipiriki was granted to returning WWI soldiers. This rugged area was a major challenge to clear – some families struggled for years to make their farms viable, but by the early 1940s only a few remained.

One of the most famous features of the river, the Bridge to Nowhere, was built in 1936 as part of a road that went from Raetihi to the river. It now stands as mute testimony to the failed efforts to settle the region. The track from the Mangapurua Landing to the bridge, though now only a walking track, used to be a 4.5m-wide roadway leading to the riverboat landing.

The Auckland–Wellington main trunk railway as well as the improved roads gradually superseded the river boats, the last of which made its final commercial voyage in 1959. Today only one vessel of the old fleet still plies the river: the *Waimarie* (p268).

WANGANUI
pop 40,700

Wanganui is a beautiful, historic town on the banks of the wide Whanganui River. The town centre and river side have been rejuvenated by the restoration of many of Wanganui's fine historic buildings.

History

Major settlement began along the riv around 1350. The first European to tra the river was Andrew Powers, in 183 European settlement at Wanganui was a celerated when the New Zealand Compa was unable to keep up with demand for la around Wellington. In 1840 many W lington settlers moved here and found permanent settlements. Initially called Pet after one of the New Zealand Company d ectors, the town's name was changed Wanganui in 1844.

When the Maoris understood that t gifts the Pakeha had given them were exchange for the permanent acquisition their land, seven years of bitter oppositi followed. The Pakeha brought in thousan of troops to occupy Queens Park, and t Rutland Stockade dominated the hill. U timately, the struggle was settled by ar tration and in the Taranaki Land Wars t Wanganui Maoris assisted the Pakeha.

Orientation & Information

Wanganui is about midway between W lington and New Plymouth. Somme P and Taupo Quay run along the weste town-centre side of the Whanganui Riv Anzac Parade runs along the east and lea to Whanganui National Park. Victoria A is the main street and contains most Wanganui's sights and eateries. Accomm dation is scattered around town.

Internet access is available at the visit centre and at **Lil Orbit donuts** (☎ 06-347 2758 Victoria Ave; ⊗ Mon-Sat). You'll find banks alo Victoria Ave and a **post office** (☎ 06-345 47 www.nzpost.co.nz; 226 Victoria Ave). Trafalgar Squa the town's main shopping centre, also ha **post office** (☎ 06-345 0014; Taupo Quay).

Automobile Association (AA; ☎ 06-348 9160; 78 V toria Ave; ⊗ 8.30am-5pm Mon & Wed-Fri, 9am-5pm T **DOC** (☎ 06-345 2402; www.doc.govt.nz; 74 Ingestre ⊗ 9.30am-4.30pm Mon-Fri)

Wanganui visitors centre (☎ 06-349 0508; www .wanganuinz.com; 101 Guyton St; ⊗ 8.30am-5pm Mo Fri, 10am-2pm Sat & Sun, 9am-3pm Sat & Sun summer

Sights
WHANGANUI RIVERBOAT CENTRE

On the river bank, the **Whanganui Riverb Centre** (☎ 0800 783 2637, 06-347 1863; www.wang .org.nz/riverboats; 1a Taupo Quay; admission free; ⊗ 9 4pm Mon-Fri, 10am-4pm Sat, 1-4pm Sun) houses

WANGANUI

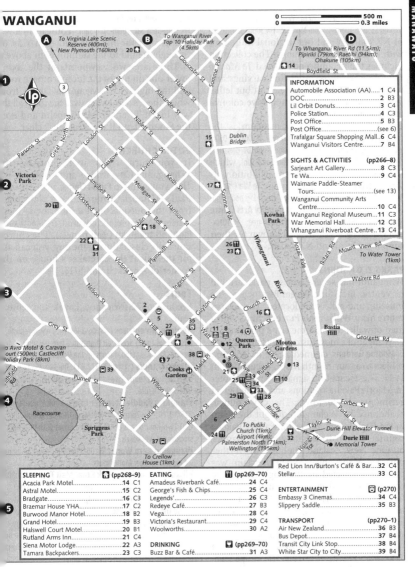

0 .... 500 m
0 .... 0.3 miles

To Virginia Lake Scenic Reserve (400m); New Plymouth (160km)

To Wanganui River Top 10 Holiday Park (4.5km)

To Whanganui River Rd (11.5km); Pipiriki (79km); Raetihi (94km); Ohakune (105km)

Boydfield St

INFORMATION
Automobile Association (AA).....1 C4
DOC...2 B3
Lil Orbit Donuts........................3 C4
Police Station............................4 C3
Post Office................................5 B3
Post Office...........................(see 6)
Trafalgar Square Shopping Mall.6 C4
Wanganui Visitors Centre........7 B4

SIGHTS & ACTIVITIES (pp266–8)
Sarjeant Art Gallery.................8 C3
Te Wa..9 C4
Waimarie Paddle-Steamer
  Tours.................................(see 13)
Wanganui Community Arts
  Centre..................................10 C4
Wanganui Regional Museum....11 C3
War Memorial Hall...................12 C3
Whanganui Riverboat Centre..13 C4

Dublin Bridge

Victoria Park

Kowhai Park

Mount View Rd
To Water Tower (1km)

Wairere Rd

To Avro Motel & Caravan Court (500m); Castlecliff Holiday Park (8km)

Grey St

Queens Park

Moutoa Gardens

Bastia Hill

Georgetti Rd

Cooks Gardens

City Bridge

Racecourse

Spriggens Park

Forbes St

To Putiki Church (1km); Airport (4km); Palmerston North (71km); Wellington (195km)

Durie Hill Elevator Tunnel
Durie Hill Memorial Tower

To Crellow House (1km)

SLEEPING	(pp268–9)		EATING	(pp269–70)
Acacia Park Motel	14 C1		Amadeus Riverbank Café	24 C4
Astral Motel	15 C2		George's Fish & Chips	25 C4
Bradgate	16 C3		Legends'	26 C3
Braemar House YHA	17 C2		Redeye Café	27 B3
Burwood Manor Hotel	18 B2		Vega	28 C4
Grand Hotel	19 B3		Victoria's Restaurant	29 C4
Halswell Court Motel	20 B1		Woolworths	30 A2
Rutland Arms Inn	21 C4			
Siena Motor Lodge	22 A3		DRINKING	(pp269–70)
Tamara Backpackers	23 C3		Buzz Bar & Café	31 A3

Red Lion Inn/Burton's Café & Bar	32 C4
Stellar	33 C4
ENTERTAINMENT	(p270)
Embassy 3 Cinemas	34 C4
Slippery Saddle	35 B3
TRANSPORT	(pp270–1)
Air New Zealand	36 B3
Bus Depot	37 B4
Transit City Link Stop	38 B4
White Star City to City	39 B4

Waimarie side-paddle steamer and has photographic and historical exhibits. The *Waimarie's* long history began in 1900, when was shipped in pieces from England and assembled at Murrays Foundry in Wananui. After plying the Whanganui River for 0 years it sank in 1952 at its original berth. remained submerged for 40 years until it

was raised and finally relaunched, restored and proud, on the first day of the 21st century. Tours (p268) on the coal-fired steamer are a dreamy reminder of yesteryear.

MUSEUMS & GALLERIES
Opposite the War Memorial Hall is the **Wanganui Regional Museum** (☎ 06-345 7443;

www.wanganui-museum.org.nz; Watt St; adult/child/family $2/60c/$5; ☉ 10am-4.30pm Mon-Sat, 1-4.30pm Sun), one of NZ's largest and best regional museums, with excellent Maori exhibits. The collection includes the magnificently carved *Te Mata o Houroa* war canoe, other fine carvings and some mean-looking *mere* (elegant but lethal greenstone clubs). It has impressive colonial and wildlife collections.

On the hill beside the museum is the neoclassical **Sarjeant Art Gallery** (☎ 06-349 0506; www.sarjeant.org.nz; Queens Park; admission by donation; ☉ 10.30am-4.30pm Mon-Fri, 1-4.30pm Sat & Sun), which has an extensive permanent exhibition, as well as frequent special exhibits. **Te Wa** (☎ 06-348 7790; 25a Drews Ave; admission free; ☉ noon-4pm Tue-Sat) and the **Wanganui Community Arts Centre** (☎ 06-345 1551; 19 Taupo Quay; admission free; ☉ 10am-4pm Mon-Sat, 1-4pm Sun) are well known for their support of local and NZ artists.

PARKS & GARDENS
Wanganui has several grassy parks around its centre, including **Queens Park**, where the museum and gallery are located. The visitors centre has a *Walking for Fun* brochure, with a map of walks through the city's parklands.

Wanganui's most historically famous park is **Moutoa Gardens**, claimed as Maori land and subject to a four-month Maori occupation in 1995. The occupation signalled a new chapter in Maori–Pakeha relations and caused great acrimony in the town. The city council, abandoned by Wellington, fought the claim in the High Court, while some angry Pakeha counter-demonstrated under the banner of 'One New Zealand'; police raids further inflamed Maori anger. When the claim was eventually rejected by the High Court, the country expected violence, but the occupation was peacefully abandoned after a moving night-long meeting addressed by Maori leaders. The gardens have acquired a sacred status in the eyes of many Maoris.

The popular **Virginia Lake Scenic Reserve** (Rotokawau; ☉ winter gardens 9am-5pm, aviary 8.30am-5pm), about 1km north from the top end of Victoria Ave, is a beautiful reserve with a lake, theme gardens, walk-in aviary, statues and the Higginbottom Fountain. The rest of the reserve is always open.

DURIE HILL
Across the Whanganui City Bridge from the town centre is the gateway to the Durie Hill

elevator (adult/child $1/50c; ☉ summer 7.30am-6pm Mo Fri, 9am-5pm Sat, 10am-5pm Sun). You can follow tunnel into the hill side and then ride u through the hill to the summit 65m above.

There are two viewpoints at the top: lower one on top of the lift machinery roor and the higher War Memorial Tower, fro which there's a fine view over the town all th way to Mt Taranaki, Mt Ruapehu and eve the South Island if the weather is clear.

PUTIKI CHURCH
If you turn right after crossing th Whanganui City Bridge and continue fo 1km you come to **Putiki Church**, also called S Paul's Memorial Church. It's a plain plac from the outside but the interior is mag nificent, completely covered in **Maori car ings** and **tukutuku** (wall panels). The churc is usually closed during the day; you can as for the key at the caretaker's house on th corner of Anaua St and SH3.

Tours
See also p272 for canoe, kayak and jetboa tours.

Remote Adventures (☎ 06-346 5747; www.remote adventures.co.nz) Scenic air flights in a five-passenger Cessna. Also has jetboat tours up the Whanganui River.

Rivercity tours (☎ 0800 377 311, 06-344 2554; www .rivercitytours.co.nz) Two- and four-day guided canoe trip Offers canoe hire.

Waimarie paddle-steamer tours (adult/child/family $25/10/70; ☉ 2pm daily Nov-May, 1pm Sat & Sun Jun-Oct) Two-hour tour weekdays, three hours with one-hour stopover at weekends.

Wanganui Aero Work (☎ 06-345 3994; www.aerowo .co.nz) Scenic Tiger Moth flights.

Whanganui National Park Rural Mail Tour (☎ 0800 377 311, 06-344 2554; www.rivercitytours.co .nz; $30; ☉ departs 7.30am, returns 3-4pm Mon-Fri) A very inter esting trip up the Whanganui River Rd, from Wanganui to Pipiriki. There's lots of social and historical commentary. Tea and coffee supplied, but bring lunch. Ask about the op tion of a 30-minute jetboat trip from Pipiriki to Drop Scer or Bridge to Nowhere (Wednesday only).

Sleeping
Accommodation in Wanganui is of a hig standard. For a room with a view head Somme Pde.

Braemar House YHA (☎ 06-347 2529; www.braem house.co.nz; 2 Plymouth St; camp sites $20, dm $20, s. cabins $40/50, s/d guesthouse $50/70, continental/cook breakfast $10/15) Braemar sits elegantly ove oking the river, surrounded by estab-shed, kempt gardens. Its guesthouse rooms re in the main heritage building, dating om around 1895 and were originally the urses' quarters. Rooms here are elegantly rnished with Victorian furniture and top alue. In the back garden, cheaper cabins are ailable and there's limited tent space.

Tamara Backpackers (☎ 06-347 6300; www.tamara dge.com; 24 Somme Pde; dm $19-20, s $32-42, tw & d $42-') Overlooking Whanganui River, Tamara a rambling place with a kitchen, pool table d lovely back garden. Though the rooms uld do with a spruce, it's a well-run, iendly place that's popular with a young, cial crowd. Bikes are free to use.

Grand Hotel (☎ 06-345 0955; the-grand-hotel@ a.co.nz; 99 Guyton St; s/d $70/80) The only old-hool survivor in Wanganui, its comfort-le rooms are authentically retro, complete ith faded bedspreads, well-loved carpet, y TV and private bathrooms. A great dget option.

Rutland Arms Inn (☎ 0800 788 5263, 06-347 7677; w.rutland-arms.co.nz; 48 Ridgway St; r $130-150, meals 4-27) Hailed as a 'luxury heritage experi-ce', the Rutland is in a restored 1849 ilding and has elegant, spotless rooms rnished in a colonial style. Each room has TV, phone, fax and plump pillows on Pos-repedic beds. Downstairs at the polished r, framed black-and-white photos adorn e walls and an English hunting scene is picted on the beer taps. Big meals are so available.

Siena Motor Lodge (☎ 0800 888 802, 06-345 9009; w.wanganui.co.nz/pages/siena; 335 Victoria Ave; s $100-5, d $110-145, units $80) Five-star motel offering otless rooms with DVD players and Sky V. Self-contained units have a kitchenette, wer rooms have spas, and room No 9 has a ivate courtyard. Guests are welcomed with owl full of free goodies.

Crellow House (☎ 06-345 0740; 274 Taupo Quay; 45-65) A lovely, cosy B&B. Pam, the delight-l owner, cooks up a substantial breakfast d claims that 'Nobody leaves my house ngry'. Her cheese-dish collection (203 in tal) is a work of dedication. Rooms are spa-us and homely – one twin has a private throom – and staying at Crellow House is ittle like staying with your nanna.

Bradgate (☎ 06-345 3634; 7 Somme Pde; s $40-50, 80, incl breakfast) This grand old home, over-oking the Whanganui River, has three

comfortable rooms: one single, one queen-sized and one double. A lovely communal lounge room has bay windows looking over the mountains.

Also recommended:

Acacia Park Motel (☎ 0800 800 225, 06-343 9093; acacia.park.motel@xtra.co.nz; 140 Anzac Pde; r from $85) Most of Acacia Park's units are set back from the road and sheltered by trees.

Astral Motel (☎ 0800 509 063, 06-347 9063; astral motel@clear.net.nz; 45 Somme Pde; s $70-75, d $70-95) Clean rooms with Sky TV. Good value.

Burwood Manor Motel (☎ 06-345 2180; fax 06-345 8711; 63-65 Dublin St; r $80-100) Eight luxury units at this inn have their own spa.

Halswell Court Motel (☎ 0800 809 107, 06-343 9848; halswell.court@clear.net.nz; 59 Halswell St; units $70-100) This motel is attractively situated on a quiet, tree-lined street at the foot of St John's Hill.

CAMPING & CAMPERVAN PARKS
There are no camping grounds in the centre of Wanganui.

Avro Motel & Caravan Court (☎ 06-345 5279; www.wanganuiaccommodation.co.nz; 36 Alma Rd; camp/ campervan sites $18/20, tourist flats $60, units $75) This place is closest to the city centre, 1.5km west. There's an indoor spa and swimming pool but no kitchen facilities.

Wanganui River Top 10 Holiday Park (☎ 0800 272 664, 06-343 8402; wrivertop10@xtra.co.nz; 460 Somme Pde; camp & campervan sites $26, cabins $40-50, units $75-90) Six kilometres north of the Dublin Bridge, this is a peaceful, parklike camp on the town-side bank of the Whanganui River. Facilities are plentiful and of a high standard.

Castlecliff Holiday Park (☎ 0800 254 947, 06-344 2227; www.castlecliffholidaypark.co.nz; 1a Rangiora St; camp/campervan sites $18/20, cabins $30-55) Castle-cliff Camp is situated by the beach and 8km northwest of Wanganui. It has great facilities, including a playground, swim-ming pool, spa and tennis court.

Eating & Drinking
The Rutland Arms (above) is a popular spot for a lager, plus it serves thumping meals.

Redeye Café (☎ 06-345 5646; 96 Guyton St; lunch $8-15, dinner $15-25; ☺ lunch & dinner Tue-Sat) This funky, arty café has colourful art, tasty light meals and snacks and more substantial meals such as laksa and chicken salad.

Amadeus Riverbank Café (☎ 06-345 1538; 69 Taupo Quay; meals $8-14; ☺ breakfast & lunch) Drop into Amadeus for a quick bite and a coffee from its all-day café menu. Seafood, steaks, chicken and pasta are all on the menu, along with sweet treats and slabs of cake.

George's Fish & Chips (☎ 06-345 7937; 40 Victoria Ave; meals $7-15; 🕑 dinner) A bustling takeaway/restaurant with delicious fresh seafood such as groper, terakihi, snapper, blue cod and, in season, whitebait.

Red Lion Inn/Burtons Café & Bar (☎ 06-345 3831; Anzac Pde; pub meals $8-18, restaurant $18-30; 🕑 lunch & dinner) Across Whanganui City Bridge, the Red Lion is a friendly spot for a drink. The front bar is populated by locals watching the races, the back bar has cosy armchairs and open fires and wide verandas overlook the river. Downstairs pub meals range from crispy tempura to steak sandwiches and roast of the day. Burtons restaurant, upstairs, is a more formal dining area with delicious meals.

Stellar (☎ 06-345 2728; 2 Victoria Ave; meals $6.50-27; 🕑 dinner) This big, popular bar and restaurant, with its friendly family atmosphere, is the town's pride and joy. In flash surrounds, punters drink premium lagers and feast on gourmet pizzas and surf'n'turf meals. Bar snacks include wedges and sausages and mash.

Vega (☎ 06-345 1082; 49 Taupo Quay; mains $20-28; 🕑 brunch Sat & Sun, dinner Tue-Sat) These guys know what they are doing, as a packed house will testify. Professional service complements a sophisticated menu featuring dishes such as Polynesian raw fish marinated in onion, lime juice, ginger, coriander and coconut cream, and there are plenty of vegetarian and children's options. There's an excellent back bar, right on the river, with a big window and works specifically designed for the space by local artists.

Victoria's Restaurant (☎ 06-347 7007; 13 Victoria Ave; meals $11-26; 🕑 lunch Tue-Fri, dinner Tue-Sun) Exposed brick and an ambience that's popular with the older local crowd. Meals include classics such as eye fillet, rack of lamb and salmon.

Legends' (☎ 06-348 7450; 25 Somme Pde; sandwiches & pastries $4-7, meals $20-30; 🕑 breakfast, lunch & dinner Wed-Sun) Next to Tamara Backpackers, in a beautifully restored Victorian house, is this convivial restaurant. The menu has international flair and delicious takeaway sandwiches. Book for dinner.

Buzz Bar & Café (☎ 06-345 8408; 345 Victoria Ave; meals $6-14; 🕑 lunch & dinner) This is a good spot for a quiet drink and a game of pool. Th menu ranges from apple shortbread to fis burgers.

Entertainment

Embassy 3 Cinemas (☎ 06-347 6774; www.embass .co.nz; 34 Victoria Ave; tickets $11) A busy cinem showing up to five films nightly. Ticke for new-release blockbusters sell out fast.

Slippery Saddle (☎ 06-348 5599; cnr Guyton St Victoria Ave) Wanganui's main nightclub, wi most of the city's under-30s congregatin here at weekends. The dance floor heats around 11.30pm. It's a slippery slope in deed if you're still dancing at closing tim

Getting There & Away

AIR

Air New Zealand (☎ 06-348 3500; www.airnz.co. 133 Victoria Ave) has direct flights to Aucklan ($120, one hour, two to three daily).

BUS

InterCity (☎ 04-472 5111; www.intercitycoach.co 🕑 7am-9pm) and **Newmans** (☎ 04-499 3261; ww .newmanscoach.co.nz; 🕑 7am-9pm) buses opera from the top end of Ridgway St. Buses r to/from Auckland ($71, eight hours, tw daily) via Taumarunui, and to New Pl mouth ($31, 2½ hours, one daily). Headi south, buses go to/from Palmerston Nor ($15, 1¾ hours, four daily) and on to We llington ($36, four hours). For services nor to Tongariro, Taupo and Rotorua, you ha to transfer at Bulls, although some buses c into Palmerston North. For Napier, Hastin and Gisborne, change at Palmerston Nort

White Star City to City (☎ 04-478 4734; Ingestre St) has buses to/from Wellingt ($27, 3 hours 20 minutes, one to two dai and New Plymouth ($22, 2½ hours, one two daily).

For details about the mail-run bus Pipiriki see p268.

CAR & MOTORCYCLE

Between Wanganui and the centre of t North Island the winding highway (SH passes through the Paraparas, an area interesting *papa* (large blue-grey mudstor hills with some beautiful views, and a passes close by the impressive Rauka Falls and along Mangawhero River Gorg

Alternatively, you can take the Whangar River Rd (opposite).

etting Around

anganui airport (☎ 06-348 9217) is about 4km
uth of town, across the river towards the
a. **Ash's Transport Services** (☎ 06-347 7444; 28
estre St) operates a shuttle to the airport,
s station and other points in town.
Transit City Link (☎ 06-343 5555; $2) operates
imited weekday service, including routes
Castlecliff and to Wanganui River Top
Holiday Park, all departing from the bus
op on Maria Pl, near Victoria Ave.

HANGANUI NATIONAL PARK & VER ROAD

hanganui National Park's main attrac-
n is the Whanganui River, which curls its
y 329km from its source on the flanks of
Tongariro (pp283–4) to the Tasman Sea
Wanganui. The fact that the river is the
gest navigable river in the country has
en shaping its destiny for centuries. His-
ically a major link between the sea and
interior of the North Island, first for the
aoris and then for the Pakeha, the route
s eventually superseded by rail and road.
any recreational canoe, kayak and jetboat
thusiasts now use it to reach the isolated
erior of Whanganui National Park.

The native bush is thick podocarp-
oadleaved forest, with many types of
es and ferns. Occasionally you will see
plar and other introduced trees along the
er, evidence of settlements that have long
ce vanished.

There are traces of former Maori settle-
nts along the river in various places, with
(fortified village) sites, old *kainga* (village)
es, and the unusual Hauhau **niu poles** of war
d peace at Maraekowhai, at the confluence
the Whanganui and Ohura Rivers. The
takura, Reinga Kokiri and Te Rerehapa
lls, all near Maraekowhai on the Ohura
ver, were popular places for Maoris to
ne to catch small *tuna riki* eels (river, or
shwater, eels found in the Whanganui).
veral of the landings along the Whanganui
ver's banks were once river-boat landings.
The Whanganui River Rd, running along
river most of the way from Wanganui to
iriki, is a scenic and historic route worth
king the detour to see.

ientation & Information

iriki and Taumarunui are the most
pular entry and exit points to the river

as they have the most facilities, though you
can also access the river from Ohinepane
and Whakahoro (Wades Landing).

The best place for information about
the national park is at Wanganui's visitors
centre (p266) and the DOC office (p266);
there's also **Pipiriki DOC** (☎ 06-385 5022; Owairua
Rd; www.doc.govt.co.nz; ☿ 8am-5pm Mon-Fri), though
it's not always staffed, and **Taumarunui DOC**
(☎ 07-895 8201; Cherry Grove Domain; ☿ 8am-5pm
Mon-Fri). For an excellent online resource,
visit www.whanganui river.co.nz.

A useful book about the river is *Guide to
the Whanganui River* by the NZ Canoeing
Association. *In and Around Whanganui
National Park,* published by DOC, is use-
ful for tramping or pick up a copy of the
Wanganui Tramping Club's *Walking Op-
portunities in the Wanganui Area* from the
Wanganui visitors centre.

Sights

Along the Whanganui River Rd, on the
way to Pipiriki, the main attraction is the
spectacular scenery, with stark mountains
and plummeting valleys to the beautiful Whanganui River. A French Catholic
missionary established the Daughters of
Our Lady of Compassion in Jerusalem in
1892 and **St Joseph's church** is still the most
prominent feature of the town. The large,
white wooden convent stands in a beautiful
garden. Other sights include the restored **Ka-
wana Flour Mill** near Matahiwi, **Operiki Pa** and
other *pa* sites and **Aramoana hill**, from where
there's a panoramic view. The Maori villages
of **Atene**, **Koriniti**, **Ranana** and **Hiruharama** along
the road are generally not open to visitors.

Pipiriki is beside the river at the north
end of Whanganui River Rd. It was once a
bustling place served by river steamers and
paddle boats. An interesting relic, the **MV
Ongarue**, is a 20m, 65-passenger river boat
that once plied the river, now on display on
land (off limits for safety reasons). **Colonial
House** (☎ 06-385 5022; adult/child $1/50c; ☿ 10am-
noon & 1-4pm Nov–Easter) has been converted to
a museum with many interesting exhibits
about the history of Pipiriki and the river.
Beside it, some old steps and foundations
are all that remain to mark the site of the
old **Pipiriki House**, a glamorous hotel once
popular with tourists. Pipiriki is the ending point for canoe trips coming down the
Whanganui River, and for jetboat rides.

Activities
CANOEING & KAYAKING

The Whanganui is a Grade II river, which is easy enough to be enjoyed by people of all ages with little canoeing experience, yet there are enough small rapids and movement to keep it interesting. The DOC leaflet *Whanganui Journey* has information about canoeing the river.

The most popular section of the river for canoeing and kayaking is between Taumarunui and Pipiriki. The stretch of river from Taumarunui south to Pipiriki has been added to the NZ Great Walks system (p80) and called the 'Whanganui Journey'.

Between 1 October and 30 April you will need a **Great Walks Hut and Campsite Pass** (adult/child $35/18) for boat trips on the river involving overnight stays between Taumarunui and Pipiriki; the rule applies only to this stretch of the river. The pass is valid for six nights and seven days and allows you to stay overnight in the huts, camp sites beside the huts or in other designated camp sites along the river. In addition to the cost of the Great Walks Hut and Campsite Pass, passes for canoeists cost adult/child $6/3; jetboaters pay adult/child $10/5. People using huts must have hut tickets or a **Backcountry Hut Pass** (adult/child $10/5). Passes are available at the Wanganui visitors centre and regional DOC offices; some canoe operators also sell them. During summer, hut wardens are on duty and conservation officers patrol the river.

Taumarunui to Pipiriki is a five-day/four-night trip, Ohinepane to Pipiriki is a four-day/three-night trip, and Whakahoro to Pipiriki is a three-day/two-night trip. Taumarunui to Whakahoro is a popular overnight trip, especially for weekenders, or you can do a one-day trip from Taumarunui to Ohinepane or Ohinepane to Whakahoro. From Whakahoro to Pipiriki, 88km downstream, there's no road access so you're committed to the river for a few days. This is the most popular trip. Most canoeists stop in Pipiriki.

The season for canoe trips is usually from around September to Easter. Up to 5000 people make the trip up the river each year, usually over the summer holidays from Christmas to the end of January. During winter the river is almost deserted – cold weather and short days deter most people, and the winter currents are swifter.

To hire a two-person Canadian cano for one/two/three/four/five days costs abo $50/100/125/130/140. To hire single-perso kayaks costs about $40 per day. Transpo isn't included and costs roughly $50 p person but operators often include the tran port fee in the cost of canoe or kayak hire f multiday trips. Operators provide you wi everything you need for the journey, inclu ing life jackets and waterproof drums, whic are essential if you capsize in the rapids.

You can also take guided canoe or kaya trips – prices start at $250 per person for two-day guided trip and $780 per perso for a five-day trip.

Operators include:

Blazing Paddles (☎ 0800 252 946; www.blazingpaddl .co.nz; Taumarunui)

Canoe Safaris (☎ 0800 272 335, 06-385 9237; www .canoesafaris.co.nz; Ohakune)

Rivercity Tours (☎ 0800 377 311, 06-344 2554; www .rivercitytours.co.nz; Wanganui; 2-/4-day guided trips $250/550; ⊗ Dec-Apr)

Taumarunui Canoe Hire (☎ 0800 226 6348; www .taumarunuicanoehire.co.nz; Taumarunui)

Wades Landing Outdoors (☎ 07-895 5995; www .whanganui.co.nz; Owhango)

Wairua Hikoi Tours (☎ 06-342 8190; Jerusalem)

Whanganui River Guides (☎ 07-896 6726; hinenga kau@xtra.co.nz; 32 Miriama St, Taumarunui) A Maori-run company that runs Hinengakau Waka tours.

Yeti Tours (☎ 0800 322 388, 06-385 8197; www.cano .co.nz; Ohakune)

JETBOATING

Jetboat trips give you a chance to see in ju a few hours parts of the river that wou take you days to cover in a canoe or kaya Jetboats depart from Pipiriki, Taumarun and Whakahoro and charge around $90 p person. All operators provide transport the river ends of the Matemateaonga ar Mangapurua Tracks (opposite).

Jetboat operators include **Riverspirit** (☎ 08 266 9437, 06-342 1718; www.riverspirit.co.nz; Wa ganui) and Bridge to Nowhere Jetboat Tou (opposite). See also Tours (p268).

TRAMPING

Probably the best-travelled track in Wha ganui National Park is the 40-minute wa from the Mangapurua Landing to the **Bridge Nowhere**, 30km upstream from Pipiriki.

The Matemateaonga and Mangapur Tracks are excellent for longer tramps. Bo re one-way tracks beginning (or ending) at emote spots on the river, so you must ar-ange for jetboat transport to or from these oints. Any jetboat operator on the river will o this; from the Matemateaonga Track it osts around $55 per person and from the Mangapurua Track it costs around $70.

Taking four days to complete, the 42km **Matemateaonga Track** has been described as ne of NZ's best walks. Nevertheless it is not videly known and, probably due to its re-noteness, does not attract the crowds that an form on some of NZ's more famous -acks. Penetrating deep into bush, wilder-ess and hill country, it follows an old Maori -ack and a disused settlers' dray road be-ween the Wanganui and Taranaki regions. : traverses the Matemateaonga Range along he route of the Whakaihuwaka Rd, started 1911 to create a more direct link from tratford to Raetihi and the main trunk rail-ay. The outbreak of WWI interrupted the lans and the road was never completed.

The track passes through thick and re-enerating bush, much of it following the rest of the Matemateaonga Range. On a ear day, a 1½-hour side trip to the sum-it of Mt Humphries affords a panoramic ew of the Wanganui region all the way Mt Taranaki and the volcanoes of Ton-ariro. There's a steep section between the Vhanganui River (75m above sea level) and he Puketotara Hut (427m), but much of the ack is easy walking. There are three huts ong the way: Omaru Hut, Pouri Hut and uketotara Hut.

The **Mangapurua Track** is a 40km track etween Whakahoro and the Mangapurua anding, both on the Whanganui River. he track runs along the Mangapurua and aiwhakauka Streams, both tributaries of he Whanganui River. Between these val-ys a side track leads to the Mangapurua rig, at 663m the highest point in the area, om where you can see all the way to the olcanoes of the Tongariro and Egmont Na-onal Parks on a clear day. The route passes rough land that was cleared for farming y settlers last century and later aban-oned. The track takes 20 hours and is usu-ly walked in three to four days. Apart from e Whakahoro Hut at the Whakahoro end the track, there are no huts, but there are any fine camping spots. Water is available om numerous small streams. There is road

access to the track at Whakahoro and from a side track leading to the end of the Ruatiti Valley–Ohura Rd (from Raetihi).

There are a couple of shorter walks branching off the Whanganui River Rd that provide a glimpse of the wilderness of the national park. The DOC booklet *In and Around Whanganui National Park* has details on these walks.

The **Atene Skyline Track** begins at Atene, on the Whanganui River Rd, about 22km north of where it meets with SH4. The 18km track takes six to eight hours and features native forest, sandstone bluffs and the Taumata Trig (523m), with its broad views as far as Mt Ruapehu, Mt Taranaki and the Tasman Sea. The track ends back on the river road, 2km downstream from the walk's start.

From the Pipiriki DOC field centre a 1km track cuts its way through native bush to the top of Pukehinau, a hill that affords pan-oramic views of the surrounding valleys.

Sleeping
WHANGANUI NATIONAL PARK
The park has several huts, a lodge and numerous camping grounds. Along the Taumarunui–Pipiriki section are three Cat-egory 2 huts classified as Great Walks Huts: the Whakahoro Hut at Whakahoro, the John Coull Hut and the Tieke Marae/Hut, which has been revived as a *marae* (Maori meeting house); you can stay here, but full *marae* protocol must be observed (see pp47–53).

Other huts in the park are simpler, with only two bunks. On the lower part of the river, Downes Hut is on the west bank, op-posite Atene.

Bridge to Nowhere Lodge (☎ 0800 480 308, 06-348 7122; www.bridgetonowhere-lodge.co.nz; camp sites $10, cabins $20, d self-catering lodges $70-90, d B&B $230) On the other side of the river, opposite the Tieke Marae, this lodge has a range of ac-commodation options deep in the national park. It's quite remote, 21km upriver from Pipiriki, near the Matemateaonga Track; the only way to get there is by river or by tramping. The lodge also runs the popular Bridge to Nowhere Jetboat Tours.

WHANGANUI RIVER ROAD
It's advisable to book the following accom-modation options in advance.

Omaka (☎ 06-342 5595; www.whanganuiriver.co.nz; 1569 Whanganui River Rd; camp sites/woolshed/lodges per person $10/15/35, tw & d lodge $90) A rural idyll flanked by hills with the river below and the intermittent bleating of sheep. Omaka is a delightful, friendly place with beds in the spacious woolshed, including a bathroom and kitchen, or the self-contained river lodge. It's adjacent to the Atene Skyline Track and about 12km north of Parikino.

Flying Fox (☎ 06-342 8160; www.theflyingfox.co.nz; Whanganui River Rd; camp sites $20, self-contained tw & d $90-110) A superb little getaway on the bank of the river across from Koriniti. You can stay in the Brewhouse or the James K, both self-contained cottages, and self-cater, or you can request dinner, bed and breakfast. You can also camp in a secluded bush clearing. Access is by boat from Wanganui or you can drive and take the cableway across the river.

Operiki Farmstay (☎ 06-342 8159; www.whanganuiriver.co.nz; Whanganui River Rd; camp sites $20, d & tw $110) At this friendly place, you can have all your meals cooked for you. It's about 3km north of Koriniti Marae.

Koriniti Marae (☎ 0800 783 2637; dm $12) This *marae* on the east bank takes prebooked visitors; offer *koha*, or a donation, plus the fee. Call Sunny Teki at the Whanganui Riverboat Centre to make a booking.

Back Country Lifestyles (☎ 06-342 8116; dm $20) This place, located on the Wanganui side of Matahiwi, has horse riding and jetboating. Accommodation is in restored shearers' quarters with linen and breakfast included. There's a kitchen and a barbecue.

Kauika Camp Site (☎ 06-342 8061; camp/campervan sites $12/20) Beside the river at Ranana, this privately owned site has hot showers, a kitchen and a laundry.

The nuns at the **Catholic church** (☎ 06-342 8190; dm $12) in Jerusalem take in travellers (you should book ahead). A large room has been divided by curtains into cubicles.

At Pipiriki there's an informal camping ground with toilets and cold water.

Getting There & Away

From Wanganui, you can catch the mail run bus (p268) to Pipiriki.

From the north, there's road access to the Whanganui River at Taumarunui, Ohinepane and Whakahoro, though the latter is a long drive through a remote area along a road that is unsealed for much of its distance. Roads leading to Whakahoro take off from Owhango and Raurimu, both on

SH4. There isn't any further road access to the river until Pipiriki.

From the south, the Whanganui River Rd meets SH4 14km north of Wanganui and at Raetihi, 91km north of Wanganui. It takes about 1½ to two hours to drive the 79km between Wanganui and Pipiriki. The full circle from Wanganui through Pipiriki and Raetihi and back along SH4 through the Paraparas and Mangawhero River Gorge takes about four hours. Petrol is available at Raetihi and Upokongaro but not in between.

Despite the steep hills and gravel road, this route is also popular with cyclists.

MANAWATU

The rich sheep- and dairy-farming district of Manawatu is centred around the provincial city of Palmerston North and includes the districts of Rangitikei to the north and Horowhenua to the south.

PALMERSTON NORTH
pop 67,400

On the banks of the Manawatu River, Palmerston North is the principal centre of the Manawatu region and a major crossroads. With Massey University, the second-largest university in NZ, and several other colleges, Palmerston North has the relaxed feel of a rural university town.

Orientation & Information

The wide open expanse of The Square is the centre of town. You can get your bearings from a lookout on top of the Civic Centre building on The Square, open weekdays. George Street is Palmerston North's main eating and entertainment strip and also where you'll find boutique clothes shops.

BOOKSHOPS
Bruce McKenzie Booksellers (☎ 06-356 9922; booksparadise.net.nz; 51 George St)

EMERGENCY
For fire, police and ambulance call ☎ 111

INTERNET ACCESS
i Cafe (☎ 06-353 7899; cnr The Square & Fitzherbert Ave; 40min/1hr $2/3)
Internet cybercity (☎ 06-353 0777; 20 The Square; per hr $3)

PALMERSTON NORTH

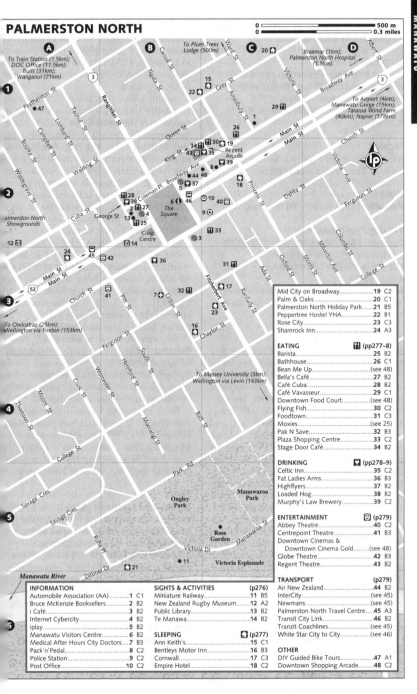

Mid City on Broadway.................**19** C2
Palm & Oaks..............................**20** C1
Palmerston North Holiday Park.....**21** B5
Peppertree Hostel YHA................**22** B1
Rose City..................................**23** C3
Shamrock Inn............................**24** A3

EATING   (pp277–8)
Barista.....................................**25** B2
Bathhouse................................**26** C1
Bean Me Up...........................(see 48)
Bella's Café..............................**27** B2
Café Cuba................................**28** B2
Café Vavasseur.........................**29** C1
Downtown Food Court.............(see 48)
Flying Fish................................**30** C2
Foodtown.................................**31** C3
Moxies..................................(see 25)
Pak N Save...............................**32** B3
Plaza Shopping Centre...............**33** C2
Stage Door Café........................**34** B2

DRINKING   (pp278–9)
Celtic Inn................................**35** C2
Fat Ladies Arms........................**36** B3
Highflyers................................**37** B2
Loaded Hog.............................**38** B2
Murphy's Law Brewery................**39** C2

ENTERTAINMENT   (p279)
Abbey Theatre..........................**40** C2
Centrepoint Theatre...................**41** B3
Downtown Cinemas &
   Downtown Cinema Gold........(see 48)
Globe Theatre...........................**42** B3
Regent Theatre.........................**43** B2

TRANSPORT   (p279)
Air New Zealand........................**44** B2
InterCity................................(see 45)
Newmans................................(see 45)
Palmerston North Travel Centre....**45** A3
Transit City Link........................**46** B2
Tranzit Coachlines...................(see 45)
White Star City to City..............(see 46)

OTHER
DIY Guided Bike Tours................**47** A1
Downtown Shopping Arcade........**48** C2

INFORMATION
Automobile Association (AA)...........**1** C1
Bruce McKenzie Booksellers...........**2** B2
i Café..**3** B2
Internet Cybercity.......................**4** B2
iplay...**5** B2
Manawatu Visitors Centre..............**6** B2
Medical After Hours City Doctors....**7** B3
Pack'n'Pedal..............................**8** C2
Police Station.............................**9** C2
Post Office................................**10** C2

SIGHTS & ACTIVITIES   (p276)
Miniature Railway......................**11** B5
New Zealand Rugby Museum.......**12** A2
Public Library............................**13** B2
Te Manawa...............................**14** B2

SLEEPING   (p277)
Ann Keith's...............................**15** C1
Bentleys Motor Inn....................**16** B3
Cornwall..................................**17** C3
Empire Hotel.............................**18** C2

iplay (☎ 06-357 4578; upstairs, 141 The Square; per hr $2) Charged by the minute, no flat rate.

MEDICAL SERVICES
Medical After Hours City Doctors (☎ 06-355 7737; www.tne-doctors.co.nz; 27 Linton St; ☺ 8am-9pm) The chemist next door is open until 10pm.
Palmerston North Hospital (☎ 06-356 9169; 50 Ruahine St)

MONEY
There are plenty of banks and ATMs around The Square and Main St.

POST
Post office (☎ 06-356 9495; 124 The Square)

TOURIST INFORMATION
Automobile Association (AA; ☎ 06-357 7039; 185 Broadway Ave; ☺ 8.30am-5pm Mon-Fri)
DOC (☎ 06-350 9700; 717 Tremaine Ave; ☺ 9.30am-4.30pm Mon-Fri)
Manawatu visitors centre (☎ 06-354 6593; www.manawatu nz.co.nz; The Square; ☺ 9am-5pm Mon-Fri, 10am-3pm Sat & Sun)

Sights & Activities
Te Manawa (☎ 06-355 5000; www.temanawa.co.nz; 396 Main St; museum & gallery admission free, Science Centre adult/child/family $6/4/15; ☺ 10am-5pm) has merged the museum, art gallery and science centre under one roof and there are substantial collections (around 55,000 items) exploring the concepts of 'life, art and mind'. Museum exhibits focus strongly on Maori culture and the gallery's emphasis is post-1960s NZ art, with installations, sculpture and photographs among other works. Stimulate your mind with interactive science and technology exhibits at the Science Centre – a popular section with children.

Victoria Esplanade (☺ 8am-6pm Apr-Sep, 8am-9pm Oct-Mar) is a beautiful park stretching along the shores of the Manawatu River. It has an excellent adventure playground with a flying fox and a small miniature railway. The **Rose Garden**, voted among the world's top-five most beautiful gardens in 2003, is magnificent if you're lucky enough to catch it in bloom. There are also plenty of peaceful nature and river walks.

Rugby fans shouldn't miss the **New Zealand Rugby Museum** (☎ 06-358 6947; www.rugby museum.co.nz; 87 Cuba St; adult/child $4/1; ☺ 10am-noon & 1.30-4pm Mon-Sat, 1.30-4pm Sun). This interesting museum contains exhibits and memora bilia relating to the history of rugby in NZ from the first game played in the country in Nelson in 1870, up to the present. It als has mementos from every country wher rugby is played.

About 15km northeast of Palmersto North the SH2 to Napier runs through th spectacular **Manawatu Gorge**. Maoris name the gorge Te Apiti (the Narrow Passage and believed that the big reddish roc in the river, near the centre of the gorg was its guardian spirit. The rock's colou is thought to change in intensity when prominent Rangitane tribe member dies o sheds blood. It takes around 3½ hours t walk the gorge and you can start at eithe end. (See also Tours, below.)

On the southeastern edge of the gorg about 40 minutes drive from Palmersto North, is the **Tararua Wind Farm** (☎ 06-574 480 Hall Block Rd), claimed to be the largest win farm in the southern hemisphere. From th top of Hall Block Rd there are spectacula views of the turbines and on a clear day yo can see both oceans and the South Island.

You can meet some native NZ owls a **Owlcatraz** (☎ 06-363 7872; www.owlcatraz.co.nz; Ma Rd South; adult/child $13/6; ☺ 9am-4pm) and wand through native bush. It's a 40 minute driv from Palmerston North and package tou are also available (see Tours, below).

Keen mountain bikers should head t **Pack'n'Pedal** (☎ 06-355 3338; www.packnpedal.co. 469 Main St). It's affiliated with the Manawat Mountain Bike Club and has maps and a vice about local cycling trails. It also se camping supplies and does bike repairs.

Tours
Big Owlcatraz Experience (☎ 06-362 7872; www.owlcatraz.co.nz; tours $60; ☺ 9am-4pm Mon-Fri) Includes door-to-door pick up, morning tea, lunch and afternoon tea, and a visit to another attraction.
DIY Guided Bike Tours (☎ 0508 440 440; 190 Featherston St; tours adult/child $25/free; ☺ 9am-4pm) Yo are supplied with a bike, map and audio commentary.
Feilding Saleyards (☎ 06-323 3318; www.feilding .nz; 10 Manchester Sq, Feilding; tours $5; ☺ 11am Fri) Local farmers show you the art of selling livestock.
Manawatu Gorge Adventures (☎ 0800 746 688; manawatugorge@xtra.co.nz; half-/full-day tours $60) Guided kayak trips along Manawatu Gorge, Rangitikei River and Whanganui River. Also has canoe and kayak hi Bookings essential.

Physical Freedom (☎ 06-329 4060; man-jet-tours@ inspire.net.nz; tours $40-140) Offers guided kayak trips through Manawatu Gorge.

Sleeping

Palmerston North has a wide range of accommodation, from budget motels and hostels, charming B&Bs and an exorbitant array of mid-range motels – just head to 'motel row' on Fitzherbert Ave, south of The Square. The visitors centre has comprehensive lists of homestays and B&Bs in the area.

BUDGET

Peppertree Hostel YHA (☎ 06-355 4054; peppertree hostel@clear.net.nz; 121 Grey St; dm/s/d $20/40/47) Decorated almost exclusively in lime green, this long-running hostel (15 years) is the best budget option – last check in at 10.30pm. Foam mattresses are thick, there's a well-appointed kitchen, open fireplace and a homey atmosphere.

Ann Keith's (☎ 06-358 6928; ak1@clear.net.nz; 123 & 146 Grey St; s/d $60/75) Next door to Peppertree Hostel is Ann Keith's B&B. Rooms here have private bathrooms, TV and tea- and coffee-making equipment, as well as electric blankets. The owners also run a relaxed hostel further down Grey St but the B&B is your best option.

Shamrock Inn (☎ 06-355 2130; www.shamrock.co.nz; 267 Main St; s $30-45, d $40-55) Classic pub accommodation at this friendly, old-fashioned boozer.

Palmerston North Holiday Park (☎ 06-358 0349; 133 Dittmer Dr; camp sites/campervan sites $20/22, cabins $30-45, tourist flats $60) Off Ruha Pl, this is a shady park with a pretty aspect beside the Victoria Esplanade. It's about 2km from The Square.

MID-RANGE

Cornwall (☎ 0800 170 000, 06-354 9010; www.corn wallmotorlodge.co.nz; 101 Fitzherbert Ave; apt $125-165) Cornwall has 27 enormous self-contained studio apartments. Rooms have a spa, Sky TV, super king-size beds and upstairs rooms have balconies. Double-glazed windows cut the noise from Fitzherbert Ave. An excellent, well-priced option.

Braemar (☎ 0800 355 805, 06-355 8053; www .braemarmotorlodge.co.nz; 177 Ruahine St; r $95-115, f $165) Studio units with TV, spa and stereo – some have a sitting area. Units on the street are noisy but those set back are great.

Palm & Oaks (☎ 06-359 0755; www.thepalm-oaks .co.nz; 183 Grey St; villa $155-250) This plush two-storey house is modern and elegant and has everything you could possibly need, including a spa, dishwasher, garage, balcony, garden and even the use of a tennis court.

Mid City on Broadway (☎ 06-357 2184; www.Mid -City.co.nz; 129 Broadway Ave; s/d from $70/80, f $120-160) Slap-bang on Broadway Ave, right in the town centre, this is a big motel with a variety of good-value, clean rooms. All units have cooking facilities and Sky TV.

Rose City (☎ 0508 356 538, 06-356 5388; fax 06-356 5085; 120 Fitzherbert Ave; units $100-125) These townhouse-style units are spacious and great value. They're comfortable and clean with a full kitchen and newish carpets.

Empire Hotel (☎ 06-357 8002, fax 06-357 7157; cnr Princess & Main Sts; s/d/f $70/75/135, meals $14-25) Clean upstairs motel rooms with private bathroom, TV, fridge, new sheets and phone. There's a wide veranda overlooking the main street. Downstairs are four separate bars, including a sports bar, and the à la carte Cobb and Co restaurant.

TOP END

Bentleys Motor Inn (☎ 0800 2368 5397; www.bentleys motorinn.co.nz; cnr Linton & Chaytor Sts; studio/apt with spa $125/150) Superb five-star modern apartments that are worth every cent. Apartments are beautiful and spacious with new appliances, stereos, contemporary furnishings, Sky TV and a spa that can heat to 39°. It often has cheaper rates.

Plum Trees Lodge (☎ 06-358 7813; www.manawatu nz.co.nz/Pages/Accommodation/44.php; 97 Russell St; s/d $200/400) Accommodation here is in a beautifully kept and secluded self-contained cottage, complete with balcony. A breakfast hamper is included in the price.

Eating

Palmerston North has a great selection of cafés and bar/restaurants serving high quality food at relatively inexpensive prices to cater for the town's student population.

Moxies (☎ 06-355 4238; cnr George & Main Sts; all-day menu $8.50-12, dinner $17-25; ☺ breakfast, lunch & dinner) This corner café is a cheerful place decked out in reds, blues and greens with big windows. Staff are equally cheerful and the all-day menu is top value – terrific omelettes. Sweet tooths will be transfixed by Moxie's lolly counter.

Café Cuba (☎ 06-356 5750; cnr George & Cuba Sts; all-day menu $7-13, dinner $13-25; ♥ breakfast, lunch & dinner) Those in search of sugar should proceed to Café Cuba (do not pass go, do not collect $200). The Galliano and Cointreau chocolate pâté is for professional chocoholics only and forget truffling in France – the Drambuie and Baileys taste explosions are all the truffle you need. This relaxed café also has a great menu with manuka-smoked salmon, venison and chicken curry served with roti bread.

Flying Fish (☎ 06-359 9270; Regent Arcade; meals $9-30; ♥ dinner) An innovative, stylish and relaxing Pacific sushi cocktail bar that 'doesn't do cream'. The emphasis here is on restorative, quality food and the flexible menu has some tantalising options – try a blackened scallop or spinach and pine nut sushi rolls, crisp sashimi sets and fresh plump oysters. The NZ-based wine list is comprehensive and alcoholic cocktails are mixed with fresh fruit juices.

Stage Door Cafe (☎ 06-359 2233; Regent Arcade; mains $6-12; ♥ lunch) A low-key affair with spiky green plants, contemporary orange plastic chairs and a retro red couch area. Stage Door is a mellow spot to while away some time with a smoothie and a sandwich.

Bella's Café (☎ 06-357 8616; 2 The Square; lunch $12-17, dinner $22-25; ♥ lunch Tue-Sat, dinner Mon-Sat) Beautifully lit with candles by night, the warm-red walls create an inviting atmosphere at this restaurant popular with a 50-something crowd. Service is professional and the Italian menu has a range of pastas such as spaghettini funghi and fettuccini pollo, with crème brûlée for dessert. The wine list is small but offers a quality selection.

Barista (☎ 06-357 2614; www.barista.co.nz; 77 George St; mains $11-18; ♥ breakfast, lunch & dinner) Big, popular and fancy café/restaurant with the menu offering such delicacies as lemon, lime and chilli prawns, kumara and corn fritters, and sautéed zucchini flower with buffalo mozzarella, asparagus, watercress and olive oil. Coffee is rich and strong. Art by local artists is exhibited on the walls.

Bathhouse (☎ 06-355 0051; 161 Broadway Ave; brunch $15-28, dinner $16-30; ♥ lunch & dinner) Furnished with gold gilt mirrors, a huge open fire and swanky couches, Bathhouse is a stylish restaurant that sometimes has jazz sessions. Thursday and Friday attract a business crowd but at weekends the Bathhouse is full of families who love to brunch.

Cafe Vavasseur (☎ 06-359 3167; 201 Broadway Ave; mains $20-30; ♥ dinner Tue-Sun) This up-market restaurant is simply and stylishly decorated with chocolate-brown walls and wooden floorboards and tables. The quality food here is extremely tasty.

Bean Me Up (☎ 06-357 1456; Downtown shopping arcade, Broadway Ave; meals $2.80-4.50; ♥ lunch) This small espresso bar/café is great for a quick bite and a superb coffee. It has two blends of coffee and cheap pies, salads, fresh sandwiches and brownies.

On Broadway Ave, Downtown Food Court offers Chinese, fish and chips, coffee etc. It's open late to cater to movie-goers. For self-caterers, the **Foodtown** (Ferguson St) supermarket is at the rear of the Plaza shopping centre. **Pak N Save** (Ferguson St) is a bit further along.

Drinking
Nightlife fluctuates according to the student year and is quieter during the holidays. Cafés and bars along George St and Broadway Ave are popular. The Regent Arcade is a fertile hunting ground for drinkers.

Fat Ladies Arms (☎ 06-358 8888; cnr Church & Linton Sts) A country-themed bar – Cowgirl's Heaven is the ladies toilet – that's packed with students during semester. Bands play from Wednesday to Saturday and 'the Fats' is definitely the place to go off. Rural types whoop it up with grunge queens, dancing until late – Friday night is techno night.

Celtic Inn (☎ 06-357 5571; Regent Arcade; meals $12-16) A classic Irish pub (note: this is not a theme pub) with darts and a pool table, red velvet chairs, green carpet and historic memorabilia everywhere. Head here for a few jars and watch live bands play Thursday to Saturday. Breakfast is served all day, and the menu ranges from Mulligan's green-lipped mussels to haggis.

Loaded Hog (☎ 06-356 5417; Coleman Pl; mains $15-25) A massive barn-like venue with pitchforks, manacles and a host of other rustic farmer art. It's busy at lunch and dinner and there's dancing later in the evening.

Murphy's Law Brewery (☎ 06-355 2337; murphys lawpn@xtra.co.nz; meals $9-20) Murphy's is replete with leather couches, a handmade granite and slate fireplace, old copper bar and big wooden barrels. It's popular with the business crowd for lunch and is full of 20-somethings Friday and Saturday nights. Live bands play Thursday to Saturday.

Highflyers (☎ 06-357 5155; cnr The Square & Main St; mains $10-25; ⊙ until 3am) In the old post office building, Highflyers is massive, with exposed brick and a big bar at its centre. DJs spin tracks from a platform and pack the house Thursday to Saturday nights. Friday happy hour (5pm to 7pm) is popular with thank-God-it's-Friday workers.

Entertainment

Downtown Cinemas & Downtown Cinema Gold (☎ 06-355 5656; www.dtcinemas.co.nz, www.cinemagold .co.nz; Downtown shopping arcade; tickets $12) The large Downtown Cinemas shows new-release flicks as well as arthouse films. For the ultimate in comfort, check out Downtown Cinema Gold.

Centrepoint Theatre (☎ 06-354 5740; www.centre point.co.nz; Church St) Hosts bigger-name professional performances, theatre sports and seasonal plays.

Globe Theatre (☎ 06-358 8699; cnr Pitt & Main Sts) A large community theatre showing a range of performances.

Abbey Theatre (☎ 06-355 0499; 369-73 Church St) Showing a range of quality amateur performances, with a predilection for musicals.

Regent Theatre (☎ 06-350 2100; Broadway Ave) This beautiful theatre hosts big events such as Peter Pan ballet and the Freddie Mercury Tribute show.

Getting There & Away

AIR

Palmerston North International Airport (☎ 06-351 4415; www.pnairport.co.nz; Airport Dr) is on the northern outskirts of town; planes are often diverted here when inclement weather prevents them landing in Wellington. From Australia, **Freedom Air** (☎ 0800 600 500, 09-523 8686; www.freedomair.com) has a direct flight one to four days per week to/from Sydney (one-way $280, 3¾ hours), Brisbane ($260, four hours) and Melbourne ($210, 4¼ hours). These flights can often be the cheapest option for getting to NZ. Flights take around 30 minutes less if departing from Australia.

Air New Zealand (☎ 06-351 8800; www.airnz.co.nz; 30 Broadway Ave) has direct flights from Palmerston North to Auckland ($110, one hour, six to seven daily), Christchurch ($120, 1¼ hours, eight daily), Hamilton ($120, 50 minutes, two daily Monday to Friday) and Wellington ($95, 30 minutes, three daily), with onward connections.

Origin Pacific (☎ 0800 302 302; www.originpacific .co.nz) has direct flights to/from Auckland (one way $120, 50 minutes, two daily) and Nelson (one way $135, 45 minutes, two daily) with onward connections to other centres.

BUS

InterCity (☎ 04-472 5111; www.intercitycoach.co.nz; ⊙ 7am-9pm), **Newmans** (☎ 04-499 3261; www.new manscoach.co.nz; ⊙ 7am-9pm) and **Tranzit Coachlines** (☎ 0800 471 227, 06-377 1227; www.tranzit.co.nz; ⊙ 8am-5pm) operate from the **Palmerston North Travel Centre** (☎ 06-355 4955; cnr Main & Pitt Sts). Some direct services between Auckland and Wellington bypass Palmerston North, stopping instead at the nearby township of Bulls.

InterCity and Newmans run frequent services from Palmerston North to most North Island destinations, including Wellington ($27, 2¼ hours, five daily), Auckland ($72, nine hours, two daily), Napier ($78, six hours 50 minutes, three daily), New Plymouth ($27, four hours, six to seven daily) and Wanganui ($15, 1¾ hours, four daily).

Tranzit Coachlines operates a service to Masterton and on to Wellington ($30, two hours).

White Star City to City (☎ 06-358 8777) operates from the Tranzit bus stop on Main St, near The Square, with regular daily services to Wellington ($20, 2¼ hours) and New Plymouth ($42, four hours).

TRAIN

The **train station** (☎ 0800 802 802; Mathews Ave) is off Tremaine Ave, about 12 blocks north of The Square. **Tranz Scenic** (☎ 0800 872 467, 04-495 0775; www.tranzscenic.co.nz; ⊙ 7am-7pm) long-distance trains between Wellington and Auckland stop at Palmerston North. On weekdays, the peak-hour *Capital Connection* travels from Palmerston North to Wellington ($20, two hours 10 minutes, one daily).

Getting Around

A taxi from the airport to the CBD takes around 12 minutes and costs between $10 and $14.

Transit City Link (☎ 06-355 4955; one way $2; ⊙ 6.45am-5.50pm Mon-Fri, 8.30am-2.55pm Sat & Sun) minibuses operate from the bus stop in the middle of Main St, on the east side of The Square. The No 12 bus goes to Massey University but none go to the airport.

Central Plateau

CONTENTS

Tongariro & Around	**282**
Tongariro National Park	282
National Park	289
Ohakune	291
Raetihi	294
Lake Rotokura	295
Waiouru	295
Lake Taupo Region	**295**
Taupo	295
Around Taupo	304
Turangi	308

The Central Plateau, with its dramatic landscapes of snow-capped volcanic peaks, extensive, lush forest and fast-flowing fish-teeming rivers, in many ways presents the most popular, and popularised, image of unspoilt, outdoorsy New Zealand. It's one of the best areas of the country to come for skiing, hiking, sailing and especially trout fishing, on the internationally renowned Tongariro River. At the heart of the region is magnificent Lake Taupo, the largest in the country, created in its present form by a massive volcanic blast some 1800 years ago. The Taupo Volcanic Zone stretches in a line from White Island, north of the Bay of Plenty, through Rotorua and down to Tongariro National Park, with its range of walking routes, including the awesome Tongariro Crossing.

The city of Taupo, on the northern shore of Lake Taupo, has long been on every backpacker's hit list, and offers all the adrenalin-pumping activities you could wish for, including jetboating, skydiving, white-water rafting, bungy jumping (the area has one of NZ's most popular spots) and quad-biking. The less-hyped-up can pass the day with a round of golf, or a spa and massage. Taupo also has a huge choice of excellent restaurants and plenty of bars and cafés in which to while away a wet afternoon.

At the southern edge of Lake Taupo, Turangi is acknowledged as one of the world's best trout-fishing centres, and attracts a steady stream of international anglers, while beyond, in the vast Tongariro National Park, lie the Whakapapa and Turoa ski fields, amongst New Zealand's finest winter-sports venues.

HIGHLIGHTS

- Visiting **Tongariro National Park** (p282), which is dominated by smoking Mt Ruapehu
- Walking the famous **Tongariro Crossing** (p284) and the **Tongariro Northern Circuit** (p284)
- Trout fishing on **Tongariro River** (p309) or boating on **Lake Taupo** (p298)
- Indulging in a spa and massage at **Taupo Hot Springs** (p297)
- Skiing at **Whakapapa** (p288) and **Turoa** (p288)
- Exploring the fascinating 'lost valley' of **Orakei Korako** (p308)
- Getting an adrenalin rush by skydiving or bungy jumping in **Taupo** (p298)

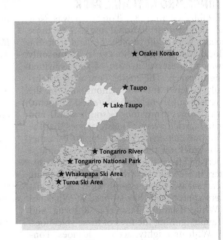

- TELEPHONE CODE: 07
- www.laketauponz.com
- www.ruapehunz.com

Climate

Due to its altitude, the Central Plateau has a generally cool climate, with temperatures ranging from around 3°C in winter up to a maximum of around 24°C in summer. Above 2500m there is a small year-round snowfield, while July to October is the skiing season in Whakapapa and Ohakune, and in places snow can linger on into spring. On the mountains, storms and freezing temperatures can occur at any time.

Getting There & Around

Air New Zealand has flights from Taupo to Auckland and Wellington; Origin Pacific flies from here to Christchurch and Nelson. There are also charter flights linking Auckland with the Whakapapa Ski Area, including those run by Mountain Air. Tranz Scenic trains on the Auckland–Wellington line stop at National Park. From Taupo, InterCity buses connect with most major destinations around New Zealand. There are several private shuttle-bus services operating around Tongariro National Park, and serving the snowfields in winter, while the Purpil People Mover Shuttle runs between Taupo and Napier on weekdays.

TONGARIRO & AROUND

TONGARIRO NATIONAL PARK

Established in 1887, Tongariro was New Zealand's first national park. The three peaks were a gift to New Zealand from the local Maori tribe who saw it as the only way to preserve an area of such spiritual significance. The name Tongariro originally covered the three mountains of the park (Tongariro, Ngauruhoe and Ruapehu) and comes from *tonga* (south wind) and *riro* (carried away). The story goes that the famous *tohunga* (priest) Ngatoro-i-rangi was stuck on the summit and had almost perished from the cold. He called to his sisters in Hawaiki for fire, saying he was being 'carried away by the south wind'. As the sisters approached they stopped at Whakaari (White Island), Tarawera, Rotorua and Taupo, igniting the fires of these volcanoes.

With its mighty, active volcanoes, Tongariro is one of NZ's most spectacular parks, recently playing the role of 'Mordor' in Peter Jackson's *Lord of the Rings* trilogy.

In summer it offers excellent walks and tramps, most notably the Tongariro Northern Circuit and the Tongariro Crossing. In winter it's a busy ski area.

Information

The **visitors centre** (☎ 07-892 3729; fax 07-892 3814; ⏰ 8am-5pm May-Nov, 8am-6pm Dec-Apr) in Whakapapa (pronounced 'fa-ka-pa-pa') Village is on the northwestern side of the park. It has maps and lots of information on the park, including walks, huts and current skiing, track and weather conditions. The many displays on the geological and human history of the park, plus a small shop, make the centre an interesting place to visit. The detailed *Tongariro National Park* map ($15) is worth buying before you go tramping. The Department of Conservation (DOC) produces a number of handy brochures on all walks in the park.

DOC centres serving the park are in Ohakune (p291) and Turangi (p308). From late December to late January DOC offers an excellent array of guided walks in and around the park; ask at park centres for brochures and information.

If you are visiting Tongariro National Park, remember that much of it experiences alpine conditions, which means that weather can change faster than you can say 'Where did all those clouds come from?' See the boxed text on p287 for safety tips before setting out on your adventure.

Mt Ruapehu

The long, multi-peaked summit of Mt Ruapehu (2797m) is the highest and most active of the volcanoes. The upper slopes were showered with hot mud and water in the volcanic activity of 1969 and 1975, and in December 1988 the volcano threw out some hot rocks. These were just tame precursors to the spectacular eruptions of September 1995, when Ruapehu sprayed volcanic rock and emitted massive clouds of ash and steam. From June to September the following year the mountain rumbled, groaned and sent ash clouds high into the sky. The 1996 ski season was pretty much a write-off, and local businesses really felt the pinch. The locals in Ohakune set up deck chairs at the end of their main street, sipped wine and observed the mountain's antics.

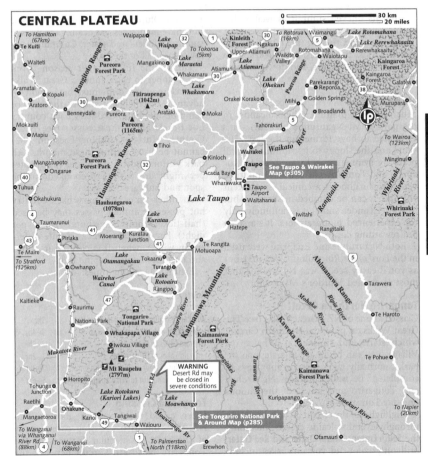

CENTRAL PLATEAU

These eruptions were not the worst of the century, however. Between 1945 and 1947 the level of Crater Lake rose dramatically when eruptions blocked the overflow. On Christmas Eve 1953 the overflow burst and the flood led to one of NZ's worst natural disasters. The volcanic mudflow (known as a lahar) swept away a railway bridge at Tangiwai (between Ohakune and Waiouru) moments before a crowded express train arrived and 153 people lost their lives in the resulting collision.

The 1995–96 eruption has once again blocked the overflow of Ruapehu's Crater Lake and has caused it to fill once more. Scientists have predicted that if the lake continues to fill at its current rate, a lahar will occur sometime in the not too distant future. A major lahar has the potential to cause damage to the road and rail bridges at Tangiwai, parts of State Highway 1 (SH1) and could possibly spill over into the headwaters of the Tongariro River. This is the worst case scenario; the Crater Lake may just leak through the dam and trickle away. DOC has set up alarm systems at Crater Lake's edge to monitor its build up so that locals and emergency teams have plenty of warning should it decide to burst its banks.

Mt Tongariro

Another old, but still active, volcano is Mt Tongariro (1967m). Red Crater last erupted in 1926. It has a number of coloured lakes dotting its uneven summit as well as hot springs gushing out of its side at Ketetahi. The Tongariro Crossing (see p284), a magnificent walk, passes beside the lakes, right through several craters, and down through lush native forest.

Mt Ngauruhoe

Much younger than the other volcanoes in the park is Mt Ngauruhoe (2287m) – it's estimated to have formed in the last 2500 years and the slopes to its summit are still perfectly symmetrical. In contrast to Ruapehu and Tongariro, which have multiple vents, Ngauruhoe is a conical, single-vent volcano. It can be climbed in summer, but in winter (under snow) it is definitely only for experienced mountaineers. It's a steep but rewarding climb.

Both Ngauruhoe and Ruapehu were used in the *Lord of the Rings* films (2001–03), but as you'll easily see, it was Ngauruhoe that most resembled Mordor's Mt Doom.

Tongariro Northern Circuit

Classed as one of NZ's Great Walks (see The Great Walks on p80), the Northern Circuit, which starts and finishes at Whakapapa Village (you can begin at Mangatepopo car park), normally takes three to four days to complete. The walk embraces Ngauruhoe and Tongariro and much of the famous one-day Tongariro Crossing.

Highlights of the circuit include tramping through several volcanic craters, including the **South Crater**, **Central Crater** and **Red Crater**; brilliantly colourful volcanic lakes including the **Emerald Lakes**, **Blue Lake** and the **Upper** and **Lower Tama Lakes**; the cold **Soda Springs** and **Ohinepango Springs**; and various other volcanic formations including **cones**, **lava flows** and **glacial valleys**.

There are several possibilities for side trips that take from a few hours to overnight. The most popular side trip from the main track is to Ngauruhoe summit (three hours), but it is also possible to climb Tongariro from Red Crater (two hours) or walk to Ohinepango Springs from New Waihohonu Hut (30 minutes).

WALKING THE TRACK

The safest and most popular time to walk the track is from December to March. The track is served by four huts: Mangatepopo,

Ketetahi, Oturere and New Waihohonu. The huts have mattresses, gas heating (cookers in summer), toilets and water. Camping is allowed near all of the huts.

During the full summer season (from late October to early June) a Great Walks Pass is required and must be bought in advance, whether you stay in the huts or camp beside them. Ordinary back-country hut tickets and annual passes (see Back-Country Hut & Camping Fees on p82) cannot be used during these months. All park visitors centres sell passes (camp sites per night are $20/25 prebooked/on the spot, and huts are $30/35).

At other times, ordinary back-country hut passes or annual passes may be used (half-ticket camp sites/huts $10/20 per night). However, this track is quite different in winter, when it is covered in snow, and becomes a tough alpine trek.

Estimated walking times:

Route	Time
Whakapapa Village to Mangatepopo Hut	3hr
Mangatepopo Hut to Emerald Lakes	3–4hr
Emerald Lakes to Ketetahi Hut	2–3hr
Emerald Lakes to Oturere Hut	1–2hr
Oturere Hut to New Waihohonu Hut	2–3hr
New Waihohonu Hut to Whakapapa Village	5–6hr

Tongariro Crossing

Often called the finest one-day walk in NZ, the Tongariro Crossing covers many of the most spectacular features of the Tongariro Northern Circuit between the Mangatepopo and Ketetahi Huts. On a clear day the views are magnificent. This is what many trampers do on day two of the Northern Circuit, with the extra walk along the Ketetahi track. Because of its popularity, shuttles are available to both ends of the track. The Tongariro Crossing can be reached from Mangatepopo Rd off SH47.

There are a couple of steep spots, but most of the track is not terribly difficult. However it is a long, exhausting day's walk. It's billed as a six- to seven-hour walk, but expect it to take longer if you're not in top condition. Some prefer to do it as a two-day walk, especially if side trips are included.

The track passes through vegetation zones ranging from alpine scrub and tussock, to places at higher altitudes where

TONGARIRO NATIONAL PARK & AROUND

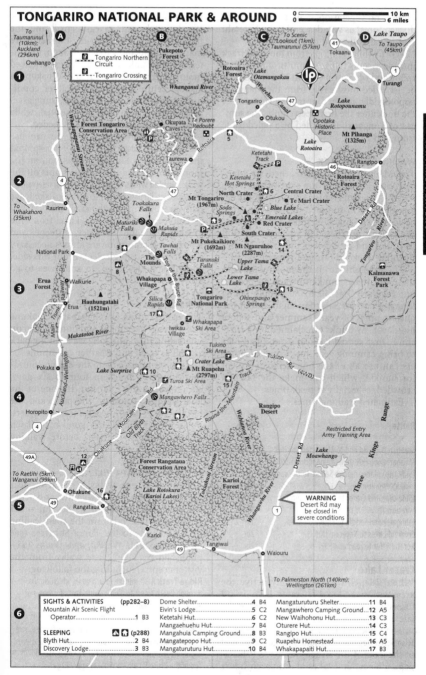

CENTRAL PLATEAU

SIGHTS & ACTIVITIES	(pp282–8)	Dome Shelter	4 B4	Mangaturuturu Shelter	11 B4
Mountain Air Scenic Flight		Eivin's Lodge	5 C2	Mangawhero Camping Ground	12 A5
Operator	1 B3	Ketetahi Hut	6 C2	New Waihohonu Hut	13 C3
		Mangaehuehu Hut	7 B4	Oturere Hut	14 C3
SLEEPING	(p288)	Mangahuia Camping Ground	8 B3	Rangipo Hut	15 C4
Blyth Hut	2 B4	Mangatepopo Hut	9 C2	Ruapehu Homestead	16 A5
Discovery Lodge	3 B3	Mangaturuturu Hut	10 B4	Whakapapaiti Hut	17 B3

there is no vegetation at all, to the lush podocarp forest as you descend from Ketetahi Hut towards the end of the track.

Worthwhile side trips from the main track include ascents to the summits of Mt Ngauruhoe and Mt Tongariro. Mt Ngauruhoe can be ascended most easily from the Mangatepopo Saddle, reached near the beginning of the track after the first steep climb. The summit of Tongariro is reached by a poled route from Red Crater.

WALKING THE TRACK

The Mangatepopo Hut, reached via Mangatepopo Rd, is near the start of the track, and the Ketetahi Hut is a couple of hours before the end. In summer, to stay at or camp beside either hut you must have a Great Walks Pass, purchased in advance and valid from the end of October until the Queen's Birthday weekend (around 1 June).

The Ketetahi Hut is the most popular in the park. It has bunks to sleep 24 people, but regularly has 50 to 60 people trying to stay there on Saturday night and at the busiest times of year (summer and school holidays). As bunks are claimed on a first-come, first-served basis, it's not a bad idea to bring camping gear, just in case. Campers can use all of the hut facilities (except for bunks), which can make the kitchen crowded, especially at peak times.

Estimated walking times:

Route	Time
Mangatepopo Rd end to Mangatepopo Hut	15min
Mangatepopo Hut to Mangatepopo Saddle	1½hr
(Side trip) Mangatepopo Saddle to the summit of Mt Ngauruhoe	3hr return
(Side trip) Red Crater to Tongariro summit return	1½hr
Mangatepopo Saddle to Emerald Lakes	1½–2hr
Emerald Lakes to Ketetahi Hut	2hr
Ketetahi Hut to road end	2hr

Crater Lake

When Ruapehu is volcanically active the area within 1.5km of Crater Lake is off limits; check with DOC park offices for the latest information.

The walk to Crater Lake in the crater of Ruapehu begins at Iwikau Village, at the end of the Top of the Bruce Rd above Whakapapa Village, and takes about seven hours

return (four hours up, three hours down). It's definitely not an easy stroll and the track isn't marked. Even in summer there may be ice and snow to get through; in winter, forget it unless you are an experienced mountaineer. Check with the Whakapapa visitors centre for current weather conditions before you set off. Boots, sunglasses and windproofs are always essential, while ice axes and crampons may be needed.

From December to April you can use the **chair lift** (adult/child $17/9; 🕙 9am-4pm) at the Whakapapa Ski Area to get you up the mountain, cutting about three hours off the walk. **Guided walks** (☎ 07-892 3738 for reservations; adult/child incl lift pass $65/45) to Crater Lake leave daily at 9.30am from the chair lift.

You can reach Crater Lake from the Ohakune side, but the track is steeper and ice axes and crampons are always necessary (to ascend a steep glacier). From this side, allow five hours to go up and three to go down.

Other Walks

The visitor centres at Whakapapa, Ohakune and Turangi have maps and information on interesting short and long walks in the park as well as track and weather conditions.

Keen trampers can do the entire Round-the-Mountain Track in four to six days, circumnavigating Ruapehu. It's one of the least-tramped tracks in the park, and the terrain varies from beech forest to desert. Be sure to get hold of a good map (such as Parkmaps No 273-04) before walking this track.

FROM WHAKAPAPA VILLAGE

A number of fine walks begin at or near the Whakapapa visitors centre and from the road leading up to it. Several other good walks take off from the road leading from Ohakune to the Turoa Ski Area (see Ohakune p291). *Whakapapa Walks* ($1), published by DOC, lists walks from the visitors centre, including the following.

Ridge Track A 30-minute return walk, which climbs through beech forest to alpine shrub lands for views of Ruapehu and Ngauruhoe.

Silica Rapids A 2½-hour, 7km loop track to the Silica Rapids, named for the silica mineral deposits formed here by the rapids on Waikare Stream. The track passes interesting alpine features and, in the final 2.5km, passes down Top of the Bruce Rd above Whakapapa Village.

TRACK SAFETY

The weather on the mountains is extremely capricious – it can change from warm, brilliant sunshine to snow, hail or wind within a few minutes. Be sure to check with one of the DOC offices for current track and weather conditions before setting out. Bring a raincoat and warm woollen clothing. Take local advice seriously: they know the mountains best and it's their time, money and effort that's going to be expended getting you back safe and sound.

Accidents occur on tracks when people misjudge loose rocks or go sliding down the volcanic slopes, so watch your step! On Ngauruhoe, watch out for loose scoria, and be careful not to dislodge rocks onto people coming up behind.

Essential equipment for walking in the park:

- waterproof raincoat and overtrousers
- warm clothing
- tramping boots
- food and drink
- first aid kit
- suncream and sunglasses
- sunhat and warm hat

In winter, alpine or mountaineering experience is essential if you are walking many tracks, especially climbing peaks. If you don't know how to use ice axes, crampons and avalanche gear, do not attempt the summits.

Tama Lakes A 17km track to the Tama Lakes (five to six hours return). On the Tama Saddle between Ruapehu and Ngauruhoe, the Tama Lakes are great for a refreshing swim. The upper lake affords fine views of Ngauruhoe and Tongariro (beware of winds on the saddle).

Taranaki Falls A two-hour, 6km loop track to the 20m Taranaki Falls on Wairere Stream.

Whakapapa Nature Walk A 15-minute loop track suitable for wheelchairs, beginning about 200m above the visitors centre and passing through beech forest and gardens typical of the park's vegetation zones.

NORTH OF WHAKAPAPA VILLAGE

Still more tracks take off from SH47, on the national park's north side, including the following.

Lake Rotoaira On the shores of Lake Rotoaira are excavations of a pre-European Maori village site.

Mahuia Rapids About 2km north of the turn-off leading to Whakapapa, SH47 crosses the Whakapapanui Stream just below the rapids.

Matariki Falls A 20-minute return track to the falls takes off from SH47 about 200m from the Mahuia Rapids car park.

Skiing

The two main ski areas are the Whakapapa Ski Area (1630m), above Whakapapa Village, and the Turoa Ski Area, to the south.

The Tukino Ski Area, on the eastern side of Ruapehu, is only accessible by a 4WD road.

The only accommodation at the ski fields is in private lodges, so most skiers stay at Whakapapa Village, National Park township or Ohakune. One pass is valid for both Whakapapa and Turoa. See Skiing on p72 for information on passes and the skiing area, or check www.whakapapa.co.nz.

Other Activities

The Grand Chateau in Whakapapa has a public nine-hole golf course and tennis courts, and hires out golf clubs, tennis rackets etc. Even if you're not staying here, stop in for a drink in the lobby just to savour the atmosphere.

Mountain Air (☎ 0800 922 812; www.mountainair .co.nz; flights from $70), with an office on SH47 near the SH48 turn-off to Whakapapa, has flights over the volcanoes.

Plateau Outdoor Adventure Guides (☎ /fax 07-892 2740) is based at Raurimu, 6km north of National Park township. It offers a wide variety of activities around Tongariro and the Whanganui River, including canoeing, kayaking, white-water rafting and tramping.

Outdoor Experiences (☎ 0800 806 369; www.tonga rironz.com) runs guided four-day canoe trips (adult/child $595/360) down the Whanganui River, departing Thursday and Saturday.

Sleeping

Whakapapa Village has a limited supply of accommodation. There are two DOC camping grounds within the park (near National Park and Ohakune), as well as huts, accessible only by walking tracks. Prices quoted here are for summer; rates are much higher in winter. National Park (p290), Ohakune (p292) and Turangi (p310) are towns near the park and offer a greater range of options.

BUDGET

Whakapapa Holiday Park (☎ 07-892 3897; whaka papaholpark@xtra.co.nz; dm/camp sites/d $20/25/55) This well-maintained and popular park is up the road from the Grand Chateau, opposite the visitors centre and 6km from the Whakapapa Ski Area. It's in a pretty spot and offers a wide range of accommodation options, including a 32-bed backpackers' lodge.

There are two basic DOC camping grounds: **Mangahuia Camping Ground** (SH47; camp sites $10) is between National Park and the SH48 turn-off heading to Whakapapa; and the **Mangawhero Camping Ground** (Ohakune Mountain Rd; camp sites $10), with a similar set-up, is near Ohakune. Both have cold water and pit toilets; and you place your fee in an honesty box.

Scattered around the park's tramping tracks are nine **huts** ($20), which have foot access only. You can camp beside the huts for $5 per person. Back-country hut tickets and annual hut passes are both acceptable. However, in the summer season a Great Walks Pass is required for the four Tongariro Northern Circuit huts: Ketetahi, Mangatepopo, New Waihohonu and Oturere. Pre-booked huts/camp sites cost $28/20, otherwise they cost $36/24.

All park visitor centres have information on huts and can sell hut tickets or Great Walks Passes. Howard's Lodge (p290) at National Park sells DOC hut tickets.

MID-RANGE

Skotel Alpine Resort (☎ 0800 756 835, 07-892 3719; www.skotel.co.nz; dm/d/chalets from $20/110/125; 💻) This is a cosy, woody hotel with a homely

and relaxing ambience. There's a choice of accommodation including self-contained chalets sleeping up to seven people, while facilities include a sauna, spa pool, gym, ski shop, games room and a licensed restaurant and bar. Prices increase during peak winter and summer periods, and you'll pay a $50 surcharge for Saturday-night stays during the winter. Bedding for dorm rooms costs $5.

TOP END

Grand Chateau Hotel (☎ 0800 242 832, 07-892 3809; www.chateau.co.nz; d/f/ste from $125/225/450; 💻 🐕) The Chateau is a grand old place. It's built in the style of an English stately home and it originally opened in 1929. Today it is undoubtedly one of New Zealand's best-known hotels, enjoying a great location and offering some quite outstanding views. The opulent building has recently been refurbished and has all the facilities you would expect, including four restaurants, two bars, a cinema, tennis courts and a nine-hole golf course. Various packages are available.

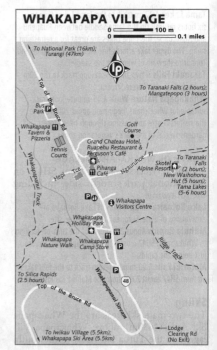

WHAKAPAPA VILLAGE

Eating

The Grand Chateau Hotel (opposite) has a good range of dining options, including the elegant á la carte **Ruapehu Restaurant** (mains around $25; ☾ dinner), **Ferguson's Café** (mains $8-10; ☾ lunch & dinner), and the convivial **Pihanga Café** (mains $15-20; ☾ lunch & dinner). The **Whakapapa Tavern & Pizzeria** (pizzas $8-10; ☾ lunch & dinner), on the main road, hosts occasional live entertainment in winter.

Skotel Alpine Resort (opposite) has a licensed **restaurant & bar** (mains around $15; ☾ dinner).

The Whakapapa Camp Store, on the main road, sells a range of takeaway snacks and food for self-catering. As usual it's more expensive from a store than a supermarket.

Getting There & Away
BUS & TRAIN

InterCity (☎ 09-913 6100) buses stop at National Park, the main gateway to Tongariro.

Tranz Scenic (☎ 0800 872 467; www.tranzscenic.co.nz) trains on the Auckland–Wellington line stop at National Park.

Alpine Scenic Tours (☎ 07-386 8918; www.alpinescenictours.co.nz; tickets $30) has a shuttle departing from Taupo (6.30am) to Whakapapa Village (arriving 8.25am) via Turangi (7.30am), Ketetahi car park (at the end of the Tongariro Crossing) and Mangatepopo car park (for the Tongariro Crossing). There are various shuttles running between Turangi, Whakapapa Village and National Park township during the day, and they go up to the ski area at Top of the Bruce Rd by request. Since seats are limited, book in advance to guarantee a spot.

Tongariro Track Transport (☎ 07-892 3716; tickets $20) is another option, specialising in the Tongariro Crossing and has buses departing from Whakapapa and National Park.

From National Park township other shuttles run to Whakapapa, Mangatepopo and Ketetahi for the Tongariro Crossing (see p291). Transport is also available from Ohakune (see p294).

CAR & MOTORCYCLE

The park is encircled by roads. SH1 (at this point it's called the Desert Road) passes down the eastern side of the park, SH4 passes down the western side, SH46 and SH47 cross the northern side and SH49 crosses the southern side. The main road up into the park is SH48, which leads to Whakapapa Village, continuing further up the mountain to Top of the Bruce Rd and the Whakapapa Ski Area. Ohakune Mountain Rd leads up to the Turoa Ski Area from Ohakune.

For the Tongariro Crossing, access is from the end of Mangatepopo Rd off SH47, and SH46 from the end of Ketetahi Rd off National Park Rd (between SH1 and SH47). Theft from parked vehicles is a problem at both ends: don't leave valuables in the car.

NATIONAL PARK
pop 460

At the gateway to Tongariro, this small settlement is at the junction of SH4 and SH47, 15km from Whakapapa Village. It caters to the ski-season crowds, with plenty of accommodation but little else apart from great views of Ruapehu. In the summer season it's one of the best bases for the walks and attractions of the park. Several daily shuttles leave from here to the start of the Tongariro Crossing and Whakapapa Village in summer, and the ski area in winter. It is also a base for other ventures, such as canoe trips on the Whanganui River.

About 20km south on SH4 at Horopito is a monument to the Last Spike – the spike that marked the completion of the Main Trunk Railway Line between Auckland and Wellington in 1908. Check out the website www.nationalpark.co.nz for more info.

Activities

Howard's Lodge (p290), Pukenui Lodge (p290) and Ski Haus (p290) hire out all necessary gear for the Tongariro Crossing and other treks. The spa pools at Ski Haus and Pukenui Lodge can be hired by non-guests as well.

Howard's Lodge takes **guided mountain-bike tours** (2hr from $20) and also provides transport and bike hire (from $20) for the 42nd Traverse – an excellent 46km mountain-bike trail through the Tongariro Forest, classed among the best one-day rides in NZ, and the 21km downhill Fishers Track.

Adrift Guided Outdoor Adventures (☎ 0800 462 374; www.adriftnz.co.nz) runs canoe adventures (adult/child one-day trip $230/200, six-day trip $800/650) and guided treks (from $135). **Tongariro River Rafting** (☎ 0800 101 024; www.tongariro-riverrafting.com) offers white-water rafting trips on the Tongariro River, as well as kayaking, fishing and mountain-biking excursions.

Horse treks can be arranged through **Tussock Trekkers** (☎ 07-892 2711). Treks range from one-hour rides to overnight excursions.

For those rainy days there's an 8m-high indoor **climbing wall** (☎ 07-892 2870; www.npbp .co.nz; Finlay St; admission $12, with own gear $9; ☙ 9am-9pm) at National Park Backpackers (below), which offers 55 different climbs.

Tongariro Track Transport (☎ 07-892 3716) provides transport for activities on the Tongariro Crossing. It runs daily to the crossing ($20 return), picking up from accommodation in National Park.

Sleeping

Prices increase dramatically in the ski season, when accommodation is tight and bookings are essential (especially on weekends). The prices following are for summer.

BUDGET

Ski Haus (☎ 07-892 2854; www.skihaus.co.nz; Carroll St; dm/camp sites/d from $20/30/70; ☐) Ski Haus is a cosy little wood-cabin affair that's been operating for a quarter of a century. It features an Alpine-style lounge with a welcoming log fire at its heart. It has a spa pool and billiards table for chilly evenings and there is a bar, kitchen and restaurant offering breakfast and dinner. Dorm rooms and doubles are simple but comfortable and there's also a 3-bedroom cottage (from $90) if you're after a bit more privacy.

Howard's Lodge (☎ /fax 07-892 2827; www.howards lodge.co.nz; 11-13 Carroll St; dm/d/ste from $20/55/120; ☐) Howard's Lodge has a spa pool, comfortable lounge and spotless, well-equipped kitchens. There's a variety of rooms to choose from, and meals are available at extra cost. Ski, snowboard, tramping gear and mountain-bike hire is available.

National Park Backpackers (☎ /fax 07-892 2870; www.npbp.co.nz; Finlay St; dm/camp sites/d from $20/25/50; ☐) This popular and welcoming backpackers next to Schnapps has basic but neat rooms, most with en-suite facilities. The big attraction is the 8m-high climbing wall (see Activities p289; discounted use for guests), and there's also a BBQ, hot tub and indoor badminton court.

Discovery Lodge (☎ 0800 122 122; www.discovery .net.nz; camp sites/dm/ste from $15/30/90; ☐) This lodge is on SH47, between National Park and Whakapapa. It has a spa pool, restaurant, bar and comfy lounge with a pool table and big-screen TV. Pricier backpacker cabins ($65) have en suite facilities and bedding, and there's room for campervans.

MID-RANGE

Adventure Lodge & Motel (☎ 07-892 2991; www .adventurenationalpark.co.nz; Carroll St; dm/d/ste from $20/80/120; ☐) Adventure Lodge is a friendly, laid-back, modern place with a wide choice of accommodation, and good package deals on offer. It has excellent facilities, including spa pools, volleyball, *boules* and a BBQ, and meals are available. Bring your own bedding for the dorm rooms or hire it for $7.

Pukenui Lodge (☎ 0800 785 368; www.tongariro.cc; Millar St; dm/d from $22/95; ☐) The picturesque Pukenui has a variety of rooms, including a smart self-contained 3-bedroom chalet (from $100). Prices rise on weekends, when dinner is included, and meals are available at other times. There is a spa, kitchen and restaurant, and the lodge sells lift passes and can organise Tongariro track transport and activities.

Mountain Heights Lodge (☎ /fax 07-892 2833; www.mountainheights.co.nz; d from $85) This friendly Swiss chalet–style lodge on SH4, 2km south of National Park, has good-quality, self-contained motel units that sleep up to six people, and comfortable en-suite rooms with TVs and tea-making facilities (breakfast included). Meals are available by arrangement, and mountain bikes can be hired (from $20 for two hours).

TOP END

Tongariro Crossing Lodge (☎ 07-892 2688; www .tongarirocrossinglodge.com; 37 Carroll St; ste from $160 ☐) This quiet, elegant colonial-style hotel offers a high standard of comfort in a very pleasant, secluded setting, with spacious tastefully furnished suites. There's a library and a restaurant that serves fine local cuisine. Dinner is $50 extra.

Eating

All of the places to stay in National Park provide meals or kitchens (or both) for their guests.

Basekamp (☎ 07-892 2872; Carroll St; burger around $6; ☙ lunch & dinner) Basekamp offers menu of 19 different hearty 'gourmet' burgers, as well as pizzas.

Eivin's Café (☎ 07-892 2844; Carroll St; mains $15-25; ☺ lunch & dinner) Eivin's is a cosy little café with a broad menu that includes pizza, pasta, steak and seafood.

Schnapps (☎ 07-892 2788; Findlay St; mains around $15; ☺ dinner) A congenial place for a drink or a meal. There are excellent pizzas, burgers, steaks and more, and in winter there are often bands on Saturday night.

Ski Haus (opposite) has a bar and restaurant that are open to both guests and non-guests in winter; and there is a licensed café at Mountain Heights Lodge (opposite).

Getting There & Away
AIR
Mountain Air (☎ 0800 922 812; www.mountainair.co.nz) runs charter flights between Auckland airport and Mt Ruapehu (same-day return per person from $1260) during the ski season. **Ski North Island Snow** (☎ 0800 854 041) does similar flights from Auckland to the Whakapapa Ski Area (from $500 per person).

BUS
InterCity (☎ 09-913 6100) buses arrive at and depart from outside Ski Haus on Carroll St daily except Saturday. Buy tickets at Ski Haus and Howard's Lodge. Journeys north to Auckland via Hamilton or south to Wellington via Palmerston North take about five hours.

Alpine Scenic Tours (☎ 07-386 8918) has twice-daily shuttles that make a round-trip between Turangi and National Park ($25), with stops at Whakapapa Village, Whakapapa Ski Area (by request), the Mangatepopo and Ketetahi car parks (Tongariro Crossing), and on from Turangi to Taupo. For the track ends, make sure you arrange transport beforehand, as there are no phones at the trail heads.

Tongariro Track Transport (☎ 07-892 3716) operates a daily shuttle from National Park to the Mangatepopo car park, stopping at Whakapapa Village on the way ($20 return). Howard's Lodge (opposite) also runs a shuttle for the Tongariro Crossing ($20 return); bookings are essential.

TRAIN
Some **trains** (☎ 0800 872 467) that run between Auckland and Wellington stop at National Park (one way from $35). Train tickets are sold not from the train station but from Ski Haus (p290) or Howard's Lodge (p290).

OHAKUNE
pop 1490

Pretty Ohakune is the closest town to the Turoa Ski Area, on the southern side of Ruapehu, and rejoices in the double honour of being the North Island's après ski capital, and NZ's Carrot Capital (the orange vegetable is grown in profusion locally). During the ski season a lot of effort goes into catering for those who've come to enjoy the snow, but visitors are discovering that there is plenty to do at other times, including hiking, canoeing, white-water rafting and horse riding.

Ohakune's main commercial district is to the south of the town on the highway. The northern end of town by the train station (known as the 'junction') comes alive during the ski season but is quiet otherwise.

Information
The Ruapehu **visitors centre** (☎ 0800 782 734, 06-385 8427; www.ruapehunz.com; 54 Clyde St; ☺ 9am-5pm Mon-Fri, 9am-3.30pm Sat & Sun) has an excellent 3D model of Tongariro National Park – great for tracing where you're going to walk. The staff make bookings for activities and accommodation, for InterCity buses, the *Interislander* ferry and for the train.

The **Ohakune Field Centre** (☎ 06-385 0010; www.ohakune.info; Ohakune Mountain Rd; ☺ 8am-3pm, to 5pm on public hols) has maps, weather reports and advice about this side of the Tongariro National Park.

The Turoa Ski Area operates a **phone line** (☎ 0900 99 333), which offers information on ski and road conditions.

Walking
Ohakune Mountain Rd stretches 17km from the northern end of Ohakune to the Turoa Ski Area on Mt Ruapehu. Several walking tracks lead off it into the national park. Stop by the Ohakune Field Centre for maps and information about the tracks. Weather on the mountains is highly changeable, so be prepared and let someone know your itinerary.

Two of the most delightful walks are the short 15-minute **Rimu Track** and the longer one-hour **Mangawhero Forest Walk**, both start from opposite the Field Centre and both pass through a lovely section of native forest. The Rimu Track is marked with plaques pointing out various features of the forest.

Popular tracks leading from Ohakune Mountain Rd include a 1½-hour return walk to the **Waitonga Falls**, beginning 11km past the Field Centre, and the five-hour return walk to **Lake Surprise**, beginning 4km further on. If you continue past the falls on the Waitonga Falls track, you'll join the Round-the-Mountain Track (see p286). Other tracks taking off from Ohakune Mountain Rd include a 10-minute return walk to the **Mangawhero Falls**, a four- to five-hour round-trip walk on the **Old Blyth Track**, and a five-hour return walk to **Lake Surprise**. Pick up the handy DOC brochure *Ohakune Walks and Mountain Road* ($1) from the Ruapehu visitors centre or Ohakune Field Centre.

Transport up Mt Ruapehu can be arranged through **Snowliner Shuttle** (☎ 06-385 8573) or **Snow Express** (☎ 06-385 4022). Expect to pay about $10 one way or $15 return. Or you could go to the top with a bicycle (see Cycling below) and do some tramping on your way down. Transport to Tongariro Crossing can be arranged through the **Ohakune Top 10 Holiday Park** (☎ 06-385 8561; return $25) or the **Ski Shed** (☎ 06-385 8887; www.skished.com; 61 Clyde St).

Cycling

Mountain bikes, as well as skis, snowboards and the like, can be rented at the **Powderhorn Ski Shop** (☎ 06-385 8888; www.powderhorn.co.nz; cnr Thames St & Mangawhero Tce), at Powderhorn Chateau, and the **Ski Shed** (☎ 06-385 8887; www.skished.com; 61 Clyde St) from around $10 per hour. Note though that bicycles are not allowed on any trails in the national park.

Other Activities

Ask at the visitors centre about activities around Ohakun: horse trekking, golf, whitewater rafting, fishing, canoeing, kayaking and jetboat trips on the nearby Whanganui River, and more. You can also take a swim in the Powderhorn Chateau's (opposite) indoor heated pool.

Ohakune is a good base to organise canoeing trips on the Whanganui River. **Canoe Safaris** (☎ 06-385 9237; www.canoesafaris.co.nz; Miro St) run two- to five-day guided trips (between $300 and $785) and also rents canoes and kayaks, from $125 for three days. **Yeti Tours** (☎ 0800 322 388; www.canoe.co.nz) do similar two- to six-day trips (between $325 and $895). Rates are cheaper for children.

Sleeping

In summer the 'junction' is a bit of a ghost town, so it may pay to stay near SH49 (unless you like ghost towns of course). The prices listed here are for summer; they're much higher in winter, when it pays to book ahead.

BUDGET

Ohakune Country Hotel (☎ 06-385 8268; www.ohakune-hotel.co.nz; 72 Clyde St; s/d/ste from $55/65/120) This is a simple and cosy hotel with a wide choice of reasonably priced accommodation, including spacious suites, located at the southern end of town. It's a sociable place and there are three ever-popular on-site bars and a restaurant, as well as a bottle shop and gaming machines, so don't come here looking for peace and seclusion.

Ohakune Top 10 Holiday Park (☎ /fax 06-385 8561; www.ohakune.net.nz; 5 Moore St; camp sites/d/ste from $25/35/50; 🖳) This is a pleasant camp with the high standards and good facilities you would expect from the Top 10 chain. There are basic cabins and smarter motel units beside a gurgling stream, with plenty of trees and green areas, a kids' playground, minigolf and free BBQ's. There's also a comfortable TV lounge/dining room.

Ohakune YHA (☎ 06-385 8724; yhaohak@yha.org.nz; 15 Clyde St; dm/d from $22/50; 🌙 Jun-Oct) This well-located hostel is near the bus stop and visitors centre, and offers simple accommodation at a good price. Sleeping options include twins, triples and bunkrooms.

MID-RANGE

Rimu Park Lodge & Chalets (☎ 06-385 9023; www.rimupark.co.nz; 27 Rimu St; dm/d from $30/70) This is a charming Edwardian villa in a secluded spot close to the centre, offering very good value. It's quiet in summer and very popular with skiers in winter. Rates vary depending on the season, and there are midweek discounts. There are chalets and units next to the house (between $130 and $300; all sleep 10). If you fancy something a little bit different, there are three restored 1934 train carriages, which cost the same as the chalets.

Hobbit Motor Lodge (☎ 0800 843 462, 06-385 8248; www.the-hobbit.co.nz; cnr Goldfinch & Wye Sts; dm/ste/f from $25/85/140) Set in pleasant but sadly Frodoless grounds, this place is popular with young families and groups. It offers a good variety of accommodation with or without

Cape Reinga (p166)

Kauri trees, Waipoua Kauri Forest
(p159)

Ruins of *Rainbow Warrior*, Cavalli
Islands (p171)

Rawhiti Point, Bay of Islands (p187)

ANDERS BLOMQVIST

Bungy jumping, Waikato River, Taupo
(p298)

GARETH MCCORMACK

Volcanic craters of Emerald Lakes,
Tongariro National Park (p282)

ROSS

Aerial view of Tongariro River and
Lake Taupo (p295)

Mt Ruapehu (p282), Tongariro National Park

PAUL

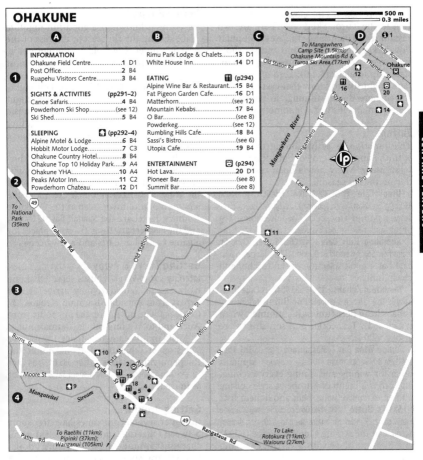

OHAKUNE

0 ————————— 500 m
0 ————————— 0.3 miles

INFORMATION
Ohakune Field Centre..............1 D1
Post Office...............................2 B4
Ruapehu Visitors Centre.........3 B4

SIGHTS & ACTIVITIES (pp291–2)
Canoe Safaris..........................4 B4
Powderhorn Ski Shop.........(see 12)
Ski Shed.................................5 B4

SLEEPING (pp292–4)
Alpine Motel & Lodge.............6 B4
Hobbit Motor Lodge................7 C3
Ohakune Country Hotel..........8 B4
Ohakune Top 10 Holiday Park...9 A4
Ohakune YHA.......................10 A4
Peaks Motor Inn...................11 C2
Powderhorn Chateau............12 D1

Rimu Park Lodge & Chalets.......13 D1
White House Inn.....................14 D1

EATING (p294)
Alpine Wine Bar & Restaurant...15 B4
Fat Pigeon Garden Cafe...........16 D1
Matterhorn...........................(see 12)
Mountain Kebabs....................17 B4
O Bar...................................(see 8)
Powderkeg............................(see 12)
Rumbling Hills Cafe................18 B4
Sassi's Bistro.........................(see 6)
Utopia Cafe...........................19 B4

ENTERTAINMENT (p294)
Hot Lava..............................20 D1
Pioneer Bar..........................(see 8)
Summit Bar...........................(see 8)

CENTRAL PLATEAU

kitchens, with good-sized units sleeping up to six people. It has a licensed restaurant, children's play area and spa pool.

Peaks Motor Inn (☎ 06-385 9144; www.thepeaks .co.nz; cnr Mangawhero Tce & Shannon St; ste from $80; 🖳) The Peaks is a sparkling new wood-cabin style motel, just under a kilometre from the centre of Ohakune. It features spacious units, all with kitchen facilities and most with spa baths. It's a little lacking in character, but it has good facilities, including two spa pools, a sauna, gym and conference room. Prices almost double in winter, though.

Alpine Motel & Lodge (☎/fax 06-385 8758; www.alpinemotel.co.nz; 7 Miro St; dm/d from $20/95; 🖳) The Alpine offers a high standard of accommodation, with neat studio units,

family units sleeping up to eight people, and a basic but decent backpackers in the rear. There's a spa pool and a popular bar-restaurant, Sassi's Bistro (p294).

White House Inn (☎/fax 06-385 8413; thewhitehouse inn@clear.net.nz; 22 Rimu St; dm/d from $45/90) The clean and cosy White House has comfortable if unspectacular accommodation in a modern building. Continental breakfast is included, and there's a nice spa and a lounge bar.

TOP END

Powderhorn Chateau (☎ 06-385 8888; www.powder horn.co.nz; cnr Thames St & Mangawhero Tce; ste from $160; 🖳 🕿) Powderhorn is *the* hotel of choice in Ohakune, a traditional European-style ski chalet with woody interiors, and is famous for its après ski; it's the closest accommodation to the Turoa Ski Area. There are two restaurants, including the very popular Powderkeg (below), a casino and ski shop. For larger groups, the 'Mansion' apartment sleeps up to eight ($700). *Lord of the Rings* fans might like to know that cast and crew stayed here during filming, so you might end up in an elf's bed. Or something.

Eating

The 'junction' is active during the winter with the après-ski crowd, but little is open in summer. Many hotels open restaurants during the ski season.

Utopia Cafe (☎ 06-385 9120; 47 Clyde St; mains around $10; ☽ breakfast, lunch & dinner) This relaxed café serves *panini* (focaccia), bagels, cakes, big breakfasts and good coffee.

Rumbling Hills Cafe (☎ 06-385 9292; Clyde St; mains from $6; ☽ breakfast & lunch) This large, open café has a good selection of sandwiches and cheap lunches.

Mountain Kebabs (☎ 06-385 9047; 29 Clyde St; kebabs $7-9; ☽ lunch & dinner) For filling takeaway kebabs head here (unless it's summer, when it's closed). Tea, coffee and soft drinks are also available.

Alpine Wine Bar & Restaurant (☎ 06-385 9183; cnr Clyde & Miro Sts; mains $10-28; ☽ dinner) Alpine is open for wining and dining every evening, and offers a menu of European-style cuisine and an extensive wine, beer and liqueur list.

Sassi's Bistro (☎ /fax 06-385 8758; www.alpine motel.co.nz; 7 Miro St; mains around $20; ☽ dinner) Sassi's, at the Alpine Motel & Lodge (p293) is a pleasant place with a varied, changing menu and welcoming owners.

Fat Pigeon Garden Cafe (☎ 06-385 9423; 2 Tyne St; mains $15-25; ☽ breakfast & lunch) The Fat Pigeon is in a charming renovated house at the end of Mountain Rd. It has pleasant seating indoors or outside in the attractive garden, and plenty of choice on the menu, plus a good wine list.

O Bar (72 Clyde St; mains from $15; ☽ lunch & dinner) At the Ohakune Country Hotel (p292), it serves up excellent wood-fired pizzas.

Powderkeg (www.powderhorn.co.nz; cnr Thames St & Mangawhero Tce; ☽ lunch & dinner) and the **Matterhorn** (www.powderhorn.co.nz; cnr Thames St & Mangawhero Tce; ☽ lunch & dinner), both restaurant-bars inside the Powderkeg Chateau (p293), are favourite après-ski hangouts. Mains at both start around $15.

Entertainment

Ohakune is known as a good-fun nightlife place during the ski season; the rest of the year it's quiet. Get hold of the gig guide, available from the visitors centre and most lodges.

Hot Lava (☎ 06-385 9232; Thames St) This nightclub is a popular spot, open every night during the ski season, with live music on weekends and disco music on other nights. (In winter it attracts some big-name bands.)

Other places that present live music during the ski season include the eternally popular **Powderkeg** (cnr Thames St & Mangawhero Tce), and the **O Bar** (Ohakune Country Hotel; 72 Clyde St), in the southern part of town. Also at the Ohakune Country Hotel are the **Summit Bar** (72 Clyde St) and the **Pioneer Bar** (72 Clyde St) – snug places for a game of pool or darts and a few beers.

Getting There & Away

InterCity (☎ 09-913 6100) buses serve Ohakune daily except Saturday; they arrive at and depart from outside Mountain Kebabs (29 Clyde St). The town is on the bus route from Auckland to Wellington via Taumarunui.

Auckland–Wellington **trains** (☎ 0800 802 802) stop at Ohakune. Buy tickets at the Ruapehu **visitors centre** (☎ 06-385 8427; 54 Clyde St; ☽ 9am-5pm Mon-Fri, 9am-3.30pm Sat & Sun), not at the station.

Getting Around

In winter several companies have transport between Ohakune and the Turoa Ski Area, charging around $15 for return door-to-door transport from wherever you're staying.

Snowliner Shuttle (☎ 06-385 8573) and **Snow Express** (☎ 06-385 4022) offer a variety of transport around the area.

RAETIHI

pop 1070

Only 11km west of Ohakune and 26km east of Pipiriki, the small town of Raetihi makes a handy base for both the Tongariro and Whanganui National Parks. The enthusiastic Raetihi **visitors centre** (☎ 06-385 4805; 48 Seddon St; ☽ 9.30am-4.30pm Mon-Fri, 1-4.30pm Sun) has details on activities and a list of farmstays and B&Bs to suit all budgets.

Kiwi Encounters (☎ 06-385 4565; adult/child $35/20) arranges night excursions (October to mid-April) to the Waimarino Forest in an attempt to spot the elusive kiwi. Bookings are essential.

Country Classic Lodge (☎ 06-385 4511; 14 Ameku Rd; s/d $50/100), a charming Victorian villa, has 10 comfortable and well-kept rooms, and offers a pleasant and quiet retreat. In addition there's a restaurant, bar and spa pools.

NZ Police Ski Club (☎ 06-385 4003; 35 Queen St; r $20) is an amenable lodge that backpackers will like as it has a spa in winter. There are four doubles, one single and dorms. Duvets and pillows are supplied, but you'll need your own bed linen.

Raetihi Holiday Park (☎ 06-385 4176; info@ruapehudc.govt.nz; Parapara Rd; camp sites/d $16/35) is a fairly basic camp ground, with only a small number of economical cabins on offer, though it's a reasonable spot to pitch your tent for the night.

LAKE ROTOKURA

About 11km southeast of Ohakune, on SH49, is Lake Rotokura, at Karioi in the Karioi Forest. It's called Lake Rotokura on the map and the sign but it's actually two lakes, not one – the locals call them the Karioi Lakes (*karioi* means 'places to linger'). It's a beautiful spot. The round-trip walk only takes an hour. Be aware that the top lake is *tapu* (sacred) to Maoris, which means no eating, fishing or swimming is allowed at the lake.

WAIOURU

pop 2600

At the junction of SH1 and SH49, 27km east of Ohakune, Waiouru is primarily an army base. In a large, grey concrete building with tanks out the front, the **Army Museum Waiouru** (☎ 06-387 6911; www.armymuseum.co.nz; adult/child $10/7; ☼ 9am-4.30pm) tells the history of the NZ army in times of war and peace, with an extensive collection of artefacts from early colonial times to the present, and an audiovisual presentation.

SH1 from Waiouru to Turangi is known as the Desert Road and is often closed in winter because of snow, but it can also close at other times of the year. It runs through the Rangipo Desert, east of Ruapehu. It's not a true desert, but was named because of its desert-like appearance, caused by a cold, exposed and windswept location.

LAKE TAUPO REGION

New Zealand's largest lake, Lake Taupo, lies in the heart of the North Island. Some 606 sq km in area and 357m above sea level, the lake was formed by one of the greatest volcanic explosions of all time (p306). The surrounding area is still volcanically active and, like Rotorua, it has thermal areas.

Today, serene Lake Taupo is proclaimed as the world's trout-fishing capital. If you thought the trout in the Rotorua springs looked large and tasty, they're nothing compared to the monsters found in Lake Taupo.

All of NZ's rainbow trout descend from a single batch of eggs brought from California's Russian River a century ago. International trout-fishing tournaments are held on Lake Taupo annually on the Anzac Day long weekend (on or around 25 April).

TAUPO

pop 21,040

Taupo lies on the northeastern corner of Lake Taupo and has scenic views across the lake to the volcanic peaks of Tongariro National Park. With a long list of attractions in close proximity to the town and a plethora of activities (ranging from fishing and boating on the lake to adrenaline-pumping bungy jumping and skydiving) it's no wonder Taupo is on most travellers' itineraries.

Lake Taupo is also the source of NZ's longest river, the Waikato, which leaves the lake at the township, flows through the Huka Falls and the Aratiatia Rapids, and then through the heart of the northern part of North Island to the west coast just south of Auckland.

History

Back in the mists of time, the Maori chief Tamatea-arikinui visited the area, noticed that the ground felt hollow and his footsteps seemed to reverberate, and called the place Tapuaeharuru (Resounding Footsteps). Another source of the name comes from the story that Tia, who discovered the lake, slept by it draped in his cloak, and it became known as Taupo-nui-a-Tia (The Great Cloak of Tia).

Taupo, as it became known, was first occupied by Europeans as a military outpost during the East Coast Land War (1868–72). Colonel JM Roberts built a redoubt in 1869 and a garrison of mounted police remained there until the defeat of the rebel warrior Te Kooti (see the boxed text on p361) later that year.

In the 1870s the government bought the land from the Maoris. Taupo has grown slowly and sedately from a lakeside village of about 750 in 1945 to a large resort town, with the population swelling considerably at peak holiday times. The town is on the lakefront where SH1, the main road from the north, first meets the lake.

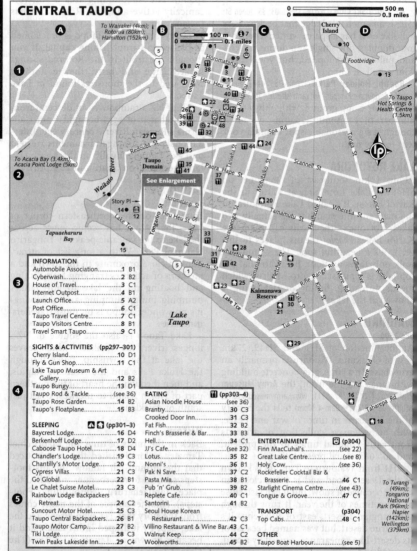

CENTRAL TAUPO

INFORMATION	
Automobile Association	1 B1
Cyberwash	2 B2
House of Travel	3 C1
Internet Outpost	4 B1
Launch Office	5 A2
Post Office	6 C1
Taupo Travel Centre	7 C1
Taupo Visitors Centre	8 B1
Travel Smart Taupo	9 C1

SIGHTS & ACTIVITIES	(pp297–301)
Cherry Island	10 D1
Fly & Gun Shop	11 C1
Lake Taupo Museum & Art Gallery	12 B2
Taupo Bungy	13 D1
Taupo Rod & Tackle	(see 36)
Taupo Rose Garden	14 B2
Taupo's Floatplane	15 B3

SLEEPING	(pp301–3)
Baycrest Lodge	16 D4
Berkenhoff Lodge	17 D2
Caboose Taupo Hotel	18 D4
Chandler's Lodge	19 C3
Chantilly's Motor Lodge	20 C2
Cypress Villas	21 C3
Go Global	22 B1
Le Chalet Suisse Motel	23 C3
Rainbow Lodge Backpackers Retreat	24 C2
Suncourt Motor Hotel	25 C3
Taupo Central Backpackers	26 B1
Taupo Motor Camp	27 B2
Tiki Lodge	28 C3
Twin Peaks Lakeside Inn	29 C4

EATING	(pp303–4)
Asian Noodle House	(see 36)
Brantry	30 C3
Crooked Door Inn	31 C3
Fat Fish	32 B2
Finch's Brasserie & Bar	33 B3
Hell	34 C1
JJ's Cafe	(see 32)
Lotus	35 B2
Nonni's	36 B1
Pak N Save	37 C2
Pasta Mia	38 B1
Pub 'n' Grub	39 B2
Replete Cafe	40 C1
Santorini	41 B2
Seoul House Korean Restaurant	42 C1
Villino Restaurant & Wine Bar	43 C1
Walnut Keep	44 C2
Woolworths	45 B2

ENTERTAINMENT	(p304)
Finn MacCuhal's	(see 22)
Great Lake Centre	(see 8)
Holy Cow	(see 36)
Rockefeller Cocktail Bar & Brasserie	46 C1
Starlight Cinema Centre	(see 43)
Tongue & Groove	47 C1

TRANSPORT	(p304)
Top Cabs	48 C1

OTHER	
Taupo Boat Harbour	(see 5)

Information

The Taupo **visitors centre** (Map p296; ☎ 07-376 0027; www.laketauponz.com; Tongariro St; ☯ 8.30am-5pm) handles bookings for all accommodation, transport and activities in the area. It has a good, free town map as well as DOC maps and information.

The Super Loo nearby is a large shower and toilet complex, with showers for $2 (for four minutes) and towels for $1.

The **Automobile Association** (AA; Map p296; ☎ 07-378 6000; 93 Tongariro St) is centrally located. The **post office** (cnr Horomatangi & Ruapehu Sts) exchanges money on Saturday morning.

Internet access is available at **Internet Outpost** (Map p296; 11 Tuwharetoa St) and **Cyberwash** (Map p296; 10 Roberts St). Prices hover around $7 to $8 per hour. Cyberwash also offers a laundry service while you check your emails.

Check out the website www.backpacklaketaupo.com for details of budget accommodation, activities, eateries and other useful information.

Sights

Taupo's main attractions, such as Wairakei Park and thermal regions, are north of town. In town, near the visitors centre, the **Lake Taupo Museum & Art Gallery** (Map p296; ☎ 07-378 4167; Story Pl; adult/child $4/free; ☯ 10.30am-4.30pm) has many historical photos and mementos of the 'old days' around Lake Taupo. The centrepiece of the collection is a Maori meeting house, Te Aroha o Rongoheikume, adorned with traditional, elaborate carvings. Other exhibits include a moa skeleton, displays on the local forestry, nautical and trout-fishing industries and a mock-up of a 19th-century shop. There are also temporary art exhibitions.

Alongside the museum is the well-tended and very pleasant **Taupo Rose Garden** (Map p296; Story Pl; admission free; ☯ 24hr), which is home to dozens of varieties of roses and has a shady pergola in the middle.

In the middle of the Waikato River, off Spa Rd and not far from the centre of town, **Cherry Island** (Map p296; ☎ 07-378 9427; adult/child $8.50/3; ☯ 9am-5pm) is a small trout and wildlife park with a café. The wildlife consists of a few goats, pigs, pheasants and ducks, which will entertain the kids. The island is reached by a footbridge.

Further out, next to the Spa Hotel, **Spa Dinosaur Valley** (Map p305; ☎ 07-378 4120; Spa Rd; adult/child $5/3; ☯ 10am-4pm) is Taupo's answer to Jurassic Park, and has giant, concrete dinosaurs.

Acacia Bay, a pleasant, peaceful beach, is a little over 5km west of Taupo.

Activities
SWIMMING & BATHING
The **AC Baths** at the **Taupo Events Centre** (Map p305; ☎ 07-376 0340; Spa Rd; adult/child $6.50/2.50; ☯ 8am-9pm), about 2km east of town, has a big, heated pool with a waterslide, indoor kids' pool, private mineral pools and a sauna. Use of the sauna/waterslide costs $4/3. There's also a **climbing wall** (adult/child $13/11; ☯ 5-9pm Mon-Fri, noon-9pm Sat & Sun).

Taupo Hot Springs & Health Spa (Map p305; ☎ 07-377 6502; www.taupohotsprings.com; Taupo-Napier Hwy (SH5); adult/child $9/3; ☯ 7am-9.30pm) is 1km from Lake Taupo. There's a variety of mineral-rich indoor/outdoor thermal pools, freshwater pools, massage spas and a giant dragon waterslide for the kids. Also on offer is a wide choice of spa and beauty treatments, including facials, waxing, acupuncture and massage. BBQ facilities are available.

FISHING
The Taupo region is world famous for its trout fly fishing. Fly fishing is the only fishing you can do on all rivers flowing into the lake, and within a 300m radius of the river mouths. Spin fishing is allowed on the Waikato River (flowing *out* of the lake) and on the Tokaanu tailrace, flowing into the lake from the Tokaanu Power Station. Several fly-fishing guides operate around Taupo, most notably in Turangi. The price of approximately $250/450 per half-/full-day, everything included, is reasonable when you consider you are paying for years of local knowledge.

An alternative way to experience the thrill of catching your own dinner is to take a boat out on the lake. A number of fishing guides and charter boats operate in Taupo, including **Te Moana Charters** (☎ 07-378 4839) and **White Striker Charters** (☎ 07-378 2736), both from $80 per hour. Check with the visitors centre for details of other operators, or head to the **launch office** (Map p296; ☎ 07-378 3444), where you can hire boats. Self-drive boats can be hired for around $30 per hour. If you take an organised trip, all equipment, plus licences, will be supplied, and a minimum

CENTRAL PLATEAU

of two to three hours is normally required (or at least suggested). Both spin fishing and fly fishing are allowed on the lake.

If you're going to do it on your own, **Taupo Rod & Tackle** (Map p296; ☎ 07-378 5337; 7 Tongariro St) by the waterfront, and the **Fly & Gun Shop** (Map p296; ☎ 07-378 4449; www.huntingandfishing.co.nz; 34 Heu Heu St), have fishing tackle for hire.

Fishing licences are available from the visitors centre or the launch office. Licences for fishing on Lake Taupo and the nearby rivers cost $12.50/27/66 per day/week/year.

Make sure you always have your fishing licence, and obey the rules listed on it when fishing – there are huge fines for violations.

WATER SPORTS

The **Sailing Centre** (Map p305; ☎ 07-378 3299; www.sailingcentre.co.nz; 75 Kurupae Rd) at Two Mile Bay, south of Taupo, hires out kayaks ($20), canoes ($25), sailboards ($25), catamarans ($40) and sailboats ($40) in summer. Rates are per hour.

Kayaking is a popular way to enjoy the lake and river; **Kayak New Zealand** (☎ 0800 529 256) has two-hour guided trips ($20) on the Waikato River, while **Kayaking Kiwi** (☎ 0800 529 255; www.kayakingkiwi.co.nz) offers three-hour trips ($69) on the lake, including refreshments. It also does combination scenic launch cruises and kayak exploration ($129).

Kiwi River Safaris (☎ 0800 723 8577; www.krs.co.nz) offers two-hour, white-water rafting trips on the Rangitaiki, Wairoa and Tongariro Rivers ($90), including free pick-up from Taupo accommodation, and lunch. It also does kayak tours down the Waikato River ($40).

Rapid Sensations (☎ 0800 353 435; www.rapids.co.nz) runs two-hour kayaking trips on the Waikato River (adult/child $40/20), as well as white-water rafting (from $55) and a 'ride 'n' raft' combo that includes a guided mountain-bike ride ($140).

Chris Jolly Outdoors (☎ 07-378 5596; www.chrisjolly.co.nz) runs a variety of activities, including water-skiing and wake boarding ($120 per hour), and it also rents out self-drive boats (from $50 per hour).

During summer there are lots of activities on Lake Taupo, including swimming, water-skiing, windsurfing, paragliding and sailing. The visitors centre has details, and gear can be hired at the lakefront.

BUNGY JUMPING

Right near Cherry Island is **Taupo Bungy** (Map p296; ☎ 0800 888 408, 07-377 1135; www.taupo bungy.com; solo/tandem jump $100/160; ☼ winter 8.30am-5pm, summer 8.30am-7pm). It's the most popular bungy-jumping operation on the North Island, largely due to its scenic setting on the Waikato River. Jumpers leap off a platform jutting 20m out over a cliff and hurtle down towards the river, 47m below. If you don't want to jump, it's a picturesque spot with plenty of vantage points. Cheap deals that combine a bungy jump, skydive with Taupo Tandem Skydiving (see below) and a jetboat ride with Huka Jet (see p306) are available; contact one of the operators for details.

SKYDIVING

This is one of the most popular Taupo adrenaline rushes. In addition to the skydiving itself, at the cheapest rate in NZ, you get a brilliant view over Lake Taupo and the entire region. The **Great Lake Skydive Centre** (☎ 0800 373 335, 07-378 4662; www.freefly.co.nz; skydives from $195, incl ground video) and **Skydive Taupo** (☎ 0800 586 766; www.skydivetaupo.co.nz; skydives from $180) do dives from 9000ft and 12,000ft, while **Taupo Tandem Skydiving** (☎ 0800 275 934; www.tts.net.nz) does skydives from between 6000ft and 15,000ft (between $169 and $299). All three companies are at Taupo Airport.

GLIDING

The **Taupo Gliding Club** (Map p305; ☎ 07-378 5627; Centennial Dr; flights from $70) goes gliding on Saturday, Sunday and Wednesday afternoons (when the weather is suitable) at Centennial Park on Centennial Dr, about 5km up Spa Rd from the town centre.

GOLF

If you're in the mood for putting a few balls around, **Taupo Golf Club** (Map p305; ☎ 07-378 6933; www.taupogolf.co.nz; 32 Centennial Dr; 9/18 holes $20/40) has two excellent, international-standard 18-hole courses, plus a golf shop, restaurant and bar.

HORSE TREKKING

Running off-road treks, **Taupo Horse Treks** (Map p305; ☎ 07-378 0356; Karapiti Rd; 1hr/2hr rides $30/50) has a good reputation. Its treks go through some fine forest with good views over the Craters of the Moon.

CYCLING

Taupo is a cyclist-friendly town, with dedicated cycle lanes along Lake Terrace and Heu Heu St, and plenty of cycle racks. Lake Taupo is also the location of two of NZ's biggest cycling events: the 160km **Lake Taupo Cycle Challenge** (www.cycle challenge.org.nz), held on the last Saturday in November each year, and the 12-hour **Day-Night Thriller** (☺ Oct), which regularly attracts over 3000 riders. The visitors centre produces an excellent free leaflet, *Cycling Around Lake Taupo*, which has suggested cycling routes.

If you don't make it to Arataki (see p307), then **Taupo Quad Adventures** (☎ 07-377 6404; www.4x4quads.com; 1hr/full-day trips $60/225) has fully guided off-road quad-bike trips. It's at the turn-off to Orakei Korako on SH1.

For self-propelled motion, all of the following places rent bikes for around $20 per day: **Rainbow Lodge** (☎ 07-378 5754; 99 Titirau-penga St), **Go Global** (☎ 07-377 0044; cnr Tongariro & Tuwharetoa Sts) and **Rent-a-Bike** (☎ 025-322 729).

Rapid Sensations (☎ 0800 353 435; www.rapids .co.nz) rents mountain bikes for $45 per day and offers guided rides from $55.

Cyberwash (☎ 0274 460 202; 10 Roberts St) rents scooters from $45 for two hours.

MOTORCYCLING

If you're looking for serious off-road action, **Kiwi Dirtbike Adventures** (☎ 021 616 707; www.kiwiad ventures.co.nz) runs full-day motorbike trips to the 42nd Traverse ($449), as well as multi-day guided tours of the South Island.

Ride New Zealand (☎ 07-377 2127; www.ridenew zealand.co.nz) has a broad range of scooters and motorbikes for rent (from $85 per day), and it offers self-guided tours.

OBSTACLE COURSES

Adrenaline junkies will enjoy the vertiginous experience offered by **Rock 'n' Ropes** (☎ 0800 244 508, 07-374 8111; www.rocknropes.co.nz; giant swing $15, adrenaline combo $35, half-day blast $59), a challenging obstacle course of swings, ropes and the like up in the swaying, teetering tree-tops. The 'adrenaline combo' involves the use of a swing, high beam and trapeze. Rock 'n' Ropes is at **Crazy Catz Adventure Park** (☎ 0800 462 7219; www.crazycatz.co.nz; activities $5-20; ☺ 9am-4.30pm winter, 9am-6pm summer) on SH5, 13km north of Taupo, which has go-carts, quad bikes, mini-golf and an animal park, among other things. Rock 'n' Ropes offers a free pick-up from Taupo.

MOUNTAINBOARDING

If you find skateboarding too tame and you're looking for a new route to grazed knees and bashed elbows, try mountainboarding – a kind of cross between snowboarding, skateboarding and mountain biking. Check out **Gravity Hill** (Map p305; ☎ 0800 472 848; www.mountainboard.co.nz; Rakanui Rd; 5 rides/half-day/full day $29/39/69), where you can career around 12 acres of tracks, slopes and jumps on mountain boards. There's a gentle grassy slope for the more cautious. All safety gear is supplied.

WALKING

An enjoyable, easy walk runs from **Taupo** to **Aratiatia** along the east bank of the Waikato River. The track follows the river to Huka Falls, crossing a hot stream and riverside marshes en route. It's about a one- to 1½-hour walk from the centre of Taupo to Huka Falls. From the falls continue straight ahead along the 7km Taupo Walkway to Aratiatia (another two-plus hours). There are good views of the river, Huka Falls and the power station across the river. From the centre of town, head up Spa Rd, passing the Taupo Bungy site. To reach the start of the walk turn left at County Ave and continue through Spa Thermal Park till the end of the street. The path heads off to the left of the car park, up over a hill and down to the hot springs by the river. Alternatively, drive out to the falls and park, cross the bridge and walk out to Aratiatia.

Another walk goes to **Mt Tauhara**, with magnificent views from the top. Take the Taupo–Napier Highway (SH5) turn-off, 2km south of the Taupo town centre. About 6km along SH5, turn left into Mountain Rd. The start of the track is signposted on the right-hand side. It will take about two hours to the top, walking slowly.

A pleasant **walkway** goes from the Taupo lakefront to Five Mile Bay. It's a flat, easy walk along public-access beaches. Heading south from Taupo, there's a hot-water beach on the way to Two Mile Bay. At Two Mile Bay the walkway connects with the Lions Walk, going from Two Mile Bay

CENTRAL PLATEAU

(4.2km south of Taupo) to Five Mile Bay (8km). Anywhere along here you can easily get back to SH1, the lakeside road.

There are plenty of other good walks and tramps in the area; the visitors centre has the relevant DOC pamphlets ($1).

Tours

Paradise Tours (☎ 07-378 9955; www.paradisetours.co.nz; tours adult/child $40/20) does three-hour tours to the Aratiatia Rapids, Geothermal Project, Craters of the Moon and Huka Falls. It also offers tours to Tongariro National Park, Orakei Korako, Rotorua, Hawkes Bay and Waitomo Caves.

Taupo Tours (☎ 07-377 0774; www.taupotours.com; tours adult/child $5/2.50) runs 20-minute sightseeing tours of Taupo in a refurbished 1950s British double-decker bus, running every half-hour (between 10am and 4pm) between Boxing Day and Easter. The bus stops behind the Super Loo and at the town end of the lakefront.

Wilderness Escapes (☎ 07-378 3413; www.wildernessescapes.co.nz) organises a wide variety of walks (from $60) and other outdoor activities, such as half-hour microlight flights ($120), kayaking (from $55), abseiling (from $60), rock climbing (from $80) and caving ($180).

Whirinaki Escape (☎ 07-377 2363; www.rainforest-treks.co.nz) runs fascinating and educational 'eco-cultural' guided walks in the Whirinaki Forest Park (one- to three-day trips between $155 and $745). Transport from Taupo, meals and accommodation are included in the price and there are reductions for children.

Kiwi Experience (☎ 09-366 9830; www.kiwiexperience.com) operates the 'East As' backpacker bus trip from Taupo around the East Cape and back again, via Gisborne and Napier. The trip takes a minimum of four days and costs $260, or $247 as an 'add on' to a Kiwi Experience National Pass. Accommodation and food are extra.

AERIAL SIGHTSEEING

Taupo's Floatplane (Map p296; ☎ 07-378 7500; www.tauposfloatplane.co.nz; flights $60-425), next to Taupo Boat Harbour, does a variety of trips, including quick flights over the lake and longer ones over Mt Ruapehu and as far afield as White Island. If you're looking for a full day out, you could try the Taupo Trifecta Combo (floatplane trip, followed by a jetboat trip and a walk through Orakei Korako; $260).

Air Charter Taupo (☎ 07-378 5467; www.aircharter-taupo.co.nz; flights $50-180), located at Taupo Airport, does scenic flights ranging from 15-minute flights to one-hour flights across Lake Taupo, Tongariro, Wairakei Park and Mt Ruapehu.

Helistar Helicopters (Map p305; ☎ 0800 435 478; www.helistar.co.nz; Huka Falls Rd; flights $75-945), about 3km northeast of town, offers a variety of scenic helicopter flights, ranging from five minutes to two hours. Also available is the Hukastar Combo, which is a helicopter flight followed by a spin on the Huka Jet (from $170).

LAKE CRUISES & JETBOATING

Four boats specialise in cruises on the lake: *Barbary*, *Ernest Kemp*, *Alice* and the *Cruise Cat*. The **Barbary** (tickets $30; ☼ 10am, 2pm & 5pm summer, 10am & 2pm rest of year), built in 1926, is a 15m ocean-going racing yacht once briefly possessed by actor Errol Flynn. 'Barbary Bill', the skipper, is much loved by tourists and locals and his trip is probably the most popular.

The **Ernest Kemp** (tickets $28; ☼ 10.30am & 2pm), built to resemble a 1920s steamboat, is named for Alfred Ernest Kemp, whose family occupied the house that still bears their name in Kerikeri, Northland. There are written commentaries in various languages for the trips.

Another steamboat plying Lake Taupo's waters is the **Alice** (adults/children $15/6; ☼ 11am, 12.30pm & 2pm Sat & Sun).

For something with a little more zip try the **Cruise Cat** (tickets $28; ☼ 11.30am Mon-Sat, 10.30am Sun), which is a large, modern launch. On Sunday you can have brunch for $42.

All the boats offer similar trips, including visiting a modern Maori rock carving beside the lake. The carving is on private land so it cannot be reached by foot; the only way to see it is by boat. Trips take between 1½ and 2½ hours.

All the boats leave from the wharves at the **Taupo Boat Harbour** (Map p296; off Redoubt St). Bookings can be made at the visitors centre or at the **launch office** (Map p296; ☼ 07-378 3444; off Redoubt St; ☼ 8.30am-5pm summer, 9am-2.30pm winter) by the wharves.

TOP 5 FREE ACTIVITIES AROUND TAUPO

- Take a wander through the eerie landscape of the **Craters of the Moon** (p307)
- Visit the **Tongariro National Trout Centre** (p308) near Turangi
- Stop for a rest in the **Taupo Rose Garden** (p297)
- Take a walk to the magnificent **Huka Falls** (p306)
- Learn about bees and sample some local honey at **Honey Hive New Zealand** (p305)

Sleeping

Taupo has a huge range of accommodation, from budget options to some of the most exclusive luxury retreats in the country. As it's on most backpackers' itineraries, there are plenty of hostel beds around, but the standard varies hugely.

BUDGET

Tiki Lodge (Map p296; ☎ 07-377 4545; www.tikilodge.co.nz; 104 Tuwharetoa St; dm/d from $26/30; 🖳) This lodge, which opened in December 2003, is a friendly, purpose-built hostel with Maori-themed décor and spotless rooms. It has comfortable, well-equipped communal areas, including a huge kitchen, TV and reading lounges and a wide balcony with a BBQ and view of the lake.

Berkenhoff Lodge (Map p296; ☎ 07-378 4909; bhoff@reap.org.nz; 75 Scannell St; dm/d $20/50; 🖳 🍸) This is a big, rambling old place in a quiet spot away from the town centre, but handy for Taupo Bungy and the AC Baths. It has good-sized, rooms (all en suite), and there's a spa pool, games room, TV lounge and kitchen, plus a BBQ and bar.

Rainbow Lodge Backpackers Retreat (Map p296; ☎ 07-378 5754; rainbowlodge@clear.net.nz; 99 Titiraupenga St; dm/d from $18/44) Rainbow Lodge is a very popular place, with clean, spacious rooms, and it books up quickly. It has a large communal area, a sauna and a games area, and can arrange lots of activities and tours. Mountain bikes, fishing tackle and camping gear are available for hire.

De Bretts Thermal Resort (Map p305; ☎ 07-378 8559; www.debrettsresort.co.nz; SH5; camp sites/s/d/ste

from $24/28/50/80; 🖳) De Bretts is a five-star-rated holiday park next to Taupo Hot Springs on the road heading to Napier. It's set in well-tended, park-like grounds and has a good choice of accommodation options, including sheltered sites, backpacker dorms and motel-style units. De Bretts is popular with families, and has plenty of kid-friendly features, such as a playground and cot and high-chair hire.

Taupo Motor Camp (Map p296; ☎ /fax 07-377 3080; www.taupomotorcamp.co.nz; 15 Redoubt St; camp sites/s/d from $24/40/46) This is Taupo's most central camp ground, occupying a pleasant and very spacious spot beside the Waikato River, and just 200m from the town centre. It has stationary caravans, with or without showers (between $45 and $75), and a playground and TV lounge.

Orange House (☎ 07-378 1934; orangehouse@ihug.co.nz; r per week $80) The Orange House is a small, private house with a pleasant garden, in a central (but secret!) location, designed to be a private, quiet, long-stay alternative to hostel accommodation (minimum stay one week). Phone ahead or ask at Go Global (below) for details.

Go Global (Map p296; ☎ 0800 464 562, 07-377 0044; www.go-global.co.nz; cnr Tongariro & Tuwharetoa Sts; dm/s/d from $21/35/48) Go Global is an ageing, knocked-about party backpackers' that has recently undergone some renovation. It's a big, sociable place, with rooms above the Finn MacCuhal's pub and TVs in most rooms, so it's not the quietest place to stay. Check out the circular pool table.

Taupo Central Backpackers (Map p296; ☎ 07-378 3206; 7 Tuwharetoa St; dm/d $23/55) This is another big old party-central backpackers that's now looking frayed around the edges, and it's all a little jaded and impersonal. There's a rooftop bar that gets lively at weekends, and all rooms have an attached bathroom.

MID-RANGE

Taupo is packed with motels, many of them strung out along Lake Terrace.

Caboose Taupo Hotel (Map p296; ☎ 0800 222 667; www.taupo.caboose.co.nz; 100-102 Lake Tce; d $99-159; 🖳 🍸) This unique hotel follows the theme of 'rail travel in colonial Africa' with a passion, and includes sloping hallways to mimic a train carriage, lots of African hardwood, leopard and zebra prints, and rooms divided into 'compartments' and 'sleepers'.

The on-site restaurant serves good quality South African cuisine.

Twin Peaks Lakeside Inn (Map p296; ☎ 07-378 8614; twinpeaks@xtra.co.nz; 76-80 Lake Tce; d $75-150; 🖳) Twin Peaks is a friendly and fairly sedate motel that is popular with families. Many of the rooms enjoy great views of the lake. Units have private spa pools and there's a sociable British-style pub on-site, the 'Jolly Good Fellows'. Children under 12 stay free and disabled-accessible units are available.

Sails Motor Lodge (Map p305; ☎ 0800 555 655; www.sailstaupo.co.nz; 138 Lake Tce; r from $125) This snazzy, nautical-themed place has a certain architectural flair about it, with spacious studios, doubles and twins, all with balconies, many with spectacular lake views, and spa baths. There are also two disabled-accessible units. It's a fair way from town though (1.5km), if you don't have your own transport. Weekend prices are marginally higher.

Chantilly's Motor Lodge (Map p296; ☎ 0800 160 700; www.chantillys.co.nz; 112 Tamamutu St; d from $95; 🖳) Chantilly's is a big, brash, new motel with a striking Art Deco/1950s Americana look and spacious units close to the centre of town. It's well geared up for business travellers, and long-term rates are also available.

Cypress Villas (Map p296; ☎ 07-378 4322; www.cypressvillas.co.nz; 37 Rifle Range Rd; ste from $105) Cypress Villas is a modern, well-designed complex. There are six self-contained, serviced units in a quiet part of town not far from the lake, composed of a studio unit, one- and two-bedroom apartments and a 'honeymoon suite'. All are spacious, open, spotlessly clean and have their own kitchen.

Le Chalet Suisse Motel (Map p296; ☎ 0800 178 378; www.lechaletsuisse.co.nz; cnr Titiraupenga & Northcroft Sts; ste from $89; 🖳) This big motel has an emphatic Alpine-chalet theme going on, and is set back from the lake. There's a selection of self-contained 'chalet-style' units, a spa pool, BBQ, games room and children's play area.

Baycrest Lodge (Map p296; ☎ 0800 229 273; www.baycrest.co.nz; 79 Mere Rd; ste from $135; 🖳 🖳) Baycrest is a relaxed, upmarket motor lodge with very neat, good-sized apartments, including two-room 'executive family units'. All have hot tubs or spa baths, and some have a private balcony or courtyard.

Chandler's Lodge (Map p296; ☎ 07-378 4927; chandlertaupo@xtra.co.nz; 135 Heu Heu St; s/d $55/80; 🖳) Could this lodge be any cosier? This is a small, friendly and intimate place, just a short walk from the town centre, with four self-contained motel units and two rooms with shared facilities. Breakfast is included and other meals can be provided at an extra cost.

Gables Motor Lodge (Map p305; ☎ 07-378 8030; gables@reap.org.nz; 130 Lake Tce; ste from $120; 🖳) Gables has attractive A-frame-style one-bedroom suites, all with private hot pools and large lounges and kitchens. There are also larger units with two bedrooms ($150). It's a quiet place a fair way from the centre of Taupo.

Suncourt Motor Hotel (Map p296; ☎ 0800 786 268; www.suncourt.co.nz; 14 Northcroft St; ste from $80; 🖳 🖳) Suncourt is a large motel and has big, comfortable, well-priced units and great facilities, including spa pool, licensed restaurant and kids' playground. It's somewhat lacking in character and doubles as a conference centre.

TOP END

Huka Lodge (Map p305; ☎ 07-378 5791; www.hukalodge.com; Huka Falls Rd; s/d/ste from $1300/1720/3110) If you're looking for discreet, understated luxury, Huka Lodge, near Huka Falls, is one of NZ's most celebrated hotels, internationally renowned for the quality of its accommodation and cuisine, and is a favourite retreat for Kiwi celebrities. There are 20 sumptuous suites and privacy is paramount. Tariffs include a five-course dinner, breakfast and airport transfer. If you want yet more seclusion, and enjoy spending money, the separate Huka Cottage can be all yours (from $3440, meals $190 extra).

Wairakei Resort (Map p305; ☎ 07-374 8021; www.wairakei.co.nz; Wairakei Park; d/ste from $155/250; 🖳) This is a huge, 187-room resort set in the beautiful surroundings of Wairakei Park, around 9km from the town, and 500m from the exclusive Wairakei International Golf Club. The superb facilities include spa pools, tennis and squash courts, gym, sauna, restaurants, bars and a nine-hole golf course. Various package deals are available.

Cove (Map p305; ☎ 07-378 7599; www.thecove.co.nz; 213 Lake Tce; d/ste $155/290) The Cove is a small, stylish lakefront hotel with smart, contemporary rooms, a high level of service and one of Taupo's best restaurants, the Landing (see below). Suites have balconies and private spa pools.

Acacia Point Lodge (☎ 07-378 9089; www.acaciapointlodgetaupo.co.nz; 11 Sylvia Pl, Acacia Bay; s/d from $670/1010) Commanding a stunning location overlooking Acacia Bay, 5km west of town, this is a truly luxurious place with large, tastefully furnished suites. Facilities include a tennis court, putting green, gym, sauna, spa, massage treatments and billiard room.

Eating

Hell (Map p296; ☎ 0800 864 355, 07-377 8181; 30 Tuwharetoa St; pizzas $6-14; ☺ dinner) Hell is an excellent takeaway pizza joint, with a huge variety of innovative pizzas, pastas and salads, including such diabolical offerings as *Mordor*, with venison pepperoni, and *Underworld*, with smoked mussels. Delivery is available ($3.50).

JJ's Cafe (Map p296; ☎ 07-377 1545; 10 Roberts St; mains $6.50-25; ☺ breakfast, lunch & dinner) JJ's has a cheap, daytime menu, including all-day breakfasts, bagels and pasta. It has indoor and outdoor seating, and it's a popular backpacker hangout.

Fat Fish (Map p296; ☎ 07-377 0086; 10 Roberts St; mains $17-26; ☺ breakfast, lunch & dinner) Right beside JJ's, Fat Fish offers, as you might expect, varied fishy dishes as well as lamb, chicken, pizzas and *panini*. It also serves good breakfasts and has outdoor seating.

Pub 'n' Grub (Map p296; ☎ 07-378 0555; Lake Tce; mains $9.50-20; ☺ breakfast & lunch) This is a friendly pub serving up traditional pub-grub standards like fish and chips, and bacon and eggs, plus a few surprises, such as oysters. It's also a good place for a beer or two.

Tongue & Groove (Map p296; ☎ 07-378 3900; 11 Tuwharetoa St; ☺ 10am-3am) The Tongue & Groove is a smart upstairs bar and brasserie that has an excellent and reasonably priced lunch and dinner menu (try the venison hotpot).

Pasta Mia (Map p296; ☎ 07-377 2930; 26 Horomatangi St; mains from $8; ☺ breakfast, lunch & dinner) Relaxed Pasta Mia serves, unsurprisingly, pasta dishes, as well as sandwiches and cakes. It's also a popular place to sit back with a coffee.

Replete Cafe (Map p296; ☎ 07-377 3011; www.replete.co.nz; 45 Heu Heu St; mains from $3.50; ☺ breakfast & lunch) This excellent and seemingly always busy café, with its menu of pies, *panini*,

burritos and sandwiches, is a great place for breakfast or brunch, and there's a well-stocked culinary shop attached.

Villino Restaurant & Wine Bar (Map p296; ☎ 07-377 4478; 45 Horomatangi St; mains $17-28; ☺ lunch & dinner) Villino is an extremely popular place serving Italian and Kiwi cuisine, including such dishes as penne with smoked salmon, vodka and lime. It has an extensive New Zealand wine list. Advance bookings for dinner, especially at weekends, are recommended.

Crooked Door Inn (Map p296; ☎ 07-376 8030; cnr Roberts & Titiraupenga Sts; mains around $25; ☺ dinner) The Tudor-style Crooked Door serves top-notch seafood dishes and big steaks, and there's also a cosy bar. It gets busy in the evenings and at weekends.

Landing (Map p305; 213 Lake Tce; mains $14-27; ☺ breakfast, lunch & dinner) This smart and romantic waterfront restaurant is at the Cove (opposite). It has an outstanding view of the lake and serves excellent fish, lamb and venison dishes. There's a predictably excellent wine list, too.

Nonni's (Map p296; ☎ 07-378 6894; 3-5 Tongariro St; mains around $20; ☺ breakfast, lunch & dinner) Nonni's is a good Italian place with pasta and speciality breads, as well as a range of hearty Italian-influenced meals.

Santorini (Map p296; ☎ 07-377 2205; 133 Tongariro St; mains $16-25; ☺ dinner Mon-Sat) Seat yourself at Santorini's first-floor balcony and enjoy Greek and Italian cuisine such as moussaka, linguini and chicken souvlaki.

Lotus (Map p296; ☎ 07-376 9497; 137 Tongariro St; mains $10-20; ☺ lunch Wed-Fri, dinner Wed-Mon) Lotus is a gaudily decorated restaurant next door to Santorini. It serves up good quality Thai food such as stir-fry and curry and it also does takeaways.

Finch's Brasserie & Bar (Map p296; ☎ 07-377 2425; 64 Tuwharetoa St; mains $15-30; ☺ dinner) Finch's is a fine-dining restaurant that serves top-notch NZ cuisine in a smart setting. It's very popular with locals – bookings are advisable on weekends.

Walnut Keep (Map p296; ☎ 07-378 0777; 77 Spa Rd; mains $20-25; ☺ dinner) The upmarket Walnut Keep has superb beef and lamb dishes and is a local favourite.

Brantry (Map p296; ☎ 07-378 0484; 45 Rifle Range Rd; mains $20-30; ☺ dinner) The formal Brantry is amongst Taupo's most refined dining choices. It specialises in high quality contemporary NZ cuisine and wine.

Seoul House Korean Restaurant (Map p296; ☎ 07-377 3344; 100 Roberts St; mains $15-25; ☯ lunch & dinner) This place has authentic barbecue-style Korean dishes, along with the usual range of Japanese specialities.

Asian Noodle House (Map p296; ☎ 07-377 6449; 9 Tongariro St; mains $7-15; ☯ lunch & dinner) A large selection of vegetarian dishes, friendly service and generous portions makes this place a good takeaway or eat-in option.

For self-caterers, **Pak N Save** (Map p296; Taniwha St) and **Woolworths** (Map p296; Spa Rd) are both open until around 9pm.

Entertainment

Holy Cow (Map p296; ☎ 07-378 7533; 11 Tongariro St) Located upstairs, the Holy Cow absolutely heaves after 11pm with much dancing and partying, mostly on table tops. People generally gravitate to the Holy Cow once other places close.

Tongue & Groove (Map p296; ☎ 07-378 3900; 11 Tuwharetoa St; ☯ 10am-3am) This bar has a balcony, pool table and occasional live bands. It's also a great place for a meal (see p303).

Finn MacCuhal's (Map p296; ☎ 07-378 6165; cnr Tongariro & Tuwharetoa Sts) This lively, dimly-lit Irish pub packs in the punters, with DJs on weekends and a large outdoor patio, though it's pretty quiet during the day.

Rockefeller Cocktail Bar & Brasserie (Map p296; ☎ 07-378 3344; Tuwharetoa St) Rockefeller is a popular local hangout, with a good-value dinner menu. It gets busy late in the evening, and is frequented by a slightly older crowd.

Great Lake Centre (Map p296; ☎ 07-376 0340; Tongariro St) There's a theatre and hall for performances, exhibitions and conventions here. The visitors centre has the current schedule.

For movies, there's the **Starlight Cinema Centre** (Map p296; ☎ 07-378 7515; Starlight Arcade, off Horomatangi St; tickets $7.50), where you can catch the latest Hollywood films.

Getting There & Away
AIR
Air New Zealand (☎ 0800 737 000) has daily direct flights to Auckland and Wellington, with onward connections.

In Taupo, ticketing is handled through travel agencies, **House of Travel** (Map p296; ☎ 07-378 2700; 37 Horomatangi St), and **Travel Smart Taupo** (Map p296; ☎ 07-378 9028; 28 Horomatangi St).

BUS
Taupo is about halfway between Auckland and Wellington. **InterCity** (☎ 09-913 6100), **Newmans** (☎ 09-913 6200) and **Alpine Scenic Tours** (☎ 07-386 8918) arrive at and depart from the **Taupo Travel Centre** (☎ 07-378 9032; 16 Gascoigne St). The travel centre also sells tickets for trains, the *Interislander* ferry and Tranz Rail.

InterCity and Newmans have several daily buses to Turangi ($18, 45 minutes), Auckland ($53, 4½ hours), Hamilton ($33, 2¾ hours), Rotorua ($23, 1 hour), Tauranga ($46, 2¾ hours), Napier ($36, 2 hours), Palmerston North ($46, 4¼ hours) and Wellington ($71, 5¾ hours). In addition, the **Purpil People Mover Shuttle** (☎ 0800 787 745; www.purpilpeoplemover.co.nz) runs to Napier on weekdays (single/return $25/35, two hours).

Shuttle services operate year-round between Taupo, Tongariro National Park and the Whakapapa Ski Area, (1½ hours). Transport to the Tongariro Crossing costs $30. During winter, shuttles travel daily and may include package deals for lift tickets and ski hire. Bookings can be made at the visitors centre or at any backpackers. **Tongariro Expeditions** (☎ 07-377 0435; www.tongariroexpeditions.com) has services departing from Taupo at 5.40am and 6.20am, and returning at 3.30pm and 4.30pm. Note though that transport can be delayed or cancelled due to changeable weather conditions.

Getting Around
Taupo's Hot Bus (☎ 07-377 1967) does an hourly circuit of all the major attractions in and around Taupo. It leaves from the visitors centre every hour, on the hour, from 10am to 6pm (each stop $4, day pass $10).

Taxi services in Taupo are provided by **Taupo Taxis** (☎ 07-378 5100) and **Top Cabs** (☎ 07-378 9250).

Bikes are forbidden on the track from Spa Park to Huka Falls due to track damage.

AROUND TAUPO
Wairakei Park
Crossing the river at Tongariro St and heading north from town on SH1, you'll arrive at the Wairakei Park area, also known as the Huka Falls Tourist Loop. Take the first right turn after you cross the river and you'll be on Huka Falls Rd, which passes along the river. When return-

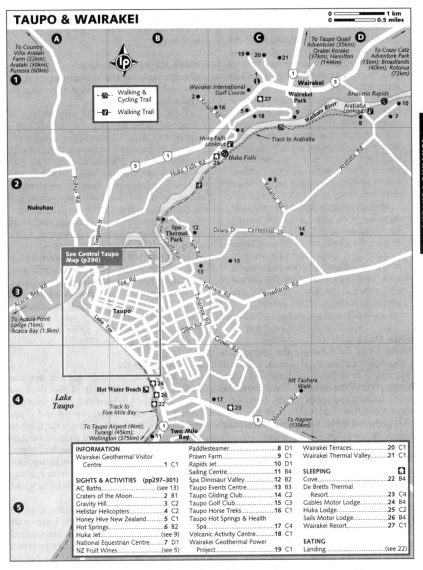

TAUPO & WAIRAKEI

To Country Villa Arataki Farm (22km); Arataki (30km); Pureora (60km)

To Taupo Quad Adventures (35km); Orakei Korako (37km); Hamilton (144km)

To Crazy Catz Adventure Park (13km); Broadlands (40km); Rotorua (72km)

Walking & Cycling Trail

Walking Trail

Wairakei International Golf Course

Wairakei

Wairakei Park

Waikato River

Aratiatia Rapids

Aratiatia Lookouts

Huka Falls Lookout

Track to Aratiatia

Huka Falls

Huka Falls Rd

Pohipi Rd

Rakanui Rd

Nukuhau

Aratiatia Rd

Spa Thermal Park

Delany Dr

Centennial Dr

Tongariro St

County Ave

Spa Rd

Spa Rd

Acacia Bay Rd

To Acacia Point Lodge (1km); Acacia Bay (1.8km)

Taupo

Taupo Rd

Tauhara Rd

Broadlands Rd

Lake Tce

Gilles Ave

Crown Rd

See Central Taupo Map (p296)

Mt Tauhara Walk

Lake Taupo

Hot Water Beach

Track to Five Mile Bay

Mountain Rd

To Napier (139km)

To Taupo Airport (4km); Turangi (45km); Wellington (375km)

Two Mile Bay

INFORMATION		Paddlesteamer	8	D1	Wairakei Terraces	20	C1
Wairakei Geothermal Visitor		Prawn Farm	9	C1	Wairakei Thermal Valley	21	C1
Centre	1 C1	Rapids Jet	10	D1			
		Sailing Centre	11	B4	SLEEPING		
SIGHTS & ACTIVITIES (pp297–301)		Spa Dinosaur Valley	12	B2	Cove	22	B4
AC Baths	(see 13)	Taupo Events Centre	13	B3	De Bretts Thermal		
Craters of the Moon	2 B1	Taupo Gliding Club	14	C2	Resort	23	C4
Gravity Hill	3 C2	Taupo Golf Club	15	C3	Gables Motor Lodge	24	B4
Helistar Helicopters	4 C2	Taupo Horse Treks	16	C1	Huka Lodge	25	C2
Honey Hive New Zealand	5 C1	Taupo Hot Springs & Health			Sails Motor Lodge	26	B4
Hot Springs	6 B2	Spa	17	C4	Wairakei Resort	27	C1
Huka Jet	(see 9)	Volcanic Activity Centre	18	C1			
National Equestrian Centre	7 D1	Wairakei Geothermal Power			EATING		
NZ Fruit Wines	(see 5)	Project	19	C1	Landing	(see 22)	

ing to Taupo, turn left back to the highway and you'll pass other interesting spots on your way back.

There's no public transport but tours go to a few places along here; otherwise walk or hire a mountain bike for the day.

En route look out for **Honey Hive New Zealand** (☎ 07-374 8553; www.honey.co.nz; Huka Falls Loop Rd; admission free; ☼ 9am-5pm Mon-Fri, 9am-5.30pm Sat & Sun), which houses NZ's largest collection of honey bee products, and a few glass-enclosed hives. In the same building is **NZ Fruit Wines** (☎ 07-374 8525; www.nzfruitwines.co.nz; ☼ 9am-5pm), where you can taste all manner of alcoholic fruit wines and liquers.

BANG!

There have been two really big eruptions in the Taupo region. The *really* big one, which created the huge hole now filled by Lake Taupo, was about 26,500 years ago and produced an estimated 800 cu km of ash and pumice. For comparison, Krakatoa (1883) produced just 8 cu km and Mt St Helens (1980) only 3. The Taupo eruption devastated the entire North Island – almost all vegetation would have been destroyed, coated with hot, poisonous ash up to 100m deep. Even the Chatham Islands (800km downwind) were covered in an 11cm-deep layer.

More recently, in AD 181, accounts of darkened skies and spectacular sunsets were recorded as far away as China and Rome – the effects of a week-long Taupo explosion that spewed out 33-billion tons of pumice and sent up an eruption column some 50km high. Fortunately, NZ was still uninhabited at the time – today the area affected is home to 200,000 people.

HUKA FALLS

Along Huka Falls Rd are the spectacular Huka Falls, known as Hukanui in Maori, meaning 'Great Body of Spray'. A footbridge crosses the Waikato River above the falls – a great torrent of water, more like a giant rapid that plunges through a narrow cleft in the rock. The water here is clear and turquoise, particularly on a sunny day.

VOLCANIC ACTIVITY CENTRE

Budding vulcanologists will love this **activity centre & bookshop** (☎ 07-374 8375; www .volcanoes.co.nz; Huka Falls Loop Rd; adult/child $6/3; ⏱ 9am-5pm Mon-Fri, 10am-4pm Sat & Sun). The observatory monitors volcanic activity in the volatile Taupo Volcanic Zone, and the visitors centre has some excellent displays on NZ's geothermal and volcanic activity.

Exhibits include a large relief map with push-button highlighters to show the volcanic regions, and old documentaries about the eruptions of Ngauruhoe and Ruapehu in 1945 – the largest NZ eruptions last century. There's also a little booth you can sit in to experience what an earthquake feels like: press a button to shudder and shake in your seat. Pick up a monitoring report to read about recent earthquakes or to see if Ruapehu is about to erupt.

HUKA JET & PRAWN FARM

On the banks of the Waikato River is the Prawn Farm, and next door, the office for Huka Jet.

Partly inspired by the engineering of riverboats like the *Waireka*, which has a draught of only 30.5cm laden, Kiwi CWF Hamilton was inspired to invent the jetboat. In the **Huka Jet** (☎ 0800 485 2538, 07-374 8572; www.hukajet.com; trips adult/child $75/45) you can take a 30-minute ride down to the Aratiatia Dam and up to Huka Falls. Trips run all day (price includes transport from Taupo). Various combined trips are available, including the 'hukastar combo' (adult/child $170/110), which includes a helicopter ride.

Prawn Farm (☎ 07-374 8474; www.prawnpark.com; tours adult/child $6/2.50) is the world's only geothermally heated fresh-water prawn farm. There are hourly tours (between 11am and 4pm), and more frequently in summer. There's a restaurant where you can try the prawns. Also on-site is Killer Prawn Golf (balls $1 each, $10 for 20).

ARATIATIA RAPIDS

Two kilometres off SH5 are the **Aratiatia Rapids**, a spectacular part of the Waikato River until the government, in its wisdom, plonked down a power house and dam, shutting off the water. To keep the tourists happy it opens the control gates at various times: from 1 October to 31 March at 10am, noon, 2pm and 4pm; from April to September at 10am, noon and 2pm. You can see the water flow through from three good vantage points (entry is free).

Rapids Jet (☎ 0800 727 437, 07-378 5828; adult/child $55/45) shoots up and down the lower part of the Aratiatia Rapids. It's a sensational 45-minute ride, rivalling the trip to Huka Falls. The jetboats depart from the end of the access road to the Aratiatia lookouts. Go down Rapids Rd; look for the signpost to the National Equestrian Centre.

The paddle steamer **Otunua** (☎ 0800 278 336, 07-378 5828; cruises adult/child $35/25) makes cruises daily to Huka Falls, at 10.30am and 2.30pm from the Aratiatia dam. The Moonlight Glowworm Cruise goes at 5.30pm in winter and 9pm in summer.

WAIRAKEI THERMAL VALLEY

This thermal valley, like Orakei Korako (p308), gets its name from the water having once been used as a mirror. It is the remains of what was once known as Geyser Valley. Before the geothermal power project started in 1958 it was one of the most active thermal areas in the world, with 22 geysers and 240 mud pools and springs.

It is now the site of **Wairakei Terraces** (☎ 07-378 0913; www.wairakeiterraces.co.nz; adult/child $18/9; ☯ tours 9am-4.30pm Apr-Sep, 9am-5pm Oct-Mar), a man-made landscape of silica terraces, pools and geysers, which attempts to recreate, in some small part, the appearance of the fabled Pink and White Terraces. There's also a **Maori Cultural Experience** (adult/child $75/37.50; ☯ 6.30pm), including a concert and *hangi*. Other attractions on the site include an animal park, carriage rides, 'Maori village' and restaurant.

WAIRAKEI GEOTHERMAL POWER PROJECT

NZ was the second country in the world to produce power from natural steam. If you dive into all of that steam you will find yourself at the **Wairakei Geothermal Power Project**, which generates about 190MW, providing about 5% of NZ's electricity.

The **visitors centre** (☎ 07-378 0913; adult/child $2/1; ☯ 9am-5pm summer, 9am-4.30pm winter) is close to the road. Information on the bore field and power house is available and a video is shown (from 9am to 4pm). You can drive up the road through the project and from a lookout see the long pipes, wreathed in steam.

Just south of here is the big Wairakei Resort and the Wairakei International Golf Club.

CRATERS OF THE MOON

An interesting and unexploited thermal area is **Craters of the Moon** (admission free, donations appreciated; ☯ dawn-dusk). It's run by DOC, so it is less touristy than other commercially exploited thermal areas. Don't miss the lookout just before the car park – it's the best place for photos.

This thermal area sprang up in the 1950s. The power station lowered underground water levels, reducing the pressure of the heated water, and causing more vigorous boiling and steam. New mud pools and steam vents appeared, and you can wander through them on a plank-walk.

There is a small kiosk staffed by volunteers at the car park (they will keep an eye on your car).

Craters of the Moon is signposted on SH1, about 5km north of Taupo.

Broadlands

This beautiful and often unseen stretch of the mighty Waikato River, equidistant (40km) from Rotorua and Taupo, is worth visiting. To get here turn off SH5 onto Homestead Rd, just south of Reporoa.

The stunning scenery of the region is best seen with **NZ Riverjet** (☎ 07-333 7111; trips $55-125). You can travel downstream by jetboat to the Orakei Korako thermal region through some magnificent steamy gorges or head upstream through the exciting Full James Rapids to Aratiatia.

Near the township of Reporoa is **Butcher's Pool** (admission free; ☯ daily), a natural thermal spring in the middle of a farmer's paddock. It's well set up, with a small parking area, changing sheds and wooden decking around the water's edge. To get here from Reporoa head south on Broadlands Rd for 2km and look for a row of trees lining a gravel driveway off to your left. This leads to the pool.

Arataki & Pureora Forest Park

The dominating western ramparts of Lake Taupo largely comprise the huge Pureora Forest. Logging was eventually stopped in the park in the 1980s after long campaigns by conservationists.

There are long and short forest treks, including tracks to the summits of Mt Pureora (1165m) and the rock pinnacle of Mt Titiraupenga (1042m).

The north section of the park is designated for recreational hunting, but you must obtain a permit from park headquarters. Pamphlets, maps and information on the park are available from the DOC offices in Taupo and Te Kuiti.

Country Villa Arataki Farm (☎ 07-882 8857; arataki .farm@xtra.co.nz; s/d $30/50), nestled beside the picturesque Mangakino Stream, is one of those rare gems. There are activities galore here, including horse trekking ($50 for two hours), mountain biking ($30 per day), tramping and trout fishing on a secluded section of the stream. The house, surrounded by a working farm (where you can participate in some of the daily activities), is well equipped with comfortable beds. On the balcony is a BBQ and heated spa pool. Phone ahead for directions on how to get there.

Orakei Korako

Between Taupo and Rotorua, **Orakei Korako** (☎ 07-378 3131; www.orakeikorako.co.nz; adult/child $21/7; ☼ 8am-5pm) receives fewer visitors than other thermal areas because of its remote location, but since the destruction of the Pink and White Terraces by the Tarawera eruption it has been possibly the best thermal area left in New Zealand, and one of the finest in the world. Although three-quarters of it now lies beneath the dam waters of Lake Ohakuri, the quarter that remains is the best part and is still very much worth seeing.

A walking track takes you around the large, colourful silica terraces for which the park is famous, as well as geysers and Ruatapu Cave – a magnificent natural cave with a pool of jade-green water. The pool may have been used by Maoris as a mirror during hairdressing ceremonies: Orakei Korako means 'the place of adorning'. Entry includes a boat ride across Lake Ohakuri.

Orakei Korako Geyserland Resort (☎ 07-378 3131; ok@reap.org.nz; dm/d from $20/80) is right on the river at Orakei Korako. There's accommodation available in a self-contained flat (it sleeps up to seven people), or in a communal lodge. Note that rates at least double on weekends and public holidays and you'll need your own linen in the lodge.

To get to Orakei Korako from Taupo, take SH1 towards Hamilton for 23km, and then travel for 14km from the signposted turn-off. From Rotorua the turn-off is on SH5, via Mihi.

TURANGI
pop 3900

Developed for the construction of the nearby hydroelectric power station in 1973, Turangi is Taupo's smaller cousin at the southern end of Lake Taupo. The town itself is 4km away from the lake, access to which is from nearby Tokaanu.

Turangi's main attractions are its world-class trout fishing, on the Tongariro River, and access to the northern trails of nearby Tongariro National Park.

Information

The Turangi **visitors centre** (☎ 07-386 8999; turangi vc@laketauponz.com; ☼ 8.30am-5pm), just off SH1, has a detailed relief model of Tongariro National Park and is the best place to stop for information about the park, Kaimanawa Forest Park, trout fishing, walks and general snow and road conditions. The office also issues hut tickets, InterCity bus tickets, ski passes and hunting and fishing licences, and acts as the Automobile Association agent for the area.

You will find the **DOC** (☎ 07-386 8607) near the junction of SH1 and Ohuanga Rd. The nearest post office and banks are in the Turangi shopping mall, opposite the visitors centre. Plenty of places in town have Internet access.

Tongariro National Trout Centre

About 4km south of Turangi on SH1 is the last DOC-managed **trout hatchery & centre** (☎ 07-386 8085; admission free; ☼ 10am-4pm). This landscaped centre has a self-guided walk to an underwater viewing chamber, hatchery, keeping ponds and a picnic area. The information centre has excellent educational displays, including a fine collection of rods and reels and a theatre showing a 14-minute film about the river. You can fish for trout in the Tongariro River, which runs close by.

Tokaanu

On the lake, about 5km west of Turangi, this settlement has a collection of motels and fishing lodges and there's plenty to do in the way of outdoor activities, especially for thrillseekers and nature lovers.

The **Tokaanu Thermal Pools** (☎ 07-386 8575; Mangaroa St; public pools adult/child $5/2.50, private pools 20min $7/3; ☼ public pools 10am-9pm, private pools till 9.30pm) is an interesting thermal area with hot baths, a trout stream, BBQ area and displays. A 20-minute walk down a boardwalk (free) leads around the mud pools and thermal springs. It is wheelchair accessible.

Walking

The DOC *Turangi Walks* ($1) leaflet outlines notable walks, such as the Tongariro River Walkway (three hours return), which is also suitable for mountain bikes; the Tongariro River Loop Track (one hour); Hinemihi's Track, near the top of Te Ponanga Saddle (15 minutes return); a walk on Mt Maunganamu (40 minutes return); and a walk around Lake Rotopounamu. This lake abounds in bird life and has some great little beaches, perfect for a summer's day picnic and swim (20 minutes to the lake, 1½ hours around it). The leaflet also lists walks in the nearby Kaimanawa Forest Park.

Trout Fishing

February and March are the best months for brown trout and June to September are the best for rainbow trout, but the fishing is good almost year-round. Don't forget that you need a fishing licence.

The visitors centre has over 20 fishing guides. The guides charge from around $50 to $65 per hour (generally a minimum of three hours), including all gear (excluding the fishing license). The other option is to hire your own gear from sports stores around town – rods cost $15 and waders $20 – but unless you're experienced it's best to hire a guide. Will Kemp, at **Tongariro Fly Fishing** (☎ 07-386 6545; www.tongariroflyfishing.co.nz) comes locally recommended.

Boats can be hired for lake fishing: aluminium dinghies cost around $25 per hour from **Motuoapa Marina** (☎ 07-386 7000), at Motuoapa.

Other Activities

River rafting is popular, and the Tongariro River has grade III rapids or, for families, grade I on the lower reaches in summer. The **Rafting Centre** (☎ 0800 101 024; Atirau Rd; rafting per person $90, family floats for 4 people $180) is the home of Tongariro River Rafting; you have the option of a four-hour trip on grade III (half that time is spent on the river), the more gentle family floats or raft fishing (only in summer). The Rafting Centre also hires out bikes for $20 for two hours.

Rock 'N' River (☎ 0800 865 226; www.raftingnew zealand.com; 203 Puanga St, Tokaanu) has a number of trips. The four-hour Tongariro River trip (grade III; $90) includes a visit to the Puketarata Falls topped off by a soak in a

CENTRAL PLATEAU

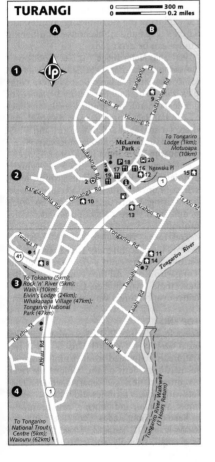

TURANGI 0 ——— 300 m 0 ——— 0.2 miles

INFORMATION	
Automobile Association	(see 4)
Banks	(see 3)
DOC	1 A3
Police Station	2 A2
Post Office	(see 3)
Turangi Shopping Mall	3 B2
Turangi Visitors Centre	4 B2

SIGHTS & ACTIVITIES	(pp308–10)
New World Supermarket	5 B2
Rafting Centre	6 A3
Tongariro Hike 'n' Bike	7 B3
Vertical Assault Climbing Wall	(see 12)

SLEEPING	(pp310–11)
Anglers Paradise Resort Motel	8 A3
Bellbird Lodge	9 B1
Club Habitat	10 A2
Creel Lodge	11 B3
Extreme Backpackers	12 B2
Parklands Motor Lodge	13 B2
Rainbow Trout Lodge	14 B3
Tongariro River Motel	15 B2

EATING	(p311)
Brew Haus	(see 10)
Grand Central Fry	16 B2
Hong Kong Chinese Restaurant	17 B2
Mustard Seed Cafe	18 B2
Red Crater Cafe	(see 12)
Valentino's	19 B2

TRANSPORT	(p311)
Turangi Bus & Travel Centre	20 B2

thermal pool. There is also an overnight trip on the Tongariro River ($250), as well as white-water kayaking (full day $95) and various rafting outings on the Wairoa, Rangitikei and Mohaka Rivers. There's a free pick up from Turangi.

Rapid Sensations (☎ 0800 227 238; www.rapids .co.nz) runs excursions on the Tongariro (from $55). It also offers activities such as raft fishing, white-water rafting on the Rangitaiki, Wairoa and Mangahao Rivers, and multiday trips on the Upper and Lower Mohaka Rivers.

Kiwi Outback Tours (☎ 07-386 6607; 2hr/3hr trips $100/145) does quad-bike trips.

On those wet days, head to the **Vertical Assault Climbing Wall** (☎ 07-386 6558; 26 Ngawaka Pl; adult/child $15/11), run by Extreme Backpackers. There's also a licensed café (see Red Crater, opposite).

Contact the visitors centre for details on horse riding (approximately $30 per hour) in the area.

Sleeping
BUDGET
Extreme Backpackers (☎ 07-386 8949; www.extreme backpackers.co.nz; 26 Ngawaka Pl; dm/d/f from $19/44/70; ▢) This is a modern, spotless backpackers' place. There's a pleasant lounge with an open fire, an inner courtyard with hammocks and a BBQ, and the rooms are spacious. There's also an indoor climbing wall (above) and a café, and it runs its own Tongariro Crossing bus.

Bellbird Lodge (☎ 07-386 8281; bellbird@reap.org .nz; 6 Rangipoia Pl; dm/s/d $18/36/40) Bellbird is a small, friendly lodge with relaxing lounges with log fires, fully equipped kitchens and a choice of rooms, including neat four- to six-bed dorms. The hosts provide transport to the Tongariro Crossing, as well as fishing licences and tackle, and are themselves well-informed anglers. There's a freezer and you can arrange to have your catch smoked.

Club Habitat (☎ 07-3867492; clubhabitat@xtra.co.nz; 25 Ohuanga Rd; dm/camp sites/d/f $19/20/70/109) This is a huge modern complex (220 beds) with rooms scattered around the grounds. It's popular with families and groups, and there is a big restaurant-bar complex (see Brew Haus, opposite), a sauna, spa and playground, plus a summer and winter activity centre on-site.

Eivin's Lodge (☎ 07-386 8062; eivins@xtra.co.nz; bed/camp sites from $20/22) Eivin's Lodge is on SH47 about halfway between Turangi and the Grand Chateau at Whakapapa (approximately 24km from either; see Map p285). It's a friendly and self-contained place, with 40 heated rooms, as well as tent and powered sites, a kitchen, lounge, spa pool, restaurant, dairy, and postal agency. There's ski hire in winter.

MID-RANGE
Anglers Paradise Resort Motel (☎ 0800 500 039; anglers@reap.org.nz; cnr SH41 & Ohuanga Rd; d/ste from $95/155; ▨) Anglers Paradise is a peaceful and relaxed place with a high standard of accommodation, including studio and one-bedroom units. It has a licensed restaurant with a cosy log fire, and makes a great base for exploring the surrounding countryside. There's a spa and smokehouse, and fishing guides can be arranged.

Parklands Motor Lodge (☎ 0800 456 284; www .parklandsmotorlodge.co.nz; cnr SH1 & Arahori St; s/d from $55/80; ▨) This is a large Best Western complex with good facilities, set in 3 hectares of gentle parkland. The ground-level units have all the standard amenities you'd expect, and there's a spa, sauna, tennis court and BBQ. There's also space for 20 campervans.

Tongariro River Motel (☎ 07-386 8555; fax 07-386 0146; cnr SH1 & Link Rd; s/d $75/95; ▨) This is a quiet place with spacious ground-level, self-contained units in an attractive park-like setting. Some units sleep up to seven people, and there's a spa pool and a playground.

Creel Lodge (☎ /fax 07-386 8081; 183 Taupahi Rd; s/d $55/85) This peaceful lodge is in a picturesque setting, backing onto a fine stretch of the Tongariro River. All the ground-level suites have their own kitchen facilities and balcony, overlooking a very attractive garden.

TOP END
Tongariro Lodge (☎ 07-386 7946; www.tongarirolodge .co.nz; Grace Rd; s/d $490/820) This is an internationally renowned trout-fishing lodge set in mature gardens on the bank of the river. Accommodation is in separate wooden chalets with private facilities and there's a tennis court, spa pool and gourmet restaurant.

Rainbow Trout Lodge (☎ 07-386 6501; www .turangi-nz.co.nz; 213 Taupahi Rd; s/d from $120/185) This is a small, friendly and relaxed homestay on the river, run by very welcoming hosts. Breakfast is included, and an excellent dinner can be arranged ($50). Host Heather Macdonald runs guided fly-fishing trips (half-day $250). The garden backs onto the river and is a perfect spot to unwind after a day flicking your rod about.

Eating

Mustard Seed Cafe (☎ 07-386 7377; Ohuanga Rd; mains $4-10; ☺ lunch) This modern café has a large selection of light meals and sandwiches, and good coffee.

Hong Kong Chinese Restaurant (☎ 07-386 7526; Ohuanga Rd; mains $15-20; ☺ lunch & dinner) Head here for sit-down or takeaway Chinese.

Red Crater Cafe (☎ 07-386 6558; 26 Ngawaka Pl; mains $6-12; ☺ breakfast & lunch) This is a bright and pleasant little café inside Extreme Backpackers (see opposite) that offers a range of light meals, snacks and drinks in an outdoor setting.

Valentino's (☎ 07-386 8821; Ohuanga Rd; mains $20-30; ☺ dinner Wed-Mon) This is a good Italian restaurant serving the usual range of pasta and pizza.

Brew Haus (☎ 07-386 7492; 25 Ohuanga Rd; mains $15-25; ☺ lunch & dinner) The Brew Haus is situated in Club Habitat (see opposite). There's a pleasant restaurant and a popular bar serving light meals and beer that is brewed on the premises.

Grand Central Fry (☎ 07-386 5344; Ohuanga Rd; burgers around $5; ☺ breakfast, lunch & dinner) This takeaway-stand's burgers and fish and chips are good value.

Getting There & Away

Both **InterCity** (☎ 09-913 6100) and **Newmans** (☎ 09-913 6200) buses arrive at and depart from the **Turangi Bus & Travel Centre** (Tautahanga Rd). Auckland–Wellington and Rotorua–Wellington buses that travel along the eastern side of the lake to and from Taupo, all stop at Turangi.

Alpine Scenic Tours (☎ 07-386 8918) runs a shuttle twice daily between Turangi and National Park township, stopping at the Ketetahi and Mangatepopo trail heads, Whakapapa and, in winter, the Whakapapa Ski Area. This is an excellent service for skiers and trampers. It also has services to and from Taupo.

Alpha Tours (☎ 0800 887 264) runs a shuttle service to Taupo activity centres, such as Huka Jet and Taupo Bungy, as well as to Orakei Korako.

Tongariro Expeditions (☎ 0800 828 763) runs shuttles from Turangi, Taupo and Whakapapa for the Tongariro Crossing and the Northern Circuit. Bellbird Lodge (opposite) and Extreme Backpackers (opposite) also provide shuttles for the Tongariro Crossing ($25 return), and sometimes for the Whakapapa Ski Area.

CENTRAL PLATEAU

Bay of Plenty

CONTENTS

Rotorua	**314**
History	314
Orientation & Information	314
Sights	316
Activities	319
Walking Tour	322
Tours	323
Sleeping	323
Eating	325
Drinking	326
Entertainment	326
Shopping	326
Getting There & Away	326
Getting Around	327
Around Rotorua	**327**
Hell's Gate	327
Waimangu Volcanic Valley	327
Wai-o-tapu Thermal Wonderland	329
Trout Springs	329
Skyline Skyrides	330
Agrodome	330
Te Ngae Park	330
Buried Village of Te Wairoa	330
Lake Tarawera	331
Whirinaki Forest Park	331
Western Bay of Plenty	**331**
Tauranga	331
Mt Maunganui	337
Around Tauranga	340
Eastern Bay of Plenty	**343**
Whakatane	343
Whakaari (White Island)	346
Motuhora	347
Whakatane to Rotorua	347
Ohope Beach	348
Opotiki	348

The Bay of Plenty, as its name suggests, is one of New Zealand's most scenic and prosperous regions, blessed with a warm and sunny climate, stunning sandy beaches and a thriving agricultural sector most noted for its kiwi fruit. The bay itself stretches from the chief city of Tauranga in the west, to Whakatane and Opotiki, the main focal points of the Eastern Bay.

Along the coast from Tauranga, the superb beaches of Mt Maunganui are a big draw for holidaying New Zealanders and surfers, while quieter stretches of pristine sand run eastwards. A wide range of water sports are on hand, and this is also a great place to go swimming with dolphins or whale-watching. Off Whakatane, meanwhile, lies the moonscape island of Whakaari (White Island), NZ's most active volcano and a breathtaking place to visit.

Inland is the remarkable 'Sulphur City' of Rotorua, which, with its unique volcanic landscape of thermal springs, geysers, bubbling mud pools and lakes, and its rich Maori heritage, is among NZ's premier tourist attractions and an unmissable experience for anyone visiting the country.

Maoris originally settled the Bay of Plenty area in the 14th century. It was Captain Cook, arriving here aboard the *Endeavour* in October 1769, who gave it this name in honour of the number of thriving settlements of friendly Maoris he encountered, and the amount of supplies they gave him. European settlement only began in the 1830s and was slowed by the land wars that ensued. Today it's one of NZ's most populous regions.

BAY OF PLENTY

HIGHLIGHTS

- Visiting the many geothermal areas in and around **Rotorua** (p314)
- Visiting the site of the **Buried Village of Te Wairoa** (p330)
- Feasting at a Maori *hangi* (meals cooked in an earth oven) and taking in a concert at **Tamaki Maori Village** (p319)
- Taking a mud bath at the **Wai Ora Spa** (p327)
- Rolling downhill inside the zorb at **Agrodome Adventure Park** (p330)
- Visiting NZ's most active marine volcano, **Whakaari** (White Island; p346)
- Spending a lazy day on the beach at **Mt Maunganui** (p337)

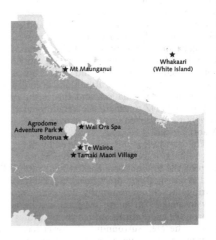

- TELEPHONE CODE: 07
- www.rotoruanz.com
- www.bayofplenty.co.nz

Climate

The Bay of Plenty is one of the sunniest regions of New Zealand, with Whakatane and the Eastern Bay recording the most sunshine hours (2350 per year on average). In summer temperatures hover between 20°C and 27°C while winter can see temperatures fall as low as 5°C, but it's slightly warmer on the coast. Rainfall is heavier inland in places such as Rotorua, which also experiences long dry spells in summer.

Getting There & Around

Air New Zealand has flights from Tauranga to Auckland, Wellington and Nelson; from Whakatane to Auckland; and from Rotorua to Auckland, Wellington, Christchurch, Queenstown and Nelson. Origin Pacific has flights between Rotorua and Auckland, Dunedin, Christchurch and Invercargill.

InterCity bus services connect Tauranga, Rotorua and Whakatane with most other main cities in NZ. Bay Coaster and Bay Hopper services run between Tauranga and Whakatane and Whakatane, and Opotiki respectively.

ROTORUA

pop 76,000

Rotorua is far and away the most popular and, inevitably, the most commercialised tourist destination on the North Island. Nicknamed 'Sulphur City', it has the most energetic thermal activity in the country, with bubbling mud pools, gurgling hot springs, gushing geysers and evil eggy smells hovering around. Rotorua also has a large Maori population, and this is the best place in NZ to experience a traditional *hangi* (meals cooked in an earth oven) and Maori concert.

The city itself is thriving, buoyed by the huge influx of tourists; Rotorua is a major stop on the international backpacker route and it can get extremely busy, especially during the summer months. It's scenically located 297m above sea level on the shores of Lake Rotorua, which teems with trout. The area surrounding Rotorua has a number of serene lakes, trout springs, wildlife parks, farm shows and adrenaline activities.

HISTORY

The Rotorua district was first settled in the 14th century when the canoe *Te Arawa*, captained by Tamatekapua, arrived from Hawaiki at Maketu in the central Bay of Plenty. The settlers took the tribal name Te Arawa to commemorate the vessel that had safely brought them so far. Much of the inland forest was explored by Tamatekapua's grandson, Ihenga, who also named many geographical features of the area. The name Rotorua means 'The Second Lake' (*roto* means 'lake' and *rua* 'two'), as it was the second lake that Ihenga discovered.

In the next few hundred years, various subtribes spread through the area and, as they grew in number, split into more subtribes and conflicts broke out over territory. In 1823 the Arawa lands were invaded by Northland's Ngapuhi chief, Hongi Hika, in the so-called Musket Wars. Both the Arawa and the Northlanders suffered heavy losses and the Ngapuhi eventually withdrew.

During the Waikato Land War (1863–67) the Arawa tribe threw in their lot with the government against their traditional enemies in the Waikato, gaining the backing of its troops and preventing East Coast reinforcements getting through to support the Maori King Movement (see p219).

With peace returning in the early 1870s, European settlement around Rotorua really took off. The army and government personnel involved in the war helped broadcast the scenic wonders of the place. People came to take the waters in the hope of cures for all sorts of diseases, and Rotorua's tourist industry was thus founded. The town's main attraction was the fabulous Pink and White Terraces, formed by the sinter deposits of silica from volcanic activity. Touted at the time as the eighth natural wonder of the world, they were destroyed in the 1886 Mt Tarawera eruption (see p329).

ORIENTATION & INFORMATION

The main shopping area is down Tutanekai St, the central part of which is a parking area and pedestrian mall. Running parallel, Fenton St starts by the Government Gardens near the lake and runs all the way to the Whakarewarewa ('Whaka') thermal area 3km away. It's lined with motels for much of its length.

BAY OF PLENTY

Tourism Rotorua (Map pp316-17; ☎ 0800 768 678; www.rotoruanz.com; 1167 Fenton St; ☀ 8am-5.30pm May-Sep, 8am-6pm Oct-Apr) makes bookings for everything around Rotorua and elsewhere in NZ, and has a travel agency and a DOC office. It also has an **exchange bureau** (☀ 8am-5.30pm), a café, and other services for travellers, including showers, luggage storage and public telephones (buy your phonecard from the exchange bureau).

Get maps and other travel information from the **Automobile Association** (AA; ☎ 07-348 3069; www.aatravel.co.nz; 1121 Eruera St). The American Express agent is **Galaxy United Travel** (Map pp316-17; ☎ 07-347 9444; cnr Amohau & Hinemoa Sts); there is a foreign exchange desk at **Thomas Cook** (Map pp316-17; ☎ 07-348 0640; cnr Fenton & Hine-

moa Sts) and there are plenty of banks that will change foreign currencies.

The **post office** (Map pp316-17; Hinemoa St) is between Tutanekai and Amohia Sts, and there is a **laundry** (Map pp316-317; 1209 Fenton St) opposite the police station.

The **Arthritis Centre** (☎ 07-348 5121) can arrange a wheelchair for disabled people. Call them between 10am and 3pm Monday to Friday. **Rotorua Taxis** (☎ 07-348 1111) has a taxi with a wheelchair hoist.

The weekly magazine *Thermal Air* is a useful and free tourist publication while the annual free *Rotorua Visitors Guide* is a more basic affair. Tourism Rotorua (above) sells a good map, *Gateway to Geyserland* ($1), of the city and surrounding area.

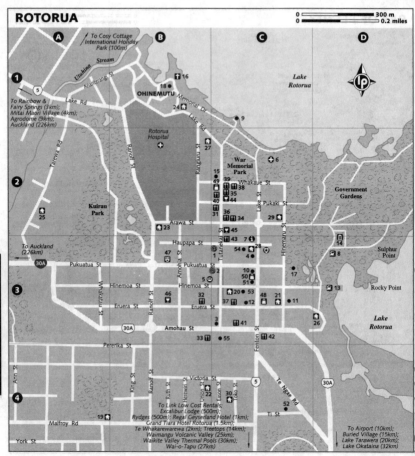

ROTORUA

There are plenty of Internet cafés around town, all charging around $5 to $6 per hour, including **Planet 4 Cyber Café** (Map above; Rotorua Central Mall, off Amohau St), **Cyber World** (Map above; 1174 Haupapa St) and **Cybershed** (Map above; ☎ 07-349 4965; 1176 Pukuatua St).

SIGHTS
Lake Rotorua
Lake Rotorua is the largest of 16 lakes in the Rotorua district. It was formed by an eruption and subsequent subsidence of the area. Two cruises on the lake depart from the Rotorua lake-front jetty, at the northern end of Tutanekai St.

The **Lakeland Queen paddle steamer** (Map above; ☎ 0800 862 784; www.lakelandqueen.co.nz)

does one-hour breakfast (adult/child $28/14), luncheon ($30/15), afternoon tea ($20/10) and dinner cruises ($55) on the lake.

Rotorua Lakes Cruises (Map above; ☎ 07-347 9852; 1-hr cruise adult/child $30/15) does a one-hour circuit of Mokoia Island. There are longer cruises available.

If you prefer to explore under your own steam, **Hamill Adventures** (☎ 07-348 4186) rents out pontoon boats ($75 per hour) and pedal boats (from $10 for 20 minutes).

Ohinemutu
Ohinemutu is a lakeside Maori village. Its name means 'Place of the Young Woman who was Killed' and was given by Ihenga in memory of his daughter.

INFORMATION		SLEEPING	(pp323–5)	DRINKING	(p326)
Cyber World	1 C3	Ann's Volcanic Rotorua	19 A4	Echo	(see 20)
Cybershed	2 C3	Base Backpackers	20 C3	Fuze	44 C2
DOC	(see 7)	Crash Palace	21 C3	Hennessy's Irish Bar	45 C2
Galaxy United Travel & American		Funky Green Voyager	22 B4	Lava Bar	(see 23)
Express Agent	3 C3	Hot Rock	23 B2	O'Malley's	46 B3
Laundry	4 C3	Jack & Di's	24 B1	Pig & Whistle	(see 43)
Money Changing Bureau	(see 7)	Kiwi Paka YHA	25 A2		
Planet 4 Cyber Café	(see 55)	Lake Plaza Rotorua	26 D3	ENTERTAINMENT	(p326)
Post Office	5 B3	Ledwich Lodge Motel	27 B2	Bar Barella	47 B3
Queen Elizabeth Hospital	6 C2	Planet Nomad		Fuze	(see 44)
Thomas Cook	(see 51)	Backpackers	28 C3	Pig & Whistle	(see 43)
Tourism Rotorua	7 C3	Princes Gate Hotel	29 C2		
Travel Agency	(see 7)	Tresco B&B	30 C4	SHOPPING	(p326)
				Best of Maori	
SIGHTS & ACTIVITIES	(pp316–22)	EATING	(pp325–6)	Tourism	(see 28)
Blue Pool	8 D3	Café Ephesus	31 C2	Jade Factory	48 C3
Indoor Climbing Wall	(see 20)	Capers Epicurean	32 B3	Madhouse Design	49 C2
Lakeland Queen Paddle Steamer	9 C1	Cocos	(see 34)	Souvenir Centre	50 C3
Map & Track Shop	10 C3	Countdown	33 B3		
Millennium	11 C3	Fat Dog	34 C2	TRANSPORT	(pp326–7)
O'Keefe's	12 C3	Herb's	35 C2	Air New Zealand	51 C3
Planet Bike	(see 20)	Indian Star	36 C2	Bus Depot	(see 7)
Polynesian Spa	13 D3	Katsubi	37 C3	Rent-a-Dent	52 C4
Rotorua Lakes Cruises	(see 9)	La Vega	38 C2	Rotorua Cycle Centre	53 C3
Rotorua Museum of Art & History	14 D3	Lady Jane's Ice Cream Parlour	39 C2		
Royal Lakeside Novotel Hotel	15 C2	Lewisham's Restaurant	40 C2	OTHER	
St Faith's Anglican Church	16 B1	Mr India	41 C3	Carey's Sightseeing	
Tamaki Maori Village	17 C3	Pak N Save	42 C3	Tours	54 C3
Tamatekapua Meeting House	18 B1	Pig & Whistle	43 C3	Rotorua Central Mall	55 C3

The historic Maori **St Faith's Anglican Church** (Map above; ☉8am-5pm) by the lake has a beautiful interior decorated with Maori carvings, *tukutuku* (woven panels), painted scrollwork and stained-glass windows. An image of Christ wearing a Maori cloak is etched on a window so that he appears to be walking on the waters of Lake Rotorua.

Opposite the church is the impressive **Tamatekapua Meeting House** (Map above), built in 1887. Named for the captain of the *Arawa* canoe, this is an important meeting house for all Arawa people (it's not open to visitors).

There's a small Maori craft shop on the site.

Rotorua Museum of Art & History

This impressive **museum** (Map above; ☎07-349 4350; www.rotoruamuseum.co.nz; Government Gardens; adult/child incl Blue Pool museum $11/5; ☉9am-5pm Apr-Sep, to 6pm Oct-Mar), better known as the Bath House, is in a grand Tudor-style edifice in the Government Gardens and originally opened as an elegant spa retreat in 1908. Displays in the former shower rooms give a fascinating insight into some of the eccentric therapies once practised here, including 'electric baths' and the Bergonie Chair, into which patients suffering from constipation were strapped, and 'vibrated rapidly'. You can also venture into the basement (hard-hats provided) for a glimpse of the complex piping system and audio-visual presentations.

The museum has an interesting exhibition of the *taonga* (treasures) of the local Arawa people, including elaborate woodcarvings and jade. Other exhibitions relate the stories of the WWII 28 Maori Battalion, with a 25-minute film, and the disastrous 1886 Mt Tarawera eruption. The survivors' stories have been preserved, as has the strange tale of the ominous, ghostly war canoe that appeared before a boatload of astonished tourists hours before the eruption. A gripping 20-minute film on the history of Rotorua, including the eruption (accompanied by shuddering seats), runs every 20 minutes in a small theatre just off reception. Other galleries host temporary exhibitions and there is also a pleasant café with good herbal teas.

In the **Government Gardens** around the Bath House are typical English touches such as croquet lawns, bowling greens and rose beds, as well as steaming thermal pools. If you fancy a game of **bowls** (☎025-245 4433; half-hour/hour $15/20; ☉4.30-6.30pm Mon-Wed, 9am-6.30pm Thu-Sun), reservations are essential. Also in the grounds is the **Blue Pool** (Map above; adult/child incl Rotorua Museum of Art & History $11/5; ☉10am-5pm), a refurbished 1930s swimming pool complex housing a small museum recalling the building's heyday, with recorded anecdotes and displays in the old changing rooms. If it all makes you feel like taking a dip yourself, there's a modern heated pool here too (adult/child $7/4).

BAY OF PLENTY

Te Whakarewarewa

This is Rotorua's largest and best-known thermal reserve and a major Maori cultural area. It's pronounced 'fa-ka-re-wa-re-wa' – most call it simply 'Whaka'. However, even Whakarewarewa is a shortening of its full name, Te Whakarewarewatanga o te Ope Taua a Wahiao, which means 'The Gathering Together of the War Party of Wahiao'.

Entry to Whaka's geyser area is through the **NZ Maori Arts & Crafts Institute** (Map p328; ☎ 07-348 9047; www.nzmaori.co.nz; Hemo Rd; adult/child $20/10; ☯ 8.15am-5.15pm winter, 8am-6pm summer). Its most spectacular geyser is **Pohutu** (Maori for 'Big Splash' or 'Explosion'), an active geyser that usually erupts between 10 and 20 times a day. Pohutu spurts hot water about 20m (sometimes over 30m) into the air. The average eruption lasts about five to 10 minutes, though the longest is reputed to have lasted for 15 hours – a world record. You get a warning because the **Prince of Wales' Feathers** geyser always starts off shortly before

Pohutu. The institute also has working crafts-people, an art gallery, a replica Maori village, kiwi house, a Maori concert held daily at 12.15pm and access to the thermal area.

Whakarewarewa Thermal Village (☎ 07-349 3463; Tryon St; adult/child incl tours & concerts $20/10; ☯ 8.30am-5pm) is on the eastern side of Whaka. There are concerts in the meeting house at 11.15am and 2pm, and guided tours every hour through the village, with its souvenir shops and café, and the thermal area daily between 9am and 4pm. There's plenty of thermal activity in the village but no access to the geysers. Whaka is 3km south of the city centre, straight down Fenton St. City buses drop you near Tryon St.

Close to the centre of Rotorua is **Kuirau Park**, an area of volcanic activity that you can wander around free of charge. Its most recent eruption in late 2003 covered much of the park (including the trees) in mud, and drew crowds of spectators hoping for more displays. It has a crater lake, pools

HINEMOA & TUTANEKAI

The story of Hinemoa and Tutanekai is one of NZ's most well-known lovers' tales. It is not a legend but a true story, though you may hear variations. The descendants of Hinemoa and Tutanekai still live in the Rotorua area today.

Hinemoa was a young woman of a subtribe that lived on the western shore of Lake Rotorua. Tutanekai was a young man of the subtribe that lived on Mokoia Island, on the lake.

The two subtribes sometimes visited one another; that was how Hinemoa and Tutanekai met. But although both were of high birth, Tutanekai was illegitimate and so, while the family of Hinemoa thought he was a fine young man and could see that the two young people loved one another, they were not in favour of them marrying.

At night Tutanekai would play his flute on the island, and sometimes the wind would carry his melody across the water to Hinemoa. In his music she could hear his declaration of love for her. Her people, meanwhile, took to tying up the canoes at night to make sure she could not go to him.

Finally, one night, as she heard Tutanekai's music wafting over the waters, Hinemoa was so overcome with longing that she could bear it no longer. She undressed and swam the long distance from the shore to the island.

When she arrived on Mokoia, Hinemoa was in a quandary. She had to shed her clothing in order to swim, but now on the island she could scarcely walk into the settlement naked! She sought refuge in a hot pool to figure out what to do next.

Eventually a man came to fetch water from a cold spring beside the hot pool. In a deep man's voice, Hinemoa called out, 'Who is it?' The man replied that he was the slave of Tutanekai, come to fetch water. Hinemoa reached out of the darkness, seized the slave's calabash gourd and broke it. This happened a few more times, until finally Tutanekai himself came to the pool and demanded that the interloper identify himself. He was amazed when it turned out to be Hinemoa.

Tutanekai stole Hinemoa into his hut. In the morning, when Tutanekai was sleeping very late, a slave was sent to wake him and came back reporting that someone else was also sleeping in Tutanekai's bed. The two lovers emerged, and when Hinemoa's efforts to reach Tutanekai had been revealed, their union was celebrated.

of boiling mud, plenty of steam and small mineral baths.

Maori Concerts & Hangi

Maori culture is a major attraction in Rotorua and, although it has been heavily commercialised, it's worth investing in the experience. The two big activities are concerts and *hangi*, and often the two are combined.

The concerts are put on by locals. Chances are, by the evening's end you'll have been dragged up on stage, experienced a Maori *hongi* (nose-to-nose contact), and also have joined hands for a group sing along. Other features of a Maori concert are *poi* dances (a women's dance where balls of woven flax are twirled) and action songs.

Elements of the performances you are likely to see here are described in the Maori Culture section (pp47–53).

There are plenty of options available to catch a concert and *hangi*. Whakarewarewa Thermal Village (see previous section) puts on daily concerts, which are included in the entry fee, and also offers the **Mai Ora concert & hangi** (adult/child $70/45; 6.15pm summer, 5.15pm winter).

For a combined concert and *hangi* one of the best options is **Tamaki Maori Village** (Map pp316-17; ☎ 07-346 2823; www.maoriculture.co.nz; 1220 Hinemaru St; adult/child $85/45; closed Christmas Day), which does an excellent Twilight Cultural Tour to a *marae* (meeting house) and Maori village complex 15km south of Rotorua. It provides transport and on the way explains the traditional protocol involved in visiting a *marae*. A 'chief' is chosen from the group to represent the visitors. The concert is followed by a *hangi*. Tours depart town at 5pm, 6pm and 7pm during the summer months and at 5pm and 7pm during the winter months.

At its city-centre location it also offers the daytime Tamaki Heritage Experience, an interesting 45-minute guided tour and performance (adult/child $26/13), giving an insight into Maori culture and mythology.

One of the latest venues to open is **Mitai Maori Village** (☎ 07-343 9132; www.mitai.co.nz; 196 Fairy Springs Rd; concert & hangi adult/child $75/35; 6.15-8.30pm), which also offers guided bush walks (8.30am to 9pm, final tour departs at 6pm).

Many of the big hotels in Rotorua offer Maori concerts and *hangi*, charging around $50/25 for adults/children, and roughly half

that for concerts alone. Some of the main venues include **Lake Plaza Rotorua** (Map pp316-17; ☎ 0800 801 440; www.lakeplazahotel.co.nz; 1000 Eruera St), **Millennium** (Map pp316-17; ☎ 07-347 1234; cnr Eruera & Hinemaru Sts), **Kingsgate Hotel** (☎ 07-348 0199; Fenton St), **Rotoiti Tours** (☎ 07-348 8969; Rakeiao Marae), **Royal Lakeside Novotel Hotel** (Map pp316-17; ☎ 07-346 3888; Tutanekai St) and **Grand Tiara Hotel Rotorua** (☎ 07-349 5200; Fenton St). Exact times and prices are liable to change, so check with the hotels or the tourist office before booking.

ACTIVITIES
Thermal Pools

The popular **Polynesian Spa** (Map pp316-17; ☎ 07-348 1328; www.polynesianspa.co.nz; off Hinemoa St; main pools adults only $14, private pools adult/child per half hr $14/5, spa therapies from $65; 6.30am-11pm, last tickets 10.15pm, spa therapies 9am-9pm) is in the Government Gardens. A bathhouse was opened at these springs in 1886 and people have been swearing by the health-giving properties of the waters ever since.

POKAREKARE ANA

Pokarekare ana is NZ's most cherished traditional song. Though most people think its origin is more ancient, the song was actually adapted from a poem by Paraire Henare Tomoana (1868–1946) of the Ngati Kahu-ngunu tribe. His original lyrics were not about Rotorua, but rather Waiapu. Nevertheless, the words seemed to fit the story of Hinemoa and Tutanekai so perfectly that in popular song the lake's name was changed to Rotorua.

Almost anyone from NZ can sing this song for you. Often you will hear only the first verse and the chorus sung, but there are several verses. If you want to sing along, the first verse and chorus go like this:

Pokarekare ana nga wai o Rotorua.
Troubled are the waters of Rotorua.
Whiti atu koe, e hine, marino ana e.
If you cross them, maiden, they will be calm.

E hine e, hoki mai ra,
Come back to me, maiden,
Ka mate ahau i te aroha e.
I will die for love of you.

BAY OF PLENTY

Remember that silver will instantly turn black on contact with the water, so be sure to remove silver jewellery. It's advisable to put all valuables in a safe-deposit box at the ticket office. The modern complex has several pools at the lake's edge that range in temperature from 36°C to 43°C, and a main pool at 38°C. Aix massage (a hydrotherapy treatment) and a variety of mud spa treatments are available. Towels and swimsuits can be hired, and there is a licensed café.

There are two open-air natural pools with medicinal mineral waters (more than 39°C) at the **Waikite Valley Thermal Pools** (Map p328; ☎ 07-333 1861; public pools adult/child $6/3, private pools $10 per 40 min; ☷ 10am-10pm). To get there, go 30km south on State Highway 5 (SH5; the highway to Taupo) to a signposted turn-off opposite the Wai-o-Tapu turn-off. The pools are another 6km down this road.

Those wishing to swim in hot water can visit **Kerosene Creek**, out on SH5. Turn left on the unsealed Old Wai-o-tapu Rd and follow it for 2km. This is one of the few places where the public can bathe in natural thermal pools for free (see also Butcher's Pool p307). Cars have been broken into in this area, so don't leave valuables in your vehicle.

Walking

Check in at the **Map & Track Shop** (Map pp316-17; ☎ 07-349 1845; 1225 Fenton St) for pamphlets and excellent maps outlining the many fine walks in the area. A handy booklet is DOC's *Your Pace, Our Place* (free).

All these walks are shown on the Around Rotorua map.

Located on the southeastern edge of town, **Whakarewarewa State Forest Park** was planted early in the 20th century as an experiment to find the most suitable species to replace NZ's rapidly dwindling and slow-growing native trees. The **Fletcher Challenge Visitor Information Centre** (Map p328; ☎ 07-346 2082; ☷ 8.30am-6pm Mon-Fri, to 5pm Apr-Sep; 10am-4pm Sat & Sun) in the park has a woodcraft shop, displays and audiovisual material on the history and development of the forest. Check in here if you want to go walking. Walks range from half an hour to four hours, including some great routes to the Blue and Green Lakes. Several walks start at the visitors centre, including a half-hour walk through the **Redwood Grove**, a grove of large Californian redwood trees.

Other walks in the Rotorua area are the 22.5km **Western Okataina Walkway**, through native bush from Lake Okareka to Ruato, on the shores of Lake Rotoiti. There's public transport past the Ruato end only; the whole walk takes about seven hours and you need good boots or stout shoes.

The **Eastern Okataina Walkway** goes along the eastern shoreline of Lake Okataina to Lake Tarawera – about a three hour, 10.5km walk. The 6km **Northern Tarawera Track** connects to the walkway and makes it possible to do a two-day walk from either Lake Okataina or Ruato to Lake Tarawera and camp overnight at a **DOC camping ground** (camp sites $12), from where you can walk another two hours to the Tarawera Falls. (see p348).

Note that as **Mt Tarawera** is a protected area and a sacred site for the local Ngati Ragitihi tribe, access is restricted and it is not possible to go tramping independently; the only access is via organised 4WD or helicopter trips (see p323).

The **Okere Falls** are about 16km northeast of Rotorua on SH33; the turn-off is well signposted. It's about a 30-minute walk through native podocarp forest to the falls. These are the 7m falls that the rafting companies take people over (see below). There are several other walks, including those up the Kaituna River to Hinemoa's Steps and to some caves.

Just north of Wai-o-Tapu on SH5, a good trail leads to **Rainbow Mountain**, with its small crater lakes and fine views. It's a short, but fairly strenuous 1½-hour walk to the top at Maungakakatamea Lookout.

Other short walks can be made around Lake Okataina, Mt Ngongotaha (just north of Rotorua) and Lake Rotorua.

White-Water Rafting

The rafting trips on the Grade V Kaituna River, off SH33 about 16km northeast of Rotorua, are the most popular. Time on the river is about 45 minutes and you go over the 7m Okere Falls, then over another 3m drop and about 14 rapids. All Rotorua's rafting companies do a Kaituna trip and it costs around $75.

Raftabout (☎ 0800 723 822; www.raftabout.co.nz), **River Rats** (☎ 0800 333 900; www.riverrats.co.nz) and **Whitewater Excitement Co** (☎ 07-349 2858; www .raftnz.co.nz) also organise white-water rafting trips on the Rangitaiki River (grade III to IV; day trips around $95) and the fast-flowing Wairoa River (grade IV to V; from $80).

The following two operators cover all of those rivers and in addition **Kaituna Cascades** (☎ 0800 524 8862; www.kaitunacascades.co.nz) does the Motu River (grade III to IV) in the East Coast region, while **Wet 'n' Wild Rafting** (☎ 0800 462 7238; www.wetnwildrafting.co.nz) do multi-day trips on the Motu (from $640) and the Mohaka (grade II to V; from $320) in the Central Plateau region. Its prices include all meals and camping equipment.

White-Water Sledging

Kaitiaki Adventures (☎ 0800 338 736, 07-357 2236; www.raft-it.com) does white-water sledging on the Kaituna River ($115). You zoom along on a sledge especially designed for manoeuvrability on the river. Also on offer are white-water rafting trips on the Kaituna ($75) and Wairoa ($80) Rivers and a sledge/raft combo on the Kaituna ($170).

Fishing

You can hire guides to trout fish or go it alone but a licence is essential and there are various regulations. Guided fishing trips cost about $80 per hour per person (minimum two people) but you are almost guaranteed to catch a fish, given enough time. Plan to spend about two to three hours on the trip. Ask at Tourism Rotorua (see p315) or at the Rotorua lakefront for fishing operators.

You can wander down to the Rotorua lakefront and fish if you have a licence. Not all lakes can be fished year-round; check with the Tourism Rotorua (see p315) before fishing other lakes. Get your fishing licence directly from a fishing guide or the **Map & Track Shop** (Map pp316-17; ☎ 07-349 1845; 1225 Fenton St; licences per day/week/season $17/34/90). Fishing gear can also be hired at **O'Keefe's** (☎ 07-346 0178; 1113 Eruera St).

Other Activities

The Whakarewarewa State Forest Park has some of the best **mountain bike trails** in the country. There are 10 tracks within the forest that will keep mountain bikers of all skill levels happy. **Planet Bike** (Map pp316-17; ☎ 07-348 9971; 1140 Hinemoa St) hires out bikes and gear ($30, 2 hours; $50, full day), does drop-offs and pick-ups, and also organises guided

rides ($60 to $100). For more information about the forest contact the **Fletcher Challenge Visitor Information Centre** (Map p328; ☎ 07-346 2082; ☺ 8.30am-6pm Mon-Fri, to 5pm Apr-Sep; 10am-4pm Sat & Sun) in the forest.

Cycling is also a good way to explore Rotorua. Other bicycle-hire places include **Lady Jane's** (Map p316-17; ☎ 07-347 9340; cnr Tutanekai & Whakaue Sts), and the **Rotorua Cycle Centre** (Map pp316-17; ☎ 07-348 6588; 1120 Hinemoa St). Expect to pay about $15 per hour for a mountain bike; a full day costs around $50. 'City bikes' (road bikes) cost around $25 a day.

For a bit of indoor exercise try the **indoor climbing wall** (Map pp316-17; ☎ 07-350 1400; thewall 1140@hotmail.com; 1140 Hinemoa St; adult without/with gear hire $10/14, student $6/10; ☺ noon-late Mon-Fri, 10am-late Sat, 10am-8pm Sun). It also organises full-day outdoor climbing trips ($100); bookings are essential.

You can go tandem skydiving with **NZOne** (☎ 07-345 7569; www.nzone.biz; dives $250-300) from Rotorua airport. The initial flight includes some amazing views over the lakes and volcanoes of the region, and dives go from 9000 or 12,000ft.

Adventure Kayaking (☎ 07-348 9451; www.adventure kayaking.co.nz) has half-day kayaking trips on Lake Rotorua and Lake Rotoiti ($55); full-day trips on Lake Tarawera ($75) or Lake Rotoiti ($80); a twilight lake paddle with a soak in a hot pool ($65); and two- and three-day trips starting at $160. They also rent kayaks from $40 per day.

Kaituna Kayaks (☎ 0800 465 292; www.kaituna kayaks.com) runs half- and full-day guided kayak trips on the Kaituna River ($95/160).

Operators doing horse treks include **Farmhouse** (Map p328; ☎ 07-332 3771), northeast of Lake Rotorua, and **Peka** (Map p328; ☎ 07-346 1755), south of Rotorua. It costs about $30 for the first hour and less for consecutive hours. **Te Urewera Adventures** (☎ 07-366 3969) offers one- to three-day horse treks ($120 to $590) in the Te Urewera National Park, based out of Ruatahuna.

Mountain Action (Map p328; ☎ 0800 682 284; www.mountainaction.co.nz) offers a wide range of activities including 4WD tours through farm and bush ($60 to $150), horse treks (half-hour to half-day $20 to $210), paintball ($40) and rides in the Argo, an 8-wheel, all-terrain amphibious vehicle (from $10). Kids are also well-catered for, with 50cc and 160cc bike rides, pony rides and a petting zoo.

BAY OF PLENTY

Off Road NZ (☎ 07-332 5748; www.offroadnz.co.nz; 193 Amoore Rd) is the place to go for self-drive tours through bush, 20km north of Rotorua. Prices start at $80 for the 4WD bush safari, and you can also try your hand at driving 'monster trucks' (from $35) and sprint cars (from $30), while other activities here include clay-pigeon shooting ($18 for five shots) and archery ($15 for 10 arrows).

Action New Zealand (Map p328; ☎ 07-348 3531; www.action-nz.co.nz; cnr Te Ngae Rd & Sala St) has an intriguing array of activities to try, mostly aimed at the corporate 'team-building' market, such as axe and knife throwing, archery, whip-cracking, pistol-shooting and electronic clay-target shooting.

WALKING TOUR

Start at the Tudor-style **Tourism Rotorua** (**1**; p315) office on Fenton Street and head west along Haupapa St, passing the **Pig & Whistle** (**2**; p325) pub, formerly the town's police station; notice the Maori-inspired carvings in the stonework. Continue to the end of the road and turn left, then left again at the roundabout onto Pukuatua St. From here, head

north into the wide expanse of Kuirau Park, an area of active volcanic activity – look out for sulphurous steam rising ethereally from the sodden ground. You might also see the results of a recent mud eruption.

Continue through the park, exiting at Lake Road, and cross to the Maori village of Ohinemutu, with its fabulously carved **Tamatekapua Meeting House** (**3**; p317), and **St Faith's Anglican Church** (**4**; p317), also decorated in traditional Maori emblems.

From here, head eastwards along Memorial Dr, which offers spectacular views across Lake Rotorua. You'll see plenty of graceful black swans here, but resist the temptation to feed them, as they can be aggressive.

Turn south and walk alongside the War Memorial Park. At Whakaue St head east then onto Hinemaru St. Opposite the **Princes Gate Hotel** (**5**; p325) you will see the magnificent Maori carvings and the Princes Gate Arches, where you can enter the Government Gardens, with their beautifully laid-out flower beds, lawns and ponds. The **Rotorua Museum of Art and History** (**6**; p317), which was once an exclusive spa, is the

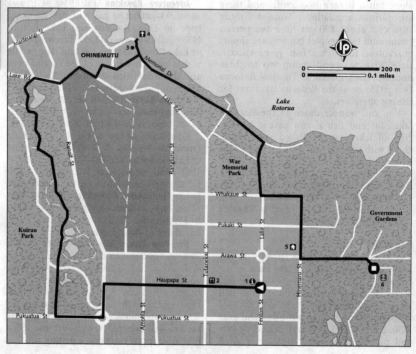

city's most awe-inspiring building. Take a look round the museum and finish your walk with tea on the veranda.

TOURS

Rotorua offers a mind-boggling array of tours. Tourism Rotorua (see p315) can book any tours, as can hostels and hotels.

Carey's Sightseeing Tours (Map pp316-17; ☎ 07-347 1197; www.careys.co.nz; 1108 Haupapa St) is the largest outfit in Rotorua. It offers trips such as a tour of the Wai-o-Tapu and Waimangu thermal areas ($85) and its 'world-famous' Waimangu Round Trip: focusing on the 1886 Mt Tarawera eruption, it includes the Waimangu Volcanic Valley, a cruise on Lake Rotomahana, a cruise on Lake Tarawera, a visit to the Buried Village and a dip in the Polynesian Spa (adult/child $190/80, full day).

Tread & River Expeditions (☎ 07-362 4399; www.treadriver.co.nz) specialises in upscale multi-day adventures involving rafting, mountain biking, walking, abseiling and more, such as the nine-day East Cape Escape ($4000), including food and accommodation. Day trips start at $185.

Mt Tarawera New Zealand Ltd (☎ 07-349 3714; www.mt-tarawera.co.nz) organises guided half-day 4WD tours to the top of Mt Tarawera ($110) as well as helicopter landings on the summit ($300) and the Volcanic Eco Tour, which combines the 4WD trip with Wai-o-Tapu and Waimangu ($195).

Tarawera Legacy (☎ 07-349 3463) runs day trips visiting the Rotorua Museum of Art & History, the Buried Village and Whakarewarewa Thermal Village (adult/child $65/32), picking up from hotels.

Waitomo Wanderers (☎ 0800 924 866) does return trips to Waitomo ($30).

Scenic Flights

Flights over the city and the lake start at around $70, Tarawera flights around $150. Otherwise you can fly further afield to Whakaari (White Island) and even down to Mts Ruapehu and Ngauruhoe in Tongariro National Park.

Volcanic Wunderflites (☎ 0800 777 359; flights $70-480) is particularly popular for flights over the awesome chasm of Mt Tarawera.

Volcanic Air Safaris (☎ 0800 800 848; www.volcanicair.co.nz; flights $55-790) has floatplane and helicopter flights, including a combined flight and jetboat experience and combined helicopter flight and guided tour of Hell's Gate.

Redcat (☎ 0800 733 228; flights $95-280) is a 1950s Grumman Ag Cat biplane; trips range from 12-minute 'city scenic' flights ($95) over the lake and city, to the 45-minute 'sulphur spectacular' over Wai-o-Tapu and other thermal areas ($280). Leather jackets, silk scarves and goggles are provided for that dashing Biggles look.

Heli-pro (☎ 07-357 2512), which is based at Rainbow Farm and the New Zealand Maori Arts and Crafts Institute, does a variety of trips including city flights ($55) and Mt Tarawera ($300).

SLEEPING
Budget

Rotorua has a huge, and expanding, supply of backpacker accommodation around town and plenty of camp sites in the surrounding countryside.

Kiwi Paka YHA (Map pp316-17; ☎ 07-347 0931; stay@kiwipaka-yha.co.nz; 60 Tarewa Rd; camp sites/dm/s/d from $18/20/35/50; 🖳 🍸) This is a well-maintained YHA hostel 1.2km from the city centre (it runs a transfer service). It's a quiet place that attracts a slightly older backpacker clientele. There are also smart en suite chalets (from $60); facilities include a thermal pool, a pleasant café (The Twisted Pippie) and a bar.

base Backpackers Rotorua (Map pp316-17; ☎ 07-350 2040; www.basebackpackers.com; 1140 Hinemoa St; dm/d from $20/55; 🖳) This is one of the newest branches of the scrupulously clean, upmarket base backpackers chain, with good-sized rooms and great communal areas. There's a female-only floor, personal lockers in each room, and mountain bikes for hire. There's a bar and climbing wall here too.

Planet Nomad Backpackers (Map pp316-17; ☎ /fax 07-346 2831; www.planetnomad.co.nz; 1193 Fenton St; dm/d from $18/45; 🖳) This clean and airy place is on a busy road near Tourism Rotorua and the bus station. The rooms are a decent size and there's a large lounge and modern kitchen, as well as barbecue facilities. Discounts on activities around NZ are on offer.

Funky Green Voyager (Map pp316-17; ☎ 07-346 1754; 4 Union St; dm/d from $18/45) This is one of the smallest and nicest of Rotorua's backpackers. In a tranquil residential neighbourhood, close to the centre, the hostel is comfortable and casual with a spacious backyard and a pleasant sunny conservatory.

Crash Palace (Map pp316-17; ☎/fax 07-348 8842; www .crashpalace.co.nz; 1271 Hinemaru St; dm/d from $18/45; 🖳) This sociable two-storey hostel is a pleasant, homely place in a fairly quiet location, but still very close to the centre of Rotorua. It has a small but well-stocked kitchen, a relaxing garden area, spa pool and lounge with pool table.

Hot Rock (Map pp316-17; ☎ 07-348 8636; hotrock@ acb.co.nz; 1286 Arawa St; dm/s/d from $20/50/60; 🖳 🐾) Hot Rock is a big and brash hostel with decent rooms and well-kept communal areas. It's a firm favourite with the party-hearty bussed-in-backpacker crowd and not exactly the place to come for quiet reflection. There are three hot pools (indoor and outdoor) and the lively Lava Bar is on the premises.

Blue Lake Top 10 Holiday Park (Map p328; ☎ 0800 808 292; www.bluelaketop10.co.nz; 723 Tarawera Rd; camp sites/d/apt from $22/40/90; 🖳) Blue Lake park is located 10km from town, and is set amid bushland near the shores of Blue Lake. It has a good choice of accommodation, including well-maintained motel units. Kayaks, canoes, fishing boats and bicycles are available for hire.

Friendly Waiteti Trout Stream Holiday Park (Map p328; ☎ 07-357 5255; www.waiteti.com; 14 Okona Cres; camp sites/dm/d/apt from $20/12/35/85) This is a secluded camping ground set in lovely mature gardens on the bank of the Waiteti stream, about 6km north of town. As the name implies, it's a friendly place popular with family groups and anglers. There's a good range of accommodation, plus spa, playground, TV room and various fishing facilities, and it's handily placed for out-of-town attractions such as the Agrodome and Rainbow Springs Nature Park.

Cosy Cottage International Holiday Park (☎ 0800 222 424; www.cosycottage.co.nz; 67 Whittaker Rd; camp sites/d from $24/45; 🐾) On the bank of the Utuhina stream, this peaceful, family-friendly park has thermally heated camp sites, a hot water beach, natural steam *hangi* cooker, hot mineral pools and an adventure playground. Canoes, bicycles and fishing tackle can be rented.

Mid-Range

Waiteti Lakeside Lodge (Map p328; ☎ /fax 07-357 2311, www.waitetilodge.co.nz; 2 Arnold St, Ngongotaha; s/d from $140/150) The luxurious Waiteti lodge enjoys an enviable location in private grounds on the lake, at the mouth of the Waiteti trout stream. There are just five spacious, wood-cabin-style rooms and the hosts can arrange fly-fishing trips and other activities.

Kotare Lodge (Map p328; ☎ 07-332 2679; www.kotare lodge.co.nz; 1000j Hamurana Rd; s/d $100/150) Kotare is a peaceful and secluded single-storey lodge overlooking Lake Rotorua, and is set in well-manicured gardens. The elegantly appointed rooms have great views and there are some nice extra touches including abundant fresh flowers and home baking.

Regal Geyserland Hotel (☎ 0800 881 882; geyser land@silveroaks.co.nz; 424 Fenton St; d from $90; 🖳 🐾) This is a big complex on the edge of the Whakarewarewa thermal reserve and opposite the international golf course. The motel-style rooms are neat, simple and good value, and there's a gym, spa, sauna and restaurant.

Excalibur Lodge (☎ 07-350 3076; www.excalibur lodge.co.nz; 12 Peace St; s/d incl breakfast from $85/100) There's a medieval ambience to the Excalibur, around 1km south of the city centre, with its four-poster beds and four themed 'Arthurian' rooms. There's also a snooker room, and fishing trips can be arranged. Other meals can be provided in addition to breakfast.

Lake Plaza Rotorua (Map pp316-17; ☎ 0800 801 440; www.lakeplazahotel.co.nz; 1000 Eruera St; d from $105; 🐾) The gigantic and outwardly uninspiring 250-room Lake Plaza is the largest hotel in town, with neat lake-facing rooms and an on-site restaurant. It's just a short walk from the centre of town too.

Rydges (☎ 0800 367 793; www.rydges.com; 272 Fenton St; d/ste from $120/340; 🖳 🐾) Rydges is one of several huge chain hotels in Rotorua with large, if fairly standardised rooms, a gym, spa, restaurant and other good-quality facilities. It's also a big conference venue.

Jack & Di's (Map pp316-17; ☎ 0800 522 526; www .jackanddis.co.nz; 21 Lake Rd; d from $145) This boutique hotel in Ohinemutu is an attractive place with tastefully decorated rooms and apartments. There's a plunge pool, lounge, kitchens and dining room for guest use.

Ann's Volcanic Rotorua (Map pp316-17; ☎ 0800 768 683; volcanic@xtra.co.nz; 107 Malfroy Rd; d $80-110) Ann's is a welcoming and friendly motel with bright, spacious ground-level units, most with private spas. The two-bedroom apartments sleep up to nine people and are good value for larger groups.

RODNEY ZANDBERGS

Traditional stick game (p319)

DENNIS JOHNSON

Prince of Wales' Feathers geyser at Te Whakarewarewa
Thermal Village (p318), Rotorua

Stalagmites and stalactites, Waitomo Caves (p235)

OLIVER STREWE

Whakaari (White Island; p346)

Zorbing (p330), near Rotorua

Mud pools, Te Whakarewarewa (p318), Rotorua

Champagne Pool, Wai-o-Tapu Thermal Wonderland (p329)

Tresco B&B (Map pp316-17; ☎ 0800 873 726; www .trescorotorua.co.nz; 3 Toko St; s/d from $50/90) This is a small and friendly B&B with simple en-suite doubles, and singles with or without facilities. There is a free pick-up from the airport or bus stop.

Birchwood Spa Motel (☎ 0800 881 800; www.birch woodspamotel.co.nz; 6 Sala St; ste from $95) Birch-wood is a quality modern motel complex that has neat studios and bright one- and two-bedroom units with private spa pools or spa baths. It's popular with families and small groups.

Ledwich Lodge Motel (Map pp316-17; ☎ 0508 730 049; ledwich@clear.net.nz; 12 Lake Rd; ste from $100; 🖳) Ledwich is a quiet, older motel in a good location very close to the lakefront, and not too far from the town centre. The units are clean and light, thermally heated and many have lake views.

Top End
Princes Gate Hotel (Map pp316-17; ☎ 07-348 1179; www.scenic-circle.co.nz; 1057 Arawa St; d/ste from $150/250; 🖳) This is a grand Victorian building dat-ing from 1897 and now housing a charming 'boutique' hotel that has a lot more charac-ter than most places in Rotorua. There are 50 individually designed rooms with elegant touches, such as crystal chandeliers and four-poster beds. There's a restaurant and bar, sauna and hot pools, and it's right opposite the entrance to the Government Gardens.

Treetops (☎ 07-333 2066; www.treetops.co.nz; 351 Kearoa Rd, Horohoro; s/d from $490/730; 🖳) Treetops is a strikingly chic, modern lodge. It's in a very quiet and secluded location in extensive parkland with private trout streams, lakes and waterfalls, off SH5, 14km south of Rotorua. There's a sumptuous lounge, library and

billiard room, complete with panelled walls and stuffed animal heads for that hunting-lodge look. There are also eight private villas on the estate (from $590 per person).

Kawaha Point Lodge (Map p328; ☎ 07-346 3602; www.kawahalodge.co.nz; 171 Kawaha Point Rd; s/d $550/800; 🖳) The luxurious but rather steeply priced Kawaha Point is a relaxed, owner-hosted lodge with stylish rooms and a spectacular lake-front location. It has lovely gardens, a conservatory and a croquet lawn; five-course dinners cost extra.

EATING
Tutanekai St has the widest selection of restaurants and cafés in Rotorua.

La Vega (Map pp316-17; ☎ 07-348 2082; 1158 Whakaue St; mains $17-55; ☺ lunch & dinner) The laid-back, Latin-style La Vega does an ex-tensive range of tasty 'gourmet' pizzas, as well as roast meat and seafood.

Café Ephesus (Map pp316-17; ☎ 07-349 1735; 1107 Tutanekai St; mains around $16-20; ☺ lunch Mon, lunch & dinner Tue-Sun) This is a small Turkish place of-fering a good range of traditional meat and fish dishes, plus pizzas and lighter meals.

Cocos (Map pp316-17; ☎ 07-348 4220; 1151 Arawa St; mains $10-18; ☺ breakfast, lunch & dinner Thu-Sun, lunch & dinner Mon-Wed) Cocos is a great value place specialising in fresh 'hot plate' meat and veggie dishes, with set lunch and din-ner menus, including an 'all you can eat Mongolian-style BBQ'.

Pig & Whistle (Map pp316-17; ☎ 07-347 3025; cnr Haupapa & Tutanekai Sts; mains $12-23; ☺ 11.30am-late) This busy restaurant/bar in the former police station has fish and chips, smoked chicken pizza, burgers and sandwiches on the menu. It also has its own microbrewery.

Katsubi (Map pp316-17; ☎ 07-349 3494; 1123 Eruera St; mains $12-45; ☺ breakfast, lunch & dinner) Drop in here to sample authentic Japanese and Ko-rean specialities, from sushi and sashimi to *golbaengi muchim* (seasoned moonsnail with noodles).

Fat Dog (Map pp316-17; ☎ 07-347 7586; 1161 Arawa St; mains $12-22; ☺ breakfast, lunch & dinner) Fat Dog is a colourful and popular café, good for a wide range of light meals at any time of the day.

Indian Star (Map pp316-17; ☎ 07-343 6222; 1118 Tutanekai St; mains $11-20; ☺ lunch & dinner) The usual broad range of meat and veggie cur-ries and tandoori dishes are on the menu at this popular Indian eatery, and there's also a takeaway service available.

Mr India (Map pp316-17; ☎ 07-349 4940; 1161 Amohau St; mains $15-20; ☺ lunch & dinner) Mr India is moderately priced and has all the authentic subcontinent favourites as well as a good selection of vegetarian dishes.

Lewisham's Restaurant (Map pp316-17; ☎ 07-346 0976; 1099 Tutanekai St; mains $23-32; ☺ breakfast, lunch & dinner) Lewisham's has a fairly limited but good menu of grilled and roasted meat, including ostrich and rack of lamb.

Herb's (Map pp316-17; ☎ 07-348 3985; Lake End 1096 Tutanekai St; mains $25-33; ☺ dinner) Herb's is a large, refined restaurant with a formal air and lots of roast and grilled meats on the menu, plus the odd curry.

Lady Jane's Ice Cream Parlour (Map pp316-17; ☎ 07-347 9340; 1092 Tutanekai St) Sweet-toothed visitors will love the extensive selection of ice creams at Lady Jane's.

DRINKING
Lava Bar (Map pp316-17; ☎ 07-348 8616; 1286 Arawa St) At this boisterous bar in the Hot Rock backpackers (see p324) you can mix with an international and local crowd, play pool and listen to good music.

Echo (Map pp316-17; 07-350 3291; 1140 Hinemoa St) In base Backpackers (see p323), Echo is another bustling hostel bar attracting a mix of locals and travellers.

Pig & Whistle (Map pp316-17; ☎ 07-347 3025; cnr Haupapa & Tutanekai Sts; ☺ 11.30am-late) A popular renovated police station with its own microbrewed beers: Snout dark ale and Swine lager. You can also eat here (see p325).

Fuze (Map pp316-17; ☎ 07-349 6306; cnr Pukaki & Tutanekai Sts; ☺ 3pm-late Tue-Sat) is a chilled-out bar attracting a more mature crowd. It has a nice ambience, good cocktails and snack food.

Inevitably, Rotorua has its share of 'Irish' theme pubs, notably **O'Malley's** (Map pp316-17; ☎ 07-347 6410; 1287 Eruera St), and **Hennessy's Irish Bar** (Map pp316-17; ☎ 07-343 7902; 1206 Tutanekai St), a dimly lit place for an evening drink, if you can bear the seemingly unceasing jolly-Irish-pub-song soundtrack.

ENTERTAINMENT
Bar Barella (Map pp316-17; ☎ 07-347 6776; 1263 Pukeuatua St) is good for drum 'n' base on the weekends.

Pig & Whistle (Map pp316-17; ☎ 07-347 3025; cnr Haupapa & Tutanekai Sts; ☺ 11.30am-late) usually has live bands on Friday and Saturday

nights and **Fuze** (Map pp316-17; ☎ 07-349 6306; cnr Pukaki & Tutanekai Sts; ☺ 3pm-late Tue-Sat) has occasional live music.

SHOPPING
Rotorua has a vast number of tourist-oriented shops, selling a range of traditional woodcarvings, greenstone, thermal mud products and more. Fenton St is a good place to start your shopping trip.

Jade Factory (Map pp316-17; ☎ 07-349 3968; jadefact @wave.co.nz; 288 Fenton St) Specialises in high-quality, high-price, hand-crafted greenstone jewellery and carvings, from small, simple pieces up to elaborate items costing thousands of dollars. You can also watch the craftsmen at work.

Best of Maori Tourism (Map pp316-17; ☎ 07-347 4226; www.nativeartsnz.com; 1189 Fenton St) Has a wide assortment of Maori craftwork for sale, including woodcarvings, greenstone jewellery and clothing.

Souvenir Centre (Map pp316-17; ☎ 07-348 9515; 1231 Fenton St) Sports a comprehensive stock of kiwiana to satisfy all your wooden tiki and tacky t-shirt needs. Paua-shell jewellery, woolly jumpers and thermal mud cosmetics can also be had.

Madhouse Design (Map pp316-17; ☎ 07-347 6066; www.madhousedesign.co.nz; 1093 Tutanekai St) A very interesting contemporary gallery shop, showcasing paintings, sculptures, glass and other works by local artists.

GETTING THERE & AWAY
Air
Air New Zealand (Rotorua Map pp316-17; ☎ 07-343 1100; cnr Fenton and Hinemoa Sts; ☺ 8.30-5pm weekdays Rotorua Airport ☎ 07-345 6175; ☺ daily) offers daily direct flights to Auckland, Christchurch, Nelson, Queenstown and Wellington, with onward connections.

Bus
All major bus companies stop at the Tourism Rotorua centre (see p315), which handles bookings.

InterCity (☎ 07-348 0366) has daily buses to and from Auckland ($45, four hours), Wellington ($80, eight hours), Tauranga ($21, 1½ hours), Palmerston North ($60, 5½ hours) and Hamilton ($20, 1½ hours). On the East Coast routes, InterCity goes daily to Gisborne ($55, 4½ hours) via Opotiki ($25, 2¼ hours) and Whakatane ($25, 1½ hours), and to Napier ($55, three hours) via Taupo ($21, one hour).

Newmans (☎ 07-348 0999) services go from Rotorua to Auckland ($38, four hours), Palmerston North ($60, 5½ hours) and Hamilton ($20, 1½ hours).

Magic Bus and Kiwi Experience backpacker buses also stop in Rotorua.

Hitching

Hitching to Rotorua is generally easy, except on SH38 from Waikaremoana – past Murupara the road is unsealed and traffic is very light. The problem hitching out of Rotorua is often the sheer number of backpackers leaving town. You may have to join the queue and wait.

GETTING AROUND
To/From the Airport

The airport is located about 10km out of town, on the eastern side of the lake. **Super Shuttle** (☎ 07-349 3444) offers a door-to-door service to and from the airport for $12 for the first person and $3 for each additional passenger after that. A taxi from the city centre costs about $18.

Bicycle

Rotorua is fairly spread out and public transport isn't good, so cycling might be a good option. See p321 for information about hiring bikes.

Bus

There are a multitude of shuttle services to many of the attractions around town. Check with Tourism Rotorua (see p315) for details.

Ritchies Coachlines (☎ 07-345 5694) operates shuttles to many of the attractions in and around Rotorua. An all-day pass costs $7; one stage costs $1.60. They also run suburban buses to Whakarewarewa (route 3) and Rainbow Springs (route 2; Ngongotaha), departing/arriving Rotorua on Pukuatua St.

Car

Rotorua has a host of car rental companies. The competition is fierce and all seem to offer 'specials' to undercut the competitors. **Rent-a-Dent** (Map pp316-17; ☎ 07-349 3993; 14 Ti St) and **Link Low Cost Rentals** (☎ 07-349 1629; 1222 Fenton St) are two economical companies.

AROUND ROTORUA

HELL'S GATE   Map p328

Known as Tikitere to Maoris, **Hell's Gate** (☎ 07-345 3151; www.hellsgate.co.nz; Te Ngae; adult/child $16/8; ☉ 9am-8.30pm) is 16km northeast of Rotorua on the road to Whakatane (SH30). George Bernard Shaw visited Hell's Gate in 1934 and said of it, 'I wish I had never seen the place, it reminds me too vividly of the fate theologians have promised me', and proceeded to give the place its English name. The reserve covers 10 hectares, with a 2.5km-walking track to the various attractions, including the largest hot thermal waterfall in the southern hemisphere.

Long regarded by Maoris as a place of healing, the site also houses the **Wai Ora Spa & Wellness Centre** (mud bath & spa adult/child $50/20; 1 hr massage $100; 'Ultimud' package $170/80) where you can relax with a variety of mud and spa treatments.

WAIMANGU VOLCANIC VALLEY
                                         Map p328

The valley is another interesting **thermal area** (☎ 07-366 6137; www.waimangu.com; valley walk adult/child $25/7.50, boat trip $25/7.50; ☉ 8.30am-5pm daily, to 6pm Jan) created during the eruption of Mt Tarawera in 1886, making it brand spanking new in geological terms. Walking through the valley (an easy downhill stroll) you'll first pass many interesting thermal and volcanic features, including the Inferno Crater Lake, where overflowing water can reach 80°C and Frying Pan Lake, the largest hot spring in the world. Waima-ngu means 'Black Water', as much of the water here was a dark, muddy colour. In this valley, the Waimangu Geyser was once active enough to be rated the 'largest geyser in the world'. Between 1900 and its extinction in 1904 it would occasionally spout jets of black water nearly 500m high.

The walk continues down to Lake Rotomahana (meaning 'Warm Lake'), from where you can either get a lift back up to where you started or take a half-hour boat trip on the lake, past steaming cliffs and the former site of the Pink and White Terraces.

Waimangu is approximately a 20-minute drive south from Rotorua, 19km along SH5 (towards Taupo) and then 5km to 6km from the marked turn-off. Last admission is at 3.45pm (4.45pm in January).

BAY OF PLENTY

AROUND ROTORUA

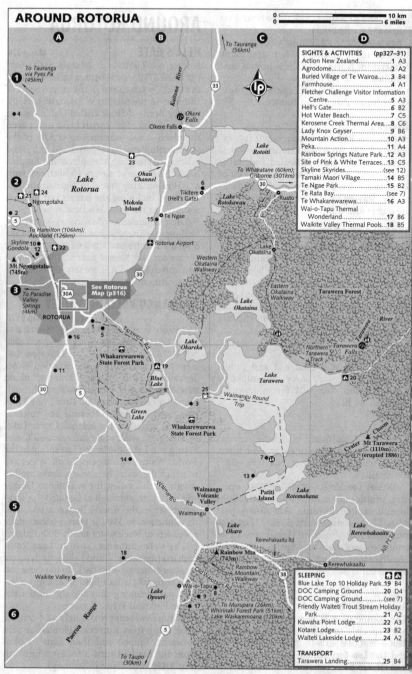

BAY OF PLENTY

SIGHTS & ACTIVITIES	(pp327–31)
Action New Zealand	1 A3
Agrodome	2 A2
Buried Village of Te Wairoa	3 B4
Farmhouse	4 A1
Fletcher Challenge Visitor Information Centre	5 A3
Hell's Gate	6 B2
Hot Water Beach	7 C5
Kerosene Creek Thermal Area	8 C6
Lady Knox Geyser	9 B6
Mountain Action	10 A3
Peka	11 A4
Rainbow Springs Nature Park	12 A3
Site of Pink & White Terraces	13 C5
Skyline Skyrides	(see 12)
Tamaki Maori Village	14 B5
Te Ngae Park	15 B2
Te Rata Bay	(see 7)
Te Whakarewarewa	16 A3
Wai-o-Tapu Thermal Wonderland	17 B6
Waikite Valley Thermal Pools	18 B5

SLEEPING	
Blue Lake Top 10 Holiday Park	19 B4
DOC Camping Ground	20 D4
DOC Camping Ground	(see 7)
Friendly Waiteti Trout Stream Holiday Park	21 A2
Kawaha Point Lodge	22 A3
Kotare Lodge	23 B2
Waiteti Lakeside Lodge	24 A2

TRANSPORT	
Tarawera Landing	25 B4

MT TARAWERA ERUPTION

In the mid-19th century Lake Rotomahana, near Rotorua, was a major tourist attraction. International visitors came to see the **Pink and White Terraces**: two large and beautiful terraces of multileveled pools, formed by silica deposits from thermal waters that had trickled over them for centuries. The Maori village of **Te Wairoa**, on the shores of nearby Lake Tarawera, was the departure point for visiting the terraces. From here a guide and rowers would take visitors by boat to the terraces. **Mt Tarawera**, which had not been active in the 500 years since Maoris arrival in the area, towered silently over the lakes.

On 31 May 1886 the principal terrace guide, Sophia Hinerangi, took a party of tourists across the lake to see the terraces. As they crossed the lake a ceremonial canoe of a kind not seen on the lake for 50 years, glided across its waters. The *waka wairua* (phantom canoe) was seen by all in the tourist boat, both Maori and Pakeha.

To Maoris, the appearance of the canoe was an omen of imminent disaster, confirming the impending calamity that Tuhoto Ariki, a 104-year-old *tohunga* (priest) living in Te Wairoa, had already prophesised.

The old *tohunga* proved to be correct: in the early hours of 10 June 1886 there were earthquakes and loud sounds, and the erupting Mt Tarawera lit up the sky with fireballs. By the time the eruption finished five hours later, over 1500 sq km had been buried in ash, lava and mud. Three Maori villages, including Te Wairoa, were obliterated, 153 people were killed, the Pink and White Terraces were destroyed and Mt Tarawera was split open along its length as if hit with a huge cleaver.

Over the following days excavations were carried out at Te Wairoa to rescue survivors. Guide Sophia became a heroine, having saved many lives by providing shelter in her well-constructed house. The old *tohunga*, however, was not so fortunate. He was trapped inside his buried house and for four days rescuers refused to dig him out, claiming he had in fact caused the eruption and not just predicted it.

Travellers can see more about the eruption at Waimangu Volcanic Valley (p327) and visit the haunting memorial of the excavated Buried Village of Te Wairoa (pp330-1).

WAI-O-TAPU THERMAL WONDERLAND
Map p328

Also south of Rotorua, **Wai-o-Tapu** (☎ 07-366 6333; www.geyserland.co.nz; adult/child $18/6; ☒ 8.30am-5pm), meaning 'Sacred Waters', is perhaps the best of the thermal areas to visit. It has many interesting features, including the large, boiling Champagne Pool, craters and blowholes, colourful mineral terraces and the **Lady Knox Geyser**, which spouts off (with a little prompting from a soap-type organic substance) punctually at 10.15am and gushes for about an hour.

Wai-o-Tapu is 27km south of Rotorua on SH5 (towards Taupo), and a further 2km from the marked turn-off.

TROUT SPRINGS
Map p328

Several springs run down to Lake Rotorua and the trout, lured by the feeds from tourists, swim up the streams to the springs. If you watch you may see a trout leaping the little falls to come up to the springs or returning to the lake.

Rainbow Springs Nature Park (☎ 0800 724 626, 07-350 0440; Fairy Springs Rd; adult/child $22/13; ☒ 8am-5pm) is the best known of the trout springs. There are a number of springs (one with an underwater viewer) and an aviary. It's a pleasant walk through the tree ferns and native bush to see the trout in the streams. Pick up your bag of trout feed at the entrance and watch the feeding frenzy. The springs also have a wildlife area with eels, wallabies, deer, birds, sheep, wild pigs and other native and introduced fauna, now all found in the wild in NZ. Also on site is a kiwi conservation project, and the **Kiwi Encounter Tour** (adult/child $30/19; ☒ tours 11am & 1pm) provides a fascinating and informative glimpse into the lives of these nocturnal birds, including egg incubation and hatching.

Across the road, the **New Zealand Farm Show** is part of Rainbow Springs and has shows at 10.30am, 11.45am, 1pm, 2.30pm and 4pm, with sheep shearing and sheepdog demonstrations.

Rainbow Springs is 4km north of central Rotorua, on the west side of Lake Rotorua – take SH5 towards Hamilton and Auckland. Admission to Rainbow Springs includes the farm show and springs.

Paradise Valley Springs (☎ 07-348 9667; www.para disev.co.nz; adult/child $18/9; ☷ 8am-5pm) are similar to Rainbow Springs. It's set in a 6-hectare park with various animals, including a pride of lions (fed at 2.30pm). The springs, 13km west of Rotorua on Paradise Valley Rd, are at the foot of Mt Ngongotaha.

SKYLINE SKYRIDES   Map p328

Skyline Skyrides (☎ 07-347 0027; www.skylineskyrides.co .nz; Fairy Springs Rd; gondola adult/child $17/7, luge $6, gondola & 5 luge rides $33/25; ☷ from 9am) is on the west side of Lake Rotorua, near the Rainbow and Fairy Springs. Here you can take a gondola ride up Mt Ngongotaha for a panoramic view of the lake area and, once there, fly back down the mountain on one of three concrete tracks on a luge (a sort of toboggan on wheels), coming back up again on a chairlift. There is a café and restaurant on top of the mountain.

There is also a flight simulator, mountain bikes, 'sky swing' and other attractions to spend your money on at the top, and there are walking tracks around the mountain.

AGRODOME   Map p328

If seeing millions of sheep in rural NZ has stimulated your interest in these animals, visit **Agrodome** (☎ 07-357 1050; www.agro dome.co.nz; Western Rd; adult/child $18/9, tour $20/10, tour & show $35/18). There's an educational and entertaining one-hour show at 9.30am, 11am and 2.30pm daily, and sheep auctions, sheep-shearing and sheepdog displays, and after all that, you may even be able to tell the difference between some of the 19 breeds of sheep on show. There's also a dairy display, farmyard nursery, cow-milking demonstration, chocolate factory and woollen mill, as well as **Ocean Pearl Farm** (admission $10/5), where you can visit a facility producing paua pearls.

You can hire horses for a guided tour or else take a farm-buggy tour of the 120-hectare farm. Agrodome is around 9km north of Rotorua on SH1.

Agrodome Adventure Park

As the name suggests, the Adventure Park is a little more adventurous than watching

sheep being shorn. Here you have the chance to zorb, bungy, swoop, experience a simulated skydive and ride the agrojet.

Like the bungy, **zorbing** (dry or wet $40) is one of those unusual Kiwi innovations. The rules are simple: climb into an inflated plastic sphere (the two spheres are held together with shock cords), strap in and then roll downhill for about 150m. You will rotate within the sphere, and eventually the sphere will come to a stop. If that's not enough for you, skip the tying in and ask for a couple of buckets of cold water to be tossed inside the sphere – you literally slip downhill.

Other system-shocking experiences include the 43m **bungy** ($80), a rather large swing called the **swoop** ($45), which reaches speeds of up to 130km/h (G-force 3), the **agrojet** ($35), allegedly NZ's fastest jetboat, that whips you around a 1km manmade course before you can even catch your breath, and **freefall xtreme** ($65), a freefall skydive simulator which floats you 5m in the air on a powerful column of wind.

TE NGAE PARK   Map p328

Three kilometres beyond the airport, **Te Ngae Park** (☎ 07-345 5275; adult/child $6/3; ☷ 9am-5pm) is a 3D, 1.7km-wooden maze similar to the original Wanaka maze in the South Island. It will entertain the kids for an hour or two.

BURIED VILLAGE OF TE WAIROA
Map p328

Fifteen kilometres from Rotorua, the **Buried Village of Te Wairoa** (☎ 07-362 8287; www.buried village.co.nz; adult/child $18/6; ☷ 9am-5.30pm Nov-Mar, 9am-4.30pm Apr-Oct) is reached by a scenic drive along Tarawera Rd, which passes the Blue and Green Lakes.

There's a museum just beyond the ticket counter that has artefacts and information on the events before and after the June 1886 eruption. There's a small theatre where you can watch a film about the eruption, seen through the eyes of the young English tourist who died in the village's hotel. Of particular interest is the story of the *tohunga* Tuhoto Ariki who, according to some, was blamed for the destruction (see the boxed text p329). The site of his *whare* (house) has been excavated and the dwelling reconstructed. It is on display in the park along with excavations of other buildings buried by volcanic debris, including the Rotomahana Hotel, the blacksmith's and a number of houses, where sealed wine bottles, smashed crockery and other grim reminders of daily domesticity cut short can be seen.

There's a peaceful bush walk through the valley to Te Wairoa Falls, which drops about 80m over a series of rocky outcrops. The last part of the track to the falls is steep and slippery and not really suitable for young children to attempt.

LAKE TARAWERA   Map p328

About 2km past the Buried Village is Tarawera Landing on the shore of Lake Tarawera. Tarawera means 'Burnt Spear', named by a visiting hunter who left his bird spears in a hut and on returning the following season found both the spears and hut had been burnt.

Tarawera Launch Services (☎ 07-362 8595; adult/child $30/15) has a cruise at 11am crossing over Lake Tarawera towards Lake Rotomahana. It stays on the other side for about 45 minutes, long enough for people to walk across to Lake Rotomahana, then returns to the landing. The trip takes 2½ hours.

A one-hour **cruise** (adult/child $18/10) on Lake Tarawera leaves at 1.30pm in winter and 1.30pm, 2.30pm and 3.30pm in summer.

Hot Water Beach on Te Rata Bay has hot thermal waters and a very basic **camping ground** (camp sites $12) run by DOC.

WHIRINAKI FOREST PARK   Map p328

About 50km southeast of Rotorua, signposted off the main road, is the 609-sq-km Whirinaki Forest Park. Access is off SH38 on the way to Te Urewera National Park; take the turn-off at Te Whaiti to Minginui. The park is noted for the sheer majesty and density of its native podocarp forests; it has walking tracks, scenic drives, camping and huts, lookouts, waterfalls, the Whirinaki River and some special areas, including Oriuwaka Ecological Reserve and Arahaki Lagoon. The booklet *Tramping & Walking in Whirinaki Forest Park* from DOC has information about the park.

The best source of information on the park is the **DOC Rangitaiki Area Office** (☎ 07-366 1080) in Murupara.

Ask for details on the fine Whirinaki Track, an easy two-day walk. This can be combined with Te Hoe Loop Walk for a four-day walk (with seven huts) that starts

in some of NZ's finest podocarp forest and proceeds along a series of river valleys.

Sleeping

Down by the Whirinaki River, at Mangamate Waterfall, there's an informal **camping area** (camp sites $12). The forest has 10 **backcountry huts** ($10). Pay at the DOC office. Murupara has all types of accommodation as well as food outlets.

WESTERN BAY OF PLENTY

The western Bay of Plenty extends from Katikati and Waihi Beach to Te Puke on the coast and south to the Kaimai Range.

The area is not as popular with tourists as the far more commercial Rotorua region, but it enjoys one of the highest proportions of sunny days in NZ, has some superb beaches, and is a major centre for a variety of water sports.

TAURANGA

pop 58,500

Tauranga is the principal city of the Bay of Plenty and one of the largest export ports in NZ, shipping out the produce of the rich surrounding region. It's also one of the country's fastest growing cities, with increasing numbers of newcomers and holiday-home buyers attracted by the temperate climate and a city well endowed with facilities. Tauranga has excellent restaurants, good shopping and an attractive waterfront, which includes two huge marinas. Fishing, sailing and other water-borne activities are all at hand. The major tourist attractions though are the beaches and headland scenery of Mt Maunganui across the harbour.

Tauranga is the centre of NZ's principal kiwi fruit region; work is available when the fruit is being picked (May and June) but you may be able to find some orchard or agricultural work at almost any time. Check with the hostels for work contacts.

Information

The Tauranga **visitors centre** (Map p332; ☎ 07-578 8103; www.tauranga.govt.nz; 95 Willow St; ☺ 7am-5.30pm Mon-Fri, 8am-4pm Sat & Sun) sells InterCity bus tickets. The public library, also located here,

BAY OF PLENTY

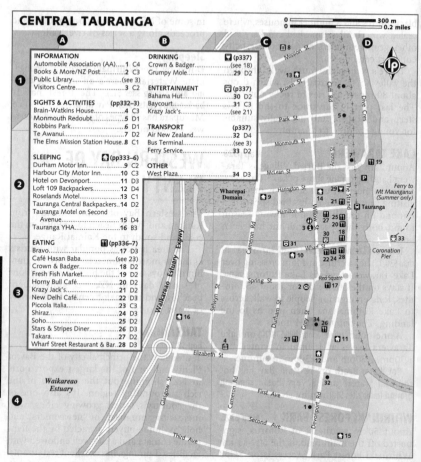

CENTRAL TAURANGA

INFORMATION
Automobile Association (AA).....**1** C4
Books & More/NZ Post............**2** C3
Public Library.........................(see 3)
Visitors Centre.........................**3** C2

SIGHTS & ACTIVITIES   (pp332–3)
Brain-Watkins House................**4** C3
Monmouth Redoubt................**5** D1
Robbins Park...........................**6** D1
Te Awanui...............................**7** D2
The Elms Mission Station House.**8** C1

SLEEPING   (pp333–6)
Durham Motor Inn.....................**9** C2
Harbour City Motor Inn...........**10** C3
Hotel on Devonport.................**11** D3
Loft 109 Backpackers...............**12** D4
Roselands Motel......................**13** C1
Tauranga Central Backpackers..**14** D2
Tauranga Motel on Second
    Avenue..............................**15** D4
Tauranga YHA..........................**16** B3

EATING   (pp336–7)
Bravo......................................**17** D3
Café Hasan Baba.................(see 23)
Crown & Badger.....................**18** D2
Fresh Fish Market....................**19** D2
Horny Bull Café.......................**20** D2
Krazy Jack's............................**21** D2
New Delhi Café........................**22** D2
Piccola Italia............................**23** C3
Shiraz.....................................**24** D3
Soho......................................**25** D2
Stars & Stripes Diner...............**26** D2
Takara....................................**27** D2
Wharf Street Restaurant & Bar..**28** D3

DRINKING   (p337)
Crown & Badger......................(see 18)
Grumpy Mole.........................**29** D2

ENTERTAINMENT   (p337)
Bahama Hut............................**30** D2
Baycourt.................................**31** C3
Krazy Jack's............................(see 21)

TRANSPORT   (p337)
Air New Zealand......................**32** D4
Bus Terminal...........................(see 3)
Ferry Service...........................**33** D2

OTHER
West Plaza..............................**34** D3

---

has Internet access, and there are plenty of Internet cafés scattered around town. You can buy books and post mail at **Books & More/NZ Post** (Map above; ☎ 07-577 9911; 17 Grey St).

The **DOC office** (☎ 07-578 7677; 253 Chadwick Rd W, Greerton) is about 10 minutes' drive from the centre of Tauranga; follow Cameron Rd. You can pick up maps from the **AA office** (Map above; ☎ 07-578 2222; cnr Devonport Rd & First Ave).

Sights

The **Elms Mission Station House** (Map above; ☎ 07-577 9772; Mission St; admission $5; ☺ 2-4pm Sun & public holidays) was founded in 1835; the present house was completed in 1847 by a pioneer missionary, the Rev AN Brown, and is the oldest building in the Bay of Plenty. It is furnished in period style, including the Mission Library.

The **Brain-Watkins House** (Map above; ☎ 07-577 7672; 233 Cameron Rd; admission $2; ☺ 2-4pm Sun) was built in 1881 from native kauri wood and is one of Tauranga's best preserved Victorian colonial homes, complete with original furnishings.

Te Awanui (Map above), a fine replica *waka* (Maori canoe), is on display in an open-sided building at the top end of The Strand, close to the centre of town. Continue uphill beyond the canoe to **Monmouth Redoubt** (Map above; Monmouth St), a fortified site during the Maori Wars. Further along is **Robbins Park** (Map opposite; Cliff Rd), with a rose garden and hothouse.

Compass Community Village (Map pp334-5; ☎ 07-571 3700; 155 Seventeenth Ave; admission free; ☻ 8am-4.30pm Mon-Fri, to 4pm Sat, 9am-4pm Sun) has restored period buildings; it is mainly used by community groups and for conferences.

Activities
WALKING
There are many walking options around Tauranga and Mt Maunganui. A good number of these are outlined in the free *Walkways of Tauranga* pamphlet, including the fascinating **Waikareao estuary** (Map pp334-5) and the popular **Mauao Base Track**. For walks further afield pick up a copy of *Short Walks of the Western Bay of Plenty* ($1). Both are available from visitors centres.

The backdrop to the western Bay of Plenty is the rugged 70km-long **Kaimai Mamaku Forest Park**, with tramps for the more adventurous. More detailed information on walks in this area is provided in the DOC pamphlet *Kaimai Mamaku Forest Park Day Walks* ($1).

McLaren Falls (admission free; ☻ 8am-5.30pm, till 7.30pm in summer), found in the Wairoa River valley, 15km southwest of Tauranga just off SH29, is a 170-hectare lakeland park, with walking tracks, barbecue sites, exotic trees and rich bird life. There are three basic modern hostels (adult/child $15/10) and camp sites ($8) if you wish to stay in the park. Contact **Tauranga District Council** (☎ 07-577 7000; www.tauranga.govt.nz) for bookings.

SEA ACTIVITIES
During summer, Tauranga comes alive with sea activities of all kinds, including swimming with dolphins, jet-skiing, parasailing, water-skiing, diving, surfing, fishing and sailing. The visitors centre (see p331) has lots of information on operators.

The **Tauranga Dolphin Company** (☎ 0800 836 574), **Dolphin Seafaris** (☎ 0800 326 8747; www.nzdolphin.com; 90 Maunganui Rd, Mt Maunganui; ☻ trips leave 8am summer, 9am winter) and **Butler's Swim with Dolphins** (☎ 0508 288 537; www.swimwithdolphins.co.nz; ☻ leaves Tauranga 9am, Mt Maunganui 9.30am) run dolphin-swimming trips. Even if you don't meet the dolphins it is good value for a day cruise and you get to snorkel on the reefs. Trips cost $100/85 for adults/children.

Tauranga Underwater Centre (Map pp334-5; ☎ 07-571 5286; www.diveunderwater.com; 50 Cross Rd; ☻ 8am-6pm Mon-Sat, 8-10am Sun if fine) operates a number of snorkelling, scuba and Professional Association of Diving Instructors (PADI) diving courses, including open water courses ($450) and speciality courses (from $130).

WHITE-WATER RAFTING
White-water rafting is popular around Tauranga, particularly on the Wairoa River, which has some of the best falls and rafting in NZ. It's definitely a rafting trip for thrill-seekers, ranging from Grade II cascades to Grade V rapids. One highlight of the trip is a plunge over a 4m waterfall! The water level is controlled by a dam, so it can only be rafted on 26 days of the year; advance bookings are essential. Contact **Wet 'N' Wild Rafting** (☎ 0800 462 7238; www.wetnwildrafting.co.nz; 2 White St, Rotorua; 1½ hr trip $85) for precise dates and reservations. It also has trips on other rivers, including the Waituna ($75). **River Rats** (☎ 0800 333 900; www.riverats.co.nz) runs similar trips on the Wairoa ($90) and Kaituna ($80).

SKYDIVING
The Tauranga airport at Mt Maunganui is the base for a number of air clubs. An 8000ft tandem skydive starts at $190 with **Tandem Skydiving** (☎ 07-576 7990; freefall@xtra.co.nz).

Tours
Scenic flights can be arranged at the airport. The **Tauranga Glider Club** (☎ 07-575 6768) flies every weekend, weather permitting. Costs start at around $27 per hour.

Island Air Charter (☎ 07-575 5795; www.island air.co.nz) at the airport does scenic flights, including over Whakaari (White Island) from $120 for one hour, the Rotorua thermal area ($120 for one hour) and around the Tauranga/Mt Maunganui area ($40 for 15 minutes). Other flights are possible on request.

Sleeping
Most of the places to stay around Tauranga are a little out of the town centre.

BUDGET
There are a number of good backpackers in town and camp grounds on the outskirts.

Tauranga Central Backpackers (Map p332; ☎ 07-571 6222; www.tgabackpack.co.nz; 64 Willow St; dm/s/d $20/40/50; ▣) This bright, well-run place is bang in the centre of town, with large TV

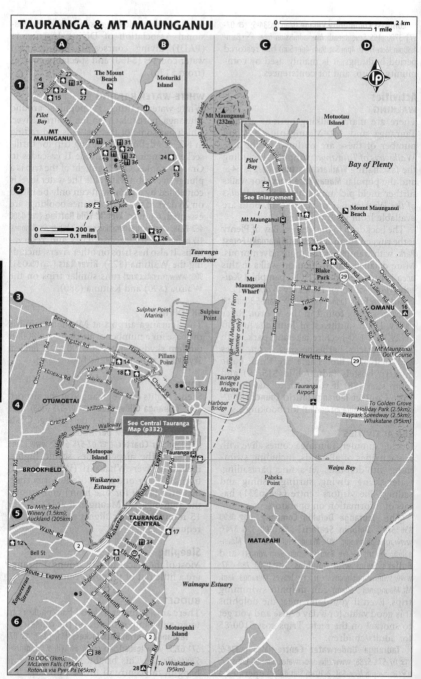

TAURANGA & MT MAUNGANUI

0 ─────────────────── 2 km
0 ─────────────────── 1 mile

A   **B**   **C**   **D**

Moturiki Island

The Mount Beach

Pilot Bay

MT MAUNGANUI

Mt Maunganui (232m)

Mauao Base Track

Motuotau Island

Bay of Plenty

Pilot Bay

See Enlargement

Mt Maunganui

Mount Maunganui Beach

0 ─────── 200 m
0 ─────── 0.1 miles

Tauranga Harbour

Mt Maunganui Wharf

Sulphur Point Marina

Sulphur Point

Tauranga–Mt Maunganui Ferry (Summer only)

Marine Pde

OMANU

Mt Maunganui Golf Course

Blake Park

Levers Rd

Beach Rd

Ngatai Rd

Vale St

Seaview Rd

Pillans Rd

Chapel St

Harbour Dr

Keith Allan Dr

Pillans Point

OTUMOETAI

Milton Rd

Hinewa Rd

Seaview Rd

Cross Rd

Tauranga Bridge Marina

Harbour Bridge

Tauranga Airport

Hewletts Rd

To Golden Grove Holiday Park (2.5km); Baypark Speedway (2.5km); Whakatane (95km)

Grange Rd

Waikareao Estuary Walkway

See Central Tauranga Map (p332)

Tauranga

Waipu Bay

BROOKFIELD

Motuopae Island

Waikareao Estuary

Waihi Rd

To Mills Reef Winery (1.5km); Auckland (205km)

Kingswood Rd

Bell St

Cameron Rd

TAURANGA CENTRAL

MATAPAHI

Paheka Point

Route J Expwy

Tenth Ave

Eleventh Ave

Fifteenth Ave

Sixteenth Ave

Seventeenth Ave

Fraser St

Edgecumbe Rd

Cameron Rd

Grace Ave

Waimapu Estuary

Motuopuhi Island

Konorewa Stream

To DOC (3km); McLaren Falls (15km); Rotorua via Pyes Pa (45km)

To Whakatane (95km)

INFORMATION	
Post Office	1 B5
Visitors Centre	2 B2
SIGHTS & ACTIVITIES	
Compass Community Village	3 A6
Hot Saltwater Pools	4 A1
Island Style Surf Shop	5 B2
Mount Surf Shop	6 B2
Rock House	7 C3
Tauranga Underwater Centre	8 B4
SLEEPING	
Apple Tree Cottage	9 B4
Avenue 11 Motel	10 B5
Baywatch Motor Inn	11 C2
Bell Lodge Motel & Backpackers	12 A5
Belle Mer	13 B2
Bureta Park Motor Inn	14 B4
Calais Mount Resort	15 A1
Cosy Corner Motor Camp	16 D3
Harbour View Motel	17 B5
Just the Ducks Nuts	18 B4
Mission Belle Motel	19 A2
Mount Backpackers	20 B2
Mount Maunganui B&B	21 D3
Ocean Sands Motel	22 A1
Oceanside Motor Lodge & Twin Towers	23 A1
Outrigger Motel	24 B2
Pacific Coast Lodge & Backpackers	25 C3
Pacific Motor Inn	26 B2
Pavilions	27 A1
Silver Birch Thermal Holiday Park	28 B6
EATING	
Astrolabe	29 B2
Bardeli's at the Mount	30 A2
Beaches Café	(see 23)
Bombay Brasserie	31 B2
Bureta Park Motor Inn Restaurant	(see 14)
Café Istanbul	32 B2
Clippers Restaurant & Bar	33 B2
Midi Café & Wine Bar	(see 28)
Pak N Save	34 B5
Sand Rock Café & Bar	35 A1
Thai-Phoon	(see 19)
Two Small Fish	36 B2
DRINKING	
Barmuda	(see 30)
Mount Mellick	37 B2
ENTERTAINMENT	
Aclantis	(see 33)
Worlds End	38 A6
TRANSPORT	
Bus Depot	(see 2)
Salisbury Wharf (ferry)	39 A2

lounge, pool table, modern kitchen and friendly staff. It can also help with work and rents out bikes for $10 a day.

Apple Tree Cottage (Map pp334-5; ☎ 07-576 7404; mark.gail@clear.net.nz; 47 Maxwell St; camp sites & dm/d $20/40) Apple Tree Cottage, at Pillans Point, Otumoetai, is a friendly, family-run backpackers in a quiet residential area close to the harbour. It has a basic wooden cottage and simple bunkrooms set in an attractive garden.

Bell Lodge Motel & Backpackers (☎ 07-578 6344; www.bell-lodge.co.nz; 39 Bell St; camp sites/dm/s/d $24/19/60/70; 🖳) Bell Lodge, 4km west of town, is a spruce, purpose-built hostel, pleasantly situated on three hectares of land. This is a well-equipped place, with a big kitchen, barbecue and a lounge.

Loft 109 Backpackers (Map p332; ☎ 07-579 5638; www.loft109.co.nz; 109 Devonport Rd; dm/s/d $19/26/45; 🖳) Loft 109 is a small centrally located hostel, with clean, simple, no-frills bunk rooms. There's a kitchen and communal areas, and all beds have individual lockers.

Just the Ducks Nuts (Map pp334-5; ☎ 07-576 1366; www.justtheducksnuts.co.nz; 6 Vale St; camp sites/dm/d $28/20/45) This six-bedroom house is in a peaceful residential area, with a good view of the harbour. It has a laid-back atmosphere, good communal areas, a library and comfy rooms. They will drop off and pick up.

Silver Birch Thermal Holiday Park (Map pp334-5; ☎ /fax 07-578 4603; silverbirch@xtra.co.nz; 101 Turret Rd; camp sites/d/apt from $22/35/65) Silver Birch is on the Waimapu Estuary, not far south of town. It's a relaxing, family-friendly place with good facilities, including thermal pools and a shop, and has a card-operated security gate entrance. Kayaks are available for rent.

Tauranga YHA (Map p332; ☎ 07-578 5064; yhataur@yha.org.nz; 171 Elizabeth St; camp sites/dm/d $22/18/50; 🖳) The YHA is a cosy, well-equipped hostel, conveniently close to the city centre. There's a large garden, spotless bunkrooms and lockers for your gear.

MID-RANGE
Tauranga has a fair number of generic but good-quality motels, popular with domestic tourists and weekenders.

Hotel on Devonport (Map p332; ☎ 07-578 2668; www.hotelondevonport.net.nz; 72 Devonport Rd; d/ste from $130/145) The Devonport is a trendy new boutique hotel in a great central location, aimed very much at business travellers. It has 38 comfortable, well-designed rooms with a contemporary, minimalist feel, and all the mod-cons and facilities you would expect.

Bureta Park Motor Inn (Map pp334-5; ☎ 07-576 2221; Vale St; www.buretapark.co.nz; s/d from $70/80; 🖳) Bureta Park is a cosy and well-maintained motel complex in a quiet part of Otumoetai, with a British-style pub and ever-popular restaurant (see p336). Good value half-board options are also available (s/d $85/110).

Tauranga Motel on Second Avenue (Map p332; ☎ 0800 109 007; www.taurangamotel.co.nz; 1 Second Ave; d from $105) The waterfront Tauranga Motel is a very smart place, which offers plush, well-designed units that all enjoy great views of the harbour. The welcoming hosts can prepare excellent breakfasts at extra cost.

Avenue 11 Motel (Map pp334-5; ☎ 07-577 1881; www.avenue11.co.nz; 26 Eleventh Ave; d from $85) This is a very smart 'boutique' motel offering just four self-contained, tastefully furnished suites with polished wood flooring. It's a relaxing place in a quiet residential area away from the city centre, and there's an attractive garden and views of the harbour.

Roselands Motel (Map p332; ☎ 07-578 2294; www.roselands.co.nz; 21 Brown St; d/ste from $85/95) Roselands Motel is an older but very well-kept complex with light, roomy units. It's a fairly small place, located in a central yet quiet spot, a little north of the city centre. Facilities include a spa pool and guest barbecue.

Durham Motor Inn (Map p332; ☎ 07-577 9691; www.durham.co.nz; cnr Cameron Rd & Harington St; d from $100; 🖧) The Durham is a modern, sparkling clean motel in an unbeatable location in the centre of town. It has 20 ground-level units with kitchens, some with disabled access, and very good facilities.

Harbour View Motel (Map pp334-5; ☎ 07-578 8621; www.harbourviewmotel.co.nz; 7 Fifth Ave; s/d $75/85) The Harbour View is a big place with large and very neat, homely units at a good price. As the name suggests, most rooms have views over the water, and kayaks are available for rent.

Harbour City Motor Inn (Map p332; ☎ 07-571 1435; www.taurangaharbourcity.co.nz; 50 Wharf St; d from $95) The Harbour City is a shiny contemporary motel with comfortable and stylishly decorated units, all with spa baths. It's in a very good location, close to the city centre.

Eating

Many good eating options can be found along The Strand. You can pick up the useful free *Dine Out* restaurant guide at the visitors centre (see p331).

Wharf Street Restaurant & Bar (Map p332; ☎ 07-578 8322; Upstairs, 8 Wharf St; mains $25-50; ☺ lunch & dinner) Wharf Street is a classy, award-winning restaurant specialising in fresh fish, with an extensive wine list, attentive service and great views over the harbour from the balcony.

Mills Reef Winery (☎ 0800 645 577; Moffat Rd, Bethlehem; mains $25-35; ☺ lunch & dinner) Mills Reef is first and foremost a winery, but it also has a very good restaurant; unsurprisingly, the accompanying wine list is superb. The winery is 7km from the town centre at Bethlehem.

Crown & Badger (Map p332; ☎ 07-571 3038; cnr The Strand & Wharf St; mains $8.50-15; ☺ breakfast, lunch & dinner) This friendly British-style pub serves up such Anglo-inspired concoctions as Nelson's nachos ($8.50), Park Lane pork ($15) and Northampton ham and eggs ($14). They also do good breakfasts and there's a kids' menu.

Horny Bull Café (Map p332; ☎ 07-578 8741; 67 The Strand; mains $18-25; ☺ lunch & dinner Mon-Fri, breakfast, lunch & dinner Sat & Sun) The Horny Bull is a vaguely Western-style bar and restaurant specialising in steaks of various sizes with various dressings, as well as other meaty dishes with corny names such as 'Stand by your Lamb' and 'All Chook up'.

Bravo (Map p332; ☎ 07-578 4700; Red Square; mains $10.50-16; ☺ breakfast, lunch & dinner) This trendy, well-regarded restaurant and bar is a pleasant spot for inexpensive light meals, bagels, pizzas and drinks, with outdoor seating on the pedestrianised street.

Piccola Italia (Map p332; ☎ 07-578 8363; 107 Grey St; mains $16-27; ☺ dinner Tue-Sun) An Italian place with a pleasant little courtyard, serving up pasta, pizza and fish dishes as Dean Martin croons away over the sound system. Bella!

Café Hasan Baba (Map p332; ☎ 07-571 1480; 107 Grey St; mains $10-25; ☺ lunch & dinner) Adjoining Piccola Italia, Hasan Baba serves good-value Middle Eastern cuisine, including couscous, salads and lamb, in an atmospheric setting.

Spinnakers (☎ 07-574 4147; Harbour Bridge Marina; mains $25-50; ☺ lunch & dinner Mon-Fri, dinner Sat & Sun) Spinnakers is a fine-dining establishment with lovely views of the marina and Tauranga Harbour. The house speciality is seafood, but pork, chicken and veggie dishes are available.

Bureta Park Motor Inn Restaurant (Map pp334-5; ☎ 07-576 2221; Vale St; mains $12-14; ☺ lunch & dinner) The popular restaurant of the Bureta Park Motor Inn (see p335) specialises in well-priced buffet lunches and three-course dinners. Hearty roast meat and veggie dishes are the stock in trade.

Soho (Map p332; ☎ 07-577 0577; 59 The Strand; mains $22-29; ☺ dinner) Soho is a stylish restaurant serving a combination of French and Italian cuisine. Excellent three-course set meals cost $40.

Shiraz (Map p332; ☎ 07-577 0059; 12 Wharf St; mains $17-20; ☺ lunch & dinner Mon-Sat) Shiraz has Mediterranean and Middle Eastern food at reasonable prices, including kebabs, felafel, meze and moussaka.

Krazy Jacks (Map p332; ☎ 07-587 4111; 47 The Strand; mains $7.50-20; ☺ lunch & dinner) Krazy Jacks is a popular bar and restaurant serving up steaks, surf 'n' turf and the like, as well as salads and pasta.

Takara (Map p332; ☎ 07-579 4177; 18 Hamilton St; mains $12-19; ☺ lunch & dinner Tue-Sun, dinner Sun)

Takara offers a good selection of Japanese sushi and tempura dishes. Set menus start at $18, and there's free green tea.

New Delhi Café (Map p332; ☎ 07-578 5533; 20 Wharf St; mains $14-20; ☼ lunch & dinner) New Delhi has a good choice of spicy and not-so-spicy Indian dishes, such as beef vindaloo, chicken korma, and vegetable biryani. A takeaway menu is available.

Stars & Stripes Diner (Map p332; ☎ 07-577 1319; West Plaza, 75 Devonport Rd; burgers from $5.80, mains from $14.; ☼ lunch Mon, breakfast lunch & dinner Tue-Sat, lunch & dinner Sun) This cheap American-style fast-food joint has lots of burgers, chilli dogs and sandwiches on the menu, plus steaks, burritos and breakfasts.

Fresh Fish Market (Map p332; ☎ 07-578 1789; 1 Dive Cres; mains from around $5; ☼ lunch & dinner) Down on the waterfront, this place serves excellent fish and chips and is a local legend.

Drinking
Crown & Badger (Map p332; ☎ 07-571 3038; cnr The Strand & Wharf St) A cosy British-style pub, which makes a nice place for a quiet drink. You can also eat here (see opposite).

Grumpy Mole (Map p332; ☎ 07-571 1222; 41 The Strand; ☼ 3pm-3am Tue-Sat) A big and very woody wild-west theme bar, adorned with cattle skulls, buffalo heads and sporting pool tables.

Entertainment
Bahama Hut (Map p332; ☎ 07-571 0839; 19 Wharf St; ☼ 4pm-late Mon-Thu, noon-late Fri-Sun) One of the more popular joints in town; it has resident DJs, a dance floor and a surfing theme.

Worlds End (Map pp334-5; ☎ 07-579 4185; 229 Fraser St) Away from the centre, Worlds End has live music on Thursday and Friday nights and various events at other times.

Baycourt (Map p332; ☎ 07-577 7189; www.baycourt .co.nz; Cnr Durham & Wharf Sts) Hosts an eclectic mix of highbrow entertainment including theatre, world-music concerts, music festivals, theatre for children and community cultural programmes.

Krazy Jack's (Map p332; ☎ 07-587 4111; 47 The Strand) has occasional live jazz and rock. You can also eat here (see opposite).

Getting There & Away
AIR
Air New Zealand (Map p332; ☎ 07-577 7300; cnr Devonport Rd & Elizabeth St) has daily direct flights

to Auckland, Nelson and Wellington, with connections to other centres. Tauranga's airport is at Mt Maunganui. **Origin Pacific** (☎ 0800 302 302) flies direct to Wellington and connects to other regional cities.

BUS
InterCity (☎ 07-578 8103) tickets and timetables are provided by the Tauranga visitors centre (see p331), where the bus terminal is located. InterCity connects Tauranga with Auckland ($35, 4½ hours), Hamilton ($24, two hours), Thames ($18, 1½ hours), Rotorua ($21, 1½ hours), Taupo ($50, 2½ hours) and Wellington ($90, nine hours).

Bay Coaster (☎ 0800 422 9287) runs a daily service to Whakatane ($11.50, 1½ hours), via Te Puke.

Supa Travel (☎ 07-571 0583) is a local company that has buses on demand to Auckland Airport ($85 one way), as does **Tauranga Airport Shuttles** (☎ 07-574 6177). Most bus lines continue to Mt Maunganui after stopping in Tauranga.

Getting Around
A taxi from Tauranga's centre to the airport costs around $11.

Tauranga's local bus service runs from Monday to Saturday to most locations around the area, including Mt Maunganui, Papamoa and Te Puke.

Several car rental agencies have offices in Tauranga, including **Avis** (☎ 07-578 4204; 325 Cameron Rd), **Budget** (☎ 07-578 5156; Dive Cr), **Hertz** (☎ 07-578 9143; 150 Elizabeth St W) and **Rent-a-Dent** (☎ 07-578 1772; 19 Fifteenth Ave).

The local taxi companies are **Citicabs** (☎ 07-577 0999), **Coastline** (☎ 07-571 8333), **Mount Taxis** (☎ 07-574 7555) as well as **Tauranga Taxis** (☎ 07-578 6086).

The **ferry service** (Map p332; ☎ 07-578 5381; adult/child one-way $6/3; ☼ 8.15am-4.15pm) to Mt Maunganui, which takes about 30 minutes, operates from Boxing Day to Waitangi Day.

MT MAUNGANUI   Map pp334-5
pop 16,800
The town of Mt Maunganui (the name means 'Large Mountain') stands at the foot of the 232m hill of the same name (also called 'the Mount', or Maumo). NZ's 'Surf City' is just across the inlet from Tauranga, and its fine beaches make it a popular holiday resort for Kiwis. The Mount attracts

large numbers of surfers, and a planned artificial reef to be constructed 250m offshore should make it a world-class surfing spot. Check out the website www.mountreef.co.nz for details and progress reports.

Information

The Mt Maunganui **visitors centre** (☎ 07-575 5099; Salisbury Ave; ⊗ 9am-5pm Mon-Fri, 9am-4pm Sat & Sun Oct-Easter) is excellent for local info.

Sights & Activities

Walking trails go around Mt Maunganui and to its top, where there are magnificent views; the walk should take about an hour, and gets steeper towards the summit. You can also climb around the rocks on **Moturiki Island**, which is actually joined to the peninsula; check out the *Walkways of Tauranga* pamphlet, available from the visitors centre (see above). The island and the base of the Mount also make up the **Crimson Trail**, offering spectacular views of the pohutukawa trees when they're in full bloom between November and January. Leaflets are available at the visitors centre, or you can log on to www.projectcrimson.org.nz.

The beach between Moturiki and Maunganui is good for surfing and swimming. If you're keen to ride a wave, contact the **Mount Surf Shop** (☎ 07-575 9133; 96 Maunganui Rd), which rents out wet suits ($15), surfboards ($30) and body boards ($20) for a full day or **Island Style Surf Shop** (☎ 07-575 3030; www.nzsurfschools.co.nz; 227 Maunganui Rd), which organises one-hour lessons from $60 (including hire of all necessary gear).

There are **hot saltwater pools** (☎ 07-575 0868; Adams Ave; adult/child $2.50/1.50; ⊗ 6am-10pm Mon-Sat, 8am-10pm Sun & holidays) at the foot of the Mount.

The **Rock House** (☎ 07-572 4920; www.therockhouse.co.nz; 9 Triton Ave; ⊗ 4-8pm Mon, noon-8pm Tue-Fri, 10am-6pm Sat & Sun) has an indoor climbing wall, which costs $12/8 for the day.

The **Baypark Speedway** (☎ 07-574 6009; adult/child $20/5), south east of the Mount, holds speed-car meetings twice a month in summer, and once a month in winter. Call for times.

Sleeping

Mt Maunganui is a hugely popular holiday destination and has plenty of accommodation. Prices tend to be slightly higher than in Tauranga.

BUDGET

Pacific Coast Lodge & Backpackers (☎ 0800 666 622; www.pacificcoastlodge.co.nz; 432 Maunganui Rd; dm/d from $20/50; 💻) This spotless, purpose-built hostel has comfy, wood-panelled bunk rooms and great facilities. It's decorated throughout with colourful murals, and the friendly staff are happy to book activities for you.

Mount Backpackers (☎ /fax 07-575 0860; www.mountbackpacker.co.nz; 87 Maunganui Rd; dm/d from $18/50; 💻) Mount Backpackers is located in the very heart of the Mount's town centre and only a few minutes' walk from the beach. Boogie boards and bikes can be hired here, and special deals are offered on a range of local activities, including surf lessons.

Mount Maunganui B&B (☎ 07-575 4013; www.mountbednbreakfast.co.nz; 463 Maunganui Rd; s/d from $45/75) The five rooms at this homely place are a bit small, but they're cheap and well cared for, and a cooked breakfast is included in the price. There's also a guest billiard lounge.

Golden Grove Holiday Park (☎ 07-575 5821; fax 07-575 5182; 73 Girven Rd; camp sites/d/ste from $24/40/65) Golden Grove is a big family-friendly camp with spruce, modern accommodation including cabins with kitchens and self-contained motel units. It's popular with school groups.

Cosy Corner Motor Camp (☎ 07-575 5899; www.cosycorner.co.nz; 40 Ocean Beach Rd; camp sites/d/ste $24/50/70; 🐾) This is another good-quality, family camping ground. It has a sociable atmosphere and is close to the beach. There's a good range of facilities on offer, including BBQ and games room.

MID-RANGE

Baywatch Motor Inn (☎ 07-574 7745; www.baywatchmotorinn.co.nz; 349a Maunganui Rd; d from $115; 🐾) Baywatch is a friendly, family-run complex on the main road, a little south of the town centre. It is modern, spacious units with big comfy beds and kitchenettes, and all the mod-cons you'd expect. It also has disabled-accessible units.

Calais Mount Resort (☎ 0800 422 524; www.calais.co.nz; 6 Adams Ave; d/ste from $120/350) Calais has 38 tastefully designed and decorated suites and studios, including two- and three-bedroom apartments, in a handy spot just below the Mount, and about 100m from the beaches. There's a good on-site restaurant (Sails) and landscaped gardens.

Mission Belle Motel (☎ 0800 202 434; www.mission bellemotel.co.nz; cnr Victoria Rd & Pacific Ave; d from $110) Mission Belle is a large and attractive Spanish Mission–style complex in an excellent central location close to restaurants and shops, and a short walk to the beach. It has smart studios and more roomy suites, and in-room dining is available.

Ocean Sands Motel (☎ 0800 726 371; www.ocean sands.co.nz; 6 Maunganui Rd; ste $120-280) Ocean Sands is a big, upscale motel close to the beach with high-quality self-contained studios, one- and two-bedroom apartments and penthouse suites.

Outrigger Motel (☎ 0800 889 966; www.nzmotels .co.nz/outrigger.mt/; 48 Marine Parade; d from $95) The modern and spacious Outrigger complex has good-sized ground-level units on the seafront, a stone's throw to the beach. Rooms are scrupulously clean and some have great sea views.

Pacific Motor Inn (☎ 0800 556 699; 261 Maunganui Rd; d from $120; ⊠) This vaguely Art Deco–style modern motel is a light and airy place on the main road, with neat, roomy units. All have kitchens and spa baths. It's popular with business travellers and there are conference facilities.

TOP END
Oceanside Motor Lodge & Twin Towers (☎ 0800 466 868; www.oceanside.co.nz; 1 Maunganui Rd; d/ste from $165/250; ⊠) This landmark hotel is split into the Motor Lodge, with big, bright studios and well-equipped apartments, and the high-rise Twin Towers, offering more luxurious two-bedroom suites. These large rooms have breathtaking sea views, enhanced by floor-to-ceiling windows. There's a two-night minimum stay here. The facilities are of a high standard and include a gym, sauna and restaurant.

Belle Mer (☎ 0800 100 235; www.bellemer.co.nz; 53 Marine Parade; ste from $165; ⊠) This is a luxury complex with an Art Deco touch. It offers well-designed two- and three-bedroom apartments, many boasting spectacular sea views. All have fully equipped kitchens, washing machines and spa baths, plus wide, sunny balconies or private patios.

Pavilions (☎ 07-572 0001; www.pavilion.net.nz; 4 Marine Parade; ste $180-510) In a superb location right opposite the beach, the Pavilions offers luxury, fully self-contained apartments with between one and three bedrooms. Rooms

have been individually designed, with a clean-cut contemporary look and polished wood floors.

Eating & Drinking
Maunganui Road has the biggest concentration of eateries in the area.

Astrolabe (☎ 07-574 8155; 82 Maunganui Rd; mains $15-32; ☽ breakfast, lunch & dinner) This smart restaurant and bar serves inventive fare such as lamb with white truffle oil mash and plenty of fish variations. Oysters, pumpkin soup and salads also feature.

Bardeli's at the Mount (☎ 07-572 0196; 19 Pacific Ave; mains $14-25; ☽ breakfast, lunch & dinner Thu-Sun, breakfast & lunch Mon-Wed) Bardeli's is a trendy, popular restaurant with an eclectic menu including salads, curries, fish and pasta.

Two Small Fish (☎ 07-575 0096; 107 Maunganui Rd; mains $10-35; ☽ breakfast, lunch & dinner) This place does good-value lunches from $10, and, as you might expect, fish dominates.

Midi Café & Wine Bar (☎ 07-574 7394; 94 Maunganui Rd; mains $13-26; ☽ breakfast, lunch & dinner) Midi is a small place with interesting items such as tea-smoked lamb rump and swordfish on the menu, alongside old favourites like fish and chips.

Thai-Phoon (☎ 07-572 3545; 14a Pacific Ave; mains $13-17; ☽ dinner) Authentic Thai specialities such as red and green curries, stir-fries and sweet and sour dishes are the order of the day here.

Beaches Café (☎ 07-574 8075; cnr Adams Ave & Marine Pde; mains around $8-10; ☽ breakfast, lunch & dinner) This pleasant spot at the base of the Mount serves light meals, sandwiches and the like and is a popular place to hang out with a coffee.

Bombay Brasserie (☎ 07-575 2539; 75-77 Maunganui Rd; mains around $18; ☽ dinner) This place has all the popular Indian dishes and a good wine list. There's also a takeaway menu.

Clippers Restaurant & Bar (☎ 07-575 3135; cnr Rata St & Maunganui Rd; mains $14-20; ☽ breakfast, lunch & dinner) This modern, nautically themed restaurant does great daily roasts, as well as seafood and steak. There's also a bar and a giant chess set for patrons on the outside decking.

Café Istanbul (☎ 07-574 1574; 91 Maunganui Rd; mains $16-25; ☽ dinner Mon-Fri, lunch & dinner Sat & Sun) Busy Café Istanbul serves up traditional Turkish dishes, plus salads, pasta and roasts.

Sand Rock Café & Bar (☎ 07-574 7554; 4 Marine Parade; mains $21-34; ☽ breakfast, lunch & dinner) This

BAY OF PLENTY

is a good place for fresh fish, fillet steaks and lighter meals such as pasta and *panini* (focaccia).

Mount Mellick (☎ 07-574 0047; 317 Maunganui Rd) An Irish pub offering standard pub grub fare all day long.

Barmuda (☎ 07-575 8363; 19c Pacific Ave) A laid-back locals' bar above Bardelli's restaurant, with pool tables, video jukebox, pokies and Sky sports.

Entertainment

Aclantis (☎ 07-575 3135; 290 Maunganui Rd) A popular place, with regular live music, three bars and a dance floor.

Mount Mellick (see above) also hosts live bands Friday nights and varied entertainment on other nights.

Getting There & Away

You can reach Mt Maunganui across the harbour bridge from Tauranga or from the south via Te Maunga on SH2. See p337 for public transport details for the Mount. Tauranga airport is at Mt Maunganui.

Newmans, Supa Travel buses and Inter-City serve Tauranga. Their buses stop at the bus depot at Mt Maunganui visitors centre. **Bay Hopper** (☎ 0800 422 9287) buses run from Wharf St in Tauranga to the Mount, stopping at the visitors centre and hot pools.

The ferry to Tauranga departs from Salisbury Wharf near the visitors centre.

AROUND TAURANGA
Matakana Island

Just across the harbour from Tauranga, this elongated island is a quiet rural retreat that shelters the harbour. Two-thirds of the island is covered in pine forest, providing the main industry, and the rest, on the western side, is farmland. Matakana Island has 24km of pristine white-sand surf beach on its eastern shore and is a good place for windsurfing, kayaking and fishing. An ideal way to explore the island is by bicycle, which you can take across on the ferry. There is a general store and social club but not much else, so bring your own supplies.

GETTING THERE & AWAY

The **main ferry** (☎ 035 927 251) departs from Omokoroa at 7.45am, 2pm and 4pm daily for the western side of the island ($3, 15 minutes). The island has no public transport.

Omokoroa

This town, 22km west of Tauranga, is a popular summer destination. It's on a promontory that protrudes well into the sheltered harbour and affords fine views of the harbour and Matakana Island. There are a couple of campervan parks, including **Omokoroa Tourist Park** (☎ 07-578 0857; www.omokoroatouristpark.co.nz; 165 Omokoroa Rd; camp sites/d/units from $28/40/70; ☎) a neat, family-oriented place with thermal hot pools and a range of accommodation. From Omokoroa you can visit Matakana on the regular ferry service.

Katikati
pop 2900

Katikati (known to some as 'Catty-Cat'), on the Uretara River, was the only planned Ulster settlement anywhere in the world, and in more recent years has reinvented itself as an open-air art gallery with many of its buildings adorned with **murals**. Pick up a free map of the town's murals from the **Mural Town Information Centre** (☎ 07-549 1658; www.katikati.co.nz; 36 Main Rd; ☼ 9am-4.30pm).

The **Katikati Heritage Museum** (☎ 07-549 0651; cnr SH2 & Wharawhara Rd; adult/child $6/3; ☼ 9am-4pm), 1km south of Katikati, is a unique place relating local history from the Maori period, but concentrating on the story of the 19th-century Ulster pioneers, with lots of photos, documents and a mock-up of an Orange Hall amongst many other things, including the largest bottle collection in the southern hemisphere. The enthusiastic custodians give personal tours through the miscellaneous displays. There's also a café and mini golf.

In the centre of town, the **Haiku Pathway** is a pleasant walking route past boulders inscribed with haiku verses down to a peaceful, landscaped park beside the river. There are two entry points off Main Rd, one beside the information centre.

Morton Estate (☎ 07-552 0795; ☼ 10.30am-5pm) is one of NZ's bigger wineries and it's located on SH2, 8km south of Katikati. Wine tastings and door sales are also available.

SLEEPING

Most accommodation is located in the countryside surrounding Katikati, and the information centre (see opposite) has a list of local home and farmstays.

Colannade Backpackers (☎ /fax 07-552 0902; colannade@actrix.co.nz; 122 Work Rd; Aongatete; dm $14)

This tranquil place is 10km south of Katikati, set in the heart of the horticultural area. The rooms are comfy and if you stay three nights or more they'll do your washing.

Sapphire Springs Holiday Park (☎ 07-549 0768; sapphire.springs@xtra.co.nz; Hot Springs Rd; camp sites/dm/s/d from $20/15/40/50) Sapphire Springs is a relaxing place set in 32 hectares of park and bushland, with thermal pools, bushwalks, playground and mini golf. It's a popular family park and a wide choice of accommodation is available.

Katikati Naturist Park (☎ 0800 456 7567; www .katikati-naturist-park.co.nz; 149 Wharawhara Rd; camp sites/campervans/d from $24/40/50; ☎) Katikati Park, 3km southeast of Katikati, is well set up for those who prefer to promenade *au naturel*. There's a spa, sauna, lounge and putting green and a variety of accommodation including self-contained chalets ($65).

Katikati Motel (☎ 07-549 0385; katikati@ihug.co.nz; cnr Main & Fairview Rds; d $70-80) This friendly motel is a quiet and relaxing place, conveniently close to the centre of town. It's an older, smallish complex with just eight ground-floor units.

Jacaranda Cottage (☎ /fax 07-549 0616; jacaranda .cottage@clear.net.nz; 230 Thompson's Track, RD2; s/d from $50/80) Jacaranda Cottage has great views of the coast, walks in the Kaimai Range and you can even try your hand at milking a cow. There is also a one-bedroom, self-contained cottage available (two-night minimum stay).

Aberfeldy Farmstay (☎ 07-549 0363; www.aberfeldy .co.nz; 164 Lindemann Rd, RD1; s/d $60/100) For privacy's sake, the friendly Aberfeldy (a peaceful sheep and cattle farm 3km north of town) only takes one party at a time, in a cosy apartment with private lounge. Breakfast is included.

Kaimai View Motel (☎ 07-549 0398; kaimaiview@ xtra.co.nz; 78 Main Rd; d from $95; ☎) This standard chalet-block complex is opposite the Katikati Motel, and just a short walk south of the town centre. The simple, comfortable accommodation includes two units with disabled-access facilities and spacious two-bedroom apartments.

Fantail Lodge (☎ 07-549 1417; www.fantaillodge .co.nz; 117 Rea Rd; s/d from $230/320) Fantail Lodge is an exclusive, Tudor-style retreat set in extensive gardens, with large comfortable rooms and a highly regarded restaurant. There's also a self-contained three-bedroom cottage (from $500, minimum three-night stay).

EATING
Landing (☎ 07-549 3218; Main Rd; mains $11-24; ☎ lunch & dinner) This smart licensed restaurant at the Talisman Hotel serves excellent roasts and pizzas.

Twickenham Homestead (☎ 07-549 0388; cnr SH2 & Mulgan St; mains around $20; ☎ lunch & dinner) For elegant afternoon teas and fine dining, try the Twickenham.

One Wild Chook (☎ 07-549 3017; Main Rd; mains around $10; ☎ breakfast & lunch) The Chook is a simple local café, with chicken, among other things, on the menu.

Tuhua (Mayor Island)

Beautiful Tuhua, commonly known as Mayor Island, is a dormant volcano located about 40km north of Tauranga. The striking features of the island include black obsidian rock and crystal-clear water. You'll find walking tracks through the now-overgrown crater valley and an interesting walk around the island. The northwest corner is a marine reserve, but specialist groups can ask for permission from the DOC to land here.

Tuhua Island Backpackers (☎ 07-579 5655; camp sites & dm from $12) is the only place to stay on the island. It's rather basic accommodation but you can't get much more off the beaten track than this. The only cooking facility is a barbecue (wood supplied). You need to bring all your own food and some way of storing it as there are no fridges.

GETTING THERE & AWAY
MV Manutere (☎ 07-544 3072) and **Tauranga Marine Charters** (☎ 07-552 6283) run to the island three or four days a week from late December until around Easter, departing from Coronation Pier in Tauranga, going via Mt Maunganui (times on demand). The trip takes about three hours one way (adult/child $40/25 return). There's also a landing fee of $10/3. You may be able to reach the island from Whangamata and Waihi Beach (see p212) on fishing boat charters.

Minden Lookout

From Minden Lookout, about 10km west of Tauranga, there's a superb view back over the Bay of Plenty. To get there, take SH2 to Te Puna and turn off south on Minden Rd; the lookout is about 4km up the road.

Papamoa

pop 7460

Papamoa, 13km east of Mt Maunganui, is blessed with miles of beaches and is not quite as urbanised as the Mount. It's a good spot for swimming and surfing and, if you have your own transport, makes a good base for exploring the Bay of Plenty region. Digging for tuatua (a type of shellfish) is popular when the tide is low.

Papamoa Beach Top 10 Holiday Resort (☎ /fax 07-572 0816; www.papamoabeach.co.nz; 535 Papamoa Beach Rd; camp sites/d/ste from $26/45/75) This resort has a perfect spot right on the beachfront, with a huge selection of accommodation options, including villas (from $140). There's an adventure playground and a restaurant and service station alongside.

Pacific Palms Resort (☎ 0800 808 835; www.pacificpalmsresort.co.nz; 21 Gravatt Rd; d $110-240; 🖵 🗩) Pacific Palms is a bright modern place next to Palm Beach Shopping Plaza, with roomy, self-contained two- and three-bedroom apartments in landscaped grounds a few minutes walk from the beach. There are tennis courts on site.

Beach House Motel (☎ 0800 429 999; www.beachhousemotel.co.nz; 224 Papamoa Beach Rd; d $85-175; 🖵 🗩) The Beach House is a comfy motel with a snazzy contemporary design, a short walk from the sea. It has sparkling self-contained studio units and one- and two-bedroom apartments, including disabled access.

Pembroke House B&B (☎ 07-572 1000; pembrokehouse@xtra.co.nz; 12 Santa Fe Key; s/d from $70/90) Pembroke is a modern villa across the road from the beach with spacious en-suite rooms and a guest lounge.

You can get takeaway food from places on Beach Rd, and the **Blue Biyou** (☎ 07-572 2099; 559 Papamoa Beach Rd; mains from $7) is known for fine meals and enormous Sunday brunches.

Te Puke

pop 6775

Hailed as the 'Kiwi Fruit Capital of the World', Te Puke has native bush near the town and it is not far from several good beaches and exciting rivers. Te Puke gets busy in the kiwi-fruit-picking season when there's plenty of work. The **visitors centre** (☎ 07-573 9172; 130 Jellicoe St; 🕑 8am-4.30pm Mon-Fri, 9am-noon Sat) has a notice board with fruit-picking vacancies.

SIGHTS & ACTIVITIES

The Bay of Plenty is kiwi fruit country and here you can learn a little more about the fruit that is so important to NZ's economy. Gardening enthusiasts can visit many private gardens in the area.

Kiwi Fruit Country (☎ 07-573 6340; www.kiwifruitcountry.co.nz; adult/child $11/5.50; 🕑 9am-5pm) is on SH2 at the turnoff for Maketu, 6km east of Te Puke and 36km from Tauranga. You can visit the orchards and the shop, watch a video about kiwi fruit and sample some of the products. The complex is also a theme park, including an informative 35-minute 'kiwi-kart' ride through the orchards and an exhibition on how the fruit is grown and packed. Tours of the park run throughout the day. Other fruit grown here include nashi pears, citrus and avocados.

Next to Kiwi Fruit Country is the **Vintage Auto Barn** (☎ 07-573 6547; www.vintagecars.nzhere.com; adult/child $7/2; 🕑 9am-5pm) with over 100 vintage and classic cars on display, such as a 1906 Cadillac and a 1923 Model T Ford. Some are for sale or hire.

The **Comvita visitors centre** (☎ 0800 504 959; Paengaroa; free; 🕑 9am-5pm) represents Comvita healthcare treatments made from honey and other bee products. There's an educational gallery, an auditorium, a shop, and tours at 10am and 2pm daily. The centre is 9km east of Te Puke on the SH33 heading towards Rotorua.

At **Longridge Park** (☎ 07-533 1515; www.longridgepark.co.nz, Paengaroa; 🕑 9am-5pm, to 4pm winter), near Te Puke, you can take a half-hour jetboat ride (adult/child $65/35) up the winding and bush-clad Kaituna River, or take a tour of a working kiwi fruit farm ($15/10), which includes a sheep-milking demonstration. There's also a petting farm ($1.50) with sheep, goats and rabbits, as well as freshwater eels. Afterwards, you can 4WD over a challenging series of tracks ($60/25). Also available is a jetboat and 4WD combo ($115/55) and clay pigeon shooting ($2 per shot).

O'Hara's Wildlife Estate (☎ 0508 723 274; Paengaroa; 🕑 by arrangement), on SH33 towards Rotorua, is a working deer farm, home to five types of deer as well as feral sheep, wallabies and pigs. It offers a variety of activities including horse treks along the Kaituna River ($50), canoe safaris ($60), rafting ($90), archery ($35) and wildlife safaris ($50). Bookings are essential.

SLEEPING

The visitors centre (opposite) has a list of home and farmstays in the area.

Lindenhof Homestay (☎ 07-573 4592; 58 Dunlop Rd; s/d incl breakfast $50/90; 🏊) The Lindenhof, 2km north of Te Puke, has comfortable rooms in a lovely homestead. It has a spa pool and tennis court.

Croeso i Hafod (☎ 07-533 1086; info@croesoihafod .co.nz; 151 Wilson Rd, Paengaroa; s/d $45/80) East of town in Paengaroa, this cosy B&B with a vaguely Welsh flavour has just a couple of rooms and is set in tranquil, beautifully tended gardens, often used for wedding ceremonies.

Maketu
pop 1000

There's a *pa* (fortified Maori village) site overlooking the water at Town Point, near the township of Maketu, northeast of Te Puke. Maketu was the landing site of the *Arawa* canoe, more than 600 years ago, and there is a stone monument on the foreshore commemorating this.

To get to Maketu from Tauranga, take SH2 through Te Puke and turn left into Maketu Rd just past Rangiuru. The **visitors centre** (☎ 07-533 2343; Maketu Rd; 🕐 noon-2pm Mon-Fri) is a useful source of information.

Beach Holiday Park (☎ 07-533 2165; www.maketu beach.co.nz; 3 Town Point Rd; camp sites/d/ste from $34/ 35/85) This beachfront campervan park is a quiet place, which also has wooden cabins overlooking a wide, safe-swimming beach, and good-value motel-style units. There's a licensed restaurant on site.

Blue Tides Beachfront Retreat (☎ 0800 359 191; 7 Te Awhe Rd; www.bluetides.co.nz; d $100-145) This small homely place commands a pleasant location facing the sea. Good quality self-contained units and B&B options are offered.

The **Seaside Café** (☎ 07-533 2381; Town Point Rd; mains from $10) is a pleasant spot for fresh fish and takeaways, or try Maketu's famous pies at **Maketu Pies** (☎ 07-533 2358; 6 Little Waihi Rd) near the visitors centre.

EASTERN BAY OF PLENTY

The Eastern Bay of Plenty extends from Maketu and Pukehina to Opotiki in the far east of the bay, taking in Whakatane and Ohope. The main feature of the region is long stretches of sandy beaches backed by cliffs covered in pohutukawa trees.

WHAKATANE
pop 17,700

Whakatane (pronounced 'fa-ka-ta-ne') lies on a natural harbour at the mouth of the Whakatane River. When the *Mataatoa* canoe landed at the mouth of the river in the 13th century, Whakatane was already an important Maori centre. The *Mataatua* (Face of God) canoe was part of the migration by the Maori people from Hawaiki to NZ. It is said that the canoe brought not only people, but soil, kumara and taro for plantation cultivation in the new land. Only around the beginning of the 20th century did Europeans discover the richness of the land and settle there in any significant numbers.

Whakatane today is the principal town for the Eastern Bay of Plenty and a service centre for the Rangitaiki agricultural district. It's a pleasant (if not particularly exciting) town with a friendly atmosphere, and it enjoys plenty of sunshine year-round. Many visitors are attracted to the nearby beaches, especially in summer. The eastern bay's major attraction is offshore: Whakaari (White Island), NZ's most active volcano.

WOMEN'S WORK

The origin of Whakatane's name goes back some eight centuries, 200 years after the original Maori settlers arrived here. The warrior Toroa, together with family members and a cargo of kumara, sailed into the estuary here, in a huge ocean-going *waka* (canoe), the *Mataatua*. The men disembarked to greet the local leaders, leaving the boat in the hands of the women and children, but the tide turned and those on shore could only watch as the *waka* drifted helplessly out to sea. Then, Toroa's daughter, Wairaka, cried out *'E! Kia whakatane au i ahau!'* (Let me act as a man!), and, breaking the traditional Maori *tapu* that women should not steer *waka*, she took the paddle and brought the boat and its company safely to shore. A statue of Wairaka today stands proudly atop a rock in Whakatane's harbour in commemoration of her brave deed and for bestowing the town's name.

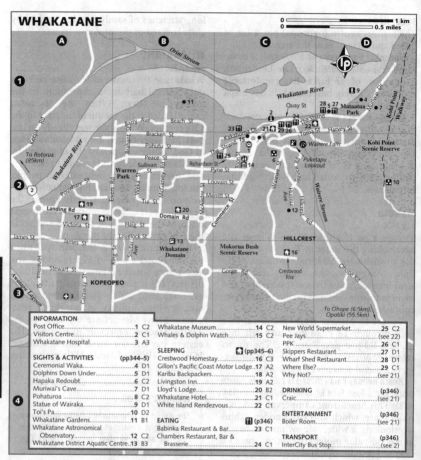

WHAKATANE

0 _____ 1 km
0 _____ 0.5 miles

INFORMATION		
Post Office	1	C2
Visitors Centre	2	C1
Whakatane Hospital	3	A3
SIGHTS & ACTIVITIES	(pp344–5)	
Ceremonial Waka	4	D1
Dolphins Down Under	5	D1
Hapaka Redoubt	6	C2
Muriwai's Cave	7	D1
Pohaturoa	8	C2
Statue of Wairaka	9	D1
Toi's Pa	10	D2
Whakatane Gardens	11	B1
Whakatane Astronomical Observatory	12	C2
Whakatane District Aquatic Centre	13	B3

Whakatane Museum	14	C2
Whales & Dolphin Watch	15	C2
SLEEPING	(pp345–6)	
Crestwood Homestay	16	C3
Gillon's Pacific Coast Motor Lodge	17	A2
Karibu Backpackers	18	A2
Livingston Inn	19	A2
Lloyd's Lodge	20	B2
Whakatane Hotel	21	C1
White Island Rendezvous	22	C1
EATING	(p346)
Babinka Restaurant & Bar	23	C1
Chambers Restaurant, Bar & Brasserie	24	A2

New World Supermarket	25	C2
Pee Jays	(see 22)	
PPK	26	C1
Skippers Restaurant	27	D1
Wharf Shed Restaurant	28	D1
Where Else?	29	C1
Why Not?	(see 21)	
DRINKING	(p346)
Craic	(see 21)	
ENTERTAINMENT	(p346)
Boiler Room	(see 21)	
TRANSPORT	(p346)
InterCity Bus Stop	(see 2)	

Information

The **visitors centre** (☎ 0800 478 674; www.whakatane
.com; Quay St; ☺ 8.30am-5pm Mon-Fri, 10am-4pm Sat &
Sun) is open longer in summer. The staff
make tour bookings and also handle general
inquiries for DOC. Nearby is a **New Zealand
Post** (☎ 07-307 1155; Commerce St) outlet. If you
need emergency medical treatment, visit the
Whakatane Hospital (07-306 0999; Stewart St).

Sights

The **Whakatane Museum** (☎ 07-306 0505; Boon
St; admission by donation; ☺ 10am-4.30pm Mon-Fri,
11am-3pm Sat & Sun) is an excellent regional
museum. It has photographic and artefact
exhibits on early Maori and European settlers as well as on the natural environment,

including the smoking Whakaari volcano
just offshore. It's also a centre of historical
research, with an archive of historical publications. Adjacent is an art gallery featuring
mostly local artists.

Just to one side of the traffic circle is
Pohaturoa (cnr The Strand & Commerce St), a large
rock outcrop and *tapu* (sacred) site, where
warriors were once tattooed. The Treaty of
Waitangi was signed here by Ngati Awa
chiefs in 1840. The coastline used to come
right up to this point and there's a tunnel
in the rock where baptisms and other rites
were performed. Also here is a monument
to the Ngati Awa chief Te Hurinui Apanui.

Muriwai's Cave (partially collapsed), beside Muriwai Dr, once provided shelter to

a famous ancestress and seer who arrived from Hawaiki on the *Mataatua*. A ceremonial **waka** (canoe), named after the original *Mataatua*, sits secure behind a grill in the reserve across the road.

The **Whakatane Astronomical Observatory** (☎ 07-308 6495; Hurinui Ave; admission $5) in Hillcrest, opens to the public every fine-weather Tuesday evening.

The small **Whakatane Gardens** are at the river end of McGarvey Rd, and comprise a rose garden and attractive Japanese Garden.

Activities
DOLPHIN SWIMMING
Dolphins Down Under (☎ 0800 354 7737; www.dolphin swim.co.nz; 2 The Strand; adult/child $100/75), **Whales & Dolphin Watch** (☎ 07-308 2001; www.whalesand dolphinwatch.co.nz; 96 The Strand; $100/80; ⏱ departs at 6am, 10.30am & 3pm) and **Blue Sky Tours** (☎ 0800 377 878; trips $130) run dolphin-swimming trips year-round (subject to weather). There's a high success rate for dolphin spotting (check with local fishing-boat operators at the wharf if you want to make sure there are dolphins around). All equipment is supplied.

WALKING
The visitors centre (opposite) stocks a good booklet *Discover the Walks Around Whakatane* ($2), which lists walks ranging from 30 minutes to half a day. The interesting 2½-hour **River Walk** is an easy and scenic introduction to Whakatane, following the course of the river past the wharf and Mataatua Reserve to the estuary, returning to town past Muriwai's Cave.

Other notable walks include the 3½-hour **Kohi Point Walkway**, Nga Tapuwae-o-Toi (The Sacred Footsteps of Toi), which extends through the Kohi Point Scenic Reserve, passing many attractive sites including lookouts and **Toi's Pa** (Kapua te Rangi), reputedly the oldest *pa* site in NZ. Other walkways are the Ohope Scenic Reserve, the Mokorua Bush Scenic Reserve, Latham's Hill Track and Puketapu Lookout and Hapaka Redoubt. The 300m **White Pine Bush Walk**, starting about 20km south of Whakatane, is suitable for wheelchairs.

OTHER ACTIVITIES
Check with the visitors centre (opposite) about the wide variety of activities in and around the Whakatane area. Possibilities include horse treks, bushwalking, trout or sea fishing, diving, windsurfing and rafting. Most trips to Whakaari leave from Whakatane (see p347). Ohope Beach also offers a range of activities.

Kiwi Jet Boat Tours (☎ 0800 800 538; www.kiwij etboattours.com; adult/child $65/55) has a 1¼-hour jetboat trip along the Rangitaiki River from Matahina Dam to Aniwhenua Falls (minimum of four people).

KG Kayaks (☎ 07-315 4005; www.kgkayaks.co.nz; tours $55) KG operates guided kayaking tours along the coastline and around Ohiwa Harbour, and also rent out kayaks ($15 for one hour, $25 for three hours).

Ohope Golf Club (☎ 07-312 4486; ohope@golf.co.nz; Harbour Rd, Ohope; 10/18 holes $15/25) This friendly golf club has a spectacular setting overlooking the sea at Ohope. Clubs can be hired at extra cost.

Whakatane District Aquatic Centre (☎ 07-308 4192; Short Street; adult/child $3/1.30; ⏱ 6am-8pm Mon-Fri, 7am-6pm Sat & Sun) This state-of-the-art modern swimming complex has indoor and outdoor pools, spa pools and a waterslide.

Sleeping
BUDGET
Budget accommodation is in short supply in Whakatane, but the visitors centre (opposite) lists homestays and farmstays in the area.

Karibu Backpackers (☎ /fax 07-307 8276; 13 Landing Rd; camp sites/dm/s/d $28/19/32/50; 🖥) This quiet and intimate hostel is in a converted house with a large garden, communal kitchen and lounge. Rooms are clean and spacious and free bike use is offered.

Lloyd's Lodge (☎ 07-307 8005; lloyds.lodge@xtra .co.nz; 10 Domain Rd; dm/d $20/50; 🖥) Lloyd's is a friendly hostel in an old wooden house, offering fascinating in-house Maori cultural evenings, including games, stories and songs; you can even try preparing your own *hangi*.

Whakatane Hotel (☎ 07-307 1670; 79 The Strand; dm/s/d $16/30/55) This old Art Deco hotel is right in the centre of town, with rooms above The Craic pub (see p346); it's not exactly the Ritz, but it has character and it's cheap and handily placed.

MID-RANGE
White Island Rendezvous (☎ 0800 242 299; www .whiteisland.co.nz; 15 The Strand East; d/f from $90/120) White Island is a spotless place with a good selection of accommodation, including two

disabled-accessible units. There's a separate
self-contained wooden cottage available
(from $120) with its own pretty garden and
big lounge. Also here is a café and Pee Jay
charters to Whakaari (see opposite).

Crestwood Homestay (☎ 07-308 7554; www
.crestwood-homestay.co.nz; 2 Crestwood Rise; d $70-110
incl breakfast) Crestwood is a friendly homestay in a quiet residential area. There are
just a couple of spotless rooms, with a large
private lounge and kitchenette. Other meals
can be arranged at extra cost.

Livingston Inn (☎ 0800 770 777; www.livingston
.co.nz; 42 Landing Rd; d from $95) The Livingston is
a superior and efficiently run motel complex, with spacious, well-kept units. All
have 'computer friendly' workstations and
either a spa bath or private spa pool.

Gillon's Pacific Coast Motor Lodge (☎ 0800 224
430; pacific.coast.lodge@xtra.co.nz; 41 Landing Rd; d from
$90; 🖳) Gillon's is another big, upscale motel
with smart and stylish studios and units,
some with spa baths. There's a well-tended
garden and a high standard of service.

Eating

Skippers Restaurant (☎ 07-307 1573; The Strand;
mains from $10; 🕑 lunch & dinner) Housed in
Whakatane Sportfishing Club, this convivial place offers good-value seafood, surrounded by numerous stuffed trophy fish.

Babinka Restaurant & Bar (☎ 07-307 0009; 14
Kakahoroa Dr; mains $20-25; 🕑 breakfast, lunch & din-
ner) Babinka is a trendy restaurant with an
interesting menu that includes a variety of
Indian, Turkish and Moroccan dishes.

Chambers Restaurant, Bar & Brasserie (☎ 07-
307 0107; 40 The Strand; mains $20-27; 🕑 lunch & din-
ner) Upmarket Chambers is in the former
council building, serving intriguing dishes
such as kingfish with kumara and banana,
as well as duck, pork and scallops.

Wharf Shed Restaurant (☎ 07-308 5698; The Strand;
mains $25-28; 🕑 lunch & dinner) The Wharf Shed's
menu is heavy on seafood, and there is a
smattering of venison and beef dishes too.

Pee Jay's (☎ 07-308 9588; 15 The Strand; meals $7-
10; 🕑 breakfast & lunch) This popular café inside
White Island Rendezvous (see pp345–6)
has hearty breakfasts and brunches, salads,
sandwiches and Cuban coffee.

PPK (☎ 07-308 5000; 60 Strand E; mains $8-13;
🕑 lunch Tue-Fri, dinner Tue-Sun) Good value
pizza, pasta and kebabs are on the menu
at this place.

Why Not? (☎ 07-308 8138; 79 The Strand; mains $14-
25; 🕑 lunch & dinner) Why Not serves big portions of pasta, salads, fish and steak and its
outdoor seating catches the afternoon and
evening sun.

Where Else? (☎ 07-308 6721; 62 The Strand; mains
$6-16; 🕑 lunch & dinner) Whakatane's other
interrogative restaurant is a wooden cabin-
style affair offering a menu of Tex-Mex
standards such as burritos and tacos, as
well as inexpensive lunches of the fish and
chips and burgers variety.

Drinking & Entertainment
Both venues are located in the Whakatane
Hotel (see p345).

Craic (☎ 07-307 1670) A busy Irish theme-
pub, which also serves cheap food.

Boiler Room (☎ 07-307 0176) Next door to the
Craic, the Boiler Room packs them in with
the occasional live band and pool tables.

Getting There & Around
Air New Zealand (☎ 07-308 8397) has daily
flights linking Whakatane to Auckland,
with connections to other centres.

Taxis (☎ 0800 421 829) to or from the airport
cost $20. There is no bus service.

InterCity buses stop outside the visitors
centre. InterCity has buses connecting
Whakatane with Rotorua ($25, 1½ hours)
and Gisborne ($35, three hours), with
connections to other places. All buses to
Gisborne go via Opotiki. Courier services
around East Cape originate in Opotiki and
Gisborne (see p353).

WHAKAARI (WHITE ISLAND)
NZ's most active volcano is Whakaari
(White Island), just 50km off the coast
from Whakatane. It's a small island of 324
hectares, formed by three separate volcanic cones, all of different ages. Erosion
has worn away most of the surface of the
two older cones and the youngest, which
rose up between the two older ones, now
occupies most of the centre of the island.
Hot water and steam continually escape
from vents over most of the crater floor
and temperatures of 600°C to 800°C have
been recorded. The highest point on the island is Mt Gisborne at 321m. Geologically,
Whakaari is related to Motuhora (Whale
Island) and Putauaki (Mt Edgecumbe), as
all lie along the same volcanic trench.

The island is privately owned and the only way you can land on it is with a helicopter or boat tour that has arranged permission. There is no jetty so boats have to land on the beach, which means that landings are not possible in rough seas. A visit to Whakaari is an unforgettable, if disconcerting, experience but the constant rumblings and plumes of steam do not necessarily mean that it is about to blow up.

History
Before the arrival of Europeans, Maoris caught sea birds on the island for food. In 1769 Captain Cook named it White Island, inspired by the dense clouds of white steam hanging above it.

The first European to land on the island was a missionary, the Reverend Henry Williams, in 1826. The island was acquired by Europeans in the late 1830s and changed ownership a number of times after that. Sulphur production began but was interrupted in 1885 by a minor eruption, and the following year the island was hurriedly abandoned in the wake of the Tarawera eruption (see p329). The island's sulphur industry resumed in 1898 but only continued until 1901, when production ceased altogether.

In the 1910s further mining operations were attempted and abandoned due to mud flows and other volcanic activity, which resulted in the deaths of several miners, and ownership of the island continued to change. In 1953 White Island was declared a Private Scenic Reserve.

The island was at its most active between 1976 and 1981, when two new craters were formed and 100,000 cubic metres of rock was ejected.

Getting There & Away
Most trips to Whakaari include a tour on foot around the island. A landing by boat is definitely dependent on the weather. All trips (except for fixed-wing aerial sightseeing) incur a $20 landing fee, which is normally included in the quoted price.

Operators include:

Dive White (☎ 0800 348 394; www.divewhite.co.nz; per person from $120) Offers diving and snorkelling trips to White Island.

Pee Jay (☎ 0800 733 529; www.whiteisland.co.nz; per person $130 incl lunch) Tours on a 23m monohull launch,

taking six hours with two hours on the island, plus extra time whale- and dolphin-spotting if you're lucky.

Scott Air (☎ 0800 535 363; www.scottair.co.nz; per person from $135) Aerial sightseeing tours over the island.

Vulcan Helicopters (☎ 0800 804 354; www.vulcanheli .co.nz; per person $380) Has 2½-hour helicopter flights (minimum of five people). The pilot will land if conditions are safe.

White Island Adventure Tours (☎ 0800 733 529; per person $100 incl lunch) Offers a 4½- to six-hour boat trip with a bit of dolphin-spotting en route. You spend about two hours on the island. The boat used is an 18m launch.

MOTUHORA
Nine kilometres north off the coast of Whakatane is Motuhora (Whale Island), so-called because of its shape, which has an area of 414 hectares. It's another volcanic island, on the same volcanic trench as Whakaari, although it's much less active. Along its shore are hot springs, which can reach 93°C. The summit is 353m high and the island has several historic sites, including an ancient *pa* site, an old quarry and a camp.

Whale Island was settled by Maoris before the 1769 landing of Captain Cook. In 1829 there was a Maori massacre of sailors from the trading vessel *Haweis* while it was anchored at Sulphur Bay. This was followed by an unsuccessful whaling venture in the 1830s. In the 1840s the island passed into European ownership and is still privately owned, although since 1965 it has been an officially protected wildlife refuge administered by DOC.

Whale Island is principally a haven for sea and shore birds, some of which are quite rare. Some of the birds use the island only for nesting at certain times of the year, while others are present year-round. The island has a large colony of grey-faced petrels, estimated to number 10,000.

The island's protected status means landing is restricted. There are only six trips to the island each year (adult/child $50/40) over the Christmas period; bookings can be made through the Whakatane DOC office or visitors centre (see p344).

WHAKATANE TO ROTORUA
Travelling along SH30 from Whakatane to Rotorua you'll come to the **Awakeri Hot Springs**, 16km from Whakatane. It has hot springs, spa pools, picnic areas and a **holiday park** (☎ 07-304 9117; camp sites/d/ste from $22/39/70), which has a selection of accommodation,

including stationary caravans ($37) and motel units ($90). The springs cost $3/1.50 for adults/children.

Lying just off SH30, **Kawerau** is a timber town surrounded by pine forest and dependent on the huge **Tasman Pulp & Paper Mill** (☎ 07-323 3456). You can visit the mill for a 1½-hour tour; bookings are essential. Kawerau has a **visitors centre** (☎ 07-323 7550; Plunkett St ⏰ 8.30am-4.40pm Mon-Fri, 10am-3pm Sat & Sun) in the centre of town, and a selection of accommodation, but the only real reason to come here is to visit the waterfalls outside town.

Tarawera Falls are a half-hour drive from Kawerau, along a well-graded road through the pine forests (watch out for the logging trucks). From the end of the road it is a 15-minute walk through native forest to the falls, which emerge from a hole in the canyon wall. The track continues another two hours up to the top of the falls and on to Lake Tarawera. This is a good walk with views of the lake and Mt Tarawera. You need a permit to visit ($2), which you can obtain from the visitors centre.

Dominating Kawerau is **Putauaki (Mt Edgecumbe)**, a volcanic cone with panoramic views of the entire Bay of Plenty. You need a permit for access ($2) but it closes periodically, generally during times of high fire risk; contact the visitors centre for permits and the latest news.

OHOPE BEACH
pop 3010
The town of Ohope, 7km 'over the hill' from Whakatane, has a great beach, perfect for long walks, lazy days and surfing, and is backed by quiet Ohiwa Harbour. Just beyond the harbour is the small Sandspit Wildlife Refuge; if you're here in September, you might see the godwits flying in from Siberia.

Ohiwa Harbour Tours (☎ 07-312 4993; per person $55) takes you on a two-hour tour of the harbour, with historical and ecological commentary along the way.

Ohope Beach Top 10 Holiday Park & Adventure Complex (☎ /fax 07-312 4460; www.ohopebeach.co.nz; 367 Harbour Rd; camp sites/d from $24/50; 🏊) The family-friendly Top 10 Park is at the eastern end of the beach overlooking the sea, offering a good standard of accommodation. There's a basketball and tennis court, mini golf, adventure playground and pool and slide complex.

Surfs Reach Motel (☎ 07-312 4159; www.surfs reachmotels.co.nz; 52 West End; d from $80) At the far western end of Ohope Beach is this quiet, friendly place. The units are light and roomy and have good sea views.

Surf and Sand Holiday Park (☎ 07-312 4884; www.surfandsand.co.nz; Harbour Rd; camp sites/ste from $32/120) Surf and Sand is normally only open between late December and February. It has campervan sites and one- and two-bedroom apartments with sea views.

Jody's on the Beach (☎ 07-312 4616; motel31@xtra.co.nz; 31 Westend Rd; s/d from $65/95) Jody's is another beachfront motel in a quiet spot, with neat ground-level units.

Eating options include **Café Addiction** (☎ 07-312 5292; 19 Pohutukawa Ave; mains $18-25; ⏰ dinner Wed-Sun), serving fish and steak dishes at the western end of Ohope, and **Stingray Café** (☎ 07-312 4005; 340 Harbour Rd; mains $11-20; ⏰ lunch & dinner Fri-Sun, dinner Mon-Thu), a popular seafood place overlooking the harbour.

On the main highway heading towards Opotiki is the **Ohiwa Oyster Farm** (☎ 07-312 4565; Wainui Rd), a roadside takeaway place. There are tables near the water where you can consume your fish and chips and oysters.

OPOTIKI
pop 7070
Opotiki, the easternmost town of the Bay of Plenty, is the gateway to the East Cape and the rugged forests and river valleys of the Raukumara and nearby ranges. The town itself is little more than a sleepy backwater, but many visitors stop over on the way to the East Coast and there are some reasonable surf beaches nearby, such as Ohiwa and Waiotahi. Opotiki is a model of Maori tradition: the main street is lined with the works of master carvers.

The Opotiki area was settled from at least 1150, some 200 years before the larger 14th-century migration. In the mid-1800s Opotiki was a centre for Hauhauism, a Maori doctrine that was grounded in Judaeo-Christian beliefs and advocated, among other things, an end to the oppression of the Maori.

Information
The Opotiki **visitors centre** (☎ 07-315 8484; www.eastlandnz.com; cnr St John & Elliott Sts; ⏰ 8am-5pm) and **DOC office** (☎ 07-315 1001) are in the same building. The centre takes bookings

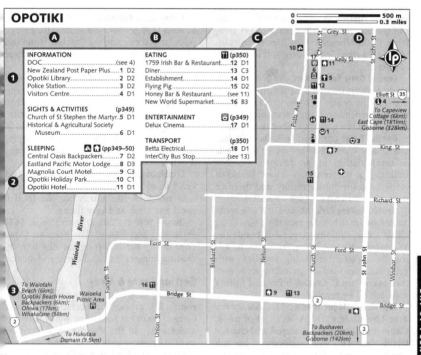

OPOTIKI

0   500 m
0   0.3 miles

INFORMATION
DOC..(see 4)
New Zealand Post Paper Plus.....1 D2
Opotiki Library..............................2 D2
Police Station................................3 D2
Visitors Centre.............................4 D1

SIGHTS & ACTIVITIES   (p349)
Church of St Stephen the Martyr.5 D1
Historical & Agricultural Society
    Museum.......................................6 D1

SLEEPING   (pp349–50)
Central Oasis Backpackers........7 D2
Eastland Pacific Motor Lodge....8 D3
Magnolia Court Motel..................9 C3
Opotiki Holiday Park..................10 C1
Opotiki Hotel..............................11 D1

EATING   (p350)
1759 Irish Bar & Restaurant.....12 D1
Diner...13 C3
Establishment.............................14 D1
Flying Pig...................................15 D2
Honey Bar & Restaurant........(see 11)
New World Supermarket........16 B3

ENTERTAINMENT   (p349)
Delux Cinema............................17 D1

TRANSPORT   (p350)
Betta Electrical..........................18 D1
InterCity Bus Stop..................(see 13)

To Capeview
Cottage (6km);
East Cape (181km);
Gisborne (328km)

To Waiotahi
Beach (6km);
Opotiki Beach House
Backpackers (6km);
Ohiwa (17km);
Whakatane (58km)

To Hukutaia
Domain (9.5km)

To Bushaven
Backpackers (20km);
Gisborne (142km)

for a variety of activities and it stocks the indispensable free booklet *Opotiki & East Cape*.

You can send mail at the **New Zealand Post Paper Plus** (☎ 07-315 6155; 106c Church St) outlet and Internet access is available at the **Opotiki Library** (cnr King & Church Sts).

Sights & Activities

Known by the local Whakatohea tribe to have acted as a government spy, Reverend Carl Volkner was murdered in 1865 in the **Church of St Stephen the Martyr** (Church St) – you can still see the blood stains near the pulpit. The church was then fortified by government troops.

Just over 7km south of the town centre is the fascinating **Hukutaia Domain** (Woodlands Rd; ☼ daily), which has one of the finest collections of native plants in NZ, many of them rare and endangered. In the domain's centre a 21m puriri tree, named Taketakerau, is estimated to be over 2000 years old. The remains of the distinguished dead of the Upokorere *hapu* (subtribe) of the Whakaohea tribe were ritually buried beneath it.

The tree is no longer *tapu* as the remains have been reinterred elsewhere.

The **Historical & Agricultural Society Museum** (☎ 07-315 5193; 123 Church St; adult/child $2/1; ☼ 10am-3.30pm Mon-Sat, 1.30-4pm Sun) is spilling over with historical items donated by the local community.

Catch the latest movies at the **Delux Cinema** (☎ 07-315 6110; Church St).

Motu River Jet Boat Tours (☎ 07-325 2735; adult/child $85/50) has as many as three 1½-hour trips daily on the Motu River. **Wet 'n' Wild** (☎ 0800 462 7238; www.wetnwildrafting.co.nz) offers two- to four-day rafting/camping/jet boating adventures on the Motu (from $640).

Sleeping

Opotiki Beach House Backpackers (☎ 07-315 5117; Appleton Rd; dm/s/d $17/23/45) This is a light and spacious place with good-sized, spotless rooms, well-placed around 5km west of Opotiki right on Waiotahi Beach. A free pick-up service is available from town.

Bushaven Backpackers (☎ 027-201 0512; dm/s/d from $15/20/40) Bushaven is in a secluded bush-clad valley beside the Te Waiti stream in the Urutawa Forest, some 19km south of Opotiki, and a perfect place to get away from it all. Home-cooked meals are available and a free pick-up/drop-off in Opotiki is offered.

Central Oasis Backpackers (☎ 07-315 5165; 30 King St; dm/tw/d $12/28/30) This small backpackers is in the centre of town in a ragged old cottage that has certainly seen better days, though it has a good, sociable atmosphere.

Opotiki Hotel (☎ 07-315 6078; Church St; dm/d $20/35) The Opotiki offers cheap and basic accommodation in an historic wooden building in the centre of town. Breakfast is included for double rooms, and there's a restaurant downstairs (see opposite).

Opotiki Holiday Park (☎ /fax 07-315 6050; opotiki .holidays@xtra.co.nz; Potts Ave; camp sites/d from $20/36; 🖳 🐾) This camping ground is beside the Waioweka River, 200m from town. It's mainly a place for young families, with great facilities for kids including an adventure playground. Kayaks, bikes and fishing rods can all be rented.

Capeview Cottage (☎ 0800 227 384; www.capeview .co.nz; Tablelands Rd; d $130) A little out of town, Capeview Cottage is a tranquil and characterful place with two bedrooms, a hot tub and lovely views of the coast. A weekly rate is also available ($800).

Magnolia Court Motel (☎ 0800 556 246; mag nolia.crt.motel@xtra.co.nz; cnr Bridge & Nelson Sts; s/d from $70/80; 🖳) Magnolia is a neat modern establishment with 10 roomy ground-level units with all the motel-style comforts you'd expect, though it's nothing out of the ordinary.

Eastland Pacific Motor Lodge (☎ 07-315 5524; www.eastlandpacific.co.nz; cnr Bridge & St John Sts; d from $80) Eastland is another clean, modern and fairly bland motel with ground-floor studios and units, some with spa baths.

Eating

Opotiki has a scattering of reasonable eateries, but it isn't exactly a gourmet carousel.

Honey Bar & Restaurant (☎ 07-315 6078; Church St; mains $3.50-25; 🕑 lunch & dinner) Honey is a popular place inside the Opotiki Hotel (see opposite), with an eclectic menu and cheap snack food.

1759 Irish Bar & Restaurant (☎ 07-315 6115; Church St; mains $10-20; 🕑 lunch & dinner) The restaurant at the Masonic hotel serves roasts and grills, as well as pub grub and snacks.

Flying Pig (☎ 07-315 7618; 95 Church St; mains $8-10; 🕑 breakfast & lunch) The licensed Flying Pig serves kebabs and the like, and has cheap lunch specials.

Establishment (☎ 07-315 6244; Church St; sandwiches around $3; 🕑 breakfast & lunch) This café may not look like much but the food is good and fresh and very filling.

Diner (☎ 07-315 5805; 77 Bridge St; mains $4-18 🕑 breakfast, lunch & dinner) The licensed Diner does hearty meals throughout the day, including burgers, fish and chips and steaks.

Getting There & Away

Travelling east from Opotiki there are two routes. SH2 crosses the spectacular Waioeka Gorge. There are some fine walks that take about a day in the **Waioeka Gorge Scenic Reserve**. The gorge gets steeper and narrower as you travel inland, before the route crosses typically green, rolling hills, dotted with sheep, on the descent to Gisborne.

The other route east from Opotiki is SH35 around the East Cape, described fully in the East Coast chapter (see p355).

InterCity buses pick up/drop off at The Diner on Bridge St, though for tickets and bookings you'll have to go to **Betta Electrical** (☎ 07-315 8555; 115 Church St).

InterCity has daily buses connecting Opotiki with Whakatane ($15, 40 minutes), Rotorua ($21, two hours, 10 minutes) and Auckland ($50, 6¾ hours). Heading south the buses connect Opotiki with Gisborne ($25, two hours) by a daily service.

The Bay Hopper runs twice daily to Whakatane ($7, 1¼ hours).

The East Coast

CONTENTS

East Cape	**353**
Opotiki to East Cape	355
Raukumara & Waioeka	356
East Cape to Gisborne	357
Poverty Bay	**358**
Gisborne	358
Gisborne to Wairoa	364
Hawkes Bay	**365**
Wairoa	365
Wairoa to Napier	366
Te Urewera National Park	366
Napier	368
Hastings	375
Havelock North	378
Around Hawkes Bay	378

The East Coast harbours some of New Zealand's most dramatic, most varied and least travelled landscapes, from the wild and rugged terrain of the East Cape to the bustling East Coast cities of Gisborne, Napier and Hastings, the rich wine country of Hawkes Bay and the primeval forests that encircle Lake Waikaremoana in Te Urewera National Park.

From Opotiki at the eastern edge of the Bay of Plenty, circling around to Gisborne, the remote East Cape remains well off the main tourist routes due to infrequent or often non-existent public transport. It's a beautiful unspoilt area, with stunning coastal scenery and dense inland forests. This isolated region has retained its strong Maori influence and community spirit, and offers an authentic taste of rural NZ life.

Gisborne, NZ's most easterly city, is a relaxed, sunny destination renowned internationally for its surf and beaches, while the seaside resort of Napier, further south on beautiful Hawke Bay, is one of the East Coast's main draws with its amazing collection of Art Deco architecture.

Inland, the lush agricultural land supports some of NZ's most productive and esteemed wineries, most of which open their doors (and cellars) to visitors. The towns of Hastings and Havelock North make good bases for exploring this region and attract large numbers of international backpackers during harvest time.

HIGHLIGHTS

- Tramping the **Lake Waikaremoana Track** (p366), one of NZ's Great Walks, in Te Urewera National Park
- Exploring Art Deco heritage in **Napier** (p368)
- Touring the wineries of **Gisborne** (p358) and the **Hawkes Bay** (p378) wine country
- Following the scenic SH35 around the **East Cape** (p357)
- Catching the sunrise at **East Cape Lighthouse** (p355), mainland NZ's most easterly point
- Sampling the local produce at Hastings **HB Food Group Farmers Market** (p380)
- Surfing at **Wainui Beach** (p362)

- TELEPHONE CODE: 07 and 06
- www.hawkesbaynz.com
- www.gisbornenz.com

Climate
The East Coast enjoys an enviably warm and sunny climate, especially around Napier and Gisborne, where temperatures rise to around 25°C in summer and rarely dip below 5°C in winter. Napier and the surrounding Hawkes Bay region are also quite dry, recording an average of just 800mm of rain annually.

Getting There & Around
Air New Zealand flies out of both Gisborne and Napier to Auckland and Wellington. Origin Pacific has flights from Napier to other NZ cities including Nelson, Dunedin and Christchurch. InterCity runs buses out of Gisborne, Wairoa, Napier and Hastings, linking each other and connecting with major cities around the country, while Bay Xpress runs between Napier and Wellington and the Purpil People Mover Shuttle links Napier with Taupo on weekdays. The remote East Cape has no public transport, but there are four private courier services operating out of Gisborne and Opotiki.

EAST CAPE

The East Cape is a scenic, isolated and little-visited region of the North Island. The small communities scattered along the coast are predominantly Maori (largely of the Ngati Porou tribe; look out for the many red-roofed *marae* or 'meeting houses') and everyone seems to know everyone else, even if perhaps they don't meet that often. The pace of life is laid-back, the way of life predominantly rural, and the locals are friendly and welcoming to strangers. Geographically, the area has few natural harbours and, until the road network was completed, goods had to be loaded off the beaches onto waiting barges. The interior is still wild bush, with the Raukumara Range extending down the centre of the cape. The western side of the range is divided into several protected forests: Raukumara Forest Park, Urutawa Forest and Waioeka Gorge Scenic Reserve.

The coast is traced by 330km of highway (State Highway 35; SH35), which took decades to build and is an excellent road (open year-round). The drive is worthwhile, if

only for the magnificent views: a wild coast dotted with little bays, inlets and coves that change aspect with the weather. On a sunny day the water is an inviting turquoise, at other times a layer of clouds hangs on the craggy mountains rising straight up from the beaches and everything turns a misty green. Dozens of fresh, clear streams flow through wild gorges to meet the sea. During summer the coastline turns crimson with the blooming of the pohutukawa trees that line the seashore.

The region is passionate about rugby and especially their rugby team, Ngati Porou East Coast. If you do get a chance to see a match, be sure not to miss it – the atmosphere is electrifying and it seems like the Cape's whole population is there to watch (in fact it might be – only 6700 people make the East Cape their home).

The **Maori Tourism Network** (☎ 06-864 4694) produces a useful leaflet on accommodation and activities around the East Cape. It is available in visitors centres in Rotorua, Gisborne and elsewhere.

Getting There & Around
Travel around the East Cape is often slow and sometimes nonexistent, especially on weekends, but transport has firmed up over the past few years and now a couple of transport operators regularly link Hicks Bay with Opotiki and Gisborne. It's essential to book on any of the shuttle services; the service will either pick you up from where you're staying or arrange a place to meet.

The four main transport operators offering their services on the East Cape are **Matakaoa Coast Line Couriers** (☎ 0800 628 252), **East Land Couriers** (☎ 07-315 6350), **Polly's Passenger Courier** (☎ 06-864 4728) and **Cook's Courier** (☎ 06-864 4711).

Three of the four operators travel up and down the west coast of the East Cape. Matakaoa departs from Opotiki for Hicks Bay at 1.45pm Monday to Friday (you can also catch them at Whakatane), while Polly's leaves at 2pm Monday to Saturday. East Land only goes as far as Cape Runaway, leaving Opotiki at 2.30pm Monday to Friday. Matakaoa makes the return journey at 6.15am Monday to Saturday, Polly's 6.30am Monday to Friday and 7.30am Saturday, and East Land at 8pm Monday to Friday.

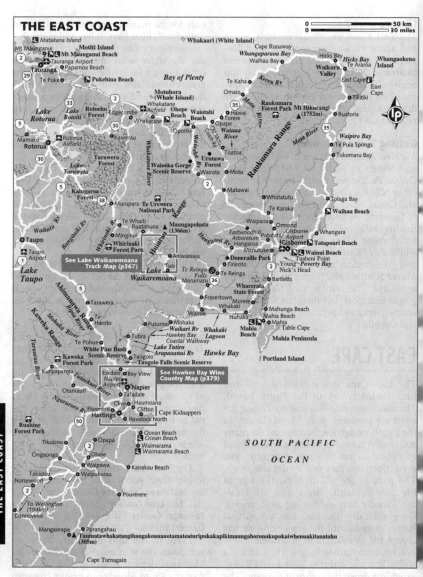

THE EAST COAST

One-way tickets cost around $20 and the trip takes around four hours (one way).

Only Polly's and Cook's operate on the eastern side of the East Cape. Polly's departs Gisborne for Hicks Bay at 1pm weekdays and Cook's at 2pm weekdays and 12.30pm Saturday. Polly's then leaves Hicks Bay for Gisborne at 6.30am weekdays, and

Cook's at 8am weekdays and 7.30am on Saturday. A one-way ticket costs around $30. Polly's also offers an unlimited-stops one-way ticket between Gisborne and Whakatane for $60.

Another option for the East Cape is to join the Kiwi Experience 'East As' **backpacker bus** (☎ 09-366 9830; www.kiwiexperience.com; $260), which does a circuit from Taupo, taking a minimum of four days.

Kiwi Trails (☎ 07-343 7922; www.kiwitrails.co.nz; $280) do round-cape trips on demand, operating out of Rotorua.

Hitching can be challenging at times due to the general lack of traffic heading around the East Cape, but your hostel or motel will usually be able to find you a ride.

OPOTIKI TO EAST CAPE

This trip is well described in *Opotiki & East Cape,* a comprehensive booklet available free from the Opotiki visitors centre (see p348). Along the first stretch of road from Opotiki there are fine views across to the steaming Whakaari (White Island) volcano. At the Waiaua River is the turn-off for the road to Gisborne via Toatoa and the Old Motu Coach Rd, probably more suited to mountain bikes than cars.

When you are travelling along this stretch of road keep an eye out for the magnificent *whakairo* (carving) on the gateway at Torere School.

The beaches at **Torere** and **Hawai** are steeply shelved and covered with driftwood; they're both good spots for seascape photography. Hawai is the boundary of the Whanau-a-Apanui tribe, whose sphere of influence extends north to Cape Runaway. About 45km from Opotiki the road crosses the **Motu River**, famed for jetboating, whitewater rafting and kayaking (see p349).

Some 25km further on is **Te Kaha**, once a whaling centre but now a small town that's popular for boating and fishing. It has a rocky beach, pub, store and accommodation. At the large *marae*, the Tukaki meeting house is magnificently carved. A succession of picturesque bays, including the beautiful **Whanarua Bay**, are passed before **Whangaparaoa Bay** and **Cape Runaway** are reached. This is the area where kumara (sweet potato) was supposedly first introduced to NZ. On the way you'll pass

TELEPHONE CODES

The telephone area code from Opotiki east to Hicks Bay, just before the East Cape itself, is ☎ 07. From Te Araroa onwards past the East Cape and south to Gisborne the code is ☎ 06.

the **Raukokore Anglican Church**, standing like a picture postcard on a lone promontory, 30km from Te Kaha. They have recently had penguins nesting under the font. Cape Runaway can only be reached on foot; seek permission before going onto private land.

Hicks Bay gets its name from a crew member of Captain Cook's *Endeavour*. It is a magnificent place, complemented by nearby Horseshoe Bay. There are a variety of **horse treks** (☎ 06-864 4634) at Hicks Bay; one-hour beach rides cost $25, 2½-hour hill treks $50, four-hour treks $60. There is also horse trekking available at Maungaroa Lodge (p356).

Nearly 10km further on is the sizable community of **Te Araroa**, which has a visitors centre. At Te Araroa there is a distinct change in geography from the volcanic rock outcrops to the sandstone cliffs standing above the town on the bay. One of NZ's largest **pohutukawa**, Te Waha o Rerekohu, reputed to be over 600 years old, stands in the school grounds. Also in Te Araroa is the **East Cape Manuka Company** (☎ 0508 626852; admission free), a manuka oil distillery with a visitors centre and a shop, which sells antibacterial soaps, oils and creams made from the particularly powerful East Cape manuka.

At Te Araroa you turn off for the **East Cape Lighthouse**, the most easterly tip of mainland NZ. The lighthouse is 21km east of Te Araroa (a 30-minute drive) along a mostly gravel road, and at the end there's a 25-minute climb to the lighthouse itself.

Sleeping & Eating

Te Kaha, the central point on the western side of the East Cape, makes a good stopping point.

Te Kaha Homestead Lodge (☎ 07-325 2194; fax 07-325 2193; dm/d/f $25/60/80) This friendly homestay sits right on the waterfront, with a view of White Island. The charming garden has ancient pohutukawa trees and a spa pool with spectacular sea views. The enthusiastic owner also runs fishing trips and can organise a variety of activities. Home-cooked meals cost $25.

Tui Lodge (☎ /fax 07-325 2922; jorex@xtra.co.nz; Copenhagen Rd; s/d incl breakfast from $75/100) Tui Lodge is a great place to stay. It's a spacious, modern guesthouse – originally intended as a fishing lodge – set in lovely gardens that attracts tuis (parson birds). Some rooms have coastal views. It's a short distance up

Copenhagen Rd from SH35. Dinner can be arranged, as can horse treks, fishing and diving trips.

Maungaroa Lodge (☎ 07-325 2727; fax 07-325 2776; s/d $20/40) This atmospheric lodge, in the Raukumara Ranges, is at the end of Maungaroa Access Rd (off Copenhagen Rd). The accommodation consists of a self-contained lodge. There's the Kereu River to splash about in, native bush to explore and horse trekking (from $25), which includes a picnic lunch.

Te Kaha Hotel (☎ /fax 07-325 2830; tekahahotel@ xtra.co.nz; Main Rd; s/d from $40/60) This hotel has clean and neat rooms above the local pub and has fantastic views up and down the coast. Meals are available in the bar, including fresh fish and chips.

Waikawa B&B (☎ /fax 07-325 2070; bnb@waikawa .net; d $90-100) Further along towards Whanarua Bay, and signposted on the main road, is Waikawa B&B, set in a delightful little spot overlooking a small bay. As well as a couple of en suite rooms, there's a three-bedroom self-contained cabin ($120). It's an extra $30 for dinner.

Maraehako Bay Retreat (☎ 07-325 2648; marae hako@xtra.co.nz; SH35 Te Kaha Opotiki; dm/d $20/50) This is a great hostel at pretty Whanarua Bay, with clean, spacious rooms. It's right on the water and the owner can arrange a number of activities such as diving, fishing, quad biking and horse riding.

Waihau Bay Holiday Park (☎ 07-325 3844; fax 07-325 3980; camp sites/s/d from $20/20/40) This basic and peaceful camp is a bit further on from Waihau Bay, at Oruati Beach, with accommodation including stationary caravans ($15 per person) and a self-contained cottage (from $80).

Lottin Point Motel (☎ /fax 06-864 4455; Lottin Point Rd; ste $80) This motel is midway between Whangaparaoa Bay and Hicks Bay, 4km north of SH35 on the coast, with units sleeping up to five people. Lottin Point is well known as a top snapper-fishing spot, and the motel can organise fishing trips.

Backpackers Homestay Hicks Bay (☎ 06-864 4634; s/tw/d $18/36/40) This small, restful place has just four neat rooms. It's signposted 4km inland from Hicks Bay and has wonderful views over farmland. Horse treks can be arranged.

Mel's Place (☎ 06-864 4964; www.eastcapefishing .co.nz; camp sites/dm $15/20) This is another quiet hostel off the beaten track. It's on an old

Maori *pa* (fortified village) site, overlooking Horseshoe Bay. The camp sites enjoy splendid views over the bay and self-contained cottages alongside are available ($80 to $100). Fishing trips can be arranged.

Hicks Bay Motel Lodge (☎ 0800 200 077, 06-864 4880; d from $85; ☳) This motel at Hicks Bay is up on the hill overlooking the bay, with great sea views. It's a big, well-managed place that offers self-serviced units as well as serviced rooms, and there's a restaurant and glow-worm caves on the premises.

Te Araroa Holiday Park (☎ 06-864 4873, 864 4473; camp sites/dm/d from $18/12/35) This park, over the hill towards Te Araroa from Hicks Bay, is another lovely spot. In a sheltered 15-hectare park-like setting near the beach, the park has lots of amenities, including a cinema (the most easterly in the world!) and fish and chip shop.

RAUKUMARA & WAIOEKA

Inland, the Raukumara Range offers tramping (the highest mountain in the range is Hikurangi, at 1752m) and white-water rafting on the Waioeka and Motu Rivers – contact **Wet 'n' Wild Rafting** (☎ 0800 462 7238; www.wetnwildrafting.co.nz) for more information. The most popular way of accessing this rugged, untamed region is via SH2 (the Waioeka Gorge Road), the 144km road that connects Opotiki to Gisborne.

There are many great walks in this region, and the Department of Conservation (DOC) offices in Opotiki (p348) and Gisborne (p360) can supply you with information. See DOC's *Raukumara Forest Park* and *Waioeka Gorge Scenic Reserve* pamphlets. The rare whio (blue duck) may be seen in Raukumara, and Hochstetter's frog (*Leio-pelma hochstetteri*) is quite common in the park. Some parts of the region are penetrable by mountain bike, while others are certainly not. This region is one of NZ's last frontiers, as wild as sections of south Westland.

The **Quarters** (☎ 07-315 7763; wairata.forest.farm@ xtra.co.nz; units $30-40; ☐) is a remote, rustic farmstay in Wairata, almost halfway between Opotiki and Gisborne, sleeping up to eight people, in one double and two bunkrooms. There's a kitchen, but you'll need your own bed linen.

Matawai Village Café (☎ 06-862 4823; Main Rd, Matawai) is a convenient place to get a bite to eat.

EAST CAPE TO GISBORNE

Heading south from Te Araroa the first place of interest you come to is **Tikitiki**. The Anglican Church is well worth visiting for its Maori architectural design.

A few kilometres off the road is **Ruatoria**, which has powerful Mt Hikurangi as a backdrop. Ruatoria is a very important Maori town – the centre of the Ngati Porou tribe. The politician Sir Apirana Ngata (an inspiring leader who became Minister of Native Affairs in 1928) lived here, as did Victoria Cross–winner Lt Moananui-a-Kiwa Ngarimu and All Black George Nepia.

About 25km south is **Te Puia Springs**, a pretty little town with hot springs nearby, and the pleasant **Waipiro Bay**. Another 11km further is **Tokomaru Bay**, a crumbling, picturesque town with a splendid beach and sweeping cliffs at the southern end of the bay. Hiking, swimming, surfing, fishing and cycling are all popular activities here.

Tolaga Bay, the largest community on the East Cape, is next. The attraction here is the beach, 3km south of the town. At the southern end of the beach is **NZ's longest pier**, a disused wharf running 660m out to sea, which is pleasant for a stroll. Close by is the start of the **Cooks Cove Walkway**, a 2½-hour return walk to a cove where Cook landed in 1769. It's a not-too-strenuous walk across farmland and through native bush; it's closed from August to Labour Day weekend (October) for lambing season. South of Tolaga Bay is the small settlement **Whangara**, the setting for Witi Ihimaera's wonderful novel *The Whale Rider*, which was also filmed here. It is a great book to read for a feel of the Maori culture and mythology of the area, and the film has won a number of international awards (see p42 for more about New Zealand cinema).

After passing Tatapouri and Wainui Beaches you reach Gisborne.

Sleeping & Eating

Eastender Farmstay (☎ 06-864 3042; eastenderfarmstay@xtra.co.nz; dm $18) This farm is close to the beach, 8km east of Tikitiki (follow the signs) and offers eight-bed backpacker huts. It's a sociable place with a great selection of activities, including horse rides (from $50) and bone carving ($30). *Hangi* meals cost $10.

Blue Boar Tavern & Mountain View Café (☎ 06-864 8619) You can get food and drink at this pleasant café 2km south of Ruatoria.

Waikawa Lodge (☎ 06-864 6719; www.waikawalodge.co.nz; Waikawa Rd; s/d $25/50) Waikawa Lodge is a small backpackers cottage (with two doubles and a kitchen), located at Waipiro Bay, and offering two-hour horse treks ($40). If you are coming from Opotiki, turn off at the Kopuaroa Rd sign. If you are coming from Gisborne, look for the signposted turn-off to Waipiro Bay. Both roads lead to Waikawa Rd and the lodge is up a farm road at the end of the road. Waikawa Rd is impassable when conditions are very wet so it's essential to ring before you come. The owners will pick you up from Te Puia Springs or Waipiro Bay.

Te Puia Springs visitors centre (☎ 06-864 6853; Main Rd) In the council chambers, this service centre can tell you about homestays in the area.

House of the Rising Sun (☎ 06-864 5858; Potae St, Tokomaru Bay; dm/d $15/36) This is a small, comfortable and homey hostel about a block from the beach.

Brian's Place (☎ 06-864 5870; Tokomaru Bay; camp sites/dm/tw/d $24/18/36/45) Brian's is in a great spot overlooking the bay, uphill from the Rising Sun. It has a double room, two lofts (sleeping four) and camp sites. You can organise horse treks here too (from $40).

IT'S A LONG WAY...TO TIKITIKI...IT'S A LONG WAY...TO GO...

State Highway 35 (SH35), the coastal route around the East Cape, may look short on a map but it really is a long way to go. It's a windy road with few opportunities to reach the open-road speed limit, and there are very few overtaking lanes to get past the plethora of milk trucks, logging trucks, and ancient cars – cars that would *never* earn a Warrant of Fitness (WoF) anywhere except the Coast. If you're in a hurry, turn inland up SH2 from Opotiki, because if you try to drive the length of SH35 in one day, you're up for an exhausting day behind the wheel. It's a good six hours – and that's without stopping to paddle in the surf at the pohutukawa-lined beaches, check out old *marae* or take short walks into the rugged bush. Much better to stop over on the way and make it at least a two-day trip. (But beware – on the Coast, two days can turn into three, into four, five...)

Tolaga Bay Holiday Park (☎ 06-862 6716; 167 Wharf Rd; camp sites/d from $20/36) Further south, this well-equipped family-oriented camp is located on a good, safe-swimming beach near the longest pier in NZ. It's a good spot for fishing.

Tolaga Bay Motel (☎ 06-862 6888; cnr Cook & Monkhouse Sts; s/d from $60/70) There are just seven pleasant units at this motel, all with cooking facilities. Fishing trips can be arranged and there's a golf course and bowling green nearby.

POVERTY BAY

This region got its name in 1769 from one of its earliest European visitors, James Cook (on his first expedition). While trying to replenish his ship, there were skirmishes with the local Maori, six of whom were killed. Cook decided the area had little to offer, hence 'poverty'.

The actual bay is quite small, a half-moon stretching from Tuahine Point to Young Nicks Head. The Poverty Bay region includes the coast from Tolaga Bay south to the Mahia Peninsula and west to the hills of the East Cape, the gem of which is Lake Waikaremoana.

GISBORNE

pop 32,700

Gisborne is NZ's most easterly city, and one of the closest in the world to the International Date Line. The Maori name for the area, Tairawhiti, means 'the coast upon which the sun shines across the water' and Gisborne is the first city in the world to see the dawn of each new day. The fertile plains around Gisborne support intensive farming of subtropical fruits, market-garden produce and vineyards.

Within easy reach of the city are a number of great surf beaches, making Gisborne something of a surfers' hotspot, while the city itself is on the coast at the confluence of two rivers: the Waimata and Taruheru (the short stretch below the junction is the Turanganui). Often described as 'the city of bridges', it is also noted for its fine parks.

History

The Gisborne region has been settled for over 1000 years. Two skippers of ancestral

migratory *waka* (canoes) – Paoa of the *Horo-uta* and Kiwa of the *Takitimu* – made an intermarriage pact that led to the founding of Turanganui a Kiwa (now Gisborne) soon after their arrival from Hawaiki. The newly introduced kumara flourished in the fertile soil and the Maori settlement spread to the hinterland.

Even though Gisborne was the site of Cook's first landing in NZ in 1769, European settlement of the region only began in 1831. A man of considerable drive, John Williams Harris, was first to purchase a small area on the west bank of the Turanganui River. He set up the region's first whaling venture and in 1839 began farming up the Waipaoa River near Manutuke.

As whaling became increasingly popular, missionaries began to move into the area. Father Baty and Rev William Colenso were the first Europeans to tramp into the heart of Te Urewera and lay eyes on Lake Waikaremoana.

Gradually more Europeans arrived but organised settlement was limited by Maori resistance. When the Treaty of Waitangi (see p29) was signed in 1840 many chiefs from the East Coast refused to acknowledge the treaty, let alone sign it.

In the 1860s numerous battles with the Maoris broke out. The Hauhau insurrection that began in Taranaki and spread to the Bay of Plenty and East Coast reached its height here at the battle of Waerenga-a-hika in late 1865. By the following year the government had crushed opposition and transported a number of the survivors, including the charismatic Te Kooti (see the boxed text on p361), to the remote Chatham Islands. This paved the way for an influx of European farmers. In 1868 Te Kooti escaped with an army of 200 and exacted revenge on the settlement at Matawhero, killing 33 Europeans and 37 Maoris.

Even today, however, much of the pasture land is leased from the Maoris and a large part of it is under their direct control. Unfortunately, the pioneer farmers were so anxious to profit from the land that they ripped out far too much forest cover with disastrous results. Massive erosion occurred as the steeply sloping land was unable to hold the soil after heavy rains.

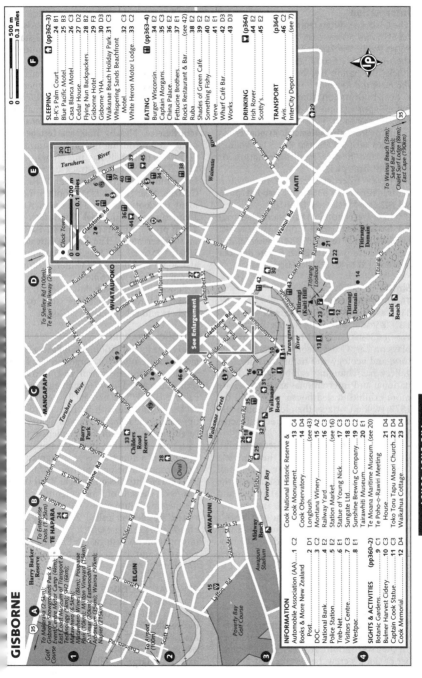

GISBORNE

INFORMATION
Automobile Association (AA)......1 C2
Books & More New Zealand
Post.................................2 D1
DOC.................................3 C2
National Bank......................4 E2
Police Station.....................5 E1
Treb-Net...........................6 E1
Visitors Centre....................7 C3
Westpac............................8 E1

SIGHTS & ACTIVITIES (pp360–2)
Botanic Gardens....................9 C1
Bulmer Harvest Cidery.............10 C3
Captain Cook Statue...............11 C3
Cook Memorial.....................12 D4
Cook National Historic Reserve &
Cook Monument.....................13 C4
Cook Observatory..................14 D4
Longbush......................(see 43)
Montana Winery...................15 A2
Railway Yard......................16 C3
Station Market................(see 16)
Statue of Young Nick..............17 C3
Sungate Ltd.......................18 C3
Sunshine Brewing Company..........19 C2
Tairawhiti Museum.............(see 20)
Te Moana Maritime Museum..........20 E1
Te Poho-o-Rawiri Meeting
House.............................21 D4
Toko Toru Tapu Maori Church.......22 D4
Waikahua Cottage..................23 D4

SLEEPING (pp362–3)
B-K's Palm Court...................24 B1
Blue Pacific Motel.................25 B3
Casa Blanca Motel..................26 C3
Cedar House........................27 D2
Flying Nun Backpackers.............28 B2
Gisborne Hotel.....................29 F3
Gisborne YHA.......................30 D3
Waikanae Beach Holiday Park........31 C3
Whispering Sands Beachfront
Motel..............................32 C3
White Heron Motor Lodge............33 C2

EATING (pp363–4)
Burger Wisconsin...................34 E2
Captain Morgans....................35 E2
China Palace.......................36 E2
Fettucine Brothers.................37 E1
RocKs Restaurant & Bar........(see 42)
Ruba...............................38 E2
Shades of Green Café...............39 E2
Something Fishy....................40 E1
Verve..............................41 E1
Wharf Café Bar.....................42 D3
Works..............................43 D3

DRINKING (p364)
Irish Rover........................44 E2
Scotty's...........................45 E2

TRANSPORT
Avis...............................46 C2
InterCity Depot................(see 7)

Information

The Gisborne **visitors centre** (☎ 0800 447 267, 06-868 6139; www.gisbornenz.com; 209 Grey St; ☺ 7.30am-5.30pm Mon-Fri, 9am-5pm Sat & Sun) is right beside the unmissable Canadian totem pole, and stocks the handy free booklet *Gisborne & the Eastland Region*.

Seek information from the visitors centre before approaching the **DOC office** (☎ 06-869 0460; 63 Carnarvon St; ☺ 8am-4.30pm Mon-Fri). Pick up maps from the **Automobile Association** (AA; ☎ 06-868 1424; 363 Gladstone Rd). The visitors centre and hostels have information on seasonal fruit picking.

There's Internet access at the visitors centre, Verve (see p364) and **Treb-Net** (☎ 06-863 3928; Shop 7 Treble Court, 17 Peel St).

There are a couple of banks on Gladstone Rd: **National Bank** (☎ 06-867 1164; 36 Gladstone Rd) and **Westpac** (☎ 06-863 1654; 101 Gladstone Rd), and nearby there is also a **Books & More New Zealand Post** (☎ 06-867 8220; 166 Gladstone Rd).

Sights

TAIRAWHITI MUSEUM

This excellent regional **museum** (☎ 06-867 3832; 18 Stout St; admission by donation; ☺ 10am-4pm Mon-Fri, 1.30-4pm Sat & Sun) has numerous displays on East Coast Maori and colonial history, and geology and natural history. The gallery has changing exhibitions of local, national and international art. Outside are more exhibits: a sled house, stable and the 1872 Wyllie Cottage, the oldest house still standing in Gisborne, with reconstructed Victorian interiors.

The **Te Moana Maritime Museum** behind the main museum is part of the complex. One wild night in 1912 the 12,000-ton *Star of Canada* was blown ashore on the reef at Gisborne. The ship's bridge and captain's cabin were salvaged, and eventually installed in what became the town's best-known home. This unique house was moved here, restored and made into a museum. There are displays on Maori canoes, early whaling and shipping, Cook's visit to Poverty Bay, and a totally awesome collection of vintage surfboards.

STATUES & VIEWS

There's a **statue of 'Young Nick'** (Nicholas Young), Cook's cabin boy, in a little park on the river mouth. A press-ganged member of Cook's crew, he was the first to sight

NZ. Across the bay are the white cliffs that Cook named Young Nick's Head. Also in this park is a **Captain Cook statue**; he's standing atop a globe etched with the routes of his voyages.

Across the river at the foot of Kaiti Hill is a **Cook monument**, near the spot where he first set foot on NZ (9 October 1769 in 'ship time' according to Cook's journal, but really the 8th). It's in the **Cook National Historic Reserve**. Nearby **Waikahua Cottage** was once a refuge during the Hauhau unrest.

Titirangi (Kaiti Hill) has fine views of the area. There's a walking track up from the Cook monument, starting near Waikahua Cottage. Near the top is yet another monument to Cook, but it's a fine one. At the 135m summit is the **Cook Observatory**, with a sign proclaiming it the 'World's Easternmost Observatory'. The **Gisborne Astronomical Society** (☎ 06-867 7901; admission $2) meets here at 7.30pm on Tuesday in winter, 8.30pm in summer; all are welcome.

Down on **Kaiti Beach**, low tide attracts a wealth of bird life, including stilts, oystercatchers and other pelagic visitors.

TE POHO-O-RAWIRI

Also at the foot of Titirangi is **Te Poho-o-Rawiri meeting house**, one of the largest in NZ. It has a richly decorated interior and its stage is framed by carved *maihi* (ornamental carved gable boards). The human figure kneeling on the right knee with its right hand held upwards is the *tekoteko* (carved figure) representing the ancestor who challenges those who enter the *marae*. It's always open, except when a function is in progress; call for permission before entering (☎ 06-868 5364). The little **Toko Toru Tapu Maori church** stands on the side of Titirangi, not far from the meeting house.

The free leaflet called *Tairawhiti Heritage Trails: Gisborne District* provides good information on historic sites in this Maori ancestral land. It's available from the visitors centre.

OTHER ATTRACTIONS

The Gisborne area has a few attractive gardens that are worth a visit. The huge **Eastwoodhill Arboretum** (☎ 06-863 9003; www.eastwoodhill.org.nz/; 2392 Wharekopae Rd, Ngatapa; adult/child $8/free; ☺ 9am-5pm), 35km west of town, has NZ's largest collection of northern hemisphere temperate trees, shrubs and climbers. To get there follow the Ngatapa-Rere Road; there's a 45-minute marked track through the trees and budget accommodation in the park (dm $25).

The **Botanic Gardens** are in town beside the Taruheru River.

Also of interest is the **Station Market** (Grey St; ☺ 10am-4pm Tue-Sat), consisting of a string of small shops and a homely café on the long-disused railway station platform. The **Gisborne City Vintage Railway** (☎ 06-867 5083; 2-hr trip $35) runs steam-train excursions on the track to Wairoa three to four times a year. The engine is kept in the adjoining **Railway Yard** (☎ 06-867 0385; admission by donation; ☺ 9am-1pm Sat).

Gisborne is a major wine-producing area, noted for its white varietals; more than a third of NZ's chardonnay grapes are grown here. Wineries to visit include: **Matawhero Wines** (☎ 06-868 8366; 185 Riverpoint Rd); **Millton Vineyard** (☎ 06-862 8680; 119 Papatu Rd, Manutuke); **Longbush** (☎ 06-863 0627; The Esplanade); **Montana** (☎ 06-867 9819; Lytton Rd); **Pouparae Park** (☎ 06-867 7931; 385 Bushmere Rd) and **Shalimar** (☎ 06-863 7776; Ngatapa Rd). The visitors centre (opposite) has details on opening hours and tours.

Trev's Tours (☎ 06-863 9815; tours $50-150) does tours of Gisborne and the surrounding area, including a wine trail.

Eastland Scenic Tours (☎ 025-413 117; tours from $55) does a round trip to Lake Waikaremoanoa and a 12-hour round trip of the East Cape (from $75).

There is also a natural beer brewery, the **Sunshine Brewing Company** (☎ 06-867 7777; 109 Disraeli St), and **Bulmer Harvest Cidery** (☎ 06-868 8300; Customhouse St), which have tastings and cellar-door sales.

TE KOOTI

The enigmatic Te Kooti was born into the Rongowhakaata tribe in Poverty Bay in the 1830s. As a young man, he was accused of assisting the Hauhau in Gisborne in a siege by government troops and in 1865, along with a number of others, was packed off to exile in the Chatham Islands. Here he experienced the visions that were to eventually lead to the establishment of the Ringatu Church.

In 1867 Te Kooti led an escape from the Chathams; more than 200 men, women and children sailed away on a captured supply ship, the *Rifleman*. They landed at Poverty Bay where during a ceremony of thanks for their safe return, Te Kooti urged his followers to raise their right hands to pay homage to God rather than kneel in submission. This is believed to be the first time the 'raised hand', from which Ringatu takes its name, was used.

The escapees intended to make their way peaceably into the interior, but resident Poverty Bay magistrate Reginald Biggs demanded they give up their arms. They refused, and skirmishes followed, during which the government troops suffered a succession of humiliating defeats.

Te Kooti attacked Matawhero, killing Biggs and, later, several chiefs, including the father of his first wife. He became both hated and feared, and some of his prisoners decided it would be prudent to become supporters.

Te Kooti became for a while the bogey man of the entire East Coast, moving his forces in and out of the Urewera region, and attacking both Poverty Bay and Bay of Plenty townships. Finally in 1872, as government forces closed in from three directions, he retreated into the King Country, at that time a vast area entirely under the reign of the Maori king, where government troops dared not venture.

Once under the protection of the king, in Te Kuiti, Te Kooti swore he'd fight no more. He devoted the rest of his life to making peace with his former enemies and formulated the rituals of the Ringatu Church. His reputation as a prophet and healer spread, and he made a series of predictions about a successor (Rua Kenana claimed this mantle in 1905).

After his pardon Te Kooti lived in the Bay of Plenty near Opotiki, and he spent much time visiting other Ringatu centres in the region. He never returned to Poverty Bay and he eventually died at Ohiwa Harbour in 1893.

His body was removed by his followers from its original burial place and to this day no-one knows for sure exactly where he was finally laid to rest.

You can visit the *marae* Te Kooti helped build for those who looked after him in Te Kuiti (p241), and the intrepid might also visit the Urewera base of Te Kooti and his successor, Rua Kenana, at Ruatahuna/Maungapohatu (p366).

THE EAST COAST

Near the A&P Showgrounds in Maka-raka is the **East Coast Museum of Technology & Transport** (ECMOT; ☎ 06-868 8254; adult/child $2/1; ⏲ 9.30am-4.30pm).

Matawhero is a few kilometres south along SH2. The historic Presbyterian Church here is the only building in town to have survived the conflicts of 1868.

Activities

You can swim at Waikanae Beach in the city. Midway Beach has a surf club and a swimming complex with a big waterslide and children's playground. **Enterprise Pools** (☎ 06-867 9249; Nelson Rd; adult/child $2.50/1.50; ⏲ 6am-3pm Mon & Fri, 6.30am-8pm Tue-Thu, 2-5pm Sat & Sun) is an indoor complex open to the public. Wainui Beach also has a surf club where you can safely swim between the flags.

Surfing is hugely popular in Gisborne due to a plethora of surf beaches close to the city. Waikanae Beach is good for learners, while more experienced surfers could choose from The Pipe, south of town, or Sponge Bay Island, just to the north. The bays of Wainui and Makrori, on SH35 heading towards East Cape, also have plenty of breaks.

Sungate Ltd (☎ 06-868 1673; 55 Salisbury Rd) hires out an array of water-sports equipment, including surfboards and boogie boards ($10/5 per hour).

Surfing with Frank (☎/fax 06-867 0823) Frank Russel gives private lessons for $40 and group lessons for $30. Suits and boards are provided.

Gisborne Quad Adventures (☎ 06-868 4394; sab batical@xtra.co.nz; 176 Valley Rd; 1 hr from $60) runs quad-bike safaris on local farmland and bush.

Whale Rider Tours (☎ 06-868 5878; tereiputald@xtra .co.nz; $50) offers guided tours around the locations used in the award-winning local film of the same name. Bookings can be made at the Gisborne visitors centre (p360).

Te Kuri Walkway is a three-hour (5.6km) walk through farmland and some forest to a commanding viewpoint. The walk starts 4km north of town at the end of Shelley Rd. It's closed from August to October for lambing.

Waimoana Horse Trekking (☎ 06-868 8218; Wainui Beach; 1-/2-hr treks $30/40) takes you up over hilly farmland and down onto sandy Wainui Beach.

DAME KIRI TE KANAWA

One of the most internationally famous Kiwis of all time is opera diva Dame Kiri Te Kanawa.

It's hard to imagine that this lyrical soprano who graces La Scala and Covent Garden with aplomb had her beginnings in the far-flung 'frontier' town of Gisborne, Poverty Bay, but it's true.

Te Kanawa's first major leading role was as the Countess in *Le Nozze di Figaro* at Covent Garden (1971), and she has since embraced the roles of Donna Elvira *(Don Giovanni)*, Marguerite *(Faust)*, Mimi *(La Bo-héme)*, Amelia *(Simon Boccanegra)* and Desdemona *(Otello)*. There have been many famous commercial recordings including *West Side Story* with José Carreras, and the haunting calls across the valley of Cante-loube's *Songs of the Auvergne*.

Hot on Dame Kiri's heels is another rising Kiwi soprano, Deborah Wai Kapohe. As well as performing with the New Zealand Symphony Orchestra and playing numerous roles with New Zealand Opera, she has won international acclaim, with appearances as far afield as China and London's Royal Albert Hall. She is also an accomplished songwriter, and gives solo performances at venues around NZ, accompanying herself on the guitar. Check out Deborah's website at www.ringtroutcds.com.

The adventurous can get close up to mako sharks ('waterborne pussycats') in submersible metal cages with **Surfit Charters** (☎ 06-867 2970; www.surfit.co.nz; 48 Awapuni Rd; per person from $165). Tamer snorkelling on the reefs around Gisborne can also be arranged.

Sleeping

BUDGET

Chalet Surf Lodge (☎ 06-868 9612; www.chaletsurf .co.nz; 62 Moana Rd, Wainui Beach; dm/d $20/50; 🖳) This mellow place is in a great spot right opposite Wainui Beach, around 8km from town, and is popular with surfies. There's a big, open communal area and a range of rooms available. Apartments start at $75, and surf lessons at $35, and there's free bike and boogie-board hire.

Flying Nun Backpackers (☎ 06-868 0461; fax 06-868 0463; 147 Roebuck Rd; dm/s/d from $17/27/45) This historic former convent was where Dame Kiri Te Kanawa (see the boxed text opposite) had her early singing lessons. They're big on security and there are spacious rooms and a big, open garden.

Waikanae Beach Holiday Park (☎ 06-867 5634; Grey St; camp sites/d/ste from $20/30/60) This family-friendly camp has an enviable location on the glorious Waikanae Beach, with 'ranch-house' style cabins, motel units and a kids' playground. Surfboards and bikes are available for hire and there's a tennis court next door.

Gisborne Showgrounds Park & Event Centre Motor Camp (☎ /fax 06-867 5299; www.gisborneshow .co.nz; 20 Main Rd; camp sites/d from $20/30) This huge park at Makaraka, 4km from the city centre, is a shady, restful place with spanking new cabins and good on-site facilities. Pets are welcome and there's even stabling and grazing for horses.

Gisborne YHA (☎ 06-867 3269; yha.gis@clear.net.nz; 32 Harris St; dm/d from $17/40; ☐) Situated 1.5km from the town centre across the river, this hostel is in a substantial and characterful old home with spacious grounds. It's a sociable place but big enough, and far enough away from the city, to be a quiet retreat too.

MID-RANGE

Gisborne has a good stock of seafront motel accommodation. All offer pretty much the same standards and facilities, though, and there's little to choose between them.

B-K's Palm Court (☎ 0800 672 000, 06-868 5601; www.palmcourt.co.nz; 671 Gladstone Rd; ste $95-160) B-K's is a good quality Best Western motel with 15 ground-level units, some with spa baths. It's very clean and well run, and so close to the beach.

Blue Pacific Motel (☎ 06-868 6099; www.seafront .co.nz; 90 Salisbury Rd; ste $80-130) This is a small, welcoming, family-run place, perfectly located right on the beach. It's an older property but still clean and comfy, and there's a sauna, spa pool and kids' playground.

Casa Blanca Motel (☎ 0800 172 000; fax 06-867 7106; 61 Salisbury Rd; ste $75-90) Casa Blanca is a rather quiet Spanish-style motel with nine ground-level units, set back from the beach. Rooms are a reasonable size and have private patio areas at the back.

White Heron Motor Lodge (☎ 0800 997 766; wheron@clear.net.nz; 474 Gladstone Rd; ste from $100)

White Heron is another quality motel with modern, well-equipped units. A cooked breakfast can be delivered to your room and there are some nice welcoming touches such as complimentary gym and golf-club passes.

Whispering Sands Beachfront Motel (☎ 06-867 1319; 22 Salisbury Rd; ste from $115) Whispering Sands has 14 well-appointed units right on Waikanae Beach and impressive views of Poverty Bay. It's popular with family groups.

Gisborne Hotel (☎ 06-868 4109; www.gisborne hotel.com; cnr Tyndall & Huxley Rds, Kaiti; d $110-150; ☐) The Gisborne is a peaceful old place with large, well-maintained rooms, though it's a little isolated and a touch old fashioned in its décor scheme.

TOP END

Cedar House (☎ 06-868 1902; www.cedarhouse.co.nz; 4 Clifford St; s/d $185/230) This Edwardian mansion, once a private school, has been turned into a sumptuous B&B with exquisite native timbers used throughout. With just four spacious rooms and a cosy guest lounge, it's a quiet and intimate place.

Eating

Ruba (☎ 06-868 6516; 14 Childers Rd; mains $12-23; ☺ breakfast, lunch & dinner Thu-Sat, breakfast & lunch Mon-Wed) Ruba is a stylish licensed restaurant and coffee bar with an eclectic menu of salads, pasta, fish and lamb. It's a pleasant stop for a drink, too, and sells packaged coffee and mugs.

Works (☎ 06-863 1285; Esplanade; mains $10-26; ☺ lunch & dinner) Housed in part of Gisborne's original freezing works, this excellent winery/restaurant serves imaginatively prepared meat, fish and vegetarian dishes. It also has a predictably extensive wine list, if you just want to sit back and sample the local produce.

Wharf Café Bar (☎ 06-868 4876; 60 The Esplanade; mains $16-25; ☺ lunch & dinner) The Wharf is a smart place on the waterfront serving excellent fish dishes. It also has outdoor seating providing a scenic spot for a drink.

Rocks Restaurant & Bar (☎ 06-868 3257; No 1 Wharf Shed, 60 The Esplanade; mains $13-31; ☺ lunch & dinner Tue-Sun, dinner Mon) The Rocks offers entertaining 'stonegrill' dining overlooking the harbour, with seafood and steaks cooked at your table.

Shades of Green Café (☎ 06-868 1450; cnr Lowe St & Reads Quay; mains from around $12; ☺ breakfast, lunch

& dinner Thu-Sat, breakfast & lunch Mon-Wed) This laid-back café with its 'ethnic' décor serves salads, pasta and organic veggie options. It's also a good place for tea and muffins.

Burger Wisconsin (☎ 06-867 6442; 26 Gladstone Rd; burgers $6.50-9.50; ☽ lunch & dinner) It's hard to beat the variety of burgers at this takeaway chain. Pumpkin and tofu, satay, and blue cheese are just some of the flavours on offer, and there's a small seating area.

Something Fishy (☎ 06-867 7457; 61 Gladstone Rd; mains $18-30; ☽ dinner) This is the place to come for grilled and fried fish, crayfish and all manner of seafood.

Captain Morgans (☎ 06-867 7821; 285 Grey St; burgers $4-7; ☽ breakfast, lunch & dinner) This popular eatery is close to Waikanae Beach. The burgers are particularly good and particularly large.

Verve (☎ 06-868 9095; 121 Gladstone Rd; mains $12-24; ☽ breakfast, lunch & dinner; ☐) This snazzy place serves up various continental-style meals, and has Internet connections.

China Palace (☎ 06-867 4911; 55 Peel St; mains $10-19; ☽ lunch & dinner) A good value smorgasbord on Friday, Saturday and Sunday evenings, but also, alas, karaoke on weekdays.

Fettucine Brothers (☎ 06-868 5700; 12 Peel St; mains $16-28; ☽ dinner) This is a well-regarded Italian restaurant serving up lots of pasta and meat dishes in a smart, formal setting.

Drinking

Irish Rover (☎ 06-867 1112; 66 Peel St) This Irish theme-pub is packed at weekends, and there's occasional live music. They also serve inexpensive pub grub such as fish and chips ($13). Watch out for the 'no hats, no undesirable tattoos' sign on the door.

Scotty's (☎ 06-867 8173; 35 Gladstone Rd) Scotty's is a popular local hangout and gets lively on the weekend. The large garden bar fills up on hot summer afternoons and there's the occasional live band.

Sand Bar (☎ 06-868 6828; Oneroa Rd) The Sand Bar is a friendly and convivial place out at Wainui. Best nights are Thursday to Saturday; a shuttle runs from the bar to the city centre at midnight.

Getting There & Away

AIR

Air New Zealand (☎ 06-868 2700; 37 Bright St) has daily direct flights to Auckland and Wellington, with onward connections to places like Rotorua and Hamilton.

BUS

The **InterCity depot** (☎ 06-868 6139) is at the visitors centre. InterCity has one bus daily (leaves at 9am) to Napier ($35, four hours) via Wairoa ($20, 1½ hours). From Napier there are connections to Palmerston North ($60, three hours) and Wellington ($80, 5¾ hours). InterCity also runs buses (leaving at 8am) between Gisborne and Auckland ($70, nine hours) via Opotiki ($25, two hours), Whakatane ($35, three hours) and Rotorua ($55, 4½ hours).

For details on public transport on the much longer, but very scenic, route to Opotiki, via the East Cape, see p353. Another route from Rotorua to Gisborne is the partly unsealed SH38, which runs through the Te Urewera National Park, past Lake Waikaremoana and joins the Napier route at Wairoa, 97km south of Gisborne; see p365.

HITCHING

Hitching is OK from the south of the city, and not too bad through Waioeka Gorge to Opotiki; it's still best to leave early. To hitch a ride out, head along Gladstone Rd to Makaraka, 6km west, for Wairoa and Napier, or the turn-off to Opotiki and Rotorua. Hitching from Wairoa to Waikaremoana is hard going.

Getting Around

Gisborne **Taxi Buses** (☎ 06-867 2222) runs the town's bus service; buses only go on weekdays and the last run is at 5.15pm. Taxis include **Gisborne Taxis** (☎ 06-867 2222) and **Eastland Taxis** (☎ 06-868 1133). **Link Taxis** (☎ 06-868 8385) runs to Gisborne airport ($10 to $12 from town).

For rentals try **Hertz** (☎ 06-867 9348; Aerodrome Rd), **Budget** (☎ 06-867 9794; 344 Ormond Rd) or **Avis** (☎ 06-868 9084; 320 Gladstone Rd).

GISBORNE TO WAIROA

Heading south towards Napier you have two choices: the SH2 follows the coast, while the SH36 skirts inland. The two routes meet in Wairoa.

Coastal Route

The coastal route runs just inland most of the way south from Gisborne, before it enters the Wharerata State Forest. At the southern edge of the state forest, 56km from Gisborne, Morere is a pretty little town noted for its hot springs. The **Morere Hot Springs** (☎ 06-837 8856; morere.hot.springs@ xtra.co.nz; adult/child $5/2.50; ⏱ 10am-6pm Mon-Thu, 10am-7pm Fri-Sun) has a series of hot and cold indoor and outdoor pools, set in a scenic reserve of lowland rainforest. Walking tracks range from 20 minute strolls to challenging three-hour hikes.

Morere Tearooms & Camping Ground (☎ 06-837 8792; SH2; camp sites/d $20/50) is located opposite the springs alongside native bush and a babbling stream.

Moonlight Cottage (☎ 06-837 8824; moonlight cottage@xtra.co.nz; Main Rd; dm/d $18/32) is another place to stay in Morere, about two minutes' walk from SH2. Follow the road next to the tearooms across the stream. This colonial farmhouse has a spacious lounge, fully equipped kitchen and wide veranda. There's also a self-contained cottage ($75). It's closed in July and August.

SH2 continues south to Nuhaka on the northern end of the sweep of Hawke Bay, where you can head west to Wairoa or east to the superb, windswept and wild **Mahia Peninsula**. There are long, curving beaches popular with surfers, clear water for diving and fishing, bird-watching at Mangawhio Lagoon and walks to a number of reserves. Mahia was once an island, but sand accumulation has formed NZ's largest tombolo landform (where a sand or shingle bar ties an island to another island or the mainland). The peninsula is a magical, atmospheric place, majestic in either sun or storm. Facilities are limited and you'll need your own transport to get around.

Mahia Beach Motel & Holiday Park (☎ 06-837 5830; mahia.beach.motels@xtra.co.nz; camp sites/d from $24/40) has camp sites, motel rooms and cabins on a safe swimming beach. There's an on-site restaurant, shop and kid's playground and miniature railway, and fishing charters are available.

Blue Bay Holiday Resort (☎ 06-837 5867; www .bluebay.co.nz; Opoutama; camp sites/d from $24/50) occupies a nice secluded spot by the beach, 12km east of Nuhaka. There is plenty of tree shelter and a licensed bar and café.

Inland Route

Along SH36, the inland route to Wairoa, there are also several things to see and do. You can climb up **Gentle Annie Hill** for a good

view over the Poverty Bay area. **Doneraille Park** (53km from Gisborne), a native bush reserve, is a popular picnic spot with good swimming when the water is clear.

There's fine trout fishing at **Tiniroto Lakes**, 61km from Gisborne; simple, comfortable accommodation can be had at the **Tiniroto Tavern** (☎ 06-863 7019; 2 School Rd, Tiniroto; dm/d $20/40). About 10km further, **Te Reinga Falls** is worth a detour off the main road.

HAWKES BAY

Hawkes Bay (note that the body of water is 'Hawke Bay') is one of NZ's richest agricultural areas and a major wine-producing region, enjoying lots of sunshine and a diverse landscape, including stunning coastal scenery, fertile plains and the busy cities of Napier and Hastings, with their fine Art Deco architecture.

Also here is the attractive township of Havelock North – a good base for touring the wineries – and unique natural attractions such as the Cape Kidnappers gannet colony.

For information on the region, check out www.hawkesbaynz.com.

WAIROA
pop 5228

The highways SH2 and SH36 meet in Wairoa, 98km south of Gisborne. Wairoa has a reasonable beach and is a gateway to Te Urewera National Park, although gang trouble has tarnished the town's image in recent years. The relocated **lighthouse** by the river, built in 1877 of solid kauri, used to shine from Portland Island at the tip of the Mahia Peninsula. Ten kilometres east of Wairoa is Whakaki Lagoon, an important wetlands area renowned for its bird populations.

The Wairoa **visitors centre** (☎ 06-838 7440; wirvin@nzhost.co.nz; cnr SH2 & Queen St; ⏱ 9am-5pm) has information on Te Urewera National Park and sells DOC passes. The **DOC field centre** (☎ 06-838 8252; 272 Marine Parade) is open by appointment only.

Sleeping & Eating
Three Oaks Motel (☎ 06-838 8204; cnr Campbell St & Clyde Rd; s/d $70/80; ⌨) This is a restful place with decent grounds, offering the usual

motel-style comforts, and ground-level units. Meals are available and there's an on-site playground.

Vista Motor Lodge (☎ 06-838 8297; vistamotor lodge@xtra.co.nz; 2 Bridge St; ste from $90; ☐ ☒) Vista has spacious and comfortable studios and one- and two-bedroom units in a scenic spot on the riverbank, and it also has a licensed restaurant.

For food, try the pleasant **Johanna's** (☎ 06-838 7410; Clyde Court; mains around $10) for fuller meals, or the excellent **Oslers Bakery** (☎ 06-838 8299; Marine Parade), for filled rolls and snacks.

Getting There & Away
All **InterCity** (☎ 06-838 7440) buses that travel between Gisborne and Napier pass through Wairoa.

WAIROA TO NAPIER
There are some good reserves along this stretch of road that break the twisting drive, all accessible from SH2. Pick up the brochure *Napier to Wairoa: Heritage Trails* at the Wairoa visitors centre; it lists all the following reserves.

Lake Tutira has a farmland setting; there are walkways around the lake and a bird sanctuary. The **Hawkes Bay Coastal Walkway** is 12km from SH2, down Waikari Rd. The walkway is 16km long, goes from the Waikari River to the Aropaoanui River, and involves equal portions of boulder hopping, track walking and beach walking.

Off Waipatiki Rd and 34km from Napier is the **Waipatiki Scenic Reserve**. The **White Pine Bush Scenic Reserve**, 29km from Napier, is notable for the dominant kahikatea (white pine). The **Tangoio Falls Scenic Reserve**, 2km south of White Pine, has Te Ana Falls, stands of ponga and wheki ponga (types of tree ferns), and podocarps. The White Pine and Tangoio Falls Scenic Reserves are linked by the **Tangoio Walkway**, which follows Kareaara Stream.

There's peaceful, rustic backpacker accommodation at **Bushdale Farm** (☎ /fax 06-838 6453; 438 Cricklewood Rd; dm/d $20/40), about 13km from Wairoa heading towards Napier. Pick-up from Wairoa can be arranged.

Glen-View Farm Hostel (☎ 06-836 6232; fax 836 6067; dm/d $15/40) Glen-View Farm is a hill-country sheep-and-cattle station, where horse riding and walking are popular. You can join in farm activities. The hostel is 31km north of Napier off SH2, 2km along the Arapaoanui Rd towards the sea.

TE UREWERA NATIONAL PARK
Home of the Tuhoe people, one of NZ's most traditional tribes, Te Urewera is rich in history. The army of Te Kooti (p361) found refuge here during its battles against the government. Te Kooti's successor, Rua Kenana, was the leader of a thriving community at Maungapohatu, beneath the sacred mountain of the same name, from 1905 until his politically inspired arrest in 1916. Maungapohatu never recovered after that and only a small settlement remains. Slightly larger is nearby Ruatahuna, where the extraordinary Mataatua Marae celebrates Te Kooti's exploits.

Te Urewera National Park is one of the country's most attractive parks. It is a marvellous area of lush forests, lakes and rivers, with lots of walks, ranging from half an hour to several days, and plenty of birds, trout, deer and other wildlife. The main focus of the park is the superbly scenic Lake Waikaremoana (Sea of Rippling Waters). Most visitors to the park come to go fishing on the lake or walk the Lake Waikaremoana Track, one of NZ's Great Walks, but other walks are possible.

The park protects part of the largest untouched native forest area on the North Island. The rivers and lakes of the park offer good trout fishing.

Information
The **Aniwaniwa visitors centre** (☎ 06-837 3803; urewerainfo@doc.govt.nz; ☉ 9am-5pm) is situated within the park on the shores of the lake. It has interesting displays on the park's natural history and supplies information on the walking tracks and accommodation around the park.

Hut and camping ground passes for the Lake Waikaremoana Track can also be bought at DOC offices and visitors centres in Gisborne, Wairoa, Whakatane and Napier.

For online information about the area check out www.lake.co.nz.

Lake Waikaremoana Track
This three- to four-day tramp is one of the most popular walks on the North Island.

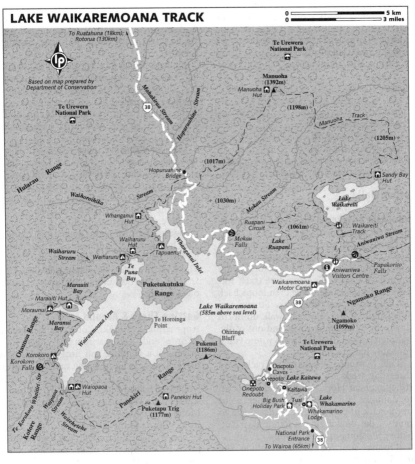

LAKE WAIKAREMOANA TRACK

Based on map prepared by Department of Conservation

The 46km track has spectacular views from the Panekiri Bluff, but all along the walk – through fern groves, beech and podocarp forest – there are vast panoramas and beautiful views of the lake. The walk is rated as easy and the only difficult section is the climb to Panekiri Bluff. It is very busy from mid-December to the end of January and at Easter.

The walk can be done year-round, but the cold and rain in winter deter most people and make conditions much more challenging. Because of the altitude, temperatures can drop quickly, even in summer. Walkers should take portable stoves and fuel as there are no cooking facilities in the huts. It's not recommended that you

park your car at either end of the track – there have been break-ins.

Five huts and five camp sites are spaced along the track. It's essential to book through DOC and if you are intending to do the walk over the Christmas/New Year period, it would be wise to book as far ahead as possible.

WALKING THE TRACK

The track can be done either clockwise from just outside Onepoto in the south or anticlockwise from Hopuruahine Bridge in the north. Starting from Onepoto, all the climbing can be done in the first few hours. Water on this section of the track is limited so make sure you fill your water bottles before heading off. For those with a car, it is safest to leave it at Waikaremoana Motor Camp and then take a boat (see p368) to the trail heads.

Estimated walking times:

Route	Time
Onepoto to Panekiri Hut	5hr
Panekiri Hut to Waiopaoa Hut	3–4hr
Waiopaoa Hut to Marauiti Hut	4½hr
Marauiti Hut to Waiharuru Hut	2hr
Waiharuru Hut to Whanganui Hut	2½hr
Whanganui Hut to Hopuruahine Bridge	1½hr

Other Walks

Other major walks in the park include the **Whakatane River Round Trip** and the **Manuoha–Waikareiti Track**.

The three- to five-day Whakatane River Round Trip starts at Ruatahuna on SH38, 45km from the Aniwaniwa visitors centre towards Rotorua. The five-hut track follows the Whakatane River then loops back via Waikare River, Motumuka Stream and Whakatane Valley. You can walk on north down the Whakatane River and out of the national park at Ruatoki (from where you'll probably have to hitch).

The Manuoha–Waikareiti Track is a three-day walk for experienced trampers. It begins near Hopuruahine and heads up to Manuoha Hut (1392m), the highest point in the park. It then follows a ridge down to pretty Lake Waikareiti via Sandy Bay Hut, before finishing up at Aniwaniwa.

Popular short/day walks include the **Old Maori Trail** (four hours return), starting at Rosie Bay and following a traditional Maori route to Lake Kaitawa; the **Waikareiti Track** (two hours return), through beech and rimu forest; and the **Ruapani Circuit** (six hours), which takes in wetlands. The DOC booklet *Lake Waikaremoana Walks* ($2.50) lists many good short walks.

Sleeping & Eating

There are various camps and cabins along SH38, including a camp, cabins and motel 67km inland from the Wairoa turn-off.

Waikaremoana Motor Camp (☎ 06-837 3826; misty@lake.co.nz; camp sites/dm/s/f from $20/20/40/80) This camping ground has a wonderful spot right on the shore of Lake Waikaremoana, with well-designed wooden chalets, 'fish-erman's cabins' sleeping up to five people and camp sites with panoramic views. There's an on-site shop, and good fishing facilities.

Big Bush Holiday Park (☎ 0800 525 392, 06-837 3777; www.lakewaikaremoana.co.nz; camp sites/dm/d from $20/20/65; 🖳) This place, between Lake Waikaremoana and Tuai is another attractively situated camp with neat cabins and backpacker rooms. It has its own small lake and licensed restaurant.

Lake Whakamarino Lodge (☎ 06-837 3876; www.lakelodge.co.nz; s/d/ste $60/70/100) This lodge is at Tuai, and overlooks peaceful Lake Whakamarino. It offers a rather higher standard of accommodation, and lunch ($19) and dinner ($25) are available.

There are more than 50 DOC huts along the walkways throughout the national park. The five Lake Waikaremoana Track **huts** (per night $28) are rated as Great Walks huts. There are five DOC **camping grounds** (camp site $20). All ranger stations have information on camping.

Getting There & Around

Approximately 105km of road between Wairoa and Rotorua remains unsealed, making it a winding and time-consuming drive. Traffic is light, which makes it slow for hitching.

Big Bush Holiday Park (☎ 06-837 3777) runs a shuttle from Wairoa through to Rotorua on Monday, Wednesday and Friday ($30) and from Wairoa to the lake daily ($25).

The Waikaremoana **Shuttle or Boat service** (☎ 06-837 3729) operates on demand from the motor camp to either Onepoto or Hopuruahine Stream ($15).

NAPIER

pop 55,000

Lying on sweeping Hawke Bay, Napier occupies a fine coastal position and, like most places in the Hawkes Bay area, enjoys its fair share of sunshine all year. The city's biggest draw card, though, is its architecture; Napier challenges Miami for the title of Art Deco Capital of the World, and there are numerous examples of the style around the city centre.

Napier also makes a good base for exploring many of the region's top wineries, which are a short distance from the city limits.

History
Long before James Cook sighted the area in October 1769, Maoris found a plentiful source of food in the bay and the hinterland. The Otatara Pa, with its barricades now rebuilt, is one of the pre-European sites of habitation. It's south of the city on Gloucester St, past the Eastern Institute of Technology.

French explorer Jules Dumont d'Urville used Cook's charts to sail the *Astrolabe* into the bay in 1827. In the 1830s whalers started using the safe Ahuriri anchorage and a trading base was established in 1839.

The town was planned in 1854, named after the British general and colonial administrator, Charles Napier, and it soon began to flourish as a commercial regional centre.

In 1931 Napier was dramatically changed when a disastrous earthquake, measuring 7.9 on the Richter scale, virtually destroyed it. In Napier and nearby Hastings 258 people died, and Napier suddenly found itself 40 sq km larger when the earthquake heaved the seabed above sea level – in some places the land level rose by over 2m. Napier's airport was built on that previously submerged area. The rebuilding programme that followed produced one of the world's best examples of an Art Deco city.

Orientation
At the northern end of town looms Bluff Hill, acting as a natural boundary between the centre and the Ahuriri and port areas. The prime commercial streets are Hastings and Emerson Sts. Emerson St has been developed into a pedestrian thoroughfare with many Art Deco features.

Information
Napier's well-informed **visitors centre** (06-834 1911; www.isitehawkesbaynz.com; 100 Marine Pde; 8.30am-5pm) is normally open later during the summer. You can pick up maps from the **AA office** (06-834 2590; 87 Dickens St).

The **DOC office** (06-834 3111; 59 Marine Parade), in the Old Courthouse, has information on walkways around Napier, the Cape Kidnappers gannet colony (p380), Te Urewera National Park (p366), and the Kaweka and Ruahine Forest Parks, both 50km west of Napier (see p381 for more information about the parks).

There's an Internet café at **And Computers** (06-834 0963; Ocean Boulevard Mall, off Dickens St) and there's a **Books & More New Zealand Post** (06-835 9800; 57 Dickens St) nearby.

Sights
ART DECO ARCHITECTURE
The earthquake and fire of 1931 resulted in the destruction of most of Napier's older brick buildings. Two frantic years of reconstruction from 1931 to 1933 meant that many of the city's buildings date from the peak years of the Art Deco architectural style, a unique assemblage that has won international acclaim.

The Napier Art Deco Trust promotes and protects the city's architectural heritage and has excellent guided Art Deco walks. The one-hour walk ($8) leaves from the visitors centre daily at 10am. The two-hour walk ($12) leaves from the **Deco Centre** (06-835 0022; www.artdeconapier.com; 163 Tennyson St; 9am-5pm) at 2pm daily during the summer months, and at 2pm on Wednesday, Saturday and Sunday in winter. The walks are preceded by an introductory talk and end with a video and refreshments.

The shop in the Deco Centre sells books, postcards and souvenirs. Walk brochures ($4) are available from the visitors centre, Deco Centre or the museum.

There's an *Art Deco Scenic Drive* map of the Art Deco and Spanish Mission–style architecture around Napier and Hastings ($4). The *Marewa Meander* ($2) leads you through a suburb transformed after the quake.

Guided tours in a 1934 Buick can be arranged through **Deco Affair Tours** (025-241 5279; tours $15-75). Tours last from 20 minutes to 2½ hours.

Fairway Tours (0800 428 687; www.fairwaytours.co.nz; tours $15) runs one-hour 'city highlights' tours, giving a good overview of town, leaving from the visitors centre.

See the boxed text on p371 for Art Deco examples in Napier.

MARINE PARADE
Lined with Norfolk pines and some fine old wooden buildings that survived the quake, Marine Parade has retained the air of an old-fashioned English seaside resort complete with pebble beach, but the strong riptide makes for hazardous swimming.

NAPIER

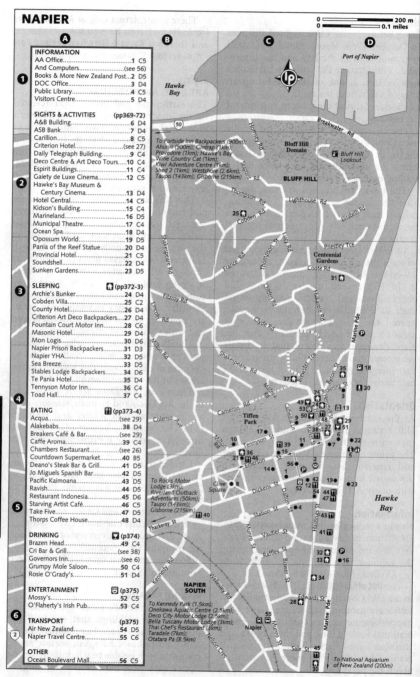

| 0 | 200 m |
| 0 | 0.1 miles |

INFORMATION
AA Office...1 C5
And Computers...........................(see 56)
Books & More New Zealand Post....2 D5
DOC Office...3 D4
Public Library.....................................4 C5
Visitors Centre...................................5 D4

SIGHTS & ACTIVITIES (pp369-72)
A&B Building.......................................6 D4
ASB Bank...7 D4
Carillion..8 C5
Criterion Hotel..............................(see 27)
Daily Telegraph Building..................9 C4
Deco Centre & Art Deco Tours......10 C4
Espirit Buildings...............................11 C4
Gaiety de Luxe Cinema...................12 C5
Hawke's Bay Museum &
    Century Cinema..........................13 D4
Hotel Central....................................14 C5
Kidson's Building.............................15 C4
Marineland.......................................16 D5
Municipal Theatre...........................17 D4
Ocean Spa...18 D4
Opossum World...............................19 D5
Pania of the Reef Statue.................20 D4
Provincial Hotel...............................21 C5
Soundshell..22 D4
Sunken Gardens...............................23 D5

SLEEPING (pp372-3)
Archie's Bunker................................24 D4
Cobden Villa.....................................25 C2
County Hotel....................................26 D4
Criterion Art Deco Backpackers.....27 D4
Fountain Court Motor Inn...............28 C6
Masonic Hotel..................................29 D4
Mon Logis...30 D6
Napier Prison Backpackers.............31 D3
Napier YHA.......................................32 D5
Sea Breeze..33 D5
Stables Lodge Backpackers.............34 D6
Te Pania Hotel..................................35 D4
Tennyson Motor Inn........................36 C4
Toad Hall..37 C4

EATING (pp373-4)
Acqua..(see 29)
Alakebabs...38 D4
Breakers Café & Bar.....................(see 29)
Caffe Aroma.....................................39 C4
Chambers Restaurant...................(see 26)
Countdown Supermarket................40 B5
Deano's Steak Bar & Grill...............41 D5
Jo Miguels Spanish Bar....................42 D5
Pacific Kaimoana..............................43 D5
Ravish..44 D5
Restaurant Indonesia.......................45 D6
Starving Artist Café.........................46 C5
Take Five...47 D5
Thorps Coffee House........................48 D4

DRINKING (p374)
Brazen Head......................................49 C4
Cri Bar & Grill...............................(see 38)
Governors Inn...............................(see 6)
Grumpy Mole Saloon.......................50 C4
Rosie O'Grady's.................................51 D4

ENTERTAINMENT (p375)
Mossy's..52 C5
O'Flaherty's Irish Pub......................53 C4

TRANSPORT (p375)
Air New Zealand...............................54 D5
Napier Travel Centre........................55 C6

OTHER
Ocean Boulevard Mall.....................56 C5

Port of Napier

Hawke
Bay

Breakwater Rd

Bluff Hill
Domain

Bluff Hill
Lookout

BLUFF HILL

Hornsey Rd

Lighthouse Rd

Priestley Tce

Cobden Rd

Centennial
Gardens

Coote Rd

Shakespeare Rd

France Rd

Thompson Rd

Lucy Rd

Elizabeth Rd

Hukarere Rd

Chaucer Rd

Fitzroy Rd

Lincoln Rd

Clyde Rd

Marine Pde

To Portside Inn Backpackers (900m);
Ahuriri (900m); Gintrap (1km);
Provedore (1km); Hawke's Bay
Wine Country Cat (1km);
Kiwi Adventure Centre (1km);
Shed 2 (1km); Westshore (2.6km);
Taupo (143km); Gisborne (215km)

Milton Rd

Shakespeare Rd

Brewster St

Byron St

Browning St

Cathedral Ln

Colenso Ave

Cameron Rd

Nelson Rd

Tiffen
Park

Tennyson St

Emerson St

Clive
Square

Dickens St

Dalton St

Station St

Munro St

Vautier St

Raffles St

Bower St

Marine Pde

Thackeray St

To Rocks Motor
Lodge (3km);
Riverland Outback
Adventures (50km);
Taupo (143km);
Gisborne (215km)

Hastings St

Hawke
Bay

Edwards St

**NAPIER
SOUTH**

Kennedy Rd

Wellesley Rd

To Kennedy Park (1.5km);
Onekawa Aquatic Centre (2.5km);
Deco City Motor Lodge (2.5km);
Bella Tuscany Motor Lodge (3km);
Thai Chef's Restaurant (3km);
Taradale (7km);
Otatara Pa (8.5km)

Nelson Cres

Munro St

Napier

Sale St

To National Aquarium
of New Zealand (200m)

Marine Parade has parks, **sunken gardens**, swimming pools, an aquarium and a marine park. The statue of **Pania of the Reef**, a tragi-romantic figure from local Maori folklore, is at the parade's northern end.

Marineland (☎ 06-834 4027; 290 Marine Parade; adult/child $9/5; 10am-4.30pm) has performing seals and dolphins; displays take place at 10.30am and 2pm, with an extra 4pm show in summer. You can also swim with dolphins ($40, wet-suit hire $10), take a tour of Marineland, which includes touching and feeding dolphins ($15), or tour the penguin recovery workshop, where you'll help feed and care for penguins ($15). Bookings are essential.

Further along the Parade, the **National Aquarium of New Zealand** (☎ 06-834 1404; www.nationalaquarium.co.nz; adult/child $12/6; 9am-9pm Jan, 9am-7pm Feb-Easter, 9am-5pm rest of year) has sharks (which you can swim with if you're a qualified diver; $40 plus $30 for gear), saltwater crocodiles, piranha, turtles and other animals, including kiwis and the unique tuatara (a prehistoric reptile). Hand feedings take place at 10am and 2pm and the 'behind the scenes' tour costs $20/10 (9am and 1pm).

If you want to find out more about the most vilified creature in NZ, head to **Opossum World** (☎ 06-835 7697; www.opossumworld.co.nz; 157 Marine Parade; 9am-5pm). There's a static display on the pesky varmint which kids might enjoy, and a shop selling all manner of possum pelt products.

HAWKES BAY MUSEUM
Also on Marine Parade is a well-presented **art gallery & museum** (☎ 06-835 7781; www.hawkesbaymuseum.co.nz; 65 Marine Parade; adult/child $7.50/free; 9am-5pm May-Sep, 9am-6pm Oct-Apr). There are exhibitions on Maori art and culture, including artefacts from the East Coast's Ngati Kahungunu tribe, and displays on the early colonial settlers. There are also interactive displays on dinosaurs and a record of the struggle of an amateur palaeontologist, Jean Wiffen, who proved professional sceptics wrong, discovering several prehistoric species when they said there were none to be found in NZ. The fascinating section on earthquakes includes a 35-minute audiovisual in which Napier quake survivors tell their stories, while upstairs, there's another video on local Maori history. Other rooms play host to temporary art exhibitions.

DECOED OUT

Art Deco is the name given to a decorative style that hit the headlines in 1925 at the International Exposition of Modern Decorative and Industrial Arts held in Paris. Zigzags, lightning flashes, geometric shapes and rising suns all characterise this distinctive style. Ancient cultures, such as the Egyptian and Mayan, were also drawn upon for inspiration. Soft pastel colours are another Art Deco giveaway, employed by restorers, though many of Napier's buildings were originally monochrome plaster.

Emerson St has some excellent examples of Art Deco, though many of the shopfronts have been modernised and you'll have to look up to the second storeys to see the fine Art Deco detail. Good examples on Emerson St are the **Provincial Hotel**, **Kidson's Building**, the **Esprit buildings**, the **Criterion Hotel & Criterion Art Deco Backpackers** and the **ASB Bank**, with its wonderfully restored interior.

On Dalton St, the **Hotel Central** is a superb example of the style. Round the corner on Dickens St, look for the extravagant Moorish and Spanish Mission–style building which used to be the **Gaiety de Luxe Cinema**. On the corner of Dickens and Dalton Sts is the former **State Cinema** (now a shopping complex).

Tennyson St has fine, preserved buildings. The restored **Municipal Theatre** stands out with its neon light fittings and wall decorations. The **Daily Telegraph building** is one of the finest examples of Art Deco in Napier and the **Deco Centre**, facing Clive Square is also impressive, despite some modifications. At the intersection of Tennyson and Hastings Sts are more fine buildings, particularly the block of Hastings St from Tennyson to Browning Sts.

On Marine Parade the **Soundshell** is Art Deco, as is the paving of the plaza. From here you can admire the **A&B building's** Art Deco clock tower (neon-lit at night) and also the **Masonic Hotel** (p373).

THE EAST COAST

Also on site is the **Century Cinema** (☎ 06-835 9248; www.centurycinema.co.nz; tickets $10) which has a regular programme of art-house movies.

BLUFF HILL LOOKOUT
There's an excellent view over all of Hawkes Bay from Bluff Hill, 102m above the Port of Napier. It's a sheer cliff-face down to the port, however, and rather a circuitous route to the top. It's open daily from sunrise to sunset.

Activities
Although the beach along Marine Parade is too dangerous for swimming, there's great swimming and surfing on the beach up past the port.

The **Onekawa Aquatic Centre** (☎ 06-834 4150; Maadi Rd; adult/child $2.50/1.50, waterslide $4 for unlimited rides; ☺ 6am-9pm), south of town, has water-slides and other attractions.

Ocean Spa (☎ 06-835 8553; 42 Marine Parade; adult/child $6/4; ☺ 6am-10pm Mon-Sat, 8am-10pm Sun) is an excellent swimming pool complex on the waterfront. There are spas ($8/4) and you can indulge in a half-hour massage for $35. There is also a restaurant.

At the **Kiwi Adventure Centre** (☎ 06-834 3500; 58 West Quay, Ahuriri; climb plus harness adult/child $15/12; ☺ 10am-9pm Tue-Fri, 10am-6pm Sat & Sun), just out of the town centre, there is a climbing wall. It also organises canyoning, caving and kayaking trips.

More activities can be found at **Riverland Outback Adventures** (☎ 06-834 9756; fax 06-834 9724), 50km north of Napier on SH5, where there's horse trekking ($25 to $50), one- and two-day white-water rafting trips ($25 to $230), and a horse trek and canoeing combo ($75). There is also accommodation, including camp sites ($18) and self-contained lodge units (s/d/f $20/50/65). There's a spa, sauna and swimming pool on site.

Riverside Jet (☎ 06-874 3841) organises trips on the scenic Ngaruroro River (adult/child from $25/15).

The **Hawkes Bay Wine Country Cat** (☎ 0800 946 322; www.hbwinecountrycat.com) runs daily lunch (adult/child $50/24) and dinner & dance ($50) cruises from West Quay out into the bay. Cruises depart at 11am and 6.30pm.

Festivals & Events
In the third week of February, Napier holds an Art Deco weekend, when there are din-ners, balls, bands and much fancy dress.

You might also encounter Bertie, Napier's Art Deco ambassador, who likes to prom-enade around town in period togs.

A popular open-air concert is also held every February at the Mission Estate Winery, the oldest winery in the country. Previous performers have included Kiri Te Kanawa, Kenny Rogers and the Doobie Brothers. Get more information at www .missionconcert.co.nz.

Sleeping
BUDGET
Archie's Bunker (☎ 06-833 7990; www.archiesbunker .co.nz; 14 Herschell St; dm/s/d from $20/25/50; 🖳) This modern and well-cared-for hostel is cen-trally located, with clean, spacious rooms and good communal areas, including TV lounges and pool table. The friendly owners help organise work and rent out bikes.

Napier Prison Backpackers (☎ 06-835 9933; www .napierprison.com; 55 Coote Rd; dm/d $20/50; 🖳) If you're looking for atmosphere, this Victor-ian prison – only decommissioned in 1993 – has plenty, from the creaking cell doors to the liberal scribbling of gang graffiti. You can even sleep on the former prisoners' bunks. Guided one-hour tours cost $10 (free for inmates).

Stables Lodge Backpackers (☎ 06-835 6242; www .stableslodge.co.nz; 370 Hastings St; dm/d from $13/50; 🖳) Stables Lodge is a charming, spotless old house with horsey décor and a quiet, relaxed atmosphere. There's a quiet inner courtyard, hammocks in the garden, a couple of friendly dogs and free Internet access.

Kennedy Park (☎ 0800 457 275; www.kennedypark .co.nz; Storkey St; camp sites/d/ste from $24/38/75; 🖳 🖳) This is a Top 10 park in Marewa, 2.5km from the centre, with a good range of simple but cosy and clean accommodation plus motel-style units. There's a restaurant and playground on site.

Portside Inn Backpackers (☎ 06-833 7292; www .portsideinn.co.nz; 52 Bridge St; camp sites/dm/f from $20/17/60; 🖳) On the other side of Bluff Hill at Ahuriri is this sociable modern hostel. There's a huge lounge bar, space for campervans and a small garden. Its main selling point is its proximity to the bars and restaurants at Ahuriri.

Napier YHA (☎ 06-835 7039; yhanapr@yha .nz; 277 Marine Parade; dm/s/d from $18/24/50) This large wooden house enjoys a good location opposite the beach, though street-facing rooms can be noisy. It's an older building, with a lot of character, and there's a sunny courtyard out the back.

Toad Hall (☎ 06-835 5555; www.toadhall.co.nz; cnr Shakespeare Rd & Brewster St; dm/s/d from $18/20/40) Toad Hall is an older building and a rare survivor of the '31 earthquake. It's now a basic hostel with simple, clean rooms, none with more than two beds. There's a bar downstairs and a great rooftop terrace.

Criterion Art Deco Backpackers (☎ 06-835 2059; www.criterionartdeco.co.nz; 48 Emerson St; dm/s/d from $20/24/45; ☐) This place is upstairs in the former Criterion Hotel, one of Napier's best examples of Spanish Mission architecture. There's a large lounge with a balcony, though some rooms are small and stuffy, and it can get noisy.

MID-RANGE

County Hotel (☎ 0800 843 468; www.countyhotel.co.nz; 12 Browning St; d/ste from $150/300) The County Hotel is an elegantly restored Edwardian building (one of very few to survive the 1931 earthquake), with 18 individually styled rooms. There's an impressive library, and the hotel runs a transfer from the airport in a Daimler once used by the Queen ($50). Even Lulu once stayed here!

Mon Logis (☎ 06-835 2125; monlogis@xtra.co.nz; 415 Marine Parade; s/d incl breakfast $120/160) The chic French-style Mon Logis was built in 1915 as a private hotel. It has three delightful en-suite rooms decorated with Gallic flair, and one room with an adjacent bathroom. There are great sea views.

Rocks Motor Lodge (☎ 0800 835 9626; info@the rocksmotel.co.nz; 27 Meeanee Quay, Westshore; ste from $105; ☐) The Rocks is a higher quality, contemporary motel with a stylish tin façade and crisp, well-designed ground-level suites, most with double spa baths. It's close to Westshore Beach and has good business facilities.

Masonic Hotel (☎ 06-835 8689; www.masonic.co.nz; cnr Marine Parade & Tennyson St; s/d/ste $75/85/120) The fine old Art Deco Masonic Hotel couldn't be more conveniently sited, right in the heart of town and part of the huge Masonic Establishment complex, which includes a pub and a couple of good restaurants. All rooms are en suite, and there's a restaurant and bar with a dance floor.

Sea Breeze (☎ 06-835 8067; seabreeze.napier@xtra .co.nz; 281 Marine Parade; s/d $75/110) This Victorian

seafront villa has three attractive rooms individually decorated in Asian styles and a comfortable upstairs sunroom with sea views.

Deco City Motor Lodge (☎ 0800 536 6339; www.decocity.co.nz; 308 Kennedy Rd; ste from $110; ☐ ☒) This upmarket Art Deco–inspired motel a couple of kilometres from the centre has a stylish exterior and spacious, spotless units, all double-glazed. It's popular with business travellers and there's a secretarial service and other business facilities.

Bella Tuscany Motor Lodge (☎ 0800 365 754; www .bellatuscany.co.nz; 451 Kennedy Rd; ste from $90) This quiet, out-of-town motel is a very clean and bright place with agreeable, neatly furnished suites decorated in a vaguely 'Mediterranean' style. All have private courtyards and there are also disabled-accessible units.

Fountain Court Motor Inn (☎ 0508 411 000; www.fountaincourt.co.nz; 411 Hastings St; ste from $110; ☐ ☒) Fountain Court is a large, smart-looking modern motel near the centre. The roomy suites come with spa baths, and there's a children's playground and the excellent Aquarium Restaurant. There's also a free pick-up service.

Tennyson Motor Inn (☎ 0800 502 122; www.tennyson .co.nz; cnr Tennyson St & Clive Sq; d from $120) Tennyson is a big place, handily located in the centre of town, with unspectacular but perfectly decent rooms. There's a good on-site restaurant serving breakfast and dinner, and a cocktail bar.

TOP END

Cobden Villa (☎ 06-835 9065; www.cobdenvilla.com; 11 Cobden Rd; d $230-400) This gorgeous Art Deco home has been lovingly restored by its current owners, and offers four stylish, period-inspired rooms. You can even be driven into town in a 1938 Buick. It's the cat's pyjamas!

Te Pania Hotel (☎ 06-833 7733; www.scenic -circle.co.nz; 45 Marine Parade; d from $220) The strikingly concave Te Pania is a very modern place in a great seafront location. Most of the spacious rooms have sea views, and there's a restaurant and gym.

Eating

Jo Miguels Spanish Bar (☎ 06-835 8477; 193 Hastings St; mains from $7.50; ☺ lunch & dinner Wed-Sun, dinner Mon-Tue) Jo Miguels is a thoroughly Spanish place – complete with guitars and matador posters on the walls – serving good tapas dishes and pizzas, and there's also a little geranium and vine-filled courtyard.

Restaurant Indonesia (☎ 06-835 8303; 409 Marine Parade; mains $20-37; ☺ dinner) Filled with Balinese artworks and Indonesian curios, this place has a good range of authentic meaty and veggie specialities on the menu, including generous smorgasbord or *rijsttafel* meals, consisting of up to 19 dishes (around $27 per person).

Pacifica Kaimoana (☎ 06-833 6335; 209 Marine Parade; mains $25-33; ☺ lunch & dinner Mon-Sat) Pacifica is a new, trendy restaurant and a choice place for top-quality seafood, as well as various grilled meat dishes.

Ravish (☎ 06-833 6040; 131 Marine Parade; mains around $20; ☺ lunch & dinner) Ravish is another stylishly modern place with friendly service, offering a changing menu of well-presented dishes from Thai green curry to fresh fish. It's also a nice spot for a coffee.

Shed 2 (☎ 06-835 2202; West Quay; mains $15-25; ☺ dinner Mon, lunch & dinner Tue-Sun) This open and very popular restaurant/bar overlooks the marina, and concentrates on seafood and meat dishes, but also has pizzas.

Provedore (☎ 06-834 0189; West Quay; mains $10-26; ☺ lunch & dinner Tue-Sun) Provedore is a trendy restaurant by day and a popular bar by night. There's an eclectic menu and a long wine list.

Gintrap (☎ 06-835 0199; West Quay; mains $16-28; ☺ lunch & dinner) This large, open bar has excellent views of the marina, and is good for bar snacks and more substantial meals such as pasta, fish and grills.

Breakers Café & Bar (☎ 06-835 8689; cnr Marine Parade & Tennyson St; mains from $6; ☺ breakfast, lunch & dinner) This is a relaxed place with outdoor seating, offering good-value all-day breakfasts, salads, steaks and seafood.

Thai Chef's Restaurant (☎ 06-843 4595; 110 Taradale Rd; mains from $18; ☺ lunch Wed-Fri, dinner daily) This constantly busy place, around 3km west of the city centre, serves excellent and authentic Thai cuisine. The menu includes such cheeky dishes as 'sexy little duck' and 'flaming chicken erection'.

Take Five (☎ 06-835 4050; 189 Marine Parade; mains $22-30; ☺ dinner Mon-Sat) Take Five has excellent organic food (lamb, steaks and seafood) with the added bonus of live jazz on Friday and Saturday nights.

Deano's Steak Bar & Grill (☎ 06-835 4944; 255 Marine Parade; mains from $12; ☺ lunch & dinner) Deano's

has a good range of steaks for reasonable prices and special $14 meal deals on Monday and Wednesday nights, including drink.

Acqua (☎ 06-835 8689; cnr Marine Parade & Emerson St; mains $22-35; ☺ dinner) A top place to sample some great, innovative seafood, including monkfish, gurnard, octopus and oysters.

Chambers (☎ 06-835 7800; 12 Browning St; mains $22-29; ☺ lunch & dinner) This highly rated place at the County Hotel (see p373) offers excellent roasts and fish dishes, and a good wine menu.

Caffe Aroma (☎ 06-835 3922; 20 Dalton St; bagels from $4; ☺ breakfast & lunch) If you're into espresso coffee, bagels and Vespas, this is definitely your place. They also do cooked breakfasts from $7.

Starving Artist Café (☎ 06-835 1646; 260 Emerson St; mains from $5; ☺ breakfast & lunch) This place does good-value breakfasts, salads and pasta, and is adorned with colourful works by local artists, most for sale.

Alakebabs (☎ 06-834 1170; 4 Market St; kebabs $3-10.50; ☺ lunch & dinner) Excellent-value takeaway place for tasty doner kebabs and filled pittas. There's also outdoor seating.

Thorps Coffee House (☎ 06-835 6699; 40 Hastings St; mains from $5; ☺ breakfast & lunch Mon-Sat) Thorps is a good spot for light snacks, *panini* (focaccia), muffins and pastries.

Drinking

Governors Inn (☎ 06-835 0088; Cnr Emerson St & Marine Parade) Governors Inn is a sedate pub with pool tables in its back bar.

Rosie O'Grady's (☎ 06-835 8689; cnr Marine Parade & Tennyson St) Rosie's is a dimly-lit 'Irish' pub that has occasional live music. It's part of the Masonic Establishment.

Brazen Head (☎ 06-834 3587; 21 Hastings St) Yet another 'Irish' pub, this is a much smarter place with a good value lunch and dinner menu and occasional live music.

Cri Bar & Grill (☎ 06-835 7162; 8 Market St) This is a lively local bar with pool tables and cheap food, popular with backpackers.

Grumpy Mole Saloon (☎ 06-835 5545; cnr Hastings & Tennyson Sts) This Wild West wood-cabin style chain-pub regularly pulls in the crowds with cheap drink offers and loud music.

Restaurants with popular bars include **Provedore** (☎ 06-834 0189; West Quay), and **Gintrap** (☎ 06-835 0199; West Quay), which has an open bar with top views and a DJ on Friday and Saturday night.

THE EAST COAST

Entertainment

O'Flaherty's Irish Pub (☎ 06-834 1235; 35 Hastings St) O'Flaherty's is a rough-edged Irish pub with mismatched furniture and stripped floorboards. They have live bands Thursday to Saturday nights.

Mossy's (☎ 06-835 6696; 88a Dickens St) Mossy's is a regular café by day and has live bands Friday and Saturday nights.

Gintrap (opposite) has a DJ twice a week.

Getting There & Away

AIR

Air New Zealand (☎ 06-833 5400; cnr Hastings & Station Sts) offers daily direct flights to Auckland, Christchurch and Wellington, with onward connections. **Origin Pacific** (☎ 0800 302 302) flies from Napier to Auckland, with connections.

BUS

InterCity and Newmans both operate from the **Napier Travel Centre** (☎ 06-834 2720; 8.30am-5pm Mon-Fri, 8am-11.30am & 12.30-1.30pm Sat & Sun) on Munro St. InterCity has services to Auckland ($80, seven hours), Hamilton ($58, five hours), Rotorua ($52, three hours), Taupo ($36, two hours), Tauranga ($80, five hours), Gisborne ($35, four hours), Palmerston North ($38, 2¾ hours) and Wellington ($60, 4¼ hours).

Newmans routes head north to Taupo, Rotorua and Tauranga, through Palmerston North and Wanganui to New Plymouth, and to Wellington via Palmerston North. Its route times and prices are similar to those of InterCity.

Bay Xpress (☎ 0800 422 997) runs daily to Wellington ($35, five hours).

The **Purpil People Mover Shuttle** (☎ 0800 787 745) runs between Napier and Taupo on weekdays (two-hour one-way trip/day return $25/35), picking up and dropping off at your accommodation.

HITCHING

If you're heading north catch a bus and get off at Westshore, or try thumbing closer in. If you're heading south stick to SH2. The alternative inland route (SH50) is much harder going, with less traffic.

Getting Around

The airport **shuttle bus** (☎ 06-844 7333) charges $10 from the airport to Napier city centre, and **Napier Taxi Service** (☎ 06-835 7777) charges about $13.

Nimbus (☎ 06-877 8133) operates the suburban bus services, with regular buses between Napier and Hastings via Taradale (Monday to Saturday; $5.20, 55 minutes), plus other local services. All local buses depart from the corner of Dickens and Dalton Sts.

HASTINGS

pop 50,200

Hastings, located only 20km south of Napier, shared the same fate as Napier in the 1931 earthquake and is also well known for its Art Deco and Spanish Mission–style architecture.

Hastings is an agricultural centre and a good base for exploring nearby wineries. During the apple harvest season, from February to April, it is popular with fruit-pickers, and accommodation is tight at this time.

Information

The Hastings **visitors centre** (Map p376; ☎ 06-873 5526; info@hastingsvic.co.nz; 8.30am-5pm Mon-Fri, 10am-3pm Sat & Sun; cnr Russell & Heretaunga Sts) is in the Westerman's Building. You can pick up maps at the **AA office** (Map p376; ☎ 06-878 4101; 337 Heretaunga St W) and post mail at **New Zealand Post Books & More** (Map p376; ☎ 06-878 9425; K Mart Plaza, Karamu Rd). Internet access is available at **Hectic Netway** (Map p376; 123 Heretaunga St E).

Sights & Activities

The legacy of the 1931 earthquake is an impressive collection of **Art Deco and Spanish Mission–style buildings**. To explore Hastings' architecture in depth get the *Heritage of Hastings* pamphlet from the visitors centre.

The highlights are undoubtedly the **Westerman's Building** (Map p376), with its impressive bronze and leadlight shopfronts that have largely survived modernisation. Then there's the magnificent **Hawkes Bay Opera House** (Map p376; ☎ 06-876 8096; Hastings St), the most imposing example of Spanish Mission style in the region. The paved Civic Square is also attractive, with an Art Deco **clock tower** (Map p376) as its centrepiece.

Children will love **Splash Planet Waterpark**

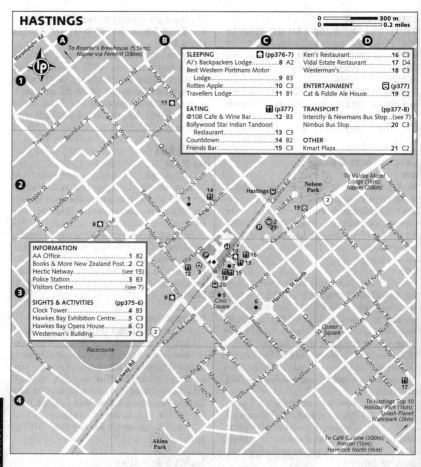

HASTINGS

0 — 300 m
0 — 0.2 miles

SLEEPING (pp376-7)
AJ's Backpackers Lodge...............8 A2
Best Western Portmans Motor
Lodge.......................................9 B3
Rotten Apple............................10 C3
Travellers Lodge.......................11 B1

EATING (p377)
@108 Cafe & Wine Bar..............12 B3
Bollywood Star Indian Tandoori
Restaurant..............................13 C3
Countdown...............................14 B2
Friends Bar...............................15 C3

Ken's Restaurant......................16 C3
Vidal Estate Restaurant............17 D4
Westerman's.............................18 C3

ENTERTAINMENT (p377)
Cat & Fiddle Ale House.............19 C3

TRANSPORT (pp377-8)
Intercity & Newmans Bus Stop...(see 7)
Nimbus Bus Stop.....................20 C3

OTHER
Kmart Plaza..............................21 C2

INFORMATION
AA Office...................................1 B2
Books & More New Zealand Post..2 C2
Hectic Netway........................(see 15)
Police Station.............................3 B3
Visitors Centre.......................(see 7)

SIGHTS & ACTIVITIES (pp375-6)
Clock Tower................................4 B3
Hawkes Bay Exhibition Centre....5 C3
Hawkes Bay Opera House............6 C3
Westerman's Building.................7 C3

(Map p379; ☎ 06-876 9856; Grove Rd; adult/child $25/20; ☼ 10am-6pm Sep-Apr) in Windsor Park, which is 2km southeast of the town centre. Splash Planet's facilities include waterslides, hot pools, a miniature castle, go-karts, minigolf, a boating lake and a paddle steamer.

The **Hawkes Bay Exhibition Centre** (Map above; ☎ 06-876 2077; Eastbourne St E; ☼ 10am-4.30pm Mon-Fri, 10am-4pm Sat & Sun) in the Civic Square, hosts a wide variety of changing exhibitions. Prices vary depending on the exhibition.

Festivals & Events
The Blossom Festival, a celebration of spring, is held in September/October, with parades, arts and crafts, and visiting artists.

Sleeping
Backpackers fill up quickly during the harvest, and all can arrange work.

Rotten Apple (Map above; ☎ 06-878 4363; www.hbtv.co.nz; 114 Heretaunga St E; dm/d $16/36; 🖳) This centrally located hostel is the pick of the crop, so to speak. It has spacious communal areas, well-kept rooms and plenty of information on picking work.

Travellers Lodge (Map above; ☎ 06-878 7108; travellers.lodge@clear.net.nz; 606 St Aubyn St W; dm/s/d from $18/28/44; 🖳) This suburban house has large grounds and is well set up for fruit pickers. There are tidy rooms, a sauna and a games room, and long-stay rates are negotiable.

AJ's Backpackers Lodge (Map above; ☎ 06-878 2302; ajbackpackers@xtra.co.nz; 405 Southland Rd; dm $23)

THE EAST COAST

AJ's is a tidy, well-run place in an old colonial villa. It's busy and sociable with a lot of character, and weekly rates are available ($135).

Hastings Top 10 Holiday Park (Map p379; ☎ 0508 427 846; www.hastingsholidaypark.co.nz; Windsor Ave; camp sites/d/ste from $22/33/70) This big camping ground has lots of shady areas in Windsor Park, adjacent to Splash Planet. Spotless cabins and self-contained motel units are also offered and there are good facilities including a playground and carwash.

Valdez Motor Lodge (Map p379; ☎ 0800 825 339; 1107 Karamu Rd N; ste from $100; ☒) The Spanish-style Valdez is in a quiet area 1.5 km from the city centre, and has large self-contained units, all with private patios. Some units have wheelchair access.

Best Western Portmans Motor Lodge (Map opposite; ☎ 0800 767 862; www.portmans.co.nz; 401 Railway Rd; ste from $100; ☒) Portmans is a big Best Western motel complex with neat and spacious ground floor units not far from the centre, though it's nothing out of the ordinary.

Greenhill The Lodge (Map p379; ☎ 06-879 9944; www.greenhill.co.nz; 103 Greenhill Rd, Raukawa; ste $470; ☒ ☒) Greenhill is a stunning colonial lodge set in extensive, secluded parkland west of Hastings near Bridge Pa, with five suites and a separate self-contained cottage ($450). There's a billiard room, library and cosy lounge, and meals and drinks are available.

Eating & Drinking

@108 Café & Wine Bar (Map opposite; ☎ 06-878 8596; 108 Market St; mains around $18; ☒ breakfast, lunch & dinner) This trendy little bar has an excellent wine selection and does a range of grills and salads.

Bollywood Star Indian Tandoori Restaurant (Map opposite; ☎ 06-876 8196; 102-106 Heretaunga St E; mains around $20; ☒ lunch & dinner) Bollywood Star is a bright, busy place with an extensive menu and TV screens playing Indian dance numbers while you dine. Takeaway and free delivery services are available.

Friends Bar (Map opposite; ☎ 06-878 6201; Heretaunga St; mains $6-10; ☒ lunch & dinner) This open, friendly café/bar has filling bar meals and cheap roast lunches. It's a popular backpacker hangout and they have live bands and karaoke at weekends.

Ken's Restaurant (Map opposite; ☎ 06-878 4131; 201 Karamu Rd N; mains $10-15; ☒ lunch & dinner) Ken's is a welcoming and informal bar and restaurant, serving up fish and chips, burgers, veggie bakes and the like. There's live music Fridays.

Sileni Estates (Map p379; ☎ 06-879 8768; www.sileni.co.nz; 2016 Maraekakaho Rd; mains $18-23; ☒ lunch Sun-Mon, dinner Tue-Sat) For a really special experience take a trip out to stunning Sileni Estates, 10 minutes' drive from the centre of Hastings. Beautifully prepared meat and fish dishes are on the menu, accompanied, of course, by an excellent wine list.

Vidal Estate Restaurant (Map oppsite; ☎ 06-876 8105; 913 St Aubyn St E; mains $18-29; ☒ lunch & dinner) This gourmet restaurant is a smart, formal place attached to the Vidal Winery. High-quality lamb, beef and seafood are served here.

Westerman's (Map opposite; ☎ 06-878 2931; 104 Russell St; mains from around $6; ☒ breakfast & lunch) This self-service café has the usual cafeteria-style quiches, sandwiches and light meals.

Café Cuisine (☎ 06-876 3798; Havelock Rd; mains from around $15; ☒ lunch & dinner) On the way to Havelock North, Café Cuisine is a highly regarded place for seafood.

Roosters Brewhouse (Map p379; ☎ 06-879 4127; 1470 Omahu Rd; ☒ 10am-7pm Mon-Sat) This brewhouse, about 10 minutes' drive northeast of Hastings, has its own superbly brewed beer on tap. There's a sunny garden and they do large lunches.

Prenzel (☎ 06-870 8524; www.prenzel.com; 180 Havelock Rd; ☒ 10am-4.30 winter, 10am-5.30 summer) Prenzel is a fruit distillery a little under 1km from Hastings. You can sample and buy liqueurs, schnapps and sparkling fruit wines, as well as olive oil.

Entertainment

Hawkes Bay Opera House (see p375) Offers a regular programme of music and theatre.

Cat & Fiddle Ale House (Map opposite; ☎ 06-878 4111; 502 Karamu Rd N; mains around $15; ☒ lunch & dinner) This popular Tudor-style place has good pub food and live Celtic music Wednesday nights.

At the end of the week you can also catch live music at Friends Bar and Ken's Restaurant (above).

Getting There & Away

Nimbus (☎ 06-877 8133) operates frequent local bus services from Hastings to both Napier and Havelock North; both run from Monday to Saturday.

All InterCity and Newmans buses going to Napier continue to Hastings, stopping at the visitors centre.

HAVELOCK NORTH
pop 8510

Havelock North, situated 5km east of Hastings, is a great holiday destination that is well worth a visit for its lovely gardens, wineries (see below), village atmosphere and the towering backdrop of Te Mata Peak. Check out www.havelocknorth.com for more information.

Play spot the queen bee at the **Arataki Honey Shop** (Map opposite; ☎ 06-877 7300; 66 Arataki Rd; $10; ☼ 8.30am-5pm Mon-Sat, 9am-4pm Sun), 3km east of Havelock North. There's a working beehive, as well as bee products and tours of the factory.

If you have kids in tow, there's the **miniature railway** (☎ 06-877 8857; per ride $1) in beautiful Keirunga Park; it operates on the first and third Sunday of the month.

Te Mata Peak

Te Mata Peak is about 16km from Havelock North. Dramatically sheer cliffs rise to the Te Mata trig (399m), commanding a spectacular view over the Heretaunga Plains to Hawke Bay. On a clear day you can see all of Hawke Bay across to the Mahia Peninsula and west to Mt Ruapehu in Tongariro National Park.

Te Mata Peak is part of the 98-hectare Te Mata Trust Park, with four walkways of varying difficulty; leaflets are available at Hastings visitors centre. You can drive right up to the trig at the summit.

The peak is naturally a favourite spot for **hang-gliding**. Gliders get remarkable possibilities from the updraughts breezing in from the South Pacific Ocean, about 5km away.

Airplay Paragliding (☎ 025-512 886; airplay@xtra .co.nz) offers tandem paragliding ($120) and one-day introduction courses ($180), weather permitting.

Sleeping, Eating & Drinking

Peak Backpackers (☎ 06-877 1170; fax 06-877 1175; 33 Havelock Rd; dm/s/d from $18/27/40) This spacious and sociable suburban house caters well for long-stay fruit pickers. There are good communal areas, including a large garden, and weekly rates are available.

Woolshed Apartments (☎ 06-877 0031; www .woolshedapartments.co.nz; 106 Te Mata Rd; ste $100-170) This modern, restful place offers studios and spacious, well-designed two-floor apartments with private barbecue decks, in a peaceful setting just north of the town centre.

Telegraph Hill Villa (Map opposite; ☎ 06-877 5140; 334 Te Mata Rd; d $170; ☑) Telegraph Hill is a peaceful hilltop retreat with great views. The villa has two en suite bedrooms and there's also a sunny veranda and tennis court. Breakfast provisions are supplied (there's a fully equipped kitchen).

Jacksons Bakery & Café (☎ 06-877 5708; 15 Middle Rd; ☼ breakfast & lunch Mon-Sat from 6am) Does a staggering array of breads, as well as excellent pies, filled bagels, sandwiches and pastries.

The Tudor-style **Rose & Shamrock** (☎ 06-877 2999; cnr Napier Rd & Porter Dr; mains $10-20; ☼ lunch & dinner) has pub-grub standards like fish and chips, and hosts live bands on Friday and Saturday nights. Just opposite, **Loading Ramp** (☎ 06-877 6820; 6 Treachers Lane; mains $22-27; ☼ lunch & dinner) is a smarter pub where you can get a better class of cuisine, including pasta and roasts.

Peak House Restaurant (Map opposite; ☎ 06-877 8663; 357 Te Mata Rd; mains $18-25; ☼ lunch & dinner Wed-Mon) has a spectacular view and is a nice place for a drink.

In the centre of town **Diva** (☎ 06-877 5149; Portere Dr; mains $20-25; ☼ dinner) serves up hearty roasts. The adjoining **Deviate** (☎ 06-877 5149; ☼ 9pm-late Thu-Sat; admission free) is a popular cocktail lounge with regular DJ nights.

Getting There & Away

Nimbus (☎ 06-877 8133) runs several buses from Monday to Saturday to Havelock North from Hastings.

AROUND HAWKES BAY
Wineries, Food, Arts & Crafts

The Hawkes Bay area is one of NZ's premier wine-producing regions, with many vineyards. It's very much the chardonnay capital of NZ, but cabernet sauvignon and merlot grapes from the area are also highly regarded and many varieties are produced.

The Hawkes Bay Winemakers produce the handy *Guide to the Wineries*, which lists an ever-increasing number of wineries open to visitors, and an excellent free map

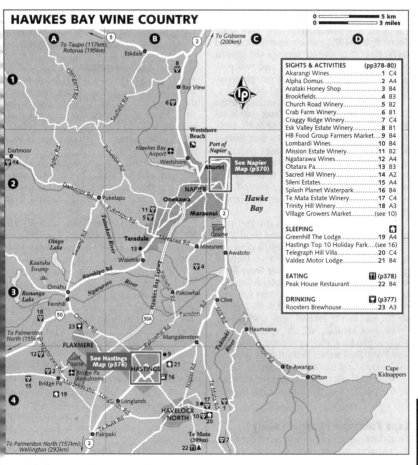

HAWKES BAY WINE COUNTRY

SIGHTS & ACTIVITIES	(pp378–80)
Akarangi Wines	1 C4
Alpha Domus	2 A4
Arataki Honey Shop	3 B4
Brookfields	4 B3
Church Road Winery	5 B2
Crab Farm Winery	6 B1
Craggy Ridge Winery	7 C4
Esk Valley Estate Winery	8 B1
HB Food Group Farmers Market	9 B4
Lombardi Wines	10 B4
Mission Estate Winery	11 B2
Ngatarawa Wines	12 A4
Otatara Pa	13 B3
Sacred Hill Winery	14 A2
Sileni Estates	15 A4
Splash Planet Waterpark	16 B4
Te Mata Estate Winery	17 C4
Trinity Hill Winery	18 A3
Village Growers Market	(see 10)

SLEEPING	⌂
Greenhill The Lodge	19 A4
Hastings Top 10 Holiday Park	(see 16)
Telegraph Hill Villa	20 C4
Valdez Motor Lodge	21 B4

EATING	(p378)
Peak House Restaurant	22 B4

DRINKING	(p377)
Roosters Brewhouse	23 A3

THE EAST COAST

More committed oenophiles can buy *The Complete Guide-Hawkes Bay Wine Country* ($25) available at visitors centres. Vineyards offering tastings include **Sileni Estates** (☎ 06-379 8768), **Sacred Hill Winery** (☎ 06-844 0138), **Crab Farm Winery** (☎ 06-836 6678), **Brookfields** (☎ 06-834 4615), **Mission Estate Winery** (☎ 06-845 9350), **Esk Valley Estate Winery** (☎ 06-836 6411), **Vidal Estate** (☎ 06-876 8105) in Hastings, **Ngatarawa Wines** (☎ 06-879 7603), **Alpha Domus** (☎ 06-879 5752), **Trinity Hill Winery** (☎ 06-879 7778), and **Church Road Winery** (☎ 06-844 2053) in Taradale. Church Road offers a very informative tour of its facilities, including a small wine museum ($7.50). There's an excellent jazz concert every February, plus Sunday jazz through the summer months.

Havelock North has a concentration of wineries, especially out on Te Mata Rd. **Te Mata Estate Winery** (☎ 06-877 4399), **Akarangi Wines** (☎ 06-877 8228), **Lombardi Wines** (☎ 06-877 9018) and **Craggy Range Winery** (☎ 06-873 7126) are all worth a visit. A number of wineries are open for lunch and offer excellent dining.

Every year around the beginning of February, **Harvest Hawkes Bay** (☎ 0800 442 946; www.harvesthawkesbay.co.nz) puts on a big show to celebrate wine and food. The weekend event of tastings and concerts involves upwards of 25 wineries.

A fine way of visiting the wineries is by bicycle (you can hire one in Napier), since most of the wineries are within easy cycling distance and it's all flat land. **Bike D'Vine** (☎ 06-833 6697; www.bikedevine.com), **Bike About Tours** (☎ 06-843 9991; www.bikeabouttours.co.nz) and **On Yer Bike** (☎ 06-879 8735) arrange self-guided bike tours of the vineyards, and will pick you, or your purchases up, if you get tired. Costs are around $40 for a full day.

Motorised tour operators include **Grape Escape** (☎ 0800 100 489), **Bay Tours** (☎ 06-843 6953), **Vince's Vineyard Tours** (☎ 06-836 6705), **Vicky's Wine Tours** (☎ 06-843 9991) and **Hawkes Bay Tours** (☎ 0800 868 742). Tours generally last around four hours and start at $40 per person, which includes a visit to four or five wineries. An all-day tour costs around $85. All tour operators will pick up in Napier, Hastings or Havelock North.

Food is also becoming an integral part of many tours to vineyards, and food markets are an extremely popular pastime for locals and tourists alike. Two markets of particular note are the **HB Food Group Farmers Market** (☎ 06-877 1001; Hawkes Bay Showgrounds, Kenilworth Rd, Hastings; ☼ 8.30am-12.30pm Sun), and the **Village Growers Market** (☎ 06-877 7985; The Sun Dial, Black Barn Rd, Lombardi Estate, Havelock North; ☼ 9am-noon Nov-Mar), which specialises in organic produce. Pick up a copy of *Hawkes Bay Food Trail* which lists produce growers in the area, and has a handy map.

Some local craftspeople open their studios to the public. Get the informative *Hawkes Bay Arts Trail* from visitors centres.

Cape Kidnappers Gannet Colony

From late September to late April the Cape Kidnappers gannet colony comes to life. Elsewhere these large birds usually make their nests on remote and inaccessible islands but here (and also at Muriwai near Auckland) they nest on the mainland; they are unphased by human spectators.

The gannets usually turn up in late July after the last heavy storm of the month. Apparently, the storm casts driftwood and other handy nest-building material high up the beach, so very little effort is needed to collect it. In October and November eggs are laid and take about six weeks to hatch. By March the gannets start to migrate and by April only the odd straggler will be left.

You don't need a permit to visit the gannet sanctuary. The best time to see the birds is between early November and late February.

Several tour operators take trips through Cape Kidnappers (so named because local Maoris tried to kidnap a Tahitian servant boy from Cook's expedition here).

Gannet Beach Adventures (☎ 0800 426 6387; www.gannets.com; adult/child $28/19) has rides on a tractor-pulled trailer along the beach, departing from the Clifton Beach car park. From where they drop you, it's a 20-minute walk to the main saddle colony. The guided return trip takes about four hours.

Gannet Safaris (☎ 0800 427 232; www.gannetsafaris.com; adult/child $45/23) has a 4WD overland trip that takes you right to the gannet colonies across farmland. It departs from Summerlee Station in Te Awanga.

Cape Kidnappers Guided Walks (☎ 06-875 0837; half-/full-day walks $45/90) offers walks over Summerlee Station, a 2000-hectare sheep-and-cattle run about 2km from Te Awanga.

Alternatively, the 10km walk along the beach from Clifton, just along from Te Awanga, takes about two hours. You must leave no earlier than three hours after high tide and start back no later than 1½ hours after low tide. It's 20km return (at least five hours) and there are no refreshment stops, so go prepared!

All trips are dependent on the tides. The tide schedule is available from the Napier visitors centre (p369). No regular buses go to Te Awanga or Clifton from Napier, but **Kiwi Shuttle** (☎ 027-459 3669) goes on demand for $20 per person. There is a rest hut at the colony.

The reserve is administered by DOC, which produces a handy leaflet and booklets on the colony ($1).

Beaches

Two popular surf beaches south of Cape Kidnappers are **Ocean Beach** and **Waimarama Beach**. To get to them, take Te Mata Rd out of Havelock North and continue east past Te Mata Peak.

Inland Ranges

The main populated area of Hawkes Bay is concentrated around Napier–Hastings. Regional Hawkes Bay, however, does extend much further than that, both to the south and inland.

The inland region provides some of the best tramping on the North Island – in

---

THE LONGEST PLACE NAME IN THE WORLD

Hold your breath and then say this name as fast as you can:

Taumatawhakatangihangakoauauotamateaturipukakapikimaungahoronukupokaiwhenuaki-
tanatahu.

The name is a shortened form of 'The Brow of a Hill Where Tamatea, the Man with the Big Knees, Who Slid, Climbed, and Swallowed Mountains, Known as Land Eater, Played his Flute to his Lover'.

Tamatea Pokaiwhenua (Land Eater) was a chief so famous for his long travels across the North Island that it was said he ate up the land as he walked. There are many other place names in the region also attributed to this ancient explorer, an inspiration to the modern traveller.

---

the remote, untamed Kaweka and Ruahine Ranges. There is an excellent series of DOC pamphlets on the ranges. See *Central Hawkes Bay, Southern Hawkes Bay, Maraetotara Plateau* and *Puketitiri Reserves* for details.

An ancient Maori track, now a road, runs inland from the bay, heading from Fernhill near Hastings via Omahu, Okawa, Otamauri, Blowhard Bush and the Gentle Annie Rd to Taihape. It is a three-hour return car journey from Fernhill to the top of the Kaweka Ranges.

Central Hawkes Bay

The two main towns of central Hawkes Bay are Waipukurau (almost always called simply 'Wai-puk') and Waipawa. The Waipukurau **visitors centre** (☎ 06-858 6488; chbinfo @xtra.co.nz; 9am-5pm Mon-Fri, 10am-2pm Sat) is on Railway Esplanade.

The prestigious Te Aute College, about 20km north of Waipukurau, was school to many influential Young Maori Party leaders (who lobbied the 1935 Labour government

for equality), such as James Carroll, Apirana Ngata, Maui Pomare and Peter Buck.

Many visit this region to see the **longest place name in the world** (yes, longer than Llanfairpwllgwyngllgogerychwyrndrobwllllantysiliogogogoch in Wales; see the boxed text above). From Waipukurau, head towards Porangahau (on the coast), following this road for 40km until you reach the Mangaorapa junction. Then follow the 'Historic Sign' indicators; the much-photographed AA road sign is a few kilometres up the hill (on private property) from Mangaorapa station.

After contemplating the name's astronomic length you can stop off at **Lochlea Farmstay** (☎ /fax 06-855 4816; lochlea.farm@xtra.co.nz; 344 Lake Rd, Wanstead; dm/s/d $20/32/40), an idyllic, laid-back and friendly farm. There are also camp sites ($24) and a self-contained cottage that sleeps four ($85).

In Waipawa stop for tea at the **Abbotslee Tearooms** (☎ 06-857 8389; 34 Great North Rd) and in Waipukurau try the Greenland Bakery or Café Supreme, both on Ruataniwha St.

Wellington Region

CONTENTS

Wellington	**384**
History	384
Orientation	386
Information	386
Sights	387
Activities	392
Wellington for Children	394
Tours	394
Festivals & Events	394
Sleeping	395
Eating	399
Drinking	402
Entertainment	403
Shopping	404
Getting There & Away	404
Getting Around	405
Hutt Valley	**407**
Kapiti Coast	**407**
Paekakariki	408
Paraparaumu	409
Kapiti Island	410
Waikanae	410
Otaki	410
The Wairarapa	**411**
Masterton	412
Mt Bruce	412
Greytown	412
Martinborough	413
Wairarapa Coast	414
Forest Parks	414

Wellington, New Zealand's capital, is on a picturesque harbour at the southeastern tip of the North Island. Approaching it from the north, you'll pass through one of two regions – either the Kapiti Coast on the western side via State Highway 1 (SH1) or the Wairarapa on the eastern side via State Highway 2 (SH2) – before entering the heavily populated Hutt Valley or the city itself.

Wellington takes part in sibling rivalry with larger Auckland, a friendly jibing that perhaps stems from the common misconception that Auckland is actually NZ's capital. Nicknamed 'Windy Welly', you won't need to spend much time in this funky, energetic city to see that it's a well-deserved moniker. Steep hills and spectacular views of rugged coastline, challenging walks, a thriving café and entertainment scene, and serious dedication to the arts make Wellington an enormously enjoyable city with much to keep you occupied and amazed.

Along the Kapiti Coast are the mystical Kapiti Island and the relaxing beach towns of Paekakariki and Paraparaumu backed by the striking Tararua Range. In the scenic Wairarapa region you can delight your palate with the delicate flavours of a pinot noir – a regional speciality – and experience some country hospitality at Martinborough and Greytown.

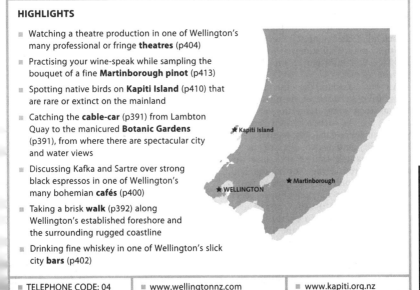

HIGHLIGHTS

- Watching a theatre production in one of Wellington's many professional or fringe **theatres** (p404)
- Practising your wine-speak while sampling the bouquet of a fine **Martinborough pinot** (p413)
- Spotting native birds on **Kapiti Island** (p410) that are rare or extinct on the mainland
- Catching the **cable-car** (p391) from Lambton Quay to the manicured **Botanic Gardens** (p391), from where there are spectacular city and water views
- Discussing Kafka and Sartre over strong black espressos in one of Wellington's many bohemian **cafés** (p400)
- Taking a brisk **walk** (p392) along Wellington's established foreshore and the surrounding rugged coastline
- Drinking fine whiskey in one of Wellington's slick city **bars** (p402)

★ Kapiti Island

★ Martinborough

★ WELLINGTON

- TELEPHONE CODE: 04
- www.wellingtonnz.com
- www.kapiti.org.nz

WELLINGTON REGION

Climate

November to April are the region's warmer months and the best time to visit – temperatures during this time hover around 20°C. During the colder months, May to August, the temperatures drop to around 5°C to 14°C. You'll often see snow on the peaks, especially along the Tararua and Ruahine Ranges.

Wellington's maritime climate catches the blustery, persistent, and often chilly, winds that whistle through the Cook Strait. Wellington city has an elevation of 147m and an average rainfall of around 130mm in July and around 80mm in January.

Getting There & Around

Wellington is an important transport hub. It has a busy international airport (p404) that is also serviced by several domestic airlines and it's where you cross the Cook Strait to travel between Wellington in the North Island to Picton in the South Island (p405). Easy train (p405) and bus (p405) connections make commuting a viable option and many people travel from Hutt Valley, the Kapiti Coast and the Wairarapa to work (or party) in Wellington city. If you're driving, you'll be coming from the north via State Highway One (SH1) on the western side of the island or State Highway Two (SH2) on the eastern side.

For comprehensive timetable and fare information check online at www.wrc.govt.nz/timetables. Call Ridewell for timetable and ticketing information for all bus and train services.

Air New Zealand has the most comprehensive network of domestic flights. Qantas runs some domestic services and smaller airlines such as Origin Pacific and Soundsair serve particular regions.

InterCity and Newman's are the main bus companies that travel just about anywhere around the North (and South) Island. In popular areas, such as national parks, there are smaller shuttle services available that are usually run by private operators. Tranz Metro operates the main commuter train lines to the Kapiti Coast and the Waiarapa and long-distance trains also run through the North Island.

Though the hills are steep and the winds strong, cycling is another popular option for traversing the region's terrain.

Cars are easy to hire in Wellington and there's a host of reliable operators. Note that it's cheaper to hire a separate car on each island, rather than pay for the ferry transport costs, if you're crossing the strait (p406).

WELLINGTON

pop 205,500

Bound by its magnificent harbour, with wooden Victorian buildings terraced up the steep hills, Wellington city prides itself as a cultural and artistic centre. There are hosts of restaurants, cafés, nightlife and activities, and it's home to the country's parliament and national treasures. Apart from Wellington's importance as the capital, it's a major travel crossroads between the North and South Islands.

The city's harbour was formed by the flooding of a huge valley. An earthquake pushed up Miramar Peninsula in 1460. The city congregates on one side of the harbour but it's so cramped for space that many workers live in the two narrow valleys leading north between the steep, rugged hills – one is the Hutt Valley and the other follows SH1 through Tawa and Porirua.

Wellington's most recent claim to fame was as host for the world premieres of *Lord of the Rings: The Two Towers* (2002) and *Return of the King* (2003).

HISTORY

Maori legend has it that the explorer Kupe was the first person to discover Wellington harbour. The original Maori name was Te Whanga-Nui-a-Tara, Tara being the son of a Maori chief named Whatonga who had settled on the Hawkes Bay coast. Whatonga sent Tara and his half-brother to explore the southern part of the North Island. When they returned over a year later, their reports were so favourable that Whatonga's followers moved there, founding the Ngati Tara tribe.

The first European settlers arrived in the New Zealand Company's ship *Aurora* on 22 January 1840, not long after Colonel William Wakefield arrived to buy land from the Maoris. The idea was to build two cities: one would be a commercial centre by the harbour (Port Nicholson) and the other, further north, would be the agricultural hub. The settlers were to be allotted two blocks: a town section of an acre and a back-country block worth £1 an acre (0.4 hectare).

However, the Maoris denied they had sold the land at Port Nicholson, or Poneke, as they called it. As it was founded on hasty and illegal buying by the NZ Company, land rights struggles followed, which were to plague the country for years, and still affect it today.

Wellington began as a settlement with very little flat land. Originally the waterfront was along Lambton Quay, but reclamation of parts of the harbour began in 1852 and it has continued ever since. In the 1850s Wellington was a thriving settlement of around 5000 people. In 1855 an earthquake razed part of Hutt Rd and the area from Te Aro flat to the Basin Reserve, which initiated the first major reclamation.

In 1865 the seat of government was moved from Auckland to Wellington.

One blustery day back in 1968 the wind blew so hard it pushed the almost-new Wellington–Christchurch car ferry *Wahine* onto Barrett's Reef just outside the harbour entrance. The disabled ship later broke loose from the reef, drifted into the harbour and slowly sank, causing the loss of 51 lives (p390).

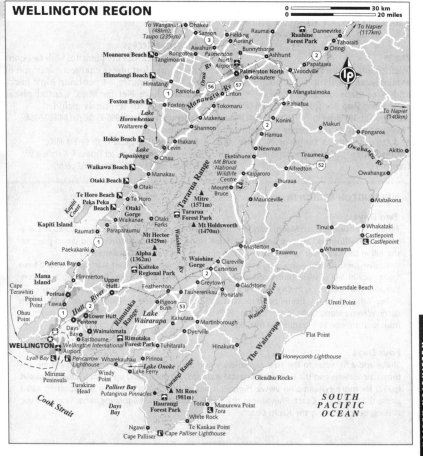

WELLINGTON REGION

ORIENTATION

Lambton Quay, the main business street, wriggles along almost parallel to the seafront (which it once was). The heart of the city stretches from the train station, at the northern end of Lambton Quay, southeast to Cambridge and Kent Terraces. Thorndon, immediately north of the centre, is the historic area and embassy district.

The waterfront along Jervois Quay, Cable St and Oriental Parade is an increasingly revitalised area and houses the futuristic Te Papa museum. Queens Wharf has been redeveloped and has some upmarket restaurants, museums and a gallery. Oriental Parade is Wellington's premier seafront boulevard.

Cuba Mall, Courtenay Pl, Manners St, Willis St and Queens Wharf, as well as Lambton Quay, are where the action is, be it for eating, drinking or shopping.

Maps

Wellington visitors centre has free maps available and sells a wide range of Kiwi and Wise maps and road atlases.

The **Map Shop** (Map pp396-7; ☎ 04-385 1462; www .mapshop.co.nz; 193 Vivian St; ⏱ 8.30am-5.30pm Mon-Fri, 10am-1pm Sat) is at the corner of Victoria St and carries a great range of NZ city and regional maps, plus topographic maps for trampers.

INFORMATION

Bookshops

Arty Bees (Map pp396-7; ☎ 04-385 1819; 17 Courtenay Pl; www.artybees.co.nz) Massive second-hand bookshop specialising in science fiction, fantasy and detective novels.

Bellamy's (Map pp396-7; ☎ 04-384 7770; 105 Cuba Mall) Second-hand bookshop. Wide selection of Maori-tonga and NZ books.

Bizy Bees (Map pp396-7; ☎ 04-384 5339; Oaks Manners St)

Dymocks (Map pp388-9; ☎ 04-472 2080; 366 Lambton Quay)

Unity Books (Map pp396-7; ☎ 04-499 4245; 57 Willis St) An institution, with an excellent fiction section, including NZ literature.

Whitcoull's (Map pp396-7; ☎ 04-801 5240; Courtenay Central)

Emergency

For police, fire and ambulance emergencies call ☎ 111.

Internet Access

Internet facilities are plentiful with fast connections. Most places charge a minimum of $1 for 15 minutes, $4 per hour. Most backpackers have Net facilities. Central places with numerous terminals include:

Cybernomad (Map pp396-7; ☎ /fax 04-801 5964; 43 Courtenay Pl)

Email Shop (Map pp396-7; ☎ 04-917 8860; www.WellingtonNZ.com; cnr Victoria & Wakefield Sts; 8.30am-6pm; $4 per hr, after 6pm $2 per hr)

WELLINGTON REGION IN...

Two Days

Explore Wellington's rich Maori, maritime and settlement history at **Te Papa** (p390) and the **Museum of Wellington City and Sea** (p390). Stroll along the windy waterfront and take a jaunt up the hill in the **cable car** (p391) for a wander through the **Botanic Gardens** (p391).

Revive from a boutique-shopping adventure with an aromatic cup of heart-starting coffee or a fresh feijoa juice at any of Wellington's cool **cafés** (p400). Explore the arts scene by checking out a contemporary art exhibition at **City Gallery Wellington** (opposite) and **Academy Galleries** (p387).

For dinner, feast on green-lipped mussels and other fresh local seafood, or a spicy Malaysian curry. Wander along Cuba St and Courtenay Pl where you can watch some live music – anything from death metal to a traditional Irish jig.

Four Days

Shake and add water to the two-day itinerary and stir in the following. Wellingtonians are enthusiastic walkers and the **Red Rock Coastal walk** (p392) rocks! Head up to **Mt Victoria lookout** (p392) for more eye-popping views. Hightail it out of Wellington city for a seal-spotting safari along the Wairarapa Coast. Plunge into the Tasman Sea for an invigorating swim at one of the striking beaches along the Kapiti Coast.

Internet@Cyber City (Map pp396-7; ☎ 04-384 3717; 97-99 Courtenay Pl; $1 per ¼hr, $4 per hr)

Medical Services
Accident & Urgent Medical Centre (Map pp388-9; ☎ 04-384 4944; 17 Adelaide St, Newtown; ⊗ 24hr) South of town; no appointment is necessary.
After-hours pharmacy (☎ Adelaide St, Newtown; ⊗ 5-11pm Mon-Fri, 9am-11pm Sat & Sun) Right next door to the Accident & Urgent Medical Centre.
Wellington Hospital (☎ 04-385 5999; Riddiford St, Newtown)

Money
There are numerous banks and ATMs around Wellington that accept international cards.
  Moneychangers include:
American Express (Map pp388-9; ☎ 04-473 7766; 280-292 Lambton Quay) At the Cable Car Complex.
City Stop (Map pp396-7; ☎ 04-801 8669; 107 Manners St) A 24-hour convenience store that exchanges travellers cheques.
Thomas Cook (Map pp388-9; ☎ 04-472 2848; 358 Lambton Quay) A foreign exchange office inside the Harvey World Travel branch.

Post
Main post office (Map pp388-9; ☎ 04-496 4065; Ground fl, NZ Post House, Waterloo Quay)
Post office (Map pp396-7; ☎ 04-473 5922; 43 Manners Mall)

Tourist Information
Airport information desk (☎ 04-385 5123; 1st fl, Main Terminal; ⊗ 7am-7pm)
Automobile Association (AA; Map pp388-9; ☎ 04-931 9999; 342-352 Lambton Quay; ⊗ 8.30am-5pm Mon-Fri, 9am-1pm Sat)
Department of Conservation (DOC; Map pp388-9; ☎ 04-472 5821; www.doc.govt.nz; Government Bldgs, Historic Reserve, Lambton Quay; ⊗ 9am-5pm Mon-Fri, 10am-3pm Sat) Offers information about walks, parks, outdoor activities, camping in the region, and it's where you organise permits for Kapiti Island (p410).
Wellington Visitors Centre (Map pp396-7; ☎ 04-802 4860; www.WellingtonNZ.com; Civic Sq, cnr Wakefield & Victoria Sts; ⊗ 8.30am-5.30pm Mon & Wed-Fri, 8.30am-5pm Tue, 9.30am-4.30pm Sat & Sun) The official and most comprehensive tourist information centre. Its friendly staff books almost everything, and provides the *Official Visitor Guide to Wellington* plus many useful brochures. There's a souvenir shop, the Email Shop and a café in the complex.

Travel Agencies
Flight Centre (Map pp396-7; ☎ 04-384 4413; cnr Cuba & Manners Sts; www.flightcentre.com.au)

STA Travel (Map pp396-7; ☎ 04-385 0561; 130 Cuba St; www.statravel.co.nz)

SIGHTS
Galleries
Wellington has a host of public, independent and dealer galleries. For a more comprehensive list pick up a copy of the Arts Map brochure from the visitors centre.
  City Gallery Wellington (Map pp396-7; ☎ 04-801 3952; www.city-gallery.org.nz; Civic Sq, 101 Wakefield St; admission NZ exhibits free, international exhibits varies; ⊗ 10am-5pm) has regularly changing contemporary exhibitions ranging from art to architecture and design. NZ artists feature but it's also where you'll find major international exhibitions, for example a photographic exhibition by German filmmaker Wim Wenders.
  Part of the New Zealand Academy of Fine Arts, **Academy Galleries** (Map pp388-9; ☎ 04-499 8807; nzafa@xtra.co.nz; 1 Queens Wharf; admission free; ⊗ 10am-5pm) is a contemporary, international space for fine arts. When the gallery isn't exhibiting Academy graduates' work it's available for hire and may have artists' paintings from Iran and Peru, embroidery, ceramics and quilts.

Historic Buildings
Completed in 1866, **Old St Paul's Cathedral** (Map pp388-9; ☎ 04-473 6722; 34 Mulgrave St; admission by donation; ⊗ 10am-5pm) looks quaint from the outside, while the striking interior is a good example of early English Gothic timber design. It features magnificent stained-glass windows and houses displays of Wellington's early history.
  Opposite the Beehive building, at the northern end of Lambton Quay, stand the 1876 **Government Buildings** (Map pp388-9), among the world's largest all-wooden buildings. With its block corners and slab wooden planking, you have to look twice to realise that it's not made of stone. The building has been restored and houses Victoria University's law department and various offices, including the DOC visitors centre.
  Dating from 1843, **Premier House** (Map pp388-9; Tinakori Rd) is the official prime ministerial residence. An early Labour prime minister, Michael Joseph Savage, spurned such luxury, however, and the house was used for a variety of purposes between 1935 and 1990 until it was restored.

WELLINGTON REGION

GREATER WELLINGTON

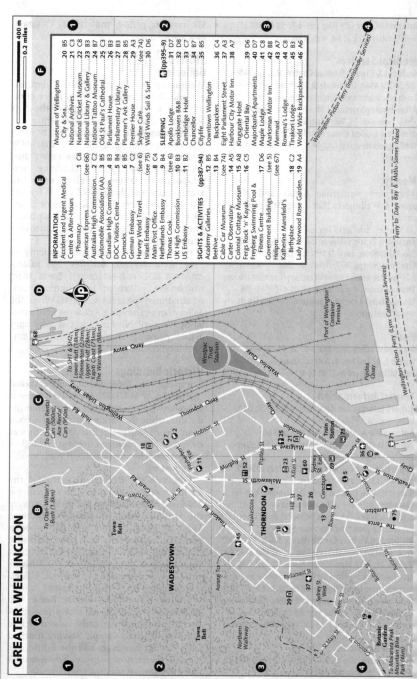

0 ———— 400 m
0 ———— 0.2 miles

INFORMATION

Accident and Urgent Medical	
Centre & After-Hours	
Pharmacy..**1** C8	
American Express....................(see 66)	
Australian High Commission.......**2** C2	
Automobile Association (AA)......**3** B5	
Canadian High Commission........**4** B3	
DOC Visitors Centre...................**5** B4	
Dymocks.....................................**6** B5	
German Embassy........................**7** C2	
Harvey World Travel................(see 6)	
Israeli Embassy.......................(see 75)	
Main Post Office.......................**8** C4	
Netherlands Embassy.................**9** B4	
Thomas Cook..........................(see 6)	
UK High Commission................**10** B3	
US Embassy................................**11** B2	

SIGHTS & ACTIVITIES   (pp387-94)

Academy Galleries.....................**12** B5	
Beehive....................................**13** B4	
Cable Car Museum...................(see 74)	
Carter Observatory....................**14** A5	
Colonial Cottage Museum..........**15** A8	
Fergs Rock 'n' Kayak.................**16** C5	
Freyberg Swimming Pool &	
Fitness Centre.........................**17** D6	
Government Buildings...............(see 5)	
Helipro..................................(see 67)	
Katherine Mansfield's	
Birthplace..............................**18** C2	
Lady Norwood Rose Garden.......**19** A4	

Museum of Wellington	
City & Sea.............................**20** B5	
National Archives......................**21** C3	
National Cricket Museum...........**22** C8	
National Library & Gallery..........**23** B3	
National Tattoo Museum............**24** B7	
Old St Paul's Cathedral..............**25** C3	
Parliament House.......................**26** B3	
Parliamentary Library.................**27** B3	
Plimmer's Ark Gallery.................**28** B5	
Premier House...........................**29** A3	
Skyline Café...........................(see 74)	
Wild Winds Sail & Surf..............**30** D6	

SLEEPING   (pp395-9)

Apollo Lodge............................**31** D7	
Booklovers B&B.........................**32** D8	
Cambridge Hotel.......................**33** C7	
Chancellor.................................**34** B7	
Citylife.....................................**35** B5	
Downtown Wellington	
Backpackers...........................**36** C4	
Eight Parliament Street...............**37** A3	
Harbour City Motor Inn..............**38** A7	
Kingsgate Hotel	
Oriental Bay............................**39** D6	
Majoribanks Apartments............**40** D7	
Maple Lodge.............................**41** C8	
Marksman Motor Inn..................**42** B8	
Mermaid...................................**43** A7	
Rowena's Lodge........................**44** C8	
Tinakori Lodge..........................**45** B3	
World Wide Backpackers............**46** A6	

To SH1 & SH2;
Lower Hutt (18km);
Plimmerton (23km);
Upper Hutt (28km);
Kapiti Coast (71km);
The Wairarapa (90km)

To Omega Rental
Cars (500m);
Ace Rental
Cars (950m)

To Otari-Wilton's
Bush (1.8km)

Town Belt

WADESTOWN

THORNDON

Town Belt

Northern Walkway

Botanic Gardens

To Makarara Peak
Mountain Bike
Park (4km)

Westpac
Trust
Stadium

Port of Wellington
Container
Terminal

Aotea Quay

Waterloo Quay

Thorndon Quay

Hobson St

Pipitea Quay

Train Station

Ferry to Picton–Picton Ferry (Lynx Catamaran Services)

Wellington–Picton Ferry (Interislander Services)

Ferry to Days Bay & Matiu-Somes Island

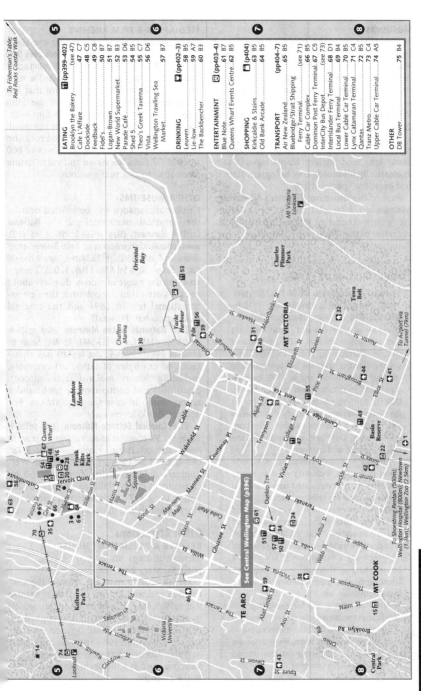

EATING 🍴 (pp399–402)
Brooklyn the Bakery ....(see 47)
Cafe L'Affare 47 C7
Dockside 48 C5
Feedback 49 C8
Fidel's 50 B7
Logan-Brown 51 B7
New World Supermarket ...52 B3
Parade Café 53 D6
Shed 5 ....54 B5
Theo's Greek Taverna 55 C7
Vista 56 D6
Wellington Trawling Sea
Market 57 B7

DRINKING 🍷 (pp402–3)
Leuven 58 B5
Lie-low 59 A7
The Backbencher 60 B3

ENTERTAINMENT (pp403–4)
Blue Note 61 B7
Queens Wharf Events Centre ..62 B5

SHOPPING 🛍 (p404)
Kirkcaldie & Stains 63 B5
Old Bank Arcade 64 B5

TRANSPORT (pp404–7)
Air New Zealand 65 B5
Bluebridge/Strait Shipping
Ferry Terminal ....(see 71)
Cable Car Complex 66 B5
Dominion Post Ferry Terminal ..67 C5
InterCity Bus Depot ....(see 73)
Interislander Ferry Terminal ..68 D1
Local Bus Terminal 69 B4
Lower Cable Car Terminal ...70 B5
Lynx Catamaran Terminal ...71 C4
Qantas 72 B5
Tranz Metro 73 C4
Upper Cable Car Terminal ...74 A5

OTHER
DB Tower 75 B4

Museums

MUSEUM OF WELLINGTON CITY & SEA

Professional exhibits in the three-storey **Museum of Wellington City & Sea** (Map pp388-9; ☎ 04-472 8904; www.museumofwellington.co.nz; Queens Wharf; admission free; ☺ 10am-5pm) offer an imaginative and interactive experience about Wellington's rich maritime history and social heritage since Maori settlement. There's a moving documentary about the tragedy of the *Wahine* (p385), an impressive lighthouse lens, and ancient Maori legends dramatically told using tiny hologram actors and excellent special effects.

Part of the museum, **Plimmer's Ark Gallery** (admission free), has solid chunks of the ship the *Inconstant* and an interesting historical overview of the 'Father of Wellington' John Plimmer.

TREASURES OF TE PAPA

Te Papa (Map pp396-7; ☎ 04-381 7000; www .tepapa .govt.nz; Cable St; admission free; ☺ 10am-6pm Mon-Wed & Fri-Sun, 10am-9pm Thu), the 'Museum of New Zealand', is an inspiring and interactive look at NZ's history and culture. Dominating the waterfront, the striking construction took five years to build (costing $317 million) and in 1998, its inaugural year, it attracted two million visitors. Quickly gaining widespread praise for its innovation and approachability, the museum has become a national symbol, affectionately dubbed 'Our Place', as it celebrates the essence of NZ and its people.

Among Te Papa's treasures, is a huge Maori collection, including its own *marae* (meeting house); dedicated hands-on 'discovery centres' for children; natural history and environment exhibits; a re-creation of a European settlement; contemporary art and culture and more. Exhibits are presented in impressive gallery spaces with a touch of high tech (eg a virtual bungy jump and a house shaking through an earthquake). Short-term changing exhibits require a small admission fee.

Allow at least a day for exploring, but don't expect to see it all. To target your areas of interest head to the information desk at level two. A café, gift shop, an auditorium and the upmarket restaurant Icon round off this impressive complex.

MEDIAPLEX & FILM ARCHIVE

Highlighting Wellington's square-eye dedication to film and television, **Mediaplex** (Map pp396-7; ☎ 04-384 7647; www.filmarchive.org.nz; 84 Taranaki St; admission free; ☺ noon-5pm Sun-Thu, noon-8pm Fri & Sat) is an innovative centre that has absorbed the film archives from the Film Centre. The complex combines a film archive, library, cinema and research centre all under one architecturally designed roof and has an extensive collection with over 90,000 titles of NZ film, television and video dating from 1895 to this year's sitcom.

OTHER MUSEUMS

Cricket aficionados will be bowled over by the historical memorabilia at the **National Cricket Museum** (Map pp388-9; ☎ 04-385 6602; www.nationalcricketmuseum.co.nz; Basin Reserve; adult/concession & child $5/2; ☺ 10.30am-3.30pm 1 Nov–30 Apr, 10.30am-3.30pm Sat & Sun 1 May–31 Oct). There's an extensive range of videos, displays about cricket's arrival in the colonies, the first international test in 1894 and the original Addington bat. Howzat!

The **National Tattoo Museum** (Map pp388-9; ☎ 04-385 6444; fax 04-385-6443; 42 Abel Smith St; admission free; ☺ noon-5.30pm Tue-Sat) has thousands of examples of tattoo art on show, including Maori *moko* (facial tattoos), traditional and contemporary tools, and a tattoo studio in case the urge strikes. For dedicated ink-lovers only.

The **Colonial Cottage Museum** (Map pp388-9; ☎ 04-384 9122; www.colonialcottagemuseum.co.nz; 68 Nairn St; adult/child $5/free; ☺ noon-4pm 26 Dec–30 Apr, noon-4pm Wed-Sun 1 May–24 Dec) is central Wellington's oldest building, built in 1858 by carpenter William Wallis and lived in by his family until 1977. The museum relates the story of family life in colonial Wellington.

Other Attractions

BEEHIVE & PARLIAMENT HOUSE

Three buildings on Bowen St form NZ's parliamentary complex.

Office workers swarm around the distinctive and well known modernist **Beehive** (Map pp388-9; Bowen St; www.beehive.govt.nz), which is exactly what it looks like. Designed by British architect Sir Basil Spence, its construction began in 1969 and was completed in 1980. Controversy surrounded its construction and it's the architectural symbol of the country.

KATHERINE MANSFIELD

Katherine Mansfield is NZ's most distinguished author, known throughout the world for her short stories and often compared to Chekhov and Maupassant.

Born Kathleen Mansfield Beauchamp in 1888, she left Wellington at 19, for Europe, where she spent the rest of her short adult life. She mixed with Europe's most famous writers, such as DH Lawrence, TS Eliot and Virginia Woolf, and married the literary critic and author John Middleton Murry in 1918. In 1923, aged 34, she died of tuberculosis at Fontainebleau in France. It was not until 1945 that her five books of short stories (*In a German Pension*, *Bliss*, the *Garden Party*, the *Dove's Nest* and *Something Childish*) were combined into a single volume, *Collected Stories of Katherine Mansfield*. She spent five years of her childhood at 25 Tinakori Rd in Wellington; it is mentioned in her stories the *Aloe* (which in its final form became *Prelude*) and *A Birthday* (a fictionalised account of her own birth).

Katherine Mansfield's birthplace (Map pp388-9; ☎ 04-473 7268; www.bookcouncil.org.nz/litevents/kmbirthplace.htm; 25 Tinakori Rd; adult/child $5.50/2; ☉ 10am-4pm) is a lovingly restored and maintained house with a restful heritage garden. The excellent video *A Portrait of Katherine Mansfield* screens here and the 'Sense of Living' exhibition displays photographs of the period alongside excerpts from her writing. A doll's house has been constructed from details in the short story of the same name. The No 14 Wilton bus stops nearby on Park St.

Next door to the Beehive is **Parliament House** (Map pp388-9; Bowen St), completed in 1922, and beside this is the neo-Gothic Parliamentary Library building, dating from 1899. The Parliament House **visitors centre** (☎ 04-471 9999; www.ps.parliament.govt.nz; ☉ 10am-4pm Mon-Sat) is in the ground-floor foyer of Parliament House. For information about tours see p394.

BOTANIC GARDENS

The tranquil, 26-hectare **Botanic Gardens** (Map pp388-9; ☎ 04-499 1400; ☉ dawn-dusk) are easily visited in conjunction with a cable-car ride. The large gardens contain native bush and

other gardens, including the Lady Norwood Rose Garden with over 100 rose species. There's also a teahouse, visitors centre and the NZ headquarters of World Wide Fund for Nature, with information and displays. The gardens are also accessible from the Glenmore St entrance.

The main entrance to **Otari-Wilton's Bush** (☎ 04-475 3245) is north of the city at the junction of Wilton Rd and Gloucester St; catch the No 14 Wilton bus. Devoted to the cultivation and preservation of indigenous NZ plants, it has a number of walks through densely forested areas and flax clearings, plus picnic areas and an information centre.

CABLE CAR

Wellington's 'must-do' attraction, the red **cable car** (Map pp388-9; ☎ 04-472 2199; www.wellingtonnz.com/CableCar; one way/return adult $1.80/3.60, concession & child $1/2, family $10; ☉ every 10 minutes, 7am-10pm Mon-Fri, 8.30am-10pm Sat & Sun) chugs up the steep hill from Lambton Quay to Kelburn. This fun, jaunty activity is well-loved by children. At the top are photo-opps galore, fresh air, Wellington's Botanic Gardens (above), Carter Observatory (below), Skyline Cafe and the small, well-presented **Cable Car Museum** (☎ 04-475 3578; admission free; ☉ 9am-5pm), which tells the cable car's tale since it began in 1902.

Central Wellington is a stroll back down through the Botanic Gardens, or by a series of steps, which interconnect with roads (a 30- to 40-minute walk).

CARTER OBSERVATORY

In the gardens near the top cable-car terminal, **Carter Observatory** (Map pp396-7; ☎ 04-472 8167; www.carterobs.ac.nz; 40 Salamanca Rd; adult/child/family $10/5/25; ☉ 10am-5pm Sun-Tue, 10am-late Wed-Sat) has displays and videos about astronomy and you can view the night sky through the telescope (weather permitting). From Wednesday to Saturday it runs shows at night, which are popular with children. The 'Night Sky' is recommended for kids aged 10 and over.

FERRY TO DAYS BAY & MATIU-SOMES ISLAND

Trips across the harbour to Days Bay are made on the **Dominion Post Ferry** (☎ 04-499 1282; www.eastbywest.co.nz; Shed 5, Queens Wharf one-way tickets adult/child $7.50/4), departing from Queens

Wharf around eight times daily weekdays and five times daily at weekends. It's a 30-minute trip to Days Bay, where there are beaches, a fine park and a boatshed offering canoes and rowboats for hire. There is also a couple of houses that Katherine Mansfield's family kept for summer homes; her story *At the Bay* recalls summer holidays here. A 10-minute walk from Days Bay brings you to the upmarket settlement of Eastbourne, with good cafés and picnic spots.

At least three Days Bay ferries per day also call in at **Matiu-Somes Island** (return fare adult/child $17/9), a former prisoner-of-war camp and quarantine station. Now a reserve managed by DOC, it has walking trails and beaches.

NATIONAL LIBRARY & ARCHIVES

Opposite the Beehive, the **National Library** (Map pp388-9; ☎ 04-474 3000; www.natlib.govt.nz; cnr Molesworth & Aitken Sts; admission free; ☉ 9am-5pm Mon-Fri, 9am-1pm Sat) houses by far the most comprehensive book collection in NZ. Also housed here is the Alexander Turnbull Library, an early colonial collection with many historical books, maps, newspapers and photographs. The library regularly hosts public lectures and cultural events and the **National Library Gallery** (admission free; ☉ 9am-5pm Mon-Fri, 9am-4.30pm Sat, 1-4.30pm Sun) has changing exhibits.

One block away, the **National Archives** (Map pp388-9; ☎ 04-499 5595, www.archives.govt.nz; 10 Mulgrave St; admission free; ☉ 9am-5pm Mon-Fri, 9am-1pm Sat), or the 'Keeper of the Public Record – the Memory of Government', displays several significant national treasures, including the original Treaty of Waitangi (p29).

SCENIC LOOKOUT

The best view of the city, harbour and surrounding region is from the lookout at the top of **Mt Victoria** (196m), east of the city centre. You can take bus No 20 (Monday to Friday) to the top or, if you're feeling particularly energetic, make the taxing walk. To drive, take Oriental Parade along the waterfront and then Carlton Gore St.

ZOO

The well-maintained **Wellington Zoo** (☎ 04-381 6750; www.zoo.wcc.govt.nz; 200 Daniel St; adult/child $9/4; ☉ 9.30am-5pm) has a commitment to conservation and research. There's a wide variety of native and non-native wildlife;

outdoor lion and chimpanzee parks; and a nocturnal kiwi house, which also houses tuatara and giant weta. The zoo is 4km south of the city; catch Stagecoach bus Nos 10 and 23.

ACTIVITIES
Mountain Biking

Makarara Peak Mountain Bike Park (www.makara peak.org.nz) is a council-run park in the hills of Karori, west of the city centre. The main entrance is on South Karori Rd (accessible on bus routes Nos 12 and 17). The 200-hectare park has numerous tracks ranging from easy to very difficult. **Mud Cycles** (☎ 04-476 4961; www.mudcycles.co.nz; 1 Allington Rd, Karori; bike hire half/full day $25/40) has mountain bikes for rent, is close to the park, offers free inner-city pick-up and drop-off (or can drop bikes to your accommodation) and has advice about track information. It also has guided tours, from $55 for a half-day. **Penny Farthing Cycles** (Map pp396-7; ☎ 04-385 2279; Penny.Farthing.wgtn@xtra.co.nz; 89 Courtenay Pl) stocks a full range of bicycles, bicycle gear and clothing. At the time of writing it also intended to rent bikes.

There are other good opportunities for mountain biking around town – the visitors centre or any of the city's bike shops can give you specific information and maps.

Walking

If Wellington has a peak hour it's along Cable St at lunchtime (BYO jogging shorts!), which is excellent for a stroll. The visitors centre is a great source of information for walks and, for guided walks, see Tours (p394).

The easy **Red Rocks Coastal Walk**, south of the city, follows the volcanic coast from Owhiro Bay to Red Rocks and Sinclair Head, where there's a seal colony. Take bus No 1 or 4 to Island Bay, then No 29 to Owhiro Bay Parade (or walk 2.5km along the Esplanade). From the start of Owhiro Bay Parade it's 1km to the quarry gate where the coastal walk starts (two to three hours' duration).

Other Activities

With all this wind and water, Wellington is a great place for **windsurfing** – choose from sheltered inlets, rough harbours and wave-beaten coastal areas, all within half an hour's drive of the city. **Wild Winds Sail & Surf** (Map pp388-9; ☎ 04-384 1010; www.wildwinds.co.nz; Chaffers

RED-CARPET WALKING TOUR

In December 2003 Wellington hosted the world premiere of *Lord of the Rings: The Return of the King*. Stars walked the 2km route from the Beehive to the Embassy Theatre, where 460m of red carpet was laid. This walking tour follows the red-carpet route.

Start at the modernist **Beehive** (**1**; p390) and head east along Bowen St to Lambton Quay. Turn right and splurge at **Kirkcaldie & Stains** (**2**; p404). After the Edwardian **Old Bank Arcade** (**3**), turn right onto Willis St and celebrate making it to central Wellington with a locally brewed beer at the **Malthouse** (**4**; p402). Turn left at Mercer St, continuing along Wakefield St. At Civic Square, check out **City Gallery Wellington** (**5**; p387) and, if you've got kids, **Capital E** (**6**; p394). Take a lunch break at **Café Lido** (**7**; p400). From Wakefield St, turn right into funky Cuba St and left at Manners St past the triangular **Te Aro park** (**8**), which was a *pa* between 1800 and 1890. Get the adrenalin pumping with a strong coffee at **Espressoholic** (**9**; p400) then cruise along vibrant Courtenay Pl to the beautifully renovated **Embassy Theatre** (**10**; p403), where you can watch a new-release flick on the biggest screen in the southern hemisphere.

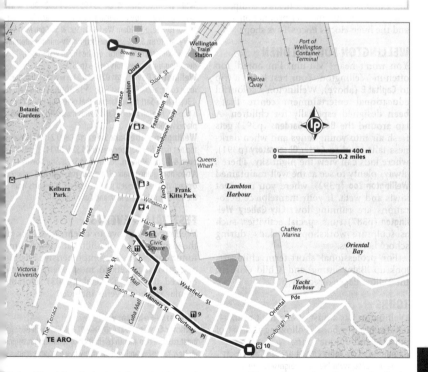

Marina, Oriental Bay; 1hr beginners lesson $40, kit rental $30; 10am-3pm Mon-Fri, 10am-3pm Sat, 11am-3pm Sun) has windsurfing lessons for beginners, prices include all equipment.

At the long-running **Fergs Rock n Kayaks** (Map pp388-9; 04-449 8807; www.fergskayaks.co.nz; shed 6, Queens Wharf; inline skates/kayak per 2hr $10/18, adult/student/child rock climbing $12/9/8; 10am-8pm Mon-Fri, 9am-8pm Sat & Sun) you can challenge your calf muscles with indoor rock-climbing, cruise the waterfront on a pair of inline skates and see the sights from a kayak. Fergs also offers a range of introductory courses and guided kayaking trips on the bay.

Gnarly surfing breaks are found at **Lyall Bay** near the airport, and **Palliser Bay**, southeast of Wellington. The visitors centre can help you with fishing and diving charters.

Freyberg Swimming Pool & Fitness Centre (Map pp388-9; ☎ 04-384 3107; www.wcc.govt.nz/recreation /pools.html; 139 Oriental Parade; adult/child $3.50/1.50; ⏲ 6am-9pm) has a heated indoor pool for lap swimming plus a spa and sauna.

For something more dramatic try a reverse **bungy rocket** (Map pp396-7; ☎ 04-382 8438; cnr Taranaki St & Courtenay Pl; per person 1st/2nd ride $35/ 15), where you sit in a capsule-like device that is flung into the air at high speed.

Kids will love colourful **Capital E** (Map pp396-7; ☎ 04-913 3720; www.capitale.org.nz, Civic Sq; admission free, admission to exhibits $2-10; ⏲ call for opening hours), the educational entertainment centre geared especially to them. It has interactive rotating exhibits, a children's theatre company, OnTV studio, multimedia production suite and the huge Hocus Pocus Toys shop.

WELLINGTON FOR CHILDREN

You won't hear, 'Mu-um, I'm bored' too often in Wellington. Your best bet is a trip to **Capital E** (above), Wellington's colourful educational entertainment centre that's been designed especially for children. A lap around the **Botanic Gardens** (p391) gets fresh air into young lungs and when darkness falls head to **Carter Observatory** (p391), where kids can view the night sky. There's always plenty to see at the well-maintained **Wellington Zoo** (p392), where you can spot kiwis and weta. If your mantelpiece decorations are running low, **City Gallery Wellington** (p387) runs special activities, such as sculpture workshops for kids, during school holidays.

For professional short-term childcare, look up 'Baby Sitting' and 'Child Care' in the Yellow Pages directory.

TOURS

Wellington has a host of excellent tours – it's essential to book. Following is a list of popular and unique tours.

Hammond's City Tours (☎ 04-472 0869, after hours ☎ 04-528 2248; www.WellingtonSightseeingTours.com; adult/child city tour $40/20, Kapiti $65/33, Wairarapa $130/65; ⏲ city tours depart 10am & 2pm, Kapiti 9am & 1.30pm, Wairarapa 9am) Runs a 2½-hour city highlights tour; 4-hour tour of the Kapiti Coast; and a full-day Wairarapa experience, which includes Palliser Bay and some Lord of the Rings (LOTR) sites. Includes pick up and drop off from your accommodation.

Helipro (Map pp388-9; ☎ 04-472 1550; www.helipro .co.nz; Shed 1, Queens Wharf; 10/20/30min flights per

person $75/135/250) Scenic helicopter flights that cover various routes – city panorama, south coaster, harbour cruise and capital views.

Parliament House tours (☎ 04-471 9503; tourguides@ parliament.govt.nz; Ground fl, Parliament House; admission free; ⏲ departs hourly 10am-4pm Mon-Fri, 10am-3pm Sat, noon-3pm Sun)

Rover Ring Tour (☎ 021-426 211; www.wellington rover.co.nz; full-day per person $150; ⏲ 8.30am-4.30pm) A fantastic LOTR tour with an enthusiastic guide who manages to bring the scene locations, minus the props, to life – lunch at the Chocolate Fish café is included. Minimum two people, maximum six. Tours run daily during high season, every three to five days (by request) otherwise.

Walk Wellington (☎ 04-384 9590, 04-802 4860; www .wellingtonnz.com/walkwellington; adult/child/child under 5 $20/10/free; ⏲ 10am Wed & Fri-Sun & 5.30pm Mon-Fri Nov-Mar, 10am Sat & Sun Apr-Oct) Ninety-minute informative walking tours that focus on the city or waterfront, departing from the visitors centre (p387).

Wellington Rover (☎ 021-426 211; www.wellington rover.co.nz; adult day pass $35; ⏲ 8.30am, 11am, 2pm & 4.30pm Mon-Sat) A popular tour that gives you the option of a hop-on, hop-off minibus and covers those tricky-to-reach places without a car.

Wellington – the Dark Side (☎ 0800 215 411; Will@ top.net.nz; adult/backpackers/child $24/20/14; ⏲ 10am-noon & 1-3pm Mon-Fri, 10am-noon Sat & Sun Nov-Mar) A two-hour guided walk of 'murder, mayhem and nefarious activity' has received positive reports. It departs from the corner of Manners Mall and Cuba Mall.

FESTIVALS & EVENTS

Wellingtonians love to celebrate. Check at the visitors centre or online at www.welling tonnz.com for a comprehensive listing of festivals; tickets to most events can be booked through Ticketek (p403). Notable regular regional events include:

January–February
Summer City Festival (☎ 04-801 3500; www.feeling great.co.nz) A two-month celebration of summer that begins on New Year's Eve and includes many free outdoor events.

Late February–March
New Zealand Festival (☎ 04-473 0149; www.nzfestival .telecom.co.nz) Late February to March. A biennial event (held in even-numbered years) involving a month of culture, including theatre, dance, music and opera performances, with many top international artists involved.
Fringe NZ (☎ 04-495 8015; www.fringe.org.nz) A month-long festival of visual arts, music, dance and theatre. It's home is Bats Theatre (p404).

April–May
International Laugh Festival (☎ 09-309 9241)
National and international comedians perform in venues
around town.

July
International Film Festival (☎ 04-385 0162; www
.enzedff.co.nz) A three-week event showcasing the best of
NZ and international cinema.

October
International Jazz Festival (☎ 04-385 9602; www
.jazzfestival.co.nz) A popular fortnight of jazz concerts,
workshops, jazz crawls and street performances.

November
Toast Martinborough Wine, Food & Music Festival
(☎ 06-306 9183; www.toastmartinborough.co.nz) Third
Sunday. A wine-tasting extravaganza when tiny Martinborough swells by around 11,000 people.

SLEEPING

Typically, accommodation in Wellington is
more expensive (around $10 to $30 extra)
than in regional areas. In saying that, the
overall standard is generally high and there
are a heap of great places to stay right in,
or within easy walking distance of, the city
centre. One hassle is the lack of inner-city
parking.

Budget accommodation is mainly in
the form of multistorey hostels or smaller
guesthouse-style hostels, costing around $60
to $80 per double. Budget accommodation is
scattered throughout the city, conglomerat-
ing around Courtenay Pl and Brougham St
at Mt Victoria, a quiet residential area at the
eastern edge of the city. From the train station, catch bus No 2 to Brougham St; Nos 1
and 4 to Basin Reserve. The area is only a
five-minute walk from Courtenay Pl.

Mid-range (around $81 to $150) and top-
end options ($151 plus) are delightful B&Bs
in renovated heritage homes, self-contained
apartments, motels and hotels. There's no
'motel alley' in Wellington, rather they are
scattered around the immediate city-centre
fringe, but Wellington is awash with hotels
and apartments. It's primarily a business
destination and rates drop dramatically (up
to half-price) from Friday to Sunday.

Camping grounds are scarce in Wellington. Rowena's Lodge can accommodate a few
tents otherwise head to Hutt Valley (p407).

GAY & LESBIAN WELLINGTON

Wellington's gay scene is tiny, but friendly and inclusive. Sovereign bar and Pound nightclub are
the main long-running contenders for best entertainment venues but there are heaps of cafés
and bars around the inner-city area, especially around Courtenay Pl, Lambton Quay and Cuba
St which are also gay friendly.

From the visitors centre you can pick up the pocket-sized quarterly *New Zealand Gay Guide*
brochure, which has details about cruise clubs, saunas, bars, restaurants and accommodation
in Wellington.

Media such as **express** (www.gayexpress.co.nz; $2.50; every 2nd Wed) and **UP Newspaper** (www.up
newspaper.com; $3.50; monthly) will keep you current with the latest happenings in the local gay scene.
The publications are free from selected venues or you can buy them from newsagents.

Around March is the **Annual Gay & Lesbian Fair** (www.gayfair.wellington.net.nz), which has a host
of stalls and entertainment, culminating in a ripsnorter dance party.

For phone information, or just to talk, contact **Wellington Gay Switchboard** (☎ 04-473 7878;
gayswitchboard@yahoo.com; 🕐 7.30-10pm) and **Lesbian Line** (☎ 04-499 5567; wgtnlesbianline@hotmail.com;
🕐 7.30-10pm Tue, Thu & Sat).

Excellent online resources include www.gaynz.com, which has comprehensive national coverage
of all things queer; www.gayline.gen.nz; and www.wellington.lesbian.net.nz.

Unity Bookshop (p386) has a wide variety of gay and lesbian titles and a queer section.

Sovereign (Map pp396-7; ☎ 04-384 5054; www.pound.co.nz; Level 1, Oaks Complex, Dixon St; 🕐 4.30pm-
late Tue-Sun) is a cosy, relaxed and retro bar with a mixed gay and lesbian clientele; just look for
the door with 'The straight route is often boring' painted above it. Thursday night from 8pm is
karaoke night at Sovereign, but for disco and drag head to the adjacent **Pound** (🕐 11pm-very
late Fri & Sat), which sparks up at around 1am.

See also Gay & Lesbian Travellers, p666.

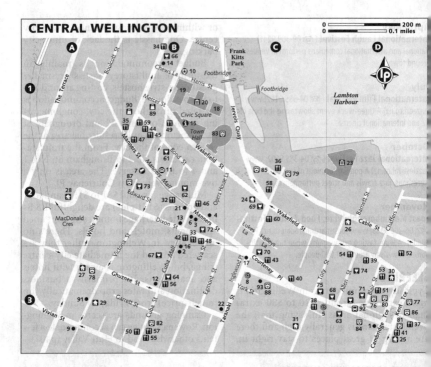

CENTRAL WELLINGTON

0 — 200 m
0 — 0.1 miles

During the peak holiday season (December to February) it's advisable to book accommodation in advance as the better places fill up quickly.

Hostels

Wellington city YHA (Map above; ☎ 04-801 7280; yhawgtn@yha.org.nz; cnr Cambridge Tce & Wakefield St; dm $25-29, tw & d $65, tw & d with bathroom $80, f with bathroom $90) These guys know how to hostel. Staff at the Wellington YHA are friendly, efficient and knowledgeable and can book anything you need with a minimum of fuss. The main communal area is excellent: a kitchen that even Jamie Oliver would call lovely jubbly, big dining area, pool table and a dedicated TV/video room. Rooms are clean and well-maintained.

Wildlife House (Map above; ☎ 04-381 3899; www .wildlifehouse.co.nz; 58 Tory St; dm $24-26, s & d $60, with bathroom $70; 🖳) You can't miss this large zebra-striped building. Rooms are spacious, many with a desk and couch. Communal areas are funkily designed with wood and corrugated iron, and include reading, TV and video rooms; a gym; and a modern kitchen. Unlimited Internet access is free. It could be cleaner.

World Wide Backpackers (Map pp388-9; ☎ 0508 04 888 555, 04-802 5590; www.worldwidenz.co.nz; 291 The Terrace; dm $25, tw $53, d $53-56) In an old house, this friendly, well-regarded backpackers is small, clean and homely and offers winning free extras like Internet, free local calls, breakfast, and wine in the evening. It's down-to-earth and chilled.

Rosemere Backpackers (Map above; ☎ 04-384 3041; www.backpackerswellington.co.nz; 6 MacDonald Cres; dm $22, s $38, tw $50, d $55) Rosemere has under-gone some serious refurbishment. It's a short walk uphill from the centre and has a fun, relaxed atmosphere and offers extras such as free city pick-up and Internet, soup in the winter, and a barbecue in the summer.

Rowena's Lodge (Map pp388-9; ☎ 0800 801 414, 04-385 7872; www.wellingtonbackpackers.co.nz; 11 Brougham St; dm/camp sites/s/d/tr $20/26/28/50/75; 🅿) It's the views that have it at Rowena's. A women's hostel during WWII, this is a rambling, friendly hostel with an outdoor barbecue area and the only place in town

INFORMATION		
Arty Bees	1	D3
Bellamy's Bookshop	2	B3
Bizy Bees	3	B2
City Stop	4	B2
Cybernomad	5	C3
Email Shop	(see 15)	
Flight Centre	6	B2
French Embassy	7	B2
Internet@Cyber City	8	C3
Japanese Embassy	(see 90)	
Map Shop	9	A3
Police Station	10	B1
Post Office	11	B2
STA Travel	12	B3
STA Travel	13	B2
STA Travel	(see 40)	
Unity Books	14	B1
Wellington Visitors Centre	15	B1
Whitcoull's	(see 40)	
Whitcoull's	16	B3

SIGHTS & ACTIVITIES	(pp387–94)	
Bungy Rocket	17	C3
Capital E	18	B1
Central Library	19	B1
City Gallery	20	B1
Dark Side Tours	21	B2
Mediaplex & Film Archive	22	B3
Te Papa	23	D2

SLEEPING	(pp395–9)	
Duxton Hotel	24	C2
Halswell Lodge	25	D3
Museum Hotel de Wheels	26	D2
Quest on Willis	27	A3
Rosemere Backpackers	28	A2
Victoria Court Motor Lodge	29	A3
Wellington City YHA	30	D3
Wildlife House	31	C3

EATING	(pp399–402)	
Abrakebabra	32	B2
Angkor	33	B2
BNZ Centre	34	B1
Bouquet Garni	35	B1
Brewery Bar & Restaurant	36	C2
Café Bastille	37	D3
Chow	38	C3
Commonsense Organics	39	D3
Courtenay Central	40	C3
Deluxe Café	41	D3
Dixon St Deli	42	B2
Espressoholic	43	C3
Fisherman's Plate Seafood	44	B1
Hell	45	B1
James Smith Corner	46	B2
Kopi	47	B2
La Casa della Pasta	48	B2
Lido	49	B1
Midnight Espresso	50	B3
Mondo Cucina	51	D3
New World Supermarket	52	C3
One Red Dog	53	D3
Pandora Panetteria	54	D3
Sushi takeaways	55	B3
Tulsi	56	B3
Vegetarian Café	57	B3
Wellington Market	58	C2
Wholly Bagels	59	B1
Zibibbo	60	C2

DRINKING	(pp402–3)	
Dubliner	(see 70)	
Ed's Juicebar	61	B2
Fluid	62	B2
Fluid	(see 40)	
Grand	63	D3
JJ Murphy & Co	64	B3

Kitty O'Shea's	65	D3
Malthouse	66	B1
Matterhorn	67	B3
Mercury Lounge	68	D3
Mojo	69	C2
Molly Malone's	70	C3
Ponderosa	71	D3
Sovereign	72	B2
Tupelo	73	B2
Vespa Lounge	74	D3
Wellington Sports Café	75	C3

ENTERTAINMENT	(pp403–4)	
Amba	76	D3
BATS Theatre	77	D3
Bodega	78	B1
Circa Theatre	79	C2
Downstage Theatre	80	D3
Embassy Theatre	81	D3
Hoyts Regent on Manners	(see 62)	
Indigo	82	B3
Michael Fowler Centre	83	B1
Paramount	84	D3
Pound	(see 72)	
Reading Cinemas	(see 40)	
Rialto	85	C2
Sandwiches	86	D3
Studio Nine	87	B2
Westpac Trust St James Theatre	88	C3

SHOPPING	(p404)	
Mainly Tramping	89	B1
Majestic Centre	90	B1

TRANSPORT	(pp404–7)	
Apex Car Rental	91	A3
Bus Stop	92	D3
Penny Farthing Cycles	93	C3

to offer camping. There are free shuttle services to ferries, buses, trains and hitching points.

Downtown Wellington Backpackers (Map pp388-9; ☎ 04-473 8482; www.downtownbackpackers.co.nz; 1 Bunny St; dm $23, s $45, tw $50-60, d $55-75) Opposite the railway station, Downtown is huge and busy. It's one of the largest Art Deco buildings in NZ and a young Queen Elizabeth II stayed here in 1953. It has a big-city feel with slightly dingy rooms, but amenities are sound: a restaurant serving cheap food; large bar with billiard table; huge kitchen and lounge; and pubs next door.

Maple Lodge (Map pp388-9; ☎ 04-385 3771; 52 Ellice St; dm/s/tw/d $21/35/45/50; [P]) Cosy and welcoming Maple Lodge offers clean accommodation with small dorms (there's bunks, dorms have the best views) and wee doubles, all with sinks except the twin. There's no TV, instead there's ambient chill-out music, board games and conversation. It's a popular option with solo travellers.

Moana Lodge (☎ 04-233 2010; www.moanalodge .co.nz; 49 Moana Rd, Plimmerton; dm $22-24, tw $50-60, d $50-60) If you'd prefer to stay out of the city this exceptional backpackers is on the beach in Plimmerton, 25km from town off SH1. It's well run and the friendly, caring owners are more than happy to share their local expertise and pick you up from the train station (suburban trains between Wellington and the Kapiti Coast stop in Plimmerton). There's free use of kayaks, bikes and golf clubs.

Guesthouses & B&Bs

Eight Parliament Street (Map pp388-9; ☎ 04-499 0808; www.boutique-bb.co.nz; 8 Parliament St, Thorndon; r $120-185, house $270-370) In historic Thorndon, this absolutely delightful house is stylishly renovated and run by a friendly German host. The three rooms, each with en suite, are comfortable and there's a great kitchen and decking area out in the country-cottage garden.

Tinakori Lodge (Map pp388-9; ☎ 0800 939 347, 04-939 3478; www.tinakorilodge.co.nz; 182 Tinakori Rd; s/tw & d $85/115, with bathroom $110/155; [P]) Tinakori Lodge, also in Thorndon, offers spotless B&B rooms in a grand Victorian house set amid bush. Children under 12 years old are discouraged from staying here.

WELLINGTON REGION

THE AUTHOR'S CHOICE

Booklovers B&B (Map pp388-9; ☎ 04-384 2714; www.bbnb.co.nz; 123 Pirie St; s with/without bathroom $120/90, d $100-120, d with bathroom $140-160) Booklovers is an elegant old home, run by award-winning NZ author Jane Tolerton. There are four inviting rooms with sweeping view, TV, CDs and CD-player, and the home is filled with books; breakfast is superb – berry compote, homemade granola. From the front gate bus No 2 runs to Courtenay Pl and the train station and there's a short bushwalk.

Mermaid (Map pp388-9; ☎ 04-384 4511; www .mermaid.co.nz; 1 Epuni St; s $75-125, d $85-140) In the cool Aro Valley neighbourhood, a mere short black away from Cuba St, the Mermaid is a small women-only guesthouse in a wonderfully restored villa. Each room is individually themed with colourful artistic flair. White robes and fluffy towels make Mermaid a luxurious experience and there's a guest kitchen, lounge and deck area.

Motels

Halswell Lodge (Map pp396-7; ☎ 04-385 0196; www .halswell.co.nz; 21 Kent Tce; s/d $85/95, units $135-160) Handy to all the central sights, Halswell has small, clean motel rooms with TV, fridge and en suite at budget rates. For singles, rooms are good value; the upmarket lodge suite with spa is a better option for doubles.

Marksman Motor Inn (Map pp388-9; ☎ 04-385 2499; www.marksmanmotel.co.nz; 40-44 Sussex St; units $100-180; P 💻) New owners have recently given Marksman a thorough facelift. The result is clean, comfortable studios and apartments with soft beds, a lounge, TV and telephone; some come with a spa. Rooms can be a little noisy but the Marksman is well positioned for airport runs.

Apollo Lodge (Map pp388-9; ☎ 0800 361 645, 04-385 1849; www.apollo-lodge.co.nz; 49 Majoribanks St; s $95-110, d $120, f $150-180; P) Within easy striking distance of Courtenay Pl, Apollo Lodge has a range of accommodation from older-style self-contained units or architecturally-designed executive suites to a three-bedroom cottage and an Edwardian house. Opposite, the owners also run **Majoribanks Apartments** (Map pp388-9; ☎ 04-385 1849; 38 Majoribanks St; s/d $95/100) with fully self-contained ex-residential flats that sleep four; check in at Apollo Lodge.

Victoria Court Motor Lodge (Map pp396-7; ☎ 04-472 4297; www.victoriacourt.co.nz; 201 Victoria St; r $135-190; P) Offers stylish apartments with spas and cooking facilities and studio units. It's right in the thick of the city centre.

Harbour City Motor Inn (Map pp388-9; ☎ 0800 332 468, 04-384 9809; www.harbourcitymotorinn.co.nz/ 92-96 Webb St; units $95-170) Harbour City has primarily studio units. Each room has a TV, phone and en suite and there's a guest spa and restaurant here.

Hotels

Cambridge Hotel (Map pp388-9; ☎ 04-385 8829, www.cambridgehotel.co.nz; 28 Cambridge Tce; dm $23-25, s $55, d & tw with bathroom $95/100) This restored heritage hotel provides quality pub accommodation at affordable prices. Its central position, well-equipped kitchen, Sky TV and cheap weekly rates make it popular with long-stays. Guests can purchase barbecue and burger-making ingredients (steak $10, burger ingredients $6) and cook downstairs on the pub grill.

Museum Hotel de Wheels (Map pp396-7; ☎ 0800 944 335, 04-385 2809; www.museumhotel.co.nz; 80 Cable St; r Mon-Fri $280-460, Sat & Sun $230-320) The 'de Wheels' part of this hotel's name refers to its amazing relocation – it was moved 120m in 1993 to vacate the space needed for construction of Te Papa. Rooms are decked out in olde-world opulence with velvet brocade and gilt trimmings, and don't forget the views.

Chancellor (Map pp388-9; ☎ 04-385 2153; www .ghihotels.com; 213 Cuba St; r $190; P 💻) Formerly Trekkers Lodge, this place has been renovated within an inch of its life and it now sports modern, boutique motel-style rooms with comfortable beds, TV, phone and en suite. Right on Cuba St, the Chancellor is a great choice. Cheaper rates are usually available.

Duxton Hotel (Map pp396-7; ☎ 04-473 3900; www .duxton.com; 148 Wakefield St; r from $290) Views over the quay, big comfortable beds with soft sheets, an abundance of European pillows, mohair rugs, simple blonde-wood furniture and cable TV. A businessperson's hotel during the week, rates are cheaper on the weekends. Clean, comfortable and quality accommodation.

Kingsgate Hotel Oriental Bay (Map pp388-9; ☎ 0800 782 548, 04-385 0279; www.kingsgateorientalbay .co.nz; 73 Roxburgh St; r $190-240; P ⬛ ⬛) Split into two wings, the Bay wing has larger rooms with harbour views, the Roxburgh wing has smaller rooms overlooking Roxburgh St and some with restricted harbour views – go the upgrade. All rooms have Sky TV, a balcony and 24-hour room service.

Quest on Willis (Map pp396-7; ☎ 04-916 0500; www .questapartments.com.au; 219 Willis St; r $135-230; P) One of the ubiquitous franchises of the prominent Quest chain. Check online if the Willis St location isn't exactly what you're after – there are a number of Quests in Wellington's CBD. Accommodation is mostly studio apartments, each with kitchen facilities.

THE AUTHOR'S CHOICE

Citylife (Map pp388-9; ☎ 0800 368 888, 04-922 2800; www.citylifewellington.nz-hotels.com; 300 Lambton Quay; r Mon-Fri $300-500, Sat & Sun $150-290; P ⬛) Excellent hotel-style apartments right in the city centre, ranging from studios to two-bedroom apartments. Features include broadband Internet, full kitchen, CD and video player, and in-room laundry facilities. Weekend rates are superb value. The vehicle entrance is from Gilmer Tce, off Boulcott St.

EATING

Wellington has a comprehensive array of cuisines. There's old-school arty cafés serving vegetarian comfort food – lasagnes, veggie burgers, burritos etc; modern restaurants dishing up Pacific Rim fare for the young professionals; pubs serving high-quality counter meals; and relaxed restaurants and takeaways selling mainly Malaysian, Indian and Chinese staples.

Cuba St is one of the best strips for food and Courtenay Pl, traditionally Chinatown, also has plenty of cafés, bars and restaurants. Not surprisingly, most of the seafood restaurants can be found on the city's waterfront.

Restaurants

Wellington's restaurants are scattered around the city centre – Courtenay Pl, the Manners Mall–Willis St area and Cuba St. There are also some winners on Tinakori Rd, Thorndon.

Kopi (Map pp396-7; ☎ 04-499 5570; 103 Willis St; roti $9-16, mains $14-16; ⊙ lunch & dinner) Malaysian for 'coffee', Kopi is consistently voted the city's best Malaysian eatery, the crowds attesting to its popularity. Choose from *roti chanai* (flat, flaky bread dipped in a creamy coconut curry); curries, such as goat korma; and *nasi kandar* (coconut rice). For dessert: feijoa ice cream.

Angkor (Map pp396-7; ☎ 04-384 9423; 43 Dixon Street; mains $15-25; ⊙ lunch Mon-Fri, dinner Mon-Sat) A highly rated Cambodian restaurant where you can sample such delights as *amok trei* (spicy steamed fish) and *yao-horn* (a charcoal broiler steam boat created for sharing).

Tulsi (Map pp396-7; ☎ 04-802 4144; 135 Cuba St; mains $16-22; ⊙ lunch & dinner) Big, bright and contemporary Indian place with a central circular bar, cheap curries, naan and rice for lunch. Lunch deals are excellent.

Chow (Map pp396-7; ☎ 04-382 8585; www.chow .co.nz; 45 Tory St; meals $11-19; ⊙ lunch & dinner) This super-stylish eatery/bar serves fresh Asian cuisines amid '70s décor – pots of spiky mothers-in-law tongues, cream-coloured retro chairs and orange low-hanging lamps. Try a fragrant broth of marinated whitefish, Japanese barbecue pork and fresh fried tofu in a spicy tomato and tamarind gravy. Motel is the fabulous lounge bar.

Fisherman's Table (Map pp388-9; ☎ 04-801 7900; Oriental Bay; mains $18-30; ⊙ lunch & dinner) Built over the water in the old Oriental Bay Sea Baths and with good harbour views, this casual, family-style eatery offers reasonably priced seafood.

Shed 5 (Map pp388-9; ☎ 04-499 9069; Queens Wharf; mains $28-35; ⊙ lunch & dinner) A big, flashy seafood restaurant, right on the water and in one of the oldest remaining wharf stores (originally a woolshed). It's popular with the business set, especially at lunch when prices for the quality seafood are lower.

Dockside (Map pp388-9; ☎ 04-499 9900; Queens Wharf; mains $22-32; ⊙ lunch & dinner) An upmarket, nautically themed restaurant with superb water frontage and quality seafood. With an emphasis on local produce you can feast on Nelson scallops or smoked groper and sweet paprika fishcakes.

La Casa della Pasta (Map pp396-7; ☎ 04-385 9057; 37 Dixon St; lunch mains $12-20, dinner mains $15-25; ⊙ lunch Mon-Fri, dinner daily) Reasonably priced, home-style Italian food is what this no-fuss place does well. Authentic pasta dishes include comforting staples such as lasagne, ravioli, tortellini and gnocchi.

Café Bastille (Map pp396-7; ☎ 04-382 9559; 16 Majoribanks St; entrees $12-16, mains $22-24; ☼ dinner) A modern French restaurant with an emphasis on local produce, an expansive wine list and knowledgeable staff. Try Lake Pukaki salmon with warm potato salad and watercress and finish with orange-caramel crepes. If you don't love the French, you will after this meal.

Theo's Greek Taverna (Map pp388-9; ☎ 04-801 8806; 13 Pirie St; mains $17-25; ☼ lunch & dinner) A whitewashed Mediterranean-style building with an outdoor courtyard and live music and dancing (Thursday, Friday and Saturday) to complement the authentic cuisine. The meze platters are a great way to sample a variety of tasty appetisers.

Mondo Cucina (Map pp396-7; ☎ 04-801 6615; 15 Blair St; meals $20-27; ☼ dinner) Mondo's curved décor, ambient dub tones and muted red lamps smooth away the kinks. The menu mixes Californian, Italian and French styles with a Kiwi twist and offers up imaginative contemporary fare such as manuka wood-fired pizzas, duck a l'orange and wild mushroom risotto.

One Red Dog (Map pp396-7; ☎ 04-384 9777; 9 Blair St; meals $16-26; ☼ dinner) A bustling, upmarket brewery pub, popular for late-night weekend drinks, with a wide selection of beers. On offer are excellent gourmet pizzas, pastas, calzones and salads. Families take the early dinner sitting and young 20-somethings create a fun, upbeat atmosphere.

Zibibbo (Map pp396-7; ☎ 04-385 6650; 25-29 Taranaki St; mains $20-27; ☼ lunch & dinner) With a menu leaning towards Italian and Spanish cuisine, this bright restaurant and bar is a great spot to relax and enjoy the scrumptious tapas or wood-fired pizzas.

Bouquet Garni (Map pp396-7; ☎ 04-499 1095; 100 Willis St; meals $23-30; ☼ lunch Mon-Fri, dinner daily) In a beautiful heritage building this elegant restaurant and wine bar (over 450 tipples) is an oasis of cool in the bustling centre. Popular for an after-work drink or excellent á la carte meals.

Logan-Brown (Map pp388-9; ☎ 04-801 5114; 192 Cuba St; mains $26-40; ☼ lunch Mon-Fri, dinner Mon-Sun) A fine-dining experience in a former 1920s bank chamber which is worth the

splurge. Service is excellent, neither fussy nor obtrusive, and the simple elegant food is delicious. The weekday lunch and pretheatre set menus are top value and the wine list extensive.

Brewery Bar & Restaurant (Map pp396-7; ☎ 04-381 2282; www.thebrewerybar.co.nz; cnr Taranaki & Cable Sts; lunch mains $11-25, dinner mains $18-27; ☼ lunch & dinner) Occupying prime water frontage in a renovated warehouse, the Wellington Brewing Company takes beer seriously. Those brewed on site include Sassy Red or Wicked Blonde. Families, tourists and businessmen come for big portions of beer battered fish and chips, sirloin and linguine.

Cafés

Wellington prides itself on its cultural heart and no literati could flourish without a decent café scene. Per capita, the city boasts more cafés than New York City. Many offer breakfast all day and a brunch menu, are licensed and open late.

Lido (Map pp396-7; ☎ 04-499 6666; cnr Victoria & Wakefield Sts; lunch mains $13-16, dinner mains $13-22; ☼ lunch & dinner) A popular corner café with curved windows and a sunny aspect. In a chilled-out unpretentious atmosphere you can dine on the likes of Mediterranean and Indochina platters, pastas, Italian-style pork and mozzarella balls and plum crumble (mmm). Service is friendly and professional.

Espressoholic (Map pp396-7; ☎ 04-384 7790; 128 Courtenay Pl; breakfast $4-16, lunch & dinner mains $12-18; ☼ until midnight Mon-Fri, until 3am Sat & Sun) A serious supporter of coffee addiction, this grungy café, with chipped black tables and colourful graffiti-art, serves strong brews of Italian coffee. There's a broad vegetarian selection such as corn fritters, and ricotta ravioli. Espressoholic keeps late hours, plays cool music and has a courtyard.

Midnight Espresso (Map pp396-7; ☎ 04-384 7014; 178 Cuba St; meals $7-14; ☼ 8am-3am Mon-Fri, 9am-3am Sat & Sun) Dine on primarily vegetarian and vegan food among the hessian-sack art and metal sculptures at this cool, high-ceilinged café. This long-running local stalwart serves food until around 2am and is an institution for paper-reading, coffee drinking and philosophising.

Fidel's (Map pp388-9; ☎ 04-801 6868; 234 Cuba St; brunch $5-16, dinner $8-20; ☼ breakfast, lunch & dinner) Fidel's is an institution for caffeine-craving, left-wing subversives, watched over by images of Castro. Terrific eggs (Benedict, Florentine, with salmon, mushrooms, hash browns – you name it) are miraculously pumped from the itsy kitchen. Pierced, tattooed staff are studiously vague, but friendly.

Vegetarian Café (Map pp396-7; ☎ 04-384 2713; 179 Cuba St; meals $6-12; ☟ lunch) A gem for noncarnivores, this cheap, cheerful and inviting place has great veggie and vegan options. Try the Tex-Mex burrito or sate your hunger with a well-priced bowl of chilli or steamed vegetables.

Deluxe Café (Map pp396-7; ☎ 04-801 5455; 10 Kent Tce; meals $4-8; ☟ lunch) At lunchtime this cosy, well-loved café is packed with funky Gen-Xers, businessmen and chilled locals. Right next to the Embassy Theatre, Deluxe serves rich, full-bodied Havana espresso, loose-leaf herbal teas, dense chocolate brownies, filos, lasagne, healthy rolls and sandwiches, and sushi.

Brooklyn the Bakery (Map pp388-9; ☎ 04-802 4111; 29 College St; meals $9-13; ☟ breakfast & lunch) The sister shop of Dixon St Deli (p402), Brooklyn has the same stylish chocolate-brown interior and makes bread, bagels and coffee.

Two very popular cafés by the water, **Parade Café** (Map pp388-9; ☎ 04-939 3935; 148 Oriental Parade; meals $8-15; ☟ lunch & dinner) and **Vista** (Map pp388-9; ☎ 04-385 7724; 106 Oriental Parade; meals $10-15; ☟ lunch & dinner) both offer mixed menus, great brunch choices, reasonable prices and outdoor seating.

Quick Eats
Pandoro Panetteria (Map pp396-7; ☎ 385 4478; 2 Allen St; meals $1.50-7; ☟ breakfast & lunch) An Italian bakery with smooth flavoursome coffee, savoury and sweet muffins, stuffed breads, pastry scrolls, cakes, tarts and brownies.

THE AUTHOR'S CHOICE

Cafe L'Affare (Map pp388-9; ☎ 04-385 9748; 27 College St; meals $6-16; ☟ breakfast & lunch, closed Sun) Doing everything right, L'Affare is a massive, atmospheric café with fast service, high communal tables, couches, a disco ball and industrial stage lights. Prominent coffee roasters and suppliers, the café smells of freshly ground Colombian. Sensational toasted baps are a bargain.

Wholly Bagels (Map pp396-7; cnr Willis & Bond Sts; bagels $1.60-8; ☟ lunch) Authentic boiled bagels, sold 'naked', or with a selection of flavoured cream cheeses and filled with the likes of tuna salad and pastrami.

Feedback (Map pp388-9; ☎ 04-385 9000; 87 Kent Tce; meals $5-10; ☟ dinner) 'One step beyond' burgers that satisfy the most deep-seated burger cravings. Buns are filled with traditional or gourmet fillings including steak, lamb, beef, chicken and veggie options such as Mexican chilli bean and chick pea. Terrific.

Hell (Map pp396-7; ☎ 0800 864 355; 14 Bond St; meals $12-14; ☟ dinner) Demon gourmet pizzas are themed after all things evil. Try the seven deadly sins range or the vegetarian 'purgatory'. Attached is Syn bar, which is fun for drinks.

Sushi takeaways (Map pp396-7; ☎ 04-385 0290; 189 Cuba St; meals $5-10; ☟ lunch) Has super-fresh Japanese treats that are cheap and tasty.

Abrakebabra (Map pp396-7; ☎ 04-473 3009; 90 Manners St; meals $6-12; ☟ lunch & dinner) Chicken and lamb kebabs and burgers on thick fluffy bread with a variety of dips, and the all-important baklava finisher. If you love a kebab, this is the place.

For lip-smacking fish and chips check out:

Wellington Trawling Sea Market (Map pp388-9; ☎ 384 8461; 220 Cuba St; meals $5-13; ☟ lunch & dinner) Sells caught-that-morning fish and wonderful fish dinners with chips and salad, and fat burgers.

Fisherman's Plate Seafood (Map pp396-7; ☎ 04-473 8375; 12 Bond St; meals $8-14; ☟ dinner) Eat straight off the butchers' paper at this classic fish 'n' chipper with its tiny 'dining' area – orange plastic swivel chairs, fake pine-wood panelling and a jaunty fish mural. Battered scallops and hand-cut chips are delicious.

Wellington Market (Map pp396-7; Wakefield St; meals $3-12; ☟ 10am-5.30pm Fri-Sun) Excellent Asian choices, including Indian and even Nepalese food. A speciality here is Maori cuisine; you can buy food prepared in a *hangi*.

For food courts, head to **Courtenay Central** (Map pp396-7; Courtenay St; meals $3.50-9; ☟ lunch & dinner), **BNZ Centre** (Map pp396-7; Willis St; meals $4-10; ☟ lunch) and **James Smith Corner** (Map pp396-7; ☎ 04-801 8813; 55 Cuba St; meals $2-9; ☟ lunch).

Self-Catering
New World supermarket (Map pp396-7; City ☎ 04-384 8054; 279 Wakefield St; ☟ 7am-midnight; Thorndon

Map pp388-9; ☎ 04-499 9041; Molesworth St; ⊗ 8am-10pm) has two convenient branches.

For something more gourmet, **Dixon St Deli** (Map pp396-7; ☎ 04-384 2436; 45 Dixon St; meals $4.50-16; ⊗ lunch) is a food shop and café selling its own range of produce.

Commonsense Organics (Map pp396-7; ☎ 04-384 3314; 260 Wakefield St) has a range of organic produce.

DRINKING

Wellingtonians drink, but stylishly, in low-lit bars, or, more boisterously, in Irish and microbrewery pubs. Most places serve bar snacks and/or meals. Courtenay Pl is the nightlife centre of Wellington. Blair and Allen Sts, running off Courtenay Pl, are fertile hunting grounds for booze and music, but here it's moody, upmarket lounge bars – wear your party frock. Cuba St has plenty to keep you entertained and arrive at Edwards St after midnight. (See also Live Music p403 and Nightclubs p403)

Matterhorn (Map pp396-7; ☎ 04-384 3359; 106 Cuba St; brunch $9-19, tapas plate $5, dinner $15-27) In a smart, architecturally designed space with low lighting and polished concrete floors, Matterhorn is way cool. Three bars dispense quality drinks to 20-somethings and its leather-bound menu reveals salty tapas such as smoked eel and warehou. DJs at weekends spin ambient funk. We love the Matterhorn.

Tupelo (Map pp396-7; ☎ 04-384 1152; 6 Edward St; ⊗ Tue-Sat) We all love a back-alley bar and intimate Tupelo, with above-average service, is warm, red and lit by chandeliers. DJs play hip-hop, jazz and housey soul Wednesday through Friday and meals include green-lip mussels in a chive sabayon and whiskey-flamed langoustine.

Lie-low (Map pp388-9; ☎ 04-385 0647; 186 Willis St; ⊗ 8pm-6am Thu-Sat) A groovy late-night opener that is kitsch, bohemian and plays a great range of music in the electroclash genre. Well-mixed cocktails are a treat. Lie-low is lots of fun.

Vespa Lounge (Map pp396-7; ☎ 04-385 2438; 21 Allen St; ⊗ until 6am) A smooth bar with low-hanging red lamps casting a moody glow, red velvet drapes, slate-grey walls a pool table, shiny polished wood bar and a DJ who plays smooth tunes in a funky house vein.

Grand (Map pp396-7; ☎ 04-801 7800; 69 Courtenay Pl; ⊗ until 3am Fri, 5am Sat) An upmarket ground-floor bar that's all chocolate-brown, exposed brick, black ottoman-style lounges and gilt mirrors. There's dancing on level two (Friday and Saturday), pool tables level three and a casino level four.

JJ Murphy & Co (Map pp396-7; ☎ 04-384 9090; 119-123 Cuba St; meals $11-16) A popular bar in Cuba Mall with outdoor tables. It's a great spot to watch sporting events. Inside it's all dark-wood booths and big barrels, with plenty of pool tables. The classic pub menu is Irish themed and there's live music Wednesday to Sunday.

Malthouse (Map pp396-7; ☎ 04-499 4355; 47 Willis St; meals $12-20) A shrine for lovers of naturally brewed beer, from local ales through to fine international drops such as Tuborg and Kronenbourg. Extremely popular with corporate types, there are a couple of big balconies, pool tables and a dining room with posh pub-grub.

Mercury Lounge (Map pp396-7; ☎ 04-384 6737; 1/46 Courtenay Pl) A slick upstairs lounge bar with faux-suede lounges, premium beers and DJs spinning happy house at weekends. Popular with young professionals.

Molly Malone's (Map pp396-7; ☎ 04-384 2896; cnr Courtenay Pl & Taranaki St) This rousing, popular pub has live music nightly. Traditional Irish fare is served upstairs in the **Dubliner** (mains $19-25) whiskey bar and restaurant (with a scary 100 whiskeys to choose from!).

Kitty O'Shea's (Map pp396-7; ☎ 04-384 7392; 28 Courtenay Pl; meals $8-15) Live music every night – catch an open jam session early in the week, some unplugged traditional Irish reels midweek and some amped-up pub rock at weekends. Oh, by the way, it's an Irish pub.

Backbencher (Map pp388-9; ☎ 04-472 3065; cnr Molesworth St & Sydney St East; lunch mains $8.50-14, dinner mains $14-22) Opposite the Beehive is the upmarket Backbencher, which popular with suits, big groups and families. Three-dimensional puppet heads of NZ pollies are mounted, trophy-room style, and there are clever satirical cartoons. Atmosphere is casual, fun and friendly.

Ponderosa (Map pp396-7; ☎ 04-384 1064; 28 Blair St; ⊗ 5pm-6am) An intimate, cowboy-themed cocktail bar with tree-stump tables and DJs spinning funk, house, hip-hop and retro from Thursday to Saturday.

Wellington Sports Café (Map pp396-7; ☎ 04-801 5115; cnr Courtenay Pl & Tory St; meals $12-15) With its big-screen TVs and cheap meals, this is the perfect spot to watch the big games. There's often a DJ when there's no big sporting contest to televise.

Leuven (Map pp388-9; ☎ 04-499 2939; 135 Featherston St) This 'beer café' (their description) is more upmarket than your everyday pub and a great place to sample hearty Belgian cuisine, such as mussels and *frites* (fries), washed down by one of a huge selection of beers.

Juice Bars & Coffee

Ed's Juicebar (Map pp396-7; ☎ 04-478 1769; Bond St; juices $3.50-7, meals $5-10; ⏰ lunch) Tiny Ed's is rude with health and has a substantial selection of pure juices and smoothies such as Floo Fighter and Liver Lover. Soups change daily and at lunch there are hot meals, fresh salads and sandwiches. Produce is locally sourced, organic and GE-free.

Fluid (Map pp396-7; Courtenay Central & Manners Mall; juices & smoothies $3.50-7.50) Rehydrate with a 'berry berry nice smoothie', a booster juice with bee pollen or spirulina, or just a straight-up OJ.

Mojo (Map pp396-7; ☎ 0800 665 626, 04-472 3434; www.mojocoffeecartel.com; 182 Wakefield St; coffee $3) Boutique coffee specialists that make full-bodied brews and also supply coffee beans.

ENTERTAINMENT

Wellington is undisputed king of NZ's nightlife with copious clubs, bars and other insomniac refuges. It also has a vibrant performing arts scene. Purchase tickets from **Ticketek** (☎ 04-384 3840; www.ticketek.com) at Queen Wharf Events Centre, Westpac St James Theatre or the Michael Fowler Centre. For gig guides pick up a copy of the free brochure the *Package*, available at venues, cafés and record shops around town. Entertainment concentrates around Cuba St, Edwards St and Courtenay Pl, where it all starts to go rambunctiously wrong in the early hours of the morning.

Cinemas

Show times for movies are listed in the local newspapers or at http://film.wellington.net .nz. Adult tickets cost around $12, children $6.50, and most cinemas have a cheap day early in the week.

Embassy Theatre (Map pp396-7; ☎ 04-384 7657; www.theembassytheatretrust.org.nz; 10 Kent Tce) Boasting the largest screen in the southern hemi-

sphere, this grand dame underwent major restoration in November 2003. It hosted the world premiere of *LOTR: The Return of the King* and the Australasian premiere of *LOTR: The Two Towers*. At other times it screens mainstream films.

Other cinemas:

Hoyts Regent on Manners (Map pp396-7; ☎ 04-472 5182; http://hoytsnz.ninemsn.com.au/cinema/1MML.asp; 73 Manners St) Screens all the latest Hollywood blockbusters.

Paramount (☎ 04-384 4080; www.paramount.co.nz; 25 Courtenay Pl) Shows mainly arthouse movies; $6 tickets Monday.

Reading Cinemas (Map pp396-7; ☎ 04-801 4600; www.readingcinemas.co.nz; Courtenay Central) Screens mainstream new-release films.

Rialto (Map pp396-7; ☎ 04-385 1864; www.rialto.co.nz; cnr Jervois Quay & Cable St) Screens independent productions.

Live Music

Bodega (Map pp396-7; ☎ 04-384 8212; 101 Ghuznee St; cover charge varies; ⏰ 4pm-3am) Welly's longest-running live music venue, cool Bodega plays music every night from around 10pm. Expect to hear dirty rock, Latin, soul, DJs and reggae-mon. There are over 17 beers on tap and the vibe here is rockin'.

Indigo (Map pp396-7; ☎ 04-801 6797; 171 Cuba St; cover charge varies; ⏰ 4pm-3am Tue-Sun) A live-music haunt with local DJs spinning experimental techno, comedy nights on Tuesday, and live music that prompts parents to say, 'What's this racket?'. It's grungy, with dreadlocked punters smoking Lucky Strikes.

Amba (Map pp396-7; ☎ 04-801 5212; 21 Blair St; cover charge varies; ⏰ 11am-late) A fancy lounge bar and popular live music venue that specialises in jazz but also incorporates styles of swing, funk and dub. On Monday nights there's free mussels at the bar.

Blue Note (Map pp388-9; ☎ 04-801 5007; 191 Cuba St; cover charge varies; ⏰ 8.30am-6am) Punters from all walks of life – gay, straight, transgender – come to the slightly seedy Blue Note to sing; Wednesday, Sunday and Monday are dedicated karaoke nights. There are also open mike nights and jam sessions.

Nightclubs

Studio Nine (Map pp396-7; ☎ 04-384 9976; 9 Edward St) A cool dance club hosting international DJs and with a fab lounge area. This is the place to head for all-night doof – make sure you bring plenty of stamina.

Sandwiches (Map pp396-7; ☎ 04-385 7698; www .sandwiches.co.nz; 8 Kent St; snacks $6, meals $12-30; ⊗ closed Sun&Mon) Funk it up at cool-man-cool Sandwiches, a bar and nightclub with live performances – comedy, jazz, electronica – from Wednesday to Saturday. Platters such as 'Mafia madness', gourmet pizzas and club sandwiches are available.

See also Gay & Lesbian Wellington, p395.

Theatre

The most active place in NZ for live theatre, Wellington's accessible performing-arts scene supports a number of professional and quality amateur companies.

Circa Theatre (Map pp396-7; ☎ 04-801 7992; www .circa.co.nz; 1 Taranaki St; adult/standby $30/16; ⊗ box office 10am-4pm Mon-Fri, performances Tue-Sun) Running for 27 years, Circa's main auditorium seats 250 people, its studio seats 100. Cheap tickets are available for preview shows – the night before opening night – and standby tickets one hour before a show.

Downstage Theatre (Map pp396-7; ☎ 04-801 6946; www.downstage.co.nz; cnr Courtenay Pl & Cambridge Tce; tickets $35-40) A professional theatre company with a strong presence in the Wellington theatre scene, Downstage is NZ's longest-running theatre, reaching 40 years of age in 2003. Its 250-seat auditorium also shows contemporary dance.

BATS Theatre (Map pp396-7; ☎ 04-802 4175; www .bats.co.nz; 1 Kent Tce; adult/concession around $15/12) Alternative, avant-garde theatre, and home of the Fringe. Reduced-price, same-day theatre tickets are available at the visitors centre, subject to availability (tickets are on sale from noon).

Westpac Trust St James Theatre (Map pp396-7; ☎ 04-802 4060; www.stjames.co.nz; 77 Courtenay Pl) A grand old heritage building often used for opera, ballet and major musical shows and major musicians (eg Jack Johnson). It provides a permanent home for the Royal New Zealand Ballet (www.nzballet.org.nz).

Michael Fowler Centre (Map pp396-7; ☎ 04-801 4231; www.wellingtonconventioncentre.com; Wakefield St) A huge centre with 19 venues. It has great acoustics and hosts all sorts of performances, from popular bands to the New Zealand Symphony Orchestra.

SHOPPING

Two publications keeping fashionistas in the loop are *Wellington's Shopping Guide*

(published twice a year) and *Fashion Map* – the guide to NZ and international designers and boutique clothes shops. For second-hand records and books, plus retro clothing and funky off-beat furniture, take a stroll along Cuba St. Shops selling outdoor equipment are found on Mercer St.

Kirkcaldie & Stains (Map pp388-9; ☎ 04-472 5899; www.kirkcaldies.co.nz; 165-177 Lambton Quay) New Z's answer to Bloomingdale's or Harrods, Kirkcaldie & Stains is an upmarket department store that's been running since 1863.

Mainly Tramping (Map pp396-7; ☎ 04-473 5353; 39 Mercer St) For all your specialist outdoor needs, be they tramping, kayaking or mountain climbing. Staff here are knowledgeable and helpful.

GETTING THERE & AWAY
Air

At **Wellington airport** (Map p385; ☎ 04-385 5100; www.wellington-airport.co.nz; PO Box 14 175; ⊗ closed 2-4am) there's an **information desk** (☎ 04-385 5123; 1st fl Main Terminal; ⊗ 7am-7pm) in the check-in hall. There's also a foreign exchange office, ATMs, storage lockers, car-rental desks, cafés and shops. Those in transit or with early flights are not permitted to stay overnight inside the airport. Departure tax on international flights is adult/child $25/10.

Air New Zealand (Map pp388-9; ☎ 0800 737 000; www.airnz.co.nz; cnr Lambton Quay & Grey St) offers direct domestic flights to/from Wellington to most major centres, including Auckland (one way $90 to $280, one hour, hourly), Christchurch (one way $70 to $220, 45 minutes, 12 daily), Dunedin (one way $105 to $300, 1¼ hour, four daily), Rotorua (one way $95 to $250, one hour 10 minutes, four to five daily) and Westport (one way $95 to $260, 55 minutes, one daily Sunday to Friday).

Origin Pacific (☎ 0800 302 302; www.originpacific .co.nz) has daily direct flights to Nelson (one way $95, 35 minutes, five daily), where you can connect to Christchurch.

Qantas (Map pp388-9; ☎ 0800 808 767; www.qantas .co.nz; 2 Hunter St) runs connections to/from Wellington to Auckland (one way $85 to $320, one hour, six daily) and Christchurch (one way $55 to $230, 55 minutes, seven daily).

Soundsair (☎ 0800 505 005, 03-520 3080; www .soundsair.co.nz) runs a service between Wellington and Picton (one way $80, 25 minutes, eight daily). Holders of backpacker and student cards are eligible for discounts.

Boat

On a clear day sailing into Wellington Harbour or navigating the Marlborough Sounds is a truly enjoyable experience. Sailing can be rough in adverse weather but the ferries are large and have lounges, cafés, bars and an information desk (some Interislander ferries even have a movie theatre).

There are three options for crossing the strait between Wellington and Picton on the South Island by boat (note that sailing times are subject to change):

Bluebridge Ferries/Strait Shipping (Map pp388-9; ☎ 0800 844 844, 04-473 1479; www.strait.co.nz; adult/child $40/25) Crossing takes three hours, 20 minutes. Departs Wellington at 3am (except Monday) and 1pm. Returns from Picton at 8am (except Monday) and 7pm. Car or campervan/motorbike/bicycle or surfboard $150/45/10.

Interislander (Map pp388-9; ☎ 0800 802 802, 04-498 3302; www.interislandline.co.nz; adult/child $60/40) Crossing takes three hours. There are roughly nine sailings per day but regular daily services depart Wellington at 1.30am (except Monday), 9.30am, 2pm and 5.30pm; and return from Picton at 5.30am (except Monday), 10am, 1.30pm, 6pm and 9.30pm. For car or campervan/motorbike/bicycle or surfboard you'll pay an extra $220/60/10. Discount fares are often available for advance bookings. Children under two travel free.

Lynx (Map pp388-9; ☎ 0800 802 802, 04-498 3302; www.interislandline.co.nz; adult/child $60/40) Crossing takes 2¼ hours. Departs Wellington at 8am and 3.30pm; returns from Picton at 11.30am and 7pm. There is a faster option for the same price on a high-speed catamaran. For car or campervan/motorbike/bicycle or surfboard you'll pay extra $220/60/10. Children under two travel free.

You can book ferries at your accommodation, by phone, online, at travel agents and directly at individual offices. Interislander services arrive and depart from the Interislander terminal. Lynx and Bluebridge/Strait Shipping services are based at Waterloo Quay, not far from the train station.

A free ferry shuttle-bus service is provided on both sides of the strait. In Wellington it operates between the ferry and train station (where long-distance buses also depart), departing from the train station 35 minutes before each sailing. A shuttle meets all arriving ferries. On the Picton side, a free shuttle runs between the ferry and the Picton-Christchurch *Tranz Coastal*

train. Car-hire companies also pick-up and drop-off at the ferry terminal; if you arrive outside business hours, arrangements can be made to collect your hire vehicle from the terminal car park.

Bus

Wellington is an important junction for bus travel, with buses to Auckland and all major towns in between. **InterCity** (☎ 04-472 5111; www.intercitycoach.co.nz; ⏰ 7am-9pm) and **Newmans** (☎ 04-499 3261; www.newmanscoach.co.nz; ⏰ 7am-9pm) buses depart from Platform 9 at the train station. Tickets are sold at the travel reservations and tickets centre in the train station.

White Star City to City (☎ 04-478 4734) has one to two buses that depart daily from Bunny St, near Downtown Wellington Backpackers, and run along the west coast of the North Island to Palmerston North (one way $20, 2¼ hours), Wanganui (one way $27, three hours 20 minutes) and New Plymouth (one way $45, six hours 20 minutes). Connect at Palmerston North for services to Masterton, Hastings, Napier and Gisborne.

Hitching

It's not easy to hitch out of Wellington – the highways heading out of the city, SH1 and SH2, are motorways for a long distance and hitching is illegal on motorways. The best option is to catch a bus or train to one of the towns on the Kapiti Coast or to Masterton and hitch from there.

Train

Wellington train station has a **travel centre** (☎ 04-498 2058; ⏰ 7.15am-5.30pm Mon-Fri, 7.15am-12.15pm Sat & Sun) that books and sells tickets for trains, buses, ferries, tours and more. Luggage lockers are also available.

Aside from the Tranz Metro (p406) suburban trains that leave from here, two long-distance trains operate between Wellington and Auckland. The daytime *Overlander* (adult $145, 11 hours, departs 8.45am) and the overnight *Northerner* (adult $130, 11 hours, departs 7.50pm) run through the central North Island.

GETTING AROUND
To/From the Airport

The airport is 7km southeast of the city centre.

Super Shuttle (☎ 0800 748 885, 04-387 8787; www.supershuttle.co.nz) provides a door-to-door minibus service at any hour between the city and the airport for $15 to $20.

The **Stagecoach Flyer** (☎ 04-387 8700; www .stagecoach.co.nz; 45 Onepu Rd, Kilbirnie; airport-city $5, StarPass $9) is a local bus running between the airport, Wellington city and Lower Hutt. Buses run from the city to the airport between 5.45am and 7.45pm weekdays, 6.15am to 8.15pm weekends; and from the airport, between 6.20am and 8.20pm weekdays, 6.50am to 8.50pm weekends.

A taxi between the city centre and airport costs $15 to $20.

Bus

Wellington has an efficient local bus system. **Stagecoach** (☎ 04-387 8700; www.stagecoach.co.nz; 45 Onepu Rd, Kilbirnie), has frequent services from 7am to 11.30pm on most routes. Most depart from beside the train station and from the major bus stop on Courtenay Pl at the intersection with Cambridge Terrace. Useful colour-coded bus route maps and timetables are available at the visitors centre.

Bus fares are determined by zones: there are eight zones, and the cheapest fare is $1.50 for rides in zone one, $2 for two zones and up in 50c increments to $5. A Single Daytripper Pass costs $8 and allows unlimited bus travel for one day (excluding the airport bus, After Midnight buses and services to Hutt Valley). An all-day StarPass for $9 allows unlimited rides on all bus services.

The City Circular is the name given to the distinctive bright yellow buses that take in Wellington's prime inner-city locations, making it very handy for travellers wishing to see the major sights. These buses loop the city every 10 minutes and the fare is $2.

The **After Midnight Bus Service** (☎ 04-801 7000) has buses departing from the central entertainment district (Courtenay Pl or Cuba St), at 1am, 2am and 3am Saturday and Sunday on a number of routes to the outer suburbs. The flat fare is $3.50.

Car

Wellington has a number of hire-car operators that will negotiate cheap deals, especially for longer-term rental of a couple of weeks or more, but overall rates aren't as competitive as in Auckland. Rack rates range from around $45 to $110 per day;

cars are usually about two or three years old and in excellent condition. Some of these companies include:

Ace Rental Cars (☎ 0800 525 500, 04-471 1178; fax 04-471 1178; 150 Hutt Rd)
Apex Car Rentals (Map pp396-7; ☎ 0800 300 110, 04-385 2163; www.apexrentals.co.nz; 186 Victoria St)
Omega Rental Cars (☎ 0800 667 722, 04-472 8465; www.omegarentals.com; 92-96 Hutt Rd)
Shoestring Rentals (☎ 0800 746 378, 04-389 2983; www.carhire.co.nz/shoestring; 138 Adelaide Rd)

For details about major car-hire companies, such as Avis and Budget, see the Transport chapter (p689).

If you plan on travelling to both the North and South Islands it's a much cheaper option to return your hire car to either Picton or Wellington and pick up another after crossing the strait. This is a common practice and car-hire companies make it a painless exercise.

There are often cheap deals on car relocation from Wellington to Auckland (most renters travel in the opposite direction) – a few companies offer very cheap rental on this route, with the catch being that you may only have 24 or 48 hours to make the journey.

For those looking to buy or sell a car, there's a **Cable St Car Fair** (☎ 04-499 3322; Cable St; ☻ 9am-noon Sat) in the car park near Te Papa museum. **Turners Auctions** (☎ 0800 282 8466, 04-587 1400; www.turners.co.nz; 120 Hutt Park Rd, Lower Hutt), not far from the camping ground, buys and sells used cars by auction. Also check noticeboards at backpackers for ridiculously cheap deals.

Taxi

Taxi ranks are conveniently placed around town (eg Cambridge Terrace, just near Courtenay Pl; outside Te Papa museum). Taxi companies include **Wellington Combined Taxis** (☎ 04-384 4444) and **Wellington Ace** (☎ 04-388 8100).

Train

Tranz Metro (☎ 04-801 7000; www.tranzmetro.co.nz) operates four suburban electric train routes. Trains run frequently from 6am to midnight, departing from Wellington train station. These routes are: Johnsonville, via Ngaio and Khandallah; Paraparaumu, via Porirua and Paekakariki; Melling, via Petone; and Upper

Hutt, going on to Masterton. Timetables are available from the train station, visitors centre or online.

HUTT VALLEY

pop 130,000

The Hutt River acts as the western boundary for land-starved Wellington's dormitory cities, Lower Hutt and Upper Hutt. Apart from some attractive forest parks for picnics and a few museums, they are fairly suburban. Both cities are easily reached by train or bus from Wellington.

Tourist information can be found at **Lower Hutt visitors information centre** (☎ 04-560 4715; www.huttcity.govt.nz; 10 Andrews Ave; ☺ 9am-5pm Mon-Fri, 10am-4pm Sat & Sun) and **Upper Hutt visitors information centre** (☎ 04-527 2141; www .upperhuttcity.com; 6 Main St; ☺ 9am-5pm Mon-Fri, 10am-4pm Sat & Sun). A useful online resource is www.huttcity.govt.nz.

Sights

Lower Hutt is home to the waterfront **Petone Settlers Museum** (☎ 04-568 8373; The Esplanade; admission by donation; ☺ noon-4pm Tue-Fri, 1-5pm Sat & Sun), with stories of migration and settlement in the area. The **Dowse Art Museum** (☎ 04-570 6500; www.huttcity.govt.nz/council/services /recreation/dowse/; 35 Laings Rd, Lower Hutt; admission free; ☺ 10am-4pm Mon-Fri, 11am-5pm Sat & Sun) is a showcase for NZ art, craft and design.

Maori Treasures (☎ 04-939 9630; www.maori treasures.com; 56-58 Guthrie St; admission by donation, self-guided/one-day tours $13/210; ☺ 9am-4pm), also in Lower Hutt, is a complex of Maori artists and craftspeople that is well worth a visit. There are two tours available – a self-guided tour and a one-day package in conjunction with Te Papa museum, which includes transport and lunch. The tours explain Maori culture and customs and demonstrate Maori arts and crafts (including weaving, wood and bone carving, and stone sculpting).

The drive from Upper Hutt to Waikanae (on the Kapiti Coast) along the scenic Akatarawa road passes the 10-hectare **Staglands Wildlife Reserve** (☎ 04-526 7529; www.staglands.co.nz; adult/child $10/5; ☺ 10am-5pm) where the rare blue duck has been successfully bred. It's 17km from SH2, 20km from SH1.

Days Bay and **Eastbourne** are to the south of the Hutt Valley and make a pleasant

afternoon excursion (see p391). It's a 7km walk or cycle from Burdans Gate at the end of Muritai Rd in Eastbourne to the 1906 **Pencarrow Lighthouse**, the country's first permanent lighthouse.

Rimutaka Forest Park is 45 minutes' drive east of Wellington. Catchpool Valley, 12km south of Wainuiomata, is the most popular entrance to the park and there's a **DOC visitors centre** (☎ 04-564 8551), just off Coast Rd. Further on from the visitors centre is a **camping ground** (adult/child $4/2) in a delightful setting. A shower block and barbecues make it better than the usual DOC camp.

Sleeping

Rates listed here are for two people.

Harcourt Holiday Park (☎ 04-526 7400; www .harcourtholidaypark.co.nz; 45 Akatarawa Rd, Upper Hutt; camp/campervan sites $18/22, cabins & tourist flats $65, units $80) A well-designed, well-maintained park, 35km northeast of Wellington, just off SH2 – from Wellington it's a 30-minute drive. The park is set in native bushland with a river nearby. Facilities aren't as many as Hutt Park, but the location is prettier.

Hutt Park Holiday Village (☎ 0800 488 872, 04-568 5913; www.huttpark.co.nz; 95 Hutt Park Rd, Seaview, Lower Hutt; camp/campervan sites $21/22, cabins $39-70, units/motels $70/90; P ☐) This busy park is 13km southwest of Wellington. Its facilities are excellent with three communal kitchens, Sky TV, trampoline, spa etc but its industrial and inconvenient location detracts. It's a 15-minute drive from the ferry, a five-minute walk from the bus stop (take the Eastbourne bus) or a 20-minute walk from Woburn train station.

KAPITI COAST

With striking, quiet beaches and water that begs to be swum in (depending on your constitution), Kapiti Coast is a summer playground of the city, as well as a suburban extension of Wellington. The region takes its name from large Kapiti Island, a bird and marine sanctuary 5km offshore from Paraparaumu. Tararua Forest Park, in the Tararua Range, forms a stunning backdrop to the coastline along its length and also has some accessible day walks and longer tramps.

A visit to the Kapiti Coast is an easy and popular day trip from Wellington but if you're after a few restful days or are on your way further north, there are some quality accommodation options for stopovers.

Orientation & Information

The Kapiti Coast stretches 30km along the west coast from Paekakariki (45km north of Wellington) to Otaki (71km north of Wellington). Most towns have two settlements – one along the highway and another by the water. Paraparaumu is the most built up town on the coast but still runs at a slow pace, especially by the beach.

The most comprehensive visitors centres are at Otaki (p411) and Paraparaumu (opposite). A useful website for the region is www.kapiti.org.nz. The main **DOC** (☎ 04-296 1112; www.doc.govt.nz; 10 Parata St, Waikanae; ☉ 9am-4.30pm Mon-Fri) for the Kapiti area is at Waikanae but your first port of call should be the visitors information centres.

Getting There & Away

Getting to the west coast from Wellington is a breeze – it's on the major route (SH1) north from Wellington and regular use by commuters means that there are convenient transport options in place. By car, it's about 45 minutes from Wellington to Paraparaumu and an hour to Otaki, much of it by motorway.

For comprehensive timetable information check online at www.gw.govt.nz or call the **Ridewell information service** (☎ 0800 801 700, 04-801 7000; ridewell@gw.govt.nz).

BUS

InterCity (☎ 04-472 5111; www.intercitycoach.co.nz) has buses between Wellington and Palmerston North (one way $27, 2¼ hours, six Monday to Friday and seven Saturday and Sunday), stopping at Paraparaumu (one way $17, 55 minutes) and Otaki (one way $18, 1¼ hour).

White Star City to City (☎ 04-478 4734) and **Bay Express** (☎ 0800 422 997; www.bayxpress.co.nz) also have services to/from the Kapiti Coast.

TRAIN

Tranz Metro (☎ 04-801 7000; www.tranzmetro.co.nz) commuter trains between Wellington and the coast are easier and more frequent than buses. There are services between Wellington and Paraparaumu (one way $8, 55 minutes, half-hourly 5.20am to 11.30pm),

stopping at Paekakariki ($7). Monday to Friday off-peak fares (9am to 3pm) are slightly cheaper.

Tranz Scenic (☎ 0800 872 467, 04-495 0775; www.tranzscenic.co.nz; ☉ 7am-7pm) Long-distance trains between Wellington and Auckland stop at Paraparaumu daily, as does the Monday to Friday, peak-hour *Capital Connection* service between Wellington and Palmerston North (one way $20, two hours 10 minutes, one daily), stopping at Paraparaumu (one way $8, 45 minutes, one daily) and Otaki (one way $12, 1¼ hour, one daily).

PAEKAKARIKI

pop 1690

Paekakariki is a tiny, friendly seaside village spread along a lovely stretch of often-deserted black-sand beach, just two blocks from the train station and the highway. Paekakariki is well within striking distance of Wellington and is a relaxing place to chill out.

Paekakariki's main attraction, the **Fly by Wire** (☎ 0800 359 259; www.flybywire.co.nz) was facing closure at the time of writing. Call to check if it's operating.

About 5km north of Paekakariki at MacKay's Crossing, just off SH1, the **Tramway Museum** (☎ 04-292 8361; Queen Elizabeth Park, MacKay's Crossing; admission free, adult/child/family tram rides $4/2/10; ☉ 11am-5pm 26 Dec–late Jan, 11am-5pm Sat, Sun & public holidays) has restored wooden trams that ran in Wellington until its tram system was shut down in 1964. A 2km track runs from the museum through **Queen Elizabeth Park** and down to the beach.

There are **horse-riding** opportunities in Queen Elizabeth Park – contact **Stables in the Park** (☎ 04-292 8787; rides/lessons from $10/20) for information.

An alternative way to travel between Wellington and Paekakariki is over the scenic Paekakariki Hill Rd. If you're cycling south, it's a steep climb for about 3km and smooth sailing after that.

Sleeping & Eating

There is no mid-range or top-end accommodation in Paekakariki.

Paekakariki Backpackers (☎ 04-902 5967; paekak backpack@paradise.net.nz; 11 Wellington Rd; dm $21, tw & d $50, with bathroom $55) What a place! Set on a steep hill covered with a beautiful garden, dorms have sea and sunset views and there's a spa pool on the lower deck of the garden. It's a small, friendly and homey place and there's free use of boogie boards and bikes.

Paekakariki Holiday Park (☎ 0800 656 699, 04-292 8292; paekakariki.holiday.park@xtra.co.nz; Wellington Rd; camp sites/tourist flats/cabins $20/39/60) A large, well-maintained park with individually hedged sites and views of Kapiti Island. It's roughly 1.6km north of the township in Queen Elizabeth Park, a mere 200m from the beach.

Paekakariki Café (☎ 04-292 8860; 7 Beach Rd; brunch $6-16, dinner $15-26; ☺ breakfast, lunch & dinner Wed-Sun) Cosy café with green-velvet and wrought-iron chairs and an exhibition space. Coffee is strong, and substantial, innovative meals range from quesadillas to udon noodles with miso.

Il Gambero (☎ 04-292 7040; 9 Wellington St; meals around $18; ☺ dinner Wed-Sun) Right next to the backpackers, Il Gambero serves up tasty Italian fare.

Salt-tea-Towers (☎ 04-292 8890; cnr Cecil & Tilley Rds; meals $6-10; ☺ dinner) An excellent fish 'n' chipper with kumara chips, oysters, scallops and burgers.

Paekakariki Hotel/Next Door restaurant (pub meals $6-13, restaurant meals $16-24; ☺ lunch & dinner) Classic country boozer on the highway with pub meals, a bottle shop and greyhounds racing on the TV. Its restaurant is family style with children's meals and a Sunday roast.

PARAPARAUMU
pop 18,900

Relaxing Paraparaumu is the principal town of the Kapiti Coast, forming a suburban satellite of Wellington, which is within commuting distance. The beautiful beach is the coast's most developed, and boat trips to Kapiti Island depart from here (note that you need to book these trips in Wellington, see p394).

The name Paraparaumu is rather a mouthful, so locally it's usually shortened to 'para-par-*am*', a corruption of the original. The correct pronunciation is 'pah-ra-pah-ra-oo-moo'; the name means 'Scraps From an Oven' and is said to have originated when a Maori war party attacked the settlement and found only scraps of food in the oven.

Orientation & Information

Coastlands Shoppingtown (☎ 04-902 9885; Coastlands Parade, SH1), the hub of Paraparaumu's highway settlement, is easily spotted on the main highway, left as you head into town from Wellington. Three kilometres west along Kapiti Rd (just past Coastlands) beautiful Paraparaumu Beach; Seaview Rd is the main road for Paraparaumu's beach settlement. Sleeping and eating options are most atmospheric along the beach.

There is a Bank of New Zealand at Coastlands Shoppingtown.

Moby Dickens' Books (☎ 04-902 6667; 17 Seaview Rd)
Paraparaumu Medical Centre (☎ 04-902 8500, emergency 04-298 2228; 92-94 Kapiti Rd)
Visitors information centre (☎ 04-298 8195; kapiti .information@kcdc.govt.nz; Coastlands Pde, SH1; ☺ 9am-4pm Mon-Sat, 10am-4pm Sun) The small office is slap bang in the middle of the Coastlands Shoppingtown car park.

Sights & Activities

Paraparaumu Beach, with its beachside park, great swimming and other water activities, is the main attraction. **Paraparaumu Beach Golf Club** (☎ 04-902 8200; www.paraparaumubeachgolfclub .co.nz; 376 Kapiti Rd; 9/18 holes $45/90; ☺ 7am-dusk) is ranked as NZ's best golf course, 99th in the world by Golf Magazine in 2003. It has hosted the NZ Golf Open. Visitors are welcome and you can book online.

On SH1, 2km north of Paraparaumu, the **Lindale Centre** (☎ 04-297 0916; www.kapiti.org.nz; ☺ 9am-5pm) is a large tourist complex where you'll find the Lindale Farm Park, with Saturday and Sunday farm shows, farm walks and speciality food shops selling the region's famous cheese, olives, honey and ice cream – definitely worth a taste.

Another kilometre or so north, just off SH1, the **Southward Car Museum** (☎ 04-297 1221; www.southward.org.nz; adult/child $5/2; ☺ 9am-4.30pm) has one of the largest collections of antique and unusual cars in Australasia.

The airport on Kapiti Rd is home to the **Kapiti Aero Club** (☎ 04-902 6536; www.kapitia eroclub.co.nz; flights $100-170), which offers Tiger Moth **aerobatic flights** and **scenic flights** in four-seater planes or helicopters; **Wellington Gliding Club** (☎ 04-297 1341; gliding joy flights $95) also operates from the aero club.

Sleeping

Barnacles Seaside Inn (☎ 04-902 5856; http://bar naclesseasideinn.tripod.com/; 3 Marine Parade; dm/s $20/33, tw & d $60; (P)) Opposite the beachside park and Paraparaumu Beach, Barnacles has sensational YHA accommodation in a 1920s heritage building. Each warm and cosy room is individually decorated with antique dressers and has a sink and heater; some have electric blankets and sea views.

Ocean Motel (☎ 04-902 6424; www.oceanmotel .co.nz; 42-44 Ocean Rd; r $70-110; (P)) There's no view but there's a range of clean, cosy units with Sky TV. Some have cooking facilities and the higher priced ones have a spa. Top value.

Copperfield Seaside Motel (☎ 0800 666 414, 04-902 6414; www.bestwestern.co.nz; 7-13 Seaview Rd; r $90-130; (P)) A clean and comfortable Best Western right next to Cookie's Restaurant. Most motel rooms have a spa.

Elliotts Motor Lodge (☎ 04-902 6070; www.ellio ttsmotorlodge.co.nz; 33 Amohia St, SH1; r $120-150; (P)) On the highway, Elliotts is an excellent option with spic'n'span self-contained studios and apartments, some with views. Heading north, it's just after Kapiti Rd on the left.

Lindale Motor Park (☎ 04-298 8046; www.holiday parks.co.nz/lindale; SH1; camp/campervan sites $20/22, cabins $55) About 2km north of town off SH1, the park is adjacent to the Lindale Centre. It offers sheltered sites and cosy, well-equipped cabins.

Eating & Drinking

Cookie's Restaurant (☎ 04-902 9111; 7-13 Seaview Rd; meals $12-16; ⊙ lunch & dinner) Cookie's is a big family-style restaurant that's popular with the grey-haired set. You'll find most of Paraparaumu here on Thursday night (roast night) and you may even need to book.

Maclean St Fish Supply (☎ 298 5041; Maclean St; meals $7-14; ⊙ lunch & dinner) Battering anything from tinned pineapple to fresh, plump scallops Maclean's does a roaring trade. All meals come wrapped in paper and a serving of the fat, hand-cut chips is essential.

Burger Wisconsin (☎ 04-902 8743; 32 Marine Parade; meals $7-11; ⊙ lunch & dinner) A small chain that whips up traditional burgers and gourmet veggie, chicken and lamb. Wash it down with a milkshake.

Beachcomber Cafe & Bar (☎ 04-902 8966; 24 Marine Parade; meals $7-14; ⊙ breakfast, lunch & dinner) A handy café if you're after a basic cooked breakfast with beach views.

Insomnia Bar & Restaurant (☎ 04-902 6084; 10 Seaview Rd) Perhaps more at home in Welly, Insomnia is a contemporary bar with clean, minimalist design. Give it a try on Friday or Saturday night.

For self-catering, you can pick up supplies at **Four Square** (☎ 04-298 4528; 16 Seaview Rd).

KAPITI ISLAND

About 10km long and 2km wide, Kapiti Island is the coastline's dominant feature. Since 1897 the island has been a protected reserve. It's a special place and many bird species that are now rare or extinct on the mainland still thrive on the island.

Access is limited to 50 people per day and it's essential that you obtain a permit. Book a permit (adult/child $9/4.50) at Wellington's DOC (p387) up to three months in advance. During summer DOC recommends booking up to one month in advance for a weekday visit, two months for a weekend visit. You can also organise permits with the Paraparaumu visitors centre (p409) but you must give them at least a days' notice.

Transport, which is booked separately, runs to/from Paraparaumu Beach daily and takes around 15 minutes each way (phone the local number in the morning to confirm weather and departure time):

Kapiti Marine Charter (☎ 0800 433 779, 04-297 2585; www.kapitimarinecharter.co.nz; 5 Knight Ave, Paraparaumu; adult/child/child under 5 $30/20/free, guided walks $10; ⊙ tours depart 9am or 9.30am, return 3pm or 4pm) Can arrange for a local shuttle from Wellington.

Kapiti Tours (☎ 0800 527 484, 04-237 7965; www.kapiti tours.co.nz; PO Box 50-079, Porirua; adult/child return transport $30/20, guided walks $10/free; ⊙ tours depart/ return 9am/3pm)

WAIKANAE
pop 9340

About 5km north of Paraparaumu at tiny Waikanae the **Nga Manu Nature Reserve** (☎ 04-293 4131; www.ngamanu.co.nz; Ngarara Rd; adult/child/family $7.50/3.50/15; ⊙ 10am-5pm) is a great 15-hectare bird sanctuary featuring picnic areas, bushwalks and a nocturnal house with kiwi, owls and tuatara, eel feeding and guided tours. To reach it, turn seawards from SH1 onto Te Moana Rd and then right down Ngarara Rd; follow the signs; the sanctuary is several kilometres from the turn-off.

OTAKI
pop 5600

Otaki is primarily a gateway to the Tararua Range. It has a strong Maori history and influence: the little town has nine *marae* and a Maori college. The historic Rangiatea Church, built under the guidance of Ngati Toa chief Te Rauparaha nearly 150 years ago, was tragically burnt to the ground in 1995 but there are plans for reconstruction. This was the original burial site of Te Rauparaha.

Orientation & Information

Most services, including the train station where buses stop, are on SH1. The main centre of Otaki, with the post office and other shops, is 2km seawards on Tasman Rd. Three kilometres further on the same road brings you to Otaki's windswept beach. Note that the telephone area code in Otaki is ☎ 06, not ☎ 04 like the rest of the Kapiti region. The **Visitors information centre** (☎ 06-364 7620; kapiti.information@kcdc.govt.nz; Centennial Park, 239 SH1; ☺ 8.30am-5pm Mon-Fri, 9am-4pm Sat & Sun) is just south of the main roundabout.

Activities

Two kilometres south of Otaki, scenic Otaki Gorge Rd heads inland from SH1 and leads 19km (5km unsealed) to **Otaki Forks**, the main western entrance to **Tararua Forest Park**. Otaki Forks has picnic, swimming and camping areas (adult/child $4/2), and there are bushwalks from 30 minutes to 3½ hours in the immediate area; longer tracks lead to huts. The visitors information centre sells detailed maps and knowledgeable staff can give information and advice about the walks. Ask at the DOC at Waikanae (p408) or Wellington (p387) for advice on longer tracks in the park – you can walk across the Tararua Range, but must bring adequate clothing and be well equipped and prepared for adverse weather. Be sure to sign the intentions book.

Sleeping & Eating

Otaki Oasis Backpackers (☎ 06-364 6860; www .otakioasis.co.nz; 33 Rahui Rd; dm $21, d $50-60) The Oasis is a friendly organic hobby farm on the inland side of the railway tracks. There is a small but adequate backpackers lodge next to the house and there's a chlorine-free spa. Horse-riding lessons and treks are also available here.

Byron's Resort (☎ 0800 800 122, 06-364 8121; www.byronsresort.co.nz; 20 Tasman Rd; camp/campervan sites $20/22, tourist flats $60-70, motel r $75-100, cottage

$110-140, meals $12-18; ☑) An older-style resort by the beach, it has the licensed Byron Brown's restaurant (head here for dinner), a pool, spa, sauna, gym, tennis court and playgrounds. There's also a self-contained cottage, separate from the resort and right on the beach.

Cottage Park (☎ 06-364-6228; www.aaguides.co.nz; 272 SH1; camp sites $22, studios $65, d $98-110; ☑) Clean and comfortable self-contained cottages with Sky TV, studios without cooking facilities, and sites for campervans. There's also an indoor pool.

Te Horo Lodge (☎ 0800 483 467, 06-364 3393; www.tehorolodge.co.nz; 109 Arcus Rd; r $190-220; ☑) For a touch of luxury, this secluded lodge in Te Horo, halfway between Otaki and Waikanae (head inland from SH1 on School Rd), has a great guest lounge with an impressive stone fireplace, plus pool, spa and lovely gardens.

Brown Sugar Cafe (☎ 06-388 1880; SH1; meals $6-12; ☺ breakfast & lunch) Just south of the township, Brown Sugar serves up great coffee, sandwiches and light meals that you can enjoy in its pretty courtyard garden.

THE WAIRARAPA

The large region east and northeast of Wellington is known as the Wairarapa, named after Lake Wairarapa (Shimmering Waters), a shallow but vast 8000-hectare lake.

This region is principally a sheep-raising district – it boasts three million sheep within a 16km radius of Masterton, the region's main town. It also features the Mt Bruce National Wildlife Centre, wineries at Martinborough and tramping tracks and camping areas in regional and forest parks. The Wairarapa region, particularly around Martinborough, is popular with weekending Wellingtonians.

The route through the Wairarapa, along SH2, is a mountainous, pleasant alternative to busy SH1 on the west coast. Budget accommodation is thin on the ground.

See www.wairarapanz.com for info about the region. Note that the telephone area code over here on the east coast is ☎ 06, not ☎ 04 like the rest of the Wellington region.

Getting There & Away

From Wellington, the **Tranz Metro** (☎ 04-801 7000; www.tranzmetro.co.nz) train to Masterton (one way $15, 1½ hours, five to six week-days and two at weekends). Also from Wellington, Hammond's City Tours (p394) runs full-day Wairarapa experience tours.

Tranzit Coachlines (☎ 0800 471 227, 06-377 1227; www.tranzit.co.nz; Queen St, Masterton; ☺ 8am-5pm) has a bus between Masterton and Palmerston North (one way $18, 1½ hours, one daily), plus a few daily services between Featherston and Masterton via Greytown and Carterton. **Wairarapa Coach Lines** (☎ 0800 666 355, 06-308 9352; www.yellowpages.co.nz/for/waicoach) operates a weekday bus between Masterton and Martinborough (one way $5, one hour, one Monday to Friday).

MASTERTON
pop 19,900

The main town of the Wairarapa is Masterton but Martinborough is a more pleasant option to use as a base for the region. Masterton's main claim to fame is the international Golden Shears competition held annually during the first week of March, in which sheep shearing is raised to the level of sport and art.

State Highway 2 runs through the centre of town. From the south SH2 is named High St, which is then named Chapel St. Queen St, to the east, is parallel to High/Chapel St and Queen Elizabeth Park is just before the river on Queen St, heading north.

Masterton visitors centre (☎ 06-377 7577; www.wairarapa.co.nz/tourism/masterton.html; 316 Queen St; ☺ 9am-5pm Mon-Fri, 10am-4pm Sat & Sun) is the main tourist information for Wairarapa.

The 32-hectare **Queen Elizabeth Park** has sports grounds, an aviary, aquarium, a small lake, minigolf, children's playgrounds and a miniature railway. Opposite the park is the well-designed **Aratoi Art & History Museum** (☎ 06-370 0001; www.aratoi.co.nz; cnr Bruce & Dixon Sts; admission free; ☺ 10am-4.30pm), an interesting museum and gallery displaying the art and cultural heritage of the region.

Sleeping, Eating & Drinking

Empire Lodge (☎ 06-377 1902; empirelodge@xtra.co.nz; 94 Queen St; dm $20-30, s $25-55, d $40-70, f $75-110) A budget hotel and backpackers with a communal kitchen, TV room and views of the Tararua Range from the outdoor balcony with a barbecue. Rooms have plenty of natural light and some have an en suite and TV.

Mid-range motels line the highway, particularly in the southern part of town.

Discovery Motor Lodge (☎ 06-378 7745; www.discovery.co.nz; 210 Chapel St; r $105-185; ☒) Discovery has clean and modern studio and two-bedroom units, and a swimming pool. It's a good option.

Cornwall Park Motel (☎ 06-378 2939; www.nzmotels.co.nz/cornwall; 119 Cornwall St; units $75-100; ☒) Roughly three minutes drive from the city centre the motel is known as 'the quiet one'. Units have a CD player and Sky TV, and there's a children's play area and a pool.

Mawley Park Motor Camp (☎ 06-378 6454; jclarke@contact.net.nz; 15 Oxford St; camp/campervan sites $18/20, cabins $27-38) Arrowed off SH2 in the northern part of town is this friendly riverside place with leafy, shaded sites, clean cabins and decent facilities.

Café Strada (☎ 06-378 8450; Queen St; meals $6.60-19; ☺ breakfast, lunch & dinner) Serves gluten- and wheat-free food and has a great vegetarian selection such as sheep-fetta tortellini, soups and rich chocolate brownies.

Café Cafe Char Char (☎ 06-378 8504; cnr Dixon & Bruce Sts; meals $7-11; ☺ lunch) An excellent lunch spot with salads, *paninis* (focaccias) and pasta.

Slug & Lettuce (☎ 06-377 3087; 94 Queen St; meals $10-14) An English-style pub and restaurant that's great for an ale and a reasonably priced counter meal.

MT BRUCE

The **Mt Bruce National Wildlife Centre** (☎ 06-375 8004; www.mtbruce.doc.govt.nz; adult/child $8/free; ☺ 9am-4.30pm), 30km north of Masterton on SH2, is an important sanctuary for native NZ wildlife, mostly birds. Large aviaries and outdoor reserves have some of the country's rarest and most endangered species, as well as more common species. There's an impressive nocturnal house with kiwi (sightings aren't guaranteed), tuatara and other endangered reptiles. You can feed eels at 1.30pm and there are four guided tours daily. Tranzit Coachlines runs buses between Masterton and Palmerston North that can pick up and drop off here (one way $9).

GREYTOWN

A number of rural communities line SH2, each with a minor attraction or two and varying degrees of appeal. Greytown is the pick of them, for its architecture and the high quality of its cafés and restaurants.

Greytown was the country's first planned inland town and intact examples of Victorian architecture line the main street. The quaint **Cobblestones Village Museum** (☎ 06-304 9687; 169 Main St; www.cobblestones.org.nz/look.htm; adult/child $2.50/1; ☺ 9am-4.30pm) is an early settlers museum.

Greytown Hotel (☎ 06-304 9138; 33 Main St; www.greytown-hotel.co.nz; s/d $45/70, meals $16-28; ☺ lunch & dinner) is purported to be the oldest pub in NZ. It's a great old-fashioned place to stay – classic pub rooms with shared facilities are comfortable, each with a TV and sink; and there's a cooked breakfast in the morning. The Victorian-decorated dining room serves tasty meals – Sunday is roast night ($13) – and there's a pub menu. There's live music Friday or Saturday night.

White Swan (☎ 06-304 8894; www.thewhiteswan .co.nz; Main St; r $155-255, mains $19-27) is painted in fresh summer pastels – blue, cream and apple green – and is easily the most elegant boutique accommodation in the region. Each room is individually, and sumptuously, decorated. It's worth popping in for a drink or meal, so sit on the breezy veranda and soak up the old-fashioned ambience.

Oak Estate (☎ 06-304 8187; oak.estate@xtra.co.nz; cnr SH2 & Hospital St; units $100-120) has stylish self-contained units and there's a basic **camping ground** (☎ /fax 06-304 9837; Kuratawhiti St; camp/campervan sites $16/14) scenically located in the park.

Main St Cafe (☎ 06-304 9022; 88 Main St; meals $6-12) serves excellent café fare, and there's an adjacent deli. **Salute!** (☎ 06-304 9825; 83 Main St; pizzas $16-25), opposite, has great gourmet pizzas and Mediterranean-inspired meals.

MARTINBOROUGH
pop 1500

Martinborough, with its many vineyard, is a prime 'mini-break' destination and the centre for tourism in the Wairarapa. At weekends, Gucci replaces gumboots as gourmands dine in the excellent restaurants, sniff the pinot, and lap up the luxurious boutique accommodation. Martinborough is 'simply delightful'.

Martinborough is famous for its **Toast Martinborough Wine, Food & Music Festival** (p395), during which winemakers save vintages to be tasted specifically for the festival and

around 8,500L of wine is consumed over the day. Around 30 small **wineries** are near the town and are detailed in the free *Martinborough & Wairarapa Wine Trails* brochure and map. The region produces around 3% of NZ's grapes but is particularly known for its pinot noir and sauvignon blanc.

Orientation & Information
Martinborough is south of Greytown, off SH2. Kitchener St is the main drag of this tiny village.

Martinborough visitors centre (☎ 06-306 9043; www.wairarapanz.com; 18 Kitchener St; ☺ 9am-5pm Mon-Fri, 10am-4pm Sat & Sun)

Activities
You can sample many wines under one gabled roof at the **Martinborough Wine Centre** (☎ 06-306 9040; www.martinboroughwinecentre.co.nz; 6 Kitchener St), which is also a food shop selling local produce and cookbooks. Its **Village Café** (meals $3-12; ☺ lunch) serves light meals and wine by the glass. A local growers market is held here every Sunday.

Patuna Farm Adventures (☎ 06-306 9966; www .patunafarm.co.nz; horse trek $30-45, pole-to-pole $15-60, chasm walkway $15) offers interesting horse treks, the challenging pole-to-pole rope course, golf cross, and a four-hour walk through native bush and a limestone gorge around the impressive Patuna Chasm Walkway.

Tours
Wet n' Wild (☎ 06-306 8252; www.wetnwild.co.nz; 3 Kitchener St; kayaking/jetboat/vineyard/tours per person $45/55/60/290) offers jetboat tours, kayaking and trout fishing trips, with all gear supplied. It also has combination Martinborough experience tours.

Sleeping
The visitors centre has a long list of B&Bs, farmstays and self-contained cottages in the area, and will book them for you. Cottages, in keeping with the weekend getaway theme, are available in town and the surrounding area, costing from around $90 to $200 per double.

Claremont Motel (☎ 06-306 9162; www.claremont -motels.co.nz; 38 Regent St; s $90-100, d $125-140, f $140-180) In a pretty, peaceful setting off Jellicoe St, the Claremont has clean, two-storey units. Rates are cheaper during the week.

Martinborough Motel (☎/fax 06-306 9048; 43 Strasbourg St; units $70-85) A basic but comfortable motel with studio units.

Margrain Vineyard Villas (☎ 06-306 9292; www .margrainvineyard.co.nz; cnr Ponatahi & Huangarua Rds; villas around $170) If you fancy staying on a vineyard, check out the spacious, modern villas on Margrain Vineyard. Extras include continental breakfast provisions in the fridge, plus views from the balcony.

Martinborough Hotel (☎ 06-306 9350; www.martin boroughhotel.co.nz; the Square; r with breakfast $250-300, meals $22-35) A grand old hotel on the main square that has been magnificently restored and is now home to 16 spacious and luxurious rooms, each individually decorated with style and flair. All open onto a wide veranda or pretty courtyard garden. Downstairs the lively Settlers Bar serves posh pub grub, such as pork and sage sausages, and the elegant Dining Room has an innovative menu and terrific wine list.

Eating & Drinking

Eating and drinking is what Martinborough's all about with award-winning restaurants and gourmet cafés, delicatessens and food shops. The unmissable Martinborough Hotel (see Sleeping) is the best place for a drink.

Ma Maison (☎ 06-306 8388; Jellicoe St; meals around $75) Ma Maison, a country cottage 4km south of town, is only open Saturday evening for dinner, and it specialises in a nine-course French degustation (tasting) menu. Bookings are essential.

Cafe Medici (☎ 06-306 9965; 9 Kitchener St; meals $5-10) This cosy and inviting café is a great spot for coffee and cake or a simple lunch of soup with homemade bread, salad, calzone or nachos.

Flying Fish Cafe (☎ 06-306 9270; the Square; meals $6-16) There's something for everyone here, from the all-day brunch to pizza and burgers (traditional and gourmet), plus lunch and dinner items from a changing blackboard menu.

WAIRARAPA COAST

The Wairarapa Coast from Palliser Bay to Castlepoint is one of the most remote and intriguing coasts in the North Island. The road to Cape Palliser is very scenic, hemmed in by the sea and the mountains of the Aorangi Range. It also offers grand views across

to the South Island, a spectacular sight in winter when the far-off hills are cloaked in snow. On the way, you pass the Wairarapa Wetlands and the Spit at Onoke – both good bird-watching sites. The coast is also the best place around Wellington for surfing.

The **Putangirua Pinnacles**, formed by rain washing silt and sand away and exposing the underlying bedrock, stand like giant organ pipes. Accessible by a track near the car park on Cape Palliser road, it's a one-hour return walk along a stream bed to the pinnacles, or take the three-hour loop track, which takes in the hills and coastal views.

Not far to the south is the archetypal fishing village of **Ngawi**. The first thing you'll notice is the old bulldozers pulling the fishing boats ashore. Continue on to the Cape Palliser **seal colony**, the North Island's largest breeding area. Whatever you do in your quest for a good photo, don't get between the seals and the sea. If you block off their escape route they're likely to have a go at you!

There are 250 steps up to the Cape Palliser **lighthouse**, from where there are even more breathtaking views of the South Island on a clear day.

Castlepoint, 68km from Masterton, with its reef and the lofty 162m-high Castle Rock, is an awesome place, with protected swimming and plenty of walking tracks. There is an easy 30-minute return walk across the reef to the lighthouse; over 70 species of fossil shells are in the rock. Another one-hour walk goes to a huge limestone cave (take a torch), or take the 1½-hour track from Deliverance Cove to Castle Rock. Keep well away from the lower reef when there are heavy seas; many lives have been lost here.

FOREST PARKS

Good opportunities for tramping in the Wairarapa are available in the Tararua, Rimutaka and Haurangi Forest Parks. There are some fine coastal walks, too. Maps and information are available from the DOC offices in Wellington (p387) and Masterton (p412).

A favourite tramping spot is **Holdsworth**, at the main eastern entrance to the Tararua Forest Park, where mountain streams run through beautiful virgin forest. The park entrance has swimming, picnic and camping areas (adult/child $4/2), and fine walks including: short, easy family walks;

excellent one- or two-day walks; and longer, challenging treks for the experienced, as far as the west coast, near Otaki. The resident **conservation officer** (☎ 06-377 0022) has maps and information about the area, and an intentions book. Ask about the current weather and track conditions before setting off, and come prepared for all types of weather – the Tararua Forest Park has a notoriously changeable climate. The turn-off to Holdsworth is just south of Masterton on SH2; from there it's about 15km to the park entrance.

Closer to Wellington, the 18km **Rimutaka Incline** offers a day walk or a few hours' cycle along the railway line that carried trains between Wellington and the Wairarapa between 1878 and 1955. One end is accessed 10km south of Featherston along Western Lake Rd, the other is on SH2 at Kaitoke, 9km north of Upper Hutt. Take a torch.

The **Kaitoke Regional Park**, 16km north of Upper Hutt on SH2, is good for swimming, rafting, camping, picnicking and walking; it has walks ranging from 20 minutes to six hours long.

Marlborough & Nelson

CONTENTS

Marlborough Region	**418**
Picton	420
Marlborough Sounds	425
Havelock	429
Blenheim	430
Renwick	435
Kaikoura	435
Nelson Region	**442**
Nelson	442
Nelson Lakes National Park	450
Nelson to Motueka	452
Motueka	452
Motueka to Abel Tasman	455
Abel Tasman National Park	456
Golden Bay	**459**
Sh60 to Takaka	459
Takaka	460
Pohara	461
Collingwood & Around	462
Kahurangi National Park	463

Crossing Cook Strait from the North Island to the South Island is an exciting prospect – a bit like entering a new country, but one where everyone still says 'fush and chups' and takes 'wee Tiki tours'. New Zealand's South Island is less populated than the North and runs at a slower pace; the Maori influence is also less apparent. Both islands have similar landscapes, but the South is more mountainous, bisected by the strikingly beautiful Southern Alps.

The massive ferries that make the sailing from Wellington to Picton carry more than just tourists and locals and it's how the respective islands receive many of their supplies. Cargo trains are shunted onto the ferries (not carriages, full-length trains) and chug away happily at the other end. Many new cars are also transported this way.

During the crossing it may feel like you're heading south but Wellington city is actually south of the sleepy port of Picton, so you're really moving east to west.

Gliding slowly past the scenic bays and inlets of Marlborough Sounds is a marvellous spectacle. In Marlborough, you'll find the incredibly popular Queen Charlotte Track, famous wineries around Blenheim, and the beautiful beach town of Kaikoura.

In the Nelson region there are some of the best tramping and kayaking possibilities in the country. Nelson itself is a relaxing city with a thriving arts community, as is nearby Motueka. Around Golden Bay, there's the mellow, alternative town of Takaka and the remote and haunting beauty of Farewell Spit.

HIGHLIGHTS

- Swimming with **seals** (p438) in the Pacific Ocean or seeing aerial views of **killer whales** (p438) in Kaikoura
- Wending your way, by bicycle, through the **Marlborough wine region** (p432) for a tipple of pinot and a gourmet feast
- Rejuvenating mind and body with lungfuls of mountain air at **Kahurangi National Park** (p463)
- Luxuriating in a romantic boutique hideaway in an inlet at **Marlborough Sounds** (p425)
- Experiencing the lush wilderness of **Abel Tasman National Park** (p458) by kayak
- Inspiring your creativity with contemporary art and design at Nelson's **Wonderful World of Wearable Art & Collectable Cars Museum** (p445)
- Discovering a colony of Australasian gannets on the remote **Farewell Spit** (p462)

★Farewell Spit · ★Abel Tasman National Park · Marlborough Sounds★ · Kahurangi National Park★ · ★Nelson · ★Marlborough Wine Region · ★Kaikoura

 TELEPHONE CODE: 03 · www.destinationmarlborough.com · www.nelsonnz.com

Climate
The forecast is good: both Marlborough and Nelson experience some of the sunniest weather in New Zealand, especially around the Nelson–Motueka area and Blenheim (around 2400 hours of NZ sunshine per year). Around Takaka, the climate is subtropical.

January and February are the warmest months, with temperatures averaging 22°C; July is the coldest month averaging 12°C.

The rainfall west of Motueka averages 2000mm to 3000mm annually whereas Nelson's average rainfall is 986mm. It's also windier on the west coast, especially at the incredibly exposed Farewell Spit.

Northwest of Nelson and around the Takaka region, there is a karst landscape, which manifests as limestone outcrops, underground streams and gorges.

Getting There & Away
Picton is the main starting point for explorations around the South Island as it's the entry and exit point for ferries crossing the Cook Strait. Three ferry companies – Bluebridge Ferries/Strait Shipping, Interislander and Lynx – make the crossing. From Picton you can pretty much connect to anywhere in the South Island.

Soundsair is a local airline that runs a service between Picton and Wellington and Air New Zealand has domestic flights between and around the two islands. Origin Pacific, based in Nelson, has flights to major destinations.

InterCity is the major bus line, servicing most destinations but there are also local services and a profusion of shuttle buses. K Bus runs buses to/from Picton to the Heaphy Track, servicing the top of the South Island; East Coast Express, runs to/from Picton to Christchurch, via Blenheim and Kaikoura; South Island Connections has buses to/from Picton to Christchurch and Dunedin, with links to Nelson and Motueka; Atomic Shuttles runs to/from Picton and Nelson to Greymouth (via Nelson Lakes) and Christchurch, and to/from Nelson to Fox Glacier; Southern Link which runs to/from Nelson to Christchurch; and Abel Tasman Coachlines and Golden Bay Coachlines, which both provide services to/from Nelson to the Heaphy track.

Renting a car is incredibly easy and there are a host of car-hire companies at Picton

ferry terminal. It's cheaper to pick up a different car at each island – car-hire companies are used to this and make it an easy and painless process.

TranzScenic has a TranzCoastal train that takes the scenic route from Picton to Christchurch, via Blenheim and Kaikoura.

Getting Around
Driving is the most flexible way to get around the South Island, but there are also plenty of bus links (see Getting There & Away, previously).

Boat is the best way to navigate Marlborough Sounds and explore Queen Charlotte Track. There are no scheduled buses that service the Sounds, apart from the mail run (p420) but numbers are limited on this service and it's a long trip. You can also take a water taxi to various points around the Sounds, or take a sea kayaking tour.

There is a variety of options for accessing and exploring Abel Tasman National Park and the Abel Tasman Coastal Track: guided tours, sea shuttles, water taxis, sea kayaking – you can even take a helicopter.

A popular way to explore the wineries near Blenheim is by bicycle (p435). There are also plenty of tours (p433) if you plan on some serious tasting.

Nelson Lakes Shuttles has a service from St Arnaud to the lakes.

MARLBOROUGH REGION

The convoluted, sheltered waterways of the Marlborough Sounds are the first sight of the South Island for many visitors. Picton is the gateway to the island and a prime spot for walking, fishing, sailing, kayaking and exploring the many hideaways in the Marlborough Sounds. A short drive to the south of Picton is Blenheim and the Marlborough wine region.

History
The first European to visit the Marlborough district was Abel Tasman, who sheltered on the east coast of D'Urville Island in 1642. It was more than 100 years before James Cook arrived in January 1770. Cook named Queen Charlotte's (now Charlotte) Sound. Cook's detailed reports made the area the best-known haven in the southern hemisphere.

MARLBOROUGH & NELSON

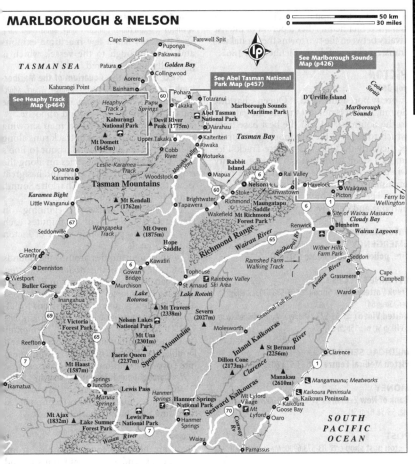

In 1827 French navigator Jules Dumont d'Urville discovered the narrow strait now known as French Pass. His officers named the island just to the north in his honour.

In the same year a whaling station was set up at Te Awaiti in Tory Channel, which brought about the first permanent European settlement in the district. In June 1840 Major Bunbury arrived on HMS *Herald* on the hunt for Maori signatures to the Treaty of Waitangi.

Not long after this, the Nelson settlers came into conflict with Maori tribes over ownership of part of the Wairau Plain, which led to the infamous Wairau Massacre (p422). One of the chiefs involved in the conflict, Te Rauparaha, was indirectly a major reason

for the British government taking control of New Zealand. He enlisted captains and crews of visiting whaling ships and set out on the horrific slaughter of other tribes. In his most gruesome raid he was aided by a Pakeha trader, who transported his warriors and then lured the opposing chiefs on board, who were attacked by Te Rauparaha's men, virtually wiping out the local tribe. When news reached Sydney, the British government finally decided to bring order to the unruly British citizens.

In March 1847 Wairau was finally bought and added to the Nelson territory. Settlers petitioned for independence and the colonial government established the region of Marlborough. Waitohi (now Picton) was approved as the capital and 'The Beaver' was renamed Blenheim. After a period of intense rivalry between the two towns the capital was transferred peacefully to Blenheim in 1865.

PICTON
pop 3600

A pretty port at the head of Queen Charlotte Sound, Picton is not just the marine gateway to the South Island, but the best base from which to explore the Marlborough Sounds, particularly the Queen Charlotte Track. Picton is a small town that is a hive of activity when the ferry docks and during the peak of summer, but slow and sleepy any other time. The town is built around an enclosed harbour and deep-water port.

Information
EMERGENCY
Fire, police and ambulance (☎ 111)

INTERNET ACCESS
Creek Pottery & Gift Shop (☎ 03-573 6313; 26 High St; per 15min $4)
United Video (☎ 03-573 7466; www.unitedvideo.co.nz; 63 High St; per 15min $3)

MEDICAL SERVICES
Picton Medical Centre (☎ 03-573 6092; 71 High St)

MONEY
Bank of New Zealand (☎ 0800 240 000; www.bnz.co .nz; 55-58 High St)

POST
Picton post shop (☎ 03-573 6900; Mariners Mall, 72 High St)

TOURIST INFORMATION
Automobile Association agent (AA; ☎ 03-573 6784; www.aaamarlinmotel.com; 33 Devon St; ⏰ 9am-6pm) Marlin Motel is the AA agent.
Picton visitors centre (☎ 03-520 3133; Foreshore; www.destinationmarlborough.com; ⏰ 8.30am-5pm) Pick up maps and information on walking in the Sounds area. The DOC counter here is staffed during summer.

Sights & Activities
The *Edwin Fox* is purportedly the ninth-oldest ship in the world. Built of teak in Bengal, the 48m, 760-ton vessel was launched in 1853. During its long and varied career it carried convicts to Perth (Australia), troops to the Crimean War and immigrants to NZ.

The **Edwin Fox Maritime Centre** (☎ 03-573 6868; edwinfoxsoc@xtra.co.nz; Dunbar Wharf; adult/child $5/1; ⏰ 8.45am-5pm) has a few maritime exhibits and leads through to the vessel, which is gradually being restored.

Next door is the **Aquarium of the Marlborough Sounds** (☎ 03-573 6030; Dunbar Wharf; adult/ child/family $8/5/20; ⏰ 9am-5pm) is a hit with the kids and there's a playground opposite.

The visitors centre has a map showing several walks. An easy 1km track runs along the eastern side of Picton Harbour to Bob's Bay. The **Snout Walkway** carries on along the ridge from the Bob's Bay path and has great views the length of Queen Charlotte Sound. Allow three hours for the walk.

The **Tirohanga Walkway**, beginning on Newgate St, takes about 45 minutes each way and offers panoramic views of Picton and the Sounds.

Diving opportunities around the Sounds include the wreck of the *Mikhail Lermontov*, a Russian cruise ship that sank in Port Gore in 1986. It's said to be the world's biggest diveable cruise shipwreck. **Diver's World** (☎ 03-573 7323; www.pictondiversworld.co.nz; London Quay; dives $90-190) has dives on *Mikhail Lermontov* (bookings essential) and to Karaka Point and Double Bay. It offers night dives, equipment hire (two-dive minimum) and courses.

Marlborough Sounds Adventure Company (☎ 03-573 6078; www.marlboroughsounds.co.nz; Waterfront; bikes per day $40) hires mountain bikes recommended for riding the Queen Charlotte Track.

Tours
There are heaps of tours to choose from, mostly cruise and walk combinations around Queen Charlotte Sound. See p427 for details about sea kayaking beside the Queen Charlotte Track.

Beachcomber Fun Cruises (☎ 0800 624 526, 03-573 6175; www.beachcombercruises.co.nz; Town Wharf; Magic Mail Run Queen Charlotte Sound/Pelorus mail run $65/95, cruises $45-55; ⏰ Magic Mail Run Queen Charlotte Sound Mon-Sat, Pelorus mail run Tue, Thu & Fri) Two-hour and four-hour cruise/walk options. Also offers full-day mail run boat cruises on Queen Charlotte and Pelorus Sounds, which are genuine NZ Post rural delivery-services.

Cougar Line (☎ 0800 504 090, 03-573 7925; www.co ugarlinecruises.co.nz; Town Wharf; cruises $55-65) Offers short cruises, cruise/walk deals and a twilight cruise from mid-December to February.

Dolphin Watch Marlborough (☎ 03-573 8040; www.dolphinwatchmarlborough.co.nz; ecotours $35-70,

PICTON

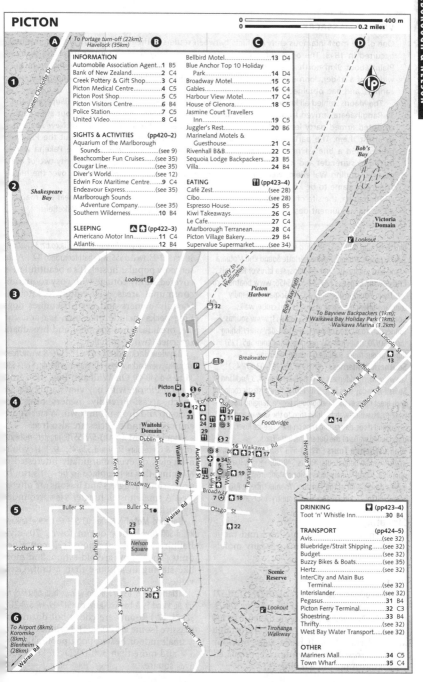

0 ————————— 400 m
0 ————————— 0.2 miles

INFORMATION
Automobile Association Agent...**1** B5
Bank of New Zealand...............**2** C4
Creek Pottery & Gift Shop...**3** C4
Picton Medical Centre.............**4** C5
Picton Post Shop......................**5** C5
Picton Visitors Centre.............**6** B4
Police Station............................**7** C5
United Video..............................**8** C4

SIGHTS & ACTIVITIES (pp420–2)
Aquarium of the Marlborough
    Sounds.............................(see 9)
Beachcomber Fun Cruises......(see 35)
Cougar Line............................(see 35)
Diver's World.........................(see 12)
Edwin Fox Maritime Centre......**9** C4
Endeavour Express.................(see 35)
Marlborough Sounds
    Adventure Company.........(see 35)
Southern Wilderness...............**10** B4

SLEEPING (pp422–3)
Americano Motor Inn.............**11** C4
Atlantis....................................**12** B4

Bellbird Motel.........................**13** D4
Blue Anchor Top 10 Holiday
    Park...................................**14** D4
Broadway Motel......................**15** C5
Gables.....................................**16** C4
Harbour View Motel...............**17** C4
House of Glenora....................**18** C5
Jasmine Court Travellers
    Inn.....................................**19** C5
Juggler's Rest..........................**20** B6
Marineland Motels &
    Guesthouse.......................**21** C4
Rivenhall B&B.........................**22** C5
Sequoia Lodge Backpackers...**23** B5
Villa..**24** B4

EATING (pp423–4)
Café Zest................................(see 28)
Cibo..(see 28)
Espresso House.......................**25** B5
Kiwi Takeaways.......................**26** C4
Le Cafe...................................**27** C4
Marlborough Terranean..........**28** C4
Picton Village Bakery.............**29** B4
Supervalue Supermarket........(see 34)

To Portage turn-off (22km);
Havelock (35km)

Shakespeare Bay

Bob's Bay

Victoria Domain

Lookout

Lookout

Picton Harbour

To Bayview Backpackers (1km);
Waikawa Bay Holiday Park (1km);
Waikawa Marina (1.2km)

Breakwater

Footbridge

Waitohi Domain

Waikawa Rd

Scenic Reserve

Nelson Square

Lookout

Tirohanga Walkway

To Airport (8km);
Koromiko (8km);
Blenheim (28km)

DRINKING (pp423–4)
Toot 'n' Whistle Inn...............**30** B4

TRANSPORT (pp424–5)
Avis..(see 32)
Bluebridge/Strait Shipping.....(see 32)
Budget....................................(see 32)
Buzzy Bikes & Boats..............(see 35)
Hertz......................................(see 32)
InterCity and Main Bus
    Terminal...........................(see 32)
Interislander...........................(see 32)
Pegasus..................................**31** B4
Picton Ferry Terminal.............**32** C3
Shoestring...............................**33** B4
Thrifty....................................(see 32)
West Bay Water Transport.....(see 32)

OTHER
Mariners Mall.........................**34** C5
Town Wharf............................**35** C4

WAIRAU MASSACRE

One of the most infamous early conflicts between settlers in the Nelson region and Maori tribes occurred in 1843. The opportunistic New Zealand Company tried to settle part of the Wairau Plain, about 9km north of Blenheim near Tuamarina, after buying the alleged rights from the widow of a trader, John Blenkinsopp. He claimed he bought the land from the Maoris for a 16lb cannon, and had obtained a dubious deed signed by local chiefs.

The Maoris denied all knowledge of the Wairau sale and two Ngati Toa chiefs, Te Rauparaha and Te Rangihaeata, arrived from Kapiti to resist survey operations. The Pakeha sent out a hurriedly co-opted armed party led by Arthur Wakefield, brother of the then governor of New Zealand, to arrest them. The party was met peacefully by the Ngati Toa at Tuamarina but the Pakeha precipitated a brief skirmish, during which Te Rangihaeata's wife was shot. The Pakeha were forced to surrender and Rangihaeata, mad with rage, demanded vengeance. Twenty two of the party, including Wakefield, were killed; the rest escaped through the scrub and over the hills. The event came to be known as the Wairau Massacre.

Tuamarina, the site of the massacre, is 19km south of Picton. In the cemetery near the road is a Pakeha monument designed by Felix Wakefield, youngest brother of Arthur Wakefield.

bird-watching tour $85; bird-watching tour Tue, Thu & Sun) Ecotours around Queen Charlotte Sound and Motuara Island bird sanctuary. Spot dolphins, sea birds or fur seals.

Endeavour Express (03-573 5456; www.boatrides.co.nz; Town Wharf; cruises $45-55) A backpacker-friendly company offering a range of cruises and cruise/walks.

Sounds Connection (03-573 8843; www.soundsconnection.co.nz; 10 London Quay; half-day wine/fishing tour $50/70, half-/full-day gourmet wine tour $65/125) Runs various tours, including fishing and wine.

Southern Wilderness (0800 266 266, 03-578 4531; www.southernwilderness.com; Railway Station, 3 Auckland St; half-/full-day trips from $90/130) An enthusiastic company with great tours of the Marlborough region, ranging from wine tours, white-water rafting trips to the Gowan and Buller Rivers and three-day rafting trips on the Clarence River. It also runs guided walks of the Queen Charlotte Track.

Waka Whenua Tours (03-573 7877; www.picton.co.nz/for/wakawhenuatours; adults $40-60; 10.30am, noon & 1.30pm) Winery tours visiting Marlborough vineyards with a descendant of the Tangata Whenua tribe Te Atiawa. Scenic/historic/cultural and 'Back Country' tours available.

Sleeping

Picton has plenty of budget and mid-range options scattered about town. Many motels are on Waikawa Rd.

BUDGET

Sequoia Lodge Backpackers (0800 222 257, 03-573 8399; www.sequoialodge.co.nz; 3a Nelson Sq; dm $20-22, tw & d $60) Named after one of the enormous trees out the front, this is a big, comfortable and well-run place. It has a giant outdoor chess set, fresh bread nightly and percolated coffee morning and evening.

Villa (03-573 6598; www.thevilla.co.nz; 34 Auckland St; dm $22-23, tw & d $55, with bathroom $60;) A deservedly popular hostel. It's a beautiful rose-covered sunny cottage with cosy rooms and communal areas, well-equipped kitchens, friendly owners and even-friendlier dogs. Free perks include bike hire, tea and coffee, breakfast, hot spa pool and broadband Internet (two terminals).

Bayview Backpackers (03-573 7668; www.truenz.co.nz/bayviewbackpackers; 318 Waikawa Rd; dm $17, s $30-36, tw & d $40-45) On Waikawa Bay, 4km from central Picton, with bay views and pleasant porch areas. Friendly owners offer free pick-up and drop-off in town. Water-sports equipment and bicycles are also free.

Juggler's Rest (03-573 5570; jugglers-rest@xtr.co.nz; 8 Canterbury St; dm/d $20/45;) If you're a juggler, or even marginally interested in learning, this is the place to be – it's run by professional jugglers and lessons are offered free. A small hostel, Juggler's is surrounded by bush.

Bellbird Motel (/fax 03-573 6912; 96 Waikawa Rd; d $60-70) Slightly out of town, '70s-style Bellbird has six spacious self-contained units. The rooms are old-school and more like staying in a house than a unit. Great value.

Atlantis (03-573 8876; www.atlantishostel.co.nz; cnr Auckland St & London Quay; dm $17-19, tw $20-21, s $21-24;) Rooms are cheap but dorms are massive (some are 30-bed). Facilities include a small indoor heated pool, pool table, Sky TV and more than 300 DVDs to keep your eyes square.

Blue Anchor Top 10 Holiday Park (☎ 03-573 7212; www.blueanchor.co.nz; 70-78 Waikawa Rd; camp sites/campervan sites $20/22, cabins $35-48, self-contained units $60-80; ☒) About 1km from the town centre, Blue Anchor is a well-kept, modern park with a range of facilities, including spa and swimming pools, playground, Internet access and a recreation room stuffed with games.

Waikawa Bay Holiday Park (☎ 0800 924 529, 03-573 7434; www.waikawa.kiwiholidayparks.com/info; 302 Waikawa Rd; camp sites & campervan sites $18, cabins $30-40, self-contained units $50-75) About 4km from Picton, this a pleasant spot to stay and has a good range of accommodation, grassy sites and a courtesy van.

MID-RANGE

Broadway Motel (☎ 0800 101 919, 03-573 6563; www .broadwaymotel.co.nz; 113 High St; r $110-160) Broadway is conveniently located, modern and clean with double-glazed windows and Sky TV. Some rooms have a balcony and a spa, and the different prices reflect size rather than standard.

Americano Motor Inn (☎ 0800 104 104, 03-573 6398; www.americano.co.nz; 32 High St; s $95, d $105-115, f $150) Central, self-contained family units with cheerful floral quilt covers and ceiling fans. The two-bedroom units have a living area and a balcony overlooking High St. A courtesy shuttle bus is offered for ferry pick-up.

Marineland Motels & Guesthouse (☎ 03-573 6429; www.marinelandaccom.co.nz; 26-28 Waikawa Rd; s $50-65, d with bathroom $65-90, self-contained units $75-95; ☒) Marineland has old-fashioned rooms in a beautiful characterful home with a guest lounge and dining room. Continental breakfasts are included, with cooked breakfast on request. Modern motel rooms are fully self-contained and have Sky TV.

House of Glenora (☎ 03-573 6966; www.glenora.co .nz; 22 Broadway; s/d $55/95, with bathroom $65/130) This attractive old house has several bright, colour-themed rooms, some with en suite. The owner runs the International Weaving School and you can see her work and even partake in weaving tuition workshops.

Rivenhall B&B (☎ 03-573 7692; rivenhall.picton@ xtra .co.nz; 118 Wellington St; s/d $55/80) Perched high on the hill overlooking Picton and the Marlborough Sounds, Rivenhall is a lovely homestay option with friendly hosts. Breakfast of your choice is provided and for an additional $25 Nan will cook you dinner.

Harbour View Motel (☎ /fax 0800 101 133, 03-573 6259; 30 Waikawa Rd; units $65-80) Harbour View has an elevated position that offers watery views of Picton's endearing harbour. Units are fully self-contained.

TOP END

Jasmine Court Travellers Inn (☎ 0800 421 999, 03-573 7110; www.jasminecourt.co.nz; 78 Wellington St; d $110-175) Beautiful and comfortable five-star accommodation at exceptionally reasonable rates. Warm, spacious self-contained studios and two-bedroom apartments are immaculate, with quality appliances, delicate German crockery, DVDs and beds that will have insomniacs snoring. Some rooms have a spa and upstairs balconies have views of the harbour.

Gables (☎ 03-573 6772; www.thegables.co.nz; 20 Waikawa Rd; s $90, d $110-150, cottages $150-170) This bright B&B has three spacious, homely en suite rooms in the main house and two cottages with kitchenettes at the back. Top value and gracious hosts.

Eating & Drinking

Most of Picton's cafés and restaurants are on High St or facing the waterfront on London Quay.

Café Zest (☎ 03-573 6616; 31 High St; meals $6-15; ⓥ breakfast & lunch) A cheery spot with blue walls and the classic black-and-white tiled floor. Food is served with a modern twist – breakfast toast may come with chunky plum jam and pesto as the condiments of choice.

Picton Village Bakery (☎ 03-573 7082; 46 Auckland St; meals $4-6) Dutch owners bake a range of European treats, including 'dark long-baked rye bread' – good for when you're tramping (as it doesn't break up). Pies here are scrumptious as are focaccias and ciabatta sandwiches. Gluten-free bread is available on request.

Le Cafe (☎ 03-573 5588; 33 High St; mains $12-15) Right on the waterfront with a slightly Bohemian character, Le Cafe is a great place for a lingering breakfast or lunch – it also has one computer with Internet access. It's a cruisey place for a coffee and a read of the paper.

Cibo (☎ 03-573 7171; 33 High St; meals $6-14; ⓥ breakfast & lunch) This licensed and BYO café offers something different, with treats such as Spanish tapas for lunch and thick pancake stacks for breakfast on weekends.

Espresso House (☎ 03-573 7112; 58 Auckland St; mains $17-24; ⓥ lunch & dinner) In a converted house, this small espresso bar has a compact wine list and serves sensational pasta and Pacific Rim fare. Food is fresh, nutritious and stylishly done. For dinner, try venison kofta on couscous, tomato and mussel fettuccini or a steaming bowl of soup with hearty slices of bread.

Marlborough Terranean (☎ 03-573 7122; 31 High St; mains $25-28; ☺ lunch & dinner summer, dinner Wed-Sun winter) This is a sophisticated restaurant with a European menu dominated by seafood dishes. It's the rack of lamb with tarragon jus and garlic mash that earns rave reviews.

Toot 'n' Whistle Inn (☎ 03-573 6086; 7 Auckland St; meals $9.50-15; ☺ 7am-3am) A classic local right by the ferry terminal. Head here for big portions of pub grub – plenty of chips – washed down with big portions of lager.

If you're hankering for fish and chips, try **Kiwi Takeaways** (☎ 03-573 5537; 14 Wellington St; meals $4-9; ☺ dinner).

Self-caterers head to **Supervalue supermarket** (☎ 03-573 6463; Mariners Mall, 71 High St).

Getting There & Away

You can make bookings for trains, ferries and buses at Picton train station and at the excellent Picton visitors centre (p420).

AIR
Soundsair (☎ 0800 505 005, 03-520 3080; www.soundsair.co.nz) runs a service between Picton and Wellington (one way $79, 25 minutes, eight daily). There are discounts for backpacker and student-card holders.

A courtesy shuttle bus to/from the airstrip at Koromiko, 8km south, is included in the price of flights.

BOAT
Ferries depart and arrive at the **Picton ferry terminal** (Auckland St), where all ferry services have booking desks. The terminal has conveniences such as public showers, a laundrette, phones and Internet access.

There are three options for crossing the strait between Picton and Wellington (note that timetables are subject to change).
Bluebridge Ferries/Strait Shipping (☎ 0800 844 844, 04-473 1479; www.strait.co.nz; adult/child $40/25, car or campervan/motorbike/bicycle or surfboard $150/45/10; ☺ departs Picton 8am & 7pm Sun-Fri, 2.30pm & 11pm Sat, departs Wellington 3am & 1pm Sun-Fri, 10am & 7pm Sat) Crossing takes three hours 20 minutes.

Interislander (☎ 0800 802 802, 04-498 3302; www.interislandline.co.nz; adult/child $60/40, child under 2 free, car or campervan/motorbike/bicycle or surfboard $220/60/10; ☺ departs Picton 10am, 1.30pm, 6pm & 9.30pm Mon, 5.30am, 10am, 1.30pm, 5pm, 6pm & 9.30pm Tue-Thu, 5.30am, 10am, 1.30pm, 6pm & 9.30pm Fri-Sun, departs Wellington 9.30am, 2pm & 5.30pm Mon, 1.30am, 9.30am, 12.15pm, 2pm & 5.30pm Tue-Thu, 1.30am, 9.30am, 2pm & 5.30pm Fri-Sun) Crossing takes three hours. Discount fares often available for advance bookings.
Lynx (☎ 0800 802 802, 04-498 3302; www.interislandline.co.nz; adult/child $60/40, child under 2 free, car or campervan/motorbike/bicycle or surfboard $220/60/10; ☺ departs Picton 11.30am & 7pm, departs Wellington 8am & 3.30pm) Crossing takes 2¼ hours. A faster option for the same price on a catamaran.

For more information about crossing the strait see p405.

BUS
Buses serving Picton operate from the ferry terminal or the visitors centre.

InterCity (☎ 03-573 7025; www.intercitycoach.co.nz; Picton ferry terminal) runs services to/from Christchurch ($50, five hours, two daily) via Kaikoura ($27, 2¼ hours) with connections to Dunedin and Invercargill. Services also run to/from Nelson ($29, two hours, three daily) with connections to Motueka ($30, one daily) and Greymouth and the glaciers, and to/from Blenheim ($10, 25 minutes, five daily). At least one bus daily on each of these routes connects with a Wellington ferry service.

A profusion of smaller shuttle buses head south to Christchurch, usually offering a door-to-door service to central accommodation places. Companies include:
Atomic Shuttles (☎ 0800 248 885, 03-573 7477; www.atomictravel.co.nz)
K Bus (☎ 03-525 9434; www.kahurangi.co.nz)
Magic Travellers Network (☎ 03-548 3290; www.magicbus.co.nz)
South Island Connections (☎ 0508 742 669, 03-366 6633; www.southislandconnections.co.nz)
Southern Link Shuttles (☎ 03-573 7477; www.yellow.co.nz/site/southernlink)

TRAIN
Tranz Scenic (☎ 0800 872 467; www.tranzscenic.co.nz; ☺ 7am-7pm) runs the scenic *TranzCoastal* service from Picton to Christchurch ($85, five hours 20 minutes, one daily), via Blenheim (30 minutes) and Kaikoura (2½ hours).

The service connects with the *Interislander* ferry. It departs from Picton at 1.40pm; from Christchurch it departs at 7.30am. A free shuttle service links the train station and ferry terminal on both sides of the strait.

Getting Around
Renting a car in Picton is easy and affordable – around $45 to $110 per day; most agencies also allow drop-offs in Christchurch. If you're planning to drive in the North Island it's a cheaper option to return your car to Picton and pick up another car in Wellington after crossing the strait.

Picton's car-hire companies include:

Avis (☎ 03-573 6363; www.avis.com; Picton ferry terminal)

Budget (☎ 03-573 6081; www.budget.com; Picton ferry terminal)

Hertz (☎ 03-520 3044; www.hertz.com; Picton ferry terminal & 12 York St)

Pegasus (☎ 03-573 7733; www.rentalcars.co.nz; 1 Auckland St) Cheaper than the major operators.

Shoestring (☎ 03-573 7788; www.carhire.co.nz/shoestring/; Picton Lodge, 9 Auckland St)

Thrifty (☎ 03-573 7387; www.thrifty.com; Picton ferry terminal)

See also p429 and p430 for details of cruises, boat connections and water taxis to the Sounds.

MARLBOROUGH SOUNDS
The Marlborough Sounds feature many delightful bays, islands, coves and waterways, which were formed by the sea flooding its deep valleys after the ice ages. Parts of the Sounds are now included in the Marlborough Sounds Maritime Park, which is actually many small reserves separated by private land, mostly pastoral leases. To get an idea of how convoluted the sounds are, Pelorus Sound is 42km long but has 379km of shoreline.

The Queen Charlotte Track is the main attraction for trampers, but there are other walks, such as the two-day Nydia Track (p429), and secluded accommodation is scattered throughout the Sounds.

Sleeping
Some sleeping options are accessible only by boat and are delightfully isolated. Prices are reasonable and most places offer free use of dinghies and water-sports equipment. Most popular are those on or just off the Queen Charlotte Track (p428) and there are places to stay along Queen Charlotte Dr between Picton and Havelock.

There are almost 30 DOC camping grounds throughout the Sounds, providing water and toilet facilities but not much else – none have cooking facilities.

Unless you're carrying a tent it's essential to book the following places in summer and some close over winter – check with the Picton visitors centre (p420).

DOC Momorangi Bay Motor Camp (☎ 03-573 7865; momorangi.camp@xtra.co.nz; Queen Charlotte Dr; camp sites $16-30, cabins $30) Momorangi Bay, 15km from Picton on the road to Havelock, is a fully serviced camping ground with a kitchen and showers. It's one of several motor camps along Queen Charlotte Dr. There are around 30 camp sites with water frontage.

Smiths Farm Holiday Park (☎ 03-574 2806; www.smithsfarm.co.nz; Queen Charlotte Dr, Linkwater; camp sites/campervan sites $18/20, cabins $40, self-contained/motel units $70/90) This is a cut above your average park with lush camping areas and new cabins (shared facilities or self-contained). It's just before the turn-off to Portage, and is part of a working beef farm.

Hopewell (☎ 03-573 4341; www.hopewell.co.nz; Kenepuru Sound; tw & d $40) Hopewell is a comfortable and highly rated backpackers hostel on a remote part of Kenepuru Sound. It's surrounded by native bush and opens onto the sea – there's also an outdoor spa. Access by road is possible but the bumpy drive makes the water taxi from Portage the best option.

D'Urville Wilderness Resort (☎ 03-576 5268; www.durvilleisland.co.nz; Catherine Cove, D'Urville Island; self-contained units $90-160) A remote beachfront lodge on D'Urville Island. You can rent a unit and self-cater (there's also an attached café-bar), or there's fully catered accommodation. To get there it's a 1½-hour drive from State Highway 6 (SH6) to French Pass (unsealed after Okiwi Bay), then a water-taxi ride across to the lodge.

Queen Charlotte Wilderness Park (☎ 03-579 9025; www.truenz.co.nz/wilderness; Cape Jackson; 2 nights & 3 days $260) North of Ship Cove and extending right up to Cape Jackson, this park is a private farming lease that allows you to explore north of the Queen Charlotte Track. The package includes accommodation, dinner and transfers from Picton. As well as opportunities for tramping on a virtually deserted track, there's boating, kayaking and horse riding.

MARLBOROUGH SOUNDS

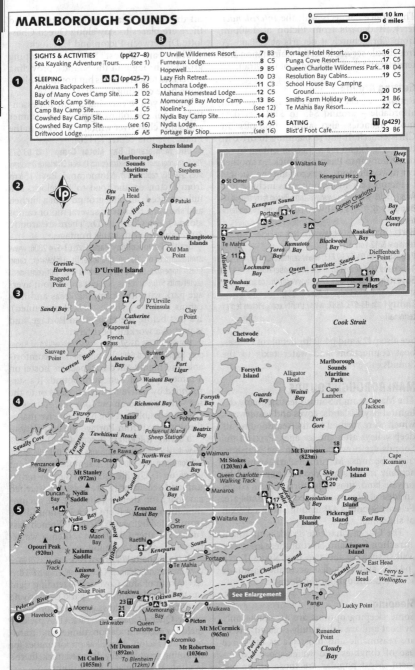

SIGHTS & ACTIVITIES (pp427–8)	D'Urville Wilderness Resort............7 B3	Portage Hotel Resort....................16 C2
Sea Kayaking Adventure Tours......(see 1)	Furneaux Lodge............................8 C5	Punga Cove Resort.......................17 C5
	Hopewell.....................................9 B5	Queen Charlotte Wilderness Park..18 D4
SLEEPING (pp425–7)	Lazy Fish Retreat..........................10 D3	Resolution Bay Cabins..................19 C5
Anakiwa Backpackers......................1 B6	Lochmara Lodge...........................11 C3	School House Bay Camping
Bay of Many Coves Camp Site........2 D2	Mahana Homestead Lodge............12 C5	Ground................................20 D5
Black Rock Camp Site....................3 C2	Momorangi Bay Motor Camp........13 B6	Smiths Farm Holiday Park.............21 B6
Camp Bay Camp Site.....................4 C5	Nydia Bay Camp Site...................14 A5	Te Mahia Bay Resort....................22 A5
Cowshed Bay Camp Site................5 C2	Nydia Lodge................................15 A5	
Cowshed Bay Camp Site.............(see 16)	Portage Bay Shop.......................(see 16)	**EATING** (p429)
Driftwood Lodge...........................6 A5	Noeline's..................................(see 12)	Blist'd Foot Cafe..........................23 B6

0 — 10 km
0 — 6 miles

Lazy Fish Retreat (☎ 03-573 5291; www.lazyfish.co
.nz; Queen Charlotte Sound; bungalows & apt $395-495)
Twelve kilometres from Picton, Lazy Fish
is accessible by boat only. It has magnificent top-end accommodation in secluded,
peaceful surrounds – you'll unwind in minutes. All fine-dining meals are included and
accommodation consists of bungalows and
a sea-view apartment, each with a veranda
and hammocks or day beds. Children under
16 are actively discouraged.

Getting There & Around
The best way to get around the Sounds is still
by boat, although the road system has been
extended. Apart from the mail run (p420),
which is run by Beachcomber Fun Cruises,
no scheduled buses service the Sounds. However, most of the Sounds is accessible by car.
The road is sealed to the head of Kenepuru
Sound but beyond that it's nothing but narrow, forever-winding gravel roads. To drive
to Punga Cove from Picton takes at least two
hours – or 45 minutes by boat.

Scheduled boats service most of the accommodation on the Queen Charlotte Track
(see p429) and are the cheapest way to get
around. Another option is **Arrow Water Taxis**
(☎ 03-573 8229, 025 444 689; www.arrowwatertaxis.co.nz;
Town Wharf, Picton), an operator servicing Queen
Charlotte Sound that takes passengers on
demand.

Queen Charlotte Track
The Queen Charlotte Track has wonderful
coastal scenery, beautiful coves and some
'great-escape' luxury, mid-range accommodation options and pristine camping spots.
The coastal forest is lush, and from the ridges
you can look down on either side to Queen
Charlotte and Kenepuru Sounds. The track is
71km long and connects historic Ship Cove
with Anakiwa. It's not through national
park and passes through privately owned
land and DOC reserves – access depends on
the cooperation of local landowners so it's
important to respect their property by staying in designated camp sites and carrying out
your rubbish.

Queen Charlotte is a well-defined track
and suitable for people of all ages of average fitness. You can do the walk in sections
using local boat transport, or walk the whole
three- to four-day journey. Sleeping options
are only half a day's walk apart. Though

there aren't the hordes that walk the Abel
Tasman Track, there's still some solid traffic. Mountain biking is also an option and
it's possible to ride the track in two or three
days – note that the section between Ship
Cove and Punga Cove is closed to cyclists
between 1 December and 28 February. At
this time you can still get dropped by boat
at Punga Cove and ride to Anakiwa. As with
Abel Tasman, you can do part of the trip by
sea kayak (p429).

Ship Cove is the usual starting point,
mainly because it's easier to arrange a boat
from Picton to Ship Cove than vice versa,
but the track can be started from Anakiwa.
There's a public phone at Anakiwa but not
at Ship Cove. Between Camp Bay and Torea
Saddle you'll find the going toughest. About
halfway along there's an excellent viewpoint,
Eatwell's Lookout, about 15 minutes off the
main track. Estimated distances and walking times have been recently revised, making
some of the DOC literature and signposting
outdated. Estimated route times:

Route	Distance	Time
Ship Cove to Resolution Bay	4.5km	2hr
Resolution Bay to Endeavour Inlet	10.5km	2½hr
Endeavour Inlet to Camp Bay/Punga Cove	12km	4hr
Camp Bay/Punga Cove to Torea Saddle/Portage	23km	8hr
Torea Saddle/Portage to Mistletoe Bay	9km	4hr
Mistletoe Bay to Anakiwa	12km	3hr

INFORMATION
The Picton visitors centre (p420) has copies
of the *Queen Charlotte Track* brochure, and
is the best spot for information; try also Rutherford YHA & Travel in Havelock (p429).

TOURS
Most of the tour companies (p420) that are
based in Picton offer guided cruises around
the Sounds and walks on the Queen Charlotte
Track. See also Track Transport (p429).

Buzzy Bikes & Boats (☎ 03-573 7853; todd.fam@xtra
.co.nz; Town Wharf; bike/kayak per day $40/50) Hires
mountain bikes, kayaks and power boats
($200 to $340 per day plus fuel). It also runs
a water taxi between Picton and the Marlborough Sounds.

Marlborough Sounds Adventure Company (☎ 0800 283 283, 03-573 6078; www.marlboroughsounds .co.nz; Town Wharf, Picton; 1-/2-/3-/4-day tours $85/145/445/965, twilight paddle $50, full-day kayak hire $40) Organises a variety of sea-kayak trips and tramps. Kayak trips range from a three-hour twilight paddle to a four-day guided tour. It also offers guided walks of the track.

Sea Kayaking Adventure Tours (☎ 03-574 2765; www.nzseakayaking.com; Anakiwa Rd, Anakiwa; day trip $75, 1-/3-/4-/5-day tours $180/280/360/480, full-day kayak hire $40) Offers environmental, nature-based paddling tours, with an emphasis on personalised service and small groups.

SLEEPING & EATING

It's strongly advised to book accommodation for the Queen Charlotte Track early, especially in summer, as the area can be solidly booked. There are **DOC camping grounds** (camp sites $10) along the track and an interesting variety of lodges and guesthouses – many charge around $5 to $10 extra for linen.

The following listings are arranged in order heading south from Ship Cove.

School House Bay Camping Ground (Ship Cove) Beautifully situated with cold water and toilets but no cooking facilities.

Resolution Bay Cabins (☎ 03-579 9411; Resolution Bay; camp sites with/without use of cooker $30/20, dm $25, cabins/cottages from $70/95) A delightfully rustic place with backpacker beds and old-fashioned cabins with kitchen and attached bathroom. They have real character, with potbelly stoves, ageing furniture and a generator provides the electricity. It's incredibly peaceful.

Furneaux Lodge (☎ 03-579 8259; www.furneaux.co .nz; Rural Bag 381; dm $30-35, chalets/studios $135/185) A century-old place set amid lovely gardens, and a godsend for thirsty trampers – it has one of the only pubs in NZ accessible by boat or foot only. The backpacker section is in an old stone cottage with a big open fire and there are comfortable, self-contained one-bedroom chalets and flash studio units. Meals are available in the bar and restaurant.

Camp Bay Camp Site (Camp Bay) On the western side of Endeavour Inlet.

Punga Cove Resort (☎ 0800 809 697, 03-579 8561; www.pungacove.co.nz; Endeavour Inlet; dm $35, chalets $160-350) A huge range of self-contained, studio, family and luxury A-frame chalets, some with gorgeous sea views. For backpackers, there's a separate area overlooking

the bay. The resort has a pool, spa, shop, bar and an excellent restaurant.

Mahana Homestead Lodge (☎ 03-579 8373; www.mahanahomestead.com; Endeavour Inlet; dm $25, d $55) Every room in this purpose-built lodge has sea views and it gets a huge rap from guests. There's only a natural water supply here so use water wisely and bring your own linen if possible. Mahana's chocolate cake is renowned throughout the Sounds.

Noeline's (☎ 03-579 8375; near Punga Cove; tw $44) Five minutes up the hill from the Homestead, Noeline's is a friendly, relaxed homestay with a handful of beds, cooking facilities and great views.

Bay of Many Coves Camp Site (Bay of Many Coves) On a saddle above the track.

Black Rock Camp Site (Kumutoto Bay) Further along past Bay of Many Coves, above Kumutoto Bay.

Portage Resort Hotel (☎ 03-573 4309; www .portage.co.nz; Kenepuru Sound; dm $25, d $160-225, ste $265) This resort is a stalwart on Kenepuru Sound. It's flash with an à la carte restaurant, casual café and bar. The backpacker section is great, with lounge and cooking facilities. Even if you're not staying, drop in for a beer. The hotel has sailboats, sailboards, fishing, spa, gym and tennis courts.

Portage Bay Shop (☎ 03-573 4445; www.portage charters.co.nz; Kenepuru Sound; s/d $30/60) Offers backpacker accommodation and hires yachts, dinghies, kayaks, bikes and fuel.

Cowshed Bay Camp Site (Cowshed Bay) East from the Portage Hotel Resort.

Lochmara Lodge (☎ 03-573 4554; www.lochmara lodge.co.nz; Lochmara Bay; dm $25-28, d $60-80, self-contained units $120; ☯ Oct-May) A superb retreat on Lochmara Bay, reached by a side track south of the Queen Charlotte Track, or by boat from Picton. Facilities include an outdoor spa, hammocks, barbecues and volleyball court. As well as a homely backpacker lodge with four- and eight-bed dorms, there are stylish en-suite rooms and units, all set in lush surroundings.

Te Mahia Bay Resort (☎ 03-573 4089; www.temahia .co.nz; Kenepuru Sound; dm $30, units $105-140) This resort is north of the track, just off the main road, in a beautiful bay facing Kenepuru Sound. It has dorm beds and very roomy self-contained units looking out over the water. There's a store and kayaks for hire.

Anakiwa Backpackers (☎ 03-574 1338; anakiwa@ ihug.co.nz; 401 Anakiwa Rd; dm $19, tw & d $50) This small place is right at the southern end of the trail. There are only six beds in the self-contained section, and there is home-made bread.

Blist'd Foot Cafe (Anakiwa) After days of walking this café is the place to rest your feet and debrief with fellow trampers. It's near the pick-up point for water transport back to Picton.

DOC Mistletoe Bay camp site (Mistletoe Bay) has an area for tents only, as does DOC Davies Bay camp site (Umungara) further along the track. Davies Bay is also a popular picnic spot.

TRACK TRANSPORT
A number of boat operators service the track, allowing you to start and finish where you like. They offer pack transfers so your gear can wait for you at your accommodation. Transport costs $55 to $65 return, and around $40 for a one-way drop off. Bikes and kayaks can be transported.

Main operators in Picton:

Beachcomber Fun Cruises (☎ 0800 624 526, 03-573 6175; www.beachcombercruises.co.nz; Town Wharf) Also offers the Queen Charlotte Sound mail boat cruises (p420).

Cougar Line (☎ 0800 504 090, 03-573 7925; www.cougar linecruises.co.nz; Town Wharf) Has a return pass and a variety of luxury 'cruise and walk' packages.

Endeavour Express (☎ 03-573 5456; www.boatrides.co .nz; Town Wharf) Picton to outer Queen Charlotte Sound, stopping at Furneaux Lodge, and Punga Cove. Pick up from Torea Bay or Anakiwa.

West Bay Water Transport (☎ 03-573 5597; west _bay@xtra.co.nz; Picton ferry terminal) Covers the south-ern end of the track (Anakiwa, Lochmara Bay and Torea Bay), leaving from the southern side of the Picton ferry terminal (West Bay jetty). West Bay has one- and two-day specials ($40) with walks from Torea Saddle or Mistletoe Bay to Anakiwa.

HAVELOCK
pop 500

Tiny Havelock, at the confluence of the Pelorus and Kaiuma Rivers 35km west of Picton, is a base from which to explore the more remote parts of Marlborough Sounds, particularly Pelorus and Kenepuru Sounds. Founded around 1860 and named after Sir Henry Havelock of Indian Mutiny fame, Havelock was once the hub of the timber milling and export trade, and later became the service centre for gold-mining in the area.

Havelock's thriving small-boat harbour and claim to fame as the 'green-shelled mussel capital of the world' pretty much sums it up.

Information
Rutherford YHA & Travel (☎ 03-574 2114; 46 Main Rd; www.marlboroughadventures.co.nz; ☼ 8am-10pm) Helpful staff book tours, particularly for the Nydia Track, and accommodation and offer heaps of regional advice. DOC and transport agents.

Activities
NYDIA TRACK
The **Nydia Track** starts at Kaiuma Bay and ends at Duncan Bay (or vice versa). The walking time is around 9½ hours. Nydia Bay was originally the site of a Maori *pa* (fortified village) called Opouri, which means 'Place of Sadness', so named after a bloody battle between members of the same tribe. The walk passes through different bird habitats.

There are **DOC camping grounds** (camp sites $10) at Nydia Bay and Duncan Bay, and the **DOC Nydia Lodge** (☎ 03-574 2019; Nydia Bay; dm $15), a 50-bed hut. About halfway along, **Driftwood Lodge** (☎ 03-579 8454; driftwood@nydiabay.co.nz; d $35) is in a farmyard setting. It has kitchen facilities and hot showers. **Te Mahoerangi Backpackers** (Nydia Bay; d $36) is a small back-packers right on the bay – book at Ruther-ford YHA & Travel (p429).

It's best to get dropped off at Shag Point, on Kaiuma Bay, by water taxi; you can ar-range a water taxi for around $60 at Duncan Bay. **Pelorus Sounds Water Taxi** (☎ 03-574 2151) is one of the main operators; phone from Driftwood Lodge.

Tours
Many water taxis operate out of Havelock and nature cruises can be organised to Maud Island.

For cruises on the Pelorus mail boat see p420.

All Season Cruises (☎ 03-574 1220; cb.chamberlain@ xtra.co.nz; day/overnight cruise $65/160) The popular three-hour lunch cruise, aboard the raunchy launch *Foxy Lady*, heads to a mussel farm. It also runs overnight cruises.

Havelock Sea Kayaking Company (☎ 03-574 2114; www.marlboroughadventures.co.nz; kayak trips $80-150, kayak hire $35) Has full-day sea-kayaking trips, including a deluxe overnight version, on the Marlborough Sounds.

Sounds Natural Adventure Holidays (☎ 03-574 2144; www.soundsnatural.co.nz; kayak trips $80-150) To fully embrace the outdoors, there's the option of naturist tours.

Sleeping & Eating

Rutherford YHA & Travel (☎ 03-574 2114; www .yha.org.nz/hostels-ind.asp?id=43; 46 Main Rd; camp sites $22, dm $20, tw & d $46) This well-equipped place is in an 1881 schoolhouse once attended by Lord Ernest Rutherford, who discovered the atomic nucleus. The enthusiastic manager has information about walks and the rooms are bright and cheery.

Havelock Garden Motel (☎ 03-574 2387; info@ gardenmotels.com; 71 Main Rd; self-contained units $75-110) As the name suggests, this small, family-run motel has a beautiful garden aspect. Some of the more expensive rooms have spas. The entrance is right before Mussel Boys.

Havelock Motor Camp (☎ 03-574 2339; www .holidayparks.co.nz/havelock; 24 Inglis St; camp sites/ campervan sites $21/22, cabins $30-70, self-contained units $45-105, motel units $60-180) Near the marina, this motor camp has shady sites and a wide variety of accommodation. There are standard camping ground facilities here.

Mussel Boys (☎ 03-574 2824; www.musselboys.co.nz; 73 Main Rd; meals $20-30; ☽ lunch & dinner) Mussel Boys specialises in fresh local mussels, especially 'steamers' (whole shell), 'flats' (half shells) and chowders. You can't miss the 'mussel' team playing rugby on the roof. The mussels are plump and fresh, the chowder, creamy and delicious.

Getting There & Away

InterCity (☎ 03-573 7025; www.intercitycoach.co.nz) has daily Picton–Blenheim–Nelson buses that pass through Havelock. Several shuttle bus operators also ply this route, including **K Bus** (☎ 03-577 8332; www.kahurangi.co.nz) and **Atomic Shuttles** (☎ 03-573 7477; www.atomictravel .co.nz). There are no buses on the more direct 35km back road to Picton (Queen Charlotte Dr), but this is a scenic route if you're driving or cycling.

BLENHEIM
pop 25,900

Blenheim is 29km south of Picton on the Wairau Plain, a contrasting landscape to the Sounds. The flatness of the town, at the junction of the Taylor and Opawa Rivers, was a problem in the early days – Blenheim grew up around a swamp, now the reclaimed Seymour Sq, which has attractive lawns and gardens.

Blenheim is the best place to access NZ's biggest wine-growing district.

During the second weekend of every February, Blenheim hosts the **BMW Wine Marlborough Festival** (☎ 03-577 9299, 04-384 8630; www .bmw-winemarlborough-festival.co.nz) at Montana's Brancott Winery.

Information
BOOKSHOPS
Whitcoulls (☎ 03-578 0479; www.whitcoulls.co.nz; 55 Market Sq)

EMERGENCY
Fire, police and ambulance (☎ 111)

INTERNET ACCESS
Blenheim Library (☎ 03-578 2784; library@ marlborough.govt.nz; cnr Arthur & Seymour Sts; per 15min $2, per hr $6)

MONEY
Bank of NZ (☎ 0800 240 000; www.bnz.co.nz; 92-94 Market St)

POST
Post office (☎ 03-578 3904; www.nzpost.co.nz; cnr Scott & Main Sts)

TOURIST INFORMATION
Automobile Association (AA; ☎ 03-578 3399; www .nzaa.co.nz; 23 Maxwell Rd; ☽ 8.30am-5pm Mon-Wed & Fri, 9am-5pm Thu)
Marlborough visitors centre (☎ 03-577 8080; train station, Sinclair St; www.destinationmarlborough.com; ☽ 8.30am-5pm Mon-Fri, 9am-4pm Sat & Sun) Friendly and efficient.

Sights
The main sights around Blenheim are the lush vineyards with their gourmet restaurants; see p432.

Near Seymour Sq are relics of Blenheim's violent early history. The tiny **Blenkinsopp's cannon** is outside the council offices on Seymour St. Originally from the whaling ship *Caroline*, which Blenkinsopp captained, it's reputedly the cannon for which Te Rauparaha was persuaded to sign over the Wairau Plain.

Opposite Seymour Sq, the **Millennium Art Gallery** (☎ 03-579 2001; Seymour St; admission by gold-coin donation; ☽ 10am-5.30pm) is a contemporary gallery with changing exhibitions by local, national and international artists.

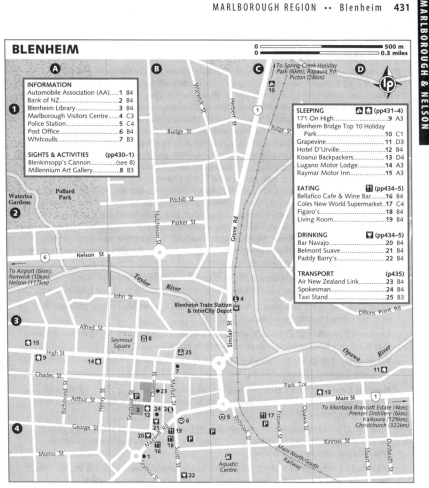

BLENHEIM

INFORMATION
Automobile Association (AA).....**1** B4
Bank of NZ.................................**2** B4
Blenheim Library.......................**3** B4
Marlborough Visitors Centre.....**4** C3
Police Station............................**5** C4
Post Office.................................**6** B4
Whitcoulls.................................**7** B3

SIGHTS & ACTIVITIES (pp430–1)
Blenkinsopp's Cannon...........(see 8)
Millennium Art Gallery..............**8** B3

SLEEPING (pp431–4)
171 On High..............................**9** A3
Blenheim Bridge Top 10 Holiday
  Park.....................................**10** C1
Grapevine................................**11** D3
Hotel D'Urville.........................**12** B4
Koanui Backpackers.................**13** D4
Lugano Motor Lodge................**14** A3
Raymar Motor Inn....................**15** A3

EATING (pp434–5)
Bellafico Cafe & Wine Bar........**16** B4
Coles New World Supermarket..**17** C4
Figaro's....................................**18** B4
Living Room..............................**19** B4

DRINKING (pp434–5)
Bar Navajo................................**20** B4
Belmont Suave..........................**21** B4
Paddy Barry's...........................**22** B4

TRANSPORT (p435)
Air New Zealand Link...............**23** B4
Spokesman................................**24** B4
Taxi Stand................................**25** B3

Tours

Back Country Safaris (☎ 03-575 7525; www.backcountry safaris.co.nz; Redwood Pass Rd; half-/full-day tours $240/390) Interesting tramping and mountain-biking tours, including high-country farm trips to Molesworth cattle station via the Awatere valley, and a wine tour.

Sleeping

As well as plenty of varied accommodation in Blenheim itself, there are lovely places scattered among the vineyards, particularly along Rapaura Rd.

BUDGET

Koanui Backpackers (☎ 03-578 7487; www.koanui.co .nz; 33 Main St; dm $20, s $45, tw & d $50-58) A bright,

friendly place with cosy rooms and a big, modern kitchen. It's a toasty place in winter with the log fire burning, electric blankets on the beds and a TV lounge with free videos. Koanui is popular with fruit-pickers. Discounted single rooms in low-season.

Grapevine (☎ 03-578 6062; rob.diana@xtra.co.nz; 29 Park Tce; dm $17, d $36-40) In an old maternity home, the Grapevine is a homely place with cot-like dorm beds. The big advantage is the Opawa River running right past the back door – you can borrow canoes for free.

Raymar Motor Inn (☎ 0800 361 362, 03-578 5104; fax 03-578 5105; 164 High St; d $70-75) A very reasonably priced motel which is central to Blenheim on the SH6. Studio rooms have comfortable beds, a TV and telephone.

MARLBOROUGH WINE TRAIL

With more than 50 wineries and acres of vineyards dotted around Blenheim and Renwick, Marlborough is NZ's biggest wine-producing area. It's particularly famous for floral sauvignon blancs, chardonnays, fruity rieslings and *méthode champenoise* sparkling wines. Wine tours are the prime attraction and wineries have cellar-door sales and tastings. Tours also visit breweries, liqueur distilleries and cottage industries where you can sample preserves and olive oil.

Wineries are clustered around Renwick, 8km west of Blenheim, and along Rapaura Rd, north of Renwick – there are 25 cellar doors in a 5km radius. It's perfect cycling distance and the bulk of riding is a thoroughly enjoyable experience. However, you'll need to take care cycling along busy highways with trucks zooming past, especially when your road sense is diminished by the grape. There are also plans to turn Rapaura Rd into a highway.

Montana Brancott Winery (☎ 03-578 2099; www.montanawines.com; Main South Rd, Blenheim; winery tours $10, meals $10-24; 9am-5pm) was the first to plant commercial vines in the region in 1973 and is NZ's largest winery (with a storage capacity of 20 million litres). It's also the host of the BMW Wine Marlborough Festival. Tours of the winery are every 30 minutes from 10am to 3pm.

The successful **BMW Wine Marlborough Festival** (www.bmw-winemarlborough-festival.co.nz; Brancott Estate; adult $35; 10am-6.45pm) is held annually to the delight of many food and wine enthusiasts. Other prominent wineries:

- **Mud House** (☎ 03-572 9374; www.mudhouse.co.nz; 197 Rapaura Rd; 10am-5pm) Fabulous winery serving beautiful food. Has an outlet for Prenzel liqueur, an olive shop and quilter's barn.
- **Saint Clair** (☎ 03-570 5280; www.saintclair.co.nz; cnr Rapaura & Selmes Rds; 9am-5pm) Award-winning wines, country preserves and a café.
- **Lawson's Dry Hills** (☎ 03-578 7674; www.lawsonsdryhills.co.nz; Alabama Rd; 10am-5pm) A winery that is proudly leading the way in screw-top wine bottles.
- **Framingham** (☎ 03-572 8884; www.framingham.co.nz; Conders Bend Rd; 10am-5pm) Specialises in aromatic, German-style white wines.
- **Nautilus Estate** (☎ 03-572 9374; www.nautilusestate.com; 12 Rapaura Rd; 10am-4.30pm) and **Cloudy Bay** (☎ 03-520 9040; www.cloudybay.co.nz; Jacksons Rd; 10am-4.30pm) Two large internationally renowned wineries (both big exporters).
- **Huia** (☎ 03-572 8326; www.huia.net.nz; Boyces Rd; 11am-4.30pm) and **Te Whare Ra** (☎ 03-572 8581; www.te-whare-ra.co.nz; 56 Anglesea St; 10am-4.30pm) Two excellent boutique wineries (Te Whare Ra has only 18 acres of vines).
- **Villa Maria Estate** (☎ 03-255 0660; www.villamaria.co.nz; cnr New Renwick & Paynters Rds; 10am-5pm) A big, highly regarded winemaker that consistently reels in major awards.
- **Prenzel Distillery** (☎ 03-578 2800; www.prenzel.com; Sheffield St; 10am-5pm) Six kilometres southeast of Blenheim, Prenzel produces a great range of liqueurs, schnapps, fruit wines and brandies.

Blenheim Bridge Top 10 Holiday Park (☎ 0800 268 666, 03-578 3667; www.blenheimtop10.co.nz; 78 Grove Rd; camp sites/campervan sites $22/24, cabins $40-50, units $60-80) About five minutes north of the town centre, this holiday park has camp sites by the river plus a range of cabins and units.

Spring Creek Holiday Park (☎ 03-570 5893; www.holidayparks.co.nz/spring; Rapaura Rd; camp sites/campervan sites $21/22, cabins $30-70, self-contained units $45-105, motel units $60-180) Spring Creek is 6km out of Blenheim towards Picton and about 500m off SH1. It's in a peaceful location near a good fishing creek.

MID-RANGE

171 On High (☎ 03-579 5098; www.171onhighmotel.co.nz; cnr High & Percy Sts; self-contained apt $95-120) An excellent mid-range option, each apartment with contemporary furnishings, full kitchen, Sky TV and some with spas. Rooms are on the smallish side but extremely comfortable.

Lugano Motor Lodge (☎ 03-577 8808; www.lugano.co.nz; cnr High & Henry Sts; self-contained units $100-160) Handy to central Blenheim, opposite Seymour Sq. Clean rooms range from studios to luxury one- and two-bedroom units. Spa baths, Sky TV and thermo mattresses.

Tours

Wine Tours by Bike (☎ 03-572 9951; www.winetoursbybike.co.nz; 106 Jeffries Rd; half-/full-day bike hire $35/50) runs a pick-up and drop-off service from Blenheim to Jeffries Rd. Its hire fees include a winery map, pannier and mobile phone so you can call to be picked up if you get too tipsy (or buy too many bottles to carry). It also offers an **Antares Homestay** (www.antareshomestay.co.nz; r $140) option at its four-acre property. There are two en-suite rooms available, a log fire, 12m swimming pool and a relaxing view overlooking the vineyards. Bike hire is included in the rates.

There are several wine tours (by minibus) available from Blenheim and a couple from Picton. Pick up from your accommodation is easily arranged.

- **Deluxe Travel Lines** (☎ 0800 500 511, 03-578 5467; www.deluxetravel.co.nz; wine tour $50) is a big operator with a six-hour tour that includes a Montana tour. Departures can be arranged from Picton.
- **Highlight Tours** (☎ 03-577 9046; www.marlborough.co.nz/highlight; half-day tours $50) offers personalised small-group tours.
- **Marlborough Wine Tours** (☎ 03-578 9515, 025-248 1231; www.marlboroughwinetours.co.nz; tours $50-70) has a range of tours.
- **Marlborough Wine Trails** (☎ 03-578 1494, 027-264 4704; www.marlboroughwinetrails.co.nz; half-/full-day tours $50/85) offers personalised tours and the host, Barry, is an effusive guide.

Food

With wine there must be food and lunch at one of the vineyards is all part of the gourmet experience. Most vineyards have attached cafés or restaurants, many with stunning views, serving fresh local produce. Expect perfectly matured cheeses, broths and consommés, plump scallops, herb-encrusted this and manuka-smoked that, so brush up on your gourmet speak. The following eateries serve delicious meals (see also Mud House, earlier).

- **Gibbs at Cairnbrae** (☎ 03-572 8048; www.cairnbrae.co.nz; 258 Jacksons Rd; meals $15-25 🕒 lunch & dinner)
- **Herzog** (☎ 03-572 8770; www.herzog.co.nz; 81 Jeffries Rd; set menu $100; 🕒 lunch & dinner) Also offers cooking classes.
- **La Veranda Vineyard Cafe** (☎ 03-572 9177; www.marlboroughwinevalley.co.nz/39.html; Domaine Georges Michel, Vintage Lane; meals $24-28; 🕒 lunch & dinner)
- **Twelve Trees** (☎ 03-572 9054; www.allanscott.com/restaurant.asp; Allan Scott winery, Jacksons Rd; meals $14-22; 🕒 lunch) Has an innovative blackboard menu.
- **Wairau River Wines** (☎ 03-572 9800; www.wairauriverwines.com; Rapaura Rd; meals $15-21; 🕒 lunch)
- **Whitehaven** (☎ 03-577 6634; www.whitehaven.co.nz/cafe.htm; 1 Dodson St; mains $26-30; 🕒 lunch)

Chardonnay Lodge (☎ 03-570 5194; www.chardonnaylodge.co.nz/index.html; 1048 Rapaura Rd; self-contained units $110-130; 🖳) Set in a big, tree-filled garden, this lodge offers two self-contained villas and a B&B homestay option in the main house. Breakfast is provided by the pool in summer. There's also a tennis court.

TOP END
Hotel D'Urville (☎ 03-577 9945; www.durville.com; 52 Queen St; r $300) In the old public trust buildings, rooms in this luxury boutique hotel are beautifully decorated and individually themed, with the impenetrable original vault doors. All rooms differ in size. Downstairs is the slick **wine bar and brasserie** (meals $15-30; 🕒 breakfast, lunch & dinner) with apple-green walls and ottomans. Food here is highly rated and there's a big selection of local wines.

Stonehaven (☎ 03-572 9730; www.stonehavenhomestay.co.nz; 414 Rapaura Rd; s $90, d $120-200; 🖳) Staying at this beautiful vineyard is a great way to absorb the viticultural atmosphere. Stonehaven is a lovely B&B with three guest rooms in a solid stone-and-cedar home. Rooms are clean and comfortable with terrific views.

MARLBOROUGH WINE TRAIL

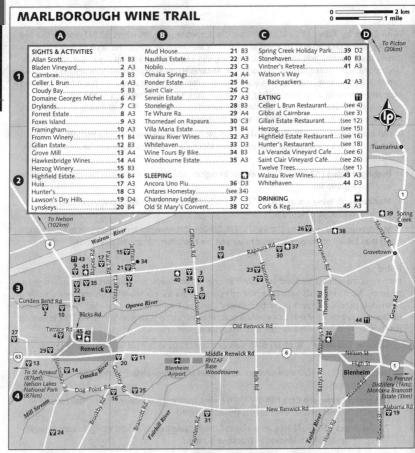

SIGHTS & ACTIVITIES
Allan Scott	1 B3
Bladen Vineyard	2 A3
Cairnbrae	3 B3
Cellier L Brun	4 A3
Cloudy Bay	5 B3
Domaine Georges Michel	6 A3
Drylands	7 C3
Forrest Estate	8 A3
Foxes Island	9 A3
Framingham	10 A3
Fromm Winery	11 B4
Gillan Estate	12 B3
Grove Mill	13 A4
Hawkesbridge Wines	14 A4
Herzog Winery	15 B3
Highfield Estate	16 B4
Huia	17 A3
Hunter's	18 C3
Lawson's Dry Hills	19 D4
Lynskeys	20 B4

Mud House	21 B3
Nautilus Estate	22 A3
Nobilo	23 C3
Omaka Springs	24 A4
Ponder Estate	25 B4
Saint Clair	26 C2
Seresin Estate	27 A3
Stoneleigh	28 B3
Te Whare Ra	29 A4
Thornedael on Rapaura	30 A3
Villa Maria Estate	31 B4
Wairau River Wines	32 A3
Whitehaven	33 D3
Wine Tours By Bike	34 B3
Woodbourne Estate	35 A3

SLEEPING
Ancora Uno Piu	36 D3
Antares Homestay	(see 34)
Chardonnay Lodge	37 C3
Old St Mary's Convent	38 D2

Spring Creek Holiday Park	39 D2
Stonehaven	40 B3
Vintner's Retreat	41 A3
Watson's Way Backpackers	42 A3

EATING
Cellier L Brun Restaurant	(see 4)
Gibbs at Cairnbrae	(see 3)
Gillan Estate Restaurant	(see 12)
Herzog	(see 15)
Highfield Estate Restaurant	(see 16)
Hunter's Restaurant	(see 18)
La Veranda Vineyard Cafe	(see 6)
Saint Clair Vineyard Café	(see 26)
Twelve Trees	(see 1)
Wairau River Wines	43 A3
Whitehaven	44 D3

DRINKING
Cork & Keg	45 A3

Old Saint Mary's Convent (☎ 03-570 5700; www
.convent.co.nz; Rapaura Rd; r $295-440) Once a convent,
now exclusive luxurious accommodation set
in a manicured garden and reached by a
lavender-lined drive. The honeymoon suite
is in the chapel and is all gothic windows and
elaborate lead lighting. The magnificent interior features a kauri staircase and full-sized
snooker table.

Ancora Uno Piu (☎ 03-578 2235; www.cottage
stays.co.nz/unopiu/cottage.htm; 75 Murphys Rd; r $270; ☑)
This Italian-run boutique homestead is
good for a romantic getaway and there's a
separate two-bedroom mud-brick cottage
for rent. There's a claw-foot bath, modern kitchen, saunas and an olive grove –
gorgeous.

Eating & Drinking

Blenheim has a thriving café and restaurant
scene, or you can dine among the vines at
some of the region's vineyards (see the
boxed text p432).

Living Room (☎ 03-579 4777; cnr Scott St & Maxwell
Rd; meals $7-20; ☒ noon-11pm Mon-Thu) The popular
Living Room is a chic café–wine bar decorated in warm tones with artistic style. It's
great for a cosy drink on the couches or for
a quality breakfast.

Figaro's (☎ 03-577 7277; 8 Scott St; meals $10-14;
☒ breakfast & lunch) Superb coffee at this stylish cream-and-brown café, perfect for a lin-
gering breakfast or just take away one of the
fat muffins stuffed with fruit. It's advisable
to book dinner at excellent Figaro's.

Bellafico Cafe & Wine Bar (☎ 03-577 6072; www
.bellafico.co.nz; 17 Maxwell Rd; brunch mains $10-30, dinner
mains $21-32; ☺ lunch & dinner Mon-Sat) Bellafico's
wine list is recommended by local wineries
and is updated bimonthly; it also stocks a
range of microbrewed beer. The menu has
an emphasis on local produce with European influences and features crayfish.

Belmont Suave (☎ 03-577 8238; 67 Queen St) A
cool, funky, split-level bar that goes off at
night, with people spilling onto the pave-
ment. A feature wall with forest wallpaper,
orange-and-green swivel chairs and mirrors complement the retro feel. DJs play at
weekends and it's the place to boogie.

Bar Navajo (☎ 03-577 7555; 70 Queen St; mains $14-
30; ☺ 8.30am-3am) A busy, American-Indian
themed bar with a colourful totem (authenticity yet to be verified), booths, pool tables,
and a rather beaten up mannequin that has
suffered the ravages of time. The varied
menu has venison sandwiches, salmon and
fettuccini. DJs from 10.30pm at weekends.

Paddy Barry's (☎ 03-578 7470; 51 Scott St; meals
$10-14; ☺ lunch & dinner) For pub food and oc-
casional live entertainment this big, vaguely
Irish pub serves filling meals and has a fun
atmosphere and an outdoor deck.

For self-catering head to the supermar-
ket, **Coles New World** (☎ 03-520 9030; Freswick St).

Getting There & Around

AIR
Blenheim airport is about 6km west of town
on Middle Renwick Rd. **Air New Zealand Link**
(☎ 0800 737 000, 03-578 4059; www.airnz.co.nz; 29 Queen
St) has direct flights to/from Wellington
(one-way $80, 25 minutes, 10 daily), with
connections to other centres.

BICYCLE
Spokesman (☎ 0800 422 453; spokes@xtra.co.nz; 61
Queen St; half-/full-day bike hire $35/60) hires bikes
and mobility scooters.

BUS
Deluxe Travel Lines (☎ 03-578 5467; blenheim.depot@
ritchies.co.nz; 45 Main St) has regular services between Blenheim and Picton ($8, 20 minutes,
two to four daily). The **InterCity** (☎ 03-577 2890;
www.intercitycoach.co.nz) Nelson–Christchurch
bus (five daily) stops at Blenheim en route.
There's also a host of shuttle buses that stop
at Blenheim on the Nelson–Christchurch
route (see p424).

TAXI
There's a **Red Band and Picton Taxis** (☎ 0800
802 225, 03-578 0225; 9 Market St) depot in the city
centre.

TRAIN
Tranz Scenic (☎ 0800 872 467; www.tranzscenic.co.nz;
☺ 7am-7pm) runs the scenic *TranzCoastal*
service between Picton ($10 to $20, 30 minutes, one daily) and Christchurch ($32 to
$75, five hours, one daily), which stops at
Blenheim.

RENWICK

Renwick is a tiny town about 10 minutes west
of Blenheim. Many of the region's wineries
are within walking distance (certainly within
cycling distance) of town. A dedicated **cycling
path** is being established around Renwick and
through the surrounding vineyards. You can
borrow bikes and get more information from
Watson's Way Backpackers.

Watson's Way Backpackers (☎ 03-572 8228; www
.watsonswaybackpackers.co.nz; 56 High St; camp sites $20,
dm $20, d $44-52) This is a lovely place to stay.
There's a purpose-built section at the back, a
leafy garden with small three- and four-bed
dorms and cheery en-suite doubles. Camping's available in the garden and there's free
bike use.

Vintner's Retreat (☎ 03-572 7420; www.thevint
nersretreat.co.nz; 55 Rapaura Rd; stables $240-275, manor
$260-290, lodge $325) Elegant Vintner's Retreat
is in the midst of the Renwick vineyards.
There are three types of self-contained
two- and three-bedroom villas, all very
roomy and tastefully decorated. Rates are
on a sliding scale for the number of guests/
nights – a group of six can have the biggest
lodge for less than $40 per person.

Cork & Keg (☎ 03-572 9328; Inkerman St) This
English-style country pub (right down to the
English guv'na) is a rip-roaring place for a
night out after wine-touring. It brews its own
draught beer and cider, as well as dispensing
Guinness. There's a big open fire, welcoming atmosphere and you can bring your own
meat and use the barbecue for free.

KAIKOURA

pop 3850
Kaikoura is a stunning town with a superb
setting on a bay backed by the steeply rising foothills of the Seaward Kaikouras, magnificently snowcapped in winter. It's 183km

KAIKOURA

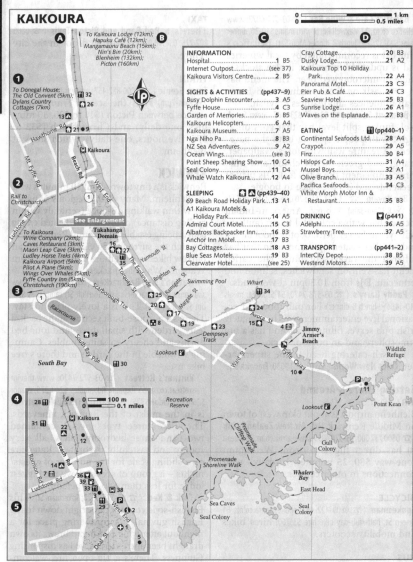

0 —————— 1 km
0 —————— 0.5 miles

To Kaikoura Lodge (12km);
Hapuku Café (12km);
Mangamaunu Beach (15km);
Blenheim (132km);
Picton (160km)

To Donegal House;
The Old Convent (5km);
Dylans Country
Cottages (7km)

Hawthorne Rd

Mt Fyffe Rd

Beach Rd

West End

Rail to
Christchurch

Ludstone Rd

To Kaikoura
Wine Company (2km);
Caves Restaurant (3km);
Maori Leap Cave (3km);
Ludley Horse Treks (4km);
Kaikoura Airport (5km);
Pilot A Plane (5km);
Wings Over Whales (5km);
Fyffe Country Inn (5km);
Christchurch (190km)

Takahanga
Domain

The Esplanade

Torquay St

Yarmouth St

Brighton St

Ramsgate St

Margate St

Scarborough Tce

Racecourse

South Bay Pde

South Bay

Swimming Pool

Wharf

Avoca St

Ward St

Fyffe Quay

Jimmy
Armer's
Beach

Dempseys
Track

Lookout

Recreation
Reserve

Wildlife
Refuge

Point Kean

Lookout

0 —————— 100 m
0 —————— 0.1 miles

Kaikoura

Beach Rd

Romson Rd

Ludstone Rd

West End

Deal St

Promenade
Clifftop Walk

Promenade
Shoreline Walk

Gull
Colony

Whalers
Bay

East Head

Sea Caves

Seal
Colony

Seal Colony

INFORMATION
Hospital...1 B5
Internet Outpost.....................(see 37)
Kaikoura Visitors Centre............2 B5

SIGHTS & ACTIVITIES   (pp437–9)
Busy Dolphin Encounter............3 A5
Fyffe House..................................4 C3
Garden of Memories...................5 B5
Kaikoura Helicopters..................6 A4
Kaikoura Museum.......................7 A5
Nga Niho Pa................................8 B3
NZ Sea Adventures.....................9 A2
Ocean Wings.........................(see 3)
Point Sheep Shearing Show.......10 C4
Seal Colony...............................11 D4
Whale Watch Kaikoura..............12 A4

SLEEPING   (pp439–40)
69 Beach Road Holiday Park....13 A1
A1 Kaikoura Motels &
   Holiday Park.........................14 A5
Admiral Court Motel..................15 C3
Albatross Backpacker Inn..........16 B3
Anchor Inn Motel......................17 B3
Bay Cottages..............................18 A3
Blue Seas Motels.......................19 B3
Clearwater Hotel..................(see 25)

Cray Cottage..............................20 B3
Dusky Lodge...............................21 A2
Kaikoura Top 10 Holiday
   Park..22 A4
Panorama Motel.........................23 C3
Pier Pub & Café..........................24 C3
Seaview Hotel.............................25 B3
Sunrise Lodge............................26 A1
Waves on the Esplanade............27 B3

EATING   (pp440–1)
Continental Seafoods Ltd...........28 A4
Craypot......................................29 A5
Finz..30 B4
Hislops Cafe...............................31 A4
Mussel Boys...............................32 A1
Olive Branch..............................33 A4
Pacifica Seafoods......................34 C3
White Morph Motor Inn &
   Restaurant.............................35 B3

DRINKING   (p441)
Adelphi......................................36 A5
Strawberry Tree.........................37 A5

TRANSPORT   (pp441–2)
InterCity Depot..........................38 B5
Westend Motors.........................39 A5

north of Christchurch on SH1, and a mecca for wildlife enthusiasts.

Kaikoura was once just a sleepy little fishing town noted mainly for its crayfish, until Nature Watch Charters began whale-watching trips in 1987. The tours' fame escalated, putting Kaikoura on the tourist map. Thousands of international visitors come

for the wildlife and during summer it pays to book the whale-watching and dolphin-swimming tours at least a few days ahead.

The 'Big Five' most likely to be seen are the sperm whale, the endemic Hectors dolphin (the smallest and rarest of dolphins), the dusky dolphin (found only in the southern hemisphere), the New Zealand fur seal and the bottlenose dolphin. Other animals frequently seen include orcas (killer whales), bottlenose dolphins, pilot whales and blue penguins. Sea birds include shearwaters, fulmars, petrels and royal and wandering albatross. Seals are readily seen on the rocks at the seal colony.

There's no guarantee of seeing any specific animal on any tour but something of interest will be sighted. Sperm whales are most likely to be seen from October to August and orcas from December to March. Most other fauna is seen year-round.

Marine animals are abundant at Kaikoura because of the currents and continental-shelf formation. From land, the shelf slopes gradually to a depth of about 90m, then plunges to more than 800m. Warm and cold currents converge here, and when the southerly current hits the continental shelf it creates an upwelling current, bringing nutrients up from the ocean floor and into the light zone. The waters are often red with great clouds of krill, the sperm whale's favourite food, attracting larger fish and squid.

History

In Maori legend, the tiny Kaikoura Peninsula (Taumanu o te Waka o Maui) was the seat where the demigod Maui sat when he fished the North Island up from the depths of the sea. The area was heavily settled before Europeans came – at least 14 Maori *pa* sites have been identified, including Nga Niho Pa.

Excavations near Fyffe House show that the area was a moa-hunter settlement about 800 to 1000 years ago. In 1857, George Fyffe came upon an early moa-hunter burial site near the present Fyffe House. He discovered the largest moa egg ever found (240mm long, 178mm in diameter).

James Cook sailed past the peninsula on 15 February 1770, but didn't land. His journal states that 57 Maoris in four double-hulled canoes came towards the *Endeavour*, but 'would not be prevail'd upon to put along side'. In 1828 the beachfront of Kaikoura, now the site of the Garden of Memories, was the scene of a tremendous battle. Here a Ngati Toa war party, led by chief Te Rauparaha, bore down on Kaikoura, killing or capturing several hundred of the Ngai Tahu tribe.

The first European to settle in Kaikoura was Robert Fyffe, who established a whaling station in 1842. Kaikoura was a whaling centre from 1843 until 1922, and sheep farming and agriculture flourished. After whaling ended, the sea and the farmland continued to support the community.

Information

Ambulance (☎ 03-319 5199; Beach Rd)
Hospital (☎ 03-319 7760; Deal St)
Internet Outpost (☎ 03-319 7970; www.internet-out post.com; 19 West End; $5.50 per hr)
Kaikoura visitors centre (☎ 03-319 5641; www .kaikoura.co.nz; West End; ☷ 9am-5.30pm Mon-Fri summer, 9pm-4.30pm Sat & Sun summer, 9am-5pm Mon-Fri winter, 9am-4pm Sat & Sun winter) By the car park (on the beach side). Staff are very helpful and can make tour bookings. There's a DOC representative here during summer.
Post office (☎ 03-319 6808; 41 West End)

Sights & Activities

George Fyffe, cousin of Kaikoura's first European settler, Robert Fyffe, came to Kaikoura from Scotland in 1854 and built **Fyffe House** (☎ 03-319 5835; fyffe.bill@xtra.co.nz; 62 Avoca St; tours adult/child $5/free; ☷ 10am-4pm) around 1860. The house is the only survivor from the whaling days.

Kaikoura Museum (☎ 03-319 7440; kk.museum@ xtra.co.nz; 14 Ludstone Rd; adult/child $3/50c; ☷ 12.30-4.30pm Mon-Fri, 2-4pm Sat & Sun) includes the old town jail (1910), historical photographs, Maori and colonial artefacts and an exhibit on the region's whaling era.

The 30-minute **Point Sheep Shearing Show** (☎ 03-319 5422; www.pointbnb.co.nz; Fyffe Quay; adult/ child $10/5; ☷ 1.30pm & 4pm) is extremely entertaining. Peter Smith does a sheep-shearing demonstration with one of his Drysdale ewes and you can feed and pat Ram Man, the show's star, and also learn a bit about wool classing. It also runs a charming **B&B** (r $90).

Just before Point Kean is a **seal colony**, with a nearby car park. From the shore, you can see seals lazing on the rocks wondering why everyone is looking at them.

For a taste of pinot, chardonnay and gewürztraminer, with striking sea views, visit the **Kaikoura Wine Company** (☎ 03-319 7966; www.kaikourawines.co.nz; tours & tasting $8.50, platters $24; ☷ 10am-5.30pm), 2km south of town off SH1. Tours leave on the hour and take in the winery plus the amazing cellar. It has delicious vineyard platters or you can bring a picnic.

On the hill at the eastern end of town is a water tower with a **lookout**; you can see both sides of the peninsula and along the coast. Take the walking track up to the tower from Torquay St or drive up Scarborough Tce.

There's a safe swimming **beach** in front of the Esplanade and a **pool**. Other beaches are on the peninsula's northeast (eg, Jimmy Armer's) and at South Bay. The whole coastline, with its rocky formations and abundant marine life, is good for **snorkelling** and **diving**. New Zealand Sea Adventures (below) offers scuba-diving opportunities. Mangamaunu Beach, about 15km north of Kaikoura, has good **surfing**.

A novel activity is offered by **Pilot A Plane** (☎ 03-319 6579; aeroclub.kaikoura@xtra.co.nz; Kaikoura airport; 30min flight $85), with no flying experience necessary. The Kaikoura Aero Club takes you on a flight and bravely lets you take the controls.

Dropping a line off the wharves is popular, particularly at the Kahutara River mouth or by surfcasting on the many beaches. For **fishing charters**, see opposite.

Two-hour guided **horse treks**, taking in farmland and either river beds or the coast, are available with **Fyffe View Horse Treks** (☎ 03-319 5069; fax 03-319 7202; Chapmans Rd) and **Ludley Horse Treks** (☎ 03-319 5925; Inland Rd). Treks cost around $45 to $50.

In winter, nearby **Mt Lyford** has skiing opportunities (p75). Shuttle buses run from Kaikoura to the mountain daily.

WALKING

There are two **walkways** starting from the seal colony, one along the seashore and one above it along the cliff top; a loop takes 2½ hours. If you go on the seashore trail, check the tides with the visitors centre beforehand (it's best to go within two hours of low tide). Both walks afford excellent views of the fur seal and red-billed seagull colonies. A trail from South Bay leads over farmland and back to the town (45 minutes).

Mt Fyffe Walking Track centres on Mt Fyffe (1602m), which dominates the narrow Kaikoura Plain and the town. Information about history, vegetation, birds and walking tracks is in the *Mt Fyffe and the Seaward Kaikoura Range* brochure.

Kaikoura Coast Track (☎ 03-319 2715; www.kaikouratrack.co.nz; $130) is a three-day walk through private farmland and along the Amuri Coast, 50km south of Kaikoura. The 43km walk has spectacular coastal views and accommo-

dation is in comfortable farm cottages. The cost includes three nights' accommodation and pack transport; bring your own sleeping bag and food. A two-day mountain-bike option is $70.

Tours

Tours are big business in Kaikoura. It's all about the marine mammals and there are some excellent opportunities to see these amazing creatures up close. For many, the main attraction is the sperm whale, and Kaikoura is an accessible spot to see one. Other whales include orcas, minke, humpback and southern right. Dolphins and sea birds are also spotted.

WHALE-WATCHING

For most a whale-watch tour is a thrilling experience, but there's one hitch: the weather. Whale Watch depends on planes to spot whales from the air, which is extremely difficult in foggy or wet conditions. The Whale Watch office then cancels line after line of disappointed customers. If this trip is a *must* for you, allow a few days.

Aerial whale-watching companies give a guarantee that you see the whole whale (as opposed to possibly only viewing a tail or flipper from a boat) as you fly overhead.

Kaikoura Aero Club (☎ 03-319 6579; kaikoura@xtra.co.nz; Kaikoura airport; 30min flight $85) Pilot A Plane flights

Kaikoura Helicopters (☎ 03-319 6609; www.kaikourahelicopters.co.nz; Railway Station; 30-40min flight $165-230)

Whale Watch Kaikoura (☎ 0800 655 121, 03-319 6767; www.whalewatch.co.nz; Whaleway Station, Whaleway Rd; tours adult/child $110/60; ☼ 3-16 trips daily) Based at the old train station, 3½-hour tours head out to sea in search of whales and other wildlife in boats equipped with hydrophones (underwater microphones) to pick up whale sounds. Book ahead.

Wings over Whales (☎ 0800 226 629, 03-319 6580; www.whales.co.nz; Kaikoura airport; 30min flight adult/child $135/75; ☼ 9am, 11am, 1pm & 3pm)

DOLPHIN & SEAL SWIMMING

Busy Dolphin Encounter (☎ 0800 733 365, 03-319 6777; www.dolphin.co.nz; 58 West End; observation adult/child $55/45, swim $115/105; ☼ 8.30am & 12.30pm, extra trip summer 5.30am) The chance to swim with huge pods of dusky dolphins. Wet suits, masks and snorkels provided for the three-hour 'dolphin encounter'. Book in advance as participants rave about this popular trip.

NZ Sea Adventures (☎ 0800 728 223, 03-319 6622; www.godive.co.nz; 114 Beach Rd; boat seal-swim adult/child

$60/50, observation $50/40, shore swim $45/40, dives $100/60; ☻ seal swim Oct-May) Boat- and shore-based seal swimming, plus diving tours. Sea-kayak tours explore the peninsula's coastline.

Seal Swim Kaikoura (☎ 03-319 6182; www.sealswim kaikoura.co.nz; 202 The Esplanade; adult/child $50/40; ☻ Nov-Apr) Two-hour guided snorkelling tours among NZ fur seals from the shore.

OTHER TOURS

Maori Leap Cave (☎ 03-319 5023; adult/child $8.50/3.50; ☻ 7am-7pm) A limestone cave discovered in 1958. Six 40-minute tours a day depart from Caves Restaurant, 3km south of town. Book at the restaurant or the visitors centre.

Maori Tours (☎ 0800 866 267, 03-319 5567; maoritours kk@xtra.co.nz; adult/child $75/35; ☻ 10.30am, extra trip summer 3pm) Advance bookings (up to one week) are essential for this popular half-day tour where you experience Maori hospitality and rituals.

Ocean Wings (☎ 0800 733 365, 03-319 6777; www.ocean wings.co.nz; 58 West End; adult/child $60/35) Bird-watchers relish the opportunity to see pelagic species, including albatross, shearwaters, shags, mollymawks and petrels.

South Bay Fishing Charters (☎ 03-319 7517; adult $70) Price includes a cray and fish lunch on this 2½-hour tour.

Victoria Lee Fishing Charters (☎ 03-319 6478; viclee@ ihug.co.nz; $750) Six- to seven-hour deep-sea crayfishing trips. Price includes all gear and a crayfish lunch.

Sleeping

For such a small place, Kaikoura has wall-to-wall accommodation – book ahead in summer. There are some excellent B&Bs and guesthouses, mostly on the outskirts of town, and plenty of motels to choose from, especially along The Esplanade.

BUDGET

Intense competition keeps the budget accommodation standard high.

Sunrise Lodge (☎ 03-319 7444; 74 Beach Rd; dm/tw $22/54; ☻ Sep-May) One of Kaikoura's newer backpackers, where the enthusiastic owners really make this place. You might be invited to help check craypots, go on a low-tide beach safari or rescue injured wildlife. The rooms are bright and comfortable (no bunks).

Cray Cottage (☎ 03-319 5152; 190 The Esplanade; dm $20-22, tw $50; ☻ Aug-May) A small, friendly and tranquil place with a self-contained hostel behind the owners' house. It's about 1km east of the town centre and free pick-up/drop-off is available.

Albatross Backpacker Inn (☎ 03-319 6090; www .albatross-kaikoura.co.nz; 1 Torquay St; dm $20-22, s $40, tw & d $52) High-quality backpackers hostel with a lovely large TV/living area, plus decks, verandas and even an aviary. Some of the dorms have 'Turkish-theme' bunks – semi-enclosed beds with a unique design.

Dusky Lodge (☎ 03-319 5959; duskyjack@hotmail .com; 67 Beach Rd; dm $20-21, tw & d $56) A busy hostel, with all the facilities to cope. There's a brilliant outdoor deck and spa with mountain views, and a good-sized kitchen and lounge.

Seaview Motel and **Clearwater Motel** (☎ 0800 456 000, 03-319 6149; 164 & 168 The Esplanade; self-contained units from $75) Two motels next to each other, both run by the same enthusiastic owner, who has a pinboard to mark your country of origin. Self-contained units are clean and nifty, many with sea views. This is a popular choice with Asian travellers.

Bay Cottages (☎ 03-319 5506; baycottages@xtra.co .nz; 29 South Bay Pde; cottages $60) Excellent-value tourist flats (with kitchenette and bathroom) capable of sleeping four to six. They're on South Bay, a few kilometres south of town, and close to swimming beaches and the excellent Finz restaurant (p441). The friendly owner may take you out crayfishing and often puts on a coffee-and-cray brunch.

Pier Pub & Café (☎ 03-319 5037; pierhotel@xtra.co .nz; 1 Avoca St; s/d $40/80, meals $9-20) A classic establishment, way down the southern end of the beach. Apart from being a friendly spot for a drink, there's cheap accommodation – many rooms have views of the water and Kaikoura Ranges, and there's a big old balcony. Rates include a continental breakfast.

69 Beach Road Holiday Park (☎ 03-319 6275; www.holidayparks.co.nz/69beach; 69 Beach Rd; camp sites/ campervan sites $21/22, cabins $30-70, self-contained units $45-105, motel units $60-180) This creek-side park is an excellent place right by a bakery. It has friendly, helpful owners and clean facilities, including a well-equipped communal kitchen.

Kaikoura Top 10 Holiday Park (☎ 03-319 5362; www.kaikouratop10.co.nz; 34 Beach Rd; camp sites/camper-van sites $24/26, cabins $43-53, units $70-80, motel r $100; ☋) Tucked away behind a large hedge is this well-maintained camping ground, with excellent facilities and a range of quality cabins.

A1 Kaikoura Motels & Holiday Park (☎ 03-319 5999; www.kiwiholidayparks.com; 11 Beach Rd; camp/ campervan sites $20, cabins $45-60, units $80-100; ☋)

About 200m from the town centre, this is a peaceful, green camping ground with a number of comfortable cabins and units. The area backs onto a creek. There's a trampoline to keep the kids bouncing.

MID-RANGE

Prices vary dramatically from low to high season. Listed here are the maximum rates.

Old Convent (☎ 03-319 6603; www.theoldconvent.co.nz; Mt Fyffe Rd; s $85, tw & d $115-175, f $195-210) This memorable B&B retains many features of the rambling old buildings. The old chapel is now an inviting guest lounge full of magazines, books and games and the rooms have lost their Acmud design and are decked out with old-fashioned furniture and crisp sheets.

Lemon Tree Lodge (☎ 03-319 7464; www.lemontree.co.nz; 31 Adelphi Tce; r $115-180, with breakfast $130-210) In a 1940s building, Lemon Tree offers boutique accommodation and receives rave reviews. The 'pacific' and 'crew' rooms have stunning views and there's a hot tub overlooking Kaikoura, the ocean and mountains.

Panorama Motel (☎ 03-319 5053; www.nzmotels.co.nz/panorama.kaikoura; 266 The Esplanade; self-contained units $90-120) Panorama wins on the view front. Comfortable, self-contained studios have views over the water to the distant mountains.

Donegal House (☎ 03-319 5083; www.donegalhouse.co.nz; Mt Fyffe Rd; s/d $100/120) Begorrah! There is some fine Irish hospitality at this simple B&B set in a huge garden. The real reason to stay here is for the proximity to the wonderful pub and restaurant (opposite).

Dylans Country Cottages (☎ 03-319 5473; www.dylanscottages.co.nz; Postmans Rd; cottages $140) Set on the lovely 'Lavendyl' lavender farm, these two private, self-contained cottages make a great escape. They're set in pretty gardens, and one cottage has a secluded outdoor bath and the other an indoor spa.

Also recommended:

Admiral Court Motel (☎ 03-319 5525; www.kaikouramotel.co.nz; 16 Avoca St; r $110-140) Clean, self-contained, motel-style units with Sky TV and a breezy aspect.

Blue Seas Motels (☎ 03-319 5441; panorama.motel@xtra.co.nz; 222 The Esplanade; studio $95-150, f from $165)

TOP END

Kaikoura Lodge (☎ 03-319 6559; Hapuku Rd; www.kaikouralodge.com; d $255-295) Twelve kilometres north of Kaikoura is this fabulously indul-

gent place, perfect for a stylish escape. It features US-imported timbers and furniture made on site, Sky TV and an olive grove. Part of the same complex is **Hapuku Café** (day menu $8-18; dinner mains $18-28; ☺ breakfast, lunch & dinner), specialising in venison and groper and with 85 varieties of South Island beer.

Anchor Inn Motel (☎ 03-319 5426; www.anchor-inn.co.nz; 208 The Esplanade; units $150-200) Anchor Inn is the top choice in town, with spacious, immaculate units. It's an award-winning motel and earns rave reviews. Extras include double-glazed tinted windows to enjoy the great water views without being seen.

Fyffe Country Inn (☎ 03-319 6869; fyffe@xtra.co.nz; SH1; d $189-330) Five kilometres south of Kaikoura, this luxurious lodge is set in magnificent gardens. Choose between studios in the inn or garden, with a huge suite available. The hospitable owners can tailor DB&B packages – well worthwhile as there's an award-winning restaurant here.

Waves on the Esplanade (☎ 03-319 5890; www.kaikouraapartments.co.nz; 78 The Esplanade; apt $180-250) Massive, beautiful, luxury apartments with balconies overlooking the ocean, shiny new appliances and furnishings, Sky TV and DVD players. Apartments have two bathrooms and a full kitchen.

Eating

If you're not into seafood you might struggle for choice in Kaikoura but if you love crustaceans and all things fishy you'll be in gastronomic heaven.

White Morph Motor Inn & Restaurant (☎ 03-319 5014; www.whitemorph.co.nz; 92-94 The Esplanade; half/full crayfish $50/95) A warm restaurant with professional service and convivial atmosphere. The inspiring menu includes wild NZ venison ('cooked no more than medium-rare and we won't be bribed') and Thai seafood broth with lemongrass and coconut. Next door are spacious, upmarket **units** ($115).

Hislops Cafe (☎ 03-319 6971; 33 Beach Rd; meals $6-15; ☺ breakfast, lunch & dinner) This smart café has a reputation for fresh, organic food. Start the morning with fruit salad, toasted muesli, omelettes or French toast and feel healthy and smug all day. There's also a daytime blackboard menu (salads, pasta, open sandwiches) and evening dining.

Craypot (☎ 03-319 6027; 70 West End; snacks $7-18, mains $20-30, half/full crayfish $50/97; ☺ lunch & dinner) This mellow, large, long-running restaurant

PICK YOUR POISSON

Among all the marine life you can encounter in Kaikoura, you certainly can't avoid one sea creature in town: the crayfish. The town's name reflects its abundance in these waters – in Maori 'kai' means food and 'koura' means crayfish. In season, crayfish is always featured in Kaikoura restaurants and local takeaways. Unfortunately, it's pricey – you'll pay the export price, which at the time of writing was hovering around $70 per kilogram. If you're not too keen on the idea of paying around $50 for a restaurant meal of half a cray ($90 to $100 for a whole), you can purchase fresh, nongarnished crays at **Pacifica Seafoods** (☎ 03-319 5817; The Wharf; 9am-5pm Mon-Fri) or from **Nin's Bin**, a rustic, beach-side caravan 20km towards Picton.

You could also take a **fishing tour** (p439) and crack into some cray that way. Alternatively, you might strike it lucky and find a local who'll kindly take you out crayfishing and allow you to share in their catch. This is an economical way to taste the local produce, not to mention fun.

and bar serves feeds of fresh, tender seafood. Try the mussel chowder or stop messing about and head directly for the cray.

Finz (☎ 03-319 6688; 103 South Bay Pde; mains $27-35; dinner daily Oct-May, Wed-Sun Jun-Sep) At South Bay, Finz is widely regarded by locals as the best restaurant in town. Try the cray, or Finz's signature dish, seafood fettuccine. Red-meat lovers will be tempted by venison, rib-eye steak and lamb. Alternatively, share a vino at the adjacent **bar** (meals $8-16).

Mussel Boys (☎ 03-319 7160; www.musselboys.co.nz; 80 Beach Rd; meals $20-30; lunch & dinner) Part of the small Mussel Boys chain, this is a bright, cheery and kid-friendly restaurant. It's a little out of town but worth the trip, especially if you're into bivalves – you can get them as 'flats' (grilled on the half-shell) or 'steamers' (whole shell). Tempting sauces include roast tomato and chilli, green curry and coconut milk.

Continental Seafoods Ltd (☎ 03-319 5509; 47 Beach Rd; meals $4-12) Heading north, just out of town, is the place for a grease hit – fish and chips, battered shellfish and fat, salty chips.

Olive Branch (☎ 03-319 6992; 54 West End; lunch mains $7-16, dinner mains $16-20, half/full cray $35/68) With the most reasonably priced cray in town, Olive Branch is classy and elegant and has a lovely balcony. The menu features venison pizza, vegetarian cannelloni, Marlborough mussels and vegetarian nachos.

For self-catering head to **Kaikoura Four Square** (☎ 03-319 5332; 31-33 West End).

Drinking

Strawberry Tree (☎ 03-319 6451; 21 West End; meals $5-9) A fun, atmospheric pub with couches, pool table and live music twice a month – jamming sessions encouraged. Snack food is

available and, on Friday nights in summer, there's free crayfish! Be sure to check out the journalistic photos taken by the owner. All the furniture and décor has been taken from demolished historical buildings.

Adelphi Lodge (☎ 03-319 6555; West End) Opposite Strawberry Tree, Adelphi is popular with punters and pool sharks as there are four pool tables.

Donegal House (☎ 03-319 5083; www.donegalhouse .co.nz; Mt Fyffe Rd; mains $23-28; lunch & dinner) An unexpected 'little Irish pub in the country' and a real gem. Guinness and Kilkenny are available and there's regular live music, plus a huge outdoor area. There's a simple menu offering well-prepared staples such as crayfish, steak, chicken and pasta.

Getting There & Away
BUS

There are **InterCity** (☎ 04-472 5111; www.intercity coach.co.nz) services operating between Kaikoura and Nelson ($50, five hours, two daily), Picton ($27, 1½ hours, two daily) and Christchurch ($25, 2½ hours, two daily). Buses arrive and depart from the town car park on West End; tickets and information are available at the visitors centre.

The following services run to/from Kaikoura to Christchurch, and to Picton, via Blenheim:

Atomic Shuttles (☎ 0800 248 885, 03-322 8883; www .atomictravel.co.nz)

East Coast Express (☎ 0508 830 900)

Hanmer Connection (☎ 0800 377 378, 03-315 7575)

South Island Connections (☎ 0508 742 669, 03-366 6633; www.southislandconnections.co.nz) Also runs to/from Kaikoura to Dunedin, Nelson and Motueka.

Southern Link (☎ 03-358 8355; www.yellow.co.nz/site /southernlink)

TRAIN
Tranz Scenic (☎ 0800 872 467, 04-495 0775; www.tranz
scenic.co.nz; ⏰ 7am-7pm) runs the *TranzCoastal*
service, which stops at Kaikoura on its run
between Picton ($20 to $45, two hours 20
minutes, one daily) and Christchurch ($20
to $45, three hours, one daily). The north-
bound train departs from Kaikoura at
10.25am, and the southbound at 4.05pm.

Getting Around
You can hire bicycles from **Westend Motors**
(☎ 03-319 5065; 48 West End; hour/half-day/full-day hire
$5/12/21), at the Shell service station.
You can hail or telephone a **taxi** (☎ 03-319
6214).

NELSON REGION

The Nelson region is one of the top destinations for travellers to NZ. It boasts an equable climate (more sunshine than any other
part of NZ), top beaches, and some of the
most popular national parks – Kahurangi,
Nelson Lakes and Abel Tasman – in the
country. It's also the home of an enthusiastic
and progressive community of artists, craftspeople, winemakers and entrepreneurs.

NELSON
pop 52,300
Nelson is a bright, active place and an obvious starting point for exploring the wonderful western coastal region. It's noted for its
fruit-growing, wineries and breweries and
its energetic arts and crafts community.

History
Maoris began to migrate to the South Island
during the 16th century, and among the first
to arrive in Nelson were the Ngati Tumatakokiri. By 1550 this tribe occupied most of
the region. Other tribes followed the Tumatakokiri, settling at the mouth of the Waimea
River. The Tumatakokiri remained supreme
in Tasman Bay until the 18th century, when
the Ngati-apa from Wanganui and the Ngai
Tahu – the largest tribe in the South Island –
combined for a devastating attack on the
Tumatakokiri, who virtually ceased to exist
as an independent tribe after 1800.
The Ngati-apa's victory was short-lived.
Between 1828 and 1830 they were practically annihilated by armed tribes from

Taranaki and Wellington who sailed into
the bay in the largest fleet of canoes ever
assembled in NZ.
By the time the European settlers arrived,
no Maoris lived at Te Wakatu – the nearest
pa being at Motueka – and the decimated
population that remained offered no resistance. The first Pakeha settlers set sail in
response to advertisements by the New
Zealand Company, set up by Edward Gibbon Wakefield to systematically colonise
the country. His grandiose scheme was to
transplant a complete slice of English life
from all social classes. In reality 'too few
gentlemen with too little money' accepted
the challenge and the new colony almost
foundered in its infancy.
The settlement was planned to consist of
small farms grouped around central towns.
However, the New Zealand Company's
entitlement to the land was disputed and it
was almost a year before this was sorted out.
Town land was distributed early, but farmland remained unallocated for so long that
landowners and labourers were forced to
live in town and whittle away their capital.
The Wairau Massacre (p422) resulted
in the deaths of 22 of Nelson's most able
citizens and plunged the colony into deep
gloom. To make matters worse, the New
Zealand Company was declared bankrupt in
April 1844 and the settlement had to endure
near-famine conditions. Only the later arrival of hard-working German immigrants
saved the region from economic ruin.

Information
BOOKSHOPS
Page Blackmore Booksellers (☎ 03-548 9992;
www.pageandblackmore.co.nz; 254 Trafalgar St)
Q Books (☎ 03-545 7555; q.books@clear.net.nz;
130 Hardy St) Second-hand book exchange.

EMERGENCY
Fire, police & ambulance (☎ 111)

INTERNET ACCESS
Aurora (☎ 03-546 6867; Trafalgar St; per 30min/1hr
$4/6)
Boots Off (☎ 03-546 8789; Bridge St; per 30min/1hr
$3.50/5) Also has second-hand and as-new books for sale.
Internet Outpost (☎ 03-539 1150; www.internet
-outpost.com; 38 Bridge St; $3.60/5 per 30min/1hr)
Kiwi Net Café (☎ 03-548 8404; 93 Hardy St; per
30min/1hr $3/4)

NELSON

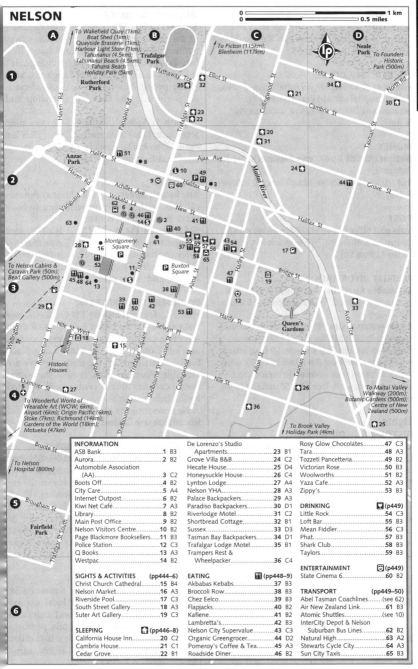

| 0 | 1 km |
| 0 | 0.5 miles |

To Wakefield Quay (1km);
Boat Shed (1km);
Quayside Brasserie (1km);
Harbour Light Store (1km);
Tahunanui (4.5km);
Tahunanui Beach (4.5km);
Tahuna Beach
Holiday Park (5km)

To Picton (115km);
Blenheim (117km)

Neale
Park To Founders
Historic
Park (500km)

To Nelson Cabins &
Caravan Park (50m);
Bead Gallery (500m)

To Wonderful World of
Wearable Art (WOW; 6km);
Airport (6km); Origin Pacific (6km);
Stoke (7km); Richmond (14km);
Gardens of the World (18km);
Motueka (47km)

To Maitai Valley
Walkway (200m);
Botanic Gardens (500m);
Centre of New
Zealand (500m)

To Brook Valley
Holiday Park (4km)

To Nelson
Hospital (800m)

Rutherford
Park

Trafalgar
Park

Anzac
Park

Montgomery
Square

Buxton
Square

Queen's
Gardens

Historic
Houses

Fairfield
Park

INFORMATION		
ASB Bank	1	B3
Aurora	2	B2
Automobile Association		
(AA)	3	C2
Boots Off	4	B3
City Care	5	A4
Internet Outpost	6	B2
Kiwi Net Café	7	A3
Library	8	B2
Main Post Office	9	B2
Nelson Visitors Centre	10	B2
Page Blackmore Booksellers	11	B3
Police Station	12	C3
Q Books	13	A3
Westpac	14	B2

SIGHTS & ACTIVITIES	(pp444–6)	
Christ Church Cathedral	15	B4
Nelson Market	16	A3
Riverside Pool	17	C3
South Street Gallery	18	A3
Suter Art Gallery	19	C3

SLEEPING	(pp446–8)	
California House Inn	20	C2
Cambria House	21	C1
Cedar Grove	22	B1

De Lorenzo's Studio		
Apartments	23	B1
Grove Villa B&B	24	C2
Hecate House	25	D4
Honeysuckle House	26	C4
Lynton Lodge	27	A4
Nelson YHA	28	A3
Palace Backpackers	29	A3
Paradiso Backpackers	30	D1
Riverlodge Motel	31	C2
Shortbread Cottage	32	B1
Sussex	33	D3
Tasman Bay Backpackers	34	D1
Trafalgar Lodge Motel	35	B1
Trampers Rest &		
Wheelpacker	36	C4

EATING	(pp448–9)	
Akbabas Kebabs	37	B3
Broccoli Row	38	B3
Chez Eelco	39	B3
Flapjacks	40	B2
Kafiene	41	B2
Lambretta's	42	B3
Nelson City Supervalue	43	C3
Organic Greengrocer	44	D2
Pomeroy's Coffee & Tea	45	A3
Roadside Diner	46	B2

Rosy Glow Chocolates	47	C3
Tara	48	A3
Tozzeti Pancetteria	49	B2
Victorian Rose	50	B3
Woolworths	51	B2
Yaza Cafe	52	A3
Zippy's	53	B3

DRINKING	(p449)	
Little Rock	54	C3
Loft Bar	55	B3
Mean Fiddler	56	C3
Phat	57	B3
Shark Club	58	B3
Taylors	59	B3

| **ENTERTAINMENT** | (p449) | |
| State Cinema 6 | 60 | B2 |

TRANSPORT	(pp449–50)	
Abel Tasman Coachlines	(see 62)	
Air New Zealand Link	61	B3
Atomic Shuttles	(see 10)	
InterCity Depot & Nelson		
Suburban Bus Lines	62	B2
Natural High	63	A2
Stewarts Cycle City	64	A3
Sun City Taxis	65	B3

LIBRARIES
Elma Turner Library (☎ 03-546 8100; library.info@ncc
.govt.nz; 27 Halifax St; ☺ 10am-6pm Mon-Thu, 10am-
7.30pm Fri, 10am-1pm Sat, 1-4pm Sun)

MEDICAL SERVICES
City Care (☎ 03-546 8881; 202 Rutherford St; ☺ 24hr)
Nelson Hospital (☎ 03-546 1800; Waimea Rd,
entrance Kawai St) Emergency doctor, ambulance and
dentist.

MONEY
Westpac (☎ 0800 400 600; www.westpac.co.nz; 168-170
Trafalgar St)
ASB (☎ 03-548 7426; www.asbbank.co.nz; cnr Trafalgar
& Hardy Sts)

POST
Main post office (☎ 03-546 7818; www.nzpost.co.nz;
cnr Trafalgar & Halifax Sts; ☺ 7.45am-5pm Mon-Fri,
9.30am-12.30pm Sat)

TOURIST INFORMATION
Automobile Association (AA; ☎ 03-548 8339; www
.nzaa.co.nz; 45 Halifax St; ☺ 8.30am-5pm Mon & Wed-
Fri, 9am-5pm Tue)
Nelson visitors centre (☎ 03-548 2304; www.nelson
nz.com; cnr Trafalgar & Halifax Sts; ☺ 8.30am-6pm summer, 8.30am-5pm Mon-Fri & 10am-4pm Sat & Sun winter)
Pick up a copy of the *Nelson Visitor Guide* here. A DOC officer
attends the visitors centre in summer for inquiries about
national parks and walks. There's a $2.50 service fee for bus
and tour bookings.

Sights
HISTORIC BUILDINGS
The traditional symbol of Nelson is its Art
Deco **Christ Church Cathedral** (☎ 03-548 1008; Trafalgar Sq; ☺ 8am-7pm), at the top of Trafalgar
St. Work began in 1925 but was delayed,
and arguments raged in the 1950s over
whether the building should be completed
according to its original design. Finally
completed in 1965 to a modified design, it
was consecrated in 1972, 47 years after the
foundation stone was laid.

Close to the cathedral, **South St** is home
to a row of restored workers' cottages,
dating from 1863–67, said to be the oldest
preserved street in NZ.

The beautiful **Isel Park gardens** are worth a
wander, and in the grounds you'll find the
historic **Isel House** (☎ 03-547 1347; isel@ihug.co.nz;
16 Hilliard St, Stoke; admission by donation; ☺ 11am-
4pm).

MUSEUMS & GALLERIES
Suter Art Gallery (☎ 03-548 4699; www.thesuter.org
.nz; 208 Bridge St; adult/child $3/50c; ☺ 10.30am-4.30pm)
adjoins Queen's Gardens and has a few
interesting lithographs and paintings. It's
the city's main repository of high art, with
changing exhibitions, musical and theatrical performances, films, a craft shop and
café.

South St Gallery (☎ 03-548 8117; www.nelson
pottery.co.nz; 10 Nile St W; admission free; ☺ 9am-5pm
Mon-Fri, 10am-4pm Sat & Sun) is noted for its extensive collection of pottery.

GARDENS
The **Botanic Gardens** has a lookout at Botanical Hill, with a spire proclaiming it NZ's
exact geographical centre.

Gardens of the World (☎ 03-542 3736; www
.gardensoftheworld.co.nz; 95 Clover Rd E, Hope; adult/child
$5/free; ☺ 10am-dusk) feature beautifully land-
scaped gardens from the Orient, America,
Europe and Australia.

FOUNDERS HISTORIC PARK
Home to **Founders Brewery** (☎ 03-548 4638; www
.biobrew.co.nz; Founders Historic Park, 87 Athawhai Dr),
NZ's first certified organic brewery, producing Tall Blonde, Red Head and Long Black
brews. Short tours of the microbrewery are
available. Founders Park is near the waterfront 1km from the city centre, easily spotted
by the large windmill.

Next door to the brewery is the beautiful
Miyazu Japanese Gardens.

MCCASHIN'S BREWERY & MALTHOUSE
Known as **Mac's Brewery** (☎ 03-547 0526; www
.macs.co.nz; 660 Main Rd, Stoke; tastings/tours $3/7;
☺ tours 11am & 2pm), it's the source of the favourite beer for many Nelsonites. Black
Mac, a dark ale, is legendary but there are
five varieties in all. Take a brewery tour or
just turn up at the bar for a tasting. It's about
6km south of Nelson in Stoke – the Stoke
Loop bus runs past.

NELSON MARKET
Nelson Market (☎ 03-546 6454; Montgomery Sq;
☺ 8am-1pm Sat) is an excellent local market
with lots of fresh produce, food stalls and
arts and crafts, such as wood, oils, possum-
fur products and glass. Sunday is the flea
market, **Monty's** (☺ 9am-1pm), at the same
place.

WONDERFUL WORLD OF WEARABLE ART & COLLECTABLE CARS MUSEUM

The Nelson and Golden Bay region exudes creativity. Artists, potters, weavers and fashion designers live and work here, so it's hardly surprising that NZ's most inspiring and successful art-meets-fashion show was born here.

It began humbly in 1987 when creator Suzie Moncrieff decided to hold an off-beat fashion show in a marquee in Wakefield. The concept was not simply to design a dress, but to create a piece of art that could be worn and modelled. Local artists and audiences loved the idea and slowly the New Zealand Wearable Art Award grew into an annual event, with traditional fabrics going out the window in favour of ever-more whacky and imaginative designs. Everything from wood, papier-mâché, paua shell, copper wire, soft-drink cans, wine bladders and food stuffs have been used to create the garments. The show also features themed entries such as the illumination section and the popular Bizarre Bra Award. Entries are now received from around NZ and abroad, and a look at some of the past winners (and entrants) shows that WOW creativity knows no limits.

The show, now called the Montana World of Wearable Art Award, is held in Nelson's Trafalgar Sq every September. The extravaganza is held over six nights and in 2003 it attracted more than 15,000 people, including Prime Minister Helen Clark and international dignitaries. Even if you can't check out the show, be sure to get along to the eye-popping **WOW gallery** (☎ 03-548 9299; www.wowcars.co.nz; 95 Quarantine Rd; adult/child $15/7; ☽ 9am-6.30pm summer, 10am-5pm winter). It opened in 2001, and showcases the bizarre and spellbinding 'garments' featured in the Wearable Art Awards. The galleries are small but hi-tech, with a carousel mimicking the usual catwalk models, and an illumination room. The artworks change every three months and there are plans to display more in future.

Equally enthralling is the **Collectable Cars** display, featuring mint-condition classics such as a 1959 pink Cadillac, a 1908 Renault made famous as a Parisienne taxi, an E-type Jaguar and an Eldorado Cadillac convertible used by Eisenhower in the 1953 US presidential parade.

There's also a **café** (meals $6-14) in the foyer of the gallery with cakes, sandwiches and platters.

Activities

There are plenty of activities on offer in this region, and although most take place some way out of the city, the following operators will pick up and drop off in Nelson. For tramping and sea kayaking see p456.

Nelson Bonecarver (☎ 03-546 4275; 87 Green St, Tahunanui; day course $55) offers instruction and materials so you can design and carve your own pendant out of bone. You can also create your own bead necklace at the **Bead Gallery** (☎ 03-546 7807; www.beads.co.nz; 18 Parere St; ☽ 9am-5pm Mon-Sat, 10am-4pm Sun).

Go paragliding with **Adventure Paragliding and Kiteboarding** (☎ 03-546 6863; www.skyout.co.nz; 6 Bridge St; ☽ 9.30am-5.30pm Mon-Fri, 9.30am-12.30pm Sat) or **Nelson Paragliding** (☎ 03-544 1182; www.nelsonparagliding.co.nz; 108 Queen St). Both charge $155 for a tandem flight and $190 for a full-day introductory course.

Tandem skydive with **Skydive Abel Tasman** (☎ 0800 422 899, 03-528 4091; www.skydive.co.nz; 16 College St, Motueka airstrip; jumps 9000ft/12,000ft $210/260). It includes transport to Motueka airstrip, 10 minutes' instruction and a certificate.

Hang-gliding with **Nelson Hang Gliding Adventures** (☎ 03-548 9151; gmeadows@clear.net.nz; 20min flight $140) is another aerial possibility at Takaka Hill and the Richmond Range.

Rock climbing on the sheer limestone cliffs of the Golden Bay and Takaka area has long been popular with local outdoor enthusiasts. **Vertical Limits** (☎ 03-545 7511; www.verticallimits.co.nz; 28 Halifax St; $130; ☽ 10am-9pm Mon-Fri, 10am-6pm Sat & Sun) has full-day rock-climbing trips – no experience necessary – and **Nelson Bays Adventure** (☎ 0800 379 842, 03-526 7842; www.whenua-iti.org.nz; Moutere Hwy, Lower Moutere; day trip $120) offers rock climbing, caving and tramping.

Another popular activity is the skywire and four-wheel motorbike tours with **Happy Valley Adventures** (☎ 0800 157 300, 03-545 0304; www.happyvalleyadventures.co.nz; 194 Cable Bay Rd; adult/child skywire $65/55, four-wheel motorbike driver $65-125, passenger $20-30), a 10-minute drive northwest along SH6.

Horse riding is handled by **Stonehurst Farm Horse Treks** (☎ 0800 487 357, 03-542 4121; www.stonehurstfarm.co.nz; RD 1, Richmond; 2hr/half-day rides $35/85), which offers one-hour farm rides, two-hour Sundowner treks and, for experienced riders, the chance to take part in a cattle muster.

There are many opportunities to go sailing in Tasman Bay. To help out on a yacht, the best option is the Wednesday night races, run by **Catamaran Sailing Charters** (☎ 03-547 6666; www.sailingcharters.co.nz; 46 Martin St; Wed night races $40, adult/child day trip from $85/40, whole boat $300). You get two hours to help crew a boat around the harbour in racing conditions.

Of the many **walks**, the riverside footpath makes a pleasant stroll through the city, and the Maitai Valley Walkway is particularly restful and beautiful. There are also fun **mountain biking** trails about the place. Natural High (p450) provides maps, information and bikes.

For **swimming**, head to the picturesque **Riverside Pool** (☎ 03-546 3221; Riverside Dr).

Tours

For sea kayaking in the Abel Tasman National Park see p456. Popular tours around Nelson include wineries in the Richmond and Upper Moutere area, and 'craft and scenic tours' and helicopter flights.

Bay Tours (☎ 0800 229 868, 03-544 4494; www.baytours nelson.co.nz; 48 Brougham St; half-/full-day wine tour $60/135, craft $50/72, scenic $50-135) A variety of tours, including combinations of wine and craft.

JJ's Scenic Tours (☎ 0800 568 568; www.jjs.co.nz; 10 Musgrave Cres, Tahunanui; half-day tour $55) Tours visit four vineyards and a brewery. Also offers a variety of other tours.

Tasman Helicopters (☎ 03-528 8075; www.tasman helicopters.co.nz; tours from $110) A host of chopper flights and tours, including *Lord of the Rings* locations, D'Urville Island sea fishing, wine tours and flights over Farewell Spit and Kahurangi and Abel Tasman National Parks.

Festivals & Events

With its enthusiastic artistic flair, Nelson stages many noteworthy events throughout the year. For the Montana World of Wearable Art Award see p445.

Arts Festival (☎ 03-546 0212; www.nelsonfestivals.co.nz) September. Events such as a masked carnivale parade, cabaret, writers, theatre and music.

Nelson Jazz Festival (☎ 03-546 9269; www.nelsonjazz .co.nz/3Festival.htm) Late December. Jazz cats from all round NZ gather for this musical extravaganza.

Sleeping

In summer Nelson swells with tourists. Book accommodation in advance or arrive early in the day.

Nelson is backpacker central, so hostel accommodation is often purpose-built and high quality. Ye olde B&Bs, furnished in convincingly Victorian style, are popular and many of these are in beautiful heritage buildings.

Many of Nelson's motels are near the beach at Tahunanui, on Beach Rd and Muritai St. Others are on the highway in from Richmond.

BUDGET
Paradiso Backpackers (☎ 03-546 6703; www.backpacke nelson.co.nz; 42 Weka St; camp sites from $12, dm $20-22, tw & d $52; 🏊) Club Med for the impoverished, Paradiso is a sprawling place in spacious grounds. There's plenty of pool-side action, watched over by the glassed-in main kitchen, a high-rotation hammock, volleyball court and sauna. Rooms are nothing special; dorms are four- and eight-bed with mezzanines, and there's heated A-frame tents. Free veggie soup in winter and an $8 barbecue in summer are big hits.

Tasman Bay Backpackers (☎ 03-548 7950; www .tasmanbaybackpackers.co.nz; 10 Weka St; dm $22, tw & d $52) This popular option is light and airy with great views, communal living areas and a well-used hammock and swing chair. Colourful rooms have four to six beds with individual reading lights and shared facilities. The kitchen is well organised and the friendly young owners cook bread in winter. Tasman is a cool place.

Shortbread Cottage (☎ 03-546 6681; 33 Trafalga St; dm/d $22/53) A small, homely, 13-bed hostel. Cosy rooms are freshly painted and bed have new mattresses; only two bedroom have en suites. There's a small kitchen and a great outdoor garden area. Home-made shortbread is served at 6pm.

Trampers Rest & Wheelpacker (☎ 03-545 7477 fax 03-548 7897; 31 Alton St; dm/d $20/50) With jus a few beds, Trampers is hard to beat fo a homely environment. The enthusiasti owner is a keen tramper and cyclist and provides information as well as free us of bikes. There's a small kitchen, book ex change, tuned piano and lots of CDs.

Nelson YHA (☎ 03-545 9988; yhanels@yha.org.n 59 Rutherford St; dm $20, tw & d $50-70) This spotless central place is purpose-built with facilitie such as a soundproof, vaultlike TV room and a well-organised modern kitchen open ing onto an outdoor terrace.

Hecate House (☎ 03-546 6890; www.brazen.co.r /hecate; 181 Nile St; dm $20, s/d $45/50, tw per person $2.

Chilled, female energy radiates from Hecate House, a women-only hostel in a lovely historic house. There's a cosy TV room, small kitchen and laundry facilities, and the cedar hot tub, in the organic garden, is a therapeutic way to iron out those tramping kinks.

Honeysuckle House (☎ 03-548 7576; 125 Tasman St; s/d/tw $35/52/54) A friendly, family-run, 11-bed backpackers in a quiet part of town. A lovely, homely environment. Twins and doubles have a TV and the back garden is the geographic centre of NZ!

Palace Backpackers (☎ 03-548 4691; www.thepalace.co.nz; 114 Rutherford St; dm $20, tw & d $50) The Palace is in an early-20th-century villa set above the street with views from the balconies. It doesn't look like much from the street but this is perhaps the nicest of the big backpackers. It has plenty of character, no bunks and lots of little common areas.

Nelson Cabins & Caravan Park (☎ 03-548 1445; www.holidayparks.co.nz/nelson; 230 Vanguard St; cabins & tourist flats $48-60) Clean, friendly and the most central caravan park in Nelson. There are no camp sites but the basic cabins are a mixture of twins, bunk beds and tourist flats.

Tahuna Beach Holiday Park (☎ 03-548 5159; www.tahunabeachholidaypark.co.nz; 70 Beach Rd; camp sites & campervan sites $22, cabins $30-55, flats $56-70, units $80-90) This is a huge park accommodating thousands – such as a mini-village with its own supermarket, on-site dairy, mini golf and *pétanque*. It's near the beach, 5km from the city, with a huge range of accommodation.

Brook Valley Holiday Park (☎ 03-548 0399; fax 03-548 7582; 584a Brook St; camp sites & campervan sites $20, cabins $23-40) This place, at the end of Tasman St in the upper Brook Valley, is in a superb forested setting by a stream. It's the same distance from the centre as Tahuna, but smaller and more personal.

MID-RANGE

Grove Villa B&B (☎ 0800 488 900, 03-548 8856; www.grovevilla.co.nz; 36 Grove St; s/d $75/90, s with bathroom $85-115, d with bathroom $100-140) Reasonably priced B&B with six rooms in a gorgeous heritage home close to town. Rooms are furnished in period style and have a TV and lots of natural light. Continental breakfast is served in the country-style dining room, which opens onto an outdoor area. The lounge has a log fire and big windows.

De Lorenzo's Studio Apartments (☎ 0508 335 673, 03-548 9774; www.delorenzos.co.nz; 51-55 Trafalgar St; r from $145; P 🖥) Central, luxurious, self-contained apartments with spa baths, cable TV with plenty of movie channels, and washing machine and dryer. It's worth the price for that little bit extra.

Sussex (☎ 03-548 9972; www.sussex.co.nz; 238 Bridge St; s $100-130, d $120-150) In a historic family home, the Sussex has four lovely en suite rooms and a fifth with a private bathroom down the hall – all named after famous composers – the owners are musicians. The Strauss room has the best views. There's a pleasant garden and buffet breakfast is included.

Lynton Lodge (☎ 03-548 7112; www.nzmotels.co.nz/lynton/index.html; 25 Examiner St; self-contained apt $90) High on the hill, with wonderful views of Nelson and the cathedral lit up at night, Lynton Lodge has excellent older-style self-contained apartments. It looks and feels more like a guesthouse than a motel, with relaxed common areas. A terrific option.

Trafalgar Lodge Motel (☎ 0800 000 051, 03-548 3980; www.trafalgarlodge.co.nz; 46 Trafalgar St; B&B $55, studios $85-92) Centrally located, Trafalgar has options for all budgets. There's cheaper B&B-style rooms in the guesthouse and classic studio rooms with phone and Sky TV in the motel section. B&B rooms have a sink, electric blankets, a couch and an area to make hot beverages, and includes breakfast.

Cedar Grove (☎ 0800 233 274, 03-545 1133; www.cedargrove.co.nz; cnr Trafalgar & Grove Sts; studio $120-200, self-contained r $140-170) A popular motel that's often full, so book ahead. Warm and spacious rooms are clean, with cooking facilities and all the business trimmings such as phone and fax. The spa, robes, CD player and video are for later.

Riverlodge Motel (☎ 03-548 3094; www.manz.co.nz/riverlodge; 31 Collingwood St; studios $79, self-contained apt $105-150) Central and accessible for walks along the river. There's a range of rooms, varying in size and newness, but generally spacious and with Sky TV. There's a quiet studio at the rear.

TOP END

California House Inn (☎ 03-548 4173; www.californiahouse.co.nz; 29 Collingwood St; r $185-240) An original manor home with six gorgeous rooms immaculately furnished with Victorian-era furniture and grace. So as not to spoil the look, TV and video and DVD players are available on request. Service is personalised and food is a big thing with an elaborate breakfast each morning – house specials include stuffed pancakes and home-made peach jam.

Cambria House (☎ 0800 548 4681, 03-548 4681; www.cambria.co.nz; 7 Cambria St; r $185-245) In a 139-year-old homestead, Cambria has seven rooms in what was once a sea captain's manor. Expect a sumptuous breakfast using local and free-range produce, eg Marlborough salmon omelette. Some of the rooms are small, making them a tad overpriced, but there's a relaxing lounge and decking area.

Eating

The wealth of local produce, particularly seafood, makes dining out in Nelson an exciting prospect. Deep-sea fish such as orange roughy and hoki, scallops from the bays, and mussels and oysters are available, complemented by well-rounded NZ wines, particularly from the Marlborough region, and microbrewed beers. Food is often organic and there are loads of vegetarian options.

RESTAURANTS

Victorian Rose (☎ 03-548 7631; 281 Trafalgar St; mains $13-18; ☼ noon-late) This place is a pastiche of English/Irish pub styles in airy, high-ceilinged premises. Substantial counter meals include mussels and cockles steamed in Mac beer and served with fresh buttered bread, lamb and chicken roast, seafood mornay and fish or chicken curry. There are backpacker specials available. (See also Drinking, opposite.)

Lambretta's (☎ 03-545 8555; 204 Hardy St; mains $22-28; ☼ 9am-late Mon-Sat, summer 6pm-late Sun) Named after the Italian scooter, this predominantly pizza-and-pasta restaurant is reasonably priced with a busy, casual atmosphere. There are no run-of-the-mill toppings here – all are interesting gourmet combinations. It's a big place with Grecian columns.

Broccoli Row (☎ 03-548 9621; 5 Buxton Sq; mains $20-25; ☼ lunch & dinner Mon-Sat) Vegetarian and seafood dishes are the speciality here, including soups, tapas platters and spinach-and-potato gnocchi. It's a lovely little BYO café, tucked away off Buxton Sq.

Boat Shed (☎ 03-546 9783; 351 Wakefield Quay; lunch mains $16-18, dinner mains $24-27; ☼ breakfast, lunch & dinner) The Boat Shed is an ambient seafood restaurant sitting on stilts over the sea. The food here is undeniably delicious. There's an interesting menu, including a range of 'breakfast cocktails' – perfect for continuing your hangover.

Tara (☎ 03-548 0881; 104 Hardy St; lunch mains $4-12, dinner mains $8.50-15; ☼ lunch Tue-Sat, dinner Mon-Sat) An affordable restaurant serving sushi, udon noodles and miso soup.

For excellent seafood by the ocean and a touch of the Cote d'Azur in sunny Nelson, head to Wakefield Quay for the **Quayside Brasserie** (☎ 03-548 3319; 309 Wakefield Quay; meals $16-30; ☼ lunch & dinner) or the casual **Harbour Light Store** (☎ 03-546 6685; 341 Wakefield Quay; meals $8-24; ☼ lunch & dinner).

CAFÉS

Kafiene (☎ 03-545 6911; 22 New St; meals $8.50-12; ☼ breakfast & lunch Mon-Sat, dinner Sat) Kid-friendly Kafiene is a chilled place, set in a pebble-covered courtyard that's dotted with well-loved couches, decorative mirror mosaics, a dedicated play area with toys and heavy-duty sandpit, and established greenery. Feast on bagels, veggie burgers, nachos, thumpin' breakfasts and delicate butterfly cupcakes. It has a range of loose-leaf herbal teas.

Rosy Glow Chocolates (☎ 03-548 3383; 20 Harley St; per chocolate $3-3.50, boxed selections $18-36; ☼ 9am-5pm Mon-Fri, 10am-1pm Sat) A sibling of the original Rosy Glow in Collingwood (p462), this is a must on any chocoholic's itinerary. Home-made logs of rich, creamy chocolate such as conquistador (hazelnut praline in dark chocolate) and ginger bar (caramel and chopped ginger).

Chez Eelco (☎ 03-548 7595; 296 Trafalgar St; brunch mains $10-16, dinner mains $12-27; ☼ breakfast, lunch & dinner) Near the cathedral, Chez Eelco is a Nelson institution. The spacious, arty café has plenty of newspapers and magazines to read and serves terrific breakfasts and light meals; the lemon meringue pies are divine. There's a small gallery at the back and art exhibited on the walls.

Flapjacks (☎ 03-548 0270; 75 Bridge St; burgers $6-10, mains $17-23; ☼ breakfast, lunch & dinner) Nelson's version of the American diner, with pine tables, booths, and an outdoor eating area. The burgers are big and extremely popular. There's a range of pancakes and toasted sandwiches. Closes early on Monday.

Zippy's (☎ 03-546 6348; 276 Hardy St; meals $4.50-7; ☼ lunch Mon-Sat) At this biorhythmically aligned vegetarian lunch spot, décor is a crazy combo of purple, teal and red and service is zippy yet earnest. Food includes risotto cakes, fabulous frittata and the 'locally famous' chocolate afghans. Drinks include ice-cream shakes, *chai* and heart-startlingly rich, full-flavoured coffee.

Yaza Cafe (☎ 03-548 2849; Montgomery Sq; meals $4-11, cover charge $3; ☉ breakfast & lunch daily, dinner Thu-Sat) At the site of the weekend markets, Yaza is a cosy, kid-friendly café with all-day breakfast and live music most Fridays and Saturdays, ranging from folk, acoustic blues and roots, punk, pop and reggae. The food is free-range and organic and patchouli lingers in the air – it's 'your lounge in town'.

Pomeroy's Coffee & Tea (☎ 03-548 7524; 276 80 Hardy St; ☉ 9am-6pm) A coffee and tea supplier that will have connoisseurs beaming. Sells the best beans and fresh, loose-leaf tea imported from overseas.

QUICK EATS

Akbabas Kebabs (☎ 03-548-8825; 130 Bridge St; meals $6.50-10.50; ☉ 11am-9pm) Tiny Turkish kebab house. Dine at low tables surrounded by rugs and carpets in the small corner lounge. Perfect for a quick bite.

Tozetti Pancetteria (☎ 03-546 8484; 41 Halifax St; $3.50-5.50; ☉ 7am-5pm Mon-Fri, 7am-noon Sat) You'll smell fresh bread baking before you see Tozetti. A tiny bakery serving beautiful breads, sandwiches and sweet treats. Strong Pomeroy's coffee.

Roadside Diner (Trafalgar St, near Bridge St; meals $6-12; ☉ 6pm-3.30am Fri & Sat) A big white pie cart that has been serving food since 1933. Reputedly the 'biggest burgers in NZ'.

SELF-CATERING

Organic Greengrocer (☎ 03-548 3650; www.organic greengrocer.co.nz; cnr Tasman & Grove Sts; pies $3; ☉ 8.30am-5pm Mon-Fri, 9am-3pm Sat) Stocking all things wheat-, dairy- and gluten-free, this organic food store has a range of fresh produce and dry goods, and vegetarian pies and cakes are baked on the premises. You can also join up for Willing Workers on Organic Farms (WWOOF) memberships here (see p677).

Head to **Woolworths** (☎ 03-546 6466; cnr Paruparu Rd & Halifax St) and **Nelson City Supervalue** (☎ 03-548 0191; 69 Collingwood St; ☉ 8am-9pm), which claims to stock more than 480 organic products.

Drinking & Entertainment

Nelson has a small but active nightlife scene. Most of the late-night pubs and bars cluster around Bridge St, where the action starts to build by around 10pm.

Victorian Rose (p448) Backpackers (and locals) often start with a meal and a few drinks at this popular spot. Guinness is served with care and there's a large selection of beers; happy hour is from 4pm to 7pm Friday. There are also regular live bands (jazz on Tuesday, blues on Thursday).

Mean Fiddler (☎ 03-546 8516; 145 Bridge St; meals $6.50-15) A real bar. This pub is traditionally Irish (owned by a Dubliner) but not obnoxiously so with leprechauns and shamrocks everywhere. It has the biggest range of whiskies in Nelson (some costing up to $1000) and a range of imported beers. There's live music daily and an outdoor courtyard.

Phat (☎ 03-548 3311; 137 Bridge St; cover charge $5-25; ☉ 10pm-late Wed-Sat) DJs at this righteous club spin techno, dub, drum and bass, breaks and hip-hop. Phat hosts big-name international acts. There's a cover charge every night, which those who worship the beats happily pay.

Shark Club (☎ 03-546 6630; 132-136 Bridge St; snacks $4-6; ☉ noon-late) If you're hankering for a game of stick, with some of the fiercest white pointers around, head to this pool hall. There's a pool comp every Wednesday and Thursday (entry $2), a jukebox for inspiration and bar snacks (nachos, wedges etc) for fuel.

The **Suter Art Gallery** (p444) has theatre, music and dance. **State Cinema 6** (☎ 03-548 3885; www.statecinema6.co.nz; 91 Trafalgar St) has six big screens and is the place to see mainstream, new-release flicks.

Other places worth checking out:

Little Rock (☎ 03-546 8800; 165 Bridge St; ☉ noon-late Mon-Fri, 3pm-late Sat & Sun) Popular bar and café, decorated in Flintstone-era décor, which turns into a dance club after about 11pm.

Taylor's (☎ 03-548 0508; 131 Bridge St) Glitzy lights and blinking slot machines. A party place popular with backpackers – there are $10 drink-and-food deals.

Loft Bar (☎ 03-545 7576; Bridge St) Cool hip-hop and funk.

Getting There & Away

AIR

Air New Zealand Link (☎ 0800 737 000; www.airnz.co.nz; cnr Trafalgar & Bridge Sts; ☉ 9am-5pm Mon-Wed & Fri, 9.30am-5pm Thu, 9.30am-12.30pm Sat) has direct flights to/from Wellington (one-way $95, 35 minutes, 10 daily), Auckland ($140, one hour 20 minutes, eight daily) and Christchurch ($100, 50 minutes, seven daily), with connections to other cities.

Origin Pacific (☎ 0800 302 302, 03-547 2020; www .originpacific.co.nz; Trent Dr), which is based in Nelson, has direct connections to several major centres, including Auckland (one way $100 to $225, 1¼ hours, two daily), Christchurch ($65 to $170, 50 minutes, two to five daily) and Wellington ($60 to $165, 35 minutes, six to 10 daily). There's a service to Hamilton ($100 to $230, two hours 20 minutes, three to four daily) via Wellington.

BUS
See also p459 for details about services to/ from Abel Tasman National Park.

Abel Tasman Coachlines (☎ 03-548 0285; www.abel tasmantravel.co.nz; 27 Bridge St) operates services to Motueka ($9, one hour, two to three daily), Takaka ($22, two hours 10 minutes, two daily) and Kaiteriteri ($14, one hour 20 minutes, one daily).

Atomic Shuttles (☎ 0800 248 885, 03-322 8883; www .atomictravel.co.nz; cnr Trafalgar & Halifax Sts) has buses to Picton ($15, two to 2½ hours, one to two daily), Greymouth ($40, 7¾ hours, one daily) and Fox Glacier ($70, 10 hours, one daily).

InterCity coaches (☎ 03-548 1538; www.intercity coach.co.nz; 27 Bridge St) runs services daily to Picton ($29, two hours, three daily), Christchurch ($70, 8½ hours, one daily) and Greymouth ($70, six hours, one daily) via Murchison and Westport, with connections to Franz Josef and Fox Glaciers.

K Bus (☎ 03-525 9434; www.kahurangi.co.nz) provides transport to/from Picton ($20, two hours, two to three daily), Collingwood ($34, three hours, one to two daily), Takaka ($22, 2½ hours, two daily) and the beginning of the Heaphy Track ($42, three hours 50 minutes, one daily).

Getting Around
TO/FROM THE AIRPORT
Super Shuttle (☎ 0800 748 885, 03-547 5782; www.super shuttle.co.nz; $10) offers 24-hour door-to-door service to and from the airport, which is 6km southwest of town. A taxi to the airport costs about $15.

BICYCLE
If you want to nip from town to the beach, or do some serious off-road touring, hire a bike from **Natural High** (☎ 03-546 6936; www.natural high.co.nz; 52 Rutherford St; bike hire per day $25-80), which has a large specialist range. **Stewarts Cycle City** (☎ 03-548 1666; www.stewartscyclecity.com;

114 Hardy St; half-/full-day hire $20/40) also hires bikes and does repairs; it offers cheap deals to travellers from abroad.

BUS
Nelson Suburban Bus Lines (☎ 03-548 3290; www .nelsoncoaches.co.nz; 27 Bridge St) operates local services from its terminal out to Richmond via Tahunanui and Stoke until about 5pm or 6pm weekdays, and until 2pm or 3pm on Saturday. These connect with two loop services in Stoke, which will get you to Isel park, Broadgreen House and Mac's Brewery

The **Bus** (☎ 03-547 5912; single trip $4) is a central bus service running every hour or so on four routes, all starting from the bus depot.

TAXI
Sun City Taxis (☎ 0800 422 666, 03-548 2666; 140 Bridge St) has a convenient rank at Bridge St. Also try **Nelson City Taxis** (☎ 0800 108 855, 03-548 8223).

NELSON LAKES NATIONAL PARK
At the pristine Nelson Lakes National Park are two beautiful glacial lakes fringed by beech forest and flax, with a backdrop of forested mountains. Part of the park, east of Lake Rotoiti, is classed as a 'mainland island' and is part of an aggressive conservation scheme to eradicate introduced pests such as possums and stoats, and recover native flora and fauna. There's excellent tramping, including short walks, lake scenery and also winter skiing at Mt Robert ski field. Lakes Rotoiti and Rotoroa are rich with bird life and famous for brown trout fishing.

Orientation & Information
The park is accessible from two different areas: Lakes Rotoiti and Rotoroa. St Arnaud village, on the shore of Lake Rotoiti (on the highway between Murchison and Blenheim) is a tiny place but the main centre. Rotoroa, about 7km off the highway, has far fewer visitors and little accommodation (mainly trampers and fishing groups).

The **DOC visitors centre** (☎ 03-521 1806; www .doc.govt.nz; View Rd, St Arnaud; ☺ 8am-4.30pm) has park information, including weather reports and hut tickets. It also has an interesting interpretive display.

Walking
An excellent three-day tramp from St Arnaud takes you south along the eastern

shore of Lake Rotoiti to Lake Head Hut, across the Travers River and up the Cascade Track to Angelus Hut on beautiful, alpine Lake Angelus. The trip back to St Arnaud goes along Robert Ridge to the Mt Robert ski field. The track descends steeply to the Mt Robert car park, from where it's a 7km road walk back to St Arnaud.

Other walks at Rotoiti, most starting from the car park and camping area at Kerr Bay, include the Bellbird Walk (10 minutes), Honeydew Walk (45 minutes), Peninsula Nature Walk (1½ hours), Black Hill Track (1½-hour return), St Arnaud Range Track (five hours), Loop Track (1½-hour return) and Lake Circuit (seven hours).

Short walks around Lake Rotoroa include the Short Loop Track (20 minutes), while medium-length ones include Porika Lookout (two- to three-hour return) at the northern end of the lake, and Braeburn Walk (two-hour return) on the western side. The long and arduous track along the eastern shore of the lake connects with the Travers-Sabine and Speargrass Tracks to Lake Rotoiti. The DOC visitors centre has brochures about all these walks and can provide current information about track conditions.

Sleeping & Eating

There are well-equipped **DOC camping grounds** (☎ 03-521 1806; camp sites/campervan sites summer $16/20, winter $10/12) on the lake shore at West Bay and Kerr Bay. Sites have toilets, hot showers and a kitchen.

St Arnaud has quite a few accommodation options, but it's a quiet place after about 8pm.

Yellow House (☎ 03-521 1887; www.nelsonlakes.co.nz; Main St; camp sites $26, dm $23, tw & d $56) A well-maintained and well-equipped YHA associate, the Yellow House has a big kitchen and relaxing sun deck, as well as a spa for bubbling away aches and pains. You can also hire tramping equipment and store luggage here and there's EFTPOS and credit card facilities.

St Arnaud Log Chalets (☎ 03-521 1887; www.nelsonlakes.co.nz; Main St; chalets $80-120) Next door to the Yellow House (and run by the same people), these are stylish timber en suite chalets. The larger one-bedroom units feature full kitchen facilities.

Alpine Lodge (☎ 03-521 1869; www.alpinelodge.co.nz; Main St; r $125-150) Expertly made chalets in

a clean alpine-style building. There's a range of accommodation, beautifully finished with natural timbers. Apartments are spacious, most with views, and it goes a long way to creating the alpine experience. It also has the monopoly on eating out in St Arnaud, with a **bar** (meals $14-18) serving bistro meals and a more upmarket **restaurant** (mains $22-31). The **Alpine Cafe** (☎ 03-521 1869; breakfast & lunch $8-13) is a tasty option.

Top House (☎ 03-521 1848; B&B from $40, cottage $90) Perched on a hill, 8km from St Arnaud, the Top House dates from 1887, when it was a hotel. Now it's a lovely B&B with a cosy fireplace, superb views of the St Arnaud Range and even a chance for a round of golf on the hill side nine-hole course. As well as rooms in the historic house, there are modern units out the back. Dinner is available for around $25.

Nelson Lakes Homestay (☎ 03-521 1191; www.nelsonlakesaccommodation.co.nz; B&B s/d $90/125) This pleasant B&B is on a property about 4km from St Arnaud, on the road to Blenheim. The en-suite rooms are comfortable and good-value evening meals are available.

Nelson Lakes Village Centre (☎ 03-521 1854; Main Rd; meals $5-12) A general store, selling fish and chips, burgers and the like.

Getting There & Around

On its Picton–Greymouth run, **Atomic Shuttles** (☎ 0800 248 885; www.atomictravel.co.nz) passes through St Arnaud. The express service, which is hours faster, runs daily December to Easter, and Monday, Wednesday and Friday from April to November. Sample fares to/from St Arnaud include Picton ($25, one hour 50 minutes express or five hours 50 minutes, one to two daily), Nelson ($20, three hours 20 minutes, one daily), Blenheim ($25, one hour 20 minutes express or five hours 20 minutes, one to two daily) and Greymouth ($40, three hours 10 minutes express or 4½ hours, one to two daily).

Nelson Lakes Shuttles (☎ 03-521 1023; www.nelsonlakesshuttles.co.nz) provides transport from St Arnaud to Mt Robert car park (per person $10) and Lake Rotoroa (per person $20).

Water taxis (☎ 03-521 1894 on Lake Rotoiti, 03-523 9199, 021-702 278 on Lake Rotoroa) operate on both lakes. At Lake Rotoiti, there's also **kayak and fishing-boat hire** (half-/full-day hire $25/35).

NELSON TO MOTUEKA

From Richmond, south of Nelson, SH60 heads northwest to Motueka. This region fringing Tasman Bay is all the rage with local holiday makers, so there's plenty of accommodation, art-and-craft outlets, vineyards, yacht charters, fishing and swimming. The area is rich with bird life, particularly Arctic migrant waders.

Sights

About 20km west of Nelson is the turn-off to **Rabbit Island**, which boasts great swimming beaches, boating, fishing and forest walks. The island has 13km of undeveloped, unspoilt beach backed by plantation forest. The bridge to the island is closed after 9pm and camping is not allowed.

Further along, the picturesque Waimea Inlet and the twin villages of **Mapua** and **Ruby Bay** are at the mouth of the Waimea River. Mapua has numerous art-and-craft outlets and there's a small aquarium, **Touch the Sea** (☎ 03-540 3557; seatouch@xtra.co.nz; Mapua Wharf; adult/senior/child/family $7/5/4/15; 🕑 10am-4pm Tue-Sun), an educational look at sea horses and other marine life. There's also a gift shop.

WINERIES

The Nelson region has a flourishing winemaking industry and although it doesn't rival the Marlborough region in size, there are enough wineries to keep you busy (around 20 at last count). Many vineyards on the **Nelson Wine Trail** can be visited by doing a loop from Nelson through Richmond to Motueka, following the SH60 coast road in one direction and the inland Motueka Valley Hwy in the other. Wineries are open for tastings and sales, and several have cafés and restaurants. See p446 for information about wine tours.

Grape Escape (☎ 03-544 4054; www.grapeescape.co .nz; McShane Rd; 🕑 10am-4.30pm) is a complex housing two wineries, Richmond Plains (certified organic wine) and Te Mania, as well as a café-bar and an art-and-craft gallery. It's on the wine-tour itineraries.

Other wineries worth a visit include:
Denton Winery (☎ 03-540 3555; alex@ dentonwinery.co.nz; Awa Awa Rd; 🕑 11am-5pm)
Neudorf Vineyards (☎ 03-543 2643; www.neudorf .co.nz; Neudorf Rd; 🕑 10am-5pm Mon-Sat Sep-May, daily 27 Dec-31 Jan)

Ruby Bay Winery (☎ 03-540 2825; rubybay@xtra.co.nz; Korepo Rd; 🕑 10am-5pm Dec-Easter, Sat & Sun only Oct-Nov)
Seifrieds (☎ 03-544 1555; www.seifried.co.nz; Redwood Rd; 🕑 10am-5pm) One of the region's biggest wineries. Restaurant has tasty lunch.

Tours

Mapua Adventures (☎ 03-540 3770; bookings@mapua magic.com; Mapua Wharf; tours $40-60) Mountain bike tours on Rabbit Island and sea-kayaking trips around Waimea Inlet.
Mapua Jet (☎ 03-540 3833; www.mapuajet.co.nz; Mapua Wharf; tours $50-150) Jetboat rides. One-hour tours of Rabbit Island and the Waimea Inlet. It also offers an ecotour with an ecologist/ornithologist explaining the diverse bird-life of the inlet.

Sleeping & Eating

Consult staff at Motueka visitors centre (opposite) for a host of out-of-the-way homestays, bachs and B&Bs in the area.

Iwa Bach (☎ 03-540 2108; barbara.blewman@actrix .co.nz; Wharf Rd; r $80) A fantastic place with a self-contained studio in an original 1950s forestry hut. It's close to Mapua Wharf, is clean and cosy and a great place to relax.

Rerenga Farm (☎ 03-543 3825; www.homestays .net.nz/rerenga.htm; Dovedale-Woodstock Rd; d $95) Explore the country in style at this 'rural retreat'. The 89-year-old homestead has lovely B&B rooms and dinner is $30. It's a very restful place and a good spot to regroup.

Mapua Leisure Park (☎ 03-540 2666; www.mapua leisurepark.co.nz; 33 Toru St, Mapua; camp sites/campervan sites $22/24, cabins $38, chalets $55-60) This park is 'NZ's first clothes-optional leisure park'. You don't *have* to bare all (many don't) and the position and facilities are superb – tennis and volleyball courts, pool, sauna, spa and a waterfront café.

Smokehouse (☎ 03-5402280; www.smokehouse.co.nz; Shed 3, Mapua Wharf; meals $20-27) Right on the Mapua waterfront, Smokehouse does delicious wood-smoked fish such as groper, tarakihi, moki and snapper.

Flax Restaurant & Bar (☎ 03-540 2028; Mapua Wharf; mains around $30; 🕑 Tue-Sun) Just along from Smokehouse, the stylish, arty Flax features magnificent fresh food.

MOTUEKA

pop 6610

Motueka is the centre of a green-tea, hops and fruit-growing area. The main picking season for apples, grapes and kiwi fruit is

March to June. The town is usually used as a base or stopover en route to Golden Bay and the Abel Tasman and Kahurangi National Parks, and in summer it's a bustling place. The inhabitants are very cosmopolitan and there's a solid community of craftspeople and some excellent cafés.

Information

Cyberworld (☎ 03-528 9877; motueka@yahoo.com; Wallace St; $5 per hr)

DOC field office (☎ 03-528 9117; www.doc.govt.nz; cnr High & King Edward Sts; 8am-4.30pm Mon-Fri)

Motueka Books & more (☎ 03-528 6600; 207 High St) This bookshop also moonlights as a post office.

Motueka visitors centre (☎ 03-528 6543; www.abel tasmangreenrush.co.nz; 20 Wallace St; 8am-5pm, until

7pm summer) An excellent visitors centre that books tours and huts for the Abel Tasman Track. Definitely check with staff here about all the different options for tackling the track.

Sights & Activities

The small **Motueka District Museum** (☎ 03-528 7660; 140 High St; adult/child $2/50c; 10am-3pm Mon-Fri, 10am-1pm Sat) has displays re-creating the region's colonial past. For tours from Motueka into Abel Tasman National Park try Abel Tasman Wilsons Experiences (p457) and Sea Kayak Company (p458).

Sleeping

Accommodation at Motueka is predominantly budget style though there are some excellent mid-range options.

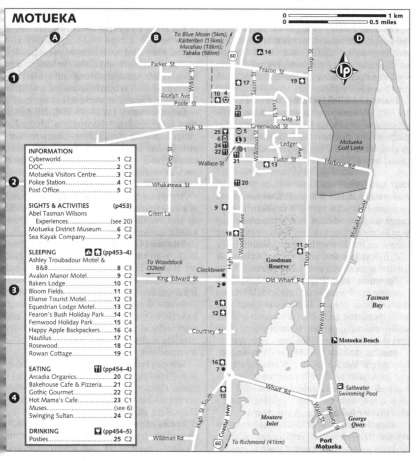

BUDGET

Bakers Lodge (☎ 03-528 0103; www.bakerslodge.co.nz; 4 Poole St; dm $22-25, s & tw & d $52, with bathroom $68, f $88-98) This YHA-associate, in a carefully renovated former bakery, is the pick of Motueka's hostels. It's spacious, immaculate and has plenty of common areas, including a large kitchen and outdoor barbecue area.

Happy Apple Backpackers (☎ 03-528 8652; happyapple@xtra.co.nz; 500 High St; camp sites $21, dm $22, tw & d 55) A friendly hostel with a number of rooms separate from the main house. There's a huge backyard for tents and it has the facilities to handle the numbers. Weekly rates available.

Ashley Troubadour Motel & B&B (☎ 0800 222 046, 03-528 7318; troubadour@xtra.co.nz; 430 High St; s/d with breakfast $52/75, motel d $75-95) Two types of accommodation – B&B and motel-style. All rooms have a washbasin.

Fernwood Holiday Park (☎ 03-528 7488; www.holidayparks.co.nz/fernwood; 519 High St South; camp sites/campervan sites $20/22, cabins $35-48) At the southern entrance to town, Fernwood is a well-kept place with all the usual facilities and some leafy sites.

Fearon's Bush Holiday Park (☎ 0800 668 835, 03-528 7189; 10 Fearon St; camp sites/campervan sites $20/21, self-contained units $60-80) Fearon's is a spacious place at the northern end of town. It has grassy camp sites, comfortable cabins and motel units.

MID-RANGE

Avalon Manor Motel (☎ 03-528 8320; www.webnz.co.nz/avalonmotel; 314 High St; r $115-170; 🖳) Terrific mid-range accommodation in a prominent highway location close to town. Massive four-star rooms are modern with cooking facilities, Sky TV, free videos and great views. 'Affordable luxury' is its slogan and it holds true.

Equestrian Lodge Motel (☎ 0800 668 782, 03-528 9369; www.equestrianlodge.co.nz; Tudor St; r $110-170; 🖳) An excellent choice. Rooms are clean and well-appointed and all look towards a large, well-manicured garden. It's a peaceful place and there's a spa and children's play area.

Nautilus (☎ 0800 628 845, 03-528 4558; www.nautiluslodge.co.nz; 67 High St; r $115-170) A similar standard to Avalon and the Equestrian, Nautilus has well-appointed modern rooms with spas and some with cooking facilities. There's also private balconies and courtyards.

Elianse Tourist Motel (☎ 03-528 6629; elianse.motel@xtra.co.nz; 432 High St; units $80) Self-contained, clean and spacious units just out of town at reason-able rates. Great family options, comfortable beds and cosy electric blankets.

Also recommended:

Bloom Fields (☎ 03-528 7083; bloom.fields@xtra.co.nz; 220 Thorp St; s/d $100/120) Lovely B&B with two rooms.

Blue Moon (☎ 03-528 6996; www.thebluemoon.co.nz; 57 School Rd, Riwaka; s/d $90/130) Luxury in a serene garden setting. The sunken bath is a treat. Vegetarian meals by arrangement.

Rosewood (☎ 03-528 6750; www.accomodation-new-zealand.co.nz/rosewood; 48 Woodland Ave; s $55, tw & d $90) A cosy homestay B&B in a straight-up NZ home.

Rowan Cottage (☎ 03-528 6492; www.rowancottage.net; 27 Fearon St; r $110-130) B&B with delicious organic breakfast – fresh fruits and berries. Stylish open-plan studio.

Eating & Drinking

High St, Motueka's seemingly endless main street, has some real gems.

Hot Mama's Cafe (☎ 03-528 7039; 195 High St; all-day menu $7-12, mains $15-22; ☻ 8am-late) Hot Mama's is a cool open-fronted place painted in vibrant colours and is the funkiest café in town. It sells tap beer, strong coffee and delicious food such as burritos, lasagne and BLTs. There's live music at weekends in summer.

Gothic Gourmet (☎ 03-528 6699; 208 High St; mains $21-29; ☻ dinner) Formerly a Methodist church, now an elegant fine-dining restaurant. It has thick carpet, brick-red walls, comfortable couches and excellent food such as ostrich steaks and scallops.

Muses (☎ 03-528 8696; 140 High St; meals $9-20; ☻ brunch) In the museum building, Muses is a café and art gallery, with dining inside or out on the covered patio. It has fresh salads, desserts and coffee.

Bakehouse Cafe & Pizzeria (☎ 03-528 5111; meals $7-28; ☻ lunch & dinner) Tucked away in a lane off Wallace St, this European-style café-bar specialises in excellent pizza and Italian food. It's unassuming but highly recommended.

Arcadia Organics (☎ 03-528 7840; 265 High St; meals $3-10; ☻ lunch) Caters to vegetarian and vegan diets. Serves quiches and savoury muffins and sells grainy breads and lots of fruit and veg.

Swinging Sultan (☎ 03-528 8909; 172 High St; kebabs $6-9; ☻ 8am-1am summer, 8am-9pm winter) Chunky meat, chicken, falafel and beef kebabs are served round the clock at this hard-working shop. Also makes a strong coffee.

Posties (☎ 03-528 9890; 122 High St; meals $8-21; ☻ breakfast, lunch & dinner) A pub with all the classics – roast of the day, schnitzel, mixed grill – and there's also a kids' menu. The public bar is open until 2am and has live bands Friday and Saturday.

Getting There & Away

Abel Tasman Coachlines (☎ 03-528 8850; www.abel tasmantravel.co.nz) buses stop at the visitors centre. There are services from Motueka to Nelson ($9, one hour, two to three daily), Takaka ($15, 1¼ hours, two daily) and the Abel Tasman National Park (both ends of the track year-round). It also operates a charter service to the Heaphy Track. Buses also link Motueka with Kaiteriteri and Marahau.

K Bus (☎ 03-525 9434; www.kahurangi.co.nz) has buses to/from Takaka ($22, two hours, three daily) and Nelson ($9, one hour, four daily); they pick up at the visitors centre. Buses also run to and from Totaranui and Marahau. See the Abel Tasman National Park (p456) for more information on transport to and from the Abel Tasman Track.

MOTUEKA TO ABEL TASMAN
Kaiteriteri

This is one of the most popular resort beaches in the area, 13km from Motueka on a sealed road (which continues on to Marahau). The beach has genuine golden sand and clear, green waters. Behind the camping ground is **Withells Walk**, a 45-minute excursion into native bush from where great views look out across the bay. Otherwise, walk to Kaka Pah Point at the end of the beach and explore some of the secluded little coves and hideaways.

Launch and kayak trips run to the Abel Tasman National Park from Kaiteriteri, though Marahau is the usual base.

TOURS

Waka Tours (☎ 03-527 8160; www.wakatours.co.nz; adult/child $135/115) Experienced Maori guides in full traditional dress run half-day tours in the Abel Tasman National Park. You paddle a traditionally carved Waka Tangata canoe.

SLEEPING & EATING

Flashpackers (☎ 03-527 8281; www.kaiteriflashpackers .co.nz; Inlet Rd; dm $30, s & d $120, f $180) Flashpackers is just that – a flash backpackers. Beds are inner-spring rather than foam, and rooms are mainly doubles, though small and spartan. A nautical navy-and-white colour scheme has been used throughout and all the rooms have

views. Communal facilities are excellent and TVs can be hired for $5 a day.

Kaiteriteri Beach Motor Camp (☎ 03-527 8010; www.holidayparks.co.nz/kaiteriteri; Inlet Rd; camp sites/ campervan sites $20/22, cabins $35-48) This well-equipped camp, across from the beach, swells with summer holiday makers but is large enough to cope and its facilities are great.

Kimi Ora Spa Resort (☎ 03-527 8027, 0508 546 4672; www.kimiora.com; Martin Farm Rd; s $190-230, d $250-310) Kimi Ora is above the town and is a place to really pamper yourself, with spa units, an indoor and outdoor pool complex, sauna and massage, as well as tennis courts, gym and a bush fitness track. Its focus is on well-being. There's also a very good vegetarian **restaurant** (meals $9-26) here, open to all.

Beached Whale (☎ 03-5278114; www.harlequin.co.nz /menu/restaurants/beachedwhale.asp; Inlet Rd; meals $15-24; ⏰ 11am-11pm) Underneath Flashpackers, the Beached Whale is a relaxed bar and restaurant with a pool table, pub-café menu and live entertainment nightly.

Shoreline Kaiteriteri (☎ 03-527 8507; cnr Inlet & Sandy Bay Rds; brunch mains $10-18, dinner mains $18-29; ⏰ 11am-11pm) This is a modern café-bar-restaurant right on the beach. Punters relax on the sunny decking and watch the day pass away.

Marahau

Further along the coast from Kaiteriteri, tiny Marahau, 18km north of Motueka, is the main gateway to the Abel Tasman National Park. From here you can book water taxis, hire kayaks, swim with seals or head on foot into the park. There are regular bus connections to/from Marahau (p459).

SLEEPING

Marahau has quite a few accommodation possibilities. The camping grounds fill up in summer.

Barn Backpackers (☎ 03-527 8043; Harvey Rd; camp sites $24, dm $19, tw & d $48, tr $66) A peaceful, tranquil place surrounded by gum and willow trees. There's a mix of accommodation, from an all-girls dorm, a big loft bunk room, outdoor tepees and camp sites on the spacious lawn. This is a comfortable, homely place.

Old MacDonald's Farm (☎ 03-527 8288; oldmacs@ xtra.co.nz; Harvey Rd; camp sites/campervan sites $20/24, caravans $45, cabins $65, studios $120-160) Towards the end of Harvey Rd, this 100-acre property has llamas, alpacas, deer and cows, as well as backpacker huts, camping and the semi-open-air **Gum Drop Cafe** (meals $6-15; ⓧ noon-4pm). There are swimming holes in the river running through the property and a volleyball court.

Ocean View Chalets (☎ 03-527 8232; Marahau Beach; www.accommodationabeltasman.co.nz; chalets $100-210) Stunning cypress chalets, 300m from the Abel Tasman Track, overlooking Sandy Bay. Placed for maximum privacy, the chalets are self-contained, some with wheelchair access, and are a beautiful option.

Marahau Lodge (☎ 03-527 8250; www.abeltasman marahaulodge.co.nz; Marahau Beach; d $130-175) On the main waterfront road, Marahau Lodge has modern, comfortable studios and self-contained units. They're lovely rooms with peaked roofs, fans, TVs, phone and microwave.

Marahau Beach Camp (☎ 0800 808 018, 03-527 8176; www.abeltasmanmarahaucamp.co.nz; Franklin St; camp sites/campervan sites $20/22, dm $18, cabins & caravans $45, chalets $65) A well-established camping ground on Marahau Beach with a range of options, from separate backpacker accommodation to chalets. There's a shop, kayak hire ($65 a day) and a water-taxi service.

Southern Exposure Backpackers (☎ 03-527 8424; www.southern-exposure.co.nz; Moss Rd; camp sites $20, dm/s/d $22/40/50) Sitting on a hill in a patch of native bush above Marahau, this small backpackers hostel is run by Southern Exposure Sea Kayaking (p458). The surroundings are rustic and the backpackers is well run.

Park Café (☎ 03-527 8270; Harvey Rd; day menu $8-12, mains $19-28; ⓧ breakfast, lunch & dinner) Near the start of the Abel Tasman Track and the park information kiosk, Park Café is bright and breezy. There are views of the beach to one side and the national park to the front. Lunch includes fettuccini, fish, vego sausages and green-lipped mussels. It's also a licensed bar.

ABEL TASMAN NATIONAL PARK

The coastal Abel Tasman National Park is an accessible and popular tramping area. The park is at the northern end of a range of marble and limestone hills extending from Kahurangi National Park, and the interior is honeycombed with caves and potholes. There are various tracks in the park, including an inland route, although the coastal track is by far the most popular.

Abel Tasman Coastal Track

This 51km, three- to five-day track is one of the most beautiful in the country, passing through pleasant native bush that overlooks beaches of golden sand lapped by gleaming blue-green water. The numerous bays, small and large, are like a travel brochure come to life.

Once little known outside the immediate area, this track has well and truly been 'discovered' and in summer hundreds of people may be on the track at any one time – far more than can be accommodated in the huts, so bring your tent. Track accommodation works on a booking system, similar to the Routeburn and Milford Tracks. If you don't have a prebooked hut ticket for a particular night in season (1 October to 30 April), you will be refused entry to a hut – check with the Abel Tasman Coastal Track booking desk (p453). Outside the season you don't need to book but you still need to purchase a pass.

Between Bark Bay and Awaroa Head, there is an area classified as the **Tonga Island Marine Reserve** and is home to a seal colony and visiting dolphins. Tonga Island itself is a small island out from Onetahuti Beach.

For a full description of the route, see Lonely Planet's *Tramping in New Zealand*.

INFORMATION

The track operates on a **Great Walks Pass** (camp sites/huts $14/28 Oct-Apr, huts $20 May-Sep, child half-price, child under 11 free) system. The **Abel Tasman Coastal Track booking desk** (☎ 03-528 0005) is at the Motueka visitors centre (p453). Staff here are experts and can offer suggestions to tailor the track to your needs and organise transport at each end. You can also obtain hut passes from Takaka DOC and Nelson visitors centre. Try to plan your trip a couple of days beforehand.

WALKING THE TRACK

Many visitors combine walking and kayaking on the track – see the boxed text on p458.

Several sections of the main track are tidal, with long deviations required during high tide. There is no alternative route around Awaroa Inlet. Check the newspaper, subtracting 20 minutes from the Nelson tide times. Tide tables and advice are available at DOC and the Moteuka visitors centre (p453).

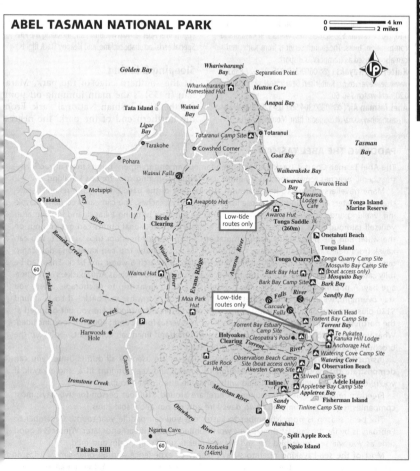

ABEL TASMAN NATIONAL PARK

Take additional food so you can stay longer should you have the inclination. Bays around all the huts are beautiful but you should definitely bring generous amounts of sandfly repellent. At the tiny, picturesque beach of Te Pukatea near Anchorage Hut there are no sandflies.

Estimated walking times are as follows, south to north: Marahau to Anchorage Hut (four hours), Anchorage Hut to Bark Bay Hut (three hours), Bark Bay Hut to Awaroa Hut (four hours), and Awaroa Hut to Totaranui (1½ hours).

Many walkers stop at Totaranui, the final stop for the boat services and a pick-up point for buses, but it is possible to keep walking around the headland from Totaranui to Whariwharangi Hut (two hours) and then on to Wainui (1½ hours), where buses service the car park.

TOURS

See also p459 for information about water taxis.

Abel Tasman Sailing Adventures (☎ 0800 467 245, 03-527 8375; www.sailingadventures.co.nz; day trips $45-115) Offers yacht rentals and private skippered charters.

Abel Tasman Seal Swim (☎ 0800 252 925; www.seal swim.com; seal swim adult/child $120/100, seal watch $60/40; ⏲ 8.45am & 1pm) Trips to the seal colony, departing from Marahau. You can also be dropped off in the park and walk back after the swim. Fun and educational experience.

Abel Tasman Wilsons Experiences (☎ 0800 223 582, 03-528 7801; www.abeltasmannz.com; High St,

Motueka; 3hr/half-day cruises $44/58, kayak & walk $85-110, cruise & walk $50-85) Cruises, walks and kayak (and combination) tours. The launch services from Kaiteriteri can also be used as trampers' transport.

Kaiteriteri Kayaks (☎ 0800 252 925, 03-527 8383; www.seakayak.co.nz; Kaiteriteri Beach; seal swim $100-120, seal watch $40-60)

Abel Tasman Air (☎ 0800 304 560, 03-528 8290; www .flytasmanbay.co.nz/pitts-special.htm; Motueka; Abel

Tasman/Pitts Special/Heaphy flights per person $95/185/155) Flights over Abel Tasman National Park, including the Pitts Special aerial acrobatic biplane, and Heaphy Track flights.

Sleeping & Eating

At the southern edge of the park, Marahau (p455) is the main jumping-off point for the Abel Tasman National Park. From the northern end of the park, the nearest

PADDLING THE ABEL TASMAN

The Abel Tasman Coastal Track has long been famous among trampers, but its main attractions – the scenic beaches, coves and bays – make it an equally alluring spot for sea kayaking.

Many travellers choose to kayak around at least part of the park, cruising the relatively safe, sheltered waters and calling in at those impossibly pretty beaches. You can easily combine kayaking, walking and camping. It needn't necessarily be a matter of hiring a kayak and looking after yourself (although it is possible to do that) – a string of professional outfits can get you out on the water and the possibilities and permutations for guided or freedom trips are vast. You can kayak from half a day to three days, camping or staying in huts. You can kayak one day, camp overnight and walk back, or walk further into the park and catch a water taxi back. Trips can be fully catered or you can arrange to stay in huts or accommodation such as Aquapackers in Anchorage Bay. A popular choice if your time is tight is a guided kayak trip to Anchorage, where you stay overnight, walk unguided to Onetahuti Beach and catch a water taxi back – it costs around $130 plus camping or hut fees. Most companies offer a three-day trip where you get dropped at the northern end of the park and paddle back (or vice versa) for around $400 with food included. What you decide to do may depend on your own time (and financial) constraints – pick up the brochures, look at the options and talk to other travellers.

Instruction is given to first-timers and double kayaks are used by all outfits unless you can demonstrate that you're competent enough to control and keep upright in a single kayak. If you're on your own you'll be matched with someone else in the group.

Freedom rentals (kayak and equipment hire) are around $100 per person for two days; most companies require a minimum of two days hire and do not allow solo hires.

The peak season is from November to Easter but you can paddle year-round. December to February is by far the busiest time, so it's worth timing your visit earlier or later. Winter is a good time as you will see more bird life and the weather is surprisingly calm and mild.

Most of the sea-kayaking operators have plenty of experience and all offer similar trips at similar prices. Marahau is the closest base but trips are also run out of Motueka, Kaiteriteri and even Nelson.

■ **Abel Tasman Kayaks** (☎ 0800 732 529, 03-527 8022; www.abeltasmankayaks.co.nz; Marahau Beach; 2-day kayak/walk & kayak $130/260, 3-day guided tour, incl meals $399)

■ **Kaiteriteri Kayaks** (☎ 0800 252 925, 03-527 8383; www.seakayak.co.nz; Kaiteriteri Beach; half-day & sunset paddle $65, full-day guided trips $95-170, overnight guided $160-310, overnight freedom $100-180)

■ **Kiwi Kayaks** (☎ 0800 695 494; www.kiwikayaks.co.nz; Main Rd, Riwaka; one-day kayak & walk $75, full-day guided tour $95-130, 2-day $145-300, 3-day $299, 3-day catered $389)

■ **Ocean River Adventure Company** (☎ 0800 732 529, 03-527 8266; www.seakayaking.co.nz; Main Rd, Marahau; 1-day $115-170, 2-day $330-595, 3-day $545-795)

■ **Sea Kayak Company** (☎ 03-528 7251, 0508 252 925; www.seakayaknz.co.nz; 506 High St, Motueka; 1-day tour $100, 2-day $200-245, 3-day $395, 5-day catered $950)

■ **Southern Exposure Sea Kayaking** (☎ 0800 695 292, 03-527 8424; www.southern-exposure.co.nz; Moss Rd, Marahau; 1-day trip $95-125, 2-day noncatered/catered $245/310, 3-day $295/385)

towns with accommodation are Pohara (p461) and Takaka (p460), plus there's the **Totaranui Campground** (☎ 03-525 8083; camp sites/campervan sites $20/24), accessible by road in the north of the park. Only sites for tents or campervans are available here.

Within the park itself there are four huts – Anchorage (24 bunks), Bark Bay (28 bunks), Awaroa (22 bunks) and Whariwharangi (19 bunks) – as well as 21 designated camp sites. None of the huts have cooking facilities, so you should carry your own stove. Some of the camp sites have fireplaces but, again, you should carry cooking equipment. Hut and camp passes should be purchased before you enter the park (see Information, p456). Note that from Christmas Day to late January these huts and camping grounds are usually full.

There are several other options in the park.

Aquapackers (☎ 0800 430 744; www.aquapackers.co .nz; dm $55) The *MV Parore* and *Catarac* are great options for backpackers, especially those who don't mind the drinking sessions that tend to eventuate on board. The former patrol boat is decked out with accommodation for 14 passengers and the cost includes a big dinner, breakfast and a packed lunch for you to take on the day's walk.

MV Etosha (☎ 0800 386 742; r $75) This has been upgraded and now has three double cabins available. The boats are moored at Anchorage Bay, so the best way to get to them is via water taxi (p459). The boats meet at prearranged points along the track so you can do day walks and then sleep onboard.

Kanuka Hill Lodge (☎ 03-548 2863; www.kanuka lodge.co.nz; the Anchorage; s/d $165/225, breakfast & lunch/dinner $15/50) When you really want to get away from it all, Kanuka Hill, accessible only by water taxi or sea kayak, is a chilled place surrounded by native bush. Dinner is usually super-fresh seafood accompanied by a fine wine. Three double en-suite rooms are available.

Awaroa Lodge & Cafe (☎ 03-528 8758; www .awaroalodge.co.nz; Awaroa Bay; r $150-320) This luxury ecolodge at the northern end of the track is roughly 300m from the water and 200m off the track. Rooms are beautifully furnished with artistic, contemporary touches. As its slogan says, 'life doesn't get much better than this'. The innovative café menu focuses on organic food. Awaroa is

accessible by water taxi or on foot but not by road.

Getting There & Away

Moteuka (p452) is your best base for accessing the Abel Tasman Coastal Track. Transport options to and from the track are extremely flexible – you can kayak one way, take a helicopter, a bus or water taxi.

Abel Tasman Coachlines (☎ 03-548 0285; ww.abel tasmantravel.co.nz) operates buses between Motueka and Marahau ($8, 40 minutes, two to three daily), Totaranui ($22, 2¼ hours, two to three daily), Takaka ($15, one hour, two to three daily) and the Wainui car park at the northern end of the track ($26, 1¾ hours, two to three daily).

K Bus (☎ 03-525 9434; www.kahurangi.co.nz) services run between Motueka and Takaka ($22, two hours, three daily), Marahau ($8, 40 minutes, two daily), Totaranui ($22, 2¼ hours, one daily) and the Wainui car park ($26, 1¾ hours).

Getting Around

The beauty of Abel Tasman is that it's easy to get to and from any point on the track by water taxi. General prices from Marahau and Kaiteriteri include Anchorage and Torrent Bay ($22), Bark Bay ($25), Tonga ($27), Awaroa ($30) and Totaranui ($32). Operators include:

Abel Tasman Sea Shuttle (☎ 0800 732 748, 03-528 9759; www.abeltasmanseashuttles.co.nz; 415 High St, Motueka)

Abel Tasman Water Taxis (☎ 0800 423 397, 03-528 7497; www.abeltasman4u.co.nz; Kaiteriteri)

Aqua Taxi (☎ 0800 278 282, 03-527 8083; www.aqua taxis.co.nz; Marahau)

Marahau Water Taxis (☎ 0800 808 018, 03-527 8176; www.abeltasmanmarahaucamp.co.nz; Marahau Beach Camp, Franklin St, Marahau)

GOLDEN BAY

SH60 TO TAKAKA

From Motueka, SH60 winds steadily up and over Takaka Hill, with magnificent, dramatic scenery, and onwards to Takaka and Collingwood.

Takaka Hill (791m) separates Tasman Bay from Golden Bay. Near the summit are the **Ngarua Caves** (☎ 03-528 8093; adult/child $12/5; ♥ 10am-4pm Sep–mid-Jun) where you can see moa bones. You can only enter the caves on a 40-minute guided tour, leaving on the hour.

Also in the area is the biggest *tomo* (cave) in the southern hemisphere, **Harwood's Hole**. It is 400m deep and 70m wide and is a 30-minute walk from the car park at the end of Canaan Rd, off SH60. Exercise caution as you approach the lip of the hole – accidents have occurred.

As you cross the crest of the hill, **Harwood Lookout** has fine views down the Takaka River Valley to Takaka and Golden Bay.

From the lookout you wind down through the beautiful Takaka Hill Scenic Reserve to the river valley. The nearby Cobb Valley is notably the site of New Zealand's biggest annual dance (rave) party, the **Gathering** (www.gathering.co.nz), held over the New Year period.

TAKAKA
pop 1230

One of the most relaxed towns in NZ, Takaka is the centre for the beautiful Golden Bay area and the last town of any size as you head towards the northwestern corner of the South Island. It's a bustling place in summer, with a local community of 'Woodstock children' and artistic types.

Information

Bites café/bar (☎ 03-525 9676; 46 Commercial St; Internet per hr $5, meals $7-19; ☽ breakfast, lunch & dinner) Internet access and buffet-style Asian and café food.

DOC (☎ 03-525 8026; www.doc.govt.co.nz; 62 Commercial St; ☽ 8am-4pm Mon-Fri) Information on Abel Tasman and Kahurangi National Parks, the Heaphy and Kaituna Tracks, Farewell Spit, Cobb Valley and the Aorere gold fields. Sells hut tickets ($28).

Golden Bay Information Centre (☎ 03-525 9136; Willow St; gb.vin@nelsonnz.com; ☽ 9am-5pm)

Golden Bay Net Cafe (☎ 03-525 9130; 37 Commercial St; per hr $5) Internet access.

Sights

The **Golden Bay Museum & Gallery** (☎ 03-525 9990; Commercial St; adult/child $2/50c; ☽ 10am-4pm, closed Sun winter) is a well-presented jumble of historical memorabilia, but the stand-out exhibit is the diorama depicting Abel Tasman's 1642 landing in Golden Bay.

Many artists and craftspeople are based in the Golden Bay area, including painters, potters, blacksmiths, screen printers, silversmiths and knitwear designers. The large **Artisans' Shop** (30 Commercial St) displays their wares. The *Arts of Golden Bay* leaflet provides directions to all the galleries and workshops in the area.

Bencari Farm & Café (☎ 03-525 8261; McCallums Rd; adult/child/f $10/5/30, meals $7-22; ☽ Christmas holidays 10am-7pm, other times 10am-5pm Thu-Mon), on the Anatoki River 6km south of town, has a variety of farm animals (including llamas) and a café, but the prime attraction at this farm is feeding the fat, tame eels in the river.

Next door, you can fish for salmon at the **Anatoki Salmon Farm** (☎ 03-525 7251; www.anatoki salmon.co.nz; McCallums Rd; per kg catch $18), a truly relaxing venture, or buy fresh or smoked fish.

TE WAIKOROPUPU SPRINGS

Simply called 'Pupu', these are the largest freshwater springs in NZ and reputedly the clearest in the world. About 14,000 litres of water a second is thrown up from a number of underground vents dotted around the Pupu Springs Scenic Reserve, including one with 'dancing sands' thrown upwards by the great volume of incredibly clear water emerging from the ground.

Three short walks lead to the main springs (some suitable for wheelchairs) and take you to a glassed viewing area, passing by 19th-century **gold-mining works** – gold was discovered in Golden Bay in 1856. To reach Pupu from Takaka, head 4km northwest on SH60, turn inland at Waitapu Bridge and continue for 3km.

Tours

Barefoot guided tours (☎ 03-525 7005, 0508 525 700; www.bare-foot.co.nz; 104 Commercial St; tours $45) Its mission is 'to see you leave Golden Bay with a big smile on your face'. Seven- to eight-hour tours to the tip of the South Island, with a one-hour cliff-top walk.

Golden Bay Kayaks (☎ 03-525 9095; www.goldenbay kayaks.co.nz; Pohara; kayak per day $55, tours from $50) Rents out kayaks (with discounts for multiple days) and has half-day guided tours.

Kahurangi Guided Walks (☎ 03-525 7177; www .kahurangiwalks.co.nz; Dodson Rd, Takaka; Rawhiti cave adult/child $25/15, day walks around $90, Heaphy Track $900) Specialises in taking small groups through Abel Tasman National Park, covering nearly every track, including a five-day walk along the Heaphy Track.

Sleeping

There's accommodation at Takaka, and the nearby beach resort of Pohara (p461) is also popular and has the closest camping ground.

Golden Bay Barefoot Backpackers (☎ 03-524 8624; www.bare-foot.co.nz; 114 Commercial St; dm $20-21, s/tw/d $25/44/45) A small, cosy, renovated house with open lounge and kitchen areas and a garden out the back. There's fresh home-made bread and you can bubble in the spa. Barefoot is a good place to hook up with travellers.

Annie's Nirvana Lodge (☎ 03-525 8766; www .nirvanalodge.co.nz; 25 Motupipi St; dm/d $24/54) Close to the town centre, on the road to Pohara, Nirvana is a small, peaceful haven with a homely atmosphere. There's a separate shared room at the bottom of the organic garden, a spa and bikes for hire.

River Inn (☎ 03-525 9425; www.riverinn.co.nz; dm $18, tw & d $36) The River Inn, 3km west of town on the road to Collingwood, is a big old two-storey pub with backpacker rooms upstairs and a large bar below.

Golden Bay Motel (☎ 0800 401 212, 03-525 9428; gold.bay@xtra.co.nz; 132 Commercial St; r $75-110) Spacious self-contained rooms are clean and breezy and furnished with older-style fixtures. Room Nos 1 and 2 have private balconies, which look onto the lush, green lawn.

Anatoki Lodge (☎ 0800 262 333, 03-525 8047; anatoki@xtra.co.nz; 87 Commercial St; r $95-130; ☒) Studios and one- and two-bedroom units with cooking facilities, lounge area, TV and phone. The solar-heated pool's a bonus.

Eating

Wholemeal Café (☎ 03-525 9426; 60 Commercial St; meals $5-25; ☒ breakfast, lunch & dinner) This is a local institution and the stand-out place to eat in Takaka. It's a Bohemian café, restaurant and art gallery, which also sells bulk natural foods and sometimes has live music in the evening. There's a dedicated curry menu, free-range runny poached eggs for breakfast, smooth coffee and fresh sandwiches and salads.

Dangerous Kitchen (☎ 03-525 8686; 48 Commercial St; pizzas $10-24; ☒ breakfast, lunch & dinner) Dedicated to Frank Zappa, the Dangerous Kitchen specialises in whacky gourmet pizzas and serves strong, aromatic coffee and hefty slabs of cake. It's a mellow, laid-back place to hang, and brightly coloured hippo and lion cushions add to that *frisson* of 'danger'.

Big Fat Moon Cafe (☎ 03-525 7490; 1 Commercial St; mains $15-18; ☒ 8am-9pm Mon-Sat) A casual Asian café-restaurant dabbling in Indian, Thai, Malaysian and Indonesian dishes.

Lunch dishes and takeaways (such as laksa) are cheap and spicy.

Milliways (☎ 03-525 9636; 90 Commercial St; mains $20-28; ☒ breakfast, lunch & dinner) A fancy licensed restaurant with fresh, creative food and a relaxed atmosphere. There are roast dinners Sunday and Monday.

Eatery on the Rock (☎ 03-525 8096; 29 Main Rd; lunch mains $8-14, dinner mains $17-32; ☒ lunch & dinner) Built atop a karst outcrop, this is the newest addition to Takaka's eating scene. It's on the right as you head into town. The menu features shellfish platters and local crab and is fine-dining with seating overlooking a garden.

Drinking & Entertainment

Catch a flick at Takaka's cinema, **Village Theatre** (☎ 03-525 8453; Commercial St; adults $12), which screens newish releases.

Telegraph Hotel (☎ 03-525 9308; Commercial St) and the **Junction Hotel** (☎ 03-525 9207; 15 Commercial St) are old-fashioned pubs if you fancy a quiet lager, but most people relax with a drink outside Wholemeal Café and Dangerous Kitchen.

See also Mussel Inn (p463).

Getting There & Around

K Bus (☎ 03-525 9434; www.kahurangi.co.nz) runs between Takaka and Collingwood ($12, 30 minutes, one daily), the beginning of the Heaphy Track ($20, 1½ hours, two daily) and Nelson ($22, 2½ hours, two daily).

Abel Tasman Coachlines (☎ 03-548 0285; www.abel tasmantravel.co.nz) also operates between Takaka and Nelson ($22, two hours 10 minutes, two daily). Both companies have daily services to Totaranui at the northern end of Abel Tasman National Park, passing Pohara on the way.

Golden Bay Coachlines (☎ /fax 03-525 8352; 98 Commercial St) runs to/from Nelson to the Heaphy Track.

Quiet Revolution Cycle Shop (☎ 03-525 9555; 7 Commercial St; bike hire per day $30) hires mountain bikes, has local track information and also does repairs and servicing.

POHARA

Tiny Pohara is a popular summer resort, 10km northeast of Takaka. The beach is on the way to the northern end of the Abel Tasman Coastal Track. The unsealed road to the park is scenic and passes by **Ligar**

MARLBOROUGH & NELSON

Bay, which has a lookout and a memorial to Abel Tasman, the first European to enter Golden Bay.

The **Rawhiti Cave** near Pohara has the largest entrance of any cave in NZ. It's well worth a look and is best seen on a guided tour as there's a rough track with limited markings. Kahurangi Guided Walks (p460) specialises in taking small groups through the cave. It's an enjoyable three-hour guided tour. Please respect the sensitive cave environment – don't take limestone as a souvenir.

Sleeping & Eating

Nook (☎ 03-525 8501; nook@clear.net.nz; Abel Tasman Dr; dm $20, s $42, tw $40-46, d $46-54, cottage $100; ☾ Sep-May) In a cutesy little cottage, the Nook is a casual backpackers, close to the beach between Clifton and Pohara. Behind the main house is a lovely self-contained straw-bale cottage.

Sans Souci Inn (☎ 03-525 8663; www.sanssouci inn.co.nz; Richmond Rd; s/d $60/80) Just off Abel Tasman Dr at Pohara Beach, Sans Souci Inn has seven stylish mud-brick rooms, done in a bright, breezy Mediterranean style. The rooms are set around a garden courtyard, simply furnished and have a private outdoor setting from which to contemplate the garden. All rooms share the ecofriendly toilet in the bathroom. Food at the **restaurant** (mains $35; ☾ breakfast & dinner) is superb.

Sandcastle (☎ 0800 433 909, 03-525 9087; www .goldenbayaccommodation.co.nz/goldenbay.htm; Haile Lane; d $95, breakfast $15) This is a delightful, ecofriendly place with a wood-fired sauna and outdoor spa pools. There are six fully self-contained and individual chalets set in native bush surroundings.

Pohara Beach Top 10 Holiday Park (☎ 03-525 9500; www.holidayparks.co.nz/pohara; Abel Tasman Dr; camp sites/campervan sites $20/22, cabins $35-48, self-contained units $70-90) Right on the beach in the middle of the village, this park has self-contained units and basic but clean cabins sleeping four. There's also a well-equipped camp kitchen.

Penguin Café & Bar (☎ 03-525 6126; Abel Tasman Dr; meals $9.50-30; ☾ lunch & dinner) A classy café with thick wood-framed windows and mosaic murals. A terrific NZ wine list and the menu features home-smoked venison with Camembert and red-onion jam.

Windjammers (☎ 03-525 7672; Abel Tasman Dr; meals $17-23; ☾ lunch & dinner) More of a classic boozer with a nautical feel – décor is thick, coiled rope and brightly coloured papier mâché fish. Classic pub grub and fresh seafood.

COLLINGWOOD & AROUND

pop 250

Tiny Collingwood is the last town in this part of the country and it certainly has that outpost feel. It's busy in summer, though for most people it's a jumping-off point for the Heaphy Track in Kahurangi National Park or a base for trips to the remarkable Farewell Spit.

No visit to Collingwood would be complete without dipping into the original **Rosy Glow Chocolate House** (☎ 03-524 8348; Beach Rd; ☾ 10am-5pm Sat-Thu). Chocoholics will go nuts here, where hand-made chocolates are lovingly produced.

As befits a frontier town, this is a place where you can get a 'hoss': **Cape Farewell Horse Treks** (☎ 03-524 8031; www.horsetreksnz.com/home.html; treks $40-80, overnight packages $170-200).

Guided kayaking trips in the Whanganui Inlet are organised by **Innlet Backpackers** (☎ 03-524 8040; tours $65-85).

Information

Paddle Crab Kitchen (☎ 03-524 8708; www.farewell -spit.co.nz; Farewell Spit; meals $7-20; ☾ 9am-6pm summer, 9am-5pm winter) provides information about the region. It's 24km from Collingwood. There's also a café with superb views of Farewell Spit and free binoculars. On the track leading down from the visitors centre is the assembled skeleton of a pilot whale, a species that often beaches here. You can walk down and look out over the eel grass flats and see many waders and sea birds such as pied and variable oystercatchers, turnstones, Caspian terns, eastern bar-tailed godwits, black and white-fronted terns, and big black shags.

Sights & Activities
FAREWELL SPIT

A wetland of international importance and a renowned bird sanctuary, Farewell Spit is the summer home of thousands of migratory waders from the Arctic tundra. On the 26km beach there are huge crescent-shaped sand dunes from where you get panoramic views of the Spit, Golden Bay and, at low tide, the vast salt marsh. It's bleak, unprotected and unusual country.

The crossing to the northern side of the Spit is made by tour companies (p463), the only vehicles allowed to visit the Spit. The trucks grind up over the beach to about 1km from Cape Farewell. Down towards the start of the sand are a number of fossilised shellfish. Many species of birds are seen along the way and the normal trip ends at the old lighthouse compound.

Further east, up on the blown shell banks that comprise the far extremity of the Spit, are colonies of Caspian terns and Australasian gannets.

WHARARIKI BEACH
This isolated beach is a further 6km from Paddle Crab Kitchen along an unsealed road, and then a 20-minute walk from the car park over farmland (part of the Puponga Farm Park, administered by DOC). It is a wild introduction to the West Coast, with unusual dune formations, two looming rock islets just out from shore and a seal colony at its eastern end. What a way to get away from the 'rat race' of Collingwood! As inviting as a swim at this usually deserted spot may seem, there are strong undertows that make the sea very dangerous.

Tours
Scheduled tours leave daily from Collingwood but departure times are dependent on the tides (departure at low tide).

Farewell Spit Nature Tours (☎ 0800 250 500, 03-524 8188; www.farewell-spit.co.nz; tours $35-75) Explores Fossil Point and the lighthouse reserve. Prices include lunch.

Farewell Spit Safari (☎ 0800 808 257, 03-524 8257; www.farewellspit.co.nz; Tasman St, Collingwood; tours from $60) Five-hour lighthouse safari that takes you up the beach in a 4WD. Also visits the gannet colony, a 1km walk from the lighthouse.

Sleeping
There's accommodation in Collingwood itself and more places scattered along the road to Farewell Spit.

Beachcomber Motel (☎ 03-524 8499; Tasman St; www.yellow.co.nz/site/collingwoodbeachcombermotel; studios $100, f $130) Clean and spacious self-contained units in excellent nick. The larger units have a mezzanine floor and are terrific value.

Skara Brae (☎ 03-524 8464; www.accommodation collingwood.co.nz; Elizabeth St; s $95, d $110-120) Built in 1908, this was the original police residence in Collingwood. Now it's a comfortable and welcoming B&B with en-suite rooms in the

main house and two self-contained units at the back.

Innlet Backpackers (☎ 03-524 8040; jhearn@xtra.co .nz; camp sites $15, dm $23, tw & d $55, cottages $60-120) The Innlet, on the way to Pakawau about 10km from Collingwood, is a top-notch backpackers. The renovated main house is comfortable, with an inviting potbelly stove in the lounge, and there are various huts outside. The owners, Jonathan and Katie, are very environmentally aware and offer kayak hire and guided kayaking and tramping trips.

Eating
Courthouse Cafe & Gallery (☎ 03-525 8472; Haven Rd; meals $6-25; ☺ lunch) This historic café prepares delicious à la carte meals from locally grown organic produce and fresh seafood. There's an alfresco area where you can enjoy a lingering lunch.

Mussel Inn (☎ 03-525 9241; Onekaka; meals $5-21; ☺ 11am-late) Located about halfway between Takaka and Collingwood, Mussel Inn is a cosy and welcoming tavern-café-brewery. There's music performed every week (twice a week in summer) and it brews its own ginger beer and lemonade. A big bowl of mussels has restorative properties, especially when washed down with a 'Captain Cooker', a brown beer brewed naturally with manuka. The Mussel Inn also offers a free beer for every fresh possum tail brought in!

Getting There & Away
Abel Tasman Coachlines (☎ 03-528 8850; www.abeltas mantravel.co.nz) has services between Collingwood and Nelson ($34, three hours, one to two daily) and Takaka ($12, 30 minutes, one to two daily).

K Bus (☎ 03-525 9434; www.kahurangi.co.nz) runs from Collingwood to Takaka ($12, 30 minutes, one daily) and on to Motueka and Nelson. The same bus goes to the Innlet and the Heaphy Track car park.

KAHURANGI NATIONAL PARK
This is the second largest of NZ's national parks and undoubtedly one of the greatest. Its 500,000 hectares comprise an ecological wonderland – more than 100 bird species, 50% of all NZ's plant species, 80% of its alpine plant species, a karst landscape and the largest known cave system in the southern

hemisphere. Kahurangi means 'treasured possession'.

For a complete track description see Lonely Planet's *Tramping in New Zealand*.

Information

The best spot to pick up detailed information, park maps and Great Walks passes for the Heaphy Track is from Golden Bay Information Centre (p460). Alternatively, you can get passes at Nelson (p444) and Motueka (p453) visitor centres.

Heaphy Track

One of the best-known tracks in NZ, the four- to six-day, 82km Heaphy Track doesn't have the spectacular scenery of the Routeburn or Milford Tracks, but it certainly has its own beauty.

The track lies almost entirely within Kahurangi National Park. Highlights include the view from the summit of Mt Perry (two-hour return walk from Perry Saddle Hut), and the coast, especially around Heaphy Hut. It's worth spending a day or two resting at Heaphy Hut. It is possible to cross the Heaphy River at its mouth at low tide.

There are seven **huts** ($28) set up for around 20 or more people, and beds are on a first-come-first-served basis. All have gas stoves, except Heaphy and Gouland Downs, which need wood. **Camp sites** ($36) are available at Gouland Downs, Aorere Shelter and Brown Hut, as well as on the coastal part of the track – Heaphy Hut, Katipo Shelter and Scotts Beach. At the time of writing it was likely that you would need to prebook huts and camp sites before setting off on the walk.

WALKING THE TRACK

Most people travel southwest from the Collingwood end to Karamea. From Brown Hut the track passes through beech forest to Perry Saddle. The country opens up to the swampy Gouland Downs, then closes in with sparse bush all the way to MacKay Hut. The bush becomes denser towards Heaphy Hut, with the beautiful nikau palm growing at lower levels.

The final section is along the coast through heavy bush and partly along the

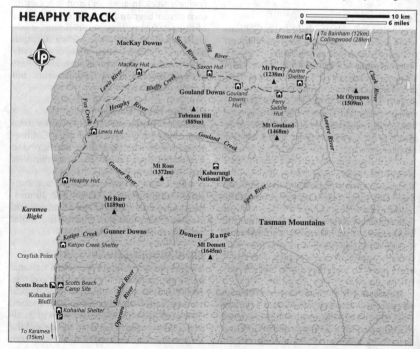

HEAPHY TRACK

beach. Unfortunately, the sandflies can be unbearable along this, the most beautiful part. The climate here is surprisingly mild, but do not swim in the sea as the undertows and currents are vicious. The lagoon at Heaphy Hut is good for swimming, and fishing is possible in the Heaphy River.

The Heaphy Track has kilometre markers; the zero marker is at the southern end of the track at the Kohaihai River near Karamea. Estimated walking times are as follows:

Route	Time
Brown Hut to Perry Saddle Hut	5hr
Perry Saddle Hut to Gouland Downs Hut	2hr
Gouland Downs Hut to Saxon Hut	1½hr
Saxon Hut to MacKay Hut	3hr
MacKay Hut to Lewis Hut	3–4hr
Lewis Hut to Heaphy Hut	2–3hr
Heaphy Hut to Kohaihai River	5hr

Wangapeka & Leslie-Karamea Tracks

After walking the Heaphy from north to south, you can return to the Nelson/Golden Bay region by the more scenic, though harder, Wangapeka Track. Although not as well known as the Heaphy, the Wangapeka is thought by many to be a more enjoyable walk. It starts 25km south of Karamea at Little Wanganui, runs 52km east to the Rolling River near Tapawera and takes about five days. There is a chain of nine **huts** ($7-14 per night) along the track.

The 91km Leslie-Karamea Track is a medium-to-hard tramp of five to seven days. It connects the Cobb Valley near Takaka with Little Wanganui, finishing on part of the Wangapeka Track.

Cobb Valley

The Cobb Valley and Mt Arthur Tablelands offer plenty of scope for trampers. The Cobb Valley is 28km along a winding road from Upper Takaka (allow 1½ hours to drive). First drive up to the power station and from there it's another 13km to the valley. Once in the valley there are a number of walks to choose from. Sylvester Hut to Diamond Lake is the best day walk (four-hour return). You can walk through the lakes at the top, leaving from Cobb Dam, or walk as far as you want along Cobb River. Other walks of a few hours' duration include Cobb Ridge to Peat Flat and Trilobite Hut to Chaffey Hut.

Aorere Gold Field

Aorere was the first major gold field in NZ. In February 1857 five ounces (142g) of Collingwood gold was auctioned in Nelson, precipitating a gold rush that lasted three years, although various companies continued to wrest gold from the soil by sluicing and stamping batteries right up until WWI. The old gold fields are now overgrown but terraces, water races and mine shafts can still be seen.

Getting There & Away

Abel Tasman Coachlines (☎ 03-528 8850, 03-548 0285) has a service from Nelson to the Heaphy Track ($42, three hours 50 minutes, one daily) via Takaka and Collingwood; in winter it runs on demand and is more expensive.

K Bus (☎ 03-525 9434; www.kahurangi.co.nz) provides transport from Nelson to the beginning of the Heaphy Track ($42, three hours 50 minutes, one daily). There's a phone at the trailhead to call buses.

Wadsworths Motors (☎ 03-522 4248; Main Rd, Tapawera) services the eastern ends of the Wangapeka and Leslie-Karamea Tracks. For details of transport at the Karamea end of all the tracks see p475.

Hitching to either the Karamea or Collingwood end of the Heaphy Track is difficult.

466

The West Coast

THE WEST COAST

CONTENTS

Murchison	468
Buller Gorge	470
Westport	470
Around Westport	473
Westport to Karamea	474
Karamea	474
Westport to Greymouth	476
Grey Valley	478
Greymouth	480
Around Greymouth	484
Hokitika	484
Around Hokitika	488
Hokitika to the Glaciers	488
Glaciers	490
South to Haast	498
Haast Region	498
Haast Pass	500

The West Coast region (also known as Westland) is a rugged, salt-sprayed stretch of wild rocky beaches and bush-clad hills sweeping up to towering icy peaks. Often the narrow coastal strip is nothing but *pakihi* (dried-up swamp) or second-class farmland, but the contrast on either side between the energetic wash of the ocean and the hilly heights is striking. Easy access to solitude is also one of the West Coast's major characteristics – a short plunge off the highway and you can be enveloped in rainforest, skipping pebbles at a mountainous snow-clad silhouette across the surface of a serene lake, or picking through the rusted debris of over a century's worth of gold mining, coal mining and timber milling.

Literally the biggest drawcards between Karamea in the north and Jackson Bay in the south are the huge icy dimensions of the Franz Josef and Fox Glaciers, framed by the dominating peaks of Mts Cook and Tasman – you can fly past them in a plane, land on them in a helicopter, or trudge up them. But there are other features that provide some competition in the scenery stakes, such as the earthquake-scarred Buller Gorge, the caves and limestone formations of Oparara Basin, the sea-gouged beaches north of Greymouth and the wonderful geological layering at Punakaiki Rocks. The West Coast is also a major source of *pounamu* (greenstone, or jade) and Hokitika is the best place in New Zealand to see it being crafted.

HIGHLIGHTS

- Heli-hiking to the blue-ice caves of **Franz Josef Glacier** (p492) and **Fox Glacier** (p495)
- Kayaking the gorgeous channels of **Okarito Lagoon** (p489)
- White-water rafting in the rivers and caves around **Westport** (p471)
- Marvelling at nature's pancake stack at **Punakaiki** (p476)
- Getting a feel for limestone in the **Oparara Basin** (p474)
- Weighing up some lovely greenstone jewellery in **Hokitika** (p487)
- Walking in seclusion around **Jackson Bay** (p500)

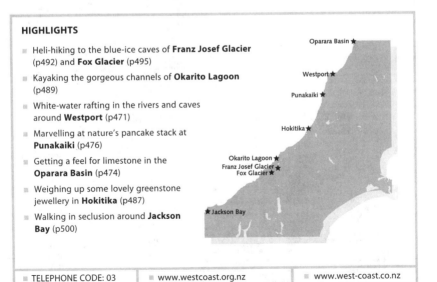

■ TELEPHONE CODE: 03　　■ www.westcoast.org.nz　　■ www.west-coast.co.nz

Climate

Most visit the region during summer (December to February) but from May to September the days can be warm and clear, with views of snow-washed peaks, less crowds and off-peak accommodation rates. With an average annual rainfall of around 5m, Westland could be called 'Wetland' – when it rains it pours. But the West Coast has as many hours of sunshine as the Christchurch region, and when it's pouring over on the east coast it's just as likely to be sunny here.

Getting There & Around

Air New Zealand Link will fly you into Westport from Wellington, and into Hokitika from Christchurch.

The West Coast is navigated by numerous coach lines and shuttles, some of which also have connections to east-coast hubs like Christchurch and Dunedin, and other significant South Island centres such as Queenstown and Nelson. Major operators include Atomic Shuttles, InterCity and Southern Link Shuttles.

For details of a spectacular train ride linking the West Coast with the folks back east in Christchurch, see the boxed text on p483.

MURCHISON
pop 850

Murchison, on the Buller Gorge Heritage Hwy (SH6) 125km south of Nelson, is the northern gateway to the West Coast. It's an

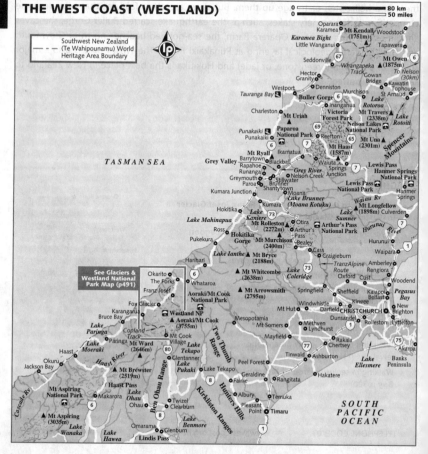

THE WEST COAST (WESTLAND)

important service centre for the surrounding region and base camp for adventure activities in the Upper Buller Gorge.

Information
The **Murchison visitors centre** (☎ 03-523 9350; www.murchisonnz.com; Waller St; 10am-5pm) either reduces its opening hours or shuts up shop over winter. There are no banks in town.

Sights & Activities
The small **Murchison Museum** (☎ 03-523 9335; 60 Fairfax St; admission by donation; 10am-4pm) is a musty warehouse of town artefacts, like 1930s electric cookers, an antique telephone exchange and sundry photos taken in the aftermaths of the 1929 Murchison and 1968 Inangahua earthquakes.

Murchison is a major centre for outdoor activities, including fishing, boating, mountain biking, rafting and kayaking. Hundreds of kayakers descend on Murchison in summer to navigate the Buller and its tributaries.

New Zealand Kayak School (☎ 03-523 9611; www.nzkayakschool.com; 111 Waller St; kayak rental per day $45, 4-day intro course $595) rents out kayaks and offers professional courses from introductory to advanced levels; price includes transport and accommodation but BYO food.

Ultimate Descents (☎ 0800 748 377, 03-523 9899; www.rivers.co.nz; 51 Fairfax St; rafting half-/full day from $105/185) is a highly regarded company that undertakes white-water rafting and kayaking trips on the Buller River, including half-day, easygoing, family rafting excursions (adult/child $95/75). Other options include full- or multi-day West Coast helirafting trips (from $295).

The area is threaded with popular **mountain bike trails**, like the one along the west bank of the Matakitaki (16km return) and the Maruia Saddle Trip (83km return). Hire bikes from Riverview Holiday Park (see Sleeping; p469).

The local river **fishing** is deemed superb – full-day guided trips in search of trout cost around $550 and the visitors centre lists guides. Back on dry land, the Tutaki Valley has good horse trekking; **Tiraumea Horse Treks** (☎ 03-523 9341; rides per hr $28) runs trips lasting from one hour to a full day.

Go **gold panning** (equipment hire $5) in Lyell Creek, the Buller River or the Howard Val-

ley; the visitors centre rents out pans and shovels (it requires a $20 bond).

Festivals & Events
The year's main event is the **Buller Festival**, a kayaking and rafting extravaganza over the first weekend in March.

Sleeping
Riverview Holiday Park (☎ 03-523 9591; riverview.hp@xtra.co.nz; Riverside Tce; camp sites & campervan sites $16, d $32-75) In a serene riverside location, 1.5km from town on the road to Nelson, this park has motel rooms and cheap cabins that look a bit like old workers' huts. Mountain bikes can be hired here for around $10 per hour.

Commercial Hotel (☎ 03-523 9696; Waller St; s/d $30/50) The front section of the Commercial was renovated several years ago, improving the place markedly. Rooms remain simple and clean, with shared facilities. Offering similar rooms is the weathered **Hampden Hotel** (☎ 03-523 9008; Fairfax St; s/d $30/50), diagonally opposite the Commercial.

Lazy Cow (☎ 0800 529 9269, 03-523 9451; Waller St; dm/d $18/50;) Clean and cosy home-style budget accommodation just south of the visitors centre, with a nice sun-deck to perch on. The rocking-horse is allegedly the best seat in the house.

Hu-Ha Bikepackers (☎ 03-548 2707; SH6; camp sites $20, dm $18) Tranquil cyclist-loving home-stay with two small dorms, located on a large property just north of Kawatiri where the highway splits to Nelson and St Arnaud. It's nearly 40km from Murchison, but nonetheless is very popular with cyclists.

Coch-y-Bondhu Lodge (☎ 03-523 9196; www.homestays.net.nz/cochybondhu.htm; 15 Grey St; s/d from $90/105) Lovely, well-crafted home-stay set on an untrammelled 1.2-hectare block overlooking the Buller River. One of the owners doubles as an experienced fishing guide and home cooking at dinnertime can be arranged.

Mataki Motel (☎ 0800 279 088, 03-523 9088; 34 Hotham St; d $60-85;) Quietly located a few blocks off the main street, this low-cost motel offers serviceable rooms, a rural backdrop, a small playground for the kids and cooked/continental brekkies by request.

Murchison Motel (☎ 0800 166 500, 03-523 9026; murchison.motels@xtra.co.nz; 53 Fairfax St; d $90-130) This motel comprises a bunch of refurbished and newly erected one- to two-bedroom units peacefully tucked away behind Rivers Cafe (see Eating; p470). Also available here is a cottage sleeping up to eight people.

Eating

Rivers Cafe (☎ 03-523 9009; Fairfax St; meals $9-18; ☺ breakfast, lunch & dinner) Cheerful licensed café set up in what appears to be an old service station adjacent to the Ultimate Descents office, where it serves steak sandwiches, Thai chicken and veg breakfasts.

Beechwoods Cafe (☎ 0800 114 211, 03-523 9571; 32 Waller St; meals $8-25; ☺ breakfast, lunch & dinner; 🖥) More like a roadhouse than a café, due to the buses that regularly belch their way into the large car park. The ready-made food ranges from lasagne to scotch fillet steak and numerous burgers (including veg).

Commercial Hotel (☎ 03-523 9696; Waller St; mains $7-18; ☺ lunch Mon & Tue, lunch & dinner Wed-Sun) Within this hotel is Stables Cafe, where you can sink your teeth into seafood baskets, quiche, steaks and salads. There's outdoor seating too.

Getting There & Away

A number of bus services pass through Murchison on the way to the West Coast, Nelson, St Arnaud, Blenheim and Picton. These include **Atomic Shuttles** (☎ 03-322 8883; www.atomictravel.co.nz) on their Picton–Greymouth service; **InterCity** (☎ 03-379 9020; www.intercitycoach.co.nz) on the Nelson–Fox Glacier run; **Southern Link Shuttles** (☎ 03-358 8355; www.yellow.co.nz/site/southernlink) on the Christchurch–Nelson route; and **Lazerline** (☎ 0800 220 001, 03-388 7652), also on the Christchurch–Nelson route. These buses stop either outside Midwest Cafe (67 Fairfax St) or Beechwoods Cafe (32 Waller St).

BULLER GORGE

The road from Murchison to the coast via the Buller Gorge is scenic, though it was damaged by the 1929 and 1968 earthquakes. The gorge itself is a watersports hub; for info on white-water rafting and kayaking, see Murchison (p469).

About 14km west of Murchison is the **Buller Gorge Swingbridge** (☎ 03-523 9809; www.bullergorge.co.nz; SH6; bridge crossing adult/child $5/2; ☺ 8am-8pm Oct-Apr, 9am-5.30pm May-Sep). It's NZ's longest swingbridge (110m) and it leads to some interesting short walks on the other side of the gorge, including White Creek's Fault-

line, epicentre of the 1929 earthquake. To get back you can ride the thrilling, 160m **Comet Line flying fox** (seated ride adult/child $25/13, 'Supaman' ride $35/20), either seated in a harness or flying Superman-style. **Buller Experience Jet** (☎ 03-523 9880; www.murchison.co.nz; adult/child $65/45) runs 20-minute jetboat trips from the swingbridge.

Further west is **Inangahua Junction**, where you can head through Lower Buller Gorge to the coast, or south via Reefton to Greymouth on the inland route (SH69); the coastal route has more to offer but is longer.

Inwood Farm Backpackers (☎ 03-789 0205; Inwoods Rd; dm/tw from $18/22) is a small farmhouse at Inangahua Junction with two small dorms and one twin. There's no TV, so you'll just have to bushwalk, swim and otherwise enjoy nature. The hostel is closed June through August. There's also a **DOC camping ground** on SH6 at **Lyell** (adult/child $5/2.50), Upper Buller Gorge, 10km northeast of Inangahua (not to be confused with Inangahua Junction).

Buller Gorge can seem dark and forbidding, especially on a murky day – primeval ferns and cabbage trees cling to steep cliffs, and toi toi (a tall native grass) flanks the road between gorge and river. The road at **Hawks Crag**, an overhang just high enough to fit a bus under, has been literally hacked out of the rock. It's named after goldminer Robert Hawks, who prospected in the area.

WESTPORT

pop 4845

Westport is the main town at the northern end of the West Coast, where the Buller River drains into the sea. It's an ordinary working town with little to capture the interest of bypassers, but makes a reasonable base for outdoor activities, particularly in the Buller Gorge and Charleston ranges, and is an obvious stopover on the way to Karamea (for the Heaphy Track). There's also a sizeable seal colony west of town (see Around Westport; p473). Its prosperity was achieved unearthing coal, although most mining takes place some distance from town at Stockton.

Information

Westport visitors centre (☎ 03-789 6658; www.westport.org.nz; 1 Brougham St; ☺ 9am-7pm daily Nov-Mar, 9am-5pm Mon-Fri & 9am-4pm Sat & Sun Apr-Oct) has information on the tracks and walkways in the area, handles bookings for tours and transport, and sells DOC hut tickets for the Heaphy Track. However, it doesn't sell tickets for the Wangapeka Track – for those, and general tramping info, visit the Buller Region office of the **DOC** (☎ 03-788 8008; 72 Russell St; 8am-noon & 1-4.30pm Mon-Fri).

The **Automobile Association office** (AA; ☎ 03-789 7379; 75-79 Palmerston St) is in the BP service station. Internet access is available at **Web Shed** (☎ 03-789 5131; 208 Palmerston St; per hr $6).

Sights

Coaltown Museum (☎ 03-789 8204; Queen St; adult/student/child $7/5/3; 9am-4.30pm) is a splendid reconstruction of coal-mining life, including a walk through a simulated mine complete with sound effects and videos. As well as original coal- and gold-mining artefacts, a brewery display and some excellent photographic exhibits, there's a section devoted to the dredging of Westport's harbour, including a huge operational steam engine (now running on electricity).

The locally owned **Miner's Brewery** (☎ 03-789 6201; 10 Lyndhurst St; 10am-5.30pm Mon-Fri, 11am-5.30pm Sat) was established in 1993 and concocts four different beers, among them the organically brewed 'Green Fern'. Tours of the brewery have been discontinued but you can still taste the output.

Activities

From Charleston, south of Westport, **Norwest Adventures** (☎ 0800 116 686, 03-789 6686; www.caverafting.com) runs cave rafting trips ($120) into what could easily be the reaches of Xanadu on Coleridge's sacred river (the Nile actually). The popular 'Underworld Rafting' experience involves a walk through ancient limestone formations and the paddling of rubber rafts through glow-worm–filled caverns. It starts with an open-carriage railway trip through rainforest, which can also be done as a separate 1½-hour train ride (adult/child $20/15). Norwest Adventures also does five-hour adventure caving trips ($230), starting with a 30m abseil into Te Tahi *tomo* (hole) followed by a worm's-eye-view of rock squeezes and waterfalls, exploring prehistoric fossils and fabulous formations as you go. Another possibility is

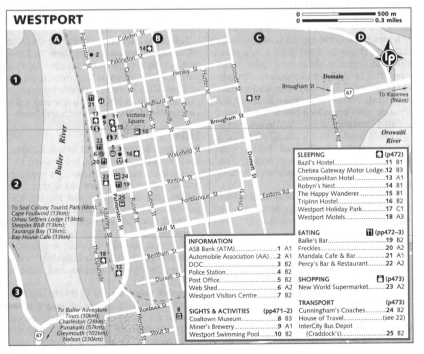

WESTPORT

0 ——— 500 m
0 ——— 0.3 miles

To Seal Colony Tourist Park (6km);
Cape Foulwind (13km);
Omau Settlers Lodge (13km);
Steeples B&B (13km);
Tauranga Bay (13km);
Bay House Cafe (13km)

To Buller Adventure
Tours (10km);
Charleston (28km);
Punakaiki (57km);
Greymouth (102km);
Nelson (230km)

To Karamea
(96km)

INFORMATION	
ASB Bank (ATM).......................1 A1	
Automobile Association (AA)....2 A1	
DOC..3 B2	
Police Station...........................4 B2	
Post Office...............................5 B2	
Web Shed................................6 A2	
Westport Visitors Centre...........7 B2	

SIGHTS & ACTIVITIES (pp471-2)	
Coaltown Museum.....................8 B3	
Miner's Brewery.......................9 A1	
Westport Swimming Pool.........10 B2	

SLEEPING	(p472)
Bazil's Hostel...........................11 B1	
Chelsea Gateway Motor Lodge.12 B3	
Cosmopolitan Hotel.................13 A1	
Robyn's Nest...........................14 B1	
The Happy Wanderer...............15 B1	
TripInn Hostel.........................16 B2	
Westport Holiday Park............17 C1	
Westport Motels.....................18 A3	

EATING	(pp472-3)
Bailie's Bar..............................19 B2	
Freckles...................................20 A2	
Mandala Cafe & Bar................21 A1	
Percy's Bar & Restaurant.........22 A2	

SHOPPING	(p473)
New World Supermarket..........23 A2	

TRANSPORT	(p473)
Cunningham's Coaches............24 B2	
House of Travel.................(see 22)	
InterCity Bus Depot	
(Craddock's)........................25 B2	

a walking tour (per person/family $60/180) through the glow-worm cave.

Buller Adventure Tours (☎ 0800 697 286, 03-789 7286; www.adventuretours.co.nz; Buller Gorge Rd), 4km east of the Greymouth turn-off, offers a variety of water- and land-based activities in the gorge area: white-water rafting ($95) on grade 3–4 'Earthquake Slip' rapids on the Buller; 1¾-hour jetboat rides ($65); and 2½-hour horse treks ($50) along the riverbank.

You can also take a relaxing dip in Westport's heated **swimming pool** (☎ 03-789 6779; Brougham St).

Events

The **Buller Gorge Marathon** finishes in Westport with a big party on the second weekend in February. The **Cape Classic Surfing Contest** is another big event on the Labour Day weekend in October.

Sleeping

HOSTELS

Robyn's Nest (☎ 03-789 6565; robyns.nest@xtra.co.nz; 42 Romilly St; dm/d $21/48; 💻) Located in the north of town and with a relaxed style that's part farmhouse and part old lodge, complete with a back porch and swirling carpets. Get the room upstairs with the balcony if you can.

TripInn Hostel (☎ 03-789 7367; tripinn@clear.net.nz; 72 Queen St; dm from $20, d $46; 💻) Set in a rambling 19th-century house on a quiet backstreet, this hostel has a nice garden, separate video lounge, ebullient owners and an unhurried air. Snooze in the main house or the separate units embedded beside it.

Happy Wanderer (☎ 03-789 8627; happywanderer@ xtra.co.nz; 56 Russell St; dm/d $22/50; 💻) This is a homely, purpose-built YHA hostel with good facilities and 24-hour access. The modern dorms have their own en suite and kitchen facilities.

Bazil's Hostel (☎ 03-789 6410; 54 Russell St; www .bazils.com; dm/d $19/45) Well appointed with a sheltered lawn and heated rooms.

MOTELS & HOTELS

Westport has dozens of motels, mostly on the highway into town where it becomes Palmerston St, while a couple of cheap options are hiding on the Esplanade, on the east bank of the Buller River.

Westport Motels (☎ 0800 805 909, 03-789 7575; 32 The Esplanade; s/d from $65/80; 🅿) One of the town's best motel deals, lying opposite the

Buller River and with thoroughly comfortable beds, plus a spa and swimming pool. They have several family units to accommodate large broods.

Chelsea Gateway Motor Lodge (☎ 0800 660 033, 03-789 6835; www.nzmotels.co.nz/chelsea.gateway/ index.html; 330 Palmerston St; s & d from $95) This well-appointed motel does a lot of corporate business during the week and is often less busy at weekends. The spa units are sometimes priced only slightly higher than the smaller standard rooms – if so, snap one up.

Cosmopolitan Hotel (☎ 03-789 6305; coshotel@ ihug.co.nz; 136 Palmerston St; s $35-42, d $68) Rooms here have been nicely done up and are better than the average pub bedroom, though give the $35 single a miss as it's a shoebox. Also note that north-facing windows look out on an unsightly processing plant.

CAMPING & CAMPERVAN PARKS

Westport Holiday Park (☎ 03-789 7043; westport holidaypark@xtra.co.nz; 31-37 Domett St; camp sites $20, campervan sites $22, dm $15, d $35-95) Situated in a pleasingly bushy locale, this park is littered with compact A-frame mini-'chalets', some super-basic bunkrooms and a range of other sheltered accommodation, from old caravans to motel units.

Seal Colony Tourist Park (☎ 0508 937 876, 03-789 8002; www.sealcolonytouristpark.co.nz; Marine Pde, Carters Beach; camp sites & campervan sites $23, d $45-110) This well-maintained park is 6km from Westport and has all the amenities suitable for a family vacation, such as BBQs, a playground and a swimmable (though fairly ordinary) beach.

Eating & Drinking

Percy's Bar & Restaurant (☎ 03-789 6648; 198 Palmerston St; meals $8-22; 🕐 breakfast, lunch & dinner) Dependable central eatery attracting a youngish crowd and serving dishes like turbot fillet cooked with vodka, lime and tomato, and pan-fried ham with gruyere cheese and mustard. Does breakfast until 2.30pm.

Freckles (☎ 03-789 8270; 216 Palmerston St; meals $6-10; 🕐 lunch Mon-Sat) Modest little café with a range of good, well-priced meals: pies and quiches, lamb kofta burgers and smoked chicken salads.

Mandala Cafe & Bar (☎ 03-789 7931; 110 Palmerston St; mains $8-18; 🕐 breakfast, lunch & dinner) Though the name hints at it, there are no mystic symbols of the universe here, just a standard café cooking up crumbed fish, pasta and burgers (a mighty porterhouse version among them).

Bailie's Bar (☎ 03-789 7289; 187 Palmerston St; mains $15-30; ☺ lunch & dinner) This beer parlour has a tentative Irish theme and lets you cook your own steak for $20, or dumps 500g of sirloin on your plate for $31. Alternatively, select one of the cheaper snacks, like pizza and burgers.

Get supplies at the **New World supermarket** (☎ 03-789 7669; Palmerston St).

Getting There & Away

Air New Zealand Link (☎ 0800 737 000, 09-357 3000; www.airnz.co.nz) has direct flights to/from Wellington (from $100), which can be booked through the **House of Travel** (☎ 03-788 8120; 196 Palmerston St). A taxi to the airport costs around $15.

InterCity (☎ 03-789 7819; www.intercitycoach.co.nz) buses passengers daily from **Craddock's Service Station** (197 Palmerston St) to Nelson ($49, 3½ hours), Greymouth ($24, two hours) and Franz Josef ($43, 6½ hours). **Atomic Shuttles** (☎ 03-322 8883; www.atomictravel.co.nz) stops at Westport on its daily Picton–Greymouth run – fares from Westport include Picton ($45), Nelson ($30), and Greymouth ($20).

The **Mainlander** (☎ 0800 836 969; 03-789 6658), based at the Cunningham's depot, travels to Christchurch ($40, five hours) via Inangahua Junction and Lewis Pass. It departs Westport at 9am Monday to Friday.

East West Coach (☎ 03-789 6251) operates a service to Christchurch (adult/child $44/ 34) departing from Craddock's at 8am daily, with the return shuttle departing Christchurch at 2pm. **Southern Link Shuttles** (☎ 03-358 8355; www.yellow.co.nz/site/southernlink) also runs to Christchurch ($35), departing Westport at 10am daily except Saturday and with a change at Springs Junction.

Karamea Express (☎ 03-782 6757; www.lastresort .co.nz) makes the trip from Westport (departing 11.30am Monday to Friday from May to October, and on Saturday between November and April) to Karamea (adult/child $20/ 15, 1½ hours). **Cunningham's Coaches** (☎ 03-789 7177; Palmerston St) does this trip in 2¾ hours ($15), as it makes more stops; it departs Westport at 3pm weekdays.

AROUND WESTPORT

Depending on the time of year, anything from 20 to over 100 NZ fur seals may be down on the rocks at the **Tauranga Bay seal colony**, 15km from Westport. Pups are born from late November to early December and for about a month afterwards the mothers stay on the rocks to tend the young before setting out to sea on feeding forays.

The **Cape Foulwind Walkway** (1½ hours return) extends along the coast 4km past the seal colony to Cape Foulwind, passing a replica of Abel Tasman's astrolabe (a navigational aid) and a lighthouse site. The northern end of this walk can be accessed by car from Cape Foulwind Rd.

The Maoris knew the cape as Tauranga, meaning a 'sheltered anchorage' or 'landing place'. The first European to reach the cape was Abel Tasman, who sighted it in December 1642 and named it Clyppygen Hoek (Rocky Point). When James Cook anchored here in March 1770, his ship, the *Endeavour*, was rocked by a furious storm, so he gave it the apt name it retains today.

From the Tauranga Bay car park it's a five-minute walk to the seal colony lookout, though you can often see the animals playing in the surf along this walk. The cliffs can be dangerous, so stick to marked areas.

Sleeping & Eating

There are some excellent B&Bs and homestays out towards Tauranga Bay; the Westport visitors centre has details.

Steeples B&B (☎ 03-789 7876; steepleshomestay@ xtra.co.nz; Lighthouse Rd; s/d from $45/85) This good, reasonably priced option in a lovely home has a pair of rooms and a huge garden running down to the clifftops.

Omau Settlers Lodge (☎ 0800 466 287, 03-789 5200; thecape@xtra.co.nz; 1054 Cape Rd; s $90-95, d $125) Within convenient stumbling distance of the tavern at Cape Foulwind is this excellent, newly built motel, which has eight casually stylish units and dishes out a buffet breakfast (included in room price).

Bay House Cafe (☎ 03-789 7133; Beach Rd; mains $28; ☺ lunch & dinner) One of the region's best restaurants, Bay House has a stylish but not overbearing interior, a front deck that's good for an extended lunch on a breezeless day, and gourmet treats like Tasman Bay mussel linguini, not to mention great views out over the breakers of Tauranga Bay. Book ahead.

WESTPORT TO KARAMEA

This trip north along State Highway 67 (SH67) is a fine drive, with the road squeezed up against the rocky shoreline by a high hill smothered in scrub and trees. The first town along the way is Waimangaroa, where there's a turn-off to **Denniston**. This town was once the largest producer of coal in NZ and can be reached via the **Denniston Walkway**, which follows the original path to the town and has great views of the fantastically steep **Denniston Incline**. In its day the Incline was a great engineering feat, as empty coal trucks were hauled back up the incline by the weight of the descending loaded trucks, sometimes at a gradient of one in one (though perhaps it's not really the 'eighth wonder of the world', as claimed in a local tourist leaflet). Four kilometres north of Waimangaroa is the **Britannia Track**, a six-hour return walk to the Britannia battery and other remnants of the gold-mining era.

At Granity, 30km north of Westport, head 5km uphill to the semi-ghost towns of **Millerton** and **Stockton**, contrasting with the activity at NZ's largest operational coal mine nearby. The **Millerton Incline Walk** (40 minutes return) takes in the old railway, a tunnel and an old dam.

Further north is another interesting walk at **Charming Creek**, an all-weather, five-hour return track following an old coal line through the picturesque Ngakawau River Gorge. You can pursue this track all the way to **Seddonville**, a small town surrounded by bush-covered hills on the Mohikinui River.

Three kilometres off the highway is the wild **Gentle Annie Beach**. At the mouth of the Mohikinui is **Gentle Annie Coastal Enclave** (☎ 03-782 1826; www.gentleannie.co.nz; Gentle Annie Rd; camp sites $18, dm $19, d $75-180), a great place for time-out, where a basic backpacker lodge peacefully coexists with a three-bedroom beach cabin and two four-bedroom houses; prices vary considerably depending on the season/choice of cabin. Another inhabitant is the BYO **Cowshed Cafe** (meals $9-23; ☽ lunch & dinner), a former dairy shed converted into an airy space filled with the smells of wholesome soups, rotis and fresh veg creations.

Between Mohikinui and Little Wanganui the road passes over the **Karamea Bluff**, making for a slow, magnificently winding drive through rata and matai forest with views of the Tasman Sea below.

KARAMEA
pop 685

Karamea is a real end-of-the-road town, at the end of SH67 and near the southern ends of the Heaphy and Wangapeka Tracks, with most facilities clustered around Market Cross. Info, maps and DOC hut tickets are available at the **Karamea Information & Resource Centre** (☎ 03-782 6652; www.karameainfo.co.nz; Market Cross; ☽ 9am-5pm).

Oparara Basin

North of Karamea in the **Oparara Basin** are spectacular limestone arch formations and the unique Honeycomb Hill Caves (ancient home of the moa) with the surrounding karst landscape blanketed by primitive rainforest. Moss-laden trees droop over the Oparara River, illuminated by light filtering through a dense forest canopy.

Ten kilometres along the road to the start of the Heaphy Track, turn off at McCallum's Mill Rd and go 15km past the sawmill along a winding gravel (sometimes rough) road to the arches. It's an easy walk (45 minutes return) through old-growth forest to the huge **Oparara Arch** that spans its namesake river – you can scramble through to the other side of the 200m-long, 37m-high formation. The smaller but equally beautiful **Moria Gate Arch** is a harder walk (one hour return) along a muddy track that is not always easy to follow.

Other interesting natural features are **Mirror Tarn** (20 minutes return) and the **Crazy Paving & Box Canyon Caves** (10 minutes return). Beyond these are the magnificent **Honeycomb Hill Caves & Arch**, which lie in a special protected area and can only be accessed by a pre-booked **guided tour** (☎ 03-782 6652; adult/child $50/25). The caves contain the bones of three of the five moa species (slender *Megalapteryx didinus*; small *Pachyornis elephantopus*; and giant *Dinornis giganteus*) and were where the bones of the now-extinct giant Haast eagle, once the world's largest, were discovered. This eagle had a 3m to 4m wingspan and preyed on the moa.

Activities

The Karamea River is good for swimming, fishing and canoeing. Canoe trips are organised by the **Last Resort** (☎ 0800 505 042, 03-782 6617; www.lastresort.co.nz; Waverley St; kayaks per person $30); see Sleeping & Eating (p475).

The Little Wanganui, Oparara and Ko-haihai Rivers also have good swimming holes. The tidal lagoons 1km north and 3km south of Karamea are sheltered and good for swimming at high tide, but otherwise swimming in the open sea is dangerous. The only drawback to the beautiful beaches around Karamea are the millions of sandflies; plenty of repellent (or wind) might save your sanity.

There are plenty of good day walks, including the **Fenian Track** (four hours return) leading to **Cavern Creek Caves** and **Adams Flat**, where there's a replica of a gold miner's hut; the trek to 1084m **Mt Stormy** (eight hours return); and the walk to **Lake Hanlon** (one hour return). The first leg of the **Wangapeka Track** also makes a good day walk.

If you're not keen on walking the whole **Heaphy Track**, or if you have a vehicle and want to retrieve it, you can walk as far as the **Heaphy Hut** (5 hr; adult/child $14/7) and stay in the hut overnight. Alternatively, follow the track only as far as **Scotts Beach** (1½ hr return), passing beautiful nikau palm groves along the way. For more information on the Heaphy and Wangapeka Tracks, see Kahurangi National Park (p463).

The area has plenty of **mountain bike trails**, from a 16km trip along the Matakitaki River past the site of the 1929 earthquake-prompted slip, to the 83km round trip to lovely Maruia Saddle. The information and resource centre has all the details.

Sleeping & Eating

Karamea Holiday Park (☎ 03-782 6758; www.karamea .com; Maori Pt; camp sites $18, campervan sites $20, s $16-50, d $22-60) Located in native bush 3km south of Market Cross, this is the place to brush up on your whitebaiting skills (see the boxed text, p499) and to otherwise wean yourself off your urban routine (in-between visits to the TV room).

Karamea Domain (☎ 03-782 6719; Waverley St; camp sites & campervan sites $24, dm $10) This camping ground at the local sports reserve has an on-site caretaker and a choice between basic sites and equally basic berths in the bunkhouse.

Punga Lodge Backpackers (☎ 03-782 6667; Waverley St; camp sites $24, dm/d $19/40) Karamea's only hostel is a casual 10-room affair with a sizeable lounge, a BBQ area and a handful of camp sites.

Last Resort (☎ 0800 505 042, 03-782 6617; www.last resort.co.nz; Waverley St; camp sites $20, dm $22, d $65-140) This fetching complex has a range of rooms connected by walkways to the impressive central building. The buildings have sod roofs and feature massive beams made of local timbers. There are modern lodge rooms and cottages, all set in a pleasant native garden. There's also a fine licensed **restaurant** (mains $15-30; ☺ breakfast & dinner) dishing up seafood chowder and flaming liver salad, and a **café-bar** (mains $7-15; ☺ lunch) serving cheaper meals like burgers and fish and chips.

Karamea Village Hotel (☎ 03-782 6800; karamea hotel@xtra.co.nz; Waverley St; dm $18, d $95-120) This is a pub where Meatloaf is played with gusto and no sense of shame. That said, it has modern en suite motel units next door and a fully-equipped backpackers' house across the road. It also does good, heavy-on-the-meat meals and does a roaring trade in the local delicacy: whitebait sandwiches.

Bridge Farm Motels (☎ 03-782 6955; www.kara meamotels.co.nz; Bridge Rd; d $80-130) The accommodation at this rural motel ranges from studios to two-bedroom units, which are bright, comfortable and spacious. A continental breakfast is included in the tariff.

Four Square Discounter supermarket (☎ 03-782 6701; Market Cross; ☺ 8.30am-6pm Mon-Fri, 9am-5pm Sat, 9am-noon Sun) The self-sufficient can buy supplies here.

Getting There & Away

Karamea Express (☎ 03-782 6757; www.lastresort .co.nz) travels between Karamea and Westport (adult/child $20/15, 1½ hours), departing 7.50am weekdays from May to October, plus Saturday from November to April.

Cunningham's Coaches (☎ 03-789 7177; Palmerston St) has an evening service to Westport ($15, 2¾ hours), departing Karamea at 6.15pm Monday to Friday.

The Karamea Express also runs to Kohaihai at the southern end of the **Heaphy Track** ($8), departing Karamea at 1.45pm and returning 2.10pm from mid-October to Easter, plus 12.30pm (returning 1pm) from December to February. At other times it runs on demand (for a higher price; ring for a quote). The Karamea Express also runs on demand to the **Wangapeka Track**. The ends of the Heaphy and Wangapeka Tracks have phones to arrange transport out to Karamea.

It's also possible to fly from Karamea to Takaka (around $130) and then walk back on the Heaphy Track – contact the information centre for details.

WESTPORT TO GREYMOUTH

The coastal road yields fine views of the Tasman Sea and a surf-pounded coastline – fill up in Westport if you're low on petrol, as there's no fuel along the road south until Runanga (92km away). The main attraction along this route is Punakaiki and the geologically brilliant Pancake Rocks.

Between Westport and Punakaiki are a number of teensy towns (10 or so inhabitants), but it was a different story 140 years ago when the gold rush was on. To see what all the fuss was about, visit **Mitchell's Gully Gold Mine** (www.mitchellsgullygoldmine.8m.com; SH6; adult/child $5/1; 9am-4pm), a wonderfully evocative site crisscrossed by old rail tracks and with a photogenic tumbledown waterwheel. Follow a narrow forest path through tunnels bored into hillsides, passing derelict mining shafts (watch the kids – the shafts are unfenced). The site, 22km south of Westport, is run by a guy whose family worked this site 100 years ago and feels far more authentic than pricey Shantytown further south (see Around Greymouth, p484).

Charleston, 28km south of Westport, was a booming town during the 1860s gold rush, with shanties all along the pack route, gold-diggers staking their claims on the Nile River and a mind-boggling 80 hotels along the main street. Today the raucous pubs are gone (bar one), but there are still some decent places to stay in and around town.

Jack's Gasthof (03-789 6501; jack.schubert@xtra.co.nz; SH6; camp sites $10, campervan sites $16, d $50) is situated north of Charleston on the Little Totara River. This nice, greenery-surrounded place is in a peaceful spot just off the highway. There are two doubles, both with colour-swirled walls, and a **café** (mains $15-23; breakfast, lunch & dinner) serving pizza and a variety of other meals. There's a discount on the room price if you have dinner here.

Pyramid Farm (03-789 8487; www.pyramid-farm.tk; SH6; dm $18-20, d from $65) is located 2km north of Charleston. This 64-hectare, rainforest-covered property has a comfortable 12-bed timber lodge with a well-equipped kitchen and a cosy lounge, including several cottages. Various activities can be organised,

including tube rafting ($105) along an underground stream.

Charleston Motel (03-789 7599; SH6; d $75-85) comprises a quartet of comfortable units looking out to the adjacent highway – inspect the rooms first if you find bright colour schemes disconcerting. Close by is **Charleston Tavern** (03-789 8862; SH6; mains $15-22; lunch & dinner), cheerfully draped in international flags and with the usual small-town pub fare, including a popular Sunday roast.

The coast from Fox River to Runanga is rugged and the road will remind West Coast Americans of California's Big Sur. Woodpecker Bay, Tiromoana, Punakaiki, Barrytown, Fourteen Mile, Motukiekie, Ten Mile, Nine Mile and Seven Mile are all **beaches** sculpted by the relentless fury of the Roaring Forties.

Right on the beach at Woodpecker Bay, 12km north of Punakaiki, is **Coastal Experience** (03-789 7830; SH6; d $70-80), a couple of rustic bachs with a million-miles-from-anywhere ambience; just sit and watch the surf crashing onto rocky outcrops.

Punakaiki & Paparoa National Park

Almost midway between Westport and Greymouth is the small settlement of Punakaiki, which has some of the West Coast's finest scenery and is on the doorstep of the beautifully rough, 30,000-hectare Paparoa National Park. The **Paparoa National Park visitors centre** (03-731 1895; punakaikivc@doc.govt.nz; SH6; 9am-6pm Oct-Apr, 9am-4.30pm May-Sep) has interesting displays on the park and supplies info on activities, accommodation and trail conditions.

Punakaiki is best known for the wondrous **Pancake Rocks** and their accompanying **blowholes**. Through a layering and weathering process known as stylobedding, the limestone rocks at Dolomite Pt have formed into what looks like stacks of thin pancakes. When a good tide is running (check at the visitors centre for times), the water surges into caverns below the rocks and squirts out from impressive geyser-like blowholes. A 15-minute **walk** loops from the highway around the rocks and blowholes.

Paparoa National Park has many other natural attractions besides its gritty pancakes. The region is blessed with other sea cliffs, fine mountains (the Paparoa Range), rivers, diverse flora and a Westland black petrel colony, the world's only nesting area of this rare sea bird.

ACTIVITIES
Interesting **walks** in the national park include the 27km **Inland Pack Track**, a two- to three-day route established by miners in 1867 to circumvent the more rugged coastal walk; they are detailed in the DOC *Paparoa National Park* pamphlet ($1). The **Croesus Track** is covered by another DOC leaflet (50c) and is an 18km, one- to two-day tramp over the Paparoa Range from Blackball to Barrytown, passing through historic gold-mining areas (see Blackball; p479). If you're planning on walking, register your intentions at the park's visitors centre. Many of the inland walks are subject to river flooding, so check conditions before setting out.

Punakaiki Canoes (☎ 03-731 1870; www.riverkayaking.co.nz; SH6; canoe hire per 2hr/day $30/50) hires out canoes and kayaks near the Pororari River bridge. **Punakaiki Horse Treks** (☎ 03-731 1839; www.pancake-rocks.co.nz; 2½hr ride $80) arranges four-legged excursions in the national park.

TOURS
Locally-based **Green Kiwi Tours** (☎ 0800 474 733; www.greenkiwitours.co.nz; tours per hr from $60, caving from $40) offer information-laden tours throughout the region, including to the Westland black petrel breeding colony, as well as caving, bouldering and heli-hiking.

SLEEPING & EATING
Punakaiki Beach Camp (☎ 03-731 1894; beachcamp@xtra.co.nz; SH6; camp sites $20, campervan sites $22, d $30-40) An appealingly landscaped plot of land beside the water, drenched with ocean smells and studded with budget cabins.

Punakaiki Beach Hostel (☎ 03-731 1852; www.punakaikibeachhostel.co.nz; Webb St; dm/s/d from $23/39/56; 🖳) Snug beach-bumming hostel sporting a large veranda and an outdoor spa; only a short trudge from Pancake Rocks and some bushy trails. There are also rooms for rent in the Seaside House on Owen St.

Rocks Homestay (☎ 03-731 1141; www.therockshomestay.com; 33 Hartmount Pl; s/d from $95/110) Three kilometres north of Punakaiki (the turn-off is 100m north of the Truman Track) is this view-blessed house, with a front porch looking out over wild shrubbery to the sea. Tasty breakfasts are part of the package and

dinners are cooked by arrangement. A good place to enjoy some secluded walks.

Hydrangea Cottages (☎ 03-731 1839; www.pancake-rocks.co.nz; SH6; d $175-275) Four lovely stand-alone cottages – each a different size – perched on a hydrangea-sprouting hillside overlooking Pancake Rocks. Breathe in the views and the air of the surrounding forest. Punakaiki Horse Treks are based here (see Activities & Tours; p477).

Punakaiki Rocks Villas (☎ 0800 786 252, 03-731 1168; www.punakaiki-resort.com; SH6; d $160-295) Several dozen luxurious self-contained rooms are on offer in this breezy complex. Get an ocean-facing room for an eyeful of sea-spray, or a room in the bush if privacy is what you're after.

Wild Coast Cafe (☎ 03-731 1873; SH6; mains $9-16; ☙ breakfast & lunch) Beside the visitors centre is this tourist-swamped café, fittingly serving a pancake stack with fruit, cream and maple syrup. The café also cooks veg lasagne and various other light meals.

Punakaiki Tavern (☎ 03-731 1188; SH6; mains $14-23; ☙ lunch & dinner) Help yourself to a glass or two of something cold in the beer garden or in front of the fireplace when the drizzle settles in. Big, hearty mains vie with cheaper bar snacks for your attention. There are also standard **units** (d $95).

GETTING THERE & AWAY
Services between Westport and Greymouth by both **InterCity** (☎ 03-789 7819; www.intercitycoach.co.nz) and **Atomic Shuttles** (☎ 03-322 8883; www.atomictravel.co.nz) stop at Punakaiki daily, allowing enough time to see the Pancake Rocks.

The Coast Road
The scenic coast road from Punakaiki to Greymouth is flanked by white-capped breakers and rugged sea rocks on one side and the steep, bush-clad Paparoa Ranges on the other.

Barrytown, 16km south of Punakaiki, is home to the historic **All Nations Hotel** (☎ 03-731 1812; allnations@xtra.co.nz; SH6; camp sites $25, dm/s/d $22/32/64), opposite the western end of the Croesus Track and thus handy for those tramping in from Blackball and desperate for a bed and a beer (not necessarily in that order). For food, try the highly recommended **Rata Cafe** (☎ 03-731 1151; SH6; mains $10-23; ☙ breakfast, lunch & dinner daily Oct-Apr, closed

Mon & Tue May-Sep), a stylish and spacious place perched up on a hillside, and blessed with a great atmosphere and excellent food like buffalo burgers and cider-poached turbot.

GREY VALLEY

From Murchison, an alternative to the SH6 route to the West Coast is to turn off at Inangahua Junction and travel inland via Reefton, then over the mountains into the Grey Valley. This makes for a pleasant valley drive, with captivating scenery along the winding road as you go.

Despite the best efforts of a century of plunderers, abundant rainfall has fuelled regenerating bush on the green-cloaked hills and the paddocks have fast become overgrown. The small towns provide a reminder of those futile attempts to tame the land and of the gold that brought diggers flooding into this area in the 1860s.

Reefton
pop 1050

Reefton is a pleasant little town in the heart of great walking country, its name derived from the region's gold-bearing quartz reefs. As early as 1888, Reefton had its own electricity supply and street lighting, beating all other towns in NZ. If you've crossed the Lewis Pass from Christchurch, this is the first town of any size you come to.

The modern **Reefton visitors centre** (☎ 03-732 8391; www.reefton.co.nz; 67 Broadway; 8.30am-6pm Oct-Apr, 8.30am-4.30pm May-Sep) has lots of information, a one-room re-creation of the **Quartzopolis Mine** (admission 50c) and Internet access.

SIGHTS & ACTIVITIES

A number of the shops on Broadway date from the 1870s; the *Historic Reefton* leaflet ($1) explains all.

At Blacks Point, 2km east of town on the road to Christchurch, is a **museum** (SH7; adult/child $4/2; 9am-noon & 1-4pm Wed-Fri & Sun, 1-4pm Sat Oct-Apr) set in a former Methodist church and crammed with prospecting paraphernalia. Next door is the **Gold Stamper Battery** (admission $1; 1-4pm Wed & Sun Oct-Apr), once used for crushing ore.

The surrounding area has many fine **walks** and the Big River Track offers great **mountain-biking** possibilities. The short walks around town include the **Powerhouse Walk**,

Reefton Walkway and the historic **Reefton Walk**. The **Blacks Point Walk** (two to three hours) takes you to abandoned coal mines.

There's also a wealth of walking in **Victoria Forest Park** – at 182,000 hectares NZ's largest such park and overgrown by five different species of beech tree. The two-day **Big River** and the three-day **Kirwans, Blue Grey River** and **Robinson Valley Tracks** are all fulfilling tramping options. The visitors centre has the requisite information and maps.

SLEEPING & EATING

DOC camping ground (SH7; adult/child $5/2.50) You can camp at Slab Creek, 7km southwest of Reefton.

Reefton Motor Camp (☎ 03-732 8477; 1 Ross St; camp sites $14, campervan sites $18, d $32) On the Inangahua River at the eastern end of the main street, this camping ground is encircled by some glorious specimens of Lawson's pine. The basic cabins more closely resemble snug shacks, with bunks, a closet and a small table.

Old Bread Shop (☎ 03-732 8420; lorettar@chc .quik.co.nz; 155 Buller Rd; dm $16-18, d & tw $40) This small, homely backpackers' has a handful of doubles and a dorm lounging inside a brightly restored old bakery. The friendly owners are lifelong Reefton residents and live next door; ask them about the great local fishing opportunities.

Reef Cottage (☎ 0800 770 440, 03-732 8440; reefton@ clear.net.nz; 51 Broadway; d $75-130) This charming, curious-looking 1867 cottage, from the outside resembles a false façade in a mock-Wild West town. It was once a solicitor's office and one of the rooms uses the old vault (complete with original door) as its en suite. The cottage can be booked for groups of up to eight people.

Dawsons (☎ 03-732 8406; 74 Broadway; s & d $80) Also called Reefton Auto Lodge, this central, no-fuss place has serviceable units huddled around a small rear courtyard. Meals are available here in the **Electric Light Cafe** (mains $16-20; breakfast & dinner), with standard pub mains like rump steak and pork chops, plus a daily roast with six (count 'em) veg for $10.

Reefton Hotel (☎ 03-732 8447; 75 Broadway; mains $10-15; lunch & dinner) Cheaper pub-meal options than Electric Light Cafe, though a similar menu.

Alfresco (☎ 03-732 8513; Broadway; mains $10-22; lunch & dinner) Serves grilled meats and a half-dozen pizzas (one topped with chicken satay and apricot sauce), to be eaten out on the front or back decks; the latter gets the wintertime sun. There are also some tables inside for when the alfresco is too fresco.

GETTING THERE & AWAY
Both **Southern Link Shuttles** (☎ 03-358 8355; www .yellow.co.nz/site/southernlink) and **East West Coach** (☎ 03-789 6251) both stop in Reefton on their regular services between Westport and Christchurch. **Atomic Shuttles** (☎ 03-322 8883; www.atomictravel.co.nz) also stops here on its Greymouth–Picton express run.

SH7 to Greymouth
At Hukarere, 21km south of Reefton, turn east and drive 17km to **Waiuta**, once the focus of a rich gold mine and now a ghost of its former self. A reef of gold was discovered here in 1905 – it was called the Birthday Reef, as it was found on the birthday of King Edward VII – and by 1906 the Blackwater Mine had been sunk. The town's population grew to around 500, but in 1951 the mine collapsed and Waiuta was abandoned virtually overnight. The drive to Waiuta through beech forest is scenic, though the last 8km or so is a winding, narrow and occasionally rough dirt road. The interpretive walks and views are worth the trip out to this lonely site.

If you feel like bedding down in a ghost town, **Waiuta Lodge** (adult/child $15/7, plus $10 key deposit) is a 30-bunk building with full kitchen facilities. Book and get a key at the **Reefton visitors centre** (☎ 03-732 8391; 67 Broadway).

BLACKBALL
Off the highway and north of the Grey River (take the Blackball–Taylorville Rd) about 25km north of Greymouth is historic Blackball, a working town established in 1866 as a service centre for the gold-diggers, which then became a coal-mining centre from 1890 until 1964. The national Federation of Labour (an organisation of trade unions) was born here after cataclysmic strikes in 1908 and 1931.

One kilometre from Blackball, on the road to Roa, is the recommended starting point for the 18km **Croesus Track** (info leaflet 50c), which crosses the Paparoa Range and ends at Barrytown on the West Coast. It can be done in a long day, or you can overnight

at the DOC's **Ces Clark Hut** (adult/child $10/5), roughly halfway along.

The hub of Blackball's social life is the extroverted **Formerly the Blackball Hilton** (☎ 03-732 4705; www.blackballhilton.co.nz; 26 Hart St; d $110-180), designated a New Zealand Historic Place. The 'formerly' was apparently added after a certain giant hotel chain challenged the original moniker. Accommodation-wise, there's a choice between B&B and DB&B ($110 and $180 per double respectively); you can also rent a miner's cottage. Things to occupy you include tramping the Croesus Track, gold panning, horse riding, fishing and regular live-music events.

The **Blackball Salami shop** (☎ 03-732 4111; 11 Hilton St) sells lovingly produced, low-fat venison and beef salami.

LAKE BRUNNER
At Stillwater you can detour to Lake Brunner, also known as Moana Kotuku (Heron Sea). Locals reckon Lake Brunner and the Arnold River which feeds it are among the world's best **trout-fishing** spots (not an uncommon boast in NZ) – as testament to this, local fishing guides use the tagline, 'Where the trout die of old age'. Fishing guides can be hired in Moana (ask at the Moana Hotel) or just collar a local for advice. **Lake Brunner Boat Hire** (☎ 03-738 0291; 66 Koe St) hires out fishing boats ($100 per day, plus fuel) and kayaks (half-/full day $40/60).

Short walks include the 20-minute **Velenski Walk**, which starts near the motor camp and leads through a stupendous tract of native totara, rimu and kahikatea, and the **Arnold River Walk**, which crosses a swingbridge over the river.

Lake Brunner Motor Camp (☎ 03-738 0600; lake.brunner@paradise.net.nz; Ahau St; camp sites $16, campervan sites $20, s $18) has good views across the lake to some impressive hills. Besides an array of sites, the camp also has small four-berth cabins. It has a general store which also sells fishing gear.

The local pub **Moana Hotel** (☎ 03-738 0083; Ahau St; s $16-18, d $60-90) has shared cabins and hillside motel units, and its **bistro** (mains from $12; ☿ lunch & dinner) has a view to the lake. This is also the place to hook up with a fishing guide.

The pleasant **Station House Cafe** (☎ 03-738 0158; Koe St; dinner mains $20-25; ☿ lunch & dinner) is on a hillside opposite the Moana Railway

Station, where the *TranzAlpine* train pulls in, and has a meat-filled dinner menu.

GREYMOUTH
pop 13,500

Greymouth was once the site of a Maori *pa* (fortified village) and was known as Mawhera (Widespread River Mouth). The Ngai Kahu people believe that the Cobden Gap north of town is where their ancestor Tuterakiwhanoa broke the side of *Te Waka o Aoraki* (The Canoe of Aoraki), releasing trapped rainwater to the sea.

Relatively small, provincial Greymouth is nonetheless the largest town on the West Coast and has a long gold-mining history. It's located at the mouth of the Grey River (hence its name) and despite the high protective wall along Mawhera Quay the river still manages to flood the town after periods of heavy rain.

Being at the other end of the coast-to-coast route from Christchurch (by road or rail), Greymouth gets a fair amount of tourist traffic, but there's not much to do in the town itself. As with Westport, however, plenty of adventure activities can be organised from here.

Information

Greymouth visitors centre (☎ 0800 473 966, 03-768 5101; cnr Herbert & Mackay Sts; ☼ 9am-7pm daily Oct-Apr, 9am-5pm Mon-Fri & 10am-4pm Sat & Sun May-Sep) is located in the Regent Theatre (see Entertainment; p483). It offers Internet access ($8 per hour), as does **DP:One Cafe** (☎ 03-768 4005; 108 Mawhera Quay; per 30min $3); see Eating p483. The **AA** (☎ 03-768 4300; 84 Tainui St) has an office here.

Sights

Monteith's Brewing Co (☎ 03-768 4149; www.monteiths .co.nz; cnr Turumaha & Herbert Sts; admission $10; tours 10am, 11.30am & 2pm Mon-Fri, 11.30am & 2pm Sat & Sun), the original West Coast brewery, distributes its beers nationwide. Styles include original ale, golden lager, Celtic Red, pilsener, Monteith's delicious black and the perky Summertime Ale. Check out the production process, which involves coal-fired boilers, before undertaking the obligatory taste test.

Left Bank Art Gallery (☎ 03-768 0038; 1 Tainui St; adult/child $2/free; ☼ 10am-7.30pm Oct-Apr, 10am-5pm May-Sep), situated within the historic Bank

of NZ building, is a small but important collection of jade carvings by contemporary West Coast artisans; temporary sculpture and painting; and a children's gallery in the old vault. You can buy various art and crafts here, including bone- and wood-carved jewellery.

History House Museum (☎ 03-768 4028; www .history-house.co.nz; Gresson St; adult/child $3/1; ☼ 10am-4pm Mon-Fri) was founded 10 years ago and details Greymouth's gold-prospecting past through numerous photos and other historical accounts.

Jade Boulder Gallery (☎ 03-768 0700; 1 Guinness St; admission free; ☼ 8.30am-9pm Oct-Apr, 8.30am-5pm May-Sep) is a pricey but impressive workshop where original jade sculpture and jewellery is crafted. There's a fascinating display of jade boulders showing the raw state of the precious *pounamu*. Free guided tours are held several times daily.

Activities

The **Point Elizabeth Walkway** (three hours return) heads north of Greymouth through the Rapahoe Range Scenic Reserve. The short **Quay Walk** from Cobden Bridge towards Blaketown is also worthwhile.

Mountain bike trails include the aptly named Kumara Mud Plug. Bikes can be rented from **Wildside Tours & Cafe** (☎ 03-768 5959; 121 Mackay St; half-/full-day hire $15/30).

Eco-Rafting Adventures NZ (☎ 03-768 4005; www .ecorafting.co.nz; 108 Mawhera Quay; rafting half-/full-day trips from $80/130), based at the DP:One Cafe, stages white-water rafting trips on the Arnold, Buller and Upper Grey Rivers, plus heli-rafting further afield.

Another river-froth enthusiast is the **Wild West Adventure Company** (☎ 0800 147 483, 03-768 6649; www.nzholidayheaven.com; 8 Whall St; trips $95-360), which does everything from three-hour trips to full-day heli-rafts. A popular 5½-hour expedition is the 'Dragons Cave' ($120), where you float on inflated tubes down through a subterranean glow-worm gallery and slide down a 30m natural hydro-slide. They also do a sedate, three-hour 'Jungle Boat' cruise ($95) down the Arnold River aboard a Maori *waka* (canoe).

On Yer Bike (☎ 0800 669 372, 03-762 7438; www .onyerbike.co.nz; 2hr ride adult/child $95/80) is based at Coal Creek, 5km north of Greymouth, where it does various quad-bike trips, including the two-hour 'Bum-Bruiser Track'.

GREYMOUTH

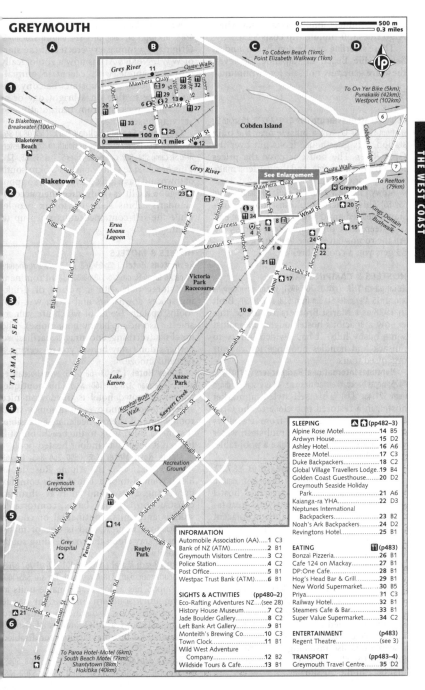

0   500 m
0   0.3 miles

Grey River 11
Quay Walk

Mawhera Quay

Albert St

Tainui St

Guinn St

Boundary St

26

6

9   29
13
Mackay

28   32

27

33

5   4
25

12

Whall St

0   100 m
0   0.1 miles

Cobden Island

To Cobden Beach (1km);
Point Elizabeth Walkway (1km)

To On Yer Bike (5km);
Punakaiki (42km);
Westport (102km)

6

Cobden Bridge

To Blaketown
Breakwater (100m)

**Blaketown
Beach**

Collins St

Coakley St

Doyle St

Blake St

Packers Quay

Rigg St

Reid St

Blake St

Preston Rd

Blaketown

**Erua
Moana
Lagoon**

Grey River

Gresson St
23

7

Johnston St

Ainsley St

Guinness St

Leonard St

Herbert St

Tarapuhi St

See Enlargement

Mawhera Quay

Albert St

Mackay St

3
34

8

18

Whall St

35

Greymouth

Smith St

Mount St

Chapel St

15

24

22

1

31

17

Puketahi St

Alexander St

Tainui St

To Reefton
(79km)

Kings Domain
Bushwalk

7

T A S M A N   S E A

**Victoria
Park
Racecourse**

10

**Lake
Karoro**

**Anzac
Park**

Anzac
Creek

Kowhai Bush
Walk

Sawyers Creek

Cowper St

Franklin St

Raleigh St

19

Buccleuch St

**Recreation
Ground**

Aerodrome Rd

**Greymouth
Aerodrome**

Water Walk Rd

Paroa Rd

High St

Shakespeare St

Palmerston St

Marlborough St

30

14

**Grey
Hospital**

**Rugby
Park**

Chesterfield St
21

Shelley St

Tasman St

6

Milton Rd

16

To Paroa Hotel-Motel (6km);
South Beach Motel (7km);
Shantytown (8km);
Hokitika (40km)

INFORMATION
Automobile Association (AA).....**1** C3
Bank of NZ (ATM)....................**2** B1
Greymouth Visitors Centre.......**3** C2
Police Station.........................**4** C2
Post Office.............................**5** B1
Westpac Trust Bank (ATM).......**6** B1

SIGHTS & ACTIVITIES   (pp480–2)
Eco-Rafting Adventures NZ....(see 28)
History House Museum............**7** C2
Jade Boulder Gallery................**8** C2
Left Bank Art Gallery................**9** B1
Monteith's Brewing Co...........**10** C3
Town Clock............................**11** B1
Wild West Adventure
  Company..........................**12** B2
Wildside Tours & Cafe.............**13** B1

SLEEPING   (pp482–3)
Alpine Rose Motel..................**14** B5
Ardwyn House.......................**15** D2
Ashley Hotel..........................**16** A6
Breeze Motel.........................**17** C3
Duke Backpackers..................**18** C2
Global Village Travellers Lodge.**19** B4
Golden Coast Guesthouse.......**20** D2
Greymouth Seaside Holiday
  Park...............................**21** A6
Kaianga-ra YHA....................**22** D3
Neptunes International
  Backpackers......................**23** B2
Noah's Ark Backpackers..........**24** D2
Revingtons Hotel...................**25** B1

EATING   (p483)
Bonzai Pizzeria......................**26** B1
Cafe 124 on Mackay...............**27** B1
DP:One Cafe.........................**28** B1
Hog's Head Bar & Grill............**29** B1
New World Supermarket.........**30** B5
Priya....................................**31** C3
Railway Hotel........................**32** B1
Steamers Cafe & Bar...............**33** B1
Super Value Supermarket........**34** C2

ENTERTAINMENT   (p483)
Regent Theatre.....................(see 3)

TRANSPORT   (pp483–4)
Greymouth Travel Centre........**35** D2

THE WEST COAST

t also conducts amphibious, eight-wheel Argo rides (30-minute trip costs $25).

There's **surfing** at Cobden Beach and at Seven Mile Beach in Rapahoe; however, these are generally not safe for swimming.

Sleeping
B&BS
Golden Coast Guesthouse (☎ 03-768 7839; 10 Smith St; s/d from $50/75) Up on a hillside near the train station, this guesthouse looks out over the Grey River. The house is cosy, the prices more than reasonable, and the gardens make a lovely floral touch.

Ardwyn House (☎ 03-768 6107; 48 Chapel St; s/d $50/80) This attractively old-fashioned home-stay is nestled amid a nice garden at the end of a steep drive on a quiet, dead-end street. All the rooms have shared facilities; an extra $5 gets you a cooked brekkie.

HOSTELS & CAMPING PARKS
Kaianga-ra YHA (☎ 03-768 4951; yha.greymouth@yha.org.nz; 15 Alexander St; dm from $18, s & d $50) Built in 1938 as a Marist Brothers' residence, this is now a spacious hostel lodged up against some bushy hills. It has a video library to ransack and handles bookings for various organised tours.

Neptunes International Backpackers (☎ 03-768 4425; nepts.backpacker@actrix.co.nz; 43 Gresson St; dm/d from $21/48; ▯) This self-styled upmarket hostel, in a restored pub close to the Grey River, gets good reviews from travellers for its bunkless dorms, helpful staff, water views and leisure facilities like a pool table, spa and BBQ.

Global Village Travellers Lodge (☎ 03-768 7272; globalvillage@minidata.co.nz; 42-54 Cowper St; dm/s/d from $21/38/48; ▯) Pristine riverside hostel determined to impress guests with great facilities, free bikes, free kayaking on adjacent Lake Karoro and soaking time in a spa. The 'international traveller' theme is enthusiastically reflected in the décor, though they could ease off the global inspiration angle a little.

Duke Backpackers (☎ 03-768 9470; dukenz@clear.net.nz; 27 Guinness St; dm/d from $20/48; ▯) This likeable, well-maintained place recently had its interior upgraded and splashed with every imaginable bright colour, and at the time of research was also installing an Internet café. Free pool is also on offer, as is a giveaway first beer in the on-site bar.

Noah's Ark Backpackers (☎ 0800 662 472, 03-768 4868; 16 Chapel St; camp sites $24, dm/s/d $20/30/45 Originally a monastery erected at the star of WWI, Noah's Ark is now a zoologically obsessed abode with eccentric animal-themed rooms. The upstairs balcony is a good place to flop on a bright day or at dusk. Free pick-up from train station on arriving buses.

Greymouth Seaside Holiday Park (☎ 0800 867 104, 03-768 6618; www.top10greymouth.co.nz; 2 Chesterfield St; camp sites $22, campervan sites $24, d $35-85; ▯) This beach-side family park is 2.5km south of town and has a kid's playground, spa poo and good facilities (with wheelchair access) Standard cabins sleep up to six people while the self-contained units sleep up to eight.

HOTELS & MOTELS
Revingtons Hotel (☎ 03-768 7055; www.revingtons.co.nz; 46 Tainui St; dm/s/d $18/60/80; ▯) Prominent two-storey pub with a warren of drinking spaces downstairs and large, well-kept rooms upstairs (some of which are vulnerable to ascending happy-hour noise). The hotel's advertising encourages barflies, so perhaps don't stay here if you're seeking a peaceful snooze.

Ashley Hotel (☎ 03-768 5135; www.hotelashley.co.nz; 74 Tasman St; d $95-160; ▣) This boutique corporate-crowd hotel is filled with nice stylistic touches and over 60 variously-sized rooms, one of them wheelchair-accessible. It's only a short walk to the beach, but still figured it needed an indoor heated pool.

Alpine Rose Motel (☎ 0800 266 835, 03-768 7586; 139 High St; d $85-130) Alpine Rose looks like it wanted to be a Tudor-style complex but changed its mind midway through construction. It has large, comfortable studios and units, continental or cooked brekkies on request, and is one of many places to stay along the road leading south to Hokitika.

South Beach Motel (☎ 0800 101 222, 03-762 6768; www.southbeach.co.nz; 318 Main South Rd; s/d $85/100) This motel has a dozen reasonable units at Greymouth's southern limits, right beside one of the coast's distinctive grey-sand beaches. There's a BBQ area, surf-fishing equipment for hire and facilities for disabled travellers.

Breeze Motel (☎ 0800 523 524, 03-768 5068; breezemotel@clear.net.nz; 125 Tainui St; s $95, d $100-125)

Old-style, low-slung motel grouping of one- and two-bedroom units, some with spa. It's a centrally located motel option, only a few hundred metres from the town centre.

Eating

Cafe 124 on Mackay (☎ 03-768 7503; 124 Mackay St; dinner $20-28; ☒ lunch & dinner Mon-Sat, lunch Sun) Jazz-flavoured café with arguably the best-value lunches in town (around $10) such as spinach and camembert pie, pumpkin lasagne and whitebait omelette, with new daily choices on a blackboard. The more expensive dinner items include mussels and chicken curry.

Priya (☎ 03-768 7377; 84 Tainui St; mains around $14; ☒ lunch & dinner Mon-Sat, dinner Sun) One of the few dedicated Indian eateries on the West Coast (like its sibling restaurant in Hokitika), with a tasty selection of veg and non-veg dishes like palak paneer (cottage cheese and spinach cooked with cream) and chicken Afghani (chicken and cashews in an almond sauce).

DP:One Cafe (☎ 03-768 4005; 108 Mawhera Quay; meals $6-9; ☒ breakfast & lunch; ☐) Bohemian, lounge-scattered café with the inspired feel of an artsy, ramshackle garage sale (minus the sale). The menu is limited to healthy pies and *panini* (focaccia) with salad, plus some tasty cakes and good coffee.

Bonzai Pizzeria (☎ 03-768 4170; 31-33 Mackay St; mains $12-22; ☒ lunch & dinner) Brisk, licensed pizzeria-café, where all menu items are available as takeaway too. Has lots of different dough toppings, plus various soups, pastas and steaks.

Hog's Head Bar & Grill (☎ 03-768 4093; 9 Tainui St; mains $15-20; ☒ lunch & dinner) We couldn't find a hog's head on the menu but there were plenty of steaks and seafood to make up for this oversight, plus cheaper lunch snacks like burgers and soups, and lots of booze to wash it all down.

Steamers Cafe & Bar (☎ 03-768 4193; cnr Mackay St & Albert Mall; mains $10-25; ☒ lunch & dinner) Committed vegetarians beware: as this place is strongly scented with the numerous meaty meals (Hawaiian ham steak to rib-eye and schnitzels) served from the carvery counter.

Low-cost, meat-dominated pub meals are available at various hotels around town, including the dirt-cheap grub offered at the

Railway Hotel (☎ 03-768 7023; Mawhera Quay; BBQ from $3; ☒ lunch & dinner).

There are several well-stocked supermarkets, including **Super Value Supermarket** (☎ 03-768 7545; cnr Guinness & Herbert Sts) and **New World Supermarket** (☎ 03-768 4442; cnr High & Marlborough Sts).

Entertainment

The Art Deco **Regent Theatre** (☎ 03-768 0920; cnr Herbert & Mackay Sts; adult/child/student/family $10/6/8/28) is a good place to catch *Lord of the Rings* re-runs.

DP:One Cafe (☎ 03-768 4005; 108 Mawhera Quay) This arts-appreciating café (see Eating above) has occasional, eclectic live music; performances are usually free.

Getting There & Away

The **Greymouth Travel Centre** (☎ 0800 767 080, 03-768 7080; Railway Station, 164 Mackay St; ☒ 9am-5pm Mon-Fri, 10am-3pm Sat & Sun) books all forms of transport, including trains and inter-island ferries, and has luggage-storage facilities. This is also the bus depot.

BUS

Coachline **InterCity** (☎ 03-768 7080; www.intercitycoach.co.nz) has daily services north to Westport ($24, two hours) and Nelson ($70, six hours), and south to Franz Josef ($45, 3½ hours) and Fox Glaciers ($50, 4¼ hours). **Atomic Shuttles** (☎ 03-322 8883; www.atomictravel.co.nz) has daily buses from Greymouth to Queenstown (10½ hours, $80) at 7.30am, as well as a separate service to Fox Glacier ($40) and a Greymouth–Picton bus ($50) via either Westport or Reefton. Atomic also has a Christchurch–Hokitika service via Greymouth ($10).

Coast to Coast (☎ 0800 800 847; www.coast2coast.co.nz) and **Alpine Coaches** (☎ 0800 274 888; www.alpinecoaches.co.nz) operate between Greymouth and Christchurch ($35) via Arthur's Pass ($20 from Greymouth, $25 from Christchurch) and also go to Hokitika.

TRAIN

TranzAlpine (☎ 0800 872 467; www.tranzscenic.co.nz) conducts its spectacular 224km, 4½-hour journey daily between Christchurch and Greymouth (see the boxed text, p484). There are various types of fares; the cheapest one-way fares start from around $70/60 per adult/child. It's possible to do the trip as a

THE TRANZALPINE

One of the world's great rail journeys is the *TranzAlpine*'s traverse of the Southern Alps between Christchurch and Greymouth – it begins near the Pacific Ocean and ends by the Tasman Sea.

Not so long ago, this popular rail journey, now made in the comfort of specially-designed carriages, was undertaken in a ramshackle railcar. In times of bad weather and road closure, it was often the only means that West Coasters had to get to the eastern side of the Divide.

The *TranzAlpine* crossing offers a bewildering variety of scenery. It leaves Christchurch at 8.15am, then speeds across the flat, alluvial Canterbury Plains to the foothills of the Alps. In the foothills it enters a labyrinth of gorges and hills known as the Staircase, and the climb here is made possible by a system of three large viaducts and most of the tunnels that will be encountered along the line.

The train emerges into the broad Waimakariri and Bealey Valleys and (on a good day) the surrounding vista is stupendous. The river valley is fringed with dense beech forest, which eventually gives way to the snow-capped peaks of Arthur's Pass National Park.

At the small alpine village of Arthur's Pass the train enters the longest of the tunnels, the 'Otira' (8.5km), and heads under the mountains to the West Coast.

There are several more gems on the western side – the valleys of the Otira, Taramakau and Grey Rivers, patches of podocarp forest, and the pleasant surprise of trout-filled Lake Brunner (Moana Kotuku), fringed with cabbage trees.

The train arrives in Greymouth around 12.45pm and departs for Christchurch an hour later, arriving at 6.05pm.

Few travellers who make this rail journey will have regrets, except when the weather is bad. Chances are if it's raining on one coast, it'll be fine on the other.

day return from Christchurch, but not from Greymouth. The train departs Greymouth at 1.45pm daily.

AROUND GREYMOUTH

The road from Greymouth to Hokitika has great views of the wild West Coast. If you deviate from the main road to the beach you'll see kilometres of salt spray and flotillas of driftwood.

Shantytown (☎ 03-762 6634; www.shantytown.co .nz; Rutherglen Rd; adult/child $12/7.50, family from $28; ❂ 8.30am-5pm), 8km south of Greymouth and 3km inland from the main road, does a pretty good job of re-creating an 1860s gold-mining town, with its own pre-aged post office, pub and lolly shop, not to mention 'Rosie's House of Ill Repute'. You can go gold panning ($3 extra for adults) and there are several locomotives to ride (included in admission price), the oldest dating from 1877 – the first steam train departs 9.45am and the last at 4pm.

Paroa Hotel-Motel (☎ 0800 762 6860, 03-762 6860; www.paroa.co.nz; 508 Main South Rd; d from $80), opposite the road to Shantytown, is a highly recommended, very relaxing motel-hotel. It has a dozen spacious, well-equipped and garden-fronted units (the family unit

sleeps seven) only a few minutes' walk from a stone-strewn beach. Its restaurant, **Ham's** (mains $14-19; ❂ lunch & dinner), serves up hearty roasts, steaks and schnitzels; there's a kid's menu too.

HOKITIKA

pop 4000

Hokitika ('Hoki' for short), 40km south of Greymouth, was settled during the 1860s goldrush and became a busy port. This is NZ's major centre for the working of greenstone, which is what attracts the bulk of its visitors, but there's more to do around here than looking at stone being mass-produced into tiki and *taniwha* bookends. Hoki is rich in history and nearby is a wealth of native forests, lakes and rivers. Although smaller and quieter than Greymouth, it arguably makes for a more interesting overnight stop.

Information

The **Westland visitors centre** (☎ 03-755 6166; hkkvin@xtra.co.nz; cnr Hamilton & Tancred Sts; ❂ 8.30am-6pm Nov-Mar, 8am-5pm Apr-Oct) is in the historic Carnegie Building, originally established as a library. There's also a local **DOC office** (☎ 03-755 8301; 10 Sewell St).

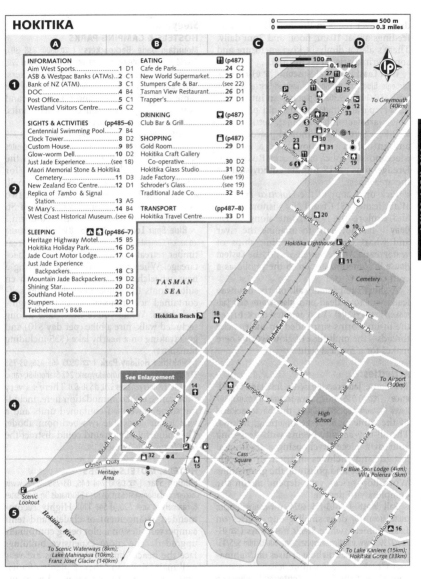

Internet access is available at **Aim West Sports** (☎ 03-755 8481; 20 Weld; $2 per 20min; ☼ 9am-8pm Mon-Fri, 9am-5pm Sat & Sun).

Sights

One of Hoki's premier attractions is its profusion of **arts and crafts outlets**; see Shopping (p487).

New Zealand Eco Centre (☎ 03-755 5251; 60 Tancred St; adult/child/family $12/6/30; ☼ 9am-5pm) is predominantly an aquarium set-up with tanks devoted to marine life such as sharks, snake-necked turtles, crayfish and square-jawed piranhas. The star attractions, however, have to be the enormous long-finned eels flopped over wooden platforms and draped over rocks in the central enclosure; feedings are at 10am, noon and 3pm daily. There's also a dimly-lit kiwi enclosure and some wrinkly tuataras (lizards).

West Coast Historical Museum (☎ 03-755 6898; Carnegie Bldg, cnr Hamilton & Tancred Sts; adult/child/ family $5/1/10; ⏰ 9.30am-5pm) has an interesting history parade that includes old photos, a Maori-artefact–filled cabinet, settlers' relics like a Scottish ceremonial powder horn and an opium pipe bowl, and a working Meccano-set replica of the Grey River Gold Dredge, plus an 18-minute audiovisual on the area's past.

Pick up a copy of the *Hokitika Heritage Walk* leaflet ($1) from the visitors centre and explore the waterfront along **Gibson Quay** – it's not hard to imagine the river and wharf choked with sailing ships of yesteryears. At the Sewell St end, the **Custom House** is sometimes open to the public as a craft centre.

A short signposted walk off the highway leads you to a dead-end **glow-worm dell** (admission free; ⏰ 24hr). Visit it after dark to see the lit-up worms suspended on their sticky threads – the multitude of glow-worms here makes for a magical sight.

Activities

Try some **jade carving** with **Just Jade Experience** (☎ 03-755 7612; www.jadecountry.co.nz; 197 Revell St; workshop $80-150) at the backpackers' of the same name (see Sleeping; below). The all-day activity begins with designing your own piece or choosing a traditional design, and includes instruction on cutting, working and polishing the greenstone. Workshop prices vary depending on the complexity of design.

Sail West (☎ 03-755 6024; www.sailwest.co.nz; cruises from $85) does small group cruises on Lake Kaniere, while **Scenic Waterways** (☎ 03-755 7239; www.paddleboatcruises.com; adult/child $25/15) has 1½-hour paddleboat cruises on Mahinapua Creek. For even more-leisurely watersports, visit the heated **Centennial Swimming Pool** (☎ 03-755 8119; 53 Weld St; adult/child/student/ family $3/1.50/2/7).

Festivals & Events

In mid-March Hokitika hosts the increasingly popular **Wildfoods Festival** in Cass Sq, a major bush food event attracting up to 20,000 curious gourmands.

Sleeping

HOSTELS & CAMPING PARKS

Mountain Jade Backpackers (☎ 0800 838 301, 03-755 8007; mtjade@minidat.co.nz; 41 Weld St; dm $20, d from $48) Spacious, open-plan backpackers' centrally located above the jade shop of the same name. It has neat and tidy dorms and doubles, and some self-contained units. Wheelchair access is provided.

Just Jade Experience Backpackers (☎ 03-755 7612; www.jadecountry.co.nz; 197 Revell St; camp sites $22, dm/d $20/44) This hostel is close to the beach and labels itself 'home-style' for good reason, as it feels a bit like a small, agreeable share-house. The pick of the two double rooms is the one facing Revell St; otherwise there's a simple four-bed dorm.

Blue Spur Lodge (☎ 03-755 8445; bluespur@xtra .co.nz; off Cement Lead Rd; dm/s $20/35, d $50-60) Great timber retreat on a large, out-of-town hectareage. When we visited, it was erecting a new, wheelchair-accessible cottage with en suite rooms to complement the other self-contained accommodation and the eight-bed dorm. While you're here, take a long secluded walk, hire a bike (per day $10) and go kayaking on a nearby lake ($35 including transport).

Hokitika Holiday Park (☎ 0800 465 436, 03-755 8172; www.hokitika.com/holidaypark; 242 Stafford St; camp sites $18, campervan sites $20, d $30-80) There's a very wide range of accommodation here, including some newer self-contained units and a wheelchair-accessible two-bedroom abode. The colourful playground could distract the kids for a little while.

HOTELS, MOTELS & B&BS

Shining Star (☎ 0800 744 646, 03-755 8921; www .accommodationwestcoast.co.nz; 11 Richards Dr; camp sites & campervan sites $20, d $40-110) Highly recommended arrangement of chalets and tent/ campervan sites on a plot being continually upgraded. The more expensive buildings face the beach, but all the cabins are very well maintained and there's plenty of adjacent pastureland to let your mind roam in.

Teichelmann's B&B (☎ 0800 743 742, 03-755 8232; www.teichelmanns.co.nz; 20 Hamilton St; d $165-180) Once home to a well-known Westland surgeon and mountaineer (Ebenezer Teichelmann), now a bright, relaxing B&B with lovely hosts. The half-dozen comfy house rooms are augmented by a new, stand-alone spa unit out back.

Southland Hotel (☎ 03-755 8344; www.southland hotel.com; 111 Revell St; d $75-90) The Southland's interior decorator obviously had a thing for wood panelling, but its rooms are big and modern enough. The priciest rooms are at the hotel's rear and allow views of the sea across a car park. You can eat on-site at the Tasman View Restaurant (see below).

Villa Polenza (☎ 0800 241 801, 03-755 7801; villa polenza@xtra.co.nz; Brickfield Rd; rooms from $400) This fine Italian villa-style guesthouse has a wonderful hilltop position overlooking the town and affording great views of the flattish coastline. Some rooms have French doors opening onto sea vistas, and dinners can be arranged. The minimum age for guests is 13 years.

Stumpers (☎ 03-755 6154; www.stumpers.co.nz; 2 Weld St; dm/s/d $22/35/45) Modern upstairs rooms are on offer in this huge, central café-hotel (see Eating; below). There's usually not much space between the end of the bed and the opposing wall in the rooms with shared facilities, but the prices are very reasonable.

Other decent motels:

Heritage Highway Motel (☎ 0800 465 484, 03-755 8098; heritage@minidata.co.nz; 12 Fitzherbert St; d from $100; 🐾) Large, high-standard units beside the highway.

Jade Court Motor Lodge (☎ 0800 755 885, 03-755 8855; www.jadecourt.co.nz; 85 Fitzherbert St; d $95-115) Clean, modern complex with several barrier-free rooms.

Eating & Drinking

Trapper's (☎ 03-755 5133; 137 Revell St; mains $25-28; 🍴 lunch & dinner) Rabbit and mushroom ragout and plated boar are two of the wildest things on the menu at this local favourite, though Trapper's has also done a reportedly delicious possum broth in the past.

Tasman View Restaurant (☎ 03-755 8344; Beach St; mains $22-26; 🍴 dinner Mon-Sat) At the rear of Southland Hotel and accessed via Beach St, this restaurant has the dry aesthetic of a slightly outdated reception centre. But, more positively, it also has ocean views and well-prepared mains like pan-fried venison and fish.

Cafe de Paris (☎ 03-755 6859; 19 Tancred St; mains $9-28 🍴 lunch & dinner) This café takes its upmarket attitude quite seriously, with the French-style treatment of oven-baked pig and pan-seared deer leg. The end result can be hit or miss, but it's worth trying and the breakfast omelettes are great.

Stumpers Cafe & Bar (☎ 03-755 6154; 2 Weld St; mains $12-25; 🍴 breakfast, lunch & dinner) Simply

prepared, filling meals like beer-battered blue-eye cod and pork parmigiana are its mainstays. The café's conspicuous size and location means it attracts its share of tourists, but locals are regularly in attendance.

Club Bar & Grill (☎ 03-755 6868; 131 Revell St) Ramshackle saloon-style bar with plenty of places along the main counter to saddle up and quench your thirst. Serves pizza to soak up the tipple.

New World Supermarket (☎ 03-755 8390; 116 Revell St) The place to go for supplies.

Shopping

Most of Hoki's craft galleries/shops lie along Tancred St. Greenstone is the primary raw material but there are also wood-carving studios and jewellery shops specialising in locally mined gold. Working greenstone is not simple and good pieces don't come cheap. In some studios you can see the carvers at work, and staff will be happy to explain the origins of the *pounamu* and the cultural significance of the designs.

Traditional Jade Co (☎ 03-755 5233; 2 Tancred St) Relatively small, personable studio where you can see artists at work. Sells lots of jadework in classic Maori designs; small tiki pendants cost around $75.

Hokitika Craft Gallery Co-operative (☎ 03-755 8802; www.hokitikacraftgallery.co.nz; 25 Tancred St) Retail gallery showing and selling the work of around 20 jade-carving, wood-turning, weaving and glass-blowing local artisans.

Jade Factory (☎ 03-755 8007; 41 Weld St) Part of the Mountain Jade complex, this outlet has a big range of well-presented jade sculpture, including golf putters with jade heads for $200 and large sculptures.

Schroder's Glass (☎ 03-755 8484; 41 Weld St) Has a workshop where you can learn terms like 'glory holes' and 'marvering', and a gallery where you can buy some of Schroder's original, craftily twisted and colourful creations, from huge platters to diminutive glasses.

Some other worthwhile shops:

Gold Room (☎ 03-755 8362; 37 Tancred St) Does a good trade in jade but is better known for gold-nugget jewellery.

Hokitika Glass Studio (☎ 03-755 7775; 28 Tancred St) Has a glass-blowing workshop, lots of colourful glass baubles and usually a tour-group bus chugging away outside.

Getting There & Away

Hokitika Travel Centre (☎ 03-755 8557; 60 Tancred St) books flights and is where most buses stop.

Air New Zealand Link (☎ 0800 737 000, 09-357 3000; www.airnz.co.nz) has regular direct flights to Christchurch (from $80), with connections to other centres.

From Hokitika there are daily **InterCity** (☎ 03-755 8557; www.intercitycoach.co.nz) services to Greymouth ($22, one hour), Nelson ($75, seven hours) and Fox Glacier ($45, 3½ hours). **Atomic Shuttles** (☎ 03-322 8883; www.atomictravel.co.nz) has services (pre-bookings are essential) to Fox Glacier ($30) and Greymouth ($10), and one to Queenstown ($70, 10 hours). **Coast to Coast** (☎ 0800 800 847; www.coast2coast.co.nz) and **Alpine Coaches** (☎ 0800 274 888; www.alpine coaches.co.nz) run to Christchurch via Arthur's Pass ($35).

AROUND HOKITIKA

A scenic drive or cycle of 33km brings you to **Hokitika Gorge**, a stunning little gorge filled with the glacial, turquoise waters of the Hokitika River. It's crossed by a swingbridge and there are several forest walkways. Ask at the visitors centre for directions.

To get to the gorge, you may pass through **Kowhitirangi**, scene of a massive 12-day manhunt involving the NZ army in 1941, staged after farmer Stanley Graham shot and killed four Hokitika policemen and subsequently three others. The incident is the subject of the 1981 film *Bad Blood*.

A loop road takes you around the scenic **Lake Kaniere**, passing by **Dorothy Falls**, **Kahikatea Forest** and **Canoe Cove**. The visitors centre and DOC have info on other walks in the area, including the 13km **Lake Kaniere Walkway** (four hours return), which follows the lake's western shore, and the **Mahinapua Walkway** (three hours return), which goes through the scenic reserve on the northeast side of Lake Mahinapua to a swamp teeming with wildlife.

There are **DOC camping grounds** at **Goldsborough** (adult/child $5/2.50), 17km from Hoki on the 1876 'gold trail'; **Hans Bay** (adult/child $5/2.50), 19km from Hoki on the east side of Lake Kaniere; and 10km away at **Lake Mahinapua** (adult/child $5/2.50). The turn-off to the latter is opposite the pale green outline of **Lake Mahinapua Hotel** (☎ 03-755 8500; SH6), where you can quench your thirst (though be warned it's often inundated by backpacker bus groups).

HOKITIKA TO THE GLACIERS

It's 140km south from Hokitika to the Franz Josef Glacier. While many travellers pass straight through, there are some good stops for walking, kayaking, watching birdlife and delving into West Coast history. **InterCity** (☎ 03-379 9020; www.intercitycoach.co.nz) and **Atomic Shuttles** (☎ 03-322 8883; www.atomictravel.co.nz) buses from Greymouth to the glaciers will stop anywhere along the highway.

Ross

Ross, 30km south of Hokitika, is a small, historic gold-mining town where the precious metal is still mined today. NZ's largest gold nugget, the 99oz 'Honourable Roddy', was found here in 1907. Grimmond House, home to the Bank of New South Wales in the gold-rush era, is now the **Ross Goldfields visitors centre** (☎ 03-755 4077; 4 Aylmer St; ☉ 9am-5pm), featuring a scale model of the town at its gold-mining peak.

Opposite is the **Miner's Cottage Museum** (admission free; ☉ 9am-5pm), in a cottage built in 1885 and containing two old pianos and a replica of Honourable Roddy. The re-creation of **Ross Gaol** next door has a very sad attempt at a 'prisoner', glimpsed through the bars.

The museum stands at the beginning of two historic goldfield **walkways**: the **Jones Flat Walk** (45 minutes return) and the **Water Race Walk** (one hour return). Behind the visitors centre is the deep-level (90m) alluvial **Birchfields Mine**, and nearby you can try your hand at **gold panning** ($6.50).

In the **Empire Hotel** (☎ 03-755 4005; 19 Aylmer St; dm/s $16/40, d from $55), threadbare four-bed backpacker rooms lie in a row to one side of the hotel, while upstairs in this friendly place are a handful of decent pub rooms. Doubles with en suite cost only $5 more than shared-facility rooms.

Roddy Nugget Cafe & Bar (☎ 03-755 4245; 5 Moorhouse St; meals $4-12; ☉ breakfast & lunch) is a country-kitchen café serving homemade venison, beef satay and steak and cheese pies and filling all-day breakfasts. The bar in back supplies liquid nutrients.

Ross to Okarito

South of Ross the rainforest becomes more dense and in parts looks as if it would be easier to walk over the top of it than to find a way through.

PUKEKURA

Just north of Lake Ianthe is this tiny place, pretty much run by one family.

The **Bushmen's Centre** (☎ 03-755 4144; SH6; admission free; ⏱ 9am-5pm) is a predictably rustic café-shop that lays on the blokey bush humour thick and fast, and has a passionate hatred of introduced animals like the possum. Inside is a souvenir shop and the **Bushmen's Museum** (adult/family $4/10), with a 20-minute video on local industry, more anti-possum displays (including some sad caged specimens) and some forlorn giant eels; think twice before paying the family admission fee.

Across the road is **Puke Pub** and adjoining it is the **Wild Foods Restaurant** (mains $20-25; ⏱ lunch & dinner), which serves 'road kill' like possum, wild pork and rabbit. If you want to stay here, try **Pukekura Lodge** (☎ 03-755 4088; SH6; camp sites $15-20, campervan sites $20, dm/d $15/40), opposite the Bushmen's Centre; there's also a house for rent ($60). Alternatively, there's a **DOC camping ground** (adult/child $5/2.50) beside Lake Ianthe, 6km south of Pukekura.

About 100m south of Lake Ianthe, on the eastern side of the highway, is a giant **matai tree**, thought to be over 1000 years old.

HARIHARI
Located 22km south of Lake Ianthe, little Harihari made headlines in 1931 when Australian Guy Menzies completed the first solo flight across the Tasman Sea from Sydney. The landing was anything but smooth as he crash-landed *Southern Cross Junior* in the La Fontaine swamp. The aircraft turned over and when Menzies undid his safety straps he fell head-first into the mud. He made the trip in 11¾ hours, 2½ hours quicker than fellow Australian Charles Kingsford Smith and his crew in 1928.

The **Hari Hari Coastal Walkway** (two to three hours return; also called the Doughboy Walk or Coastal Pack Track) is a popular loop taking in the Poerua and Wanganui Rivers. The start of the walk is about 16km from the main highway – follow Wanganui Flats Rd then La Fontaine Drive.

Units at the friendly **Tomasi Motels** (☎ 0800 753 3116, 03-753 3116; SH6; twd $40/80) are popular with passing cyclists. They are several decades old but still make for reasonably priced accommodation. Budget twins all have en suites.

The welcoming **Hari Hari Motor Inn** (☎ 0800 833 026, 03-753 3026; hhmi@xtra.co.nz; SH6; camp sites $15, campervan sites $17.50, dm/d $17.50/75) has no kitchen facilities for campers, but there is a pub **bistro** (mains $12-23; ⏱ lunch & dinner) with pizzas, steaks and Pacific oysters.

WHATAROA & THE KOTUKU SANCTUARY
Near Whataroa, 35km south of Harihari, is NZ's only nesting site for the kotuku (white heron), which appears from November to the end of February. The herons then fly off individually to spend winter throughout the country. Access is possible only with a DOC permit.

White Heron Sanctuary Tours (☎ 0800 523 456, 03-753 4120; SH6; www.whiteherontours.co.nz; adult/child $90/40) stages 2½-hour 'jetboat eco-tours' (the jetboat doesn't enter or disturb the nesting area) into the sanctuary from late October to March. After navigating a boardwalk you spend 30 to 40 minutes at the hide. Adjacent to the tours office is **Sanctuary Tours Motel** (camp sites & campervan sites $20, d $45-85), offering a choice between basic whitewashed cabins with shared facilities ($8 extra for linen) or motel units.

Okarito
Another 15km south of Whataroa is The Forks and the turn-off to peaceful Okarito, 13km away on the coast. Much of Keri Hulme's bestseller, *The Bone People*, is set in this wild, isolated region and the author is one of the 30 permanent residents in the tiny community. There are lots of **walks** along the coast from here, including to **Three Mile Lagoon** (2½ hours return; at low tide) and **Okarito Trig** (one hour return), where there are magnificent views of the Southern Alps and back across the lagoon.

Okarito Nature Tours (☎ 0800 524 666, 03-753 4014; www.okarito.co.nz; kayak rental per half-/full day $45/55) rents kayaks for highly recommended paddles into the beautiful, placid channels of **Okarito Lagoon**, a feeding ground for the kotuku and other waterbirds. The lagoon is NZ's largest unmodified wetland and consists of shallow open water and tidal flats, with surrounding rimu and kahikatea rainforest. Guided trips are also possible (from $65) as are overnight camping trips ($80) on deserted North Beach or Lake Windemere.

Okarito camping ground (off Russell St; adult/child $7.50/free) is an oasis of greenery near the sea, with barbecues, toilets, showers and a card-operated telephone. Fees are paid into an honesty box and hot showers cost $1.

Okarito YHA Hostel (☎ 03-752 0754; The Strand; dm $15) is a classic YHA original – it's an 1892 school building which became a youth hostel in 1960. Six of the 12 bunks are in the renovated lounge-cum-kitchen and hot showers are available at the camping ground across the road. Bring lots of insect repellent to dissuade the local mosquitoes and sandflies.

Royal Hostel (☎ 03-753 4080; www.okaritohostel .com; The Strand; dm $20, d $50-70; 🖳) has lovely, semi-rustic, bach-like accommodation that is spread over two houses and a self-contained unit called the 'Hutel' – it's worth getting the latter yourself for $70. There are also some crafty touches like the enormous hand-hewn table-top in the main house.

Okarito has no shops, so bring in your own food and supplies.

GLACIERS

The two most famous glaciers in the Westland National Park – the Franz Josef and the Fox – are among the major attractions in a country full of natural wonders. Nowhere else at this latitude have glaciers advanced so close to the sea. Unlike the Tasman Glacier, on the other side of the dividing range in Mt Cook National Park, these two are just what you expect glaciers to be – mighty cascades of ice, tumbling down a valley towards the sea.

The glaciers' stunning development is partly due to the West Coast being subject to prevailing rain-drenched westerlies, which fall as snow high up in the névés – the snow crystals fuse to form clear ice at a depth of about 20m. Also, ice-accumulation zones on the glaciers are very large, meaning there's a lot of ice to push down the valley. Finally, the glaciers are very steep, so the ice can get a long way before it finally melts.

The rate of descent is staggering: wreckage of a plane that crashed on the Franz Josef in 1943, 3.5km from the terminal face, made it down to the bottom 6½ years later – a speed of 1.5m per day. At times the Franz Josef can move at up to 5m per day, over 10 times as fast as glaciers in the Swiss Alps, but it usually advances about 1m per day.

GLACIER-SPEAK

It's a little-known fact that glaciers always advance and never really retreat. However, sometimes the ice melts faster than it advances, which is when the end face of the glacier moves backwards up the mountain and the glacier appears to be retreating.

The last ice age (15,000 to 20,000 years ago) saw the Franz Josef and Fox glaciers reach right down to the sea. Then warmer weather came and they may have retreated even further than their current position. In the 14th century a new mini-ice age started and for centuries the glaciers advanced, reaching their greatest extent around 1750; the terminal moraines from this time can be clearly seen. But in the 250-odd years since then, the glaciers have steadily retreated and the terminal face is now several kilometres further back.

If you want to impress/bore new friends with some more glacial knowledge while you're all comparing exploits on the West Coast's magnificent glaciers, refer to the following:
ablation zone – where the glacier melts
accumulation zone – where the snow collects
bergschrund – large crevasse in the ice near the headwall or starting point of the glacier
blue ice – as the accumulation zone or névé snow is compressed by subsequent snowfalls, it becomes firn and then blue ice
crevasse – cracks in the glacial ice as it crosses obstacles and moves down the mountain
dead ice – as a glacier retreats, isolated chunks of ice may be left behind
firn – partly compressed snow on the way to becoming glacial ice
glacial flour – the river of melted ice that flows off glaciers is a milky colour from the suspension of finely ground rocks
icefall – when a glacier descends so steeply that the upper ice breaks up in a jumble of iceblocks
kettle lake – lake formed by the melt of an area of isolated dead ice
moraine – walls of debris formed at the glacier's sides (lateral moraine) or end (terminal moraine)
névé – snowfield area where firn is formed
seracs – ice pinnacles formed, like crevasses, by the glacier passing over obstacles
terminal – the final ice face at the end of the glacier

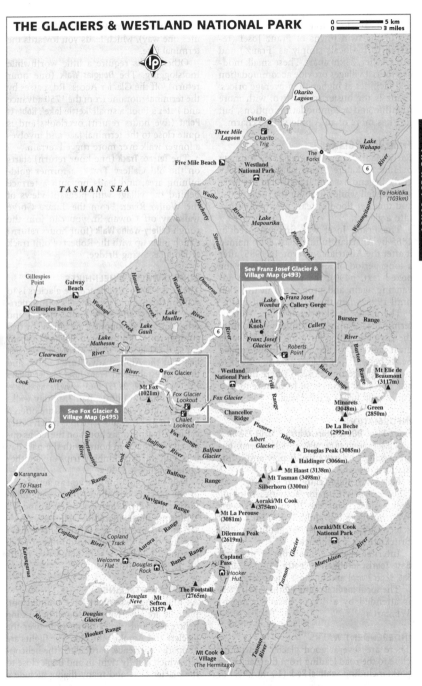

THE GLACIERS & WESTLAND NATIONAL PARK

0 — 5 km
0 — 3 miles

The heavy local tourist traffic is catered for in the twin towns of Franz Josef (referred to by locals simply as 'Franz') and Fox Glacier, 23km apart. These small, modern tourist villages provide accommodation and facilities at higher-than-average prices. Franz is the busier of the two, with more nightlife and accommodation options, but Fox has more of an Alpine-village charm.

Franz Josef Glacier

Early Maoris knew this area as Ka Roimata o Hine Hukatere (Tears of the Avalanche Girl). Legend has it that a girl lost her lover after he fell while climbing the local peaks, and that her flood of tears eventually froze into a glacier.

The Franz Josef was first explored in 1865 by Austrian Julius Haast, who named it after the Austrian emperor. In 1985, after a long period of apparent retreat (see the boxed text, p490), the glacier started advancing again and progressed nearly 2km until 1996, when the retreat started again.

The glacier is 5km from Franz, with its terminal face only a 20-minute walk from the car park. Hope for a fine day for some great views of the ice and the snow-capped peaks behind. The glaciers are roped off to stop people getting close to where there is a risk of icefall; if you want to venture further you should take a guided walk.

INFORMATION

Franz Josef DOC visitors centre (☎ 03-752 0796; www.glaciercountry.co.nz; SH6; ☽ 8.30am-6pm) has an excellent interpretive display and information on walks in the area.

Alpine Adventure Centre (☎ 0800 800 793, 03-752 0793; SH6) is a major activities booking agent and screens the 20-minute *Flowing West* movie (adult/child $10/5) on a giant screen (great visuals, shame about the Jerry Bruckheimer soundtrack).

Internet access is available at the **Scott Base Tourist Information Centre** (☎ 03-752 0288; SH6; $2 per 20min) and at most backpackers'.

The local **medical centre** (☎ 03-753 4172; SH6) is attended by a doctor based in nearby Whataroa.

INDEPENDENT WALKS

There are several good glacier viewpoints close to the road leading from the glacier car park, including **Sentinel Rock** (10 minutes) or the **Ka Roimata o Hine Hukatere Walk** (40 minutes one way), which leads you towards the terminal face.

Other walks require a little worthwhile footslogging. The **Douglas Walk** (one hour return), off the Glacier Access Rd, passes by the terminal moraine from the 1750 advance and Peter's Pool, a small 'kettle lake'. **Roberts Point** (five hours return) overlooks and is quite close to the terminal face and involves a longer walk over more rugged terrain.

The **Terrace Track** (one hour return) starts on the old Callery Track, a former gold-mining area, and leads up onto a terrace behind the village with pleasant views of the Waiho River. From the Tatare Gorge walkway off Cowan St, you can join the rough **Callery-Waiho Walk** (four hours return) which joins up with the Roberts Point track at Douglas Swing Bridge.

GUIDED WALKS & HELI-HIKES

The best way to experience the glaciers is to walk on them. Small group walks with experienced guides, and with boots, jackets and other equipment supplied, are offered by two companies at Franz Josef: **Guiding Company** (☎ 0800 800 102, 03-752 00467; www.nzguides.com), based at the Alpine Adventure Centre, and the well-established **Franz Josef Glacier Guides** (☎ 0800 484 337, 03-752 0763; www.franzjosefglacier .com). With both outfits, half-/full-day walks cost $65/110 per adult (discounts are offered to children) – the full-day trip is much better value with around six hours on the ice, as opposed to about two hours with the half-day trip. Full-day ice-climbing trips are another option and cost $200.

Heli-hikes not only give you an aerial view of the glacier, but allow you to get much further up where there's a better chance of exploring those incredible blue-ice caves, seracs and pristine ice formations – don't pass up the opportunity to do one if at all possible. A heli-hike with about two hours on the glacier costs $260.

AERIAL SIGHTSEEING

As Julie Andrews might have pointed out, the hills are alive with the sound of buzzing helicopters and planes doing runs over the glaciers and Aoraki/Mt Cook. The flights are a superb experience, particularly the helicopters which can fly right in and bank close to the glacier face, and many flights include a snow landing. A 10-minute flight without a snow landing costs between $100 and $145, while a 20-minute flight to the head of the Franz Josef or Fox costs between $150 and $180. Flights past both of the glaciers and to Mt Cook cost around $310 per person. Prices quoted are for adults; kids under 15 will pay between 50% and 70% of the adult price.

Some recommended local operators:

Air Safaris (☎ 0800 723 274, 03-680 6880; www.air safaris.co.nz)

Fox & Franz Josef Heliservices (☎ 0800 800 793, 03-752 0793; www.scenic-flights.co.nz)

Glacier Southern Lakes Helicopters (☎ 0800 800 732, 03-752 0755; www.heli-flights.co.nz)

Helicopter Line (☎ 0800 807 767, 03-752 0767; www.helicopter.co.nz)

Mount Cook Ski Planes (☎ 0800 800 702, 03-752 0714; www.mtcookskiplanes.com)

Mountain Helicopters (☎ 0800 369 423, 03-752 0046; www.mountainhelicopters.co.nz)

OTHER ACTIVITIES

For a lower-altitude experience, try one of the three-hour guided kayaking trips on Lake Mapourika (10km north of Franz) offered by **Ferg's Kayaks** (☎ 0800 423 262, 03-752 0230; www.glacierkayaks.com; 20 Cron St; $55). Trips include mountain views and a detour down a serene channel.

Bikes can only be hired from various accommodation options in Franz. The average price is around $10/20 per half-/full-day hire.

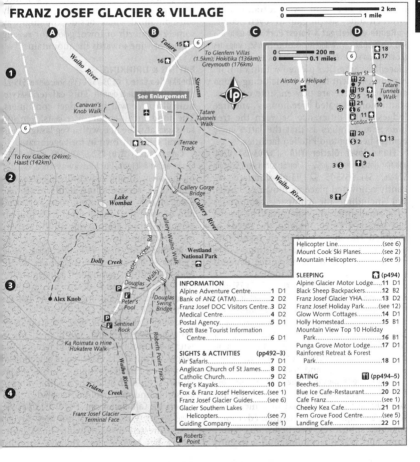

FRANZ JOSEF GLACIER & VILLAGE

Helicopter Line	(see 6)
Mount Cook Ski Planes	(see 2)
Mountain Helicopters	(see 5)

SLEEPING	🛏 (p494)
Alpine Glacier Motor Lodge	11 D1
Black Sheep Backpackers	12 B2
Franz Josef Glacier YHA	13 D2
Franz Josef Holiday Park	(see 12)
Glow Worm Cottages	14 D1
Holly Homestead	15 B1
Mountain View Top 10 Holiday Park	16 B1
Punga Grove Motor Lodge	17 D1
Rainforest Retreat & Forest Park	18 D1

EATING	🍴 (pp494–5)
Beeches	19 D1
Blue Ice Cafe-Restaurant	20 D2
Cafe Franz	(see 1)
Cheeky Kea Cafe	21 D1
Fern Grove Food Centre	(see 5)
Landing Cafe	22 D1

INFORMATION	
Alpine Adventure Centre	1 D1
Bank of ANZ (ATM)	2 D2
Franz Josef DOC Visitors Centre	3 D2
Medical Centre	4 D2
Postal Agency	5 D1
Scott Base Tourist Information Centre	6 D1

SIGHTS & ACTIVITIES	(pp492–3)
Air Safaris	7 D1
Anglican Church of St James	8 D2
Catholic Church	9 D2
Ferg's Kayaks	10 D1
Fox & Franz Josef Heliservices	(see 1)
Franz Josef Glacier Guides	(see 6)
Glacier Southern Lakes Helicopters	(see 7)
Guiding Company	(see 1)

SLEEPING

Franz Josef Holiday Park (☎ 03-752 0766; www.franzjosef.co.nz; SH6; camp sites & campervan sites from $16, dm/d $21/70; 🖳) This park is just south of town and home to the Black Sheep Backpackers, which opts for facilities and cleanliness over aesthetics (there's enough of that in the surrounding countryside); the backpackers' is often filled up by tour buses, so try to book ahead at peak times. The park and the hostel seem pleasant enough, but they do get mixed reviews from travellers.

Mountain View Top 10 Holiday Park (☎ 0800 467 897, 03-752 0735; www.mountainview.co.nz; SH6; camp sites & campervan sites $26, d $45-125; 🖳) Spread out over a big highwayside plot and fitted out with BBQs and a spa pool. Cabin-wise, they have everything from standard BYO-linen models to one- and two-bedroom units (with en suite) sleeping up to seven people.

Rainforest Retreat & Forest Park (☎ 0800 873 346, 03-752 0220; www.forestpark.co.nz; Cron St; camp sites & campervan sites $24, d $60-125) This exceptional place has camp sites plotted within rainforest and excellent facilities (including sauna and spa). There are tidy en suite cottages, stand-alone elevated 'tree houses', and tree lodges – the difference between the tree houses and lodges is that the latter have central heating and kitchen facilities.

Franz Josef Glacier YHA (☎ 03-752 0754; yha.franzjosef@yha.org.nz; 2-4 Cron St; camp sites $20, dm $24-26, s $41, d $55-75; 🖳) High-standard, recently renovated place with over 100 beds, not including the compact camp sites in a small interior courtyard. The hostel has barrier-free rooms and the needs of disabled travellers have been taken into account throughout the building. There are also two family rooms (price depends on family size and age of kids).

Glow Worm Cottages (☎ 0800 151 027, 03-752 0172; www.glowwormcottages.co.nz; 27 Cron St; dm from $22, s from $50, d $50-90) The service here can be dismissive but the rooms and facilities are pretty impressive and you can hire bikes (half-day $10). There are three- to five-bed dorms and motel units, and numerous distractions like a spa, video library and pool table.

Punga Grove Motor Lodge (☎ 0800 437 269, 03-752 0001; www.pungagrove.co.nz; Cron St; d $100-200; 🖳) Quality motel located in a nice rainforest setting. The self-contained rooms include split-level two-bedroom family units and spacious studios, and a recently installed grouping of luxury bush-hidden apartments.

Alpine Glacier Motor Lodge (☎ 0800 757 111, 03-752 0224; 14 Cron St; d $120-150) Has roomy studios (on the left as you enter the driveway) and more expensive spa-equipped units with a tiny deck bolted onto the back, plus two-bedroom units available from $180.

Holly Homestead (☎ 03-752 0299; www.holly homestead.co.nz; SH6; s $120-190, d $150-220) Lovely two-storey, cream-coloured abode with an architectural character dating back to the 1920s and four tastefully furnished rooms (two with en suite). Note that this is a self-nominated child-free zone (a child being anyone under 12 years of age).

Glenfern Villas (☎ 0800 453 633, 03-752 0054; www.glenfern.co.nz; SH6; d $120-225) Going comfortably upmarket, these units are stylish, fully self-contained villas beside the highway some 2km north of town, good for raising a glass of wine towards the mountains.

EATING & DRINKING

Cheeky Kea Cafe (☎ 03-752 0139; SH6; dinner $15-22 ⏰ breakfast, lunch & dinner) This cafeteria-style no-frills place will suit budget consumers. The food includes lots of roasts, venison sausages and the like, with a veg lasagne and several salads thrown in for vegetarians.

Cafe Franz (☎ 03-752 0793; SH6; meals $9-15 ⏰ breakfast & lunch) Tucked away in a corner of the busy Alpine Adventure Centre, this small café serves filling light meals like bangers and mash, *panini*, roast veg salad and nachos. It's usually filled with tourists exhausted from considering all the activity options around town.

Beeches (☎ 03-752 0721; SH6; mains $22-28 ⏰ lunch & dinner) Beeches specialises in NZ meats (beef fillet, lamb fillet, salmon steak). The ambience and décor are nothing special, but the food and the wine list are pretty good.

Landing Cafe (☎ 03-752 0229; SH6; mains $10-27 ⏰ lunch & dinner) Casual, tile-floored place with a big modern interior and tables flung across a front deck. Has a good selection of alcohol, regularly-changing soups, pastas and risotto, and other dishes like venison casserole and marinated fetta salad.

Blue Ice Cafe-Restaurant (☎ 03-752 0707; SH6; mains $15-28; ⏰ dinner, lunch at peak times) Stylish eatery dressed up with white linen tablecloths; but beyond the extensive wine list nd well-presented meals still down-to-earth enough to cook up several styles of pizza. The upstairs bar has a pool table and is licensed to mix cocktails until late – it stays open if there's a decent (invariably young) crowd.

Fern Grove Food Centre (☎ 03-752 0731; SH6) This well-stocked store is good for self-caterers.

GETTING THERE & AROUND

North and southbound buses operated by **InterCity** (☎ 03-752 0242; www.intercitycoach.co.nz) cross between the two glaciers, with daily buses south to Fox Glacier ($20, 40 minutes) and Queenstown ($93, eight hours), and north to Nelson ($84, 10 hours). You can also get to Franz Josef from Christchurch via Arthur's Pass) in a day. In the high season (summer) these buses can be heavily booked, so plan and book well ahead or be prepared to wait until there's space.

Atomic Shuttles (☎ 03-322 8883; www.atomictravel.co.nz) has daily services to Queenstown ($50, 7½ hours) and Greymouth ($30, 3½ hours). A ticket on the bus to Fox costs $10.

Glacier Valley Eco Tours (☎ 03-752 0699; www.glacier valley.co.nz) runs shuttles to the glacier (return

trip $10) and guided walks up the river valley to the terminal face ($30).

Fox Glacier

This glacier was named in 1872 in the wake of a visit by Sir William Fox, NZ's then-prime minister. Even if you've already visited Franz Josef Glacier, 25km up the road, it's worth stopping at Fox to see this particular mass of mountain-descending ice. At the very least, you should take the beautiful walk around Lake Matheson. The same activities offered at Franz Josef are offered in Fox township: glacier walks, flights and so on.

INFORMATION

The **DOC Fox Glacier visitors centre** (☎ 03-751 0807; SH6; 9am-12.30pm & 1-4.30pm) has a small display on the glacier environment and leaflets on short walks around the ice.

Alpine Guides (☎ 0800 111 600, 03-751 0825; www.foxguides.co.nz; SH6; 7.30am-9pm Oct-Apr, reduced hrs winter) books most activities and bus services. It's also the local **postal agency** and **money exchange**.

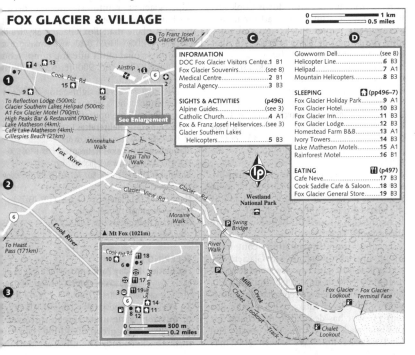

FOX GLACIER & VILLAGE

Internet access is provided at various booking centres/shops and places to stay, but the fastest connection in town is offered by **Fox Glacier Souvenirs** (☎ 03-751 0765; SH6; $2 per 12min).

Consultations at the **medical centre** (☎ 03-753 4172; SH6) are provided by a doctor based in nearby Whataroa.

The petrol station here is the last fuel stop until you reach Haast, 120km further south.

INDEPENDENT WALKS

About 6km down Cook Flat Rd is the turn-off to **Lake Matheson** and one of the most famous panoramas in NZ. It's an hour's walk around the lake and at the far end (assuming it's a fine day) are unforgettable postcard views of Mt Tasman and Mt Cook reflected in the water. The best time to catch the view is very early in the morning, when the lake is at its calmest, but late in the afternoon when the setting sun illuminates the mountains is also a great time.

Other than from the air, the best view of Fox Glacier and the neighbouring mountains is from further west down Cook Flat Rd – follow this unsealed road for its full 21km to the remote black sand and stunning rimu forest of **Gillespies Beach**. Another excellent viewpoint is **Mt Fox** (1021m; six hours return), off the highway 3km south of town, but this rugged hike is recommended only for equipped trampers.

Other good walks around the glacier include the **moraine walk** over a major 18th-century advance, the short **Minnehaha Walk** or the **River Walk**. The **Chalet Lookout Track** (1½ hours return) leads to a lookout over the terminal face.

It's 1.5km from Fox to the glacier turn-off, and the ice is another 5km from the main road. From the car park you can follow the marked track to the glacier, but as with Franz Josef it's roped off before you get to the terminal face.

Leading from the building containing Mountain Helicopters and Fox Glacier Souvenirs is a short path to a **glow-worm dell** (adult/child $4/free; 🕑 for 1hr from nightfall). But unlike sites in Hokitika, which has a freely accessible glow-worm dell (see Hokitika; p485), some Fox entrepreneur has decided to overcharge for this brief walk (across private property) and limit the access times. We've been told it may

also be possible to see glow-worms by taking the Minnehaha Walk path at night, crossing the bridge, and turning off your torch.

GLACIER WALKS & HELI-HIKES

Guided walks with all equipment provided are organised by **Alpine Guides** (☎ 0800 111 600 03-751 0825; www.foxguides.co.nz; SH6). Half-/full-day walks cost $50/80 per adult ($31/80 per child). If you're reasonably fit consider doing the full-day jaunt, because it takes you much further up the glacier; pack your own lunch.

Heli-hikes cost $240/220 per adult/child while a day-long introduction to ice climbing on the lower Fox Glacier costs $190 per person. From November to April, Alpine Guides also conducts an easygoing two-hour walk to the glacier terminal (adult/child $29/15). Various guided mountaineering excursions are also possible – contact Alpine Guides to discuss the options for tailored high-altitude trips.

SKYDIVING & AERIAL SIGHTSEEING

With a backdrop comprising the Southern Alps, glaciers, rainforest and the ocean, it's hard to imagine a better place to jump out of a plane than Fox Glacier. **Skydive NZ** (☎ 0800 751 0080, 03-751 0080; www.skydiving.co.nz) is a professional outfit offering jumps from 12,000ft ($270) and 9000ft ($230). Jump videos cost $145.

The cost of aerial sightseeing at Fox is pretty much the same as at Franz Josef. Some dependable operators:

Fox & Franz Josef Heliservices (☎ 0800 800 793, 03-751 0866; www.scenic-flights.co.nz)

Glacier Southern Lakes Helicopters (☎ 0800 800 732, 03-751 0803; www.heli-flights.co.nz)

Helicopter Line (☎ 0800 807 767, 03-751 0767; www.helicopter.co.nz)

Mount Cook Ski Planes (☎ 0800 800 702, 03-752 0714; www.mtcookskiplanes.com)

Mountain Helicopters (☎ 0800 369 423, 03-751 0045 www.mountainhelicopters.co.nz)

SLEEPING

Fox Glacier Holiday Park (☎ 0800 154 366, 03-751 0821; www.holidayparks.co.nz/fox; Cook Flat Rd; camp sites $20, campervan sites $22, dm $18, s $35-70, d $55-80) Well-equipped park with a mish-mash of different-style units spread out over a rural area, with green-clad hills rising up in the background. The units are nothing lash but there's something to suit all budgets here.

Ivory Towers (☎ 03-751 0838; www.ivorytowers lodge.co.nz; Sullivan Rd; dm/s $20/38, tw & d $50-90; 🖵) As a backpackers' should be: tidy, laid-back, draped in greenery and with good facilities, plus most of the small dorms have single beds (rather than bunks) with duvets supplied. There's also a spa, videos and a book exchange.

Fox Glacier Inn (☎ 0508 369 466, 03-751 0022; www.foxglacierinn.co.nz; 39 Sullivan Rd; dm/s $20/50, $50-85) In the last few years this inn has refreshed the look of its standard rooms and added a block of appealing motel units. B&B and DB&B packages are also available.

Homestead Farm B&B (☎ 03-751 0835; foxhomstd@ xtra.co.nz; Cook Flat Rd; tw & d $130-145) Three quaint rooms are available in this century-old farmhouse: two have en suites and one a private shower. A continental breakfast is provided; cooked breakfasts cost an extra $7 per person. Young children (under seven) are excluded from this B&B's guest list.

Fox Glacier Hotel (☎ 0800 273 769, 03-751 0839; fox.resort@xtra.co.nz; Cook Flat Rd; s $25-30, d $85-130; 🖵) Builders managed to get this two-storey structure up just in time to mark the beginning of the Great Depression at the end of the 1920s. The hotel has a gracious old-world air but with touches of modernity, like a relatively new café-bar. The budget singles come with or without shower.

Rainforest Motel (☎ 0800 724 636, 03-751 0140; www.rainforestmotel.co.nz; Cook Flat Rd; d $95-110) The pleasingly light and bright rooms here probably had the best feel of any motel we checked out in the area. Also on-site are two-bedroom units that can fit up to four people and cost $150.

Lake Matheson Motels (☎ 0800 452 2437, 03-751 0830; Cook Flat Rd; s & d $90-120) Has very clean motel units with old-fashioned innards, as well as a house that sleeps seven people (from $155, with a minimum of five people needed to book it). The management is extremely helpful and the place has all the requisite facilities.

Other recommended accommodation:

A1 Fox Glacier Motel (☎ 0800 187 900, 03-751 0804; Cook Flat Rd; d $95-125) Relaxed and friendly complex with great Mt Cook views on a clear day.

Fox Glacier Lodge (☎ 03-751 0888; foxglacierlodge@ hotmail.com; Sullivan Rd; campervan sites $24, d $130-190)

Handsome-looking buildings with solid mountain views out back.

Reflection Lodge (☎ 03-751 0707; www.reflection lodge.co.nz; Cook Flat Rd; d $130-150) Spacious, appealingly modern house and fantastic mountain views from the guest lounge.

EATING & DRINKING

Cafe Neve (☎ 03-751 0110; SH6; mains $14-30; ☽ lunch & dinner) Good food and outdoor seating are the staples here. The lunch menu mixes Asian noodles (veg or chicken), lamb hot pot, pizzas and breakfast bagels, while dinner dishes include chicken supreme and venison loin.

Cook Saddle Cafe & Saloon (☎ 03-751 0700; SH6; meals $8-25; ☽ breakfast, lunch & dinner) Overtly rustic yet still cosy eatery, where the roughly-hewn tables are piled high with burgers, seafood, chargrilled meats and Mexican-slanted food like enchiladas and nachos. Once the food is downed, there's plenty of beer and wine to follow it.

High Peaks Bar & Restaurant (☎ 03-751 0131; Cooks Flat Rd; mains $12-30; ☽ dinner) Newish, fresh looking complex with a back-corner restaurant and a front-of-house bar-café with a pool table. The café has cheaper meals like bangers & mash and T-bone steak, while the more expensive restaurant serves pan-fried scallops and rack of lamb.

Cafe Lake Matheson (☎ 03-751 0878; Lake Matheson Rd; mains $14-18; ☽ breakfast to dinner) Hybrid café and shop at the edge of the Lake Matheson car park, where it pleases the tourist hordes with calamari salad, Thai red curry chicken, and seafood laksa. Also has a sunset BBQ nightly ($25; 6pm to 9pm rain or shine).

Fox Glacier General Store (☎ 03-751 0829; SH6; ☽ 8am-8pm) Has a reasonable selection of vittles, plus beer and wine takeaways.

For pub-style meals:

Fox Glacier Hotel (☎ 03-751 0839; Cook Flat Rd; mains $14-18; ☽ dinner) Past-era dining room serving venison casserole and good old roast of the day.

Fox Glacier Inn (☎ 03-751 0022; 39 Sullivan Rd; mains $15-25; ☽ dinner) Steaks and seafood.

GETTING THERE & AROUND

Most buses stop outside the Alpine Guides building.

The services offered by **InterCity** (☎ 03-751 0701; www.intercitycoach.co.nz) overlap; southbound services from Greymouth go to Fox Glacier, while northbound ones from Queenstown continue on to Franz Josef ($20, 40 minutes). Both north and southbound services from Fox village depart around 8.45am daily. Services also run to and from Nelson ($90, 11 hours) and Queenstown ($90, seven hours).

Atomic Shuttles (☎ 03-322 8883; www.atomic travel.co.nz) also runs between Queenstown and Greymouth daily. Fares include Queenstown ($50), Greymouth ($40) and Franz Josef ($10). There's an additional northbound service to Punakaiki ($40).

Fox Glacier Shuttle/Tours (☎ 0800 369 287) will drive you to Lake Matheson or Fox Glacier ($10 return).

SOUTH TO HAAST

About 26km south of Fox Glacier is the **Copland Valley**, the western end of the difficult but spectacular **Copland Track** (three days one-way). The full walk should be tackled east to west (starting from Mt Cook) but from the SH6 you can still do a very pleasant six- to seven-hour walk up Copland Valley to overnight at the DOC hut at **Welcome Flat** ($10), where there are some great thermal springs; pay hut fees at the DOC visitors centres in Haast or Fox village. Eight kilometres south of the Copland Track terminus is **Pine Grove Motel** (☎ 03-751 0898; pine_grove@xtra.co.nz; SH6; camp sites & campervan sites $20, d $35-70), which despite its well-worn persona has inexpensive units in reasonable condition, plus some picturesque scenery.

On the edge of a forest just north of the Paringa River is the **Salmon Farm Cafe & Shop** (☎ 03-751 0837; SH6; meals $10-25; ☼ lunch), selling salmon-garnished omelettes, platters, pastas and fresh pâté and smoked meat.

Lake Paringa, 70km south of Fox Glacier, is a tranquil little trout-filled lake surrounded by forest. Stay at **Heritage Lodge Lake Paringa** (☎ 0800 727 464, 03-751 0894; www.lakeparinga.co.nz; campervan sites $25, d $85-95), which has modern units, kayak hire (two-hour hire $30) and a **café-bar** (mains $10-25; ☼ breakfast, lunch & dinner) serving burgers and strawberry chicken. There's also a basic **DOC camping ground** (adult/child $5/2) 1km south of the lodge.

The historic **Haast–Paringa Cattle Track** starts from SH6 some 43km north of Haast (just south of Lake Paringa) and emerges on the coast by the Waita River, a few kilometres north of Haast. Before the Haast Hwy

opened in 1965, this was the main stock route between Haast and the Whataroa markets. The first leg of the track to **Blowfly Hut** and back makes for a flat, pleasant half-day hike. The full walk takes three days, with stops at **Maori Saddle Hut** and **Coppermine Creek Hut**. Track info is available from the Haast visitors centre; hut fees are $5 per night.

Lake Moeraki, 31km north of Haast, is another peaceful forest lake with good fishing. A 40-minute walk from here along a stream brings you to **Monro Beach**, where there's a breeding colony of Fiordland crested penguins (July to November) and fur seals. **Wilderness Lodge Lake Moeraki** (☎ 03-750 0881; www.wildernesslodge.co.nz; SH6; d $360-790) is a plush private B&B lodge (no public facilities) with well-appointed rooms and cooked breakfasts; though you're really paying a premium for the waterside location and the privilege as a guest to undertake free activities like guided nature walks and canoe trips.

About 5km south of Lake Moeraki is the much-photographed **Knights Point**, which is the coastal region where the Haast road was eventually opened in 1965. And who was Knight? He was a surveyor's dog.

HAAST REGION

The Haast region is the centre of a major nature refuge, where enormous stands of rainforest survive alongside extensive wetlands. The area's kahikatea swamp forests sand-dune forests, seal and penguin colonies, kaka and vast sweeps of beach ensured its inclusion in the Southwest New Zealand (Te Wahipounamu) World Heritage Area. The forests yield flaming red rimu in flower and kahikatea thriving in swampy lagoons, while observant twitchers might see fantails, bellbirds, kereru (NZ pigeons) falcons, kaka, kiwi and morepork.

Haast
pop 295

The tiny community of Haast is at the ocean mouth of the wide Haast River, 120km south of Fox Glacier. After the magnificent scenery of the glaciers or Haast Pass, this modern service town doesn't make a big impression but it can be a convenient base for exploring the surrounding World Heritage Area.

Haast is a big West Coast whitebaiting centre and during the fishing season local rivers are lined with eager whitebaiters.

The DOC Haast visitors centre (☎ 03-750 0809; haastfc@doc.govt.nz; cnr SH6 & Jackson Bay Rd; ☼ 9am-5pm Nov-Mar, 9am-4.30pm Apr-Oct) has comprehensive regional info and every half-hour it screens the brief Haast landscape film *Edge of Wilderness* (adult/child $3/free).

JETBOATING

Exhilarating 1½-hour jetboat trips along the wild Waiatoto River are conducted by Haast River Safari (☎ 0800 865 382, 03-750 0101; www.haastriver.co.nz; adult/child $110/50; ☼ 8.45am & 2.45pm), based at the Red Barn between Haast township and the visitors centre. A similar trip is offered by Waiatoto River Safaris (☎ 0800 538 723, 03-750 0780; www.riversafaris.co.nz; Jackson Bay Rd; adult/child $110/75; ☼ 8.45am, noon & 3.15pm), which advertises a two-hour 'sea to mountain' jetboat experience.

SLEEPING & EATING

Accommodation is divided between Haast township, 3km east of the visitors centre, and the road to Jackson Bay.

Wilderness Accommodation (☎ 03-750 0029; Pauareka Rd; dm $20, d $45-80; ☐) Sprawling dark-brown timber complex with hostel and motel wings. The backpackers' has functional four-bed dorms, spacious doubles and a marvellous sheltered courtyard-garden, perfect for slouching no matter the weather.

Haast Highway Accommodation (☎ 03-750 0703; Marks Rd; campervan sites $24, dm from $22, d $50) This YHA-associated hostel has small, squeezy doubles with shared facilities, an airy high-ceilinged lounge/kitchen space, a 'motorpark' with campervan sites and an on-site store. Next door are the standard units of Aspiring Court Motel (☎ 0800 500 703, 03-750 0777; haastway@xtra.co.nz; Marks Rd; d $70-130), which offers good off-season rates.

Haast Beach Holiday Park (☎ 0800 843 226, 03-750 0860; haastpark@xtra.co.nz; Jackson Bay Rd; camp sites & campervan sites $22, dm $18, d $36-95) This park has good facilities and is 15km off the highway on a peaceful patch of ground close to a beach and a nice estuary walk.

McGuires Lodge (☎ 0800 624 847, 03-750 0020; www.mcguireslodge.co.nz; SH6; d $100-155) McGuires has lots of well-equipped, timber-fronted rooms, some of them perhaps a little too snug. Its restaurant (mains $28-30; ☼ dinner) serves venison, whitebait and lobster and has been recommended by travellers.

Haast World Heritage Hotel (☎ 0800 502 444, 03-750 0828; www.world-heritage-hotel.com; cnr SH6 & Jackson Bay Rd; dm $20, s $30-55, d $70-110; ☐) This grandiosely-titled place has seen better days, and those better days have seen better days, nonetheless its 50 centrally-heated en suite rooms are well kept, and good rates are often available. The restaurant (mains $14-25) opens for dinner when guest numbers warrant it.

Okuru Beach B&B (☎ 03-750 0719; www.okuru beach.co.nz; off Jackson Bay Rd; s $50, d $75-85) You'll find this low-key, nicely-situated house (it's only a short walk from a swathe of sand and rainforest) 14km south of Haast in the hamlet of Okuru – turn right at the blue B&B sign.

Smithy's Tavern (☎ 03-750 0034; Marks Rd; dinner $18-22; ☼ lunch & dinner) Sounds like a hole-in-the-wall bar, but it's actually a spacious

WHITEBAIT

Whitebait are small, translucent, elongated fish – the imago (immature) stage of the river smelt. They swarm up West Coast rivers in dense schools and are caught in set seine-net traps or large, round scoop nets. Many an argument has been had along a riverbank or near a river mouth about the best rock to position yourself on to catch the biggest haul.

The fishing season has been limited in recent times to allow the declining whitebait stocks to re-group. The breeding season is usually from September to mid-November, but varies from year to year. Cooked in batter, these small fish are delicious and highly prized by locals.

One of the West Coast's culinary doyennes provided this recipe for whitebait patties: Take a pint of whitebait (about a half-litre – yes, the fish are measured as a liquid rather than a solid, as they used to be piled into pint-size glass milk bottles for sale) and pour into a bowl. For the batter take one egg, three tablespoons of flour, a pinch of salt and a little milk to make a smooth paste. Mix this and then pour over the whitebait. Cook in smoking-hot fat until golden brown and serve immediately with mint sauce and hot potato chips (fries). Pickled onions are a fine accompaniment.

bistro-style place with various soup, fish and roast offerings. There are usually lots of locals chewing under the tavern's antler-strewn rafters.

Haast supermarket (☎ 03-750 0030; Paua Reka Rd; ⏰ 9am-7pm) Filled with supplies.

GETTING THERE & AWAY

InterCity (☎ 03-379 9020; www.intercitycoach.co.nz) and **Atomic Shuttles** (☎ 03-322 8883; www.atomic travel.co.nz) buses stop on Pauareka Rd on their way between Fox and Wanaka.

Haast to Jackson Bay & Cascade River

From Haast a side-road heads to the Arawhata River and Jackson Bay with numerous wilderness walks along the way.

Near Okuru is the **Hapuka Estuary Walk** (20 minutes return), a boardwalk loop through this soporific estuary.

After crossing the Arawhata Bridge, turn onto the narrow, unsealed gravel road that follows the Jackson River to **Martyr Saddle**, with views of the Cascade River valley and the incredible **Red Hills** – their distinctive colour is due to high concentrations of magnesium and iron in rocks forced up by the meeting of the Australo and Pacific tectonic plates. Three kilometres after Martyr Saddle is a lookout over the flats of the **Cascade River**, a true wilderness region.

The main road continues west from the Arawhata Bridge to the remote fishing hamlet of **Jackson Bay**. The views from here across to the Southern Alps are unforgettable and there are colonies of Fiordland crested penguins near the road. Migrants settled here in 1875 under a doomed assisted-immigration programme. Dreams of establishing a farming district were shattered by rain and the lack of a wharf, not built until 1938. Today,

fishing boats gather lobster, tuna, tarakih and gurnard.

Walks at Jackson Bay include the **Smooth-water Bay Track** (three hours return) and the **Wharekai Te Kau Walk** (40 minutes return) to Ocean Beach, a secluded bay with interesting rock formations. **Round About Haast** (☎ 03-750 0890; tours $65-100) does dolphin- and penguin-viewing excursions in Jackson Bay.

The **Craypot** (☎ 03-750 0035; meals $5-18 ⏰ 9am-7pm Oct-Apr, reduced hrs winter) is a classic mobile-home café parked by Jackson Bay's wharf, serving whitebait burgers, fish and chips, venison meal and mixed grills.

HAAST PASS

Turning inland at Haast, SH6 snakes alongside the wide Haast River and climbs up the pass into Mt Aspiring National Park. As you head further inland the vegetation becomes more sparse until the 563m summit is reached, where you reach snow country covered in tussock and scrub. Along the Haast Pass, en route to Wanaka (145km, 2½ hours), are several picturesque waterfalls only a few minutes' walk off the highway, including the **Fantail** and **Thunder Creek** falls. There's also the **Bridle Track** (1½ hours one-way) between the pass and Davis Flat. See the DOC booklet *Haast Pass/Tioripatea Highway: Short Walks* ($1).

The present roadway over Haast Pass (Tioripatea or 'clear path' in Maori) was opened in 1965, but before that this route was used by Maoris carrying greenstone from the West Coast to the Makarora River in Otago. The pass got its European name from geologist Julius Haast, who passed through it in 1863.

There are food and fuel stops at Makarora and Lake Hawea. If driving north, check your fuel gauge: the petrol station at Haast is the last before Fox Glacier, 120km north.

Baby fur seal, South Bay, Kaikoura (p435)

Swingbridge, Sandfly Bay Lagoon, Abel Tasman National Park (p456)

Leslie-Karamea Track (p465), Kahurangi National Park

Farewell Spit (p462)

DAV

Kayaker, Mosquito Bay, Abel Tasman National Park (p456)

Wine barrels, Montana
Brancott Winery (p432),
Blenheim

RODNEY ZANDBERGS

Marlborough Sounds (p425)

JON DAVISON

Canterbury

CONTENTS

Christchurch	**503**
History	504
Orientation	504
Information	504
Sights	505
Activities	511
Christchurch for Children	513
Tours	513
Festivals & Events	513
Sleeping	513
Eating	517
Drinking	519
Entertainment	520
Shopping	521
Getting There & Away	523
Getting Around	524
Around Christchurch	**524**
Lyttelton	524
Banks Peninsula	526
North Canterbury	**530**
Hanmer Springs	530
Lewis Pass Highway	533
Central Canterbury	**534**
Craigieburn Forest Park	534
Arthur's Pass	535
Ashburton	536
Methven	537
Mt Somers	540
South Canterbury	**540**
Temuka	540
Timaru	540
To Mackenzie Country	543
Mackenzie Country	545
Aoraki/Mt Cook National Park	549

CANTERBURY

Canterbury, the epicentre of the South Island's commercial activity, has a physical presence that slowly builds from the volcanically uplifted hills of Banks Peninsula and the expansive, well-farmed flatlands of Canterbury Plain to the mountaineer-calling pinnacles of the Southern Alps. It's the stuff of classic New Zealand holiday snaps and still-life videos: emerald, sheep-strewn pastures backed by jagged, snow-tipped mountains.

The region's urban centrepoint (and the island's largest human enclave) is Christchurch, a city with puritan roots but an energetic enthusiasm for the trappings of modern life, where fulfilling distractions range from absorbing art galleries and Gothic rooflines to formal gardens, shopper-trampled boutiques and eccentrically fashionable bars and restaurants. The region's environmental treats include the dolphin-cruised harbour just off the Francophile town of Akaroa, the sulphur pools and jetboat-happy canyons at Hanmer Springs, the forested terraces lining Lewis and Arthur Passes, and the vivid hues of Mackenzie Country lakes. One of NZ's most inspiring sights is of the highest peak in Aoraki/Mt Cook National Park on a bright day, with the névé's and seracs of nearby Tasman Glacier providing impressive scenic support.

The Canterbury region technically includes the town of Kaikoura in the north, but we've included Kaikoura (p435) in the Marlborough & Nelson chapter due to its proximity to Blenheim and Picton, and the ease of travelling between these coastal towns.

CANTERBURY

HIGHLIGHTS

- Letting your eyes scale the spectacular faces of the Cloud Piercer in **Aoraki/Mt Cook National Park** (p549)
- Strolling, tramming, punting and dining your way around charming yet cosmopolitan **Christchurch** (p503)
- Treading the alpine ways around spurs and peaks in **Arthur's Pass National Park** (p535)
- Exploring the gentrified wilds of **Banks Peninsula** (p526)
- Enjoying the blues at **Lake Tekapo** (p545) and **Lake Pukaki** (p548)
- Getting a dose of organised adventure around **Hanmer Springs** (p530)
- Taking a soothing soak in the Japanese bathhouse at **Maruia Springs** (p533)

- TELEPHONE CODE: 03
- www.christchurchnz.net

Climate

Canterbury is one of the driest and flattest regions of New Zealand – the moisture-laden westerlies from the Tasman Sea hit the Southern Alps and dump their rainfall on the West Coast well before reaching the eastern environs of the South Island. The statistics say it all: Canterbury has an annual rainfall of only 0.75m, compared with a soaking 5m on the West Coast.

Getting There & Around

Air New Zealand embarks on direct flights between Christchurch and other key NZ cities and towns such as Auckland, Dunedin, Queenstown and Wellington, with onward connections to other centres. Qantas also flies from Christchurch to the cities listed above. Origin Pacific Airways flies directly between Christchurch and Dunedin, Invercargill, Nelson and Wellington.

A long list of bus and shuttle operators scurry along the east coast, connecting Canterbury's coastal (and near-coastal) settlements with northern destinations such as Picton and southern places such as Dunedin – major operators include Inter-City, Southern Link Shuttles, Atomic Shuttles and South Island Connections. Some of the above connect Christchurch with points west such as Arthur's Pass, the West Coast and Mt Cook, as do Coast to Coast, Alpine Coaches and Cook Connection.

Rail options for east-coast and coast-to-coast travel are provided by Tranz Scenic; its *TranzAlpine* service connects Christchurch and Greymouth, while its *TranzCoastal* trains chug north to Picton, with connections to the North Island.

CHRISTCHURCH

pop 331,400

Christchurch is often described as the most English of NZ's cities, a description bolstered somewhat by the punts gliding down the picturesque Avon River, a grand Anglican cathedral rising above the city's central square, and the trams rattling past the streets with oh-so-British names. Even the tranquil suburbia to the west, with its manicured gardens

CANTERBURY

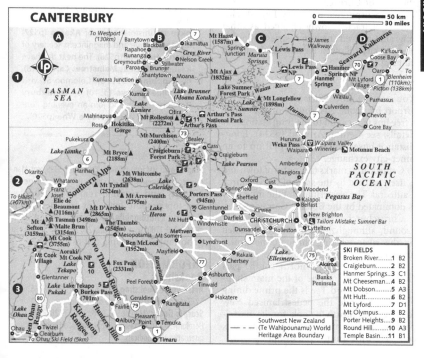

dotted with geraniums, chrysanthemums and crisply cut lawns with nary a blade of grass out of place, do little to challenge this.

But for all its self-consciously inherited charm, Christchurch should not be dismissed as simply a facsimile of somewhere else. This is also a thoroughly modern NZ city, as exemplified by the Kiwi art that has pride of place in the city's newish gallery, the wildlife reserves teeming with native animals, and a multitude of great cafés, restaurants and bars.

HISTORY

Though it still has the Gothic architecture and wooden villas bequeathed by its founders, Christchurch has strayed from the original urban vision. The settlement of Christchurch in 1850 was an ordered Church of England enterprise, and the fertile farming land was deliberately placed in the hands of the gentry. Christchurch was meant to be a model of class-structured England in the South Pacific, not just another scruffy colonial outpost. Churches were built rather than pubs, and wool made the elite of Christchurch wealthy. In 1862 it was incorporated as a very English city, but its character slowly changed as other migrants arrived, new industries followed, and the city followed its own aesthetic and cultural notions.

ORIENTATION

You can get into Christchurch from the airport by public bus, shuttle or taxi, while a free bus ferries you to the train station; for details, see Getting Around (p524). Long-distance buses conveniently pull up to an inner-city exchange.

Cathedral Sq marks the centre of town and is itself marked by the spire of Christchurch Cathedral. The western half of the inner-city is dominated by the Botanic Gardens.

Christchurch is compact and easy to walk around, although it's slightly complicated by the river twisting through the centre and constantly crossing your path.

Colombo St runs north–south past Cathedral Sq and is one of the main shopping strips. Oxford Tce is the prime dining boulevard, while the pedestrianised New Regent St is worth a look for its pastel-painted Spanish mission–style architecture, complete with stunted fire escapes.

CANTERBURY

CHRISTCHURCH IN...

Two Days

After a heart-starting espresso, head to **Cathedral Sq** (opposite) to see its church and idiosyncratic human traffic. Jump on the **tramway** (p510) for an inner-city tour and get off at the **Arts Centre** (p509) to browse historic grounds and craft shops. Grab lunch at **Dux de Lux** (p519), then lose yourself inside a brushstroke at **Christchurch Art Gallery** (p509). Have a late-afternoon **Avon punt** (p508) before getting acquainted with restaurants and drinking spots on **Oxford Tce** (p519). The next morning, ride the **gondola** (p510) and do some mountaintop walking. Take a lazy picnic in the **Botanic Gardens** (p508) and an equally relaxed look at **Canterbury Museum** (p508), or visit the **International Antarctic Centre** (p510) to really chill out. Eat at one of the many good local **Asian restaurants** (p517) before hitting a club in **Lichfield St** (p520) or a cocktail list at a riverside bar.

Four Days

Follow the two-day itinerary, then take a day-trip to **Banks Peninsula** (p526) to explore the historic town of **Akaroa** (p527) and the wildlife and magnificent scenery of **Akaroa Harbour** (p528). The next day have a late breakfast at **Mainstreet Cafe** (p518), go **shopping** (p521) on Colombo St, visit a **wildlife reserve** (p510) or **Canterbury Brewery** (p510), and join an evening concert and feast at **Nga Hau e Wha** (p510).

Maps

Map World (Map pp506-8; ☎ 03-374 5399; cnr Manchester & Gloucester Sts) carries a wide range of NZ city and regional maps, guidebooks, and topographic maps for trampers. New Zealand's **Automobile Association** (AA; Map pp506-8; ☎ 03-379 1280; www.aa.co.nz; 210 Hereford St) has a good range of touring and town maps.

INFORMATION
Bookshops

Arts Centre Bookshop (Map pp506-8; ☎ 03-365 5277; Arts Centre) Great range of NZ titles.

Scorpio Books (Map pp506-8; ☎ 03-379 2882; 79 Hereford St) Lots of travel, history and Maori culture, plus international periodicals.

Smith's Bookshop (Map pp506-8; ☎ 03-379 7976; 133 Manchester St) Excellent second-hand bookshop with unruly book-squashed shelves over three floors.
Whitcoulls (Map pp506-8; ☎ 03-379 4580; 111 Cashel St) Veritable hangar of all-ages books.

Emergency
Police, Ambulance & Fire (☎ 111)
Safecare (☎ 03-364 8791) 24-hour help for victims of rape/sexual assault

Internet Access
The going Internet-access rate in Christchurch's Internet cafés is often as low as $3 an hour. Most hostels also have Internet terminals or kiosks, while data points are common in hotels and becoming more widespread in motels.
Cyber Cafe Christchurch (Map pp506-8; ☎ 03-365 5183; 166 Gloucester St; ☽ 10am-10pm Mon-Fri, 10am-9pm Sat)
E-caf (Map pp506-8; ☎ 03-365 6480; Arts Centre; ☽ 8am-11pm)
Netopia (Map pp506-8; ☎ 03-365 2612; 728 Colombo St; ☽ 11am-11pm Sun-Thu, 11am-late Fri & Sat)
Vadal Internet Fone Shop (Map pp506-8; ☎ 03-377 2381; 57 Cathedral Sq; ☽ 8am-late)

Internet Resources
For info on Christchurch, visit www.christchurch.org.nz and www.localeye.info.

Medical Services
24 Hour Surgery (Bealey Ave Medical Centre; Map pp506-8; ☎ 03-365 7777; cnr Bealey Ave & Colombo St)
Christchurch Hospital (Map pp506-8; ☎ 03-364 0640, emergency dept 364 0270; Riccarton Ave)

Money
Hereford St is home to several major banks.
Thomas Cook (Map pp506-8; ☎ 03-366 2087; cnr Colombo & Armagh Sts) Inside a branch of Harvey World Travel.

Post
There are two central post offices.
Cathedral Sq (Map pp506-8; ☎ 03-377 5411; 3 Cathedral Sq; ☽ 8am-6pm Mon-Fri, 10am-4pm Sat)
Christchurch Mail Centre (Map pp506-8; ☎ 03-353 1758; 53-59 Hereford St; ☽ 7am-5pm Mon-Fri)

Telephone
You'll find numerous pay phones in the southwestern corner of Cathedral Sq.
Vodafone (Map p522; ☎ 0800 300 021; www.vodafone.co.nz; Christchurch airport) Has a counter at the airport.

Tourist Information
Christchurch & Canterbury visitors centre (Map pp506-8; ☎ 03-379 9629; www.christchurchnz.net; Cathedral Sq; ☽ 8.30am-5pm Mon-Fri, 8.30am-4.30pm Sat & Sun) Loads of information and books transport, activities and accommodation; also here is the Southern Encounter Aquarium & Kiwi House (see Cathedral Sq below).
Department of Conservation (DOC; ☎ 03-379 9758; 133 Victoria St; ☽ 8.30am-5pm Mon-Fri) Has information on South Island national parks and walkways.
Information desks (☎ 03-353 7774; travel&info@cial.co.nz) At both terminals of the airport; can book transport and accommodation.

SIGHTS
Cathedral Square
Cathedral Sq, named after the building that dominates it, is where locals and tourists continually crisscross each other's paths, giving the city's flat centrepiece a lively bustle. In the centre of the square is the 18m-high **Metal Chalice** sculpture, created by Neil Dawson to acknowledge the new millennium. A human landmark is provided by local eccentric the **Wizard**, who dresses like a Harry Potter film extra and harangues crowds with his soapbox philosophy. His pseudo-celebrity status is entrenched by regular appearances in *The Press* newspaper and by invitations to open conferences and take part in city festivals.

The Gothic **Christchurch Cathedral** (Map pp506-8; ☎ 03-366 0046; www.christchurchcathedral.co.nz; admission free; ☽ 8.30am-7pm Mon-Fri, 9am-6pm Sat & Sun) was consecrated in 1881 and has an impressive rose window, wooden-ribbed ceiling and tilework emblazoned with the distinctive Fylfot Cross. You can also climb halfway up the 63m-high **spire** (adult/child/family $4/1.50/8). Administrators are keen to charge for whatever they can (eg a camera or video permit costs $2.50), but the proceeds help maintain this wonderful building.

Southern Encounter Aquarium & Kiwi House (Map pp506-8; ☎ 03-359 0581; www.southernencounter.co.nz; Cathedral Sq; adult/child/student/family $10/5/8/25; ☽ 9am-4.30pm), accessed through the visitors centre, exposes you to disturbingly large eels, seahorses, red-eared slider turtles and other marine life. It also has a touch tank and a small swaying bridge that kids will love. Don't expect much from the kiwi enclosure; these endangered birds don't like light and are hypersensitive to sound.

CENTRAL CHRISTCHURCH

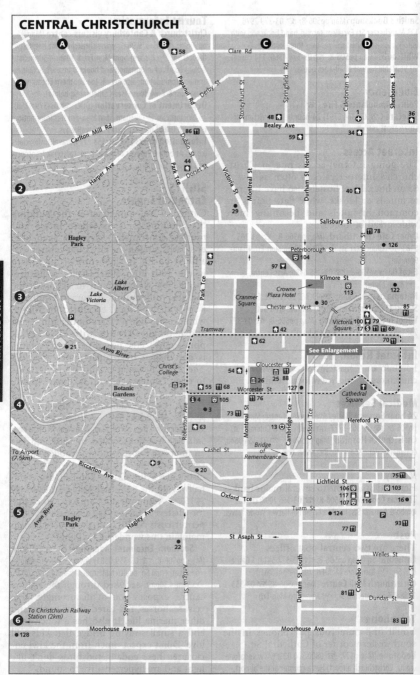

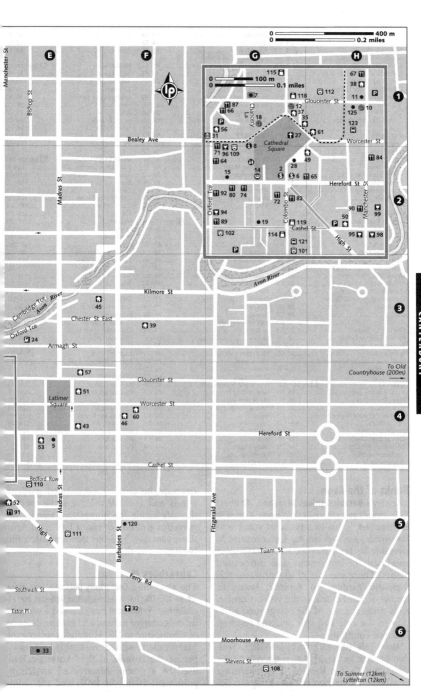

CANTERBURY

INFORMATION
24 Hour Surgery..............................1 D1
ANZ Bank (ATM)............................2 G2
Arts Centre Bookshop.....................3 B4
Arts Centre Information..................4 B4
Automobile Association (AA)............5 E4
Bank of NZ (ATM)..........................6 G2
Canterbury Public Library...............7 G1
Christchurch & Canterbury Visitors
  Centre.......................................8 G1
Christchurch Hospital....................9 B5
Cyber Cafe Christchurch...............10 H1
E-caf................................(see 3)
Map World..................................11 H1
Netopia......................................12 G1
Police Station..............................13 C4
Post Office..................................14 G2
Scorpio Books.............................15 G2
Smith's Bookshop.........................16 D5
Thomas Cook..............................17 D3
Vadal Internet Fone Shop..............18 G1
Whitcoulls...................................19 G2

SIGHTS & ACTIVITIES (pp505–13)
Antigua Boatsheds........................20 B5
Arts Centre................................(see 3)
Botanic Gardens Visitors
  Centre & Cafe............................21 A3
Canterbury Brewery.....................22 B5
Canterbury Museum......................23 B4
Centennial Leisure Centre.............24 E3
Centre of Contemporary Art..........25 C4
Christchurch Art Gallery................26 C4
Christchurch Cathedral.................27 G1
Christchurch Personal Guiding
  Service.....................................28 G2
DOC...29 C2
Floral Clock................................30 D3
Our City O-Tautahi......................31 G1
Roman Catholic Cathedral............32 F6
Rutherford's Den.....................(see 4)
Science Alive!..............................33 E6
Southern Encounter Aquarium &
  Kiwi House............................(see 8)

SLEEPING (pp513–17)
Avenue Motor Lodge.....................34 D1
Base Backpackers.........................35 G1
Bella Vista..................................36 D1
Camelot Cathedral Square Hotel....37 G1
Casino Court.........................(see 58)
Central City YHA.........................38 H1
Chester Street Backpackers............39 F3
Colombo in the City....................40 D2
Copthorne Hotel..........................41 D3
Croydon House............................42 C3

Dorothy's Boutique Hotel..............43 E4
Dorset House...............................44 B2
Foley Towers...............................45 E3
Frauenreisehaus Women's
  Hostel......................................46 F4
George..47 B3
Hambledon.................................48 C1
Heritage.....................................49 H2
Hotel Grand Chancellor.................50 H2
Kingsgate Hotel....................(see 58)
Latimer Hotel..............................51 E4
New Excelsior Backpackers............52 E5
Occidental Backpackers.................53 E4
Orari B&B...................................54 C4
Rolleston House YHA....................55 B4
Rydges Hotel...............................56 G1
Stonehurst..................................57 E4
Strathern Motor Lodge..................58 B1
Turret House...............................59 C2
Vagabond Backpackers..................60 F4
Warners......................................61 H1
Windsor Hotel.............................62 C3
YMCA...63 B4

EATING (pp517–19)
Azure...................................(see 89)
Barcelona...................................64 G2
Cafe d'Fafo.................................65 H2
Caffe Roma.................................66 G1
City Seafood Market.....................67 H1
Cook 'n' with Gas........................68 C4
Copenhagen Bakery & Cafe...........69 D3
Daily Grind.................................70 D3
Daily Grind.................................71 G1
Dimitris......................................72 G2
Dux de Lux.................................73 C4
Ebisu..74 G2
Java Coffee House.........................75 D5
Le Bon Bolli...............................76 C4
Le Cafe.................................(see 4)
Lotus Heart................................77 D5
Mainstreet Cafe & Bar..................78 D2
Matsu Sushi................................79 D3
Mum's..................................(see 12)
Mythai..80 G2
New World Supermarket................81 D6
New Zealand Natural.....................82 G2
Pak N Save Supermarket...............83 D6
Penang Noodle House...................84 H2
Retour.......................................85 D3
Saggio di Vino.............................86 B1
Sala Sala.....................................87 G1
Santorini....................................88 C4
Sticky Fingers.......................(see 64)
Tap Room...................................89 G2
Topkapi......................................90 H2

Two Fat Indians...........................91 E5
Viaduct......................................92 G2
Zydeco.......................................93 D5

DRINKING (pp519–20)
All Bar One.................................94 G2
Bailie's.................................(see 61)
Coyote.................................(see 94)
Grumpy Mole Saloon....................95 H2
Holy Grail..................................96 G2
Jolly Poacher..............................97 C3
Le Bar Bruxelle....................(see 61)
Loaded Hog................................98 H2
Sullivans.....................................99 H2
Vic and Whale............................100 D3

ENTERTAINMENT (pp520–21)
Arts Centre Cinemas................(see 3)
Base...101 G2
Bog...102 G2
Carbon.....................................103 D5
Christchurch Casino....................104 C3
Court Theatre............................105 C4
eye spy.....................................106 C4
Heaven......................................107 D5
Hoyts..................................(see 33)
Jade Stadium.............................108 G6
Ministry/Smile.....................(see 103)
Regent on Worcester...................109 G2
Sammy's Jazz Review...................110 E5
Southern Blues Bar......................111 E5
Theatre Royal.............................112 H1
Town Hall..................................113 D3

SHOPPING (pp521–23)
Arts Centre Market..................(see 3)
Ballantynes................................114 G2
Cave Rock Gallery....................(see 3)
Champions of the World..............115 G2
Mountain Designs........................116 D5
Snowgum...................................117 D5
Swanndri Shop...........................118 G1
Triangle Centre..........................119 G2

TRANSPORT (pp523–4)
Air New Zealand.....................(see 81)
Backpackers Bazaar.....................120 F5
Bus Exchange.............................121 D2
First Choice...............................122 D3
InterCity Bus Depot....................123 H1
Mac's Rent-A-Car.......................124 D5
New Zealand Motorcycle Rentals...125 H1
Pegasus Rental Cars....................126 D3
Punting on the Avon...................127 C4
Qantas.................................(see 69)
Turners Auctions........................128 A6

Banks of the Avon

The city's **Botanic Gardens** (Map above; ☎ 03-941 7590; www.ccc.govt.nz/parks/botanicgardens; Armagh St; admission free; ☑ 7am-1hr before sunset, visitors centre 10am-4pm Sep-Apr, 11am-3pm May-Aug) comprise 30 riverside hectares planted with 10,000-plus specimens of indigenous and introduced plants. There are lots of greenhouses and thematic gardens to explore, lawns to sprawl on, and a café at the visitors centre. Kids make full use of the playground adjacent to the café and will ogle the restored Peacock Fountain.

Mona Vale (Map p522; ☎ 03-348 9660; 63 Fendalton Rd; admission free; ☑ 9.30am-4pm daily Oct-Apr, 10am-3.30pm Wed-Sun May-Sep) is a charming Elizabethan-style homestead sitting on 5.5 riverside hectares of landscaped gardens, ponds and fountains. Have some food in the café inside the homestead, wander the gorgeous grounds, or take a half-hour Avon River **punt** ($16; ☑ operates 10am-5pm Jun-Apr). Bus No 9 gets you there.

Canterbury Museum

The absorbing **Canterbury Museum** (Map above; ☎ 03-366 5000; info@cantmus.govt.nz; Rolleston Ave; admission free; ☑ 9am-5pm) has amassed a wonderful collection of natural and manmade items of significance to NZ. Highlights include the Maori gallery, with some stunning *pounamu* pieces; the coracle in the 'Antarctic Hall' used by a group shipwrecked on Disappointment Island in 1907; and the child-

oriented Discovery ($2), with interactive displays and living exhibits like some docile tarantulas. The 4th-floor café has good views of botanic greenery.

Christchurch Art Gallery
Set in an eye-catching metal-and-glass collage, the city's new **Art Gallery** (Te Puna o Waiwhetu; Map opposite; ☎ 03-941 7300; www.christ churchartgallery.org.nz; cnr Worcester St & Montreal St; admission free, audio guide $2.50; ☒ 10am-5pm Thu-Tue, 10am-9pm Wed) has an engrossing permanent collection divided into pre–20th century, 20th-century and contemporary galleries, plus temporary exhibitions featuring modern NZ artists like Margaret Hudson-Ware, Margaret Elliott and Peter Siddell. Thematic guided tours are regularly held (ask at the information desk) and there's also a spacious café/wine bar on-site.

Other Museums & Galleries
Nearly 30 classic aircraft and exhaustive detail of NZ's military aviation history are warehoused at **Air Force World** (Map p522; ☎ 03-343 9532; www.airforcemuseum.co.nz; 45 Harvard Ave, Sockburn; adult/child/student/family $10/5/7/25; ☒ 10am-5pm; tours 11am, 1pm & 3pm). After exploring the underbelly of a Vampire, Skyhawk or the rather less scary-sounding Beaver, take the one-hour tour (included in admission price) of the hangars and restoration workshops. Bus Nos 5, 51 and 81 take you there.

Ferrymead Historic Park (Map p522; ☎ 03-384 1970; www.ferrymead.org.nz; Ferrymead Park Dr; adult/child/family $10/5/25; ☒ 10am-4.30pm) is a heritage complex fitted out with a mock-Edwardian township and museum-piece rail transportation. Tram rides are usually held on Saturday and Sunday, while train rides are less frequent (contact the park for details); all rides are covered by the admission price.

Science Alive! (Map opposite; ☎ 03-365 5199; www.sciencealive.co.nz; 392 Moorhouse Ave; adult/child/child under 5/family $10/7/5/24; ☒ 10am-5pm) is located in the city's old train station and is crammed with ever-changing interactive exhibits – stuff with a scientific bent, from optical illusions to things that kiddies can push, pull and climb. There's a free shuttle bus from Cathedral Sq.

Centre of Contemporary Art (CoCA; Map opposite; ☎ 03-366 7261; www.coca.org.nz; 66 Gloucester St; admission by donation; ☒ 10am-5pm Mon-Fri, noon-4pm

---

THE ATOMIC MAN
Should you happen to have a NZ $100 bill loitering in your wallet, you'll find that staring out from it is the face of Ernest Rutherford, the first person to split the atom. He achieved this feat in 1917 at Manchester University, after picking up a Nobel Prize for Chemistry in 1908 and later discovering that atoms were not thin, easily penetrated objects but in fact had a small, heavy nucleus. After firing alpha particles at a thin strip of foil and observing the end result, he exclaimed that 'It was as if you fired a 15-inch shell at a sheet of tissue paper and it came back to hit you'. (He also once said that 'All science is either physics or stamp collecting', which perhaps explains his limited fan base in the wider scientific community.)

Before these discoveries, though, he was a student at Canterbury College in Christchurch, where his future career was inspired by the teachings of Professor Alexander Bickerton. Have a look at an evocative old lecture theatre, with its graffiti-carved desks, and one of Rutherford's early work spaces in the exhibit 'Rutherford's Den' (below).

Sat & Sun) is a big white canvas of a place that was about to undergo major renovations at the time of writing. In the meantime, it will continue to showcase the work of creative modern-day NZ photographers, painters and sculptors (including recent fine arts graduates and the work of younger artists, the latter in the 'ArtZone' gallery), as well as multi-hued exhibitions of international works.

Our City O-Tautahi (Map opposite; ☎ 03-941 7460; www.ccc.govt.nz/ourcity; Cambridge Tce; admission free; ☒ 10am-4pm Mon-Fri) is a Christchurch-focussed exhibition in the old Municipal Chambers, revealing interesting facets of the city's history. There are diplomatic gifts like a gold scimitar from the Amir of Bahrain, an antique ejector seat salvaged from an air race between London and Christchurch in 1953, and displays on current and future developments.

Arts Centre
The former Canterbury College site (later Canterbury University), with its enclave of

wonderful Gothic Revival buildings, has been transformed into the excellent **Arts Centre** (Map pp506-8; ☎ 03-363 2836; www.artscentre.org.nz; 2 Worcester St; admission to site free; visitors centre ☉ 9.30am-5pm), where arts and craft outlets (see Shopping p521) share the premises with theatres, restaurants and cafés. The visitors centre, located in the clock tower on Worcester St, provides details of free guided tours of the complex. From here, you can also access the interesting **Rutherford's Den** (www.rutherfordsden .org.nz; admission gold coin donation; ☉ 10am-5pm); see the boxed text, p509.

International Antarctic Centre

The **International Antarctic Centre** (Map p522; ☎ 03-358 9896; www.iceberg.co.nz; Orchard Rd; adult/child/family $20/10/50, audioguide $5; ☉ 9am-8pm Oct-Apr, 9am-5.30pm May-Sep) is part of a huge complex built for the administration of the NZ, US and Italian Antarctic programmes. Learn all about the icy continent via historical, geological and zoological exhibits, including videos of life on Scott Base, an aquarium of creatures gathered under the ice in McMurdo Sound, and an 'Antarctic Storm' chamber where you get a first-hand taste of -18°C wind chill (check at reception for 'storm' forecasts). The 15-minute **Hägglund Ride** (per person $12, admission & ride adult/child/family $30/20/90) involves a zip around the centre's back blocks in an all-terrain vehicle. Visiting the centre is expensive, but worthwhile if you make the most of the Antarctic education on offer. You can reach it on the airport bus, or it's a short walk from the airport.

Maori Culture

The country's largest *marae*, **Nga Hau e Wha** (The Four Winds; Map p522; ☎ 03-388 7685; www .nationalmarae.co.nz; 250 Pages Rd; marae admission free, concert-tour-hangi package adult/child $65/36; ☉ marae 9am-4.30pm Mon-Fri, concert 6.45pm daily), is a multicultural facility where you can see carvings, weavings and paintings in the *whare nui* (meeting house) and the *whare wananga* (house of learning). Tours (adult/child $30/19) must be booked in advance and are taken in conjunction with a nightly concert; an optional extra is a *hangi* (traditional feast).

There's another Maori cultural experience at Willowbank Wildlife Reserve (see Wildlife Reserves opposite) called **Ko Tane** (Map p522; ☎ 03-359 6226; www.kotane.co.nz; Hussey Rd; dancing-tour-hangi package adult/child $65/38; hourly 5.30-8.30pm

Oct-Apr, 6.30pm & 7.30pm May-Sep), featuring traditional dancing and a wildlife tour (adult/child $25/12), also with an optional *hangi*.

Canterbury Brewery

Established in 1854, this **brewery** (Map pp506-8; ☎ 03-379 4940; 36 St Asaph St; adult/child $12/6; ☉ tours 10am & 12.30pm Mon-Fri, 1pm Sat) is the region's largest and produces Canterbury Draught. Bookings are essential for the interesting 1½-hour tours, which take in historical exhibits and the brewing and bottling/canning areas, and end with someone waving a glass of beer under your nose.

Tramway

Trams were first introduced to Christchurch streets in 1905 but were discontinued as a means of transport 50 years later. However, restored **trams** (☎ 03-366 7830; adult/child $12.50/free; ☉ 9am-9pm Nov-Mar, 9am-6pm Apr-Oct) now operate a 2.5km inner-city loop that takes in prime local features and shopping areas; tickets are valid for two consecutive days and can be bought from the driver. One tram is fitted out as a **restaurant** (☎ 03-366 7511; mains $30; ☉ dinner), which means you can chew while you view.

Gondola

The **gondola** (Map p522; ☎ 03-384 0700; www.gondola .co.nz; 10 Bridle Path Rd; return fares adult/child/student/family $17/8/16/45; ☉ 10am-late) takes 10 minutes to whisk you up from the Heathcote Valley terminal to the café-restaurant complex on Mt Cavendish (500m), which yields great views over Lyttelton Harbour and towards the Southern Alps. Paths lead to the **Crater Rim Walkway** (see Activities opposite). The No 28 Lyttelton bus travels here.

Wildlife Reserves

Orana Wildlife Park (Map p522; ☎ 03-359 7109; www .oranawildlifepark.co.nz; McLeans Island Rd; adult/child $14/6; ☉ 10am-5pm) has an excellent walk-through native bird aviary, a nocturnal kiwi house, and a reptile exhibit featuring the wrinkly tuatara. But most of the grounds are devoted to Africana, including lions, rhinos, giraffes, zebras, oryx and cheetahs. Animal feeding times are scheduled daily and there's a 'farmyard' area where children can pet the more-domesticated animals.

Willowbank Wildlife Reserve (Map p522; ☎ 03-359 6226; www.willowbank.co.nz; Hussey Rd; adult/child/

family $16/8/36; ☺10am-10pm) is another good
faunal reserve, with a focus on native NZ
animals and hands-on enclosures that contain alpacas, wallabies and deer. Tours are
held several times a day and also at night,
for spotting nocturnal critters. Maori performances also take place here (see Maori
Culture opposite).

ACTIVITIES

The most popular activities around Christchurch are rather gentler than the high-powered pursuits of places such as Wanaka
and Queenstown. Punting down the Avon
River is a good example, as are the inner-city
walks and the trails further south at Lyttelton Harbour, and the swimming off New
Brighton and Sumner beaches. But there are
a few up-tempo activities too, such as skiing,
sky diving and jetboating the Waimakariri.

Boating

The historic green-and-white **Antigua Boatsheds** (Map pp506-8; ☎03-366 5885; www.boatsheds.co
.nz; 2 Cambridge Tce) rent out canoes ($7 per
hour), rowboats ($12 per 30 minutes) and
paddle boats ($14 per 30 minutes) for Avon
River exploration. Alternatively, the boatsheds are also the starting point for **Punting in the Park** (☎03-366 0337; adult/child $13/5;
☺10am-dusk), where someone else does all
the elbow work during a 30-minute trip in
a flat-bottomed boat.

A similar experience is offered by **Punting on the Avon** (☎03-379 9629; 20min trip per person
$18; ☺10am-dusk Mon-Fri, by arrangement Sat & Sun)
from the landing stage at the Worcester
St bridge.

Cycling

City Cycle Hire (Map pp506-8; ☎0800 343 848, 03-339
4020; www.cyclehire-tours.co.nz; bikes per half/full day
from $20/30) will deliver bikes to where you're
staying. It also runs half- and full-day tours
(per person $75 to $135) to Port Hills and
Akaroa.

You can pedal downhill from the gondola terminal with the **Mountain Bike Adventure Company** (☎0800 424 534; ride $45). Price
includes the gondola ride up the mountain;
bookings are essential.

Walking

The visitors centre has information on
Christchurch walks. Within the city are the

Riverside Walk and various historical strolls,
while further afield is the excellent clifftop
walk to **Taylors Mistake** (2½ hours).

For great views of the city, take the
walkway from the **Sign of the Takahe** (Map
p522) on Dyers Pass Rd. The various 'Sign
of the...' places in this area were originally
roadhouses built during the Depression as
rest stops. Now they vary from the impressive tearooms at the Sign of the Takahe to
a simple shelter at the Sign of the Bellbird
and are referred to primarily as landmarks.
This walk leads up to the **Sign of the Kiwi**
(Map p522) through Victoria Park and then
along Summit Rd to Scotts Reserve, with
several lookout points along the way.

You can walk to Lyttelton on the **Bridle Path**
(1½ hours), which starts at Heathcote Valley
(take bus No 28). The **Godley Head Walkway**
(two hours return) begins at Taylors Mistake,
crossing and recrossing Summit Rd, and offers beautiful views on a clear day.

The **Crater Rim Walkway** (nine hours)
around Lyttelton Harbour goes some 20km
from Evans Pass to the Ahuriri Scenic Reserve. From the gondola terminal on Mt
Cavendish, walk to Cavendish Bluff Lookout
(30 minutes return) or the Pioneer Women's
Memorial (one hour return).

Other Activities

Queen Elizabeth II Park (Map p522; ☎03-941 6849;
www.qeiipark.org.nz; Travis Rd, Burwood; adult/child/family
$5/2/10; ☺6am-9pm Mon-Fri, 7am-8pm Sat & Sun) is a
huge sports complex with indoor pools
(including a 40m wave pool), waterslides,
a gym and squash courts; take bus No 43.
Closer to town is the **Centennial Leisure Centre**
(Map pp506-8; ☎03-941 6853; www.centennial.org.nz;
181 Armagh St; pool adult/child/family $5/2/10; ☺6am-
9pm Mon-Thu, 7am-7pm Fri-Sun), with a heated
indoor pool.

The closest **beaches** to the city are Waimairi,
North, New Brighton and South Brighton;
bus Nos 5, 49 and 60 head here. Sumner, to
the city's southeast, is also popular (bus No
30 or 31), while further east at Taylors Mistake are some good surfing breaks.

Several **skiing** areas lie within a two-hour
drive of Christchurch. See Skiing & Snowboarding (p73), and also Hanmer Springs
(p530), Craigieburn Forest Park (p534) and
Methven (p537).

Other active options in and around
Christchurch include **jetboating** (from $55) the

CHRISTCHURCH WALKING TOUR

This walking tour is 3.84km and should take you around two hours to complete. Warm up your feet by lapping **Cathedral Sq (1**; p505), with a side-trip into the Gothic ambience of **Christchurch Cathedral (2**; p505). Head north up Colombo St and turn right onto Gloucester St, then turn left to follow the **Tramway's (3**; p510) restored tracks up **New Regent St (4**; p504) – take a look above the shopfronts to spy some lovely Spanish mission pastels.

Swill some energising coffee at the **Daily Grind (5**; p518), then turn left down Armagh St and right up Colombo St. To your left is the greenery of **Victoria Sq (6**). Head left down the path opposite Oxford Tce and cross the bridge over the gentle **Avon River (7**; p508) to smell the time at the **Floral Clock (8**).

Ignore the looming ugliness of the Mayan-temple-style **Crowne Plaza (9**) and turn left onto Durham St North, then go left down Gloucester St and right along sociable **Oxford Tce (10**; p517). Prowl the terrace to select a bar-restaurant for an evening indulgence, then backtrack to Worcester St and head west. A right up Montreal St leads to the shining artistry of **Christchurch Art Gallery (11**; p509).

Back on Worcester St, continue west to the historic ex-university confines of the **Arts Centre (12**; p509), with its inspired retail galleries and the interesting **Rutherford's Den (13**; p509), then turn left down Rolleston Ave to reach **Antigua Boatsheds (14**; p511), where a soporific punt down the Avon is on offer.

Head back to the corner of Rolleston Ave and Worcester St to the **Canterbury Museum (15**; p508), housed in a fine Benjamin Mountfort-designed building, then lose yourself in the **Botanic Gardens' (16**; p508) blooming beauty.

Now celebrate your high-stepping exploits by turning right on Rolleston Ave and then left on Hereford St to buy yourself a drink at the convivial **Dux de Lux (17**; p519).

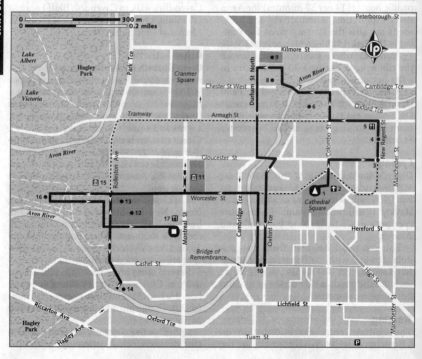

Waimakariri River, **tandem skydiving** ($250), **tandem paragliding** ($120), **ballooning** ($220), **rafting** ($145) on the Rangitata River and **horse trekking** (from $35); ask at the visitors centre.

CHRISTCHURCH FOR CHILDREN

There's no shortage of kid-friendly places and activities in Christchurch, some of them fairly pricey but most with a low-level impact on your wallet.

For picnics and open-air frolicking, visit the **Botanic Gardens** (p508); there's a handy playground beside the café. Extend your nature-based experience with a trip to Orana or Willowbank Wildlife Reserves (p510), a ride on the **Gondola** (p510), or a look around the **Southern Encounter Aquarium** (p505) – and don't forget the ecological delights of nearby **Banks Peninsula** (p526).

Educational and attention-getting factors are high at **Science Alive** (p509) and **Canterbury Museum's Discovery centre** (p508), while young mouths can hang open during a Maori **cultural show** (p510).

To exhaust a young person's energy supplies, head for the waterslides of **Queen Elizabeth II Park** (p511), or hit the **beaches** (p511) at Sumner or New Brighton, the latter with a concrete pier where kids ride the foam on boogie boards. At the engrossing **International Antarctic Centre** (p510), kids will love the storm chamber and the Hägglund Ride. When sweet tooth's demand some attention, go to **New Zealand Natural** (Map pp506-8; ☎ 03-365 0501; cnr Colombo & High St) for multi-flavoured ice-cream and shakes.

For professional short-term childcare, look up 'Baby Sitting' and 'Child Care' in the *Yellow Pages* directory.

TOURS

As the visitors centre can tell you, numerous companies conduct tours of the city and will also trundle you out to nearby towns (Lyttelton, Akaroa) and sites further afield (Arthur's Pass, Hanmer Springs, the wineries of the Waipara).

The nonprofit **Christchurch Personal Guiding Service** (Map pp506-8; ☎ 03-379 9629; tours $8; ☺ tours 10am & 1pm Oct-Apr, 1pm May-Sep) does informative, two-hour city walks. Get tickets from the visitors centre; during summer, tickets are also available from a red-and-black kiosk in the southeast of the square. **Christchurch Bike Tours** (☎ 03-366 0337; www.chchbiketours.co.nz; tours

$28; ☺ 2pm Nov-Apr) pedal around the city on informative two-hour tours.

Christchurch Sightseeing Tours (☎ 0508 669 660, 03-366 9660; www.christchurchtours.co.nz; tours from $30) offers comprehensive 3½-hour city tours year-round; a three-hour circuit of private gardens in spring and summer; and twice-weekly tours of heritage homes from September to May.

For a host of touring options in and around Christchurch, try **Canterbury Leisure Tours** (☎ 0800 484 485, 03-384 0999; www.leisure tours.co.nz; tours from $40). You can do everything from three-hour city tours to full-day Akaroa, Mt Cook, Arthur's Pass and Kaikoura outings (the day tours are fine if you're short on time, but otherwise try to spend longer in these fine places).

Canterbury Vin de Pays (☎ 03-357 8262; www .vindepays.co.nz; tours from $65) combines sightseeing with regional wine and cheese tasting, including a nicely flavoured reconnaissance of Waipara Valley wineries. In a similar vein (most likely blue), **Taste Canterbury** (☎ 03-326 6753; www.goodthings.co.nz /taste_canterbury.htm; tours from $80) takes small groups of people out into the countryside to pleasure their palates.

FESTIVALS & EVENTS

The **World Buskers Festival** (www.worldbuskers festival.com) entertains the city streets from mid- to late-January, concentrated around Cathedral Sq and the Arts Centre. Mid-February sees the **Flowers & Romance Festival** (www.festivalofflowers.co.nz) – the city provides gardens in full bloom, the romance is up to you. **Showtime Canterbury** (www.showtimecante rbury.co.nz) dominates the first half of November with major horse races such as the New Zealand Cup, fashion shows, fireworks and the centrepiece **A&P Show** (Agricultural & Pastoral Show; www.theshow.co.nz).

SLEEPING

Christchurch has a growing population of hostels, most of them within a 10-minute shuffle of Cathedral Sq. Several budget stalwarts are found around Latimer Sq, with some smaller, homelier options to the east of here. There are also several well-established options close to the foliage of the Botanic Gardens.

The city is overrun by motels (over 120 of them), with their preferred habitats being

Bealey Ave, north of the centre, and Riccarton Rd, west of town beyond Hagley Park. A number of top-end hotels are clustered on or around Cathedral Sq.

A fair number of motels and hotels can supply cots and highchairs, and they can also accommodate wheelchairs, though full barrier-free rooms are relatively scarce.

Budget
HOSTELS

Stonehurst (Map pp506-8; ☎ 0508 786 633, 03-379 4620; www.stonehurst.com; 241 Gloucester St; dm $22, s from $55, d $60-85; P ☒ ☒) Well-managed, all-budget complex opposite Latimer Sq where you can rent everything from a dorm bunk to a three-bedroom tourist flat (see Motels & Hotels opposite), and then celebrate your arrival with a dip in the heated swimming pool or a drink at the bar. Decide in advance what you're after (eg don't get a poolside bunk room if you want peace and quiet) and book ahead at peak times.

Foley Towers (Map pp506-8; ☎ 03-366 9720; foley.towers@backpack.co.nz; 208 Kilmore St; dm/d from $19/48; P ☒) Friendly Foley Towers provides lots of well-maintained rooms encircling quiet inner courtyards, and a warm welcome in dorms de-chilled by underfloor heating. It's a great spot to stay in if you need a break from places specialising in mass off-the-bus arrivals.

Frauenreisehaus Women's Hostel (Map pp506-8; ☎ 03-366 2585; jesse-sandra@quicksilver.net.nz; 272 Barbadoes St; dm/s $23/35; ☒) The refreshing, welcoming Frauenreisehaus is a women-only hostel that offers free bikes, a well-equipped kitchen and the opportunity to plunder fresh herbs and spices from the garden. It's essential you reconfirm your booking before arrival.

Vagabond Backpackers (Map pp506-8; ☎ 03-379 9677; vagabondbackpackers@hotmail.com; 232 Worcester St; dm $19-22, s/d $32/50; P ☒) Small, homely place with an appealing garden that accentuates Vagabond's peaceful, unruffled air. Its pinkish façade is only a short walk from Cathedral Sq.

Old Countryhouse (Map pp506-8; ☎ 03-381 5504; http://homepages.ihug.co.nz/~oldhouse; 437 Gloucester St; dm $21-28, d $50-70; P ☒) Popular for its cosiness and taking-it-easy ambience, the Countryhouse has split itself into two separate, very clean villas. It's a bit further out than other hostels, but is still only 1km east

of Latimer Sq; if you don't feel like walking, bus No 30 stops opposite.

Chester Street Backpackers (Map pp506-8; ☎ 03-377 1897; chesterst@free.net.nz; 148 Chester St E; dm/d from $20/50; ☒) It has a suburban location but definitely not a suburban feel. Rather, this small and welcoming backpackers' has an enticingly cosy atmosphere, and the barbecue set up in the boot of an old Anglia Deluxe is a nice touch.

Occidental Backpackers (Map pp506-8; ☎ 03-379 9284; www.occidental.co.nz; 208 Hereford St; dm $19-22, s/tw/d $35/45/50; P ☒) The Occidental rarely gets rave reviews from backpackers, as not everyone finds the tatty lounge and the sometimes violent colour scheme endearing. But you could do worse than one of the balcony-equipped front-facing rooms, and we found it irrepressibly friendly. It supplies a free breakfast and cheap bar food (meals $4 to $12).

Central City YHA (Map pp506-8; ☎ 03-379 9535; yha.christchurchcity@yha.org.nz; 273 Manchester St; dm/d from $26/60; P ☒) Comfortable bunks and beds, huge, spotless lounges and kitchens (of which there are two), a pool table and helpful staff are some of the characteristics of this well-equipped, central hostel.

Warners (Map pp506-8; ☎ 03-377 0550; www.warnerscentral.co.nz; 50 Cathedral Sq; dm/s/d $22/55/60; P ☒) The hostel section of the Warners Hotel was recently spruced up and has a pleasant feel to it, though the TV room and kitchen have aged facilities. At the time of writing, the building's western arm was being transformed into a luxury hotel.

Base Backpackers (Map pp506-8; ☎ 0800 942 225, 03-300 9999; www.basebackpackers.com; 56 Cathedral Sq; dm $22-25, s $35-45, d & tw $50-75; P ☒) A well-kept, equally central, place with good kitchen and laundry facilities.

New Excelsior Backpackers (Map pp506-8; ☎ 0800 666 237, 03-366 7570; www.newexcelsior.co.nz; cnr Manchester & High Sts; dm $22-25, s $35-40, d $55; ☒) This revamped pub (which has a history as a hotel dating back to the 1860s) is a decent, central and well-equipped backpackers', with its own café-bar and great outdoor deck.

Dorset House (Map pp506-8; ☎ 03-366 8268; www.dorsethouse.co.nz; 1 Dorset St; dm/s $23/50, d $55-60; P ☒) Lovely 130-year-old weatherboard home with a nice atmosphere, a large regal lounge, a pool table and single beds instead of bunks. It's only a short stroll from expansive parklands.

Rolleston House YHA (Map pp506-8; ☎ 03-366 6564; yha.rollestonhouse@yha.org.nz; 5 Worcester St; dm/ tw $22/50; ⓟ 🖵) Pleasant Rolleston House is in an excellent position beside the tramline and can count both the Arts Centre and the Botanic Gardens as neighbours. It's a good choice for those who don't have the energy or the inclination for a party-til-you-drop hostel.

YMCA (Map pp506-8; ☎ 0508 962 224, 03-365 0502; www.ymcachch.org.nz; 12 Hereford St; dm $18, s $45-70, d $55-90; ⓟ 🖵) Functional accommodation that focuses on facilities and cleanliness rather than style or character, with a choice of en-suite rooms or shared bathroom. You can get cheap breakfasts and dinners ($6 to $12) in the dining room, and also hire time in the adjoining gym or on the climbing wall.

CAMPING & CAMPERVAN PARKS
Meadow Park Holiday Park (Map p522; ☎ 0800 396 323, 03-352 9176; meadowpark@xtra.co.nz; 39 Meadow St; camp sites & campervan sites $22, d $36-85; ⓟ 🐕) Good place to pitch a tent or a campervan. It's also well equipped for leisure activities, with an indoor pool, spa and a big playground for the kids to unleash their energies on. Accommodation with a roof ranges from old 'standard' cabins to plain motel units.

North South Holiday Park (Map p522; ☎ 0800 567 765, 03-359 5993; www.northsouth.co.nz; 530 Sawyers Arms Rd; camp sites $19, campervan sites $21, d $37-60; ⓟ) If you don't want to travel too far after picking your campervan up at the airport, consider driving here. The many facilities include a pool, sauna, tennis courts and playground. If you don't have your own transport, airport transfers can be arranged.

South New Brighton Motor Camp (Map p522; ☎ 03-388 9844; www.holidayparks.co.nz/southnewbrighton; 59 Halsey St; camp sites $18, campervan sites $20, d $35-60; ⓟ) The cabins are nothing special and we got an unexpectedly gruff reception when we visited, but the sheltered grounds and the location – a short walk from South Brighton Beach – are why people come here.

Mid-Range
B&BS
There are two central guesthouses on Armagh St, both in old buildings with lots of character. **Croydon House** (Map pp506-8; ☎ 0800 276 936, 03-366 5111; www.croydon.co.nz; 63 Armagh St;

s $90-105, d $120-145) offers B&B (including a full cooked breakfast) in a charming 1920s building, its 1st-floor balcony brightened up by flower boxes; it has a family room that can fit four people and also rents self-contained apartments. The nearby **Windsor Hotel** (Map pp506-8; ☎ 0800 366 1503, 03-366 1503; www.windsorhotel.co.nz; 52 Armagh St; s/d $75/110; ⓟ) is another classic old abode, this one with several wings and around 40 similarly styled rooms; note that all facilities here are shared.

Turret House (Map pp506-8; ☎ 0800 488 773, 03-365 3900; www.turrethouse.co.nz; 435 Durham St North; s $75-100, d $95-135; ⓟ) Behind the concrete stubble of this 1905 home is a cosy interior with seven en-suite rooms of varying size. It's located on a reasonably busy intersection but most rooms seem fairly well insulated from street noise.

Orari B&B (Map pp506-8; ☎ 03-365 6569; www.orari.net.nz; 42 Gloucester St; s/d from $135/150; ⓟ) Orari is a fine late-19th-century home that has been stylishly updated with light-filled rooms, inviting guest areas and a front garden that is lovely in full bloom. Art connoisseurs note: it's located across the road from Christchurch Art Gallery.

MOTELS & HOTELS
Stonehurst (Map pp506-8; ☎ 0508 786 633, 03-379 4620; www.stonehurst.com; 241 Gloucester St; motel d $95-165, apt per week from $500; ⓟ 🖵 🐕) The place to go for some good deals on a variety of motel rooms (from studios to two-bedroom units) and fully self-contained tourist flats. The accommodation is central, comfortable and modern, staff are exceedingly helpful, and reception is manned around the clock.

Colombo in the City (Map pp506-8; ☎ 0800 265 662, 03-366 8775; www.motelcolombo.co.nz; 863 Colombo St; d $95-150; ⓟ) It may sound like a Peter Falk telemovie, but it's actually a bunch of roomy ultra-modern units only a few blocks north of Oxford Tce, handy if you feel like sampling some late-night culture. Wheelchairs are accommodated here.

Bella Vista (Map pp506-8; ☎ 0800 235 528, 03-377 3363; www.bellavistamotel.co.nz; 193 Bealey Ave; rooms $85-180; ⓟ) This line-up of well-equipped units has plenty of internal space to make yourself comfortable in, and an outside spa in which to soak off a hard day's sightseeing; it can also provide highchairs, portable cots and baby baths. Another good option on Bealey Ave is **Avenue Motor Lodge** (Map pp506-8; ☎ 0800 500 283, 03-366 0582; www.avenuemotorlodge.co.nz; 136 Bealey Ave; rooms $75-170; Ⓟ), which has wheelchair-accessible rooms and will pick up from the airport by arrangement.

Casino Court (Map pp506-8; ☎ 0800 109 388, 03-355 6863; www.casinocourtmotorlodge.co.nz; 76 Papanui Rd; d $95-140; Ⓟ) Located just north of Hagley Park is this nicely maintained motel complex, with uniformly modern units (some with spa bath) and a decent list of mod-cons.

Kingsgate Hotel (Map pp506-8; ☎ 03-355 6109; www.kingsgateautochristchurch.co.nz; 72 Papanui Rd; d from $125; Ⓟ) The Kingsgate is another option on this accommodation-crowded street. Its balconies are arranged around a garden courtyard.

Strathern Motor Lodge (Map pp506-8; ☎ 0800 766 624, 03-355 4411; www.strathern.com; 54 Papanui Rd; d from $100; Ⓟ) A curious mixture of brick and timber, but with comfortable rooms.

Clyde on Riccarton (Map p522; ☎ 0800 280 282, 03-341 1280; www.clydemotel.co.nz; 280 Riccarton Rd; s/d from $90/100; Ⓟ) Neat and functional double-storey motel set up on busy Riccarton Rd, with units ranging in size from studios to three bedrooms. Has a playground for littlies and a spa for biggies.

Apollo Motel (Map p522; ☎ 03-348 8786; www.apollomotel.co.nz; 288 Riccarton Rd; d from $85; Ⓟ) A few doors down from Clyde on Riccarton is this motel, with similarly sturdy rooms; it's worth paying a bit more for the bigger units.

Airport Gateway Motor Lodge (Map p522; ☎ 0800 2428 3929, 03-358 7093; www.airportgateway.co.nz; 45 Roydvale Ave; rooms from $105; Ⓟ 🖳) One of a number of motels located near the airport, handy for those early flights. Has a sizeable arrangement of good-standard rooms and no lack of facilities.

Camelot Cathedral Square Hotel (Map pp506-8; ☎ 0800 258 858, 03-365 2898; www.thecamelot.co.nz; 66 Cathedral Sq; d $95-150; Ⓟ) Camelot offers some attractive rates for its well-outfitted rooms, considering its location is a mere pillow's toss from the foundations of Christchurch Cathedral. Needless to say, try for a room with a view of the square.

Top End
Dorothy's Boutique Hotel (Map pp506-8; ☎ 03-365 6034; www.dorothys.co.nz; 2 Latimer Sq; d from

$180) This elegant brown-brick Edwardian mansion was built in 1916 and features a lovely courtyard, a bar with *Wizard of Oz* mementos (ruby slippers and an affinity for Kansas aren't compulsory for guests, though) and some exceedingly cosy chambers. If you need more convincing, there's also an award-winning on-site **restaurant** (mains $17-30; ☼ lunch Tue-Fri, dinner nightly).

Heritage (Map pp506-8; ☎ 0800 368 888, 03-377 9722; www.heritagehotels.co.nz; 28-30 Cathedral Sq; d from $250; Ⓟ 🏊) The Heritage goes all out to impress with deluxe hotel rooms and plush suites installed in the restored innards of the adjacent Old Government Building. When you get tired of doing laps of your open-plan lounge, do laps of the heated pool instead.

Latimer Hotel (Map pp506-8; ☎ 0800 176 176, 03-379 6760; www.latimerhotel.co.nz; 30 Latimer Sq; s/d from $100/120; Ⓟ 🖳) This large, grey-roofed hotel is located opposite the flat greenery of Latimer Sq, where it busies itself with conferences and other guests. Its plainly modern rooms are accompanied by a gym and sauna. All the ground-floor rooms are wheelchair accessible.

Rydges Hotel (Map pp506-8; ☎ 03-379 4700; www.rydges.com; cnr Worcester St & Oxford Tce; d from $160; Ⓟ) The curved concrete façade of this structure could do with a face-lift, but inside there's plenty of modern comforts to distract you from the exterior aesthetics. Rydges regularly offers excellent walk-in rates, and for less than $20 extra per person it'll chip in a decent breakfast.

Hambledon (Map pp506-8; ☎ 03-379 0723; www.hambledon.co.nz; 103 Bealey Ave; suites from $230; Ⓟ) Sumptuous antique-furnished mansion with elegantly old-fashioned en-suite rooms (some with four-poster beds) that will take your mind off modern-day worries. You can also rent out one of three garden-view cottages on the mansion's grounds.

Copthorne Hotel (Map pp506-8; ☎ 0800 267 846, 03-379 5880; www.copthornecentral.co.nz; 776 Colombo St; rooms from $120; Ⓟ) The façade and foyer of this low-rise hotel have a strangely dated feel, but it's in a good location opposite the greenery of Victoria Sq and has comfortable modern rooms. Guests also get complimentary use of the nearby Centennial Leisure Centre (see Other Activities p511).

CHRISTCHURCH •• Eating **517**

Other top-bracket hotels:

George (Map pp506-8; ☎ 0800 100 220, 03-379 4560; www.thegeorge.com; 50 Park Tce; rooms from $350; **P**) Parkside hotel with an oversupply of luxury.

Hotel Grand Chancellor (Map pp506-8; ☎ 0800 275 337, 03-379 2999; www.grandhotelsinternational.com; 161 Cashel St; rooms from $200; **P**) First-rate facilities.

EATING

Christchurch offers a pleasing variety of cuisines and eateries, and the quality is generally high. Cafés range from minimalist caffeine specialists to upmarket European-style places and less-polished, more-Bohemian joints. Restaurants dish up a hearty mixture of Asian and European food, and some of the best establishments are mod-NZ specialists who dote over local produce.

The largest concentration of cafés and restaurants is found along 'the Strip' – the eastern side of Oxford Tce between Hereford and Cashel Sts. The common characteristics here are good vantage points, outdoor tables and meat-heavy international dishes, not to mention the kind of intense rivalry that sees a fair bit of culinary innovation.

Most places make an effort to list one or two decent veg meals on their menus. Eateries either dedicated to plant food or with impressive vegetarian offerings include Mainstreet Cafe & Bar (p518), Lotus Heart (p518) and Dux de Lux (p519).

Restaurants   Map pp506-8

Cook 'n' with Gas (☎ 03-377 9166; 23 Worcester St; mains $27-30; ☺ dinner Mon-Sat) Exuberant cottage restaurant serving up NZ produce with prize-winning flair and the help of a great wine list. They take their cooking seriously here, so expect a slow-paced dining experience. For a taste of the ocean, perhaps give the smoked salmon with a seafood bouillabaisse a try.

Topkapi (☎ 03-379 4447; 185 Manchester St; mains $9.50-18; ☺ lunch & dinner Mon-Sat) Grab yourself a cushioned, low-slung bench in the tapestry-draped interior and enjoy some great Turkish food, including a wide range of meat or veg kebabs. The takeaway counter does brisk business.

Zydeco (☎ 03-365 4556; 113 Manchester St; mains $20-28; ☺ dinner) Blackened lamb, wild venison ragout and a hearty gumbo are just some of the Creole/Cajun dishes you can sample in this laidback eatery. They couldn't resist some kitsch deep-South embellishments, such as the 'gator stapled to one wall.

Retour (☎ 03-365 2888; Cambridge Tce; mains $15-30; ☺ dinner Tue-Sun) Raised splendidly above the banks of the Avon on a small rotunda, such as some culinary lighthouse, Retour is an accomplished practitioner of modern NZ cooking. Eat your way through prawn and crayfish ravioli, braised leg of wild hare or confit of duck.

Viaduct (☎ 03-377 9968; 136 Oxford Tce; mains $15-30; ☺ lunch & dinner) Has meaty fresh-from-the-farm mains such as 'beef fillet musketeer' (three medallions, obviously) and funky mix-it-up décor, though the alabaster Roman pillars may be testing the limits of chic-dom.

Tap Room (☎ 03-365 0547; 124 Oxford Tce; mains $18-28; ☺ breakfast, lunch & dinner) A mixture of historic building (with industrial embellishments), upmarket café and beer garden where business types dine out on gumbo, Canterbury lamb and an assortment of pasta dishes.

Azure (☎ 03-365 6088; 128 Oxford Tce; mains $14-30; ☺ lunch & dinner) Worth checking out for its NZ-focussed cookery.

Sala Sala (☎ 03-366 6755; 184 Oxford Tce; mains $16-30; ☺ lunch Mon-Fri, dinner) This spacious, orderly restaurant serves all the usual Japanese standards, from tempura to sashimi and sushi platters (the latter for around $20). The service is so soothingly mild-mannered it would give Clark Kent an anxiety attack.

Barcelona (☎ 03-377 2100; Clarendon Towers, Oxford Tce; mains $10-30; ☺ lunch & dinner) Yet another accomplished member of the Oxford Tce restaurant clan, this one dealing out delicious light meals such as Spanish paella and pea and goat's cheese soufflé, plus stomach-stretching mains such as beef sirloin.

Sticky Fingers (☎ 03-366 6451; Clarendon Towers, Oxford Tce; mains $15-30; ☺ breakfast, lunch & dinner) Carnivore's can go crazy here on teriyaki rib-eye and double-braised pork bellies, or on numerous pizzas and pastas. Follow main course with the aptly named dessert 'Love Handles' (kiwifruit pavlova).

Mythai (☎ 03-365 1295; 84 Hereford St; mains $15-18; ☺ lunch & dinner Mon-Sat) The cuisine of playfully exotic Mythai includes some flavoursome seafood, noodle and rice meals, with several veg choices. A memorable dish is the *pha sarm lot* (fish of the day in garlic and hot chilli sauce).

CANTERBURY

Ebisu (☎ 03-374 9375; 96 Hereford St; mains $10-18; ⏰ lunch Fri, dinner nightly) This *izakaya* (Japanese-style pub) is outfitted with long bars and tables, and murals on the walls. It serves sashimi and other traditional fare, plus grilled dishes ideal for a group feast.

Two Fat Indians (☎ 03-371 7273; 112-114 Manchester St; mains $13-20; ⏰ lunch & dinner) Drawing young backpackers and mixed-age locals alike, this polished twin-room eatery lives by the tagline, 'The art of pint & curry'. The extensive menu pleases both carnivores and vegetarians, and includes *palak kofta* (spinach dumplings) and a reliable chicken tikka masala. A minimum order of $15 per person often applies.

Mum's (☎ 03-365 2211; cnr Colombo & Gloucester Sts; mains $10-18; ⏰ lunch & dinner) Get a double hit of Asian flavours (Japanese and Korean) at this maternal restaurant. Korean meals include octopus and *sundae gugbab* (pork soup), while sushi and noodles round out the Japanese tastes, including a half-dozen veg options.

Saggio di Vino (☎ 03-379 4006; 185 Victoria St; mains $15-35; ⏰ dinner) Some find the service here too slow and the food portions too small and costly. But meals such as the lobster bisque and rack of lamb, plus an outstanding wine list, still seem to satisfy their devotees.

Santorini (☎ 03-379 6975; cnr Gloucester St & Cambridge Tce; mains around $25; ⏰ dinner Tue-Sat) Santorini is a double-storey wood-soaked place with an atmosphere that often imitates the outside mural of an impromptu Greek party. It serves up great moussaka, *brizola* (marinated rib-eye steak) and a range of *mezedakia* (appetisers), sometimes accompanied by live bouzouki music.

Le Bon Bolli (☎ 03-374 9444; cnr Worcester St & Montreal St; mains $15-26; ⏰ lunch & dinner) A French-influenced menu is served within this restaurant's inspired interior, with one room daubed with frescoes; upstairs is a more formal dining space. The antipasto platter is excellent, as is their crème brulée (even if they do say so themselves).

Cafés

Mainstreet Cafe & Bar (Map pp506-8; ☎ 03-365 0421; 840 Colombo St; meals $5-13; ⏰ breakfast & lunch) This bright, airy, upstairs/downstairs affair serves vegan and veg food with panache; it's good for breakfast with the works or teriyaki tofu wraps after a late night. Mainstreet

also has an eclectic live-music programme (see Live Music p520).

Cafe d'Fafo (Map pp506-8; ☎ 03-366 6083; 13. Hereford St; meals $8-14; ⏰ breakfast & lunch) Claim to cater to the coffee connoisseur and back it up by delivering large, tasty, pumped-up double-shot lattes. The extensive breakfast menu includes a veg eggs Benedict with pesto hollandaise.

Java Coffee House (Map pp506-8; ☎ 03-366 0195; cnr High & Lichfield Sts; mains $9-13; ⏰ breakfast & lunch) Funky, bright-paint-splattered place with groovin' music, hungover staff and leaflets for upcoming dance events. It's a good place for a late-morning serve of eggs on pancakes, and you can get your latte or chai tea in a cup or bowl.

Le Cafe (Map pp506-8; ☎ 03-366 7722; Clock Tower Worcester St; meals $11-17; ⏰ breakfast, lunch & dinner) Only a restaurant set in an arts centre would choose a name of such simple pretentiousness. That said, the nice fresh food is decidedly mainstream – pizza, pasta, focaccias, fish and chips, chicken Caesar salad – and the surroundings pleasantly historic.

Caffe Roma (Map pp506-8; ☎ 03-379 3879; 176 Oxford Tce; mains $10-18; ⏰ breakfast & lunch) This imitation European café has a refined persona, making it a relatively quiet, semi-formal place for breakfast. Savour a plateful of lamb kidneys or rosemary brioche.

On the Beach (Map p522; ☎ 03-326 7090; 25 The Esplanade) Out of town and on the sand at Sumner, beside the prominent Cave Rock. Serves good but pricey all-day breakfasts and seafood treats.

Quick Eats   Map pp506-8

A variety of food stalls set themselves up daily in Cathedral Sq, or you can accost one of the many food vans selling everything from Lebanese to Thai at the **Arts Centre market**. For reliable souvlaki, try **Dimitris** (☎ 03-377 7110; 709 Colombo St).

Daily Grind (☎ 03-377 4959; cnr New Regent & Armagh Sts; meals from $5; ⏰ lunch & dinner) Provides express delivery of coffee, juices (including a 'flu chaser') and smoothies, plus tasty solids such as *panini* (focaccia), bagels and salads. There's a second **Daily Grind** (☎ 03-377 6288) on the corner of Worcester St and Oxford Tce.

Lotus Heart (☎ 03-379 0324; 595 Colombo St; mains $7-13; ⏰ breakfast & lunch Mon-Fri, dinner Fri, lunch & Sun) Meditative meat-free eatery, where

Buddhist chanting or ethereal melodies may accompany your delicious Cajun veg stew, mushroom stroganoff or African beans. Also has organic coffee and great smoothies.

City Seafood Market (☎ 03-377 3377; 277 Manchester St; ☺ lunch Mon-Fri) The place to go to browse a variety of fresh, ice-packed seafood, or to pick up some consistently cheap fish and chips ($3).

Matsu Sushi (☎ 03-365 3822; 105 Armagh St; meals $5-9; ☺ lunch Mon-Fri) This atmospheric little Japanese eatery doles out a sushi lunch box for $5, plus noodle soups and other dishes for under $10.

Penang Noodle House (☎ 03-377 2638; 172 Manchester St; meals $6.50-14; ☺ lunch & dinner Mon-Sat) Don't be put off by the tattered menu out front and the brow-beaten interior. This place serves good-value Malaysian food, including veg choices and the uncommon option of ostrich with satay sauce.

Copenhagen Bakery & Cafe (☎ 03-379 3935; PricewaterhouseCoopers Centre, 119 Armagh St; ☺ breakfast & lunch) If the medals strung proudly above the display counter are anything to go by, you can snaffle some multi-award-winning tarts, quiches, cakes and breads here; don't pass up the apple pie.

Self-Catering   Map pp506-8
Self-caterers should head to the large **Pak N Save supermarket** (☎ 03-377 1000; 297 Moorhouse Ave) or the **New World supermarket** (☎ 03-377 6778; South City Centre, Colombo St).

DRINKING   Map pp506-8
The chameleonic nature of the city's eating and drinking scene sees numerous restaurants and cafés packing away their dinner menus later in the evening and distributing cocktail, wine and beer lists. Predictably, the fashionable Oxford Tce is a prime area for after-dark bar-hopping, but there are plenty of other places to drink at, from crusty old pubs to upgraded taverns with thick knots of people around their pool tables.

Holy Grail (☎ 03-365 9816; 88 Worcester St) Set in a converted Art Deco theatre, the Holy Grail is a mutilevel complex that includes a 10m screen with its own set of padded bleachers, pool tables, balcony bars and a minimalist dance floor. Caters mainly to sports lovers but there are also free DJs most nights.

Bailie's and the Belgian beer-themed **Le Bar Bruxelle** are both inside **Warners Hotel** (☎ 03-366 5159; 50 Cathedral Sq), with access to a good beer garden.

Sullivans (☎ 03-379 7790; 150 Manchester St) Unsurprisingly, lots of Guinness and Kilkenny are downed here amid the usual Irish-pub décor. But surprisingly, the bar doesn't usually open until 4pm and has been known to close on Sunday.

Loaded Hog (☎ 03-366 6674; cnr Manchester & Cashel Sts) Surprisingly nonrustic place with brewery equipment strewn along the walls (in testimony to its naturally brewed beers) and a fondness for major sports events.

Grumpy Mole Saloon (☎ 03-371 9301; cnr Manchester & Cashel Sts) Unapologetically hewn from all manner of Wild West kitsch.

Jolly Poacher (☎ 03-379 5635; 31 Victoria St) Keeps dangerously long hours – noon til dawn daily – and so what starts off as a casual lunch could become a gruelling liquid marathon. The comfortable booths can get packed out by groups, particularly when a sporting contest is in the offing.

Vic and Whale (☎ 03-366 6355; 772 Colombo St) Large one-room saloon equipped with pool tables and oversized TVs. All the drinking action takes place around the big central bar and spilt drinks are not uncommon when things get busy.

There are numerous establishments on Oxford Tce that swap their knives and forks for tumblers, wine glasses and beer goggles once mealtime is over, including **All Bar One** (☎ 03-377 9898; 130 Oxford Tce), which has a subdued interior and a manic outdoor area once the cocktail hour kicks in; **Coyote** (☎ 03-366 6055; 126 Oxford Tce), ostensibly a Tex-Mex eatery but with well-established bar credentials with younger night-owls; **Viaduct** (☎ 03-366

6055; 126 Oxford Tce), popular for its food and its bar service; and the **Tap Room** (☎ 03-365 0547; 124 Oxford Tce), where the long-lunch and after-work crowds like to hang out.

ENTERTAINMENT   Map pp506-8

Christchurch's vigorous bar/club scene is centred on Lichfield St (usually from 10pm Wednesday through Saturday), while many Oxford Tce restaurants transform into late-night watering holes with DJs and impromptu dance floors. Nightclub admission ranges from free to $10, though big-name DJ events can cost upwards of $20; live music in pubs, bars and cafés is mostly free. For information on clubbing events and live gigs, get the free weekly flier *The Package* (www.thepackage.co.nz) and the free fortnightly leaflet *J.A.G.G.* (www.jagg.co.nz), available from Java Coffee House (see Cafés p518) and other nightlife-conscious cafés, shops and venues. Also check out entertainment listings in *The Press* newspaper.

Christchurch is the hub of the South Island's performing arts scene, with several excellent theatres; a major concert ticketing company is **Ticketek** (☎ 03-377 8899; www.ticketek.co.nz). Average movie ticket prices are $13/11/7.50 per adult/concession/child, with cheaper matinee sessions.

Casino

Christchurch Casino (☎ 03-365 9999; www.christchurchcasino.co.nz; 30 Victoria St) The country's oldest casino is actually only a decade old, but has quickly come to grips with the rewards of round-the-clock gambling.

Cinemas

Hoyts (☎ 03-366 6367; www.hoyts.co.nz; 392 Moorhouse Ave) *American Pie* and *Matrix* sequels will probably keep appearing in years to come.

Regent on Worcester (☎ 03-366 0140; 94 Worcester St) This classic old cinema favours middling films: not quite arthouse, but not blockbusters either.

Arts Centre Cinemas (☎ 03-366 0167; Arts Centre) Comprises two venues (the Academy and Cloisters) and, appropriately enough, they show arthouse films.

Live Music

Sammy's Jazz Review (☎ 03-377 8618; www.sammys .co.nz; 14 Bedford Row; admission free) This great, brick-walled, wooden-floored jazz den is

patronised nightly by notable local singers such as Gennine Bailey and also accommodates the odd funk outfit. When the weather allows it, retreat to the outdoor courtyard for some alfresco listening. There may be an admission charge for big-name acts.

Dux de Lux (☎ 03-366 6919; cnr Hereford & Montreal Sts) Invites ska, reggae, rock, pop and dub artists to cater to demanding crowds at least several nights a week. It's also one of the city's busiest watering holes, particularly on a sunny day when the outdoor areas are a mass of raised glasses.

Southern Blues Bar (☎ 03-365 1654; 198 Madras St; admission free) This lively blues bar has nightly gigs (starting around 10.30pm) and a dance floor for aficionados of good blues music. It pulls a mixed, loquacious crowd of musicians, office workers and the terminally fashionable.

Vic and Whale (☎ 03-366 6355; 772 Colombo St; admission free) The wood-panelled walls of this saloon resound with the noise of bands and DJs on Saturday night, sometimes Friday night, too.

Mainstreet Cafe & Bar (☎ 03-365 0421; www.mainstreetcafe.co.nz; 840 Colombo St; admission free) Acoustic gigs and laid-back electronica can be heard in this casual café-bar space, as well as regular open mic nights (usually Tuesday).

Other places where you can catch live sounds:

Bailie's (☎ 03-366 5159; 50 Cathedral Sq) In Warners Hotel and with free end-of-week gigs.

Bog (☎ 03-379 7141; 82 Cashel St) Pub programme of DJs, live music and quiz nights.

Sullivans (☎ 03-379 7790; 150 Manchester St) Free bands and regular Irish dancing.

Nightclubs

eye spy (☎ 03-379 6634; 56 Lichfield St) One of the better bar-club hybrids on the Lichfield St clubbing strip, infused with a chilled-out orange glow and with some cute little seats in back and funky DJ sounds from around 11pm. Good place for early-evening cocktail slurping.

Base (☎ 03-377 7149; www.thebase.co.nz; 1st fl, 674 Colombo St) Specialises in drum 'n' bass, hard house and trance nights, with some nights seeing up to half-a-dozen DJs sharing the turntables. Occasionally this multilevel club lowers its colours with something tacky, like a 'Night in Ibiza' party.

Carbon (downstairs, 76 Lichfield St) Prominent, cocktail-shaking underground club that regularly hauls in DJs from around NZ and the UK, resulting in some huge house, jazz, hip-hop, dub and broken-beat gigs.

Other clubs to try:

Heaven (☎ 03-377 9879; 633 Colombo St; 🕙 11pm-late Fri & Sat) Techno is the aural weapon of choice here.

Ministry/Smile (☎ 03-379 2910; 90 Lichfield St) Two venues in one big space, with all-star DJs often in attendance.

Performing Arts

Town Hall (☎ 03-377 8899; www.ticketek.com; 86 Kilmore St; adult from $20, child & student from $10; box office 🕙 9am-5.30pm Mon-Fri, 10am-5pm Sat, later when events are on) The riverside town hall is one of the main venues for local performing arts, where you can hear a chamber or symphony orchestra, choirs and bands, or catch some theatre and the odd visiting hypnotist.

Theatre Royal (☎ 0800 205 050, 03-377 0100; 145 Gloucester St; admission $25-85) Another stalwart of the local scene, where the Royal New Zealand Ballet might stage *Peter Pan* before being upstaged by the Canterbury Opera doing *La Traviata*.

Court Theatre (☎ 0800 333 100, 03-963 0870; www.courttheatre.org.nz; 20 Worcester St; tickets adult/child/student/family from $30/10/20/75; box office 🕙 9am-8pm Mon-Fri, 10am-8pm Sat) Located within the Arts Centre, the Court Theatre hosts year-round performances of everything from Samuel Beckett to *My Fair Lady*. The resident Court Jesters troupe stage its long-running improvised comedy show, *Scared Scriptless*, every Friday night at 11pm.

Sport

Jade Stadium (☎ 03-379 1765; tickets 03-377 8899; 30 Stevens St) This stadium has been known to host cricket internationals. But it's best-known as Canterbury's rugby heartland, where you can see the Crusaders in action in the Super 12 competition.

SHOPPING

Colombo St, High St and Cashel St (including its pedestrianised mall) are all crammed with cash- and credit-card-hungry places, particularly the fashion and accessories stores where the creative output of reputable NZ designers is on display. For a wider

range of arts and crafts, visit the Arts Centre and the shops in the city's art galleries. A handy (though obviously commercially biased) guide to upmarket retailers is the *Little Black Book of Christchurch's Best Shopping*, free from the visitors centre.

The Arts Centre has dozens of craft shops and art galleries selling pottery, jewellery, woollen goods, Maori carvings, handmade toys and more; in some cases you can see the craftspeople at work. One of the best shops is **Cave Rock Gallery** (Map pp506-8; ☎ 03-365 1634), with an excellent range of ceramics, glassware, fabrics (including kaleidoscopic blouses) and jewellery carved from jade and paua shells. Every weekend the Arts Centre also has a lively craft and produce **market** (🕙 10am-4pm Sat & Sun), with buskers regularly in attendance.

For camping gear, hiking boots and other outdoors equipment, trek over to **Snowgum** (Map pp506-8; ☎ 03-365 4336; 637 Colombo St) or to **Mountain Designs** (Map pp506-8; ☎ 03-377 8522; 654 Colombo St).

Ballantynes (Map pp506-8; ☎ 03-379 7400; cnr Colombo St & City Mall) Venerable Christchurch department store with a respectful hushed atmosphere, selling everything from men's and women's fashions to cosmetics, travel goods and specialty NZ gifts.

Triangle Centre (Map pp506-8; cnr Colombo St & Cashel Mall) This modern, relatively low-key collective of two dozen shops is across the road from Cathedral Sq. Stuff sold here includes CDs, fashion, jewellery, sports goods and food.

Swanndri Shop (Map pp506-8; ☎ 03-379 8674; 123 Gloucester St) Fans of the 'Swannie', NZ's ubiquitous woollen checked shirt, will find what they're looking for here. Swanndri has also branched out into upmarket 'streetwise' garments, which presumably means your clothes can find their way home by themselves if necessary.

Champions of the World (Map pp506-8; ☎ 03-377 4100; 767 Colombo St) All Blacks merchandise outlet, whose rather immodest choice of name has haunted them since the most recent World Cup. Snap up the NZ rugby union team's official jerseys, socks, ties, shorts, scarves...

Untouched World (Map p522; ☎ 03-357 9399; 155 Roydvale Ave) If you find yourself out by the airport, consider buying into the concept of this classy 'lifestyle store', where you can procure

CANTERBURY

GREATER CHRISTCHURCH

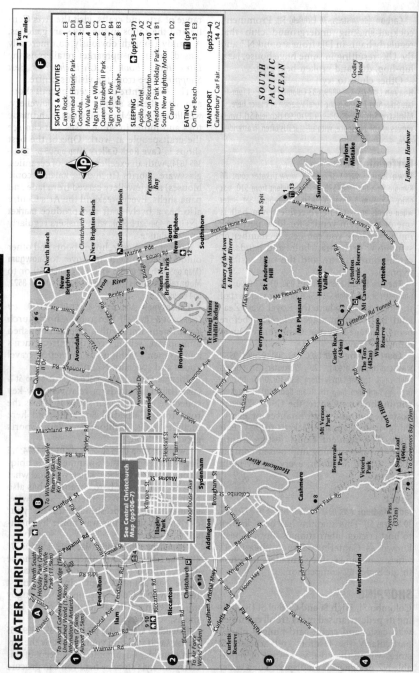

SIGHTS & ACTIVITIES

Cave Rock	1 E3
Ferrymead Historic Park	2 D3
Gondola	3 D4
Mona Vale	4 B2
Nga Hau e Wha	5 C2
Queen Elizabeth II Park	6 D1
Sign of the Kiwi	7 B4
Sign of the Takahe	8 B3

SLEEPING (pp513-17)

Apollo Motel	9 A2
Clyde on Riccarton	10 A2
Meadow Park Holiday Park	11 B1
South New Brighton Motor Camp	12 D2

EATING (p518)

On The Beach	13 E3

TRANSPORT (pp523-4)

Canterbury Car Fair	14 A2

3 km
2 miles

SOUTH PACIFIC OCEAN

some quality NZ-made clothing and eat well-prepared food in the sunny courtyard.

GETTING THERE & AWAY

Air

Christchurch airport (Map opposite; ☎ 03-358 5029; www.christchurch-airport.co.nz) is the main international gateway to the South Island; for details of international flights and the carriers who provide them, see the Transport chapter (p678). The airport has excellent facilities, including a foreign exchange, ATMs, baggage storage, car-rental desks, cafés and shops, plus **travel & information centres** (☎ 03-353 7754; travel&info@cial.co.nz) in both the domestic terminal (open 7.30am to 8pm) and the international terminal (open for all international flight arrivals). Passengers on international flights are charged a departure tax of $25.

Christchurch is directly connected with several overseas destinations, including key Australian cities; for details, see the Transport chapter (p678).

In conjunction with small affiliated airlines under the collective banner Air New Zealand Link, **Air New Zealand** (☎ 0800 737 000; www.airnz.co.nz) also offers numerous direct domestic flights with connections to other centres. There are direct flights to and from Auckland (from $90), Blenheim (from $85), Dunedin (from $75), Hamilton (from $120), Hokitika (from $65), Invercargill (from $85), Nelson (from $75), Queenstown (from $75), Wanaka (from $80) and Wellington (from $65). The airline has a large inner-city **travel centre** (Map pp506-8; ☎ 03-363 0600; 549 Colombo St).

Qantas (Map pp506-8; ☎ 0800 808 767, 03-379 6504; www.qantas.co.nz; Price Waterhouse Centre, 119 Armagh St) offers direct flights to Auckland (from $90), Dunedin (from $95), Invercargill (from $150), Nelson (from $125), Queenstown (from $75), Rotorua (from $105) and Wellington (from $65).

Origin Pacific Airways (☎ 0800 302 302, 03-547 2020; www.originpacific.co.nz) has direct flights to Dunedin (from $75), Invercargill (from $85), Nelson (from $75) and Wellington (from $65), with connections to other places.

Bus

InterCity (☎ 03-379 9020; www.intercitycoach.co.nz) buses depart from Worcester St, between the cathedral and Manchester St. North-bound buses go to Kaikoura ($32, three hours), Blenheim ($60, five hours) and Picton ($65, 5½ hours), with connections to Nelson ($75, eight hours). Buses also go west to Queenstown direct ($60, 7½ hours), or to Queenstown ($135, 10 hours) via Mt Cook ($75, 5½ hours); there are also direct services to Wanaka ($95, seven hours). Heading south, buses run along the coast via the towns along State Highway 1 (SH1) to Dunedin ($55, six hours), with connections to Invercargill ($75, 9¾ hours) and Te Anau ($75, 10½ hours).

Coast to Coast (☎ 0800 800 847; www.coast2coast.co.nz) and **Alpine Coaches** (☎ 0800 274 888; www.alpinecoaches.co.nz) run from Christchurch to Greymouth and Hokitika (both $35) via Arthur's Pass ($25).

Myriad shuttle buses run to destinations such as Akaroa, Dunedin, Hanmer Springs, Picton, Queenstown, Wanaka, Westport and points in-between, most of them bookable at the visitors centre; see the sections on the respective towns for details.

For information on backpacker buses rumbling through Christchurch, see the Transport chapter (p678).

Car, Campervan & Motorcycle

Major car and campervan rental companies all have offices in Christchurch, as do numerous smaller local companies; see the lengthy list in the *Yellow Pages*. Operators with national networks often want cars to be returned from Christchurch to Auckland because most renters travel in the opposite direction, so special rates may apply. For reliable national rental companies, see the Transport chapter (p678).

Smaller-scale rental companies:

First Choice (Map pp506-8; ☎ 0800 736 822, 03-365 9261; www.firstchoice.co.nz; 132 Kilmore St)

Mac's Rent-A-Car (Map pp506-8; ☎ 0800 154 155, 03-377 9660; www.macsrentals.co.nz; 156 Tuam St)

New Zealand Motorcycle Rentals (Map pp506-8; ☎ 03-377 0663; www.nzbike.com; 166 Gloucester St) Also does guided tours.

Pegasus Rental Cars (Map pp506-8; ☎ 0800 803 580, 03-365 1100; www.rentalcars.co.nz; 127 Peterborough St)

If you want to buy or sell a car, check out **Backpackers Bazaar** (Map pp506-8; ☎ 03-379 3700; www.backpackercars.co.nz; cnr Tuam & Barbadoes Sts). The **Canterbury Car Fair** (Map opposite; ☎ 03-338 5525; Wrights Rd entrance; ⊗ 9am-noon Sun) is held at Addington

Raceway; sellers fee is $20. **Turners Auctions** (Map pp506-8; ☎ 03-366 1807; www.turners.co.nz; 32 Moorhouse Ave) buys and sells used cars by auction; vehicles priced under $6000 usually go under the hammer (metaphorically) at 6pm on Tuesday and Thursday.

Train
Christchurch railway station (Map pp506-8; ☎ 0800 872 467, 03-341 2588; Troup Dr, Addington; ☒ ticket office 7am-4.30pm) is serviced by a free shuttle that picks up from various accommodation; ring the visitors centre to request pick-up.

The *TranzCoastal* runs daily each way between Christchurch and Picton via Kaikoura and Blenheim, departing from Christchurch at 7.30am and arriving at Picton at 12.50pm; fares to Picton start at around $40 per person. The *TranzAlpine* runs daily between Christchurch and Greymouth via Arthur's Pass (see the boxed text, p484); there are various types of fares, with the cheapest one-way tickets starting at around $70. For more information on both these services and the various fares available, contact **Tranz Scenic** (☎ 0800 872 467; www.tranzscenic.co.nz).

GETTING AROUND
To/From the Airport
Christchurch airport (Map p522; ☎ 03-358 5029; www.christchurch-airport.co.nz), at the northwestern end of Memorial Ave, is 12km from the city centre. **Super Shuttle** (☎ 0800 748 885, 03-357 9950) is one of several airport shuttles operating 24 hours and charging $12 to $18 depending on the pick-up/drop-off point. The airport is also serviced by public bus, the **City Flyer** (☎ 03-366 8855; adult/child $5/3), which runs from Cathedral Sq between 6am and 11pm Monday to Friday and 7.30am to 10.30pm Saturday and Sunday; it departs every 20 to 30 minutes up to 5pm or 6pm, then every hour. A taxi to/from the airport costs between $25 to $30.

Car, Campervan & Motorcycle
For drivers, Christchurch's network of one-way streets can create confusion, particularly for those whose sense of direction deserts them once they leave their own driveway. Be sure to equip yourself with a decent map. If you want to avoid the metered parking or car parks of the inner-city streets, check out the all-day parking a half-dozen blocks out of the centre (eg east of Latimer Sq).

Public Transport
The Christchurch **bus network** (Metro; ☎ info line 03-366 8855; www.metroinfo.org.nz; ☒ info line 6.30am-10.30pm Mon-Sat, 9am-9pm Sun) is operated by a government/private business consortium and is inexpensive and efficient. Most buses run from the City Exchange, with its pedestrian entrance on Colombo St opposite Ballantynes department store. The exchange has an information desk here; alternatively, get timetables from the visitors centre. A cash fare to anywhere in the city proper is $2. New metrocards allow two-hour/full-day travel for $1.50/3, but the catch is that the cards must be loaded up with a minimum of $10 before you can use them.

For information on the following two services, contact **Red Bus** (☎ 0800 733 287; www.redbus.co.nz). The Shuttle is a free inner-city service (as far north as Kilmore St, south to Moorhouse Ave) with about 20 pick-up points; it runs every 10 to 15 minutes from 8am to 10.30pm Monday to Thursday, to midnight Friday, from 9.30am to midnight Saturday, and 10am to 8pm Sunday. The After Midnight Express ($4) operates on four suburban routes, most of them departing Oxford Tce; it departs hourly between midnight and 4am Friday and Saturday.

The **'Best Attractions Shuttle'** (24-hr pass adult/child $15/10) is operated by **Canterbury Leisure Tours** (☎ 0800 484 485, 03-384 0999) and links major attractions such as the International Antarctic Centre, the Gondola and Willowbank Wildlife Reserve. It departs Cathedral Sq every 1½ to two hours from 9am to 7pm late December to late April, and 10am to 5.10pm the rest of the year.

Taxi
Christchurch's main taxi companies:
Blue Star (☎ 03-379 9799)
First Direct (☎ 03-377 5555)
Gold Band (☎ 03-379 5795)

AROUND CHRISTCHURCH

LYTTELTON
pop 3100
Southeast of Christchurch are the prominent Port Hills which slope down to the city's port, Lyttelton Harbour. Christchurch's first European settlers landed here in 1850 to embark on their historic trek over the hills,

and this is where you'll find the historic port of Lyttelton, only 12km from Christchurch. It is popular with weekend day-trippers because of its scenic setting, attractive old buildings and some good café-bars.

The very helpful **Lyttelton visitors centre** (☎ 03-328 9093; lyttinfo@ihug.co.nz; 20 Oxford St; ⊙ 9am-5pm) has numerous information leaflets on the town and surrounding area.

Sights

You can drive straight to Lyttelton via a **road tunnel**, an impressive piece of engineering with gleaming tiles reminiscent of a huge, elongated public toilet. But there's a much more scenic (and 10km longer) route along the narrow **Summit Rd**, which has some breathtaking city, hill and harbour views, as well as vistas of the Southern Alps; see the *Lyttelton Port Hills Drive* pamphlet ($1).

Lyttelton Museum (☎ 03-328 8972; Gladstone Quay; admission by donation; ⊙ 2-4pm Tue, Thu, Sat & Sun) has interesting maritime exhibits such as wreck-recovered artefacts and ship models (there's a 6ft version of the *Queen Mary*), plus Lyttelton historical paraphernalia such as a 19th-century pipe organ and an Antarctic gallery (both Scott and Shackleton used the port as a base).

The neo-Gothic **Timeball Station** (☎ 03-328 7311; 2 Reserve Tce; adult/child $5/1; ⊙ 10am-5pm), built in 1876, was where (for 58 years) a huge timeball was hoisted on a mast and then dropped at exactly 1pm, Greenwich Mean Time, allowing ships in the harbour to set their clocks and thereby accurately calculate longitude. Be aware that it requires a short, steep climb, and that the wind can really rip across the tower's top.

Tours

Black Cat (☎ 0800 436 574, 03-328 9078; www.blackcat .co.nz; 17 Norwich Quay; cruises adult/child $45/15) operates two-hour 'Christchurch Wildlife Cruises' on Lyttelton Harbour, where you may (but may not) see rare Hector's dolphins, blue penguins and various seabirds.

Sleeping & Eating

Most local pubs offer budget accommodation. There are also a few B&Bs sprinkled around town and the surrounding hills; the visitors centre can help with bookings.

Tunnel Vision Backpackers (☎ 03-328 7576; www .tunnelvision.co.nz; 44 London St; dm/tw/d $18/20/24)

It may have an emblematic backpack dangling over the entrance, but families are also welcome in this inviting old former hotel. The interior is smart and colourful, filled with standard-issue bunks and beds, and there's a small deck off the kitchen. The hostel is closed June through August.

Royal Hotel (☎ 03-328 7114; cnr Norwich & Canterbury Sts; s/d $40/70) Rooms tend to be on the small side but are clean and cheap. The **pub** (mains $10-17; ⊙ lunch & dinner) also serves decent grub, heavy on the meat.

Shonagh O'Hagan's (☎ 03-328 8577; shonagh.ohag an@xtra.co.nz; 16 Godley Quay; s/d $85/110) Super-comfy B&B in the old schoolmaster's house. Rooms vary in size and style, but all are well kept and have shared facilities. The cooking-proficient owner does dinners by arrangement.

Volcano Cafe (☎ 03-328 7077; 42 London St; mains $19-25; ⊙ dinner) Within popular Volcano's blinding yellow walls is a friendly, festive, laminex-heavy café serving seafood risotto, enchiladas and variable but consistently delicious curries and pastas.

Satchmo (☎ 03-328 8348; 8 London St; mains $8-25; ⊙ lunch & dinner) Mellow little place with some small inner alcoves and a great leafy courtyard. Does a good trade in meaty meals such as surf 'n' turf (beef fillet topped with prawns and hollandaise) and pizzas dedicated to music icons such as Billie Holiday and Satchmo himself: Louis Armstrong.

Entertainment

Wunderbar (☎ 03-328 8818; above the supermarket, 19 London St; ⊙ 1pm-late) Head down the laneway off London St, walk behind the supermarket, clamber up the stairway and enter this decidedly uplifting place. Have a drink on the balcony, nurture a glass in a red-velvet booth, or have an eventful time in the fabulously eccentric upholstered backroom, which hosts everything from discos to trannie shows and live music.

Door Cafe (☎ 03-328 8855; 36 London St; films adult/child $10/5) Not just *the* place for a morning cuppa and a bagel, but also a bright little mezzanine-equipped venue for occasional live music, film screenings and bellydancing shows.

Lava Bar (☎ 03-328 7077; 42 London St) Adjoining Volcano Cafe (naturally) and open for sociable boozing nightly. Has an outdoor terrace and is crammed with quirky artistic touches, which seem less quirky the more you drink.

Getting There & Away

Bus No 28 runs regularly from Christchurch to Lyttelton. From Lyttelton by car you can continue around Lyttelton Harbour and eventually on to Akaroa. This is a very scenic, longer and occasionally trying route than via SH75, between Christchurch and Akaroa.

BANKS PENINSULA

Banks Peninsula and its appealing hills were formed by two giant volcanic eruptions. Small harbours such as Le Bons, Pigeon and Little Akaroa Bays radiate out from the peninsula's centre, giving it a cogwheel shape. The historic town of Akaroa is a highlight, as is the absurdly beautiful drive down the spine of the peninsula.

History

James Cook sighted the peninsula in 1770 and thought it was an island, promptly naming it after naturalist Sir Joseph Banks. The Ngai Tahu tribe, who occupied the peninsula at the time, were attacked at the fortified Onawe *pa* by the Ngati Toa chief Te Rauparaha in 1831 and their population was dramatically reduced.

In 1838 whaling captain Jean Langlois negotiated the purchase of Banks Peninsula from local Maoris and returned to France to form a trading company. With French-government backing, 63 settlers headed for the peninsula in 1840. But only days before they arrived, panicked British officials sent their own warship to raise the flag at

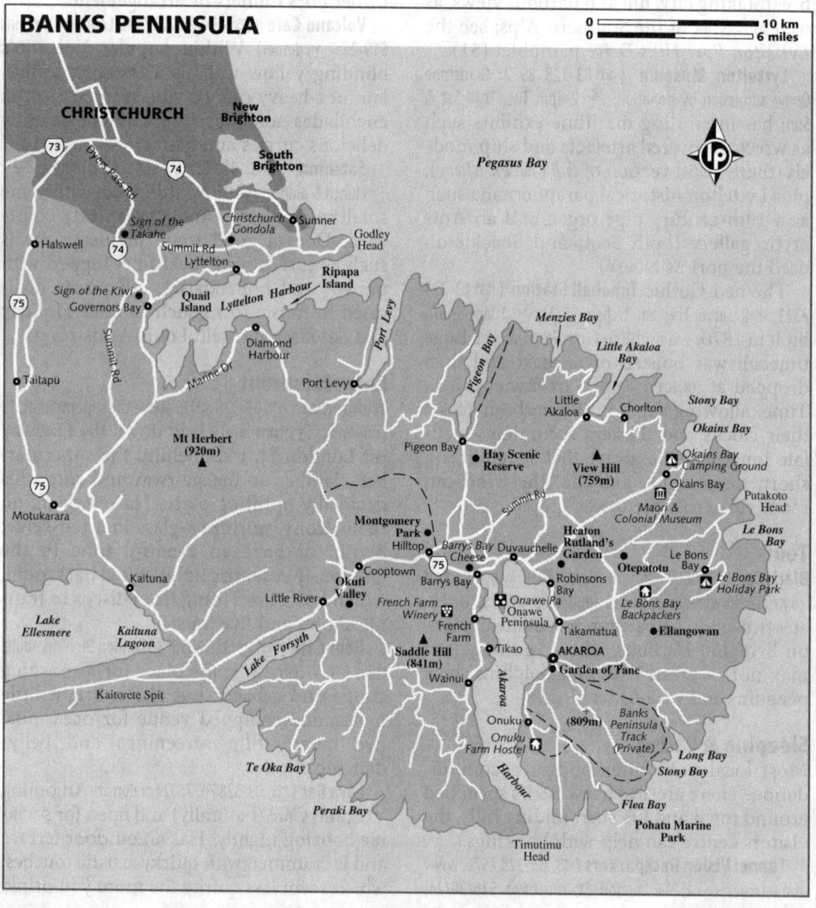

Akaroa, claiming British sovereignty under the Treaty of Waitangi. Had the settlers arrived two years earlier, the South Island may well have become a French colony.

The French did settle at Akaroa, but in 1849 their land claim was sold to the New Zealand Company and the following year a large group of British settlers arrived. The heavily forested land was cleared and soon dairy farming (later supplanted by sheep farming) became the peninsula's main industry.

Sleeping

Onuku Farm Hostel (☎ 03-304 7066; Onuku Rd; dm $14-22, d $45) Wonderful backpackers' on a 340-hectare sheep farm near Onuku, 5km south of Akaroa. The owners also organise swimming-with-dolphins tours ($80) and kayaking trips ($25) for guests, and will lob a free fishing line your way; they pick up from Akaroa. The hostel is closed May through August.

Le Bons Bay Backpackers (☎ 03-304 8582; Le Bons Bay Rd; dm/d $20/50) Six kilometres before Le Bons Bay is this excellent, restored farmhouse, wedged in a glorious valley. Besides bucolic splendour, you can also enjoy gourmet dinners ($12; including veg options) and two-hour wildlife-spotting bay tours ($22). The owners will pick up from Akaroa. Book ahead as beds here are in demand; the hostel is closed June to September.

Le Bons Bay Holiday Park (☎ 03-304 8533; lebonsholiday@xtra.co.nz; Le Bons Bay Rd; camp sites & campervan sites $22, d $50) Speaking of things bucolic, take a stream-side camp site or one of the trim little cabins at this secluded holiday park

Okains Bay Camping Ground (☎ 03-304 8789; 1162 Okains Bay Rd; camp sites from $12) Nice, pine tree-peppered place. Permits to unfold and erect your sheets of canvas are available from the house at the camping ground's entrance.

The basic **Duvauchelle Reserve Board Motor Camp** (☎ 03-304 5777; Seafield Rd; camp sites & campervan sites $20, cabins $30) is ten kilometres before Akaroa at Duvauchelle, with pleasant foreshore sites and ultra-simple cabins backed by green hills. The friendly **Hotel des Pecheurs** (☎ 03-304 5803; Duvauchelle; dm $15, d $75-85) has plain motel rooms, scuffed backpacker accommodation across the road (add $5 for linen) and good-value meals.

Akaroa
pop 650

Akaroa means 'Long Harbour' in Maori and is the site of the country's first French settlement; in fact, descendants of the original French settlers still reside here. Located 82km from Christchurch, this is a charming town that strives to re-create the feel of a French provincial village, down to the names of its streets (rues Lavaud, Balguerie, Jolie) and houses (Langlois-Eteveneaux).

INFORMATION

The information stockpiled at **Akaroa visitors centre** (☎ 03-304 8600; www.akaroa.com; 80 Rue Lavaud; ☼ 9am-5pm) includes details of the peninsula's many farmstays. There's an ATM-equipped Bank of New Zealand opposite the visitors centre and Internet access at **Bon-E-Mail** (☎ 03-304 7447; 41 Rue Lavaud; $2 per 20min; ☼ 9am-8pm).

SIGHTS & ACTIVITIES

The interesting **Akaroa Museum** (☎ 03-304 1013; cnr Rues Lavaud & Balguerie; adult/child/student/family $4/1/3.50/8; ☼ 10.30am-4.30pm Oct-Apr, 10.30am-4pm May-Sep) is spread over several historic buildings, including the old courthouse, the tiny Custom House by Daly's Wharf, and one of NZ's oldest houses, Langlois-Eteveneaux. It has modest displays on the peninsula's once-significant Maori population, a courtroom diorama, a 20-minute audiovisual on peninsular history, and Akaroa community relics and archives (check out the weird timeline entwining major global events with NZ history).

Maori & Colonial Museum (Map opposite; ☎ 03-304 8611; Okains Bay; adult/child $5/1; ☼ 10am-5pm) started life as a private collection of indigenous and pioneer artefacts but went public 25 years ago. It features a reproduction Maori meeting house, a sacred 15th-century god stick and a war canoe.

The *Akaroa Historic Area Walk* booklet ($5) details an excellent **walking tour**, starting at the 1876 Waeckerle Cottage and finishing at the old Taylor's Emporium premises near the wharf, along the way taking in all the wonderful old wooden buildings and churches that give the town its character.

To really break into stride, tackle the **Banks Peninsula Track** (Map opposite; ☎ 03-304 7612; www.bankstrack.co.nz; $180), a 35km, four-day walk across private farmland and then around the dramatic coastline of Banks Peninsula; cost includes transport from Akaroa and hut accommodation. There's also a more-leisurely two-day option ($120).

Dolphins Up Close (www.swimmingwithdolphins .co.nz; cruise & swim adult/child $95/65, cruise only $45/30) attempts to get you swimming alongside harbour-cruising dolphins, assuming they're feeling sociable; it's cheaper if you just like to watch. **Dolphin Experience** (☎ 0508-365 744, 03-304 7726; cruise & swim adult/child $80/55, cruise only $35) also has popular dolphin-swimming tours.

TOURS

To go in search of Hector's dolphins and blue penguins, take a two-hour harbour cruise with **Akaroa Harbour Cruises** (☎ 0800 436 574, 03-304 7641; www.canterburycat.co.nz; adult/child $39/15; ☒ 1.30pm daily, plus 11am Nov-Mar).

Bayline Services (☎ 03-304 7207; 108 Rue Jolie; $20; ☒ 8.20am Mon-Sat) operates the Eastern Bays Scenic Mail Run, a 140km, five-hour delivery service to remote parts of the peninsula, and visitors can come along to visit isolated communities and bays. It departs the visitors centre; bookings are essential. It also does a 2½-hour tour of the inner bays ($20; departs at 2pm with a minimum of four people).

SLEEPING

Most of the accommodation located on Banks Peninsula is in or near Akaroa, but

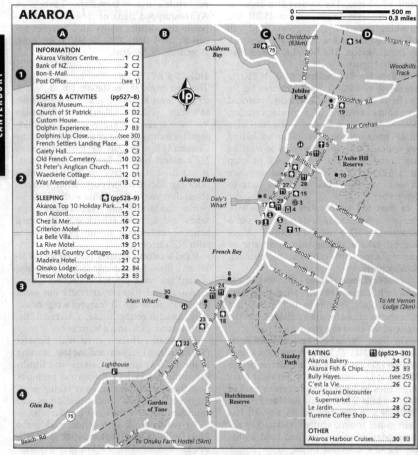

AKAROA

0 — 500 m
0 — 0.3 miles

INFORMATION
Akaroa Visitors Centre..............1 C2
Bank of NZ..............................2 C2
Bon-E-Mail...............................3 C2
Post Office.........................(see 1)

SIGHTS & ACTIVITIES (pp527-8)
Akaroa Museum.........................4 C2
Church of St Patrick....................5 D2
Custom House............................6 C2
Dolphin Experience......................7 B3
Dolphins Up Close...................(see 30)
French Settlers Landing Place....8 C3
Gaiety Hall................................9 C3
Old French Cemetery.................10 D2
St Peter's Anglican Church.........11 C2
Waeckerle Cottage....................12 D1
War Memorial...........................13 C2

SLEEPING (pp528-9)
Akaroa Top 10 Holiday Park....14 D1
Bon Accord..............................15 C2
Chez la Mer.............................16 C2
Criterion Motel.........................17 C2
La Belle Villa............................18 C3
La Rive Motel...........................19 D1
Loch Hill Country Cottages.....20 C1
Madeira Hotel..........................21 C2
Oinako Lodge...........................22 B4
Tresori Motor Lodge...............23 B3

EATING (pp529-30)
Akaroa Bakery..........................24 C3
Akaroa Fish & Chips..................25 B3
Bully Hayes.........................(see 25)
C'est la Vie...............................26 C2
Four Square Discounter
  Supermarket...........................27 C2
Le Jardin.................................28 C2
Turenne Coffee Shop...............29 C2

OTHER
Akaroa Harbour Cruises...........30 B3

To Christchurch (83km)
Morgans Rd
Childrens Bay
Woodhills Track
Jubilee Park
Woodhills Rd
Rue Grehan
Rue Ward
Rue Brittan
L'Aube Hill Reserve
Akaroa Harbour
Daly's Wharf
Settlers Hill
Rue Balguerie
French Bay
Rue Benoit
Smith St
Julius Armstrong St
Main Wharf
Watson St
To Mt Vernon Lodge (2km)
Rue Jolie
Rue Lavaud
Stanley Park
Aubrey Rd
Bruce Tce
Selwyn Ave
Percy St
Hutchinson Reserve
Lighthouse
Garden of Tane
Glen Bay
Beach Rd
Onuku Rd
To Onuku Farm Hostel (5km)

CANTERBURY

ther possibilities are scattered around the various bays (see p527).

Akaroa Top 10 Holiday Park (☎ 03-304 7471; karoa.holidaypark@xtra.co.nz; 96 Morgans Rd; camp sites campervan sites $24, d $40-70) Up on a hillside above town but connected by a pathway to Woodhills Rd, this pleasant park has some good harbour views and options for every budget, including recently installed low-cost cabins.

Bon Accord (☎ 03-304 7782; www.bon-accord.co.nz; 7 Rue Lavaud; dm/d $22/50; 🖳) Friendly backpackers' in a compact 150-year-old house, complete with a garden to empty your mind in and summer barbecues to occupy your stomach.

Chez la Mer (☎ 03-304 7024; chez_la_mer@clear net.nz; 50 Rue Lavaud; dm $20, s/d from $35/50) Nearby Bon Accord is this similarly historic and garden-equipped backpackers, which also offers free mountain bikes.

Mt Vernon Lodge (☎ 03-304 7180; Rue Balguerie; camp sites $30, dm/d from $18/50; 🖳) Laid-back Mt Vernon is a YHA-associated lodge 2km from town (free pick-up is offered), set in the middle of extensive rural grounds where you can choose between dorms and self-contained cabins. Nature walks and horse treks are two of the possible distractions here.

Madeira Hotel (☎ 03-304 7009; 48 Rue Lavaud; s/d $20/40) Excellent accommodation deal provided in this big, atmospheric hotel, with dirt-cheap prices being charged for clean, well-kept rooms.

La Rive Motel (☎ 0800 247 651, 03-304 7651; larive@paradise.net.nz; 1 Rue Lavaud; d from $75) This is an old-style motel with big, light-filled rooms and good facilities; well priced considering each unit is fully self-contained.

Criterion Motel (☎ 0800 252 762, 03-304 7775; www.akaroacriterion.co.nz; 75 Rue Jolie; d $100-165) Crop of modern units near the waterfront, with harbour-view balconies and plenty of mod-cons to take for granted while on holiday. Bills itself as 'Luxury Mediterranean Accommodation' – fortunately its sense of style is better than its sense of geography. For more designer-conscious lodgings, try the nearby **Tresori Motor Lodge** (☎ 0800 273 747, 03-304 7500; www.tresori.co.nz; s/d from $100/125).

Loch Hill Country Cottages (☎ 0800 456 244, 03-304 7195; www.lochhill.co.nz; d $125-160) On the highway 1km north of Akaroa and designed to overflow with country style. All but one of the private, self-contained stone retreats have a view to the harbour, and several come with spa and log fire.

La Belle Villa (☎ 03-304 7084; 113 Rue Jolie; s/d from $80/110; 🖳) Charming B&B in a classic old home, the private grounds outfitted with a sizeable swimming pool and lovely gardens. It only has a handful of rooms so try to book ahead if possible.

Oinako Lodge (☎ 03-304 8787; www.oinako.co.nz; 99 Beach Rd; d $165-220) Dignified old retreat built near the beach in 1865 for the then-British Magistrate, and still a place to kick back in style. Offers individually themed rooms (most with spas) and a gourmet breakfast.

EATING

Le Jardin (☎ 03-304 7447; 41 Rue Lavaud; meals $6-15; 🕙 lunch & dinner Wed-Sun) Set in a converted old house cradled by delightful gardens, Le Jardin has good light meals such as chicken laksa and ricotta, rice and spinach cakes; munch at a table out front or in the stylish interior.

Madeira Hotel (☎ 03-304 7009; 48 Rue Lavaud; mains $13-17; 🕙 lunch & dinner) Good NZ pub fare such as pork bangers in brown onion sauce is served in the Madeira's red-boothed dining room. There's a pleasant beer garden here and live bands often play on summer weekends.

C'est la Vie (☎ 03-304 7314; 33 Rue Lavaud; mains $26-30; 🕙 dinner Wed-Sun) Diminutive place that welcomes diner 'reviews' in the form of comments scrawled over several walls. Go classic French with duck l'orange, or maybe brie, avocado and artichoke-stuffed chook breast.

Bully Hayes (☎ 03-304 7533; 57 Beach Rd; mains $10-17; 🕙 breakfast, lunch & dinner) Brasserie-style waterfront café-bar with a small outdoor terrace and a menu consisting of pesto chicken, chargrilled beef salad, green-lipped mussels and breakfast pancakes.

French Farm Winery (Map p526; ☎ 03-304 5784; www.frenchfarm.co.nz; French Farm Valley Rd; mains $14-22; 🕙 lunch) Through the lavender-wreathed entrance of the winery's main house, set amid beautiful grounds on the western side of Akaroa Harbour, is a good restaurant. A cheese board for two costs $22, and in summer pizzas are served alfresco. Try one of the winery's white wines, or its orange-steeped liqueur. Nearby is **Barrys Bay Cheese** (Map p526; ☎ 03-304 5809; Barrys Bay; 🕙 9.30am-5.30pm), where

CANTERBURY

you can pick up fine cheddar, havarti, gouda and flavoured cheeses.

Akaroa Bakery (☎ 03-304 7663; 51 Beach Rd; ⊗ breakfast & lunch) For pastries, sandwiches and cakes.

Akaroa Fish & Chips (☎ 03-304 7464; 59 Beach Rd) Serves up marine takeaway.

Turenne Coffee Shop (☎ 03-304 7005; 74 Rue Lavard; meals $4-8; ⊗ breakfast & lunch; ⬚) Inventive tearoom fare such as gado gado flan and pumpkin and mushroom pie.

Four Square Discounter supermarket (Rue Lavaud; ⊗ 9am-6pm Mon-Sat) Self-caterers should head here.

GETTING THERE & AWAY

The **Akaroa Shuttle** (☎ 0800 500 929; www.akaroa shuttle.co.nz) departs from outside Christchurch visitors centre at 8.30am and 2pm from November to April, and 8.30am Saturday to Thursday (plus 4.30pm on Friday) from May to October (bookings essential in winter), returning from Akaroa two to three times daily; return fare $20. **French Connection** (☎ 0800 800 575; one way $15, return $20) leaves from Christchurch visitors centre at 8.45am, returning from Akaroa at 2.30pm daily (plus 3.45pm April to August, and 4.15pm September to March); bicycles cost $5 extra and must be pre-booked.

NORTH CANTERBURY

From Christchurch, SH1 heads north for 57km through Woodend and Amberley to Waipara. From here SH1 continues northeast to Kaikoura, while SH7 branches due north to Hurunui through flat farming country and itself splits a few kilometres north of Culverden – the northeastern route terminates at the whale-watching capital of Kaikoura and the westerly path (the continuation of SH7) leads to the Lewis Pass, Maruia Springs and eventually either the West Coast or Nelson. About 27km from Culverden is the turn-off from SH7 to Hanmer Springs, a well-known thermal area and activity resort. The *Alpine Pacific Triangle Touring Guide*, free at visitors centres, outlines things to see and do in this region.

The scenic Waipara Valley has over a dozen wineries, all outlined in the free *Waipara Valley Vineyards* brochure. Sample

a Mountford pinot noir or prize-winning Canterbury House Sauvignon Blanc, and stop for lunch in the lovely restaurants a Pegasus Bay or Waipara Springs. **Waipara Springs** (www.waiparasprings.co.nz), **Pegasus Bay** (www.pegasusbay.com) and **Canterbury House** (www .canterburyhouse.com) are open daily for wine tasting and sales; most other wineries are open by appointment. See Tours (p513 in the Christchurch section for details of companies offering tours of the area.

If you turn onto the SH7 at Waipara and then take the first right, you'll quickly find the novel **Waipara Sleepers** (☎ 03-314 6003; www.inet.net.nz/~waipara.sleepers; 12 Glenmark Dr; camp sites $20, caravan sites $24, dm/s/d from $20/27/47), where you can bunk down in converted train guards' vans, camp among a small clutch of sites and cook meals in the 'station house', all of it on a pastoral plot conveniently close to the local pub and general store.

HANMER SPRINGS
pop 750

Hanmer Springs, the main thermal resort on the South Island, is 10km off SH7. Apart from its hot pools, it's popular for outdoor activities that include forest walks, horse treks, fishing, jetboating, rafting, bungy jumping and skiing. Visitors swell the population year-round, as Hanmer is a favourite weekend destination for Christchurch folk.

Information

Hurunui visitors centre (☎ 0800 442 663, 03-315 7128; www.hurunui.com; Amuri Ave; ⊗ 10am-5pm) can book accommodation, transport and local activities. Also here is a **Bank of New Zealand ATM** (⊗ 9am-9pm).

Hanmer Springs Adventure Centre (☎ 03-315 7233; 20 Conical Hill Rd; bike rental per hr/half-day/full day $15/25/35, fishing rods per day $25, scooters per hr $28; ⊗ 9am-5pm) also supplies information on (and handles bookings for) various activities, and rents equipment such as mountain bikes, fishing rods, scooters and ski and snowboard gear.

For health issues, contact the **Hanmer Springs Medical Centre** (☎ 03-315 7503; 20 Amuri Ave).

Sights
THERMAL RESERVE

Visitors have been soaking in the waters of **Hanmer Springs Thermal Reserve** (☎ 03-315 7511;

www.hotfun.co.nz; cnr Jacks Pass Rd & Amuri Ave; adult/
child $10/5; ⊙ 10am-9pm) for over 100 years.
Local legend has it that the thermal springs
are a piece of the fires of Tamatea that
dropped from the sky after an eruption of
Mt Ngauruhoe on the North Island; Maoris
call the springs Waitapu (Sacred Waters).

The hot spring water mixes with
freshwater to produce pools of varying
temperatures. In addition to the mineral
pools, there are landscaped rock pools,
sulphur pools, a freshwater 25m lap pool,
private sauna/steam suites ($17 per half-
hour), massage facilities, a restaurant (see
Eating p533), and a family activity area that
includes a waterslide ($5).

MOLESWORTH STATION
North of Hanmer Springs, the **Molesworth
Station** (admission $10 per car; ⊙ independent visits
late-Dec–mid-Feb), at 180,500 hectares, is NZ's
largest farm with the country's largest
cattle herd. Inquire at the visitors centre
about independent visits to Molesworth,
usually only possible during a six-week
period at the beginning of each year. Al-

ternatively, **Trailways Safaris** (☎ 03-315 7401;
www.molesworth.co.nz; tours $80-200) offers 4WD
tours of the station and the remote private
land stretching north to St Arnaud; the day
tour includes a picnic lunch.

Activities
There are two main skiing areas near
Hanmer Springs. **Hanmer Springs Field** is the
closest, 17km (unsealed) from town, and **Mt
Lyford** is some 60km away. They aren't as
expensive as the larger resorts (see Skiing
& Snowboarding p75). The **Adventure Centre**
(☎ 03-315 7233; 20 Conical Hill Rd; fare to Hanmer Springs
Field adult/child $19/16, to Mt Lyford $29/25) operates
shuttle buses to the mountains.

The pamphlet *Hanmer Forest Recreation*
($1) outlines pleasant short **walks** near
town, mostly through picturesque forest.
The easy Woodland Walk starts from
Jollies Pass Rd, 1km from town, and goes
through Douglas fir, poplar and redwood
stands. It joins the Majuba Walk, which
leads to Conical Hill Lookout and then
back to Conical Hill Rd, about 1½ hours
all up. The visitors centre has details of

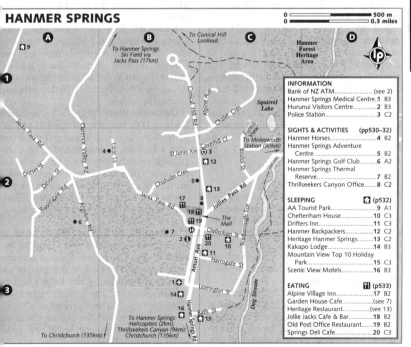

HANMER SPRINGS

0 — 500 m
0 — 0.3 miles

To Conical Hill Lookout
To Hanmer Springs Ski Field via Jacks Pass (17km)
Hanmer Forest Heritage Area
Squirrel Lake
To Molesworth Station (80km)
The Mall
To Hanmer Springs Helicopters (2km); Thrillseekers Canyon (9km); Christchurch (135km)
To Christchurch (135km)

INFORMATION
Bank of NZ ATM.....................(see 2)
Hanmer Springs Medical Centre.**1** B3
Hurunui Visitors Centre............**2** B3
Police Station..........................**3** C2

SIGHTS & ACTIVITIES (pp530–32)
Hanmer Horses........................**4** B2
Hanmer Springs Adventure
    Centre................................**5** B2
Hanmer Springs Golf Club......**6** A2
Hanmer Springs Thermal
    Reserve...............................**7** B2
Thrillseekers Canyon Office......**8** C2

SLEEPING (p532)
AA Tourist Park........................**9** A1
Cheltenham House...................**10** C3
Drifters Inn...............................**11** C3
Hanmer Backpackers................**12** C2
Heritage Hanmer Springs........**13** C2
Kakapo Lodge..........................**14** B3
Mountain View Top 10 Holiday
    Park....................................**15** C3
Scenic View Motels.................**16** B3

EATING (p533)
Alpine Village Inn....................**17** B2
Garden House Cafe...............(see 7)
Heritage Restaurant.............(see 13)
Jollie Jacks Cafe & Bar...........**18** B2
Old Post Office Restaurant......**19** B2
Springs Deli Cafe....................**20** C3

longer tramps, including Lake Sumner Forest Park.

In case the name isn't a big enough hint, **Thrillseekers Canyon** (☎ 03-315 7046; www.thrillseeker.co.nz; bungy jump $115; jetboating adult/child/family from $70/35/180, rafting adult/child $85/45) is the adrenalin centre of Hanmer Springs. You can hurl yourself off a 35m-high ferry bridge with a bungy cord, jetboat through the Waiau Gorge or go white-water rafting (grade 2 to 3) down the Waiau River. Book at the Thrillseekers Canyon centre, next to the bridge where the Hanmer Springs turn-off meets SH7. There's also an information/booking **office** (☎ 03-315 7346; the Mall) in town.

Hanmer Springs Helicopters (☎ 0800 888 308, 03-315 7758; hanmerheli@xtra.co.nz; 10min flight adult/child $155/90, 30min flight $240/135) hovers over the surrounding forest and the Clarence Valley, and on longer flights will land at the high-country St James Station.

Hanmer Horses (☎ 0800 873 546, 03-315 7444; www.hanmerhorses.co.nz; Lucas Lane; 1hr rides adult/child $40/35) will go riding over hill, dale, tussock and mountain, should they be required to. They'll even lead littlies on a 20-minute pony ride ($10).

BackTrax (☎ 0800 422 258, 03-315 7684; www .backtrax.co.nz; 2½hr trips $130) organises quad-bike trips up into the hills and along (and across) the Hanmer River; minimum age is 16. The region is also popular for mountain biking – the **Hanmer Springs Adventure Centre** (☎ 03-315 7233; 20 Conical Hill Rd) offers trail maps, advice and bike rental, and also does an organised ride ($75) up over Jacks and Jollies Passes.

Drivers and putters should head to **Hanmer Springs Golf Club** (☎ 03-315 7110; Argelins Rd).

Sleeping

Mountain View Top 10 Holiday Park (☎ 0800 904 545, 03-315 7113; www.holidayparks.co.nz/mtnview; Bath St; camp sites $20, campervan sites $24, d $40-80) Fresh-aired, amenity-ridden and fairly busy park located only a few minutes' walk from the thermal reserve. You'll need your own linen and towels for all accommodation bar some self-contained units.

AA Tourist Park (☎ 03-315 7112; aatouristpark@ xtra.co.nz; 200 Jacks Pass Rd; camp sites $18, campervan sites $24, d $26-65) This large, well-run park is 3km from town and will appeal more to the budget-minded, as the accommodation

includes cheap no-frills caravans and als cabins with the power unplugged. Cam and campervan sites are sizeable.

Hanmer Backpackers (☎ 03-315 7196; hanmerl ckpackers@hotmail.com; 41 Conical Hill Rd; dm/d $20/5 ▢) The township's original backpacker has had some good work done to its sma dimensions in recent times and now spor a bigger kitchen and a mezzanine loung It's inviting and comfortable, and has a ba becue area to hang about in summer and log fire to huddle next to in winter.

Kakapo Lodge (☎ 03-315 7472; stay-kakapo@xt .co.nz; 14 Amuri Ave; dm $20-24, d $55-80; ▢) YHA affiliated Kakapo has a simple, uncluttere aesthetic enhanced by a roomy kitchen an lounge, underfloor heating to banish winte chill, and an outdoor deck. Besides room in the main lodge, there are also severa motel-style units.

Scenic View Motels (☎ 0800 843 974, 03-315 741 www.hanmerscenicviews.co.nz; 10 Amuri Ave; d $100-18 Scenic View is a relatively new and attrac tive stone complex with modern, colourf studios and two-bedroom apartments, wit mountain views as an added extra. Makes nice change from the bland breed of mot room.

Drifters Inn (☎ 03-315 7554; www.driftersinn.co.r 2 Harrogate St; d from $100) Facilities at this exce lent inn include a cosy lounge area an a large, modern kitchen that's availabl round-the-clock for those with nocturn. stomachs. Prices include a buffet-style cor tinental breakfast.

Cheltenham House (☎ 03-315 7545; www.chelt ham.co.nz; 13 Cheltenham St; s/d from $115/140) St perb B&B close to the thermal pools an with a half-dozen snooze-inducing suite all with en suite or private bathroom an two of them in garden cottages. Cooke breakfasts can be delivered direct to you doona and there's also a full-sized billia table and grand piano to pose next to wit aperitif in hand.

Heritage Hanmer Springs (☎ 0800 368 888, 0 315 7021; www.heritagehotels.co.nz; 1 Conical Hill Rd; from $150; ▨) The broad, Spanish-accente façade of the Heritage is deceptively ur assuming, considering the lodge's luxury studded interior. The garden rooms an villas live up to their promises of flora scented privacy, and the on-site restaura (see review for Heritage Restaurant p532 won't disappoint.

Pancake Rocks (p476), Punakaiki National Park

Swamp forest, Haast (p498)

Greenstone carving, Hokitika (p484)

Fox Glacier (p495)

PAUL K

Banks Peninsula (p526)

Tram, Christchurch (p510)

KRZYSZTOF DYDYNSKI

FERGUS BLAKISTON

Hikers, Aoraki/Mt Cook National Park (p549)

Church of the Good Shepherd (p545), Lake Tekapo

DAVID WALL

Eating

The eating scene in the Hanmer Springs area has ballooned in recent times. At the time of writing, there were a number of new eateries gearing up to open in the vicinity of the Mall, while a wood-and-timber restaurant and shopping complex that's located adjacent to the Hermitage Hotel was still getting established.

Springs Deli Cafe (☎ 03-315 7430; 47 Amuri Ave; meals $9-15; ☺ breakfast & lunch) Cruisy mainstreet café with great breakfast selections and a variety of quiches, focaccias and sweet nibbles for lunch. One of Hanmer Springs better-value cafés, and usually crowded for this reason.

Jollie Jacks Cafe & Bar (☎ 03-315 7388; 12a Conical Hill Rd; mains $13-25; ☺ lunch & dinner) This café is a decent spot for an extended meal, with its pleasant, high-ceilinged interior and scattering of outdoor tables. Daytime fare is along the lines of pizza, Asian beef salad, and corn and crab fritters.

Alpine Village Inn (☎ 03-315 7005; 10 Jacks Pass Rd; mains $12-20; ☺ lunch & dinner) Timber-clad place better known as the local boozer, but doing a sideline in reasonably priced bistro meals, such as a giant T-bone steak and chicken 'cordon bleu'.

Garden House Cafe (☎ 03-315 7115; Amuri Ave; mains $10-14; ☺ lunch & dinner) This café in the thermal reserve has an outside deck on which you can dry out your wrinkly skin and fill your stomach with burgers, omelettes, salads and pastas; also has a kids' menu.

Old Post Office Restaurant (☎ 03-315 7461; 2 Jacks Pass Rd; mains $30; ☺ dinner) This restaurant is much awarded for the way in which the chef wields beef and lamb on a plate. The drool-prompting desserts include meringue roulade with choc mousse.

Heritage Restaurant (☎ 03-315 7021; 1 Conical Hill Rd; mains $25-30; ☺ dinner) The lofty dining room of the upmarket Heritage hotel specialises in NZ produce and has witnessed the devouring of many lamb shanks, pork cutlets and beef steaks in its lifetime, not to mention the guzzling of many Waipara region wines.

Getting There & Away

Hanmer Connection (☎ 0800 377 378) runs from Hanmer Springs to Christchurch ($25) and Kaikoura ($30).

LEWIS PASS HIGHWAY

The Lewis Pass Hwy (SH7) wiggles its way west from the Hanmer Springs turn-off to Lewis Pass, Maruia Springs and Springs Junction. This is a beautiful route, though as it lies at the northern end of the Southern Alps, the 907m-high **Lewis Pass** is not as steep or the forest as dense as on the routes through Arthur's and Haast Passes. The forest near Lewis Pass is mainly red and silver beech, and the kowhai trees that grow along the river terraces are spectacular in spring.

The Lewis Pass area has some interesting walks; pick up the DOC-produced pamphlets *Lewis Pass Region* and *Lake Sumner Conservation Park* (each 50c). Most tracks pass through beech forest. Snow-capped mountains form the backdrop and there are lakes, alpine tarns and mountain rivers. The most popular tramps are those around **Lake Sumner** in the Lake Sumner Conservation Park and the **St James Walkway** in the Lewis Pass National Reserve. Subalpine conditions apply; sign the intentions book at the start of the St James Walkway and at Windy Point for the Lake Sumner area before heading off.

Maruia Springs (☎ 03-523 8840; www.maruia.co.nz; SH7; camp sites $40, d from $130) is a small, highway-side thermal resort on the banks of the Maruia River, 69km from the Hanmer turn-off and 15km east of Springs Junction. It has modern, pricey units (camping and room rates all include admission to the pools) and several eateries, including the **Hot Rocks Cafe** (mains $18-23; ☺ lunch & dinner), which serves upmarket café food such as salmon and polenta patties. But the **thermal pools** (adult/child/family $10/5/25; ☺ 9am-9pm) are the main drawcard here – thermal water is pumped into a sex-segregated traditional Japanese bathhouse and outdoor rock pools that you can relax in no matter what the weather; magic in winter as snowflakes drift down. There are also **private spa houses** (per hr for 2 people $30; ☺ 10.30am-6pm).

From the resort, SH7 continues to **Springs Junction**, where the Shenandoah Hwy (SH65) branches north to meet SH6 near Murchison, while SH7 continues west to Reefton and then down to Greymouth. At the junction of these two highways is the **Alpine Inn** (☎ 03-523 8813; SH7; dm without/with linen $20/33, s/d $60/90), an unusual arrangement of large stone-and-timber units beside a small stream, with rural smells wafting over from nearby paddocks; there's basic backpacker accommodation across the road.

The DOC camping grounds along SH7 include **Marble Hill** (adult/child $5/2.50), 6.5km east of Springs Junction (start of the Lake Daniells walk) and **Deer Valley** (free) at Lewis Pass, 10km east of Maruia Springs.

CENTRAL CANTERBURY

It's about two hours west from Christchurch on SH73 to Arthur's Pass National Park. The trans-island crossing from Christchurch to Greymouth, over Arthur's Pass, is a scenic route covered by buses and the *TranzAlpine* train (see the boxed text, p484).

Nowhere else in NZ do you get a better picture of the climb from sea to mountains. From Christchurch, almost at sea level, the road heads over the flat Canterbury Plains, through rural towns such as Kirwee, Darfield, Sheffield and Springfield. It then winds up into the skiing areas of Porter Heights and Craigieburn before following the Waimakariri and Bealey Rivers to Arthur's Pass, passing good-looking lakes such as Pearson and Grasmere along the way.

To the southwest of Christchurch (reached by SH73 and SH77) is the Mt Hutt ski resort and Methven.

CRAIGIEBURN FOREST PARK

Accessed from SH73, this forest park is 110km northwest of Christchurch and 42km south of Arthur's Pass. The park has a significant system of walking tracks, with longer tramps possible in the valleys west of the Craigieburn Range – see the DOC pamphlet *Craigieburn Forest Park: Day Walks* ($1). Some of the surrounding country is also suitable for skiing and rock climbing (particularly at Castle Hill). Dominating the vegetation is beech, tussock, totara and turpentine scrub; if you're lucky, you may see patches of South Island edelweiss (*Leucogenes grandiceps*).

Craigieburn has a rise of 503m and so is one of NZ's best skiing areas. Its wild-country slopes suit the advanced skier; see Skiing & Snowboarding (p75).

Located between the entrance to the forest park and the Broken River bridge to the south is **Cave Stream Scenic Reserve**, where you can explore a 362m-long cave with a small waterfall at one end; be sure to take all the necessary precautions (two light sources per person etc) if doing the one-hour walk through the pitch-black cave. For details, get the DOC brochure *Cave Stream Scenic Reserve* (50c).

Sleeping & Eating

Smylie's Accommodation (☎ 03-318 4740; www.smylies .co.nz; Main Rd, Springfield; s $20-45, d $65) YHA-associated hostel in the town of Springfield, around 30km southeast of Craigieburn and run by a family whose surname is fortunately not Simpson. There's a strong Japanese influence here, most evident in the food, the popular Japanese bath, *kotatsu* (foot warmer) and some futon-equipped rooms. In winter, ski equipment, meals and ski field transport are provided.

Flock Hill Lodge (☎ 03-318 8196; www.flockhill .co.nz; SH73; dm/d $18/120) High-country sheep station 44km east of Arthur's Pass, adjacent to Lake Pearson and the Craigieburn Forest Park. Backpackers after a rustic experience can stay in old shearers' quarters, while large groups can opt for two-bedroom motel units or large cottages with kitchenette; one room is fully equipped for disabled travellers. When you're not renting mountain bikes or fishing gear, feed your face in the restaurant or bar.

Bealey Hotel (☎ 03-318 9277; www.bealeyhotel .co.nz; dm $20, d $85-95) This hotel is located 12km east of Arthur's Pass at Bealey, a tiny settlement famous for a hoax by the local publican in 1993, which led New Zealanders to believe that a live moa had been sighted in the area. There are self-contained motel units and the budget Moa Lodge with 10 double rooms, plus there's a restaurant and bar.

Wilderness Lodge (☎ 03-318 9246; www.wilderness lodge.co.nz; SH73; d $390-590) Luxurious 20-room lodge on a mountain-beech-speckled sheep station (2,400 hectares worth), 16km east of Arthur's Pass. Alpine views from the bedrooms and daily guided nature walks add to the great outdoors appeal of this stream-threaded property. Breakfast and a gourmet four-course dinner are included in the room price.

ARTHUR'S PASS

The settlement of Arthur's Pass is 4km from the pass of the same name and is the highest-altitude NZ town. The 924m pass was on the route used by Maoris to reach Westland, but its European discovery was made by Arthur Dobson in 1864, when the Westland gold rush created enormous pressure to find a crossing over the Southern Alps from Christchurch. A coach road was completed within a year of Dobson's discovery, but later on the coal and timber trade demanded a railway, duly completed in 1923.

The town is a handy base for walks, climbs, views and winter-time skiing in Arthur's Pass National Park, and makes a good (though long) day trip from Greymouth or Christchurch.

Information

DOC Arthur's Pass visitors centre (☎ 03-318 9211; SH73; ⏱ 8.30am-5pm) has information on all park walks, including route guides for longer hut-lined tramps. It doesn't make onward bookings or reservations, but can help with local accommodation and transport information. The centre also screens a 17-minute video (adult/child $1/free) on the history of Arthur's Pass and has excellent displays – check out the 1888 Cobb & Co coach in a back room.

Trampers can hire detailed topo maps ($1 per day, with $20 refundable deposit) from the visitors centre. Staff also offer invaluable advice on the park's often savagely changeable weather conditions. Check conditions here and fill out an intentions card before going on any walk; be sure to sign out again after returning, otherwise they'll send a search party to find you!

For online information, visit www.softrock.co.nz/apis. There's Internet access at the **Sanctuary** (SH73; per hr $5), a gift shop with a couple of terminals stowed away in a small annex.

About 150m from the visitors centre is the local chapel – make time for a visit and enjoy a lovely surprise inside.

Arthur's Pass National Park

Day walks in this glorious national park offer 360-degree views of snowcapped peaks, many of them over 2000m; the highest is Mt Murchison (2400m). There are huts on the tramping tracks and several areas suitable for camping. The leaflet *Walks in Arthur's Pass National Park* ($1) details walks to scenic places including **Temple Basin** (three hours return), **Mt Bealey**, **Mt Aicken** and **Avalanche Peak** (all six to eight hours return). There's also skiing at Temple Basin; see Skiing & Snowboarding (p75).

Longer tramps with superb alpine backdrops include the two-day **Goat Pass Track** and the difficult **Harman Pass** and **Harpers Pass Tracks**. Such tracks require previous tramping experience – flooding can make the rivers dangerous to cross and the weather is extremely changeable; seek advice from DOC first.

ARTHUR'S PASS

0 —— 200 m
0 —— 0.1 miles

To Temple Basin (4km);
Greymouth (100km)

Devils Punchbowl Creek

Mt Aicken Track

Arthur's Pass National Park

Scotts Track

West Coast Rd

Bealey River

Southern Alps

Chalet Accommodation & Restaurant

Sanctuary
Oscar's Haus
Alpine Cafe

Arthur's Pass Store & Tearooms
Mountain House Backpackers
Outdoor Education Centre
Chapel

Entrance to Otira Tunnel (8.5km)

Arthur's Pass Alpine YHA

Public Telephones

Avalanche Creek

Public Shelter

Avalanche Peak Track

DOC Arthur's Pass Visitors Centre

Start of Bealey/Lyell/ Avalanche Traverse

73

Arthur's Pass

Mountain House Cottages

Transalpine Railway

Southern Alps

Alpine Motel

Rough Creek

Mt Bealey Track

Police Station

To Bealey (12km); Christchurch (158km)

Sleeping & Eating

You can camp within Arthur's Pass township at the basic **public shelter** (adult/child $5/free) where there's stream water, a sink, tables and toilets. Camping is free at **Klondyke Corner**, 8km south of Arthur's Pass, and **Kelly Shelter**, 17km to the northwest; both have toilets and the water must be boiled before drinking.

Arthur's Pass Alpine YHA (☎ 03-318 9230; yha.art hurspass@yha.org.nz; SH73; camp sites $20, dm/d from $20/50) Friendly, well-maintained hostel, with a near-permanent log fire blazing away due to the Southern Alps chill. Offers lots of advice on regional walks and there's plenty of room to stow your gear and bikes.

Mountain House Backpackers (☎ 03-318 9258; www.trampers.co.nz; SH73; camp sites $24, dm/d $21/55) This lodge gets the thumbs up from many travellers for its cosy feel, good facilities and predisposition towards local walks and tramps. The owners also rent some self-contained **cottages** ($150-250) set well back from the roadside, which you can share with strangers or rent out entirely for yourself.

Alpine Motel (☎ 03-318 9233; alpine.motels@xtra .co.nz; SH73; d $70-95) Tucked away in the southern part of town is this small complex of comfortable motel units. Car storage is available if you're going to disappear into the wilderness for a while.

Chalet (☎ 0800 506 550, 03-318 9236; www.arthurs pass.co.nz; SH73; d $110-120; 💻) This large accommodation complex has decent, centrally heated rooms (rate includes breakfast) and an outdoor spa. Downstairs is the **Chalet Restaurant** (mains $13-30; 🕙 lunch & dinner), where you can eat the likes of chicken or veg hot pot and lamb shanks in the bistro or á la carte restaurant. It's the settlement's most upmarket eatery, but the food and service aren't always reliable.

Other dining choices are limited. The **Arthur's Pass Store & Tearooms** (☎ 03-318 9235; SH73; 🕙 7.30am-7pm) sells sandwiches, pies, other hot snacks, basic groceries and expensive petrol; at the time of writing it was expanding its premises. **Oscar's Haus Alpine Cafe** (☎ 03-318 9234; SH73; mains from $10; 🕙 lunch & dinner) is a licensed café serving good-value meals (open until late in summer).

Getting There & Around

Arthur's Pass is on the main run for buses travelling between Christchurch ($25) and Greymouth ($20); **Atomic Shuttles** (☎ 03-322 8883; www.atomictravel.co.nz), **Alpine Coaches** (☎ 0800 274 888; www.alpinecoaches.co.nz) and **Coast to Coast** (☎ 0800 800 847; www.coast2coast.co.nz) stop here.

The *TranzAlpine* train operated by **Tranz Scenic** (☎ 0800 872 467; www.tranzscenic.co.nz) runs between Christchurch and Greymouth via Arthur's Pass. It leaves Arthur's Pass for Greymouth (from $40) at 10.45am and for Christchurch (from $50) at 4pm. Bus and train tickets are sold at the **Arthur's Pass Store** (☎ 03-318 9235; SH73).

The road over the pass was once winding and very steep – the most tortuous of all the passes – but a new, spectacular viaduct has removed many of the treacherous hairpin bends. It's slowly being extended to eliminate areas prone to rockfall.

Mountain House Taxi (☎ 03-318 9258), based at Mountain House Backpackers (above), offers a transport service to the walking tracks and to Temple Basin ski field.

ASHBURTON
pop 15,800

Ashburton, 85km from Christchurch, is the service centre for the surrounding district. There's little reason to linger here, although the nearby Rakaia and Rangitata Rivers attract jetboats and white-water rafters respectively.

As it passes through Ashburton, SH1 is known as West St. Go east over the train line onto parallel East St for the town's main businesses (post office, banks etc). **Ashburton visitors centre** (☎ 03-308 1064; www.ashburton.co.nz; cnr Burnett & East Sts; 🕙 8.30am-5pm Mon-Fri, 10am-3pm Sat, 10am-1pm Sun) handles transport and accommodation bookings.

Ashburton Art Gallery & Museum (☎ 03-308 3167/1133; Baring Sq E; admission by donation; 🕙 10am-4pm Tue-Fri, 1-4pm Sat & Sun) is worth a look for its ever-changing art exhibitions and regional history displays. Beside the highway is the **Ashford Craft Village** (☎ 03-308 9085; 427 West St), a retail showroom of pottery, restored furniture, weaving loomoutput and antiques.

Sleeping & Eating

Coronation Holiday Park (☎ 03-308 6603; 780 East St; camp sites & campervan sites $22, d $34-70; 💻) Two tree-littered hectares of sheltered camp sites and a variety of cabins and tourist flats. Budget travellers can rent one of two backpacker rooms (a double and a twin), which cost $22 for one person and $34 per double; linen not supplied. The adjacent **Coronation Park Motels** (s $70-100, d $85-120) is run by the same people.

Academy Lodge Motel (☎ 0800 107 699, 03-308 5503; 782 East St; s from $70, d $80-95) One of the cheaper motel deals in Ashburton, particularly if you're travelling solo and don't want to stay at a holiday park. Units are old-style but roomy; continental breakfast is provided.

Jesters (☎ 03-308 9983; 9 Mona Sq; mains $12-25; ⟲ dinner Mon-Sat) Locally recommended for its innovative cookery, from home-made chicken liver pâté and oven-baked field mushrooms to the lamb loin marinated in cumin and honey. Ring and check if it's open for lunch.

Cactus Jack's (☎ 03-308 0495; 209 Wills St; mains $18-22; ⟲ dinner) Lively but casual restaurant-bar with a mixture of fajitas, pork and spinach pies, and 'Wanda the Fish' (crumbed catch of the day).

Getting There & Away

InterCity (☎ 03-308 8219; www.intercitycoach.co.nz) stops its buses outside Ashburton's visitors centre on their way between Dunedin and Christchurch. Shuttles such as **South Island Connections** (☎ 0508 742 669, 03-366 6633; www.southislandconnections.co.nz) do the same.

METHVEN

pop 1070

Inland from Ashburton on SH77 is Methven, a good base for the Canterbury Plains or the nearby mountains. Resting for most of the year, Methven wakes up in winter when it fills up with skiers heading to/from Mt Hutt and other ski areas. But there are non-winter activities here too, including excellent hot-air ballooning, fishing and golf.

Information

Methven visitors centre (☎ 03-302 8955; www.methven.net.nz; Main St; ⟲ 7.30am-8pm daily winter, 9am-5pm Mon-Fri & 10am-4.30pm Sat & Sun summer) will book accommodation, skiing packages, transport and activities (also see the website www.nz-holiday.co.nz/methven). Opposite it is the town's **Medical Centre** (☎ 03-302 8105; Main St).

There's a Bank of New Zealand next to the visitors centre. Get online at the visitors centre or **E-mail Shop** (☎ 03-302 8982; Forest Dr).

Activities

It's **skiing** that keeps Methven busy. Nearby **Mt Hutt** (see Skiing & Snowboarding p74) offers five months of skiing (June to October), perhaps the longest ski season of any resort in NZ.

The place to go in Methven for ski rental and advice is **Big Al's Ski & Sport** (☎ 03-302 8003; www.bigals.co.nz; cnr Main St & Forest Dr). It also rents out golf clubs, mountain bikes and fishing gear.

Methven Heliski (☎ 03-435 1834; www.heliskiing.co.nz/methven/about.htm; day trips from $750) operates from July to September, offering trips that include five powder runs (at least 3000 vertical metres), guide service, safety equipment and lunch. Another wintertime business is **Black Diamond Safaris** (☎ 03-302 9696; www.blackdiamondsafaris.co.nz), which takes you to the area's uncrowded club ski fields by 4WD. Prices start at $50 for 4WD transport only; $125 gets you transport, a lift pass and lunch.

Mt Hutt Bungy (☎ 03-302 9969; bungy $100) provides the opportunity for an exhilarating bungy jump from a cantilevered platform at Kea Rock. It markets itself misleadingly as 'NZ's highest bungy', true in terms of the altitude where the jump takes place, but not in terms of the bungy height (43m; Queenstown has much higher jumps). It usually operates only over winter.

The **Mt Hutt Forest** is predominantly mountain beech; it's 14km west of Methven. Adjoining it are the **Awa Awa Rata Reserve** and the **Pudding Hill Scenic Reserve**. There are two access roads: Pudding Hill Rd leads to foot access for Pudding Hill Stream, and McLennan's Bush Rd leads to both reserves. There are many walking trails, including the water-crossing **Pudding Hill Stream Route** (2½ hours) and the **Awa Awa Rata Reserve Loop Track** (1½ hours).

There's a good, easy walk through farmland and the impressive **Rakaia River Gorge** (three to four hours return), beginning at the car park just south of the bridge on SH77. **Rakaia Gorge Alpine Jet** (☎ 03-318 6574; www.rivertours.co.nz; $70) and **Rakaia Gorge Scenic Jet** (☎ 03-318 6515; $60) both do 40-minute jetboat trips to the gorge.

For a sedate aerial experience, try a balloon flight with **Aoraki Balloon Safaris** (☎ 03-302 8172; www.nzballooning.com; flights from $260), which ends with a champagne breakfast.

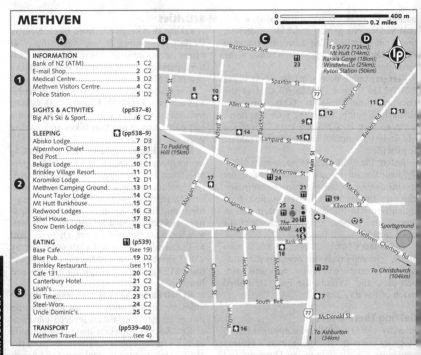

METHVEN

INFORMATION
Bank of NZ (ATM)............................1 C2
E-mail Shop.....................................2 C2
Medical Centre................................3 D2
Methven Visitors Centre..................4 C2
Police Station..................................5 D2

SIGHTS & ACTIVITIES (pp537–8)
Big Al's Ski & Sport.........................6 C2

SLEEPING (pp538–9)
Abisko Lodge...................................7 D3
Alpernhorn Chalet...........................8 B1
Bed Post...9 C1
Beluga Lodge.................................10 C1
Brinkley Village Resort...................11 D1
Koromiko Lodge.............................12 D1
Methven Camping Ground.............13 D1
Mount Taylor Lodge.......................14 C2
Mt Hutt Bunkhouse........................15 C2
Redwood Lodges............................16 C3
Skiwi House....................................17 B2
Snow Denn Lodge..........................18 C3

EATING (p539)
Base Cafe....................................(see 19)
Blue Pub...19 D2
Brinkley Restaurant.....................(see 11)
Cafe 131...20 C2
Canterbury Hotel............................21 C2
Lisah's..22 D3
Ski Time...23 C1
Steel-Worx.....................................24 C2
Uncle Dominic's.............................25 C2

TRANSPORT (pp539–40)
Methven Travel............................(see 4)

Terrace Downs (☎ 0800 465 373, 03-318 6943; www.terracedowns.co.nz; SH72; green fees $90, club hire $30), 25km from Methven near Windwhistle, is a 'high-country resort' with a world-class 18-hole golf course.

Sleeping

Due to the influx of skiers in winter, many places have drying rooms and ski storage. Some are closed in summer, but the following are open year-round, with lowest prices applicable only outside the ski season.

Methven Camping Ground (☎ 03-302 8005; Barkers Rd; camp sites $19, campervan sites $20, d $30-50) Small park keeping to itself off Barkers Rd, close to the centre of town. It's in a scenic location, and the facilities (including a TV room) and cabins are serviceable.

Mt Hutt Bunkhouse (☎ 03-302 8894; mthutt bunks@xtra.co.nz; 8 Lampard St; dm/d from $17/34; 🖳) Offers simple accommodation just off Methven's main street, as well as all the requisite wintertime facilities: ski tuning, boot drying, storage and room heating, and a barbecue for when the snow thaws.

More good facilities and a backpacker-friendly atmosphere are provided at **Skiwi House** (☎ 03-302 8772; www.skiwihouse.co.nz; 30 Chapman St; dm/d from $17/40).

Redwood Lodges (☎ 03-302 8964; www.meth vennzcom; 5 Wayne Pl; s $20-25, d $50) Transformed from a one-time vicarage into two well-appointed travellers' lodges with a communal kitchen area and brightly decorated rooms. You can choose between bunks, quads, doubles and twins (some rooms have an en suite).

Alpernhorn Chalet (☎ 03-302 8779; nzbcoutfitters@ xtra.co.nz; 44 Allen St; per person from $25) Small and inviting budget chalet, with a wonderful conservatory housing an indoor garden and spa pool, and other nice alpine touches such as rimu-carved kitchen benches. Rooms come in double or twin variations and all have shared facilities.

Snow Denn Lodge (☎ 03-302 8999; info@methven accommodation.co.nz; cnr McMillan & Bank Sts; dm/d $25. 65) This centrally located YHA-associated lodge is a modern, purpose-built house with lots of room to lounge in and some appealing dining-living areas, a large kitchen and a spa pool. Prices are a bit higher than your average hostel.

Bed Post (☎ 03-302 8508; www.mthuttbeds.com; 177 Main St; dm $18-22, d $70-95) The Bed Post has room in its lodge for 20 budget-conscious souls, who can make the most of full kitchen and laundry facilities. Others can opt for the fully furnished one- to three-bedroom motel units; larger units can sleep up to eight.

Beluga Lodge (☎ 03-302 8290; www.beluga.co.nz; 40 Allen St; s/d from $150/175) Highly relaxing B&B is on offer at the Beluga Lodge in the form of king-sized beds, an in-house masseur and a garden-sited hydrotherapy pool. Those in need of real de-stressing should consider the garden suite which has its own outdoor spa. A four-bedroom cottage is also available ($300; minimum three-night stay).

Brinkley Village Resort (☎ 0800 161 223, 03-302 8885; www.brinkleyvillage.co.nz; Barkers Rd; d $95-200) Stylish apartment complex with hot tubs, barbecue areas and over 80 rooms to cater to weary post-skiing hordes. The studios are not overly large but are well appointed, and the management is exceptionally helpful. The resort has an á la carte restaurant (see Eating & Drinking below).

Ryton Station (☎ 0800 926 868, 03-318 5818; www.ryton.co.nz; camp sites & campervan sites $5, dm $25, d $120-135) Beautifully isolated 14,800-hectare sheep station, 50km northwest of Methven on the north shore of Lake Coleridge. The high-country accommodation ranges from a wilderness camping ground and 16-bed budget lodge (bedding and meals available from the homestead) to DB&B lakeview chalets. There are also great activities including fishing, walking, horse riding, mountain biking and golf.

Some cosy, friendly, hotel-style lodges:

Abisko Lodge (☎ 03-302 8875; www.abisko.co.nz; 74 Main St; d $90-105) A spa, sauna, pool table, bar and restaurant enhance the enjoyment.

Koromiko Lodge (☎ 03-302 8165; 182 Main St; d from $80) Nice B&B, with two-course dinners by arrangement.

Mount Taylor Lodge (☎ 03-302 9699; www.mount taylorlodge.co.nz; 32 Lampard St; d $90-130) Stylish 11-room lodge only a few years old and with great views of the Alps.

Eating & Drinking

In winter, most of Methven's eateries do a roaring trade nightly but are often open only three to five nights a week in summer; some close down for the entire sunny season.

Canterbury Hotel (☎ 03-302 8045; cnr Main St & Forest Dr; mains $10-20; ☺ lunch & dinner) One of Methven's two pubs, known for obvious reasons as the Brown Pub. This is where locals tend to hang out, either conversing at the bar or eating one of the many solid pub grills, including sausages, schnitzel and 'brontosaurus steak' (500g of rump steak).

Blue Pub (☎ 03-302 8046) The other of the town's pub options, a favourite of the visiting ski crowd for discussing the day's exploits on the mountain. Its **Base Cafe** (mains from $15; ☺ lunch & dinner) goes for slightly more upmarket fare than its counterpart pub across Main St.

Lisah's (☎ 03-302 8070; Main St; mains $15-21; ☺ dinner Wed-Sat) Mellow, red-walled Lisah's is a top local choice. Satisfy your stomach with lemongrass chicken, or carpet bag steak (stuffed with oysters). It's also an intimate wine bar and cocktail lounge.

Ski Time (☎ 03-302 8398; Racecourse Ave; mains $22-27; ☺ dinner) Eye-catching lodge with a stylish dining room, the main features of which are an open fire and a rockpile bar; there's also a pool table in back. The menu is pretty good too, with the Moroccan lamb a quality choice.

Brinkley Restaurant (☎ 03-302 8885; Barkers Rd; mains $17-26; ☺ dinner) This classy restaurant at Brinkley Village Resort does á la carte with panache when guest numbers make it worthwhile. Try the salmon on horserad-ish mash, or the eggplant, zucchini and capsicum torte.

For good pizzas and kebabs, pay a visit to **Uncle Dominic's** (☎ 03-302 8237; the Sq; pizzas $11-21; ☺ lunch Sat & Sun, dinner nightly), while **Cafe 131** (☎ 03-302 9131; Main St; meals $9-14; ☺ lunch summer) has reasonably priced salads, roast veg filo and BLTs.

Several restaurants are open over winter but usually closed over summer. One such place is **Steel-Worx** (☎ 03-302 9900; 36 Forest Dr; meals from $10), with standard mains complemented by cheaper bar snacks such as burgers and pizza.

Getting There & Around

Methven Travel (☎ 03-302 8106) picks up from Christchurch city and airport and delivers you to your accommodation (adult/child

$27/14); other companies also offer this service during the ski season.

InterCity (☎ 03-379 9020; www.intercitycoach.co .nz) has daily buses between Methven and Christchurch ($21).

Many shuttles operate to Mt Hutt ski field in winter for around $20 to $25; inquiries and pick-ups are from the visitors centre.

MT SOMERS

Mt Somers is a small settlement just off SH72, the main road between Geraldine and Mt Hutt. The 17km **Mt Somers Subalpine Walkway** (10 hours) traverses the northern face of Mt Somers, linking the popular picnic spots of Sharplin Falls and Woolshed Creek. Trail highlights include volcanic formations, Maori rock drawings, deep river canyons and botanical diversity. There are two huts on the walk: **Pinnacles Hut** and **Mt Somers Hut** (both $10). Be warned that this route is subject to sudden changes in weather and all tramping precautions should be taken. Hut tickets and information are available at the well-stocked **Mt Somers General Store** (☎ 03-303 9831; Pattons Rd).

Campers and campervan pilots can stay at the small, well-kept **Mt Somers Holiday Park** (☎ 03-303 9719; www.mountsomers.co.nz; Hoods Rd; camp sites $18, campervan sites $20, d $36-55).

At the highway turn-off to Mt Somers is **Stronechrubie** (☎ 03-303 9814; www.strone chrubie.co.nz; SH72; rooms $90-200), with studio and luxury chalets scattered across one hectare of gardens. Its á la carte **restaurant** (mains from $25; ☼ dinner Wed-Sun) has a great reputation for meat and veg meals; if you stay here, consider one of the DB&B packages.

SOUTH CANTERBURY

The SH1 heading south from Christchurch along the coast passes through the port city of Timaru on its way to Dunedin and so gets a lot of traffic. But so does the inland SH8, which weaves towards the bright lakes (Tekapo, Pukaki, Ohau) of Mackenzie Country before veering south through Twizel – it's at this bend in the highway that SH80 branches off north up to the magnificent heights of Aoraki/Mt Cook National Park.

TEMUKA
pop 3950

In 1853 William Hornbrook settled on his run Arowhenua, on the south bank of the Temuka River, with his wife joining him a year later. Arowhenua had long been a *pa* site of the Ngai Tahu people. Their earth ovens, *te umu kaha* (the fierce ovens), gave Te-umu-kaha its name, which later became Temuka.

Temuka visitors centre (☎ 03-615 9537; 72-74 King St; ☼ 8.30am-5.30pm Mon-Fri, 10am-1pm Sat summer, shorter hrs winter) is inside the library.

The site of pioneer aviator Richard Pearse's first attempted flight and a replica of his plane are out on Main Waitohi Rd, 13.5km west of Temuka (signposted from King St) towards Hanging Rock Bridge (see the boxed text, p543).

Located around five kilometres southwest of Waitohi is **Pleasant Point**, which has an interesting **railway museum** (☎ 03-614 8323; www.timaru.com/railway; adult/child/family $6/3/18) at the old train station and a restored railcar that runs along 3km of track mainly on Sunday and public holidays throughout the year.

The central **Temuka Holiday Park** (☎ 03-615 7241; temukaholiday@xtra.co.nz; 1 Fergusson Dr; camp sites $18, campervan sites $20, d $30-40) is planted in the middle of Temuka Domain, and also happens to be next to a mini-golf place and a swimming pool, which makes it highly appealing to park-happy families. Temuka's small collection of motels includes the Elmore Leonard-sounding **Benny's Getaway Motel** (☎ 03-615 8004; www.nzmotels.co.nz/bennys; 54 King St; d $65-75), with dated but clean and well-priced rooms.

About 7km north of Temuka at Winchester is the elegant **Kavanagh House** (☎ 03-615 6150; www.kavanaghhouse.co.nz; SH1; d $250-270), where you can relax by staring up at your king-sized bedroom's ornate ceiling roses, sitting out on your private veranda with a glass of wine, or perhaps sliding across the polished floorboards in your socks. The onsite café-restaurant will keep you well-fed.

TIMARU
pop 27,350

Timaru, an important port city for the surrounding agricultural region, is also a convenient stopping point halfway between Christchurch and Dunedin. Its moniker comes from the Maori name Te Maru, meaning 'The Place of Shelter'. However, no permanent settlement existed here when the first European arrivals, the Weller brothers of Sydney, set up a whaling station in 1839. The *Caroline*, a sailing ship that picked up whale oil, gave the picturesque bay its name.

The town began to boom when a landing service was established at the foot of Strathallan St. It was moved in 1868 to George St and is now a restaurant called the Loaded Hog (see Eating & Drinking p543). After about 30 vessels were wrecked attempting to berth near Timaru between the mid-1860s and 1880s, an artificial harbour was built. Hence today's excellent port and Caroline Bay's beach, a result of breakwater construction.

Orientation & Information

SH1 is known by many names as it passes through Timaru: the Hilton Hwy north of town, Evans St as it enters town and then Theodosia St and Craigie Ave as it bypasses the central business district around Stafford

St. Continuing south, the highway becomes King St and then SH1 again after emerging from town.

The **Timaru visitors centre** (☎ 03-688 6163; info@timaru.com; 14 George St; ⏰ 8.30am-5pm Mon-Fri, 10am-3pm Sat & Sun), diagonally across from the train station, has enthusiastic staff, street maps and information on local walks; it also handles transport bookings. You'll find the **post office** (☎ 03-686 6040; 19 Strathallan St; ⏰ 8.30am-5.30pm Mon-Fri, 9.30am-1pm Sat) in the Books & More store.

For Internet access, try either **Danny's Internet Cafe** (☎ 101 Stafford St; per hr $6) or the pricey Internet café in the **Movie Max 5 cinema** (☎ 03-684 6987; Canon St; Internet access per 10min $2, movies adult/child/student $10/7/8).

Sights

South Canterbury Museum (☎ 03-684 2212; www .timaru.govt.nz; Perth St; admission by donation; ⏰ 10am-4.30pm Tues-Fri, 1.30-4.30pm Sat & Sun) has an interesting collection of historical and natural artefacts of the region, from hand-worked washing machines to fossils. It is housed in a building with the interior look of a

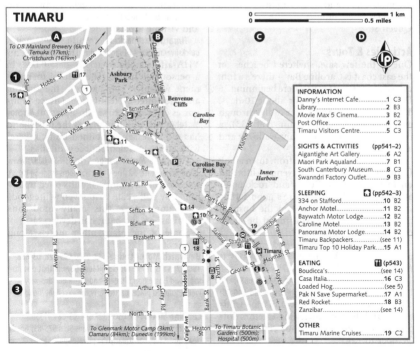

TIMARU

0 — 1 km
0 — 0.5 miles

To DB Mainland Brewery (6km);
Temuka (17km);
Christchurch (163km)

Evans St
Hobbs St
Selwyn St
Grasmere St
White St
Selwyn St
Preston St
Avenue Rd
Wilson St
Le Cren St
Craigie Ave

Ashbury Park
Park View Tce
Benvenue Ave
Virtue Ave
Beverley Rd
Wai-iti Rd
Sefton St
Bidwill St
Elizabeth St
Church St
Arthur St
North St

Dashing Rocks Walk
Benvenue Cliffs
Caroline Bay
Marine Pde
Caroline Bay Park
Inner Harbour
Port Loop Rd
The Terrace
Sophia St
Stafford St
Strathallan St
Ritchie St
Fraser St
Perth St
George St
Hayman St
Hayes St
Bank St
Theodosia St

To Glenmark Motor Camp (3km);
Oamaru (84km); Dunedin (199km)
Heaton St
To Timaru Botanic Gardens (500m);
Hospital (500m)

INFORMATION
Danny's Internet Cafe.............1 C3
Library...................................2 B3
Movie Max 5 Cinema..............3 B2
Post Office............................4 C2
Timaru Visitors Centre...........5 C3

SIGHTS & ACTIVITIES (pp541–2)
Aigantighe Art Gallery.............6 A2
Maori Park Aqualand...............7 B1
South Canterbury Museum......8 C3
Swanndri Factory Outlet..........9 B3

SLEEPING (pp542–3)
334 on Stafford....................10 B2
Anchor Motel.......................11 B2
Baywatch Motor Lodge.........12 B2
Caroline Motel.....................13 B2
Panorama Motor Lodge.........14 B2
Timaru Backpackers.......(see 11)
Timaru Top 10 Holiday Park....15 A1

EATING (p543)
Boudicca's.....................(see 14)
Casa Italia..........................16 C3
Loaded Hog....................(see 5)
Pak N Save Supermarket.......17 A1
Red Rocket..........................18 B3
Zanzibar........................(see 14)

OTHER
Timaru Marine Cruises..........19 C2

circus big-top. Hanging from the ceiling á la trapeze is a replica of the aeroplane designed and flown by Richard Pearse (see the boxed text, opposite).

Aigantighe Art Gallery (☎ 03-688 4424; 49 Wai-iti Rd; admission free; ⓨ 11am-4pm Tue-Fri, noon-4pm Sat & Sun) is one of the South Island's largest public galleries, a 900-piece collection of NZ and European art from the previous four centuries set up in a 1908 mansion, and adorned externally by a sculpture garden. The gallery's Gaelic name means 'at home'.

DB Mainland Brewery (☎ 03-688 2059; Sheffield St; tours free; ⓨ tours 10.30am Mon-Fri), 6km north of town, offers free tours of its brewing and bottling plant. Enclosed footwear (no sandals or thongs) must be worn; bookings required.

If you're in need of woollens or oilskins, drop by the trademark **Swanndri Factory Outlet** (☎ 03-684 9037; 24 Church St; ⓨ 10am-4.30pm Mon-Fri, 10am-2pm Sat), where discounted high-quality clothing is in abundance.

The lovely **Botanic Gardens** (admission free; ⓨ 8am-dusk), established in 1864, have ponds, a conservatory and NZ's largest collection of species roses (numbering 50); enter from Queen St.

Activities & Tours

One of the few safe, sheltered beaches on the east coast is Caroline Bay – there's a fun, crowded **Christmas Carnival** here beginning 26 December and running for about 10 days. The beachside **park** has a walk-through aviary, a wading pool, mini-golf ($3), a roller-skating rink, a pleasant walkway and a landscaped 'piazza'.

A good **walk** heads north from town along Caroline Bay, past the Benvenue Cliffs and on to the Dashing Rocks and rock pools at the end of the bay. There's good **surfing** in the south of town, east of the hospital at Patiti Point, where you might be lucky enough to spot sea lions.

The calmest waters around are in the pool at **Maori Park Aqualand** (☎ 03-688 4504; Te Weka St; adult/child $3/1.50).

Timaru Marine Cruises (☎ 03-688 6881; No 1 Wharf, cnr Loop Rd & Ritchie St; adult/child $40/20) checks out the wide variety of marine wildlife around the port, including Hectors dolphins and seals, on 1½-hour cruises from October to April.

Sleeping

Timaru Top 10 Holiday Park (☎ 0800 242 121, 03-684 7690; www.timaruholidaypark.co.nz; 8 Glen St; camp sites $22, campervan sites $24, d $37-75) Satisfyingly green parkland site with an excellent amenities block and a golf course next door where you can swing clubs without paying any green fees. If budgeting, you could squeeze five people into a standard cabin for less than $75.

Glenmark Motor Camp (☎ 03-684 3682; www .timarumotorcamp.co.nz; Beaconsfield Rd; camp sites $18, campervan sites $20, d $30-60; ▣) Glenmark is a spread-out park with modern cabins lazing near a river 3km south of the centre. It's a generally peaceful place, except when kids discover the small on-site swimming pool.

334 On Stafford (☎ 03-684 4729; www.334 onstafford.co.nz; 334 Stafford St; dm $20-22, d $50-65; ▣) This renovated neoclassical building has some attractive features and excellent facilities (free Internet, pool table, videos, piano), though the hostel within it is yet to develop its own independent character. The more-expensive dorms are bigger and newer; there's also on **art gallery** (admission free; ⓨ 10am-4pm Mon-Sat, 1-4pm Sun) exhibiting local and visiting artists.

Timaru Backpackers (☎ 03-684 5067; rotty@ quicksilver.net.nz; 44 Evans St; dm/d from $17/40) This YHA-affiliated backpackers' has 40 beds in a personable house. The helpful management will pick you up from the station, and they offer cycle hire too. Direct all inquires (and check in) at the adjacent **Anchor Motel** (d $65), which manages the hostel and has old-style self-contained units, several with either wheelchair access or spas.

Panorama Motor Lodge (☎ 03-688 0097; www .panorama.net.nz; 52 The Bay Hill; rooms from $110) A selection of ultramodern units piled up behind Bay Hill's café strip. Even whitegoods sales don't have this many mod-cons (dishwasher, spa bath, hairdryers...).

Some of the many other motels along Evans St:

Baywatch Motor Lodge (☎ 0800 929 828, 03-688 1886; 7 Evans St; d $100-135) Move beyond that disturbing David Hasselhoff imagery and check out this very well-equipped place, particularly the excellent 'deluxe' units.

Caroline Motel (☎ 0508-227 654, 03-684 4155; www.carolinemotel.co.nz; 46-48 Evans St; d $75-85) Good clean motel fun, particularly the private spa.

The visitors centre has details of B&Bs and farmstays in the area.

Eating & Drinking

Zanzibar (☎ 03-688 4367; 56 The Bay Hill; mains $12-25; ☺ lunch & dinner) One of several refreshingly casual, well-patronised café-restaurants on The Bay Hill, Zanzibar has a great breakfast menu and later-in-the-day dishes such as lamb curry. The light, airy interior is a good place for morning conversation or an afternoon drink around the copper-hued bar.

Boudicca's (☎ 03-688 8550; 64 The Bay Hill; mains $14-25; ☺ lunch & dinner) Another popular Bay Hill eatery, this one with a plain interior but a fair range of kebabs, and fish dishes such as blue bayou gumbo and gurnard fillets with paella. Also does good espressos and doubles as an evening wine bar.

Red Rocket (☎ 03-688 8313; 4 Elizabeth St; mains $11-19; ☺ lunch & dinner) Eat simple pasta dishes and gourmet science-fiction-styled pizzas ('light saber lamb', 'cling-on gourmet chicken') in a nicely converted old church. The attempted connection between pizzas, space travel and a house of worship is rather odd, but the food (particularly the seafood pizza) is great.

Loaded Hog (☎ 03-684 9999; 2 George St; meals $5-18; ☺ lunch & dinner) Located in the lava-built (basalt bluestone) former Landing Service building adjacent to the visitors centre, this casual barn of a place has a $5 lunchtime pig-out (quiche, *panini*, stuffed spud) and sizeable meaty meals for dinner.

Casa Italia (☎ 03-684 5528; 2 Strathallan St; mains $19-25; ☺ lunch & dinner) The historic 1902 Customs House makes a fine setting for Casa Italia's fine Italian food. Try the beef-filled ravioli pomodoro or the pork funghi in hollandaise sauce, accompanied by a drop of red or white.

Pak N Save supermarket (☎ 03-688 6011; Northtown Mall, cnr Ranui & Evans Sts; ☺ 8am-9pm Mon-Fri, 8am-7pm Sat & Sun) The self-sufficient will be able to shop here.

Getting There & Away

InterCity (☎ 03-684 7195; www.intercitycoach.co.nz) stops outside the train station, from where its buses head to Christchurch ($26), Dunedin ($31) and Invercargill ($55). There are also numerous shuttle buses running between Christchurch and Dunedin that

---

FLIGHTS OF FANCY

Richard Pearse (1877–1953), a farmer and inventor, was born at Waitohi, northwest of Timaru. Once known to locals as 'Mad Pearse' and 'Bamboo Dick' (because he employed bamboo in his inventions), he may well have been the first human to fly in a heavier-than-air machine.

Pearse was a loner who tinkered away in his shed, building aircraft with home-made tools. His first plane, 8m wide, was made of scrap metal and bamboo braced by wire and powered by a simple two-cylinder engine which he designed himself; underneath were bicycle wheels.

It's reputed that he first flew about 1km in 1902 or 1903 before crash-landing in gorse near the Ophir River. The flight was supposedly witnessed by several people, but no exact date has been ascertained. Many believe his attempts were before the Wright brothers flew at Kittyhawk, North Carolina, on 17 December 1903.

Pearse disappeared into obscurity and died a recluse in a psychiatric hospital in Christchurch. But interest in his inventions grew after his death and he is remembered in Auckland's **Museum of Transport & Technology** (p101) and in the **South Canterbury Museum** (p541), where there's a reconstruction of his first aircraft. There's also a memorial at the point where his first flight supposedly commenced.

---

stop at Timaru, including **Atomic Shuttles** (☎ 03-322 8883; www.atomictravel.co.nz); the average fare to Christchurch or Dunedin is $20 to $25.

Cook Connection (☎ 0800 266 526, 0274-583 211; www.cookconnect.co.nz) runs between Timaru and Mt Cook ($45) via Fairlie ($15), Lake Tekapo ($25) and Twizel ($27). On alternate days it connects Mt Cook and Oamaru.

TO MACKENZIE COUNTRY

Those heading to Queenstown and the southern lakes from Christchurch will probably turn off SH1 onto SH79, along a scenic route towards the high country (p545) that signals the rise of Aoraki/Mt Cook National Park's eastern foothills. The road passes through the small towns of Geraldine and Fairlie before joining SH8, which heads over Burkes Pass to the blue intensity of Lake Tekapo.

Geraldine

pop 2325

Geraldine has an affable country-village atmosphere due in part to its pretty private gardens and active craft scene. For information, contact the **Geraldine visitors centre** (☎ 03-693 1006; information@geraldine.co.nz; Talbot St; ⊗ 8.30am-5pm Mon-Fri, 10am-4pm Sat & Sun). The town also has a **DOC office** (☎ 03-693 1010; Nth Tce).

The **Vintage Car & Machinery Museum** (☎ 03-693 8005; 178 Talbot St; adult/child $5/free; ⊗ 10am-4pm daily from late Oct–early Jun, 10am-4pm Sat & Sun winter) has over 30 vintage and veteran cars from 1907 onwards, while a huge shed at the back houses 100 tractors dating from 1912. There's also a rare 1929 Spartan Biplane and tonnes of heavy-duty farm equipment.

In the second week of January, there's boot-scootin' mayhem to acts like the Coal Rangers and the Dusty Spittle show during the annual **Geraldine Country Music Festival** (concert tickets $5-15).

SLEEPING & EATING

You'll find basic DOC camping grounds at **Orari Gorge** (Yates Rd; camp sites $8), 12km northwest of Geraldine, and **Waihi Gorge** (Waihi Gorge Rd; per person $4), 14km northwest of Geraldine; both have good swimming spots and picnic areas.

Geraldine Motor Camp (☎ 03-693 8147; geraldine .motor.camp@xtra.co.nz; 39 Hislop St; camp sites & campervan sites $20, d $30-80) Triangular, well-treed slice of greenery across the road from a large oval (just in case you needed more room to roam). Besides budget cabins and self-contained units, staff can also set you up in a two-bedroom house.

Olde Presbytery Backpackers (☎ 03-693 9644; pkoelet@hotmail.com; 13 Jollie St; dm/s/d $20/30/50) Splendid place across the road from Talbot Forest Scenic Reserve and with its own serene garden. This snug house has only three rooms (one single, one double and a four-bed dorm), so come here if you're seeking salvation from overcrowded hostels.

Crown Hotel (☎ 03-693 8458; geraldine-crown@ xtra.co.nz; 31 Talbot St; s & d $45-90) This 1906 hotel has a dozen above-average pub rooms and a big guest balcony. Gets bonus points for being one of the few hotels that was honest

enough to warn us away from rooms above the bar when a band was due to play that night.

Geraldine Motels (☎ 0800 400 404, 03-693 8501; www.nzmotels.co.nz/geraldine; 97 Talbot St; s/d from $65/75) The most central motel option, with a range of old-style units and a couple of newish, nicely outfitted studios. There's also a spa pool, kids' playground and a pleasant yard out back.

Totara Restaurant (☎ 03-693 8458; 31 Talbot St; mains $13-25; ⊗ lunch & dinner) Totara is inside the Crown Hotel and serves filling, good-value meals such as country roast and crumbed herb chicken; it has a popular stonegrill, where ostrich, lamb and beef are cooked over very hot rocks.

Also part of the Crown Hotel is the nearby **Village Inn Cafe Bar** (☎ 03-693 1004; 41 Talbot St; mains $10-20; ⊗ lunch & dinner), dominated by a long bar and serving mains such as ostrich framboesia (seared fillet with raspberry demiglace) and a separate kids' menu.

Berry Barn Complex (☎ 03-693 9900; cnr Cox & Talbot Sts) caters to hungry blow-ins with a bakery, cafés and a cheese shop selling tasty Talbot Forest Cheeses. Also here is **Barker's** (☎ 03-693 9727), a reputable fruit-products emporium selling fine juices, sauces, smoothies and jams.

Peel Forest

The Peel Forest, 19km north of Geraldine (signposted off SH72), is among NZ's most important indigenous podocarp (conifer) forests. A road from nearby Mt Peel station leads to **Mesopotamia**, the run of English writer Samuel Butler (author of the satire *Erewhon*) in the 1860s.

Get information such as the *Peel Forest Park: Track Information* brochure ($1) at **Peel Forest Store** (☎ 03-696 3567; Rd 20; ⊗ from 8am Mon-Sat, from 10am Sun), which stocks petrol, groceries and takeaway food. The store also manages the DOC camping ground beside the **Rangitata River** (camp sites $14, campervan sites $17, dm adult/child $15/6), about 3km beyond the store and equipped with two- to four-berth cabins, showers, a kitchen, laundry and cardphone.

The magnificent podocarp forest consists of totara, kahikatea and matai. One fine example of totara on the **Big Tree Walk** has a circumference of 9m and is over 1000 years old. Local bird life includes the rifleman,

NZ pigeon (kereru), bellbird, fantail and grey warbler. There are also trails to several picturesque waterfalls: **Emily Falls** (1½ hours return), **Rata Falls** (two hours return) and **Acland Falls** (one hour return).

Rangitata Rafts (☎ 0800 251 251, 03-696 3534; www.rafts.co.nz) goes white-water rafting on the Rangitata River, which contains exhilarating grade V rapids. The company's base is at Mt Peel, about 11km past the camping ground, where there's some budget lodge **accommodation** (dm/d $12/34). Rafting trips can be taken from either Peel Forest ($135) or Christchurch ($145) and include hot showers and a barbecue; time spent on the river is three hours.

Fairlie
pop 845
Fairlie is often described as 'the gateway to the Mackenzie' because west of here the landscape changes dramatically as the road mounts Burkes Pass to the open spaces of Mackenzie Country.

The **Resource Centre** (☎ 03-685 8496; www.fairlie.co.nz; 64 Main St; ☜ 10am-4pm Mon-Fri) is the local visitors centre. Buses and shuttles pass through town on the Christchurch–Queenstown route.

There's skiing 37km northwest of here at **Fox Peak** in the Two Thumb Range. **Mt Dobson**, 26km northwest of Fairlie, is in a 3km-wide basin (see Skiing & Snowboarding p74). The **Ski Shack** (☎ 03-685 8088; SH8) has information and gear rental.

SLEEPING & EATING
Fairlie Gateway Top 10 Holiday Park (☎ 03-685 8375; www.fairlietop10.co.nz; 10 Allandale Rd; camp sites & campervan sites $22, d $35-75) Tranquil, creekside park that is perfect for families, as it has a large playground for children to hurl themselves around and can also provide baby baths, cots and highchairs.

Rimuwhare Country Retreat (☎ 03-685 8058; rimuwhare@xtra.co.nz; 53 Mt Cook Rd; d $75) This commendable place has old-fashioned but spacious units well off the main road and a well-established garden to frolic in, plus a licensed **restaurant** (mains $21-28; ☜ lunch & dinner) that can supply good veg meals. You can also rent reasonable units at **Pinewood Motels** (☎ 03-685 8599; www.pinewoodmotels.co.nz; 25-27 Mt Cook Rd; d from $70), including one that's wheelchair-accessible.

Old Library Cafe (☎ 03-685 8999; 6 Allandale Rd; mains $15-25; ☜ lunch & dinner) Has elegant touches like an old pressed-metal ceiling and serves fresh, tasty food such as chicken roesti (sautéed chook in a brandy-mushroom sauce on a potato cake). The wine selection is great and includes some Aussie reds.

MACKENZIE COUNTRY
The expansive high ground from which the peaks of Aoraki/Mt Cook National Park grow is known as Mackenzie Country after the legendary James 'Jock' McKenzie, who's said to have run his stolen flocks around 1843 in this then-uninhabited region (nobody's sure why the region and the chap himself have different spellings). When he was finally caught, other settlers realised the potential of the land and followed in his footsteps. The first people to traverse the Mackenzie were Maoris, who used to trek from Banks Peninsula to Otago hundreds of years ago.

Lake Tekapo
pop 295
This small township at the southern end of its namesake lake has unobstructed views across turquoise water, with hills and snow-capped mountains as a backdrop – for an explanation of why this and other lakes in the region have such striking coats of blue, see the boxed text below. Tekapo derives its name from the Maori words *taka* (sleeping mat) and *po* (night), though it's not clear if this refers to indigenous sleeping habits or a Maori encounter with early explorers.

BLUE CRUSH
The blazing turquoise colour of Lake Tekapo, a characteristic it shares with other regional bodies of water such as Lake Pukaki, is due to 'rock flour' (sediment) in the water. This so-called flour was created when the lake's basin was gouged out by a stony-bottomed glacier moving across the land's surface, with the rock-on-rock action grinding out fine particles that ended up being suspended in the glacial melt water. This sediment gives the water a milky quality and refracts the sunlight beaming down, hence the brilliant colour.

CANTERBURY

Lake Tekapo is a popular first stop on tours of the Southern Alps, with Mt Cook and Queenstown buses chugging up to the cluster of main-road tourist shops to create some short-lived retail chaos.

Kiwi Treasures (☎ 03-680 6686; SH8; ☼ 7.30am-8pm summer, limited hrs winter) is both souvenir shop and visitors centre; for Web-based information visit www.laketekapountouched .co.nz.

Located nearby is the town's **post office** (SH8; ☼ 8.30am-5.30pm). There's **Internet access** (per 20min $2) at the Tekapo Helicopters office (p547).

SIGHTS & ACTIVITIES

The diminutive, picturesque **Church of the Good Shepherd** beside the lake was built of stone and oak in 1935. Further along is a **statue** of a collie dog, a tribute to the sheepdogs that helped develop the Mackenzie Country. It's a good idea to visit after the last bus group leaves, otherwise the place is swarming with rubberneckers.

Popular **walks** include the track to the summit of **Mt John** (three hours) from just beyond the camping ground. From there, continue on to **Alexandrina** and **McGregor Lakes**, making it an all-day walk. Other walks are detailed in the brochure *Lake Tekapo Walkway* ($1).

Lake Tekapo Adventures & Cruises (☎ 0800 528 624, 021-680 650; www.laketekapo.co.nz; cruise from $38) organises activities in the vicinity of the Godley Glacier ranging from 4WD safaris and mountain-bike runs to fishing and lake cruises. **Mackenzie Alpine Trekking Company** (☎ 0800 628 269, 03-680 6760; www.laketekapo.cc/matc; 1hr ride $45, full-day ride $220) organises four-footed high-country transport.

In winter, Lake Tekapo is a base for **downhill skiing** at Mt Dobson or Round Hill and **cross-country skiing** on the Two Thumb Range, providing ski area transport and ski hire. Lake Tekapo also has an open-air **ice-skating rink** (☼ Jun-Sep).

Alpine Recreation (☎ 0800 006 096, 03-680 6736; www.alpinerecreation.co.nz) organises mountaineering and climbing courses, guided treks and ski touring in Aoraki/Mt Cook National Park. The challenging three-day Ball Pass Trek between the Tasman and Hooker Valleys costs $700.

LAKE TEKAPO

0 — 300 m
0 — 0.2 miles

To Mt John Track (200m);
Lake Tekapo Motels (200m);
Motor Camp (200m)

Lake Tekapo

To Airport (3km);
Twizel (58km);
Mt Cook (99km)

Simpson La

Boat Ramp

Tekapo River

Pioneer Dr

Roto Pl

Aorangi Cres

Mackenzie St

Scally St

Alpine Garden

Alexandra Pl

Greta St

To Burkes Pass (18km);
Fairlie (42km)

Allan St

INFORMATION	
Kiwi Treasures.......................1 B2	
Police Station.......................2 C2	
Post Office...........................3 B2	

SIGHTS & ACTIVITIES	(p546)
Church of the Good Shepherd...4 D1	
Sheepdog Statue....................5 D1	

SLEEPING	(p547)
Godley Resort Hotel................6 C2	
Lake Tekapo Lodge.................7 B2	
Lake Tekapo Scenic Resort.......8 B2	
Lake Tekapo YHA...................9 B1	
Tailor-Made-Tekapo	
Backpackers.......................10 B3	
The Chalet..........................11 D2	

EATING	(p547)
Four Square Discounter	
Supermarket.......................12 B2	
Kohan................................13 C2	
Pepe's...............................14 C2	
Reflections..........................15 B2	

TRANSPORT	(pp547-8)
Tekapo High Country Crafts.....16 B2	

OTHER	
Air Safaris...........................17 B2	
Tekapo Helicopters................18 C2	

TOURS

Air Safaris (☎ 0800 806 880, 03-680 6880; www.air
safaris.co.nz) does 50-minute flights over Mt
Cook and its glaciers (adult/child $240/
160), taking you up the Tasman Glacier,
over the upper part of the Fox and Franz
Josef Glaciers, and by Mts Cook, Tasman
and Elie de Beaumont. It does a similar
flight from Glentanner Park (see Aoraki/
Mt Cook National Park, p552) for an extra
$20 per person.

Tekapo Helicopters (☎ 0800 359 835, 03-680 6229;
www.tekapohelicopters.co.nz) has 25-minute flights
($180) and 45-minute trips ($320) that all
include icefield landings and grand viewings
of Mt Cook and the glaciers.

SLEEPING

Lake Tekapo Motels & Motor Camp (☎ 0800 853 853,
03-680 6825; laketekapo-accommodation.co.nz; camp sites &
campervan sites $24, d $45-120) Has an exception-
ally pretty and peaceful lakeside locale, plus
everything from cabins to motel units. Bedding hire for the cabins costs $10.

Lake Tekapo YHA (☎ 03-680 6857; yha.laketekapo@
yha.org.nz; 3 Simpson Lane; camp sites $20, dm/d from $21/
50) Friendly, well-equipped little place, its
living room adorned with open fireplaces
and outstanding views across the lake to the
mountains beyond, but with no TV to dominate proceedings. There are limited camp
sites here; book ahead if you want one.

Tailor-Made-Tekapo Backpackers (☎ 03-680 6700;
www.tailor-made-backpackers.co.nz; 9-11 Aorangi Cres;
dm/d from $19/45; 🖳) This hostel favours beds
rather than bunks and is spread over a pair of
well-tended houses on a peaceful side-street,
well away from the main-road traffic. An
effort has been made to brighten up the interior and there's a barbecue-equipped garden; couch potatoes note there's no TV.

Godley Resort Hotel (☎ 0800 835 276, 03-680
6848; www.tekapo.co.nz; d $90-160; 🏊) This large
hotel is favoured by tour groups and has
older-style budget rooms as well as smarter
refurbished rooms with lake views. A gym,
spa and swimming pool are among the attractive facilities, and the hotel also rents
bikes and organises fishing and golfing
excursions.

Lake Tekapo Scenic Resort (☎ 03-680 6808; www
.laketekapo.com; SH8; d $150-220) Not so much a
self-contained resort as a centrally located
complex of attractively modern studio and
family units, with only bare parkland separ-

ating it from the lake. Breakfast is an added
extra ($10 per person).

Chalet (☎ 0800 843 242, 03-680 6774; speck@xtra
.co.nz; 14 Pioneer Dr; d $120-200) The lakefront Cha-
let is on a property that stretches well back
from the road and has some lovely, well-
designed studios and one-/two-bedroom
units with access to a back garden. It also
rents out local holiday houses.

Lake Tekapo Lodge (☎ 0800 525 383, 03-680 6566;
www.laketekapolodge.co.nz; 24 Aorangi Cres; d $200-295)
Luxurious hilltop B&B set in a youthful
brick home with a monasterial entryway.
Three of its four rooms have direct access
to the great views from the back decking.
Apparently the star gazing is good out here
at night.

EATING

Pepe's (☎ 03-680 6677; SH8; meals from $12; 🍽 lunch
& dinner) Filled with large booths and its walls
decorated with skiing paraphernalia, Pepe's
is an atmospheric little place in which to
attack various pastas and gourmet pizzas
such as their specialty pepperoni, a 'smoked
salmon siesta', or the 'vegetarian vintage'
(fired up with horseradish sauce).

Reflections (☎ 03-680 6808; SH8; mains $15-27;
🍽 lunch & dinner) The bistro section of Lake
Tekapo Scenic Resort has nicely prepared
meals such as salmon roulade and venison
pie, which you can eat in the plain interior
or at an outside table that looks down to
the lake.

Kohan (☎ 03-680 6688; SH8; mains $13-25; 🍽 lunch
& dinner Mon-Sat, lunch Sun) You'll find the truly
clinical décor of this Japanese restaurant
down a path beside the Godley Resort
Hotel. It caters mainly to transient tour
groups, hence the lack of attention to interior niceties, but on the plus side it offers
a full range of sushi treats and dishes such
as teriyaki chicken and tempura seafood;
takeaway is an option.

Four Square Discounter supermarket (SH8;
🍽 7.30am-9pm) Pick up supplies here.

GETTING THERE & AWAY

Southbound services to Queenstown ($40),
Wanaka ($50), Mt Cook ($25), and north-
bound services to Christchurch ($40), are
offered by **InterCity** (☎ 03-379 9020; www.intercity
coach.co.nz). **Southern Link Shuttles** (☎ 03-358
8355; www.yellow.co.nz/site/southernlink), **Atomic Shuttles** (☎ 03-322 8883; www.atomictravel.co.nz) and

Cook Connection (☎ 0800 266 526, 0274-583 211; www.cookconnect.co.nz) include Lake Tekapo on their routes; ticket prices range from $20 to $45 for most destinations.

Between them, **Kiwi Treasures** (☎ 03-680 6686; SH8) and **Tekapo High Country Crafts** (☎ 03-680 6656; SH8) handle bookings for visiting buses.

Lake Pukaki

On the southern shore of Lake Pukaki, 45km southwest of Lake Tekapo and 2km northeast of the turn-off to Mt Cook, is the **Lake Pukaki visitors centre** (☎ 03-435 3280; lake.pukaki@xtra.co.nz; SH8; ☼ 9.30am-5pm Mon-Sat, 10am-5pm Sun), with reams of information on Mackenzie Country. But the highlight here is the sterling **lookout** that on a clear day gives a picture-perfect view of Mt Cook and its surrounding peaks, with the ultra-blue lake in the foreground. For an explanation of the lake's colour, see the boxed text on p545.

Twizel

pop 1140

The uneventful town of Twizel, just south of Lake Pukaki and rather vaguely self-labelled the 'Town of Trees', only came into existence in 1968, when it was built to service construction of the nearby hydroelectric power station. The town's survival beyond that project is thanks to the tenacity of residents and its handy proximity to Mt Cook (a 45-minute drive away).

Right in town is the **Twizel visitors centre** (☎ 03-435 3124; www.twizel.com; Market Pl; ☼ 9am-6pm daily Oct-Apr, 10am-4pm Mon-Sat May-Sep).

ACTIVITIES

Nearby **Lake Ruataniwha** is popular for rowing, boating and windsurfing. **Fishing** in local rivers, canals and lakes is also big business; ask at the visitors centre.

Helibikes (☎ 0800 435 424, 03-435 0626; www.helibike.com) flies you by helicopter up a mountain, which you then ride down on two wheels; one such trip is the 3½-hour Benmore descent ($220). There are also regular mountain-biking trips (no helicopters involved), such as a two-hour ride along farm tracks ($55).

The black stilt is the rarest wader species in the world (only found in the Mackenzie Basin). You can do a one-hour tour of the **Kaki Visitor Hide** (☎ 03-435 3124; adult/child $13/5),

which is adjacent to a DOC-run captive breeding centre. Bookings are essential and tours depart Twizel visitors centre (you need your own transport).

TOURS

Glacier Southern Lakes Helicopters (☎ 03-435 0370; www.heli-flights.co.nz) flies over the Mt Cook region from a helipad beside Mackenzie Country Inn. Flights last from 25 minutes ($210) to 70 minutes ($510) and include either a snow or glacier landing.

SLEEPING

Lake Ruataniwha Holiday Park (☎ 03-435 0613; holidaypark2000@xtra.co.nz; Max Smith Dr; camp sites $20, campervan sites $22, d $36-50) Four kilometres south of Twizel is this 20-hectare park. The cabins look a bit shabby but are OK inside. Canoes and waterbikes can usually be hired, otherwise you can sun yourself on the lake-top pontoon.

Parklands Alpine Tourist Park (☎ 03-435 0507; parklands1@xtra.co.nz; 122 Mackenzie Dr; camp sites $20, campervan sites $22, dm $18, d $40-85) Another park option, offering some very good accommodation in a colourfully refurbished maternity hospital set on pretty grounds.

Omahau Downs (☎ 03-435 0199; omahaudowns@xtra.co.nz; SH8; dm $18-20, d $45-85) Thoroughly relaxing rural homestead on a soporific plot just north of Twizel, where guests suspend plans and obligations to soak themselves in the unique wood-fired alfresco bathtub, or just gaze across the fields at Mt Cook. Three-bed dorms, cottage rooms and main-house B&B are all on offer.

High Country Lodge (☎ 03-435 0671; www.highcountrylodge.co.nz; Mackenzie Dr; dm $18, s from $35, d $50-80) Cabins originally built for hydro-scheme workers are now put to work accommodating out-of-towners. There's a large range of sturdy, good-value accommodation, beginning with two-bed dorms, plus an on-site bar-restaurant, games room and a nine-hole golf course opposite.

Mackenzie Country Inn (☎ 03-435 0869; bookings@mackenzie.co.nz; cnr Ostler & Wairepo Rds; rooms from $145) Prominent log-and-rock hotel with large, comfortable rooms that gets business by the bus-load (literally) during peak times. Rents bikes to guests and nonguests alike from $10.

Mountain Chalet Motels (☎ 0800 629 999, 03-435 0785; www.mountainchalets.co.nz; Wairepo Rd; dm/d from

$18/95) Highly recommended place to stay, with well-equipped A-frame chalets. The cheapest units are studios, but there are a number of two-bedroom beasts for larger groups/families, too.

EATING
Korner Kafe (☎ 03-435 0501; 1/20 Market Pl; mains $10-25; ☺ lunch & dinner) Poor spelling aside, this is a locally recommended place with plenty of veg options such as frittata, roast veg platters and filo, plus several salads. It also serves lots of T-bone and porterhouse with various sauces.

Hunter's Cafe & Bar (☎ 03-435 0303; 2 Market Pl; mains $13-24; ☺ lunch & dinner) This café is also locally recommended. It's a light, open space with benches around the walls and sundry tables bordering a large bar space. It supplies generous mains and has cheaper bar snacks for small-stomached folk, as well as lots of wine by the bottle or glass.

GETTING THERE & AWAY
Buses belonging to **InterCity** (☎ 03-379 9020; www.intercitycoach.co.nz) stop at Twizel on route to Mt Cook. The Christchurch–Queenstown shuttles such as **Southern Link Shuttles** (☎ 03-358 8355; www.yellow.co.nz/site/southernlink) and **Atomic Shuttles** (☎ 03-322 8883; www.atomictravel.co.nz) also stop here. The **Cook Connection** (☎ 0800 266 526, 0274-583 211; www.cookconnect.co.nz) calls in at Twizel on its way from Mt Cook (one-way/return $15/25) to Timaru ($27) and Oamaru ($27).

High Country Shuttles (☎ 0800 435 050, 03-435 0506) also has services between Twizel and Mt Cook (one-way/return $15/25).

Lake Ohau & Ohau Forests
Six forests in the Lake Ohau area (Dobson, Hopkins, Huxley, Temple, Ohau and Ahuriri) are administered by DOC. The numerous walks in this vast recreation grove are detailed in the DOC pamphlet *Ohau Conservation Area* ($1); huts and camping areas are also scattered throughout for adventurous trampers. There's a DOC camping ground in **Temple Forest** (adult/child $5/2) on Lake Ohau Rd, 50km southwest of Twizel.

Lake Ohau Lodge (☎ 03-438 9885; www.ohau.co.nz; Lake Ohau Rd; dm $20, s $80-125, d $90-135) is in an idyllic setting on the western shore of the rower-friendly Lake Ohau, though its popularity means you can't expect to get it all to yourself. To include breakfast, you'll pay an extra $10 to $15; set three-course dinners are an extra $30 per person (give advance notice if you have any special dietary requirements).

The lodge is the wintertime service centre for the **Ohau snowfields** (equipment hire per day $30, lift passes per day $50).

AORAKI/MT COOK NATIONAL PARK
The spectacular 700-sq-km Aoraki/Mt Cook National Park, along with Fiordland, Aspiring and Westland National Parks, has been incorporated into the Southwest New Zealand (Te Wahipounamu) World Heritage Area, which extends from Westland's Cook River down to the chilly toes of Fiordland. Fenced in by the Southern Alps and the Two Thumb, Liebig and Ben Ohau Ranges, more than one-third of the park has a blanket of permanent snow and glacial ice.

Of the 27 NZ mountains stretching over 3050m high, 22 are in this park. The peak that all the others look up to is the mighty Mt Cook, which at 3755m is the highest peak in Australasia. Known to Maoris as Aoraki (Cloud Piercer), after an ancestral deity in Maori mythology, the tent-shaped Mt Cook was named after James Cook by Captain Stokes of the survey ship HMS *Acheron*.

The Mt Cook region has always been the focus of climbing in NZ. On 2 March 1882, William Spotswood Green and two Swiss alpinists failed to reach the summit of Cook after an epic 62-hour ascent. But two years later a trio of local climbers – Tom Fyfe, George Graham and Jack Clarke – were spurred into action by the news that two well-known European alpinists, Edward Fitzgerald and Matthias Zurbriggen, were coming to attempt Cook, and set off to climb it before the visitors. On Christmas Day 1884 they ascended the Hooker Glacier and north ridge, a brilliant climb in those days, and stood on the summit.

In 1913, Australian climber Freda du Faur became the first woman to reach the summit. In 1948 Edmund Hillary's party along with Tenzing Norgay climbed the south ridge – Hillary went on to become the first to reach the summit of Mt Everest. Since then, most of the daunting face routes have been climbed. Among the region's many great peaks are Sefton, the beguiling Tasman, Silberhorn, Elie de Beaumont,

CANTERBURY

Malte Brun, Aiguilles Rouges, Nazomi, La Perouse, Hicks, De la Beche, Douglas and the Minarets. Many can be ascended from Westland National Park, and there's a system of climbers' huts on both sides of the divide.

In the early hours of 14 December 1991, a substantial piece of Mt Cook's east face (around 14 million cubic metres) fell away in a massive landslide. Debris spewed out over the surrounding glaciers for 7.3km, cleaving a path down the Grand Plateau and Hochstetter Icefall and reaching as far as the Tasman Glacier.

Mt Cook is a wonderful sight – assuming there's no cloud in the way. Most visitors arrive on tour buses, jump out at the Hermitage hotel for photos, and then zoom off back down SH80. Those who choose not to take this awesome peak and its glorious surrounding landscape for granted stick around and try some of the excellent short walks. While on the trails, look out for the thar, a goat-like creature and excellent climber; the chamois, smaller and of lighter build than the thar but an agile

climber; and red deer. In summer, you'll see the large mountain buttercup, often called the Mt Cook lily, as well as mountain daisies, gentians and edelweiss.

Information

The **DOC Aoraki/Mt Cook visitors centre** (☎ 03-435 1186; mtcookvc@doc.govt.nz; Bowen Dr; ☉ 8.30am-6pm Oct-Apr, 8.30am-5pm May-Sep) will be able to advise on weather conditions, guided tours and tramping routes, and screens a 20-minute audiovisual on the history and mountaineering of the Mt Cook region ($3). Online information is available at www.mount-cook.com.

The Hermitage's souvenir shop handles post; it's open from 7am until 10pm in summer. The hotel's coffee shop sells some groceries, as does the YHA (see Sleeping p553), but you'd fare better by stocking up before turning off the SH8. And remember that Mt Cook has no banking facilities.

The **Alpine Guides Shop** (☎ 03-435 1834; Bowen Dr) sells skiing and mountaineering gear; you can also rent equipment such as ice axes, crampons, day-packs and sleeping bags.

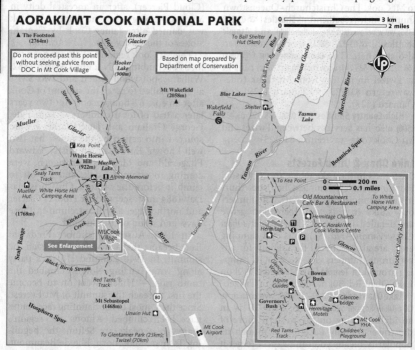

Sights

TASMAN GLACIER

Higher up, the Tasman Glacier is a predictably spectacular sweep of ice, but further down it's downright ugly. Glaciers in NZ (and elsewhere in the world) have generally been retreating over the past century, although they are advancing now. Normally as a glacier retreats it melts back up the mountain, but the Tasman is unusual because its last few kilometres are almost horizontal. So in recent decades it has melted from the top down, exposing a jumble of stones, rocks and boulders. In other words, in its 'ablation zone' (where it melts) the Tasman is covered in a more or less solid mass of debris, which slows down its melting rate and makes it unsightly.

Despite this considerable melt, the ice by the site of the old Ball Hut is still estimated to be over 600m thick. In its last major advance (17,000 years ago), the glacier crept south far enough to carve out Lake Pukaki. A later advance did not reach out to the valley sides, so the old Ball Hut Rd runs between the outer valley walls and the lateral moraines of this later advance.

Like the Fox and Franz Josef Glaciers on the other side of the divide, the Mt Cook glaciers move fast. The Alpine Memorial, located near the old Hermitage site on the Hooker Valley Track and commemorating one of the mountain's first climbing disasters, illustrates the glaciers' speed. Three climbers were killed by an avalanche in 1914. Only one of the bodies was recovered at the time but 12 years later a second one melted out of the bottom of the Hochstetter Icefall, 2000m below where the party was buried.

HERMITAGE

This is arguably the most famous hotel in NZ, principally for its location and the fantastic views of Mt Cook. Originally constructed in 1884, when the trip up from Christchurch took several days, the first hotel was destroyed in a flash flood in 1913; you can see the foundations in Hooker Valley, 2km from the current Hermitage. Rebuilt, it survived until 1957, when it was completely burnt out; the present Hermitage was built on the same site and was recently given a new wing.

Even if you're not staying at the Hermitage, you can still sample the bar and restaurants here and look out the huge windows up at Mt Cook's indomitable face.

Activities

WALKING

Various easy walks from the Hermitage area are outlined in the brochure *Walks in Aoraki/ Mt Cook National Park* ($1), available from the visitors centre. Always be prepared for sudden weather changes.

The trail to **Kea Point** (two hours return) is lined with native plant life and kea, and ends at a platform with excellent views of Mt Cook, the Hooker Valley and the ice faces of Mt Sefton and the Footstool. The walk to **Sealy Tarns** (three to four hours return) branches off the Kea Pt Track and continues up the ridge to **Mueller Hut** (dm $22); a new 28-bunk hut was opened here mid-2003, 300m south of the old hut and with its own gas.

It's a four-hour return walk up the **Hooker Valley** across a couple of swing bridges to Stocking Stream and the terminus of the Hooker Glacier. After the second swing bridge Mt Cook totally dominates the valley.

The **Tasman Valley** walks are popular for their views of the Tasman Glacier. Walks start at the end of the unsealed Tasman Valley Rd, 8km from the village. The **Tasman Glacier View** track (40 minutes return) leads to a viewpoint on the moraine wall, passing the **Blue Lakes** (more green than blue these days) on the way. Views of Mt Cook and the surrounding area are spectacular, but the view of the glacier is limited mostly to the icy grey sludge of the Terminal Lake and the Tasman River. To approach the snub of the glacier, take the route to Ball Shelter (three to four hours one-way) from the car park; you can stay here at **Ball Shelter Hut** (dm $5).

If you intend staying at any of the park's huts, register your intentions at the visitors centre and pay the hut fee; besides the aforementioned two, most huts cost $20 per night.

Longer Walks

Longer walks are only recommended for those with mountaineering experience (see Mountaineering p552), as conditions at higher altitudes are severe, the tracks dangerous and many people have died here; the majority of walkers shouldn't even consider tackling these trails.

Guided Walks

From November to March, **Alpine Guides Trekking** (☎ 03-435 1809; www.ultimatehikes.co.nz; full-day walk adult/child $95/65) offers a day-long 8km walk from the Hermitage through the Hooker Valley to the terminal lake of the Hooker Glacier; half-day walks can also be organised.

Alpine Recreation offers high-altitude guided treks in the area, as well as mountaineering courses; see Lake Tekapo (p546).

MOUNTAINEERING

For the experienced, there's unlimited scope here for climbing. But regardless of your aptitude, take every precaution: over 200 people have died in climbing accidents in the park. These are recorded in the bleak 'In Memoriam' book in the visitors centre, which begins with the first death on Mt Cook in 1907. Several tragedies in December 2003 showed just how terribly capricious the mountains can be – a total of eight climbers died on Mt Tasman and Mt Cook, three of them experienced mountain guides who were well known in Mt Cook village.

The highly changeable weather is an important factor around here – Mt Cook is only 44km from the coast and bears the brunt of weather conditions blowing in over the Tasman Sea, which can mean sudden storms. Unless you know what you're doing in such conditions, don't attempt to climb anywhere without a guide.

It's important to check with the park rangers before attempting any climb, and to heed their advice. You must fill in a climber's intentions card before starting out on any climb, so rangers can check on you if you're overdue coming out. And make sure you sign out again when you return.

Alpine Guides (☎ 03-435 1834; www.alpineguides .co.nz; Bowen Dr) has guided climbs in summer, ranging from eight-day introductory courses ($2250) through to week-long ascents of Mt Cook ($4150).

SKIING & HELI-HIKING

Alpine Guides (☎ 03-435 1834; www.alpineguides.co.nz; Bowen Dr), over the winter months, does tai-lored ski-touring trips and ski-mountaineering and alpine snowboarding courses. One of its specialties is glacier heli-skiing (www.heliskiing.co.nz) – there are day trips on Tasman Glacier involving two 8km to 10km runs and three skiplane flights ($650), and a 'Wilderness Heli-Skiing' trip with a minimum of 3000 vertical metres and four to five runs in the Liebig or Malte Brun Ranges ($735).

Cloud 9 Helihiking (☎ 03-435 1077; www.glacier explorers.com; adult/child from $300/220) does summer trips to the 'Dark Side': you're flown to Mt Dark (approximately 2000m) and walk back down. The guided trip takes around four hours.

AERIAL SIGHTSEEING

Mount Cook Ski Planes (☎ 0800 800 702, 03-435 1026; www.mtcookskiplanes.com) buzzes over this magnificent iced-in terrain during 40-minute (adult/child $280/210) and 55-minute flights ($370/280), both with glacier landings. Flights without a landing are much cheaper, such as the 25-minute 'Mini Tasman' trip ($190/150).

From Glentanner Park, the **Helicopter Line** (☎ 0800 650 651, 03-435 1801; www.helicopter.co.nz) does 20-minute 'Alpine Vista' flights ($185), an exhilarating 30-minute flight over the Ben Ohau Range ($280), and a 45-minute 'Mountain High' flight over the Tasman Glacier and by Mt Cook ($390). All flights feature snow landings.

Other airborne operators who fly around the region include **Air Safaris** (see Lake Tekapo p547) and **Glacier Southern Lakes Helicopters** (see Twizel p548).

OTHER ACTIVITIES

The visitors centre, the Hermitage, the YHA and Glentanner Park provide information and make bookings for a multitude of activities and tours in the area, though be aware that most of them are weather-dependent.

The highly rated **Glacier Explorers** (☎ 03-435 1077; www.glacierexplorers.com; adult/child $85/40) heads out on the terminal lake of the Tasman Glacier. It starts with a half-hour walk to the shore of Lake Tasman, where you board a small motorised inflatable and get up close and personal with the ice for an hour.

The three-hour trips conducted by **Glacier Sea-kayaking** (☎ 03-435 1890; www.mtcook.com; $75) enable you to sea kayak across glacial bays, circumnavigating the odd iceberg as you paddle.

Another way of checking out the area is with **Glentanner Horse Trekking** (☎ 03-435 1855; 1-/2-hr rides $50/70), which does sumguided treks on a high-country sheep station, in summer only. **Alan's 4WD Tours** (☎ 03-435 0441; www.mountcooktours.co.nz; adult/child $85/45; tours from Oct-Apr) runs 2½-hour 4WD trips from The Hermitage up to Husky Flat, from where it's a 15-minute walk to a glacier viewpoint; there's plenty of interesting commentary and alpine flora to gaze at along the way.

Sleeping

White Horse Hill Camping Area (☎ 03-435 1186; Hooker Valley; per night adult/child $5/3) This basic DOC-run camping ground is at the old Hermitage site, 2km from Aoraki/Mt Cook village and the starting point for the Hooker Valley Track. There's running water and toilets but no electricity, showers or cooking facilities. Book at the visitors centre. There's also a handy public shelter in the village, with running water, toilets and coin-operated showers.

Glentanner Park Centre (☎ 0800 453 682, 03-435 1855; www.glentanner.co.nz; camp sites $20, campervan sites $22, dm $20, d $50-80) Located on the northern shore of Lake Pukaki, this is the nearest camping ground to the national park and has great views of Mt Cook, 25km to the north. It's well set up with various cabins, a **dormitory** (☺ October to April only), a restaurant and a booking service for the aforementioned Air Safaris, The Helicopter Line and Glentanner Horse Trekking.

Unwin Hut (☎ 03-435 1100, 435 1840; SH80; dm $25) This lodge is about 3.5km before the village and belongs to the New Zealand Alpine Club (NZAC). Members get preference, but beds are usually available for climbing groupies. There are basic bunks and a big common room with a fireplace, kitchen and excellent views up the Tasman Glacier to the Minarets and Elie de Beaumont.

Mt Cook YHA (☎ 03-435 1820; yha.mtcook@yha.org .nz; cnr Bowen & Kitchener Dr; dm/d from $24/65) This excellent hostel comes equipped with a free sauna, drying room, a decent video collection, warming log fires and – for those who haven't expended all their energy on local trails – an in-house boul-dering wall. Book at least a few days in advance in the high season.

Hermitage (☎ 0800 686 800, 03-435 1809; www .mount-cook.com; Terrace Rd; rooms $180-820) The enormous Hermitage complex has long had a monopoly on mid-range and top-end accommodation in the village. The least-expensive beds are in well-equipped A-frame chalets that can sleep up to four people (they have one double and two single beds each). Priced up from these are the motel units, the hotel-style rooms of Glencoe Lodge (the double rate of $410 includes a buffet dinner; lodge is closed over winter), and finally rooms in various wings of the hotel proper – a luxurious upper-level room in the new Aoraki Wing (doubles from $790) comes with an outdoor terrace, binoculars and four-course dinners in the Panorama Restaurant.

Eating & Drinking

Hermitage (☎ 03-435 1809; Terrace Rd) Eating options in the hotel include the mezzanine-level coffee shop that dispenses daytime snacks and the extensive buffets of the **Alpine Restaurant** (lunch $37, dinner $50). But the pride of place goes to the **Panorama Room** (mains $25-40), a top-notch à la carte restaurant with such fine Kiwi treats as groper steak and rack of Canterbury lamb, plus a separate veg menu. The view from here is outrageously good – you see Sefton to your left, Cook in the centre and the Ben Ohau Ranges, dark brown and forbidding, to your right. Adjacent to the Panorama Room is the Snowline Lounge Bar, with its well-upholstered lounges in which to woo a wine glass.

The smaller, less-formal Chamois Bar is upstairs in Glencoe Lodge, 500m from the main hotel near the YHA, where it entertains with a pool table and big-screen TV; beer-drinking food such as nachos, burgers and steak sandwiches are also served here.

Old Mountaineers Cafe Bar & Restaurant (☎ 03-435 1890; Bowen Dr; mains $15-25; ☺ from 10.30am; 🖳) Sitting next to the visitors centre is this relatively new, attractive café-bar, with a cosy interior, outdoor seating, some good meals and views straight up the mountain. In a village that has been dominated by the high-priced Hermitage for more than a century, this place is a real breath of fresh, independent air.

Glentanner Restaurant (☎ 03-435 1855; SH80; meals $11-17; ◷ breakfast & lunch) The cafeteria-style eatery at Glentanner Park throws together basic cooked and continental breakfasts, and lunchtime burgers, BLTs and *panini*. Dinners (usually only served over summer) are just as simple: veg quiche and steak sandwiches.

Getting There & Away

The village's small, modern airport only serves aerial sightseeing companies. Some of these may be willing to combine transport to, say, the West Coast (ie Franz Josef) with a scenic flight, but the flights are heavily weather-dependent.

InterCity (☎ 03-435 1809; www.intercitycoach.co. nz) heads to Mt Cook from Christchurch ($75), Queenstown ($65) and Wanaka ($55); buses stop at the YHA and the Hermitage, both of which handle bookings. **High Country Shuttles** (☎ 0800 435 050, 03-435

0506) runs between Mt Cook and Twizel (one way/return $15/25). You can usually connect with **Southern Link Shuttles** (☎ 03-358 8355; www.yellow.co.nz/site/southernlink) and **Atomic Shuttles** (☎ 03-322 8883; www.atomictravel.co.nz) to travel on to Christchurch, Queenstown or Wanaka. The **Cook Connection** (☎ 0800 266 526, 0274-583 211; www.cookconnect.co.nz) shuttles to Timaru and Oamaru (both $45).

InterCity subsidiary **Newmans Coach Lines** (☎ 03-379 9020; www.newmanscoach.co.nz) offers the 'Mt Cook Wanderer', a Christchurch–Mt Cook–Queenstown sightseeing trip costing $130/90 per adult/child from Christchurch and $115/80 from Queenstown.

If you're driving up here, it's best to fill up at Lake Tekapo or Twizel. There is petrol at Mt Cook, but it's expensive and involves summoning an attendant from the Hermitage.

Otago

CONTENTS

Dunedin & the Otago
  Peninsula   **557**
Dunedin   557
Otago Peninsula   567
Central Otago   **570**
Cromwell   570
Alexandra   571
Clyde   572
Alexandra to Palmerston   574
Alexandra to Dunedin   575
Clutha District   576
North Otago   **577**
Oamaru   577
Waitaki Valley   580
Oamaru to Dunedin   581
Queenstown Region   **581**
Queenstown   581
Arrowtown   597
Glenorchy   598
Lake Wakatipu Region
  Tramps   600
Wanaka Region   **602**
Makarora   602
Hawea   603
Wanaka   604
Cardrona   611

OTAGO

The large scoop of South Island terra firma known as Otago has a wonderfully restless landscape distinguished in the east by coastal wildlife havens and a Victorian-era city with a youthful vibe; in the centre by vineyard-nurturing soil, broad plains and former gold-mining sites where the once-rich dust has well and truly settled; and in the west by lake-moated peaks, rainforest trails and several self-obsessed towns that take outdoor activities to daunting new heights.

The city of Dunedin is a fine place to spend a few days absorbing the high culture of several notable museums and galleries, and the popular culture of indie gigs, cruisy bars and clamouring cafés. Nearby castle-crowned Otago Peninsula provides a beautiful natural counterpoint, with the lives of penguins, seals, albatross and sea lions under constant tourist scrutiny. The small hardy towns of Central Otago are historical microcosms, from the 'Art Deco in a paddock' curiosity of Ranfurly to the stately gold-mining-era hotels of Clyde and St Bathans, while fine-wine making is prompting contemporary recognition of the region. Queenstown (aided and abetted by Wanaka) has become the open-air action centre of New Zealand, with outdoors entrepreneurs spending every waking moment thinking of new ways of challenging gravity and notions of common sense. Respite lies to the west, where the Routeburn, Greenstone and other tracks lead into imperturbable wilderness, such as the greenery-clogged Mt Aspiring National Park.

HIGHLIGHTS

- Letting your adrenaline go wild in the hurly-burly of **Queenstown** (p581) or **Wanaka** (p604)

- Doing the exact opposite in the loungy bars and cafés of **Dunedin** (p564)

- Eyeballing yellow-eyed penguins on **Otago Peninsula** (p567)

- Cycling or walking the **Otago Central Rail Trail** (p573) across the gold-mined Maniototo

- Tasting your way through the home-brewed stocks of Pinot Noir from **Central Otago** (p576)

- Striding down the subalpine splendour of the **Routeburn Track** (p600)

- Doing some **Remarkables** (p588) skiing

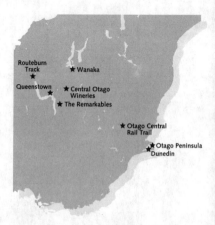

Climate

Due to the way the Southern Alps block the wet winds whistling in from the Tasman Sea, the east coast of Otago (including Dunedin and the Otago Peninsula) has a relatively dry climate. In Central Otago, summer days are generally warm to hot and rainfall is very low, while in winter temperatures can drop to well below freezing. This climatic spectrum is greatest in the town of Ophir, which reputedly has the widest temperature range of any NZ town – from -20°C in winter to 35°C in summer.

Getting There & Around

Air New Zealand flies from Dunedin to the major centres of Christchurch, Wellington and Auckland, and also connects these last two cities with Queenstown. The airline has also just established a new Christchurch–Wanaka route.

Numerous bus/shuttle companies crisscross Otago, driving from Dunedin to Queenstown and/or Wanaka. Several also divert south to Te Anau and Invercargill, and others migrate north to Christchurch or wind through the Haast Pass and up the West Coast. Major operators include Inter-City, Atomic Shuttles, Wanaka Connexions, Southern Link Shuttles and Catch-A-Bus.

DUNEDIN & THE OTAGO PENINSULA

The attractive, increasingly urbane city of Dunedin is wedged at the southwestern end of fiord-like Otago Harbour. This tidal harbour's southern shoreline is defined by the fauna-rich, raggedly-shaped mass of Otago Peninsula, and between them these two places host a wealth of ecotourism activities. One of the most engaging things about this region is the highly enjoyable contrast between arts-loving city and animal-loving peninsula.

DUNEDIN

pop 110,800

Dunedin is the South Island's second city (after Christchurch) and home of NZ's first university. The city has a statue of Robert Burns guarding its centre, echoing its foundation by Scottish settlers – 'Dunedin' is Celtic for 'Edinburgh'.

Gold-rush wealth in the latter half of the 19th century produced a grand Victorian city in the South Pacific. Though central Dunedin now has modern intrusions, much of the fetching Victorian architecture survives: solid public buildings dot the city and wooden villas are scattered across the hilly suburbs. The city is cultured, graceful and lively for its size, with its 20,000-plus tertiary students helping drive the local arts, entertainment, café and pub scenes.

History

The area's early Maori history was particularly bloody, involving a three-way feud between peninsular tribes. *Utu* (revenge) followed attack as the Ngai Tahu and Ngati Mamoe tribes' feud escalated in the early 19th century. Coastal sealing and whaling then brought ravaging diseases, and by 1848 the once considerable population of Otakau Pa was just over 100.

The first permanent European settlers arrived at Port Chalmers in March 1848, six years after a plan for a Presbyterian settlement on the South Island's east coast was mooted. Gold was soon discovered in Otago and the province quickly became the colony's richest, most influential entity. But after its heady start, Dunedin declined economically and much of its population drifted away. Contemporary life in the city is more stabilised, with well-tended suburbs surrounding a socially busy centre.

Information

Dunedin visitors centre (☎ 03-474 3300; www.cityofdunedin.com; 48 the Octagon; ☷ 8.30am-5.30pm Mon-Fri, 9am-5.30pm Sat & Sun) is in the magnificently restored municipal chambers. The **DOC** (☎ 03-477 0677; 1st fl, 77 Stuart St; ☷ 8.30am-5pm Mon-Fri) has info on regional walking tracks, and there's an office of the **Automobile Association** (AA; ☎ 03-477 5945; 450 Moray Pl; ☷ 8.30am-5pm Mon-Fri).

The **GPO** (☎ 03-477 3517; 243 Princes St; ☷ 8.30am-5.30pm Mon-Fri) handles poste restante; a little north is another inner-city **post office** (☎ 03-474 0932; 233 Moray Pl; ☷ 8.30am-5.30pm Mon-Fri, 10am-12.30pm Sat).

Internet access costs between $3 and $5 per hour and is available at several hostels

and cafés. **Friendly Cyberlounge** (☎ 03-477 8433; 1st fl, 434 George St), above Khmer Satay Noodle House, has high-performance, high-speed machines (and low rates). The big, clean **Internet Depot** (☎ 03-470 1730; 18 George St; ☻ 9am-11pm Mon-Thu, 9am-midnight Fri & Sat, 10am-11pm Sun) has lots of terminals.

Dunedin's finest paper emporium is **University Book Shop** (☎ 03-477 6976; 378 Great King St; ☻ 8.30am-5.30pm Mon-Fri, 9.30am-3pm Sat, 11am-3pm Sun). Upstairs is a great range of discounted books.

For medical help, there's **Dunedin Hospital** (☎ 03-474 0999; 201 Great King St). The **Urgent Doctors & Accident Centre** (☎ 03-479 2900; 95 Hanover St) has a pharmacy open outside normal business hours.

Sights

TAIERI GORGE RAILWAY

Some visitors rate the **Taieri Gorge Railway** (☎ 03-477 4449; www.taieri.co.nz; Dunedin Railway Station, Anzac Ave; ☻ 2.30pm Oct-Mar, 12.30pm Apr-Sep, extra 9.30am summer services) one of the great train journeys, similar to Colorado's Silverton–Durango line. While winding through the rocky gorge, the train crosses a dozen viaducts, one of them 50m above the creek bed. The four-hour excursion involves a 58km trip to Pukerangi and back again ($60); some trains continue a further 19km to Middlemarch ($65).

Most people take the train as a day trip, but you can travel one way and continue by bus to Queenstown (adult/child $110/55).

Another option is to bring your bike along and cycle from Middlemarch to Clyde along a rail-line extension; see the 'Otago Central Rail Trail' boxed text (p573). Before boarding the train, take some time to inspect Dunedin station's striking Edwardian façade and Royal Doulton mosaic-tile floors.

OTAGO MUSEUM

Give yourself a few hours to roam the wonderful **Otago Museum** (☎ 03-474 7474; www.otago museum.govt.nz; 419 Great King St; admission by donation; ☺ 10am-5pm). In the Tangata Whenua Gallery is a Maori war canoe, grand meeting-house carvings and a Kiribati warrior carrying a shark-tooth sword. Exhibits in the Nature Galleries include a large wasp's nest and a rather terrifying specimen of the Japanese spider crab, the world's largest. The nature theme continues in the excellent hands-on science of **Discovery World** (adult/child/family $6/3/14), where kids can peer at live animals like tarantulas and frogs.

DUNEDIN PUBLIC ART GALLERY

Dunedin's **Public Art Gallery** (☎ 03-474 3240; www.dunedin.art.museum; 30 the Octagon; permanent exhibition free; ☺ 10am-5pm) is an excellent fine arts exhibition space that has an appropriately airy, sky-lit foyer. The permanent exhibition showcases NZ art of the past 150 years (such as a corrugated-steel piece from Ralph Hotere and a room dedicated to Frances Hodgkins), plus the odd Monet, Turner and a prominent Goldie. Temporary exhibitions (admission is charged) have included 'The Pre-Raphaelite Dream', a 19th-century collection borrowed from London's Tate Gallery.

OTHER MUSEUMS & GALLERIES

Even if you're not into old steam locomotives like the 1872-built *Josephine*, it's worth visiting the **Otago Settlers Museum** (☎ 03-477 4000; 31 Queens Gardens; adult/child/concession $4/free/$3; ☺ 10am-5pm) just to see the fantastic old Art Deco bus depot foyer that's now the museum's southern wing. There are also some great pioneer exhibits, including the eerie Smith Gallery, its walls crammed with the stolid faces of immigrants from the 19th century.

New Zealand Sports Hall of Fame (☎ 03-477 7775; www.nzhalloffame.co.nz; Dunedin Railway Station, Anzac Ave; adult/child/student $5/2/3; ☺ 10am-4pm) is

for sports buffs who want to read cricketer Richard Hadlee's motivational mottoes and know which wrestler patented the 'octopus clamp' (Lofty Blomfield) and who won gold in the long-jump at Helsinki (Yvette Williams).

OLVESTON

Designed by a London architect and completed in 1906, grandiose **Olveston** (☎ 03-477 3320; www.visit-dunedin.co.nz/olveston.html; 42 Royal Tce; adult/child $14/4; ☺ guided tours 9.30am-4pm) looks as it did when lived in by the ostentatious Theomin family in the early 1900s. Though the building itself is not overwhelmingly impressive, the lavish furnishings and artworks are. To see it, you must book a place on a one-hour guided tour.

OTHER SIGHTS

The **First Church of Otago** (☎ 03-477 7150; 415 Moray Pl; admission free) is a fine Presbyterian edifice, with a limestone outer skin and 56m-high spire built in 1873. It has a nice rose window and a tapestry in the right transept that depicts Otago's settlement 25 years prior to the church's inauguration. Duck into the visitors centre behind the pulpit to admire more stained glasswork.

One-hour tours of Dunedin's **Cadbury World** (☎ 0800 223 287, 03-467 7967; www.cadbury world.co.nz; 280 Cumberland St; adult/child/student/family $14/8/12/36; ☺ tours every half-hour 9am-3.30pm) will expose you to a Willy Wonka–style foyer and details of the choc making that has been conducted in this factory since the 1930s. It handles 85% of NZ chocolate production.

To see the production of a different kind of confection, take a 1½-hour tour of **Speight's Brewery** (☎ 03-477 7697; www.speights.co.nz; 200 Rattray St; adult/child/concession/family $15/5/12/35; ☺ tours 10am, 11.45am & 2pm daily, plus 4.30pm Sat & Sun), at the end of which you can try each of the six beers brewed here. For $50, follow the tour with a three-course lunch or dinner at the adjacent Ale House.

Dating from 1868, the 28-hectare **Dunedin Botanic Gardens** (☎ 03-477 4000; cnr Great King St & Opoho Rd; admission free; ☺ gardens dawn-dusk, visitors centre 9.30am-4.30pm) has cultivated clusters of azaleas, camellias, roses and native plants, plus a four-hectare rhododendron dell and an aviary with 50 species of bird. For a man-made contrast, visit the **University of Otago**

OTAGO

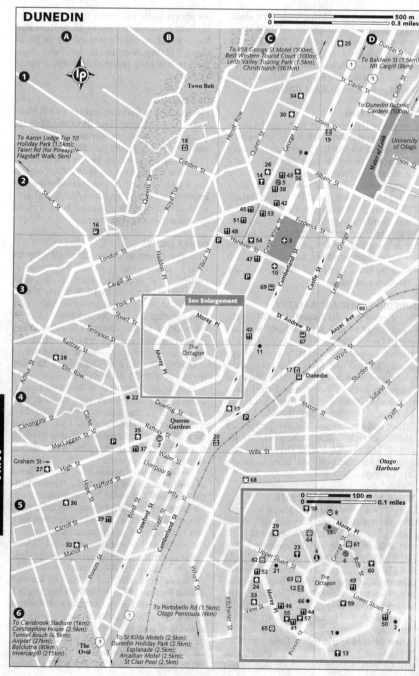

DUNEDIN

| 0 | 500 m |
| 0 | 0.3 miles |

Town Belt

To 858 George St Motel (100m);
Best Western Tourist Court (100m);
Leith Valley Touring Park (1.5km);
Christchurch (361km)

To Baldwin St (1.5km);
Mt Cargill (8km)

To Dunedin Botanic
Gardens (500m)

To Aaron Lodge Top 10
Holiday Park (1.5km);
Taieri Rd (for Pineapple-
Flagstaff Walk; 5km)

University
of Otago

Water of Leith

See Enlargement

The Octagon

Dunedin

Otago
Harbour

To Portobello Rd (1.5km);
Otago Peninsula (4km)

To Carisbrook Stadium (1km);
Corstorphine House (2.5km);
Tunnel Beach (6.5km);
Airport (27km);
Balclutha (80km);
Invercargill (215km)

The
Oval

To St Kilda Motels (2.5km);
Dunedin Holiday Park (2.5km);
Esplanade (2.5km);
Arcadian Motel (2.5km);
St Clair Pool (2.5km)

OTAGO

| 0 | 100 m |
| 0 | 0.1 miles |

The
Octagon

Moray Pl

Upper Stuart St

George St

Bath St

Lower Stuart St

Moray Pl

View St

Princes St

INFORMATION			SLEEPING	(pp562–4)		Percolator	49 D6
Automobile Association (AA)	1 D6		97 Motel Moray Place	24 C6		Potpourri	50 D6
DOC	2 D6		Albatross Inn	25 D1		Reef	51 C2
Dunedin Hospital	3 C3		Alexis Motor Lodge	26 C2		Tangenté	52 C6
Dunedin Visitors Centre	4 D5		Chalet Backpackers	27 A5		Thai Over	53 C2
Friendly Cyberlounge	5 C2		Elm Lodge Backpackers	28 A4			
Internet Depot	6 D5		Kingsgate Hotel	29 C5		DRINKING	(p565)
Main Post Office	7 B4		Kiwis Nest	30 C1		Abalone	54 C3
Post Office	8 D5		Leviathan Heritage Hotel	31 C4		Albert Arms	(see 45)
University Book Shop	9 C2		Manor House Backpackers	32 A5		Bennu Cafe & Bar	55 C6
Urgent Doctors &			Next Stop Dunedin Backpackers	33 C6		Captain Cook	56 C2
Accident Centre	10 C3		Sahara Guesthouse & Motel	34 C1		Di Lusso	(see 59)
			Southern Cross Hotel	35 B4		Isis	57 C6
SIGHTS & ACTIVITIES	(pp558–62)		Stafford Gables YHA	36 A5		Poolhouse	58 C5
Cadbury World	11 C4					Pop Bar	59 D6
Cycle Surgery	(see 2)		EATING	(pp564–5)		Woolshed	60 D6
Dunedin Public Art Gallery	12 C6		Arc Cafe	37 B4			
First Church of Otago	13 D6		Azi Jaan	38 C2		ENTERTAINMENT	(pp565–6)
Knox Church	14 C2		Bell Pepper Blues	39 A5		Bath St	61 D5
Library	15 D5		Countdown Supermarket	40 C3		Dunedin Casino	(see 35)
Moana Pool	16 A2		Etrusco at the Savoy	41 C6		Fortune Theatre	62 C5
New Zealand Sports			Fix	42 C2		Hoyts Cinemas	63 C6
Hall of Fame	17 C4		Governors Cafe	43 C2		Metro Cinema	64 C5
Olveston	18 B2		Hungry Frenchman	(see 44)		Rialto Cinemas	65 C6
Otago Museum	19 D2		Jizo Japanese Cafe & Bar	44 C6			
Otago Settlers Museum	20 C4		London Lounge	45 C2		TRANSPORT	(pp566–7)
Records Records	21 C6		Mazagran Espresso Bar	46 C6		Air New Zealand	66 C6
Speight's Brewery	22 B4		Mission	47 C3		InterCity Depot	67 C3
St Paul's Church	23 C5		New Satay Noodle House	48 C2		Monarch Wildlife Cruises & Tours	68 C5
Taieri Gorge Railway	(see 17)		Nova Cafe	(see 12)		Suburban Bus Stop	69 C3

☎ 03-479 1100; www.otago.ac.nz), founded with 81 students in 1869 and with an interesting mish-mash of old and new architecture.

Baldwin St is listed in the *Guinness Book of Records* as the world's steepest street, with a gradient of 1 in 1.266. From the city centre, head north up Great King St for 2km to where the road branches left to Timaru, get in the right-hand lane and then keep going straight rather than taking the sharp right-hand turn. The road you're on becomes North Rd; Baldwin St will be on the right after 1km. The annual 'Gutbuster' race (February) sees the winner run up and back in around two minutes.

If you'd like an education in NZ indie music, dive into the piles of predominantly second-hand vinyl and CDs at **Records Records** (☎ 03-474 0789; www.recordsrecords.co.nz; 213 Stuart St), an iconic Dunedin music store that has been in business in the same building for over 30 years.

Activities

SWIMMING & SURFING

St Clair and St Kilda are popular swimming beaches, the former equipped with the heated, saltwater **St Clair Pool** (☎ 03-455 5352; Esplanade, St Clair Beach; adult/child $4.50/2; late-Oct–late-Mar). Based at St Clair Pool is **Southern Coast Surf Clinic** (☎ 03-455 6007; www.surfcoachnz.com), which teaches surfing to beginners, organises trips for the experienced, and rents out surfboards, boogie

boards and wet suits; the western end of St Clair Beach also happens to have swell surfing. Alternatively, swim at **Moana Pool** (☎ 03-471 9780; 60 Littlebourne Rd; adult/child per swim $4.50/2, swim & waterslide $8.50/5).

WALKING

There's a short walkway across farmland to **Tunnel Beach**, southwest of central Dunedin. Catch a Corstorphine bus from the Octagon to Stenhope Cres and walk 1.4km along Blackhead Rd to Tunnel Beach Rd, then 400m to the start of the walkway (45 minutes return; closed August to October by lambing). The hand-hewn stone tunnel was built by John Cargill to enable secluded, beachside family picnics. The impressive sandstone cliffs contain small fossils.

Catch a Normanby bus to the start of Norwood Rd, then walk two hours uphill (90 minutes down) to the **Mt Cargill–Bethunes Gully Walkway**. The highlight is the view from Mt Cargill (also accessible by car). In Maori legend the three peaks of Cargill (named after a leader of early Otago colonists) represent the petrified head and feet of a princess of an early Otakau tribe. From Mt Cargill, a trail continues to the 10-million-year-old lava-formed **Organ Pipes** and, after another half-hour, to Mt Cargill Rd on the other side of the mountain.

Northwest of Dunedin, the 5km-long **Pineapple–Flagstaff Walk** (two hours) has great views of the harbour, coastline and

OTAGO

inland ranges; look out for the signpost at Flagstaff–Whare Flat Rd, off Taieri Rd.

The **Otago Tramping & Mountaineering Club** (www.otmc.co.nz) organises full-day and weekend tramping trips and meets every Thursday evening at 3 Young St, St Kilda; nonmembers most welcome.

OTHER ACTIVITIES

Mainland Air (☎ 0800 284 284, 03-486 2200; www.mainlandair.com) and **Alpine Air** (☎ 03-486 2283; www.alpineair.co.nz) are both based at Dunedin airport and offer regional aerial sightseeing; half an hour's air time costs from $125.

Local horse-trekkers include **Hare Hill** (☎ 0800 437 837, 03-472 8496; www.horseriding-dunedin.co.nz), based north of Dunedin and offering beach and hill-trail rides from $50/95 per half-/full day.

Cycle Surgery (☎ 03-477 7473; 67 Stuart St; per day $25) hires bikes and is a good source of mountain biking info. For details of some rides in and around Dunedin, pick up the free brochure *Fat Tyre Trails* from the visitors centre.

See under Otago Peninsula (p569) for more activity options.

Tours

Dunedin City Explorer (☎ 0800 322 240; day ticket adult/child $15/7.50; ☺ buses depart the Octagon 9.45am, 11.30am, 1pm, 2.30pm & 4pm) is a hop-on, hop-off bus service that loops around the city's main sights, including Otago Museum, Olveston, Botanical Gardens and Baldwin St.

Hair Raiser (☎ 03-477 2258; adult/child $15/10; ☺ 6pm Wed & Fri) is a factual evening tour of the city's darker side, which departs outside the visitors centre.

Newton Tours (☎ 03-477 5577; www.transportplace.co.nz; adult/child $15/7.50) does one-hour double-decker tours of Dunedin five times daily, taking in historic homes, the First Church of Otago, the university and the railway station. Newton also runs numerous other double-decker routes and peninsula wildlife tours.

Monarch Wildlife Cruises & Tours (☎ 03-477 4276; www.wildlife.co.nz; wharf, cnr Wharf & Fryatt Sts) ships out daily on the MV *Monarch* for tours of the harbour and peninsula. The half-day 'Peninsula' cruise (adult/child from $70/23) passes fur seal, shag and gull colonies, and the albatross colony at

Taiaroa Head. You can also join the cruise for an hour's sail at Wellers Rock on the peninsula ($30/10).

For more wildlife-centric tours, see under Otago Peninsula (p569).

Sleeping
B&BS

Sahara Guesthouse & Motel (☎ 03-477 6662; 619 George St; r from $85) The healthy mission-green trim of this place is at odds with its arid-sounding name. B&B includes cooked breakfast and is in the main house, in spacious though slightly worn rooms. There are also two levels of old-style but very clean motel units out back.

Albatross Inn (☎ 0800 441 441, 03-477 2727; www.albatross.inn.co.nz; 770 George St; d $95-125) B&B in an Edwardian house with a seductive historic atmosphere. The continental breakfast brims with muffins and other fresh selections, and noon checkouts can be arranged. The upper-end price gets you a king-size bed.

Corstorphine House (☎ 03-487 1000; www.corstorphine.co.nz; Milburn St; s/d from $610/800) Eight luxurious themed rooms are on offer in this gracious old manor, so that you can get a taste of Japanese, French or Moroccan décor while staying in Dunedin; prices can drop by over one-third during winter. Meals are provided in the Conservatory Restaurant, which has a fine range of central Otago wines.

HOSTELS

Stafford Gables YHA (☎ 03-474 1919; yha.dunedin@yha.org.nz; 71 Stafford St; dm/d from $23/55; ☐) Set in a late-19th-century former private hotel, this is a large-roomed, relatively peaceful hostel with a rooftop garden and balconies attached to some rooms. Staff happily give the lowdown on Dunedin activities.

Chalet Backpackers (☎ 03-479 2075; kirsti@paradise.net.nz; 296 High St; dm/d $20/50) Small, homely brick building that adds to its character with a games room (with pool table), an expansive kitchen, a piano and rumours of a resident ghost. Has opted for comfy single beds rather than bunks in all dorms.

Elm Lodge Backpackers (☎ 0800 356 563, 03-474 1872; www.elmwildlifetours.co.nz; 74 Elm Row; dm from $18, d $40; ☐) Good place to stay if you feel like looking down on Dunedin and the harbour from a nearby hilltop, and if you appreciate cosiness and quick access to a sheltered garden. It's a short walk up from the Octagon, or they'll pick up. They also do wildlife tours (see under Otago Peninsula; p569).

Kiwis Nest (☎ 03-471 9540; kiwisnest@ihug.co.nz; 597 George St; dm/s $20/40, d $50-80) It's quite an accomplishment for such a rambling place to retain a cosy, personal feel, but Kiwis Nest somehow manages this trick. If privacy is a priority, try for the self-contained unit with its own small piece of outdoor decking. Doubles come with or without en suite; there's a $10 difference between the two.

Manor House Backpackers (☎ 0800 477 0484, 03-477 0484; www.manorhousebackpackers.co.nz; 28 Manor Pl; dm/d $20/48) Another of Dunedin's trademark warm, well-aged hostels, set in twin historic homes overlooking some parkland. The dorms are smallish but tidy affairs and staff are pretty relaxed.

Next Stop Dunedin Backpackers (☎ 0800 463 987, 03-477 0447; www.nextstop.co.nz; 2 View St; dm/d $18/45; ☐) This mural-daubed hostel clings to the side of a steep street, with most of its rooms arranged around a nice fire-warmed central space. The doubles are small but upper-level rooms are brightened by skylights (only one dorm has this feature). There's also a small rooftop terrace.

HOTELS

Leviathan Heritage Hotel (☎ 0800 773 773, 03-477 3160; leviathan@xtra.co.nz; 27 Queens Gardens; d $70-135) This landmark building is in pretty good nick despite its years of toil and its well-appointed rooms are very popular with visitors. There's an on-site bar and café to encourage you not to leave the premises; continental/cooked breakfast is an extra $10/14 per person.

Kingsgate Hotel (☎ 0800 782 548, 03-477 6784; dunedin@kingsgatehotels.co.nz; 10 Smith St; d from $120; ☐) Centrally located on the steeper side of the Octagon, only a downhill roll away from numerous eateries and bars. Has big modern rooms and 24-hour room service. You can often get good weekend deals (usually from $105 per night).

Southern Cross Hotel (☎ 0800 696 963, 03-477 0752; www.scenic-circle.co.nz; cnr Princes & High Sts; rooms from $160; ☐) For something more sumptuous try here.

MOTELS

Alexis Motor Lodge (☎ 0800 425 394, 03-471 7268; www.alexis.co.nz; 475 George St; d $100-130; ☐) Well-equipped motel with contemporary rooms adjacent to the impressive Knox Church, and only a short stroll to Otago Museum. It's also within smelling distance of several eateries across George St.

97 Motel Moray Place (☎ 0800 909 797, 03-477 1991; info@97motel.co.nz; 97 Moray Pl; d $95-150) The outside of this place has weathered a few aesthetic storms over the years, but the rooms look a lot better than the façade. Here you pay for the central location, not the view, which from some rooms is dominated by deteriorating inner-city buildings.

St Kilda Motels (☎ 03-455 1151; stkildamotels@xtra.co.nz; cnr Queens Dr & Victoria Rd; s/d from $55/65) Cheap suburban option, appealingly close to St Kilda beach but at a busy intersection. Due to its price and location, its two one-bedroom units and several two-bedroom models can book out well in advance at peak times.

Other motel recommendations:

858 George Street Motel (☎ 0800 858 999, 03-474 0047; www.858georgestreetmotel.co.nz; 858 George St; d $95-140) Plush townhouse apartments make a refreshing change from your standard squat motel block.

Arcadian Motel (Map p568; ☎ 0508 272 234, 03-455 0992; www.dunedinmotel.co.nz; 85 Musselburgh Rise; d from $75) Good range of accommodation on the way to the peninsula, from studios to three-bedroom family units.

Best Western Tourist Court (☎ 0800 244 664, 03-477 4270; www.bestwestern.co.nz/touristcourt; 842 George St; s & d $70-120) Very hospitable and comfortable motel, with management that goes out of the way to be helpful.

CAMPING & CAMPERVAN PARKS

Leith Valley Touring Park (☎ 03-467 9936; lvtpdun@southnet.co.nz; 103 Malvern St; camp sites & campervan sites $22, d $32-64) Lovely little park snuggled up against a cliff face north of town; take Duke St, at the top end of George St. Some camp sites lie beside a small creek and it has a very cosy timber lounge-dining-kitchen area. Continental breakfast costs an extra $5 per person.

Dunedin Holiday Park (☎ 0800 945 455, 03-455 4690; www.dunedinholidaypark.co.nz; 41 Victoria Rd; camp sites $20, campervan sites $22, d $30-65) This sizeable park is several hundred metres east along Victoria Rd from St Kilda Motels (see p563), over a hill from St Kilda Beach. It has

OTAGO

a kids' playground and around 100 camp sites, and can get pretty crowded at peak times. The cheapest en suite accommodation is in a lodge room.

Aaron Lodge Top 10 Holiday Park (☎ 0800 879 227, 03-476 4725; www.aaronlodgetop10.co.nz; 162 Kaikorai Valley Rd; camp sites $24, campervan sites $26, d $40-78; ☐ ☒ ☒) Well-tended holiday plot 2.5km northwest of the city, with good bus access (take a Bradford or Brockville bus from the Octagon). It has great gardens climbing the hill behind reception, where secluded camp sites are secreted. Kids are well catered for, with everything from play equipment to a pool and an 'under 5s playroom'.

Eating
RESTAURANTS
Bell Pepper Blues (☎ 03-474 0973; 474 Princes St; dinner mains $27-34; ☯ lunch Wed-Fri, dinner Mon-Sat) Lunch at this highly-regarded restaurant comprises what's called the 'Chile Club', where light lunches in the order of duck liver pâté with ginger relish are served. Full-on dinner mains involve char-grilled swordfish, masala-dusted cervena and vegetarian polenta.

Etrusco at the Savoy (☎ 03-477 3737; 1st fl, 8a Moray Pl; mains $12-15; ☯ dinner) Reasonably priced Italian (pizza, pasta, antipasto) is served in a lovely pillar-supported room within the grand old Savoy building. Small circles of stained glass in the windows add colour to the wood-heavy atmosphere. Diners tend to dress semi-formal to partake of the elegance.

Mission (☎ 03-477 1637; 65 Hanover St; mains $13-25; ☯ lunch & dinner) Extraordinary venue – an old church, which became a club and was then turned into an immaculate conception of a restaurant/bar. Menu includes pizza, calzone and various pastas (including roast veg and pesto), plus hoy sin pork and pumpkin-cheese fritters.

Hungry Frenchman (☎ 03-477 5748; 38 the Octagon; mains $22-27; ☯ lunch & dinner) Wonderful downstairs eatery modelled on a classic French brasserie, complete with dark tones and mellow music. Try the baked ravioli of mushroom and blue cheese, or the Coquilles St Jacques (scallops in a white wine sauce with cheese and bacon). Among the desserts is a delicious dark berry parfait. Book ahead.

Thai Over (☎ 03-477 7815; 388 George St; mains $17; ☯ dinner) Good central Thai restaurant with familiar Asian dishes like pad Thai, but also newcomers like lamb shank curry (though the 'spaghetti drunken' Thai/Italian fusion leaves us baffled).

Esplanade (☎ 03-456 2544; Esplanade; mains $15-25; ☯ brunch & dinner) In the old Hydro Hotel overlooking St Clair Beach, where oceanfront views are accompanied by jazzy background music to get you in the mood to munch a hearty brunch. Of the mains choices, spaghetti chicken livers is one of the more unusual offerings.

Reef (☎ 03-471 7185; 333 George St; mains $19-24; ☯ lunch & dinner) Wade into the Reef's deep-blue interior and try the excellent chilli crab or share a seafood platter between two for around $60. The 'express' lunches ($10, served within 15 minutes) include prawns, calamari rings and seafood chowder.

CAFÉS
Nova Cafe (☎ 03-479 0808; 29 the Octagon; mains $13-25; ☯ breakfast, lunch & dinner) Chew over what you just perused in the Public Art Gallery in neighbouring Nova Cafe, a red-walled eatery with good coffee and a menu filled with venison osso bucco, roast veg stacks, burgers and seafood gumbo.

Governors Cafe (☎ 03-477 6871; 438 George St; meals $8-15; ☯ lunch & dinner) Cool, happening café decorated with student notices and serving all-day breakfasts for late-risers, plus an array of milkshakes and light meals like pizzas and nachos.

Mazagran Espresso Bar (☎ 03-477 9959; 36 Moray Pl; ☯ 8am-6pm Mon-Fri, 10am-2pm Sat & Sun) International coffee-bean emporium, roughly the size of a large espresso machine and usually with a queue of addicts reading *The Socialist Review* and *Real Groove*.

Fix (☎ 03-479 2660; 15 Frederick St; ☯ early Mon-Thu, later Fri-Sun) Another good espresso place where you're welcome to BYO food to accompany their coffee; the courtyard is always crammed with uni folk.

Tangenté (☎ 03-477 0232; 111 Moray Pl; meals $10-25; ☯ lunch daily, dinner Fri & Sat) Overdoes the 'casual funk' and 'designer cuisine' angles, but this taste-conscious bakery-café nonetheless serves a delicious range of brunch fare and various seafood, meat and pasta dishes. The café also does organic breads and serves coffee in towering ceramic goblets.

Percolator (☎ 03-477 5462; 142 Lower Stuart St; meals $7-14; ☼ breakfast, lunch & dinner) Hip little place with a relaxed young crowd and ironically grandiose touches like an opulent paint job. Egg-heavy brunches are the big deal here and there's lots of arts-related material to browse.

Tasty veg and vegan food ($7 to $15) is offered at the highly entertaining **Arc Cafe**; see under Live Music & Nightclubs (p566).

QUICK EATS

London Lounge (☎ 03-477 8035; 387 George St; mains $9-15; ☼ lunch & dinner) Upstairs in the Albert Arms tavern is this student-popular local, dishing out gourmet pub fodder like MacDuff sausages and Rob Roy roast of the day, all at heavily deflated prices.

Jizo Japanese Cafe & Bar (☎ 03-479 2692; 56 Princes St; meals $6-15; ☼ lunch & dinner Mon-Sat) Good-value Japanese eatery with a black-cloaked interior and a small mezzanine level. Try the squid teriyaki or any of the excellent udon noodle dishes.

New Satay Noodle House (☎ 03-479 2235; 16 Hanover St; meals $6-9; ☼ lunch & dinner) Dirt-cheap, no-frills place serving a wide variety of Chinese and Thai dishes, plus some kormas and vindaloos too. Judging by the consistently full tables, the food is popular.

Azi Jaan (☎ 03-477 0505; 424 George St; ☼ lunch & dinner) Turkish takeaway selling tasty shwarmas, shish kebabs and burgers. On either side of it is a strip of cheap noodle, curry and pizza places.

Potpourri (☎ 03-477 9983; 97 Lower Stuart St; meals $6-9; ☼ breakfast & lunch) Wolf down organic pizzas, burritos, pies and quiches in this wholefoods-cooking café while something groovy like James Brown plays in the background.

SELF-CATERING

Head to **Countdown supermarket** (☎ 03-477 7283; 309 Cumberland St) for 24-hour supplies.

Drinking

Pop Bar (☎ 03-474 0842; 14 the Octagon) Booth-sized downstairs bar-club that gets going late, with vinyl benches and plenty of barstools to warm while you're waiting for the music to start.

Di Lusso (☎ 03-477 3776; 12 the Octagon) This is a loungy hideaway dressed to impress at night and fond of its vodka and its aquarium.

Abalone (☎ 03-477 6877; cnr George & Hanover Sts) Shiny first-floor restaurant-bar that stays open until late for cocktails and other refined boozing against a background of chic muzak once the dinner crowds have been packed away. There are lots of chairs to sink into and a long elegant bar to slump over.

Bennu Cafe & Bar (☎ 03-474 5055; 12 Moray Pl) Rich-décor establishment in the Savoy building, all burgundy and gold leaf. The bar dominates the far end of the room under a glass atrium and attracts a mellow, older crowd for late-night glass-clinking. For more of the same – lavish interior, huge cocktail list – try the piano-bar ambience of **Isis** (☎ 03-477 8001; 68 Princes St).

Captain Cook (☎ 03-474 1935; 354 Great King St) The 'Cook' is a classic hang-out for procrastinating students during term, supplying them with a beer garden, big-screen TV, cheap food and plenty of freshly-filled glasses.

Albert Arms (Royal Albert Mine Host Bar; ☎ 03-477 2952; 387 George St) This Flatiron-shaped pub has recently been refurbished. It attracts low-key locals and the odd student grouping.

Woolshed (☎ 03-477 3246; 318 Moray Pl) This country-comfort drinking spot is full of alcohol-soaked good cheer, rural wall-hung paraphernalia and several pool tables. Can get quite raucous when the crowd starts to build.

Poolhouse (☎ 03-477 6121; 12 Filleul St; pool per hr $6-9) Not one of your run-of-the-mill seedy poolhalls, but a clean, well-run, relatively quiet place where you can knock balls around on 7ft and 9ft tables, sipping a skill-lowering ale in between pots. A new backpackers' was being installed upstairs when we visited, which may change the ambience somewhat.

Entertainment

The *Otago Daily Times* newspaper lists what's on around the city. So does the free weekly pamphlet *f*INK*, available at cafés and bars around town or online (www.fink.net.nz). A number of nightspots close on Sunday and Monday.

CINEMAS

For commercial releases, get down to **Hoyts** (☎ 03-477 3250; info line 03-477 7019; 33 the Octagon; adult/child/student $13/7.50/10.50). The **Rialto Cinemas** (☎ 03-474 2200; www.rialto.co.nz; 11 Moray Pl;

OTAGO

adult/child/student \$13/7.50/11) shows a mixture of mainstream and independent releases in a halcyon-era cinema. **Metro** (☎ 03-474 3350; www.metrocinema.co.nz; Town Hall, Moray Pl; admission before/after 5pm \$8.50/10) resides in the Town Hall and prefers arthouse titles.

LIVE MUSIC & NIGHTCLUBS

Arc Cafe (☎ 03-474 1135; www.arc.org.nz; 135 High St; gigs free-\$10; 🖳) The pick of the local live-music scene is the ultra-diverse Arc Cafe. Within the space of a week, you can catch acoustic gigs, funk, jazz, stand-up comedy, DJs and drumming circles while surrounded by a mainly young, laid-back crowd.

Bath St (☎ 03-477 6750; 1 Bath St; admission free-\$8) Like all respectable late-night clubs, the perennial Bath St is accessed through a small unsigned doorway and down a bare corridor. It's not that big, but the dance floor is bigger than most other clubs around town and hosts popular hip-hop and house gigs.

Bars/restaurants that are keen on musical inspiration (most events free):

Abalone (☎ 03-477 6877; cnr George & Hanover Sts) Makes clubbing sounds from 10pm Friday and Saturday.

Bennu Cafe & Bar (☎ 03-474 5055; 12 Moray Pl) At the time of research, Bennu was planning to open a downstairs space for jazz and other live music.

Mission (☎ 03-477 1637; 65 Hanover St; 🕑 from 11pm Fri & Sat) Play pool under the stained glass, drink beer sitting on an old pew or just hang about staring at the organ pipes until the post-dinner DJs take over.

Pop Bar (☎ 03-474 0842; 14 the Octagon) DJs usually play Thursday to Saturday, progressing from soul to house as the days pass.

Woolshed (☎ 03-477 3246; 318 Moray Pl) Rustic live music (like bush bands) from midweek onwards.

SPORT

Carisbrook Stadium (☎ 03-455 1191; http://otago rugby.com; Burns St; tickets \$15-30) The so-called 'home of NZ rugby' (also known less congenially as the 'House of Pain'). Attending a rugby game here (season runs February to October) is a great way to expose yourself to the Kiwi passion for this sport. Terrace tickets to low-key games are usually available at the ground.

Bottom Bus (☎ 03-434 7370; www.bottombus.co.nz) Runs rugby trips combining meals, drinks, face painting and transport (with/without bus pass \$175/230). Transport can also be arranged from Queenstown (from \$195).

THEATRE

Fortune Theatre (☎ 03-477 8323; www.fortunethea tre.co.nz; 231 Stuart St; adult/child \$25/15; 🕑 box office 9am-5pm Mon-Fri, also 4.30-8.30pm Sat & 1.30-4pm Sun when shows are on) Local company that has been treading the floorboards in a graceful old church for over 25 years. Surprisingly, tickets are \$2 more expensive when booked online.

OTHER

Dunedin Casino (☎ 0800 477 4545; www.dunedincasino .co.nz; 118 High St) Part of the Southern Cross Hotel, Dunedin's casino has engulfed the former Grand Hotel building's ostentatiously refurbished architecture, from the gilded grand staircase right up to the glass dome.

Getting There & Away

AIR

Direct, budget-priced flights between Dunedin and eastern Australia destinations are offered by **Freedom Air** (☎ 0800 600 500, 09-523 8686; www.freedomair.co.nz); see the Transport chapter (p678).

Air New Zealand (☎ 0800 737 000, 03-479 6594; www.airnz.co.nz; cnr Princes St & the Octagon) conducts direct flights to/from Auckland (from \$165), Christchurch (from \$75) and Wellington (from \$100). **Qantas** (☎ 0800 808 767, 03-379 6504; www.qantas.co.nz) also offers direct flights to Christchurch (from \$95). **Origin Pacific Airways** (☎ 0800 302 302, 03-547 2020; www.originpacific.co.nz) flies direct to Christchurch too (from \$75).

BUS

Major bus line **InterCity** (☎ 03-474 9600; www .intercitycoach.co.nz; 205 St Andrew St) has direct services to Christchurch (\$60), Queenstown (\$55) and Te Anau (\$45).

Several door-to-door shuttles service Dunedin, arriving and departing at Dunedin Railway Station on Anzac Ave; you can make inquiries and bookings at the station's **travel desk** (☎ 03-477 4449; 🕑 8.30am-5pm Mon-Fri, 9am-5pm Sat & Sun). **Atomic Shuttles** (☎ 03-322 8883; www.atomictravel.co.nz) runs to/from Christchurch (\$30), Invercargill (\$25) and Queenstown or Wanaka (\$30). Knightrider operates a night-time service on the Christchurch–Dunedin–Invercargill route (\$35 each segment). **Catch-A-Bus** (☎ 03-479 9960) operates daily between Dunedin and Te Anau (\$45), and also has services to

Christchurch ($45), Queenstown ($30) and Wanaka ($38). **Wanaka Connexions** (☎ 03-443 9122; www.wanakaconnexions.co.nz) shuttles from Dunedin to Wanaka and then Queenstown (both $35).

From Dunedin, **Bottom Bus** (☎ 03-434 7370; www.bottombus.co.nz) and **Catlins Coaster** (☎ 0800 304 333, 021 682 461; www.catlinscoaster.co.nz) both do the scenic route through the Catlins; see under The Catlins (p638).

TRAIN
The magnificent **Dunedin Railway Station** (Anzac Ave) is visited by the Taieri Gorge Railway (p558).

Getting Around
Dunedin Airport (☎ 03-486 2879; www.dnairport.co.nz) is located 27km southwest of the city. **Kiwi Shuttles** (☎ 03-473 7017; http://kiwishuttles.co.nz) handles airport transfers (around $15). **Dunedin Taxis** (☎ 03-477 7777) and **City Taxis** (☎ 03-477 1771) also operate door-to-door shuttles for a similar price; a standard taxi ride between the city and airport costs around $50 to $60.

City buses (www.orc.govt.nz/bustt/bus.asp) leave from stops in the Octagon, while buses to districts around Dunedin leave from Cumberland St. Buses run regularly during the week, but routes combine on Saturday and Sunday to form limited services, or they simply stop running. The visitors centre has timetables and the average trip costs under $2.

For details of the hop-on, hop-off Dunedin City Explorer (see under Tours p562).

OTAGO PENINSULA
Otago Peninsula has a reputation as the most accessible wildlife area on the South Island – albatross, yellow-eyed penguins, blue penguins, fur seals and sea lions all thrive here – and also harbours a score of historical sites, walkways and natural formations. For an overview, pick up the *Otago Peninsula* brochure and map from Dunedin's visitors centre and check out www.otago-peninsula.co.nz.

Sights
ALBATROSS
Taiaroa Head, at the peninsula's eastern end, has the world's only mainland royal albatross colony. The birds arrive at the nesting site in September, court and mate in October, lay eggs in November, then incubate the eggs until January, when the chicks hatch. Between March and September parents leave their chicks while collecting food, returning only for feeding. By September the fledged chicks leave.

The **Royal Albatross Centre** (☎ 03-478 0499; www.albatrosses.com; Taiaroa Head; ☼ 9am-7pm summer, shorter hrs winter) has excellent displays on the albatross and other peninsular wildlife, as well as a pretty good **café** (mains $11-17). The only public access to the colony is from the centre, with tours offered half-hourly (bookings essential). The one-hour 'Royal Albatross' tour (adult/child/family $25/12/65) includes a 30-minute video and talk at the centre, then heads up the hill to a glassed-in viewing area overlooking the nesting sites.

In calm weather it's unlikely you'll see an albatross flying, but chances are better later in the day when the wind picks up; ask if the birds are around before you pay. The centre is open year-round but the main viewing area is closed to the public during the breeding season (mid-September to late November). At this time you can still attend the 'Albatross Insight' introductory talk and video confined to the centre (adult/child/family $8/4/20).

Also here are the tunnels of historic 1886 **Fort Taiaroa**, featuring a 150mm Armstrong Disappearing Gun. The gun was installed during the late 19th century to counter the improbable threat of attack from Tsarist Russia, and was so named because it could be withdrawn into its bunker after firing. 'Fort Taiaroa' tours (adult/child/family $12/6/33) depart the albatross centre; there's also a 1½-hour 'Unique Taiaroa' tour (adult/child/family $30/15/75) combining albatross colony and fort.

PENGUINS
The yellow-eyed penguin (*hoiho* in Maori), one of the rarest penguin species, is faced with an ongoing loss of habitat, especially the low-lying coastal vegetation in which the birds nest. Sadly, many farmers in Southland and Otago allow cattle to trample the remaining patches of vegetation favoured by these birds.

On the peninsula, a private conservation reserve called **Penguin Place** (☎ 03-478 0286;

OTAGO

Harrington Pt Rd; tours adult/child/family $30/15/75; tours every half-hour) has been set-up by the owners of Penguin Place Lodge (see p570), who have replanted the breeding habitat, built nesting sites, cared for sick and injured birds and trapped predators. From the lodge, you can do tours of the reserve, comprising a talk on penguin conservation and close-up viewing from a system of trenches and hides; these trips are very popular, so book ahead. For accommodation, see p569.

Several tour operators (see opposite) go to other yellow-eyed penguin beaches via land owned by farmers who charge for the privilege. Yellow-eyed penguins also nest at other public beaches, including Sandfly Bay which has a DOC hide; follow all signs, don't approach the penguins, and view them only from the hide. Unfortunately, the penguins have been badly disturbed at some beaches by first-class idiots wielding flash photography and car headlights, to the point where (according to some concerned locals) the birds are moving further down the coast.

SEA LIONS

The New Zealand (or Hooker's) sea lions can usually only be seen on a tour (see opposite) to a 'secret' beach where the first pup was born on the NZ mainland after a breeding absence of 700 years. They are also often present at Allans and Victory Beaches. The sea lions, visitors from Campbell Island and the Auckland Islands, are predominantly bachelor males.

LARNACH CASTLE

This **castle** (☎ 03-476 1616; www.larnachcastle.co.nz; Camp Rd; castle & grounds adult/child $15/6, grounds only $8/3; ☺ 9am-5pm) is a monumental extravagance, a mashing of architectural styles and fantasies on the highest point of the peninsula, funded (to the tune of £125,000, or about $25 million by today's standards) by one William Larnach in 1871 to impress his French nobility-descended wife. Larnach, a merchant and politician, committed suicide in a Parliament House committee room in 1898, one of the many scandals presented inside the castle for tourist titillation.

OTAGO PENINSULA

	0	5 km
	0	3 miles

SIGHTS & ACTIVITIES	(pp567-9)
Glenfalloch Woodland Garden	1 B3
Larnach Castle	2 B2
Marine Studies Centre	3 C2
Natures Wonders	4 D1
Penguin Place	5 D1
Royal Albatross Centre & Fort Taiaroa	6 D1

SLEEPING	(pp569-70)
Arcadian Motel	7 A3
Cottage	8 B2
Dunedin Holiday Park	9 A3
Harington Point Village Motel	10 D1
Homestead	11 C2
Larnach Lodge	(see 2)
McFarmers Backpackers	12 C2
Penguin Place Lodge	(see 5)
St Kilda Motels	13 A3

EATING	(pp569-70)
Whalers Arms Cafe	14 B3

See Dunedin Map (p560)

Larnach Castle can be reached from Dunedin by guided tour or by taking the Portobello bus to Company Bay and walking 4km uphill. If you buy access to the gardens only, you can still visit the café in the castle's ballroom. There's also some wonderful accommodation here (see below).

OTHER SIGHTS

Glenfalloch Woodland Garden (☎ 03-476 1775; 430 Portobello Rd; admission by donation; ⏰ 9.30am-dusk) is a gorgeous florescent landscape covering 12 hectares, with walking tracks leading through a profusion of rhododendrons, azaleas, magnolias and fuchsias. The café-wine bar here is open over summer. The Portobello bus stops out the front.

The University of Otago–run **Marine Studies Centre** (☎ 03-479 5826; www.otago.ac.nz/marine studies; Hatchery Rd; adult/child/family $8/4/16; ⏰ noon-4.30pm) showcases the work of the adjacent marine laboratory. The main attraction is a one-room aquarium displaying octopus, crayfish and seahorses, plus a rockpool-style touch-tank. There are guided tours of the facility (adult/child/family $16/8/32) at 10.30am daily.

Activities

WALKING

The peninsula has numerous scenic farmland and beach walks, accessible with your own transport and detailed in the free brochure *Otago Peninsula Tracks*.

From the car park at the end of Seal Point Rd, trudge down huge sand dunes to the beautiful beach at **Sandfly Bay** (40 minutes). From the end of Sandymount Rd, there's a walk to the impressive cliff scenery of the **Chasm** and **Lovers Leap** (40 minutes return), plus a one-hour side-trail to Sandfly Bay.

OTHER ACTIVITIES

Natures Wonders (☎ 0800 246 446; www.natures wondersnaturally.com; adult/child $30/25; ⏰ 9am-7pm summer, shorter hrs winter) does 45-minute round-trips in an 8WD amphibious vehicle through property at Taiaroa Head, taking in great coastal scenery and wildlife. It's based not far from the albatross centre, on a site where an all-day café with a large outdoor deck was about to open when we visited.

E-Tours (☎ 03-476 1960; www.inmark.co.nz/e-tours; $95) operates full-day cycling trips along rural

tracks and beach, plus admission to either the albatross or penguin centres, or a cruise. Price includes pick-up from Dunedin.

Wild Earth Adventures (☎ 03-473 6535; www .wildearth.co.nz; from $80) takes sea-kayaking trips in the area, spending about two hours in the water. It also picks up from Dunedin. More sea kayaking options, including trips out to Quarantine Island, are offered by **Just Kayaking** (☎ 0800 867 325; info@justkayaking.co.nz; from $79).

Those keen on sinking to new depths in the harbour should contact **Dive Otago** (☎ 03-466 4370; www.diveotago.co.nz; day dives from $135), which also heads further afield to plunge into places like Milford Sound.

Tours

Otago Nature Guides (☎ 03-454 5169; www.nznature guides.com) offers small-group ecotours (maximum four people) where walks, wildlife viewing, knowledgeable commentary, most food and accommodation is provided – one such package includes a sunrise walk to see yellow-eyed penguins, a day-long tour of Dunedin and the Otago Peninsula, lunch and two nights B&B ($420).

Newton Tours (☎ 03-477 5577; www.transport place.co.nz) heads from Dunedin to Larnach Castle along Highcliff Rd (adult/child $32/ 16, including castle entry), and does various wildlife on and around Taiaroa Head (from $50/25).

Otago Explorer (☎ 0800 322 240, 03-474 3300; from $35; ⏰ 9am & 3pm) is the only peninsula operator to offer guided tours inside Larnach Castle, with the guide giving a good spin on the Larnach family history.

Elm Wildlife Tours (☎ 0800 356 563, 03-474 1872; www.elmwildlifetours.co.nz; standard tour $65) conducts small-group wildlife-spotting tours of up to six hours out of Dunedin, with pick-up and drop-off included in the cost.

Back to Nature Tours (☎ 0800 477 0484, 03-477 0484; www.backtonaturetours.co.nz; from $50), based out of Manor House Backpackers (see p563), does a similar trip, departing Dunedin in the afternoon.

Sleeping & Eating

Portobello Village Tourist Park (☎ 03-478 0359; portobellotp@xtra.co.nz; 27 Hereweka St; camp sites $20, campervan sites $24, d $30-65) Pretty little park in Portobello township, with a fine removed-from-it-all feel, bike hire, basic bunkrooms and

OTAGO

fully equipped tourist flats. It's a short walk from the bright lights of Portobello's CBD.

McFarmers Backpackers (☎ 03-478 0389; mcfarmersbackpackers@hotmail.com; 774 Portobello Rd; dm/d $20/45) Friendly, highly-rated hilltop farmstay combining a harbourside position with a rural nature. Backpackers are well catered for and families can vie for the separate self-contained cottage. Located 1km from Portobello village; the local bus usually stops out the front.

Portobello Hotel (☎ 03-478 0759; 2 Harington Pt Rd; s/d $35/70) The township's old pub has a pair of decent rooms, one with en suite. There are plans to embellish the hotel with some outdoor decking and a bistro in the future; in the meantime, you'll find plenty of locals yabbering away in the front bar.

Larnach Lodge (☎ 03-476 1616; www.larnachcastle .co.nz; Camp Rd; rooms $200-240) A dozen plush, historically themed rooms in the begardened grounds of Larnach Castle. Stalk the estate as if it's your own and order tea in the ballroom with the appropriate flourish; dinners by arrangement. Room and breakfast are also available in the 125-year-old Coach House (Stablestay; doubles $95).

Penguin Place Lodge (☎ 03-478 0286; Harington Pt Rd; adult/child $20/10) Simple but well-maintained lodge accommodation with shared facilities on private farmland. Linen is $5 extra but the harbour and pasture views come free of charge.

Harington Point Village Motel (☎ 03-478 0287; www.wildlifetours.co.nz; 932 Harington Pt Rd; d $85-120) Close to the albatross centre and imbued with an appreciation of natural beauty (thanks to the wildlife-savvy owners), this motel has spacious, self-contained units.

Bayways Motel (☎ 03-478 0181; bayways@clear .net.nz; cnr Portobello & Highcliff Rds; d $85-110) Another good option, this place is located in Portobello and has a couple of deck-sporting units looking out towards the harbour.

Cottage (☎ 03-476 1877; www.visit-dunedin.co.nz /thecottage.html; 748 Portobello Rd; d $120-155) Charming, old-world cottage in a private setting at Broad Bay, built as a fisherman's getaway and now a modern retreat with generous breakfasts.

Homestead (☎ 03-478 0384; thehomestead@clear.net .nz; 238 Harington Point Rd; d $100-120) Has three likeable self-contained units a few kilometres from Portobello.

1908 Cafe (☎ 03-478 0801; 7 Harington Pt Rd; mains $10-25; ☺ breakfast, lunch & dinner) The best dining choice on the peninsula, in Portobello and with a mod-NZ à la carte menu and gourmet blackboard specials. Families won't go hungry here, and neither will those with dietary requirements, who will be accommodated wherever possible.

Whalers Arms Cafe (☎ 03-476 1357; 494 Portobello Rd; mains from $10; ☺ lunch & dinner) Something-for-everyone café and bar, with a watery vista at Macandrew Bay and a good range of light and heavy meals, as well as a variety of wine to choose from.

Getting There & Around

There are a half-dozen bus services each weekday between Dunedin and Portobello ($4), several continuing on to Harington Pt, though weekend services are limited. Once you get to the peninsula, however, you'll find it's tough to get around without your own transport.

Note that the petrol station in Portobello keeps unpredictable hours, so it's best to fill up in Dunedin before driving out.

CENTRAL OTAGO

Much of Central Otago lies on a rugged and dry plateau sheltered by the Southern Alps. A multitude of towns here owe their origin to a 40-year gold mining era during the late 19th century. The old goldfields extend from Wanaka south to Queenstown and Glenorchy, east through Alexandra to the coast at Palmerston, and southeast from Alexandra to Milton. Interpretative pamphlets such as *Otago Goldfields: Heritage Trail* pinpoint areas where stone buildings, mining equipment and miles of tailings (left-over mining waste) can be found. In places like Queenstown, a different sort of gold is now being mined – tourism. This region is also becoming more prominent for its fine wine making; see the 'Top Otago Tipples' boxed text (p576).

For good regional information, visit www .tco.org.nz.

CROMWELL

pop 2610

This modern but low-on-character waystation on the main route between Wanaka and Queenstown is at the heart of stone fruit country, as testified to by the giant Carmen Miranda hat-piece display in front of the town and the many roadside fruit stalls.

The **Cromwell & Districts visitors centre** (☎ 03-445 0212; cromwellvin@xtra.co.nz; 47 the Mall; ☺ 10am-4pm) has displays on the Clutha Valley hydroelectricity projects and local mining artefacts.

The town's historic precinct, **Old Cromwell Town**, is a row of historic buildings on Melmore Tce overlooking Dunstan Dam; they were painstakingly removed and restored from the original Cromwell, now flooded by the waters of the dam. It's a disappointingly lifeless area, home to a few craft shops, though the buildings are interesting. The *Old Cromwell Town Historic Precinct* brochure details a self-guided tour.

Nearby gold-mining sites include Bannockburn, crumbling Bendigo and the Kawarau. About 7km towards Queenstown and across a footbridge spanning the spectacular Kawarau Gorge is the **Goldfields Mining Centre** (☎ 03-445 1038; www .goldfieldsmining.co.nz; SH6; adult/child $14/6; ☺ 9am-5pm), a rather commercial operation offering tours of the tailings and old mine machinery, including the opportunity to pan for gold or buy their gold jewellery. There are also 40-minute jetboat rides here on the Kawarau River with **Goldfields Jet** (☎ 03-445 3105; www.shotoverjet.co.nz; adult/child $75/45).

Further along the road to Queenstown are some excellent **wineries**, plus there's **bungy jumping** at the old Kawarau suspension bridge (see p585).

Sleeping & Eating

Cromwell Top 10 Holiday Park (☎ 0800 107 275, 03-445 0164; www.cromwellholidaypark.co.nz; 1 Alpha St; camp sites & campervan sites $24, d $40-90; ▣) This huge park, 2km from the town centre, is a friendly place with excellent modern facilities; the new units are a particularly good deal. There's also a playground to occupy the kids and a BBQ area clouded by cooking smells.

Chalets Holiday Park (☎ 0800 830 231, 03-445 1260; www.thechalets.co.nz; 102 Barry Ave; camp sites & campervan sites $18, s $25, d $40-60) Large lodges owned by the local polytechnic, once the quarters for dam workers. Each chalet has its own lounge, kitchen and grouping of

well-equipped rooms, and there's a bar-restaurant on-site.

Golden Gate Lodge (☎ 0800 104 451, 03-445 1777; www.goldengate.co.nz; Barry Ave; rooms $95-180) Complex of nearly 50 rooms that's partial to large conferences. It overlooks Lake Dunstan and also has its own restaurant and bar. Several units are wheelchair-accessible or have spa baths.

Pub (☎ 03-445 0725; 71 the Mall; meals $8-17; ☺ lunch & dinner) Not hard to guess what this former café has transformed into. Think big-screen TV playing music 'hits', pool table and a menu governed by pizza, steak sandwiches and rissoles, mash and gravy.

Bannockburn Heights Cafe (☎ 03-445 3211; Cairnmuir Rd, Bannockburn; mains from$12; ☺ lunch & dinner) Situated 8km from Cromwell, this adjunct to a prominent Central Otago vineyard serves a variety of seafood and other meat dishes. It provides a 'courtesy coach' to pick up and drop off in Cromwell, so you can enjoy as much wine with your meal as you please.

ALEXANDRA

pop 4620

Southeast of Cromwell is Alexandra, Central Otago's service hub and an oasis of trees among barren, rocky hills. The lure of gold brought thousands to the Dunstan goldfields, but the town owes its permanence to the post-rush dredging boom of the 1890s. The orchardists followed and built Alexandra's current prosperity.

There's a **DOC office** (☎ 03-440 2040; 43 Dunstan Rd) on the town's outskirts. The informative **Central Otago visitors centre** (☎ 03-448 9515; www.alexandra.co.nz; 22 Centennial Ave; ☺ 9am-5pm) is planning to relocate to yet-to-be-built premises across the road in Pioneer Park, which will also house the local museum.

Speaking of which, the **Alexandra Museum** (☎ 03-448 6230; Dunorling St; admission by donation; ☺ 10am-4.30pm Mon-Fri, 2-4pm Sun) is currently in temporary lodgings, awaiting its new home. A lot of stuff is in storage, but there are still viewable historical photos and mining-days artefacts, including a piece of staircase salvaged from the historic 1862 Bendigo Hotel that was demolished in 2001.

On a hill above town is the austere, 11m-diameter **Alexandra Clock** (the local reply to the Hollywood Hills sign), which can be

OTAGO

reached by walking track (one hour return) or by driving to a nearby viewpoint.

Activities

Alexandra is mountain bike heaven, with many old gold trails weaving through the Old Man, Dunstan, Raggedy and Knobby Ranges. A highlight for enthusiasts is the **Dunstan Trail**, and another is the subject of the 'Otago Central Rail Trail' boxed text (opposite). A series of pamphlets, *Mountain Biking*, at the visitors centre detail many exhilarating rides; check track conditions first. Rent bikes from **Kayak & Outdoor** (☎ 03-448 8149; 21 Shannon St; bike hire per day $12-40), or take one of their guided 20km to 48km trips.

Safari Excursions (☎ 03-448 7474; half-day tour per person $25-35) offers 4WD explorations of craggy canyons and tussocked hills.

Sleeping

Alexandra Holiday Park (☎ 03-448 8297; Manuherikia Rd; camp sites & campervan sites $19, d $28-60) One of two fairly tired-looking parks in town, though it does have some shady sites and a scenic setting.

Fruitlands (☎ 03-449 2192; www.fruitlandscountry lodge.co.nz; SH8; d $95) This restored historic lodge is 13km south of town, where its stony walls shoulder a gallery of local crafts, café, outdoor terrace and three great modern units.

Rocky Range (☎ 0800 153 293, 03-448 6150; www.rockyrange.co.nz; s/d $195/310; 🖳) Right up the upscale reposing on the highpoint of a 40-hectare property and with four luxurious rooms and a rock-wedged spa pool.

Motels worth an inspection include **Kiwi Motel** (☎ 03-448 8258; 115 Centennial Ave; d $68-80), with its decent-sized grey-brick units and kids' equipment (including cots, highchairs and playground), and **Almond Court Motel** (☎ 0800 256 663, 03-448 7667; 53 Killarney St; d $75-95; 🐾), with some king-size beds.

Eating

La Strada Caffe (☎ 03-448 9021; 72 Centennial Ave; meals $8-13; 🕑 breakfast & lunch) Relaxed, brunch-proficient café where pancakes and other filling dishes like the tasty 'hen grenade' (sautéed chicken, onions and peanut sauce) are carried with panache across the black-and-white tiled floor.

Nuno's (☎ 03-448 5444; 73 Centennial Ave; mains $10-22; 🕑 lunch Wed-Sun, dinner daily) Portuguese isn't the most prominent cuisine in NZ, but Nuno's is one place where you can tuck into an authentic fish stew, plus lots of other seafood and land-dwelling meats.

Getting There & Away

The visitors centre handles bookings for InterCity, Atomic, Wanaka Connexions and Catch-a-Bus, which all pass through Alexandra with connections to Wanaka, Queenstown and Dunedin.

CLYDE

pop 850

This evocative little town, 10km west of Alexandra, was once the centre of the Dunstan goldfields and historic stone buildings line its streets. Regional visitors centres should stock the free brochure *Walk Around Our Historic Town: Clyde*, detailing a self-guided town walk. **Lookout Point** allows great views over the once-bustling gold diggings.

Sleeping & Eating

Clyde Holiday & Sporting Complex (☎ 03-449 2713; crrc@ihug.co.nz; Whitby St; camp sites & campervan sites $17, d $36-40) As befits its name, the camping ground is punctuated by a large rugby oval and is near a swimming pool. There are on-site caravans and 'cabins', with the look of very basic little huts.

Hartley Arms Backpackers (☎ 03-449 2700; hartleyarms@xtra.co.nz; 25 Sunderland St; dm/d $20/45) The dorm rooms are a tight squeeze but the refreshing, garden-enhanced ambience more than compensates. All of the accommodation, including the sole double, is behind the lovely main house. Also check out the doorway of the Masonic lodge across the street.

Dunstan Hotel (☎ 03-449 2869; 35 Sunderland St; s/d $30/55) This Dam Pub (that's its nickname) is a good, clean place with well-priced upstairs rooms and a cute lounge with psychedelic carpet. Continental/cooked breakfasts cost $7/13 extra (by arrangement).

Dunstan House (☎ 03-449 2295; www.dunstan house.co.nz; 29 Sunderland St; d $90-160) Built at the turn of the 20th century, this old coaching inn (a Cobb & Co stopover) has had its history-saturated Victorian interior refurbished with great attention to period detail. The in-house restaurant seems to favour Italianate recipes.

Olivers (☎ 03-449 2860; www.olivers.co.nz; 34 Sunderland St; d $125-275) Collection of 1860s buildings

OTAGO CENTRAL RAIL TRAIL

The Central Otago rail branch line was originally built to provide reliable transport from goldfield towns to Dunedin, the region's commercial centre. Construction began near Dunedin in 1879 and by 1907 was opened as far as Clyde.

As cars became more prevalent and roads improved throughout the 20th century, railway use waned and in 1990 the 150km stretch of rail between Middlemarch and Clyde was permanently closed. DOC acquired the line and set about ripping up tracks and resurfacing the trail, including the old rail bridges, viaducts and tunnels. The old railway line is now a year-round recreational facility, designed especially for walkers, mountain-bikers and horse-riders. The total number of annual trail-users is now well over 10,000 and not surprisingly many new business have sprung up to service them.

The trail can be biked or walked in either direction, although a popular option is to travel from Dunedin on the scenic Taieri Gorge Railway (p558) and then cycle from Pukerangi to Middlemarch (19km by road), to begin the trail the following day. The entire trail takes approximately three to five days to complete (alternatively, many people choose to do a section of the trail as a day-trip). The trail caters for all fitness levels as there are no steep hills, and exposes users to wonderful scenery and a profound sense of remoteness. The towns passed though include reasonably-sized settlements like Ranfurly, Omakau and Alexandra, and tiny villages like Waipiata, Wedderburn, Oturehua and Lauder; even the latter now have a place where you can grab a bite to eat and doss down for the night. Mountain bikes can be rented for the journey from Alexandra or Dunedin.

Any of the area's major visitors centres (Alexandra, Cromwell, Dunedin) should be able to provide detailed information on the trail, and everything you need to know is also online at www.otagocentralrailtrail.co.nz.

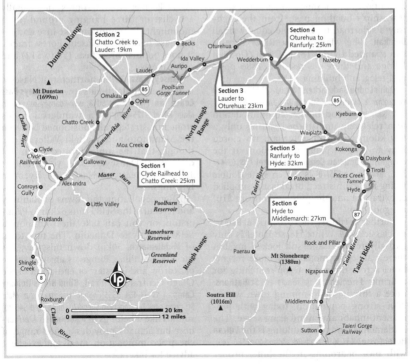

amid private gardens, with accommodation in converted stables, lodge, barn and smokehouse – in order of ascending price. The smokehouse has a four-poster bed and sunken bath. Olivers also has a fine brick-floored **restaurant** (dinner $26-30; lunch & dinner); sample the ginger-flavoured duck breast, smoked venison or the good wine list.

Post Office Cafe & Bar (☎ 03-449 2488; 2 Blyth St; meals $11-20; 10am-late) The old PO has a new career as a commendable eatery, with a menu including lamb and pesto lasagne, falafel salad and rich homemade pies, along with desserts like plum duff with brandy sauce.

ALEXANDRA TO PALMERSTON

Northeast of Alexandra, the Manuherikia Valley bears rich evidence of Otago's golden age. At Blackstone Hill the State Hwy 85 (SH85) swings southeast to the Maniototo plain and heads via a scenic section called the 'Pig Root' (hinting at the early road's condition) to Palmerston and the sea.

The peacefulness of contemporary **Ophir**, 27km north of Alexandra, belies this small township's bustling past; from the highway a side-road leads to the equally small **Omakau**. The Manuherikia River here is still spanned by the 1870s Dan O'Connell Bridge and there's a restored 1886 post-and-telegraph building.

Ophir Lodge Backpackers (☎ 03-447 3339; blgaler@ xtra.co.nz; 1 Macdonald St; dm & s from $16, d from $32;) has good budget accommodation in a relatively undisturbed setting only a few kilometres from Omakau; it's closed May to August. The nicest room at the congenial **Omakau Commercial Hotel** (☎ 03-447 3715; Main Rd; s/d $35/70) is the en suite double facing the main street; breakfast is supplied at extra cost and the pub meals (from $10) are good too.

Further northeast, the road forks at **Becks** – its classic 1864 White Horse Hotel is only partially restored and still locked up, but there's an eponymous (and more recent) hotel across the road if you're itching for a drink. The left fork leads to **St Bathans**, once a thriving gold-mining town with a 2000-strong population, today with permanent inhabitants numbering seven. The settlement's landmark building is the **Vulcan Hotel** (☎ 03-447 3629; Main Rd; s from $40, d $80-240), with nice bedrooms in the hotel proper

and more expensive cottages round back; be warned it often books out for weekend weddings due to its isolation and charm. Its **restaurant** (mains $19-23) is a cut above regular hotel eateries. No, Leonard Nimoy has never stayed here.

There's a five-minute walk here to **Blue Lake**, coloured by sluicing activity and popular for picnics. You can also walk around the lake's edge to a lookout (30 minutes).

Back on SH85, eastbound past Blackstone Hill, is **Naseby**, once the largest gold-mining town on the Maniototo and a great area for walks and mountain biking. From May to September the **Maniototo Ice Rink** (☎ 03-444 9270; Channel Rd) is used for skating, curling and ice hockey; when we visited, a large indoor rink was being developed for year-round cool sports.

At Naseby is the large, pine-scented **Larchview Holiday Park** (☎ 03-444 9904; johnsjoy naseby@paradise.net.nz; Swimming Dam Rd; camp sites & campervan sites $20, d $30-55), located next to a swimmable dam. The **Royal Hotel** (☎ 0800 262 7329, 03-444 9990; www.naseby.co.nz; 1 Earne St; s/d $25/40) has simple rooms and usually a cyclist or three hanging around, as it moonlights in mountain bike hire and repair; ask here about Naseby Forest tracks. It does popular breakfasts ($8 to $12) and other meals.

Danseys Pass, 39km northeast of Naseby, is another old goldfields town. **Danseys Pass Coach Inn** (☎ 03-444 9048; www.danseyspass.co.nz; Main Rd; d $125-140) is a wonderful 1860s stone inn, strategically positioned between the Maniototo and Waitaki Valley. Note, though, that the inn is located southwest of (not at) Danseys Pass – you'll find it 16km northeast of Naseby at Kyeburn Diggings.

After negotiating the towns of Ranfurly and Kyeburn, the SH85 runs 62km to Palmerston, or you can take the southbound SH87 directly to Dunedin. The tiny town of **Middlemarch**, 50km down this way, has the Rock & Pillar Range as an impressive backdrop, and is a start or end-point of the Otago Central Rail Trail. **Blind Billy's Holiday Camp** (☎ 03-464 3355; blindbillys@xtra.co.nz; Mold St; camp sites & campervan sites $20, dm $15, d $40-70) sounds like it belongs in a sequel to *Deliverance* but actually provides a good range of cheap accommodation, meals and excellent advice for bikers.

OTAGO

Ranfurly
pop 840

Quiet Ranfurly is the hub of the vast inland Maniototo plain and is also keen to harness the tourism opportunities provided by the rail trail. Its main asset is its rural Art Deco architecture. Similar to Napier on the North Island, Ranfurly suffered catastrophe in the 1930s, this time by a series of fires and the town was rebuilt in the style of the time; many buildings have recently been restored.

The old train station houses the helpful **Maniototo visitors centre** (☎ 03-444 1005; Charlemont St; ☽ 10am-4pm summer, shorter hrs winter), which has a free back-room photographic display and audiovisual presentation on Ranfurly and its old railway. Next door in the old Centennial Milk Bar is the **Art Deco Exhibition** (☎ 03-444 9963; Charlemont St; admission $2 'donation'; ☽ 10.30am-4pm), containing several Art Deco furniture pieces and a wall of fetching crockery.

SLEEPING & EATING

Peter's Farm Hostel (☎ 03-444 9083; www.petersfarm.co.nz; Waipiata; dm/s/d $20/33/40) Just the ticket if you want to stay in a relaxed farmhouse thrown together using mud bricks and sundry rocks in 1880. It's signposted 3km from Waipiata, which is 12km southeast of Ranfurly, off the highway. Main attractions are kayaking, gold-panning, fishing, cycling (free equipment supplied) and a nearby walking loop. They'll pick up from Ranfurly. If visiting in winter, ring ahead to check that the hostel is open.

Ranfurly Motel (☎ 03-444 9383; robbieandjoan@xtra.co.nz; 1 Davis Ave; s/d $55/70) Located on a peaceful side-street, the Ranfurly Motel has a big yard fronting its units where families can spread themselves out a bit. The units are all quite big and fully self-contained.

Ranfurly Lion Hotel (☎ 03-444 9140; 10 Charlemont St; dm $10-15, s/d $45/75; ☐) Arguably the mainstay of Ranfurly social life. The singles are a bit squeezy, while doubles/twins have a bit more room around the beds. The much-vaunted Art Deco **dining room** (dinner mains from $15; ☽ lunch & dinner) isn't that impressive, but the food is fine; lunchtime roast of the day and veg costs $9.

Old Po Backpackers (☎ 03-444 9588; oldpobackpackers@hotmail.com; 11 Pery St; beds $15-30) At the time of research, this rambling renovated hostel was being established; might be worth checking out.

GETTING THERE & AWAY

A daily shuttle passing through Ranfurly on its way between Wanaka and Dunedin is operated by **Catch-a-Bus** (☎ 03-479 9960).

Macraes Flat
Not all the gold has disappeared. Tiny Macraes Flat, on a minor road linking SH85 with SH87, is the gateway to the huge **Macraes Gold Mine**, NZ's largest open-cut diggings. Two-hour tours are arranged through **Stanley's Hotel** (☎ 03-465 2400; tours $15) in Macraes Flat.

ALEXANDRA TO DUNEDIN
South along SH8 from Alexandra towards Dunedin lies more evidence of 19th-century gold-seeking and some great rough-hills scenery.

Roxburgh township is surrounded by pretty hills in a productive fruit-growing area. Here you'll find **Villa Rose Backpackers** (☎ 03-446 8761; 79 Scotland St; dm/d from $16/36), an old-fashioned house with high-ceilinged rooms and the possibility of seasonal fruit-picking work (though this also means itinerant fruit pickers tend to fill the place up). For food, try **Succulents Cafe & Wine Bar** (☎ 03-446 8757; SH8; light meals $8; ☽ lunch Tue-Sat, dinner Thu & Fri), identifiable by the wrought-iron flowers in the windows and serving *panini* (focaccia), spinach cannelloni and fine wine.

About 7km south of Roxburgh is the **Seed Farm** (☎ 03-446 6824; www.theseedfarm.co.nz; SH8; s/d $95/110), which has four rooms in lovely converted stables, as well as continental breakfasts with homemade jam, and fresh-produce dinners.

In quaint **Lawrence** is the well-run **Oban House Backpackers** (☎ 03-485 9259; obanhouse@xtra.co.nz; 1 Oban St; dm $18), an attractive brick-and-timber place behind a rock garden; turn up Lismore St from the highway, go to the end, and the hostel is diagonally opposite. **Jazzed on Java** (☎ 03-485 9234; 26 Ross St; mains $8-20; ☽ lunch Thu-Tue, dinner Thu-Sun) serves rib-eye, laksa and bagel burgers, and decent coffee.

Near Lawrence is **Gabriels Gully**, site of a gold stampede involving 10,000 miners in 1861, after Gabriel Read discovered the mineral in the Tuapeka River.

OTAGO

TOP OTAGO TIPPLES

Central Otago has long had a reputation for wonderful scenery and high-adrenaline activities, but it's also NZ's fastest-growing wine region.

The area is not new to grape-growing. A Frenchman named John Feraud came here in 1862, drawn by the Dunstan gold rush, and set about growing his own grapes. He produced a variety of wines, but after his departure from the area commercial wine making ceased. It wasn't revived until the 1980s, when experimental grapes were planted around Queenstown, Wanaka and Alexandra. The first modern commercial wines were produced in 1987 and it's estimated there are now some 70 vineyards in Central Otago, with at least 10 open to the public.

To sample these wineries and learn more of the area's viticulture, pick up the excellent, free 'Central Otago Wine Map' from a local visitors centre, or check out www.otagowine.com. Various winery tours are also conducted from major tourist towns like Queenstown and Wanaka.

You don't have to venture too far out of Queenstown to begin your taste test. On SH6, near the historic Kawarau Suspension Bridge and bungy jump, there are three excellent wineries open to the public for tastings from 10am to 5pm daily. **Peregrine** (Map p582; ☎ 03-442 4000; www.peregrinewines.co.nz) is about 5km east of the bridge and produces excellent sauvignon blanc, pinot noir and pinot gris. **Chard Farm** (Map p582; ☎ 03-442 6110; www.chardfarm.co.nz) is accessed by a truly hair-raising road off the highway, almost opposite the bridge. Finally, **Gibbston Valley** (Map p582; ☎ 03-442 6910; www.gvwines.co.nz), 700m from the Kawarau Bridge, is the region's largest wine producer; its pinot noir is a multi-award-winner. You can do a half-hour tour of the impressive wine cave here ($9.50, including tastings), plus there's a cheese factory and a great restaurant with outdoor courtyard.

CLUTHA DISTRICT

The mighty Clutha River is not NZ's longest river (the Waikato is 16km longer) but it carries the most water, after draining a huge area that includes Lakes Hawea, Wanaka and Wakitipu. It's dammed in several places to feed hydroelectric power stations. The Clyde Dam holds back the waters of Lake Dunstan; in the 1980s it generated great controversy at the drowning of such natural beauty. The towns of Clinton, Lawrence, Milton, Waihola, Tapanui, Owaka (see under the Catlins; p638) and Balclutha are all part of this region.

Balclutha

pop 4130

The largest town in South Otago, Balclutha is dominated by an impressive arched concrete bridge across the Clutha River. There isn't very much to the town and little reason to linger, although it may be a convenient point from which to take a guided tour of the Catlins (p638), or a place to stock up on supplies before embarking on the Southern Scenic Route (p630).

Drop into the **Clutha visitors centre** (☎ 03-418 0088; balvin@nzhost.co.nz; 4 Clyde St; ☑ 8.30am-5pm Mon-Fri, 9.30am-3pm Sat & Sun) and afterwards visit the wonderful **South Otago Historical Society Museum** (Renfrew St; admission by donation; ☑ 10am-4pm Mon-Fri, 1-4pm Sun), a warehouse of regional history with old buggies, hand-worked washing machines and other old domestic and farming equipment; have a chat to the attendant about the old way of life.

SLEEPING & EATING

Naish Park Motor Camp (☎ 03-418 0088; 56 Charlotte St; camp sites $18, campervan sites $20, d $30-45) This is a compact, well-treed enclosure with a handful of basic cabins and adequate kitchen facilities. You'll find it a few turns off the main street.

Rosebank Lodge (☎ 03-418 1490; reception@rosebanklodge.co.nz; 265 Clyde St; d $90) Friendly place with a clutch of big, recently refurbished units, each with its own piece of outdoor decking. Also on-site is the worthwhile **265 on Clyde Restaurant** (mains $10-30; ☑ lunch & dinner).

Garvan Homestead (☎ 03-417 8407; www.garvan-homestead.co.nz; Lovells Flat; d $95-120) Charming 1915 Tudor-style homestead set in magnificent gardens 13km north of Balclutha on SH1. The old-world B&B rooms here make way for modern à la carte dining at mealtimes.

NORTH OTAGO

The Waitaki River marks out the northern boundary of North Otago. South of this relatively wide watercourse is Oamaru, the region's largest town. Follow either SH82 from Waimate or SH83 from Pukeuri Junction (8km north of Oamaru) to reach Kurow and the Waitaki Valley. From here SH83 continues to Omarama via the hydroelectric lakes of Waitaki, Aviemore and Benmore.

A good source of information on the area is www.tourismwaitaki.co.nz.

OAMARU
pop 12,000

Architecturally-exotic Oamaru was first settled by the Europeans in 1853 and within 25 years had become one of NZ's largest towns. A glamorous trade in refrigerated meat shipping made it prosperous, and local limestone was subsequently used to erect the many imposing buildings that still grace the town. Oamaru has an affinity with the arts which extends well beyond the fact that writer Janet Frame lived here and used the town as the setting for some of her novels (see the 'Oamaru In Frame' boxed text; p579) – indeed, the town is home to numerous 'artists, craftspeople and eccentrics' (in the words of one rather eccentric local). It also has fine public gardens and there's access to colonies of blue penguins and the rare yellow-eyed penguin.

There's loads of information at **Oamaru visitors centre** (☎ 03-434 1656; info@tourismwaitaki .co.nz; 1 Thames St; ☼ 9am-6pm Mon-Fri, 10am-5pm Sat & Sun). The **post office** (☎ 03-433 1190; cnr Coquet & Severn Sts; ☼ 8.30am-5pm Mon-Fri) is only open weekdays.

Sights
HARBOUR-TYNE HISTORIC PRECINCT

Oamaru has NZ's best-preserved collection of historic commercial buildings, particularly in the harbour area and around Tyne St, where there are dozens of classified buildings. The architecture is a mosaic of styles from Gothic revival to neoclassical Italianate and Venetian palazzo. Local limestone was soft enough to saw but hardened when exposed to the air, and so was a convenient and enduring building

material. Pick up the free *Historic Oamaru* pamphlet.

Several small businesses have set up here, including a bookbinder, bookshop, antique vendors, cafés and the beer-friendly Criterion Hotel. The **Woolstore** (1 Tyne St) has a good café (see p580), souvenirs and the **Auto Museum** (☎ 03-434 8336; adult/child $4/free; ☼ 10am-4pm), a garage exhibit that includes a Jag, a Bentley, a 1968 Monaro GTS and a 1952 Cooper speedster. A market is held here on Sunday.

The one-hour **Whitestone Walking Tours** (person/family $8/20; ☼ tours 11am, noon, 2pm & 3pm) can be booked at (and leave from) the visitors centre.

PENGUINS

You can walk from town to the yellow-eyed penguin and blue penguin colonies at Cape Wanbrow Reserve. Note that there's been recent slippage on the foreshore walk between the two colonies, and you may not be able to walk all the way around.

Blue penguins are numerous here, nesting off Oamaru Harbour. Once considered a pest for nesting under buildings and on council reserves, they're now Oamaru's mascot and the town's biggest attraction. The fenced-off nesting site has a **visitors centre** (☎ 03-433 1195; www.penguins.co.nz; Waterfront Rd; viewings adult/child $13/8) as well as a large-capacity viewing grandstand. Penguins waddle ashore just after dusk year-round; numbers are higher in summer.

The loss of their coastal forest breeding grounds has made yellow-eyed penguins one of the world's rarest. The nesting site at Bushy Beach is equipped with a hide allowing unobtrusive observation of these beautiful birds. Yellow-eyeds are best seen a few hours before sunset, when they come ashore to feed their chicks. But they're shy and easily upset, so avoid loud noises and stick to the trail and hide.

Penguin Express (☎ 03-434 1656; www.coastline -tours.co.nz; adult/child $20/5) does 2½-hour tours taking in both penguin colonies; price includes admission to blue penguin colony.

OTHER SIGHTS

In the old Athenaeum (a one-time subscription library) is the **North Otago Museum** (☎ 03-434 1652; www.northotagomuseum.co.nz; 60 Thames St; admission free; ☼ 1-4.30pm Sun-Fri, 10am-1pm Sat), a museum highlighting the history

OTAGO

of the Waitaki district with displays on everything from the local impact of the Boer War to early photography. Donations are appreciated.

Forrester Gallery (☎ 03-434 1653; www.forrestergallery.com; 9 Thames St; admission free; ⌚ 10.30am-4.30pm Mon-Fri, 10.30am-1pm Sat, 1-4.30pm Sun), set in a former bank building fronted by some impressive Corinthian columns, has displays of regional and visiting artistry. A recent exhibition showcased the work of six artists on the topic of Doubtful Sound.

The **public gardens** (main entry Severn St) date from 1876 and make for a delightful stroll. Look out for the red **Japanese bridge** crossing Oamaru Creek, and the lovely *Wonderland* statue.

Oamaru livens up with penny-farthing races and other events during **Victorian Heritage Celebrations** in late-November.

Sleeping

Oamaru Top 10 Holiday Park (☎ 0800 280 202, 03-434 7666; Chelmer St; www.top10.co.nz; camp sites & campervan sites $23, d $38-75) Has a prime position beside Oamaru public gardens and is ideal for greenery- and birdsong-seeking families. The park is well looked after and has a kids' playground.

Red Kettle YHA (☎ 03-434 5008; yha.oamaru@yha.org.nz; cnr Reed & Cross Sts; dm/d $22/55) This snug, red-roofed YHA has an atmosphere enhanced by a log fire and is also close to the gardens, a few blocks from the main

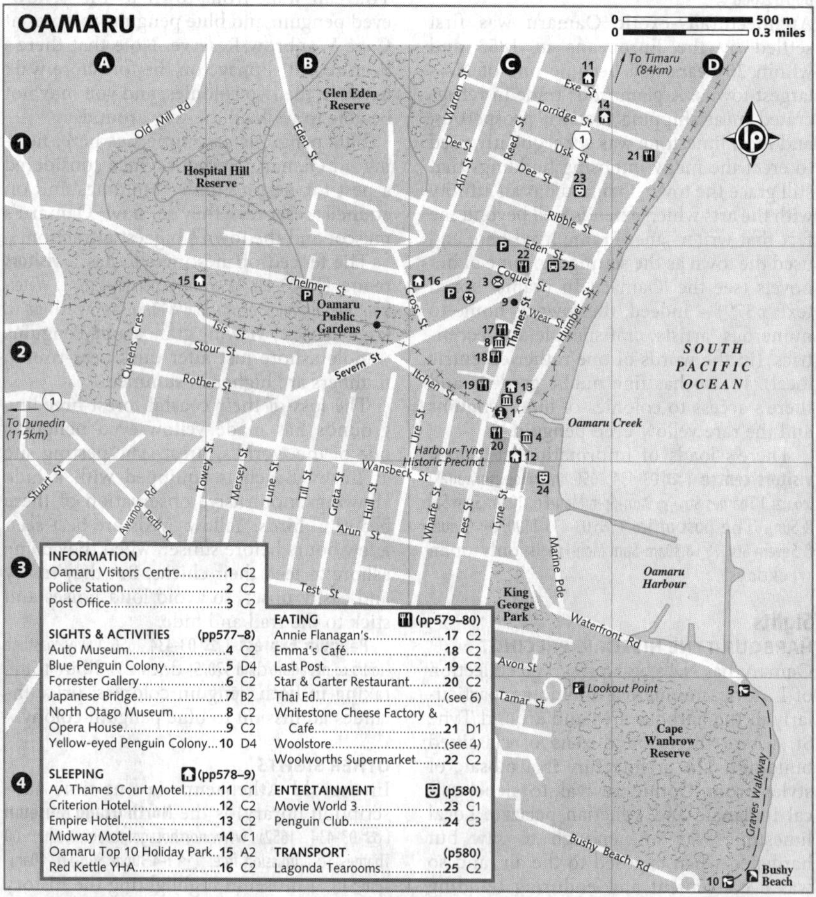
OAMARU
0 500 m
0 0.3 miles
A
B
C
D
1
2
3
4
To Timaru (84km)
To Dunedin (115km)
Glen Eden Reserve
Hospital Hill Reserve
Oamaru Public Gardens
Old Mill Rd
Eden St
Warren St
Aln St
Reed St
Exe St
Torridge St
Usk St
Dee St
Ribble St
Coquet St
Wear St
Chelmer St
Cross St
Thames St
Humber St
Isis St
Stour St
Rother St
Severn St
Itchen St
Queens Cres
Stuart St
Awamoa Rd
Perth St
Towey St
Mersey St
Lune St
Till St
Greta St
Hull St
Ure St
Wansbeck St
Arun St
Wharfe St
Tees St
Tyne St
Test St
Harbour-Tyne Historic Precinct
Oamaru Creek
SOUTH PACIFIC OCEAN
Marine Pde
Oamaru Harbour
King George Park
Waterfront Rd
Avon St
Tamar St
Lookout Point
Cape Wanbrow Reserve
Graves Walkway
Bushy Beach Rd
Bushy Beach
INFORMATION
Oamaru Visitors Centre.............1 C2
Police Station.............2 C2
Post Office.............3 C2
SIGHTS & ACTIVITIES (pp577–8)
Auto Museum.............4 C2
Blue Penguin Colony.............5 D4
Forrester Gallery.............6 C2
Japanese Bridge.............7 B2
North Otago Museum.............8 C2
Opera House.............9 C2
Yellow-eyed Penguin Colony...10 D4
SLEEPING (pp578–9)
AA Thames Court Motel.............11 C1
Criterion Hotel.............12 C2
Empire Hotel.............13 C2
Midway Motel.............14 C1
Oamaru Top 10 Holiday Park..15 A2
Red Kettle YHA.............16 C2
EATING (pp579–80)
Annie Flanagan's.............17 C2
Emma's Café.............18 C2
Last Post.............19 C2
Star & Garter Restaurant.............20 C2
Thai Ed.............(see 6)
Whitestone Cheese Factory & Café.............21 D1
Woolstore.............(see 4)
Woolworths Supermarket.............22 C2
ENTERTAINMENT (p580)
Movie World 3.............23 C1
Penguin Club.............24 C3
TRANSPORT (p580)
Lagonda Tearooms.............25 C2

drag of Thames St. It's only open September to May.

Empire Hotel (☎ 03-434 3446; empirehotel@hotmail.com; 13 Thames St; dm/s/d $18/30/45; 💻) Right on the main street is this 1867-built former hotel. Some of the rooms are a bit squishy, but the location and facilities – free Internet access and bike use, reading room – are good.

Criterion Hotel (☎ 03-434 6247; www.criterion.net.nz; 3 Tyne St; s from $80, d $125-150) Very much a Victorian 'heritage-style' place with the requisite décor and atmosphere, though it tends to overcharge for its not-so-large rooms with shared facilities (the one en suite room is the exception).

Midway Motel (☎ 0800 447 744, 03-434 5388; 289 Thames St; d $70-90) Two-storey peach-coloured units in a quiet street, with a kids' play area, access to a gym for fitness-minded adults, and a courtesy vehicle to ferry you to attractions.

Another good motel option is **AA Thames Court Motel** (☎ 0800 223 644, 03-434 6963; aathamescourt@hotmail.com; 252 Thames St; s/d from $65/70), with largish rooms and a couple of separate family units.

Eating

Emma's Cafe (☎ 03-434 1165; 30 Thames St; meals $8-15; 🕐 lunch) Relaxed, uncluttered place with plenty of room in which to digest goulash soup, asparagus strudel, quiches and some large salads.

Whitestone Cheese Factory & Cafe (☎ 03-434 8098; www.whitestonecheese.co.nz; 3 Torridge St; light meals from $4; 🕐 lunch) Exemplary organic cheeses are produced here, including the ultra-rich Mt Domet Double Cream and the wonderful sheep's milk 'Island Stream', plus a brie, camembert, blue cheeses and more. Buy cheese to takeaway or munch a cheese-smothered *panini*, pasta or melt.

Last Post (☎ 03-434 8080; 12 Thames St; mains $10-22; 🕐 lunch & dinner) Meals in the cosy interior of Oamaru's old post office include the 'rib-eye rumble' and a chicken, brie and cranberry melt. Also has a covered (and heated) courtyard in which to eat and drink.

Annie Flanagan's (☎ 03-434 8828; 84 Thames St; mains $10-22; 🕐 lunch & dinner) This bar does Irish-themed food like Curragh (Guinness-battered) fish of the day and non-Irish fare like Cajun chicken salad. There's a 'steak challenge' ($30) for famished carnivores.

Star & Garter Restaurant (☎ 03-434 5246; 9 Itchen St; mains $10-22; 🕐 lunch & dinner) Cheerful, in-demand restaurant serving up lots of lamb roasts and chicken dishes, as well as fine desserts like steamed fig pudding and the enigmatic 'knickerbocker glory'.

Thai Ed (☎ 03-434 3449; 7 Thames St; mains $13-15; 🕐 lunch Wed-Sat, dinner) This colourful place does decent soups and curries to takeaway or eat inside. The sweet peanut sauce stirfry is a stomach-filler, as is the spicy, lime-flavoured panang curry (spicy meats in a creamy coconut sauce with lots of vegetables).

Criterion Hotel (☎ 03-434 6247; 3 Tyne St; meals $8-15) The bar here is good for a drink, as many older locals will testify. Has a limited pub menu with stuff like beef hotpot and bangers and mash.

OAMARU IN FRAME

Renowned novelist Janet Frame was born in Dunedin in 1924 but spent most of her early school years in Oamaru. Her home at 56 Eden St is mentioned in her autobiographies. She uses the name 'Waimaru' as a pseudonym for the town and it appears in some of her novels.

Frame first gained international recognition in 1957 with *Owls Do Cry*. The places alluded to in this novel include the clock tower, the Opera House ('Miami' in the book), the Majestic (the 'Regent'), the local dump (now the site of the Red Kettle YHA) and the Duck Pond.

All these places are visited on the 1½-hour Janet Frame Trail outlined in the free *Heritage Trails of North Otago* booklet. Other sites relate to the novels *Faces in the Water* (1961), *The Edge of the Alphabet* (1962), *Scented Gardens for the Blind* (1963), *A State of Siege* (1967) and *Intensive Care* (1970).

It was Jane Campion's film version of *An Angel at my Table*, based on the second volume of Janet Frame's autobiographical trilogy, that renewed interest in her works. Frame had a somewhat difficult life as a young woman and became rather reclusive. She was short-listed for the Nobel Prize for literature in 2003. Sadly, Janet Frame died on 29 January 2004, shortly after announcing that she was terminally ill with leukaemia.

Light meals (and breakfasts) are available at the **Woolstore** (☎ 03-434 8336; 1 Tyne St; meals $11-17; ☺ breakfast & lunch).

Woolworths supermarket (☎ 03-434 8127; 108-116 Thames St; ☺ 7am-7pm, liquor section closes midnight) is large and central.

Entertainment

Movie World 3 (☎ 03-434 1077, info line 03-434 1070; www.movieworld3.com; 239 Thames St; adult/child $12/6) Get big-screen entertainment here.

Penguin Club (admission free; ☺ Fri 8pm-1am) Signposted down an industrially bruised alley off Harbour St is this fine club where local musicians gather for jam sessions. It sometimes gets visiting acts, for which the cover charge can be as high as $15; ask at the visitors centre for a programme.

Annie Flanagan's (☎ 03-434 8828; 84 Thames St; gigs free) Live end-of-week music also takes place here; it has a beer garden.

Getting There & Around

InterCity (☎ 03-474 9600; www.intercitycoach.co.nz) stops in Oamaru while running between Christchurch ($32) and Dunedin ($20). So do shuttles like **Atomic Shuttles** (☎ 03-322 8883; www.atomictravel.co.nz) and **South Island Connections** (☎ 03-366 6633; www.southislandconnections.co.nz), both charging around $15 to Dunedin and $30 to Christchurch. Buses arrive/depart from InterCity agent **Lagonda Tearooms** (☎ 03-434 8716; 191 Thames St); bookings for all buses can be done through the visitors centre.

Cook Connection (☎ 0800 266 526, 0274-583 211; www.cookconnect.co.nz) runs three times weekly from October to April (twice-weekly May to September) between Oamaru and Mt Cook (one-way/return $45/80) via Kurow, Omarama and Twizel.

WAITAKI VALLEY

The Waitaki Valley cradles some interesting towns and sights between the turn-offs of SH1 and Omarama.

Duntroon has an authentic blacksmith shop, and trout- and salmon-fishing nearby. There are Maori limestone cliff drawings at **Takiroa**, signposted off the highway about 2km west of Duntroon; these were done with red ochre and charcoal and may date back to the moa-hunting period (AD 1000–1500).

Kurow is at the junction of the Waitaki and Hakataramea Rivers. Since the

Waitaki power station was built in 1928, Kurow has serviced local hydroelectric schemes like Benmore power station and Aviemore.

Instead of continuing west on SH83 to Otematata, take the **scenic detour** over the dam at Lake Aviemore, around the lakeshore, then over the huge Benmore Dam earthworks; this 21km route disgorges you just north of Otematata.

You can **camp** (per vehicle $10) at various council-run places on the northern edge of Lakes Aviemore and Benmore. For something less natural but more refined, grab some B&B at **Tokarahi Homestead** (☎ 03-431 2500; www.homestead.co.nz; 47 Dip Hill Rd; d $190-290), an elegant limestone lodge shadowed by a giant redwood; it's 11km from Duntroon on the road to Danseys Pass.

Glenmac Farmstay (☎ 03-436 0200; www.farmstaynewzealand.co.nz; Gards Rd; camp sites & campervan sites $15, dm/s/d $18, d $80-100), 10km east of Kurow, has a backpackers' and B&B rooms on a 1600-hectare property among rolling hills. The highly accommodating **Otematata Country Inn** (☎ 03-438 7797; enquiries@otematatacountryinn.co.nz; 11-12 Rata Dr, Otematata; dm & s $25, d $40-65) has great-value cottages (families can get an entire three-bedroom house to themselves) and good dinners ($11 to $19) of the chicken kiev and shrimp cocktail variety; turn off the highway on West Rd, then turn right into Rata Dr.

Omarama
pop 355

Omarama is at the head of the Waitaki Valley, 119km northwest of Oamaru. The **Omarama visitors centre** (☎ 03-438 9816; 6 Chain Hills Hwy; ☺ 8.30am-4.45pm) is in 'Glen Craig's', a tourist souvenir place adjacent to the Mobil station.

The **Clay Cliffs** (admission $5) were formed by the active Osler fault line that continually exposes clay and gravel cliffs. They're on private land; the turn-off is 3.5km north of Omarama. Make sure you leave all gates as you found them.

The area's northwest thermals allow fantastic gliding, which is why the world championships were held here a decade ago. **Alpine Soaring** (☎ 03-438 9600; www.soaring.co.nz; 30min/1hr flights $210/290) provides hang time.

SLEEPING & EATING

Omarama Top 10 Holiday Park (☎ 0800 662 726, 03-438 9875; omarama.holiday@xtra.co.nz; SH8; camp sites & campervan sites $24, d $38-80) Covering four hectares of streamside greenery, this park has plenty of roaming territory and a playground to herd the kids into.

Omarama Hotel (☎ 03-438 9713; cnr SH8 & SH83; s/d $35/70) OK, older-style pub rooms with shared facilities, though be aware that the pub gets pretty busy over the weekend. Big portions of food are available in the bistro.

Clay Cliffs Estate (☎ 03-438 9654; SH8; mains $15-28; ☻ lunch & dinner) Try one of this small vineyard's fetta, brie or blue cheese platters accompanied by a glass of their finest (the pinot gris is splendid). Alternatively, eat Caesar or Greek salad, or Mt Cook salmon, with pecan pie for dessert. Eat beside the pond or in the large whitewashed interior.

On either side of Omarama along SH8 are farmstays offering budget accommodation and usually some camp sites, including **Buscot Station** (☎ 03-438 9646; camp sites & campervan sites $15, dm $15, tw & d $20), 8km north of town, and **Killermont Station** (☎ 03-438 9864; camp sites & campervan sites $24, dm $20), 13km west of Omarama but closed June to August.

OAMARU TO DUNEDIN

The ocean-hugging road south from Oamaru provides a peaceful break from SH1, with some fine coastal views; take Wharfe St out of town (following signs for Kakanui). Situated on extensive beachside acreage 16km down this road is the **Hall Coastal Backpackers** (☎ 03-439 5411; coastalback packer@ihug.co.nz; All Day Bay; dm $23, d $55-70), where it's obligatory to take advantage of the swimming, surfing, BBQs, fishing, kayaking, wildlife-watching and on-site tavern; it's closed June to September.

SH1 from Oamaru to Dunedin is a pleasant stretch of town-lined bitumen. The big attractions along here are the small, ancient boulders at **Moeraki**, 30km south of Oamaru, and again further south at **Katiki** and **Shag Point**. You can walk to them along the beach from Moeraki (40 minutes) or closer, or pay $2 to access them via a stairway from the highway-side tourist complex. Scientists believe the boulders were not washed up onto the beach but eroded from the mudstone cliffs behind. Subsequent erosion has exposed a fascinating internal

network of veins – sit on the beach awhile and contemplate their age.

A gravel road leads from the back of Moeraki to a lighthouse for great views of the coast, and trails lead down the cliffs to a seal colony and a yellow-eyed penguin hide.

Moeraki Motor Camp (☎ 03-439 4759; moerakimo torcamp@xtra.co.nz; 114 Haven St; camp sites & campervan sites $20, d $34-80) has a range of cabins, sites and updated facilities, while **Moeraki Motel** (☎ 03-439 4862; cnr Beach & Haven Sts; d $80-100) has popular balcony-laden units.

For food and atmosphere, it's hard to beat **Fleur's Place** (☎ 03-439 5980; Old Jetty, Moeraki; mains $12-25; ☻ lunch & dinner), usually swamped by locals and tourists indulging in fresh seafood (like deep sea dory with mustard and caper sauce), conversing around the artful bar, or sitting at an outside table or on the upstairs decking and gazing over the bay.

QUEENSTOWN REGION

Queenstown is NZ's self-styled outdoor-adventure capital, but when the adrenaline ebbs and the party-goers have called it a night (or morning), stunning Lake Wakatipu and the surrounding mountains materialise as the truly intoxicating attractions. The aptly-named Remarkables and the Eyre Mountains form a breathtaking backdrop to this super-active town – superlatives can't do justice to the sight of the snow-capped peaks at sunrise or in the afterglow of dusk.

QUEENSTOWN
pop 7500
Queenstown, on the northern shore of the serpentine Lake Wakatipu, is the epitome of the big-budget resort town, awash with organised tour groups and plenty of hustling for the tourist dollar. There's great skiing in winter and plenty of substitute summer pastimes. Most activities are centred on the lake and many nearby rivers, with white-water rafting, sledging and jetboating all great ways to get wet, while bungy jumping and tandem parachuting are exciting ways to fly. The town is also well-equipped for more earth-bound pursuits, like wine-sipping, boutique-browsing and dinner-digesting.

OTAGO

This is not an irredeemably brash place – in fact some of the cafés, bars and other places to hang out are remarkably laid-back – but with its innumerable exciting activities, great facilities and magnificent scenery, Queenstown is understandably a huge destination for travellers. So be forewarned that its streets are often paved with humanity – if you're averse to major crowds or have long-held illusions about the sacredness of your personal space, you probably won't like it.

History

The region was deserted when the first Pakeha arrived in the mid-1850s, although there is evidence of previous Maori settlement. Sheep farmers came first, but in 1862 two shearers discovered gold on the banks of the Shotover River, precipitating a deluge of prospectors. A year later Queenstown was a mining town with streets and permanent buildings. Then the gold petered out and by 1900 the population had dropped from several thousand to a mere 190.

The lake was the principal means of transport and at the height of the mining boom there were four paddle-steamers and 30 other craft plying the waters.

Orientation & Information

This compact town slopes up steep hills from the lakeside. The main streets are the pedestrian-only Mall and Shotover St, with its activity-booking offices.

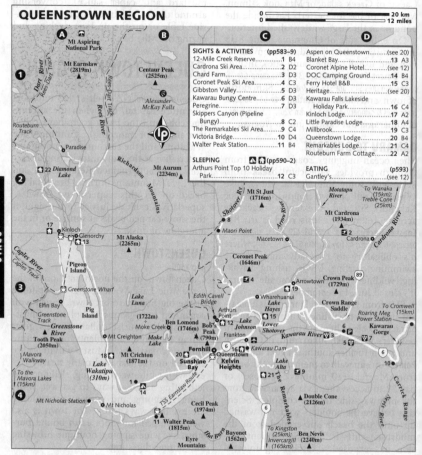

QUEENSTOWN REGION

SIGHTS & ACTIVITIES	(pp583–9)
12-Mile Creek Reserve	1 B4
Cardrona Ski Area	2 D2
Chard Farm	3 D3
Coronet Peak Ski Area	4 C3
Gibbston Valley	5 D3
Kawarau Bungy Centre	6 D3
Peregrine	7 D3
Skippers Canyon (Pipeline Bungy)	8 C2
The Remarkables Ski Area	9 C4
Victoria Bridge	10 D4
Walter Peak Station	11 B4

SLEEPING	
Arthurs Point Top 10 Holiday Park	12 C3

Aspen on Queenstown	(see 20)
Blanket Bay	13 A3
Coronet Alpine Hotel	(see 12)
DOC Camping Ground	14 B4
Ferry Hotel B&B	15 C3
Heritage	(see 20)
Kawarau Falls Lakeside Holiday Park	16 C4
Kinloch Lodge	17 A2
Little Paradise Lodge	18 A4
Millbrook	19 C3
Queenstown Lodge	20 B4
Remarkables Lodge	21 C4
Routeburn Farm Cottage	22 A2

EATING	(p593)
Gantley's	(see 12)

QUEENSTOWN IN...

Two Days

Have a wake-up feast at **Vudu Cafe** (p593) before riding the **Skyline Gondola** (p583). After disembarking high above town, get some fresh air on the loop track, then dare yourself to try the **Ledge Bungy** (p586) or **Sky Swing** (p586). Extend the adrenaline rush with a high-speed ride on the **Shotover Jet** (p586), or calm yourself down with a relaxing lake cruise on the **TSS Earnslaw** (p589). Toast your efforts with afternoon drinks on the waterfront, then try to decide between seafood at **Wai Waterfront** (p593) or pizza at **Winnie Bagoes** (p594). Devote the next day to thrills and spills by doing more bungy jumping, or white-water rafting, river surfing, sky diving, skiing, mountain biking... After dinner, settle into a long night with microbrews at raucous **Dux de Lux** (p593) or fine liquor in the suave confines of the **Bunker** (p593).

Four Days

Follow the two-day itinerary, then head to nearby **Arrowtown** (p596) to wander the enigmatic **Chinese settlement** (p597), browse the local crafts, and eat a gourmet lunch. The following day, take a leisurely, scenic drive along the shore of Lake Wakatipu to the serene hamlet of **Glenorchy** (p598), where you can ride a jetboat up the remote **Dart River** (p586) or head into **Mt Aspiring National Park** (p606) to do some wonderful short tramps in the vicinity of the **Routeburn Track** (p600).

The busy **Queenstown visitors centre** (Map pp584-5; ☎ 0800 668 888, 03-442 4100; info@qvc.co.nz; Clocktower Centre, cnr Shotover & Camp Sts; ☽ 7am-7pm Dec-Apr, 7am-6pm May-Nov) is the biggest booking agent in town.

Destination Queenstown (☎ 0800 478 336, 03-441 1800; 44 Stanley St; www.queenstown-nz.co.nz; ☽ 8.30am-5.30pm Mon-Fri) doesn't do bookings but is very informative.

The **DOC visitors centre** (Map pp584-5; ☎ 03-442 7935; queenstownvc@doc.govt.nz; 37 Shotover St; ☽ 9am-5pm May-Nov, 9am-6pm Dec-Apr) details the area's natural attractions. Next door is the **Info & Track Centre** (Map pp584-5; ☎ 03-442 9708; www.infotrack.co.nz; 37 Shotover St; ☽ 7am-9pm), handling tramper transport to the Routeburn, Greenstone, Caples, Kepler, Milford and Rees-Dart trailheads.

Kiwi Discovery (Map pp584-5; ☎ 0800 505 504, 03-442 7340; www.kiwidiscovery.com; 37 Camp St; ☽ 7am-8.30pm peak times) also organises summertime track transport and wintertime ski transport and hire.

One of the prime activity-booking offices is the **Station** (Map pp584-5; ☎ 03-442 5252; www.thestation.co.nz; cnr Camp & Shotover Sts; ☽ 8am-7.30pm), which houses AJ Hackett Bungy and various other operators.

Real Journeys (Map pp584-5; ☎ 0800 656 503, 03-442 7500; www.realjourneys.co.nz; Steamer Wharf, Beach St; ☽ 7.30am-8.30pm) is a subsidiary of the prominent South Island travel firm

Fiordland Travel and books a huge range of lake trips and tours.

The main **post office** (Map pp584-5; ☎ 03-442 7670; Camp St; ☽ 8.30am-6pm Mon-Fri, 9am-4pm Sat) has poste restante facilities. For health issues, visit the **Queenstown Medical Centre** (Map pp584-5; ☎ 03-441 0500; 9 Isle St).

Most hostels have Internet access, and there are several cybercafés charging around 10c per minute:

Budget Communications (Map pp584-5; ☎ 03-441 1562; 2nd fl, O'Connells Shopping Centre, cnr Camp & Beach Sts; ☽ 9am-11pm) Not the quickest connection, but has $3 per hour early-morning and late-night deals.

Ecafe (Map pp584-5; ☎ 03-442 9888; 50 Shotover St; ☽ 9am-11pm) Super-quick connection.

Internet Laundry (Map pp584-5; 1 Shotover St; ☽ 8am-10pm) Rates as low as $4 per hour, but only four machines.

Internet Outpost (Map pp584-5; ☎ 03-441 3018; 27 Shotover St; ☽ 10am-11pm)

Sights

The **Skyline Gondola** (Map pp584-5; ☎ 03-441 0101; www.skyline.co.nz; Brecon St; return fare adult/child/family $17/7/36; ☽ 9am-6.30pm) is a cable-car ride to the summit of a hill where there are excellent views and various cash-hungry features, namely a restaurant, the 30-minute hi-tech film **Kiwi Magic** (adult/child/family $9/4.50/20) and a **luge** (see under Other Activities; p588). You can, however,

OTAGO

QUEENSTOWN

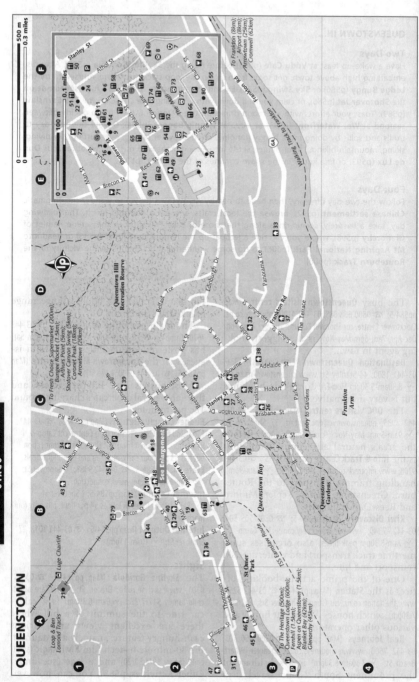

INFORMATION		
Budget Communications	1	F2
DOC	(see 3)	
Ecafe	2	E2
Info & Track Centre	3	E1
Internet Laundry	4	C2
Internet Outpost	5	E1
Kiwi Discovery	6	F1
Police Station	7	F2
Post Office	8	F2
Queenstown Accommodation Centre	9	E1
Queenstown Medical Centre	10	B2
Queenstown Visitors Centre	11	F1
Real Journeys	12	B2
Station	13	F1

SIGHTS & ACTIVITIES	(pp583–9)	
AJ Hackett Bungy	(see 13)	
Alpine Sports	14	F1
Caddyshack City	15	B2
Extreme Green Rafting	(see 6)	
Gravity Action	16	E1
Kawarau Jet	(see 20)	
Kiwi & Birdlife Park	17	B2
Kiwi Magic	(see 21)	
Ledge Bungy	(see 21)	
Ledge Sky Swing	(see 21)	
Luge	(see 21)	
Maori Concert & Hangi	18	C2
NZONE	(see 16)	
Off Road Adventures	19	B2
Parabungy	20	E2
Paraflights NZ	(see 20)	
Queenstown Rafting	(see 16)	
Skyline Gondola	21	A1
Small Planet Sports Co	22	F1
Tandem Paragliding	(see 21)	
TSS Earnslaw	(see 12)	
Twin Rivers Jet	23	E2
Underwater World	(see 20)	
Vertigo	24	F1

SLEEPING	(pp590–2)	
Bella Vista	25	B1
Black Sheep Lodge	26	C3
Blue Peaks Apartments	27	C3
Blue Peaks Lodge	28	C3
Browns Boutique Hotel	29	B2
Bungi Backpackers	30	C3
Butterfli Lodge	31	A3
Chalet Queenstown B&B	32	D3
Colonial Village Motels	33	E3
Creeksyde Top 10 Holiday Park	34	C1
Dairy Guesthouse	35	B2
Deco Backpackers	36	B2
Earnslaw Lodge	37	D3
Garden Court	38	C3
Hippo Lodge	39	C1
Lomond Lodge Motor Inn	40	B2
McFees	41	E2
Melbourne Motor Lodge	42	C2
Pinewood Lodge	43	B1
Queenstown Lakeview Holiday Park	44	B2
Queenstown YHA	45	A3
Rydges	46	A3
Scallywags Travellers Guesthouse	47	A2
Southern Laughter	48	B2
Thomas's Hotel	49	E2

EATING	(pp593–5)	
Alpine Supermarket	50	F1
Bakery	51	F1
Bunker	52	F2
Coronation Bathhouse Cafe & Restaurant	53	C3
Cow	54	E2
Dux de Lux	55	F2
Fergburger	56	F2
Fishbone Bar & Grill	57	F1
Freiya's	58	F1
Habebe's	59	E2
Kappa Sushi Cafe	60	F2
Ken's Noodles	(see 58)	

Leonardo's	61	F1
Minami Jujisei	62	E2
Naff Caff	63	B2
Night 'n Day	(see 59)	
O'Connell's Food Hall	(see 1)	
Planet 1	64	F2
Solera Vino	65	E2
Tatler Restaurant	66	F2
Turkish Kebabs	67	E2
Vudu Cafe	(see 65)	
Wai Waterfront Restaurant & Wine Bar	(see 12)	

DRINKING	(p595)	
Cigar Bar	(see 12)	
Loaded Hog	(see 12)	
Monty's	68	F2
Pig & Whistle	69	F2
Pog Mahones	70	E2
Rattlesnake Room	71	E1
Red Rock Bar & Grill	72	E1
Shooters	(see 71)	
Spectator	(see 66)	
Tardis Bar	(see 52)	

ENTERTAINMENT	(p595)	
Chico's	73	F2
Debajo	74	F2
Embassy Cinemas	75	F2
Sky Alpine Casino	76	E2
Subculture	(see 68)	
Surreal	77	F2
Wharf Casino	(see 12)	
Winnie Bagoe's	(see 66)	
World Bar	(see 5)	

TRANSPORT	(pp595–6)	
Bus Stop (Shopper Bus, Arrow Express)	78	F1
Gondola Terminal	79	B1
InterCity Booking Office	(see 11)	
Queenstown Bike Hire	80	F2

walk the summit **loop track** (30 minutes) for free.

Kiwi & Birdlife Park (Map above; ☎ 03-442 8059; www.kiwibird.co.nz; Brecon St; adult/child/family $16/6/33; ☻ 9am-5pm) is a large, peaceful bird sanctuary with two kiwi houses, a nursery where endangered birds are raised, and a free-range duck pond. The birdlife also includes the rare black stilt, keas, moreporks and parakeets.

The **Maori Concert & Hangi** (Map above; ☎ 03-442 8878; qtownmaori@paradise.net.nz; 1 Memorial St; adult/child $50/30; ☻ dining & concert 7-9.30pm), involving a show and a *hangi*-style feast, is something of a rarity on the South Island, but this Queenstown version does its best to cater to throngs of tourists. Bookings are essential.

Underwater World (Map above; ☎ 03-442 8538; Jetty; adult/child/family $5/3/10; ☻ 8.30am-6pm) is a submerged observation gallery that's overpriced and has streaky windows, though the agile little scaup or 'diving' ducks do make quite a sight. Perhaps save your money for the Milford Deep underwater observatory (p625).

Activities
BUNGY JUMPING

Queenstown is famous for its bungy jumping and the activity's local master of ceremonies is **AJ Hackett Bungy** (Map above; ☎ 03-442 7100; www.ajhackett.com; The Station, cnr Camp & Shotover Sts). Prices for the following options include transport out of town and gondola rides where relevant.

The historic 1880 Kawarau Bridge 23km from Queenstown on SH6, became the world's first commercial bungy site in 1988 and offers a 43m-high leap ($130). The eight-million-dollar **Kawarau Bungy Centre** (Map p582; ☎ 03-442 1177; adult/child $5/ free; ☻ 8am-8pm) opened here at the beginning of 2004 and includes the multimedia Bungy Dome theatre, a bungy museum, café and bar.

At the top of the gondola, 400m above Queenstown, is the **Ledge Bungy** (adult/child $130/90), the most scenic of the latex-rubber cord options and one you can do at night.

If these aren't high enough, then do the 102m-high **Pipeline** (Map p582; $160), a rather dramatic jump off a single-span suspension

OTAGO

NERVOUS ON NEVIS

No safety-standard reassurances can remove trepidation prior to leaping from the gondola jump pod of the 134m-high Nevis Highwire bungy. The world's first gondola jump is an engineering marvel, with 30 international patents on its many innovations. It spans a remote gorge on the Nevis River and the gondola is suspended by 380m-long cables.

Several aspects of the construction have been deliberately designed to maximise exposure and titillate the 'fear factor'. This fear increases when, bedecked in a safety harness, you take the airy cable-car out to the pod, and literally thunders when you peer through the glass-bottomed floor to watch the reactions of the first jumpers.

Your turn comes. You're briefed while sitting in a chair and adjustments are made to the bungy cords based on your weight. The chair is turned and you shuffle towards the abyss.

Countdown, then six-plus seconds of free-fall with the riverbed far beneath hurtling towards you – what an incredible ground-rush! Relief as the bungy extends and you're catapulted to the top of the first bounce. At the top of the second bounce you release a rip cord and swing over into a sitting position. Now you can enjoy the bouncing and admire the view. A short bump, the clever recovery system swings into action, and you are winched back to the safety of the pod.

A relieved jumper quipped: 'This is great, you don't have to walk up from the river'.

bridge across Skippers Canyon (a 45-minute trip from town), on the site of an 1864 gold-sluicing water pipeline. Higher still is the **Nevis Highwire** ($195); see the 'Nervous on Nevis' boxed text (p586). If you're a true masochist, you can do AJ Hackett's **'Thrillogy'** ($290), combining the Kawarau, Ledge and Nevis jumps.

The highest of the local bungy plummets, however, takes place between 150m and 180m above Lake Wakatipu courtesy of **Parabungy** (☎ 03-409 0712; www.parabungy.co.nz; $230), using a speedboat to tow you up in the air with a parasail and then have you take a long-distance plunge towards the lake.

Bungy Variations

The new **Shotover Canyon Swing** (☎ 0800 279 464, 03-442 6990; www.canyonswing.co.nz; $110) is touted as the world's highest rope swing (109m), where you jump from a cliff-mounted platform in a full body harness and take a wild swing across the canyon at 150km per hour.

On a similar theme, at Hackett's Ledge bungy site is the **Ledge Sky Swing** (adult/child $85/65), where you go into free-fall in a harness before soaring through the air on a huge arc. Another option is the **Bungee Rocket** (☎ 03-442 9894; Gorge Rd; $65), which one local said was 'for couch potatoes yearning for an adrenaline rush' – you're strapped into a seat in a cage-like device that's flung into the air at high speed, then bounces around on the end of bungy cords.

JETBOATING

The Shotover and Kawarau are the preferred rivers to hurtle along near Queenstown, with the Dart River less travelled, lengthier and more scenic (see under Glenorchy; p599). Trips either depart from Queenstown or go via minibus to the river in question before boarding the jetboat.

Shotover Jet (☎ 0800 746 868; www.shotoverjet .co.nz; adult/child $90/50) does half-hour trips through the rocky Shotover Canyons, with an emphasis on 360° spins; the thrill factor of these trips is loudly trumpeted, but in reality they're very safe.

Twin Rivers Jet (☎ 03-442 3257; www.twinrivers jet.co.nz; adult/child $75/39) and **Kawarau Jet** (☎ 03-442 6142; www.kjet.co.nz; adult/child $75/39) both do one-hour trips on the Kawarau and Lower Shotover Rivers.

WHITE-WATER RAFTING

The Shotover and Kawarau Rivers are equally good for rafting. For rafting purposes, rivers are graded from I (easy) to VI (unraftable). The Shotover canyon varies from III to V+, depending on the time of year, and includes shooting the Oxenbridge Tunnel, while the Kawarau River is IV and is fine for first-time rafters. On some of the rougher stretches there's usually a minimum age of 12 or 13 years. Trips typically take four to five hours, but half of this time is spent getting there and back by minibus.

OTAGO

Rafting companies include **Queenstown Rafting** (☎ 0800 723 8464, 03-442 9792; www.rafting .co.nz; 35 Shotover St), **Extreme Green Rafting** (☎ 03-442 8517; www.nzraft.com; 39 Camp St) and **Challenge Rafting** (☎ 0800 423 836, 03-442 7318; www.raft .co.nz); prices for all three operators start at $135.

RIVER SURFING & WHITE-WATER SLEDGING

Serious Fun (☎ 0800 737 468, 03-442 5262; www.riversurfing.co.nz; $129) leads exhilarating trips down sections of the Kawarau River, surfing river waves, running rapids and riding whirlpools using modified bodyboards. **Mad Dog River Boarding** (☎ 03-442 7797; www.river boarding.co.nz; $130) does likewise.

Frogz Have More Fun (☎ 0800 338 738, 03-443 9130; www.frogz.co.nz; $120) gets you to steer buoyant, highly manoeuvrable sleds through rapids on the Clutha and Hawea Rivers (both good for beginners) and the Kawarau River (more challenging).

CANYONING

XII-Mile Delta Canyoning (☎ 0800 222 696; www .xiimile.co.nz; $135) has half-day trips in the 12-Mile Delta Canyons that expose you to all canyoning fundamentals: waterslides, rock jumps, swimming through narrow channels, abseiling and a few surprises. Canyoning in the remote Routeburn Valley is possible with **Routeburn Canyoning** (☎ 0800 222 696; $250); price includes transport from Queenstown.

FLYING & SKYDIVING

Tandem Paragliding (☎ 0800 759 688, 03-441 8581; www.paraglide.net.nz; $185) takes off from the top of the gondola for dreamy aerial cruises, though note that the trips only last 10 minutes. **Flight Park Tandems** (☎ 0800 467 325; www.tandemparagliding.com; $170) does similar flights from Coronet Peak.

Lazy paraflights over 100m above the lake can be done with **Paraflights NZ** (☎ 03-442 8507; www.parasail.co.nz; solo per adult/child $75/70, tandem $65/55). For those who prefer a delta wing there's **Skytrek Hang Gliding** (☎ 03-442 6311; $165) and **Antigravity** (☎ 0800 426 445, 03-441 8898; www.antigravity.co.nz; $185).

Fly by Wire (☎ 0800 359 299, 03-442 2116; www.fly bywire.co.nz; $155) is a unique experience that allows you to control a high-speed tethered plane to speeds of up to 170km/h for a six-minute flight.

NZONE (☎ 0800 376 796, 03-442 5867; www.nzone .biz) lets you tandem freefall to terminal

---

ACTIVITIES AU-GO-GO

There really is a bewildering array of activities in Queenstown, suitable for the old and young, the timid and the true adrenaline junkie. Sifting through all the options and choosing your preferred mode of fun can be a daunting task, but there are some things you can do to make your life easier. A handy activity overview is offered by **ITAG** (Independent Traveller's Adventure Guide; www.itag.co.nz) in one of their free booklets, widely available in Queenstown and elsewhere in NZ. If possible, get online and check the websites mentioned in this section to get the latest information on what tour operators are offering. Another good website is www.queenstownadventure.com.

Unless you have weeks up your sleeve, you probably won't be able to squeeze in (or afford) every single appealing activity. So work out a rough budget and list your top priorities. You might even choose to stay in local budget accommodation to free up cash for more activities.

Once in Queenstown you can either book directly with activity companies, at your accommodation (most backpackers', hotels and motels have a booking service) or at one of the town's many booking agencies, located mainly on Camp and Shotover Sts. Choose the most convenient, as prices won't vary from place to place. Also bear in mind that countless activity combinations ('combos') are arranged between major operators – one example is the 'Ultimate Trio' ($450), which comprises a jetboat ride, white-water rafting trip and tandem skydive from 9000ft.

Also note that in Queenstown (and throughout NZ), participation in all adventure activities involves a degree of risk – they wouldn't be half as much fun if the adrenaline wasn't pumping. Most operators do everything in their power to ensure that participants are safe and have a great time, but accidents do happen and Lonely Planet receives many letters from travellers with sad tales of broken bones and the like. So if you plan to dive head-first into the aforementioned activities, consider the appropriate travel insurance to cover any potential mishap.

OTAGO

velocity (up to 200km/h) before your parachute opens and you're nursed safely to ground.

SKIING
In winter the Remarkables (p73) and Coronet Peak ski fields (p73) are the region's key snowsport centres.

Those who prefer motorised mobility to skis can churn up the white stuff in the Garvie Mountains with **Nevis Snowmobile Adventure** (☎ 0800 442 4250, 03-442 4250; www.snowmobile nz.com; adult/child $420/320); three-hour trips include a scenic helicopter flight over the Remarkables to the base.

Heli-skiing is also popular and a full day with three runs costs around $680. **Heli Ski Queenstown** (☎ 03-442 7733) and **Harris Mountains Heli-Ski** (☎ 03-442 6722; www.heliski.co.nz) are local operators.

MOUNTAIN BIKING
There's some great mountain biking around Queenstown. **Adventure Biking** (House of Safari; ☎ 03-441 0065; 48 Camp St; from $80) organises uphill/downhill riding action from Moke Lake along Moke Creek Gorge, taking in river crossings along the way.

If you're not fit enough for any strenuous uphill pedalling, choose an operator who'll take you and your bike to a suitable high-point. **Gravity Action** (☎ 03-441 1021; www.gravityaction.com; adult/child from $100/80) does a trip into Skippers Canyon, while **Vertigo** (Map pp584-5; ☎ 0800 837 8446, 03-442 8378; www .heli-adventures.co.nz; 14 Shotover St; from $100) has guided downhill trips. Both operators also have heli-biking options.

Queenstown Bike Hire (Map pp584-5; ☎ 03-442 6039; Marine Pde; bikes per day from $20, kayaks 2hr $18) has a wide variety of bikes (and some kayaks) and suggestions on where to cycle. **Small Planet Sports Co** (Map pp584-5; ☎ 03-442 6393; 17 Shotover St; bikes per half/full day $25/35) also hires mountain bikes.

WALKING
Stroll along the waterfront through town and into the peaceful **Queenstown Gardens** (Map pp584-5) on the peninsula. One of the shortest local climbs is up **Queenstown Hill** (900m; 2-3hr return); access is from Belfast Tce.

For a more spectacular view, climb **Ben Lomond** (Map pp584-5; 1746m; 6-8hr return). It's a difficult walk requiring high-level fitness

and shouldn't be underestimated; consult the DOC on this and the region's many other walks.

Alpine Sports (Map pp584-5; ☎ 03-442 7099; 28 Shotover St) hires packs, sleeping bags and boots for $6 per day; tents cost $10 per day. **Kiwi Discovery** (Map pp584-5; ☎ 03-442 7340; 37 Camp St) and **Info & Track Centre** (Map pp584-5; ☎ 03-442 9708; 37 Shotover St) also rent equipment. **Small Planet Sports Co** (Map pp584-5; ☎ 03-442 6393; 17 Shotover St) sells new and used outdoor equipment for tramping, skiing and biking.

Guided Nature Walks (☎ 03-442 7126; www.nz walks.com; adult/child $85/40) conducts excellent half-day walks in the area. **Encounter Guided Day Walks** (☎ 03-442 8200; www.ultimatehikes.co.nz; adult/child $125/75; ☑ Oct-Apr) offers a day on the Routeburn Track.

OTHER ACTIVITIES
There are plenty of wild trails heading to otherwise inaccessible historical areas amid the region's canyons and hills. **Off Road Adventures** (Map pp584-5; ☎ 03-442 7858; www.offroad.co.nz; 61a Shotover St; 2½hr tour from $140) offers guided biking (motorbikes or quads) through this challenging back-country terrain.

Via Ferrata (☎ 03-409 0696; dave@viaferrata.co.nz; 3 hr climbs $110) guides inexperienced climbers via rock-embedded rungs and wire ropes up stony faces and ledges above Queenstown.

The **Luge** (Map pp584-5; ☎ 03-441 0101; www .skyline.co.nz; Brecon St; $6) involves taking to one of two 800m-long tracks at the top of the gondola in a three-wheel cart.

Mini-golf enthusiasts will enjoy the intricacy of the model-decorated 'course' at **Caddyshack City** (Map pp584-5; ☎ 03-442 6642; 25 Brecon St; adult/child/family $15/10/45; ☑ 10am-5.30pm), though prices are steep.

You can also do life-size golfing, fishing, horse riding, mountain climbing, diving and more, including just collapsing in an exhausted heap. See the visitors centre or any of the major booking agencies for details.

Queenstown for Children
Queenstown specialises in the kinds of breathtakingly fun activities that have children clamouring for more – until they're too exhausted to clamour any further.

For a wild (and wet) experience, treat the kids to the full-circle spins of the **Shotover Jet** (p586) or to a rapid-threading **white-**

water rafting trip (p586). Tamer variations on the classic bungy jump include the **Bungee Rocket** (p586) and the **Sky Swing** (p586), while several places in town hire **mountain bikes** (opposite).

The **Skyline Gondola** (p583) is a scenic, slow-moving family option, though at the top of the hill lies a zippy twin-track **luge** (p588). Lake cruises on the **TSS Earnslaw** (below), steam train excursions on the vintage **Kingston Flyer** (p590) and 4WD tours of narrow, snaking **Skippers Canyon** (below) are also good if you feel like slowing down the pace a little. An engrossing indoor attraction is the intricate mini-golf course at **Caddyshack City** (opposite).

The **Kiwi & Birdlife Park** (p585) has plenty of natural attractions for youthful nature lovers, while fascinating NZ culture is on show during the **Maori Concert & Hangi** (p585).

For short-term childcare, look up 'Baby Sitting' and 'Child Care' in the *Yellow Pages* directory.

Tours

SKIPPERS CANYON   Map p582
Popular Skippers Canyon trips take the scenic, winding (some would say hair-raising) 4WD-only road from Arthurs Point towards Coronet Peak and then above the Shotover River, passing sights left over from the gold-mining days. **Nomad Safaris** (☎ 03-442 6699; www.outback.org.nz; adult/child $110/60) heads out this way on four-hour tours.

Skippers Canyon Heritage Tours (☎ 03-442 5949; qtown.heritage.tours@clear.net.nz; tours adult/child $95/50) does four-hour tours brimming with gold-mining facts, and is owned by a descendant of the area's early settlers.

AERIAL SIGHTSEEING
No possibility is ignored in Queenstown – if you can't boat up it, down it or across it, or walk around it, then you can fly over it. **Over The Top Helicopters** (☎ 03-442 2233; www.flynz.co.nz; from $135), **Queenstown Air** (☎ 03-442 2244; www.queenstownair.co.nz; adult/child from $130/80), **Air Fiordland** (☎ 0800 103 404, 03-442 3404; www.airfiordland.com; 1hr flight $280) and **Milford Sound Scenic Flights** (☎ 0800 207 206, 03-442 3065; www.milfordflights.co.nz; adult/child from $280/165) are all local operators.

For a little more excitement, take a 15-minute aerobatic flight in a Pitts Special biplane with **Actionflite** (☎ 03-442 9708; www.actionflite.co.nz; $240). For a little less, take

a one-hour flight in a hot-air balloon with **Sunrise Balloons** (☎ 0800 468 247, 03-442 0781; www.ballooningnz.com; adult/child $300/195).

LAKE CRUISES
The stately, steel-hulled **TSS Earnslaw** is the most famous of the lake's many cruise boats. Built over a century ago and licensed to carry over 800 passengers, it churns across the lake at 13 knots, burns a tonne of coal an hour and was once the lake's major means of transport. It has been used for lake cruises since 1969. In case you're wondering, 'TSS' stands for Twin Screw Steamer'. Book trips through **Real Journeys** (Map pp584-5; ☎ 0800 656 503, 03-442 7500; www.realjourneys.co.nz; Steamer Wharf, Beach St).

Cruise options include the standard 1½-hour Lake Wakatipu navigation (adult/child $36/15) and 3½-hour excursions to the high-country Walter Peak Farm (adult/child $55/15), which includes sheep-shearing demonstration and sheep-dog performances. Dinner cruises (adult/child $95/50) also visit this farm, where a buffet dinner is served at the Colonel's Homestead.

MILFORD SOUND
Day trips via Te Anau to Milford Sound take 12 to 13 hours and cost around $180/90 per adult/child, including a two-hour cruise on the sound; bus-cruise-flight options are also available. Operators include **Real Journeys** (Map pp584-5; ☎ 0800 656 503, 03-442 7500; Steamer Wharf, Beach St), **Great Sights** (☎ 0800 744 487; www.greatsights.co.nz), **Kiwi Discovery** (Map pp584-5; ☎ 03-442 7340; 37 Camp St) and **InterCity** (☎ 03-442 8238; www.intercitycoach.co.nz). The **BBQ Bus** (☎ 03-442 1045; www.milford.net.nz) takes groups of no more than 20 people and throws in a BBQ lunch.

To save on tour travel time and cost, consider visiting Milford from Te Anau (p622). The same applies to Doubtful Sound tours, which cost around $270/130 from Queenstown.

WINERY TOURS
Taking a guided tour of the region's fine wineries means being able to enjoy a drink or three without having to drive yourself. **Queenstown Wine Trail** (☎ 03-442 3799; www.queenstownwinetrail.co.nz; adult/child from $80/40) offers a personalised, informative five-hour tour with tastings at four wineries,

OTAGO

while **Central Otago Wine Tours** (☎ 03-442 0246; www.winetoursnz.com; from $125) does small-group excursions of varying length. **It's Wine Time** (☎ 0508 946 384; www.winetime.co.nz; $75-165) is also recommend for its tours of Central Otago vineyards.

KINGSTON FLYER

At Kingston, 45km from Queenstown on the southern tip of Lake Wakatipu, is the **Kingston Flyer** (☎ 0800 435 937, 03-248 8848; www.kingstonflyer.co.nz; return fare adult/child/family $30/10/70; ☯ 3 times daily Sep-May), a heritage steam train plying a 14km stretch of track between Kingston and Fairlight – the original flyer ran between Kingston and Gore from 1878 to the mid-1950s. Transport to/from Queenstown by bus, catamaran or helicopter can be arranged.

Sleeping

Accommodation prices tend to rocket during the peak summer and ski seasons; book well in advance at these times. You'll pay extra for rooms with guaranteed lake views.

A good resource for bedroom-seeking families or groups is the **Queenstown Accommodation Centre** (Map pp584-5; ☎ 03-442 7518; www.qac.co.nz; 30 Shotover St), which offers a range of holiday homes and apartments (sleeping four to 12 people) on its books. Prices range from around $110 to $700 per week and there's a minimum stay of three days (one week at peak times such as Christmas).

B&BS & GUESTHOUSES

Melbourne Motor Lodge (Map pp584-5; ☎ 0800 741 444, 03-442 8431; stay@mmlodge.co.nz; 35 Melbourne St;

AUTHOR'S CHOICE

Thomas's Hotel (Map pp584-5; ☎ 03-442 7180; www.thomashotel.co.nz; 50 Beach St; dm $22, d $70-120) The central, lakeside location is a real winner, the rooms (all en suites) are spacious, and car parking can be arranged in a nearby underground lot. Rooms on the building's back corner come with large windows along two walls and thus have grand views over the harbour, mere metres away. The hotel's eponymous mascot is a sleepy, much-petted cat.

---

d $85-120) Welcoming place with a barn-sized lounge that has terrific views of the lake. It has B&B rooms (ordinary-looking but excellent value) with breakfasts that won't leave you hungry, and more-expensive motel rooms at the rear.

Little Paradise Lodge (Map p582; ☎ 03-442 6196; www.littleparadise.com; Glenorchy-Queenstown Rd; s $45, d $100-120) Handmade, environmentally dedicated house 28km from Queenstown, with the owner having hewn the bed headboards, various carvings and adornments around the idiosyncratic house, created a duck pond and a wade-in pool, and established beautiful gardens. Fantastic location opposite the lake.

Chalet Queenstown B&B (Map pp584-5; ☎ 0800 222 457, 03-442 7117; www.chalet.co.nz; 1 Dublin St; s/d from $95/125) Soothing, highly welcoming B&B. The front three rooms face the lake and have access to a lofty balcony, and double-glazing helps keep out traffic noise. There's also a collection of second-hand paperbacks to rifle through and free mountain bike use.

Ferry Hotel B&B (Map p582; ☎ 03-442 2194; www.ferry.co.nz; Spence Rd; d $155-185) About 11km out of town (signposted off SH6 at the Lower Shotover Rd) is this engaging 1870s building, chock-full of history and with topnotch rooms and gardens.

Dairy Guesthouse (Map pp584-5; ☎ 0800 333 393, 03-442 5164; www.thedairy.co.nz; 10 Isle St; d from $300) Upmarket guesthouse that amalgamates several abutting historic buildings, including a 1920s general store. A charmer of a place with some large, well-appointed rooms and further refurbishments on the drawing board.

Remarkables Lodge (Map p582; ☎ 03-442 2720; www.remarkables.co.nz; SH6; d from $500; ⚡) Exclusive four-bedroom lodge in the foothills of the Remarkables, only a few kilometres south of the ski field entrance on SH6. The superb, guest-spoiling facilities include a pool, hot tub, log fire and bar.

HOSTELS & BUDGET HOTELS

Queenstown YHA (Map pp584-5; ☎ 03-442 8413; yha.queenstown@yha.org.nz; 88-90 Lake Esplanade; dm from $25, s/d $50/65; 🖵) Big, rambling, chalet-style place, though without much character inside. If you're going to take one of the smallish doubles, try for one of the two rooms with lake views; no such views accompany any single rooms. Staff in this ever-busy place are exceedingly helpful.

Hippo Lodge (Map pp584-5; ☎ 03-442 5785; www .hippolodge.co.nz; 4 Anderson Heights; dm from $23, s/d from $33/60; ▣) Relaxed, good-quality, multi-level lodge recently subjected to appealing renovations. The lodge doesn't offer town pick-ups, which means those with back-packs face a steep climb, but it's worth it. Note to optimistic wildlife lovers: 'Hippo' is the name of the owner's dog.

McFees (Map pp584-5; ☎ 03-442 7400; www .megalo.co.nz/mcfees; 48a Shotover St; dm $22, d $70-80) McFees is an old-style place with some unusual design features (one room we saw had a nicely carpeted wall), an extremely amenable front desk and good facilities (particularly the kitchen), and is excellent value considering the location. There are two room rates, for lake view and non–lake view rooms; some of the latter come with their own courtyard.

Butterfli Lodge (Map pp584-5; ☎ 03-442 6367; www.butterfli.co.nz; 62 Thompson St; dm/d $23/60) But-terfli has positioned itself on a hillside so that it has great lake views from an outside deck and an above-it-all feel, though the interior is fairly plain. The cheapest beds are in a four-bed room.

Pinewood Lodge (Map pp584-5; ☎ 0800 7463 9663, 03-442 8273; www.pinewood.co.nz; 48 Hamilton Rd; dm $22, d $50-110; ▣) Scattered enclave of budget to family lodges, each with its own lounge. There's free pick-up from town, a spa and a small shop at reception, plus a 24-hour TV and pool room.

Black Sheep Lodge (Map pp584-5; ☎ 03-442 7289; theblacksheep@queenstown.co.nz; 13 Frankton Rd; dm/d $23/55; ▣) This former motel is now a good-standard backpackers' with the air of a large bunkhouse, particularly in the rooms adjacent to the front entry. It's at-tractively casual and has central heating, a fire-stoked lounge and a spa.

Deco Backpackers (Map pp584-5; ☎ 03-442 7384; www.decobackpackers.co.nz; 52 Man St; dm/d $20/50) Two semi-detached ex-residential Deco places joined forces to create this distinc-tive backpackers'. The rooms are nothing special, but the hillside aspect lends it some good views and there's freshly percolated coffee to wake up to in the morning.

Bungi Backpackers (Map pp584-5; ☎ 03-442 8725; www.bungibackpackers.co.nz; 15 Sydney St; dm/d $19/50; ▣) This exuberant hostel has overdosed

on colour and has so much paraphernalia plastered to the walls you can't actually see what's holding the roof up. One of several local hostels offering a 'smoking room' to fume-starved travellers.

Southern Laughter (Map pp584-5; ☎ 03-441 8828; www.southernlaughter.co.nz; 4 Isle St; dm/s from $21/50, d $55-65; ▣) The balconies, hammocks and clinging foliage in parts of this place give it almost a tropical retreat feel. Smallish share rooms range from four-bed dorms to eight-bed 'units', and there's a pool table, spa and videos. You'll need an affinity with pink to stay here.

Scallywags Travellers Guesthouse (Map pp584-5; ☎ 03-442 7083; 27 Lomond Cres; dm/d $24/60) Small view-blessed backpackers' up a steep hill, with a jumble of odds and ends inside that give it a lived-in atmosphere rather than a sense of transience. Free pick-up is offered from town.

HOTELS

Queenstown Lodge (Map p582; ☎ 0800 756 343, 03-442 7107; www.fernhillapartments.co.nz; Sainsbury Rd, Fernhill; dm $29, s & d $105; ▣) Located up on the hill behind the Heritage hotel land-grab, this was originally built as a Contiki lodge but has since transformed into an agreeable accommodation complex with an on-site bar/eatery, **Peppers** (mains around $15). The shuttle heads into town hourly from 8am to 11pm.

Coronet Alpine Hotel (Map p582; ☎ 0800 877 999, 03-442 7850; www.coronetalpinehotel.co.nz; 161 Arthurs Point; d from $130; ▣ ▣) Large hotel in spacious grounds north of town at Arthurs Point. It's the closest hotel to Coronet Peak and offers great facilities for skiers, plus summer extras like a swimming pool. Has a van shuttling to/from Queenstown.

Browns Boutique Hotel (Map pp584-5; ☎ 03-441 2050; www.brownshotel.co.nz; 26 Isle St; s/d $200/240) Intimate hotel modelled on a European pen-sion. There are only 10 rooms, each with a balcony to hang out on and with a comfort factor raised by huge beds. Often booked out well in advance, so get in early.

Aspen on Queenstown (Map p582; ☎ 0800 427 688, 03-442 7688; www.queenstownhotel.com; 139 Fernhill Rd, Fernhill; d $130-300; ▣) This Colorado wannabe has a range of suites and one- and two-bedroom apartments, with suitably plush fittings and a choice of courtyard or lake views. The indoor heated pool and pool

OTAGO

table–equipped bar may eat into your leisure time.

Heritage (Map p582; ☎ 0800 368 888, 03-442 4988; www.heritagehotels.co.nz; 91 Fernhill Rd, Fernhill; from $300;) First-rate stone-and-cedar resort the size of a small village, where rates vary according to room size, the view from your window and the season. The mod-cons and leisure facilities are predictably numerous and the luxury is more thickly applied than Marilyn Manson's make-up.

Rydges (Map pp584–5; ☎ 0800 478 847, 03-442 7600; www.rydges.com; 38-54 Lake Esplanade; d from $130;) Upgraded in the past few years, this big white foreshore structure looks more like an apartment complex than a hotel. Upper balconies have great lake views and there's 24-hour room service so you won't go hungry in the wee hours.

MOTELS
Colonial Village Motels (Map pp584–5; ☎ 03-442 7629; www.colonialvillage.co.nz; 136 Frankton Rd; d from $100) Get a different view of Queenstown's watery locale from this highly recommended motel, which has units piled up on a hillside looking out across Frankton Arm. If the units closest to the busy road don't appeal, there are other rooms more removed from the roadside (and with king-size beds).

Earnslaw Lodge (Map pp584–5; ☎ 0508 3276 7529, 03-442 8728; www.earnslawlodge.co.nz; 77 Frankton Rd; d $100-135) This is another exceptionally friendly place, with a choice of standard highway-facing rooms or dearer units with a less-trafficked aspect. They also have one downstairs budget cubbyhole with a double bed in it ($75).

Garden Court (Map pp584–5; ☎ 0800 427 336, 03-442 9713; www.gardencourt.co.nz; 41 Frankton Rd; d $130-195;) Modern motel with efficient staff, room service, wheelchair-accessible rooms and a supply of cots and highchairs. At time of research, a new block of lake-facing units was being erected.

Lomond Lodge Motor Inn (Map pp584–5; ☎ 03-442 8235; 33 Man St; www.lomondlodge.com; d $100-180;) Quietly-situated complex with garden-facing studios and 'superior' apartments with open fire-warmed lounges and mod-cons like video players. Apartments without their own kitchens all have access to a communal cooking area.

Bella Vista (Map pp584–5; ☎ 0800 610 171, 03-442 4468; www.bellavistamotels.co.nz; 36 Robins Rd; r from

$100) This relative newcomer to the Queenstown motel scene has spacious units to leap into and the added extra of continental or cooked breakfasts.

Blue Peaks Lodge & Apartments (Map pp584–5; ☎ 0800 162 122, 03-442 9224; www.bluepeaks.co.nz; cnr Stanley & Sydney Sts; d $130-185) The outside of this lodge looks a little bit dated, but inside it's nicely detailed and it's well and truly up-to-date facility-wise. Luxury two-bedroom apartments are also available nearby from $300; refer all inquiries to the lodge.

CAMPING & CAMPERVAN PARKS
Queenstown Lakeview Holiday Park (Map pp584–5; ☎ 0800 482 7352; 03-442 7252; www.holidaypark.net.nz; Brecon St; camp sites & campervan sites $24, d $70-100) Only a short stroll from the gondola, this park has exposed camping sites, very good facilities and an arc of tall luxury flats keeping sentinel-like watch over the lake. You have to admire the restrained immodesty of their advertising slogan: 'Arguably New Zealand's No 1 Holiday Park'.

Creeksyde Top 10 Holiday Park (Map pp584–5; ☎ 0800 786 222, 03-442 9447; www.camp.co.nz; 54 Robins Rd; camp sites & campervan sites $27, d $50-135) Creeksyde's pine needle-covered grounds contain everything from plain lodge rooms to tourist flats and motel units; most end-of-year sites and rooms are booked out by the start of December. The reception area is impaled on a 10-tonne boiler tube salvaged from an old wool mill.

Kawarau Falls Lakeside Holiday Park (Map p582; ☎ 0800 226 774, 03-442 3510; www.campsite.co.nz; SH6; camp sites & campervan sites $26, dm $19, d $50-90;) Foreshore camp sites and a six-bedroom lodge (three rooms have balconies and views of the lake) are two overnight options here. There's also a three-bedroom house that sleeps 10 (from $120). Great waterside location.

Arthurs Point Top 10 Holiday Park (Map p582; ☎ 0800 462 267, 03-442 9311; top10.queenstown@xtra.co.nz; Gorge Rd; camp sites & campervan sites $24, d $40-90) Located about 5km from town towards Arrowtown, where it's right outside the well-trafficked bustle of Queenstown and is scenically hemmed in by some chunky hills.

Located fifteen kilometres from Queenstown towards Glenorchy is a DOC camping ground at **12-Mile Creek Reserve** (Map p582; adult/child $5/2.50).

Eating

RESTAURANTS

Bunker (Map pp584-5; ☎ 03-441 8030; Cow Lane; mains $39; ⓥ dinner) Set in a former ski tuning den, the Bunker is a low-lit restaurant with terrific food, an equally terrific selection of Australian and NZ wines, and a couple of framed James Bond photos on the wall. There's only a handful of tables so book ahead. Mains have included horopito-rubbed roast venison, twice-cooked duck leg and seared rare tuna. After dinner it becomes a cosy bar (see p594).

Solera Vino (Map pp584-5; ☎ 03-442 6082; 25 Beach St; mains $28-35; ⓥ dinner) Upmarket eatery dressed down in earthy tones, but with enough white linen to hint at formality. Its motto is 'No fast food – no loud music' and mains include a good bouillabaisse and a signature French onion soup with gruyere cheese. Make reservations for the end of the week.

Coronation Bathhouse Cafe & Restaurant (Map pp584-5; ☎ 03-442 5625; Marine Pde; lunch $15-21, dinner $27-38; ⓥ lunch & dinner) Treat yourself to brunch, lunch or dinner in this restored historic bathhouse (built 1911) in lakeside gardens. Dinner mains include ragout of rabbit, roasted spatchcock and terrine of wild venison.

Wai Waterfront Restaurant & Wine Bar (Map pp584-5; ☎ 03-442 5969; Steamer Wharf, Beach St; mains $30-38; ⓥ dinner) Chic waterfront restaurant and wine bar combination. Serves confit of duck and beefy mains, but it's the seafood that's really in demand here, like game fish and an extensive oyster menu (done about 16 different ways). There's a seven-course degustation menu ($130/85 with/without wine).

Fishbone Bar & Grill (Map pp584-5; ☎ 03-442 6768; 7 Beach St; mains $15-30; ⓥ lunch & dinner) A bright spray of colour in a town full of sombre stylishness. Mains include calamari in chilli-plum sauce, wine-steamed mussels and char-grilled cod, and ocean-going calypso sometimes accompanies your meals. There's a kids' menu too.

Minami Jujisei (Map pp584-5; ☎ 03-442 9854; 45 Beach St; mains $15-30; ⓥ lunch Mon-Sat, dinner) Accomplished Japanese restaurant with various dishes cooked *nabe mono* (hotpot-style) and lots of seafood to choose from. A delicious choice is the venison *tatati* (the venison is briefly seared then put into ice and served).

Gantley's (Map p582; ☎ 03-442 8999; Arthurs Pt Rd; mains $29-39; ⓥ dinner) Fine contemporary NZ dining in a historic 1863 stone-and-timber building at Arthurs Point, with a highly-regarded wine list and plenty of candlelight at dinnertime. Reservations are essential; a courtesy bus is run to/from town.

Freiya's (Map pp584-5; ☎ 03-442 7979; 33 Camp St; mains $12-18; ⓥ lunch & dinner) Well-prepared dine-in (and takeaway) Indian. Start with the usual array of samosas and pakoras, followed by a good rogan josh or dal makhani (lentils) simmered with ginger, onions and garlic. There are a half-dozen veg selections.

Tatler Restaurant (Map pp584-5; ☎ 03-442 8372; 5 the Mall; mains $24-30; ⓥ breakfast, lunch & dinner) Tatler's self-consciously cool interior is a little too effective, with a style that's slightly cold. But it specialises in solid NZ fare: venison, tuna, salmon and beef. The upstairs extension of the restaurant becomes the **Spectator** bar during the peak summer/winter seasons.

Cow (Map pp584-5; ☎ 03-442 8588; Cow Lane; mains $15-26; ⓥ noon-11pm) The dark, cosy, stone-walled interior of the Cow takes a little getting used to, particularly if you've just entered from bright sunlight. It's popular with locals for its tasty range of pizzas and pastas, but has been more hit-and-miss with travellers. The laneway it's on was where cows were brought in to be milked from nearby paddocks during the 1860s gold rush.

Dux de Lux (Map pp584-5; ☎ 03-442 9688; 14 Church St) At the time of research, the stony old McNeill's Cottage Brewery was being transformed into a sister branch of Christchurch's ultra-popular Dux de Lux veg/seafood restaurant-cum-brewer and live-music spot. You'll want to check it out.

CAFÉS & QUICK EATS

Vudu Cafe (Map pp584-5; ☎ 03-442 5357; 23 Beach St; breakfast $9-12, lunch $13-15; ⓥ breakfast, lunch & dinner) Head to this always-crowded café for an early-morning cholesterol fix via the brekkie *quesadillas* (with pesto, cheese, avocado and sour cream). This cool but by no means pretentious place also does great creative light lunches and dinettes like potato and dill pikelets, a chicken and cashew noodle bowl, and venison sausages and mash.

OTAGO

Naff Caff (Map pp584-5; ☎ 03-442 8211; 1/66 Shotover St; meals $3-12; ☺ breakfast & lunch) Small, welcoming place with bagels, muffins, pain au chocolat, homemade muesli, great coffee and various teas (which can be purchased in 100g bunches). Not so naff after all.

Leonardo's (Map pp584-5; ☎ 03-442 8542; 22 Shotover St; meals $8-14; ☺ breakfast & lunch) The main drawcards in Leonardo's mellow interior are the organic, freshly roasted coffee and sweet tastes like chunks of tiramisu, ginger crunch and baked cheesecake.

Ken's Noodles (Map pp584-5; ☎ 03-442 8628; 37 Camp St; meals $4-12; ☺ lunch & dinner Mon-Sat, lunch Sun) Udon and ramen noodle meals like miso-ramen (noodles in miso soup) and six-piece sushi packs ($4) are efficiently dished out in Ken's Noodles sparse, no-fuss interior.

Kappa Sushi Cafe (Map pp584-5; ☎ 03-441 1423; Level 1, 36a the Mall; mains $10-25; ☺ lunch) Established upstairs café with a small weatherproof balcony where you can tuck into sushi, sashimi, tempura, noodles – all the Japanese standards.

Fergburger (Map pp584-5; ☎ 03-441 1232; Cow Lane; burgers $8-15; ☺ noon-5am) High-quality gourmet burger counter hidden down Cow Lane, with bun-enclosed offerings ranging from the classic 'Fergburger' to the 'Sweet Bambi' (with cervena) and the whopping 'Big Al'.

Inside the shopping centre is **O'Connell's Food Hall** (Map pp584-5; ☎ 03-442 7760; cnr Camp & Beach Sts; ☺ 8am-8pm), a basement food court with budget nosh, including Turkish, fish and chips, Thai, Japanese and burgers. Get standard bakery treats at the **Bakery** (Map pp584-5; ☎ 03-442 8698; 15 Shotover St; ☺ breakfast & lunch), with some tables on an upstairs terrace. **Habebes** (Map pp584-5; ☎ 03-442 9861; Wakatipu Arcade; meals $5-11; ☺ lunch) has a fresh assortment of quiches, delicious pita rolls and impressive pies (lentil, chicken), with plenty of veg options, while falafels, kebabs, shish kebabs and mixed grills are on the menu at **Turkish Kebabs** (Map pp584-5; ☎ 03-441 3180; 31 Beach St; meals $8-15; ☺ breakfast, lunch & dinner). For cheap Japanese takeaway, head to the waterfront van called **Planet 1** (Map pp584-5; cnr Church St & Marine Pde; ☺ lunch).

SELF-CATERING

The 24-hour **Night 'n Day** (Map pp584-5; ☎ 03-442 8289; 24 Rees St) convenience store has lots of goodies, including pies, sandwiches, wine and beer. For some fully-fledged self-catering, head to the **Alpine Supermarket** (Map pp584-5; ☎ 03-442 8961; cnr Stanley & Shotover Sts; ☺ 8am-9pm Mon-Fri, 9am-9pm Sat & Sun).

Drinking

Cigar Bar (Map pp584-5; ☎ 03-441 8066; Steamer Wharf, Beach St) Classy waterfront bar with a low-lit room in back with leather couches to slump into while clutching a balloon of Remy Martin and a Cohiba, Cuaba, Montecristo or one of the other cigars locked away in the humidor.

Winnie Bagoes (Winnie's; Map pp584-5; ☎ 03-442 8635; 1st fl, 7 the Mall) Deservedly popular place for a beer, with its laid-back ambience and retractable roof. Lounge in front of the log fire on cold afternoons, play pool, or eat in a booth or on the outside balcony; meals ($15 to $28) include gourmet pizzas, Mexican, seafood and Thai-flavoured fare.

Bunker (Map pp584-5; ☎ 03-441 8030; Cow Lane) After the dinner dishes are cleared away, the Bunker becomes a great bar space with a club lounge, open fire and a secretive, just-discovered feel, especially in the wee hours (it closes at 5am). There's another bar area further down the side-alley and up some stairs.

Monty's (Map pp584-5; ☎ 03-441 1081; Church Lane) The front bar here is so rustic you half-expect to see a bunch of fur-trappers having a fist fight over a card game. Monteith's is its preferred beer-verage. It's next door to Dux de Lux (see p593).

Pog Mahones (Map pp584-5; ☎ 03-442 5382; 14 Rees St) Wood-saturated Irish pub right by the lake, where it gets a multitude of bay view–seeking drinkers. Has a cosy upstairs bar with a teensy first-come, first-seated balcony.

Pig & Whistle (Map pp584-5; ☎ 03-442 9055; 19 Camp St) Escape the boisterous crowds elsewhere by heading to this sedate pub with an older, quieter crowd, low-key music and a large beer garden out front.

Loaded Hog (Map pp584-5; ☎ 03-441 2969; Steamer Wharf, Beach St) Cavernous bar, a bit less rustic than its English-tavern name suggests, although it has enough farming paraphernalia nailed to the ceiling and floors to start up several agricultural ventures. Also has outside tables and a long list of NZ wines to drink up.

Red Rock Bar & Grill (Map pp584-5; ☎ 03-442 6850; 48 Camp St) In the same mould as many other places around town: alcove-riddled interior, pock-marked floors, some outside seating, light daytime meals and little to make a lasting impression except when a sizeable drinking crowd gathers.

Rattlesnake Room (Map pp584-5; ☎ 03-442 9995; 14 Brecon St) One of NZ's many saloon-style places attempting to invoke some rough-and-ready spirit by looking like the set of a cowboy film, this one even more distinctive for its Santa Fe adobe design, the enormous six-shooter hanging from the ceiling and decorative long-horn skulls. In keeping with the anachronistic interior, they were blasting ancient David Bowie when we visited. Next door is a big generic sports bar, **Shooters** (Map pp584-5; ☎ 03-442 4144; 10 Brecon St).

Entertainment

The free weekly flyer *The Source* details many of the entertaining goings-on around Queenstown. Rare is the night when there's no music or clubbing on offer, and many bars are open until 2am or 3am as a matter of course during busier times. Most DJ and live music gigs are free, though some nightclubs (Subculture, Debajo) charge $3 to $5 admission post-midnight from Thursday to Saturday; a few dollars more for out-of-town DJs.

CINEMA

Embassy Cinemas (Map pp584-5; ☎ 03-442 9994; www.embassymovies.co.nz; 11 the Mall; adult/child/student $13/6.50/9) There's a programme of new-release movies here; the pre-5pm sessions are cheaper.

LIVE MUSIC

Several bars listed under Drinking (opposite) have live music and DJs:

Cigar Bar (Map pp584-5; ☎ 03-441 8066; Steamer Wharf, Beach St; music 9.30pm Fri & Sat) Smoker's bar with live jazz and acoustic performances.

Pog Mahones (Map pp584-5; ☎ 03-442 5382; 14 Rees St) Occasional live (and loud) Irish music and solo musicians.

Winnie Bagoes (Winnie's; Map pp584-5; ☎ 03-442 8635; 1st fl, 7 the Mall) Acoustic shows and DJs over summer/winter.

NIGHTCLUBS

Subculture (Map pp584-5; ☎ 03-442 7685; downstairs, 12-14 Church St) Friendly, underground

Subculture has some skilful locals and out-of-towners toying with the turntable to make drum 'n' bass, hip-hop, dub and reggae noises.

Debajo (Map pp584-5; ☎ 03-442 6099; Cow Lane) Smallish downstairs affair with a tentative Latin décor (a couple of toreador posters) but a solid reputation for house beats and decent cocktails.

Tardis Bar (Map pp584-5; ☎ 03-441 8397; Skyline Arcade) Seems an ill-fitting name, as it's no bigger on the inside than it looks on the outside. It is, however, a good dance-bar with regular DJs and a foot-weathered floor.

World Bar (Map pp584-5; ☎ 03-442 6757; 27 Shotover St) Usually wall-to-wall with boozing, DJ-listening backpackers, this place was being entirely re-fitted when we visited. Go and see how this particular world is shaping up.

Several restaurants and bars quick-change into late-night clubs:

Chico's (Map pp584-5; ☎ 03-442 8439; 1st fl, the Mall) Grill above Old Man Rock café-bar that turns into a classic-hits disco.

Rattlesnake Room (Map pp584-5; ☎ 03-442 9995; 14 Brecon St) DJs usually mosey on in on Friday and Saturday nights.

Surreal (Map pp584-5; ☎ 03-441 8492; 7 Rees St) A mixture of drum 'n' bass, hip-hop, trance, garage and soul, plus great food and vivacious staff.

CASINOS

The low-rolling **Sky Alpine Casino** (Map pp584-5; ☎ 03-441 0400; www.skyalpine.co.nz; Beach St; noon-4am) has several bars and gaming areas, with the main tables squeezed into one large room. Another place to put your money at stake is the **Wharf Casino** (Map pp584-5; ☎ 03-441 1495; Steamer Wharf, Beach St; 11am-3am).

Getting There & Away
AIR

Direct daily flights are offered by **Air New Zealand** (Map pp584-5; ☎ 0800 737 000, 03-441 1900; www.airnz.co.nz; 8 Church St) between Queenstown and both Auckland (from $150) and Christchurch (from $75), with connections to other major centres. **Qantas** (☎ 0800 808 767, 03-379 6504; www.qantas.co.nz) also has direct flights to Christchurch (from $75), with connections to Auckland and Rotorua.

OTAGO

BUS

The booking office for **InterCity** (Map pp584-5; ☎ 03-442 8238; www.intercitycoach.co.nz; cnr Camp & Shotover Sts), in the Queenstown visitors centre, has details of daily bus services from Queenstown, including to Christchurch (from $60), Te Anau ($35), Milford Sound ($70), Dunedin ($55) and Invercargill ($38), plus a daily West Coast service to the glaciers ($95) via Wanaka ($26) and Haast Pass.

'Alternative' bus tours such as the West Coast Express, Kiwi Experience, Magic Bus or the Flying Kiwi also go up the West Coast to Nelson; see under Backpackers Buses (p685).

The **Bottom Bus** (www.bottombus.co.nz) does a loop service around the south of the South Island (see under The Catlins; p638). Book tickets at the **Info & Track Centre** (Map pp584-5; ☎ 03-442 9708; 37 Shotover St).

Myriad shuttle buses can also be booked at the visitors centre. Shuttles to Wanaka charge between $15 and $25, to Dunedin the price is $25 to $30, to Te Anau it's $25 to $35, to Christchurch $45 to $50. Providers include Wanaka Connexions, offering regular services to Wanaka; **Atomic Shuttles** (☎ 03-322 8883; www.atomictravel.co.nz) goes to Christchurch, Dunedin and Invercargill; **Southern Link Shuttles** (☎ 03-358 8355) has services to Dunedin, Christchurch and Wanaka; **Catch-a-Bus** (☎ 03-479 9960) goes to Dunedin and Topline Tours goes to Te Anau.

TRAMPERS & SKIERS TRANSPORT

Both the **Info & Track Centre** (Map pp584-5; ☎ 03-442 9708; 37 Shotover St) and **Kiwi Discovery** (Map pp584-5; ☎ 0800 505 504, 03-442 7340; 37 Camp St) can arrange transport to the tracks. **Backpacker Express** (Map pp584-5; ☎ 03-442 9939; www.glenorchyinfocentre.co.nz; 2 Oban St) runs to/from the Routeburn, Greenstone, Caples and Rees-Dart Tracks, all via Glenorchy. The morning bus picks up at various accommodation points around Queenstown. Prices are $15 between Queenstown and Glenorchy, and $15 between Glenorchy and any of the tracks.

Bus services between Queenstown and Milford Sound via Te Anau can be used for track transport. See under Te Anau (p621) for information on the tramper-servicing company Tracknet.

Kiwi Discovery (Map pp584-5; ☎ 0800 505 504, 03-442 7340; 37 Camp St) also operates ski-season shuttles to Coronet Peak and the Remarkables (adult/child $25/17) and to Cardrona and Treble Cone ($35/24).

Getting Around
TO/FROM THE AIRPORT

Located 8km from town is **Queenstown Airport** (Map p582; ☎ 03-442 3505; www.queenstownairport.co.nz; Frankton). **Super Shuttle** (☎ 0800 748 8853, 03-442 3639) picks up and drops off in Queenstown (from $8). The **Shopper Bus** (☎ 03-442 6647) runs to the airport ($3.50) hourly from 8.15am to 5.15pm. **Alpine Taxis** (☎ 03-442 6666) or **Queenstown Taxis** (☎ 03-442 7788) charge around $20.

PUBLIC TRANSPORT

The **Shopper Bus** (☎ 03-442 6647) has services to Fernhill and Frankton accommodation ($2.50).

ARROWTOWN
pop 1700

Off the highway between Cromwell and Queenstown is the loop road to Arrowtown, which grew from the discovery of gold in the Arrow River in 1862. It has a beautiful avenue lined with deciduous trees (especially pretty in autumn) and much-photographed wooden buildings, over 60 of them from the 19th century and faithfully restored. Some people find the town a bit too self-consciously upmarket *nouveau*-quaint, while others adore its history- and arts-enriched personality. It's less than a half-hour drive from Queenstown, which means it gets completely jammed with rubberneckers on weekends.

The **visitors centre** (☎ 03-442 1824; www.arrowtown.com; 49 Buckingham St; ☒ 8.30am-5pm) is officed by some very helpful locals. Sharing its premises (and phone line) is the **Lake District Museum & Gallery** (www.museumqueenstown.com; adult/child $5/50c; ☒ 8.30am-5pm), which has exhibits on the region's early Maori inhabitants and the gold-rush era. Get a copy of the leaflet 'Arrowtown Walks' (free); it has information on getting to Macetown (opposite) and historic notes on the area.

Also equip yourself with the attractive booklet *Historic Buildings of Arrowtown* ($2.50), detailing self-guided walks in the township.

GARETH MCCORMACK

Tent among mountain daisies, Aoraki/Mt Cook National Park (p549)

WES WALKER

Waimakariri River Valley, Arthur's Pass
National Park (p535)

North Quad and aerial sculpture, Arts
Centre (p509), Christchurch

KRZYSZTOF DYDYNSKI

DAVID WALL

Mountain bikers, the Remarkables (p588)

DAVID WALL

Snowboarder, Cardrona
(p611)

White-water rafters, Queenstown (p586)

PAUL KE

Jetboat, Shotover River (p586),
Queenstown

DAVID WALL

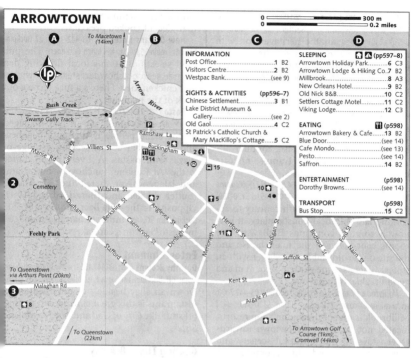

ARROWTOWN

Arrowtown has the best example of a gold-era **Chinese settlement** (off Buckingham St; admission free; 24hr) in NZ. Several restored huts provide an evocative reminder of the role of Chinese 'diggers' during and after the gold rush, while interpretive signs explain the lives of residents. The Chinese were subjected to much prejudice, especially during the 1880s economic depression. They often did not seek new claims but worked through tailings looking for the fine gold undetected by earlier miners.

Arrowtown Golf Course (03-442 1719; www.arrowtown.nzgolf.net; green fees $40, club hire $17) is picturesque and challenging, with narrow defiles and rock obstacles adding to the fun.

Macetown

Fourteen kilometres north of Arrowtown is Macetown, a ghost town reached via a long, unimproved and flood-prone road (the original miners' wagon track), which crosses the Arrow River over 25 times! Four-hour trips are made from Queenstown by 4WD vehicle, and gold panning time is included. The main operator is

Nomad Safaris (03-442 6699; www.nomadsafaris.co.nz; adult/child from $110/60), which has a pick-up service for passengers located in Arrowtown.

Sleeping

Arrowtown Holiday Park (03-442 1876; 11 Suffolk St; camp sites $19, campervan sites $20, d $35-75) This large ground is the only choice in town for campers. The mountain views are magnificent and there's a tennis court and kids' playground.

New Orleans Hotel (03-442 1745; neworleanshotel@xtra.co.nz; 27 Buckingham St; s $50-70, d $70-95) This homesick hotel is a long way from Louisiana, but has pulled itself together enough to offer recently-refurbished accommodation, including a couple of rooms overlooking the river.

Viking Lodge (03-442 1765; www.vikinglodge.co.nz; 21 Inverness Cres; d $90-125;) Has a collection of self-contained A-frame 'chalet units', each sleeping up to six people. The upstairs/downstairs sleeping arrangements and the swimming pool are big hits with families.

OTAGO

Settlers Cottage Motel (☎ 0800 803 801, 03-442 1734; www.arrowtown.co.nz/settlers; 22 Hertford St; d $100-130) Goes for the heritage look with a decidedly yesteryear style (heavily-patterned carpets and prim furnishings) and a pretty garden setting. Wheelchair-accessible rooms are available.

Arrowtown Lodge & Hiking Co (☎ 0800 258 802, 03-442 1101; www.arrowtownlodge.co.nz; 7 Anglesea St; s $80-110, d $130-160) B&B establishment with four cottage-style suites and full cooked breakfasts. The owners also conduct all-inclusive guided alpine tramps, historic hikes and scenic bushwalks.

Old Nick B&B (☎ 0800 653 642, 03-442 0066; www .oldnick.co.nz; 79 Buckingham St; s $100-145, d $120-180) Built at the turn of the 20th century to accommodate the local constabulary, this is now a comfort-conscious B&B with five rooms split between the main house and the site of the old stables (the latter with en suites). There's a fine garden to roam in and good breakfasts to devour.

Millbrook (Map p582; ☎ 0800 800 604, 03-441 7000; www.millbrook.co.nz; Malaghan Rd; d $300-510; 🏊) Millbrook is one of the region's top resorts, located not far from Arrowtown towards Queenstown. It has beautiful scenery and luxurious accommodation (rooms, suites, villas and cottages of varying sizes) and its grounds contain restored historic buildings, a health spa, sports facilities and good restaurants. Non-guests can buy a great-value day pass ($30) allowing use of the resort's gymnasium, spa and sauna, pool and tennis courts.

Eating

Saffron (☎ 03-442 0131; 18 Buckingham St; mains $16-22; 🕑 lunch & dinner) Small and simple place but with a style-savvy air, patrons dressed in expensive casual-wear, and a reputation as a fine restaurant. The salmon is excellent, as is the long list of desserts (and dessert wines).

Cafe Mondo (☎ 03-442 0227; Ballarat Arcade, Buckingham St; meals $10-15; 🕑 breakfast & lunch; 🖥) Licensed place accessed off the courtyard behind the bakery, and with a good selection of light food such as sweetcorn fritters, ploughmans lunch and Caesar salad, plus lots of sweet things to nibble.

Arrowtown Bakery & Cafe (☎ 03-442 1587; Buckingham St; 🕑 lunch) Among the standard bakery fare is a great selection of pies, including

lamb satay and mince bolognaise, and more than decent cooked breakfasts.

New Orleans Hotel (☎ 03-442 1745; 27 Buckingham St; mains $10-20; 🕑 lunch & dinner) The pub food selections at this local drinking den include seafood chowder, steak sandwiches and chicken kiev. There's a nice terrace out back of the main bar.

Pesto (☎ 03-442 0885; 18 Buckingham St; mains $15-20; 🕑 dinner) Behind Saffron and managed by the same people is this cosy benches-and-booths bar space, serving a range of pizzas and pastas. A lively pizza choice is the 'Al Capone' (anchovies, hot salami and jalapenos) or there's the 'Taj Mahal' (butter chicken and chargrilled eggplant). Opposite is the **Blue Door** (☎ 03-442 0415; 18 Buckingham St), an intimate bar also managed by Pesto/Saffron's caretakers.

Entertainment

Dorothy Browns (☎ 03-442 1968; www.dorothybrowns .com; off Buckingham St; adult/child/student $15/5/10) Down an alley beside the aforementioned restaurants is this great cinema/bar, reeling off stuff like *City of God* and *The Magdalene Sisters*.

Getting There & Away

From Queenstown, the **Double Decker Bus** (☎ 03-441 4421) does a three-hour round-trip to Arrowtown (adult/child return $34/15) at 10am and 2pm daily. **Arrow Express** (☎ 03-442 1900; www.arrowtownbus.co.nz) has three services daily (adult/child $10/6, return $18/10) stopping outside the museum in Arrowtown and the McDonald's on Camp St in Queenstown.

The buses of **InterCity** (☎ 03-442 8238; www .intercitycoach.co.nz) running to Dunedin and Christchurch can also stop at Arrowtown for prebooked passengers.

GLENORCHY

pop 215

The very small, beautifully-situated hamlet of Glenorchy lies at the head of Lake Wakatipu 47km, or a scenic 40-minute drive from Queenstown. Regrettably, most people rush through to knock off the Routeburn Track and end up bypassing some other great tramping opportunities in the Rees and Dart River Valleys.

The **DOC visitors centre** (☎ 03-442 9937; glenorchy vc@doc.govt.nz; cnr Mull & Oban Sts; 🕑 8.30am-4pm

has the latest walking track conditions and
hut tickets; get camping gear and supplies
in Queenstown or Te Anau.

The town has an 18-hole **golf course** (cnr
Oban & Mull Sts; green fees $5); for club hire, in-
quire at Glenorchy Hotel or Glen-Roydon
Lodge (see p599).

Activities

WALKING & SCENIC DRIVING

The DOC leaflet *Glenorchy Walkway* (free)
details an easy waterside walk around the
outskirts of town, with several picnic areas
along the way.

Those with wheels should explore
the superb valleys north of Glenorchy.
Paradise, in case you've been seeking it,
lies 15km northwest of town just before
the start of the Dart Track. Paradise is just
a paddock but the gravel road there runs
through beautiful farmland surrounded by
majestic mountains (there are several small
creek crossings). Alternatively, you can explore the Rees Valley or take the road to
Routeburn, which goes via the Dart River
Bridge. Near the start of the Routeburn
Track in Mt Aspiring National Park is a
day hut and the short **Double Barrel** and the
Lake Sylvan walks.

JETBOATING & KAYAKING

Dart River Safaris (☎ 0800 327 853, 03-442 9992;
www.dartriver.co.nz; Mull St; adult/child $160/80) jour-
neys by jetboat into the heart of the glorious Dart River wilderness, where you can
savour the grandeur of Mt Earnslaw and
the bush-clad mountain walls that sandwich the river before taking a 4WD trip
down a back road to Paradise. The round
trip from Glenorchy takes three hours.
Transfers from Queenstown cost an extra
$20/10 per adult/child and add three hours
to the package. Shuttles leave Queenstown
at 8am and noon daily.

Dart River Safaris also offer trips starting with a 75-minute jetboat ride up the
Dart and then a river descent in an inflatable three-seater canoe called a **'funyak'**
(www.funyaks.co.nz); from Glenorchy the whole
ride takes 6½ hours (adult/child $240/175);
for transfers from Queenstown add $20/15
per adult/child.

Dart Wilderness Adventures (☎ 0800 109 139,
03-442 9939; www.glenorchyinfocentre.co.nz; adult/child
$160/80) also jetboats along the Dart River

between Glenorchy and Sandy Bluff, a
three-hour, 80km round-trip. Shuttles from
Queenstown (adult/child $20/10) depart at
9.30am and 1.30pm daily.

OTHER ACTIVITIES

Catering to all levels of horse-riding experience is **Dart Stables** (☎ 0800 474 3464; 03-442 5688;
www.dartstables.com; Coll St), with options that include a two-hour ride at the head of Lake
Wakatipu ($85; $105 from Queenstown), a
full-day hoof ($160) or an overnight trek
with a sleepover in Paradise ($380). **High
Country Horses** (☎ 03-442 9915; www.high-country
-horses.co.nz) does guided one- and two-hour
rides for beginners ($40 and $60 respectively), full-day rides ($110) and various
overnighters.

Locally recommended guide Stuart Trip-
ney was **Born to Fish** (☎ 03-441 2000; www.bornto
fish.co.nz; half-/full-day trips $350/600) and can take
you on fly-fishing excursions (including
heli-fishing and multi-day jaunts), all
equipment supplied.

Tours

Glenorchy Air (☎ 0800 676 264, 03-442 2207; www
.glenorchy.net.nz) does a 2½-hour flight over
Mt Cook and the glaciers, bypassing Mt
Aspiring on the way and with a Fox or Franz
Josef landing as an added extra ($430). It
also heads out to Taiaroa Head for a tour
of royal albatross and yellow-eyed penguin
colonies ($430, five hours), and has a Mil-
ford Sound fly-cruise deal ($345).

Sleeping & Eating

Glenorchy Holiday Park (☎ 03-442 7171; 2 Oban St;
camp sites $18, campervan sites $20, dm $16, d $32-80)
Spread-out park that's well set up for trampers, fronted by a jetboat and track shuttle-
booking office and a mall shop with limited
supplies. It has rustic bunks and cabins, and
a self-contained villa.

Glenorchy Hotel (☎ 0800 453 667, 03-442 9902;
relax@glenorchynz.com; Mull St; d from $70) Very
comfortable shared-facility and en suite
rooms are available in this pub.

Kinloch Lodge (Map p582; ☎ 03-442 4900; www
.kinlochlodge.co.nz; Kinloch Rd; dm $24, d $55-160)
Across Lake Wakatipu from Glenorchy is
this excellent retreat, a great place to unwind or prepare for a tramp (track transfers
can be organised). Stay in the main house's
'Heritage' rooms (top choices are the two

front-facing rooms) and have a three-course meal in the fine **restaurant** for an all-inclusive $220 per two people. There's also a bar and hot tub. Kinloch is a 26km drive from Glenorchy or you can organise a three-minute boat ride ($5).

Glen-Roydon Lodge (☎ 03-442 9968; www.glen roydon.com; Argyle St; d from $95) This lodge is stocked with well-appointed, hotel-style rooms and has informative hosts. It also has a family room with one double and one single bed, though this is prone to noise from in-house residents. There's a front-of-house **café** (lunch $8-15; ☼ lunch) and an expansive **restaurant** (dinner $20-25; ☼ dinner) with good meals like the delicious blue cod with wasabi and beetroot sauce.

Mt Earnslaw Motels (☎ 03-442 6993; www.earnslaw .bizland.com; Mull St; d $85-100) Modern units (some with wheelchair access) with large, spread-yourself-out beds and well-equipped kitchens. The sauna is a good place to steam away your cares.

Routeburn Farm Cottage (Map p582; ☎ 03-442 9901; elfinbay@queenstown.co.nz; Routeburn Rd; d $85) The rural grounds of Routeburn Farm are on the road to the Routeburn Track, 6km before the start of the walk and 21km from Glenorchy. Here you'll find a comfortable three-bedroom self-contained cottage surround by walking opportunities. The owners conduct one-on-one horse rides ($90).

Blanket Bay (Map p582; ☎ 03-442 9442; www .blanketbay.com; Glenorchy Rd; rooms $1190-2390; ☒) World-class resort on the shores of Lake Wakatipu just south of Glenorchy. Constructed of native timber and local schist stone, it's a breathtaking place, a good match for its stunning setting. The lodge has luxurious facilities, including an open-fire-warmed lounge, dining room, bar and outdoor heated pool.

Glenorchy Cafe (☎ 03-442 9958; Mull St; meals $8-15; ☼ breakfast & lunch, dinner over summer) Eating here is like eating in someone's warm living room, a feeling accentuated by the artful domestic décor, complete with carpet and the well-aged sounds of some old vinyl 45s.

Out back of the Glenorchy Hotel is the simple **Backpackers Retreat** (dm $18). The pub also has a **café-restaurant** (mains $15-30; ☼ breakfast, lunch & dinner) serving broccoli and blue cheese penne and the 'Lord of the

Locals' (dish of grilled meats like chicken beef and venison).

Stock up on groceries in Queenstown.

Getting There & Away
The sealed Glenorchy–Queenstown Rd is wonderfully scenic, but its constant hills are a killer for cyclists. In summer, trampers' buses like **Backpacker Express** (☎ 03-442 9939; www.glenorchyinfocentre.co.nz; 2 Oban St), based at the Glenorchy Holiday Park, travel this road daily and also drive from Glenorchy to the start of the Routeburn, Rees-Dart Greenstone and Caples Tracks (all $15); the Routeburn Track service can be caught from Queenstown ($30), with first departures around 8am. Prices quoted are for pre-booked trips; there'll be an extra $5 levy if you just turn up.

LAKE WAKATIPU REGION TRAMPS
The mountainous region at the northern head of Lake Wakatipu has some of the greatest scenery in NZ, which you can view while tramping along the famous Routeburn and lesser-known Greenstone Caples, and Rees-Dart Tracks. Also see the DOC brochure *Lake Wakatipu walks and trails* ($1) for shorter tracks. Glenorchy is a convenient base for all these tramps.

Routeburn Walk Ltd (☎ 03-442 8200; www.rout burn.co.nz) has a three-day guided walk on the Routeburn ($950/1050 low/high season and a six-day 'Grand Traverse' ($1330/1480) which combines walks on the Routeburn and Greenstone Tracks. Prices include return transport, accommodation and all meals.

Track Information
For details of accommodation, transport to/from all trailheads and DOC information offices and ranger stations, see under Queenstown (p583), Glenorchy (p598) and Te Anau (p615).

DOC staff advise on maps and track conditions, and sell hut and Great Walks passes For more details on all these tracks see Lonely Planet's *Tramping in New Zealand*.

Routeburn Track
The three- to four-day Routeburn Track is one of the most popular rainforest/subalpine tracks in NZ for the great variety of landscape it passes through. Unfortunately, it's become the surrogate for those who've missed out on

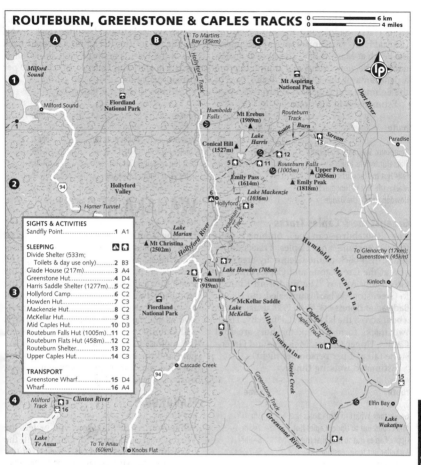

ROUTEBURN, GREENSTONE & CAPLES TRACKS

SIGHTS & ACTIVITIES
Sandfly Point.................................1 A1

SLEEPING
Divide Shelter (533m;
  Toilets & day use only)...........2 B3
Glade House (217m)...................3 A4
Greenstone Hut...........................4 D4
Harris Saddle Shelter (1277m)...5 C2
Hollyford Camp............................6 C2
Howden Hut.................................7 C3
Mackenzie Hut.............................8 C2
McKellar Hut...............................9 C3
Mid Caples Hut...........................10 D3
Routeburn Falls Hut (1005m)...11 C2
Routeburn Flats Hut (458m)....12 C2
Routeburn Shelter.....................13 D2
Upper Caples Hut......................14 C3

TRANSPORT
Greenstone Wharf.....................15 D4
Wharf...16 A4

the Milford Track and pressures on the track have necessitated the introduction of a booking system, similar to Milford's.

Advance bookings are required throughout the main season (late-October to April), either through DOC offices in Te Anau, Queenstown or Glenorchy, or by emailing greatwalksbooking@doc.govt.nz. The **Great Walks huts pass** (per night adult/child $35/18) allows you to stay at Routeburn Flats, Routeburn Falls, Mackenzie Hut and Howden Hut; various 'family' passes are also available. A **camping pass** (per night adult/child $15/7.50) allows you to pitch a tent only at Routeburn Flats and Lake Mackenzie.

Outside the main season, hut passes are still required (adult/child $10/5 per night);

camping is free. Note that the Routeburn Track is often closed by snow in winter and stretches of the track are very exposed and dangerous in bad weather; always check conditions with the DOC.

There are car parks at the Divide and Glenorchy ends of the Routeburn; they're unattended, so don't leave valuables in your car. **Glenorchy Holiday Park** (☎ 03-442 7171; 2 Oban St, Glenorchy) stores gear for free if you use its transport, otherwise it charges $3 per day.

WALKING THE TRACK

The track can be started from either end. Many people travelling from the Queenstown end try to reach the Divide in time to catch the bus to Milford and connect with a cruise

OTAGO

on the sound. Highlights include the views from Harris Saddle and the top of nearby Conical Hill – you can see waves breaking on the beach at Martins Bay. These are almost as good as the view from Key Summit, offering a panorama of the Hollyford Valley, and of the Eglinton and Greenstone River valleys.

Estimated walking times:

route	time
Routeburn Shelter to Flats Hut	3hr
Flats Hut to Falls Hut	1–1½hr
Falls Hut to Mackenzie Hut	4½–6hr
Mackenzie Hut to Howden Hut	3–4hr
Howden Hut to the Divide	1–1½hr

Greenstone & Caples Tracks

The Routeburn can be combined with the Greenstone and Caples Tracks for a round-trip back to the Glenorchy area. Access at the Greenstone and Caples end is at Greenstone Wharf. The road from Kinloch to Greenstone Wharf is unsealed and rough; **Backpacker Express** (☎ 03-442 9939) usually runs a boat across the lake from Glenorchy. These two tracks form a loop; the huts are Mid Caples, Upper Caples, McKellar and Greenstone (all $10 per person per night).

Estimated walking times:

route	time
Greenstone Wharf to Mid Caples Hut	3hr
Mid Caples Hut to Upper Caples Hut	2–3hr
Upper Caples Hut to McKellar Hut	6–8hr
McKellar Hut to Greenstone Hut	5–7½hr
Greenstone Hut to road end	3–5hr

From McKellar Hut you can walk two to 2½ hours to Howden Hut on the Routeburn Track (you'll need to book this hut from late-October to April). Other options from McKellar Hut include turning off for the Divide before reaching Howden Hut.

Rees-Dart Track

This difficult four- to five-day circular route goes from the head of Lake Wakatipu by way of Dart River, Rees Saddle and Rees River valley, with the possibility of a side-trip to the Dart Glacier if you're suitably equipped. Access by vehicle is possible as far as Muddy Creek on the Rees side, from where it's two hours to 25-Mile Hut.

You can park at Muddy Creek; transport is also available to and from the tracks. Most people go up the Rees first and then back down the Dart. The three DOC huts (Shelter Rock, Dart and Daleys Flat) cost $10 per person per night.

Estimated walking times:

route	time
Muddy Creek to Shelter Rock Hut	6hr
Shelter Rock Hut to Dart Hut	5–7hr
Dart Hut to Daleys Flat Hut	6–8hr
Daleys Flat Hut to Paradise	6–7½hr

WANAKA REGION

Driving south into Otago via the Haast Pass, you pass between the region's centre-piece lakes, Wanaka and Hawea, a grand freshwater pairing wedged among some awesome hills and cliffs. While driving alongside these lakes, you'll be distracted by some glorious watery vistas. As impressive as the lakes are, though, this area is still dominated by Mt Aspiring (Tititea), the highest peak outside the Mt Cook region and the highpoint of the surrounding national park, with its overgrown valleys, unspoiled rivers and glaciers.

MAKARORA
pop 40

When you reach Makarora you've left the West Coast and entered Otago, but the township still has a West Coast frontier feel. The **DOC visitors centre** (☎ 03-443 8365; www.makarora.co.nz; SH6; ☺ 8am-4.45pm daily Nov-Apr, 8am-4.45pm Mon-Fri May-Oct) should be consulted before undertaking any regional tramps.

Activities
'SIBERIA EXPERIENCE'

Makarora is the base for one of NZ's great outdoor adventures, the **'Siberia Experience'** (☎ 0800 345 666, 03-443 8666; www.siberiaexperience.co.nz; adult/child $230/170), offered by Southern Alps Air. This thrill-seeking extravaganza combines a half-hour scenic small-plane flight, a three-hour bushwalk through a remote mountain valley and a half-hour jetboat trip down a river valley in Mt Aspiring National Park. Make sure you follow the markers as you descend from Siberia

Valley, as people have become lost and have had to spend the night in the open – as an aside, the inappropriate name of this utterly beautiful valley was bequeathed by an (obviously short-sighted) early traveller, who as an encore called some nearby Matterhornesque peaks Dreadful and Awful. Consider spreading the experience out over two days and overnighting in Siberia, which has a 20-bed **DOC hut** ($10) and nearby **camp sites** ($5).

Southern Alps Air (☎ 0800 345 666, 03-443 4385; www.southernalpsair.co.nz) also has 40-minute scenic flights over Mt Aspiring (adult/child $170/85), 75-minute trips to Mt Cook and the glaciers ($330/150) and landings at Milford Sound ($300/160); reductions of up to $35 are offered for dawn/dusk flights on some trips and kids under three travel free.

JETBOATING
Wilkin River Jets (☎ 0800 538 945, 03-443 8351; www.wilkinriverjets.co.nz; adult/child $65/30) does a superb 50km, one-hour jetboating trip into Mt Aspiring National Park on the Makarora and Wilkin Rivers. The ride is piloted by companionable, informative drivers and gives you the chance to see remote river valleys at their pristine best, plus it's a fair bit cheaper than Queenstown trips.

WALKING
Shorter walks in the area include the 5km-long **Bridal Track** (1½ hours one-way), from the top of Haast Pass to Davis Flat, and the **Blue Pools Walk** (30 minutes return), where you can see huge rainbow trout.

Longer tramps go through magnificent countryside but shouldn't be undertaken lightly. Alpine conditions, flooding and the possibility of avalanches mean you must be well prepared; consult with the DOC before heading off. The *Tramping Guide to the Makarora Region* ($3.50), published by DOC, is a good investment.

The three-day **Gillespie Pass** tramp goes via the Young, Siberia and Wilkin Rivers; this is a high pass with avalanche danger. With a jetboat ride down the Wilkin to complete it, this rates alongside the Milford Track as one of the great tramps. The **Wilkin Valley Track** heads off from Kerin Forks Hut or you can fly in to Top Forks. From Kerin Forks, at

the top of the Wilkin River, the track leads to Top Forks Hut, then the north branch of the Wilkin. Here are the picturesque **Lakes Diana**, **Lucidus** and **Castalia** (one hour, 1½ hours and 3 to 4 hours respectively from Top Forks Hut).

Jetboats go to Kerin Forks and a service goes across the Young River mouth when the Makarora floods; inquire at Wilkin River Jets or the visitors centre.

Sleeping & Eating
The nearest DOC camping grounds are on SH6 at **Cameron Flat**, 10km north of Makarora, and at **Boundary Creek Reserve**, 18km south of Makarora on the shores of Lake Wanaka; both charge $5/2.50 per adult/child.

Makarora Tourist Centre (☎ 03-443 8372; tourist centre@makarora.co.nz; SH6; camp sites $18, campervan sites $20, dm $20, d $60-90; 🖳) This large complex offers good accommodation in a peaceful bush setting; the small A-frame cabins have a real snowed-in feeling. There's also a **café** (meals under $7; 🕙 9am-5pm, longer in summer), serving basic fare like pies, quiche and sandwiches, plus a grocery store and petrol.

Larrivee Homestay (☎ 03-443 9177; www.larrivee homestay.co.nz; off SH6; s $80, d $100-120) Situated down a side-road between the DOC and the Tourist Centre, Larrivee is an attractive sight, with a house and cottage made of local stone and hand-split cedar. There's a choice between friendly B&B or a very comfortable self-contained cottage that sleeps four. Dinners can also be arranged.

Getting There & Away
West Coast Express, Magic Bus and Kiwi Experience buses stop here regularly, while **InterCity** (☎ 03-442 8238; www.intercitycoach.co.nz) has one northbound bus (to the glaciers) and one southbound bus (to Hawea, Wanaka and Queenstown) per day.

If you're driving from the south, you'll first pass a tiny settlement, but you need to continue on for a few kilometres to reach the main village (if you can call it that).

HAWEA
Lake Hawea, separated from Lake Wanaka by a narrow isthmus called the Neck, is 35km long and 410m deep. The lake was raised 20m in 1958 to provide those important cusecs for power stations downriver. A

OTAGO

viewpoint here looks across to the indomitable Corner Peak on the western shore and the distant Barrier Range, and trout and landlocked salmon can be caught in its waters.

The small town of Hawea, 15km north of Wanaka, is mostly a collection of holiday and retiree homes, which are afforded some spectacular lake and mountain views.

On the lakeshore is the sprawling, relatively peaceful **Lake Hawea Holiday Park** (☎ 03-443 1767; www.lakehawea.web-nz.com; SH6; camp sites & campervan sites $22, d $40-80), a favourite of fishing and boating enthusiasts; standard cabins are nothing flash but are an OK budget deal. The more-expensive motel rooms at **Lake Hawea Motor Inn** (☎ 0800 429 324,

03-443 1224; www.lakehawea.co.nz; 1 Capell Ave; dm $25, d $95-125) have a deck out back with unbeatable views across the lake; there's also a restaurant (lunch and dinner mains $16-25).

WANAKA
pop 3500

Map below

Wanaka is a popular summer and winter resort town, known for its New Year revelries. But the splendour of the surrounding mountains and lakes, plus the long list of adrenaline-inducing outdoor activities, make it a favoured tourist destination year-round.

Wanaka is located just over 100km from Queenstown, at the southern end of Lake Wanaka, and is the gateway to Mt Aspiring National Park and the Treble Cone, Card-

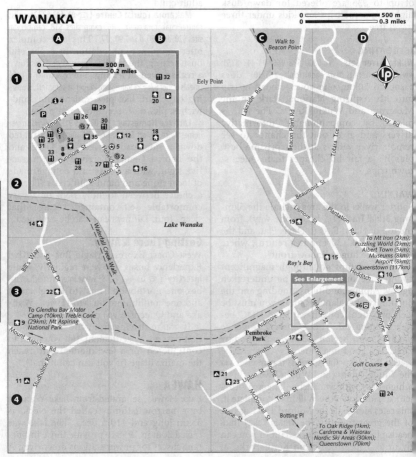

rona, Harris Mountains and Pisa Range ski areas. This sporty, laid-back town offers a sharp contrast to the hype of Queenstown, though many locals fear that all the development taking place here will ultimately change that.

Information

Lake Wanaka visitors centre (☎ 03-443 1233; www.lakewanaka.co.nz; off Ardmore St; ☻ 8.30am-6pm) is in a conspicuous log cabin down on the waterfront. The building is also home to **Lakeland Adventures** (☎ 03-443 7495; www.lakelandadventures.co.nz), which rents out kayaks (from $10 per hour) and bikes (from $25/35 per half-/full day), and manages some local jetboating and lake cruises – see p606 and p607.

The **DOC Wanaka visitors centre** (☎ 03-443 7660; Ardmore St; ☻ 8am-4.45pm Mon-Fri year-round, 9.30am-3.45pm Sat May-Oct, 8am-4.45pm Sat & Sun Nov-Apr) is the place to inquire about walks and tramps, including those in Mt Aspiring National Park.

Cybercafés include **Budget Communications** (☎ 03-443 4440; 38 Helwick St; 10c per minute; ☻ 10am-10pm) and **Wanakaweb** (☎ 03-443 7429; 1st fl, 3 Helwick St; $1 per 10 min; ☻ 9am-late).

Sights

PUZZLING WORLD

The **Puzzling World complex** (☎ 03-443 7489; www .puzzlingworld.com; adult/child $9/6; ☻ 8am-5.30pm) harbours the three-dimensional 'Great Maze', where you must navigate 1.5km of passages to the towers at each corner and then back to the exit; it's more difficult than you think. The 'Puzzling World' section has lots of illusional treats to keep kids (and adults) amused and engrossed, including

a series of holographic photographs, the unsettling Hall of Following Faces and a balance-testing tilted room. It's on the road to Cromwell, 2km from Wanaka, and is reasonably priced considering the engaging exhibits. To choose between 'Puzzling World' or the maze, rather than doing both, costs $6/4 per adult/child.

MUSEUMS

New Zealand Fighter Pilots Museum (☎ 0800 927 247, 03-443 7010; www.nzfpm.co.nz; Wanaka Airport; adult/child/family $8/4/20; ☻ 9am-4pm Feb-Dec, 9am-6pm Jan), located 8km out of town at the airport, is dedicated to NZ combat pilots, their wartime experiences and the aircraft they flew. Besides the well-preserved collection of Hawker Hurricanes, de Havilland Vampires and the odd-sounding Chipmunk, there's also a desktop aerial combat game to try out.

Wanaka Transport & Toy Museum (☎ 03-443 8765; SH6; adult/child/family $6/2/15; ☻ 8.30am-5pm) is the end result of one man's obsessive collecting of 40 years and will make spouses who complain about unruly tool sheds think differently from now on. The transport section has a movie-starring Cadillac, antique motorcycles and aircraft – just how the MIG jet fighter was acquired is anyone's guess. The toy section provides nostalgic moments for just about everyone.

At **Wanaka Beerworks** (☎ 03-443 1865; SH6; $5; ☻ 9.30am-6pm, tours 2pm) you can taste this small brewery's three carefully brewed products – a malt lager, a dark ale and the tasty bitter 'Brewski' – for a total cost of around $5. No additives or preservatives are thrown into this naturally brewed mix.

OTAGO

INFORMATION		
Bank of NZ (ATM)	1	A2
Budget Communications	2	B2
DOC Wanaka Visitors Centre	3	D3
Lake Wanaka Visitors Centre	4	A1
Police Station	5	B2
Post Office	6	D3
Wanakaweb	7	A1

SIGHTS & ACTIVITIES	(pp605-7)	
Aspiring Guides	(see 29)	
Good Sports	8	A2
Lakeland Adventures	(see 4)	

SLEEPING	🅰 🏠 (pp607-9)	
Altamont Lodge	9	A3
Archway Motel	10	D3
Aspiring Campervan Park	(see 11)	
Bay View Motel	11	A4
Bella Vista Motel	12	B2

Brook Vale	13	B2
Edgewater Resort	14	A2
Lakeside Serviced Apartments	15	D3
Matterhorn South	16	B2
Purple Cow Backpackers	17	C3
Te Wanaka Lodge	18	B2
Wanaka Bakpaka	19	C2
Wanaka Hotel	20	B1
Wanaka Lakeview Holiday		
Park	21	C4
Wanaka Stonehouse	22	A3
Wanaka YHA	23	C4

EATING	🍴 (pp609-10)	
Ambrosia	24	D4
Bombay Palace	(see 1)	
Capriccio	(see 1)	
Doughbin Bakery	(see 25)	
Hula Cafe	25	A2
Kai Whakapai	26	A1

Muzza's Bar & Cafe	27	A2
New World Supermarket	28	A2
Relishes	29	A1
Ritual Espresso Bar	30	A1
Sasanoki	31	A2
Soulfood Store & Cafe	32	B1
Tuatara Pizza	(see 32)	
White House	33	A2

DRINKING	🍺 (p610)	
Paddy's Bar	34	A2
Shooters	(see 31)	
Slainte	35	A2

ENTERTAINMENT	🎬 (p610)	
Apartment One	(see 29)	
Cinema Paradiso	36	D3

TRANSPORT	(pp610-11)	
InterCity Bus Stop	(see 27)	

MT ASPIRING NATIONAL PARK

In 1964 a mountainous area in northwestern Otago and southern Westland was earmarked as a national park named after its highest peak, Mt Aspiring (3027m). The park now blankets over 3500 sq km along the Southern Alps, from the Haast River in the north to its border with Fiordland National Park in the south.

The park has wide valleys, secluded flats, over 100 glaciers and sheer mountains. The southern end of the park around Glenorchy is well-trafficked by visitors and includes popular tramps such as the Routeburn Track (p600). But there are great short walks and more-demanding tramps in the Matukituki Valley, close to Wanaka; see the DOC leaflet 'Matukituki Valley Tracks' ($1). Tracks are reached from Raspberry Creek at the end of Mt Aspiring Rd, 54km from Wanaka; for details of shuttle services, see under Getting Around (p610).

The popular three- to four-hour return **Rob Roy Valley Track** has dramatic scenery and is highly recommended. From Raspberry Creek follow the West Matukituki Valley path and turn off to head up the Rob Roy Stream to a point below the Rob Roy Glacier.

The **West Matukituki Valley** track goes on to Aspiring Hut (4 to 5 hours return), a scenic walk over mostly grassy flats. For overnight or multi-day tramps, continue up the valley to **Liverpool Hut** for great views of Mt Aspiring, or over the very scenic but difficult **Cascade Saddle** to link up with the Rees-Dart Track (p602) north of Glenorchy.

The longer tramps are subject to snow and can be treacherous in adverse weather. Register intentions and seek advice from the DOC in Wanaka before heading off.

This snowy-peaked national park is utilised by several mountaineering and alpine-climbing companies. Between them, **Aspiring Guides** (☎ 03-443 9422; www.aspiringguides.com; Level 1, 99 Ardmore St), **Adventure Consultants** (☎ 03-443 8711; www.adventure.co.nz) and **Alpinism & Ski** (☎ 03-443 6593; www.alpinismski.co.nz) offer beginner courses (week-long instruction from around $2000) and, for the more experienced, Southern Alps ski-mountaineering tours and guided ascents of Mts Aspiring, Tasman and Tutoko.

Wanaka Rock Climbing & Abseil Adventures (☎ 03-443 6411; www.wanakarock.co.nz) has an introductory one-day rock-climbing course ($165), a half-day abseiling intro ($95) and bouldering and multi-pitch climbs for the experienced.

Activities
WALKING

The DOC brochure *Wanaka Walks and Trails* ($1) outlines walks around town, including the easy lakeside stroll to **Eely Point** (20 minutes) and on to **Beacon Point** (30 minutes), and the **Waterfall Creek Walk** (one hour return).

The fairly gentle climb to the top of **Mt Iron** (549m, 1½ hours return) reveals panoramic views. Speaking of knockout panoramas, if you're fit then consider doing the taxing, winding 8km trek up **Mt Roy** (1578m, 5 to 6 hours return), starting 6km from Wanaka on the Mt Aspiring Rd. The track crosses private land and is closed from October to mid-November for the lambing season.

JETBOATING, RAFTING & KAYAKING

Lakeland Adventures (☎ 03-443 7495; www.lakeland adventures.co.nz; off Ardmore St; adult/child $70/35) does 50-minute jetboat trips that speed across the lake and then up the Clutha River, while **Pioneer Rafting** (☎ 03-443 1246; ecoraft@xtra.co.nz; half-day rafts per adult/child $115/75, full-day $165/95) has easy white-water trips on the high-volume Clutha.

Alpine Kayak Guides (☎ 03-443 9023; www.alpine kayaks.co.nz; half-/full-day trips $99/145) paddle down the Hawea, Clutha and Matukituki Rivers from October to April.

CANYONING & RIVER SLEDGING

Adventurous souls will love canyoning, a summertime-only activity staged by **Deep Canyon** (☎ 03-443 7922; www.deepcanyon.co.nz; trips from $195; ⊙ Nov-Apr) and involving climbing, swimming and waterfall-abseiling through confined, steep and wild gorges. Transport to the canyon, lunch, instruction and equipment are included.

Frogz Have More Fun (☎ 0800 338 737, 03-443 9130; $100-120) offers white-water sledging on boogie-board-style rafts. The cheaper trips are on gentler rivers like the Clutha and Hawea, the more-expensive on the challenging Kawarau.

SKYDIVING & PARAGLIDING

Tandem Skydive Wanaka (☎ 03-443 7207; www.sky divenz.com) does jumps at 9000ft ($250) and 12,000ft ($300); the latter takes 45 seconds and will have the atmosphere whistling past your ears at 200km/h.

Wanaka Paragliding School (☎ 03-443 9193; www .wanakaparagliding.co.nz) will take you on tandem flights at 800m ($160) and 1500m ($200); the higher glide is at Matukituki Bowl.

OTHER ACTIVITIES

Lakes Wanaka and Hawea (16km away) have excellent trout fishing and numerous guides are based in Wanaka.

Lakeland Adventures (☎ 03-443 7495; www.lake landadventures.co.nz; off Ardmore St) does 2½-hour guided trips for $250, including boat hire for three people.

Alternatively, you could just hire a motorised runabout for $40 per hour and a rod for $20 per day; a 24-hour licence costs $17 ($34 per week).

Lakeland Adventures also offers **'Wild Wanaka'**, a combo experience that can include jetboat, helicopter, rally car and quad-bike rides; the all-inclusive experience costs $450, or you can reduce the price by customising the itinerary.

DOC produces a brochure *Mountainbiking around Wanaka* (50c), describing mountain-bike rides ranging from 2km (the steep Mt Iron track) to 20km (West Matukituki Valley).

For high-altitude guided mountain biking, contact **Alpine & Heli Mountain Biking** (☎ 03-443 8943; www.mountainbiking.co.nz; $130-300), which does heli-biking trips at Treble Cone and Mt Pisa, and 4WD tours of the Pisa Range.

Criffel Peak Safaris (☎ 0800 102 122, 03-443 1711; www.criffelpeaksafaris.com; 2-/4-hr trips $110/250) has quad-bike excursions up into the Criffel Range. Their four-hour trip includes a BBQ and a visit to 19th-century gold diggings.

Nearby skiing areas include **Treble Cone** (p73), **Cardrona** (p74), the **Waiorau Nordic Ski Area** (for cross-country skiing, p74) and **Harris Mountain** (for heli-skiing, p76).

Good Sports (☎ 03-443 7966; www.good-sports .co.nz; Dunmore St) hires out a vast array of sports equipment, including bikes, camping and hiking accessories, fishing rods and watersports gear.

Tours

Lakeland Adventures (☎ 03-443 7495; www.lake landadventures.co.nz) has one-hour lake cruises (adult/child $50/25) and also has a three-hour trip with a guided walk on Mou Waho ($90/45).

Wanaka Sightseeing (☎ 03-443 1855; www.wana sightseeing.co.nz; full-day winery tour $260) will bus you out on various Central Otago tours, including a winery excursion with lunch provided on the day-long option. The bus will do pick ups and drop offs at your place of accommodation.

AERIAL SIGHTSEEING

The following companies are all based at Wanaka Airport.

Aspiring Air (☎ 0800 100 943, 03-443 7943; www .nz-flights.com) has a range of scenic flights, including a 50-minute flight over Mt Aspiring (adult/child $155), a Milford Sound fly-over and landing ($300/180) and a buzz around Mt Cook including the West Coast glaciers ($330/200).

Wanaka Flightseeing (☎ 0800 105 105, 03-443 8787; www.flightseeing.co.nz; flights per adult $175-340, per child $110-200) offers a similarly wide range of flights, several with an 'early bird' discount of around $35 for early-morning departures.

Chopper outfits include **Wanaka Helicopters** (☎ 03-443 1085; www.heliflights.co.nz), which has a 20-minute flight around Wanaka ($145) and a 45-minute tour of Mt Aspiring and a number of glaciers ($400). They also do *Lord of the Rings* tours.

Another option is **Aspiring Helicopters** (☎ 03-443 1454; www.aspiringhelicopters.co.nz) with similar journeys and prices.

Festivals

Every second Easter (even-numbered years), Wanaka hosts the incredibly popular **Warbirds Over Wanaka** (☎ 0800 496 920, 03-443 8619; www .warbirdsoverwanaka.com; Wanaka Airport; three-day admission adult/child $110/15, first day only $30/5, each of last two days $50/5), a huge international air show that can attract over 100,000 people to the town.

Sleeping

B&BS

Wanaka Stonehouse (☎ 03-443 1933; www.wana kastonehouse.co.nz; 21 Sargood Dr; d $350-400) Noteworthy English-style manor where comfort and gourmet tastes are both well catered for. Energise yourself with a hearty cooked breakfast, then immediately yield to lethargy in the spa and sauna. The hosts live in a cottage elsewhere on the grounds.

Te Wanaka Lodge (☎ 0800 926 252, 03-443 9224; www.tewanaka.co.nz; 23 Brownston St, d $160-180; 🖳) Superb place with a distinctive alpine lodge flavour, lots of nooks to lounge in, a hot tub to soak in, and drinks you can buy from a small bar. All rooms are very comfortable, but it's worth paying an extra $20 or so for one of the upper-level rooms, which have slightly higher ceilings and better views than their ground-floor siblings.

Oak Ridge (☎ 0800 869 262, 03-443 7707; www.oakridge.co.nz; cnr Cardrona Valley & Studholme Rds; d $140-160; 🖳) Luxury lodge mere minutes out of town on the way to Cardrona. The slightly more expensive ground-floor rooms are the most spacious and are worth the extra cash. Besides being spoiled with a pool, spa and tennis court, guests also have quick access to the respected restaurant/wine bar **Tea Thyme** (mains $20-25; ⌣ dinner).

Lady Pembroke (☎ 03-443 4978; www.houseboats .co.nz; 2-day hire $1400-1600) The perfect way to see the lake: on a self-contained houseboat with two king-size bedrooms and two bunkrooms (each sleeping two people). Bookings usually require a minimum of two nights and all provisions are supplied by passengers; price doesn't include fuel.

HOSTELS
Purple Cow Backpackers (☎ 03-443 1880; www .purplecow.co.nz; 94 Brownston St; dm from $19, d & tw $55-70) Very popular, roomy and comfortable hostel with a definite ski-lodge feel thanks partly to its chalet-style frontage, and with the great views that seem standard for most Wanaka hostels. Facilities include a separate video lounge, efficient front desk, outdoor decks and rental of bikes and kayaks.

Wanaka Bakpaka (☎ 03-443 7837; wanakabakpak a@xtra.co.nz; 117 Lakeside Rd; dm/d $21/50) Opposite the jetty on the northern side of Roy's Bay, with great views of the lake and mountains from lounging areas. The cosiest double is the room facing the lake, to the left of the main entrance. Eschews large backpacker bus groups (and TVs) for a constant flow of travel-happy individuals.

Matterhorn South (☎ 03-443 1119; www.matter hornsouth.co.nz; 56 Brownston St; dm $25, s & d $80; 🖳) Judging by its name, this place is keen on the snow-capped mountain persona, an impression bolstered by its stark-white paint job. Large en suite dorms and a pleasant deck and BBQ area make this a nice place to stay.

Wanaka YHA (☎ 03-443 7405; yha.wanaka@yha .org.nz; 181 Upton St; camp sites $20, dm/d $24/60; 🖳) Appealing, slightly rough-around-the-edges YHA, far less boisterous and traveller-jammed than many other hostels around town. Has good storage facilities and provides advice on the abundance of activity options.

Altamont Lodge (☎ 03-443 8864; altamontlodge@ xtra.co.nz; 121 Mt Aspiring Rd; s/d $35/55) Excellent, friendly budget place on a tree-lined main road, with tennis court, spa pool and video lounge. At peak times (like winter, when skiers make the most of its drying room and ski storage) it can be booked out by selfishly large groups, so book ahead. There's a one-off linen charge of $5.

HOTELS & MOTELS
Archway Motel (☎ 0800 427 249, 03-443 7698; www .archwaymotels.co.nz; 64 Hedditch St; d from $95) The units here have a plain, low-impact style but are big and well-equipped, and two of the back units are wheelchair-accessible. Attentive service is another commendable feature of this place.

Brook Vale (☎ 0800 438 333, 03-443 8333; www.brookvale.co.nz; 35 Brownston St; d $100-115; 🖳) Choice accommodation with balcony- or terrace-equipped rooms facing a picturesque gully with a creek dribbling through it (and a path meandering alongside). There are only 10 units, so you won't feel besieged by the neighbours.

Bay View Motel (☎ 0800 229 8439, 03-443 7766; www.bayviewwanaka.co.nz; Studholme Rd; rooms $120-150; 🖳) Water-view units and very friendly owners make this one of the most appealing motel choices. The spa gets a bit of use in winter and mountain bikes are also available for hire.

Edgewater Resort (☎ 0800 108 311, 03-443 8311; www.edgewater.co.nz; Sargood Dr; d $190-480) Flash lakefront hotel with a huge range of activities and facilities, including restaurant and bar, outdoor dining area, spa, sauna and tennis court. Accommodation ranges from hotel-style rooms to deluxe two-bedroom apartments that sleep four people.

Other mid-range and top-end options:

Bella Vista Motel (☎ 0800 201 420, 03-443 6066; www.bellavistamotels.co.nz; 2 Dunmore St; d $95-125) Right in the centre of town and with good facilities.

Lakeside Serviced Apartments (☎ 0800 002 211, 03-443 0188; www.lakesidewanaka.co.nz; 9 Lakeside Rd; rooms $300-700; ☒) One of several apartment complexes along the lake, this one a plush affair with a heated pool to bob in.

Wanaka Hotel (☎ 03-443 7826; wanakahotel@xtra.co .nz; 71 Ardmore St; d $95) Dated 1960s-built place but with decent rooms, those upstairs have balconies looking onto some greenery.

CAMPING & CAMPERVAN PARKS

Aspiring Campervan Park (☎ 0800 229 8439, 03-443 6603; www.campervanpark.co.nz; Studholme Rd; campervan sites $31) Adjacent to the Bay View Motel is this modern, well-equipped campervan park. Guests have access to a spa and sauna, and there's a fine BBQ area.

Wanaka Lakeview Holiday Park (☎ 03-443 7883; www.kiwitravelchannel.co.nz; 212 Brownston St; camp sites & campervan sites $20, d $35-65) No prizes for guessing Lakeview's chief characteristic. This sprawling park is Wanaka's most central outdoor accommodation centre, and also has a range of cabins (with and without bathroom).

Glendhu Bay Motor Camp (☎ 03-443 7243; glendhu camp@xtra.co.nz; Mt Aspiring Rd; camp sites & campervan sites $19, d $30-36) Glendhu is located 10km out of town, where its spacious grounds also have a lovely lakeside aspect. The cheapest doubles are in a 16-bed lodge.

Albert Town reserve (adult/child $5/2.50) This is a DOC camping ground adjacent to SH6, 5km northeast of Wanaka.

Eating

RESTAURANTS

Relishes (☎ 03-443 9018; 99 Ardmore St; mains $17-27; ☸ dinner) Highly recommended by locals, and with creative fare such as vegetarian Japanese curries and Asian-spiced confit of duck. Has a low-key interior so you can concentrate on the quality food and good wine list.

White House (☎ 03-443 9595; cnr Dunmore & Dungarvon Sts; mains $15-25; ☸ lunch & dinner) No political connections, rather a literal one – this place belongs by all rights on a Cycladic island and has a breezy, feel-good interior.

Be tempted by numerous veg dishes like baked polenta and aubergine, as well as tiger prawns and mutton tajine (lean-meat casserole).

Sasanoki (☎ 03-443 1188; 1st fl, 145 Ardmore St; mains $20-26; ☸ dinner) Classy Japanese restaurant trying hard to combine NZ and Asian flavours in its upstairs eating space, hence a menu with soy-simmered lamb shank and chicken teriyaki.

Capriccio (☎ 03-443 8579; 1st fl, 123 Ardmore St; mains $14-30; ☸ dinner) This well-established second-storey restaurant gazes out over the lake as it dishes out spaghetti and meatballs, pumpkin and basil *pan soti*, as well as seafood meals such as tuna steak and greenlip mussels.

Tuatara Pizza (☎ 03-443 8186; 72 Ardmore St; pizzas $15-25; ☸ lunch & dinner) Some of the more interesting gourmet combinations in this fresh-food pizzeria are chicken and cranberry, Cajun chicken with chilli, and tofu with teriyaki sauce – reassuringly, tuatara is not one of the official toppings.

Bombay Palace (☎ 03-443 6086; Level 1, Pembroke Mall; mains $15-20; ☸ dinner) Serves large, satisfying portions of all the usual Indian suspects, including a half-dozen veg options. Let them know when making a booking if you're a coeliac sufferer or have other food-related allergies and they'll do their best to accommodate you.

Ambrosia (☎ 03-443 1255; 76 Golf Course Rd; dinner meals $28-30; ☸ lunch Thu-Sun, dinner Tue-Sun) The Ambrosia is a cottage-sized, Mexican villa–style place looking out over the golf course to the lake. The meals here are locally recommended and have included dishes such as flounder rolls with wasabi butter sauce and venison with cabernet sauvignon glaze.

Muzza's Cafe & Bar (☎ 03-443 7296, 57 Helwick St; mains $10-25; ☸ lunch & dinner) With a name like that, this couldn't be anything but a laid-back, unassuming place with a family-friendly atmosphere and standard pub/tavern meals, plus a kids' menu.

CAFÉS & QUICK EATS

Ritual Espresso Bar (☎ 03-443 6662; 18 Helwick St; meals $10-16; ☸ lunch) Popular dispenser of decent coffee and very good filos, focaccias, quiches and other light fare.

Kai Whakapai (☎ 03-443 7795; cnr Helwick & Ardmore Sts; meals $10-28; ☸ lunch & dinner) Cooking

OTAGO

with flair, from roast couscous and fetta to some good salads (like a great chilli beef version), pancake and egg brekkies, focaccias and pastas. This perennially popular place always seems to have a sizeable crowd packed within or hanging around outside.

Soulfood Store & Cafe (☎ 03-443 7885; 74 Ardmore St; mains $8-13; ☺ breakfast & lunch) The fairly cheap pancakes, padang-style noodle and rice meals, soups, salads and smoothies here are very wholesome and delicious, particularly the breakfast omelettes. This place also doubles as an organic food store.

Hula Cafe (☎ 03-443 9220; Pembroke Mall; meals $9-15; ☺ breakfast & lunch) Cool café tucked in behind the bakery, doing fine coffee and light food like toasted bagels. Just to be eclectic, it also serves up 'porker' schnitzels.

Doughbin Bakery (☎ 03-443 7290; Ardmore St; ☺ breakfast & lunch) For cheap baked goods on the lake front.

SELF-CATERING
New World supermarket (☎ 03-443 7168; Dunmore St; ☺ 8am-8pm) For self-caterers.

Drinking
Slainte (☎ 03-443 6755; 21 Helwick St; ☺ noon-10pm) The place to go for a lively Irish atmosphere, with Irish-jig background music and Emerald Isle–slanted food (mains $18–22) such as Irish stew and *cruibins* (grilled pigs trotters). Gets an older crowd which prefers to converse over a Guinness and hence closes relatively early to dissuade all-night drinkers.

Paddy's Bar (☎ 03-443 7645; 21 Dunmore St), Wanaka's more youthful and louder carousers go to Paddy's, which has few real Irish touches other than a preponderance of green paint and dual happy hours (5pm to 6pm and 9pm to 10pm).

Shooters (☎ 03-443 4345; 145 Ardmore St) Not the spot for a *Melrose Place* flashback, but rather an alcohol-flushed, barn-sized tavern catering to a ready-to-drink crowd. DJs usually spin something here from 10pm on Friday and Saturday (free).

Entertainment
Cinema Paradiso (☎ 03-443 1505; www.paradiso.net.nz; 1 Ardmore St; adult/child $12/8) The former town hall has been turned into a wonderful, character-filled cinema decked out with old lounge chairs and sofas. Doors open one hour before film screenings. Dinner can be pre-ordered and is served during intermission. Here you can catch satires like *A Mighty Wind* and more-mainstream fare like that flick with Johnny Depp wearing way too much mascara.

Apartment One (☎ 03-443 4911; Level 1, 99 Ardmore St; admission 11pm-3am $3, other times free; ☺ 6pm-4am Tue-Sun) Up a stairway round the back of Relishes (see p609) you'll find some relaxed people slurping cocktails or shuffling to house, deep house and drum 'n' bass dance nights.

Getting There & Away
AIR
Flights between Wanaka and Christchurch (from $80) are now offered by **Air New Zealand** (☎ 0800 737 000; www.airnz.co.nz).

Aspiring Air (☎ 0800 100 943, 03-443 7943; www.nz-flights.com) has up to three flights daily between Queenstown and Wanaka ($120, 20 minutes).

BUS
The bus stop for **InterCity** (☎ 03-443 7885; www.intercitycoach.co.nz) is on Helwick St outside Muzza's Cafe & Bar. Wanaka receives daily buses from Queenstown ($26), which motor on to Franz Josef ($70) via Haast Pass. From here, buses also go via Mt Cook ($55) to Christchurch ($130), and a daily bus to Cromwell ($10) connects with the Queenstown–Dunedin route.

The town is well serviced by door-to-door shuttles, nearly all of which can be booked at **Lake Wanaka visitors centre** (☎ 03-443 1233; off Ardmore St). **Southern Link Shuttles** (☎ 03-358 8355) goes to Queenstown ($15) and Christchurch ($35), while Wanaka Connexions goes regularly to Queenstown ($25), and Atomic Shuttles goes to Queenstown ($15), Dunedin ($30), Invercargill ($35) and Greymouth ($70).

Getting Around
Alpine Coachlines (☎ 03-443 7966; www.good-sports.co.nz; Dunmore St), operating from Good Sports, has regular transport to Raspberry Creek at Mt Aspiring National Park (adult/child $25/18), and to the ski fields of Cardrona, Waiorau and Treble Cone (adult/child return $22/15). **Mount Aspiring Express** (☎ 03-443 8422; www.adventure.net.nz) has daily services to

Raspberry Creek ($25, return $45) from October to May.

CARDRONA

Although the sealed Crown Range Rd from Wanaka to Queenstown via Cardrona looks much shorter on the map than the route via Cromwell, it's actually a twisting-and-turning mountain road that needs to be tackled with care, especially in poor weather. That said, the drive is well worth doing for its outstanding views.

The 1863-built **Cardrona Hotel** (☎ 03-443 8153; www.cardronahotel.co.nz; Crown Range Rd; d $135-185) proves that appearances can be deceiving: what looks from the outside like a squat, rather unattractive (though undoubtedly historic) building masks a cosy, painstakingly refurbished high-country hotel interior. It has recently renovated rooms and a **restaurant** (mains $15-19; ⓨ lunch & dinner) serving tasty combinations like linguini marinara, ostrich sausages, and chickpea and lentil burgers.

The hotel is near the turn-off for the **Waiorau Snow Farm** (☎ 03-443 7542; www.snowfarmnz.com; Crown Range Rd), a cross-country skiing area with 55km of trails, lodge accommodation and ski-hire facilities. During the warmer months from December to April you can ride mountain bikes or hike along these trails; bikes can be hired for $35/45 per half-/full day, plus $10 trail-use fee.

Southland

CONTENTS

Fiordland	**615**
Te Anau	615
Te Anau to Milford	622
Milford Sound	624
Manapouri	627
Southern Scenic Route	630
Central Southland	**632**
Invercargill	632
Bluff	636
Invercargill to Dunedin	637
The Catlins	**638**
Invercargill to Papatowai	640
Papatowai to Balclutha	641

The southern chunk of the South Island is a glorious collage of undisturbed mountain-rimmed fiords, sleepy beachside towns, enigmatic coastal forests and ocean bays. Fiordland National Park stakes its claim across most of the southwest region, a landscape of highs and lows from its misty peaks to its lake-filled troughs; the serenely forested hills and coastal dunes of the Catlins are in the southeast, with the urban spread of Invercargill in between. Southland has a predominantly Scottish heritage, but there's also a considerable Maori population whose *marae* (traditional ancestral villages) are gradually being re-established.

Milford Sound hogs most of the tourist attention in these parts, not just for its high cliffs and deep-water calm but also for the magnificent wilderness-surrounded road that carries people here from Te Anau. Doubtful Sound is another splendid natural outpost, where cruise boats plough around Bauza Island to get a glimpse of the Tasman Sea. You've probably also heard of the Milford Track, definitely not your average walk in the (national) park. The Catlins is threaded with beguiling side roads and is also well worth an extended exploration, particularly if you're keen on the sundry animals that occupy the local waters and dry land.

HIGHLIGHTS

- Pitting your feet against the **Milford Track** (p624) and **Kepler Track** (p617)
- Sea kayaking the coves of **Milford Sound** (p625)
- Cruising to the ocean mouth of **Doubtful Sound** (p627)
- Staring across **Lake Manapouri** (p627) from Frasers Beach
- Browsing the artistic décor of **Southland Museum & Art Gallery** (p632) in Invercargill
- Searching for *maeroero* in the wonderful **Catlins** (p638)
- Waving at fur seals on **Nugget Point** (p642)

- TELEPHONE CODE: 03
- www.southland.org.nz
- www.fiordland.org.nz

SOUTHLAND

SOUTHLAND

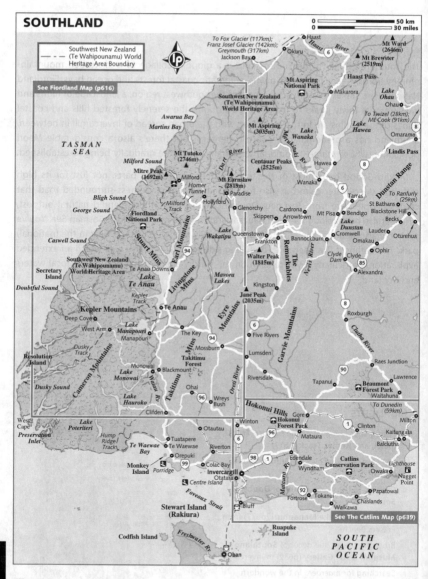

Southwest New Zealand
(Te Wahipounamu) World
Heritage Area Boundary

Climate

Southland has a temperamental climate – you'll find that even in the depths of summer, downpours or cloudy days are not uncommon (particularly in the west) and this is something you should resign yourself to while preparing for a cruise on one of the sounds (where the average rainfall is 6m), a bushwalk or any other type of outdoor activity.

Simply because of its unpredictability though, the reverse is also true, in that the colder months can still yield crisp, sunny days. One constant is that it's generally a few degrees cooler here than areas to the north.

Getting There & Around

Air New Zealand connects Invercargill with Christchurch and Wellington, while Stewart Island Flights connects Invercargill with Oban.

Major bus operators shuttle to Te Anau and Invercargill from Queenstown or Dunedin, and some also ply the Southern Scenic Route and take in Milford Sound. These include InterCity, Topline Tours, Atomic Shuttles and Bottom Bus. Companies confining themselves more or less to Southland include TrackNet and Scenic Shuttle.

FIORDLAND

The spectacular Fiordland National Park, part of the Southwest New Zealand (Te Wahipounamu) World Heritage Area (see the boxed text), is a raw wilderness area sliced by numerous deeply recessed sounds, of which the best known are Milford and Doubtful. Fiordland also has several sublime walks, including the Milford Track, which make tentative inroads into this fantastically remote region. Fiordland's immensity can only really be appreciated from the air or from a boat or kayak out on the sounds.

Some of the best examples of animals and plants, once found on the ancient supercontinent Gondwana, live in the World Heritage Area.

TE ANAU

pop 1785

Lake Te Anau was gouged out by a huge glacier and has several arms that penetrate into the mountainous forested shore. Its deepest point is 417m and it's 53km long and 10km across at its widest point, making it NZ's second-largest lake after Taupo on the North Island. The lake takes its name from the caves called Te Ana-au (Cave with a Current of Swirling Water), which were discovered on its western shore.

The township is beautifully situated by the lake and is the region's main tourist centre. It offers all manner of activities, though many visitors treat it merely as a jumping-off point for Milford and the Kepler, Dusky, Routeburn and Hollyford Tracks.

Information

The **Department of Conservation (DOC) Fiordland National Park visitors centre** (☎ 03-249 7924; fiordlandvc@doc.govt.nz; Lakefront Dr; 🕑 8.30am-6pm) is an excellent resource centre. It has a one-room exhibit of pioneering artefacts, including a massive trypot used for boiling whale blubber, and a 17-minute multimedia display ($3) on the national park. Those planning to walk the Milford, Routeburn or Kepler Tracks can book here at the **Great Walks counter** (☎ 03-249 8514; greatwalksbooking@doc.govt.nz).

The **Te Anau visitors centre** (☎ 03-249 8900; vin@realjourneys.co.nz; Steamer Wharf, Lakefront Dr; 🕑 8.30am-5.30pm) is inside the offices of **Real Journeys** (☎ 0800 656 501, 03-249 7416; www.realjourneys.co.nz; 🕑 7.30am-8.30pm), a subsidiary of the prominent South Island travel firm Fiordland Travel – it operates various cruises and tours in the region.

The office of **Air Fiordland** (☎ 03-249 7505; www.airfiordland.com; 70 Town Centre; 🕑 8.30am-6pm) is another good place to research or book activities and transport, and is also the town's InterCity bus depot.

The town has a **medical centre** (☎ 03-249 7007; Luxmore Dr) and there's a **post office** (☎ 03-249 7348;

SOUTHWEST NEW ZEALAND WORLD HERITAGE AREA

In the southwest corner of New Zealand four huge national parks together make up the Southwest New Zealand World Heritage Area. Known in Maori as 'Te Wahipounamu' (The Place of Greenstone), the region covers 2.6 million hectares and is recognised internationally for its cultural importance as well as the unique vegetation and wildlife of the area. Te Wahipounamu incorporates the following:

- Aoraki/Mt Cook National Park (p549)
- Westland National Park/Tai Poutini (p490)
- Fiordland National Park
- Mount Aspiring National Park (p606)

FIORDLAND

0 —————————— 40 km
0 —————————— 20 miles

Southwest New Zealand
(Te Wahipounamu) World
Heritage Area Boundary

Southwest New Zealand
(Te Wahipounamu)
World Heritage Area

Awarua Point

Awarua Bay
(Big Bay)

Pyke

Martins
Bay

Jamestown

Lake
Wilmot

Hollyford
Track

Lake
McKerrow

Tutoko
River

Shippers
Range

Lake
Alabaster

Mt Aspiring
National
Park

Dart
River

Dart
Track

Milford Sound

Harrison
Cove

Mt Tutoko
(2746m)

Hollyford
River

Humboldt
Falls

Mt Earnshaw
(2819m)

Mitre Peak
(1692m)

Milford

Routeburn
Track

Paradise

Poison
Bay

Sandfly Point

Lake
Ada

Hollyford
Camp

Humboldt
Mountains

Kinloch

Sutherland Sound

Lake
Quill

Ardur River

Cleddau
River

Lake Marian

Hollyford

Key Summit
(919m)

Glenorchy

Bligh Sound

Mackinnon
Pass (1073m)

Clinton River

Homer
Tunnel

94

The Divide

Lake
Gunn

Caples Track

Alisa
Mountains

To Queenstown
(20km)

George Sound

Franklin Mountains

Milford Track

Glade
House

Cascade
Creek

See Milford Track Map (p624)

Knobs Flat

Caswell Sound

Stuart
Mountains

North
Fiord

Mirror
Lakes

Greenstone
Track

Lake
Wakatipu

Mt Nicholas

Charles Sound

Nancy Sound

Thompson Sound

Secretary
Island

Fiordland
National
Park

Murchison
Mountains

Middle Fiord

Lake Te
Anau

Te Anau
Downs

Earl Mountains

Eglinton River

North
Mavora
Lake

Marora Walkway

Thomson
Mountains

To Walter
Peak Station
(7km)

Jane
Peak
(2035m)

Bradshaw
Sound

Southwest New Zealand
(Te Wahipounamu)
World Heritage Area

Te Anau
Glowworm Caves

South
Mavora
Lake

Livingstone Mountains

Eyre
Mountains

Doubtful Sound

Malaspina
Reach

Kepler
Mountains

South Fiord

94

See Kepler Track
Map (p619)

Bauza
Island

Deep Cove

Kepler
Track

Te Anau

To Queenstown
(106km)

Dagg Sound

Deep Cove
Hostel

Deep Cove

West Arm
Power Station

West
Arm

Wilmot
Pass

Lake
Manapouri

95

Manapouri

The Key

94

Mossburn

Breaksea
Sound

Mackenzie
Pass

Dusky
Track

Pillans
Pass

Hope
Arm

Hunter
Mountains

Takitumu
Forest

To Invercargill (99km);
Dunedin (232km)

Resolution
Island

Wet Jacket Arm

Harrison
Cove

Monowai

Blackmount

Waiau River

Takitumu
Mountains

Dusky
Sound

Cameron
Mountains

Lake
Monowai

Southern Scenic Route

Ohai

To Winton (32km);
Invercargill (63km)

Edwardson Sound

Cunaris
Sound

Long Sound

Lake
Hauroko

Lake
Poteriteri

99

Wreys Bush

96

To Tuatapere (13km);
Invercargill (90km)

Clifden

SOUTHLAND

102 Town Centre; ☺ 8.30am-6pm Mon-Fri, 9.30am-6pm Sat) inside the newsagency. Internet access is available via a dozen coin-operated terminals at **E-Stop** (50 Town Centre; ☺ 9am-8.30pm).

If you need topographical maps or tramping or camping equipment, try **Bev's Tramping Gear** (☎ 03-249 7389; 16 Homer St; ☺ 9am-noon & 6-8pm); tents, packs and boots can each be hired from $7 per day.

Te Anau's main shopping strip is referred to as 'Town Centre'.

Te Anau Glowworm Caves

Once present only in Maori legends, these impressive caves were rediscovered on the lake's western shore in 1948. Accessible only by boat and a part of the Aurora Caves, the 200m cave system is a magical place with waterfalls, whirlpools and a glow-worm grotto in its inner reaches; the heart of the caves is reached by walkways and two short punt journeys. **Real Journeys** (☎ 0800 656 501, 03-249 7416; Steamer Wharf, Lakefront Dr; tours per adult/child from $46/15; ☺ tours 2pm & 6.15pm, plus 5pm Nov-Mar & 8.15pm Oct–mid-May) conducts 2½-hour trips to this enigmatic place.

Te Anau Wildlife Centre

This DOC-run **wildlife centre** (☎ 03-249 7924; Te Anau-Manapouri Rd; admission free, donations welcome; ☺ 24hr), on the road to Manapouri, harbours a number of native bird species, including the rare flightless *takahe* (see the Environment chapter; p57), NZ pigeons, *kaka*, *weka*, the diminutive orange-fronted parakeet and various waterfowl. Across the road is the landscaped **Ivon Wilson Park**, with its own small lake.

Activities

WALKING

Kepler Track

This 60km Great Walk starts just outside Te Anau and heads west to the Kepler Mountains. Like any Fiordland track, the weather has a major impact on the walk; when it's wet, it's *very* wet. The alpine sections of the track require a good level of fitness and may be closed in winter due to bad weather conditions; other sections are much easier.

During the main walking season (late-October to April), advance bookings must be made by all trampers through the Te Anau DOC. Over this period, a Great Walks huts pass (per night adult/child $25/13) buys

you accommodation in the track's three well-maintained huts – Luxmoore, Iris Burn and Moturau, each of which have heating and cooking facilities. Family discounts and a 'three-night package' are also available. A **camping pass** (per night adult/child $12/6) permits you to camp only at the designated sites at Brod Bay and adjacent to Iris Burn Hut. Outside this main season, hut passes still need to be pre-purchased (per night adult/child $10/5) but no heating or cooking is on offer. Off-season camping is free.

The walk can be done over four days and features a variety of vegetation and both lakeside and riverside terrain, then a climb out of beech forest to the tree line and panoramic views. The alpine stretch between Luxmoore and Iris Burn Huts goes along a high ridge, well above the bush and offers fantastic views when it's clear. Other sections cross over U-shaped, glacier-carved valleys. It's recommended that the track be done in the Luxmoore–Iris Burn–Moturau direction. Estimated walking times:

Route	Time
DOC Fiordland visitors centre to control gates	50min
Control gates to Brod Bay	1½hr
Brod Bay to Luxmoore Hut	3½–4½hr
Luxmoore Hut to Iris Burn Hut	5–6hr
Iris Burn Hut to Moturau Hut	5–6hr
Moturau Hut to Rainbow Reach	1½–2hr
Rainbow Reach to control gates	2½–3½hr

See under Trampers' Transport (p612) for details of services to Rainbow Reach and Brod Bay.

KAYAKING & JETBOATING

Guided kayaking trips in the enthralling waterways of the World Heritage Area are run by **Fiordland Wilderness Experiences** (☎ 0800 200 434, 03-249 7700; www.fiordlandseakayak.co.nz; 66 Quintin Dr). Day paddles on Milford Sound (including transport to/from Te Anau) cost $115, or $95 if you meet at Milford. Two-day trips on Doubtful Sound cost $300 (three- to five-day Doubtful tours are also available). Independent kayak rental costs around $50 per day.

Luxmore Jet (☎ 0800 253 826, 03-249 6951; www.luxmorejet.co.nz; adult/child/family $75/40/190) sets off on a one-hour ride from Queens Reach on the Upper Waiau River; its bus will pick up at your door.

TE ANAU

INFORMATION	
Bank of NZ & Westpac Bank (ATMs)..................................**1** C2	
Bev's Tramping Gear...............**2** D3	
DOC Fiordland National Park Visitors Centre........................**3** C3	
E-Stop..................................(see 31)	
Medical Centre.......................**4** C2	
Police Station.........................**5** D2	
Post Office.............................**6** C2	
Te Anau Visitors Centre...........**7** B2	

SIGHTS & ACTIVITIES (pp617–19)	
Fiordland Community Pool.......**8** D1	
Fiordland Wilderness Experiences...........................**9** C3	
Ivon Wilson Park...................**10** C4	
Lakeland Boat Hire.................**11** B2	
Luxmore Jet..........................(see 37)	
Real Journeys......................(see 7)	
Te Anau Bike Hire.................**12** B2	
Te Anau Wildlife Centre.........**13** C4	

SLEEPING (pp619–20)	
Antler Lodge.........................**14** C1	
Cat's Whiskers......................**15** C3	
Cosy Kiwi B&B......................**16** D2	
Edgewater XL Motel...............**17** C3	
Lakefront Lodge....................**18** C3	
Lakeside Motel......................**19** C3	
Luxmore Hotel......................**20** C2	
Steamers Beach Lodge..........(see 24)	
Te Anau Great Lakes Holiday Park...................................**21** C2	
Te Anau Hotel & Villas...........**22** C3	
Te Anau Lakefront Backpackers......................**23** C3	
Te Anau Lakeview Holiday Park...................................**24** D4	
Te Anau Mountain View Top 10 Holiday Park............**25** B2	
Te Anau YHA........................**26** B2	

EATING (pp620–1)	
Fiordland Bakery...................**27** C2	
Keplers................................**28** C2	
La Toscana..........................**29** C2	
Ming Garden Chinese Restaurant.........................**30** C2	
Olive Tree Cafe.....................**31** C2	
Ranch Cafe, Bar & Grill..........**32** C2	

Redcliffe Cafe & Bar...............**33** C2	
Supervalue Supermarket.......(see 30)	

DRINKING (pp620–1)	
Moose.................................**34** C2	

TRANSPORT (p621)	
InterCity Depot....................(see 35)	

OTHER	
Air Fiordland........................**35** C2	
Southern Lakes Helicopters.....**36** B3	
Wings & Water Te Anau.........**37** C3	

0 — 500 m
0 — 0.3 miles

To Fiordland Holiday Park (1.7km); Te Anau Downs (29km); Milford Sound (120km)

Lake Te Anau

Steamer Wharf

Te Anau Memorial Gardens

Fire Station

To Mossburn (58km); Lumsden (72km); Invercargill (152km)

To Kepler Track (3km); Barnyard Backpackers (9km); Manapouri (20km)

OTHER ACTIVITIES

Trips'n'Tramps (☎ 03-249 7081; www.milfordtours walks.co.nz) offers small-group guided hikes, including an 11km Milford Track day walk (adult/child $125/80) and a 2½-hour Milford Sound cruise followed by a three-hour walk on the Routeburn Track up to Key Summit (adult/child $145/90).

High Ride Four Wheeler Adventures (☎ 03-249 8591; www.highride.co.nz; $120) does three-hour back-country trips on quad-bikes, with great views over the lakes.

The visitors centre provides information on the abundance of guided trout fishing (fly, trolling or spinning). River and stream fishing takes place roughly October through May, while lake fishing occurs year round.

For more easily accessible watersports, try the chlorine-scented **Fiordland Community Pool** (Howden St; adult/child $3/1.50; ⏱ 3.30-5pm & 7-8.30pm Mon-Fri, 2-5pm & 7-8.30pm Sat & Sun). Roughly from December to March, **Lakeland Boat Hire** (☎ 03-249 8364; Te Anau Tce) rents out rowing boats, pedal boats and canoes from a lakeside caravan.

Te Anau Bike Hire (☎ 0800 483 2628, 03-249 7211; 7 Mokonui St; bike hire per hr/day from $10/25) hires mountain bikes and quadricycles.

Tours

AERIAL SIGHTSEEING

Wings & Water Te Anau (Waterwings Airways; ☎ 03-249 7405; wingsandwater@teanau.co.nz) has seaplane flights right off Te Anau Tce. It does a

SOUTHLAND

KEPLER TRACK

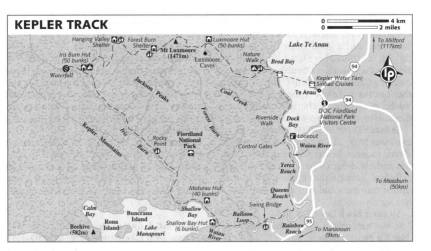

10-minute zip around the local area (adult/child $65/40), a 20-minute Kepler Track overfly (adult/child $125/75), a 40-minute Doubtful Sound flight (adult/child $230/135) and one-hour flights over Milford Sound (adult/child $320/190). There's also a 1¼-hour 'Fiordland Fantastic' trip over the remote Dusky and Doubtful Sounds (adult/child $380/190).

Air Fiordland (☎ 03-249 7505; www.airfiordland.co.nz; 70 Town Centre) offers scenic flights including a 10-minute trip over Te Anau (adult/child $100/60), a 40-minute visit to Doubtful Sound (adult/child $180/110) and a 70-minute Milford Sound flight (adult/child $280/165). It also does 4½-hour Milford Sound flight-and-cruise packages (adult/child $310/185).

Southern Lakes Helicopters (☎ 0508 249 7167, 03-249 7167; www.southernlakeshelicopters.co.nz; Lakefront Dr) has a 'triple buzz' heli-hike-cruise package ($140) and also does one-hour hovers over Doubtful Sound ($240) and a 1½-hour Doubtful and Dusky Sounds flight ($600).

CRUISES
Cruises on Lake Te Anau are popular. As well as Te Anau Glowworm Caves trips (p617), **Real Journeys** (☎ 0800 656 501, 03-249 7416; Steamer Wharf, Lakefront Dr) runs boat transfers from November to March from Te Anau Downs to Glade Wharf, the Milford Track's starting point. You can do the trip one way ($45 or $55 per adult, earlier departures are cheaper; $15 per child) if

you're walking the track, or the return cruise (adult/child $75/30).

Sinbad Cruises (☎ 03-249 7106; www.sinbadcruises.co.nz) offers yacht charters and scenic cruises on a 36ft gaff ketch, *Manuska*. You can cruise on Lake Te Anau (cruises from $50) and sail to Glade Wharf for the Milford Track ($70) or to Brod Bay for the Kepler ($20).

Sleeping
B&BS
Cat's Whiskers (☎ 03-249 8112; 2 Lakefront Dr; s/d $95/145) The congenial Cat's Whiskers has four en-suite rooms (one of them facing the lake and priced at $150) and full cooked brekkies. Despite the 'Beware of the Cat' sign, you have little to worry about from the pair of resident prowling Burmese.

Cosy Kiwi B&B (☎ 0800 249 700, 03-249 7475; www.cosykiwi.com; 186 Milford Rd; s $70-100, d $100-145; 🖳) New-fashioned, peace-abiding place with a nice domesticated atmosphere and energy-supplying breakfasts served up in the morning, including sweet and savoury pancakes.

Antler Lodge (☎ 03-249 8188; www.antlerlodgeteanau.co.nz; 44 Matai St; s $100, d $120-155) Obscured by an appealingly cluttered front garden, this new place has three en-suite cottage rooms, the upstairs one with views of Mt Luxmore. One room has wheelchair access.

HOSTELS
Te Anau Lakefront Backpackers (☎ 03-249 7713; info@teanaubackpackers.co.nz; 48-50 Lakefront Dr; dm from $23, d & tw from $54; 🖳) The ad-hoc collection

of buildings that make up this backpackers comes with attentive staff, a spa pool, BBQ area and a good waterfront location, though its atmosphere is a little lacklustre. Beware the charmless doubles in a pair of buildings across Quintin Dr, particularly the 'Southern Lakes' annex which had a washing machine lathering noisily away beneath its two rooms when we visited.

Te Anau YHA (☎ 03-249 7847; yhatanau@yha.org.nz; 29 Mokonui St; dm $24-26, s/d $36/54; 🖳) Bright, clean, modern hostel with excellent facilities and a laid-back vibe – you can be physically laid-back on the sundeck. It's well set up for trampers and will store gear; it also has family rooms.

Steamers Beach Lodge (☎ 0800 483 2628, 03-249 7457; www.teanauholidaypark.co.nz/steamers_beach_lodge .htm; 1 Te Anau-Manapouri Rd; dm $21-23, d $55; 🖳) Roughly steamboat-shaped lodge with comfortable rooms (BYO or hire bedding) and roomy communal areas, including a newish kitchen, dining room and lounge. Extras include car and gear storage, plus track transport.

Barnyard Backpackers (☎ 03-249 8006; rainbow downs@xtra.co.nz; Rainbow Downs, 80 Mt York Rd; dm from $20, s & d $50) This tranquil backpackers, on a deer farm 9km south of Te Anau, offers great trans-valley views and horse rides for $25 per hour. The main building is very cosy, with a wood heater and has a mezzanine level with pool table.

HOTELS & MOTELS

Edgewater XL Motel (☎ 0800 433 439, 03-249 7258; edgewater.xl.motels@xtra.co.nz; 52 Lakefront Dr; s/d $80/90) Doesn't have the most appealing frontage on the street, but it's excellent value considering you get a well-equipped, one-bedroom unit a mere daypack's throw from the water.

Lakeside Motel (☎ 0800 452 537, 03-249 7435; www .lakesideteanau.com; 36 Lakefront Dr; d $95-120) True to its name, this two-storey motel is opposite the water, though set back a way from the road. Lake-facing rooms are considerably more expensive than rooms facing inland; only fork out the extra cash if you really desire a watery vista.

Te Anau Hotel & Villas (☎ 03-249 9700; www.teanau hotel.co.nz; Lakefront Dr; r $220-260; 🖳 🐕) A hotel of some description has been on this site since 1890. You get a long list of mod cons for your money, from room service to pool, spa and sauna use, not to mention stretch-

yourself-out bedrooms. Good walk-in rates are sometimes available.

Lakefront Lodge (☎ 0800 525 337, 03-249 7728; www.lakefrontlodge.co.nz; 58 Lakefront Dr; r $135-185) These smart timber units face across Mokoroa St rather than towards the lake, but the lack of an immediate lakeview is balanced out by a high comfort factor. The standard units are very modern and bigger than the average motel room.

Luxmore Hotel (☎ 0800 589 667, 03-249 7526; www .luxmorehotel.co.nz; Town Centre; r $120-160) The Luxmore has 150 well-appointed rooms right in the middle of town. If you appreciate some extra space, pay more for one of the bigger, newer 'superior' rooms.

CAMPING & CAMPERVAN PARKS

Te Anau Great Lakes Holiday Park (☎ 0800 249 555, 03-249 8538; www.teanaugreatlakes.co.nz; cnr Luxmore Dr & Milford Rd; camp & campervan sites $24, dm $19, d $50-100; 🖳) Expansive park fronted by an appealing low-slung building with well-serviced rooms and facilities. It is fairly new and makes a good base. It also has a range of cabins.

Te Anau Lakeview Holiday Park (☎ 0800 483 2628, 03-249 7457; www.teanauholidaypark.co.nz; 1 Te Anau-Manapouri Rd; camp sites $22, campervan sites $25, s from $30, d $50-100; 🖳) Another large, well-equipped park, this one opposite the lake. Besides a hostel bed (see review for Steamers Beach Lodge; p620), you can get budget singles in the West Arm Lodge (they're tiny but you can't complain about the price or their condition) and roomy camp sites, some yielding great water views.

Te Anau Mountain View Top 10 Holiday Park (☎ 0800 249 746, 03-249 7462; www.teanautop10.co.nz; Te Anau Tce; camp & campervan sites $27, d $50-125; 🖳) Well-managed park with pristine units, gas BBQ, kids' playground, picnic tables, guest lounge and spa, plus lots of information on activities. Linen and bedding for the cabins cost an extra $7.

The State Hwy 94 (SH94) to Milford is lined with DOC camping grounds; see under Te Anau to Milford (p623).

Eating & Drinking

Olive Tree Cafe (☎ 03-249 8496; 52 Town Centre; lunch $8-18, dinner $23-30; 🕑 breakfast, lunch & dinner) At the end of a tiny arcade, the licensed Olive Tree has great food and a courtyard in which to sip coffee in the sun. Lunch menus have included Kashmiri lamb curry and baked ricotta, while dinner time has seen mushroom ravioli and 'roti of ocean blue nose'.

Redcliffe Cafe & Bar (☎ 03-249 7431; 12 Mokonui St; mains $16-30; ☺ dinner) Cottage restaurant with a semi-formal air and meaty dinners like green Thai fish curry, and chicken breast stuffed with mushrooms and bocconcini. Also has fine desserts like chocolate and passionfruit brûlée, and a nice garden bar.

La Toscana (☎ 03-249 7756; Town Centre; mains $10-20; ☺ dinner) Italian eatery doing brisk business with various rich pastas (including several veg versions) and a sizable list of pizzas. Has lots of booths lining the walls to slide into. Very popular towards the end of the week.

Keplers (☎ 03-249 7909; Town Centre; mains $18-27; ☺ lunch & dinner) Beef Wellington and lamb cutlets are the staple diet in this family restaurant, as is a short list of seafood offerings such as oven-grilled orange roughie. Separate kids menu available.

Ming Garden Chinese Restaurant (☎ 03-249 7770; Loop Rd; mains $14-20; ☺ dinner) Convivial place with a long list of Chinese standards and several set meals (from $42 for two people).

Ranch Cafe, Bar & Grill (☎ 03-249 8801; Town Centre) Pioneer-style establishment with a popular happy hour (8pm to 9pm) and an upstairs bar with pool tables where a younger generation hangs out. Also has appalling musical tastes, unless you happen to think *Me and You and a Dog Named Boo* is a great song. Food-wise, it does a decent $12 Sunday roast and good-value schnitzels.

Moose (☎ 03-249 7100; Lakefront Dr) Has the standard NZ small-town tavern trifecta: pokies, pool and TAB. It's a cavernous place that usually has some kind of sport blaring loudly from its big-screen TV.

Fiordland Bakery (☎ 03-249 8899; Town Centre; ☺ breakfast & lunch) has a ready supply of fresh-baked cakes, biscuits and pies. For do-it-yourself meals, there's the **Supervalue Supermarket** (☎ 03-249 9600; 1 The Lane; ☺ 8am-8pm Mon-Fri, 8.30am-7pm Sat, 10am-7pm Sun).

Getting There & Away

InterCity (☎ 03-249 7559; www.intercitycoach.co.nz) has daily bus services between Queenstown and Te Anau ($35) and on to Milford

($35), plus daily runs to Invercargill ($40) and to Dunedin ($45), continuing to Christchurch ($73).

Topline Tours (☎ 03-249 8059; www.toplinetours.co.nz) operates a daily shuttle between Te Anau and Queenstown, departing Te Anau at 10am and Queenstown at 2pm (adult/child $35/23). **TrackNet** (☎ 0800 483 2628, 03-249 7777; www.tracknet.net) also operates on this route ($35), and runs between Te Anau and Milford Sound (adult/child $38/26).

Running between Te Anau and Invercargill (adult/child $40/25) is **Scenic Shuttle** (☎ 0800 277 483, 03-249 7654; reservations@scenicshuttle.com), which departs Te Anau 8.15am daily and Invercargill 1pm (May to October) or 2pm (November to April) daily. Travelling 4½ hours to Dunedin ($45) is **Catch-A-Bus** (☎ 03-249 8900), leaving Te Anau at 1pm and Dunedin at 8.15am; bookings essential. These buses sometimes depart from the InterCity depot or they pick travellers up at their accommodation. Call for details.

Fill up with petrol in Te Anau before setting off for Milford Sound. Chains should be carried in winter and can be hired from most service stations.

TRAMPERS' TRANSPORT

A shuttle operated by **TrackNet** (☎ 0800 483 2628, 03-249 7777; www.tracknet.net) runs daily from October to April to the Routeburn, Kepler, Hollyford and Milford Tracks (call to inquire about winter services). The shuttle to Milford passes the Divide at the start/end of the Routeburn and Greenstone Tracks. For the Kepler Track, it operates a shuttle between Te Anau and the control gates ($5) and then Rainbow Reach ($8).

Kiwi Discovery (☎ 03-249 7505; 70 Town Centre) shuttles between Queenstown and Milford via Te Anau; from Te Anau to Milford and back costs $120. Book through Air Fiordland.

The **Kepler Water Taxi** (☎ 03-249 8364) runs regularly to Brod Bay ($20, return $35) from the jetty adjacent to the Lakeland Boat Hire caravan. **Sinbad Cruises** (☎ 03-249 7106) also operates a service to Brod Bay ($20).

Wings & Water Te Anau (Waterwings Airways; ☎ 03-249 7405) provides transport to Supper Cove ($230) for Dusky Sound trampers.

TE ANAU TO MILFORD

It's 119km from Te Anau to Milford on one of the most scenic roads you could hope for. The first part veers through undulating farmland atop the lateral moraine of the glacier that gouged out Lake Te Anau. At 16km the road enters a patch of mountain beech forest, passes **Te Anau Downs** at 29km and heads towards the entrance of Fiordland National Park and the Eglinton Valley. Again, you pass patches of beech (red, silver and mountain) as well as alluvial flats and meadows.

There's a wheelchair-accessible walk at **Mirror Lakes** (five minutes), 58km from Te Anau; you need clear weather to enjoy the lakes. **Knobs Flat**, 5km on, has an unmanned visitors centre with toilets, a telephone, dumping station, water and exhibits on local fauna and Milford road avalanches.

At the 77km mark is the area now referred to as O Tapara, but known more commonly as **Cascade Creek**. O Tapara is the original name of nearby Lake Gunn and refers to a Ngai Tahu ancestor, Tapara. The lake was a stopover for parties heading to Anita Bay in search of greenstone. A 45-minute walking track passes through tall red beech forest that shelters a variety of bird life. Paradise ducks and NZ scaup are often seen on the lake, while the forest floor is an array of mosses, ferns and lichens. Lake Gunn is the largest of the Eglinton Valley lakes but Fergus and Lochie are higher in altitude. In Cascade Creek you may see long-tail bats, which are NZ's only native land mammals.

The vegetation alters significantly as the **Divide** is approached. The size of the bush is reduced and ribbonwood and fuchsia are prominent. The Divide is the lowest east–west pass in the Southern Alps and there's a shelter here for walkers either finishing or starting the Routeburn, Greenstone or Caples Tracks. A 1½-hour walk along the Routeburn brings you to **Key Summit**, where there are numerous tarns and patches of alpine bog. Three river systems (the Hollyford, the Greenstone/Clutha and the Eglinton/Waiau) start from the sides of this feature and radiate to the island's west, east and south coasts.

From the Divide, the road falls into the beech forest of the **Hollyford Valley** and there's an interesting turn-off to Hollyford

NATURE STRIKES BACK

Once you leave Te Anau, you encounter two of the menaces of Fiordland: rain and sandflies. Rain in this area is very heavy – Milford gets over 6m annually. Sandflies, for those who haven't (yet) met them, are nasty little biting insects. They're actually blackflies, but were christened 'sandflies' by Captain Cook after he encountered them in Dusky Sound – the local Maori name for them is Te Namu. They're smaller than mosquitoes, with a similar bite, and you'll see clouds of them at Milford.

Don't be put off sightseeing during a downpour; the masses of water hurtling down the sheer walls of Milford Sound are an incredible sight and the rain tends to keep the sandflies away. For walking and tramping it's a different story, as the rain means flooded rivers and poor visibility.

Camp and the start of the Hollyford Track. At the end of the unsealed road is a walk to the high **Humboldt Falls** (30 minutes return). One kilometre down the Lower Hollyford Rd from Marian Corner is a track leading to **Lake Marian**; take the three-hour return tramp or, alternatively, the pleasant 20-minute return walk to view the rapids.

Back at the corner, the road to Milford rises up to the east portal of the **Homer Tunnel**, 101km from Te Anau and preceded by a spectacular, high-walled, ice-carved amphitheatre. The tunnel is named after Harry Homer, who discovered the Homer Saddle in 1889. Work on the tunnel didn't begin until 1935, providing work for the otherwise unemployed during the Depression, and wasn't finished until 1953.

At the east portal is a short **nature walk**, which has descriptions of the alpine species found here. The road may be closed in winter by high snowfalls and avalanches. Rough-hewn, the tunnel has a steep east-to-west gradient but emerges after 1207m into the spectacular **Cleddau Canyon** on its Milford side.

About 10km before Milford is the wheelchair-accessible **Chasm Walk** (20 minutes return). The Cleddau River plunges through eroded boulders in a narrow chasm, the 22m-deep Upper Fall. About 16m lower it cascades under a natural rock bridge to another waterfall. Views of **Mt Tutoko** (2746m), Fiordland's highest peak, are glimpsed above the beech forest just before you arrive in Milford. A track leads from the western side of the bridge over Tutoko River. After a two-hour walk through bush, the scenery here is overpowering. Don't venture any further unless you're a competent tramper and well equipped.

Hollyford Track

This well-known track travels along the broad Hollyford Valley through rainforest to the Tasman Sea at Martins Bay. Because of its length (four days one way), it should not be undertaken lightly. Be sure to check with the DOC in Te Anau for detailed information and the latest track and weather conditions.

Hollyford Track Guided Walks (☎ 0800 832 226, 03-442 3760; www.hollyfordtrack.com; 3-day trip adult/child $1860/1400) guides walks down this track that include a flight to Milford Sound and a jetboat trip on Lake McKerrow. It avoids the hardest, most tedious part of the walk: Demon Trail.

TrackNet (☎ 0800 483 2628, 03-249 7777; www.tracknet.net) has a regular shuttle from Te Anau to the Hollyford Rd turn-off ($25) and the start of the trail ($38).

You can also charter **Air Fiordland** (☎ 03-249 7505; www.airfiordland.com) to fly between Milford and Martins Bay ($420) or between Te Anau and Martins Bay ($830). The charge is per load; four people can be transported.

There are six DOC huts (Hidden Falls, Alabaster, McKerrow Island, Demon Trail, Hokuri and Martins Bay Hut), each costing $5 per night.

Estimated walking times:

Route	Time
Lower Hollyford Rd car park to Hidden Falls Hut	2–3hr
Hidden Falls Hut to Alabaster Hut	3–4hr
Alabaster Hut to McKerrow Island Hut	3hr
McKerrow Island Hut to Demon Trail Hut	1½hr
Demon Trail Hut to Hokuri Hut	5–6hr
Hokuri Hut to Martins Bay Hut	4–5hr

Sleeping & Eating

Along SH94 are many basic **DOC camping grounds** (camp sites $10), which operate on an honesty system. Their distances from Te Anau:

Location	Distance (km)
Ten Mile Bush	17
Henry Creek	25
Boyd Creek	45
Walker Creek	49
Totara Creek	53
McKay Creek	53
East Branch Eglinton	56
Deer Flat	62
Kiosk Creek	65
Smithy Creek	67
Upper Eglinton	71
Cascade Creek	78
Lake Gunn	81

There are several good accommodation options at Te Anau Downs, 27km from Te Anau on the SH94, near where boats depart for Glade Wharf and the Milford Track. Inquiries for the backpackers, the B&B and the motor inn can be directed to grumpys@xtra.co.nz, but specify which one you're interested in; also visit www.teanau-milfordsound.co.nz. Staff can help with local travel arrangements.

Grumpy's Backpackers (☎ 0800 478 6797, 03-249 8133) is outfitted with decent four- to six-bed dorms, each equipped with en suite, TV, fridge and heater. The ebullient owner's sense of humour shows in his choice of nickname.

Te Anau Downs B&B & Hotel (☎ 0800 500 706, 03-249 7510; SH94; d $100-110 incl breakfast; ☐) has decent-sized, well-maintained hotel rooms. The piano in the log-fire lounge is often surrounded by elderly tour groups singing boastfully about having the whole world in their hands. The adjoining **Grumpy's Restaurant 'n' Bar** (mains $14-24; ☼ lunch & dinner) has a standard pub-hotel menu; vegetarians shouldn't get their hopes up.

Te Anau Downs Motor Inn (☎ 0800 500 805, 03-249 7811; SH94; d from $110; ☐) has modern units complete the Te Anau Downs accommodation picture. Many of them have good views.

Hollyford Camp (Hollyford Rd; camp sites/s/d $10/17/28) is eight kilometres down Hollyford Rd from the highway. Hollyford Camp is also known as Gunn's Camp. Cabins here are ultra-rustic: you need your own linen (not available for hire), and cooking and heating is via a coal/wood-fired stove, with fuel provided. A generator supplies limited electricity each night. There's also a small shop and a **museum** (admission adult/child $1/30c, guests free) with pioneering memorabilia and historical flotsam like some pumice from the 1883 eruption of Krakatoa that washed up in Martins Bay.

MILFORD SOUND
pop 170

Milford Sound is the most visited of all the Southland fiords and is one of NZ's biggest tourist attractions. The calm 22km-long fiord is dominated by the sheer weather-scuffed cliffs and peaks that surround it, in particular the stunning 1692m-high Mitre Peak. Visitors should prepare themselves for an absence of blue sky, as Milford is synonymous with rain (an average of 6m per year). Although clear weather means crystal-clear exposure to Milford's beauty, a deluge also creates an unforgettable vista, thanks to the water cascading spectacularly down the rock faces. Occasionally Milford experiences an earthquake-triggered landslide, and a relatively recent one bulldozed its way down a 700m cliff.

Milford Sound receives tens of thousands of visitors each year. Some 14,000 arrive annually on the Milford Track, which ends at the sound, but most hitch a ride on the buses that pull into the cruise wharf; at peak times, the visitors centre here resembles a busy international air terminal.

Milford Track

The famous Milford Track is a four-day, 53.5km walk often described as one of the finest in the world, and many visitors make a special effort to do it. The number of walkers is limited each year; accommodation is only in huts (camping isn't allowed) and you must follow a set itinerary. Some walkers resent these restrictions, but the benefits far outweigh the inconvenience: keeping numbers down protects the environment and, though it's a hassle to book, you're guaranteed the track won't be overcrowded.

In the off-season it's still possible to walk the track, but there's limited trail transport, the huts aren't staffed and some of the bridges are removed. In the height of winter, snow and avalanches make it unwise.

Expect lots of rain, in the wake of which water will cascade *everywhere* and small streams will become raging torrents within

minutes. Remember to bring wet-weather gear and pack belongings in an extra plastic bag or two.

BOOKINGS

You can walk the track independently or with a guided tour. For independent bookings contact the Great Walks counter at DOC Fiordland National Park visitors centre (see p615). The track can only be done in one direction: Lake Te Anau to Milford. Your DOC permit allows you to enter the track on a particular day and no other. The track must be booked from November to April, and it pays to book as far ahead as possible (bookings commence on 1 July for the following season). A Great Walks pass (adult/child $105/55) allows you three nights in the huts.

The Great Walks counter in Te Anau can also book transport: bus from Te Anau to Te Anau Downs (adult/child $15/10), ferry to Glade House (adult $45 to $55, child $15), launch from Sandfly Point (the track's end) to the Milford Sound cruise terminal (adult/child $26/16) and bus back to Te

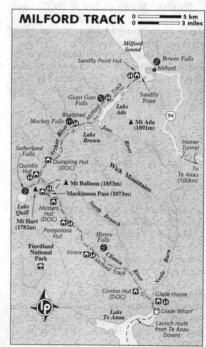

Anau (adult/child $38/26). The total transport cost is from $125/70 per adult/child.

Milford Track Guided Walk (☎ 03-441 1138; www.milfordtrack.co.nz) has guided walks for $1490/850 per adult/child in the low season (during November and from early to mid-April) and $1750/850 in the high season (December to March). These organised parties stay at a different chain of huts from the independent walkers. The guided walk is all-inclusive for five days and four nights, but walkers still only get three days on the trail. The final night is spent at Mitre Peak Lodge at Milford Sound.

WALKING THE TRACK

The trail starts at Glade House, at the northern end of Lake Te Anau and accessed by boat from Te Anau Downs or Te Anau. The track follows the fairly flat Clinton River valley up to Mintaro Hut, passing through rainforest. From Mintaro it passes over the scenic **Mackinnon Pass**, down to Quintin and Dumpling Huts and through the rainforest in the Arthur River valley to Milford Sound. You can leave your pack at the Quintin public shelter while you make the return walk to **Sutherland Falls**, NZ's highest. If the pass appears clear when you arrive at Mintaro Hut, make the effort to climb it, as it may not be clear the next day. The highlights of Milford are the beautiful views from Mackinnon Pass, the 630m-high Sutherland Falls, the rainforest and the crystal-clear streams. An intricate and highly unnatural staircase has been built beside the rapids on the descent from Mackinnon Pass. Estimated walking times:

Route	Time
Glade House to Clinton Hut	1–1½hr
Clinton Hut to Mintaro Hut	6hr
Mintaro Hut to Dumpling Hut	6hr
Side-trip to Sutherland Falls	1½hr return
Dumpling Hut to Sandfly Point	5½–6hr

Guided walkers stop at their own huts: Glade House, Pompolona and Quintin.

TRANSPORT TO GLADE WHARF

Buses operated by **TrackNet** (☎ 0800 483 2628, 03-249 7777; www.tracknet.net) drive from Te Anau to Te Anau Downs (adult/child $15/10). **Real Journeys** (☎ 0800 656 501, 03-249 7416;

www.realjourneys.co.nz) runs boat transfers from November to March from Te Anau Downs to Glade Wharf; the 10.30am service costs $45/15 per adult/child, and the 2pm service $55/15. Alternatively, **Sinbad Cruises** (☎ 03-249 7106; www.sinbadcruises.co.nz) sails from Te Anau to Glade Wharf ($68).

TRANSPORT FROM SANDFLY POINT

There are ferries leaving Sandfly Point at 2.30pm and 3.15pm for the Milford Sound cruise wharf (adult/child $25.50/14.50).

Fiordland Wilderness Experiences (☎ 0800 200 434, 03-249 7700; www.fiordlandseakayak.co.nz; 66 Quintin Dr, Te Anau) has guided kayaking from Sandfly Point to Milford ($65).

Activities
SEA KAYAKING

One of the most memorable perspectives you can have on Milford Sound is to be had sitting in a plastic shell at water level in the sound's awesome natural amphitheatre. **Rosco's Milford Sound Sea Kayaks** (☎ 0800 476 726, 03-249 8500; www.kayakmilford.co.nz) has a trip that takes in Bowen Falls, Stirling Falls and Harrison Cove beneath the bulk of Pembroke Glacier – with/without return transport to Te Anau $130/100. Trips are good value and doable by those with average fitness. There's also an afternoon trip involving a short paddle to Sandfly Point and a walk on Milford Track ($60).

Fiordland Wilderness Experiences (☎ 0800 200 434, 03-249 7700; www.fiordlandseakayak.co.nz) offers similar guided trips on the sound; see under Te Anau (p617).

UNDERWATER EXPLORATION

Unique environmental circumstances have allowed the sound to become home to some rarely glimpsed marine life. Heavy rainfall creates a permanent tannin-stained freshwater layer above the warmer seawater. This layer filters out much of the sunlight and, coupled with the sound's calm, protected waters, replicates deep-ocean conditions. The result is that deep-water species such as black coral (which is actually white while it's still alive) thrive here not far below the surface. A similar situation exists at Doubtful Sound (p627).

Milford Deep underwater observatory (☎ 03-249 9442; www.milforddeep.co.nz) dangles from a system of interlinked pontoons attached to

SOUTHLAND

Milford's rock face. Here, in a circular chamber 10.5m underwater and accompanied by an informative commentary, you can check out the resident corals, tube anemones, large horse mussels, bottom-dwelling sea perch and other diverse creatures. The half-hour observatory visits are highly recommended, even though the often-large size of accompanying tour groups may dilute the experience. You can stop over here with various cruise operators (adult/child from $20/13) or catch the **observatory shuttle** (☎ 0800 326 969; adult/child/family $45/23/100) from Milford wharf.

Tawaki Dive (☎ 03-249 9006; www.tawakidive.co.nz) explores the depths of the sound. Day trips from Te Anau include two dives and cost $240 using their gear, or $185 with your own. The cost is $40 less if you take your own transport to Milford.

Tours
AERIAL SIGHTSEEING
Numerous scenic flights are also offered in Milford. **Milford Sound Flightseeing** (☎ 0800 656 503, 03-249 7416; www.realjourneys.co.nz), owned by Real Journeys, flies over the sound for periods ranging from 10 minutes (from $70) to 40 minutes (from $280), and prices drop the more passengers there are.

MILFORD SOUND CRUISES
Cruises on Milford Sound are hugely popular; it's a good idea to book a few days ahead. On all trips you can expect to see Bowen Falls, Mitre Peak, Anita Bay and Stirling Falls, with the added possibility of glimpsing wildlife such as the hoiho or yellow-eyed penguin (one of the world's rarest). All cruises leave from the huge wharf visitors centre, a five-minute walk from the café and car park on an elevated walkway through a patch of Fiordland bush; the boardwalk goes beyond the visitors centre to **Bowen Falls** (30 minutes return).

Real Journeys (☎ 0800 656 501, 03-249 7416; www.realjourneys.co.nz) operates 1½-hour scenic cruises (adult/child $50/15); opportunistically, it charges $60/15 for the 1pm cruises simply because they're more popular. It also stages 2½-hour nature cruises ($60/15; 12.30pm and 1.30pm sailings $65/15) with a nature guide on board for commentary and to answer questions. During its months of operation (September to May), the small MV *Friendship* is a good choice because

its capacity is only 45 people; the 10am cruise costs $50/15 per adult/child and the 12.45pm trip $60/15. The larger boats can supply pre-ordered picnic lunches ($14) or a buffet spread (adult/child from $26/17).

Mitre Peak Cruises (☎ 03-249 8110; www.mitrepeak.com) has small boats with a maximum capacity of 60. Its 1¾-hour cruises cost $50/25 per adult/child, while 2¼-hour trips venturing out to the Tasman Sea cost $56/25 (noon sailing $60/25). The 4.30pm summer cruise is an excellent choice as many of the larger boats are heading back at this time.

Red Boat Cruises (☎ 0800 264 536, 03-441 1137; www.redboats.co.nz) recently added a prominent new catamaran to its fleet, the *Pride of Milford*. Sailings lasting 1¾ hours cost $46/12 per adult/child (note that the noon cruise lasts only 1½ hours but adults pay $50). Cruises lasting 2¼ hours and taking in the observatory cost $66/20. Picnic and buffet lunches are available here too.

Between them, these operators have more than a dozen cruises between 9am and 3pm daily over summer; try to go on the day's first or last cruise (or an overnight cruise) to avoid the middle-of-the-day crowds and extra cost.

OVERNIGHT CRUISES
Three boats operated by Real Journeys undertake overnight cruises, letting you appreciate the fiord when all other traffic has ceased. Kayaking, shore visits, swimming and wildlife viewing are possibilities as the boats sail the full length of the sound.

The budget-oriented *Milford Wanderer*, modelled on an old trading scow, carries 60 passengers overnight from November to April, departing around 4.30 or 4.45pm and returning the next morning at 9.15 or 9.30am. Accommodation in tiny four-bunk cabins (with shared bathrooms) costs $195/100 per adult/child if departing Milford, $260/130 from Te Anau and $320/160 from Queenstown; linen and meals provided. The *Wanderer* is YHA-affiliated, so 10% member discounts apply.

The *Milford Mariner* also sleeps 60 but has more upmarket, en-suite, twin-share cabins. Between November and April, it departs Milford at either 4.30 or 5pm and returns the following day at 9.15am. The cost is $310/155 per adult/child from Milford, $380/190 from Te Anau and $440/220 from Queenstown.

The MV *Friendship* departs between November and March at either 4.45pm or 5pm, returning 9.30am the next day. The multishare bunk rooms cost $195/100 per adult/child from Milford, $260/130 from Te Anau and $320/160 from Queenstown.

Cheaper overnight cruises take place in May, September and October, when the weather is the least dependable.

Sleeping & Eating

Independent walkers seeking a bit of luxury after completing the Milford Track will be disappointed. The Mitre Peak Lodge caters only to those doing the guided walk.

Milford Sound Lodge (☎ 03-249 8071; milford.sound .lodge@xtra.co.nz; SH94; dm/camp sites/campervan sites/d $22/24/28/60; ▣) is Milford's main accommodation and is beside the Cleddau River, 1km from the Mitre Peak Cafe. At the time of research it was still powered by a generator that was switched off between 11pm and 6.30am, but was on the verge of (finally) plugging into the region's mains supply. There's a small shop selling supplies and a **café** (mains $16-22; ☼ 7-8.30pm) plying pizza, apricot chicken and various 'vegetation' meals.

Also see Overnight Cruises (opposite) for details of floating accommodation options.

Milford Cafe (☎ 03-249 7931; SH94; ☼ lunch) on the edge of the car park and sells a basic menu of sandwiches, pies and packaged snacks; there's also a tour booking counter here. Next door is **Milford Tavern** (☎ 03-249 7427; SH94; mains $12-23; ☼ lunch & dinner) with limited snacks, beer and a smattering of local workers, but not much else.

Getting There & Away

You can reach Milford Sound by hike, flight, bus or drive. The most spectacular involves flying from Queenstown (p589) or Te Anau (p618). A good combination trip is to visit Milford by bus and return by air, or vice versa.

The 119km road trip is also spectacular, with the added excitement of the section ploughing through the lightless, water-dripping Homer Tunnel. **InterCity** (☎ 03-249 7559; www.intercitycoach.co.nz) runs daily bus services from Queenstown ($70) and Te Anau ($35), but most passengers come on day trips that include a cruise. Trampers' buses also operate from Te Anau (p621) and Queenstown (p596) and will pick up at the

Milford Sound Lodge. All these buses pass the Divide and the start/end of the Routeburn, Greenstone and Caples Tracks.

Many visitors make the return trip from Queenstown in one 12- to 13-hour day. Te Anau is a better starting point as it's only five hours return by bus. **Real Journeys** (☎ 0800 656 501, 03-249 7416; www.realjourneys.co.nz) has a coach-cruise-coach excursion that leaves Te Anau at 8am and returns 4.30pm, costing $110/55 per adult/child for the scenic cruise and $125/65 for the nature cruise. **InterCity** (☎ 03-249 7559; www.intercitycoach.co.nz) has basically the same excursion for a similar price, except the cruise is with Red Boat. **Trips'n'Tramps** (☎ 03-249 7081; www.milfordtourswalks.co.nz) also has a coach-and-cruise option out of Te Anau (adult/child $130/75). The **BBQ Bus** (☎ 03-442 1045; www.milford.net.nz) offers small, personalised trips from Queenstown (adult/child $170/95); price includes a BBQ lunch (veg option by request).

By car, the drive from Te Anau should take about 2½ hours, not allowing for stops. Fill up with petrol in Te Anau.

MANAPOURI

pop 210

Situated beside Lake Manapouri, 19km south of Te Anau, this town is a popular base for Fiordland cruises, walking expeditions and other trips, with the emphasis on excursions to the naturally fantastic environs of Doubtful Sound. The lake is the second deepest in NZ after nearby Lake Hauroko and is in a spectacular setting, surrounded by mountains the lower reaches of which are covered with native bush. On the shoreline near town is the picturesque Frasers Beach.

Information

The **Real Journeys visitors centre** (☎ 0800 656 502, 03-249 6602; www.realjourneys.co.nz; Pearl Harbour; ☼ 7.30am-8pm Oct-Apr, 8.30am-6pm May-Sep) organises most West Arm Power Station and Doubtful Sound trips.

Doubtful Sound

Cliff-hemmed Milford Sound may be visually more spectacular, but Doubtful Sound is larger, gets much less tourist traffic and is an equally magnificent wilderness area of rugged peaks, dense forest and thundering post-rain waterfalls. Some of the topsoil-lacking cliffs are marked with huge chalky

---

SAVING MANAPOURI

The original proposal to build the West Arm Power Station included a plan to raise the level of Lake Manapouri by 30m so it would join with Lake Te Anau. The possibility that this pristine lake and the ecological beauty around it would be swamped by a hydro-electricity scheme led to the initiation of what's been called New Zealand's first major environmental campaign in 1969. A year later, a staggering 265,000 signatures had been added to the Save Manapouri petition (the longest such document in the country's history), and by 1972 NZ had elected a new federal government based in no small part on the support of the party in question for the lake's protection.

---

swathes where tree avalanches or rock slides triggered by earthquakes have passed. At the sea-roughed mouth of the sound is Nee Island, inhabited by seals.

Until relatively recently, only the most intrepid tramper or sailor entered Doubtful Sound's inner reaches. Even Captain Cook, who named it, did not enter – observing it from off the coast in 1770, that he was 'doubtful' whether the winds in the sound would be sufficient to blow the ship back out to sea – and sailed on. In 1793 the Spanish sailed in, naming Malsapina Reach after one of the expedition's leaders and Bauza Island after another.

Doubtful Sound became more accessible when the road over Wilmot Pass opened in 1959 to facilitate construction of the West Arm Power Station, built to provide electricity for the aluminium smelter near Bluff. A tunnel was dug through the mountain from Lake Manapouri to Doubtful, and the massive flow of water from lake to sound drives the power station's turbines. The project did not go entirely smoothly, however, and early plans to raise the level of Lake Manapouri met with fierce resistance (see the 'Saving Manapouri' boxed text; above). Hydroelectricity generation and tourism are uneasy bedfellows in the region.

Fortunately, Doubtful Sound remains exquisitely peaceful. Bottlenose and dusky dolphins and fur seals can be glimpsed in its waters, and Fiordland crested penguins nest in October and November. As in Milford

Sound, black coral and other deep-sea life exist at unusually shallow levels at Doubtful because sunlight is filtered out by a permanent layer of tannin-stained fresh water on top of the seawater. As well as the water pumped in from Lake Manapouri, the sound receives some 6m of rain annually.

Activities

Adventure Kayak & Cruise (☎ 0800 324 966, 03-249 6626; www.fiordlandadventure.co.nz), beside the garage in Manapouri, rents kayaks (from $45 per person per day, minimum two people) for paddles on Lake Manapouri. It also has Doubtful Sound day trips combining a cruise and kayaking ($170).

With a kayak you can cross the Waiau River for some fine walks, detailed in the DOC brochure *Manapouri Tracks* ($1). A walk along the **Circle Track** (three hours return) can be extended to **Hope Arm** (five to six hours return). Although Te Anau is the usual access point for the **Kepler Track** (p617), the trail touches the northern end of Lake Manapouri and part of it can be done as a day walk from Manapouri; access is via the swing bridge at Rainbow Reach, 10km north of town. From Pearl Harbour there's also a walk along the river to **Frasers Beach** (1½ hours return), where you can find an undisturbed plot of sand from which to gaze across the beautiful lake.

Manapouri is also a staging point for the remote **Dusky Track**, a walk that takes eight days if you tramp between Lakes Manapouri and Hauroko and do the track from Loch Maree Hut to Supper Cove on Dusky Sound as a side trip along the way. This is a challenging wilderness walk, suitable only for well-equipped, experienced trampers. Contact the DOC and see Lonely Planet's *Tramping in New Zealand* for more details.

For fishing tours contact **FishFiordland** (☎ 03-249 8070; www.fishfiordland.co.nz; per hr/day $70/550), which also offers dinghy hire, scenic trips on Lake Manapouri and guided nature walks.

Tours

Real Journeys (☎ 0800 656 502, 03-249 6602; www.realjourneys.co.nz; Pearl Harbour) has a 'Wilderness Cruise', beginning with a half-hour ride across Lake Manapouri, followed by a bus ride that ventures 2km underground (by road) to the West Arm Power Station. After a

Barrels of wine, Gibbston
Valley winery (p576)

Trampers, Routeburn Track (p600), Queens-
town region

Yellow-eyed penguins, Otago
Peninsula (p567)

George St, Dunedin (p557)

Milford Sound (p624)

Tramper, Milford Track (p624)

Nugget Point (p642)

tour of the power station, the bus travels over Wilmot Pass to the sound, which you explore on a three-hour cruise. The eight-hour trip costs $195/45 per adult/child from Manapouri, $210/55 from Te Anau and $270/135 from Queenstown; picnic lunches can be pre-ordered ($20). It's possible to restrict your trip to the Lake Manapouri cruise and the power station tour and to not visit Doubtful Sound, but seriously, why would you?

From November to April, Real Journeys also has a Doubtful Sound **overnight cruise**, departing Manapouri at 12.30pm and returning noon the next day. The *Fiordland Navigator* sleeps 70 and offers twin-share en-suite cabins (adult/child $450/230 from Manapouri, $460/230 from Te Anau, $520/260 from Queenstown) or quad-share bunkrooms (adult/child $290/150 from Manapouri, $300/150 from Te Anau, $360/180 from Queenstown); 10% YHA discounts are available. Fares include meals and kayaking.

Fiordland Ecology Holidays (☎ 03-249 6600; www.fiordland.gen.nz; 5 Waianu St) has small-group tours (maximum 12 guests) led by people very familiar with the area's flora and fauna, and who sail a superbly equipped yacht into remote parts of the World Heritage Area. Three-day, two-night trips on Doubtful Sound cost around $780, while six-day, five-night trips around Doubtful and Dusky Sounds cost $1230. Other voyages take in Stewart Island and even NZ's Subantarctic Islands (p655). Book all trips well in advance.

Fiordland Explorer Charters (☎ 0800 434 673, 03-249 6616; explorercharters@xtra.co.nz; Pearl Harbour) also does 12-people-maximum trips of Doubtful Sound. A 7½-hour trip costs $160/80 per adult/child and pick up from Te Anau can be arranged. This environmentally committed operation also sells berths on scientific research vessels to independent travellers to help offset the costs of such expeditions.

Sleeping & Eating

Manapouri Glade Motel & Motor Park (☎ 03-249 6623; Murrell Ave; camp & campervan sites $24, dm $20, d $55-75) Peacefully located by the lake, this small park was undergoing redevelopment at the time of research, including the establishment of a new backpackers called Possum Lodge, so prices may rise in the near future. Sandflies are well represented here, so bring something to deter them.

Manapouri Lakeview Chalets & Motor Park (☎ 03-249 6624; www.holidayparks.co.nz/manapouri; SH95; camp & campervan sites $20, d $35-100) Quirky motor park decorated with a collection of old Morris Minors and a range of distinctive cabins. Stand-alone budget shacks have a bed, table, chairs and strip heater; we got one to ourselves for $20 (plus $5 for linen).

Freestone Backpackers (☎ 03-249 6893; freestone@xtra.co.nz; Manapouri-Hillside Rd; dm $20, d $50-60) Excellent place to stay, with several four-bunk cabins arrayed along a serene, view-blessed hill some 3km east of town. The personable owner has equipped each cabin with a wood-fired stove for cooking and heating.

Deep Cove Hostel (☎ 03-216 1340, 03-249 6602; d/tw $22/50) This remote hostel is right on Doubtful Sound; it's predominantly used by school groups, but independent travellers can stay here from mid-December to mid-February. Arrangements must be made well in advance.

Manapouri Lakeview Motor Inn (☎ 03-249 6652; manapouri@clear.net.nz; 68 Cathedral Dr; dm from $21, d $75; 🖳) This friendly motor inn's three-bed budget rooms (no bunks) look a little bit tatty but comprise a great deal, as they all come with en suites and lake views.

Cottage (☎ 03-249 6838; www.thecottagefiordland .co.nz; Waiau St; s/d from $75/95) Garden-backed en-suite rooms are on offer in this quaint cottage. The front gateway is so encrusted with flowers you have to stoop to get in.

Murrell's Grand View House (☎ 03-249 6642; www .murrells.co.nz; 7 Murrell Ave; d $250-270) This grand, late-19th-century building is hidden behind a rather formidable hedgerow off the road opposite the post office, and has been in the same house-proud family's hands for several generations. It has flower-scented, heritage-style rooms, and bookings must be made at least a month in advance. Be certain about staying here before booking, as there's a rather harsh cancellation policy.

Cathedral Cafe (☎ 03-249 6619; Waiau St; meals $5-20; 🕓 breakfast, lunch & dinner) Attached to Hay's Store, this café serves everything from veg soup to chops and schnitzel. Ask for a coffee here and you'll get it in a cup the size of a mini salad bowl. Last orders taken at 6.30pm.

Beehive Cafe (☎ 03-249 6652; 68 Cathedral Dr; mains $12-29; 🕓 lunch & dinner) This extension of the public bar at the motor inn has ostrich medallions, venison hot pot and seafood lasagne among its heartier mains, plus lighter bar snacks.

Getting There & Away

Scenic Shuttle (☎ 0800 277 483, 03-249 7654; reservations@scenicshuttle.com) drives between Manapouri and both Te Anau (adult/child $15/10) and Invercargill ($35/20). Alternatively, ask **Real Journeys** (☎ 0800 656 502, 03-249 6602; Pearl Harbour) if there are spare seats on its coaches to Te Anau.

SOUTHERN SCENIC ROUTE

The well-named Southern Scenic Route starts in Te Anau and goes via Manapouri, Blackmount and Clifden to Tuatapere, from where it follows SH99 to Invercargill via Colac Bay and Riverton. Public transport is limited but the **Bottom Bus** (☎ 03-442 9708; www.bottombus.co.nz) provides a good backpacker shuttle.

Near Clifden is the Clifden Suspension Bridge, built 1899, and the **Clifden (Waiau) Caves**, where you can undertake an exhilarating underground scramble: heaving yourself over rocks, shimmying through crawl spaces and climbing ladders provided in steep sections. This is an undeveloped cave so take all advised precautions: go with at least one other person and bring spare batteries for your torch (to be switched off occasionally to spot glow-worms). The caves are signposted on the Otautau Rd, 2km from the Clifden Rd corner; see the Tuatapere visitors centre (p630) for information and a map beforehand.

Just south of the suspension bridge is a turn-off to a walking track through a reserve of 1000-year-old *totara* trees (23km off the main road). From Clifden you can also drive 30km of mostly unsealed road to **Lake Hauroko**, the deepest lake in NZ and in a beautiful bush setting with precipitous slopes. In 1967 an interesting example of a Maori cave burial was discovered on Mary Island. In this *tapu* place a woman of high rank was buried (sitting upright) in about 1660.

One end of the challenging, 84km **Dusky Track** starts at Hauroko Burn and leads to Lake Manapouri, with a two-day detour to Supper Cove on Dusky Sound. This is a rugged tramp for experienced, well-prepared walkers. Consult the DOC and Lonely Planet's *Tramping in New Zealand*. **Lake Hauroko Tours** (☎ 03-226 6681; www.duskytrack.co.nz) has five-hour round trips (adult/child $80/40)

from Tuatapere, including light lunch, and will also drive you from Tuatapere to the start of Dusky Track ($60).

Tuatapere

pop 740

Once a timber milling town, Tuatapere is now a sleepy farming centre on the banks of the Waiau River. The woodcutters were so determined and active that only a small remnant of a once large tract of native forest in the town's domain remains. Tuatapere's profile as NZ's 'sausage capital' is not as high as it once was, but the town can still be used as a base for trips to Lake Hauroko or Te Waewae Bay.

Tuatapere visitors centre (☎ 03-226 6399; www.atoz-nz.com/tuatapere.asp; Orama Rd; ⏱ 8.30am-6pm Oct-Apr, 9am-5pm May-Sep) is extremely helpful when it comes to Clifden Caves info, hut passes and transport for walks, plus details of other local activities.

HUMP RIDGE TRACK

The 53km Hump Ridge Track begins and ends at Bluecliffs Beach on Te Waewae Bay, 20km from Tuatapere, and was inaugurated late in 2001. It's an excellent walk that takes three days to complete and passes along rugged coastline and through forests of podocarp and beech, subalpine settings and sandstone outcrops. Estimated walking times:

Route	Time
Bluecliffs Beach Car Park to Okaka Hut	8–9hr
Okaka Hut to Port Craig Village	8–9hr
Port Craig Village to Bluecliffs Beach Car Park	5–6hr

It's essential to book for this track, which is administered by a local trust rather than the DOC. Contact the **Tuatapere Hump Ridge Track Trust** (☎ 0800 486 774, 03-226 6739; www.humpridgetrack.co.nz). Summer bookings cost $40/20 per adult/child per night; winter bookings cost $25/10.

JETBOATING

Jetboat rides typically cross Lake Hauroko and go up the Wairahurahiri River. Operators include **W-Jet** (☎ 0800 376 174, 03-226 6845; www.wjet.co.nz; 6hr rides adult/child $190/90) and **Humpridge Jet** (☎ 0800 270 556, 03-225 8174 www.humpridgejet.com; 3hr rides adult/child $140/70).

SLEEPING & EATING

Tuatapere Domain Camping Ground (☎ 03-226 6650; Half-Mile Rd; camp sites/campervan sites/d $10/12/20) This camping ground is on the edge of the river-threaded Tuatapere Scenic Reserve, adjacent to a rugby oval. Its 'cabins' are a couple of bunkrooms within the one building, and you need to pick up room and amenities-block keys from 8 Grave Burn Rd.

Hump Track Backpackers (☎ 03-226 6418; 6 Clifden Rd; camp & campervan sites $20, dm $15) In partnership with the Five Mountains Holiday Park, this backpackers offers dozens of beds and sites set well back from the road on a treeless plot. There are six-bed dorms and two-bed units, both with shared facilities. Walking track transport can be arranged here.

Waiau Hotel (☎ 03-226 6409; www.waiauhotel.co.nz; 47 Main St; s/d $45/90) The hotel's comfortable rooms come with continental breakfast, though the price of doubles is a little steep. Its **bistro** (mains $9-15; ☺ lunch & dinner) serves schnitzels and bangers-and-mash, while a separate café handles pies and the mysterious local delicacy called 'mouse trap'.

The visitors centre has lists of B&Bs and farmstays. Tourist numbers are growing due to the Hump Ridge Track and this will spark more development.

Tuatapere to Riverton

About 10km south of Tuatapere the scenic route reaches the cliffs above **Te Waewae Bay**, where Hector's dolphins and southern right whales are sometimes seen. At the eastern end of the bay is tiny **Monkey Island**, or Te Poka a Takatimu (Anchor Stone of the *Taka-timu* Canoe), once a Maori whale lookout; the 'island' is accessible at low tide, when you can climb to the viewing platform, and there's good surfing and swimming here. Nearby is **Orepuki**, where strong southerlies have had a dramatic effect on the growth of macrocarpas, trees so windblown that they grow in a direction away from the shore.

Seven kilometres past Orepuki is **Hillcrest** (☎ 03-234 5129; hillcrestbackpackers@xtra.co.nz; SH99; dm/s/d from $20/23/50). A handful of rooms are available in this farm-stationed house, with a resident cat and background noises provided by cows and sheep. The best room is the front-of-house one with a double bed and rolling-hill views. It's closed May to September.

Detour off the highway to check out **Cosy Nook**, a wee picturesque settlement of bach (holiday homes). The next point of interest is **Colac Bay**, an old Maori settlement and now a popular Southlander holiday and surfing spot. You can surf at the eastern end of the beach, but serious surfers go to **Porridge**; ask locally, as getting there involves crossing a paddock.

Colac Bay Tavern & Camping Ground (☎ 03-234 8399; dustez@xtra.co.nz; off SH99; camp & campervan sites $18-20, dm $18, s $20-25, d $50) offers sheltered sites, functional rooms, a big kitchen, BBQ and hospitable owners. There's a small list of cooked food in the bistro.

Riverton
pop 1850

Riverton, located 38km west of Invercargill, is considered one of NZ's oldest European settlements, dating from the sealing and whaling days. This pretty town has good beaches and big-notes itself as the 'Riviera of the South' – perhaps not, but it is a pleasant, relaxed place. The **Riverton Rocks** area is a popular (if cold) local beach and **Taramea Bay** is a safe place to swim. Visit the lookout at **Mores Reserve** to see the wind-sheared canopy of coastal southern rata.

Riverton visitors centre (☎ 03-234 9991; www.riverton-aparima.co.nz; 172 Palmerston St; ☺ 10am-4pm Nov-Apr) takes bookings for the **Bottom Bus** (www.bottombus.co.nz), which overnights in Riverton, and is set in the town's old courthouse. It shares the building with the **Wallace Early Settlers Museum** (☎ 03-234 8520; admission by gold coin donation; ☺ 10.30am-4pm Nov-Apr, 1.30-4pm May-Oct) and its colonial-themed displays.

SLEEPING & EATING

Riverton Caravan Park & Holiday Homes (☎ 03-234 8526; Hamlet St; camp & campervan sites $16, dm $10, d $30-50) Has some very cheap caravans and cabins for rent. Also has a large (though slightly musty) kitchen-lounge and is a short walk away from a beach and a small grocery store.

Globe Backpackers (☎ 03-234 8527; www.theglobe.co.nz; 144 Palmerston St; dm $18-20, d $45) Good place that's being continually spruced up by its hands-on owners. Avoid the two downstairs dorms (one has 11 beds in it) and opt for a smaller, quieter one upstairs. For doubles,

SOUTHLAND

snaffle the upstairs room looking out over the estuary. Tends to get major backpacker bus traffic at peak times.

Riverton Rock (☎ 03-234 8886; www.riverton.co.nz; 136 Palmerston St; dm $22, d $65-95) Nicely renovated guesthouse with plenty of character and a choice of continental/cooked breakfasts for $9/15 extra. The upstairs kitchen-cum-lounge has good views and gets the afternoon sun.

Country Nostalgia (☎ 03-234 9154; 108 Palmerston St; lunch $11-15, dinner $25; ☽ lunch Tue-Sun, dinner Wed-Sat) The bright inside paint job is conspicuous, as is the quality of the food served here. Meals include risotto of mussels with mascarpone and baked pumpkin pie.

CENTRAL SOUTHLAND

To the west of SH1 between Invercargill and Gore, the Hokonui Hills point the way to the mountainous jumble of coastal Fiordland, while to the southeast is the Catlins Conservation Park, which pushes its bushy beauty right up against the island's remote southern coastline. The majority of Southland's population is concentrated in the centre of the province along SH1, and in the city of Invercargill.

INVERCARGILL
pop 49,300
The southernmost city in NZ has a fairly low skyline, which gives it the impression of being bigger than it actually is. Scattered throughout the orderly street grid of this farm-servicing community are some attractive old buildings and a worthwhile museum and art gallery, but there's little else to hold the interest of transients keen on hightailing it for nearby natural attractions like Stewart Island, the Catlins and Lake Manapouri. The opposite is true of the local student population, which has grown steadily thanks largely to the local polytechnic's clever initiative to lure them with fee-free tuition.

A number of hotels, bars and restaurants that were in business the last time we visited have now closed their doors, though it wasn't clear whether this was due to lack of clientele or in preparation for re-birthing as brand-new concerns.

Information
The **Invercargill visitors centre** (☎ 03-214 6243; www.invercargill.org.nz; Victoria Ave, Queens Park; ☽ 8am-7pm Oct-Apr, 8am-5pm May-Sep) is in the same building as the Southland Museum & Art Gallery (p632).

There's a local representative of the **DOC** (☎ 03-214 4589; 7th fl, State Insurance Bldg, 33 Don St; ☽ 9am-5pm Mon-Fri), a centrally located **post office** (☎ 03-214 7700; Don St; ☽ 8.30am-5pm Mon-Fri, 10am-12.30pm Sat) and an office of the **Automobile Association** (AA; ☎ 03-218 9033; 47 Gala St; ☽ 8.30am-5pm Mon-Fri).

Internet access costs $4 to $5 per hour and is available at the recommended **Comzone.net** (☎ 03-214 0007; 45 Dee St; ☽ 9.30am-10pm), as well as at **Global Byte Cafe** (☎ 03-214 4724; 150 Dee St; ☽ 7.30am-5pm Mon-Fri, 9am-4pm Sat & Sun), the **library** (☎ 03-218 7025; 50 Dee St; ☽ 9am-8pm Mon-Fri, 10am-1pm Sat, 1-4pm Sun) and the visitors centre.

Sights
SOUTHLAND MUSEUM & ART GALLERY
Opposite the main entrance to Queens Park, this **museum and gallery** (☎ 03-218 9753; www.southlandmuseum.com; Victoria Ave, Queens Park; admission by gold coin donation; ☽ 9am-5pm Mon-Fri, 10am-5pm Sat & Sun) has permanent exhibits featuring Maori tools and ornamentation (along with a long, old canoe), Victorian scenes, old colonial artefacts like a grand old printing press, and the Roaring 40s sub-Antarctic islands exhibit which has the skeleton of a rather awesome 'giant spider crab' (plus a rather primitive animatronic seal). Among recent exhibits were the intriguing photos, paintings and multimedia creations of 12 contemporary Ngai Tahu artists.

A prime attraction here is the *tuatara* enclosure, which you can also peer into through a glass window on the north side of the building. One of the resident lizards is Henry, more than 100 years old and apparently still going strong.

OTHER SIGHTS
Anderson Park Art Gallery (☎ 03-215 7432; anderson parkgallery@xtra.co.nz; McIvor Rd; admission by donation; ☽ 10.30am-5pm) is an attractive Georgian house built in 1925 and surrounded by 24 hectares of beautiful formal gardens, part of it taken up by a kids' playground. It contains a growing collection of New Zealand art hanging above splendid antique furniture in some gracious old rooms.

INVERCARGILL

INFORMATION
Automobile
  Association (AA)...................1 B3
Comzone.net...........................2 C4
DOC...3 D4
Global Byte Cafe.....................4 A3
Invercargill Visitors Centre....5 B3
Library.....................................6 C3
Post Office..............................7 D4

SIGHTS & ACTIVITIES (pp632–3)
Queens Park Golf Course.......8 B3
Southland Aquatic Centre......9 B4
Southland Museum & Art
  Gallery...............................(see 5)
Water Tower..........................10 A3
Wensley's Cycles...................11 D4

SLEEPING (pp633–4)
Ascot Park Hotel...................12 D3
Birchwood Manor..................13 B4
Coachmans Inn......................14 D3
Homestead Villa Motel..........15 A3
Invercargill Caravan Park &
  Camping Ground.................16 A3
Queens Park Motel.................17 B2

Southern Comfort Backpackers..18 A3
Tuatara Lodge YHA................19 C4

EATING (pp634–5)
Bonsai....................................20 C4
Cafe Amici.............................21 C4
Cod Pot..................................22 A3
Fat Indian...............................23 C4
In A Pickle.............................24 D4
Louie's...................................25 A3
Pak N Save Supermarket........26 D4
Picadilly Capers Cafe & Bar....27 C4
Thai Dee................................28 C4
Zookeepers Cafe....................29 D4

DRINKING (p635)
Frog 'n' Firkin.......................30 C4

ENTERTAINMENT (p635)
Embassy Theatre.....................31 A3
Globe.....................................32 D4
Movieland 5.........................(see 28)
Stadium Southland.................33 C3

TRANSPORT (p635)
Air New Zealand....................34 D4

Wander around delightful **Queens Park**, with its aviary, duck ponds, rose gardens and kiosk, and climb the curious **water tower** (Lee St; adult/child $1/50c; 1.30-4.30pm Sun) for a bird's-eye view of town. Sweeping **Oreti Beach** is 10km west of the city; warm currents make the water milder than expected and you can drive on the hard sands (but take care).

Activities

For details of a one-hour self-guided walk, get the free *Invercargill City Spirit Walk* brochure from the visitors centre. **Thomson's Bush**, 1km north along Queen's Dr, is the last remnant of Taurakitewaru Wood, the forest that once covered Invercargill. There are short walks 7km from town at **Sandy Point Recreation Reserve**, which has a mixture of *totara* scrub forest, fern gullies, coastal views and bird life.

For family fun, the **Southland Aquatic Centre** (Splash Palace; 03-217 3838; Elles Rd; adult/child/student/family $3.80/2.80/1.90/9.50) has a 50m pool, a kids' pool, waterslide and steam room.

The Queens Park **golf course** (03-218 8371; 215 Kelvin St; green fees $15) is an 18-holer in the heart of town.

Wensley's Cycles (03-218 6206; cnr Tay & Nith Sts) hires bikes for $20 per day.

Sleeping

A number of places will store your luggage if you intend traipsing off to Stewart Island; ask when you make your booking.

SOUTHLAND

HOSTELS

Southern Comfort Backpackers (☎ 03-218 3838; 30 Thomson St; dm/s/d $21/45/50) Set in a vintage villa with a calming colour scheme and a nice little garden, this is a consistently excellent hostel. Stay in one of the pleasant dorms or in the 'Playhouse', a little shed out the back which costs $21/34 per single/double. Only accepts payment in cash.

Tuatara Lodge YHA (☎ 0800 4882 8272, 03-214 0954; tuataralodge@xtra.co.nz; 30-32 Dee St; dm/d from $20/50; 🖳) Makes a big deal about being the world's southernmost YHA, though we didn't meet anyone who'd come here solely for that reason. It has a spacious, modern interior, very good facilities, a range of rooms (including 'executive suites' with stereos, towels etc) and efficient staff, and does a fair trade in passing backpackers.

HOTELS, MOTELS & B&BS

Ascot Park Hotel (☎ 0800 272 687, 03-217 6195; ascot@ilt.co.nz; cnr Tay St & Racecourse Rd; r $80-140; 🍸) On the eastern edge of town, this is a virtual mini-civilisation of accommodation, with close to 100 roomy studios on offer. The impressive facilities include an indoor pool (heated), a bar and onsite restaurant.

Queens Park Motel (☎ 0800 800 504, 03-214 4504; www.queensparkmotels.co.nz; d $90-130) On a quiet side street tucked into the northwestern corner of the expansive Queens Park. Has large, well-equipped units (some upstairs ones with small balconies) and comfortable beds to sink into. There's free bike use for guests, and ask about club hire for the adjacent golf course.

Coachmans Inn (☎ 03-217 6046; www.coachmans.co.nz; 705 Tay St; campervan sites $15, d $25-95) Good value motor lodge, with modernised motel units and a double-storey block of budget 'cabins' available from $15 per person. Also has a restaurant with a $13 roast.

Bella Retreat B&B (☎ 03-215 7688; www.bella retreat.co.nz; 70 Retreat Rd; d $160; 🖳) Pleasingly modern, woodland-surrounded hideaway with several airy rooms, cooked breakfasts, plenty of spots around the house to just sit and read, and a tennis court for the more active. The turn-off to Retreat Rd is 500m past Anderson Park Art Gallery, then it's another 500m to the house.

Other recommended central motels include **Birchwood Manor** (☎ 0800 888 234, 03-218 8881; www.birchwoodmanor.co.nz; 189 Tay St; d $90-130),

with several dozen newish motel rooms/apartments, and the highly hospitable **Homestead Villa Motel** (☎ 0800 488 588, 03-214 0408; villa@southnet.co.nz; cnr Dee & Avenal Sts; r $100-120), which has some huge units, at least one of which is wheelchair-accessible; if possible, avoid the rooms closest to busy Dee St.

CAMPING & CAMPERVAN PARKS

Lorneville Holiday Park (☎ 03-235 8031; www.holidayparks.co.nz/lorneville/; SH98; camp & campervan sites $20, d $36-69) Good-quality camping ground on its own large farmed plot. From town, head north along SH6 for 8km, then turn right on SH98 and travel a further 3.5km.

Gum Tree Farm Motor Park (☎ 03-215 9032; gumtreefarmmp@xtra.co.nz; 77 McIvor Rd; camp sites $18, campervan sites $20, d from $70) Appealing, carefully cultivated motor park. The three units planted here are a good deal, being big and well equipped (one has wheelchair access). The turn-off to McIvor Rd is about 7km north of the town centre.

Invercargill Caravan Park & Camping Ground (☎ 03-218 8787; 20 Victoria Ave; camp sites $15, campervan sites $17, d $28-36) Has an unusual location at the edge of Invercargill's showgrounds. Lacks the ambience of the aforementioned parks, but if it's really pouring you can pitch a tent indoors here, on a sawdust-covered dirt floor. Guests get free bike use.

Eating
RESTAURANTS

Cabbage Tree (☎ 03-213 1443; 379 Dunns Rd, Otatara; mains $12-32; 🕑 lunch & dinner Tue-Sun) Much-awarded restaurant that's no stranger to rave reviews. Caters to hungry loners and families in its beautifully renovated restaurant and wine bar, a short drive away at Otatara (past the airport). Its uncomplicated fine food includes kebabs, *panini* (focaccia), battered blue cod, Vietnamese lamb salad and a vegetable 'tower'.

Fat Indian (☎ 03-218 9933; laneway off 38 Dee St; mains $14-18; 🕑 lunch & dinner) Laneway Indian food dispenser, laying on some good vindaloos, kormas and baltis. You can get a 'tandoori sampler' (mixed tandoori platter) for $15, and there are several veg options.

Bonsai (☎ 03-218 1292; 35 Esk St; mains $7-14; 🕑 lunch & dinner Mon-Sat) Idiosyncratic restaurant with a splash of Japanese decoration but the feel of a Western café. Start with the chicken and udon noodles, then attack some teriyaki salmon or ginger beef steak.

Thai Dee (☎ 03-214 5112; 9 Dee St; mains $10-16; ☺ lunch Mon-Fri, dinner daily) Saffron-coloured Thai Dee serves up well-spiced Thai salads and soups, plus plenty of noodle and curry dishes. Try the yummy coconut cream, ginger and peanut–flavoured Musuaman curry (either meat or veg-style).

CAFÉS

Zookeepers Cafe (☎ 03-218 3373; 50 Tay St; meals $7-15; ☺ breakfast, lunch & dinner) Brightly coloured café with an enthusiastically applied zoological theme, hence the cheetah pedalling away on a bicycle suspended from the ceiling. Serves hearty breakfasts and various pastas and focaccias, and seems to be a hang-out for young locals in tune with local arts.

In a Pickle (☎ 03-218 7340; 16 Don St; meals $4-12; ☺ breakfast Mon-Fri, lunch Mon-Sat) The place to go for a late breakfast, and one of Invercargill's busiest lunch spots through the week. Has a big list of breakfast treats and lots of *panini*, quiches and cakes, plus good coffee and lots of teas to round it all out. Golden walls give it a healthy glow.

Picadilly Capers Cafe & Bar (☎ 03-218 1044; 38 Dee St; mains $10-25; ☺ lunch & dinner) This place is rather overwrought with coloured glass, brasswork and some statuary, as if keen on making an impression but not sure what that impression should be. Style aside, the mod-NZ menu is impressive and ranges from lamb burritos to peppered cervena. The non-smoking bar is a tame extension of the restaurant and closes relatively early.

Other café options:

Cafe Amici (☎ 03-214 1914; 73 Dee St; meals $5-13; ☺ breakfast & lunch) Mixed-age conversational crowds stuffing their faces with sun-dried tomato and olive chicken strudel.

Global Byte Cafe (☎ 03-214 4724; 150 Dee St; meals $5-14; ☺ breakfast & lunch) Arc-shaped, crowded space with big breakfasts.

Louie's (☎ 03-214 2913; 142 Dee St; mains $12-25; ☺ dinner) Lively, fashionable café-cum-tapas-bar with great taste in food.

QUICK EATS

If you need a break from café culture, try the fish and chips or burgers at the **Cod Pot** (☎ 03-218 2354; 136 Dee St; meals $5-15; ☺ lunch & dinner) or the gourmet pizza place at the back

of **Frog 'n' Firkin** (☎ 03-214 4001; 31 Dee St; medium pizzas from $12; ☺ dinner).

SELF-CATERING

For supermarket fare, try **Pak N Save** (☎ 03-214 4864; 95 Tay St; ☺ 8.30am-10pm Mon-Fri, 8.30am-8pm Sat & Sun).

Drinking

The **Frog 'n' Firkin** (☎ 03-214 4001; 31 Dee St) is a warm place for a beer due to the piles of exposed brickwork and an interior not too cluttered with tables or paraphernalia. But for a truly intoxicating atmosphere sample the laid-back scene at **Zookeepers Cafe** (☎ 03-218 3373; 50 Tay St) or settle yourself at the bar or in one of the booths at casually hip **Louie's** (☎ 03-214 2913; 142 Dee St).

Entertainment

Frog 'n' Firkin (☎ 03-214 4001; 31 Dee St) When it's not busy setting up beers and other beverages for drink-starved patrons, this bar hosts free DJ events on end-of-week nights.

Globe (☎ 03-214 3938; www.theglobe.net.nz; 25 Tay St) One of the biggest club-bars in town, capturing crowds from Thursday to Saturday nights in the DJ-attended main space and the upstairs Thirsty Kiwi bar. Bands that have played here have included the NZ-based outfits Panichicken and 8 Foot Sativa.

Embassy Theatre (☎ 03-214 0050; 112 Dee St) Open as a club-bar on roughly the same nights as the Globe, and also doubling on occasion as a large live-music, comedy and thespian venue.

Movieland 5 (☎ 03-211 1555; www.movie5.co.nz; 29 Dee St; adult/child/student/family $12/7/9/30) is purpose-built for the mainstream cinema experience.

The Southern Sting (www.sting.co.nz) is Invercargill's rampantly popular women's netball team – they're also rampantly successful, having won their fifth consecutive national title in 2003. You can see them play at **Stadium Southland** (☎ 03-217 1200; www.stadiumsouth.co.nz; Surrey Park, Isabella St); the season runs late March to late May.

Getting There & Away
AIR

Direct daily flights to Christchurch (from $85) and Wellington (from $120) are offered by **Air New Zealand** (☎ 0800 737 000, 03-215 0000; www.airnz.co.nz; 46 Esk St), with connections to other major centres. **Origin Pacific Airways**

(☎ 0800 302 302, 03-547 2020; www.originpacific.co.nz) has direct flights to Christchurch (from $85). **Qantas** (☎ 0800 808 767, 03-379 6504; www.qantas .co.nz) also flies direct to Christchurch (from $150).

Stewart Island Flights (☎ 03-218 9129; www .stewartislandflights.com) flies to Oban from Invercargill (adult/child one way $75/45, return $145/80) three times daily.

BUS
Based at the train station on Leven St, **InterCity** (☎ 03-214 6243; www.intercitycoach.co.nz) buses run at 3.25pm daily from Invercargill to Te Anau ($40) and at 8.45am daily to Dunedin ($43) and then Christchurch ($90). **Hazlett Tours** (☎ 03-216 0717) does the leg to Queenstown ($38) for InterCity, departing at 2.15pm daily except Sunday.

Scenic Shuttle (☎ 0800 277 483, 03-249 7654; reservations@scenicshuttle.com) operates daily between Invercargill and Te Anau (adult/child $40/25). **Catch-A-Bus** (☎ 03-249 8900) and **Atomic Shuttles** (☎ 03-214 6243; www.atomictravel.co.nz) run buses between Invercargill and Dunedin (both from $25), and **Knightrider** (☎ 03-342 8055) operates a night-time service on the Christchurch–Dunedin–Invercargill route. Most of these shuttles pick passengers up from their accommodation or at a pre-arranged point along their routes.

Campbelltown Passenger Services (☎ 03-212 7404; cps.bluff@southnet.co.nz) has door-to-door services between Invercargill and Bluff (one-way $10 to $15) connecting with the Stewart Island ferry.

Catlins Coaster and Bottom Bus services pass through Invercargill; see under the Catlins (p638).

Getting Around
Invercargill Airport (☎ 03-218 6920; 106 Airport Ave) is 2km west of central Invercargill. **Spitfire Shuttle** (☎ 03-214 1851) charges from $8 for trips between the airport and town, depending on which part of Invercargill you need to be dropped in or picked up from. By taxi it's between $10 and $15; try **Blue Star Taxis** (☎ 03-218 6079) or **Taxi Co** (☎ 03-214 4478).

The **Southland Express** runs a free bus service around the town centre (Dee, Tay, Esk, Kelvin and Gala Sts), departing every 15 minutes from 10am to 4.30pm weekdays, and 10am to 2.30pm Saturday. Otherwise, regular **city buses** (☎ 03-218 2320)

run to the suburbs (single trip $1.50, day pass $3.50; 7am to 6pm weekdays, 9am to 3pm Saturday); these buses are free from 9am to 2.30pm weekdays and from 9am to 3pm Saturday.

BLUFF
pop 2100

The rundown industrial town of Bluff is Invercargill's port, 27km south of the city and the departure point for the Stewart Island catamaran. The best place for visitors information is in a room off the café at **Land's End** (see under Sleeping & Eating; opposite), or visit www.bluff.co.nz.

Popular folklore has it that Bluff is the Land's End of NZ, though it's not the South Island's southernmost point (this claim to fame belongs to Slope Point in the Catlins). 'From Cape Reinga to Bluff' is an oft-quoted phrase signifying the entire length of NZ – the country's main highway, SH1, runs between the two and terminates near Bluff at the **Stirling Point signpost**, which indicates distances to the South Pole and elsewhere in the world.

Bluff Maritime Museum (☎ 03-212 7534; 241 Foreshore Rd; adult/child $2/free; ☺ 10am-4.30pm Mon-Fri, 1-5pm Sat & Sun) is a diorama of local industry, with exhibits on local whaling, mutton-birding and Bluff's shipwreck-littered bay. **Paua Shell House** (258 Marine Pde; admission by donation; ☺ 9am-5pm) has an amazing array of kitsch statuary and shells from all over the world, including over 1000 wall-decorating paua shells.

It's possible to tour the huge **Tiwai Aluminium Smelter** (☎ 03-218 5999; Bluff Harbour; tours free; ☺ tours 10am-Mon-Fri by arrangement only), a major employer of Invercargill townfolk, though the word locally is that the smelter isn't actively encouraging such visits.

The **Foveaux Walk** is a 6.6km (2½-hour) coastal walkway from the signpost to Ocean Beach; alternatively, follow it for 1km and return by the 1.5km **Glory Track**. Drive or walk the 3km to the observation point on top of 265m-high **Bluff Hill** (accessed off Lee St) for unobstructed views of surrounding flatlands and across to Stewart Island.

The **Bluff Oyster & Southland Seafood Festival** celebrates Bluff's famous delicacy and is held annually either late April or early May. The oysters are in season from late March to late August.

Sleeping & Eating

Bluff Camping Ground (☎ 03-212 8774; Gregory St; s/camp sites/campervan sites $8/10/12) Keys for the ultra-basic cabins and facilities (kitchen and showers each cost $2 to access via an honesty box) can be collected from 15 Parrett St. Sites have views out to the bay.

Bayview Hotel (☎ 03-212 8615; 48 Gore St; s/d incl breakfast $30/60) Has basic but comfortable and reasonably sized rooms above the bar.

Land's End (☎ 03-212 7575; www.landsend.net.nz; Stirling Pt; s $95, d $115-125) The prominent house opposite the signpost at Stirling Pt has nice cosy en-suite rooms, with either cooked or continental brekkie thrown in. You pay less for the doubles at the back of the house (facing away from the ocean). There's also a **café** (mains from $12; ☺ lunch & dinner), with freshly caught fish, oysters (in season) and plentiful wine.

Drunken Sailor Cafe & Bar (☎ 03-212 8855; Stirling Pt; lunch $8-20; ☺ lunch daily, dinner Sat) Next door to Land's End and with a decent ocean view this roomy place provides meals and beers at the limit of local terra firma. Seafood combos, salmon stacks and baked blue cod or flounder are all available.

Big Oyster Seafood Restaurant (☎ 03-212 8180; Ocean Beach Rd; mains $15-25; ☺ lunch & dinner Tue-Sun) Meal-serving adjunct to the Fowler's Oysters company, on the edge of town as you head to Invercargill and with fresh oysters galore, lobster mornay and also non-seafood mains.

Getting There & Away

Campbelltown Passenger Services (☎ 03-212 7404; cps.bluff@southnet.co.nz) has weekday door-to-door services between Invercargill and Bluff (one way $10 to $15), connecting with the Stewart Island ferry (see p651). It also offers secure vehicle storage down by the wharf ($5 per day).

INVERCARGILL TO DUNEDIN

The quickest, most direct route from Invercargill to Dunedin is along the SH1 via Gore and Balclutha. However, a much more scenic route is the continuation of the Southern Scenic Route via the coastal road through the Catlins (p638), rejoining SH1 at Balclutha.

The inland SH1 route passes through **Mataura**, site of a huge freezing works; **Gore**, home to trout fishing and country music aficionados; and **Balclutha** (p641), southern

Otago's biggest town. Some US visitors may get nostalgic on the 'Presidential Highway', a 44km stretch of SH1 linking the towns of Clinton and Gore.

Gore

pop 8500

This farming service town, Southland's second largest, spans the Mataura River and has the Hokonui Hills as a great backdrop. **Gore visitors centre** (☎ 03-208 9908; Norfolk St; ☺ 9am-5pm Mon-Fri, 10am-4pm Sat & Sun) is inside the **Hokonui Heritage Centre**, a complex that includes the **Gore Historical Museum** (admission free) and the **Hokonui Moonshine Museum** (admission $5), which explores a half century of Prohibition in this area.

The **Eastern Southland Gallery** (☎ 03-208 9907; cnr Hokonui Dr & Norfolk St; admission free; ☺ 10am-5pm Mon-Fri, 2-4.30pm Sun) is set in Gore's old public library (built 1881) and has a significant collection of NZ art, including paintings by Ralph Hotere. The new John Money wing opened in December 2003 to display the world-class collection he bequeathed, such as works by Theo Schoon and Rita Angus.

Croydon Aircraft Company (☎ 03-208 9755; www.themoth.co.nz; SH94, Mandeville; 10min flights $60, 30min $175), 16km down the road to Queenstown, restores vintage aircraft and offers weekday Tiger Moth flights.

The Mataura River and numerous other rivers and streams in the region are famous for their stocks of brown trout, hence Gore's 'World Capital of Brown Trout Fishing' claim and the overblown fish statue in town. The visitors centre can put you in touch with one of the area's many fishing guides.

In early June, Gore hosts the **NZ Gold Guitar Awards**, an annual 10-day country-music festival, during which the town is booked out. And this less than a month after the **NZ Line Dancing Championships**!

SLEEPING & EATING

Gore Motor Camp (☎ 03-208 4919; gorecamp@xtra.co.nz; 35 Broughton St; camp sites $20, campervan sites $22, d $32-60) This well-maintained park is at the southern end of town next to the showgrounds. Choose between sheltered camp sites, onsite caravans, cabins and two self-contained units.

Old Fire Station Backpackers (☎ 03-208 1925; oldfirestation@ispnz.co.nz; 19 Hokonui Dr; dm from $23, d $60) This small, friendly backpackers lies opposite the visitors centre. Stylishly renovated, it sports bright, comfortable rooms (enough to squeeze a dozen or so people inside) and an attractive courtyard and BBQ area.

There are several motels, including the older-style **Charlton Motel** (☎ 0800 929 733, 03-208 9733; charlton.motel@xtra.co.nz; 9 Charlton Rd; r $65-90) and the more contemporary **Riverlea Motel** (☎ 0508 202 780, 03-208 3130; www.nzmotels.co.nz/riverlea; 46-48 Hokonui Dr; s/d from $80/85).

Howl at the Moon (☎ 03-208 3851; 2 Main St; mains from $10; ⊙ lunch & dinner; 🖵) Sizeable café-bar with a variety of mains, cheaper bar snacks and a children's menu, not to mention a well-trafficked bottleshop.

THE CATLINS

The longer coastal route between Invercargill and Balclutha is well worth taking a slow drive along, not least because it passes through the enigmatic Catlins, a region of beautifully isolated forests and wildlife-filled bays stretching from Waipapa Point in Southland to Nugget Point in South Otago. The distance is similar to the inland route which sticks to SH1, but you travel much slower as 22km is unsealed; slow progress is being made on sealing this stretch of road, with the work unlikely to be completed until 2005.

History
The Catlins was once inhabited by moa hunters and evidence of their camp sites and middens has been found at Papatowai. Between AD 1600 and 1800 the Maori population thinned out because of the decline of the moa and the lack of kumara cultivation – they also feared wild, legendary, yeti-like creatures called *maeroero* ('wild man of the forest'), who they believed lived in the area. Later, whalers occupied sites along the shoreline, including Waikawa Harbour, Tautuku Peninsula and Port Molyneaux. Timber millers then moved into the dense stands of beech forest in the 1860s (at the height of logging there were about 30 mills in the area), followed by a wave of settling pastoralists.

Flora & Fauna
...re are still reserves of podocarp forests ... Catlins, containing trees such as

kahikatea, totara, rimu and *miro*. Behind the sand dunes of Tahakopa and Tautuku Bays are swathes of native forest extending several kilometres inland. The vegetation zones are best seen at Tautuku: sand-dune plants (marram, lupin, flax) are found near the beach; behind these are low trees, such as *rata, kamahi* and five-finger; in the peaty sands behind the dunes is young podocarp forest; and there's mature forest with emergent *rimu* and *miro* and a main canopy of *kamahi* beyond. A good example of young forest is found near Lake Wilkie, where growth has occurred on the sediments that have gradually filled in the lagoon.

The fauna includes abundant New Zealand fur seals and Hooker's sea lions, while elephant seals breed at Nugget Point (p642). The variety of bird life is an ornithologist's delight, with many sea, estuary and forest birds, plus the endangered yellow-eyed penguin, the *kaka*, blue ducks and the rare *mohua* (yellowhead).

Information
Contact the main Owaka-based **Catlins visitors centre** (☎ 03-415 8371; info@catlins-nz.com; 20 Ryley St; ⊙ 9am-5pm Mon-Fri) or the smaller **Waikawa visitors centre** (☎ 03-246 8444; dolphinmagic@xtra.co.nz; Main Rd; ⊙ 9am-5pm), and check the websites www.catlins.org.nz and www.catlins-nz.com. The DOC pamphlet *The Catlins – Walking & Tramping Opportunities* ($2.50) is useful, though the number of trails has been halved in recent years due to a lack of track maintenance. A good general guide to the Catlins environment, written by a local wildlife ranger, is *Stay a While in the Catlins* by K Widdowson ($2), available at Nugget Lodge (see under Owaka To Balclutha; p642) and local info centres.

The Catlins has no banks, few petrol stations and limited options for eating out or grocery shopping. So if you plan to spend some time there, make the most of the facilities at Invercargill, Dunedin or Balclutha first.

Tours
Bottom Bus (☎ 03-434 7370 Dunedin, ☎ 03-442 9708 Queenstown; www.bottombus.co.nz) motors along a regular loop that visits Queenstown, Dunedin, Te Anau and Milford Sound via the Catlins, Invercargill and the Southern Scenic Route. It stops at all main points of interest

THE CATLINS

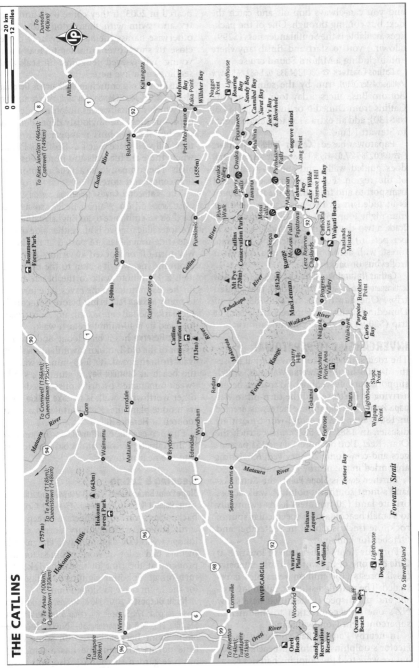

and you can always hop off and catch the next bus coming through. One of the packages available is the Southlander pass ($299), allowing you to start and finish anywhere and including a Milford Sound cruise.

Catlins Coaster (☎ 0800 304 333, 021-682 461; www .catlinscoaster.co.nz), run by the same folks as Bottom Bus, offers a day tour through the Catlins from Dunedin or Invercargill ($120 to $130); add an extra $130 to include flights to Stewart Island.

Papatowai-based **Catlins Wildlife Trackers** (☎ 0800 228 5467, 03-415 8613; www.catlins-ecotours.co.nz) does guided walks and specialist ecotours of the region. Food, accommodation and transport to and from Balclutha (if required) is included in its two-night tour ($290) or four-night tour ($580). It also manages **Top Track**, a two-day, 26km self-guided walk ($35 per person) through beaches and a private forest, with accommodation in a converted trolleybus or backpackers.

Catlins Natural Wonders (☎ 0800 353 941; www .catlinsnatural.co.nz) also offers first-rate guided trips. One-day trips cost $130/85 out of Dunedin/Balclutha, or there's an overnight trip ($200/150, plus accommodation).

INVERCARGILL TO PAPATOWAI

The road southeast from Invercargill passes the 14,000-hectare **Awarua Wetlands**, which supports various wading bird species, before arriving at Fortrose and the turn-off to **Waipapa Point**. The lighthouse here was erected in 1884, after NZ's second-worst maritime disaster. In 1881 the SS *Tararua* struck the Otara Reef, 1km offshore. Of the 151 passengers and crew, only 20 survived; 65 victims are buried in the nearby graveyard.

Further east is **Slope Point**, the South Island's most southerly point. A walk across private land (20 minutes) leads eventually to a small beacon atop a spectacular spur of rock; the track is closed in September and October for lambing.

For four hours either side of low tide at **Curio Bay**, one of the world's most extensive fossil forests (160 million years old) is revealed. The petrified stumps, fallen log fossils and plant species identified here show NZ's one-time connection to the ancient supercontinent Gondwanaland.

In nearby **Porpoise Bay** you used to see Hector's dolphins surfing in beach breaks, but we were told the dolphins had not reap-

peared in 2003. If they come back and you try and swim with them, don't touch or otherwise harass them, as they only come close to shore over summer to rear their young. Yellow-eyed penguins, fur seals and sea lions also live here.

Inside the old church in **Waikawa** is **Dolphin Magic** (☎ 03-246 8444; dolphinmagic@xtra.co.nz; Main Rd), which normally does dolphin-watching trips, but these are obviously dependent on whether the dolphins reappear. However, they still visit places such as Brothers Point, where there are fur seals and numerous seabirds. The company also acts as an information centre and store.

The **Cathedral Caves** (admission per car $5, per cyclist/tramper $2) on Waipati Beach, so-named for their resemblance to an English cathedral, are accessible for two hours either side of low tide (tide timetables are posted at the highway turn-off or stocked at visitors centres). From the highway it's 2km to the car park, then a 15-minute walk to the beach and a further 25 minutes to the caves. The turn-off to pretty **McLean Falls** is just before Cathedral's car park; the falls are 3.5km up a dirt road, followed by a 40-minute return walk.

Lenz Reserve has a bird lodge and the remains of the old Tautuku sawmill just a short walk from the road. It's a 15-minute walk to the beach at **Tautuku Bay**, a stunning sandy sweep punctuated by drifts of seaweed. Another worthwhile walk is to **Lake Wilkie** with its unique plant life. Past Tautuku is a great lookout at **Florence Hill**.

Further east is **Papatowai**, at the mouth of the Tahakopa River and a base for forays into the nearby forests.

Sleeping & Eating

Slope Point Backpackers (☎ 03-246 8420; justherb@xtra .co.nz; Slope Pt Rd; dm/camp sites/d $15/16/35) Cottage backpackers on a 140-hectare sheep and cattle station, with ordinary dorms and a lounge well lit by daytime rays. The newish owners had a lot of work planned for the property at the time of research. Take the turn-off at Tokonui signposted 'Haldane' for the 13km drive to Slope Point.

Nadir Outpost (☎ 03-246 8544; www.geocities.com /nadir_outpost; 174 Slope Pt Rd; camp & campervan sites $16, dm $15, B&B per person $50) Next door to Slope Point Backpackers, with some dark little dorms (though one has a window) but nice garden surrounds. Also sells basic supplies and snacks like microwaved sausage rolls and mini-pizzas.

Curio Bay Camping Ground (☎ 03-246 8897; 601 Curio Bay Rd; camp sites/campervan sites $10/15) Has pleasant sites staked out right on the beach, and a small onsite store.

Curio Bay Accommodation (☎ 03-246 8797; 501 Curio Bay Rd; dm $20, d $50-70) This is a modern cottage with two doubles (one with en suite), some bunks and water views.

Catlins Farmstay (☎ 03-246 8843; www.nzhomestay .co.nz/pages/Southland/HO_94.html; 174 Progress Valley Rd; d $120-220) This is a cosily rural B&B accommodation on a 400-hectare farm not far from Waikawa, with a flower-filled garden to stare at and dinners ($40) and free farm tours by arrangement.

Papatowai Scenic Highway Motels & Store (☎ 03-415 8147; b.bevin@paradise.net.nz; Main Rd, Papatowai; d $80) Mouthful of a name, but has well-appointed motel units lying behind a well-stocked grocery, fuel and takeaway shop (which sports the world's trickiest public phone).

Hilltop (☎ 03-415 8028; hilltop@ihug.co.nz; 77 Tahakopa Valley Rd, Papatowai; dm $20, d $55-60) Exceptional backpackers reached via the road just before the bridge near Papatowai, offering fantastic views and two beautifully furnished farmhouses. Mountain bikes and canoes are available for those who prefer activity to just sitting still and drinking in the peace and quiet.

Behind the motels is the simple **Papatowai Motor Camp** (☎ 03-415 8500; pest@es.co.nz; camp & campervan sites $14, dm/d $12/30), with doubles in basic cabins. Another Papatowai option is **Southern Secrets Motel** (☎ 03-415 8600; catlinsbb@xtra.co.nz; Main Rd; d $90), with four modern, balcony-equipped units.

PAPATOWAI TO BALCLUTHA

From Papatowai, follow the highway north to **Matai Falls** on the Maclennan River, then head southeast on the signposted road to the more scenic, tiered **Purakaunui Falls**, accessible along a short bush-parting walk.

Five minutes beyond Purakaunui Falls is the peaceful **Falls Backpackers** (☎ 03-415 8724; sparx@es.co.nz; Purakaunui Falls Rd; dm/d $20/50), where you bed down in one of two doubles, a twin or a two-bed dorm (all bedding supplied) in a lovely old farmhouse. Down on the water, there's a **DOC camping ground** (camp sites $4) at Purakaunui Bay.

In the **Catlins Conservation Park** you can do the **River Walk** (five hours) through silver beech forest. There's a **DOC camping ground** (camp sites $4) at Tawanui at one end of the walk.

In the middle of paddocks on the southern side of the Catlins River's mouth is the 55m-deep **Jack's Blowhole** (✂ closed Sep & Oct for lambing), 200m from the sea but connected by a subterranean cavern.

On the river mouth's northern side is the **Pounawea Nature Walk** (45 minutes return), looping through *kahikatea*, ferns, *kamahi*, *rimu*, *totara* and southern *rata*.

Owaka
pop 395
Owaka is the Catlins' main town. **Catlins visitors centre** (☎ 03-415 8371; info@catlins-nz.com; ✂ 9am-5pm Mon-Fri) and the **DOC** (☎ 03-419 1000) are both at 20 Ryley St; the visitors centre lists accommodation, including the area's many farmstays.

SLEEPING & EATING
Keswick Park Camping Ground (☎ 03-419 1110; pounawea@ihug.co.nz; Park Lane; camp sites $16, campervan sites $20, dm $15, d $24-60) In a lovely setting at nearby Pounawea, with ramshackle cabins and functional old-style tourist flats. Follow the signs to Surat Bay down Royal Tce but veer right instead of crossing the river.

Blowhole Backpackers (☎ 03-415 8998; catlinsbb@ xtra.co.nz; 24 Main Rd; dm/d $20/45) Attractive-looking reddish-brown cottage warmed by a fire and with a sunny veranda to exploit in summer.

Surat Bay Lodge (☎ 03-415 8099; www.suratbay .co.nz; Surat Bay Rd; dm/d $21/50; 🖳) Very inviting hostel in a great beachside spot at Newhaven, 5km east of Owaka. On the adjacent Catlins estuary is a resident sea lion colony, and there's a variety of tours and mountain bike hire (half-/full day $15/25) to make use of. Far removed from the daily grind.

Catlins Retreat Guesthouse (☎ 03-415 8830; 27 Main Rd; d incl breakfast $110-120) Subtle wider-world theme rooms (French touches, African hints) in an atmospheric, century-old home lounging behind a blue picket fence. The friendly owners can do lunches and dinners.

Kepplestone-by-the-sea (☎ 03-415 8134; kepple stone@xtra.co.nz; Surat Bay Rd; r $85-100) Another worthwhile B&B, Kepplestone is a cute, flower-dotted place with three rooms, near Surat Bay Lodge.

Lumberjack Bar & Café (☎ 03-415 8747; 3 Saunders St; mains from $12; ☻ lunch & dinner) An inviting spot with a good-looking timber bar (made from a 6m-long piece of macrocarpa), open fire and comfy lounge, plus some reputable lunch and dinner selections.

Some convenient motels:

Catlins Area Motel (☎ 03-415 8821; www.nzmotels .co.nz/catlins; cnr Clark & Ryley Sts; d $90) Large one-bedroom units with dishwasher, microwave and other mod-cons.

Catlins Gateway Motels (☎ 0800 320 242, 03-415 8592; cnr Main Rd & Royal Tce; s/d $70/80) Conjoined self-contained units on the town's main road.

Owaka to Balclutha

Cannibal Bay, east of Owaka, is the breeding ground of the Hooker's sea lion. The bay got its name from a surveyor who discovered human bones in a midden and assumed a cannibalistic feast. There's a **walk** (30 minutes) between here and Surat Bay.

Further around the coast, on a not-to-be-missed side track from the Kaka Point road, is **Nugget Point**. The wave-thumped rocky outcrops off the lighthouse-topped promontory, a 15-minute walk from the car park, lead off into the ocean's vast deep-blue; the rocks were so-named because they're apparently shaped like gold nuggets, which is interesting considering nuggets have no definable shape. Fur seals, sea lions and elephant seals occasionally bask together on the rocks; it's the only place on the NZ mainland where these species coexist. There's also a wealth of birdlife, with yellow-eyed and blue penguins, gannets,

shags and sooty shearwaters all breeding here. On your way to the 1869 lighthouse, you'll pass **Roaring Bay**, with a well-placed hide occasionally allowing observation of yellow-eyed penguins coming ashore (usually two hours before sunset).

Nugget Lodge (☎ 03-412 8783; www.nuggetlodge .co.nz; Nugget Rd; d $95), 3.5km before the lighthouse, has two units in a great setting. The upstairs pad has the best view and breakfasts are provided for an extra $15 per person. One of the owners is also the local wildlife ranger and can provide a wealth of local naturalist information.

From Nugget Point the road loops back through **Kaka Point** and Port Molyneaux towards Balclutha (p576). **Kaka Point Camping Ground** (☎ 03-412 8818; 39 Tarata St; camp & campervan sites $20, d $30) has a sheltered grove of sites and basic cabins located a way from the beach, on a hill behind the main road; the caretaker's residence is at 21 The Esplanade. The compact, hilltop **Fernlea Backpackers** (☎ 03-412 8834; Moana St; s/d $15/30) is for those who like the sound of crashing surf being carried to them on the breeze; head up the steps from Moana St.

Nugget View & Kaka Point Motels (☎ 0800 525 278, 03-412 8602; www.catlins.co.nz; 11 Rata St; d $65-170) has an impressive collection of ocean-viewing units, some are spa-equipped, and it's only a few minutes' walk from the sand. Operating from here is **Nugget Point Ecotours** (1hr tours $50, 4hr fishing tours $110).

Beachfront eatery the **Point** (☎ 03-412 8800; 58 Esplanade, Kaka Pt; mains $11-28; ☻ lunch & dinner) has a standard upmarket tavern menu and a driftwood bar attached.

Stewart Island
& Outer Islands

643

STEWART ISLAND &
OUTER ISLANDS

CONTENTS

Stewart Island	**645**
Chatham Islands	**651**
Other Islands	**655**
Subantarctic Islands	655
The Kermadecs	656
Tokelau	656

New Zealand's island culture doesn't just thrive on the North and South Islands, but has also flung itself out across the expansive waters of the South Pacific.

Often referred to as NZ's 'third island', the roughly triangular Stewart Island lies less than 40km from the underside of the South Island and is one of the country's great escapes, a wildlife-dense destination brimming with native birds and thick bush circumnavigated by long tramping tracks. When you're not lifting your walking boots through the undergrowth or eyeing the next forkful of fresh seafood, try taking a water taxi out to the undisturbed beauty of Ulva Island or just whiling away the hours in the coves of Halfmoon Bay.

If that's just not far enough away for you, take the two-hour flight to the Chatham Islands, 850km east of NZ's main islands, and have a first-hand encounter with descendants of the hardy Moriori and their enigmatic carvings, as well as the flocks of endemic birds that have found sanctuary here. Further still are the Kermadec Islands, pegging out the boundaries of the country's biggest marine reserve some 1000km northeast of NZ. Or how about the Subantarctic Islands, deep-south nature reserves dealing admirably with life in the Roaring 40s. The lagoon-surrounded atolls of Tokelau are nearly 500km north of Samoa – just getting out there is an adventure in itself.

HIGHLIGHTS

- Hunting (in the nonviolent sense) for indigenous birdlife on **Ulva Island** (p647)
- Taking a Great Walk along the **Rakiura Track** (p647) on Stewart Island
- Paddling the placid waterways of Stewart Island's **Paterson Inlet** (p649)
- Tracing Moriori dendroglyphs (tree carvings) at Te Hapupu on the **Chathams** (p652)
- Cruising the wild extremities of the **Subantarctic Islands** (p655)
- Diving into the coral around the **Kermadecs** (p656)
- Immersing yourself in Polynesian culture on **Tokelau** (p656)

★ Tokelau

★ Kermadec Islands

Stewart & Ulva Islands ★

★ Chatham Islands

Subantarctic Islands

- TELEPHONE CODE: 03
- www.stewartisland.co.nz

Climate

The weather on Stewart Island is incredibly changeable, with brilliant sunshine one minute and pouring rain the next. It can get very muddy underfoot and you'll need boots and waterproof clothing, but the temperature is milder than you'd expect: winter average is around 10°C; summer is 16.5°C.

The Chatham Islands are very exposed but have a temperate climate. Average daily temperatures vary from 12°C to 18°C in February and 6°C to 10°C in July. The best time to visit is in December and January, when temperatures often reach 23°C to 24°C.

Tokelau has a tropical climate with an average temperature of 28°C and heavy but irregular rainfall. It's at the northern limit of the South Pacific cyclone zone, so tropical storms are rare, but they do occasionally wreak havoc. Of greater long-term concern is the effect that rising sea levels will have on the islands' habitability.

Climatic forecasts for the utterly remote Kermadecs and NZ's Subantarctic Islands are fairly pointless, but if you insist, try the words 'wet', 'cold' and 'windy'.

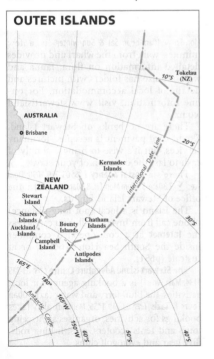

OUTER ISLANDS

STEWART ISLAND

pop 420

NZ's third-largest island, due south of Invercargill, is an increasingly popular wilderness destination. Maoris call it Rakiura (Glowing Skies), perhaps referring to the *aurora australis* often seen in this southern sky, or the spectacular blood-red sunrises and sunsets. In March 2002, 85% of Stewart Island was designated Rakiura National Park. It's often thought of as being isolated and battered by harsh southern winds – actually it's not so inhospitable, but it certainly is unspoilt.

The minuscule population of hardy, independent islanders is congregated in Oban, the only sizeable township, situated on Halfmoon Bay. Half an hour's walk away is a sanctuary of forest, beaches and hills. There are also good bathing beaches here, some easily accessible off Kamahi Rd in Oban; that said, the water is invariably chilly.

History

According to myth, NZ was hauled up from the ocean by Maui (see p47), who said 'Let us go out of sight of land, far out in the open sea, and when we have quite lost sight of land, then let the anchor be dropped'. The North Island was the fish that Maui caught; the South Island his canoe and Rakiura was the anchor – 'Te Punga o te Waka o Maui'.

There is evidence that parts of Rakiura were occupied by moa hunters as early as the 13th century. The *titi* (mutton birds) on adjacent islands were an important seasonal food source for the southern Maoris. Today's southern Maori population is predominantly Ngai Tahu, with their lineage traceable to Kati Mamoe and Waitaho.

The first European visitor was Captain Cook, who sailed around the eastern, southern and western coasts in 1770 but couldn't figure out if it was an island or a peninsula. Deciding it was attached to the South Island, he called it South Cape. In 1809 the sealing vessel *Pegasus*, under the command of Captain Chase, circumnavigated Rakiura and proved it to be an island. It was named after William Stewart, first officer of the *Pegasus*, who charted the southern coast of the island in detail.

In June 1864, Stewart and the adjacent islets were bought from the Maoris for £6000.

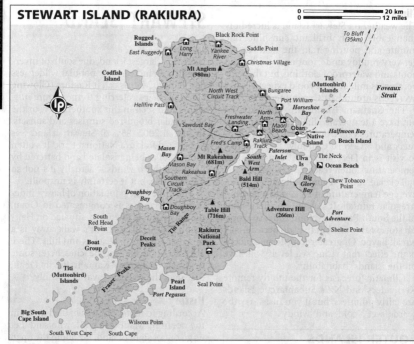

STEWART ISLAND (RAKIURA)

Early industries consisted of sealing, timber milling, fish curing and ship building. The discovery of gold and tin towards the end of the 19th century led to an increase in settlers, but the rush didn't last long. Today the island's economy is dependent on tourism and fishing – crayfish (lobster), paua (abalone), salmon, mussels and cod.

Orientation

Stewart Island is roughly 65km long and 40km across at its widest point. It has less than 20km of roads and a rocky coastline incised by numerous inlets, the largest of which is Paterson. The highest point on the island is Mt Anglem (980m). The principal settlement is Oban on the shores of Halfmoon Bay. It's named after a place in Scotland and the name means 'many coves' in Gaelic. There are some 360 homes on the island, many of them holiday homes.

Information

The **DOC Stewart Island visitors centre** (☎ 03-219 0009; stewartislandfc@doc.govt.nz; Main Rd; ☺ 8.30am-7pm Mon-Fri & 9am-7pm Sat & Sun summer, 8.30am-5pm Mon-Fri & 10am-noon Sat & Sun winter) is a few minutes' walk from the wharf and provides detailed information on flora, fauna and walks; it also has folders with pictures and details of local accommodation. For online information, visit www.stewartisland .co.nz.

There are no banks on Stewart Island. Credit card payment is accepted for many services, but it's wise to bring a supply of cash to last the duration of your stay.

There's a **postal agency** (☎ 03-219 1090; Elgin Tce; ☺ 7.30am-5.45pm Mon-Fri, 8.30am-1pm Sat) at the office of Stewart Island Flights.

The island is a local (not long-distance) phone call from Invercargill. You can access the **Internet** at a coin-operated computer inside the South Sea Hotel (p650), or at Justcafe (p651).

The **Stewart Island Adventure Centre** (☎ 03-219 1134; Main Wharf) is a booking agency for local activities, the Bluff ferry and water taxis. **Oban Tours & Taxis** (☎ 03-219 1456; Main Rd) also takes bookings for activities, organises sightseeing tours and rents scooters, cars, fishing rods, dive gear and even golf clubs.

Sights
FLORA & FAUNA
Unlike NZ's North and South Islands, there is no beech forest on Stewart Island. The predominant lowland vegetation is hardwood but there are also lots of tree ferns, a variety of ground ferns and several different kinds of orchid. Along the coast the vegetation consists of mutton bird scrub, grass tree, tree daisies, supplejack and leatherwood, but there are warnings not to go tramping off the beaten track, as the bush is impenetrable in most places. Around the shores are clusters of bull kelp, common kelp, fine red weeds, delicate green thallus and bladders of all shapes and sizes.

Ornithologists will have many field days here, examining locally bred sea birds and abundant bush birds such as tui, parakeets, kaka, bellbirds, fernbirds, robins, dotterels and kiwis. The weka can sometimes be spotted, as well as Fiordland crested, yellow-eyed and blue penguins.

Two species of deer, the red and the Virginia (whitetail), were introduced to the island in the early 20th century. Also introduced were brush-tailed possums, which are numerous in the northern half of the island and highly destructive to the native bush. Stewart Island has lots of NZ fur seals too.

ULVA ISLAND
The paradisiacal Ulva Island in Paterson Inlet is only 250 hectares, but a lot of natural splendour is packed onto it. An early naturalist, Charles Traill, was honorary postmaster here. He would hoist a flag to signal to other islands (including Stewart) that the mail had arrived and hopefuls would stream in from everywhere. His postal service fell out of favour in 1921, however, and was replaced by one at Oban. A year later, Ulva Island was declared a bird sanctuary.

Bird-watchers go all woozy here. As soon as you get off the launch the air is alive with the song of tui and bellbirds, and you'll see kaka, weka, kakariki and NZ pigeon *(kereru)*; some birds come so close that you don't need a telephoto lens to snap them. The abundance of birdlife here is due mainly to the absence of predators.

Good walking tracks have been developed in the island's northwest and are detailed in DOC leaflets, including walks to **Flagstaff Point Lookout** (20 minutes return) and **Boulder Beach** (1½ hours return). The forest has a mossy floor and many such paths intersect beautiful stands of rimu, miro, totara and rata.

You can get to Ulva by water taxi for a return fare of about $20 to $25 (p651).

OTHER SIGHTS
Rakiura Museum (Ayr St; adult/child $2/50c; ☺ 10am-noon Mon-Sat, noon-2pm Sun) shares its building with the Southland District Council office and is worth a look if you're interested in the island's history. It has information on whaling, sealing, tin mining, timber milling and fishing, and a particularly interesting section on Maori heritage.

Empress Pearl Visitors Centre (☎ 03-219 1123; 45 Elgin Tce; adult/child/family $8.50/5/25; ☺ 10am-5pm) was in the throes of establishing itself when we visited. It has a makeshift, work-in-progress aquarium comprising numerous small tanks (without explanatory labels) set up in one large room, though you do get unusually close looks at starfish, urchins, seahorses and sea slugs, plus more-unusual fish such as the spotted stargazer and southern pigfish. You can buy paua and pearl jewellery here, and there are plans for an ocean-viewing restaurant.

In a bush setting north of the waterfront is a pretty craft shop and gallery, the **Fernery** (☎ 03-219 1453; cnr Golden Bay Rd & Leonard St), selling island-themed books, paintings and etchings.

At Harrold Bay, about 2.5km southwest of town, is a **stone house** built by Lewis Acker around 1835. It's one of the oldest stone buildings in NZ.

Despite Stewart Island's isolation, world events do reach this far, as revealed by the modest **world wars memorial** on the waterfront, dedicated to the 11 islanders who died over both campaigns.

Activities
WALKING
Stewart Island is tramper's heaven, but although some walks take only a few hours, a day trip to the island is hardly worthwhile. Plan on spending at least a few days here so you can really enjoy the beaches and rare bird and plant life. The **visitors centre** (☎ 03-219 0002 for DOC-specific inquiries; Main Rd) sells hut passes and has detailed pamphlets on local

tramps. Gear can be stored here in small/large lockers for $2.50/5 per day.

There's a good network of tracks and huts in the northern part of the island, but the southern part is undeveloped and has desolate, isolated areas. You're advised not to go off on your own, particularly from the established walks, unless you've discussed your itinerary with someone else beforehand.

Each hut has foam rubber mattresses, wood stoves, running water and toilet facilities, but you need to take food, sleeping bags, ground sheets, eating and cooking

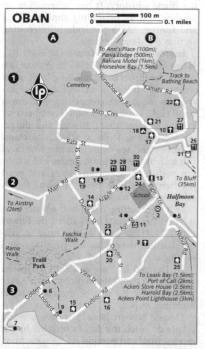

OBAN

utensils, and first-aid equipment with you. A tent and portable gas stove can be very useful over the summer holidays and at Easter, when the huts tend to fill up.

The 29km, three-day **Rakiura Track** is one of NZ's Great Walks (see Tramping p80), a well-defined, easy circuit starting and ending at Oban. Partly because of its undemanding and scenic nature, this extensively board-walked track gets very crowded in summer. Besides the shelter of huts at Port William and North Arm (both with room for 30 trampers), there are camping grounds at Sawdust Bay, Maori Beach and Port William. Overnight trampers need to buy either a date-stamped **Great Walks huts pass** (per night adult/child $10/5) or **camping pass** (per night adult/child $6/3); there's a limit of two consecutive nights in any one hut. For more info, see the DOC pamphlet *Rakiura Track* ($1).

In the island's north is the **North West Circuit Track**, a 125km trail that takes between 10 and 12 days to complete. This walk is only suitable for well-equipped and experienced trampers, as is the 56km **Southern Circuit Track** that branches off it. A **North West Circuit Pass** ($38) gives you a night in each of that track's huts. Alternatively, you can use **Back Country Hut tickets** (per night $5) or an **Annual Hut Pass** ($65) to stay in huts on either circuit track, but you'll still have to buy a **Great Walks huts pass** (per night adult/child $10/5) for use at Port William and North Arm. See the DOC brochure *North West & Southern Circuit Tracks* ($1) for full details.

Both the Rakiura and North West Circuit Tracks are detailed in Lonely Planet's *Tramping in New Zealand*.

The various short walks in the vicinity of Halfmoon Bay are outlined in the DOC pamphlet *Day Walks* ($1). The walk to **Observation Rock** (30 minutes return) has good

INFORMATION		
DOC Stewart Island		
Visitors Centre	1	A2
Postal Agency	2	B2
SIGHTS & ACTIVITIES	(pp647–9)	
Anglican Church	3	B3
Community Centre	4	B2
Empress Pearl		
Visitors Centre	5	B2
Fernery	6	A3
Golden Bay Wharf	7	A3
Oban Tours & Taxis	8	B2
Observation Rock	9	A3
Presbyterian Church	10	B2
Rakiura Museum	11	B2
Seabuzz Tours	12	B2

Stewart Island Adventure Centre	(see 26)	
World Wars Memorial	13	B2
SLEEPING	(pp649–50)	
Bay Motel	14	A2
Bayview Apartment	15	A3
Bellbird Cottage	16	B3
Dave's Place	17	B2
Ferndale Campsites	18	A2
Joy's Place	19	A2
Michael's House Hostel	20	B3
Pilgrim Cottage	21	B1
Room With a View	22	B1
Shearwater Inn/Stewart Island		
Backpackers	23	B2
South Sea Hotel	24	B2
Stewart Island Lodge	25	B3

EATING	(pp650–1)	
Boardwalk		
Cafe & Bar	26	B2
Church Hill Cafe Bar &		
Restaurant	27	B1
Fishermen's Co-op	(see 31)	
Justcafe	28	B2
Kai Kart	(see 11)	
Lighthouse Wine Bar	29	B2
Ship to Shore	30	B2
TRANSPORT	(p651)	
Foveaux Express	31	B2
Stewart Island Flights	(see 2)	
OTHER		
Wharf	(see 31)	

views over Paterson Inlet. Continue past the old stone house at Harrold Bay to **Acker's Point Lighthouse** (three hours return), where there are good views of Foveaux Strait; blue penguins and a colony of shearwaters (mutton birds) can be seen near the rocks here.

OTHER ACTIVITIES & TOURS
Paterson Inlet consists of 100 sq km of sheltered, kayak-friendly waterways, with 20 islands, DOC huts and two navigable rivers. A popular trip is a paddle to Freshwater Landing (7km upriver from the inlet) followed by a three- to four-hour walk to Mason Bay to see kiwis in the wild. **Rakiura Kayaks** (☎ 03-219 1368) rents kayaks from $40 a day, and also runs guided trips around the inlet (half-/full-day trips $45/70).

Ruggedy Range Wilderness Experience (☎ 03-219 1066; www.ruggedyrange.com) is an excellent ecotourism operator offering nature tours and guided walks. Excursions vary from a half-day trip to Ulva Island ($65) to a three-day tramp taking in Freshwater Valley and Mason Bay (from $630), with food and equipment supplied.

Oban Tours & Taxis (☎ 03-219 1456; Main Rd) zips around Halfmoon Bay, Horseshoe Bay and various other places on 1½-hour minibus tours (adult/child $20/10). You can also take out full-day hire of snorkel/scuba gear ($40/80; add $18 for scuba tank hire and fill).

Bravo Adventure Cruises (☎ 03-219 1144; philldismith@xtra.co.nz) is one of many charter outfits available for sightseeing and fishing trips – as long as you have a decent-sized group (six or more people), you can organise half-day trips from $60/30 per adult/child. A similar operator is **Thorfinn Charters** (☎ 03-219 1210; www.thorfinn.co.nz), which has an 11m launch that does half- to full-day wildlife-viewing cruises (mutton birds, seals, penguins) and fishing trips, also from around $60/30 per adult/child.

Talisker Charters (☎ 03-219 1151; www.talisker charter.co.nz) has a 17m steel sailing ketch available for half-day cruises around Paterson Inlet ($55 per person), day trips to Port Adventure ($100), dive charters ($100 per hour, including tanks and fills), and 'live aboard' charters along the Fiordland coast (from $90 per night).

Seabuzzz Tours (☎ 03-219 1282; www.seabuzz.co .nz; 5 Argyle St) runs one-hour glass-bottom boat trips (adult/child $25/12.50) and two-

hour tours of the mussel and salmon farms at Big Glory Bay ($50).

The island's **Community Centre** (☎ 03-219 1477; 10 Ayr St) houses a gym, a coin-operated sauna, squash courts and the library (seldom open), all of which are open to visitors.

Kiwi Spotting
The search for *Apteryx australis lawryi* is a highly rewarding eco-activity, particularly when you know where to look. The Stewart Island kiwi is a distinct subspecies of the brown kiwi, and has a larger beak and legs than its northern cousins. These kiwi are common over much of Stewart Island, particularly around beaches, where they forage for sandhoppers under the washed-up kelp. Unusually, Stewart Island's kiwi are active during the day as well as at night – the birds are forced to forage for longer to attain breeding condition. Many trampers on the North West Circuit Track spot them, especially at Mason Bay.

Bravo Adventure Cruises (☎ 03-219 1144; philldi smith@xtra.co.nz; tours $90) runs night-time tours to spot these flightless marvels. Numbers are limited for protection of the kiwi; a maximum of 15 people travel on the MV *Volantis*. Tour demand outstrips supply and trips only run on alternate nights, so make sure you book *well* ahead to avoid disappointment.

Sleeping
Several homes in and around Oban offer backpacker-style accommodation. Usually no advance booking is possible and for most you'll need your own sleeping bag and food. Some places are open only over summer.

There is ongoing concern on the NZ backpacker circuit about the safety of female travellers in one or two of Oban's hostels, which are not listed here. Check with the visitors centre first, and if you don't feel comfortable in the place you're staying, move on.

Another accommodation option is to hire one of the many self-contained flats or holiday homes, which often represent good value, especially if there are a few of you sharing.

B&BS
Port of Call (☎ 03-219 1394; www.portofcall.co.nz; Leask Bay Rd; s/d $200/270) Run by a family with a six-generation connection to the island,

this well-catered B&B is located 1.5km southwest of Oban, beyond Leask Bay and on the way to Ackers Pt. You get fantastic water views from the breakfast table (including of Foveaux Strait) and access to an isolated beach. There's only one guest room here though, so book well ahead. The owners also rent out a nearby studio unit (self-catering) called the **Bach** (d $220-270).

Stewart Island Lodge (☎ 03-219 1085; www.stewart islandlodge.co.nz; Nichol Rd; s/d $245/390) Modern luxury up a very steep hill on the edge of town, a locale yielding great views of the bay. The lodge has five centrally heated ensuite rooms and a comfortable timber-lined lounge. The tariff quoted is for B&B – for the DB&B package, which includes fine seafood dinners and a 'cocktail hour', add around $80/150 per single/double.

HOTELS & MOTELS
South Sea Hotel (☎ 03-219 1059; www.stewartisland lodge.co.nz; 26 Elgin Tce; s $40-80, d $80-120; ☒) Ostensibly a gregarious waterfront place with decent rooms, an upstairs balcony and separate detached motel units out back. But think twice if offered an upstairs room on a Friday or Saturday night; we weren't forewarned that a band was playing downstairs, and had music playing from under our mattress until very early in the morning.

Rakiura Motel (☎ 03-219 1096; Horseshoe Bay Rd; d $130) Small motel situated to the northeast of Oban, where it has a peaceful outlook over the contours of Halfmoon Bay. There are five older-style self-contained units here. Price includes transfers, and breakfasts and packed lunches can be pre-arranged.

Bay Motel (☎ 03-219 1119; www.baymotel.co.nz; 9 Dundee St; d $130-160) Residing here are 12 fully equipped motel units hell-bent on modernity. Sizes range from studios to two bedrooms, and two units are wheelchair-accessible. Cots and highchairs are also available.

Room With A View (☎ 03-214 9040; Kamahi Rd; topshop@xtra.co.nz; d $75) More ocean scenery is on offer in this self-contained motel-style unit, on a site tucked away around a headland from Oban's wharf (only a few minutes' walk from town though) and opposite a path leading down to a bathing beach.

HOLIDAY HOMES & FLATS
There are numerous self-contained options, usually charging between $10 and $20 for

each extra adult ($10 to $15 per child) beyond the first two people:

Bayview Apartment (☎ 03-219 1465; Excelsior Rd; d $120) Usually available only over summer, and near the sunset-conducive Observation Rock viewpoint.

Bellbird Cottage (☎ 03-219 1330; Excelsior Rd; d $95) Three-bedroom place surrounded by bush and birdlife.

Pania Lodge (☎ 03-215 7733; halstead@xtra.co.nz; off Horseshoe Bay Rd; d $125) Ten people can fit into this cosy house on a bushy 4-hectare plot near Butterfield Beach.

Pilgrim Cottage (☎ 03-219 1144; Horseshoe Bay Rd; d $95) Attractive weatherboard cottage accessible down a short bush track.

HOSTELS & CAMPING PARKS
Shearwater Inn/Stewart Island Backpackers (☎ 03-219 1114; www.stewart-island.co.nz/shearwater; cnr Dundee & Ayr Sts; camp sites/dm $16/20, s $26-36, d $44-60; ☒) Neat and clean rooms, attractive camp sites and a well-equipped kitchen are some of the features of this prominent establishment. A splash of colour brightens many of the rooms up, and there's a big, sociable collection of lounge chairs in the main communal hanging-out space.

Ferndale Campsites (☎ 03-219 1176; Horseshoe Bay Rd; camp sites $16) Ferndale has plenty of room on a well-maintained swathe of lawn near the waterfront. The ablution block has a cooking shelter (cookers can also be hired), washing machine ($2) and coin-operated showers ($2). The shower and laundry facilities are open to the general public.

Some good backpacker-accommodating homes:

Ann's Place (☎ 03-219 1065; off Mapau Rd; dm $14) Across Mill Creek from the township and offering tramping-style accommodation in a family house.

Dave's Place (☎ 03-219 1427; Elgin Tce; dm $20)

Joy's Place (☎ 03-219 1376; Main Rd; dm $20) Has bunk-rooms and a restraining order on drinking and smoking.

Michael's House Hostel (☎ 03-219 1425; Golden Bay Rd; dm $20) Basic accommodation.

Eating & Drinking
Church Hill Cafe Bar & Restaurant (☎ 03-219 1323; 36 Kamahi Rd; lunch $15, dinner $25; ☺ lunch & dinner) Accomplished eatery with several stylish interior rooms and an outdoor deck from which to enjoy the ocean view on a fine day. Specialises in the island's fresh seafood but also does stonegrilled meats and non-salted mutton bird.

Boardwalk Cafe & Bar (☎ 03-219 1470; Wharf; lunch $7-14, dinner $15-27; ☺ lunch & dinner) Amenable café upstairs in the ferry wharf terminal, with all-round water views and a menu of whitebait fritters, mutton bird fillets and pan-fried cod. There's also a pool table and many places to lounge with a drink in hand.

South Sea Hotel (☎ 03-219 1059; 26 Elgin Tce; mains $10-25; ☽ lunch & dinner) Chicken, cod or beef burgers, herbed mussels, crayfish omelettes and the occasional mutton bird dish are all de-voured in this big, light-filled space, normally lined table-to-table with tourists and locals. It's also the town's main drinking den and gets raucous crowds when bands occasionally turn up on end-of-week nights.

Justcafe (☎ 03-219 1567; Main Rd; meals $5-10; ☽ lunch; ▯) Warm little place with Inter-net access and plenty of benches to sit on. Provides muffins, quiche, soup, toasted sandwiches and caffeine fixes.

Kai Kart (☎ 03-219 1225; Ayr St; meals $6-15; ☽ lunch & dinner) Bacon and eggs, chook bur-gers, mussel melts and seafood patties are all served from this blue van outside the Rakiura Museum. In season, you can also buy green-lipped mussels for around $4 per kilo.

Lighthouse Wine Bar (Main Rd) At the time of research this place was getting an extensive makeover. We were told it would retain its old name, continue to serve gourmet pizzas and good wines, and possibly have an art-house cinema erected next door.

Self-caterers can get groceries from Oban's general store, **Ship to Shore** (☎ 03-219 1069; Elgin Tce; ☽ 7.30am-7pm Mon-Fri, 8am-7pm Sat & Sun), which sells fresh fruit and vegetables, dried foods, toiletries, beer and wine, and gas canisters.

The Fishermen's Co-op down at the main wharf often has fresh fish and crayfish for sale; you can, of course, go and catch your own seafood.

Getting There & Away
If you have limited time to spend on the island, **Invercargill visitors centre** (☎ 03-214 6243; www.invercargill.org.nz) has information on decent-value packages that often include air fares, accommodation and tours.

AIR
Stewart Island Flights (☎ 03-218 9129; www.stewart islandflights.com; Elgin Tce) handles flights between the island and Invercargill (adult/child $80/45, return $145/75). There are sometimes discount standby fares but phone ahead.

Flights depart three times daily year-round and it only takes 20 minutes to cross nar-row Foveaux Strait. The bus trip from the island's Ryan's Creek airstrip to Oban is included in the air fare.

BOAT
The passenger-only **Foveaux Express** (☎ 03-212 7660; www.foveauxexpress.co.nz) runs between Bluff and Oban (adult/child $45/23, return $85/45), departing Bluff at 9.30am and 5pm September to April, and 9.30am and 4.30pm May to August. Definitely book a few days ahead in summer; YHA members are eligible for a 10% fare discount. The strait crossing takes one hour and can often experience rough, stormy conditions.

Campbelltown Passenger Services (☎ 03-212 7404; cps.bluff@southnet.co.nz) runs a door-to-door shuttle service ($10 to $15) connecting with the ferry; it picks up from anywhere in Invercargill.

Getting Around
Oban Tours & Taxis (☎ 03-219 1456; Main Rd) rents cars for $55/75 per half-/full day (petrol and mileage included) and hires motor scooters for $25/45/50 per hour/half-day/day. Hand-ily for trampers, they also do pick-ups and drop-offs to remote parts of the island, as do a number of other charter boats including **Seaview Water Taxi** (☎ 03-219 1014), **Stewart Is-land Water Taxi & Eco Guiding** (☎ 03-219 1394) and **Seabuzzz Tours** (☎ 03-219 1282). Several oper-ators are based at Golden Bay Wharf, about a 10-minute walk from the township.

All the aforementioned charter outfits offer a water taxi service to **Ulva Island**; return fares cost $20 to $25.

CHATHAM ISLANDS

pop 770
Named Rekohu (Misty Sun) by the Mori-ori, the Chathams lie way out in the South Pacific Ocean, 850km due east of Christ-church. These remote islands comprise the first human habitation over the international dateline, and a few years ago marketed them-selves as the first to see the dawn of the new millennium. There are 10 islands in the group but apart from the 35 or so people on Pitt Island, only Chatham Island, with close to 800 people, is significantly populated.

STEWART ISLAND &
OUTER ISLANDS

The group's environmental contrasts are striking: rugged coastlines and towering cliffs; volcanic peaks; lagoons and peat bogs; sweeping beaches devoid of human footprints; isolated farms; wind-stunted vegetation and dense patches of forest. The main industry besides farming and tourism (particularly ecotourism) is crayfish processing, and there are plants at Waitangi, Kaingaroa, Owenga and Port Hutt. These four towns have been described as choking in the flotsam and jetsam of their raison d'être – in other words they're not too flash – but they do have a dilapidated charm.

History

The Chatham Islands were formed eons ago by volcanic upthrust and were first inhabited by the Moriori tribe, who it's believed travelled here from NZ's South Island between 500 and 1100 years ago. Due to their isolation from mainland Maori tribes, the Moriori maintained a more ancient Polynesian culture. But their situation began to change for the worse with the arrival of Europeans in 1791 and groups of mainland Maoris in the mid-1800s, and by the beginning of the 20th century there were just 12 full-blooded Moriori left. See the boxed text below.

THE LAST OF THE MORIORI

One of the most fascinating aspects of the Chathams is the cultural legacy of the Moriori. Moriori descendants still live here, alongside several remnants of their once-flourishing culture.

Often confused with a mythical, pre-Maori race on mainland NZ (see p26), it's now scientifically accepted that the Moriori were Maoris who sailed to the Chathams from NZ. The date of their arrival remains in dispute, but it was some time between AD 900 and AD 1500.

Once in the Chathams, the Moriori began to develop a separate identity from mainland Maoris. They did not have rigid social divisions, they forbade tribal warfare and settled disputes on a one-to-one basis with hand-to-hand combat, and their language acquired subtle differences. They carved their symbols into trees (dendroglyphs) and into the rocks (petroglyphs) fringing Te Whanga Lagoon. When the HMS *Chatham* arrived in 1791 and claimed the islands for Britain's King George III, there were believed to be about 2000 Moriori on the islands. But the establishment of whaling and sealing industries and the consequent depletion of two of the Moriori's main sources of food soon took its toll on the local population.

From about 1835, groups of mainland Maoris began to arrive in the Chathams and soon there were about 900 new residents made up of the Ngati Tama and Ngati Mutunga of the Taranaki Ati-awa. They began to occupy the land in a process known as *takahi*, killing about 300 resisting Moriori and enslaving others. By 1841 there were believed to be only 160 Moriori and over 400 Maoris, and it wasn't until two years later that the Ngati Tama and Te Ati-awa released the last of the Moriori slaves. In 1870 the Native Land Court Hearings recognised that the two mainland tribes had sovereignty over 97% of the Chathams by right of conquest, and small reserves were created for the 90 surviving Moriori. In time, the Moriori intermarried and slowly their unique culture and identity faded. Their language died with the last great Moriori scholar, Hirawanu Tapu, in 1900. At this stage, full-blood Moriori numbered 12.

Today, Moriori, Pakeha and descendants of the mainland Maoris live side by side as Chatham Islanders. The last full-blood Moriori was Tommy Solomon, who died in 1933. His passing was seen at the time as the extinction of the race, but it was far from that. His three sons and two daughters were identified as Moriori and there were many other families on the island who claimed Moriori ancestry. There are now believed to be over 300 Moriori descendants in the Chathams and there has been a revival of Moriori consciousness, particularly strong after the building of the Solomon monument at Manukau Point near Owenga in the southeast of the island.

In August 2001 the Waitangi Tribunal, charged with investigating Maori land claims, decided that the ancestral rights to the Chatham Islands belong to the Moriori. The Tribunal found that Moriori should receive compensation for the lasting impact of the Crown's failure to intervene after the 1835 mainland Maori invasion, and called the 1870 decision to award Maori sovereignty over the Chathams by right of conquest 'patently wrong'. Justice is still a long time coming, however – by early 2004, Moriori descendants had only just begun to negotiate their redress in earnest with the NZ government.

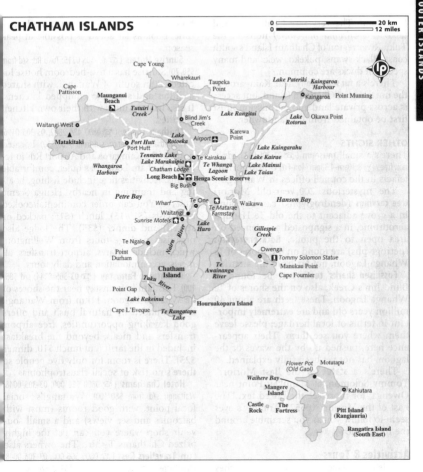

CHATHAM ISLANDS

0 ——— 20 km
0 ——— 12 miles

Cape Young

Wharekauri

Cape Pattisson

Maunganui Beach

Taupeka Point

Lake Pateriki   Kaingaroa Harbour

Kaingaroa   Point Munning

Tutuiri Creek

Blind Jim's Creek

Lake Rangitai

Lake Rotorua

Okawa Point

Waitangi West

Matakitaki

Port Hutt
Port Hutt

Lake Rotoeka

Airport

Karewa Point

Tennants Lake
Lake Marakipia
Chatham Lodge

Te Kairakau

Te Whanga Lagoon

Lake Kaingarahu

Lake Kairae

Lake Mainui

Lake Taiau

Whangaroa Harbour

Long Beach

Big Bush

Henga Scenic Reserve

Petre Bay

Wharf

Te One

Waikawa

Hanson Bay

Waitangi

Te Matarae Farmstay

Sunrise Motels

Lake Huro

Gillespie Creek

Te Ngaio

Nairn River

Point Durham

Owenga

Tommy Solomon Statue
Manukau Point

Chatham Island

Te Awainanga River

Cape Fournier

Tuku River

Point Gap

Lake Rakeinui

Cape L'Eveque

Te Rangatapu Lake

Houruakopara Island

Flower Pot (Old Gaol)

Motutapu

Waihere Bay

Mangere Island

Kahiutara

Castle Rock

The Fortress

Pitt Island (Rangiauria)

Rangatira Island (South East)

Information

Information on the islands is available from the **Te Iwi Moriori Trust Board** (☎ 03-305 0466; info@chathams.govt.nz; Waitangi Wharf, Oweng Rd, Waitangi), **Air Chathams** (☎ 03-305 0209; chatsoffice@xtra.co.nz); or the local **council** (☎ 03-305 0033; chathamcouncil@xtra.co.nz; PO Box 24, Waitangi). Once you're on Chatham Island, the best way to get informed is to talk to the locals. The **DOC office** (☎ 03-305 0098; Te One) may be unattended, so call before you visit.

The website www.chathams.com is worth a look. *A Land Apart,* by Michael King & Robin Morrison, also provides a wealth of information about the islands.

Waitangi is the islands' only sizeable town and has a couple of shops, a hotel, a small

hospital and a golf course. There's an ANZ bank here (which doubles as a post office) but no ATM, so bring enough cash with you.

Sights

BIRDS & SEALS

There are 18 species of **bird** unique to these islands and, because of their isolation, there is a large degree of endemism, as with the local tomtit, pigeon and robin. Entry to sanctuaries such as those at Pitt and Rangatira (South East) Islands is prohibited, but many species can still be seen outside these; DOC staff can outline the best viewing spots for twitchers. Endangered birds include the black robin, which was once perilously close to extinction in its last refuge, Mangere Island near

Pitt Island. The very rare Chatham Island taiko *(Pterodroma magentae)* nests in the Tuku River region of Chatham Island's south coast. Black swans, pukeko, weka and many species of ducks are common.

There's a **fur seal colony** near Kaingaroa in the northeast of Chatham Island, but access is across private land and permission must first be obtained from the landowner.

OTHER SIGHTS

There's a small **museum** (☎ 03-305 0033; admission free; ⊙ 8.30am-4.30pm Mon-Fri) of Moriori artefacts in the council offices in Waitangi.

The mysterious 200-year-old Moriori **tree carvings** (dendroglyphs) can be found in a grove adjacent to the old Te Hapupu aerodrome, in a signposted and fenced-off area open to the public. **Rock engravings** (petroglyphs) are found on the shores of Te Whanga Lagoon, not far from the airstrip.

Fossilised sharks' teeth can be found at Blind Jim's Creek, also on the shores of Te Whanga Lagoon. These teeth are about 40 million years old and are extremely important in terms of local heritage; please leave them where you see them. Their appearance here, pushed up by the waves of the lagoon, has not yet been fully explained.

There's a **statue** of the 'last Moriori', Tommy Solomon, at Manukau Point near Owenga; for more see the boxed text 'The Last of the Moriori' (p652). Tommy's eyes seem to follow you as you scramble around the rocks below.

Activities & Tours

The islands have plenty of fine beaches where you can **fish** and catch crayfish. Crays are a major industry in the Chatham Islands, and they are exported to North America and Japan. There are daily per-person quotas for cray and paua hauls; be sure to check with the DOC.

Divers can explore **shipwrecks** around the islands. Trampers can strike out on the **walking tracks** in DOC-established reserves.

Tours are organised by Hotel Chathams and Chatham Lodge (see Sleeping following), with prices given on application.

Sleeping

Over summer, the hotel and the lodge are often filled by tour groups, and this means other accommodation subsequently gets booked out too, sometimes for months at a time. Book as far ahead as possible in peak season.

Sunrise Motels (☎ 03-305 0215; Tuku Rd; s/d from $50/70) Sunrise has a five-bedroom house located 500m south of Waitangi, with shared facilities and access to equipped kitchens. It also has two units with their own kitchen facilities.

Chatham Lodge (☎ 0800 424 2842, 03-305 0196; www.chathamlodge.net.nz; s/d from $100/110) Located north of the Kaingaroa and Airport Rds junction, Chatham Lodge has quiet, comfortable rooms. Activities here include fishing, boating and tramping in nearby Henga Scenic Reserve. You can order continental/cooked breakfasts ($10/15), lunch ($15; packed or served) and dinner ($35). The lodge also organises package tours from Wellington, which include airfares, airport transfers, all meals, accommodation and daily tours.

Te Matarae Farmstay (☎ 03-305 0144; s/d $85/100) This family farmstay near the shores of Te Whanga Lagoon, 11km from Waitangi, is surrounded by natural bush and offers good kayaking opportunities, free airport transfers and meals, beyond the breakfast included in the tariff (cut lunch $10, dinner $25). There is room for only five people so there's no risk of social claustrophobia.

Hotel Chathams (☎ 0800 566 000, 03-305 0048; Waitangi; s/d from $80/100) Waitangi's social focal point, with good rooms (most with balconies and sea views) and a small souvenir shop where you can get the highly prized Chathams T-shirt. The owners also run **Travellers Rest** (☎ 0800 566 000, 03-305 0048; travellersrest@xtra.co.nz; Waitangi; s/d $110/120), which has more upmarket rooms, all with TV, phone and en suite.

There's a small **camping area** (☎ 03-305 0271; dm $20) on a family property at Owenga. You can pitch a tent (payment by *koha* or donation) or snooze in the sleepout and use the house's cooking and bathroom facilities. The friendly owners usually help arrange access to local properties.

Eating

Most places to stay offer meals. Central eating options include the **Hotel Chathams** (☎ 03-305 0048; Waitangi), with a restaurant specialising in seafood, and **Petre Bay Takeaways** (☎ 03-305 0132; Waitangi). Self-caterers will become familiar with the **Waitangi General**

Store (☎ 03-305 0041; Wharf Rd, Waitangi), which stocks a decent range of food and assorted household goods.

You can buy crayfish and blue cod at the packaging factory in Waitangi. Flounder and whitebait can be caught in the lagoon, and paua and kina gathered just offshore.

Getting There & Away
Air Chathams (☎ 03-305 0209; chatsoffice@xtra.co.nz) has services to the islands from Wellington and Christchurch (both return from $600), and can also be booked through **Air New Zealand** (☎ 0800 737 000, 03-363 0600; www.airnz.co.nz). The flight takes two hours and it's wise to book well ahead since seats are limited.

Getting Around
The airport is 21km north of Waitangi on Chatham Island and isn't serviced by any regular transport. Accommodation owners do pre-arranged airport pick-ups, usually for a fee of $10 to $20.

Air Chathams (☎ 03-305 0209; chatsoffice@xtra .co.nz) operates a light aircraft for aerial sightseeing (base charter rate $550 per hour) and transport to Pitt Island (from $360), 19km from Chatham Island. It may also be possible to hitch a ride with fishing vessels across to Pitt, but the seas in the area are very rough.

Beyond Waitangi most roads are unsealed and there's no public transport. **Chatham Motors** (☎ 03-305 0093; Reserve Rd, Waitangi) hires cars ($65 to $90 per day; airport delivery costs extra) and 4WD vehicles (from $85 per day). Prices include insurance but not kilometres, fuel or GST. Chatham Lodge, Te Matarae Farmstay and Hotel Chathams also hire out vehicles; expect to pay from $80/100 for a car/4WD.

OTHER ISLANDS

New Zealand fully or partially administers a number of outlying islands, namely the Subantarctic Islands to the south, and the Kermadecs and Tokelau in the Pacific Ocean to the north.

SUBANTARCTIC ISLANDS
The Snares, Auckland, Bounty and Antipodes Islands and Campbell Island are established nature reserves run by the Invercargill office of **DOC** (☎ 03-214 4589; www.doc.govt.nz) and can be visited only by permit. To get some idea of this wild environment, visit the Roaring 40s exhibit at Invercargill's Southland Museum & Art Gallery (p632).

The islands have a spectacularly unrewarding human history of sealing, shipwrecks and forlorn attempts at farming. But they have since discovered their true calling as a reserve for the remaining areas of vegetation unmodified by humans and as breeding grounds for sea birds, penguins and mammals such as the elephant seal. The Subantarctic Islands' remarkable wealth of birdlife led to their Unesco gazetting as a World Heritage Site in 1998, recognising their outstanding value not only to NZ but to the whole world.

Visiting these remote islands is possible via several expensive, well-managed ecotourism boat trips, which are strictly controlled by DOC.

Fiordland Ecology Holidays (☎ 03-249 6600; www .fiordland.gen.nz), based in Manapouri, is chartered for scientific trips to the Subantarctic Islands and helps fund such expeditions by selling leftover berths. Spaces on these trips are limited and there's often a long waiting list of interested casual explorers. A good level of fitness is required of those who sign up for the sail. Email or call them about upcoming possibilities.

Heritage Expeditions NZ (☎ 0800 262 8873, 03-338 9944; www.heritage-expeditions.com) has a range of lengthy, upmarket tours taking in the New Zealand and Australian subantarctic islands.

Snares Islands
The Snares Islands are famous for the incredible number of *titi* shearwaters (mutton birds) that breed there. It's been estimated that on any one evening during the breeding season (November to April), there will be five million birds in the air before they crash-land while returning to their burrows.

Other birds found here are the Snares crested penguin, cape pigeon and Buller's mollymawks.

Auckland Islands
Discovered in 1806, the Auckland Islands posed a shipwreck risk in the 19th century. Settlement was once attempted in Erebus

Cove, and it wasn't until 1992 that the last of the introduced cattle were destroyed.

Many species of birds make Enderby Island their temporary or permanent home, including endemic shags, the flightless teal and the royal albatross. Skuas (gull-like birds) are ever-present in the skies above the sea lion colony.

On Disappointment Island there are over 60,000 white-capped mollymawks.

Campbell Island

Campbell Island is the true domain of pelagic bird species. It's estimated there are over 7500 pairs of southern royal albatross based here, not to mention sizeable colonies of greyheaded and blackbrowed mollymawks. The Campbell Island teal is one of NZ's rarest birds, with perhaps only 50 to 100 remaining.

Antipodes Islands

These islands get their name from the fact that their position at latitude 180° puts them opposite latitude 0° at Greenwich, England. The real treat here is the endemic Antipodes Island parakeet, which is found with (but does not breed with) the red-crowned parakeet, a bird similar to the NZ main islands species of parakeet. Wandering albatross nest in the short grass on the islands' higher ground.

Bounty Islands

Landing is not permitted on any of the 13 Bounty Islands – there's a good chance that you would step on wildlife, as the 135 hectares of land that makes up these granite islands is soaked in mammals and birds. There are literally thousands of erect crested penguins, fulmar prions and salvins mollymawks clustered in crevices near the lower slopes and on all other available pieces of real estate.

THE KERMADECS

These islands, which have the Polynesian name Rangitahua, lie 1000km northeast of NZ and were annexed to NZ in 1887. The group consists of Raoul, McCauley and Curtis Islands, L'Esperance Rock and several other rocky outcrops. Only Raoul has water and has been settled periodically, most notably in the early 19th century when whaling was conducted here, so it has a number of

protected archaeological and historical sites. Most of the islands have boulder-strewn beaches and steep, rocky cliffs.

These islands cannot usually be reached without great difficulty and permits to do so are not readily granted because of the frequency of earthquakes and volcanic eruptions, common in this part of the Pacific's 'ring of fire'. That said, **Heritage Expeditions NZ** (☎ 0800 262 8873, 03-338 9944; www .heritage-expeditions.com) were planning a trip out this way at the time of writing.

The Kermadec Islands constitute NZ's largest marine reserve, created in 1990 and significant as a transitional zone between temperate and tropical waters. Diving is popular in the reserve, which has corals but not reefs, and an elusive goal is the rare spotted black groper.

TOKELAU
pop 1500

The trio of atolls that make up Tokelau (Atafu, Nukunonu and Fakaofo), with their tiny populations and covering only 10 sq km, lie about halfway between NZ and Hawaii. They have been administered by NZ since 1925; in more recent times, Samoa has also aided in their administration and Tokelau has steadily been moving towards self-determination and a degree of independence from Wellington.

Tokelau's small atolls cannot support a large population and there has been a steady stream of Tokelauans departing for overseas (Samoa or NZ) for many years – there are now many more Tokelauans living in NZ than on the atolls themselves. In NZ, these former atoll dwellers maintain their culture and language through various social and church groups.

Along with other low-lying Pacific nations such as Tuvalu, Kiribati and the Marshall Islands, Tokelau is at extreme risk from the effects of global warming, with rising sea levels, increased severity of storms and the death of coral reefs all frighteningly predicted for the not-too-distant future. United Nations study teams do not expect Tokelau to be inhabitable beyond the 21st century.

It's tough to visit Tokelau because there's only one cargo/passenger ship roughly every month – the MV *Tokelau*, which departs from Samoa and takes around 30 hours to reach Tokelau – and it's usually fully booked with islanders returning home from Samoa or NZ. There's no tourism to speak of and almost no established facilities for visitors, although there are a couple of places to stay and a fortnightly inter-atoll catamaran called the *Tu Tolu*.

The **Tokelau Apia Liaison Office** (TALO; ☎ 685-20822; PO Box 865, Apia), based in Samoa, deals with inquiries and issues visitors' permits (NZ$20 for one month), stipulating that consent to visit must be given by village elders, accommodation must be arranged prior to departure, and a return ticket to Samoa must be booked. Two basic (despite their names) accommodation options on Nukunonu are the **Hotel Luana Liki** (☎ 690-4140) and **Falefa Resort** (☎ 690-4137). Confirm rates with TALO; they start from around NZ$10 per person on Fakaofo and NZ$25 on Nukunonu.

Read about Tokelau online at www.tokelau.org.nz, www.nukunonu.tk and www.fakaofo.tk, and also check out Lonely Planet's *South Pacific* guide, which has a chapter on Tokelau.

DIRECTORY

Directory

CONTENTS

Accommodation	658
Business Hours	661
Children	661
Climate	662
Customs	663
Dangers & Annoyances	663
Disabled Travellers	664
Discount Cards	664
Embassies & Consulates	665
Festivals & Events	665
Food	666
Gay & Lesbian Travellers	666
Holidays	667
Insurance	667
Internet Access	667
Legal Matters	668
Maps	668
Money	669
Post	670
Shopping	671
Solo Travellers	672
Telephone	672
Time	674
Tourist Information	674
Visas	674
Women Travellers	675
Work	675

PRACTICALITIES

- Use the metric system for weights and measures
- Videos you buy or watch will be based on the PAL system
- Use a three-pin adaptor (different to British three-pin adaptors) to plug yourself into the electricity supply (230V AC, 50Hz)
- Leaf through Auckland's *New Zealand Herald*, Wellington's *Dominion Post* or Christchurch's *Press* newspapers
- Tune in to National Radio for current affairs and Concert FM for classical and jazz (see www.radionz.co.nz for frequencies), or one of the many regional or local commercial stations crowding the airwaves
- Thumb a remote to see one of the four national commercial TV stations or the subscriber television service Sky TV

ACCOMMODATION

Across New Zealand, you can tuck yourself in at night in guesthouses that creak with history, facility-laden hotels, comfortably uniform motel units, beautifully situated camp and campervan sites, and hostels that range in character from the refreshingly relaxed to the tirelessly extroverted.

The listings in this guidebook's accommodation sections are ordered from budget to mid-range to top-end options. We generally designate a place as budget accommodation if it charges up to $65 per single or $80 per double. Accommodation qualifies as mid-range if it costs roughly between $80 and $150 per double, while we've given the top-end tag to any double room costing over $150.

If you're travelling during peak tourist seasons, you'll need to book a bed well in advance. The periods when accommodation is most in demand (and at its priciest) include the summer holidays from Christmas to the end of January, Easter, and winter in snowy resort towns such as Queenstown and Wanaka. At other times of the year, you'll find that weekday rates are cheaper than weekend rates, and that special low-season rates abound. When they're not run off their feet, many hotels offer walk-in rates that are significantly reduced from their advertised rates.

Visitors centres usually have reams of information on accommodation in their areas, often in the form of folders detailing places to stay and up-to-date room prices; many can also make bookings on your behalf. Alternatively, flick through one of NZ's free, widely available and often-hefty accommodation directories, including the annual *New Zealand Accommodation Guide* published by the **Automobile Association** (AA; www.aatravel.co.nz/accom/about.shtml), the *B&B Directory of New*

Zealand (www.bed-and-breakfast.co.nz) and the *Holiday Parks & Campgrounds* and *Motels, Motor Lodges & Apartments* directories produced by **Jasons** (www.jasons.com).

B&Bs & Guesthouses

Bed and breakfast (B&B) accommodation in private homes is a growth industry in NZ, with bedrooms on offer in everything from suburban bungalows and weatherboard cottages to stately manors that have been owned by generations of one family. Location-wise, B&Bs are ubiquitous establishments, popping up in the middle of cities, rural hamlets and stretches of isolated coastline. It's an unwritten law that NZ B&B brochures must depict a dog of some description, often a vacant-eyed golden retriever.

Guesthouses are usually spartan, cheap, 'private' (unlicensed) hotels, mostly low-key places patronised by people who eschew the impersonal atmosphere of many motels. However, some are quite fancy and offer self-contained rooms.

Although breakfast is part of the deal at genuine B&B places, it may or may not feature at guesthouses. Your morning meal may be 'continental' (cereal, toast, tea or coffee), 'hearty continental' (add stuff such as yoghurt, fruit, home-baked bread or muffins), or a stomach-loading cooked meal that includes eggs, bacon, sausages and toast. Dinner is often also available, hence places with DB&B (dinner, bed and breakfast) packages.

Tariffs are typically in the $80 to $150 (per double) bracket, though some places charge upwards of $300 per double. Many upmarket B&Bs demand bookings and deposits at least a month in advance, and enforce strict and expensive cancellation policies – ie cancel within a week of your arrival date and you'll forfeit your deposit plus the balance of the room rate. Check such conditions before making a booking.

Camping & Campervan Parks

Campers and campervan drivers alike are thrown together in 'holiday parks' (previously known as motor camps) that provide powered and unpowered sites, as well as cheap bunkrooms (dorm rooms), a range of cabins, and self-contained units that are often called tourist flats. They also have well-equipped communal kitchens and din-

ing areas, and often games and TV rooms too. In cities, such parks are usually located away from the centre, but in smaller townships they can be very central or near lakes, beaches, rivers and forests.

The nightly cost of holiday park camping is usually between $10 and $12 per adult, with children charged half-price; powered sites are slightly more expensive. Prices given for camp sites, campervan sites, huts and cabins in this book are for two people. Sheltered accommodation normally ranges from $30 to $80 per double.

If you'll gladly swap facilities for wilder, less-developed locations such as national parks, head for one of the 200-plus, vehicle-accessible camping grounds managed by the **Department of Conservation** (DOC; www.doc.govt.nz). The DOC also looks after hundreds of back-country huts, most of which can only be reached on foot. For more information, see Tramping (p77).

Farmstays

Farmstays enable you to learn about the significant agricultural side of NZ life, with guests encouraged to 'have a go' at typical activities on dairy, sheep, high-country, cattle or mixed-farming spreads, as well as orchards. Costs vary widely, with B&B generally around $70 to $110. Some farms have separate cottages where you fix your own food, while others have low-cost, shared, backpacker-style accommodation.

Farm Helpers in NZ (FHINZ; www.fhinz.co.nz) produces a booklet ($25) that lists around 190 farms throughout NZ providing lodging in exchange for four to six hours work per day. **Rural Holidays NZ** (☎ 03-355 6218; www.ruralhols.co.nz) lists farmstays and homestays throughout the country on its website.

Hotels & Motels

The least-expensive form of hotel accommodation is the humble pub, which gets its name from the term 'public house'. These are older-style establishments which purvey beer and assorted social moments, but do a sideline in relatively cheap upstairs beds. Some old pubs are full of character and local characters, while some are grotty, ramshackle places that are best avoided, especially by solo women travellers. If you're considering renting a room above a pub's bar towards the end of the week, always check whether live music is scheduled for that night, or you could find yourself listening to the muted thump of a sound system until the early hours. In the cheapest pubs, singles/doubles might cost as little as $25/40 (with a shared bathroom that's probably a long trek down the hall), though $40/55 is more common.

At the other end of the hotel scale are five-star international chains, resort complexes and boutique heritage places, all of which charge a hefty premium for their mod-cons, snappy service and/or historic opulence. We quote 'rack rates' (official advertised rates) for such places throughout this book, but regular discounts and special deals mean you rarely have to pay such high rates.

There are plenty of mid-range hotels around the country that charge between $80 and $150 for their double rooms, but they face stiff competition from NZ's glut of nondescript low-rise motels, most of which have similar facilities (tea and coffee making, fridge, TV, air-con, bathroom) – the price will indicate the standard.

Hostels

NZ practically overflows with backpacker hostels, ranging from small, homestay-style affairs with a handful of beds to refurbished hotels with scuffed façades and the towering modern structures you'll find blocking the skyline in the big cities. The prices given for hostel beds throughout this guidebook are the nonmembership rates.

HOSTEL ORGANISATIONS

The biggest hostel group (and growing all the time) is **Budget Backpacker Hostels** (BBH; ☎ 03-379 3014; www.bbh.co.nz), which has around 325 hostels on its books, including homestays and farmstays. Membership costs $40 (the membership card doubles as a phonecard with $20 worth of calls) and entitles you to stay at any of the member hostels at a cost no greater than the rates advertised in the annual (free) *BBH Backpacker Accommodation* booklet. Nonmembers pay an extra fee of between $1 and $4, though not all hostel owners charge the difference. The membership card can be bought at any member hostel, or you can have it sent overseas for $45 (including postage; see the website for details). BBH rates each hostel according to traveller feedback, using a percentage figure

which supposedly tells you how good (or at least how popular) each hostel is. While the system is generally pretty accurate, our experience is that some highly rated hostels are not that great, and some low-rated places are not that bad.

VIP Backpacker Resorts (☎ 09-816 8903; www .vip.co.nz) represents over 80 hostels, particularly in the cities and major tourist spots. An advantage with VIP is that it's international, with a huge network of hostels in Australia, Southern Africa, Europe, America and some in Fiji. For $39 you'll receive a 12-month membership, entitling you to a $1 discount on accommodation. You can join online, at VIP hostels or at larger agencies dealing in backpacker travel.

Nomads Backpackers (www.nomadsworld.com) also has franchisees in NZ. Membership costs A$34 for 12 months and like VIP results in NZ$1 off the cost of nightly accommodation. You can join at participating hostels, backpacker travel agencies or online.

All of the aforementioned membership cards, including that of the YHA, also entitle the user to sundry discounts on transport, tours, activities and dining.

INDEPENDENT HOSTELS

NZ is an incubator for independent hostels, hatching them across both islands at an impressive rate. With so many places vying for the overnight attention of backpackers and other travellers, it's no surprise that these businesses try hard to differentiate themselves from their competitors. Some promote themselves purely on low-key ambience, lazy gardens, personable owners and managers and avoidance of noisy bus groups of backpackers, while others bury you in extras such as free breakfasts, free videos, spa pools, use of bikes and kayaks, shuttle buses, theme nights and tour bookings. If possible, check out your chosen place to stay before committing to a night there, to make sure the atmosphere and facilities correspond at least roughly to your expectations. If travelling with your family, note that a number of hostels designate themselves 'unsuitable for children'.

Independent backpacker establishments typically charge $19 to $25 for a dorm bed, $38 to $45 for a single and $45 to $65 for a twin or double room (usually without bathroom), with a small discount if you're a member of BBH, VIP or Nomads (see Hostel Organisations p660). Some also have space for a few tents.

If you're a Kiwi travelling in your own country, be warned that some hostels only admit overseas travellers, typically inner-city places that cite problems they've had with locals bothering their guests. If you encounter such discrimination, either try another hostel or insist that you're a genuine traveller and not a bedless neighbour.

YHA HOSTELS

NZ has over 60 Youth Hostels Association (YHA) hostels, which accommodate individuals, families and groups. The **YHA** (☎ 0800 278 299, 03-379 9970; www.stayyha.com) is part of the International Youth Hostel Federation (IYHF; also known as Hostelling International or HI), so if you're already a member of that organisation in your own country, your membership entitles you to use NZ hostels. Nightly charges are between $18 and $35 per person for members; hostels also take non-YHA members for around an extra $4 per night. Visitors to NZ should preferably purchase an HI card in their country of residence, but can also buy one at major local YHA hostels at a cost of $40 for 12 months; see the HI website for further details (www.hihostels.com). Join online, at any youth hostel or at most visitors centres.

YHA hostels provide basic accommodation in small dorms (bunk rooms, usually with four to six beds) and most also have a limited supply of single, twin, double and rooms with bathroom. They have 24-hour access, cooking facilities, a communal area with a TV, laundry facilities and, in larger hostels, travel offices. There's often a maximum-stay period (usually five to seven days). NZ YHA hostels supply all bed linen; you don't need to bring a sleeping bag.

The annual *YHA New Zealand Hostel & Discount Guide* booklet details all Kiwi hostels and the discounts (transport, activities etc) members are entitled to.

Rental Accommodation

The basic Kiwi holiday home is called a 'bach', short for 'bachelor' (and pronounced 'batch') as they were often used by single men as hunting and fishing retreats; in Canterbury and Otago they're known as 'cribs'. These are simple self-contained cottages that can be rented in rural and coastal areas, often in a soothingly private location. They can be good for longer stays in a region, although many are only available for one or two nights at a time. Prices are typically $70 to $130, which isn't bad for a whole house or self-contained bungalow.

For more-upmarket holiday houses, the current trend is to throw rusticity to the wind and erect luxury-filled cottages on beautiful nature-surrounded plots. Expect to pay anything from $120 to $400 a double.

BUSINESS HOURS

Most shops and businesses open their doors at 9am and close at 5.30pm Monday to Friday and either 12.30pm or 5pm on Saturday. Late-night shopping usually occurs on Thursday and/or Friday, when hours are extended until 9pm. Supermarkets are usually open from 9am until at least 7pm, often until 9pm or later in big towns and cities. Dairies (corner stores) and superettes (small supermarkets) close later than most other shops.

Banks normally open from 9.30am to 4.30pm Monday to Friday. Post offices are open 8.30am to 5pm Monday to Friday, with main branches also open 9.30am to 1pm Saturday; postal outlets situated in other businesses such as newsagencies may be open longer than these hours.

Restaurants are typically open until at least 9pm but tend to serve food until 11pm or later on Friday and Saturday night – the main restaurant strips in large cities keep longer hours throughout the week. Cafés can open as early as 7.30am and close around 5pm, though café-bar hybrids tend to their patrons until well into the night. Pubs usually serve food from noon to 2pm and from 6pm to 8pm. Pubs and bars often start pouring drinks at noon and stay open until late, particularly from Thursday to Saturday.

Don't count on any attractions being open on Christmas Day.

CHILDREN
Practicalities

All cities and most major towns should have centrally located public rooms where mothers (and sometimes fathers) can go to nurse their baby or change its nappy (diaper);

check with the local tourist office or city council for details.

Many motels and most holiday parks have playgrounds, fenced swimming pools, and games and video equipment. Cots, highchairs and baby baths aren't always easy to obtain at budget and mid-range accommodation, but the majority of top-end hotels will be able to supply them – the plushest places will have child-minding services. B&Bs are not usually amenable to families, as many of these businesses promote themselves as grown-up getaways where peace and quiet is valued above all else. Hostels that want to concentrate on the young backpacker demographic don't welcome kids either, but there are plenty of other hostels (including YHA affiliates) that do.

There are lots of so-called family restaurants in NZ where children can peruse their own menus. Pubs often serve kids' meals, and most cafés and restaurants (with the exception of adult-focused upmarket eateries) can handle the idea of child-sized portions.

For specialised childcare, look under 'Baby Sitters' and 'Child Care Centres' in the *Yellow Pages* telephone book, or try phoning the local council.

Child concessions (and family rates) are often available for such things as accommodation, tours, attraction entry fees and air, bus and train transport, with some discounts as high as 50% of the adult rate. However, the definition of 'child' can vary from under 12 to under 18 years; toddlers (under four years old) usually get free admission and transport.

Medical services and facilities in NZ are of a high standard, and goods such as formula and disposable nappies are widely available in urban centres. Many hire-car companies struggle with the concept of baby seats – always double-check that the company in question can supply the right size of seat for your offspring, and that the seat will be properly fitted before you pick the vehicle up.

For more information, see Lonely Planet's *Travel with Children*. Some regions are the subject of free, family-oriented information booklets, with one example being *Kidz Go!* (www.kidzgo.co.nz), which details child-friendly activities and restaurants in Queenstown and Wanaka; pick it up at local

visitors centres. Another handy site presenting information for city-bound families is www.kidsnewzealand.com.

Sights & Activities

How to keep kids occupied in NZ is not the issue. The real issue is how to keep up with them as they plead their way from one attraction and activity to the next. The free-ranging environs of national reserves and urban parkland, swathes of ocean beaches, eye-widening vistas of massive mountains and glaciers, vibrant Maori cultural shows, interactive exhibit-filled museums, high-speed jetboat rides and gold-panning jaunts are just some of the things that harness the energies and imaginations of kids across this country.

For specific ideas on how to keep your kids occupied see p20, and check out the 'For Children' text in the sections on Auckland (p109), Wellington (p394) and Christchurch (p513).

CLIMATE

NZ's location within the Roaring Forties means it gets freshened (and sometimes blasted) by relatively warm, damp winds blowing in from the Tasman Sea – Wellington is the Chicago of the southern hemisphere, getting slapped by the winds whistling through Cook Strait.

In the South Island, the Southern Alps act as a barrier for these moisture-laden easterlies, creating a wet climate on the western side of the mountains (over 7500mm annually) and a dry climate on the eastern side (about 330mm). After losing their moisture, the now-dry winds continue east, gathering heat and speed as they blow downhill and across the Canterbury Plains towards the Pacific coast; in summer this katabatic or föhn wind can be hot and fierce. In the Grey River Valley, on the South Island's West Coast, there is another kind of downhill wind called the Barber.

In the North Island, the western sides of the high volcanoes get a lot more rain than the eastern sides but the rain shadow isn't as pronounced, as the barrier here isn't as formidable as the Alps. Rainfall is more evenly distributed over this island, averaging around 1300mm annually.

Also see When to Go, p13.

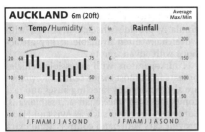

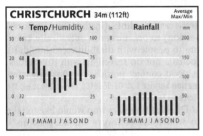

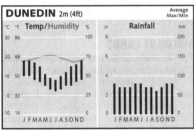

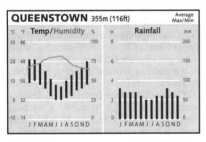

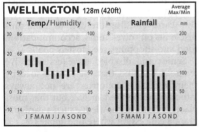

CUSTOMS

For the full story on what you can and can't bring into NZ, see the website of the **New Zealand Customs Service** (www.customs.govt.nz).

When entering New Zealand you can bring most articles in free of duty provided that Customs is satisfied they are for personal use and that you'll be taking them with you when you leave. There's also a duty-free quota per person of 1125mL of spirits or liqueur, 4.5L of wine or beer, 200 cigarettes (or 50 cigars or 250g of tobacco) and dutiable goods up to the value of $700.

Customs people are obviously fussy about drugs – declare all medicines and leave any bongs, hookahs and roach clips at home. Biosecurity is another customs buzzword, with authorities serious about keeping out any diseases that may harm the country's significant agricultural industry. Tramping gear such as boots and tents will be checked and may need to be cleaned before being allowed in; ditto golf clubs and bicycles. You must declare any plant or animal products (including anything made of wood), and food of any kind. You'll also come in for extra scrutiny if you've arrived via Africa, Southeast Asia or South America. Weapons and firearms are either prohibited or require a permit and safety testing.

DANGERS & ANNOYANCES

Though often reported in loud and salacious detail by headline-hungry broadsheets (eg the bikie gang violence that flared up several times in Wairoa in Hawkes Bay during 2003), violent crime is not common in NZ. Auckland is considered the 'crime capital' of the country, but it's very safe by most international city standards.

Theft, primarily from cars, is a major problem. Avoid leaving any valuables in a vehicle no matter where it's parked – the worst places to tempt fate are tourist parking areas and the car parks at the start of walks. If the crown jewels simply must be left behind, pack them out of sight in the boot.

Don't underestimate the risks posed by NZ's unpredictable, ever-changing maritime climate in high-altitude areas; see Tramping p77 for more information.

NZ has thankfully been spared from the proliferation of venomous creatures found in neighbouring Australia (poisonous spiders, snakes, jellyfish, Collingwood supporters

SANDFLIES *Sir Ian McKellen*

As an unpaid but enthusiastic proselytiser on behalf of all things Kiwi, including the New Zealand tourist industry, I hesitate to mention the well-kept secret of sandflies. I first met them en masse at the glorious Milford Sound, where visitors (after the most beautiful drive in the world) are met, at least during the summer, by crowds of the little buggers. There are patent unctions that cope, and tobacco repels them too, but I would hope that travellers find them an insignificant pest compared with the glory of their habitat.

Oddly, when actually filming scenes for *Lord of the Rings*, I don't recall being bothered by sandflies at all. Honestly. Had there been, we would have set the Orcs on them.

Sir Ian is a UK-based actor who spent several years in NZ filming and has become something of an unofficial ambassador for NZ tourism.

etc). Sharks exist in NZ waters but are well fed by the abundant marine life and rarely pose a threat to humans; that said, attacks on humans do occasionally occur. Much greater hazards in the ocean, however, are the rips or undertows that haunt some beaches and are capable of dragging swimmers right out to sea – take notice of any local warnings when swimming, surfing or diving.

The islands' byways are often made hazardous by speeding locals, wide-cornering campervans and traffic-ignorant sheep. Set yourself a reasonable itinerary instead of careering around the country at top speed, and try to stay alert on the road despite the distractingly beautiful scenery.

In the annoyances category, it's hard to top a sandfly visitation (see above). Equip yourself with insect repellent in coastal areas unless you're keen to imitate a whirling dervish when these little bastards start biting.

DISABLED TRAVELLERS

Kiwi accommodation generally caters fairly well for disabled travellers, with a significant number of hostels, hotels, motels and B&Bs equipped with wheelchair-accessible rooms and disabled bathrooms; rooms that are truly barrier-free, however, are few and far between. Many tourist attractions similarly provide wheelchair access, with wheelchairs often available at key attractions with advance notice.

Tour operators with accessible vehicles operate from most major centres. Key cities are also serviced by kneeling buses and taxi companies with wheelchair-accessible vans. Large car-hire firms such as Avis and Hertz provide cars with hand controls at no extra charge; advance notice is required.

The website of **Enable New Zealand** (www .enable.co.nz) has links (in the 'Kiwi Explorer' section) to organisations specifically catering to people with disabilities, although its focus is not on travelling with disabilities. A good contact point is the **Disability Information Service** (☎ 03-366 6189; dis@disinfo.co.nz; 314 Worcester St, Christchurch).

Disabled travellers who would like to take to wilderness pathways should pick up a copy of *Accessible Walks* by Anna Jameson and Andrew Jameson, which offers firsthand descriptions of over 100 South Island walks.

DISCOUNT CARDS

The **International Student Travel Confederation** (ISTC; www.istc.org) is an international collective of specialist student travel organisations, and the body behind the internationally recognised International Student Identity Card (ISIC), issued to full-time students aged 12 years and over, and giving carriers discounts on accommodation, transport and admission to various attractions. The ISTC also produces the International Youth Travel Card (IYTC or Go25), which is issued to people who are between 12 and 26 years of age and not fulltime students, and gives equivalent benefits to the ISIC. A similar ISTC brainchild is the International Teacher Identity Card (ITIC), available to teaching professionals. All three cards are chiefly available from student travel companies.

For details of hostel organisations such as YHA, BBH and VIP that issue membership cards entitling the user to numerous discounts on travel, tours, accommodation, food and shopping, see Hostels p660.

Senior and disabled travellers who live overseas will find that the cards issued by their respective countries are not always 'officially' recognised in NZ, but that most places will still acknowledge such a card and grant a concession where one applies.

EMBASSIES & CONSULATES
New Zealand Embassies & Consulates
There's a full listing of all NZ diplomatic missions overseas at www.nzembassy.com. They include:

Australia Canberra (☎ 02-6270 4211; nzhccba@austarmetro.com.au; Commonwealth Ave, Canberra, ACT 2600); Sydney (☎ 02-8256 2000; nzcgsydney@bigpond.com.au; Lvl 10, 55 Hunter St, Sydney, NSW 2000) Also in Melbourne.

Canada Ottawa (☎ 613-238 5991; info@nzhcottawa.org; Suite 727, 99 Bank St, Ottawa, Ontario K1P 6G3) Also in Vancouver and Toronto.

France Paris (☎ 01-45 01 43 43; nzembassy.paris@wanadoo.fr; 7ter, rue Léonard de Vinci, 75116 Paris)

Germany Berlin (☎ 030-206 210; nzembassy.berlin@t-online.de; Friedrichstrasse 60, 10117, Berlin) Also in Hamburg.

Ireland Dublin (☎ 01-660 4233; nzconsul@indigo.ie; 37 Leeson Park, Dublin 6) Also in Belfast.

Netherlands The Hague (☎ 070-346 93 24; nzemb@xs4all.nl; Carnegielaan 10, 2517 KH The Hague)

UK London (☎ 020-7930 8422; email@newzealandhc.org.uk; New Zealand House, 80 Haymarket, London SW1Y 4TQ)

USA Washington DC (☎ 202-328-4800; nz@nzemb.org; 37 Observatory Circle NW, Washington DC 20008); Los Angeles (☎ 310-207-1605; www.nzcgla.com; Suite 1150, 12400 Wilshire Blvd, Los Angeles, CA 90025) Also in New York.

Embassies & Consulates in New Zealand
Most principal diplomatic representations to NZ are in Wellington. Addresses of major offices include the following. Have a look in the *Yellow Pages* phone directories of main Kiwi cities for a more extensive listing.

Australia Wellington (☎ 04-473 6411; www.australia.org.nz; 72-78 Hobson St, Thorndon, Wellington)

Canada Wellington (☎ 04-473 9577; www.dfait-maeci.gc.ca/newzealand; 3rd fl, 61 Molesworth St, Wellington)

France Wellington (☎ 04-384 2555; www.ambafrance-nz.org; 34-42 Manners St, Wellington)

Germany Wellington (☎ 04-473 6063; www.deutsche botschaftwellington.co.nz; 90-92 Hobson St, Thorndon, Wellington)

Ireland Auckland (☎ 09-977 2252; consul@ireland.co.nz; 6th fl, 18 Shortland St, Auckland)

Netherlands Wellington (☎ 04-471 6390; www.neth erlandsembassy.co.nz; 10th fl, Investment Centre, cnr Featherston & Ballance Sts, Wellington)

UK Wellington (☎ 04-924 2888; www.britain.org.nz /thebhc.html; 44 Hill St, Thorndon, Wellington)

USA Wellington (☎ 04-462 6000; http://wellington.usembassy.gov; 29 Fitzherbert Tce, Thorndon, Wellington)

It's important to realise what your own embassy – the embassy of the country of which you are a citizen – can and can't do to help you if you get into trouble. Generally speaking, it won't be much help in emergencies if the trouble you're in is even remotely your own fault. Remember that while in NZ you are bound by NZ laws. Your embassy will not be sympathetic if you end up in jail after committing a crime locally, even if such actions are legal in your own country.

In genuine emergencies you might get some assistance, but only if other channels have been exhausted. For example, if you need to get home urgently, a free ticket is exceedingly unlikely – the embassy would expect you to have insurance. If you have all your money and documents stolen, it might assist with getting a new passport, but a loan for onward travel is out of the question.

FESTIVALS & EVENTS
Details of major festivals and events that take place in a single city or town are provided throughout the destination chapters of this book. The following events, however, are pursued across several cities, throughout a particular region or even around the country.

FEBRUARY
Harvest Hawke's Bay (www.harvesthawkesbay.co.nz) Appropriately indulgent wine and food celebration, with participating wineries scattered around Napier and Hastings.
NZ Masters Games (www.nzmastersgames.com) The country's biggest multisport event, held in Dunedin (even-numbered years) and Wanganui (odd-numbered years).
Waitangi Day Commemorates the signing of the Treaty of Waitangi on 6 February 1840 with various services and functions around the country.

MARCH
Twin Coast Mizone Cycle Challenge (www.twincoast -cycle.co.nz) Four-day cycling event catering to all skill levels and looping around Northland on sealed highways.

MAY
New Zealand International Comedy Festival (www.comedyfestival.co.nz) Three-week laugh-fest in venues across Auckland and Wellington.

JULY
New Zealand International Film Festival (www.enzedff.co.nz) After separate film festivals in Wellington, Auckland, Dunedin and Christchurch, a selection of flicks

takes to the road to screen themselves in major provincial towns over the next three months.

NOVEMBER & DECEMBER
Coromandel Pohutukawa Festival (www.pohutukawa fest.com) Biennial event dedicated to the conservation of the crimson, coast-dwelling pohutukawa tree, and featuring numerous concerts, exhibitions and sports events over 10 days.

FOOD

The preparation of food in NZ was once ruled by strict adherence to the *Edmond's Cookery Book*, a slavish reflection of Anglo-Saxon stodge. But nowadays the country's restaurants and cafés are adept at throwing together local staples such as lamb, beef, venison, green-lipped mussels, eels and many other island-harvested meats, and adding a dash of Asian, European and pan-Pacific culinary innovation – the end result is often referred to as Pacific Rim, a term as broad in its definition as Mediterranean or Asian.

The eateries themselves are represented by everything from butcher paper–littered fish and chip shops and no-fuss pub bistros to cafés drowned in faux-European style or artsy decoration, restaurant-bars that do full à la carte before toasting themselves with numerous late-night drinks, and fine-dining establishments where waiters always defer to your judgement (even if it's poor) and the linen is so crisp you're afraid of leaning on it in case it shatters. The website www.dineout.co.nz is worth browsing for customers' comments on NZ restaurants.

Vegetarian offerings – particularly in cities and towns with a resident food-infatuated bourgeoisie – have become quite creative, a world apart from the salad or roasted vegetable mains that used to be the norm. Urban centres and tourist-popular towns usually have at least one (often several) dedicated vegetarian cafés/restaurants, a number of them catering to vegans and those with dietary requirements such as coeliac-sufferers (advance notice is almost always required for the preparation of such meals). A good source of info is the Auckland-based **New Zealand Vegetarian Society** (☎ 09-523 4686; www.ivu.org/nzvs).

New legislation will see smoking banned in all restaurants, pubs and bars by December 2004. This edict may take a while to bed down though, so don't be surprised if smokers continue to indulge themselves in some places for a while yet.

When it comes to cities, the eating recommendations provided in this book are ordered from cafés to quick eats to restaurants. Meal prices in modern cafés (as opposed to old-style tearooms) are usually in the order of $8 to $18, while mid-range restaurants can charge as high as $25 per main. Pub meals rarely cost more than $20, and you'll often come across Sunday roasts and other bargain-basement food for less than $10.

Tipping in restaurants and cafés is widespread, but it's not expected and is only given when the service warrants it – a gratuity of between 5% and 10% of the bill is the norm.

Also see the Food & Drink chapter (p85).

GAY & LESBIAN TRAVELLERS

The gay and lesbian tourism industry in NZ is not as high-profile as in that other country across the Tasman Sea, but homosexual communities are prominent in the main cities of Auckland and Wellington, and there is a multitude of organisations throughout both islands.

The **NZ Gay & Lesbian Tourism Association** (☎ 0800 123 429, 09-917 9184; www.nzglta.org.nz) in Auckland promotes gay and lesbian tourism to NZ, while **Travel Gay New Zealand** (www.gaytravel.net.nz) is an information and reservation service covering gay destinations and accommodation. Other useful queer websites include www.gaynz.com, www.gayline.gen.nz and www.gaynz.net.nz. Several free pocket-sized booklets calling themselves the *New Zealand Gay Guide* have been published recently, one of them a quarterly produced by Pride Holdings and the other a six-monthly publication by AMA Media – at the time of writing it wasn't clear if both publications would be continued.

Gay festivals include the huge **HERO Festival** (www.gaynz.com/hero/) held every February in Auckland and the **Gay & Lesbian Fair** (www.gayfair .wellington.net.nz) staged in Wellington in March. Queenstown stages the annual mid-winter **Gay Ski Week** (www.gayskiweeknewzealand.com).

The legal minimum age for sex between consenting persons in NZ is 16.

For more information, see Gay & Lesbian Auckland (p111) and Gay & Lesbian Wellington (p395).

HOLIDAYS
Public Holidays
The following is a list of NZ's main public holidays.

New Year 1 & 2 January
Waitangi Day 6 February
Easter March/April
Anzac Day 25 April
Queen's Birthday First Monday in June
Labour Day Fourth Monday in October
Christmas Day 25 December
Boxing Day 26 December

In addition, each province in NZ has its own anniversary day holiday, a hangover from the old days when each was separately administered. The dates of provincial holidays can vary – when these holidays fall between Friday and Sunday, they are usually observed on the following Monday; if they fall between Tuesday and Thursday, they are held on the preceding Monday, enabling the great Kiwi tradition of the 'long weekend' to continue.

These holidays include the following.

Southland 17 January
Wellington 22 January
Auckland 29 January
Northland 29 January
Nelson 1 February
Otago 23 March
Taranaki 31 March
South Canterbury 25 September
Hawkes Bay 1 November
Marlborough 1 November
Chatham Islands 30 November
Westland 1 December
Canterbury 16 December

School Holidays
The Christmas holiday season, from mid-December to late January, is part of the summer school vacation – it's the time you are most likely to find transport and accommodation booked out, and long, restless queues at tourist attractions. There are three shorter school holiday periods during the year, falling roughly from mid- to late April, early to mid-July, and mid-September to early October.

INSURANCE
Don't underestimate the importance of a good travel-insurance policy covering theft, loss and medical problems; nothing will ruin your holiday plans quicker than an accident or having that brand new digital camera stolen. Most policies offer lower and higher medical-expense options; the higher ones are chiefly for countries that have extremely high medical costs, such as the USA. There is a wide variety of policies available, so compare the small print.

Some policies specifically exclude designated 'dangerous activities' such as scuba diving, parasailing, bungy jumping, whitewater rafting, motorcycling, skiing and even bushwalking. If you plan on doing any of these things (a distinct possibility in NZ), make absolutely sure that the policy you choose fully covers you for your activities of choice.

You may prefer a policy that pays doctors or hospitals direct rather than you having to pay on the spot and claim later. If you have to claim later make sure you keep all documentation. Some policies ask you to call back (reverse charges) to a centre in your home country where an immediate assessment of your problem is made. Check that the policy covers ambulances and emergency medical evacuations by air.

It's worth mentioning that under NZ law, you cannot sue for personal injury (other than exemplary damages). Rather, the country's **Accident Compensation Corporation** (ACC; www.acc.co.nz) administers an accident compensation scheme that provides accident insurance for NZ residents and temporary visitors to the country, regardless of who is at fault.

While some people cry foul of this arrangement, others point to the hugely expensive litigation 'industries' in other countries and raise a silent cheer. This scheme does not, however, cancel out the necessity for your own comprehensive travel insurance policy, as it doesn't cover you for such things as loss of income or treatment in your home country, as well as other possible eventualities such as illness.

Also see notes about medical insurance in the Health chapter (p694). For information on insurance matters relating to cars that are bought or rented, see p687.

INTERNET ACCESS
Getting connected in New Zealand is relatively simple in all but the most remote locales.

Internet Cafés

Internet cafés are usually brimming with terminals, high-speed connections and a bit of independent character in the bigger urban centres or other places where tourists sweep through in numbers. But facilities are a lot more haphazard in small, out-of-the-way towns, where a so-called Internet café could turn out to be a single terminal in an unkempt corner of a video or stationery store.

Most hostels also make an effort to hook you up, with the Internet sometimes thrown in as a freebie for guests. Many public libraries have Internet access too, but generally there are a limited number of terminals and these are provided for research needs, so not for travellers to check their emails – so head for a Internet café first.

The cost of access ranges anywhere from $2 to $10 per hour, with the lowest rates found in cities where competition and traveller numbers generate dirt-cheap prices. There's often a minimum period of access, usually in the vicinity of 10 minutes.

Free Web-based email services include **ekno** (www.ekno.lonelyplanet.com), **Yahoo** (www.yahoo.com), **MSN Hotmail** (www.hotmail.com) and **Excite** (www.excite.com).

Hooking Up

If you've brought your palmtop or notebook computer and want to get connected to a local ISP (Internet Service Provider), there are plenty of options, though some limit their dial-up areas to major cities or particular regions. Whatever enticements a particular ISP offers, make sure it has local dial-up numbers for the places where you intend to use it – the last thing you want is to be making timed long-distance calls every time you connect to the Internet. If you're based in a large city there's no problem. Major ISPs:

Clear.Net (☎ 0508 888 800; www.clear.net.nz)
CompuServe Pacific (☎ 0800 446 113; www.compuserve.com.au)
Telecom New Zealand (☎ 03-374 0253; www.telecom.co.nz)

NZ uses British BT431A and RJ-11 telephone plugs, but neither are universal – local electronics shops should be able to help. You'll also need a plug adaptor, and a universal AC adaptor will enable you to plug in without frying the innards of your machine.

A lot of mid-range accommodation and nearly all top-end hotels will have sockets, but you'll be hit with expensive call charges. In most cheaper places you'll probably find that phones are hardwired into the wall.

Keep in mind that your PC-card modem may not work in NZ. The safest option is to buy a reputable 'global' modem before you leave home or buy a local PC-card modem once you get to NZ.

For a list of useful NZ websites, see p14.

LEGAL MATTERS

Marijuana (aka 'New Zealand Green', 'electric puha' or 'dac') is widely indulged in but illegal, and anyone caught carrying this or other illicit drugs faces stiff penalties. Even if the amount of drugs is small and the fine not too onerous, a conviction will still be recorded against your name and this may affect your visa status.

Always carry your licence or IDP when driving; for more info, see p687. Drink-driving is a serious offence and remains a significant problem in NZ despite widespread campaigns and an increase in the severity of penalties. The legal blood alcohol limit is 80mg per 100mL of blood (0.08%).

If you are arrested, it's your right to consult a lawyer before any formal questioning begins.

COMING OF AGE

For the record:

- The legal age for voting in NZ is 18
- You can drive when you're 15, but you can't rent a car until you're 21
- The legal age of consent (for heterosexuals and homosexuals) is 16
- The legal drinking age is 18

MAPS

Good-quality maps are widely available in NZ, everything from street maps and road atlases to detailed topographical cartography.

The **AA** (www.aatravel.co.nz) produces excellent city, town, regional, island and highway maps, available from any of their local offices; members of affiliated overseas automobile associations will be able to obtain free maps and discounts on presentation of a membership card. The AA also produces a detailed *New Zealand Road Atlas*. Other reliable countrywide atlases, available from visitors centres and bookshops, are produced by Kiwimaps and Wises.

Land Information New Zealand (www.linz.govt.nz) publishes several exhaustive map series, including street, country and holiday maps, maps of national parks and forest parks, and handy topographical maps for trampers. You can find some of these publications in bookshops, but a better bet would be LINZ's own map-sales offices in main cities and towns; for the topo maps, try the nearest DOC office or visitors centre.

MONEY

The relatively strong NZ dollar has appreciated significantly against the US dollar and less dramatically against other prime currencies such as the euro in recent times, but over the past year or so it has nonetheless lost a little ground to the high-flying Australian dollar. See the Quick Reference section on the inside front cover for a list of exchange rates that were current just prior to publication.

New Zealand's currency is the NZ dollar, made up of 100 cents – there are 5c, 10c, 20c and 50c, $1 and $2 coins, and $5, $10, $20, $50 and $100 notes. Unless otherwise noted, all prices quoted in this book are in NZ dollars.

There are no notable restrictions on importing or exporting travellers cheques. Though not prohibited, cash amounts equal to or in excess of the equivalent of NZ$10,000 (in any currency) must be declared on arrival or departure – you'll need to fill out a Border Cash Report.

For an idea of the money required to travel around the islands, see p13.

ATMs, EFTPOS & Bank Accounts

The country's major banks, including the Bank of New Zealand, ANZ, Westpac and ASB, have 24-hour Automated Teller Machines (ATMs) attached to various branches, which accept cards from other banks and provide access to overseas accounts. You won't find ATMs everywhere, but they're widespread across both islands.

Many NZ businesses use EFTPOS (Electronic Funds Transfer At Point Of Sale), a convenient service that allows you to use your bank card (credit or debit) to pay for services or purchases direct, and often withdraw cash as well. EFTPOS is available practically everywhere these days, even in places where it's a long way between banks. Just like an ATM, you need to know your Personal Identification Number (PIN) to use it.

OPENING A BANK ACCOUNT

We've heard mixed reports on how easy it is for nonresidents to open a bank account in New Zealand. Some sources say it's as simple as flashing a few pieces of identification, providing a temporary postal address (or your permanent address) and then waiting a few days while your request is processed. Other sources say that many banks won't allow visitors to open an account with them unless they're planning to stay in NZ for at least six months, or unless the application is accompanied by some proof of employment. The websites of the banks in question are also rather vague on the services offered to short-term visitors. Needless to say, if you think you'll need to open an account, do your homework before you arrive in the country. Also be prepared to shop around to get the best banking deal – avoid banks that attempt to charge you for every imaginable transaction.

Credit & Debit Cards

Perhaps the best way to carry most of your money is within the electronic imprint of a plastic card. Credit cards such as Visa and MasterCard are widely accepted for everything from a hostel bed or a restaurant meal to a bungy jump or a bus ticket, and such cards are pretty much essential (in lieu of a large deposit) if you want to hire a car. They can also be used to get cash advances over the counter at banks and from ATMs, depending on the card, but be aware that such transactions incur immediate interest. Charge cards such as Diners Club and AmEx are not as widely accepted.

Apart from losing them, the obvious danger with credit cards is maxing out your limit and going home to a steaming pile of debt and interest charges. A safer option is a debit card with which you can draw money directly from your home bank account using ATMs, banks or EFTPOS machines around the country. Any card connected to the international banking network – Cirrus,

Maestro, Plus and Eurocard – should work, provided you know your PIN. Fees for using your card at a foreign bank or ATM vary depending on your home bank; ask before you leave.

The most flexible option is to carry both a credit and a debit card.

Moneychangers

Changing foreign currency or travellers cheques is usually no problem at banks throughout NZ or at licensed moneychangers such as Thomas Cook or American Express (AmEx) in the major cities. Moneychangers can be found in all major tourist areas, cities and airports, and conveniently tend to stay open beyond normal business hours during the week (often until 9pm).

Taxes & Refunds

The Goods and Services Tax (GST) is a flat 12.5% tax on all domestic goods and services. Prices in this book almost invariably include GST, but look out for any small print announcing that the price is GST-exclusive. There is no refund of GST paid when you leave NZ.

Travellers Cheques

Travellers cheques are a safe form of currency for short-term stays and generally enjoy a better exchange rate than foreign cash in NZ. They can also be readily replaced if they're stolen or you lose them. There is, however, a fee for buying travellers cheques (usually 1% of the total amount) and there may be fees or commissions when you exchange them. The ubiquity of debit and credit card access in this country also tend to make travellers cheques seem rather clumsy.

AmEx, Thomas Cook and other well-known international brands of travellers cheques are easily exchanged. You need to present your passport for identification when cashing them.

Fees per transaction for changing foreign-currency travellers cheques vary from bank to bank, while AmEx or Thomas Cook perform the task commission-free if you use their cheques. Private moneychangers found in the larger cities are sometimes commission free, but shop around for the best rates.

Buying travellers cheques in NZ dollars is an option worth looking at. These can be exchanged immediately at banks without

being converted from a foreign currency or incurring commissions, fees and exchange-rate fluctuations.

POST
Letters

The services offered by **New Zealand Post** (www.nzpost.co.nz) are reliable and reasonably inexpensive. Within NZ, standard post costs 45c for medium letters and postcards, and 90c for letters larger than 120mm by 235mm. FastPost promises next-day delivery between main towns and cities (longer for rural areas), and costs 90c/$1.35 for medium/large letters.

International destinations are divided into five zones: Australia (zone A); South Pacific (B); East Asia and North America (C); UK and Europe (D); and 'Rest of World' (E). Airmail postcards (up to 10g) cost $1.50 to anywhere in the world. Airmail letters (up to 200g) cost $1.50 to zones A and B, and $2 to zones C, D and E. Approximate delivery times are three to six days for zone A, three to 10 days for zone B, four to 10 days for zones C and D, and five to 10 days for zone E.

Parcels

Parcels weighing up to 1.5kg can be sent nationwide for $3.50 ($4.25 by FastPost). Large parcels weighing from 1.5kg to 25kg can be sent: up to 150km within an island for $5.95 for the first 15kg and $4 for the next 10kg; over 150km on the same island for $7.95 for the first 10kg and $4.50 for each additional 5kg; and between islands for $10.95 for the first 5kg and $9 for each additional 5kg.

International parcel zones are the same as for letters; price depends on weight and whether you send the parcel 'economy' (three to five weeks), 'air' (one to two weeks) or 'express' (within a matter of days). You can send a parcel weighing 1/2/5kg by 'economy' to Australia for $11/19/35, to North America and East Asia for $23/42/83, and to the UK and the rest of Europe for $25/47/92. To send such parcels by 'air' is roughly 20% more expensive, and by 'express' at least 50% more.

Sending & Receiving Mail

NZ post offices are generally called 'post shops' now, as most have been removed from their traditional old buildings and set up in modern shop-style premises, but we still stubbornly refer to them as post offices throughout this guidebook. You can have mail addressed to you care of 'Poste Restante, Main Post Shop' in whichever town you require. Mail is usually held for 30 days and you need to provide some form of identification (such as a passport) to collect it. For standard post office opening hours, see p661.

SHOPPING

NZ isn't one of those countries where it's necessary to buy some sort of souvenir in order to remember where you've just been – the spectacular island landscapes are mementoes in themselves, to later be plucked out of the depths of memory or the innards of a camera. But there are numerous locally crafted items you can purchase for their own unique qualities.

Clothing

The main cities of Auckland (p125), Wellington (p404) and Christchurch (p521) boast fashion-conscious sidewalk boutiques filled with the sartorial flair of young and well-established NZ designers – from the girly designs of Kristen and the leather-loving Eleanor Young, to the updated retro of Nom*D and the manly/womanly cuts of Morrison Hotel. In Auckland, head to places such as Newmarket, Ponsonby Rd and High St, while Wellington offers some retrospective mix-and-match style along Cuba St. In Christchurch, pick up new duds on Colombo, High or Cashel Sts and then show them off on self-important Oxford Tce. To see just how far New Zealanders are prepared to push the boundaries of fashionable creativity, visit the Wonderful World of Wearable Art (p445) in Nelson.

A spin-off from the backs of NZ sheep is beautiful woollen gear, particularly jumpers (sweaters) made from hand-spun, hand-dyed wool. Hand-knitted jumpers are something of a rural art form in NZ and are of the highest quality, as are other knitted goods such as hats, gloves, scarves and mufflers.

Woollen Swanndri jackets, shirts and pullovers are so well-made that they're just about the national garment in the countryside. Most common are the red-and-black or blue-and-black plaid ones. You can buy long-lasting Swanndri products (colloquially called 'Swannies') in outdoor-gear shops.

Crafts

The fine wares of NZ craftspeople can be purchased in almost every sizeable town – it appears that few (if any) places in this country are devoid of someone who's been inspired to hand-shape items for sale to passing visitors. In Christchurch head to the Arts Centre (p509), where you'll find dozens of shops and galleries selling locally designed and crafted jewellery, ceramics, glassware and accessories such as colourful silk scarves. The Nelson region (p442) is another very crafty place, heavily populated by shops and with the odd market to wander around. Ditto Devonport (p103), within striking distance of downtown Auckland and replete with galleries, and Arrowtown (p596), an artistic enclave near Queenstown.

Maori Arts

For some fine examples of Maori *whakairo rakau* (woodcarving), check out the efforts of artisans at Te Whakarewarewa cultural area in Rotorua (p318), then browse the town's large collection of Maori craft and souvenir shops; in some cases you may be able to buy direct from the artists. Carvers produce tremendous forms such as leaping dolphins, as well as the sometimes highly intricate traditional Maori carvings. Expect to pay a small fortune for high-quality work; unfortunately, you may also unwittingly pay top dollar for the poor examples of the craft that are turned out for the tourist trade and end up lining souvenir shops in Auckland.

Maori bone carvings are another fine art form undergoing something of a renaissance. Maori artisans have always made bone carvings in the shape of humans and animals, but nowadays they feed the tourist industry. Bone fish-hook pendants, carved in traditional Maori and modernised styles, are most common and worn on a thong or a chain around the neck.

One way of confirming the authenticity of any Maori-made piece is to see if it's accompanied by the trademark **toi iho** (www.toiiho.com), represented by a symbol created by a Maori arts board to identify the output of individual artists or groups of artists of Maori descent. There are also modified versions of the trademark which identify items produced by groups of 'mainly Maori' artists and via 'co-productions' between Maori and non-Maori

DIRECTORY

artists. Note, though, that not all Maori artists are registered with this scheme.

Paua

Abalone shell, called paua in NZ, is carved into some beautiful ornaments and jewellery, and is used as an inlay in many Maori carvings. Lovers of kitsch and general tackiness will find that it's also incorporated into generic souvenirs, often in the most unattractive ways. Shells are used as ashtrays in places where paua is plentiful, but it's illegal to take natural paua shells out of the country; only processed ornaments can be taken with you.

Pounamu

Maoris consider *pounamu* (greenstone, or jade or nephrite) to be a culturally invaluable raw material. It's found predominantly on the West Coast of the South Island – Maoris called the island Te Wahi Pounamu (The Place of Greenstone) or Te Wai Pounamu (The Water of Greenstone).

You're unlikely to come across any *mere* (war clubs) in contemporary greenstone studios or souvenir shops, but you will find lots of stony green incarnations of Maori motifs. One of the most popular is the *heitiki*, the name of which literally means 'hanging human form', as Tiki was the first man created and *hei* is 'to hang'. They are tiny, stylised Maori figures, usually depicted with their tongue stuck out in a warlike challenge, worn on a thong or chain around the neck. They've got great *mana* or power, but they also serve as fertility symbols. Other popular motifs are the *taniwha* (monster) and the *marakihau* (sea monster).

The best place to buy greenstone items is Hokitika (p487), which is strewn with jade workshops and gift shops. Rotorua (p326) also has its fair share of greenstone crafts. To see impressive collections of both ancient and modern pieces, visit the Otago Museum (p559) in Dunedin, Te Papa museum (p390) in Wellington, Auckland Museum (p99), and Canterbury Museum (p508) in Christchurch. Traditionally, greenstone is bought as a gift for another person, not for yourself.

SOLO TRAVELLERS

Probably due to the waves of independent travellers continually swamping NZ year-round, no one will think it unusual if you're travelling on your own. New Zealanders have also developed enough cultural confidence in recent decades to go about their own thing without being self-conscious about what visitors think of their homeland, so you'll usually find that your privacy is respected. That said, locals can be unusually loquacious once they get a head of steam up – rewarding conviviality at its best, an irritating harangue at its worst.

Women travelling on their own should exercise caution when in less-populated areas, and will find that guys can sometimes get annoyingly attentive in drinking establishments; also see p675.

TELEPHONE

Telecom New Zealand (www.telecom.co.nz) is the country's key domestic player and also has a stake in the local mobile (cell) market. The other mobile network option is **Vodafone** (www.vodafone.co.nz).

Domestic & International Calls
INFORMATION & TOLL-FREE CALLS

Numbers starting with ☎ 0900 are usually recorded information services, charging upwards of $1 per minute (more from mobiles); these numbers cannot be dialled from payphones.

Toll-free numbers in NZ have the prefix ☎ 0800 or ☎ 0508 and can be called free of charge from anywhere in the country, though they may not be accessible from certain areas or from mobile phones. Telephone numbers beginning with ☎ 0508, ☎ 0800 or ☎ 0900 cannot be dialled from outside NZ.

INTERNATIONAL CALLS

Payphones allow international calls, the cost and international dialling code of which will vary depending on which provider you're using. International calls from NZ are relatively inexpensive and subject to specials that reduce the rates even more, so it's worth shopping around – look in the *Yellow Pages* for a list of providers.

The toll-free **Country Direct service** connects callers in NZ with overseas operators to make reverse-charge (collect) or credit-card calls. Details, including Country Direct numbers, are listed in the front of telephone directories or are available from the NZ international operator. The access number varies, depending on the number of phone companies in the country you call, but is usually ☎ 000-9 (followed by the country code).

To make international calls from NZ you need to dial the international access code (☎ 00), the country code and the area code (without the initial 0). So for a London number you'd dial ☎ 00-44-20, then the number. Certain operators will have you dial a special code to access their service.

Following is a list of some country codes:

Country	International Country Code
Australia	☎ 61
Canada	☎ 1
France	☎ 33
Germany	☎ 49
Ireland	☎ 353
Netherlands	☎ 31
UK	☎ 44
USA	☎ 1

If dialling New Zealand from overseas, the country code is ☎ 64 and you need to drop the 0 (zero) in the area codes.

LOCAL CALLS

Local calls from private phones are free, while local calls from payphones cost 50c; both involve unlimited talk time. Calls to mobile phones attract higher rates and are timed.

LONG-DISTANCE CALLS & AREA CODES

For long-distance calls, NZ uses four regional area codes. National calls can be made from any payphone. The main area codes are:

Region	Area Code
Auckland	☎ 09
Bay of Plenty	☎ 07
Central Plateau	☎ 07
Coromandel	☎ 07
East Coast	☎ 06
Hawkes Bay	☎ 06
King Country	☎ 07
Manawatu	☎ 06
Northland	☎ 09
South Island	☎ 03
Taranaki	☎ 06
Waikato	☎ 07
Wanganui	☎ 06
Wellington Region	☎ 04

If you're making a local call (ie to someone else in the same town), you don't need to dial the area code. But if you're dialling within a region (even if it's to a nearby town) you do have to dial the area code, regardless of the fact that the place you're calling has the same code as the place you're dialling from. All the numbers in this book are listed with their relevant area codes.

Mobile Phones

Local mobile phone numbers are preceded by the prefix ☎ 021, ☎ 025 or ☎ 027. Mobile phone coverage is good in cities/towns and most parts of the North Island, but can be patchy away from urban centres on the South Island.

If you want to bring your own phone and go on a prepaid service using a local SIM card, Vodafone is the one. Any Vodafone shop (found in most major towns) will set you up with a SIM card and phone number (about $35, including up to $15 worth of calls), and prepaid cards can be purchased at newsagencies and shops practically anywhere. Telecom also has a prepaid system, but you must buy one of its phones to get on the network (there are no SIM cards).

Phonecards

New Zealand has a wide range of phonecards available, and these can be bought at hostels, newsagencies and post offices for a fixed dollar value (usually $5, $10, $20 and $50), to be used with any public or private phone by dialling a toll-free access number and then the PIN number on the card. It's worth shopping around, as call rates vary from company to company.

The **ekit** (www.ekit.com) global communication service provides low-cost international calls – for local calls you're usually better off with a local phonecard. ekno also offers free messaging services, email, travel information and an online travel vault, where you can securely store details of all your important documents. You can join online, where you'll find the local-access numbers for the 24-hour customer-service centre. Once you've joined, always check the ekno website for the latest access numbers for each country and updates on new features. The current dial-in numbers (toll-free), accessible anywhere in NZ, are ☎ 0800 445 108 or ☎ 0800 006 731.

TIME

Being close to the international date line, NZ is one of the first places in the world to start the new day (Pitt Island in the Chatham Islands gets the first sunrise each new year). NZ is 12 hours ahead of GMT/UTC and two hours ahead of Australian Eastern Standard Time.

In summer NZ observes daylight-saving time, where clocks are put forward by one hour on the first Sunday in October; clocks are wound back on the first Sunday of the following March.

So (excluding the effects of daylight saving) when it's noon in NZ it's 10am in Sydney, 8am in Singapore, midnight in London and 5pm the previous day in San Francisco. The Chathams are 45 minutes ahead of NZ's main islands. For more on international timing, see the map of world time zones (p697).

TOURIST INFORMATION

Even before the success of recent aggressive international marketing campaigns and the country's new-found cult status as a pseudo–Middle-earth, NZ had a highly developed tourism infrastructure busily generating mountains of brochures and booklets, plus information-packed Internet pages.

Local Tourist Offices

Almost every Kiwi city or town – whether it has any worthwhile attractions or not – seems to have a visitor information centre. The bigger centres stand united within the **i-SITE Network** (www.i-site.org), which is affiliated with Tourism New Zealand (the official national tourism body), and have trained staff, abundant information on local activities and attractions, and free brochures and maps. Staff in such centres can also act as travel agents, booking most activities, transport and accommodation. Not to be outdone, staff at smaller centres are often overwhelmingly helpful.

Bear in mind, though, that many information centres only promote accommodation and tour operators who are paying members of the local tourist association, while others are ironically hamstrung by the demands of local operators that they be represented equally – in other words, sometimes visitor centre staff aren't supposed to recommend one activity or accommodation provider

over another, a curious situation that exists in highly competitive environments such as Te Anau.

Details of local tourism offices are given in the relevant city and town sections.

Tourist Offices Abroad

Tourism New Zealand (☎ 04-917 5400; www.purenz .com; Lvl 16, 80 The Terrace, Wellington) has representatives in various countries around the world. A good place to start some pre-trip research is the commission's website, which has information in four languages (including German and Japanese). Overseas offices include:

Australia (☎ 02-8220 9000; Suite 3, Lvl 24, 1 Alfred St, Sydney, NSW 2000)

China (☎ 0852-2526 0141; 3108 China Merchants Tower, Shun Tak Centre, 168 Connaught Rd, Central, Hong Kong)

UK (☎ 020-7930 1662; New Zealand House, Haymarket, London SW1Y 4TQ)

USA (☎ 310-395-7480; Suite 300, 501 Santa Monica Blvd, Santa Monica, CA 90401)

VISAS

Visa application forms are available from NZ diplomatic missions overseas, travel agents or the website of the **New Zealand Immigration service** (NZIS; ☎ 0508 558 855; www.immigration .govt.nz). The NZIS also has over a dozen offices overseas; see the website for details.

Visitor's Visa

A visitor's visa is an endorsement in your passport allowing you to visit NZ, where (unless there's a major problem) you'll be granted a visitor's permit confirming your ability to stay in the country. These visas come with a standard validity of three months and cost around NZ$85 if processed in Australia or certain South Pacific countries such as Samoa and Fiji, and NZ$120 if processed elsewhere in the world.

Citizens of Australia do not need a visa or permit to visit NZ and can stay indefinitely (if they don't have any criminal convictions). UK citizens don't need a visa either and can stay in the country for up to six months.

Citizens of another 48 countries that have visa-waiver agreements with NZ do not require a visa for stays of up to three months, provided they can show an onward ticket, sufficient funds to support their stay (NZ$1000 per month, or NZ$400 per month if accommodation has been pre-paid), and a passport valid for three months beyond the date of their planned departure from NZ – nations in this group include Canada, France, Germany, Ireland, Japan, the Netherlands and the USA.

VISA EXTENSIONS

Visitors' visas can be extended for stays of up to nine months within one 18-month period. Some visitors, however, may be granted a further extension of three months, if they meet such criteria as proof of financial self-support or an inability to leave NZ due to circumstances beyond their control. Apply for extensions at any NZIS office.

Work Visa & Working Holiday Scheme

It's illegal for foreign nationals to work in NZ on a visitor's visa, except for Australians who can legally gain work without a visa or permit. If your primary reason for visiting NZ is to seek work (you need to be a 'bona fide applicant'), or you already have an offer of employment, you'll need to apply for a work visa, which paves the way for the granting of a work permit once you arrive – this will be valid for up to three years from the date of arrival. You can still apply for a work permit once you're in NZ, but the validity will be backdated to when you entered the country. The fee for a work visa ranges from NZ$150 to NZ$290 depending on where it's processed and the type of application.

Travellers only interested in short-term employment to supplement their travels should, if they're eligible, take part in one of NZ's Working Holiday Scheme (WHS). Under these schemes, citizens aged 18 to 30 years from 17 countries – including Canada, France, Germany, Ireland, Malaysia, the Netherlands, Sweden and the UK – can apply for a 12-month visa. It's only issued to those seeking a genuine working holiday, not for permanent work, so you're not supposed to work for one employer for more than three months.

Most eligible nationals must apply for this visa in (or from) their own country, and must be able to show an onward ticket, a passport valid for at least another three months from the date they will leave NZ and evidence of at least NZ$4200 in accessible funds. However, citizens of Canada, Malaysia, the Netherlands and Singapore

can apply once they're in NZ, so long as they have a valid visitor's permit. A limited number of visas are issued each year, so apply early if you're interested.

The application fee is NZ$120 regardless of where you apply (refunded if your application is unsuccessful). The rules differ slightly for different nationalities, so check out the relevant section of the NZIS website (www.immigration.govt.nz/Work/Working+Holiday+Schemes.htm); also see Work below for information on possible jobs and opportunities with BUNAC, through which US citizens (who aren't eligible for a WHS) can apply for a work permit.

WOMEN TRAVELLERS

NZ is generally a very safe place for women travellers, although the usual sensible precautions apply. It's best to avoid walking alone late at night in any of the major cities and towns. And if you're out on the town, always keep enough money aside for a taxi back to your accommodation. The same applies to rural towns where there may be a lot of unlit, semideserted streets between you and your temporary home. When the pubs and bars close and there are inebriated people tottering around, it's not a great time to be out and about. Lone women should also be wary of staying in basic pub accommodation unless it looks safe and well managed.

Sexual harassment is not a widely reported problem in NZ, but it does happen. Don't presume that male chauvinism or downright aggressive attitudes are the preserve of so-called rural backwaters – urban/suburban males can also be adept at making fools of themselves. Lone female hitchers will lessen the risk factor when hitching with a male companion.

Check out the following websites for more information: www.womentravel.co.nz and www.womenstravel.co.nz. See p649 for a warning about one or two Stewart Island hostels.

WORK

If you arrive in NZ on a visitor's visa, then you're not allowed to work for pay. If you're caught breaching this (or another) visa condition, you could be expelled from the country.

If you've been approved for a Working Holiday Scheme (p675), you can begin to

DIRECTORY

check out the possibilities for temporary employment. There's usually quite a bit of casual or temp work around, mainly in the fields of agriculture (fruit picking, farming etc), hospitality, ski resorts and, in Auckland at least, office-based work in IT, banking and finance, and telemarketing. Registering with an agency is your best bet for inner-city office work.

Seasonal fruit picking, thinning, pruning and harvesting is readily available short-term work for visitors. Apples, kiwi fruit and other types of fruit and vegetables are picked in summer and early autumn; pay rates are low (you can usually expect to earn between $10 and $15 each hour) and the work is hard, so the demand for workers is usually high – you're usually paid by how much you pick (per bin, bucket or kilo). The main picking season is from December to May, though there's some form of agricultural work in the country year-round. Places where you may find picking work include the Bay of Islands (Kerikeri and Paihia), rural Auckland, Tauranga, Gisborne and Hawkes Bay (Napier and Hastings) in the North Island; Nelson (Tapawera and Golden Bay), Marlborough (around Blenheim) and Central Otago (Alexandra and Roxburgh) in the South Island. Approach prospective employers directly where you can, or stay at hostels or holiday parks in the picking areas that specialise in helping travellers to find work.

The winter work available at ski resorts, or in the towns that service them, includes bar tending, waiting tables, cleaning, working on ski tows and, if you're properly qualified, ski or snowboard instructing. Have a look at the website for each resort (p71) for signs of prospective work.

There are certainly many possibilities for picking up short-term work in NZ, but finding something suitable will not always be easy, regardless of how straightforward it may look from afar on work-touting websites. Be prepared to hunt around for worthwhile opportunities, and to make your own well-being the priority if you find yourself coping with unsatisfactory conditions such as exploitative pay.

Information

Seasonal Work NZ (www.seasonalwork.co.nz) has a database of thousands of casual jobs. It gives the contact details of employers looking for workers, rates of pay and nearby accommodation.

Another worthwhile resource, specialising in temporary positions in the heartland of the South Island, is the website of **Mid Canterbury Employment** (www.amoj.staffcv.com/mce /public/login.asp).

The website of the **New Zealand Fruitgrowers Federation** (☎ 04-472 6559; www.fruitgrowers.org.nz) yields lots of info on fruit-picking possibilities, including contact details for people charged with coordinating seasonal employment opportunities in various regions.

New Zealand Job Search (☎ 09-357 3996; www .nzjobs.go.to) is a handy employment service run out of Auckland Central Backpackers.

Other hostels and backpacker publications (not to mention word of mouth) are also good sources of information for local work possibilities.

IRD Number

Tourists undertaking paid work in NZ are required to get an IRD number. Apply on the website of the **Inland Revenue Department** (www.ird.govt.nz/library/publications/irdnumber.html). The issuing of an IRD number normally takes eight to 10 working days.

Paying Tax

For the vast majority of travellers, any money they earn while working in NZ will have income tax deducted from it by their employer, a process called Pay As You Earn (PAYE). Standard NZ income tax rates are 19.5% for annual salaries up to $38,000 ($730 per week), then 33% up to $60,000 and 39% for all higher amounts. A NZ accident compensation scheme premium will also be deducted from your pay packet.

A minority of travellers may face a different tax scenario if their country has a Double Tax Agreement (DTA) with NZ, and may be entitled to a tax refund when they leave NZ. Interest earned in bank accounts may also be subject to nonresident withholding tax deductions. For information on all these scenarios, contact the **Inland Revenue Non-Resident Centre** (☎ 03-467 7020; nonres@ird.govt.nz; Private Bag 1932, Dunedin).

Organised Work
AGRIVENTURE

AgriVenture (☎ 03-359 0407; www.agriventure.com; PO Box 20113 Bishopdale, Christchurch) organises farming and horticultural exchanges for people aged 18 to 30 from Australia, North America, Europe and Japan, for stays of between four and 15 months. Visas, jobs (which are regarded as 'traineeships') and accommodation with a host family are arranged in advance and you don't necessarily need an agricultural background to apply.

BUNAC
For citizens of the USA, who are unable to take part in Working Holiday Schemes, **BUNAC** (www.bunac.com) is an alternative. Its 'Work New Zealand' programme is similar to the WHS in that American citizens aged 18 to 30 can apply for a 12-month visa that allows work and travel; see also p675. It costs US$475 to apply for the programme, which includes support such as arrival orientation, help with finding jobs, accommodation (the first two nights are included) and getting the visa in the first place. Application forms can be ordered online; the NZ scheme is very popular and books out well in advance, so get your application in early. Nationals of numerous other countries can also take part in this programme.

WWOOF
An economical way of travelling around NZ which involves doing some voluntary work is to join **Willing Workers on Organic Farms** (WWOOF; ☎ 03-544 9890; www.wwoof.co.nz; PO Box 1172, Nelson). Membership of this well-established international organisation – which has representatives in Africa, Asia, North America, Europe and Australia – provides you with a book of some 800 organic farms, permaculture farms, market gardens and other environmentally sound cottage industries throughout the country where, in exchange for daily work, the owner will provide food, accommodation and some hands-on experience in organic farming. You must contact the farm owner or manager beforehand to arrange your stay; don't turn up at a farm without warning.

Membership costs NZ$40/50 per single/double (a 'double' meaning two people travelling together) if you join within NZ; to have your book sent overseas costs NZ$45/55. It doesn't hurt to be part of a Working Holiday Scheme when you join.

For details of a similar arrangement, see p659.

Transport

CONTENTS

Getting There & Away	**678**
Entering the Country	678
Air	678
Sea	682
Getting Around	**682**
Air	682
Bicycle	684
Boat	684
Bus	685
Car & Motorcycle	687
Hitching	691
Local Transport	691
Train	691

New Zealand's peaceably isolated location in a distant patch of South Pacific Ocean is one of its drawcards, but it also means that unless you come over from Australia, you have to contend with a long-haul flight to get here. As NZ is serviced by pretty good airline and bus networks, travelling around the country is a much less taxing endeavour – unless, that is, you visit any of the outer islands (with the exception of nearby Stewart Island).

GETTING THERE & AWAY

ENTERING THE COUNTRY

Disembarkation in NZ is generally a straightforward affair, with only the usual customs declarations to endure (see Customs; p663) and the inevitable scramble to get to the luggage carousel first. However, recent global instability has resulted in conspicuously increased security in NZ airports, both in domestic and international terminals, and you may find that customs procedures are now more time-consuming. One newly introduced procedure has the Orwellian title 'Advance Passenger Screening', a system whereby documents that used to be checked after

> **THINGS CHANGE...**
> The information in this chapter is particularly vulnerable to change. Check directly with the airline or a travel agent to make sure you understand how a fare (and ticket you may buy) works and be aware of the security requirements for international travel. Shop carefully. The details given in this chapter should be regarded as pointers and are not a substitute for your own careful, up-to-date research.

you touched down in NZ (passport, visa etc) are now checked before you board the flight that will transport you there – make sure all your documentation is in order so that your check-in is as smooth as possible.

Passport

There are no restrictions when it comes to citizens of foreign countries entering NZ. If you have a visa (see p674), you should be fine.

AIR

There's a large number of competing airlines servicing NZ and thus a wide variety of air fares to choose from if you're flying in from Asia, Europe or North America, though ultimately you'll still pay a lot for a flight unless you jet in across the Tasman Sea from Australia. NZ's inordinate popularity and abundance of year-round activities (tramping in summer, skiing and snowboarding in winter) means that almost any time of year can prove to be busy for inbound tourists – if you want to fly at a particularly popular time of year (eg Christmas) then make your arrangements well in advance.

Airports & Airlines

Seven NZ airports receive and farewell international flights, with Auckland handling most of the overseas traffic. The airports are:

Auckland (☎ 0800 247 767, 09-256 8899; www.auckland -airport.co.nz; airport code AKL)

Christchurch (☎ 03-358 5029; www.christchurch-airport
.co.nz; airport code CHC)
Dunedin (☎ 03-486 2879; www.dnairport.co.nz; airport
code DUD)
Hamilton (☎ 07-843 3623; www.hamiltonairport.co.nz;
airport code HLZ)
Palmerston North (☎ 06-351 4415; www.pnairport.co
.nz; airport code PMR)
Queenstown (☎ 03-442 3505; www.queenstownairport
.co.nz; airport code ZQN)
Wellington (☎ 04-385 5100; www.wlg-airport.co.nz;
airport code WLG)

AIRLINES FLYING TO & FROM NEW ZEALAND

NZ's own overseas carrier is Air New
Zealand, which flies to runways across
Europe, North America, eastern Asia
and the Pacific. Airlines that connect NZ
with international destinations include
the following (note all phone numbers
mentioned here are for dialling from
within NZ):

Air Canada (☎ 09-379 3371; www.aircanada.ca; airline
code AC; hub Pearson International Airport, Toronto)
Air New Zealand (☎ 0800 737 000; www.airnz.co.nz;
airline code NZ; hub Auckland International Airport)
British Airways (☎ 0800 274 847; www.britishairways
.com; airline code BA; hub Heathrow Airport, London)
Cathay Pacific (☎ 0508 800 454; www.cathaypacific
.com; airline code CX; hub Hong Kong International Airport)
Emirates (☎ 0508 364 728; www.emirates.com; airline
code EK; hub Dubai International Airport)
Freedom Air (☎ 0800 600 500; www.freedomair.com;
airline code SJ; hub Auckland International Airport)
Garuda Indonesia (☎ 09-366 1862; www.garuda-indo
nesia.com; airline code GA; hub Soekarno-Hatta International
Airport, Jakarta)
Japan Airlines (☎ 09-379 9906; www.jal.com; airline
code JL; hub Narita Airport, Tokyo)
KLM (☎ 09-309 1782; www.klm.com; airline code KL;
hub Schiphol Airport, Amsterdam)
Lufthansa (☎ 09-303 1529; www.lufthansa.com; airline
code LH; hub Frankfurt Airport)
Malaysia Airlines (☎ 0800 777 747; www.malaysiaair
lines.com; airline code MH; hub Kuala Lumpur International
Airport)
Pacific Blue (☎ 0800 670 000; www.flypacificblue.com;
airline code DJ; hub Brisbane Airport)
Qantas (☎ 0800 808 767; www.qantas.com.au; airline
code QF; hub Kingsford-Smith Airport, Sydney)
Royal Brunei Airlines (☎ 09-302 1524; www.bruneiair
.com; airline code BI; hub Bandar Seri Begawan Airport)
Singapore Airlines (☎ 09-303 2129; www.singapore
air.com; airline code SQ; hub Changi International
Airport)

Thai Airways International (☎ 09-377 3886; www
.thaiairways.com; airline code TG; hub Bangkok International
Airport)
United Airlines (☎ 09-379 3800; www.unitedairlines
.com; airline code UA; hub Los Angeles International Airport)

Tickets

Generally there's nothing to be gained by
buying a ticket direct from the airline –
discounted tickets are released to selected
travel agents and specialist discount agencies, and these are usually the cheapest
deals going. An exception is booking on
the Internet, where reduced administrative
costs (ie no customer service salaries) are
often reflected in cheap fares.

Automated online ticket sales work well
if you're doing a simple one-way or return
trip on specified dates, but are no substitute
for a travel agent with the lowdown on special deals, strategies for avoiding layovers
and other useful advice.

Paying by credit card offers some protection if you unwittingly end up dealing
with a rogue fly-by-night agency in your
search for the cheapest fare, as most card
issuers provide refunds if you can prove
you didn't get what you paid for. Alternatively, buy a ticket from a bonded agent,
such as one covered by the **Air Travel Or-
ganiser's Licence** (ATOL; www.atol.org.uk) scheme
in the UK. If you have doubts about the
service provider, at the very least call the
airline and confirm that your booking has
been made.

For online bookings, start with the following websites:
Airbrokers (www.airbrokers.com) This US company
specialises in cheaper tickets. To fly LA–Tokyo–Beijing–
Shanghai–Hong Kong–Auckland–Christchurch–Sydney–
LA will cost around US$2500.
Cheap Flights (www.cheapflight.com) Very informative
site with specials, airline information and flight searches
from the USA and other regions.
Cheapest Flights (www.cheapestflights.co.uk) Cheap
worldwide flights from the UK; get in early for the
bargains.
Expedia (www.expedia.msn.com) Microsoft's travel site,
also mainly USA-related.
Flight Centre International (www.flightcentre.com)
Respected operator handling direct flights, with sites for
New Zealand, Australia, the UK, the USA and Canada.
Flights.com (www.tiss.com) Truly international site
for flight-only tickets; cheap fares and an easy-to-search
database.

Roundtheworld.com (www.roundtheworldflights.com) This excellent site allows you to build your own trips from the UK with up to six stops. A four-stop trip including Asia, Australia, New Zealand and the USA costs from £900.

STA (www.statravel.com) Prominent in world student travel but you don't have to be a student; site linked to worldwide STA sites.

Travel Online (www.travelonline.co.nz) Good place to check worldwide flights from New Zealand.

Travel.com (www.travel.com.au) Good Australian site; look up fares and flights out of and into the country.

Travelocity (www.travelocity.com) US site that allows you to search fares (in US$) from/to practically anywhere.

INTERCONTINENTAL (RTW) TICKETS

If you're flying to NZ from the other side of the world, round-the-world (RTW) tickets can be real bargains. They are generally put together by the two biggest airline alliances, **Star Alliance** (www.staralliance.com) and **Oneworld** (www.oneworldalliance.com), and give you a limited period (usually a year) in which to circumnavigate the globe. You can go anywhere the carrying airlines go, as long as you stay within the set mileage or number of stops and don't backtrack when flying between continents (backtracking is generally permitted within a single continent, though with certain restrictions – see the relevant websites for details).

An alternative type of RTW ticket is one put together by a travel agent. These are usually more expensive than airline RTW fares but allow you to devise your own itinerary.

RTW tickets start from around £850 from the UK or around US$1850 from the USA.

CIRCLE PACIFIC TICKETS

A Circle Pacific ticket is similar to a RTW ticket but covers a more limited region, using a combination of airlines to connect Australia, New Zealand, North America and Asia, with stopover options in the Pacific Islands. As with RTW tickets, there

---

are restrictions and limits as to how many stopovers you can take.

Asia

Most Asian countries offer fairly competitive air fare deals, with Bangkok, Singapore and Hong Kong being the best places to shop around for discount tickets.

Common one-way fares to Auckland are US$600 from Singapore, US$800 from Penang, Kuala Lumpur, Bangkok and Hong Kong, and US$650 from Tokyo.

Going the other way, one-way fares from Auckland to Singapore cost around NZ$1000, and around NZ$1200 to Kuala Lumpur, Bangkok, Hong Kong and Tokyo, depending on the airline.

Hong Kong's travel market can be unpredictable, but excellent bargains are sometimes available. **Phoenix Services** (☎ 2722 7378) is recommended.

STA Travel (Bangkok ☎ 02-236 0262; www.statravel.co .th; Singapore ☎ 6737 7188; www.statravel.com.sg; Tokyo ☎ 03-5391 3205; www.statravel.co.jp) has offices in numerous major cities of the region.

Australia

Air New Zealand and Qantas operate a network of flights linking key NZ cities with most major Australian gateway cities, while quite a few other international airlines include NZ and Australia on their Asia-Pacific routes.

Another trans-Tasman option is the no-frills budget airline Freedom Air, an Air New Zealand subsidiary that offers direct flights between destinations on Australia's east coast (Gold Coast, Brisbane, Sydney and Melbourne) and the NZ centres of Dunedin, Wellington, Palmerston North and Hamilton – note that not all cities are connected to each other.

In early 2004, Pacific Blue, a subsidiary of budget airline Virgin Blue, commenced flights between Christchurch and numerous Australian cities, including Perth, Hobart and Adelaide; the carrier also flies between Wellington and both Sydney and Perth.

If you book early enough, you'll rarely pay more than A$200 for a one-way fare from either Sydney or Melbourne to Auckland, Christchurch or Wellington. You can fly into Auckland and out of Christchurch to save backtracking, but you

---

> **DEPARTURE TAX**
>
> There is a departure tax of between NZ$22 and NZ$25 (depending on the airport) when leaving NZ. This tax is not included in the price of airline tickets, but must be paid separately at the airport before you board your flight.

probably won't get the cheapest fares with this itinerary.

From key NZ cities, you'll pay between NZ$220 and NZ$270 for a one-way ticket to an Australian east-coast city.

There's usually not a significant difference in price between seasons, as this is a popular route pretty much year-round. The intense trans-Tasman competition, however, inevitably results in some attractive discounting.

For reasonably priced fares, try one of the numerous Australian capital-city branches of **STA Travel** (☎ 1300 733 035; www.statravel.com.au). Another good option, also with dozens of offices around the country, is **Flight Centre** (☎ 13 31 33; www.flightcentre.com.au).

Canada

The routes flown from Canada are similar to those from mainland USA, with most Toronto and Vancouver flights stopping in one US city such as Los Angeles or Honolulu before heading on to NZ.

One-way fares out of Vancouver to Auckland cost between C$1600 and C$1900 via the US west coast. From Toronto, one-way fares cost around C$1800. One-way fares from NZ start around NZ$1500 to Toronto and NZ$1400 to Vancouver.

Canadian discount air ticket sellers are known as consolidators (although you won't see a sign on the door saying 'Consolidator') and their air fares tend to be about 10% higher than those sold in the USA. **Travel CUTS** (☎ 866-246-9762; www.travelcuts.com) is Canada's national student travel agency and has offices in all major cities.

Continental Europe

Frankfurt and London are the major arrival and departure points for flights to and from NZ, both with extensive connections to other European cities. From these two launching pads, most flights to NZ travel via one of the Asian capitals.

A good option in the Dutch travel industry is **Holland International** (☎ 0900-8858; www.hollandinternational.nl). From Amsterdam, return fares start at around €1600.

In Germany, good travel agencies include the Berlin branch of **STA Travel** (☎ 030-311 0950; www.statravel.de). Fares start at around €1100.

In France (more specifically, Paris), try **Usit Connect Voyages** (☎ 01 43 29 69 50; www.usit

connections.fr) or **OTU Voyages** (☎ 01 40 29 12 12; www.otu.fr) – both companies are student/youth specialists and have offices in many French cities. Other recommendations include **Voyageurs du Monde** (☎ 01 42 86 16 00; www.vdm.com/vdm) and **Nouvelles Frontières** (☎ 08 25 00 08 25; www.nouvellesfrontieres.fr); the details given are for offices in Paris, but again both companies have branches elsewhere. Fares from Paris start from €1200.

UK & Ireland

Depending on which airline you travel with from the UK, flights to NZ go via Asia or the USA. If you fly via Asia you can often make stopovers in countries like India, Thailand, Singapore and Australia; in the other direction, stopover possibilities include New York, Los Angeles, Honolulu or a variety of Pacific islands.

Discount air travel is big business in London. Advertisements for many travel agencies appear in the travel pages of the weekend broadsheet newspapers, in *Time Out*, the *Evening Standard* and in the free magazine *TNT*.

Typical one-way fares from London to Auckland start at around £450; note that June–July and mid-December fares can go up by as much as 30%. From NZ you can expect to pay around NZ$1600 for one-way fares to London.

Popular agencies in the UK include the ubiquitous **STA Travel** (☎ 0870 160 0599; www.statravel.co.uk), **Trailfinders** (☎ 020-7628 7628; www.trailfinders.co.uk) and **Flight Centre** (☎ 0870 499 0040; www.flightcentre.co.uk).

USA

Most flights between the North American mainland and NZ are to/from the USA's west coast, with the bulk routed through Los Angeles but some going through San Francisco. If you're coming from some other part of the USA, your travel agent should be able to arrange a discounted 'add-on' fare to get you to the city of departure.

Typically you can get a one-way ticket to NZ from the US west coast for US$1300, or from the east coast for US$1700.

One-way fares from NZ to the US west coast are around NZ$1200, and to New York NZ$1700.

As in Canada, discount travel agents in the USA are usually known as consolidators.

San Francisco is the ticket consolidator capital of America, although some good deals can be found in Los Angeles, New York and other big cities.

STA Travel (☎ 800-777 0112; www.statravel.com) has offices all over the USA.

SEA

It's possible (though by no means easy or safe) to make your way to/from Australia and smaller Pacific islands, if not further afield, by hitching rides or crewing on yachts – usually you have to at least contribute something towards food. Try asking around at harbours, marinas and yacht and sailing clubs. Popular yachting harbours in NZ include the Bay of Islands and Whangarei (both in Northland), Auckland and Wellington. March and April are the best months to look for boats heading to Australia. From Fiji, October to November is a peak departure season as cyclones are on their way.

There are no passenger liners operating to/from NZ and finding a berth on a cargo ship (much less enjoying the experience) is no easy task.

GETTING AROUND

AIR

Those who have limited time to get between NZ's attractions can make the most of a widespread network of intra- and inter-island flights.

All domestic flights are nonsmoking.

Airlines in New Zealand

The country's major domestic carrier, Air New Zealand, has an aerial network covering most of the country. It achieves this with the help of several smaller airlines (including Eagle Air and Air Nelson) that are partly owned or booked by Air New Zealand and are collectively represented under the banner Air New Zealand Link.

The next biggest carrier is regional airline Origin Pacific, which has services to most major centres (with the exception of Queenstown and Greymouth) between Auckland and Invercargill. Australia-based Qantas also maintains routes between main urban areas, mostly using other airlines' planes.

Providing essential transport services to the small outlying islands such as Great

Barrier Island in Hauraki Gulf, Stewart Island and the Chathams are several small-scale outfits.

NZ regional airlines include the following:
Air Chathams (☎ 03-305 0209; chatsoffice@xtra.co.nz) Provides two-hour flights to the remote Chatham Islands from Wellington and Christchurch.
Air New Zealand (☎ 0800 737 000; www.airnz.co.nz) Offers direct flights between main destinations in conjunction with a couple of small affiliated airlines under the banner Air New Zealand Link.
Great Barrier Airlines (☎ 0800 900 600, 09-275 9120; www.greatbarrierairlines.co.nz) Connects Great Barrier Island with Auckland, Whangarei and the Coromandel Peninsula; also flies direct between Auckland and the Coromandel (Whitianga and Matarangi).
Mountain Air (☎ 0800 222 123, 09-256 7025; www .mountainair.co.nz) Flies regularly between Auckland, Whangarei and Great Barrier Island.
Origin Pacific (☎ 0800 302 302; www.originpacific.co .nz) Flies to 10 locations across both islands.
Qantas (☎ 0800 808 767; www.qantas.co.nz) Joins the dots between nine key cities, including Auckland, Wellington, Christchurch and Queenstown.
Soundsair (☎ 0800 505 005; www.soundsair.co.nz) Hops across Cook Strait between Wellington and Picton up to 16 times per day.
Stewart Island Flights (☎ 03-218 9129; www.stewartis land flights.com) Flies between Invercargill and Stewart Island.

Air Passes

With discounting being the norm these days, air passes are generally not great value.

Air New Zealand offers an Explore New Zealand Pass for residents of other countries. Valid for all Air New Zealand/Link flights, it can be bought overseas or in NZ on presentation of an international ticket (in NZ a 12.5% GST is added).

The tickets are in the form of coupons and represent one sector (ie a single flight with just one flight number). Flights use between one and three coupons, depending on how many transfers are involved. The pass can be excellent value for long-distance, direct or through flights (eg Auckland to Dunedin), but shorter hops involving transfers make it less attractive. Passes are issued in conjunction with an international ticket (with any airline) and are valid for the life of that ticket.

The cost of passes varies according to the number of coupons involved – to purchase three/four/five/six/seven/eight coupons costs from NZ$520/690/858/1030/1210/1380.

TRANSPORT

AIR FARES

From	To	One way (from NZ$)	From	To	One way (from NZ$)
Auckland	Christchurch	90	Christchurch	Hokitika	75
Auckland	Dunedin	170	Christchurch	Invercargill	85
Auckland	Great Barrier Island	100	Christchurch	Napier	140
Auckland	Hamilton	55	Christchurch	Nelson	80
Auckland	Kaitaia	100	Christchurch	New Plymouth	130
Auckland	Kerikeri	80	Christchurch	Queenstown	120
Auckland	Napier	90	Christchurch	Rotorua	130
Auckland	Nelson	120	Wellington	Blenheim	60
Auckland	New Plymouth	95	Wellington	Chatham Is	600 (return)
Auckland	Palmerston North	85	Wellington	Christchurch	75
Auckland	Rotorua	80	Wellington	Gisborne	100
Auckland	Queenstown	150	Wellington	Dunedin	110
Auckland	Taupo	85	Wellington	Hamilton	90
Auckland	Wellington	85	Wellington	Nelson	70
Auckland	Whakatane	80	Wellington	Napier	80
Auckland	Whangarei	80	Wellington	Palmerston North	80
Christchurch	Chatham Is	600 (return)	Wellington	Rotorua	90
Christchurch	Dunedin	85	Wellington	Westport	90
Christchurch	Hamilton	135	Wellington	Whakatane	130

BUS FARES

From	To	One way (from NZ$)	From	To	One way (from NZ$)
Auckland	Hamilton	20	Paihia	Kaitaia	30
Auckland	New Plymouth	55	Picton	Kaikoura	27
Auckland	Paihia	45	Picton	Nelson	30
Auckland	Rotorua	45	Queenstown	Dunedin	30
Auckland	Taupo	55	Queenstown	Greymouth	80
Auckland	Tauranga	35	Queenstown	Invercargill	38
Auckland	Thames	20	Queenstown	Milford	70
Auckland	Wellington	90	Queenstown	Mt Cook	65
Christchurch	Dunedin	55	Queenstown	Te Anau	35
Christchurch	Greymouth	35	Queenstown	Wanaka	25
Christchurch	Kaikoura	32	Rotorua	Gisborne	50
Christchurch	Nelson	65	Rotorua	Taupo	21
Christchurch	Picton	60	Te Anau	Dunedin	45
Christchurch	Queenstown	60	Te Anau	Invercargill	40
Dunedin	Invercargill	25	Wellington	Napier	60
Nelson	Greymouth	70	Wellington	New Plymouth	70
New Plymouth	Wanganui	32	Wellington	Rotorua	80

TRAIN FARES

From	To	One way (from NZ$)	From	To	One way (from NZ$)
Auckland	Hamilton	40	Picton	Blenheim	20
Auckland	Palmerston North	120	Picton	Kaikoura	40
Auckland	Wellington	140	Picton	Christchurch	70
Christchurch	Greymouth	85	Wellington	Palmerston North	40
Kaikoura	Christchurch	40			

TRANSPORT

BICYCLE

Touring cyclists in NZ are so numerous, particularly over summer, that it's as if the Kiwis have initiated some secret breeding program for creatures with brightly coloured plumage and aerodynamic heads. The country is popular with bikers because it's clean, green, relatively uncrowded, friendly, and has lots of cheap accommodation (including camping options) and easily accessible fresh water. The roads are also good and the climate generally not too hot or too cold, except on the rain-loving west coast (particularly on the South Island). The abundant hills make for hard going at times, but there are plenty of flats and lows to accompany the highs. Bikes and cycling gear (to rent or buy) are readily available in the main centres, as are bicycle repair services.

Needless to say, the choice of itineraries is limited only by your imagination. Cycling along the extensive coastline is an obvious highlight for helmeted visitors, but the inland routes have their share of devotees. One increasingly popular expedition is to follow an upgraded path along an old railway line into the former gold-mining heartland of Otago – for details, see the boxed text (p573).

By law you must wear an approved safety helmet (or risk a fine) and it's also good to have reflective gear for cycling at night or on dull days. Cyclists who use public transport will find that major bus lines and trains only take bicycles on a 'space available' basis (meaning bikes may not be allowed on) and charge up to $10. Some of the shuttle or backpackers buses, on the other hand, make sure they always have storage space for bikes, which they carry for a reasonable surcharge.

If importing your own bike or transporting it by plane within NZ, check with the relevant airline for costs and the degree of dismantling and packing required.

Carry plenty of water to avoid the possibility of dehydration. Cycling in summer heat can be made more endurable by wearing a helmet with a peak (or a cap under your helmet) and plenty of sunscreen, not cycling in the middle of the day, and drinking lots of water (not soft drinks). It can get very cold in the mountains, so pack appropriate clothing. On the South Island, the hot katabatic or föhn wind that sweeps across the Canterbury Plains during summer can cause a lot of discomfort.

The national bicycle-promotion body is **Cycling New Zealand** (www.cyclingnz.org.nz). Lonely Planet's *Cycling New Zealand* is a comprehensive guide to two-wheel tours of the country, with detailed maps, route descriptions and elevation profiles. The *Pedallers' Paradise* booklets by Nigel Rushton cover the North and South Islands. *Classic New Zealand Mountain Bike Rides* by the Kennett brothers, Paul, Simon and Jonathan, suggests a wide variety of short and long rides all over NZ.

Hire

The rates charged by most outfits for renting road or mountain bikes – not including the discounted fees or freebies offered by accommodation places to their guests – are anywhere from $10 to $20 per hour and $20 to $35 per day.

Purchase

Bicycles can be readily bought in NZ's larger cities, but prices for newer models are high. For a decent hybrid bike or rigid mountain bike you'll pay anywhere from $700 to $1500, though you can get a cheap one for around $400 to $500 – however, then you still need to get panniers, a helmet and other essential touring gear, and the cost quickly climbs. Arguably you're better off buying a used bike (assuming you can't bring your own over), but finding something that's in good enough shape for a long road trip is not always as easy as it sounds. Other options include the post-Christmas sales and mid-year stocktakes when newish cycles can be heavily discounted.

BOAT

NZ may be an island nation but there's virtually no long-distance water transport around the country. Obvious exceptions include the boat services between Auckland and various islands in Hauraki Gulf (see p133), the interisland ferries that chug over Cook Strait between the North and South Islands – for details, see under Wellington (p405) or Picton (p424) – and the passenger ferry that negotiates the width of Foveaux Strait between Bluff and the town of Oban on Stewart Island (see p651).

BUS

Bus travel in NZ is relatively easy and well organised, with services transporting you to the far reaches of both islands (including the start/end of various walking tracks), but it can be expensive, tedious and time consuming. The bus 'terminals' in smaller places usually comprise a parking spot outside a prominent local business.

The dominant bus company is **InterCity Coachlines** (☎ 09-913 6100, 03-379 9020; www.intercity coach.co.nz), which also has an extra-comfort travel and sightseeing arm called **Newmans Coach Lines** (www.newmanscoach.co.nz). InterCity can drive you to just about anywhere on the North and South Islands, from Invercargill and Milford Sound in the south to Paihia and Kaitaia in the north.

Smaller regional operators running key routes or covering a lot of ground on the North Island include the following:

Alpine Scenic Tours (☎ 07-386 8397; www.alpines cenictours.co.nz) Has services between Turangi and the National Park, with useful stops for trampers in Tongariro National Park and extension services up to Taupo.

Go Kiwi Shuttles (☎ 0800 446 549, 07-866 0336; www .go-kiwi.co.nz) Links places like Auckland, Rotorua and Hamilton with various towns across the Coromandel Peninsula.

Northliner (☎ 09-307 5873; www.northliner.co.nz) Runs from Auckland up to Paihia in the Bay of Islands.

Waitomo Wanderer (☎ 07-349 2509; www.waitomo tours.co.nz) Does a daily loop from Rotorua to Waitomo.

White Star City to City (☎ 04-478 4734) Shuttles between Wanganui, Wellington and New Plymouth.

South Island shuttle bus companies include the following:

Abel Tasman Coachlines (☎ 03-548 0285; www.abel tasmantravel.co.nz) Runs services between Nelson and the neighbouring national parks of Kahurangi and Abel Tasman.

Alpine Coaches (☎ 0800 274 888; www.alpinecoaches .co.nz) Heads from Christchurch to Hokitika/Greymouth via Arthur's Pass.

Atomic Shuttles (☎ 03-322 8883; www.atomictravel .co.nz) Has daily services throughout the South Island, including to Christchurch, Dunedin, Invercargill, Picton, Nelson, Greymouth and Queenstown/Wanaka.

Coast to Coast (☎ 0800 800 847; coast.coast@xtra.co .nz) Travels from Christchurch to Hokitika/Greymouth via Arthur's Pass.

Cook Connection (☎ 0800 266 526, 0274-583 211; www.cookconnect.co.nz) Runs between Mt Cook and both Timaru and Oamaru several times a week.

Hanmer Connection (☎ 0800 377 378, 03-315 7575) Daily services from Hanmer to Christchurch and Kaikoura.

K Bus (☎ 03-525 9434; www.kahurangi.co.nz) Roams across the top of the South Island from Blenheim to Picton.

Knightrider (☎ 03-342 8055) Runs from Christchurch to Invercargill via Dunedin.

Lazerline (☎ 0800 220 001, 03-388 7652) Heads from Christchurch to Nelson via Lewis Pass daily.

Scenic Shuttle (☎ 0800 277 483, 03-249 7654; reservations@scenicshuttle.com) Runs between Te Anau and Invercargill via Manapouri.

South Island Connections (☎ 0508 742 669, 03-366 6633; www.southislandconnections.co.nz) Operates daily shuttles between Dunedin, Christchurch and Picton.

Southern Link Shuttles (☎ 03-358 8355; www.yellow.co.nz/site/southernlink/) Runs from Christchurch to Queenstown, Nelson, Westport and Dunedin.

Topline Tours (☎ 03-249 8059; www.toplinetours .co.nz) Connects Te Anau and Queenstown.

Wanaka Connexions (☎ 03-443 9122; www.wanaka connexions.co.nz) Links Wanaka, Queenstown, Christchurch and Dunedin.

Backpacker Buses

While the bus companies offering transport options for budget travellers in various parts of NZ are pretty much organised tours, they do also get you from A to B (usually with hop-on, hop-off services) and so can be a cost-effective alternative to the big bus companies. The buses are usually smaller, you'll meet lots of other travellers, and the drivers sometimes double as tour guides; conversely, some travellers find the tour-group mentality (which sometimes includes being stuck in 'life is a party' mode) and inherent limitations don't suit them. Discounts for card-carrying students and members of hostel organisations are regularly available.

We get lots of feedback about such companies, a real mixed bag of rave reviews and lengthy criticisms of services provided. It's a good idea to compare outfits and the deals they offer when you arrive in NZ, particularly by talking to other travellers – you're bound to see them piling out of such buses at hostels.

Prominent operators:

Bottom Bus (www.bottombus.co.nz; Dunedin ☎ 03-434 7370, Queenstown ☎ 03-442 9708) Affiliated with Kiwi Experience (see following), this hop-on, hop-off service runs a deep-south loop taking in Queenstown, Dunedin, Te Anau and Milford Sound via the Catlins, Invercargill and the Southern Scenic Route. Subroutes include Dunedin to Te Anau ($260 including Milford Sound), Dunedin to Queenstown ($410 including Milford and Stewart Island)

and the 'In a Stew' route ($499 including visits to Milford, Stewart Island and either Otago Peninsula or Te Anau Caves).

Flying Kiwi (☎ 0800 693 296, 03-547 0171; www .flyingkiwi.com) The Flying Kiwi is a tour rather than a bus service. With an emphasis on outdoor activities, its 'rolling travellers' home' includes hot showers and a kitchen and carries mountain bikes, a Canadian canoe, a windsurfer, fishing gear and more. Accommodation is camping – you can bring you own tent or hire one. There's an additional food fund and the group takes turns at cooking. South Island excursions include eight-day ($430) and 10-day ($650) trips. North Island options include nine-day comprehensive ($510) and two-day 'Northern Express' ($110) trips. The 27-day, trans-NZ 'Ultimate Explorer' costs from $1300.

Kiwi Experience (☎ 09-366 9830; www.kiwiexperience .com) The biggest of the hop-on-hop-off backpacker/tour buses, Kiwi Experience's familiar pea-green buses operate a comprehensive service around the North and South Islands. There are 18 routes, and most passes are valid for one year. Trips include: 'Northern Roundup' ($340, eight-day minimum); 'Southern Roundup' ($400, 10-day minimum); all-NZ tours ($540 to $930, from 10 to 23 days); and the 'Full Monty' trip ($1540, minimum 31 days in summer and 38 days in winter). Useful small loops where other services are limited include the 'Awesome & Top Bit' route around Northland, the 'Southlander' (run by Bottom Bus) through the Catlins and along the Southern Scenic Route, 'East Cape Escape' and 'Milford Overland'.

Magic Travellers Network (☎ 09-358 5600; www .magicbus.co.nz) Magic Bus is another hop-on, hop-off bus operating an extensive network on the North and South Islands, with 16 main trips from a minimum of four days. Trips range from the basic 'Top of the North' ($210) or 'Top of the South' ($290) to the countrywide 'Spirit of NZ' (minimum 23 days) for $1110.

Bus Passes

InterCity offers numerous bus passes, either covering the whole country, or the North and South Islands separately. If you're planning to cover a lot of ground, the passes can work out cheaper than paying as you go, but they lock you into using InterCity buses (rather than, say, the convenient shuttle buses that cover much of the country). There's a 15% discount for members of YHA (Youth Hostels Association) and VIP.

Northliner offers discount backpackers passes for Northland.

INTERCITY

The appropriately named **Flexi-Pass** (www.flexi pass. co.nz) is valid for one year and allows you to travel pretty much anywhere (and in any direction) on the InterCity network;

you can get on and off wherever you like and can change bookings up to two hours before departure without penalty. The pass is purchased in five-hour blocks of travel time, from a minimum of 15 hours ($150) up to a maximum of 60 hours ($540) – the average cost of each block becomes cheaper the more hours you buy. You can top up the pass if you need more time.

InterCity offers a range of other passes tailored to travel on each island and across the country, most with a maximum life of three months. North Island passes include: 'Coromandel Loop' (adult/child $55/36), allowing travel from Thames to Whitianga and Tairua, then back to Thames; 'Coromandel Trail' (adult/child $90/60), starting from Auckland and heading to Rotorua via the Coromandel Peninsula; and 'Forests, Islands and Geysers' (adult/child $350/240), combining parts of Northland with flights to Great Barrier Island and Whitianga.

South Island passes include: 'West Coast Passport' (adult/child $150/100), which allows travel from Picton to Queenstown via the West Coast; 'Milford Sound Adventurer' (adult/child $180/120), going from Christchurch to Milford via Queenstown and Mt Cook; and 'South Island Extreme' (adult/child $470/320), allowing a loop from Picton to Picton or Christchurch to Christchurch.

There may be a reservation charge of $3 per sector (depending on the agent), or you can check to see if stand-by seats are available.

Dual-island passes include: 'Pathfinder' (adult/child $540/360), taking you from Auckland to Christchurch or vice versa, including along the South Island's West Coast and to Milford Sound; 'Trail Blazer' (adult/child $560/380), describing a loop that starts/finishes at Auckland; and 'Total New Zealand Experience' (adult/child $680/ 460), the kitchen sink of coach passes.

For details of a pass combining travel on InterCity coaches, Tranz Scenic trains and Interisland ferries, see Train Passes (p692) later in this chapter.

NORTHLINER

Northliner offers card-carrying backpackers (YHA, VIP, BBH and Nomads; for details of these organisations see p660) various passes enabling unlimited travel on different routes.

The 'Bay of Islands' ($55), 'Loop' ($85) and 'Northland Freedom' ($115) passes are all valid for one month from date of purchase, while the 'Top Half' ($80) pass is valid for two months.

Classes

There are no separate classes on buses and smoking is not permitted.

Reservations

Over summer, school holidays and public holidays, you should book well ahead on the more popular routes. At other times you should have few problems getting on to your preferred service. But if your long-term travel plans rely on catching a particular bus, book at least a day or two ahead just to be safe.

Intercity fares vary widely according to how far ahead they're booked and their availability, and the best prices are generally obtained a few weeks in advance.

CAR & MOTORCYCLE

The best way to explore NZ in depth is to have your own transport, as it allows you to create your own leisurely, flexible itinerary. Good-value car- and campervan-hire rates are not hard to track down; alternatively, consider buying your own set of wheels. If you're tempted to bring your own motorcycle into the country, be aware that this will entail an expensive shipping exercise, valid registration in the country of origin and a *Carnet De Passages en Douanes*; you'll also need a rider's licence and a helmet.

Automobile Association (AA)

New Zealand's **Automobile Association** (AA; ☎ 0800 500 444; www.aa.co.nz) provides emergency breakdown services, Kiwi literature, excellent touring maps and detailed guides to accommodation (from holiday parks to motels and B&Bs). It also maintains links with similar bodies throughout the world, so if you're a member of an affiliated organisation in your home country, bring proof of membership with you.

Driving Licence

International visitors to NZ can use their home-country's driving licence – if your

NORTH ISLAND ROAD DISTANCES (KM)

	Auckland	Cape Reinga	Dargaville	Gisborne	Hamilton	Hicks Bay	Kaitaia	Napier	New Plymouth	Paihia	Palmerston North	Rotorua	Taupo	Tauranga	Thames	Waitomo Caves	Wanganui	Wellington	Whakatane	Whangarei
Auckland	---																			
Cape Reinga	440	---																		
Dargaville	185	285	---																	
Gisborne	511	943	690	---																
Hamilton	127	566	312	399	---															
Hicks Bay	513	946	691	180	400	---														
Kaitaia	325	114	169	831	450	833	---													
Napier	421	861	606	215	252	395	748	---												
New Plymouth	371	789	554	585	242	590	699	413	---											
Paihia	241	220	130	750	368	748	109	664	597	---										
Palmerston North	531	969	541	390	402	574	853	176	236	779	---									
Rotorua	235	672	420	292	109	290	560	229	299	475	341	---								
Taupo	280	720	466	333	153	373	604	147	300	520	259	82	---							
Tauranga	210	645	390	300	108	302	537	300	306	447	424	83	165	---						
Thames	115	555	300	413	106	416	440	349	348	356	470	167	211	114	---					
Waitomo Caves	198	640	390	437	75	441	526	307	183	443	341	166	166	151	182	---				
Wanganui	454	893	640	466	329	644	780	250	163	706	74	307	225	440	479	268	---			
Wellington	666	1105	845	534	521	720	970	319	356	970	143	460	378	543	591	463	193	---		
Whakatane	301	740	487	206	195	204	630	315	354	550	421	86	168	94	208	239	358	545	---	
Whangarei	170	270	58	668	295	678	154	597	526	71	697	406	450	381	286	372	625	820	476	---

TRANSPORT

TRANSPORT

SOUTH ISLAND ROAD DISTANCES (KM)

	Aoraki/Mt Cook	Arthur's Pass	Blenheim	Christchurch	Dunedin	Franz Josef Glacier	Greymouth	Hanmer Springs	Hokitika	Invercargill	Kaikoura	Milford Sound	Nelson	Oamaru	Picton	Queenstown	Te Anau	Timaru	Wanaka	Westport
Aoraki/Mt Cook	---																			
Arthur's Pass	408	---																		
Blenheim	640	420	---																	
Christchurch	330	149	308	---																
Dunedin	331	478	674	360	---															
Franz Josef Glacier	493	248	486	395	562	---														
Greymouth	510	99	333	258	551	181	---													
Hanmer Springs	466	264	260	135	495	395	214	---												
Hokitika	530	104	370	260	570	140	41	256	---											
Invercargill	449	694	888	578	217	575	769	714	690	---										
Kaikoura	518	337	132	187	545	550	338	133	420	767	---									
Milford Sound	550	922	1075	768	410	678	860	910	810	280	960	---								
Nelson	744	384	117	418	786	470	290	305	334	1018	250	1145	---							
Oamaru	215	334	556	247	114	506	448	380	456	330	436	524	671	---						
Picton	667	458	29	336	701	531	360	300	400	918	160	1121	114	583	---					
Queenstown	271	645	794	489	280	404	583	620	513	190	676	291	693	321	822	---				
Te Anau	434	798	960	650	289	560	732	785	690	158	840	122	1025	410	988	168	---			
Timaru	212	470	162	200	492	352	300	365	417	351	610	588	85	499	336	486		---		
Wanaka	214	528	745	424	276	285	469	560	426	285	612	394	588	234	774	119	273	280	---	
Westport	666	200	266	334	695	280	102	218	145	869	340	958	230	580	292	659	828	497	592	---

licence isn't in English, it's a good idea to carry a certified translation with you. Alternatively, use an International Driving Permit (IDP), which will usually be issued on the spot (valid for 12 months) by your home country's automobile association.

Members of foreign automobile associations should bring their membership cards, as many of these bodies have reciprocal agreements with New Zealand's AA.

Fuel

Fuel (super, diesel and unleaded) is available from service stations with the well-known international brand names. LPG (gas) is not always stocked by rural suppliers; if you're on gas it's safer to have dual fuel capability. Prices vary from place to place, but basically petrol (gasoline) isn't pumped cheaply in NZ, with per-litre costs averaging around $1.05. More-remote destinations may charge a smallish fortune to fill your tank and you're better off getting fuel before you reach them – places in this category include Milford Sound (fill up at Te Anau) and Mt Cook (buy fuel at Twizel or Lake Tekapo).

Hire

CAMPERVAN

Campervans (also known as mobile homes, motor homes or RVs) are an enormously popular form of transport for those doing slow-paced tours of NZ, so popular that in well-trafficked parts of the South Island during peak tourist season you can feel socially inadequate if you're driving anything else.

You can hire campervans from an assortment of companies for an assortment of prices, depending on the time of year and how big you want your home-on-wheels to be. **Maui** (☎ 0800 651 080, 09-275 3013; www.maui.co.nz) and **Britz** (☎ 0800 831 900, 09-275 9090; www.britz.co.nz) are two of the biggest operators. Other (cheaper) operators include **Kea Campers** (☎ 09-441 7833; www.kea.co.nz), **Auto Rentals** (☎ 0800 736 893, 03-371 7343; www.autorentals.co.nz) and the budget **Backpacker Campervans** (☎ 0800 422 267, 09-275 0200; www.backpackercampervans.com).

A small van suitable for two people typically has a well-equipped mini-kitchen and fold-out dining table, the latter transforms into a double bed when mealtime is over.

Four- to six-berth campervans are the size of light trucks (and similarly sluggish) and besides the extra space usually contain a toilet and shower.

Over summer, rates offered by the main rental firms for two-/four-/six-berth vans are usually around $200/250/280 per day, dropping to as low as $60/75/90 in winter; industry in-fighting often sees even lower rates. Smaller operators' rates start at around $40 per day for kitted-out minivans.

CAR
Competition between car-rental companies in NZ is pretty fierce, so rates tend to be variable and lots of special deals come and go; car rental is most competitive in Auckland, Christchurch, Wellington and Picton. The main thing to remember when assessing your options is distance – if you want to travel far, you need unlimited kilometres. You need to be at least 21 years old to hire a vehicle.

Some sizeable companies include **Budget** (☎ 0800 652 227; www.budget.co.nz), **Hertz** (☎ 0800 654 321; www.hertz.co.nz), **Thrifty** (☎ 09-256 1405; www.thrifty.com) and **Avis** (☎ 09-275 7239; www.avis.com), which all have offices or agents in most major cities and towns. There's a vast number of local firms, or firms with outlets in a limited number of locations, which we detail throughout this guide. These are almost always cheaper than the big operators – sometimes half the price – but the cheapest car hire often comes with serious restrictions. Some less-expensive operators have national networks, including the highly recommended **Omega Rental Cars** (☎ 0800 525 210; www.omegarental.com), as well as **Pegasus** (☎ 0800 803 580; www.rentalcars.co.nz) and **Shoestring** (☎ 0800 808 708; http://carhire.co.nz /shoestring/).

The big firms sometimes offer one-way rentals (eg pick up a car in Auckland and leave it in Christchurch) but there are a variety of restrictions and sometimes a substantial drop-off fee may apply if you're not returning the car to the city of hire; however, on rental of a month or more this should be waived between Auckland and Wellington or Christchurch. On the other hand, an operator in Christchurch may need to get a vehicle back to Auckland and will offer an amazing one-way deal (Budget is one company that lists relocation specials on their website).

Some car-hire firms will not allow you to take their vehicles on the ferries that cross Cook Strait. Instead, you drop your car off at either the Wellington or Picton terminal and pick up another car once you've crossed the strait.

The major companies offer a choice of either unlimited kilometres, or 100km or so a day free plus so many cents per kilometre over this. Daily rates in main cities typically start around $75 per day for a compact, late-model, Japanese car, and around $90 for medium-sized cars (including GST, unlimited kilometres and insurance). It's obviously cheaper if you rent for a week or more and there are often low-season and weekend discounts. Credit cards are the usual payment method.

MOTORCYCLE
NZ has great terrain for motorcycle touring, despite the changeable weather in parts of the islands. Most of the country's motorcycle-hire shops are in Auckland and Christchurch, where you can hire anything from a little 50cc moped (nifty-fifty) for zipping around town to a big 750cc touring motorcycle and beyond.

New Zealand Motorcycle Rentals (Auckland ☎ 09-377 2005, Christchurch ☎ 03-377 0663; www.nzbike.com) rents out Yamahas, BMWs, touring and enduro bikes from $80 to $240 a day (as low as $60 per day for rentals of the less-powerful bikes for three weeks or more). You can also climb on a Harley 1450cc for $340 per day. High-powered sports bikes are also available to riders over 30 years of age; there's a minimum rental of six days for these bikes.

Insurance
When it comes to renting a vehicle, know exactly what your liability is in the event of an accident. Rather than risk paying out a large amount of cash if you do have an accident (minor bingles are common in NZ), you can take out your own comprehensive insurance policy, or (the usual option) pay an additional daily amount to the rental company for an 'insurance excess reduction' policy. This brings the amount of excess you must pay in the event of an accident down from around $1500 or $2000 to around $150 or $200. Smaller operators offering cheap rates often have

a compulsory insurance excess, taken as a credit-card bond, of around $900.

Most insurance agreements won't cover the cost of damage to glass (including the windscreen) or tyres, and insurance coverage is often invalidated on beaches and certain rough (4WD) unsealed roads, so always read the small print.

Purchase

For a longer stay and/or for groups, buying a car and then selling it at the end of your travels can be one of the cheapest and best ways to see NZ. You can often pick up a car as cheap as (or cheaper than) a one- or two-month rental, and you should be able to get back most of your money when you sell it. The danger, of course, is that you'll buy a lemon and it will break down every five minutes.

Auckland is the easiest place for travellers to buy a car, followed by Christchurch. An easy option for a cheap car is to scour the notice boards of backpacker places, where other travellers sell their cars before moving on; you can pick up an old car for only a few hundred dollars. Some backpackers specials are so cheap it may be worth taking the risk that they will finally die on you. Besides, these vehicles often come complete with water containers, tools, road maps and even camping gear.

Car markets and car auctions are also worth investigating. There are two weekly car markets/fairs in Auckland, the Canterbury Car Fair (held on Sunday morning) in Christchurch and a smaller market, the Cable St Car Fair (held on Saturday morning) in central Wellington.

At auctions you can pick up cheap cars from around $1000 to $4500, but you don't have the luxury of a test drive – **Turners Auctions** (☎ 0800 282 8466, 04-587 1400; www.turners.co.nz) is the country's largest such outfit with 11 locations. For details of all the aforementioned places, see the Getting There & Away sections under Auckland (p127), Wellington (p406) and Christchurch (p523).

Make sure any car you buy has a WoF (Warrant of Fitness) and that the registration lasts for a reasonable period. A WoF certificate, proving that the car is roadworthy, is valid for six months but must be less than 28 days old when you buy a car. To transfer registration, both you and the seller fill out a form which can be filed at any post office. Papers are sent by mail within 10 days. It is the seller's responsibility to transfer ownership and pay the costs involved. If needed, registration can be purchased for three months ($60), six months ($115) or a year ($220). Third-party insurance, covering the cost of repairs to another vehicle in an accident that is your fault, is also a wise investment.

Car inspections are highly recommended as they'll protect you against any dodgy WoFs (such scams have been reported in the past) and may well save you a lot of money in repair bills later. Various car inspection services will check any car you intend to buy for less than $100. They stand by at car fairs and auctions for on-the-spot inspections, or will come to you. The AA also offers a mobile inspection service – it's slightly cheaper if you bring the car to an AA-approved mechanic. AA checks are thorough, but most garages will look over the car for less.

It's wise before you buy a car to confirm the ownership of the vehicle, and find out if there are any outstanding debts on it, by registering with the online **Personal Properties Securities** (www.ppsr.govt.nz) and conducting a search; searches cost $3 and are done using the Vehicle Identification Number (VIN; found on a plate near the engine block), licence plate or chassis number.

If you don't have your own motorcycle but do have a little bit of time up your sleeve, getting mobile on two wheels in NZ is quite feasible. The beginning of winter (June) is quite a good time to start looking. Regional newspapers and the local bike press have classified advertisement sections. The main drawback of buying a bike is obviously that you'll have to try to sell it again afterwards.

BUY-BACK DEALS

One way of getting around the hassles of buying and selling a vehicle privately is to enter into a buy-back arrangement with a car or motorcycle dealer. However, dealers may find ways of knocking down the price when you return the vehicle (even if it was agreed to in writing), often by pointing out expensive repairs that allegedly will be required to gain the WoF certificate needed to transfer the registration. The buy-back amount varies, but may be 50% less than the purchase price – in a strictly financial sense, hiring or buying ınd selling the vehicle yourself (if you have he time) is usually much better value.

Road Hazards

The full spectrum of drivers and driving 1abits is represented on NZ roads, from the 10-fuss motorist who doesn't mind pulling)ver to let you past, to back-roads tailgaters vho believe they know a particular stretch)f bitumen so well that they can go as fast ıs they like – and this despite narrow, twistng roads. Traffic is usually pretty light, but t's easy to get stuck behind a slow-moving truck or campervan on uphill climbs, so)ring plenty of patience with you for your time on the road. There are also lots of gravel)r dirt roads to explore, which require a very different driving approach from sealed roads.

Road Rules

Kiwis drive on the left-hand side of the road and all cars are right-hand drive. A 'give way to the right' rule applies and is interpreted to a rather strange extreme here – if you're turning left and an oncoming vehicle is turning right into the same street, you have to give way to it.

Speed limits on the open road are generally 100km/h; in built-up areas the limit is usually 50km/h. An 'LSZ' sign stands for 'Limited Speed Zone', which means that the speed limit is 50km/h (although the speed limit in that zone is normally 100km/h) when conditions are unsafe due to bad weather, limited visibility, pedestrians, cyclists or animals on the road, excessive traffic, or poor road conditions. Speed cameras and radars are used extensively. At single-lane bridges (of which there are a surprisingly large number), a smaller red arrow pointing in your direction of travel means that *you* give way, so slow down as you approach and pull a little to the side if you see a car approaching the bridge from the other end.

All new cars in NZ have seat belts back and front and it's the law to wear yours – you're risking a fine if you don't. Small children must be belted into an approved safety seat.

Buy a copy of the *New Zealand Road Code*, a wise investment that will tell you all you need to know about life on the road. Versions applicable to both cars and motorcycles are available at AA offices and bookshops, or check the online rundown of road rules on the website of the **Land Transport Safety Authority** (www.ltsa.govt.nz/roadcode /index.html).

HITCHING

Hitching is never entirely safe in any country in the world, and we don't recommend it. Travellers who decide to hitch should understand that they are taking a small but potentially serious risk. People who do choose to hitch will be safer if they travel in pairs and let someone know where they are planning to go.

LOCAL TRANSPORT
Bus, Train & Tram

Most of NZ's urban buses have been privatised. Larger cities have fairly extensive bus services but, with a few honourable exceptions, they are mainly daytime, weekday operations; on weekends, particularly on Sunday, bus services can be hard to find or may stop altogether. Negotiating the inner-city area in Auckland is made easier by the Link and City Circuit buses, and in Christchurch by The Shuttle bus service and the historic Tramway. Most main cities have a late-night bus service roaming central entertainment districts on social, end-of-week nights.

The only city with a decent train service is Wellington, comprising four suburban routes.

Taxi

The main cities have plenty of taxis and even small towns may have a local service. Taxis cruise the busy areas in Auckland, Wellington and Christchurch, but elsewhere you usually either have to phone for one or go to a taxi rank.

TRAIN

In NZ you travel on the train for the journey, not in order to get anywhere (with the exception of the single commuter service detailed below). The company **Tranz Scenic** (☎ 0800 872 467, 04-495 0775; www.tranzscenic.co.nz) operates several visually stunning routes, namely the *Overlander/Northener* between Auckland and Wellington (the *Northener* does the route overnight), the *TranzCoastal* between Christchurch and Picton, and the *TranzAlpine* which rattles over the Southern Alps between Christchurch and Greymouth.

TRANSPORT

It also operates the weekday *Capital Connection* commuter service between Palmerston North and Wellington.

Reservations can be made by contacting Tranz Scenic and at most train stations, travel agents and visitor centres, where you can also pick up booklets detailing timetables. A variety of discount and concession fares are available for purchase within NZ, usually available during off-peak periods only – these include discounts of between 30% and 50% off standard fares for a seat in a 'backpacker carriage', which has smaller viewing windows than other carriages.

Train Passes
Tranz Scenic's **Best of New Zealand Pass** (☎ 0800 692 378; www.bestpass.co.nz), offered in conjunc-

tion with several coach and ferry operators, enables you to undertake a variety of land and sea trips throughout NZ – if you plan your itinerary well enough, you could save as much as 30% on the cost of booking each bus, train or ferry leg independently. Valid for six months, the pass works on a points system, with each leg of your trip 'costing' you a certain number of points. You can buy 600 points for $500/340 per adult/child, 800 points costs $650/440 and 1000 points costs $790/530; you can top-up points when you need them (100 extra points costs $85/60 per adult/child). A 1000-point trip could include Auckland to Wellington by train and coach, the *Interislander*, and a fair whack of the South Island by train (including the *TranzAlpine*) and coach.

Health Dr David Millar

CONTENTS

Before You Go	**693**
Insurance	693
Recommended Vaccinations	693
Medical Checklist	693
Internet Resources	694
In Transit	**694**
Deep Vein Thrombosis (DVT)	694
Jet Lag & Motion Sickness	694
In New Zealand	**694**
Availability & Cost of Health Care	694
Infectious Diseases	695
Traveller's Diarrhoea	695
Environmental Hazards	695

New Zealand is one of the healthiest countries in the world in which to travel. The risk of diseases such as malaria and typhoid are unheard of, and thanks to NZ's quarantine standards, even some animal diseases such as rabies have yet to be recorded. The absence of poisonous snakes or other dangerous animals makes this a very safe region to get off the beaten track and out into the beautiful countryside.

BEFORE YOU GO

Since most vaccines don't produce immunity until at least two weeks after they're given, visit a physician four to eight weeks before departure. Ask your doctor for an International Certificate of Vaccination (otherwise known as the yellow booklet), which will list all the vaccinations you've received. This is mandatory for countries that require proof of yellow fever vaccination upon entry, but it's a good idea to carry it wherever you travel.

Bring medications in their original, clearly labelled containers. A signed and dated letter from your physician describing your medical conditions and medications, including generic names, is also a good idea. If carrying syringes or needles, be sure to have a physician's letter documenting their medical necessity.

INSURANCE

If your health insurance doesn't cover you for medical expenses abroad, you should consider getting extra insurance – check out the Subwwway section of the **Lonely Planet website** (www.lonelyplanet.com/subwwway) for more information. Find out in advance if your insurance plan will make payments directly to providers or reimburse you later for overseas health expenditures. (In many countries doctors expect payment in cash.)

RECOMMENDED VACCINATIONS

NZ has no vaccination requirements for any traveller. The World Health Organization recommends that all travellers should be covered for diphtheria, tetanus, measles, mumps, rubella, chickenpox and polio, as well as hepatitis B, regardless of their destination. Planning to travel is a great time to ensure that all routine vaccination cover is complete. The consequences of these diseases can be severe and while NZ has high levels of childhood vaccination coverage, outbreaks of these diseases do occur.

MEDICAL CHECKLIST

- acetaminophen/paracetamol (Tylenol/Panadol) or aspirin
- adhesive or paper tape
- antibacterial ointment (eg Bactroban) for cuts and abrasions
- antibiotics
- antidiarrhoeal drugs (eg loperamide)
- antihistamines for hay fever and allergic reactions
- anti-inflammatory drugs (eg ibuprofen)
- bandages, gauze, gauze rolls
- DEET-containing insect repellent for the skin
- iodine tablets or water filter for water purification
- oral rehydration salts
- permethrin-containing insect spray for clothing, tents and bed nets
- pocketknife
- scissors, safety pins, tweezers
- steroid cream or cortisone for poison ivy and other allergic rashes
- sun block
- thermometer

INTERNET RESOURCES

You'll find that there's a wealth of travel health advice on the Internet. For further information on health, the **Lonely Planet website** (www.lonelyplanet.com) is a good place to start. The **World Health Organization** (www.who.int/ith/) publishes an excellent book called *International Travel and Health*, which is revised annually and is available online at no cost. Another good website of general interest is **MD Travel Health** (www.mdtravelhealth.com), which provides complete travel health recommendations for every country and is updated daily.

IN TRANSIT

DEEP VEIN THROMBOSIS (DVT)

Blood clots may form in the legs during plane flights, chiefly because of a prolonged period of immobility. The longer the flight, the greater the risk. The chief symptom of Deep Vein Thrombosis (DVT) is swelling or pain of the foot, ankle or calf, usually – but not always – on just one side. When a blood clot travels to the lungs, it may result in chest pain and difficulty breathing. Travellers with any of these symptoms should seek medical attention immediately.

To prevent the development of DVT on long flights, you should walk about the cabin, perform compressions of the leg muscles (ie flex the leg muscles while sitting), drink plenty of fluids and avoid alcohol and tobacco.

JET LAG & MOTION SICKNESS

Jet lag is common when crossing more than five time zones, resulting in insomnia, fatigue, malaise and/or nausea. To avoid the effects of jet lag, try drinking plenty of nonalcoholic fluids and eating light meals. Upon arrival to your destination, get exposure to natural sunlight and readjust your schedule (for meals, sleep etc) as soon as possible.

Antihistamines such as dimenhydrinate (Dramamine) and meclizine (Antivert, Bonine) are usually the first choice for treating motion sickness. Their main side effect is drowsiness. A herbal alternative is ginger, which works like a charm for some people.

IN NEW ZEALAND

AVAILABILITY & COST OF HEALTH CARE

Health insurance is essential for all travellers. While health care in NZ is of a high standard and not overly expensive by international standards, considerable costs can be built up and repatriation can be extremely expensive. See p693 for insurance information.

Health Care in New Zealand

NZ does not have a government-funded system of public hospitals. All travellers are, however, covered for medical care resulting from accidents that occur while in NZ (eg motor vehicle accidents, adventure activity accidents) by the Accident Compensation Corporation (ACC). Costs incurred by treatment of a medical illness that occurs while in NZ will only be covered by travel insurance. For more details see www.moh.govt.nz.

NZ has excellent specialised public health facilities for women and children in the major centres. No specific health concerns exist for women but greater care for children is recommended to avoid environmental hazards such as heat, sunburn, cold and marine hazards.

Self-care in New Zealand

In NZ it is possible to find yourself in a remote location where there may well be a significant delay in emergency services getting to you in the event of a serious accident or illness. This is usually the result of weather and rugged terrain, particularly on the South Island. Therefore, an increased level of self-reliance and preparation is essential. Consider taking a wilderness first-aid course (such as the one from the Wilderness Medicine Institute). In addition, you should carry a comprehensive first-aid kit that is appropriate for the activities planned. To be really safe, ensure that you have adequate means of communication. (NZ has extensive mobile-phone coverage, but additional radio communication equipment is important for remote areas.)

Pharmaceutical Supplies

Over-the-counter medications are widely available in NZ through private chemists.

These include pain killers, antihistamines for allergies, and skin care products.

Some medications that are available over-the-counter in other countries are only available by a prescription obtained from a general practitioner. These include the oral contraceptive pill, most medications for asthma and all antibiotics. If you take a medication on a regular basis, bring an adequate supply and ensure you have details of the generic name as brand names differ between countries. The majority of medications in use outside of the region are available.

INFECTIOUS DISEASES
Amoebic Meningitis
There is a small risk of developing amoebic meningitis as a result of bathing or swimming in geothermal pools in NZ – mostly in regions such as Rotorua and Taupo. In such pools, keeping the head above water to prevent movement of the organism up the nasal passage reduces the risk (which is pretty low to start with). Symptoms usually start three to seven days after swimming in a geothermal pool and early symptoms of this serious disease include headache, fever and vomiting. Urgent medical care is essential to differentiate the disease from other causes of meningitis and for appropriate treatment.

Giardiasis
The giardia parasite is widespread in the waterways of NZ. Drinking untreated water from streams and lakes is not recommended. Using water filters and boiling or treating water with iodine are effective ways of preventing the disease. Symptoms consist of intermittent bad-smelling diarrhoea, abdominal bloating and wind. Effective treatment is available (tinidazole or metronidazole).

Hepatitis C
This disease is still a growing problem among intravenous drug users. Blood-transfusion services fully screen all blood before use.

HIV
The country's HIV rates have stabilised after major media campaigns, and levels are similar to other Western countries. Clean needles and syringes are widely available.

Meningococcal Disease
This occurs worldwide and is a risk with prolonged dormitory-style accommodation. A vaccine exists for some types of the disease (meningococcal A, C, Y and W).

Sexually Transmitted Diseases (STDs)
In NZ STDs (including gonorrhoea, chlamydia and herpes) occur at rates similar to most Western countries. The most common symptoms are pain on passing urine and a discharge. Infection can be present without symptoms, so seek medical screening after any unprotected sex with a new partner. Sexual health clinics are run as part of major hospitals.

TRAVELLER'S DIARRHOEA
If you develop diarrhoea, be sure to drink plenty of fluids, preferably an oral rehydration solution containing lots of salt and sugar. A few loose stools don't require treatment but if you start having more than four or five stools a day, you should start taking an antibiotic (usually a quinolone drug) and an antidiarrhoeal agent (such as loperamide). If diarrhoea is bloody, persists for more than 72 hours and/or is accompanied by fever, shaking chills or severe abdominal pain you should seek medical attention.

ENVIRONMENTAL HAZARDS
Hypothermia
This is a significant risk, especially during the winter months, or year-round in the mountains of the North Island and all of the South Island. Mountain ranges and/or strong winds produce a high chill factor that can result in hypothermia even in moderately cool temperatures. Early signs include the inability to perform fine movements (such as doing up buttons), shivering and a bad case of the 'umbles' (fumbles, mumbles, grumbles, stumbles). The key elements of treatment are changing the environment to one where heat loss is minimised, changing out of any wet clothing, adding dry clothes with wind- and water-proof layers, adding insulation and providing fuel (water and carbohydrate) to allow shivering to build the internal temperature. In severe hypothermia, shivering actually stops; this is a medical emergency requiring rapid evacuation in addition to the above measures.

HEALTH

HEALTH

Spider Bites
NZ has two poisonous spiders, the native katipo (not very poisonous and uncommon to the point of being endangered) and the introduced (thanks, Australia) white-tailed spider (also uncommon). White-tailed spider bites have been known to cause ulcers that are very difficult to heal. Clean the wound thoroughly and seek medical assistance if an ulcer develops.

Surf Beaches & Drowning
NZ has exceptional surf beaches, particularly on the western, southern and eastern coasts. The power of the surf can fluctuate as a result of the varying slope of the seabed at many beaches. Check with local surf lifesaving organisations before entering the surf and be aware of your own limitations and expertise.

Ultraviolet Light Exposure
NZ has one of the highest rates of skin cancer in the world, so you should monitor UV exposure closely. UV exposure is greatest between 10am and 4pm, so avoid skin

exposure during these times. Always use 30+ sunscreen, making sure you apply it 30 minutes before exposure and that you reapply regularly to minimise sun damage.

Water
Tap water is universally safe in NZ. Increasing numbers of streams, rivers and lakes, however, are being contaminated by bugs that cause diarrhoea, making water purification essential when tramping. The simplest way of purifying water is to boil it thoroughly. You should also consider purchasing a water filter. It's very important when buying a filter to read the specifications so that you know exactly what it removes from the water and what it doesn't. Simple filtering will not remove all dangerous organisms, so if you cannot boil water it should be treated chemically. Chlorine tablets will kill many pathogens, but not parasites such as giardia or amoebic cysts. Iodine is more effective in purifying water. Follow the directions carefully and remember that too much iodine can be harmful.

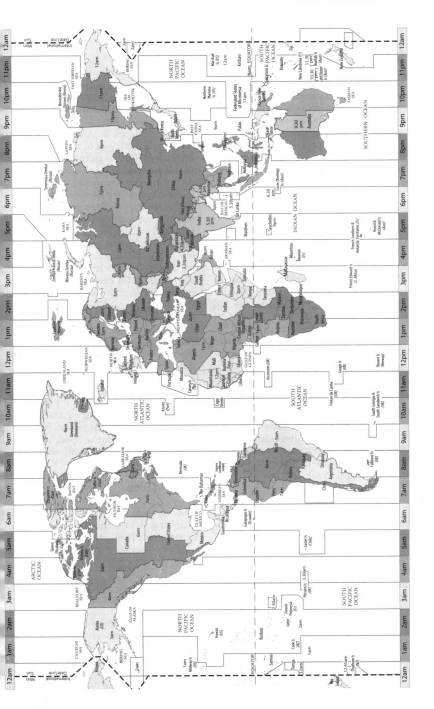

Language

New Zealand has two official languages: English and Maori. English is the language you'll usually hear spoken, but Maori, long on the decline, is making a comeback. You can use English to speak to anyone in NZ – all Maori people speak English. There are some occasions, though, when knowing a little Maori would be useful, such as visiting a marae, where often only Maori is spoken. Maori is also useful to know since many places in NZ have Maori names.

KIWI ENGLISH

Like the people of other countries in the world who speak English, New Zealanders have a unique way of speaking the language. The flattening (some would call it slaughtering) of vowels is the most distinctive feature of Kiwi pronunciation. The NZ treatment of 'fish and chips' – 'fush and chups' – is an endless source of delight for Australians. In the North Island sentences often have 'eh!' attached to the end. In the far south a rolled 'r' is practised widely, a holdover from that region's Scottish heritage – it's especially noticeable in Southland. See the Glossary on p701 for an explanation of Kiwi English words and phrases.

A Personal Kiwi-Yankee Dictionary by Louis S. Leland Jr is a fine and often hilarious book of translations and explanations of quirks between the Kiwi and American ways of speaking English. Yanks will love it.

MAORI

The Maori have a vividly chronicled history, recorded in songs and chants which dramatically recall the migration to NZ from Polynesian Hawaiki and other important events. Early missionaries were the first to record the language in a written form, and achieved this with only 15 letters of the English alphabet.

Maori is closely related to other Polynesian languages (including Hawaiian, Tahitian and Cook Islands Maori). In fact, NZ Maori and Hawaiian have the same lexical similarity as Spanish and French, although over 7000km separates Honolulu and Auckland.

The Maori language was never dead – it was always used in Maori ceremonies – but over time familiarity with it was definitely on the decline. Recent years have seen a revival of interest in it, however, and this forms an integral part of the renaissance of Maoritanga (Maori culture). Many Maori people who had heard the language spoken on the marae for years but had not used it in their day-to-day lives are now studying it and speaking it fluently. Maori is now taught in schools throughout NZ, some TV programs and news reports are broadcast in it and many English place names are being renamed in Maori. Even government departments have been rechristened with Maori names: for example the Inland Revenue Department is also known as Te Tari Taake (the last word is actually *take*, meaning 'levy', but the department has chosen to stress the long 'a' by spelling it 'aa').

In many places, Maori people have come together to provide instruction in their language and culture to young children; the idea is for them to grow up speaking both Maori and English, and to develop a familiarity with Maori tradition. It's a matter of some pride to have fluency in the language. On some marae only Maori can be spoken, encouraging everyone to speak it and emphasising the distinct Maori character of the marae.

Pronunciation

Maori is a fluid, poetic language and surprisingly easy to pronounce once you remember to split each word (and some can be amazingly long) into separate syllables.

Most consonants in Maori – **h**, **k**, **m**, **n**, **p**, **t** and **w** – are pronounced much the same as in English. The Maori **r** is a flapped sound (not rolled) with the tongue near the front of the mouth. It's closer to the English 'l' in pronunciation.

Two combinations of consonants require special attention: **ng**, pronounced as in the English words 'singing' or 'running', can be used at the beginning of words as well as at the end. To practise, just say 'ing' over and over, isolate the 'ng' part of it and then

MAORI GEOGRAPHICAL TERMS

The following words form part of many place names in NZ:

a – of
ana – cave
ara – way, path, road
awa – river or valley
heke – descend
hiku – end, tail
hine – girl, daughter
ika – fish
iti – small
kahurangi – treasured possession; special greenstone
kai – food
kainga – village
kaka – parrot
kare – rippling
kati – shut or close
koura – crayfish
makariri – cold
manga – stream or tributary
manu – bird
maunga – mountain
moana – sea or lake
moko – tattoo
motu – island
mutu – finished, ended, over
nga – the (plural)
noa – ordinary; not *tapu*
nui – big, great
nuku – distance
o – of, place of ...
one – beach, sand or mud
pa – fortified village
papa – flat land, broad slab
pipi – shellfish
pohatu – stone
poto – short

pouri – sad, dark, gloomy
puke – hill
puna – spring, hole, fountain
rangi – sky, heavens
raro – north
rei – cherished possesion
roa – long
roto – lake
rua – hole in the ground, two
runga – above
tahuna – beach, sandbank
tane – man
tangata – people
tapu – sacred, forbidden, taboo
tata – close to; dash against; twin islands
tawaha – entrance, opening
tawahi – the other side (of a river or lake)
te – the (singular)
tonga – south
ure – male genitals
uru – west
wahine – woman
wai – water
waingaro – lost; waters that disappear in certain seasons
waha – broken
waka – canoe
wera – burnt or warm; floating
wero – challenge
whaka... – to act as ...
whanau – extended family
whanga – harbour, bay or inlet
whare – house
whenua – land or country
whiti – east

Knowledge of just a few such words can help you make sense of many Maori place names. For example: Waikaremoana is the Sea *(moana)* of Rippling *(kare)* Waters *(wai)*; Rotorua means the Second *(rua)* Lake *(roto)*; and Taumatawhakatangihangakoauauotamateaturipukakapikimaunga-horonukupokaiwhenuakitanatahu means ... well ... perhaps you'd better read 'The Longest Place Name in the World' in the East Coast chapter (p381) for that translation. Some easier place names composed of words in this list are:

Aramoana – Sea *(moana)* Path *(ara)*
Awaroa – Long *(roa)* River *(awa)*
Kaitangata – Eat *(kai)* People *(tangata)*
Maunganui – Great *(nui)* Mountain *(maunga)*
Opouri – Place of *(o)* Sadness *(pouri)*
Te Araroa – The *(te)* Long *(roa)* Path *(ara)*

Te Puke – The *(te)* Hill *(puke)*
Urewera – Burnt *(wera)* Penis *(ure)*
Waimakariri – Cold *(makariri)* Water *(wai)*
Wainui – Great *(nui)* Waters *(wai)*
Whakatane – To Act *(whaka)* As A Man *(tane)*
Whangarei – Cherished *(rei)* Harbour *(whanga)*

(Note that the adjective comes after the noun in Maori constructions. Thus 'cold water' is *wai makariri* not *makariri wai*.)

practise using it to begin a word rather than end one. The **wh** also has a unique pronunciation in Maori – generally as a soft English 'f'. This pronunciation is used in many place names in NZ, eg Whakatane, Whangaroa and Whakapapa (all pronounced as if they begin with a soft 'f'). There is some local variation, however: in the region around the Whanganui River, for example, the **wh** is pronounced as in the English words 'when' and 'why'.

When learning to speak Maori the correct pronunciation of the vowels is very important. The examples below are only a rough guideline – to really get it right you'll have to listen carefully to someone who knows how to pronounce the language correctly. Each vowel has both a long and a short sound with long vowels often denoted in text by a macron (a line over the letter) or a double vowel. We have not indicated long/short vowel forms in this book.

VOWELS

a	as in 'large', with no 'r' sound
e	as in 'get'
i	as in 'marine'
o	as in 'pork'
u	as the 'oo' in 'moon'

DIPHTHONGS

ae, ai	as the 'y' in 'sky'
ao, au	as the 'ow' in 'how'
ea	as in 'bear'
ei	as in 'vein'
eo	as 'eh-oh'
eu	as 'eh-oo'
ia	as in the name 'Ian'
ie	as the 'ye' in 'yet'
io	as the 'ye o' in 'ye old'
iu	as the 'ue' in 'cue'
oa	as in 'roar'
oe	as in 'toe'
oi	as in 'toil'
ou	as the 'ow' in 'sow'
ua	as the 'ewe' in 'fewer'

Each syllable ends in a vowel and there is never more than one vowel in a syllable. There are no silent letters.

There are many Maori phrasebooks, grammar books and Maori-English dictionaries if you want to take a closer look at the language. Learning a few basic greetings is an excellent thing to do, especially if you plan to go onto a marae, where you'll be greeted in Maori.

The *Collins Maori Phrase Book* by Patricia Tauroa is an excellent book for starting to speak the language, with sections on every-day conversation and also on how the language is used in a cultural context (such as on a marae). Lonely Planet's *South Pacific Phrasebook* has a useful section on the Maori language as well as several Pacific languages (Tongan, Samoan, Cook Island Maori) that you may hear spoken around Wellington or South Auckland.

Other English-Maori dictionaries include the *English-Maori Maori-English Dictionary* by Bruce Biggs, and the *Reed Dictionary* of Modern Maori by PM Ryan, which is one of the most authoritative.

Greetings & Small Talk

Maori greetings are finding increased popularity; don't be surprised if you're greeted on the phone or on the street with *Kia ora*. Try these ones:

Haere mai!	Welcome!
E noho ra.	Goodbye. (to person staying)
Haere ra.	Goodbye. (to person going)
Kia ora.	Hello/Good luck/ Good health.
Tena koe.	Hello. (to one person)
Tena korua.	Hello. (to two people)
Tena koutou.	Hello. (to three or more people)

Kei te pehea koe?
How are you? (to one person)
Kei te pehea korua?
How are you? (to two people)
Kei te pehea koutou?
How are you? (to three or more)
Kei te pai.
Very well, thanks/That's fine.

Glossary

This glossary is a list of 'Kiwi English' and Maori terms and phrases you may come across in New Zealand. Also see the 'Maori Geographical Terms' boxed text (p699) in the Language chapter for some Maori words that pop up again and again in NZ place names.

AA – New Zealand Automobile Association, which provides road information and roadside assistance

afghan – popular homemade chocolate biscuit

All Blacks – NZ's revered national rugby union team (the name comes from 'All Backs', which is what the press called the NZ rugby team on an early visit to England)

Aoraki – Maori name for Mt Cook, meaning 'Cloud Piercer' (Aoraki is the South Island spelling; otherwise it would be Aorangi)

Aotearoa – Maori name for NZ, most often translated as 'Land of the Long White Cloud'

atua – spirits or gods

B&B – 'bed and breakfast' accommodation

bach – holiday home, usually a wooden cottage (pronounced 'batch'); see *crib*

Barrier, the – local name for Great Barrier Island in the Hauraki Gulf

baths – swimming pool, often referred to as municipal baths

Beehive – Parliament House in Wellington, so-called because of its distinctive shape

Black Power – large, well-organised and mainly Maori bikie-style gang

black-water rafting – rafting or tubing underground in a cave or *tomo*

boozer – public bar

box of birds – an expression meaning 'on top of the world', usually uttered in response to 'How are you?'

bro' – literally 'brother'; usually meaning mate, as in 'just off to see the bros'

bush – heavily forested areas

Buzzy Bee – a child's toy; a wooden bee dragged along by a string to produce a whirring noise

BYO – 'bring your own' (usually applies to alcohol at a restaurant or café)

BYOW – 'bring your own wine'

Captain Cooker – large feral pig, introduced by Captain Cook and now roaming wild over most of NZ's bush land

cervena – farmed deer

CHE – not the revolutionary but Crown Health Enterprise (regional, privatised health authorities)

chillie bin – cooler; esky; large insulated box for keeping food and drink cold

choice – fantastic; great

ciggies – cigarettes

crib – the name for a *bach* in Otago and Southland

cuzzie or cuz' – cousin; relative or mate; see *bro'*

dairy – small corner store that sells milk, bread, newspapers, ice cream and pretty much everything else

Dalmatian – a term applied to the predominantly Yugoslav gum diggers who fossicked for kauri gum (used as furniture polish) in the gum fields of Northland

DB&B – 'dinner, bed and breakfast' accommodation

DOC – Department of Conservation (or *Te Papa Atawhai*); government department which administers national parks and thus all tracks and huts

domain – open grassed area in a town or city, often the focus of civic amenities such as gardens, picnic areas and bowling clubs

doss house – temporary accommodation

DPB – 'Domestic Purposes Benefit', a government allowance, increasingly used in the vernacular as more families struggle in the free market economy

dropkick – a certain method of kicking a rugby ball; a personal insult

farmstay – accommodation on a Kiwi farm where you're encouraged to join in the typical day-to-day activities

fiscal envelope – money set aside by the NZ government to make financial reparation for injustices to Maori people since the Treaty of Waitangi

football – rugby, either union or league

freezing works – slaughterhouse or abattoir for sheep and/or cattle

Gilbert – the most popular brand of rugby football

Godzone – New Zealand (from Richard Seddon who referred to NZ as 'God's own country')

good as gold, good as – very good; no problem

greenstone – jade; *pounamu*

haka – any dance, but usually refers to the traditional challenge; war dance

hakari – feast

handle – beer glass with a handle

hangi – oven made by digging a hole and steaming food in baskets over embers in the hole; a feast of Maori food

hapu – sub-tribe or smaller tribal grouping

hard case – unusual or strong-willed character

Hawaiki – Polynesian homeland from where the Maori tribes migrated by canoe (probably Ra'iatea in the Society Islands); also a name for the Afterworld

hei tiki – carved, stylised human figure worn around the neck, often a carved representation of an ancestor; also called a *tiki*

hoa – friend; usually pronounced 'e hoa'

hokey pokey – delicious variety of ice cream with butterscotch chips

hoki – type of fish common in fish and chip shops

homestay – accommodation in a family house where you're treated as one of the family

hongi – Maori greeting; the pressing of noses and sharing of life breath

hui – gathering; meeting

huntaway – loud-barking sheep dog, usually a sturdy black-and-brown hound

Ika a Maui, Te – 'The Fish of Maui', the North Island

Instant Kiwi – state-run lottery

Interislander – any of the big old ferries that cross Cook Strait between Wellington and Picton

'Is it what!' – strong affirmation or agreement; 'Yes isn't it!'

iwi – large tribal grouping with common lineage back to the original migration from Hawaiki; people; tribe

jandals – sandals; flip-flops; thongs; usually rubber footwear

jersey – jumper, usually woollen; the shirt worn by rugby players

judder bars – bumps in the road to make you drive slowly; speed humps

kai – food; almost any word with *kai* in it has a connection with food

kainga – village; pre-European unfortified Maori village

ka pai – good; excellent

karakia – prayer

K Rd – Karangahape Rd in Auckland

kaumatua – highly respected members of a tribe; the people you would ask for permission to enter a *marae*

kina – sea urchins; a Maori delicacy

kiwi – the flightless, nocturnal brown bird with a long beak that is the national symbol; the NZ dollar; a New Zealander; a member of the national rugby league team; an adjective to mean anything relating to NZ

kiwi bear – the introduced Australian brush-tailed possum

kiwi fruit – small, succulent fruit with fuzzy brown skin and juicy green flesh; a Chinese gooseberry

koe – you (singular)

koha – donation

kohanga reo – schools where Maori language and culture are at the forefront of the education process; also called 'language nest' schools

korua – you (two people)

koutou – you (more than two people)

kumara – Polynesian sweet potato; a Maori staple food

kunekune – type of wild pig introduced by Chinese gold diggers in the 19th century

Kupe – early Polynesian navigator from Hawaiki, credited with the discovery of the islands that are now NZ

league – rugby league football

lounge bar – more upmarket bar than a public bar; called a 'ladies bar' in some countries

mana – spiritual quality of a person or object; prestige; authority of a chief or priest

manaia – traditional carving design; literally means 'bird-headed man'

manuhiri – visitor; guest

Maori – indigenous people of NZ

Maoritanga – Maori culture

marae – literally refers to the sacred ground in front of the Maori meeting house, more commonly used to refer to the entire complex of buildings

Maui – a figure in Maori (Polynesian) mythology

mere – flat, *greenstone* war club

metal/metalled road – gravel (unsealed) road

MMP – Mixed Member Proportional; a cumbersome electoral system used in NZ and Germany; a limited form of proportional voting

moa – large, extinct flightless bird

moko – tattoo; usually refers to facial tattoos

Mongrel Mob – large, well-organised and mainly Maori bikie-style gang

Moriori – isolated Polynesian group; inhabitants of the Chatham Islands

motorway – freeway or expressway

naiad – rigid-hull inflatable boat (used for dolphin swimming, whale-watching etc)

nga – the (plural); see *te*

Ngati – literally 'the people of' or 'the descendants of'; tribe; (on the South Island, it's pronounced 'kai')

nifty-fifty – 50cc motorcycle

NZ – the universal term for New Zealand; pronounced 'enzed'

pa – fortified Maori village, usually on a hill top

Pacific Rim – term used to describe modern NZ cuisine; cuisine with an innovative use of local produce, especially seafood, with imported styles

Pakeha – Maori for a white or European person; once derogatory, and still considered so by some, this term is now widely used for white New Zealanders

pakihi – unproductive and often swampy land on the South Island's west coast; pronounced 'par-kee'

papa – large blue-grey mudstones; the word comes from the Maori for Earth Mother

Papa, Te – literally 'our place', the name of the national museum in Wellington

parapenting – paragliding

paua – abalone; tough shellfish pounded, minced, then made into patties (fritters), which are available in almost every NZ fish and chip shop

PC – 'politically correct'

peneplain – area worn almost flat by erosion

pig islander – derogatory term used by a person from one island for someone from the other island

pillocking – 'surfing' across mud flats on a rubbish-bin lid

Plunket – adjective to describe the Plunket Society's services to promote the health of babies, eg Plunket rooms (baby clinics), Plunket nurses (baby nurses)

poi – ball of woven flax

poi dance – women's formation dance that involves singing and manipulating a poi

polly – politician

ponga – the silver fern; called a bungy (pronounced 'bungee', with a soft 'g', in parts of the South Island)

pounamu – Maori name for *greenstone*

powhiri – traditional Maori welcome onto a *marae*

quad bikes – four-wheel farm bikes

Rakiura – literally 'Land of Glowing Skies'; Maori name for Stewart Island, which is important in Maori mythology as the anchor of Maui's canoe

rap jump – face-down abseil

Ratana – a Protestant Maori church; adherents of the Ratana faith

raupo – bullrush

Rheiny – affectionate term for Rheineck beer

rigger – a refillable half-gallon plastic bottle for holding draught beer

Ringatu – an East Coast Maori church formed by Te Kooti

riptide – dangerously strong current running away from the shore at a beach

Roaring Forties – the ocean between 40° and 50° south, known for very strong winds

scrap – a fight

section – small block of land

silver fern – the symbol worn by the All Blacks and other national sportsfolk on their jerseys, representative of the underside of a *ponga* leaf; the national netball team are called the Silver Ferns

Steinie – affectionate term for Steinlager beer

superette – grocery store or small supermarket open outside normal business hours

sweet – all-purpose term like *choice*: fantastic; great

Tamaki Makaurau – Maori name for Auckland

tane – man

tangata – people

tangata whenua – people of the land; local people

taniwha – fear-inspiring water spirit

taonga – something of great value; a treasure

tapu – sacred; forbidden; taboo

te – the (singular); see *nga*

Te Kooti – prominent East Coast Maori prophet and rebellion leader

Te Papa Atawhai – Maori name for *DOC*

tiki – short for *hei tiki*

toheroa – large clam

tohunga – priest; wizard; general expert

toi toi – tall native grass

tomo – hole; entrance to a cave

tramp – bushwalk; trek; hike; a more serious undertaking than an ordinary walk, requiring some experience and equipment

tuatara – prehistoric reptile dating back to the age of dinosaurs (perhaps 260 million years)

tua tua – type of shellfish

tukutuku – Maori wall panellings in *marae* and churches

tuna – eel

umu – earth oven

varsity – university

VIN – Visitor Information Network; the umbrella organisation of the visitors centres and offices

wahine – woman

wai – water

waiata – song

Waikikamukau – mythical NZ town; somewhere in the *wopwops*

Wai Pounamu, Te – 'The Water of Greenstone'; Maori for the South Island

Waitangi – short way of referring to the Treaty of Waitangi

waka – canoe

Watties – the NZ food and canning giant; NZ's answer to Heinz (until Heinz took over the company)

whakapapa – genealogy

whare – house

whare runanga – meeting house

whare taonga – treasure house; museum

whare whakairo – carved house

whenua – land

whitebait – translucent fish that is scooped up in nets and eaten whole (head, eyes and all!) or made into patties

wopwops – remote; 'out in the wopwops' is out in the middle of nowhere

Behind the Scenes

THIS BOOK

Lonely Planet's *New Zealand* guide has been around since 1977, when Lonely Planet co-founder Tony Wheeler wrote the very first edition. Since then subsequent editions have been coordinated by Simon Hayman, Mary Coverton, Tony Wheeler (again), Robin Tinker, Nancy Keller and Jeff Williams. The previous (11th) edition was coordinated by Paul Harding, who shared regional chapters with Neal Bedford and Carolyn Bain.

This 12th edition was coordinated by über-author Paul Smitz and, as well as regional-chapter travel-writers Martin Robinson, Nina Rousseau and Richard Watkins, we drew on substantial expert contributions from Prof James Belich, Russell Brown, Julie Biuso, Vaughan Yarwood and Dr David Millar. Smaller sections were contributed to by (Pulitzer-winning author) Tony Horowitz, (Greens MP) Nandor Tanczos and (ex-All Black) Josh Kronfeld. See p21 for an explanation of what each author wrote. Elsewhere, the NZ's *Lord of the Rings* and Land Wars boxed texts were written by Errol Hunt, who also updated the 'Maori Culture' special section. Sir Ian McKellen wrote the boxed text on sandflies (one of NZ's very few annoyances; p664).

THANKS from the Authors

Paul Smitz Thanks to everyone who helped out during the frenetic research and time-stretching write-up of this book, including all the hospitable, affable and opinionated Kiwis and travellers who put up with my supersonic questions and lack of personal grooming, all the hard-working LP bods who clung to this book like flies (note to self: improve use of metaphors), and the sheep on the road to Arthur's Pass that chose discretion over valour. Special thanks to the enigmatic woman who can never be allowed to know that Crash Test Dummies have actually done seven albums (and counting).

Martin Robinson A big thank you to Aussie Malcolm, Barbara Doyle, Shirley Preston, Giorgio Allemano, Peter and Kerry from Kaitaia and a bus driver on Waiheke Island, to the staff at the visitors centres, especially Raglan, and to all the Kiwis who (generally patiently) answered all my questions. Mega thanks to my wife, Marie.

Nina Rousseau Thanks to Lucas McKenna for generally being excellent, providing substantial moral support, and for putting up with me with such good humour during this obsessive guidebook process. Immeasurable thanks to all the incredibly helpful and knowledgeable DOC staff and staff from the visitors centres around NZ: particularly, Lois from New Plymouth, Grace from Mt Egmont visitors centre, Sean from Takaka, Rudy from Motueka, Pearl Hewson from Wellington; Beryl and Jan from the Picton visitors centre, and Sandra from Moteuka visitors centre. Enormous thanks to Simon Cleary, Jill Winfield and George Dunford. Thanks to Sean Parker for showing me the best bar in Wellington. Thanks to Jay Leckie, for the winery tour that might have been. Thanks to Alan Harding for his helpful local tips. Thanks to Paul Smitz for being an understanding and rippa coordinating author, and to Errol Hunt for commissioning this sucker in the first place. Onyas all.

THE LONELY PLANET STORY

The story begins with a classic travel adventure: Tony and Maureen Wheeler's 1972 journey across Europe and Asia to Australia. There was no useful information about the overland trail then, so Tony and Maureen published the first Lonely Planet guidebook to meet a growing need.

From a kitchen table, Lonely Planet has grown to become the largest independent travel publisher in the world, with offices in Melbourne (Australia), Oakland (USA), London (UK) and Paris (France).

Today Lonely Planet guidebooks cover the globe. There is an ever-growing list of books and information in a variety of media. Some things haven't changed. The main aim is still to make it possible for adventurous travellers to get out there – to explore and better understand the world.

At Lonely Planet we believe travellers can make a positive contribution to the countries they visit – if they respect their host communities and spend their money wisely.

Richard Watkins Many thanks are due to all the tourism professionals in the Bay of Plenty, Central Plateau and East Coast regions for their cheerful and efficient assistance during my research, and to the helpful folks at the New Zealand High Commission and Tourism New Zealand in London. Thanks also to Errol and Paul for their patience. Special thanks go to Kris at Hawkes Bay Tourism, Esther, Melissa and Jim at Tourism Bay of Plenty, Melissa and Gina at Tourism Rotorua, Megan at Destination Lake Taupo, Tina at Opotiki visitors centre and Mary at Whakatane visitors centre. Thanks to Paul and Reg O'Brien in Te Kaha for their Maori-Irish hospitality, to Mark and Gail in Tauranga, Craig and Lyn in Mount Maunganui, Tim for the rainy Buried Village tour and Nadine for the mud bath at Hell's Gate. In Taupo, thanks to Barry Kirkland, Bruce Lilburn, Neil Kemp, Naomi Robinson and Tiki Lodge, to Heather and Jenny in Turangi, Bruce, Janet and Peter in Whakatane, Peter, Jenny and Matt (Pee Jay Charters), Greg Beachen and the Archies in Napier, Neil and Craig at Greenhill, Tony and Jude in Gisborne, Debbie and David at base Backpackers and Fiona Macdonald in Auckland.

CREDITS

New Zealand 12 was commissioned and developed in Lonely Planet's Melbourne office by Errol Hunt. Cartography for this guide was developed by Anthony Phelan. Editing was coordinated by Carolyn Boicos, with assistance from Charlotte Keown; Birgit Jordan coordinated the mapping and Yvonne Bischofberger coordinated layout and put together the splendid colour wraps. Our team of editors and proofers included Holly Alexander, Andrew Bain, Tony Davidson, Kate Evans, Carly Hall, Charlotte Harrison, John Hinman, Martine Lleonart, Katie Lynch, Kate McLeod, Lucy Monie, Simon Sellars, Suzannah Shwer, Louise Stirling, Elizabeth Swan and Katrina Webb. Quentin Frayne prepared the Language chapter, and Gina Tsarouhas, Kyla Gillzan and Barbara Delissen indexed the book.

Assisting with mapping were Barbara Benson, Piotr Czajkowski, James Ellis, Huw Fowles, Jack Gavran, Anneka Imkamp, Kim McDonald, Sarah Sloane, Andrew Smith, Chris Thomas, Chris Tsismetzis and Bonnie Wintle. Layout was assisted by Vicki Beale, Adam Bextream, Steven Cann, Laura Jane, Katherine Marsh, Jacqui Saunders, and Tamsin Wilson. Thanks to Adriana Mammarella and Kate McDonald for layout checks. Cover design was by Brendan Dempsey and James Hardy did the cover art and series design.

Ray Thomson managed the project, with help early on from Rachel Imeson, and overseeing production were Darren O'Connell (managing editor) and Corie Waddell (managing cartographer). The regional publishing managers were Kate Cody and Virginia Maxwell.

Vital readers' letters support came from Katharine Day, Jen Mundy-Nordin and Shannon Kardi. Thanks to Fiona Siseman for her work in arranging permissions, and Jodie Farrelly for assistance with contracting. Also thanks to Aimée Goggins, Anna Bolger and Malcolm O'Brien for feedback and market advice.

Thanks, for their invaluable suggestions and/or assistance with contacting expert New Zealanders of various flavours, to: Vanessa Alexander, Matthew Sullivan, Rosemary Manning, Manya Mayes, Peta Mathias and Andy Hayden, the Hunt *whanau*, Jane Harris, Kristen Prescott, David Collins, Jeff Trounce, Tourism NZ's Cas Carter and Tessa Lawrence, Witi Ihimaera, Clair Dobbs and the late Michael King (a sad farewell).

THANKS from Lonely Planet

Many thanks to the hundreds of travellers who used the last edition and wrote to us with helpful hints, useful advice and interesting anecdotes:

A Gep Aadriaanse, Hannah Aagaard-Jensen, Mark Aberkrom, Claire Adams, Heather Adams, Leah Adams, Natalie Adams, Sharon Agar, Friederike Albrecht, Tim Alexander, Chris Allitt, Roger Almond, Carla Ambrose, Pam Amos, Heath Anderson, Jamie Anderson, Maria Andersson, Richard Anthony, Nan Crystal Arens, Mark Armstrong, Stephen Armstrong, David Arnby, David Arnold, Phyllis Arthu, Michael Arthur, Dr James T Aslanis, Elizabeth Ayarra, Robert Ayres **B** Ken Bailey, Tanya Bailey, Ana Bailey-Brown, Chris Bain, Lyndon & Sarah Banbury, Brad Barr, Geoff Barton, Cris Bastianello, Stefan Baum, Cornelia Baumermann, Leslie Beard, Eric Beeby, Michael Beech, Andrew Bell, Claire Bell, Graeme Bell, Gordon Bennett, Lene Berge, Pamela Berghegen, David Bertram, Kim Bestic, Simon & Joanne Betney, Shaun Bigg, Itai Birger, David M Blakemore, Richard Blakey, Danielle Blanchard, Jeannine Blarer, Alexander Bleha, Iris Blok, Henk J Boerrigter, Sue & Tony Borer, Nick Borg, Katharina & Daniel Borszik, Mireille Bouclin, Christine Bourgeois, Benedicte Bourreau, Sharn Bowley, Vicki Bowman, Louise Bowsher, Harriet Boyce, Kieran Boyde, Tammy Boyer, D Braam, Julie & Glenn Bradley, Chris Brady, Silvia Brandl, Bob & Nancy Breslin, Sarah & Tim Bresseleers, Jayne Bretherton, Shona Brethouwer, Andy Brice, Eleanor Bridger, Pat Bridges, Helen Bright, Robin Brisker, Mary Britton, Ben Brock, Carolyn Brown, David Brown, Jens Brueggemann, Brenda Brugts, Carola Bruhn, Angela & Jason Buckley, Helen Bufton, Claire Bullock, Con Bullot, Andrew Bunbury, Leila Buni, Miranda Burger, Belinda Burgmann, Mary Burrows, Damian Bush, John Byrne **C** Rachel Cameron, Puhi & James Campbell, Mandy Cantle, Tim & Liz Capon, Marie Cappuccio, Gavin Carey, Fiona Carruthers, Nicholas Carson, Katrina

Casey, Robert Catto, Xavier Cazauran, Brook Chambers, Nila Chambers, Erica Champ, David C Chang, Matthew Channon, Anthony Chant, Sonia Chapman, Marion Chappel, Joelle Chaubeau, Ivar Christensen, Jillian Christoff, Maria Christofi, Stephanie Chua, Chan Wai Chung, William Clarke, Bjorn Clasen, Gesa Classen, Jodi & Rob Clayson, Anthony Graham Clough, Chris Coffey, Les Colbourne-Creak, Ka Colby, Rich & Sally Coleman, Berna Collier, Kendall Collier, Becca Collins, Carol Collins, Marie Collins, Furio Coltri, Tamra & Damien Coman, Anna Compton, Salvatore Consalvi, Paul Coopersmith, E Copping, Paul Corbett, Claire Cordell, Steve Cotter, Linda Cotton, Lynda Cotton, Steven Coverdale, Katrina Cowen, Jo Coyne, Ian Crawford, Paul Crofskey, Richard Cross, Brian Crowley, Sarah Cruickshank, Jena Curtis, Rebecca Curtis **D** Luisa D'Accione, Paul Dale, Jerry & Cobi Daley, Ryan Daly, Angela Danyluk, Lisa Darby, Arjan Dasselaar, Anthony Davenport, Dorothy Davies, Laura Davies, Alice Davis, Lee Dawson, Phil Day, Tim Day, Anton & Kathy de Luc, Jean & Bernadette de Maulmin, Brenda de Ruiter, Steve Deadman, Bronwen Dean, John & Trudy Dean, Sheldon Dean, Eddie Deevy, RoseMarie Deevy, Rangimarie Delamere, Kim Dellaca, Karin Demidoff, Ali Dent, Kaye deRoss, Peter Deuart, Amit Deutrscher, Daniel Di Giusto, Rebecca Dick, R Dickinson, Beverly & Michael Diggins, Nicole Dijkstra, Derek Distin, Mathew Doidge, Tina Dombek, Mike Doonan, WF Doran, Stephen Doughty, Murray Downs, Jason Drake, Roger Drake, Erik Duerr, Jodi Dunbar, Ray Dunn, Fred Duprat, Helen & Chris Dussling, Bruce Dyer **E** Helen & Paul Eagles, Sarah Eales, Christina Echols, Richard Eckman, Roger Paul Edmonds, Susan Edwards, Dorit Efrat, James Eivers, April Evans, Jan Evans, Sarah Evans, Jane Everex, Alwin Evers **F** Michael Falk, Paula Fallows, Ken Farrance, Julie Farrell, Jean Farrelly, Paul Farrelly, Vonny Fast, Simon Fathers, Jurjen Feikens, Martin Feldmann, Frank Felten, Nicolas Fevrier, Antoinette Figliola-Kaderli, Nick Fisher, Bette Flagler, Nigel Foster, Marit Frank, Louise Franklin, Reto & Sandra Frei, Nichlas Friman, Holger Funk, Erika Furger **G** Daniele Galli, Anne Garber, Chris Gardner, Jean Garelick, Dorothy Gay, John Gay, David & Barbara Geary, John Geisen-Kisch, Graham Gibson, Erik & Anja Gielen-Jabaay, Julie & Maurice Gilligan, Bernadette Girlich, Jan Glas, Sandra Glasglow, Christian Glossner, Val Goddard, Ralph Goldstein, Rosalie Goldsworthy, Virginia Gonzales, Julian Gonzalez, Nicola Goodanew, Karen Goodlet, Hattie Goodman, Annemarie Gordon, Leisa Gordon, Matthew & Adrian Gough, Sala'am Grant, Wendy Gray, Lyn Green, Andrew Greenhill, Angela Griffiths, Myles Griffiths, Scott Grossman, Andrea Gryak, Antoinette Gussenhoven **H** Yutaka Hagino, Mary Hall, Mike & Diana Hall, Richard Hall, Jane Hammet, Katrina Hammond, Alan Harding, Dorie & Lee Harmon, Lynn Harris, Rebecca Harrison, Robert Hart, Ed Harte, Frans Hartman, Geoff Hawthorn, Richard Hayton, Christopher Hayward, Marjorie Heasman, Gemma Hebertson, Kelly Hedstrom, Carol & Dennis Hegarty, Heidi Heidi, Anna Heino, Nancy Heinz-Sader, Anna Heiro, Paul Hellyer, SK Hendy, Elaine Heney, Jenny Henman, Patrick Hennessy, Mark & Emma Herbert, Judith Hereford, Joelle Hervy, Rob Herwson, Joy Hewgill, Alex Hewlett, Sarah Higgins, Alyson Higgs, Andy Hill, Belinda Hill, Brian Hill, Tom Hill, Eva Himmelberg, Duncan & Natalie Hind, John Hinde, Catia Hirsch, Amber Hobson, Rob

Hocking, Werner Hoelzl, Rita & Gerd Hofmann-Credner, Grainne Hogan, Kay & Glenn Hogg, Adrian Holliday, Jason Hollinger, Malcolm Holmes, Craig Holz, Michael Hopkins, Andy Hopko, Jennifer Hough, Alan Howarth, Graeme Howie, Jenny Howson, Rachel Hucknall, Sherrie Hudson, Cate Hughes, Janet Hughes, Marina Hughes, Emma Humphreys, Chris Hunt, Kathrin Hunziker, Warren Hurley, Trudi Hurren, Stuart Hutchings **I** Fermin Iglesias, Barbara Ingendae, Stephen Ireland, Anja Issbruecker **J** Gemma Jackson, Kristina Jacob, Libby James, Keith & Trish Janes, Alienke Jansen, Patrick Jansen, Neil Jebb, Mike Jeffcoat, Robby Jennings, Joan Jewett, Dave (JE) Johnson, Michele Johnson, Rachel Johnson, Peggy Jonckheere, Cerys Jones, Giff & Mary Jones, Kelly Jones, Louise Jones, Ilma Joukes, Bernd Juhre, Tim Julou **K** William Kaderli, Timon Kampschulte, Sue Karutz, Richard Kay, Jenny Kerr, Carla Kersten, John B King, Melissa King, Sarah Jane King, Trish King, Ken Kirkman, Lucas Klamert, Andrea Kleemann, Anne-Marie Kleijberg, Maureen Klijn, Henry Klos, Jeremy Knight, Kati Knuuttila, Megan Konar, Silke Korbl, Laura & Steve Koulish, Joe Krampel, Tatiana Krause, Christopher Kruzel, Judy Kullberg **L** Suzanne LaBarre, Bernadette Lahme, Peter Laight, Mag. Michaela Lambauer, Malcolm Lambert, Marty Lampard, Louise Langhorn, Martin Langsch, Tony Lansdowne, Chris LaRoche, Tony Laskey, Joanna Lau, Michael Laufersweiler, Nick Laugier, Markus Laux, Glen Lawrence, Rob Lawrence, Ian Leak, Vivian Lee, Jane Lehmann, Peter Leichliter, Vanessa & Lucas Leonardi, Meredith Lepore, Elizabeth J Leppman, Katharine Lequesne, Martin Lerner, Jeannie-Marie Leroi, Janet Lewis, Wayne Lewis, Ulrich Lichtenthaler, Marina Lieber, Kim Lim, Sean Limpens, Ola Lindberg, Gunilla Lindblad, Sidsel Christy Lindgaard, Elizabeth & David Lindsey, Paul Lintott, Lindsay Lipson, Gill Logan, Jo Logan, MK Loh, Lorraine Lohan, Ditte Lokon, Mette Loland, Roberto Longi, Margaret Longsbrough, Inge Loo, Lai Kit Looi, Sarah Lopez, Melanie Loriz, Nick Lott, Graham Love, Debbie Lovell, Nicky Lovf, William Lucas, Bas Lugtigheid, Kelsi Luhnow, Thomas Lynnerup **M** Andrea Macfarlane, Helen Macmullins, Bernhard Maenner, Abbey Magargee, William & T Maguire, Jane Maree Maher, Claude Malet, Leane Malone, Alison Maloney, Chalin Malz, Evy Mandikos, J Marcovecchio, Lilee Marer, Anne Margrethe, Raymond J Mark, Peter Marko, Michelle Maro, Harry Marotto, Michael Marsh, Mike Marshall, Daniel Martin, Christian Massetti, Scott Mather, Fionnuala Matthews, Mary Maynard, Trevor Mazzucchelli, Craig McAllister, Jamie McCormack, Grant Mcdonnell, Steve McFadyen, Magnus McGillivray, Pamela Ann McGinn, Fraser McInnes, Alan McKinnon, Lucy McLoughlin, Cathryn McNamara, Neil McRae, Philip Meehan, Nick Meeten, Mark Melman, Scott Menzies, Shane Merchant, Brenda Merz, Karen Metcalf, Bjoern Meyburg, Rita Mezei, Gaspard Michardiere, Marco Miersemann, Kristian Mikkelsen, Robert Miley, Janet Mills, William & Rebecca Minchin, Helen Minogue, Nicki Miquel, Steve Mitchell, Sue Mobley, Knut Moen, Paul Mohme, Marjolijn Molenaar, Bob & Sandra Mooney, Tom Mooney, Anne Lloyd Morris, Sallie Morris, Ted & Wendy Morris, Hugh & Eileen Morton, Friedi Moschner, Wolfgang Moser, James Mulhern, Ronaldo Müller, George G Mulligan, Andrew Mulrenan, Ole Munk, Vicki Munro, Heather Murphy, Tim Musclow **N** Elad Nachman, Christina Nagel, Dr Chris Nash, Regina Natsch,

Corinne Nedelec, Frank Neff, Ai-Ling Neo, Emma Newton, Simon Niblett, Martin & Helen Nicholas, Geoff Nichols, Louisa Nichols, Hanne Nielsen, Erwin & Hennie Nijkeuter, Andy Nilsson, Shohei Nimomiya, Chuck Nip, Elvi Rohde Nissen, Bethan Nolan, Kelly Norfolk, Gisela Nurcahyanti **O** Philip Obergfell, Christopher O'Brien, Mel O'Connell, Lynda O'Dea, Mr & Mrs KL O'Dea, Julie Odell, Cindy Oehmig, Stewart Oilver, Liz Oldham, Tim O'Neill, Sarah & Adrian Orchard, Michelle O'Riordan, Jack & Nancy Ostheimer, Dennis OSullivan, Brian O'Sullivan, Lynn O'Sullivan, Suzanne Owen, Bill Ozanne **P** Maria Pacheco, Melissa Paddick, Stu Padget, Kaye & Trevor Painter, Shannon Pantages, Diana Parr, Emma Parsons, Mary Jane & Walter Pawlowski, Virginia Pawlyn, Stephanie Payen, Olivia Payne, Paul Pelczar, Edwin Perkins, Patricia Perry, Stephanie Pettigrew, Rosemarie Pforter, Abby Philips, Sue Picard, Adi Pieper, Stephanie Pietruszynski, Sandra Pijl, Roger Pike, Sarah Pike, C Pillemer, Barry & Sarah Pitt, Heike Plotz, Jan-Eric Plusingrid, Anne Pohl, Jan Poker, Essi Pölhö, Kerstin Pomplun, Maggie Ponder, Dianne Pornish, S Poteet, Arne Poulsen, Zoe Poulton, Maggie Pressley, Sarah Pritchard, Michael Prys-William, Victoria Purdie, Phyllis Purdy **Q** Katy Quévillon, Rohan Quinby, John Quinn **R** Michael Raffaele, Amir Rahimzadeh, Poorani Ramalingam, Riju Ramrakha, Emma Ramsay, Thomas Rau, Nigel Rayner, Joy Rebello, Janis Redmond, Bruce Reed, Peter Reeder, Caroline Rees, Andy & Becky Reeves, Alenka Remec, Jean-Daniel Renevey, Charlotte Renner, Frank & Louise Richards, Laurie Richards, Jennifer Rickett, Matthew Ridd, Mary Riemens, Michael Riggs, Luke Riley, Rory Riley-Gillespie, Anne Rimmer, Thorsten Rinner, Mary Rios, Lutz Ritter, Janet Roach, Grahame Roberts, Victoria Roberts, James & Tania Roberts-Thomson, Neil & Sarah Robertson, Connie Robinson, Kerrie Rogers, Andrea Rogge, MacKinzie Rogge, Susan Rolph, Elizabeth Romhild, Judith Rosendahl, Petra Rossback, Clive Rowe, Zoe Rowe, Marie Royd, Gil Rozen, Ken Rubin, Jim Rucker, Jackie Rumble, Carol Russell, Disler Meier Ruth, Jonathan Ryan, Sue Ryan **S** Kate Sabey, Martin Sackett, Keith Safey, Amy Sagan, Darren Salter, Michelle Sampson, Mischa Sander, Brenda Sandilands, Peter Sapper, Alex Sas, Chiko Sato, Yoshiki Sato, Barry Sayer, Ian Scales, Sandra Scheidtmann, Jacques Schildknecht, Hans Schiltmans, John Schindler, Ursula Schmidt, Axel Schmidtke, David Schmidtke, Luree Schneider, Ursula Schober, Ann Schofield, Apollonia Schreiber, Edwin Schuurman, Ann-Christin Schwab, Emilie Scott, Janette Seal, Mike & Claire Sealey, Kerstin Seja, Sanjib Sen, Kim Senini, Maarian Senior, Lorenza Severi, Nitzan Shadmi, Eyal Shaman, Rod Shapland, Andrew Sharp, Geoff Shaw, Jodie Shaw, Jon Shaw, Trent Shepard, Michael Siefert, Simone Siemons, Ingrid Siemonsma, Anne Siikanen, Arend & Lous Sijpestein, DP Silliss, Alisha Simpson, Kenneth Simpson, Debbie Singer, James Sington, Patrick Sinke, Anneke Sips, Brian Sisk, Kristoffer Sletten, Craig Smart, Danny Smith, Dr Roger Smith, GH Smith, Jayne Smith, Moira Smith, Peter Smolka, Bella & Peter Snook, Trina So, Markus Sodergren, Brenda Soloman, Maria Sotiropoulos, Sally Sparkes, Claire Speedy, Jo Spencer, Claudia Spiegel, Freek Spits, Catherine Spratt, Abi Stafford, Robert JH Stagg, Bert & Nicole Stamsnieder, John Stansberry, Jane Stearns, Clare Steele, Annelies Steen, Jorrit Steinz, Fay Stenhouse, Judith Stettner,

Andrew Stevenson, Andrew & Emmeline Stevenson, Jonny Stevenson, Rik Stewart, William Steyn, Laurie & Daph Stokes, Bill & Ann Stoughton, Shane Straiko, Sarah Street, Karen Strehlow, The Strosbergs, Greg Sullivan, Rinko Suzuki, Bonar Swale, Petra Swalue, Kathrine Switzer, Kathi Swolinzky, Lucy & Bev Sydney, Eileen Synnott, Christian Szeglat, Queenie Szeto **T** Konia Tack, Julie Talbot, Brenda Tan, Larissa Tandy, Donna Tang, Brian Tanner, Chas Tanner, Anna Tapp, Kelly Tarbuck, Vanessa Tasker, David Taylor, Mary Taylor, Steve Taylor, James Teare, Garry Telford, Stuart Templeton, Ray & Leahn Theedam Parry, Rebecca Thiessen, A Thomas, Paul Thomas, Sally Thomas, Stephen Thompson, William Thompson, Romuald Thoraval, Michael Thorn, Nopporn Thummanond, Patricia Tierney, Edmund Ting, Maarten Tip, Luke Tolson, Jochen Topf, Karen Towns, Gillian Trotter, Paul Tuckwell, Toni & Rick Tuttle, Rob Twamley, Rachel Tyler **U** Andy Ulery, Harkiran Uppal **V** Ivan Valencic, Koosje van Bergen, Mariska van den Akker, Stefan van den Bos, Tiny Van Den Brink, Suzanne van der Kolk, Bart van Dongen, Leondra van Hattum, Teun van Metelen, Chris van Namen, Luke Vanguns, Liz Vaughan, Zoe Veater, Gerben Veneman, Frans Verhoef, Brice Villion, Nate Vinatelli, Michael & C Vink, Erna Jansen Vledder, H Plenter Vledder, Jacqueline Vlotman, Fiona Vorrink, Caspar Vroonland **W** Michael W, Parani Waaka, Reto Wagner, Ollie Waite, Jim & Jill Waits, Catriona Walker, Steve Walker, Emma Walmsley, Katharina Wandt, Lek Warawut, Andy Ward, Lucille Warlow, Diana Warr, Adrian Warren, Beth Wasgatt, Etsuko Watanabe, David Watkin, Natalie Watson, Chris Webb, Angelika Weber, Christine Weber, M Weber, Mary Weeder, Harald Wegele,

---

SEND US YOUR FEEDBACK

We love to hear from travellers – your comments keep us on our toes and help make our books better. Our well-travelled team reads every word on what you loved or loathed about this book. Although we cannot reply individually to postal submissions, we always guarantee that your feedback goes straight to the appropriate authors, in time for the next edition. Each person who sends us information is thanked in the next edition – and the most useful submissions are rewarded with a free book.

To send us your updates – and find out about LP events, newsletters and travel news – visit our award-winning website: **www.lonelyplanet.com**.

Note: We may edit, reproduce and incorporate your comments in Lonely Planet products such as guidebooks, websites and digital products, so let us know if you don't want your comments reproduced or your name acknowledged. For a copy of our privacy policy visit www.lonelyplanet.com/privacy.

Helmut & Karin Wermbter, Karen West, Bastiaan Westerhout, Laura Weston, Zoe Wharnsby, David Wheeler, David Whelan, Georgina Whetham, Elva & Peter Whitaker, Heather White, Matt Whitehead, Lorna Whitfield, David Whiting, Naomi Whitney, Laura Whittle, Julie Wilchins, Louise Wilkinson, Tanya Wilkinson, Catrin Williams, Hannah & Metua Williams, Katie Williams, Lynne Willimott, Lee Wills, Andy Wilson, Keith Winders, Marilynn Windust, Jennie Winroth, Zuzanna Wojcik, Eugene Wojcinski, John Wormington, Valerie Wotton, Craig Wright, Maureen Wright, Mandy Wuendsch Y Lesley Yamauchi, Kaori Yasukochi, Barbara Yates, Emma Yates, Johnnie Yates, Man Yau, Terry Yoshimura, DC Young, EM Young Z Junaid Zaman, Marc Zangwill, William P Zasoba, Oliver Zoellner, Amy Zuber

ACKNOWLEDGEMENTS

Many thanks to the following for the use of their content:

Globe on back cover © Mountain High Maps 1993 Digital Wisdom, Inc.

Alexander Turnbull Library, Wellington, NZ for use of images.

Index

309 Road 204
4WD activities 108-9

A
abalone 86
    shells 672
Abbey Caves 190
Abel Tasman Coastal Track 80, 456-8
Abel Tasman National Park 456-9,
    457, 7, 500-1
abseiling 237
Academy Galleries 387
accommodation 658-61, *see also indi-*
    vidual locations
Achilles Point lookout 105
Acker, Lewis 647
Acker's Point Lighthouse 649
activities 61-84, *see also individual*
    activities
aerial sightseeing 61, 137, 618-19, 626
Agrodome 330
Ahipara 165
Ahuriri Forest 549
Aigantighe Art Gallery 542
air travel 678-83
    air fares 680-2, 683
    airlines 678-9, 682
    airports 678-9
    to/from New Zealand 678-82
    within New Zealand 682-3
Akaroa 527-30, **528**
Akaroa Museum 527
albatross 567
Albatross Point 228
Alberton House 102
Albert Park 105
alcohol 87-8, 89
Alexandra 571-2
Alexandra Museum 571
Ambury Farm Park 106
Ancient Kauri Kingdom 166
Anderson Park Art Gallery 632
animals 56-7, 57-8, 59, 638, 647, *see*
    also individual species
Antipodes Islands 656
Aoraki/Mt Cook National Park 59,
    549-54, 615, **7, 532-3, 596-7,**
    550
Aorangi Ski Club 72
Aorere Gold Field 465
Aotea Centre 125
Aotea Square Market 126
Aotearoa Maori Performing Arts

000 Map pages
000 Location of colour photographs

Festival 111
Aranui Cave 236
Arataki 307-8
Aratiatia Rapids 306
area codes 673, *see also inside front*
    cover
Arrowtown 596-8, **597**
Art Deco 369, 371, 375
art galleries, *see* galleries
Arthur's Pass 535-6, **535**
Arthur's Pass National Park 75, 81,
    535, **596-7**
arts 41-6, 52-3, *see also individual arts*
Arts Centre 509-10
ASB Open Tennis Championships 111
Ashburton 536-7
Ashburton Art Gallery & Museum 536
Asian Lantern Festival 111
Atene Skyline Track 273
Athenree Hot Springs 213
Atkinson, Harry 256
ATMs 669-70
Auckland 94-129, **96, 98, 130, 10,**
    116-17
    accommodation 112-14, 114-16,
        117-18
    activities 106-9
    attractions 97-106
    city centre 112-13, 114-15, 117,
        118-19, 123
    Devonport 103, 115-16, 117-18,
        122, **104**
    drinking 123
    emergency services 95
    entertainment 123-5
    festivals 111-12
    food 118-23
    history 94
    Internet access 95
    itineraries 95
    K Rd 104, 120-1, 123
    medical services 95-7
    Mission Bay 123
    Mt Eden 114, 115, 122-3, **102**
    Newmarket 122, **102**
    Parnell 113-14, 115, 117, 120,
        123, **100**
    Ponsonby 104, 114, 115, 117,
        121-2, 123, **105**
    Princes Wharf 119-20, 123
    shopping 125-6
    tourist offices 97
    travel to/from 126-8
    travel within 128-9
    Viaduct Harbour 119-20, 123
    walking tours 109
Auckland Anniversary Day Regatta 111

Auckland Art Gallery 101
Auckland Botanical Gardens 106
Auckland Cup 112
Auckland Domain 105
Auckland Islands 655-6
Auckland Museum 99-100, **116-17**
Auckland Speleo Group 64
Auckland to Russell Yacht Race 112
Auckland Town Hall 125
Auckland Zoo 101
aurora australis 645
Australasian gannet 62
Avondale Market 126
Awa Awa Rata Reserve 537
Awakeri Hot Springs 347-8
Awakino 242-3
Awakino Gorge 242
Awana Bay 141
Awarua Wetlands 640

B
B&Bs 659
back-country huts 82
Balclutha 576, 641, 642
ballooning 513, 537-8
bank accounts 669-70
Banks Peninsula 526-30, **526, 532-3**
Banks Peninsula Walk 81
Barrytown 477-8
bars 89
base jumping 107
Bastion Point 104
Bauza Island 628
Bay of Islands 172-92, **173, 61,**
    292-3
Bay of Plenty 312-50, **315**
Baylys Beach 157-8
beaches
    Awana Bay 141
    Baylys Beach 157-8
    Bethells Beach 108
    Boulder Beach 647
    Christchurch 511
    Doubtless Bay 169
    Dunedin 561
    Frasers Beach 628
    Gannet Colony 132
    Goat Island 153-4
    Hahei 207-8
    Harataonga 141
    Hot Water Beach 209
    Kaiteriteri 455
    Kaitoke 141
    Karekare Beach 131
    Kawhia 228
    Little Oneroa Beach 135
    Manu Bay 227

Medlands Beach 141
Mokau 243
Muriwai Beach 108, 132
New Chum's Beach 204
Ngarunui Beach 227
Ninety Mile Beach 166-8
Oakura 256-7
Ocean Beach 228
Ohope Beach 348
Okiwi Bar 141
Oneroa Beach 135
Opito Bay 204
Opoutere Beach 211
Oreti Beach 633
Otama Beach 204
Pakiri 154
Palm Beach 135
Paraparaumu Beach 409
Piha Beach 108, 131
Raglan 226
Rainbow Reach 628
Rangipu Beach 227
Ruapuke Beach 227
Sandfly Bay 569
Urenui 256
Waihi Beach 212-13
Whangapoua 141
Whatipu Beach 132
Becks 574
beer 87-8, see also breweries
bellbirds 57, 145
Bethells Beach 108
bicycle travel, see cycling
bird-watching 61-2
    Ambury Farm Park 106
    Awarua Wetlands 640
    Campbell Island 656
    Cape Kidnappers Gannet Colony
        380
    Catlins 638
    Chatham Islands 653-4
    Disappointment Island 656
    Enderby Island 656
    Farewell Spit 462-3
    Kapiti Island 410
    Miranda 213
    Motuhora 347
    Mt Bruce 412
    Nga Manu Nature Reserve 410
    Nugget Point 642
    Otago Peninsula 567-8
    Otorohanga Kiwi House & Native
        Bird Park 235
    Peel Forest 544-5
    Shakespear Regional Park 149
    Snares Islands 655
    Stewart Island 647
    Sugar Loaf Islands Marine Park
        250, 251
    Takapu Refuge 132
    Tiritiri Matangi Island 58, 145
    Trounson Kauri Park 159
    Ulva Island 647
    Wharekawa Wildlife Refuge 211

birds 56, 57-8
    books 57, 62
black coral 625, 628
black-water rafting 62, 238
Blackball 479
Blenheim 430-5, **431**
Blue Lake 574
Bluecliffs Beach 630
Bluff 636-7
Bluff Hill 636
Bluff Oyster & Southland Seafood
    Festival 636
boat travel
    to/from New Zealand 682
    within New Zealand 684
boat trips, see cruises
boating, see sailing
books 14, 15, 57, see also literature
    birds 57, 62
    fishing 65
    flora 56
    food 90
    geography 56
    Internet resources 41
    New Zealand Wars 29
    tramping 78
    travel 14
Botanic Gardens 391
Boulder Beach 647
Bounty Islands 656
Bowen Falls 626
Bream Bay 154-5
breweries
    Canterbury Brewery 510
    DB Mainland Brewery 542
    Lion Breweries 101-2
    Speight's Brewery 559
    Wanaka Beerworks 605
Bridal Veil Falls 228
Britannia Track 474
Broadlands 307
Brod Bay 617
Brooklands Park 251
brush-tailed possum 58, 647
Buller Gorge 470
bungy jumping 63
    Auckland 107
    Hanmer Springs 532
    Methven 537
    Queenstown 585-6, 586
    Taupo 298, 292-3
bungy rocket 62, 63
Buried Village of Te Wairoa 54, 330-1
bus travel 685-7
bush-tailed rock wallabies 152
bushwalking, see walking
business hours 661
Butler, Samuel 544
Butterfly & Orchid Garden 197

C
cafés 89
Cambridge 231-2
Campbell Island 656

campervan travel 687-91
    driving licence 687-8
    insurance 689-90
    parks 659
    rental 688-9
    road distance chart 687, **687**, **688**
    road rules 691
camping 82, 659
Cannibal Bay 642
canoeing, see kayaking
Canterbury 501-54, **503**
Canterbury Brewery 510
Canterbury Museum 508-9
canyon swinging 62
canyoning
    Auckland 106
    Queenstown 587
    Wanaka 606
Cape Brett 176, 187
Cape Foulwind 473
Cape Kidnappers 380
Cape Reinga 166-8, **292-3**
Caples Track 81, 602, **601**
car travel 687-91
    driving licence 687-8
    insurance 689-90
    rental 689
    road distance chart 687, **687**, **688**
    road rules 691
    safety 664
Cardrona 74, 611, **75**, **76**, **596-7**
carving 52-3
Cascade Creek 622
Cascade River 500
Cascade Saddle **78**
Castle Rock 204
Castle Rock Winery 204
Cathedral Caves 640
Cathedral Cove 207
Cathedral Square 505
Catholicism 40
Catlins Conservation Park 632, 641
Catlins, the 638-42, **639**
cave rafting 62, 238
caves
    Abbey Caves 190
    Cave Stream Scenic Reserve 534
    Harwood's Hole 460
    Honeycomb Hill Caves & Arch 474
    Ngarua Caves 459-60
    Rawhiti Cave 462
    Ruatapu Cave 308
caving 64
    Aranui Cave 236
    Aurora Caves 617
    Cathedral Caves 640
    Clifden (Waiau) Caves 630
    Glowworm Cave 235-6
    Lost World Cave 237
    Museum of Caves 236-7
    Nikau Cave 220
    Piripiri Caves Scenic Reserve 240
    Ruakuri Cave 236, 238

St Benedict's Cavern 238
Te Anau Glowworm Caves 617
Waitomo Caves 235-6, **236**
Central Plateau 280-311, **283**
cervena 86
Charleston 476
Charming Creek 474
Chasm Walk 622
Chatham Islands 651-5, **653**
children, travel with 661-2
  Auckland 109
  Christchurch 513
  food 89-90
  Franz Josef Glacier 492-5
  itineraries 20
  Kelly Tarlton's Antarctic Encounter
    & Underwater World 101
  Queen Elizabeth Park 412
  Queenstown 588-9
  Rainbow's End Adventure Park 106
  Southwest New Zealand (Te
    Wahipounamu) World Heritage
    Area 549, 615
  Summer City Festival 394
  Te Ngae Park 330
  Te Whakarewarewa 318-19
  Tramway 510
  TranzAlpine railway 484
  Wellington 394
Christchurch 503-24, **506, 507, 522,
  532-3, 596-7**
  accommodation 513-17
  attractions 505-11
  drinking 519-20
  emergency services 505
  entertainment 520-1
  festivals 513
  food 517-19
  history 504
  itineraries 504
  medical services 505
  shopping 521-3
  tourist offices 505
  tours 513
  travel to/from 523-4
  travel within 524
  walking tour 512
Christchurch Art Gallery 509
Christchurch Cathedral 505
Christianity 40
Christmas in the Park 112
Christmas tree 58, 200
Circle Track 628
City Gallery Wellington 387
Clark, Helen 33
Clarke Island 211
Clay Cliffs 580

Cleddau Canyon 622
Cleddau River 622-3
Clifden (Waiau) Caves 630
Clifden Suspension Bridge 630
climate 13, 56, 662
  Auckland region 94
  Bay of Plenty 314
  Canterbury 503
  Central Plateau 282
  Coromandel region 196
  East Coast 353
  Manawatu 264
  Northland region 148
  Otago 557
  safety 663
  Southland 614
  Stewart Island 645
  Taranaki 248
  tramping 56
  Wanganui region 264
  Wellington region 384
  West Coast 468
clothing 671
Clutha district 576
Clyde 572-4
Coast to Coast Walkway 109
Cobb Valley 465
coffee 88
Colac Bay 631
Collingwood 462-3
Colville 203
Comedy Festival 111
conservation 55
consulates 665
Cook, James 28
Copland Track 498
Copland Valley 498, 6
Cornwall Park 105
Coromandel 193-215
Coromandel Coastal Walkway 200,
  203
Coromandel Forest Park 200
Coromandel Peninsula 196-213
Coromandel Pohutukawa Festival 666
Coromandel Town 201-3, **201**
Coromandel Track 81
Coronet Peak 73
costs 13-14
Cosy Nook 631
Cotton, Shane 46
courses
  Buddhist 203
  cooking 90-1
  kayaking 84
Covert Theatre 125
crafts 671
Craigieburn Forest Park 534
Craigieburn Valley 75
Crater Lake 286
Craters of the Moon 307
crayfish 441
credit cards 669-70

cricket 39
Croesus Track 479
Cromwell 570-1
cruises
  Auckland 106
  Bay of Islands 173
  Doubtful Sound 628-9
  Dusky Sound 629
  Lake Manapouri 628
  Milford Sound 626-7
  Queenstown 589
  Stewart Island 649
  Te Anau 619
  Timaru 542
culture 32, 34-46
  etiquette 90
  food 90
  haka 52, 53
  King Movement 219, 234
  Maori arts 52-3, 671-2
  Maori people 47-53, 510
  marae 50-1
  mythology 47-8, 49
  number-eight wire 35
  NZ–UK relations 32
  population 38-9
  religion 40
  Maori spirituality *(wairua)* 48-9
  women 40-1
Curio Bay 640
customs regulations 663-5
cycling 39, 67, 684, *see also* mountain
  biking
  Auckland 128, **96, 98, 130**
  Blenheim 432, **431**
  Christchurch 511 **506, 507, 522**
  Hawkes Bay 379-80
  Otago 573, **558**
  Renwick 435
  Rotorua 321, **316, 328**
  Taupo 299, **296, 305**

D
Danseys Pass 574
Dargaville 156-7, **157**
Dawson Falls 258
Days Bay 391-2, 407
de Surville, Jean 27
Deep Vein Thrombosis 694
deers 647
dendroglyphs 652, 654
Denniston 474
Desert Alpine Club 72
Devonport 103, 115-16, 117-18,
  122, **104**
Devonport Food & Wine Festival 111
disabled travellers 66, 664
Disappointment Island 656
Divide, the 622
diving, *see* scuba diving
Dobson Forest 549
dolphin swimming
  Auckland 106

Bay of Islands 174
Kaikoura 438-9
Tauranga 333
Whakatane 345
dolphins 58, 66, 528, 628, **132-3**
Doneraille Park 365
dotterel 62
Doubtless Bay 169-70
drinks 87-8
customs 90
Driving Creek Railway 201-2
du Fresne, Marion 27
Dunedin 557-67, 637, **560**, **628-9**
accommodation 562-4
attractions 558-61
drinking 565
entertainment 565-6
food 564-5
tours 562
travel to/from 566-7
travel within 567
Duntroon 580
Durie Hill 268
Dusky Sound 628
Dusky Track 628, 630
DVT 694

E
earthquakes 56
East Cape 353-8
East Cape Lighthouse 355
East Coast 351-81, **354**
East Coast war 30
Eastbourne 407
Eastern Southland Gallery 46
economy 24, 31-2, 33, 35, 37
Eden Gardens 105
Eden Park 125
Edge 125
Eftpos 669-70
Egmont National Park 81, 257, 258
electricity 658
elephant seals 638
Ellerslie Flower Show 112
email services 668
embassies 665
emergencies, *see inside front cover*
Enderby Island 656
energy consumption 55, 256
environmental issues 55
geology 54-6
Internet resources 38
land rights 24
Maori people 49-50
responsible tramping 83
Save Manapouri petition 628
Ericsson Stadium 125
events & festivals 665-6, 11
Auckland 111-12
Christchurch 513
food 88
Gore 637

Hamilton 220
Wellington 394-5
Ewelme Cottage 102-3

F
Fairlie 545
fantails 57
Fantham's Peak 257
Farewell Spit 462-3, **500-1**
farmstays 659
Ferry Landing 207
festivals, *see* events & festivals
film 15, 42-4, *see also Lord of the Rings*
New Zealand International Film
Festival 665-6
Fiordland 615-32, **616**
Fiordland crested penguin 62
Fiordland National Park 59, 615
fiords 627-8
Milford Sound 624-7
Te Anau 615-21
First Church of Otago 559
First Night 112
First Taranaki war 30
Firth of Thames 196, 213
Firth Tower 233
fishing 64-5
Bay of Islands 175
books 65
Chatham Islands 654
Glenorchy 599
Gore 637-8
Internet resources 64, 65
Lake Brunner 479
Lake Manapouri 628
Mokau 243
permits 59, 65
Rotorua 321
Ruapuke Beach 227
Sugar Loaf Islands Marine Park
250, 251
Tairua 209
Taupo 297-8
Te Anau 618
Turangi 309
Whangamata 211
whitebait 499
Whitianga 206
Fitzroy Pole 250
Flagstaff Point Lookout 647
flora 56
Florence Hill 640
food 86-7, 89-90, 91, 666, 11
books 90
courses 90-1
customs 90
festivals 88
vegetarian travellers 89
whitebait 499
Footrot Flats 234
forest parks, *see also* national parks,
regional parks
Craigieburn Forest Park 534

Haurangi Forest Park 414-15
Kaimai Mamaku Forest Park 333
Lake Sumner Forest Park 81
Omahuta Forest 163
Opua Forest 178
Pirongia Forest Park 230-1
Puketi Forest 163
Pureora Forest Park 307-8
Rimutaka Forest Park 414-15
Tararua Forest Park 411, 414-15
Victoria Forest Park 478
Waipoua Kauri Forest 159-60, **160**
Whirinaki Forest Park 331
fossilised sharks' teeth 654
Four Brothers Scenic Reserve 227
Foveaux Walk 636
Fox Glacier 495-8, **495**, **532-3**
Fox Peak 74
Frame, Janet 41, 579
Franz Josef Glacier 492-5, **493**
Frizzell, Dick 46
Froggate Edge 230
fur seals 628, 638, 640, 647, 654

G
Gabriels Gully 575
galleries 46
Academy Galleries 387
Aigantighe Art Gallery 542
Anderson Park Art Gallery 632
Auckland Art Gallery 101
Christchurch Art Gallery 509
City Gallery Wellington 387
Dunedin Public Art Gallery 559
Eastern Southland Gallery 46
Forrester Gallery 578
Govett-Brewster Art Gallery 46, 250
Southland Museum & Art
Gallery 632
gannets 132, 380
gardens
Botanic Gardens 391
Christchurch Botanic Gardens 508
Moutoa Gardens 268
Gay & Lesbian Fair 666
Gay Ski Week 666
gay travellers 666
Auckland 111
Wellington 395
Gemstone Bay 207
genetic engineering 55
Gentle Annie Beach 474
geography 54-9
books 56
environmental issues 55
geology 54-6
Geraldine 544
Gisborne 358-64, **359**
glacier skiing 76-7
glaciers 490-8
Fox Glacier 495-8, **495**
Franz Josef Glacier 492-5, **493**

Glade House 625
Glade Wharf 619, 625
Glenbrook Vintage Railway 219
Glenorchy 598-600
gliding 298
Glory Track 636
glossary 701-4
    food 87
    glacier-speak 490
glow-worms 220, 237, 486, 630
    Glowworm Cave 235-6
    Te Anau Glowworm Caves 617
Goat Island 153-4
gods 47-8, 49
gold mining 212
Golden Bay 459-65
golf 65
    Auckland 109
    Hanmer Springs 532
    Invercargill 633
    Mokau 243
Goods and Services Tax (GST) 670
Gore 637-8
Govett-Brewster Art Gallery 46, 250
Great Barrier Island 139-45, **140**, **132-3**
Great Walks 77, 80-1, **80**
    Abel Tasman Coastal Track 80, 456-8
    Heaphy Track 80, 464-5, **464**
    Kepler Track 80, 617, **619**
    Lake Waikaremoana 80, 366-8
    Mangapurua Track 273
    Matemateaonga Track 273
    Milford Track 80, 624-5, **624**
    Rakiura Track 81, 648-9
    Routeburn Track 81, 600-2, **601**
    Tongariro Northern Circuit 81, 284
    travel to/from 82
    Whanganui Journey 81
greenstone 672, **532-3**
Greenstone Track 81, 602, **601**
Grey Valley 478-80
Greymouth 480-4, **481**
Greytown 412-13
guesthouses 659
Gumdiggers Park 165-6

H
Haast-Paringa Cattle Track 498
Haast Pass 500
Haast region 498-500, **532-3**
Hahei 207-8
haka 52, 53
Hakarimata Walkway 220
Halfmoon Bay 645, 646
Hamilton 220-4, **221**

Hamilton Gardens 221
Hamilton Zoo 222
hang-gliding 378
hangi 319
Hanmer Springs 75-6, 530-3, **531**
Harataonga 141
Hari Hari Coastal Walkway 489
Harihari 488
Harrold Bay 647, 649
Haruru Falls 178
Harvest Hawke's Bay 665
Harwood's Hole 460
Hastings 375-8, **376**
Haumia-tike-tike 47
Hauraki Gulf 196
Hauraki Gulf Islands 133-45
Hauraki Gulf Maritime Park 133
Hauraki Region 213-15
Hauturu (Clarke) Island 211
Havelock 429-30
Havelock North 378
Hawai 355
Hawea 603-4
Hawera 260-1
Hawkes Bay 365-81
health 693-6
    insurance 693
    vaccinations 693
Heaphy Track 80, 464-5, **464**
Hector's dolphins 631, 640
Heineken Open Tennis Championships 111
Heke, Hone 30
Helensville 132
heli-hiking
    Aoraki/Mt Cook National Park 552, **550**
    Fox Glacier 496, **495**
    Franz Josef Glacier 492, **493**
    Te Anau 619
heli-skiing 76
helicopter tours
    Aoraki/Mt Cook National Park 552
    Hanmer Springs 532
    Lake Tekapo 547
    Queenstown 589
    Wanaka 607
Hell's Gate 327
Hermitage Hotel 551
HERO Festival 111, 666
Hicks Bay 355
Highwic House 102
hiking, *see* walking
Hillary, Edmund 67, 549-50
Hine-ahuone 47
Hine-titama 47
Hinemoa & Tutanekai 318
Hirakimata 142
Hirawanu Tapu 652
history 25-33
    European settlement 26-7
    immigration 29

King Movement 219, 234
Maori 526, 557
Musket Wars 27
NZ–UK relations 32
Polynesian settlement 25-6
Rotorua 314
Tainui canoe 229
Treaty of Waitangi 29
warfare 27, 30, 31-2, 51-2
Wellington 384-5
hitching 691
Hobbiton 232, 233
hoiho 626
Hokianga 160-3
Hokianga-Waipoua Coastal Track 160-1
Hokitika 484-8, **485**
Hokitika Gorge 488
Hokonui Hills 632, 637
Hokonui Moonshine Museum 637
holidays 13, 667
Hollyford Camp 622
Hollyford Track 623-4
Hollyford Valley 622
Holy Trinity Cathedral 103
Homer Tunnel 622
Honeycomb Hill Caves & Arch 474
Hooker's sea lions 638
Hope Arm 628
Hopkins Forest 549
horse riding 65-6
    Christchurch 513
    Glenorchy 599
    Great Barrier Island 142
    Hanmer Springs 532
    Pirongia Forest Park 230-1
    Sunset Corral 137
    Taupo 298
hostels 660-1
hot-air ballooning 61
    Auckland 109
    Hamilton 220
hot springs
    Kaitote Hot Springs Track 142
    Opal Hot Springs 233
    Te Puia Hot Springs 228
    Waingaro Hot Springs 225
Hot Water Beach 209
hotels 659-60
Hotere, Ralph 637
Howarth Wetlands Reserve 214
Howick Historical Village 103
Huka Falls 306
Huka Falls Tourist Loop 304-7
Hukanui 306
Humboldt Falls 622
Hump Ridge Track 81, 630
Hundertwasser, Freidensreich 187
hunting 59
Hurworth 256
Hutt Valley 407
Huxley Forest 549
hypothermia 695

I

immigration 29, 38-9
Inangahua Junction 470
Inglewood 256
Inland Pack Track 81
insurance
    health 693
    travel 667
    vehicle 689-90
International Antarctic Centre 510
International League for the Protection of Horses 66
Internet access 667-8
Internet resources 14-15, 38, 40, 64, 67, 68
    air tickets 679-80
    architecture 41
    arts 46
    books 41
    cinema 44
    fishing 64, 65
    gay & lesbian travellers 666
    history 33
    Maori people 48
    music 44, 45
    sports 39
    surfing 70, 71
    tramping 76
Invercargill 632-6, 640, **633**
Iris Burn Hut 617
islands
    Antipodes Islands 656
    Auckland Islands 655-6
    Bauza Island 628
    Bounty Islands 656
    Campbell Island 656
    Disappointment Island 656
    Enderby Island 656
    Goat Island 153-4
    Great Barrier Island 139-45, **140**
    Hauraki Gulf Islands 133-45
    Hauturu (Clarke) Island 211
    Kapiti Island 410
    Kawau Island 152-3
    Kermadecs, the 656
    Little Barrier 145
    Matakana Island 340
    Matiu-Somes Island 391-2
    Monkey Island 631
    Motuihe Island 145
    Motuora 145
    Moturiki Island 338
    Motutapu Island 133-4, **134**
    Nee Island 628
    Poor Knights Islands 188-9
    Rabbit Island 452
    Rangatahua 656
    Rangitoto Island 133-4, **134**
    Slipper Island 210
    Snares Islands 655
    Stewart Island 81, 645-51, **646**
    Subantarctic Islands 655-6

    Tiritiri Matangi Island 58, 145
    Tokelau 656-7
    Ulva Island 647
    Waiheke Island 134-9, **136**
    Whakaari 346-7
itineraries 16-20, 21
    Auckland 95
    children 20
    North Island 18
    South Island 17
    wineries 20
Ivon Wilson Park 617

J

Jack's Blowhole 641
Jackson, Peter 42
Jackson Bay 500
jade 672
jetboating 66, 511
    Aratiatia Rapids 306-7
    Bay of Islands 173-4
    Glenorchy 599
    Haast 499
    Hanmer Springs 532
    Lake Hauroko 630
    Lake McKerrow 623
    Mt Aspiring National Park 603
    Queenstown 586
    Rakaia River Gorge 537
    Taupo 299-300
    Te Anau 617
    Wanaka 606
    Whanganui River 272

K

K Rd 104, 120-1, 123
Kahurangi National Park 463-5, **500-1**
Kai Iwi Lakes 158
Kaikohe 162
Kaikoura 435-42, **436**
Kaikoura Coast Track 81
Kaimai Mamaku Forest Park 333
Kaingaroa Forest 59
Kaipara Lighthouse 158
Kaitaia 163-5, **164**
Kaiteriteri 455
Kaitoke 141
Kaitoke Hot Springs Track 142
Kaitoke Regional Park 415
Kaka Point 642
Kapiti Coast 407-11
Kapiti Island 410
Kapowairua 167
Kapua te Rangi 345
Karamea 474-6
Karamu Walkway 227
Karangahake Gorge 214
Karekare Beach 131, **132-3**
Karikari Peninsula 168-9
Kati Mamoe 645
Katikati 340-1

Katiki 581
Kauaeranga Valley 200
Kauri Coast 155-60
kauri trees 58-9
    Kauri Coast 155-60
    Waipoua Kauri Forest 159-60, **160**
    Warkworth 151
Kawakawa 187
Kawau Island 152-3
Kawerau 348
Kawhia 228-9
kayaking 63-4, 84
    Abel Tasman National Park 458
    Aoraki/Mt Cook National Park 552-3
    Auckland 108
    Doubtful Sound 617
    Glenorchy 599
    Great Barrier Island 142
    Kawhia 228
    Kayak Company 137
    Lake Karapiro 232
    Lake Manapouri 628
    Milford Sound 617
    Otago Peninsula 569
    Raglan 226
    Rotorua 321
    Stewart Island 649
    Taumarunui 243
    Taupo 298
    Te Anau 617
    Wanaka 606
    Whanganui River 272
kea 57
Kelly Tarlton's Antarctic Encounter & Underwater World 101
Kepler Track 80, 617, **619**
Kerikeri 183-7, **184**
Kermadecs, the 656
Key Summit 622
Kinder House 103
King Country 234-45, **218**
King Movement 219, 234
King Tawhiao 219, 234
Kingston Flyer 590
Kiri Te Kanawa, Dame 362
kite surfing 227
kiteboarding 62
kiwi 56, 57, 58, 62
    Otorohanga 234
    Stewart Island 649
    Tiritiri Matangi Island 145
kiwi fruit 342
Kiwi House 58
Knights Point 498
Knobs Flat 622
Ko Tongariro te Maunga 49
Kohukohu 162-3
kokoda 89
Koroki-mahuta 219
kotuku 489
kowhai 58

INDEX

INDEX

Kowhitirangi 488
Kuaotunu 204
Kuirau Park 318-19
Kupe 204
Kurow 580

L
Lake Brunner 479-80
Lake Castalia 603
Lake District Museum & Gallery 596-7
Lake Gunn 622
Lake Hakanoa 220
Lake Hauroko 627, 630
Lake Hawea 603
Lake Kaniere 488
Lake Karapiro 232
Lake Lucidus 603
Lake Manapouri 627, 628
Lake Mangamahoe 256
Lake Marian 622
Lake McKerrow 623
Lake Moeraki 498
Lake Ohau 549
Lake Paringa 498
Lake Pukaki 545, 548
Lake Rotokura 295
Lake Rotomanu 251
Lake Rotorua 316
Lake Ruataniwha 548
Lake Sumner Forest Park 81
Lake Tarawera 331
Lake Taupo 54, 230, 295-311, **292-3**
Lake Te Anau 615, 619, 628
Lake Tekapo 545-8, **546**, **532-3**
Lake Waikaremoana Track 80, 366-8, **367**
Lake Wakatipu 581-2, 598
Lake Wilkie 640
Lakes Diana 603
Land Information New Zealand 78
land rights 24
Land Wars 30
Lange, David 33
language 698-700
Larnach Castle 568-9
Lawrence 575
legal matters 668
Leigh 153
Lenz Reserve 640
lesbian travellers 666
   Auckland 111
   Wellington 395
Leslie-Karamea Track 81, 465
Lewis Pass 533
Lewis Pass Highway 533-4
Lewis Pass Reserve 81
Lion Breweries 101-2
Lion Rock 131

000 Map pages
000 Location of colour photographs

literature 41, see also books
Little Barrier 145
Little Oneroa Beach 135
local transport 691
Loch Maree Hut 628
long-tail bats 622
Lord of the Rings 42-3
   Matamata 232
   Tongariro National Park 282, 284
   Wellington 393
Lost World Cave 237
Luxmoore Hut 617
Lyttelton 524-6
Lyttelton Museum 525

M
Macetown 597
Mackenzie Country 545-9
Mackinnon Pass 625
Maclennan River 641
Macraes Flat 575
Macraes Gold Mine 575
macrocarpas 631
maeroero 638
magazines 39
Mahamudra Centre 203
Mahia Peninsula 365
Mahoenui 242
Makarora 602-3
Maketu 343
Maketu Marae 228
Malsapina Reach 628
mamuka 59
manaia 53
Manapouri 627-30
Manawatu 262-3, 274-9, **267**
Manawatu Gorge 276
Manganui ski area 72-3
Mangapohue Natural Bridge Scenic Reserve 240
Mangapurua Track 273
Mangawhai 154
Manhire, Bill 41
Manioroa Marae 243
Mansfield, Katherine 391
Manu Bay 225, 227
Maori & Colonial Museum 527
Maori
   arts 52-3, 671-2
   culture 47-53, 510, **8**, **324-5**
   haka 52, 53
   history 526, 557
   Internet resources 48
   King Movement 219, 234
   marae 50-1
   music 44
   mythology 47-8, 49
   population 38
   visual art 46
   spirituality 40, 48-9
   warfare 51-2
Maori Wars 30
maps 78, 668-9

marae 50-1
   Maketu Marae 228
   Manioroa Marae 243
   Nga Hau a Wha 510
   Te Tokanganui-o-noho Marae 241
   Turangawaewae Marae 220
Marahau 455-6
Marine Parade 369-71
Marlborough Region 416-42, **419**
Marlborough Sounds 425-9, **426**, **500-1**
Marlborough Wine Trail 432
Marokopa Falls 240
Marokopa Rd 240-1
Marsland Hill 250
Martha Mine 212
Martinborough 413-14
Martyr Saddle 500
Masterton 412
Matai Falls 641
Matakana Island 340
Matakohe 155-6
Matamata 232-3
Mataura 637
Mataura River 637
Matauri Bay 172
Matemateaonga Track 273
Matiu-Somes Island 391-2
Matukituki Valley walks 81
Matutaera-te-wherowhero 219
Maui 47-8
Mayor Island 341
McCahon, Colin 36, 46
McCashin's Brewery & Malthouse 444
McKellen, Ian 664
McKenzie, James 'Jock' 545
McLaren Falls 333
McLean Falls 640
Mediaplex & Film Archive 390
medical services 694-5
Medlands Beach 141
Mercer 219
Methanex NZ's Motunui Plant 256
Methven 537-40, **538**
Middlemarch 574
Mikhail Lermontov 71
Milford Deep underwater observatory 625-6
Milford Sound 589, 622, 624-7
   cruises 626-7, **628-9**
Milford Track 80, 624-5, **624**, **628-9**
Mimiwhangata Coastal Park 192
Minden Lookout 341
Minus 5° Bar 109
Miranda 213
Mirror Lakes 622
Mission Bay 104, 123, **116-17**
Mission Bay Jazz & Blues Street Fest 111
Mitimiti 163
Mitre Peak 624
moa 56

Moana Kotuku 479-80
mobile phones 673
Moeraki 581
mohua 638
Mokau 242, 243
Mokena Geyser 214
moko 53
Molesworth Station 531
money 13-14, 669-70, *see also inside front cover*
moneychangers 670
Monkey Island 631
Morere 365
Mores Reserve 631
Moriori people 26, 652
Motat (Museum of Transport & Technology) 101
motels 659-60
motorcycle travel 687-91
    rental 689-90
    road distance chart 687, **687**, **688**
    road rules 691
    safety 664
Motu River 355
Motueka 452-5, **453**
Motuhora 347
Motuihe Island 145
Motuora 145
Moturau Hut 617
Moturiki Island 338
Motutapu Island 133-4, **134**
Mt Anglem 646
Mt Aspiring 602
Mt Aspiring National Park 606, 615, **7, 78**
Mt Bruce 412
Mt Cheeseman 75
Mt Cook 549-50
Mt Cook National Park, *see* Aoraki/Mt Cook National Park
Mt Dobson 74
Mt Eden (Maungawhau) 103, 114, 115, 122-3
Mt Edgecumbe 348
Mt Egmont 257-9
Mt Holdsworth Circuit 81
Mt Hutt 74
Mt Hutt Forest 537
Mt Karioi 228
Mt Lyford 76
Mt Maunganui 337-40, **334**
Mt Ngauruhoe 284, **6**
Mt Olympus 75
Mt Pirongia 230-1
Mt Potts 74
Mt Robert 76
Mt Ruapehu 72, 282-3, **292-3**
Mt Somers 540
Mt Taranaki (Mt Egmont) 257-9, **12**
Mt Tarawera 329
Mt Te Aroha 214
Mt Tongariro 283-4

Mt Tutoko 623
Mt Victoria 103
mountain biking 67, 511, 684, **9**
    Alexandra 572
    Auckland 109
    Dunedin 562, **560**
    Great Barrier Island 142
    Hanmer Springs 532, **531**
    Internet resources 39
    Ohakune 292, **293**
    Otago 573, **568**
    Queenstown 588, **582**, **584**
    Rotorua 321, **316**, **328**
    Taupo 299, **296**, **305**
    Te Anau 618
    Tongariro 289
    Wellington 392, **385**, **388**, **389**, **396**
    Whangamata 211
mountainboarding 62
mountaineering 67-8, *see also* rock climbing
    Aoraki/Mt Cook National Park 552
mountains 54, 56, *see also individual mountains*
Moutoa Gardens 268
Murchison 468-70
Muriwai Beach 108, 132
Muriwai Regional Park 132
museums
    Auckland Museum 99-100
    Canterbury Museum 508-9
    Hokonui Moonshine Museum 637
    Mediaplex & Film Archive 390
    Motat (Museum of Transport & Technology) 101
    Museum of Caves 236-7
    Museum of Wellington City & Sea 390
    National Maritime Museum 100
    New Zealand Fighter Pilots Museum 605
    New Zealand Rugby Museum 276
    Otago Museum 559
    Puke Ariki 250
    railway museum 540
    Rotorua Museum of Art & History 317
    School of Mines & Mineralogical Museum 197
    Southland Museum & Art Gallery 632
    Tairawhiti Museum 360
    Taranaki Aviation, Transport & Technology Museum 256
    Tatatm 256
    Tawhiti Museum 260
    Te Papa 390
    Wanganui Regional Museum 267-8
    Whakatane Museum 344
    WOW Art & Collectable Cars Museum 445

music 44-5
mussels 86
mythology 47-8, 49

N
Napier 368-75, **370**, **10**
Naseby 574
National Maritime Museum 100, 116-17
National Park 289-91
national parks 59-60, **60**, *see also* forest parks, regional parks
    Abel Tasman National Park 456-9, **457**
    Aoraki/Mt Cook National Park 59, 549-54, 615, **550**
    Arthur's Pass 75, 81, 535
    Egmont National Park 81, 257, 258
    Fiordland National Park 59, 615
    Kahurangi National Park 463-5
    Mount Aspiring National Park 615, **78**
    Nelson Lakes National Park 76, 450-1
    Paparoa National Park 81, 476-7
    Rakiura National Park 645
    Southwest New Zealand (Te Wahipounamu) World Heritage Area 59, 549, 615
    Te Urewera National Park 59, 366-8
    Tongariro National Park 59, 81, 282-9, **285**
    Waitangi National Reserve 178
    Westland National Park/Tai Poutini 615, **491**
    Whanganui National Park 59, 81, 271-4
Native Land Court Hearings 652
Nee Island 628
Nelson 442-50, **419, 443**
Nelson Lakes National Park 76, 450-1
Nelson region 416-18, 442-59
nephrite 672
netball 39
New Chum's Beach 204
New Plymouth 248-55, **252**
New Plymouth Coastal Walkway 251
New Plymouth Observatory 250
New Zealand Alpine Club 68
New Zealand Fighter Pilots Museum 605
New Zealand International Comedy Festival 665
New Zealand International Film Festival 665-6
New Zealand Kayak School 84
New Zealand Rugby Museum 276
New Zealand Sports Hall of Fame 559
New Zealand Underwater Association 71
New Zealand Wars 30

Newmarket 122, **102**
newspapers 658
Nga Hau a Wha 510
Nga Manu Nature Reserve 410
Ngaiotonga Scenic Reserve 187
Ngai Tahu 645
Ngaruawahia 220
Ngarua Caves 459-60
Ngarunui Beach 227
Nikau Cave 220
Ninety Mile Beach 166-8
Ninety Mile Beach–Cape Reinga
    Walkway 81
Norgay, Tenzing 67
North Head 103
North Otago Museum 577-8
North-West Circuit 81
Northland 146-92, **148**
Northland war 30
Nugget Point 638, 642, **628-9**
number-eight wire 35
Nydia Track 429
NZ–UK relations 32
NZ Boat Show 111
NZ Forest Accord 55
NZ Gold Guitar Awards 637
NZ Line Dancing Championships 637
NZ Masters Games 665

O
O Tapara 622
Oakura 256-7
Oamaru 577-80, **578**
Oban 645, 646, **648**
Ocean Beach 228
Ohakune 291-4, **293**
Ohau 74
Ohau Forests 549
Ohinemutu 316-17
Ohope 348
Okahutiti Pa 260-1
Okarito 489-90
Okiwi Bar 141
Omahuta Forest 163
Omakau 574
Omapere 160-2
Omarama 580-1
Omokoroa 340
One Tree Hill 103
Oneroa Beach 135
Ongarue River 243
Opal Hot Springs 233
Oparara Basin 474
Ophir 574
Opito Bay 204
Opononi 160-2
Opotiki 348-50, **349**
Opoutere Beach 211

000 Map pages
000 Location of colour photographs

Opua Forest 178
Opunake 261
Orakei 104
Orakei Korako 308
Orepuki 631
Oreti Beach 633
Orewa 149-50
Orokawa Bay 212
Ostend market 135
Otago 555-611, **558**
Otago Central Rail Trail 573, **573**
Otago Museum 559
Otago Peninsula 567-70, **568**
Otago Settlers Museum 559
Otaki 410-11
Otama Beach 204
Otara Markets 126
Otorohanga 234-5, **234**
Otorohanga Kiwi House & Native Bird
    Park 235
Owaka 641-2
oystercatcher 62

P
Pacific Ring of Fire 54
Paekakariki 408-9
Paeroa 213-14
Paihia 176-81, **177**
Pakiri 154
Paku 209
Palm Beach 135
Palmerston North 274-9, **275**
Pancake Rocks 476-7, **532-3**
Papamoa 342
Paparoa National Park 81, 476-7
Papatowai 640, 641
Papatuanuku 47
paragliding 68, 137, 513, 607
Parakai 132-3
Paraparaumu 409-10
parapenting 68
Parihaka 261
Paritutu 250
Parnell 113-14, 115, 117, 120, 123,
    100
Parnell Rose Gardens 105
Pasifika Festival 111
passports 678
Pataua 192
Paterson Inlet 646, 649
paua 86, 672
Paua Shell House 636
Pauanui 210-11
Pearse, Richard 543
Peel Forest 544-5
penguins 145, 528, 567-8, 577, 642,
    647, **628-9**
petroglyphs 652, 654
Pewhairangi 176
phonecards 673
Picton 420-5, **421**
pigeon-gram service 141

Piha Beach 108, 131, **12**
pine plantations 59
Pink and White Terraces 329
Pinnacles 200
Piopio 242
Pipiriki 271-2
Piripiri Caves Scenic Reserve 240
Pirongia Forest Park 230-1
planning 13-15, 77-8
    holidays 667
plants 56, 59
    Catlins 638
    Pukeiti Rhododendron Trust 255
    Stewart Island 647
podocarp forests 544-5, 638
Pohara 461-2
pohutukawa 58, 200
poi 52
Pokarekare Ana 319
politics 24, 31-2, 33
ponga 59
Ponsonby 104, 114, 115, 117, 121-2,
    123, **105**
Poor Knights Islands 188-9
population 24, 38-9
Porpoise Bay 640
Porter Heights 75
postal sevices 670-1
Potatau-te-wherowhero 219
Pounamu 672
Pounawea Nature Walk 641
Pouto 158
Poverty Bay 358-65
Princes Wharf 119-20, 123
Pudding Hill Scenic Reserve 537
Puhoi 151
Puke Ariki 250
Pukeiti Rhododendron Trust 255
pukeko 57
Pukekura 250, 488-9
Puketi Forest 163
Puketui Valley 210
Punakaiki 476-7
Pupu 460
Purakaunui Falls 641
Purangi Winery 209
Pureora Forest Park 307-8
Putauaki 348
Putiki Church 268-9

Q
quad biking 62, see also mountain
    biking
    Auckland 109
    Hanmer Springs 532
    Kawhia 228
Queen Charlotte Track 81, 427-9
Queenstown 581-96, **582**, **584**,
    596-7
    accommodation 590-2
    activities 585-8
    attractions 583-5
    drinking 594-5

entertainment 595
food 593-4
travel to/from 595-6
travel within 596

R
Rabbit Island 452
radio 40, 658
Raetihi 294-5
Raglan 225-7, **225**
railway museum 540
Rainbow's End Adventure Park 106
Rainbow Reach 617, 628
Rainbow Valley 76
Rainbow Warrior 32, 33, 71, 171, **292-3**
Rakaia 536
Rakiura, *see* Stewart Island
Rakiura National Park 645
Rakiura Track 81, 648-9
Ranfurly 575
Ranginui 47
Rangipu Beach 227
Rangiriri Battle Site Heritage Centre 220
Rangitahua 656
Rangitata River 536
Rangitoto Island 133-4, **134**, **132-3**
Raukumara 356
Raurimu Spiral 243
Rawene 162
Rawhiti 187, **292-3**
Rawhiti Cave 462
recycling 55
Red Hills 500
red pine 59
Red Rocks Coastal Walk 392
Reefton 478-9
Rees-Dart Track 81, 602
regional parks, *see also* national parks, forest parks
    Auckland region 129
    Muriwai Regional Park 132
    Shakespear Regional Park 149
    Waitakere Ranges Regional Park 130-1
    Wenderholme Regional Park 150
Rekohu 651
religion 40, *see also* mythology
Remarkables, the 73, **63**, **596-7**
rental accommodation 661
Renwick 435
responsible tramping 83
responsible travel 55, 58
restaurants 89
Riding for the Disabled 66
rimu 59
rips 209
river cruises 222, 243
river sledging 62, 260
rivers 84
Riverton 631-2
Riverton Rocks 631

Roaring Bay 642
Robinson, Peter 46
rock climbing 68
    Froggate Edge 230
    Nelson 445
    Whanganui Bay 230
    Wharepapa South 230
Rongo-matane 47
Ross 488
Rotorua 314-27, **316**, **328**
    accommodation 323-5
    activities 319-22
    attractions 316-19
    concerts 319
    drinking 326
    entertainment 326
    food 325-6
    shopping 326
    tours 323
    travel to/from 326-7
    travel within 327
    walking tour 322-3, **322**
Rotorua Museum of Art & History 317
Routeburn Track 81, 600-2, **601**, **628-9**
Roxburgh 575
royal albatross 62
Royal NZ Easter Show 111
Ruakuri Cave 236, 238
Ruapuke Beach 227
Ruatapu Cave 308
Ruatoria 357
rugby 24
    New Zealand Rugby Museum 276
rugby union 39
Russell 181-3, **181**
Russell Road 187
Rutherford, Ernest 32, 509

S
safe travel 78, 695-6
    Hot Water Beach 209
    tramping 287
sailing 68-9
    Auckland 107
    Auckland to Russell Yacht Race 112
    Bay of Islands 174
    Christchurch 510-11
    Flying Carpet 137
    Milford Sound 626-7
    Sugar Loaf Islands Marine Park 250, 251
St Andrew's Anglican Church 231
St Bathans 574
St Benedict's Cavern 238
St Heliers Bay 104
St James Walkway 81
St John's Anglican Church 229
St Mary's Church 103, 250
sandflies 664
Sandy Bay 188
scallops 86

School of Mines & Mineralogical Museum 197
scenic flights, *see also* aerial sightseeing, hot-air ballooning
    Dunedin 562
    Glenorchy 599
    Queenstown 589
    Wanaka 607
scuba diving 69-71
    Auckland 108
    Bay of Islands 175
    Great Barrier Island 142
    Milford Sound 626
    Otago Peninsula 569
    Poor Knights Islands 188
    Tairua 209
sea kayaking 64, 174, *see also* kayaking
sea lions 568, 640, **500-1**
seal swimming 438-9
seals 67
    Chatham Island 653-4
    Doubtful Sound 628
    Kaikoura 437
    Tauranga Bay seal colony 473
Second Taranaki war 30
Seddonville 474
senior travellers 664
settler populations 29-31
Shag Point 581
Shakespear Regional Park 149
shark-cage diving 67, *see also* scuba diving
sharks 664
Shoal Bay 141
shopping 671-2
skiing 71-84, **73**, **75**
    Aoraki/Mt Cook National Park 552, **550**
    Cardrona 611
    Mt Taranaki (Mt Egmont) National Park 257-8
    Hanmer Springs Field 531, **531**
    Internet resources 71
    Lake Tekapo 546, **546**
    Methven 537, **538**
    Mt Aspiring National Park 606
    Mt Lyford 531
    Ohakune 291-4, **293**
    Queenstown 588, **582**, **584**
    Tongariro National Park 287, **285**
Skippers Canyon 589
Sky City 125
sky jumping 62
Sky Tower 97-9, **116-17**
skydiving 77
    Auckland 107
    Fox Glacier 496
    Matamata 233
    Mercer 219
    Parakai 133
    Queenstown 587-8

Taupo 298
Tauranga 333
Wanaka 607
Skyline Skyrides 330
sledging
    Queenstown 587
    Wanaka 606
Slipper Island 210
Slope Point 640
smoking 90, 666
Smugglers Bay 192
Snares Islands 655
snorkelling
    Gemstone Bay 207, 208
    Hahei 208
    Hauturu (Clarke) Island 211
snowboarding 71-6, **76**
Solomon, Tommy 652, 654
South Canterbury Museum 541-2
South Otago Historical Society
    Museum 576
South Taranaki Bight 248
southern right whales 631
Southern Scenic Route 630-2
Southland 612-42, **614**
Southland Museum & Art Gallery 632
Southwest New Zealand (Te Wahipou-
    namu) World Heritage Area 59,
    549, 615
Speight's Brewery 559
sperm whales 58, 66
spirituality, *see* mythology
sports 39, 62, *see also individual sports*
SS *Rangiriri* 222
Stanley St Tennis Courts 125
Stardome Observatory 102
State Highway 25 204
Stewart Island 81, 645-51, **646**, 6
Stewart Island kiwi 649
Stingray Bay 207
Stirling Falls 626
Stirling Point signpost 636
Stony Batter 135
Stony Batter Walk 135
Stratford 260
Stratford-Taumarunui Heritage Trail
    260
Subantarctic Islands 655-6
Sugar Loaf Islands Marine Park 250,
    251
Supper Cove 628
surfing 69, 70, **69**, **70**, **132-3**
    Awana Bay 141
    Bay of Islands 175
    Bethells Beach 108
    Dunedin 561
    Fitzroy Beach 251
    Gisborne 362

Harataonga 141
Kaitoke 141
Manu Bay 225, 227
Medlands Beach 141
Mokau 243
Monkey Island 631
Muriwai Beach 108
Ngarunui Beach 227
Oakura 251, 256-7
Okiwi Bar 141
Opunake 261
Piha Beach 108, 131
Queenstown 587
Raglan 226
Sugar Loaf Islands Marine Park 251
Timaru 542
Urenui 256
Whale Bay 227
Whangamata 211
Whangapoua 141
Whitianga 206
Sutherland Falls 625
swimming
    Auckland 108
    Awana Bay 141
    Harataonga 141
    Kaitoke 141
    Medlands Beach 141
    Monkey Island 631
    Okiwi Bar 141
    Opunake 261
    Raglan 226
    safety 664
    Taupo 297
    Whangapoua 141

T
Taieri Gorge Railway 558-9
Tainui canoe 229
Tainui Kawhia Pine Forest 228
Tairawhiti Museum 360
Tairua 209-10
takahe 57, 617
Takaka 460-1
Takapu Refuge 132
Takiroa 580
Tamatea Pokaiwhenua 381
tammar wallaby 152
tandem skydiving 513, *see also*
    skydiving
Tane-mahuta 59
Tangaroa 47
Tapotupotu Bay 167
Taramea Bay 631
Taranaki 246-61, **249**
Taranaki Aviation, Transport &
    Technology Museum 256
Tararua Forest Park 411, 414-15
Tarawera Falls 348
Tasman, Abel 26
Tasman Glacier 551, 552
Tatatm 256
tattoos 53

Taumarunui 243-5, **244**
Taupo 295-304, **296**, **305**
Taupo Volcanic Zone 54
Taurakitewaru Wood 633
Tauranga 331-7, **332**, **334**
Tauranga Bay 172
Tautuku Bay 640
Tawarau Forest 240
Tawhiri-matea 47
Tawhiti Museum 260
taxes 670
Taylor, Chad 41
Te Anau 618, 622, **618**
Te Anau Downs 619, 622
Te Anau Glowworm Caves 617
Te Anau Wildlife Centre 617
Te Apiti 276
Te Araroa 355
Te Aroha 214-15
Te Awamutu 229-30
Te Henga (Bethells Beach) 108, 132
Te Kaha 355
Te Kooti 361
Te Kuiti 241-2, **241**
Te Kuiti Muster 241
Te Mata Peak 378
Te Ngae Park 330
Te Papa 390
Te Poho-o-Rawiri meeting house 360
Te Poka a Takatimu 631
Te Puia Hot Springs 228
Te Puia Springs 357
Te Puke 342-3
Te Rauparaha 30
Te Tokanganui-o-noho Marae 241
Te Urewera National Park 59, 366-8
Te Waewae Bay 630, 631
Te Wahipounamu 549, 615
Te Waikoropupu Springs 460
Te Wairoa 54, 329, 330-1
Te Whakarewarewa 318-19, 324-5
Te Whanga Lagoon 652
Te Whiti 261
Te-arikinui-dame-te-atairangikaahu
    219
Teddy Bears Picnic 111
telephone services 672-3
Temple Basin 75
Temple Forest 549
Temuka 540
Thames 196-200, **198**
theft 663
thermal pools
    Morere 365
    Rotorua 319-20
    Taupo 297
    Tokaanu 308
thermal springs
    Hanmer Springs 530-1
    Maruia 533
Thomson's Bush 633
Tikitere 327

Tikitiki 357
Timaru 540-3, **541**
time 674
Tirau 233-4
Tiritiri Matangi Island 58, 145
Tohu Kakahi 261
Toi's Pa 345
Tokaanu 308
Tokelau 656-7
Tokomaru Bay 357
Tolaga Bay 357
Tongaporutu River 256
Tongariro Crossing 81
Tongariro National Park 59, 81, 282-9, **285**, 12, **292-3**
Tongariro Northern Circuit 81, 284
Torere 355
totara 59, 630
Totara Flats Track 81
tourism 24
tourist information 674
tours 88, 109-11, 589-90
track classification 78
Traill, Charles 647
train travel 691-2
  rail passes 692
  TranzAlpine railway 484
Tramline Track 142
tramping, *see* walking
TranzAlpine 484, 536
travel insurance 667
Treaty of Waitangi 29, 35
Treble Cone 73
tree ferns 59
trees 58-9
  Catlins 638
  dendroglyph 654
  Stewart Island 647
trekking, *see* tramping
Trounson Kauri Park 158-9
trout fishing, *see* fishing
Trout Springs 329-30
Tryphena 141
Tu-matauenga 47
Tuatapere 630-1, 631
tuatara 56
Tuhoe people 366
Tuhua 341
tui 57
Tukino 72
Tupare 255
Turangawaewae Marae 220
Turangi 308-11, **309**
Turoa 72
Turuturumokai Pa 261
Tutanekai 318
Tutukaka 188-9
TV 40, 658
Twin Coast Mizone Cycle Challenge 665
Twizel 548-9

U
Ulva Island 647
undertows 209
Upper Waiau River 617
Urenui 256

V
vegan travellers 666
vegetarian travellers 89, 666
Viaduct Basin 109
Viaduct Harbour 119-20, 123, **116-17**
Victoria Esplanade 276
Victoria Forest Park 478
Victoria Park Market 126
video systems 658
Vintage Car & Machinery Museum 544
visas 674-5, *see also* passports
visual arts 46
Vogel, Julius 29
volcanoes 54-6
  Auckland 103-4
  Lake Taupo region 306
  Motuhora 347
  Motutapu Island 133-4
  Mt Eden (Maungawhau) 103
  Mt Ruapehu 282-3
  Mt Taranaki (Mt Egmont) 257-9
  Mt Tongariro 283-4
  Mt Victoria 103
  North Head 103
  One Tree Hill 103
  Putauaki 348
  Rangitoto Island 133-4
  Tongariro National Park 81, 284
  Volcanic Activity Centre 306
  walks 110
  Whakaari 346-7

W
Waddell, Rob 231
Wai-o-Tapu Thermal Wonderland 329, **324-5**
waiata 52
Waiau Caves 630
Waiau Falls 204
Waiau River 630
Waiheke Island 134-9, **136**, **132-3**
  Windsurfing Waiheke 137
Waiheke Jazz Festival 111, 134
Waihi 212
Waihi Beach 212-13
Waikanae 410
Waikato 219-34, **218**
Waikato Land War 219
Waikato River 231, 232, 295, 307, **292-3**
Waikato War 30, 31
Waimangu Volcanic Valley 327
Waingaro Hot Springs 225
Waioeka 356
Waiorau 74
Waiouru 295
Waipapa Point 640

Waipara Valley 530
Waipawa 381
Waipoua Kauri Forest 159-60, **160**, **292-3**
Waipu 154-5
Waipukurau 381
Wairahurahiri River 630
Wairaka 343
Wairakei Geothermal Power Project 307
Wairakei Park 304-7
Wairakei Terraces 307
Wairakei Thermal Valley 307
Wairake Track 228
Wairarapa, the 411-15
Wairau Massacre 422
Wairere Falls 233
Wairoa 365-6
wairua 40, 48-9
Waitaho 645
Waitakere Ranges 130-1, **132-3**
Waitakere Ranges Regional Park 130-1
Waitaki Valley 580-1
Waitangi 176-81, **177**
Waitangi Day 665
Waitangi National Reserve 178
Waitomo 235-40
Waitomo Caves 235-6, **9**, **324-5**
Waitomo Walkway 238
Waiuta 479
Wakefield, Edward Gibbon 29
walking 77-84
  Abel Tasman Coastal Track 456-8
  Akaroa 527, **528**
  Aoraki/Mt Cook National Park 551-2, **550**
  Arthur's Pass National Park 535
  back-country huts 82
  Banks Peninsula Track 527
  Bluff 636
  books 78
  Britannia Track 474
  Cape Brett hike 176, 187
  Caples Track 602, **601**
  Charming Creek 474
  Chasm Walk 622-3
  Christchurch 511, 512, **506**, **507**, **522**
  Circle Track 628
  Coast to Coast Walkway 109
  Copland Track 498
  Coromandel Coastal Walkway 200, 203
  Croesus Track 479-80
  Dunedin 561-2, **560**
  Dusky Track 628, 630
  Egmont National Park 257, 258
  Fiordland 618, **616**
  Fox Glacier 496, **495**
  Franz Josef Glacier 492, **493**
  Glenorchy 599

INDEX

Great Barrier Island 142
Great Walks 77, 80-1, **80**
Greenstone Track 602, **601**
Haast-Paringa Cattle Track 498
Hanmer Springs 531, **531**
Hokianga-Waipoua Coastal Track 160-1
Holdsworth 414-15
Hollyford Track 623-4
Hope Arm 628
Hump Ridge Track 630
Internet resources 76
Kahurangi National Park 464-5
Kaikoura 438
Kaitoke Hot Springs Track 142
Kauaeranga Valley 200
Kepler Track 617, **619**
Lake Sumner 533
Lake Tekapo 546, **546**
Lake Wakatipu 600-2
Makarora 603
maps 78
Methven 537, **538**
Milford Track 624-5
Mt Pirongia 230-1
Mt Somers 540
Mt Taranaki (Mt Egmont) 257-8
Nelson Lakes National Park 450-1
New Plymouth's Coastal Walkway 251
Nydia Track 429
Ohakune 291-2, **293**
Ohau Forests 549
Opua Forest 178
Otago 569, 573, **558**
Peel Forest 544-5
Pinnacles 200
Pirongia Forest Park 230-1
Pounawea Nature Walk 641
Queenstown 588, **582, 584**
Queen Charlotte Track 427-9
Rakiura Track 648-9
Raukumara 356
Rees-Dart Track 602
responsible tramping 83
Rimutaka Incline 415
Rob Roy Valley Track 606
Rotorua 320, **316, 328**
Routeburn Track 600-2, **601**
safety 287
St James Walkway 533
Southern Scenic Route 630-2
Stony Batter Walk 135
Stewart Island 647-9, **646**
Stratford-Taumarunui Heritage Trail 260
Taupo 299-300, **296, 305**
Tauranga 333, **332, 334**

000 Map pages
000 Location of colour photographs

Te Anau 617
Te Urewera National Park 366-8
Timaru 542, **541**
Tongariro National Park 284-7, **285**
track classification 78
track safety 78
Tramline Track 142
travel to/from 82
Turangi 308-9, **309**
Tawarau Forest 240
Ulva Island 647
Waiheke 135
Wairake Track 228
Waitomo 238-9
Wanaka 606, **604**
Wellington 392, **385, 388, 389, 396**
West Matukituki Valley 606
Whakatane 345, **344**
Whangamata 211
Whanganui National Park 272-3
Whareorino Forest 240
Whirinaki Forest Park 331
Wilkin Valley Track 603
York Loop Track 258
Walters, Gordon 46
Wanaka 604-11, **604**
Wanaka Beerworks 605
Wanaka Paragliding School 68
Wanaka Transport & Toy Museum 605
Wanganui 262-3, 266-71, **265, 267**
Wanganui region 264-74
Wanganui Regional Museum 267-8
Wangapeka Track 81, 465
warfare 27, 30, 31-2, 51-2
    Land Wars 30
    Musket Wars 27
    Taranaki Land Wars 250
    Waikato Land War 219
Warkworth 151-2
water sports, *see individual sports, activities*
waterfalls
    Acland Falls 545
    Bowen Falls 626
    Bridal Veil Falls 228
    Dawson Falls 258
    Emily Falls 545
    Huka Falls 306
    Humboldt Falls 622
    Marokopa Falls 240
    Matai Falls 641
    McLean Falls 640
    Purakaunui Falls 641
    Rata Falls 545
    Stirling Falls 626
    Sutherland Falls 625
    Waiau Falls 204
    Wairere Falls 233
weights and measures 658, *see also inside front cover*

Wellington 384-407, **385, 388, 389, 396, 10**
    accommodation 395-9
    attractions 387-92
    drinking 402-3
    emergency services 386
    entertainment 403-4
    food 399-402
    medical services 387
    shopping 404
    tourist offices 387
    travel to/from 404-5
    travel within 405-7
Wellington Caving Group 64
Wenderholme Regional Park 150
Wentworth Falls walk 211
West Arm Power Station 628
West Coast 466-500, **468**
Western Bay of Plenty 331-43
Westland National Park/Tai Poutini 615, **491**
Westport 470-3, **471**
Whakaari 346-7, **324-5**
Whakapapa 72, 286-7, **288**
Whakatane 343-6, **344**
Whakatane Museum 344
whale-watching 66, 438
Whale Bay 227
Whale Island 347
Whale Rider 362
Whangamata 211-12
Whangamomona village 260
Whangamumu Scenic Reserve 187
Whanganui a Hei Marine Reserve 207
Whanganui Bay 230
Whanganui Journey 81
Whanganui National Park 59, 81, 271-4
Whanganui River 243
Whanganui River Road 271-4
Whangaparaoa Peninsula 149
Whangapoua 141
Whangara 357
Whangarei 189-92, **190**
Whangarei Falls 190
Whangarei Heads 192
Whangaroa Harbour 170-2
Whangaruru North Head Scenic Reserve 187
Wharariki Beach 463
Wharekawa Wildlife Refuge 62, 211
Whareorino Forest 240
Wharepapa South 230
Whataroa 489
Whatipu Beach 132
Whirinaki Forest Park 331
white heron 62, 489
White Island 346-7
white-water rafting 84, 513, 9
    Hanmer Springs 532
    Queenstown 586-7, **596-7**
    Rangitata River 545

Rotorua 320-1
Tauranga 333
Wanaka 606
white-water sledging, see river
    sledging
    Rotorua 321
whitebait 499
Whitecliffs 256
Whitianga 204-7, **205**
wildlife reserves 510-11
wildlife sanctuaries
    Kiwi House 58
    Otorohanga Kiwi House & Native
        Bird Park 235
    Takapu Refuge 132
    Te Anau Wildlife Centre 617
    Tiritiri Matangi Island 58, 145
    Ulva Island 647
    Wharekawa Wildlife Refuge
        62, 211
Wilmot Pass 628

windsurfing 84,
    see also surfing
    Fitzroy Beach 251
    Flying Carpet 137
    Oakura 251, 256-7
    Rangipu Beach 227
    Wellington 392-4
    Whitianga 206
    Windsurfing Waiheke 137
Windy Canyon 142
wine 85, 87
wine-touring 88
wineries
    Auckland region 129-30
    Central Otago 576, 589-90
    Hawkes Bay 378-80, **379**
    itineraries 20
    Marlborough 432, **434**
    Martinborough 413-14
    Nelson region 452
    tours 88

Waiheke Island 135
Waipara Valley 530
Wine Waitakere 112
Wintergarden 105
women in New Zealand 40-1
women travellers 672, 675
woodcarving, see carving
Woollaston, Toss 46
work 675-7
World Heritage areas 59
WOW Art & Collectable Cars
    Museum 445
wrybill 62
WWI 31-3
WWII 32

Y
yachting, see sailing
yellow-eyed penguins 62, 626, 638,
    640
York Loop Track 258

INDEX

MAP LEGEND

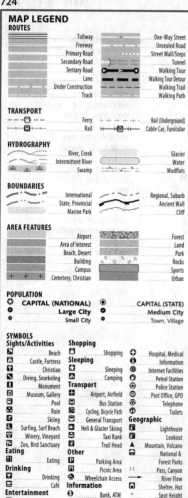

LONELY PLANET OFFICES

Australia
Head Office
Locked Bag 1, Footscray, Victoria 3011
☎ 03 8379 8000, fax 03 8379 8111
talk2us@lonelyplanet.com.au

USA
150 Linden St, Oakland, CA 94607
☎ 510 893 8555, toll free 800 275 8555
fax 510 893 8572, info@lonelyplanet.com

UK
72–82 Rosebery Ave,
Clerkenwell, London EC1R 4RW
☎ 020 7841 9000, fax 020 7841 9001
go@lonelyplanet.co.uk

France
1 rue du Dahomey, 75011 Paris
☎ 01 55 25 33 00, fax 01 55 25 33 01
bip@lonelyplanet.fr, www.lonelyplanet.fr

Published by Lonely Planet Publications Pty Ltd
ABN 36 005 607 983

© Lonely Planet 2004

© photographers as indicated 2004

Cover photographs by Lonely Planet Images: Fluke waving to the snow-capped mountains outside Kaikoura, David Wall (front); Maori warrior performing a *haka* at Te Whakarewarewa Thermal Village, Manfred Gottschalk (back). Many of the images in this guide are available for licensing from Lonely Planet Images: www.lonelyplanetimages.com.

Printed through SNP SPrint Singapore Pte Ltd at
KHL Printing Co Sdn Bhd Malaysia